EVIDENCE:
TEXT AND MATERIALS

AUSTRALIA
Law Book Co.
Sydney

CANADA and USA
Carswell
Toronto

HONG KONG
Sweet & Maxwell
Asia

NEW ZEALAND
Brookers
Auckland

SINGAPORE and MALAYSIA
Sweet & Maxwell Asia
Singapore and Kuala Lumpur

EVIDENCE:
TEXT AND MATERIALS

Second Edition

by

STEVE UGLOW

*Professor of Criminal Justice, Kent Law School,
University of Kent*

LONDON
SWEET & MAXWELL
2006

Published in 1997 by
Sweet & Maxwell Limited of
100 Avenue Road
London NW3 3PF

Typeset by LBJ Typesetting Ltd
of Kingsclere
Printed and bound in Great Britain by
TJ International Ltd, Padstow, Cornwall

No natural forests were destroyed to make this product;
only farmed timber was used and replanted

First Edition 1997

ISBN–10 0–421–92510–8
ISBN–13 978–0421–92510–6

A CIP catalogue record for this book is available from the British Library

IN THE MEMORY OF EMMA SMITH WHO DIED OF
EPILEPSY IN JULY 1995 AGED 25

PREFACE

The rules of evidence are often given a bad name—as I write this, I have just read a discussion on an e-mail list of evidence teachers. The case involved a stolen cockatoo who the thief alleged was known as Billy but who, on meeting its true owner, squawked "Hallo, I'm Primrose". Could the owner testify as to the bird's statement as evidence of its identity or should such testimony be excluded as hearsay! It is not surprising that the public (and more vocally the police) are often amazed (and sometimes angered) that what they see as relevant information, such as the accused's previous convictions, is not allowed to be given in evidence. Acquittals which are on the basis of excluded evidence are often referred to as an acquittal on a 'technicality".

Some 25 years ago, I listened, somewhat bemused, to Rupert Cross patiently explaining the law of evidence. At that time, it appeared to me as a mass of ancient cases with arcane names with some, deeply obscure, statutes occasionally intervening.

Undoubtedly it was my own shortcomings that led me to the conclusion that evidence was rather like a ball of wool that was no longer capable of being unravelled. It was woolly as well in its apparent absence of underlying structure and basic principles.

But like a good student, I took my notes and passed the exams. Nowadays I concede that this early judgment on the coherence of the subject was probably (but only probably) wrong. To treat the field simply as a matter of technicalities is also (probably) unfair.

Like football, evidence can be a simple game if the key concepts of relevance, probative value and fairness are adhered to. It is only too easy to lose sight of those basic precepts and the principles of procedural justice that underlie them. Certainly the rules are complex, but that is the result of putting those principles into practice. Returning to my lecture notes over a decade later as a prelude to teaching the subject, I was struck by how well Cross achieved that balance between simplicity and sophistication. His lectures were still fresh, clear and brimming with intellectual curiosity and insight. At the time I may not have understood, but my notes reveal that at least I knew what passages to write down! Rupert Cross is still the modern collossus in the field, with his work ably carried on by Colin Tapper. His book is both bible and goldmine for any researcher in the subject. But opening the volume is a daunting prospect even for the final year law student; the book is an essential reference too! but perhaps not the starting point for one's first steps into the subject. It is here that I find the justification for this book. Despite the erudition and scholarship of modern evidence scholars such as Zuckerman, Birch, Twining, Choo, Pattenden, John Smith and Keane among many others, in teaching evidence I have felt the lack of a book which is accessible to and easily digested by law students. Primarily aimed at students, the "text and materials" format was pioneered, in the criminal law area, by Heather Keating and Chris Clarkson and I have, unashamedly, copied their approach and objectives, namely to produce a book which has the "flow and coherence" of a textbook but which seeks to expose students to a variety of material from a diversity of sources. It is a format which lends itself to exploring evidence from a range of perspectives. It is not a topic, unlike criminal law, that lends itself naturally to a contextual approach. But wherever possible, I have sought to achieve this, especially in sections on the nature of adversarial trial, on the reliability of witnesses, on confession and identification evidence. It has been much harder to achieve when discussing estoppel! I owe a great deal to my long term colleagues at Kent Law School—Wade Mansell, Richard de Friend, Ian Grigg-Spall, Alan Thomson and Peter Firzpatrick among others—who have created an ethos of openness towards the study of law which is occasionally (although not enough) reflected in this text. I also would like to record the considerable help of the Kent Law School Office team, headed by Liz Cable. Jenny, Tom, Hannah, Jamie and Luke showed their normal and admirable forbearance during the long months of preparation and writing. But most of all, I owe a huge debt of gratitude to Venous Telford, who, despite claims of family and bar school, worked so hard gathering material, reading drafts, checking references and making constructive suggestions. Without her, the book would contain less of value and more errors. She deserves credit for the former but I alone am responsible for any mistakes that remain.

October 1996
Steve Uglow

The last decade has seen great change in the law of evidence. This text has been substantially rewritten in the light of statutory reform, especially the 1999 Youth Justice and Criminal Evidence Act and the 2003 Criminal Justice Act. Much more attention has been given to the implications of the European Convention on Human Rights as a result of the Human Rights Act 1998. These key principles underlying the rules of evidence need restating, especially at a period when politicians and police officers present themselves as better custodians of truth than judges and juries.

June 2006
Steve Uglow

ACKNOWLEDGEMENTS

Grateful acknowledgement is made for permission to reproduce from the undermentioned works:

BLACKWELL PUBLISHERS:
Cross, 'Some Proposals for Reform in the Law of Evidence' 24 *MLR* (1961)
Greer, 'Miscarriages of Criminal Justice Reconsidered' 57 *MLR* (1994)
Redmayne, 'Science, Evidence and Logic' 59 *MLR* (1996)
Stephenson, *The Psychology of Criminal Justice* 1992

CORNELL LAW REVIEW:
Dewey, *Logical Method and Law 10*, Cornell LQ 17

HART PUBLISHING LTD:
McEwan, *Evidence and the Adversarial Process* (1998)

GUARDIAN NEWSPAPERS LTD:
Campbell, *Victims Without a Voice* 2005

LEXISNEXIS BUTTERWORTHS:
Heydon, *Evidence* (1984)
The All England Law Reports
Tapper, *Crime, Proof and Punishment* (1981)

OXFORD UNIVERSITY PRESS:
Blackburn, *Truth* (2005)
Zuckerman, *The Principles of Criminal Evidence* (1989)

PALGRAVE MACMILLAN:
McBarnett, *Conviction* (1983)

PENGUIN:
Blackburn, *Truth* (2005)

PRINCETON:
Frank, *Courts on Trial* (1973)

TAYLOR & FRANCIS BOOKS (UK):
Mansell, Meteyard and Thomson, *A Critical Introduction to Law*, Cavendish, 2004, ch.3

Acknowledgement is made for extracts from the following works:

HARBINGER:
Arnold, *The Symbols of Government* (1962)

OXFORD UNVERSITY PRESS:
Spencer and Flin, *The Law and the Psychology* (1993)
Temkin, *Rape and the Legal Process* (2002)
Tapper, *Cross on Evidence* (1990)

PELICAN:
Harding, *A Social History of English Law* (1966)

SPRINGFIELD:
Wall, *Eyewitness Identification of Criminal Cases* (1965)

TIMES NEWSPAPERS LTD:
The Times, leader comment, August 23, 1996

WIEDENFELD:
Eggleston, *Evidence, Proof and Probability* (1983)

While every care has been taken to establish and acknowledge copyright and contact the copyright owners, the publishers tender their apologies for any accidental infringement. They would be pleased to come to a suitable arrangement with the rightful owners in each case.

CONTENTS

3. THE BURDEN AND STANDARD OF PROOF

4. DISCRETION TO EXCLUDE EVIDENCE: JUDICIAL OVERSIGHT OVER POLICE INVESTIGATIONS

5. DOCUMENTARY AND REAL EVIDENCE

6. DISCLOSURE OF EVIDENCE: PROVIDING INFORMATION BEFORE THE TRIAL

7. IMMUNITIES FROM TESTIFYING PUBLIC INTEREST IMMUNITY

8. IMMUNITIES FROM TESTIFYING PRIVATE PRIVILEGES AND CONFIDENTIAL INFORMATION

9. RELIABILITY, COMPETENCE AND COMPELLABILITY

10. VULNERABLE AND INTIMIDATED WITNESSES

11. REINFORCING SUSPECT EVIDENCE

12. ORAL TESTIMONY: EVIDENCE IN CHIEF

13. THE HOSTILE WITNESS AND CROSS-EXAMINATION

14. CHARACTER EVIDENCE

15. BAD CHARACTER

16. HEARSAY—ITS SCOPE AND RATIONALE

17. SECTION 118—COMMON LAW EXCEPTIONS TO HEARSAY

18. HEARSAY IN CRIMINAL PROCEEDINGS—THE CRIMINAL JUSTIVE ACT 2003

19. HEARSAY IN CIVIL PROCEEDINGS—THE CIVIL EVIDENCE ACT 1995

20. OPINIONS AND THE EVIDENCE OF EXPERTS

21. MATTERS NOT REQUIRING FULL PROOF

TABLE OF CASES

TABLE OF STATUTES

TABLE OF STATUTORY INSTRUMENTS

1

ADVERSARIAL, FAIR AND LOGICAL

I: INTRODUCTION

The rules of evidence provide a novel experience for students accustomed to more familiar areas of substantive law. When studying property rights, tort or criminal offences, legal rules are at their most visible and understandable, prescribing how things are to be done and laying down the *consequences* of breaking the rules: if there has been a road accident and a driver has been negligent, damages for personal injuries will be paid to any plaintiff; if a sane defendant intentionally kills another person, they will be prosecuted and generally receive a life sentence. Damages, imprisonment and other civil and criminal remedies are the sanctions accompanying rules which require, prohibit or regulate certain types of conduct. Within most contested trials, such substantive rules form the background to the case but otherwise play little part since only rarely is there conflict over the content of the rule. We know what the rule says and what the consequences of a breach will be.

For the practising lawyer, the immediate problem is to establish the facts: was the driver negligent? did the defendant cause the victim's death? what happened? The law of evidence is about *establishing those facts*. In a contested trial, under the common law system of justice, the opposing parties will present differing, sometimes diametrically opposed, views of the same event. Having listened to these accounts, the trier of fact[1] must decide what the facts are. The rules of evidence deal with this process: what information can be presented to the court? through what means? when can we be satisfied that a particular incident happened in a particular way? This process and its accompanying rules do not lay down any substantive law and are equally applicable whether the court is dealing with a personal injury claim, unfair dismissal or a criminal case. These rules, alongside the rules of civil and criminal procedure, have been described as *adjectival* law. This means that these rules attach themselves to and qualify the operation of a substantive rule but never, by themselves, directly decide the rights and wrongs of any issue. The law of evidence qualifies the operation of a substantive rule because it controls the flow and nature of the information which can be presented to the court. Indirectly, of course, the law of evidence can be decisive since the outcome of a case can depend on whether a particular item

---

[1] This means the magistrates in summary trials, juries in Crown Court cases and, normally, the judge in the county court or High Court.

of evidence is allowed to be presented to the court or not. For example, a guilty verdict or an acquittal can hang on whether the prosecution can meet the preconditions for the admissibility of a confession in a criminal trial; in a civil case where the weight of the evidence is evenly balanced, the decision may hinge on the question as to where the burden of proof rests.

This chapter explores three key aspects of the study of evidence, which set in context the rules and discretionary principles, the analysis of which form the substance of this book.

1. The principles of evidence are applied within contested trials where a resolution to the dispute has to be reached. The common law trial shapes the dispute into a predominantly adversarial form and adversarialism has dominated the development of the rules of evidence. Understanding the underlying structure is a prerequisite to understanding the rules of evidence which aim to produce information on which to base a decision. The nature of those rules cannot be separated from the manner in which the investigative and court process is structured. Legal cultures create particular structures and conditions within which information is discovered, argument takes place and disputes resolved.

2. Evidence and procedure are among the most technical and abstruse areas of law. But the rules are based, not on ancient historical doctrine, but on key principles of human rights, predominantly the concept of a fair trial, which permeates every aspect of the process—whether the disclosure of evidence, the protection accorded to the defendant's character or the cross-examination of a child witness. The overriding principle behind a contested trial is that the proceedings should be fair to all parties. But what does fairness consist of? Should we give fairness greater priority than discovering the truth?

3. Finally, as a student of evidence, it is essential that you take facts seriously. What is a fact to a court of law? What are its key characteristics? How are facts to be used in a valid fashion to resolve a dispute? You cannot divorce a study of the rules of evidence from a grounding in basic concepts of logic and in clear fact analysis—those processes by which (we hope) judges, magistrates and juries establish facts, draw inferences from those facts and reach decisions.

II. RESOLVING DISPUTES: EVIDENCE, ARGUMENTS AND DECISIONS

A trial is an argument—any contested trial consists of parties presenting different accounts or interpretations of the same event. Unlike daily life where we may beg to differ, the court needs to resolve that argument and come to a decision.

J. Dewey, "Logical Method and Law" (1924–5) Cornell L.Q. 17:

Human conduct, broadly viewed, falls into two sorts. . . . Sometimes human beings act with a minimum of foresight, without examination of what they are doing and of probable consequences. They act not upon deliberation but from routine, instinct, the direct pressure of appetite, or a blind 'hunch'. It would be a mistake to suppose that such behaviour is always inefficient or unsuccessful. . .

In the other sort of case, action follows upon a decision, and the decision is the outcome of inquiry, comparison of alternatives, weighing of facts; deliberation or thinking has intervened. Considerations which have weight in reaching the conclusion as to what is to be done, or which are employed to justify it when it is questioned, are called 'reasons'. If they are stated in sufficiently general terms they are 'principles'. When the operation is formulated in a compact way, the decision is called a conclusion, and the considerations which led up to it are called the premises. Decisions of the first type may be reasonable: that is, they may be adapted to good results; those of the second type are reasoned or rational, increasingly so in the degree of care and thoroughness with which inquiry has been conducted and the order in which connections have been established between the considerations dealt with.

Courts, whether trial or appellate courts, whether acting as finders of fact or finders of law, are decision-makers of Dewey's second category: they give reasoned or rational decisions. The rules of evidence require that the fact-finder, be it judge, magistrate or jury, must work from the evidence presented to them in court, from argument based on that evidence towards proof of a proposition. They may be described as 'logical agents'.

It should go without saying that the rules of evidence are shaped by the need for a decision to have a foundation in reason and logic. This preliminary point is that, as a starting point, the evidence lawyer needs to be positivist in approach, in the sense that there are objective facts and phenomena that it is possible to *know*. We are able to discover what happened at a particular time and a particular place. We discover the truth through a system of rational inquiry in the courtroom in which assertions are put forward by a party, assertions that can be proved or disproved. They may be supported by evidence and tested by argument or evidence from the other party who is able to put forward alternative assertions. Conclusions are determined on the strength of the evidence and the arguments that are put forward. The analogy here is with scientific method so that we treat reasoned inquiry as authoritative rather than intuitive or based on faith.

For the trial lawyer, the starting point is that we are able to reconstruct and know the truth about past events. But this starting point has significant limits—it is a useful but not necessarily attainable objective. We aim for truth but are aware that the best that can be achieved is a statement of probabilities.

S. Blackburn, Truth (Penguin, 2005), pp.29–30:

As well as the norm of truth or hitting the target, there are norms of right procedure. These govern whether you have done your stuff properly: taken the right observations, made the right inferences, hedged in the right places, weighed the evidence carefully and, in short, made yourself immune to procedural criticism. It may not follow that you arrive at the truth. The evidence may be poor, or misleading, or the interpretation which everyone supposes reasonable may be based on insufficient science or general misunderstanding. A trial may be fairly conducted, yet unhappily arrive at the wrong verdict. Still, there is nothing better that we can do. We act under the conviction that our best procedures, although they may let us down, markedly increase the chance that we get things right. Provided there was nothing better which we should have done then we may be immune from charges of irrationality, negligence or carelessness. Our procedures accord with reason and it is only bad luck that might stop us hitting the truth.

We can believe that the truth is out there and we can aim to discover it through rational inquiry. But, unlike science, lawyers cannot test and retest propositions in laboratory conditions. There is a single 'day in court' and we may discover that incontrovertible truth is beyond us and that we must fall back on the proposition that we followed the right process and have achieved the best truth that we can.

A. *Alternative Processes*

Dispute resolution can take different forms. Western European trials are presented as formally rational proceedings. But the Inuit, for example, use several, apparently irrational, techniques,

W. Mansell, B. Meteyard and A. Thompson. A Critical Introduction to Law (3rd ed. Cavendish, 2004), Ch.3:

. . . the Inuit used what at first sight seems a ludicrous method of dispute resolution: dispute resolution by so-called song-duel. Boxing and head-butting contests were other means of resolving disputes not involving homicide. Clearly in both boxing and head-butting competitions the facts which have led to the dispute are completely irrelevant. Like trial by battle there is no concern with issues of justice but only with a resolution, whatever that might be. He who wins acquires vindication and esteem, he who loses, loses standing in the eyes of the community. Song-duels are altogether more subtle in their operation. . . . a typical song-duel occurred in a public gathering with each of the disputants (or his representative) singing in turn a song of contempt and abuse directed at the opponent. Like the boxing or buffeting contest the song need have no relevance to the dispute in hand or its facts. Rather it was concerned to score points through ridicule and it was said that singing skill may equal or outrank gross physical prowess. . .
There are a number of features of the song-duels which are relevant to our consideration of law. . . . Even more significantly the winner of the song-duel wins the dispute even though neither the case itself nor the facts of the case are ever alluded to. The rights and wrongs of the social dispute are determined not by a discussion of the merits of the case but by talking about something which *can* be decided.
The great advantage of this process is that a social dispute to which there is simply no ready or obvious solution which would be accepted as correct by both parties is translated into a form which is amenable to decision. The social problem is not faced but rather sidestepped. . .
Admittedly at first sight this bizarre process for resolving disputes seems to be of little relevance to our perception of our way of dealing with disputes but several points need to be made. The most obvious is that in our experience most law students

on first visiting the courts, and particularly courts hearing appeals are immediately impressed (as often are the litigants themselves) by the fact that the court does not seem to be hearing argument 'about the real issue'. Rather what they experience is a debate over what seems to be a technical point of law. It is of course just such legal points that determine cases.

For the Inuit, the "facts", the "truth" or the "evidence" play no part. Analogies can be found in English history—in Anglo–Norman and Angevin England, disputes were settled through trial by battle,[2] compurgation or by ordeals such as that of hot water where the accused would put their hand in boiling water while swearing on oath. The hand would immediately be bandaged and if, after a week, it was found to be not badly blistered, the person was considered innocent. This relied upon the notion of *judicium dei*, the "judgment of god". As with the Inuit, such processes may seem irrational and ineffective if the aim is to determine the truth but these are communities which do not accept the authoritative status of reason as opposed to, say, that of faith. Alternatively the dispute may be irresoluble and any attempt to deal with it on a 'truth' basis could threaten social cohesion. The dispute is translated into different terms ("who is the best singer?") and subjected to a process (a song contest) that all find acceptable.

Do modern legal systems, which seem so obvious and sensible, differ that fundamentally? Western European courts place considerable emphasis on the discovery of "truth" in a positivist, cognitive sense of establishing precisely what happened. Through the rules of procedure and evidence, we aspire to reconstruct a past event. But we would be right to be very sceptical about such aims—more often than not contested trials conclude with no more than a partial and incomplete account. That very account is distorted by arguments about technical points of law, sometimes substantive but often evidential. To the participant or the outsider, these do not appear to be about "the real issue". Yet the outcome frequently depends on the outcome of that argument. Even when the "real" issue is centre stage, the role of the modern trial lawyer is about presenting the most plausible account of events, an analogy here with the Inuit singing champion.

We should not take our own legal systems or techniques as self–evidently correct. Indeed, across the world, there is an important split about trial structures between common law and civilian jurisdictions, with significant differences in the way in which information is brought before the court and the manner in which the dialogue between the parties, the lawyers and the court is regulated. The former jurisdictions, such as England and the USA, employ the *adversarial* mode of trial and possess a sophisticated jurisprudence on the rules of evidence. The latter jurisdictions, such as France and Germany, adopt an *investigative* or *inquisitorial* mode of trial and as a result place much less emphasis on *formal* rules of proof which are so significant in common law proceedings.

1. Adversarialism—origins and characteristics

In countries with the common law tradition, the adversarial form still dominates criminal proceedings and, to a lesser extent, civil actions. In this

---

[2] Availability of wager by battle was discussed in *Ashford v Thornton* (1818) 106 E.R. 149.

section, the emphasis will be on the criminal case as the paradigm of the common law trial. In brief, the presentation of information (evidence), the argument and the decision all take place within a trial which is separated, geographically, chronologically and formally, from all the previous events such as the police investigation, the review of the evidence by the prosecution, or any preliminary hearings before judges or magistrates. It is only the information which is given in evidence at the trial itself which can form the basis of any decision. The judge, in common with the jury and the spectators in the public gallery, will be hearing the evidence for the first time. Common law judges have no investigative functions, such as instructing the police to undertake specific inquiries or calling and examining witnesses on their own initiative.[3] The judge plays a formally passive role, listening to evidence which is advanced by the prosecution and the defence.[4] This is a major difference between common law countries and other European jurisdictions. The civilian approach for criminal proceedings is an investigative process, leading to a trial which is as much a review of that process as a dispute. The common law trial is a partisan dispute: both parties only call those witnesses likely to advance their cause and both are permitted to attack the credibility and reliability of the witnesses testifying for the other side. The criminal case is prepared for trial by the Crown Prosecution Service (CPS) or defence lawyers and in court, the lawyers decide which evidence is to be produced and which witnesses are to be called.

The rules of evidence draw their significance from this process since it is solely on the evidence retailed in court, usually by formal oral testimony, that the decision is based. This autonomy of the trial verges on quarantine: the court's decision is not allowed to be infected by information that derives from any source other than through the formal rules of evidence, except the assistance that the court can obtain in interpreting the law from appellate court decisions; once the jury has retired, they remain together[5] incommunicado and their discussions are absolutely privileged.[6]

The adversarial trial is one of the major constitutional institutions of the common law and the modern composition, jurisdiction and procedures are significantly the product of its history.[7] In its origins, a central question of any hearing lay in discovering the truth of an accusation.[8] But truth was not a matter of witnesses and evidence and instead might be found through ordeal, trial by battle[9] or by compurgation.[10] But in 1166, the Assize of Clarendon provided for a "jury of presentment"[11] which was a group of local people put

---

[3] A judge does have discretion to call and question a witness but the power should only be used sparingly in the interests of justice: *Oliva* [1965] 3 All E.R. 116; *Roberts* (1984) 80 Cr.App.R. 89.

[4] See Ch.2 on the functions of the judge in a trial.

[5] *Alexander* [1974] 1 All E.R. 539.

[6] *Attorney General v Scotcher* [2005] 3 All E.R. 1.

[7] J. Langbein, *The Origins of Adversary Criminal Trial* (Oxford 2003).

[8] S. Milsom, *Historical Foundations of the Common Law* (Butterworths, 1981) Ch.14; T. Plucknett, *A Concise History of the Common Law* (5th ed., Butterworths, 1956).

[9] Initially introduced after the Conquest for appeals of felony where a Norman was the accused.

[10] Suspicion was often the basis of accusation and proof by compurgation involved the accused producing a set number of neighbours to swear to his or her overall good character.

[11] This was later known as the grand jury which was not abolished in England until 1933 to be replaced by committal proceedings. It still survives in the USA.

on their oath to tell the truth about local crimes. This was not a trial jury but one of accusation. The allegations were tested through the ordeal of water[12] which was the only means of proof for those indicted by the presenting jury.

The ordeal was the *judicium dei*, the legitimacy of which came from God and as such the proceeding required the presence of a priest. But at the Lateran Council in 1215, the Church declared the ordeal to be mere superstition.[13] Without the religious imprimatur, other methods of proof had to be found. Continental Europe turned to the Roman–canonical law of proof[14] with its calculus of evidence ranging from the full confession to eye-witnesses down to mere circumstantial evidence or *indicia*. There was a formal, objective logic to this approach which sought to assess the weight of each item of evidence and to aggregate these to judge whether there was a "full proof". This approach still has its modern adherents, not least in Scotland. But this logical calculus did not take hold in England which turned instead to the jury of trial. This was known as a petty jury, distinguishable from the "grand jury" of accusation. The petty jury who could decide on the truth of the allegations was initially apparently the choice of the accused. But it slowly became the custom of the royal courts and after the Statute of Westminster in 1275, those who refused to "put themselves upon the country" could be imprisoned.[15] The trial was still not a fact–finding forum, however, since the jurors were people who already knew the circumstances of the accusation.[16]

In small, rural, homogenous communities, juries may well have been an effective means for the determination of the truth, let alone the resolution of quarrels and disputes amongst members of the community. For centuries, the initiation of criminal prosecution was a matter for grand juries or private individuals with little involvement by the State. How the accused was to confront or refute accusations (except through the knowledge of the local jury) remains shrouded in mystery:

S. Milsom, Historical Foundations of the Common Law (Butterworths, 1981), Ch.14:

Of the actual conduct of a trial we know almost nothing before the sixteenth century, not nearly enough until the eighteenth. How the jury informed itself or was informed, how rules of evidence emerged, when and in what detail directions were given by the justices, these are things we do not know.

---

[12] The accused was bound and lowered by a rope into a deep pool—if they sank to the level of a knot tied in the rope at the distance of his or her hair, they were declared innocent but if he or she floated, the water would not receive them and they were judged guilty. W. Warren. *The Governance of Norman and Angevin England 1086–1272* (Arnold, 1987), p.109.

[13] Warren: *ibid.*, 213.

[14] J. Langbein, *Torture and the Law of Proof* (Chicago, 1977).

[15] In 1649, Charles I refused to plead to the charges again him and was taken to have pleaded guilty—the confessor rule: G. Robertson, *The Tyrannicide Brief* (Chatto, 2005) p.164.

[16] Milsom, *op.cit.* p.411. It is not until after the 17th century that personal knowledge of the case becomes a disqualification for a juror. Lord Justice Coke talked of trial being by jury and not by evidence.

The embryonic roots of the adversarial system were challenged during the absolutist monarchies of the Tudors and Stuarts which developed "inquisitorial" courts such as Star Chamber, which operated without juries, on a basis of unidentified accusation and with the defendant interrogated by the judges under oath and perhaps under torture.[17] Political and popular reaction in the seventeenth century to such courts was to delineate the conditions under which the monarch or state has the power to restrict a person's freedom and to inflict punishment. The common law trial was a significant element of this and adversarialism was the technique which emerged. The two basic building blocks were the two principles of natural justice: *nemo iudex in suam causam*, a man should not be a judge in his own cause, and *audi alteram partem*, the court should hear both sides of a case. Progress was slow. The neutrality of the court was embedded in Chief Justice Coke's declaration in 1610 that a man should not be judge in his own cause.[18] The second cardinal principle was recognised by the early 18th century.[19] But the criminal defendant had no means of getting their story heard since it was not possible to compel witnesses to testify (although they might do so voluntarily) nor was there professional assistance to examine witnesses or to speak on the accused's behalf until 1836. Furthermore the defendant could not give sworn testimony until 1898.[20] Even the "bulwark of freedom", the jury, could not be relied on to be impartial.[21] But the central elements of the adversarial trial were in place by the end of the 19th century. These may be summarized as follows.

1. The court (judge and jury) in making decisions, does not act as an investigative body, calling and examining witnesses on its own initiative. It plays a passive role, listening to evidence which is advanced by the prosecution and the defence.
2. Both parties only call those witnesses likely to advance their cause and both parties are permitted to attack the credibility and reliability of the witnesses testifying for the other side. In court, the lawyers decide which evidence is to be produced and which witnesses are to be called. The judge should not interfere or act as an investigator.
3. The issues between the parties will be decided by the 'day–in–court' and, in criminal cases, mainly by oral testimony. This derives from perhaps the main rationale underlying adversarial trial, namely that any party has the right to confront their accuser and the evidence against them. Confrontation implies that the witness should be there in person in order that the reliability of the evidence and the

[17] Radcliffe and Cross, *The English Legal System* (5th ed., Butterworths 1971), p.107; Milsom, *op.cit.* pp.418–9; W. Holdsworth, *History of English Law* (Vol. V, Methuen, 1936–72) 155 ff.

[18] *Dr. Bonham's Case* (1610) 8 Co.Rep. 113b

[19] *The King v University of Cambridge* (1723), 1 St Tr 557.

[20] The accused was not a competent witness until Criminal Evidence Act 1898, s.1

[21] After the trial of the Quakers, Penn and Mead, in 1670, for a 'conspiratorial gathering', the jury were fined and imprisoned until eventually released by the Chief Justice who declared 'the right of juries to give their verdict by their conscience'. H. Harman and J. Griffith, *"Justice Deserted"* (NCCL 1979) p.11.

credibility of the witness can be tested. This can lengthen trials because, even where the evidence to be given is uncontroversial, the witness is normally present. Criminal trials still do not use pre-trial written pleadings, although this occurs in civil cases. Such a process would reduce trial length by concentrating on those matters in dispute.

4. The judge acts as umpire, ensuring that the rules on procedure and evidence are followed, directing the jury on the law to be applied and reminding them of the evidence that they have heard.

5. The jury's role is firstly to decide questions of fact—that is, to make up their minds between conflicting accounts as to what happened— and then to decide on the guilt or innocence of the defendant.

The common law trial is regarded as the single, public proceeding, both the beginning and end of the affair. It is difficult to explain why the adversarial process rather than the investigative process should have emerged in England: the relatively short period of absolutist monarchy and the impact of the puritan revolution in reaction to that experience of undiluted state power is one factor; the historical dominance of the local state over the national may be another. It is undoubtedly linked to the retention of private prosecution and the image of a society that was the product of the actions of its more powerful members and not of an interventionist government. But the existence of the adversarial form and of the jury system has always meant that judges have needed to exercise considerable caution and control over the information that could be properly placed before a court.

2. Civil law jurisdictions

In contrast, civilian jurisdictions do not distinguish between the gathering of information and its presentation.[22] These jurisdictions, such as France and Germany, adopt an *investigative* or *inquisitorial* mode of trial and as a result place much less emphasis on *formal* rules of proof which are so significant in common law proceedings. The final trial date is also less pivotal—in France the judge in a criminal trial will have a full *dossier* prepared by the *juge d'instruction*, who may well have conducted several hearings, taken relevant witness statements and interrogated the defendant. The trial will be on the basis of these documents and is merely the final stage of a *judicial* process.

In Europe, several jurisdictions are considering reforms which would allow the defence lawyer to question prosecution witnesses directly—at present questions have to be asked indirectly through the presiding judge. This was one of the reforms in Italy's new Code of Criminal Procedure in 1989.[23] It has been suggested that we are witnessing a rapprochement of, or convergence

---

[22] C. Bradley, "The Convergence of the Continental and the Common Law Model of Criminal Procedure" (1996) 7 Criminal Law Forum 471; P. Fennell (ed.), *Criminal Justice in Europe: A Comparative Study* (Oxford, 1995); G. Brouwer, "Inquisitorial and Adversary Procedures—a Comparative Analysis" (1981) 55 A.L.J.R. 207.

[23] M. Zander, "From Inquisitorial to Adversarial—the Italian Experiment" (1991) 141 N.L.J. 678.

between, the two traditions, prompted by the European Court of Human Rights and a broader emerging recognition that the right of individuals to participate in state processes that affect them are fundamental human rights—that there is a possible emergence of a "European vision of the criminal trial process".[24]

In civilian jurisdictions, there is in theory judicial supervision of the process from the beginning of the investigation which is seen as much more desirable. In 1999, in an address to the Senate, the then French Minister of Justice, Elisabeth Guigou, affirmed her opposition to all things adversarial.

J. Hodgson, "Constructing the Pre-trial Role of the Defence in French Criminal Procedure" (2002) 6 I.J.E.P. 1:

The adversarial system of justice is by nature unfair and unjust. It favours the strong over the weak. It accentuates social and cultural differences, favouring the rich who are able to engage and pay for the services of one or more lawyers. Our own system is better, both in terms of efficiency and of the rights of the individual.[25]

In France, the trial judge will have a full dossier prepared by the *juge d'instruction*, including witness statements and the interrogation of the defendant. The examination of witnesses will be on the basis of these documents. In contrast, the English trial judge will usually know nothing about the case before the trial, will not have been engaged in supervising any investigation, in taking statements from witnesses or the accused or in making bail decisions.

J. Cooper, "Criminal Investigations in France" (1991) 141 N.L.J. 381:

The French system of investigation of serious criminal charges differs from our system in two fundamental respects: in the person who has control over the investigation, and in the way in which the evidence collected in the course of investigation is made available to the ultimate adjudicator, the Cour d'Assises. . .

The police investigative powers are . . . far more limited in France than in this country, and it normal for the police to relinquish control of an investigation within one or two days of arrest, even in the most serious cases. At this stage, the investigation of the case can be taken over by . . . an examining magistrate, the Juge d'instruction. It is when we examine both the training and the powers of the Juge d'instruction that it immediately becomes apparent why the French process of criminal investigation and adjudication of serious criminal charges is so fundamentally different from our own.

---

[24] Mireille Delmas-Marty cited in S. Field and A. West, "Dialogue and the Inquisitorial Tradition: French Defence Lawyers in the Pre-Trial Criminal Process", (2003) 14 Criminal Law Forum 261–316; J. Jackson, "The Effect of Human Rights on Criminal Evidentiary Processes: Towards Convergence, Divergence or Realignment?" 68 Mod. 737.

[25] (2002) 61. J.E. p.1.

Juges d'instruction are young judges recruited on graduation from the National School of the Magistracy . . . All French judges are career judges who have passed through the same route, though not all serve as examining magistrates before taking higher judicial offices. They are not recruited from the senior ranks of practising advocates as in the United Kingdom, and have not themselves been advocates. Their training is in the art of interrogation, criminal investigation, forensic analysis, the sifting and preparation of evidence, psychology and the conduct of a trial. . .

It is important when evaluating the role, value and effect of the Juge d' instruction in the criminal justice process to be clear as to what he or she is setting out to do. . . All civil law systems are grounded in a philosophy of state responsibility and the French system is no exception. Thus, with an infallible Cartesian logic, it is axiomatic to the French system that the Juge d' Instruction, who is charged by the state with establishing the truth, should suffer no procedural or technical hindrance in investigating any matter that may be relevant to establishing guilt or innocence. In this respect individuals' right to a high level of freedom from state intrusion upon their civil liberties can be said to be less important in France than in the United Kingdom. At the same time, it is felt by many observers that fewer guilty people are acquitted in France and more significantly, fewer innocent people are convicted. The investigative powers are so wide, that few stones can be left unturned. . .

The powers seem awesome, and to the civil libertarian brought up in the British system, oppressive, but there are safeguards. First, the suspect is entitled to be represented by a lawyer at all stages of the investigation. Second, the relatively informal and extended nature of the investigation paradoxically allows the defendant far more scope for establishing his or her innocence than under the tightly regulated, formalistic, controlled contact that exists in England or Wales in the investigation of crime, limited as it is to the period before charge, and the occasion of the trial.

Third, the Juge d'instruction is not partie prise. He or she is neither prosecutor (police/CPS) nor defence solicitor. The task of the Juge is to establish whether the state can satisfactorily perform its constitutional function of establishing guilt at a level of "inner certainty". The fact that a Juge d'instruction does not appear in court and has not been trained in the adversarial process cannot be overemphasised. The independence of the office of the Juge from the trial process is quite genuine.

. . . It is not, of course, the Juge d'instruction who determines the guilt of the accused in the French system, nor is it the accused themselves, by pleading guilty. It is the court. Because of the extensive nature of the investigation, however, and the availability to the court of all the findings of that investigation, court hearings in France are relatively short. The only court that sits with a jury is the Cour d'Assises, the lower courts being presided over exclusively by professional judges. As it is a principle of the French system that the adjudicators should have access to all the available evidence, as sifted and analysed by the Juge d' Instruction, the rules of evidence in the Cour d' Assises are scant. The procedure is formal and very much under the direction of the presiding judge (who sits with two assessors). But it lacks the drama and tension of an English criminal trial as there is scant scope for cross-examination or surprise at such an advanced stage of the investigation. There is little eloquent advocacy, and it is normally only the judge who asks questions.

Judicial supervision in France is intended to seek out all relevant information and recent research[26] suggests that there is a cultural commitment to seek out exculpatory as well as inculpatory evidence. But that research also suggests that the inquisitorial tradition based on judicial supervision of police investigations is vulnerable to caseload pressures with magistrates and prosecutors failing to thoroughly scrutinize apparently straightforward cases.

---

[26] S. Field and A. West, *op.cit.* at 316; ; J. Hodgson, (2002) *op.cit.*: J. Hodgson, "The Police, the Prosecutor and the Juge d'Instruction" (2001) 41 Brit J Criminal p.342.

The defence role in the adversarial system is critical in both police station and court, in prompting investigators and magistrates to look below the surface. This is not the way in which the French system routinely operates. Despite some reforms, expansion of custodial legal advice has been resisted as an inappropriate distortion of the judicial search for the truth, privileging the interests of the accused over those of the victim and the public. The adversarial form of trial and the jury system led to significant legal controls to ensure that, at least in theory, only relevant and reliable information reached a trial court. The civilian jurisdictions placed their faith in an official of the state, overseeing the investigation and with many fewer constraints on what evidence may be received. There is an importance of dialogue between the accused, the lawyer and the state in both traditions, designed to bring out a full picture for the final trial. But this dialogue remains an ideal within the French inquisitorial pre-trial process and there are potential challenges to that process as the European Court of Human Rights develops its model of fair trial.

II. Fairness

The law relating to evidence is a technical subject—not only can the legal rules seem (and are) complex but also the pervading discretion given to judges makes the boundaries of those rules seem unclear. But for those studying the subject, it is of primary importance to recognise that these rules and discretions are not simply technical but exist to give substance to certain fundamental principles. Such principles have had a long, albeit chequered, history in the common law but conveniently those principles are now neatly packaged in the European Convention on Human Rights, given statutory expression in English law by the Human Rights Act 1998. As we will see at various points, the rules of evidence seek to prevent information reaching the court which has been obtained by inhumane treatment (Art.3), by breaches of an individual's right to liberty (Art.5) or privacy (Art.8) or where it offends our notions of what constitutes just and fair proceedings (Art.6).

The major principle that affects the rules of evidence and is a characteristic of any legitimate trial is the priority given to fairness—the right to a fair trial. An adversarial/fight model requires rules of engagement based on fairness whereas the inquisitorial model will often emphasise the search for truth as the primary objective. Fairness and justice are abstractions which present great difficulties of definition but have fascinated philosophers ever since Plato rebuked the young Sophist, Thrasymachus, for asserting that justice was whatever the strongest decided it would be. Whatever the substance of "justice" may be, for our purposes there are three categories to which the word may be applied: the justice of the rule, of the outcome and of the procedure. It is the third which is of most importance in studying evidence.

The justice of a particular substantive rule can have political, economic or philosophical overtones. Just because a law has been passed does not render it just. For instance, laws that once supported slavery or that enforced the apartheid regime in South Africa are now considered unjust. Social justice movements with an agenda of redistribution of wealth may question the morality of laws that protect property rights without adequate protection of the poor. But in English courts, the doctrine of sovereignty of Parliament has meant that, until the passage of the Human Rights Act 1998, the courts did not interfere in the substance of a statute. Even now they are limited to declaring that a particular provision is incompatible with the European Convention on Human Rights.

The justice of the outcome may be of two types—the verdict itself may be criticised for being unfair but this often means that it is considered to be wrong and against the weight of the evidence. There is little intervention of any kind with jury deliberations or verdict.[27] But the sanction imposed may also be criticised for its lack of justice—the victim or the victim's relatives often see the punishment as inadequate whereas the defendant may see the same sentence as disproportionate. This raises issues that are beyond the scope of this book.

The justice of the process is immediately relevant and more tangible. When we discuss fairness in the courtroom, we mean that there should be "due process of law" and assume that truth is more likely to emerge from confrontation mediated through identifiable procedures that are compatible with generally accepted standards of fairness, such as the principle of equality of arms enunciated by the European Court of Human Rights. Of course, a fair trial may still arrive at the wrong verdict and due process requires that there be access to a system of appeal. Interestingly, the common law appeal system does not directly address the correctness of the decision itself but is a review of the process by which the decision is reached. If the decision is one which could reasonably have been reached, the Court of Appeal will not interfere.

The root values of procedural justice are encapsulated in the House of Lords' decision in *Woolmington v D.P.P.*

Woolmington v D.P.P. [1935] A.C. 462, *per* Lord Sankey:

Throughout the web of English criminal law one golden thread is always to be seen that it is the duty of the prosecution to prove the prisoner's guilt. . . . If, at the end of and on the whole of the case, there is a reasonable doubt, created by the evidence given by either the prosecution or the prisoner, as to whether the prisoner killed the deceased with a malicious intention, the prosecution has not made out the case and the prisoner is entitled to an acquittal. No matter what the charge or where the trial, the principle that the prosecution must prove the guilt of the prisoner is part of the common law of England and no attempt to whittle it down can be entertained.[28]

Lord Sankey's "golden thread" of justice is that the prosecution have to prove every element in a criminal charge beyond reasonable doubt. In civil

---

[27] But see the criticisms by the Royal Commission on Criminal Justice that the Court of Appeal has been too heavily influenced by the jury decision in its reconsideration of cases, especially those alleging miscarriages of justice: Report Cm. 2263 (1993) Ch.10.

[28] [1935] A.C. 462 at 481.

proceedings, the burden of proof is normally on the claimant. In both, the defendant normally has to prove nothing. This burden of proof is a key element but it is one among many such values, especially in criminal proceedings, such as the right to know the nature of the charges and evidence against you, the right to be represented by a lawyer and the right to cross-examine and test the prosecution evidence.

These procedural rights are now underpinned by s.2 of the Human Rights Act 1998 which provides that courts must take into account rights under the European Convention on Human Rights. Article 6 provides for a "fair and public hearing".

Human Rights Act 1988, Art.6:

1. In the determination of his civil rights and obligations or of any criminal charge against him, everyone is entitled to a fair and public hearing within a reasonable time by an independent and impartial tribunal established by law. Judgment shall be pronounced publicly but the press and public may be excluded from all or part of the trial in the interest of morals, public order or national security in a democratic society, where the interests of juveniles or the protection of the private life of the parties so require, or to the extent strictly necessary in the opinion of the court in special circumstances where publicity would prejudice the interests of justice.
2. Everyone charged with a criminal offence shall be presumed innocent until proved guilty according to law.
3. Everyone charged with a criminal offence has the following minimum rights:
    (a) to be informed promptly, in a language which he understands and in detail, of the nature and cause of the accusation against him;
    (b) to have adequate time and facilities for the preparation of his defence;
    (c) to defend himself in person or through legal assistance of his own choosing or, if he has not sufficient means to pay for legal assistance, to be given it free when the interests of justice so require;
    (d) to examine or have examined witnesses against him and to obtain the attendance and examination of witnesses on his behalf under the same conditions as witnesses against him;
    (e) to have the free assistance of an interpreter if he cannot understand or speak the language used in court

Article 6(1) applies to all proceedings whereas Articles 6(2) and 6(3) apply only to those charged with criminal offences. This is a strong but not an absolute right and can be derogated from where this is necessary and proportional—for example, a trial which involves issues of national security can be held *in camera*.

Article 6 is the central text in discussing pre-trial and trial procedure—everyone is entitled to a fair hearing in front of an independent and impartial court and to a reasoned judgment. But the fairness of a hearing is not to be judged solely by what takes place within the walls of a courtroom. Events and decisions that occur at the investigation stage necessarily affect what goes on in court and hence the fairness of the hearing. For example, if the State were to lead evidence of a confession which is perhaps the result of police coercion or has been made without access to legal advice, this may mean that there has been a breach of Art.3 or 5. This violation will be relevant to the issue whether in such circumstances the hearing can be fair.

A recent example can be seen in the use of evidence obtained by torture. The common law has always forbidden the use of torture to obtain evidence but torture was routinely practised in England in the 16th and early 17th centuries under royal warrants. It was an issue that was important in the struggle between the Crown and the parliamentary common lawyers prior to the English civil war. One of the first acts of the Long Parliament in 1640 was, accordingly, to abolish the Court of Star Chamber, where torture evidence had been received, and in that year the last torture warrant in our history was issued. Holdsworth summarised it in his *History of English Law*.

W. Holdsworth, A History of English Law Vol. 5 (3rd ed. Methuen 1945), pp.194–195:

When we consider the revolting brutality of the continental criminal procedure, when we remember that this brutality was sometimes practised in England by the authority of the extraordinary power of the crown, we cannot but agree that this single result of the rejection of any authority other than that of the common law is almost the most valuable of the many consequences of that rejection. Torture was not indeed practised so systematically in England as on the continent; but the fact that it was possible to have recourse to it, the fact that the most powerful court in the land sanctioned it, was bound sooner or later to have a demoralising effect upon all those who had prisoners in their power. Once torture has become acclimatized in a legal system it spreads like an infectious disease. It saves the labour of investigation. It hardens and brutalizes those who have become accustomed to use it.[29]

It would be reasonable to suppose that such a fundamental principle would not need to be revisited but 400 years later, the government sought to allow the Special Immigrations Appeal Tribunal to rely on evidence obtained by governments abroad using torture in making decisions about indeterminate detention without trial of those suspected of terrorist offences under the Anti-terrorism, Crime and Security Act 2001. In *A v Secretary of State for the Home Department*, the House of Lords held that the principles of common law, standing alone, compelled the exclusion of evidence obtained by torture by a third party as unreliable, unfair, offensive to ordinary standards of humanity and decency, and incompatible with the principles that should animate a tribunal seeking to administer justice. This was an affirmation that rules of evidence rest firmly upon constitutional principles.

Although a breach of other rights may constitute evidence of unfairness, the ultimate issue is the concept of a "fair hearing". The European Court of Human Rights has developed the general themes underlying the concept of a fair hearing which may be applied generally:

[29] Cited by Lord Bingham in *A and v Secretary of State for the Home Department* [2005] UKHL 71 at para.12.

    i. the key constituents of fairness are the independence and impartiality of the court, the openness of the proceedings and the reasoned decision–making;

    ii. Article 6 does not impose a standard code of criminal procedure—different legal cultures have different needs and there is a wide margin of appreciation for States to determine their own procedural requirements and rules of evidence;

    iii. admissibility of evidence is a matter of regulation by national law and it is for the national courts to assess the evidence before them. The Court's task is not to give rulings on whether the evidence was properly admitted but whether the proceedings, taken as a whole, were fair;

    iv. fairness is not simply a matter whether a specific rule is compatible or whether the trial judge has addressed the correct issue. The fairness of a hearing can only be explored by looking at the process as a whole—although the State has infringed some right of the defendant, that does not automatically mean that the cumulative effect of the hearing is unfair;[30]

    v. applicants should show that they have suffered actual detriment as a result of the infringement;

    vi. although Art.6 concerns itself with the rights of the accused, victims and witnesses may well have rights that also need to be protected and the Court may have to balance competing rights;

    vii. crucially the Court judges the fairness of a hearing by the test of 'equality of arms'—that the defendant is put, so far as is possible, on the same level in terms of access to legal advice, to information or to services. The State should not abuse its dominant position so as to gain a substantial advantage vis-à-vis the accused.

Article 6 reinforces rather than merely replicates the common law's requirements for a fair trial. At common law, the judges were reluctant to use their inherent discretion to ensure that the basic elements of a fair trial were met, particularly in relation to pre-trial issues and the manner in which disputed evidence had been obtained. The discretion was very limited as explained by the House of Lords in *Sang*.[31] Here the court was concerned with evidence obtained as a result of the activities of an *agent provocateur*. The House held that the power of the judge to exclude unfairly obtained evidence was restricted to situations where the prejudicial effect of the evidence outweighed any probative weight and to excluding confessions (and analogous evidence) that have been obtained unfairly. The House considered that it was the function of judge to ensure the accused had a fair trial but not to exercise disciplinary powers over the police or prosecution, even where they had acted improperly or even illegally. Dissenting, Lord Scarman's judgment in *Sang* predicted the demands that Art.6 would make.

---

[30] *Barbera, Messegue and Jabardo v Spain* Application No. 10590/83, A 146, (1988) 11 E.H.R.R. 360.
[31] [1979] 2 All E.R. 1222.

Sang [1979] 2 All E.R. 1222, per Lord Scarman:

If the accused is misled or tricked into providing evidence (whether it be an admission or the provision of fingerprints or medical evidence or some other evidence), the rule against self-incrimination, nemo tenetur se ipsum prodere, is likely to be infringed. Each case must, of course, depend on its circumstances. All I would say is that the principle of fairness, though concerned exclusively with the use of evidence at trial, is not susceptible to categorisation or classification, and is wide enough in some circumstances to embrace the way in which, after the crime, evidence is obtained from the accused. . . .[32]

These issues in relation to judicial discretion to exclude evidence are discussed in Ch.4.

Modern law has broadened the scope for judicial intervention—where there has been a significant breach of the right to a fair trial, an English criminal court has two options—it may either halt the proceedings as an abuse of process[33] or it can exclude the specific item of evidence under s.78 of the Police and Criminal Evidence Act 1984 which states:

Police and Criminal Evidence Act 1983, s.78:

In any proceedings the court may refuse to allow evidence on which the prosecution proposes to rely if it appears to the court that, having regard to all the circumstances in which the evidence was obtained, the admission of that evidence would have such an adverse effect on the fairness of the proceedings that the court ought not to admit it.

This section was the result of an initial amendment tabled by Lord Scarman to enable courts to exclude evidence on the basis of police malpractice. Judicial concern with the fairness of the proceedings is now no longer limited to the courtroom. The discretion to exclude evidence in the interests of fairness should encompass the treatment of the accused from the start of the investigation and any abuse of their position by the state agencies involved.

Discovering the Truth or Doing Justice?

Procedural rights, especially in relation to the rules of evidence, are often seen to take precedence over the justice of the decision itself and over more pragmatic aims such as the determination of truth or law enforcement.

J. Frank, Courts on Trial (Princeton, 1973), pp.103–104:

[Substantive] rules, it is said, state what a man may or may not lawfully do out of court, before any litigation occurs. The orthodox theory holds that, from those rules,

---

[32] *ibid.* at 1247d.
[33] *Loosely* [2001] 4 All E.R. 897.

grow 'substantive legal rights', such as the right not to have others trespass on one's land or the right to have a contract performed. . .

But if one of a man's 'substantive' rights has been invaded, or threatened with invasion, and he does bring a law-suit, the suit is supposed to be governed by another kind of rules, rules of 'procedure', which relate to what must be done in court. Those conduct-in-court rules cover such subjects as the way a suit must be commenced, the way in which a party must state ('plead') his claim or defence, the sort of evidence the courts will receive or reject. These 'procedural' rules are customarily designated as 'adjective', or 'remedial', or 'dependent' or 'subordinate'. These labels indicate that these rules are really subordinate, are mere means or 'machinery', used in vindicating the rights given by the 'substantive' rules, rules which supposedly pre-exist and are independent of what any court may do about them.

That notion of the 'subordinate' character of 'procedure' may easily mislead. For the failure of a lawyer to comply with a procedural rule. . . . may spell a litigant's defeat in a law-suit, completely frustrating his 'substantive' right. Such a defeat, for 'procedural' errors, is fully as disastrous to him as if the court held that he had no such right.

Instead, then, of saying, 'If certain facts occur, a court will attach to them certain legal consequences,' we might say, 'If certain facts occur, and if the procedural rules are complied with, a court will attach these consequences.' A more accurate way of stating the matter is this: 'If certain facts are 'proved', in accordance with the requirements and within the limits allowed by the procedural rules, then a favourable decision should result.' Which is to say that, practically, 'procedure' shows up as fully as important as the 'substantive' rules. Indeed, the differentiation between the 'substantive' and 'procedural' rules, although useful for some purposes, is artificial from at least one viewpoint: All the rules, including the 'substantive' may be looked at as 'procedural' in the sense that they are all merely weapons in the courtroom fight.

Were we to start from scratch and invent a mechanism to find out facts and allocate blame, the solution would not be an adversarial system, with partisan advocates, untrained judges, reliant heavily on cross-examination and where the final decision is left to 12 people plucked arbitrarily off the street. The goal of discovering the truth and making a reliable decision might require a trained chairperson with investigative powers, sitting with assessors expert in the relevant field and with the parties' representatives having a much lower profile. Lord Woolf's review[34] of the impact of adversarialism in civil process made much of the need for more effective and efficient procedures:

Lord Woolf, Access to Justice: Interim Report (Lord Chancellor's Dept. June 1995), Ch.3:

3. By tradition the conduct of civil litigation in England and Wales, as in other common law jurisdictions, is adversarial. Within a framework of substantive and procedural law established by the state for the resolution of civil disputes, the main responsibility for the initiation and conduct of proceedings rests with the parties to each individual case, and it is normally the plaintiff who sets the pace. The role of the judge is to adjudicate on issues selected by the parties when they choose to present them to the court.

[34] Lord Woolf, *Access to Justice Interim Report* (Lord Chancellor's Dept. June 1995)— *www.dca.gov.uk/civil/interim/woolf.htm*; the final report was published in July 1996—*dca.gov.uk/ civil/final/index.htm*

4. Without effective judicial control, however, the adversarial process is likely to encourage an adversarial culture and to degenerate into an environment in which the litigation process is too often seen as a battlefield where no rules apply. In this environment, questions of expense, delay, compromise and fairness may have only low priority. The consequence is that expense is often excessive, disproportionate and unpredictable; and delay is frequently unreasonable.

5. This situation arises precisely because the conduct, pace and extent of litigation are left almost completely to the parties. There is no effective control of their worst excesses. Indeed, the complexity of the present rules facilitates the use of adversarial tactics and is considered by many to require it. As Lord Williams, a former Chairman of the Bar Council, said in responding to the announcement of this Inquiry, the process of law has moved from being "servant to master, due to cost, length and uncertainty".

6. It is often said that the existing rules and practice directions contain the solution to the present problems, if only litigation were to be conducted in accordance with them. But the present system does not ensure this. Instead the rules are flouted on a vast scale. The timetables they contain are generally ignored and their other requirements are complied with when convenient to the interests of one of the parties and not otherwise.

7. The powers of the courts have fallen behind the more sophisticated and aggressive tactics of some litigators. The orders for costs which are made are an ineffective sanction applied after the damage is done. The delay in being able to obtain effective intervention by the court both encourages rule-breaking and discourages the party who would be prejudiced from applying for preventive measures.

8. It is significant that the main procedural tools for conducting litigation efficiently have each become subverted from their proper purpose. Whether through incompetence or deliberation, pleadings often fail to state the facts as the rules require. This leads to a fundamental deficiency, namely the failure to establish the issues in the case at a reasonably early stage, from which many problems result.

9. Witness statements, a sensible innovation aimed at a "cards on the table" approach, have in a very short time begun to follow the same route as pleadings, with the draftsman's skill often used to obscure the original words of the witness.

10. The scale of discovery, at least in the larger cases, is completely out of control. The principle of full, candid disclosure in the interests of justice has been devalued because discovery is pursued without sufficient regard to economy and efficiency in terms of the usefulness of the information which is likely to be obtained from the documents disclosed.

11. The approach to expert evidence also shows the characteristic range of difficulties: instead of the expert assisting the court to resolve technical problems, delay is caused by the unreasonable insistence on going to unduly eminent members of the profession and evidence is undermined by the partisan pressure to which party experts are subjected.[35]

Many of the issues raised by Lord Woolf have been addressed, not least in the reformed Civil Procedure Rules issued under the Civil Procedure Act 1997.[36] The main points were:

1. Litigation was to be a last resort, with litigants given financial incentives to settle.
2. Judges to become trial managers, setting timetables, capping costs and imposing sanctions.

---

[35] *ibid.*, ch.3.
[36] *www.dca.gov.uk/civil/procrules_fin/menus/rules.htm*

3. Alternative dispute resolution to be encouraged through information points and legal aid funding.
4. Single set of rules for all civil courts and new trial centres.

Effectiveness and efficiency are the key words in public sector management and civil procedure has not been immune.

In criminal procedure, some[37] have followed Frank in attacking the ritual formality of the trial, arguing that priority is not given to truth determination and the substantive justice of the decision itself. For such commentators, the most sacred of cows is not immune: where is the logic in the presumption of innocence, even, when an accused's very appearance before a court makes it more likely than not (as most defendants plead guilty) that they committed the offence?[38] It was suggested that the Anglo–American criminal procedure detracts from the discovery of the truth. The Labour government accepted the premise that the criminal justice system was tilted towards the interests of the defendant and set out to tilt the scales in favour of the victim—in the Criminal Justice Act 2003, they provided for non-jury trials, for re-trials after acquittals, for easier introduction of the defendant's previous convictions and for the relaxation of the rules excluding hearsay evidence.

But do such arguments, especially in relation to criminal proceedings, ignore the symbolic force which lies in a trial's procedural justice? The rules of evidence and procedure emphasise the distinction between the trial as a logical function and the trial as a symbol. In its outward form, the trial is about the determination of truth and the application of that truth to legal rules. Were we to compare the courtroom with a police station, what would be the public reaction if a court were to interrogate a defendant over days and nights with limited rest, no legal assistance, perhaps using the threat of violence or the inducement of release to obtain responses to questions? In the court, the accused's rights are paramount because the covert function of the trial is its concrete illustration of a fair and just society. An example of this is the Scottsboro case[39] which involved an alleged gang rape of two white girls by nine black teenagers on the Southern Railroad freight run from Chattanooga to Memphis on March 25, 1931. No crime in American history—let alone a crime that never occurred—produced as many trials, convictions, reversals, and retrials.

T. Arnold, The Symbols of Government (Harbinger, 1962), pp.141–143:

. . .If the Alabama court in the Scottsboro case dared to say as a matter of principle negroes were not entitled to sit on juries and that negroes who had intercourse with

---

[37] R. Mark, *Minority Verdict* (Dimbleby Lecture BBC, 1973)

[38] R. Cross, "The Right to Silence and the Presumption of Innocence—Sacred Cows or Safeguards of Liberty" (1970) 11 J.S.P.T.L. 66.

[39] *www.pbs.org/wgbh/amex/scottsboro/*; Horne, G., *Powell v. Alabama: The Scottsboro Boys and American Justice* (1997).

white women were to be treated as white men who had committed rape, we would find a calm atmosphere about the trial which is now completely lacking. The negroes might be convicted but the trial would have been fair. The Southern court, however, did not have that confidence in the reasonableness of its conduct which permitted it to spread frankly on the record. Therefore the trial became a maze of attempts to keep relevant material out of the record. Blunders occurred so obviously against the accepted form of a trial that the Supreme Court of the United States reversed the case.[40]

Yet the cultural value of the ideal of a fair trial is advanced as much by its failure as it is by its success. Any violation of the symbol of a ceremonial trial rouses persons who would be left unmoved by an ordinary non-ceremonial injustice. Thus the Scottsboro Case gained nationwide attention. The defendants may finally be hanged, but the cause of tolerance has been dramatised in a way no one will quite forget. Harmless anarchists may be shot by the police in a strike. Liberals will be sorry and forget. But let them be unfairly treated by a court. . . . and, before the dissatisfaction has died away, the prejudice or phobia which created the unfair atmosphere of the trial will receive a public analysis and examination which otherwise it would not get. . .

It is of course true that all the machinery surrounding the ideal of a fair trial has its social cost in delays, technicalities and injustices in the judicial process. It is equally true that in times of public fear and intolerance this machinery is seldom strong enough to prevent the conviction of weak and harmless persons. Yet the cultural effect of these failures on mass psychology is probably worth everything it costs because of its contribution to the ultimate survival of a great humanitarian ideal.

A miscarriage of justice in any country always calls into question whether that society can characterise itself as a just society. It also questions the adequacy of the constitutional constraints on state power. Unlike civil process, criminal justice has functions other than the simply instrumental and, as Thurman Arnold argues, the ideal of the fair trial needs maintaining and protecting.

IV. TAKING FACTS SERIOUSLY

When mobilised, the legal process contains several distinct stages—parties will gather and marshal information, they will reveal that information to the other parties and engage in formal and informal pre-trial meetings to negotiate an outcome or to shape the trial proceedings. The final act is to participate in the contested trial itself. In all of these stages, "facts" play a key part. The substantive law (of crime or tort) will determine what needs to be proved and parties need to gather their witness statements, their documentary paper trail, and any forensic evidence. In gathering together this information, two complementary issues need to be borne in mind.

1. The first is the rules used by the courts themselves as to what information may be presented to the courts.
2. The second deals with the principles of proof—what does the information available prove? Decisions should be reached by a process of rational inquiry and it is necessary to explore those logical

---

[40] *Powell v Alabama* (1932) 278 US 45, *Patterson v Alabama* (1934) 294 US 600.

processes by which inferences drawn from the information presented to the court, facts are established and decisions reached.

For both, it is necessary to define the terms and establish clear categories
and concepts.

A. *Basic Concepts*

1. Evidence.

At its most general level, this term means those items of information which
are gathered by the parties as part of the fact–investigation process and then
presented to the court as a step towards persuading the court that their
argument is correct—in other words, information collected and advanced to
prove a case. The court does not permit all information to be placed before
it—it must be relevant, have probative weight, be non–prejudicial and not
subject to any rule of exclusion. If the information possesses these characteristics, it is *admissible evidence*, often known as judicial evidence.

The information placed before the court can be of different types: oral
testimony by witnesses, normally of their perceptions, especially what they
have seen or heard, but perhaps also the opinions of expert witnesses;
documents, often written but now frequently containing visual or sound
recordings or electronic data; real evidence, namely material objects such as
fingerprints, automatic recordings or a witness's demeanour.

(i) *direct*: evidence can also be divided into *direct* and *circumstantial* evidence.
Direct evidence is evidence which, if believed, establishes a *fact in issue*. For
example, an eyewitness to a stabbing testifies to the fact of the wounding, an
element of the offence. Such testimony, if believed, would constitute direct
evidence, as would other items such as the accused's confession

(ii) *circumstantial*: this consists of evidence of circumstances, none of which
speak directly to the facts in issue but from which those facts may be inferred.
Circumstantial evidence is usually not as good as direct evidence because it is
easy to make the wrong inference—scientists would normally use it only to
support other forms of evidence. Circumstantial evidence has to be evaluated
with care—where items of evidence point in one direction, it can be highly
persuasive but it may be a false trail and the prosecution must establish that
the evidence points only to one conclusion, excluding all other reasonable
possibilities consistent with the evidence. Were someone to be charged with
theft of money, and were then shown to have bought expensive items, those
purchases might be regarded as circumstantial evidence of the individual's
guilt. Feelings of animosity towards the victim, presence in the area of the
attack, the victim's blood on the accused's clothing—all of these can build up
into a strong but inferential case. Individual items of information may be of

greater or lesser weight, but the jury must take a view of the combination of circumstances. The classic statement is by Pollock CB in *Exall*.

Exall [1866] 4 F.&F. 922 at 929, *per* Pollock C.B.:

It has been said that circumstantial evidence is to be considered as a chain, and each piece of evidence as a link in the chain, but this is not so, for then, if any one link break, the chain would fall. It is more like the case of a rope comprised of several cords. One strand of the cord might be insufficient to sustain the weight, but three stranded together may be quite of sufficient strength. Thus it may be in circumstantial evidence—there may be a combination of circumstances, no one of which would raise a reasonable conviction or more than a reasonable suspicion; but the three taken together may create a conclusion of guilt with as much certainty as human affairs can require or admit of.

(iii) *collateral*: collateral evidence is information which does not in itself seek to prove any of the facts in issue in a case. In any trial there is the question of credibility, namely whether the direct or circumstantial evidence which has been adduced is to be believed. This depends on several factors, such as the testimony's consistency with the other evidence in the case. But very significantly we weigh the probative value of evidence by the credibility that we attach to its source. The word of a priest is treated with greater weight than that of a convicted confidence trickster. In cross-examining witnesses, a party is entitled to question on such collateral issues such as character, not because it bears on any fact in issue but because it affects the weight which the trier of fact will attach to the testimony.

2. Facts.

The Oxford English Dictionary tells us that a fact is,

Something that has really occurred or is actually the case; something certainly known to be of this character; hence, a particular truth known by actual observation or authentic testimony, as opposed to what is merely inferred, or to a conjecture or fiction; a datum of experience, as distinguished from the conclusions that may be based upon it.

The legal use of the word "fact" is more cloudy than this—not least in the sense that lawyers would regard an inference, properly drawn, as a fact to be relied on. The word is used in three distinct contexts.

(1) *information*:
the first of these corresponds to the term "evidence" discussed above. It is the information provided by oral testimony and other evidence. Who was where when? and with whom? what did they do? Often police witnesses have been

known to start their testimony with, *"The facts in this case are. . ."*. While the witnesses may be sincere in what they say, such testimony is not 'facts', let alone proof. What the witness provides for the court is simply items of information, data, which the trier of fact has to assess. The trier may or may not believe the testimony, may draw inferences from it but must decide what the facts in the case are, in other words, "What happened".

(2) *facts as found*:
the second context is where the trier of fact evaluates the information presented in court and comes to a conclusion as to what happened. Here we are close to the dictionary sense of *"something that has really occurred or is actually the case"*. But a court determines this as a matter of probability—that it is "more probable than not" that this happened or that they are sure "beyond reasonable doubt". What the trier of fact has done is to create an authoritative version, namely legally established facts which will not be litigated again.[41]

(3) *facts in issue*:
the final use of "fact" is in the phrase, facts in issue. This phrase does not approach the dictionary definition as here we are dealing with the legal concepts that are to be found in the substantive law, in the statute or precedent which creates the offence or the cause of action. These must be established if a particular party to legal proceedings is to succeed. For example, on a theft charge, the prosecution must prove five elements: that the defendant appropriated property belonging to another, dishonestly and with the intention to permanently deprive. These are the facts in issue.[42] In a simple theft case, if the prosecution can show that the accused walked out of a shop with goods which were not paid for, the court is likely to conclude from these, intermediate, facts that all the elements of the offence, the facts in issue, are satisfied. In a civil action, there may be an issue as to whether there was a contract in existence and the court would have to be satisfied that there had been an offer, an acceptance, consideration and any necessary intention. Such notions are not facts but abstractions—you do not see, hear or taste offer and acceptance although you may well hear words from which the law will infer that these exist. The party bearing the burden of proof must persuade the court of the existence of these if they wish to have a favourable finding.

In the shoplifting example, the jury can hear a store detective's information about a shoplifter taking whisky from the shelf, concealing it under a coat and leaving the shop. They may hear the defendant explain how she had simply forgotten the bottle when she paid for other items. This is straightfor-

---

[41] There are exceptions to this—appeals from magistrates' courts to Crown Court will be a rehearing of the facts of the case; new evidence may be presented in some criminal appeals to the Court of Appeal.

[42] A fact in issue is often known as "factum probandum" or (plural) "facta probanda", those legal elements that need to be proved.

wardly evidence, some of which may be believed by the jury, some of which may be disbelieved. From the evidence, the jury may conclude that she did take the bottle and that she never intended to pay for it. These are now the facts as found by the court and both are clearly important and relevant but logically they are intermediary facts since there is a further step to be taken since the jury must use these facts to determine whether they establish the facts in issue. The taking of the bottle and the intent not to pay are not in themselves the facts in issue but are facts which are relevant to the facts in issue.[43] The jury must now use those facts to consider whether there was a dishonest appropriation contrary to section 1 of the Theft Act 1968.

3. Admissibility.

In an ideal world with unlimited resources of time and money, there should perhaps be a principle of free proof, whereby litigants are free to put any information that they choose before the court which then applies basic principles of inferential reasoning to them. Rules of evidence, exceptions to such a principle, would then be unnecessary. More pragmatically constraints are placed on parties as to the information which they wish to place before the court to establish their case. The information must be admissible evidence, often referred to as judicial evidence. The following criteria must be satisfied if evidence is to be admissable.

  (a) be relevant,
  (b) have sufficient weight,
  (c) have probative value that outweighs any prejudicial effect,
  (d) not have an adverse effect on the fairness of the proceedings,
  (e) not be excluded by any specific rule of evidence.

4. Relevance.

This is a central concept. Relevant evidence is prima facie admissible unless excluded for some other reason whereas irrelevant evidence is not admissible. The probative value of evidence depends on its relevance allied to the weight accorded to it. We define relevant information as information which tends to make the existence or non-existence of another relevant fact or fact in issue more or less probable. Under the US Federal Rules of Evidence, r.401 states,

Federal Rules of Evidence, r.401:

'Relevant evidence' means evidence having any tendency to make the existence of any fact that is of consequence to the determination of the action more probable or less probable than it would be without the evidence.

---

[43] They are referred to as facta probantes—facts from which we derive facts in issue

Relevance is not an inherent characteristic of any item of evidence but exists only as a relation between an item of evidence and some other matter which requires to be proved. It is sufficiently relevant when it renders the existence of the other matter 'more probable or less probable'. But any item of evidence should not be considered in isolation but its relevance considered in the context of the evidence as a whole.

The appeal courts have tended not to lay down guidelines as to what constitutes relevance, leaving it to the trial judge's judgment. But they will interfere with that discretion when the evidence excluded is relevant or that admitted is irrelevant. There is an example of the proper exclusion of irrelevant evidence in *Gadsby*,[44] where the appellant had been convicted of attempting to murder his wife through arson. G sought to adduce evidence that another person, L, had the opportunity to place the device, and had a previous conviction for arson. The trial judge refused to admit evidence on the grounds that it was not relevant. The Court of Appeal agreed pointing out that the offence had occurred when L was a teenager, more than 20 years earlier, and that she had set fire to a box of toys in her bedroom after an argument with her mother. That conviction did not make it more probable that L had set the device and tried to kill her sister-in-law.

To decide whether an item of evidence is relevant, it is essential to identify both the item of evidence AND the fact in issue that it is adduced to prove. Diametrically opposed views on whether an item was relevant were expressed by members of the House of Lords in *Kearley*.[45] The Dorset police raided a flat occupied by the appellant, his wife and one other person. In the course of the raid they recovered a relatively small quantity of amphetamine. While on the premises, the police encountered visitors to the flat and answered the phone. Many of the callers requested drugs from "Chippie", the appellant's nickname. Since the actual amount of drugs and money discovered in the flat were not enough to raise an irresistible presumption that the accused was in possession of the drugs "with intent to supply", the prosecution sought to rely on the testimony of police officers who had heard these requests. The testimony in *Kearley* is objectionable on several grounds, not least that it was hearsay from an unidentified source and opinion evidence. The appeal raised issues of hearsay but also the question whether a telephone caller's belief that the accused was a drug supplier was at all relevant to proving the accused's intent to supply? The majority of the House regarded the evidence as irrelevant and would exclude it.

Kearley [1992] 2 All E.R. 345, at 370 *per* Lord Oliver:

The first inquiry must be: is it relevant evidence? For nothing that is not relevant is admissible. 'Relevant' cannot, I think, be better defined than in art. 1 of Stephen's Digest of the Law of Evidence[46], that is to say that the word means that–

---

[44] [2005] EWCA Crim 3206.
[45] [1992] 2 All E.R. 345; see also *Harry* (1988) 86 Cr.App.R. 105.
[46] 12th ed., (1936) p.4.

Any two facts to which it is applied are so related to each other that according to the common course of events one either taken by itself or in connection with other facts proves or renders probable the past, present or future existence or non-existence of the other

To put it, perhaps more succinctly, a fact to be relevant must be probative, and if one asks whether the fact that a large number of persons called at the premises seeking to purchase from 'Chippie' renders probable the existence of a person at the premises called 'Chippie' who is willing to supply drugs, the answer can, I think, only be in the affirmative. But the difficulty here is that it is only the combination of the facts (a) that persons called, (b) that they asked for 'Chippie' and (c) that they requested drugs which renders the evidence relevant. The mere fact that people telephoned or called, in itself, is irrelevant, for it neither proves nor renders probable any other fact. In order to render evidence of the calls relevant and therefore admissible there has to be added the additional element of what the callers said, and it is here that the difficulty arises. What was said—in each case a request for drugs—is, of course probative of the state of mind of the caller. But the state of mind of the caller is not the fact in issue and is, in itself, irrelevant, for it is not probative of anything other than its own existence. It becomes relevant only if and so far as the existence of other facts can be inferred from it. .

The first item to note is Lord Oliver's use of Stephen's definition of relevance which talks of the existence of one fact which "... *proves or renders probable*. . . " another fact. This appears a higher threshold of relevance than the Federal Rules of Evidence which would see a fact as relevant if it changes the probabilities of the existence of another fact. Thus if a student were to tell me that another student were a drug dealer, I would conclude that it is more likely that the latter were a drug dealer than it had been five minutes ago. Although the first student's statement does not "... *prove or render probable*. . . " that fact, it certainly changes (albeit ever so slightly) the probabilities.

Their Lordships also felt that, if the relevance of one caller's evidence was zero, the relevance of a dozen callers was also zero. If the entire seminar group all tell me that the particular student is the local drug dealer, I conclude much more readily that this is the case. A single person's belief might have little probative weight but it does have some. When many witnesses are willing to testify that you possess that characteristic, not only is such testimony sufficiently relevant but it has much more weight. Would the House have reached the same conclusion if the evidence related not to the accused possessing intent to supply but a violent temper?[47]

The minority in the House also agreed that the callers' beliefs were irrelevant as a means of directly proving the accused's intent but argued that the majority were focusing on the wrong issue—the correct issue was that the premises were resorted to by people seeking to buy drugs and the evidence of the requests for drugs was very relevant to establishing the use of the premises. Although the use of the premises was not a fact in issue in the case, it was immediately relevant to a fact in issue—if the premises were being used to sell drugs, there had to be a dealer with intent to supply on those premises.

---

[47] But note that even if you were to conclude that such evidence is *relevant*, there are other compelling reasons not to admit such an unverified police account.

Kearley [1992] 2 All E.R. 345, at 383–384 *per* Lord Browne-Wilkinson:

The evidence was, in my judgment, relevant because it showed that there were people resorting to the premises for the purposes of obtaining drugs from Chippie. Although evidence of the existence of such would-be buyers is not, by itself, conclusive, the existence of a substantial body of potential customers provides some evidence which a jury could take into account in deciding whether the accused had an intent to supply. The existence of a contemporaneous potential market to buy drugs from Chippie, by itself, shows that there was an opportunity for the accused to supply drugs.

In order to eliminate, for the purpose of considering relevance only, the complication that the purpose of the callers can only be demonstrated by the words that the callers use, I will seek to demonstrate the position by reference to a case where no such recourse is necessary. Suppose a shop which has a sole proprietor and sells only coffee. Say the issue is whether the proprietor had an intent to supply coffee. On a particular day there was a long queue of persons at the door of the shop waiting for it to open. Evidence of the existence of the queue would surely be admissible towards proving an intent to supply. The presence of potential purchasers is circumstantial evidence from which a jury can draw the inference that the shopkeeper was going to supply coffee. There can be no supply without persons to whom supply is made: if the existence of such persons is shown, that provides evidence of the opportunity for supply. . .

. . . In my view therefore the fact that there were a number of people seeking to buy drugs was legally relevant and admissible as showing that there was a market to which the accused could sell, even though such evidence was also capable of giving rise to an impermissible secondary inference, viz that the callers believed Chippie supplied drugs. If the callers themselves had given evidence at the trial and said only that on the relevant day they had made a call for the purpose of obtaining drugs from Chippie, I can see no ground on which such evidence could have been excluded as being irrelevant.

This is a satisfactory way of admitting the evidence—the relevance of the evidence is not to the fact in issue but to a fact relevant to that fact in issue. A chain of inference establishes the ultimate intent: the caller's opinion is not evidence of intent but merely evidence of the existence of the use of the premises for selling drugs; the fact that a market for drugs exists at those premises compels the inference that there is a person supplying drugs at the flat. From that subsequent fact, a juror may infer that it was the accused that possessed the intent to supply drugs.[48]

The threshold that an item of evidence must overcome to be sufficiently relevant is not a high one and allows considerable leeway to admit items that are essentially background in character and which are offered as an aid to understanding. But this can encompass marginal circumstantial evidence and the Royal Commission on Criminal Justice felt that the criterion of relevance was too widely interpreted by judges, allowing time-wasting by counsel and forcing juries to sit through evidence which adds little to what was already before them. A more "robust" approach would be encouraged by the powers under r.403 of the US Federal Rules of Evidence.

---

[48] The testimony may be relevant and probative but these aspects must be weighed against other key principles, namely the prejudicial effect of introducing the evidence of the callers' requests. Although not told expressly, a sensible juror will inevitably conclude that the defendant has supplied drugs before and is doing it again.

Federal Rules of Evidence, r.403:

Although relevant, evidence may be excluded if its probative value is substantially outweighed by the danger of unfair prejudice, confusion of the issues or misleading the jury, or by considerations of undue delay, waste of time, or needless presentation of cumulative evidence.

A more limited reform has been introduced by s.126 of the Criminal Justice Act 2003 to prevent the proliferation of marginal hearsay evidence,

Criminal Justice Act 2003, s.126:

(1) In criminal proceedings the court may refuse to admit a statement as evidence of a matter stated if–
    (a) the statement was made otherwise than in oral evidence in the proceedings, and
    (b) the court is satisfied that the case for excluding the statement, taking account of the danger that to admit it would result in undue waste of time, substantially outweighs the case for admitting it, taking account of the value of the evidence.

5. Weight.

Weight and relevance make up the probative value of evidence. The weight given to any item of evidence is a matter for the jury. It is for them to assess the credibility of a witness, the extent to which the information is consistent with other evidence in the case and the reliance that can be placed upon it. Although weight and relevance are logically distinct, the more direct and relevant an item of information, the greater weight attaches to it and the harder it is to rebut. For example, incriminating statements made in the police station are very difficult to retract at any later stage in the proceedings as judges and juries give such weight to the fact of a confession that they appear willing to overlook internal inconsistencies in the statement or evidence of oppressive circumstances in which it was made.

6. Prejudice.

The term "prejudice" has several meanings, the first of which revolves around the idea of a preconceived opinion, bias or leaning. For a trial court to be prejudiced in the sense of lacking impartiality or favouring one party against another is an obvious breach of the right to a fair trial. For example, jurors may be biased. The test is not one of actual bias but of apparent bias. This may be a ground for quashing the conviction if a reasonable person would consider that there was a real danger of bias on the part of the trier of fact.[49] The European Court of Human Rights applies a similar test but one

---

[49] *Gough* [1993] 2 All E.R. 724.

which would appear to place a heavy burden of proof on the applicant to displace the presumption that a tribunal has acted impartially. In *Pullar v UK*[50] one of the jurors was an employee of the main prosecution witness and knew another of the prosecution witnesses and yet the Court held that the risk of bias was not objectively justified. The same outcome occurred in *Gregory v UK*[51] where the judge received a note from a juror suggesting that some of the jurors were racially prejudiced. The judge investigated the matter and gave a clear direction to the jury on the issue and no violation occurred.

The issue of potential prejudice also affects the question whether evidence should be placed before the jury. The general common law rule was stated in *Sang*.

Sang [1979] 2 All E.R. 1222 at 1230, *per* Lord Diplock:

A fair trial according to law involves, in the case of a trial on indictment, that it should take place before a judge and a jury; that the case against the accused should be proved to the satisfaction of the jury beyond all reasonable doubt on evidence that is admissible in law; and, as a corollary to this, that there should be excluded from the jury information about the accused which is likely to have an influence on their minds prejudicial to the accused which is out of proportion to the true probative value of admissible evidence conveying that information.

Here we must distinguish two other meanings of 'prejudice.' The first of these is that of general detriment or harm but Lord Diplock is not using the term in this sense as all evidence produced by one party should be detrimental to the other party's position. He is referring to a more specific idea, namely where a court forms a judgment before proper consideration— pre-judging the issues. The traditional example of the exclusion of such evidence is that of bad character—the rule was that previous convictions were normally not admissible evidence against the accused. The rationale was that where the defendant was charged with burglary, proof of previous convictions for burglary may well lead the jury to conclude that they are guilty of this offence as well without proper consideration of the strength of the prosecution case on this particular charge.

A. Zuckerman, The Principles of Criminal Evidence (OUP, Oxford, 1989), pp.222–223:

At the simplest level such proof may lead to an exaggerated estimation of the probative value of previous crimes and other deviant conduct. . . Evidence of previous

---

[50] Application No. 22399/93 (1996) 22 E.H.R.R. 39.
[51] Application No.22299/93 (1997) 25 E.H.R.R. 57; see in *Sanders v UK* Application No.34129/96 [2000] Crim. L.R. 767.

crimes might not only distort the inferential process; it could also threaten two central principles of our criminal justice. The first is that in any criminal trial the accused stands to be tried, acquitted or convicted only in respect of the offence with which he is charged. The second is that conviction must take place only if the jury are persuaded of the accused's guilt beyond all reasonable doubt. . .

On being informed that the accused has committed other crimes in the past a jury may decide that the accused deserves punishment whether or not he is guilty of the offence charged. As Wigmore put it, the 'deep tendency of human nature to punish, not because our victim is guilty this time, but because he is a bad man and may as well be condemned now that he is caught, is a tendency which cannot fail to operate with any jury, in or out of court.'[52] This could happen where there is a feeling that the accused got away on previous occasions without conviction or with unduly light punishment; or where the accused is charged with a particular act of prohibited homosexual conduct but a stigma attaches to the sexual inclination as such. In these situations—and there may be many others—there is a real possibility that the jury's verdict will reflect their judgment about the accused's character rather than their findings about the commission of the offence charged.

The admissibility of the accused's previous convictions (or other evidence of bad character) is now determined under s.101(1) of the Criminal Justice Act 2003, in particular (1)(d) which talks of the information being ". . . *relevant to an important matter in issue.*" In *Weir*[53] the Court of Appeal stated that the previous test, which balanced probative value against prejudicial effect, was obsolete in the sense that the trial court must initially decide whether the evidence is relevant. But, having made that decision, the trial judge must then apply s.101(3) which requires that the admission of the evidence shall not have an adverse effect on the fairness of the proceedings—here, of course, the prejudicial impact in relation to any true probative value must be considered.

Prejudice is a particular problem in criminal proceedings, with lay magistrates or juries. Traditionally, the rules of evidence sought to combat prejudice by excluding those specific items of information that were considered to be prejudicial. However, the 2003 reforms mean that the accused's past disreputable conduct will be presented as part of the prosecution case in many more trials.

A. Zuckerman. The Principles of Criminal Evidence (OUP, Oxford, 1989), p.245:

Since in common sense a criminal record would often be relevant to guilty, such a direction suggests that there is some special legal rule to be observed here. By creating a conflict between the normal standards familiar to the jury and legal standards, the judges have limited their own ability to guide the jury because juries are unlikely to defer to a legal standard which they do not understand or for which they have no sympathy.

A more effective way of combating prejudice would be to bring into the open the scope of prejudice created by evidence of past criminal record and strive to persuade

---

[52] *Wigmore on Evidence*, (3rd ed., 1940), Vol.1; s.57.
[53] [2005] EWCA Crim 2866 at para.36 *per* Lord Kennedy.

juries that the principles of criminal justice, which require resisting prejudice, reflect their own perceptions of justice. . .[54]

Juries need to be given more help in assessing their own prejudice.

Hanson [2005] EWCA Crim. 824, *per* Rose L.J.:

18. . . in any case in which evidence of bad character is admitted to show propensity, whether to commit offences or to be untruthful the Judge in summing-up should warn the jury clearly against placing undue reliance on previous convictions. Evidence of bad character cannot be used simply to bolster a weak case, or to prejudice the minds of a jury against a defendant. In particular, the jury should be directed; that they should not conclude that the defendant is guilty or untruthful merely because he has these convictions. That, although the convictions may show a propensity, this does not mean that he has committed this offence or been untruthful in this case; that whether they in fact show a propensity is for them to decide; that they must take into account what the defendant has said about his previous convictions; and that, although they are entitled, if they find propensity as shown, to take this into account when determining guilt, propensity is only one relevant factor and they must assess its significance in the light of all the other evidence in the case.

7. Exclusionary rules.

Even where the evidence proferred is relevant, with sufficient probative weight and non-prejudicial, it might still be the subject of an exclusionary rule. The major rules of exclusion are ones dealing with opinion, character, public interest and hearsay and are discussed in detail later. The first three are perhaps self-explanatory. Hearsay, though, is the one of the most important concepts in evidence.

The common law rule prohibits adducing hearsay statements as evidence. The classic statement of the rule was formulated by Cross.

C. Tapper, Cross and Tapper on Evidence (10th ed., Butterworths, 2004), p.578:

an assertion other than one made by a person while giving oral evidence in the proceedings is inadmissible as evidence of any fact asserted.[55]

Despite considerable criticism, until 2005, the rule remained stubbornly in force.[56] Even after the reforms introduced by s.114 of the Criminal Justice Act

---

[54] Zuckerman, *op.cit.* p.245.

[55] C. Tapper, *Cross and Tapper on Evidence* (10th ed., Butterworths, 2004), p.578. This formula was approved by the House of Lords in *Sharp* [1988] 1 All E.R. 65 at 68b-c.

[56] *Kearley* above; after the Civil Evidence Act 1995 the rule was limited to criminal trials. This is still the case despite the passage of the Criminal Justice Act 2003.

2003, witnesses are still expected to testify from their own knowledge or belief. They are not expected to testify as to what they think others might know or believe. They give evidence of what they themselves perceived: what they saw, heard, felt, tasted or heard. A witness cannot testify about another's perceptions. Were a witness permitted to retail another, absent, person's statement, the court could not investigate the probative value of that statement. It would, of course, be able to inquire whether those actual words were spoken because that is within the witness's own perceptions. But the court could not explore other factors such as the absent witness's reliability or credibility. The court cannot assess whether the contents of the statement were likely to be true. The testimony is hearsay and is not admissible evidence.

The hearsay rule is mainly about excluding the evidence of an absent witness. But the rule does not only apply to repeating other people's statements. Witnesses cannot testify as to what they themselves said prior to the court proceedings. It does show the witness's consistency but there are considerable limitations on introducing such prior consistent statements. Thus the common law rule against hearsay is very broad, its rationale seemingly unclear to the judiciary and thus its boundaries poorly defined. It was a *rule* of exclusion and the judge had no discretion to admit a hearsay statement simply on the grounds that, as evidence, it was relevant, reliable and probative. However there are exceptions to the rule which have been broadened by the 2003 Act. Furthermore s.1114(1)(d) of the Act has introduced a residual discretion so that a hearsay statement may be introduced into evidence, although it falls outside the statutory exceptions, if the judge concludes that it is in the interests of justice for the statement to be admitted.

8. Proof.

Evidence is not proof. Simply presenting information to a court proves nothing. The trier of fact should now go through three stages:

(1) weigh up the information/evidence presented in court;
(2) decide, in a factual sense, what happened;
(3) having determined those facts, conclude whether the facts in issue exist or not.

The last two stages are invariably conflated—on a burglary charge, the jury is unlikely to draw distinctions between the facts (the accused entering Number 32 without permission and taking £100) and the facts in issue (entering as a trespasser with intent to steal). The key issue is whether the court been persuaded of the correctness of a particular case? If yes, the case has been proved. The job of persuasion can be divided into two stages.

(i) *burden of proof:*
which party has the task of persuading the trier? Must the accused satisfy the jury of their innocence or is it for the prosecution to convince them of their

guilt? Does the claimant have to persuade the judge of the correctness of their suit or is it for the defence to rebut the allegations? This is the question of the *burden of proof*. In a criminal trial, it almost invariably rests upon the prosecution. In civil proceedings, the principle is that the party who asserts a particular fact must prove it.

(ii) *standard of proof:*
what level of proof is needed? Total certainty rarely happens and when lawyers talk about proof, they refer to the probability of a state of affairs existing. In a criminal trial with an individual's liberty at stake, a high standard is required and that occurs when the jury is satisfied "beyond reasonable doubt". In theory this seems a proper formula but in practice there are significant inadequacies. For example, juries are still allowed to convict even when the prosecution case rests wholly or mainly on an uncorroborated confession, on a single identification or on accomplice evidence. In *Silcott*[57] the appellant had been convicted of the murder of a police officer in the course of a riot in north London. The evidence against him consisted only of verbal admissions, "You ain't got enough evidence", "I ain't saying no more and you've got a big surprise coming" and "No one will give evidence against me". The conviction was only quashed when forensic evidence showed these statements not to have been contemporaneously recorded as stated by the police witnesses and the page containing Silcott's damaging comments had been substituted. Yet it is difficult to see that a jury could decide that such statements, even if accepted as having been made by the accused, constituted proof beyond reasonable doubt.

The jury is not necessarily to blame and in many cases where justice has miscarried, the quality of evidence, accepted by the judge as evidence on which a reasonable jury might convict, has nowhere approached the requisite standard of proof. The ready acceptance of circumstantial evidence has meant that sometimes not only the quality but the quantity of the evidence is wanting. The English legal system has always prided itself on its rules on proof of guilt but there remain real problems as to whether judicial super-vision over the sufficiency of evidence is adequate.

In civil cases, the standard of proof is on the balance of probabilities: that is, whether a fact is more likely than not.

B. *Analysing the Facts*

The official version is that the courtroom is the forum where the truth will out. Those who might be described as "fact–sceptics" might point to the difficulties of establishing facts beyond argument—this is particularly so when you are dealing with "fuzzy" concepts such as negligence or intention.

---

[57] The Guardian, December 11, 1991.

But the trial is designed to recreate the past and establish an authoritative version of events. It does so through an amalgam of argument and advocacy: the latter is not the subject of this book but the power of persuasion through rhetoric has always been important. John Mortimer recalled Sir Edward Marshall Hall, addressing a jury on behalf of a young prostitute accused of murder, shivering in the dock, pointed at her and said to the jury: "God never gave her a chance, so will you?"[58] Emotion has always played its part in court but so has logical argument. The construction of a coherent narrative is a key part of the advocate's role:

R. Posner, "Narrative and Narratology in Classroom and Courtroom" (1997) Philosophy and Literature, 21.1, pp.292–305:

A story is a sequence of events invented, selected, emphasized, or arranged in such a way as to vivify, explain, inform, or edify. Stories "must have beginnings, middles, and ends" and must be "so constructed that the mind of the listener, viewer, or reader [can] take in the relation of beginning, middle, and end" and "see the end as entailed by a process." The story need not be true, but it must be coherent, intelligible, significant.

Ubiquitous in history, biography, literature, myth, and most religions, storytelling plays a smaller but still important role in other fields as well. One of these fields, surprisingly, is economics, where "story," contrasted with a formal model, denotes the informal, intuitive explanation—often indeed story-like—of an economic phenomenon. Stories play a big role in the legal process quite apart from the new oppositionist legal storytelling. In a trial, the plaintiff and the defendant each tell a story—actually a translation of their "real" story into the narrative and rhetorical forms authorized by law—and the jury chooses the story it likes better. (If it is a criminal case and the defendant's confession is placed in evidence, there is a story within the story.) This is not how the law conceptualizes the trial process. The law requires the plaintiff to prove each element of his claim by a preponderance of the evidence (beyond a reasonable doubt if it is a criminal case), and likewise the defendant if he pleads any affirmative defenses. . . .

The Supreme Court has magnified the story element in the sentencing phase of capital trials by holding that the defendant must be permitted to tell a no-holds-barred story of his life in an effort to persuade the jury that he should not be put to death, while the victim's family must be permitted to tell the jury the absent victim's story in order to offset the impact of the defendant's story.

The study of the courtroom is the study of practical argument. Unlike arguments on the street, this argument takes place within a formal structure with formal rules of engagement, namely evidentiary rules that tell us what can be said and how it can be said. But, just like everyday argument, developing a persuasive narrative is an important part as the advocate needs to establish in the mind of the court an overall theory of the case—what happened, how it happened and why it happened.

But alongside legal rules and the advocate's rhetoric are more analytic questions. How do we make sense of the information being presented? What

[58] *The Guardian*, February 14, 2002.

can we rationally conclude from that information? Are we persuaded of the rightness of a particular assertion? And, of course, which party wins? We need to assess evidence, draw inferences, make conclusions, perhaps sub-consciously but more or less logically and we need to bring these principles of proof to sit alongside the legal rules. Making this process transparent is central to the study of evidence

The principles of proof involve the application of logic. This is the science of reasoning, proof, thinking, or inference, allowing us to analyse a piece of reasoning, and determine whether it is correct or not. A little basic knowledge of logic is often helpful when constructing or analysing an argument.[59] The initial building block of a logical argument is a proposition which is a statement which can be either true or false. In criminal proceedings, the prosecution will make such an assertion in the indictment—for example, "The accused murdered the victim by stabbing him at a particular time and place". First, to decide on the truth or otherwise of this statement, we need to define "murder" which, at its most basic, it requires proof that the accused caused the death of the victim with the intention of causing death or serious harm. As we have seen, technically these are the facts in issue. In a criminal case, the charge is the proposition and we now need an argument to establish this.

The argument is built from individual items of evidence—for each, there are three connected stages: premises, inference, and conclusion. The premises in a trial are the items of evidence that are produced, *i.e.* "The witness stated that she saw the accused stab the victim".

In this case, this is direct evidence of the *actus reus*—there is no space here for inference. The witness saw the stabbing take place and identifies the defendant as the perpetrator. The only question for the jury is whether the witness is correct on either of these points. The defendant can challenge the truth or reliability of the statement, possibly suggesting that the witness is deranged, has poor eyesight or malicious feelings towards him. The jury has perhaps three possible conclusions:

1. that it is sure that the witness is correct and that it will rely on the testimony;
2. that the doubts about the reliability or honesty of the witness are such that it cannot in any circumstances use the testimony;
3. that there are doubts about the reliability or honesty of the witness but the testimony must be considered alongside the other evidence which may resolve those doubts.

With direct evidence, the trier of fact merely has to decide whether to accept it. That item is then established as a fact. Often the testimony will be more circumstantial and the trier has a supplementary question, "What does it mean?" For example, "Another witness saw the accused running from the scene of the stabbing". If the jury accept that the witness is honest and correct, they have established that the defendant was running. But what can be inferred from that?

---

[59] A detailed and valuable study of the principles of proof is to be found in T. Anderson and W. Twining, *Analysis of Evidence* (2nd ed., Cambridge, 2005), Ch.2.

1. the jury may find that the witness is correct and that it was the accused running;
2. the jury may also find that the accused was running away from the scene of the crime and not towards some other place;
3. the jury may infer from 2) that the accused did not wish to be found at the scene;
4. the jury may infer from 3) that this was because the accused was involved in the stabbing;
5. the jury may infer from 4) that the accused was in fact the assailant.

The jury are using the premise (the item of fact that they have established) to develop further propositions. This process is known as inference. In inference, we start with one or more propositions which have been accepted. We then derive a new proposition. The propositions arrived at by inference may then be used in further inference. As the simple example above shows, the court may often be dealing with chains of inferences.[60] Evidence leads the jury to an inferred fact from which a further inference can be drawn and so on through a series of intermediate stages until we reach the ultimate issue which has to be decided. A court has to careful to distinguish between a valid process of inference based on reliable circumstantial evidence, and mere speculation.

The evidence about the running man is purely circumstantial. Such evidence is admissible if relevant and if it does not infringe any exclusionary rules. It can be very powerful evidence, especially when looked at cumulatively, although a judge in a criminal case should hesitate before allowing a case to go to a jury based on a single piece of circumstantial evidence. Normally, however, there are a number of different items of circumstantial evidence. One individual item of evidence may well support the inference that the jury wishes to draw from another piece, *e.g.* "A police search of the road that the accused ran along revealed the weapon used in the stabbing in a rubbish bin". This new item of evidence reinforces the inference that the accused had been at the scene and was running away. The fact that the defendant had had a major quarrel with the victim might also reinforce the inference that not only had he been at the scene, he was in fact the assailant.

The jury may draw inferences from circumstantial evidence. But they are not compelled to. There are always competing inferences—the jury may decide that there were other reasons why the accused was running. Clearly the process of inference can vary in strength and validity. Not least is the fact that there may be alternative valid explanations or inferences that can be drawn from the same information or that there may be other evidence which might contradict that inference. The chain of inference above (running suggests a reluctance to be seen at the scene, therefore some link to the stabbing, perhaps being the assailant) is scarcely one to be fully confident about. Alternative explanations on the basis of coincidence can easily be

---

[60] Harry Kemelman's short story 'The Nine Mile Walk' is an entertaining example of a chain of inference. It is reprinted in Anderson and Twining, *op.cit.* p.9.

suggested: the accused was training for a marathon or rushing to catch a train. Wigmore has suggested that there may be four stages to this process.

J. Wigmore. The Science of Judicial Proof (1937), para.15:

The first process, Assertion, consists in offering a fact tending to prove a specific conclusion of Probandum. This is subject to the test whether the claimed conclusion is a probable or a more probable one, having regard to conceivable other interpretations of the fact. . .

The second process, Explanation, consists in explaining away the original fact's force by showing the existence and probability of other hypotheses; for this purpose other facts affording such explanation are receivable from the opponent. . .

The third process, Denial, consists in negating the original proponent's evidentiary fact as such, either testimonially or circumstantially; and thus [the opponent]. . .offers a new witness or circumstance. . .

The fourth process, Rivalry, consists in adducing a new fact, circumstantial or testimonial, which by a rival inference tends to disprove the proponent's Probandum. . . . . Such are the forms of probative processes available for each single fact as offered. For each additional new fact the processes may be repeated, though they may not be actually used in each instance. . . . .amidst the multifarious varieties of evidence, our mental processes thereon are reducible to four fundamental types, constantly repeated.

A party asserts a particular fact which is relevant to the proof of the case. The opposition will seek undermine the force of that assertion by explanation or denial or countering the fact by other evidence. Any inference that the accused was running away from the scene of the stabbing can be strengthened or weakened by other items of evidence which may deny, explain or produce a rival to any particular inference. The function of the trier of fact is to choose the right inference from all the possible rivals and as Wigmore suggests, any particular piece of information may gain significance when taken with the evidence as a whole.

Judges often describe the process of drawing inferences from evidence as one of common sense logic. But it might be argued that logic merely tells us whether an inference is valid or not. Whether it is the correct inference to draw is a more difficult exercise. A juror has to decide on the value of the evidence and the weight which they are is willing to put on the inference. Did the witness really see the accused? Is it justified to conclude that he was running away? The process of inference necessarily involves recourse to generalizations.

T. Anderson and W. Twining, Analysis of Evidence (2nd ed., Cambridge, 2005) p.68:

Generalisations range over a broad spectrum. At one end are scientific laws (such as the law of gravity); well-founded scientific opinions (such as the conclusion of a qualified forensic expert based upon comparisons of handwriting alleged to have been written by the same individual); and widely shared conclusions based upon common experience (for instance, everyone knows that a driver must stop for a red light). In the middle are commonly held, but unproven or unprovable beliefs (for instance, fleeing the scene of a crime is evidence of a guilty conscience). At the other end are biases or prejudices that may be strongly held irrespective of available data (for instance, women do not make good trial lawyers; men are generally poor single parents; whites cannot fairly sit as jurors when a black is on trial, etc) and less strongly held but still operative beliefs (for instance, men's fixed designs are probably carried out). Some or all of these types of background generalisations are involved in factual adjudications.

It is probably better not to refer to "common sense" reasoning but to recognise that the trial court uses inductive argument, so-called to distinguish it from the other traditional type of argument, deductive argument. A deductive argument provides conclusive proof of its conclusions; if the premises are true, the conclusion must also be true. A deductive argument is either valid or invalid. A valid argument is defined as one where, if the premises are true, then the conclusion is true. On the other hand, an inductive argument is one where the premises provide some evidence for the truth of the conclusion. Inductive arguments are neither valid nor invalid, but we can talk about whether they are better or worse than other arguments. We can also discuss how probable their premises are. In a court of law, verdicts are thus never "true" but are more or less probable. For lawyers to talk about the proof of a proposition is to discuss probabilities. This is discussed further in Ch.3.

2

THE TRIAL—JUDGE AND THE JURY

There are many issues of procedure that provide the context in which the rules of evidence operate, including investigation of the issues and the instigation of the action, disclosure of relevant information, preliminary hearings and the organisation and running of the trial.

Issues of investigation and disclosure are discussed in later chapters. This chapter will consider preliminary hearings, the basic stages of the trial itself and the specific functions of the judge and jury.

1. Preliminary Hearings

The finder of fact, whether judge or jury, is entitled to a proper definition of the issues and clear exposition of the evidence. Pre-trial hearings should be an essential means in achieving this.[1] In civil proceedings, these have been standard procedure—in county courts, there will be pre-trial reviews to ensure such matters as discovery of relevant documents, disclosure of expert reports or exchange of written statements of evidence. In the High Court, the claimant will take out a "summons for directions" which leads to a hearing analogous to the pre-trial review in county court.

In criminal cases, pre-trial review has never been a standard procedural stage but there are opportunities for such preliminary hearings.

(a) In magistrates' courts in cases where it is needed there can be a "pre-trial review"[2] of different sorts. These have developed piece-meal, and differ in practice and procedure from area to area.

(i) In 1999, as a result of the Narey Report,[3] *"early first hearings"* were introduced for those cases which are likely to be an early guilty plea. This is not a preliminary hearing but an expedited trial. If the case turns out to be more complex, the

---

[1] See Court of Appeal dicta in *Thorn* (1977) 66 C.App R 6.
[2] For a study of pre-trial review in magistrates' courts, J. Baldwin: *Pre-Trial Justice* (Blackwell, 1985).
[3] M. Narey, *Review of Delay in the Criminal Justice System* (Home Office, 1997).

court will put it over to an *"early administrative hearing"* where the court takes a plea before venue, determines mode of trial and sets pre-trial review and trial dates as necessary. This can be heard before a justices' clerk.

(ii) a "pre-trial review" can be held where it is needed to assess the state of readiness. The Clerk to the Justices can hold a pre-trial review and has all the powers of a single magistrate when doing so.

(b) In the Crown Court, there are four separate forms of procedure.

(i) non-statutory "plea and directions hearing", in which the judge can make non-binding rulings before the start of trial.[4] The magistrates' court should commit the defendant to appear in the Crown Court on a specific date fixed in liaison with the Crown Court listing officer for an initial plea and directions hearing where pleas will be taken and, in contested cases, prosecution and defence will be expected to assist the judge in identifying the key issues, and to provide any additional information required for the proper listing of the case. Local practice varies but Auld described these as *". . . perfunctory proceedings"*.[5]

(ii) "pre-trial hearing" under Part IV of the Criminal Procedure and Investigations Act 1996 which gives judges power to make binding rulings on points of law before the start of a trial. For example, the judge might be invited to make a ruling in law as to whether or not the facts support a particular charge. Trial judges are able to discharge or vary any such ruling if they consider it in the interests of justice to do so.

(iii) "preparatory hearings" under the Criminal Justice Act 1987, as the start and part of the trial, for serious or complex fraud cases, in which the judge can make binding rulings on any issue of the admissibility of evidence or law which relates to the case.

(iv) "preparatory hearings" introduced by Part III of the 1996 Act for cases in which the indictment reveals *"a case of such complexity, or a case whose trial is likely to be of such length, that substantial benefits are likely to accrue"* from such a hearing. Again the judge can make binding rulings and appeal from such rulings lies to the Court of Appeal.

These statutory preliminary hearings are part of the trial, with the judge able to rule on such matters as the admissibility of evidence. The trial judge, if

[4] Royal Commission on Criminal Justice: *Report* (Cm 2263)(1993) paras 7.12ff; Practice Direction (Crown Court: Plea and Directions Hearings) [1995] 1 W.L.R. 1318
[5] Lord Justice Auld: *A Review of the Criminal Courts of England and Wales* (2001), Ch.10, para.209.

different, should be bound by such rulings. These changes signal a move towards the point when criminal trials will be properly and judicially supervised from the institution of proceedings. But at the moment, as Auld puts it.

Lord Justice Auld, A Review of the Criminal Courts of England and Wales (2001). Ch.10, para.209:

. . . there are no fewer than four separate, but largely similar forms of preliminary hearing for Crown Court cases. They are a good example of the unsystematic and overlapping way in which the legislature, when it intervenes in matters of criminal law, burdens and confuses its procedures. In all of them arraignment may take place and, if there is an acceptable plea of guilty and the case is ready for it, the judge can proceed to sentence. Where the matter is to be contested and there are substantial outstanding issues, the hearings can be of real utility, for example as to the adequacy of mutual or third party disclosure or in ruling on claims of public interest immunity or on matters of law on agreed facts. But in all of them, there is little difference in effect between the 'binding' orders made in the statutory procedures and those made in the non-statutory plea and directions hearings. And, in all of them the court has little effective sanction to enforce its directions if the parties are unable or unwilling to comply.[6]

However, in this chapter we will be mainly concerned with the organisation and running of the contested trial rather than preliminary hearings. It is the trial which provides the most significant context within which the rules of evidence operate. The key component of a trial is interrogation and response—the process of questioning witnesses by which evidence is produced. The other element is argument by advocates about what that evidence shows. Through evidence, the parties seek to establish facts. The opposing parties challenge some or all of these. Both need to persuade the jury or court that their assertions are correct, that their 'theory of the case' is supported by facts as found and by the inferences which necessarily have to be drawn from those facts.

2. Speeches

While the building blocks of a successful trial are patient and detailed examination and cross-examination, the process of persuading the court or jury of the rightness of your case is dealt with through speeches. In brief, in civil proceedings, there will be an opening speech by the claimant outlining the case. The claimant will then produce evidence and call witnesses to be examined and cross-examined. If, at the close of the claimant's case, the defendant does not call any witnesses in reply, the claimant will sum up, to

---

[6] *ibid.*, para.211.

which the defendant has the right of reply. If the defence does call witnesses, there is no summing up at the conclusion of the claimant's case: the defence sums up at the conclusion of their case and the claimant is given the right to reply.

In criminal proceedings, there will be an opening speech by the prosecution which will be an overview of the issues and of the evidence supporting the allegations in the indictment. Whether such, often lengthy, openings are necessary was questioned by the Runciman Commission on Criminal Justice, which supported the Law Commission's proposals for particularised indictments which would remove the need for opening speeches in routine cases.

Law Commission, Counts in an Indictment (1992), para.8.7:

We considered the practice in Scotland whereby the prosecution does not make an opening speech. There the judge, aided by narrative indictments,[7] may make a brief opening statement to the jury of the issues that they will be called upon to decide at the end of the trial. The prosecution then calls the first witness. If the Law Commission's proposals on particularised indictments are enacted, there will be no need for a prosecution opening speech in many trials in England and Wales. In the more complex cases an opening speech will almost certainly continue to be necessary. On the other hand, all that will be needed in routine and straightforward cases is the opening statement from the judge explaining the burden and standard of proof and such matters of law as he or she thinks necessary for the jury's understanding of the case. The judge should not, however, do more that identify, without discussing, the factual issues to be decided in the case. Those should be set out in the indictment.

Although Runciman accepted a need for an opening address in more complex cases, best practice should be to review the issues involved in the trial and not a comprehensive rehearsal of the evidence to be given by each witness.

The prosecution should present the case in an impartial manner, without the use of emotive language. Counsel should omit reference to any evidence where the defence has given notice that it will be contested as inadmissible, especially confessions.[8] Where the prosecution cannot sensibly open the case without reference to such evidence, it is possible for there to be a preliminary hearing to settle the issue. In *Hammond*[9] in the opening speech for the prosecution, counsel referred to the defendant's confession. The defence immediately objected and the judge heard the objection to the admissibility of the confession in the absence of the jury. The Court of Criminal Appeal felt that the appropriate time to hear objections to evidence was just before the evidence was called.

---

[7] A narrative indictment sets out each offence charged by giving an account of the facts alleged to constitute it. The facts are sometimes set out at some length.

[8] *Swatkins* (1831) 4 C. & P. 548; in civil proceedings claimant must not mention facts with regard to which they cannot call evidence.

[9] [1941] 3 All E.R. 318.

Hammond [1941] 3 All E.R. 318 at 320, *per* **Humphreys J.:**

The ordinary practice in such a case, if there is any objection on the part of the counsel for the defence to the admissibility of a piece of evidence, is that he should inform the prosecution of that fact beforehand, and that that piece of evidence should not be opened to the jury . . . The court cannot lay down as a rule of practice that in no case should the judge decide to hear in advance arguments as to the admissibility of evidence. There may be cases in which it is convenient, and in which it cannot possibly result in any harm in its being done.

Under the Criminal Procedure and Investigations Act 1996, there can be preparatory hearings in criminal cases at which time rulings may be made on the admissibility of evidence.[10]

It is much rarer for there to be an opening speech for the defence. This is an option (after the close of the prosecution case) where defendants intend to call witnesses as to facts in addition to testifying themselves but not otherwise. At the close of defence evidence but before any closing speech, the prosecution will have a right to reply. The defence does have the right to the last word, (other than the judge's summing up).[11]

3. Calling and Examining Witnesses

Under the adversarial system, in civil and criminal proceedings, it is the parties who decide what to litigate, what witnesses to call and what evidence to present. All parties have the opportunity to call and examine witnesses favourable to their case. This is known as examination-in-chief. The parties also have the opportunity to test the strength of the other side's evidence by examining their witnesses and this is known as cross-examination.

In civil cases, parties have to provide written proofs of evidence of the witnesses on which they intend to rely. But there is no obligation on a party in a civil case to call any witness or to be stopped from calling witnesses. If unnecessary and repetitious witnesses are called, there are sanctions, not least in the award of costs.[12] Witnesses do not have to be called in any particular order nor do judges have the power to call witnesses on their own initiative.

In criminal proceedings, the prosecution must inform the defence (in trials on indictment) of the witnesses and other evidence on which they intend to rely. The accused also has certain obligations to reveal the line of the defence to the prosecution.[13] The prosecution's obligation to call witnesses is tempered by a discretion whether to call witnesses when counsel no longer believe them to be worthy of belief. This discretion is based on *Oliva*[14] where the

---

[10] s.31.

[11] Criminal Procedure (Right of Reply) Act 1964, s.1.

[12] *Connelly v DPP* [1964] A.C. 1254 at 1301 *per* Lord Morris of Borth-y-Gest who suggests that the court has the inherent power to 'act effectively within its jurisdiction' to prevent abuse of its own proceedings.

[13] Both prosecution and defence obligations of disclosure are under the provisions of the Criminal Procedure and Investigations Act 1996, as amended by the Criminal Justice Act 2003—see Ch.6.

[14] [1965] 3 All E.R. 116.

witness was not called to testify, since he had testified at the committal hearing in a contradictory fashion.

Oliva [1965] 3 All E.R. 116 at 122, *per* Lord Parker C.J.:

The prosecution do not, of course, put forward every witness as a witness of truth, but where the witness's evidence is capable of belief then it is their duty, well recognised, that he should be called, even though the evidence that he is going to give is inconsistent with the case sought to be proved. Their discretion must be exercised in a manner which is calculated to further the interest of justice, and at the same time be fair to the defence. If the prosecution appear to be exercising that discretion improperly, it is open to the judge of trial to interfere and in his discretion in turn to invite the prosecution to call a particular witness . . .

This was considered in *Russell-Jones*.

Russell-Jones [1995] 1 Cr.App.R. 538 at 545, *per* Kennedy L.J.:

The principles which emerge from the authorities and from rules of practice appear to be:

(1) Generally speaking the prosecution must have at court all the witnesses named on the back of the indictment (nowadays those whose statements have been served as witnesses on whom the prosecution intend to rely), if the defence want those witnesses to attend. In deciding which statements to serve, the prosecution has an unfettered discretion, but must normally disclose material statements not served.

(2) The prosecution enjoy a discretion whether to call, or tender, any witness it requires to attend, but the discretion is not unfettered.

(3) The first principle which limits this discretion is that it must be exercised in the interests of justice, so as to promote a fair trial . . . "The present case, however, seems to me to call for a reminder that the discretion should be exercised with due regard to traditional considerations of fairness."[15] . . .

(4) The next principle is that the prosecution ought normally to call or offer to call all the witnesses who give direct evidence of the primary facts of the case, unless for good reason, in any instance, the prosecutor regards the witness's evidence as unworthy of belief. In most cases the jury should have available all of that evidence as to what actually happened, which the prosecution, when serving statements, considered to be material, even if there are inconsistencies between one witness and another. The defence cannot always be expected to call for themselves witnesses of the primary facts whom the prosecution has discarded . . .

(5) It is for the prosecution to decide which witnesses give direct evidence of the primary facts of the case. A prosecutor may reasonably take the view that what a particular witness has to say is at best marginal.

(6) The prosecutor is also, as we have said, the primary judge of whether or not a witness to the material events is incredible, or unworthy of belief . . .

---

[15] *Ziems v The Prothonotary of the Supreme Court of New South Wales* (1957) 97 C.L.R. 279, 292, *per* Fullager J.

(7) A prosecutor properly exercising his discretion will not therefore be obliged to proffer a witness merely in order to give the defence material with which to attack the credit of other witnesses on whom the Crown relies. To hold otherwise would, in truth, be to assert that the prosecution are obliged to call a witness for no purpose other than to assist the defence in its endeavour to destroy the Crown's own case . . . in every case, it is important to emphasise, the judgment to be made is primarily that of the prosecutor, and, in general, the court will only interfere with it if he has gone wrong in principle.

Defence witnesses should be called by the defence. In *Nugent*[16] it was argued that alibi witnesses for the defence (whose statements to the police had been included in the committal papers) should be called by the prosecution since the defendant's interests would otherwise be prejudiced. The trial judge held that there was no such obligation citing the judgment of Lord Roche in *Seneviratne*.

Seneviratne [1936] 3 All E.R. 36 at 48, *per* Lord Roche.:

. . . [Their Lordships] cannot, speaking generally, approve of an idea that a prosecution must call witnesses irrespective of considerations of number and of reliability, or that a prosecution ought to discharge the functions of both prosecution and defence. If it does so confusion is very apt to result, and never is it more likely to result than if the prosecution calls witnesses and then proceeds almost automatically to discredit them by cross-examination. Witnesses essential to the unfolding of narratives on which the prosecution is based, must, of course, be called by the prosecution, whether in the result the effect of their testimony is for or against the case for the prosecution.

The prosecution's discretion as to which witnesses to call is, to a limited extent, fettered and there is an obligation to call all witnesses whose testimony is essential to the narrative and who are capable of belief. Obviously the statements of witnesses on whom the Crown does not wish to rely should not find their way into the trial documents. If they do, the prosecution might well have to call such witnesses and tender them to the defence for cross–examination.[17]

Defence discretion is less restricted and they are able to call which witnesses they choose and in whatever order. The exception is that, when defendants testify, they must do so before other defence witnesses under s.79 of the Police and Criminal Evidence Act 1984.

a. The ex improviso rule

Once any litigant has presented their evidence-in-chief, that is normally the end of the matter. In both civil and criminal proceedings, the parties should

---

[16] [1977] 3 All E.R. 662.
[17] *Balmforth* [1992] Crim.L.R. 825; *Armstrong* [1995] Crim.L.R. 831; *Russell-Jones* [1995] Crim.L.R. 832.

adduce all their evidence when presenting their case. Any opportunity to call further witnesses or present further evidence is very limited. In civil matters, there is a general discretion to allow evidence to be led at a later stage. In criminal proceedings, there is a limited discretion on the part of the judge to allow the prosecution to call further evidence at the close of the defence case. This is known as the *ex improviso* rule. This principle permits a judge to "improvise" and not follow the normal rules. But within the overall duty of the judge to ensure a fair trial occurs within the spirit of the system.[18]

The principle is restrictively interpreted in relation to additional evidence, allowing the prosecution to adduce further evidence in rebuttal of the defence case only where no human ingenuity could have anticipated the line of the defence. However these constraints have recently been loosened. In *Milliken*,[19] the defence was based on allegations of fabrication of evidence by the police. The judge allowed the prosecution to call evidence in rebuttal and this course of action was upheld by the Court of Appeal. Rebuttal is permitted where a line of defence has emerged that could not have reasonably been foreseen. In *Hutchinson*[20] the defendant, accused of murder, dramatically pointed out a journalist sitting in the gallery as the murderer. The prosecution had some inkling that such an allegation might be made but this did not prevent evidence being called in rebuttal. The court said,

Hutchinson (1986) 82 Cr.App.R. 59:

The ex improviso principle has to be applied by the court with a recognition that the prosecution are expected to react reasonably to what may be suggested as pre-trial warnings of evidence likely to be given which calls for denial beforehand, and for that matter to suggestions put in cross-examination of their witnesses. They are not expected to take notice of fanciful or unreal statements no matter from what source they emanate . . .[21]

There can be said to be two exceptions to the rule prohibiting the adducing of rebuttal evidence by the prosecution: first the modified *ex improviso* rule and secondly where the matter omitted is a mere formality. Apart from these, the prosecution should not seek to remedy defects in its own case after the close of their case. But in *Francis*,[22] a prosecution witness testified to picking out position 20 at an identity parade. However the prosecution failed to call evidence that the man standing at that position was in fact the accused. In making a submission of "no case to answer", defence counsel drew attention to this deficiency. The judge allowed the prosecution to recall the police inspector in charge of the parade in order to remedy the omission. The Court of Appeal upheld the conviction, stating:

---

[18] *Cameron* [2001] Crim.L.R. 587 where judge takes over cross-examination of 14-year-old rape victim who had refused to be examined by defence counsel.
[19] (1969) 53 Cr.App.R 330.
[20] (1986) 82 Cr.App.R 51.
[21] *ibid.*, at 59.
[22] [1991] 1 All E.R. 225.

Francis [1991] 1 All E.R. 225:

The discretion of the judge to admit evidence after the close of the prosecution case is not confined to the two well established exceptions. There is a wider discretion. We refrain from defining precisely the limit of that discretion since we cannot foresee all the circumstances in which it might fall to be exercised. It is of the essence of any discretion that it should be kept flexible. But lest there be any misunderstanding and lest it be thought that we are opening the door too wide . . . the discretion is one which should only be exercised outside the two established exceptions on the rarest of occasions.[23]

In a criminal trial, the judge has the power to call witnesses but these powers are very seldom used.[24] The Runciman Commission found that in 19% of contested cases, the trial judge considered that there were one or more important witnesses that had not been called. The Commission recommended that judges should use their power more often to ensure that all relevant witnesses were heard by the jury.[25] The Auld Report was less sure, ". . . so long as we retain our essentially adversarial system, I consider that judges should use this power only in exceptional cases, where justice demands it. Even then they should be cautious about its use because one or other side may have very good reasons, that they cannot divulge, consistent with justice and in the interests of a fair trial, for not calling the witness themselves."[26]

b. The role of the victim

Although not a matter of evidence, one glaring omission from the running order of a criminal trial is the victim: there is no right to speak, to be represented[27] or even a place to sit. The crime is conceptualised as a wrong against society and once the complaint has been made, control is relinquished. The victim's wishes whether to prosecute or not may be taken into account by the police or the prosecution.[28] But the lack of protection may be seen when there are attacks by the defence on the victim's character—the less sympathy the jury has for the victim, the more likely it is to acquit—so the defence has every incentive to paint the victim in as harsh a light as possible.

The adversarial trial is seen at its worst in sexual assault cases where the defence is often a thinly-veiled attack on the character of the victim. The need for representation can become acute when the defendant asks for leave to cross-examine the rape victim on her past sexual history. In such situations,

---

[23] *ibid.* at 229F per Lloyd LJ.

[24] *Roberts* (1984) 80 Cr.App.R.89.

[25] Royal Commission on Criminal Justice: *op.cit.* para.8.18.

[26] Lord Justice Auld: *op.cit.* Ch.11, para.36.

[27] This is not the case in certain European jurisdictions where the victim has a right to legal representation. In France, the victim can be joined to an action as 'une partie civile' and has locus standi in all preliminary matters and at the trial, able to argue that the charge is insufficient, to object to a certain line of questioning or to ask that certain questions be put to a witness.

[28] *e.g.* Code for Crown Prosecutors (2004) para.5.12 '. . . should always take into account the consequences for the victim of whether or not to prosecute, and any views expressed by the victim.'

the tactical interests of the prosecutor do not necessarily overlap with those of the victim.[29] However rape shield legislation limiting such examination has recently been improved.[30] Further examples can be seen in homicide cases. Where the plea is one of provocation, this may involve an attack on the victim's character. The victim's relatives might well object to the portrayal of the victim.

D. Campbell, "Victims without a voice", Guardian, January 11, 2005:

In one of the leading cases on provocation, Sara Thornton pleaded not guilty to murdering her husband, Malcolm, after killing him while he slept in a drunken stupor on the sofa. She was originally convicted of murder but had her conviction reduced to manslaughter on appeal. Vital to her case was the allegation that he was drunkenly violent towards her. His family disputed this portrayal and later protested vociferously about the way he had been presented in court. He had been married twice before and both ex-wives denied that he was violent. One said: "Yes, he was a drunk, but he was a happy drunk."

The protection of victims through evidentiary devices such as rape shield legislation has recently been improved by the restrictions on adducing evidence of the bad character of victims and witnesses which were brought in under s.100 of the Criminal Justice Act 2003. There remain exceptions to these—victims also have a right to a fair trial and that balance might be achieved by allowing independent representation in order, for example, to challenge the acceptance by the prosecution of a plea bargain or to examine witnesses or adduce contrary evidence.

II. THE ROLE OF THE JUDGE

Within the court itself, the judge is, if not king, still a constitutional monarch. In civil proceedings, amendments to the pleadings, admissibility of evidence and control of the proceedings are all in the hands of the judge, although actions can be halted at any time by the claimant by giving due notice to the defendant and to the court. Similarly, once a criminal case has been transferred to the Crown Court, issues such as discontinuance of the prosecution, *e.g.* by offering no evidence, amendment of the indictment or even the acceptance of a plea of guilty are always subject to the consent of the judge,[31] although there is an over-riding power of the Attorney-General to stop a prosecution by entering a *nolle prosequi*. Those judicial powers have been recently trimmed—in *Grafton*,[32] prosecution counsel sought to discon-

---

[29] J. Temkin: *Rape and the Legal Process* (2nd ed., OUP, Oxford, 2002), Ch.3.

[30] Under Youth Justice and Criminal Evidence Act 1999 s.41—this is discussed in Ch.10.

[31] *Broad* (1979) 68 Cr.App.R.281.

[32] [1992] 4 All E.R. 609—the Crown Prosecution Service is able to discontinue prosecutions before committal under Prosecution of Offences Act 1985, s.23. In magistrates' courts, they are also able to halt proceedings at any time—*R. v Canterbury Justices Ex p. Klisiak* [1981] 2 All E.R. 129.

tinue after part of the prosecution evidence had been heard. The Court of Appeal held that there was a common law power to discontinue proceedings even at this late stage and that the judge in such circumstances can only order an acquittal. Save in exceptional circumstances, the judge should not direct the prosecutor on what to do.[33]

Judges act as umpire, ensuring that the rules on procedure and evidence are followed. Thus, in a criminal case, they exercise control over the indictment, over the taking of the plea, over the admission of evidence. They act as the ultimate arbiter of any issue of law. They summarise the evidence for the jury, explain the law and draw their attention to the issues. Judges do not normally call or question witnesses and, as discussed above, this can mean that the jury do not hear significant witnesses. But, as discussed earlier, the *ex improviso* principle permits a judge to "improvise" to ensure a fair trial occurs.

The judge's functions can be put under three main headings: the admissibility of evidence; control over the issues to be considered by the trier of fact; summing up and directing the jury.

A. *Admissibility of Evidence*

Parties to a case will put forward items of information (through witnesses, documents or objects) which they wish to have included in the case as evidence. Before any item is admitted as evidence, it must satisfy certain conditions. These may be conditions which generally pertain to all evidence, namely, that the evidence is relevant, of sufficient weight and does not adversely affect the fairness of the trial. The conditions may be more specific to the particular class of evidence that is being offered: for example, if a party seeks to rely on a statement in a document, that document must satisfy the (not onerous) conditions of s.33 of the Criminal Justice Act 2003 or s.133 the Civil Evidence Act 1995, s.8.

An illustration of such specific conditions comes in criminal cases where it is common for the prosecution to rely on incriminating statements, confessions, made by the defendant. Such statements are only admissible if the conditions laid down by s.76 of the Police and Criminal Evidence Act 1984 are satisfied. The Crown must satisfy the court that these have been complied with. Those conditions are, namely, that the confession was obtained in circumstances which would not render it unreliable and that it was not obtained by oppression.[34]

Usually such conditions for admissibility present no problems. However the judge will often have to consider whether the necessary conditions exist for evidence to be admitted. This is a preliminary question of fact for the judge and normally the question whether an item of evidence is admissible is

---

[33] *Okotie* (unreported November 12, 1998, CA).
[34] This is discussed in Ch.4.

a wholly different question to that which needs to be decided in the action itself. But sometimes it can replicate the very question that the trier of fact later needs to decide. In *Doe d. Jenkins v Davies*,[35] the issue in an action of ejectment was whether a dead person was legitimate. Before her death, she had made a declaration about this to her solicitor, at a time when she was handing him a document concerning her parents' marriage. The admissibility of that declaration, as an exception to hearsay, depended on whether it was made by a legitimate member of the family. Although her legitimacy was the substantive issue in the case, the judge can still decide on that very matter.

Doe d. Jenkins v Davies (1847) 10 Q.B. 314 at 323, *per* Lord Denman C.J.:

There are conditions precedent which are required to be fulfilled before evidence is admissible for the jury. Thus, an oath, or its equivalent, and competence, are conditions precedent to admitting viva voce evidence; and the apprehension of immediate death to admitting evidence of dying declarations; a search to secondary evidence of lost writings; and stamps to certain written instruments; and so is consanguinity or affinity in the declarant to declarations of deceased relatives. The judge alone has to decide whether the condition has been fulfilled. If the proof is by witnesses, he must decide on their credibility. If counter-evidence is offered, he must receive it before he decides; and he has no right to ask the opinion of the jury on the fact of a condition precedent.

Where the issue is the very one that has to be decided by the jury, the judge ought to come to a *prima facie* decision: whether sufficient evidence has been produced to admit the evidence or whether the objections are well founded. But this would not be a full hearing as the foundation of the defence could be heard in front of the jury who should decide the main question. In *Stowe v Querner*,[36] the plaintiff sued on an insurance policy. The defence was that the policy had never been executed. The plaintiff sought to introduce, not the original policy which had been allegedly lost, but secondary evidence of its contents. To admit secondary evidence required the judge to decide whether the original had ever in fact existed. He admitted the evidence but still left to the jury the defence claim that the policy had never existed.

1. The voir dire

Disputes arise over the admissibility of evidence, especially in criminal proceedings where the defence object to proposed prosecution evidence. The argument as to admissibility often only involves points of law and can be disposed of on the basis of depositions and submissions of counsel. But the judge may have to conduct a factual inquiry to determine the question whether the conditions of admissibility exist. These inquiries can take place at a preparatory hearing[37] or at the trial itself.

---

[35] [1847] 10 Q.B. 314.
[36] (1870) L.R. 5 Ex. 155.
[37] *e.g.* in *R. v Z* [2000] 3 All E.R. 385 where the admissibility of the accused's previous acquittals was heard in a preparatory hearing under Criminal Procedure and Investigations Act 1996, s.29.

At a trial, when the point is reached when the disputed material would have been introduced, a hearing on admissibility would take place. These "trials within trials" are also known as hearings on the *voir dire*[38] and take their name from the special oath sworn by any witness testifying in such an inquiry: "I swear by almighty God that I will true answer make to all such questions as the court shall demand of me." Such hearings should be in open court, not in the judge's chambers, and in the presence of the parties and their legal advisers.[39] The jury would be normally asked to leave the courtroom— such a hearing should be conducted in the jury's absence. They should not be present where, for example, the subject of the *voir dire* is whether a confession should be admitted into evidence. To allow the jury to know at this stage that there was an incriminating statement, regardless of its details, would be prejudicial.

If the admissibility of a confession is in issue, a *voir dire* is always required, even where the proceedings are in a magistrates' or youth court. In *Liverpool Juvenile Court Ex p. R*,[40] the only evidence against a juvenile charged with burglary was the child's confession. The justices refused to consider its admissibility as a preliminary issue, presumably reasoning that, as triers of both law and fact who would hear all the evidence anyway, there was no reason to separate questions of admissibility from those of weight. The justices ruled that matters pertaining to the statement could be raised in the hearing proper and they could give appropriate weight to the statement. But the justices overlooked the fact that there were two advantages for a defendant in having a preliminary hearing. First, the accused could testify about the circumstances in which the confession was obtained but could not be questioned about the truth of the statement.[41] This would not be possible in the trial. Secondly, the preliminary hearing allows the accused to assess the strength of the Crown case and decide whether or not to testify in the hearing proper. As a result, the Divisional Court held that the justices should hold a preliminary hearing if it is represented to them that the confession is in breach of s.76. At that stage, the defendant may give evidence which is confined to the question of admissibility.

In contrast, it has been held to be wrong to hold a trial within a trial where the issue was the quality of identification evidence. A special warning should be given to the jury where identification evidence was relied on.[42] The issue becomes one of the weight that the jury attaches to the witness's testimony and not one of admissibility.[43] The Court of Appeal in *Davies*[44] again showed a reluctance to use a hearing on the *voir dire* in identification cases, even where the evidence is of limited value. The court suggested that there was no realistic basis on which the trial judge could have been invited to exclude the proposed oral evidence of the witness before it was given. A different

---

[38] In the USA, the term "voir dire" is used for the process of jury selection.
[39] *Lawrence* [1933] A.C. 699—the accused should be present throughout a trial.
[40] [1987] 2 All E.R. 668.
[41] *Wong Kam-ming* [1979] 1 All E.R. 939—this is discussed later in this chapter.
[42] *Turnbull* [1977] Q.B. 224.
[43] *Flemming* (1987) 86 Cr.App.R.32.
[44] [2004] EWHC 2422.

approach would apply if the issue was whether the identification procedures had been carried out fairly and in accordance with Code D of the Police and Criminal Evidence Act 1984.

A proceeding similar to a hearing on the *voir dire* is a competency hearing to decide whether a witness is competent to testify. The substantive aspects of this are discussed later,[45] but it is an issue that demonstrates the different functions of the judge and jury in a trial. The judge must decide whether the witness, for example a young child, is capable of understanding questions and giving understandable answers.[46] Should the jury be excluded from such hearings when the proceedings might disclose information which the jury could take into account in their overall assessment of the evidence? In *Hampshire*,[47] the witness was the child victim of a sexual assault whom the judge examined, in the presence of the jury, and satisfied himself that she was a competent witness. On appeal.

Hampshire [1995] 2 All E.R. 1019, *per* Auld J.:

The central question in this appeal is whether, when a judge considers it necessary to investigate a child's competence as a witness, he must do so in the presence of the jury. The rationale for the established practice of conducting such an exercise in their presence is said to be that, although the judge decides the issue of competence, they should see and hear the investigation, in addition to the evidence that follows it, to assist them in assessing the weight of that evidence. In our view, such authority as there is on the matter suggests that the practice is based more on the principle that an exercise of that sort is part of the trial and should, as a matter of openness and fairness, take place in open court and in the presence of the accused, rather than on its function in assisting the jury to determine the weight of the evidence given . . .

It follows, in our judgment, that a judge who considers it necessary to investigate a child's competence to give evidence in addition to or without the benefit of an earlier view of a videotaped interview . . . should do so in open court in the presence of the accused because it is part of the trial, but need not do so in the presence of the jury. The jury's function is to assess the child's evidence, including its weight, from the evidence he or she gives on the facts of the case after the child has been found competent to give it. The exercise of determining competence is not a necessary aid to that function . . .

This particular issue is now governed by s.54 of the Youth Justice and Criminal Evidence Act 1999, which is quite specific that such hearings would always exclude the jury. This emphasises not only the judge's gatekeeper role in regard to witnesses and evidence but also the principle of the adversarial trial that the trier of fact should only use that information which is provided in the full trial through the witness box.

At the *voir dire*, the burden of proving that the conditions of admissibility have been met must lie on the party wishing to adduce the evidence. In

---

[45] Ch.9.
[46] Youth Justice and Criminal Evidence Act 1999, s.53.
[47] [1995] 2 All E.R. 1019.

criminal proceedings, where the prosecution bear the onus of proof, the evidence will not be admissible unless the conditions for admissibility are proved beyond reasonable doubt. However the standard of proof for the defence is on the preponderance of probabilities and this would be the same for parties in civil proceedings.[48]

2. The voir dire and the admissibility of confessions

One of the commonest issues for the judge in a criminal case is the admissibility of a confession. The most common situation is where such an incriminating statement has allegedly been made to a police officer. Under the conditions laid down by the Police and Criminal Evidence Act 1984, s.76, the confession must not have been obtained in circumstances which would render it unreliable nor must it have been obtained by oppression.

Police and Criminal Evidence Act 1984, s.76(2):

76.—(2) If, in any proceedings where the prosecution proposes to give in evidence a confession made by an accused person, it is represented to the court that the confession was or may have been obtained—
(a) by oppression of the person who made it; or
(b) in consequence of anything said or done which was likely, in the circumstances existing at the time, to render unreliable any confession which might be made by him in consequence thereof,
the court shall not allow the confession to be given in evidence against him except in so far as the prosecution proves to the court beyond reasonable doubt that the confession (notwithstanding that it may be true) was not obtained as aforesaid.

Even if the prosecution satisfies the conditions laid down in s.76, there may be a further hurdle in s.78.[49] This provision (which is not limited to confessions) requires that evidence should be excluded if its admission would have an adverse effect on the fairness of the proceedings—for example, a confession, however reliable, will be excluded if the police have wrongfully denied the defendant access to legal advice before interview.

Section 76 (and s.78) lay down conditions of admissibility for confessions. Where the prosecution proposes to offer a confession in evidence, normally defence counsel will object at an early stage in order to prevent any reference to it in the prosecution opening speech. However, even if there is no objection, trial judges can act on their own initiative. Under the Police and Criminal Evidence Act 1984,

Police and Criminal Evidence Act 1984, s.76(3):

76.—(3) In any proceedings where the prosecution proposes to give in evidence a confession made by an accused person, the court may of its own motion require the

---

[48] See Ch.3.
[49] Ch.4.

prosecution as a condition of allowing it do so, to prove that the confession was not obtained as mentioned in subsection (2) above.

At the conclusion of the *voir dire*, the judge may exclude the confession. In this case, nothing more is heard of it.[50] But, if the confession is admitted, the jury must still decide whether the confession was in fact made and what weight to put on it. The same witnesses, often police officers, who testified in the *voir dire*, will be cross-examined by the defence again on the same issues, but this time in front of the jury with the objective of undermining the weight that the jury might place on that confession.[51]

A tactical problem confronts the defence. Should it actively seek to exclude the confession? This may give the prosecution witnesses an advantage as their testimony will have been rehearsed in the *voir dire* before they testify before the jury. Or should the defence recognise that there is likelihood that the judge will admit the statement and keep its powder under wraps in order to cross-examine the police witnesses more effectively in the trial proper?

When the statement is admitted, the *voir dire* decision is not necessarily the end of the matter as the judge retains discretion at common law[52] to take steps to prevent injustice. In *Sat-Bhambra*,[53] the defendant was charged with drug-smuggling. There were several taped interviews, some of which were excluded because of the possible effect of medication given to the defendant who was diabetic. However, some of the tapes were admitted. During the course of the trial proper, the doctor, who had previously testified on *voir dire*, was more robust in his view that the defendant could have been suffering from hypoglycaemia at the time of the interviews. The judge declined to reconsider the question of the admissibility of the tapes on the grounds that the terms of s.76 precluded him from doing so. The Court of Appeal, although dismissing the appeal, did say that a judge has power to take such steps as are necessary to prevent injustice. This might involve either directing the jury to disregard the statement or discharging the jury and ordering a new trial.

The prosecution must adduce evidence that the confession was not obtained in breach of s.76 conditions. To challenge the prosecution case, the defendant would necessarily need to give evidence in the *voir dire* as to the circumstances in which the statement was made. There may be circumstances where the breaches of the codes of practice are so clear that the evidence of the defendant may add little weight.

3. Proceedings in the voir dire

Two issues arise about the proceedings at *voir dire*:

---

[50] The position in *Myers* [1998] A.C. 124—that one defendant may cross-examine another defendant on an excluded confession to undermine the latter's credibility—has been changed by Criminal Justice Act 2003, s.128.

[51] In magistrates' court, it should never be necessary to call prosecution evidence relating to the obtaining of a confession twice—*R. v Liverpool Juvenile Court Ex p. R* [1987] 2 All E.R. 668 at 673b.

[52] Preserved by Police and Criminal Evidence Act 1984, s.82(3).

[53] [1988] Crim.L.R. 453.

(i) Where the defendant testifies, what questions can be put by the prosecution in cross examination?

(ii) The defendant's evidence may well be relevant (and incriminating) to the issues in the trial proper. What use can the prosecution make of this testimony later in the trial?

The key point is that, in the *voir dire*, the fact in issue is the existence or non-existence of the conditions of admissibility. In the context of confessions, this means was the statement obtained by oppression or in circumstances that might make it unreliable? The issue is not the truth or falsity of the confession but the conditions under which that confession was obtained. Consequently in the *voir dire*, any question must be relevant to the fact in issue. The prosecution cannot examine the defendant on the truth or falsity of a confession because, even if it is true, the confession may still have been obtained by oppression and the state should not be permitted to rely on it.

In *Wong Kam-ming*,[54] six men were charged with murder and malicious wounding. The only evidence against the accused was a signed statement that he had been present at the scene and had 'chopped' someone with a penknife. At *voir dire*, he admitted that he had been present at the attack but that he had been forced to copy out the statement and sign it. The confession was excluded but in the trial proper, the prosecution called two shorthand writers who had recorded the *voir dire* to testify that the defendant had admitted to being present. Also the accused was cross-examined on the discrepancies between what he had said at *voir dire* and what he was now saying in the course of his examination in chief. The Privy Council quashed the conviction.

Wong Kam-ming [1979] 1 All E.R. 939 at 942a–946d, *per* Lord Edmund-Davies:

. . . Questions 1 and 2: relevance of truth of extra-judicial statements. In *R v Hammond*[55] prosecuting counsel was held entitled to ask the accused, when cross-examining him during the voir dire, whether a police statement which the accused alleged had been extorted by gross maltreatment was in fact true, and elicited the answer that it was . . . Although much criticised, that decision has frequently been followed in England and Wales and in many other jurisdictions . . .

But the basis of this assertion [that questions as to the truth of the confession go to the credibility of the defendant] is unclear. If the accused denies the truth of the confession or some self-incriminating admission contained in it, the question whether his denial is itself true or false cannot be ascertained until after the voir dire is over and the accused's guilt or innocence has been determined by the jury, an issue which the judge has no jurisdiction to decide. If, on the other hand, the accused made a self-incriminating admission that the statement is true, then, as one critic has expressed it, 'If the confession is true, this presumably shows that the accused tends to tell the truth, which suggests that he is telling the truth in saying the police were violent'.

[54] [1979] 1 All E.R. 939.
[55] [1941] 3 All E.R. 318.

The sole object of the voir dire was to determine the voluntariness[56] of the alleged confession in accordance with principles long established . . . [T]he startling consequences of adopting the Hammond approach were well illustrated in the Canadian case of *R v Hnedish*[57] where Hall CJ said,

'. . . I do not see how under the guise of 'credibility' the court can transmute what is initially an inquiry as to the 'admissibility' of the confession into an inquisition of an accused. That would be repugnant to our accepted standards and principles of justice; it would invite and encourage brutality in the handling of persons suspected of having committed offences.'

It is right to point out that learned counsel for the Crown did not seek to submit that the prosecution could in every case properly cross-examine the accused during the voir dire regarding the truth of his challenged statement . . . But he was unable to formulate an acceptable test of its propriety, and their Lordships have been driven to the conclusion that none exists. In other words, in their Lordships' view, *R v Hammond* was wrongly decided . . .

Their Lordships turn to questions 3 and 4. As part of its case on the main issue, may the prosecution lead evidence regarding the testimony given by the accused on the voir dire? . . . in the instant appeal, counsel for the Crown felt constrained to submit that, even were the trial judge to exclude a confession on the ground that torture had been used to extort it, any damaging statements made by the accused on the voir dire could nevertheless properly be adduced as part of the prosecution's case. Boldness could go no further.

Fortunately for justice, their Lordships have concluded that, where the confession has been excluded, the argument against ever admitting such evidence as part of the Crown case must prevail . . . But what if the confession is held admissible? . . . their Lordships have . . . concluded that the same exclusion of evidence regarding the voir dire proceedings from the main trial must be observed, regardless of whether the challenged confession be excluded or admitted . . .

Question 5 remains for consideration by their Lordships. Notwithstanding the answer to question 3, in the event of the accused giving evidence in the main trial, may he be cross-examined in respect of statements made by him during that voir dire? . . . In *R v Treacy*,[58] where the accused's answers under police interrogation were held inadmissible, it was held that he could not be cross-examined to elicit that he had in fact given those answers . . . *R v Treacy* was undoubtedly correct in prohibiting cross-examination as to the contents of confessions which the court has ruled inadmissible. But what if during the voir dire the accused has made self-incriminating statements not strictly related to the confession itself but which nevertheless have relevance to the issue of guilt or innocence of the charge preferred? May the accused be cross-examined so as to elicit those matters? In the light of their Lordships' earlier conclusion that the Crown may not adduce as part of its case evidence of what the accused said during a voir dire culminating in the exclusion of an impugned confession, can a different approach here be permitted from that condemned in *R v Treacy*?

Subject to what was said to be the court's discretion to exclude it in proper circumstances, counsel for the Crown submitted that it can be, citing in support section 13 of the Hong Kong Evidence Ordinance, which was based on the familiar provision in section 4 of the Criminal Procedure Act 1865 of the United Kingdom, relating to the confrontation of a witness with his previous inconsistent statements. But these statutory provisions have no relevance if the earlier statements cannot be put in evidence. And, having already concluded that the voir dire statements of the accused are not admissible during the presentation of the prosecution's case, their Lordships find it impossible in principle to distinguish between such cross-examination of the accused on the basis of the voir dire as was permitted in the instant case by the trial

---

[56] This test has been replaced by the provisions of Police and Criminal Evidence Act 1984, s.76.
[57] (1958) 26 W.W.R. 685.
[58] [1944] 2 All E.R. 229.

judge and upheld by the majority of the Court of Appeal and that cross-examination based on the contents of an excluded confession which, it is common ground, was rightly condemned in *R v Treacy*.

But what if the voir dire resulted in the impugned confession being admitted, and the accused later elects to give evidence? If he then testifies to matters relating, for example, to the reliability of the confession (as opposed to its voluntariness, which ex hypothesi, is no longer in issue) and in so doing gives answers which are markedly different from his testimony given during the voir dire, may he be cross-examined so as to establish that at the earlier stage of the trial he had told a different story? Great injustice could well result from the exclusion of such cross-examination, and their Lordships can see no justification in legal principle or on any other ground which renders it impermissible. As has already been observed, an accused seeking to challenge the admissibility of a confession may for all practical purposes be obliged to testify in the voir dire if his challenge is to have any chance of succeeding, and his evidence is then (or certainly should be) restricted solely to the issue of the admissibility of the confession. But the situation is quite different where, the confession having been admitted despite his challenge, the accused later elects to give evidence during the main trial and, in doing so, departs materially from the testimony he gave in the voir dire. Having so chosen to testify, why should the discrepancies not be elicited and demonstrated by cross-examination? In their Lordships' view, his earlier statements made in the voir dire provide as acceptable as basis for this cross-examination to that end as any other earlier statements made by him, including, of course, his confession which, though challenged, had been ruled admissible . . .

In the instant case, however, the challenged confession was excluded. It therefore follows that in the judgment of their Lordships no less than three substantial irregularities occurred in the trial: (1) in the voir dire the accused was cross-examined with a view to establishing that his extra-judicial statement was true; (2) in the trial proper, the Crown was permitted to call as part of its case evidence regarding answers given by the accused during the voir dire; and (3) the accused was permitted to be cross-examined so as to demonstrate that what he had said in chief was inconsistent with his statement in the voir dire . . .

Wong Kam-Ming is persuasive authority that:

(i) during cross-examination on the *voir dire*, the accused may not be asked questions as to the truth of the challenged statement,

(ii) whether or not the judge has admitted the statement, the prosecution may not lead evidence of what the accused said on the *voir dire* as part of the Crown case,

(iii) where the judge has excluded the statement and the accused subsequently gives evidence in the trial, the accused may not be cross-examined as to discrepancies between present evidence and what was said on the *voir dire*,

(iv) where the judge has admitted the statement and the accused subsequently gives evidence in the trial, the accused may be cross-examined by prosecuting counsel as to discrepancies between present evidence and what was said on the *voir dire*—the defendant's statements on oath on the *voir dire* are not to be differentiated by any other earlier statements made the accused.

Incriminating statements made by the accused at the *voir dire* are not admissible evidence in the trial proper, whether as evidence-in-chief or on cross-examination. This was supported by the House of Lords in *Brophy*[59]

---

[59] [1981] 2 All E.R. 705; followed in Scotland in *Thompson (Andrew) v Crowe*, (2000) J.C. 173.

where the defendant was tried on charges of murder, of causing explosions and of being a member of the IRA. The only evidence against him was statements made to police officers. After a *voir dire* hearing, all these statements were excluded. During examination-in-chief at the *voir dire*, the accused had admitted to being a member of the IRA and the trial judge had allowed the prosecution to advance evidence of that statement. On appeal to the House of Lords.

Brophy [1981] 2 All E.R. 705 at 709, *per* Lord Fraser:

I would rest my opinion of relevance also on a wider ground. Where, as in this case, evidence is given at the voir dire by an accused person in answer to questions by his counsel, and without objection by counsel for the Crown, his evidence ought in my opinion to be treated as relevant to the issue at the voir dire, unless it is clearly and obviously irrelevant. The accused should be given the benefit of any reasonable doubt. Of course, if the accused, whether in answer to questions from his own counsel or not, goes out of his way to boast of having committed the crimes with which he is charged, or if he uses the witness box as a platform for a political speech, his evidence so far as it relates to those matters will almost certainly be irrelevant to the issue at the voir dire, and different considerations will apply to its admissibility at the substantive trial. But on any reasonable view of the respondent's evidence in this case it cannot be said to be clearly and obviously irrelevant.

Once it has been held that the material part of the respondent's evidence was relevant to the issue at the voir dire, a necessary consequence is, in my opinion, that it is not admissible in the substantive trial. Indeed, counsel for the Crown did not argue to the contrary. If such evidence, being relevant, were admissible at the substantive trial, an accused person would not enjoy the complete freedom that he ought to have at the voir dire to contest the admissibility of his previous statements. It is of the first importance for the administration of justice that an accused person should feel completely free to give evidence at the voir dire of any improper methods by which a confession or an admission has been extracted from him, for he can almost never make an effective challenge of its admissibility without giving evidence himself. He is virtually compelled to give evidence at the voir dire, and if his evidence were admissible at the substantive trial, the result might be a significant impairment of his so-called 'right of silence' at the trial . . .

The result of these decisions is that, at common law, there are significant constraints on the prosecution on using any part of the *voir dire* proceedings as part of the Crown case. But it has been argued[60] that decisions before 1984 could be reconsidered in light of the wording of s.76, since there is no question that a statement made in the course of a *voir dire*, such as that in *Brophy*, was obtained by oppression or in circumstances conducive to its unreliability. Such "judicial confessions" are consequently admissible under s.76. Even were this argument to be correct on strict construction of the statute, it is possible that the policy behind *Brophy* could be maintained by invoking s.78, an approach favoured in Australia,[61] but rejected by Lord Fraser.

---

[60] C. Tapper, *Cross and Tapper on Evidence* (10th ed., Butterworths 2004, p.199.
[61] *Wright* [1969] S.A.S.R. 256.

Brophy [1981] 2 All E.R. 710d–e, *per* Lord Fraser:

With all respect, I cannot regard that as satisfactory solution. The right of the accused to give evidence at the voir dire without affecting his right to remain silent at the substantive trial is in my opinion absolute and is not to be made conditional on an exercise of judicial discretion.[62]

4. Judicial discretion to exclude evidence

The judge not only has the capacity to exclude evidence as a matter of law but also can exercise a discretion to exclude otherwise admissible evidence. This power arises as part of a general supervisory function over the trial and an obligation to ensure a fair trial. At common law, judges could exercise an exclusionary discretion but there was no corresponding inclusionary discretion—in other words, while judges could exclude admissible evidence, they did not have the power to admit inadmissible evidence. If evidence is inadmissible, that was the end of the matter, regardless of any considerations that may be put forward regarding the public interest or the administration of justice. However, by s.114(1)(d) of the Criminal Justice Act 2003 there is now a limited exception—a judge is permitted to admit otherwise inadmissible hearsay evidence if the court is satisfied that it is in the interests of justice to do so.[63]

The discretion to exclude concerns evidence which is otherwise relevant, has sufficient probative value in relation to the time and trouble caused by its admission and is not subject to any other exclusionary rule. But even where these conditions exist, evidence may still be excluded. The power to do so exists both at common law and under statute.

At common law, this can occur where the prejudicial effect of the evidence is so great as to outweigh any probative value. The scope of the judge's discretion at common law is discussed by the House of Lords in *Sang*.[64] This discretion has been retained by s.82 of the Police and Criminal Evidence Act 1984.

Police and Criminal Evidence Act 1984, s.82:

82.—(3) Nothing in this part of the Act shall prejudice any power of a court to exclude evidence (whether by preventing questions from being put or otherwise) at its discretion.

---

[62] *Brophy* at 710d-e *per* Lord Fraser. This principle is not affected by the derogation from the right of silence contained in Criminal Justice and Public Order Act 1994 s.35, since the right must remain until, in the substantive trial itself, the prosecution has adduced sufficient admissible evidence.

[63] Ch.18.

[64] [1979] 2 All E.R. 46.

But the judgment in *Sang* has been substantially overtaken by the impact of s.78 of the Police and Criminal Evidence Act 1984 which requires a judge to take account of all the circumstances, including those in which the evidence was obtained, in deciding whether the admission of the evidence would have "an adverse effect on the fairness of the proceedings". This is discussed later.[65]

B. *Control Over the Issues Before the Court*

The ultimate decision in any case rests with the trier of fact who must decide whether to find for the claimant or defendant or to convict or acquit the accused. The issues that have to be decided are normally laid out in the statement of case or in the indictment but the judge must decide whether there is sufficient evidence to support those issues going before the trier of fact or whether new issues (such as a defence to a criminal charge) have been sufficiently established.

1. Withdrawal of issues

Judges exercise significant control by their ability to withdraw either specific issues or the whole case from the jury. This involves a judgment as to whether sufficient evidence has been produced for that issue to be decided by the jury.[66] For example, in *Metropolitan Railway Co. v Jackson*, the plaintiff sued for damages, having crushed a thumb in a carriage door. There was evidence of the injury and that the train had been overcrowded but none that the overcrowding had caused the plaintiff's thumb to be in the wrong place at the wrong time. The judge correctly withdrew the issue from the jury.

Metropolitan Railway Co. v Jackson [1877] 3 A.C. 193 at 196, *per* Lord Cairns L.C.:

The question is, was there at the trial any evidence of this negligence which ought to have been left to the jury? . . . the judge has a certain duty to discharge and the jurors have another and a different duty. The judge has to say whether any facts have been established by evidence from which negligence may be reasonably inferred; the jurors have to say whether, from those facts, when submitted to them, negligence ought to be inferred. It is, in my opinion, of the greatest importance to the administration of justice that these separate functions should be maintained, and should be maintained distinct. It would be a serious inroad on the province of the jury, if, in a case where there are facts from which negligence may reasonably be inferred, the judge were to withdraw the case from the jury upon the ground that, in his opinion, negligence ought not to be

---

[65] See Ch.4.
[66] This is discussed further in Ch.4 in relation to the evidential burden of proof.

inferred; and it would, on the other hand, place in the hands of the jurors a power which might be exercised in the most arbitrary manner, if they were at liberty to hold that negligence might be inferred from any state of facts whatever . . .

This again defines the different functions of the judge and jury—it is the judicial function to decide whether sufficient evidence has been presented on any issue to leave the matter to the jury; it then becomes the jury's function to decide whether they are persuaded by that evidence. As *Metropolitan Railway* shows, the power to withdraw a particular issue effectively disposes of the case.

In *Metropolitan Railway*, the judge was withdrawing an issue from the consideration of the jury. In *Acott*,[67] the issue was whether a further issue should placed before them. The accused denied murdering his mother but was convicted. He argued on appeal that the judge should have left the defence of provocation to the jury after the Crown had raised the issue in cross-examination, suggesting that he had lost his self-control, having been angered by his mother treating him like a little boy. Allegations put in the form of questions are not evidence and the judge refused to allow the jury to consider the issue of provocation. It was for the judge to decide whether there was evidence of provoking conduct and loss of self control. There must be sufficient evidence to find a reasonable possibility, rather than a merely speculative possibility.

Acott [1997] 1 All E.R. 706 at 713b–d, *per* Lord Steyn:

. . . there can only be an issue of provocation to be considered by the jury if the judge considers that there is some evidence of a specific act or words of provocation resulting in a loss of self-control. It does not matter from what source that evidence emerges or whether it is relied on at trial by the defendant or not. If there is such evidence, the judge must leave the issue to the jury. If there is no such evidence, but merely the speculative possibility that there had been an act of provocation, it is wrong for the judge to direct the jury to consider provocation. In such a case there is simply no triable issue of provocation. I would hold that in such circumstances our law of provocation knows no principle that 'the jury must not be deprived of their opportunity to return a perverse verdict' . . .

2. "No case to answer"

At the close of the prosecution or claimant's case, the defence might argue that the evidence which has been brought forward is not sufficient in quantity or quality to permit the trier of fact to convict or to hold in the claimant's favour. If this assertion of "no case to answer" is upheld, that is the end of the case. The judge must decide whether the case is to be left to the jury as the trier of fact. But nowadays, in civil proceedings, a judge rarely sits with a

---

[67] (1997) 1 All E.R. 706; *Miao* [2003] EWCA 3486.

jury. If, at the end of the claimant's case, the defendant makes a submission of "no case to answer", the judge would normally not rule on this unless the defendant elects not to call evidence.[68] The reasoning behind such a requirement to elect is that the judge in a civil matter is trier of fact as well as of law and a party should not expect the judge to express an opinion on the evidence until it is complete. However, there is no such requirement for election where the judge sits with a jury.[69]

In criminal matters, it is a different matter. At the end of the prosecution case, it is common practice for the defence to argue that there is no case to answer because the prosecution had failed to produce sufficient evidence on a constituent element of the offence. But what is "sufficient"? The leading authority is *Galbraith*.

Galbraith [1981] 2 All E.R. 1060 at 1062e–g, *per* Lord Lane C.J.:

How then should the judge approach a submission of 'no case'?

(1) If there is no evidence that the crime alleged has been committed by the defendant, there is no difficulty. The judge will of course stop the case.

(2) The difficulty arises where there is some evidence but it is of a tenuous character, for example, because of inherent weakness or vagueness or because it is inconsistent with other evidence. (a) Where the judge comes to the conclusion that the prosecution evidence, taken at its highest, is such that a jury properly directed could not properly convict upon it, it is his duty, upon a submission being made, to stop the case. (b) Where, however, the prosecution evidence is such that its strength or weakness depends on the view to be taken of a witness's reliability, or other matters which are generally speaking within the province of the jury and where on one possible view of the facts there is evidence upon which a jury could properly come to the conclusion that the defendant is guilty, then the judge should allow the matter to be tried by the jury . . .

This approach applies not only to defence submissions of 'no case to answer' but also to arguments whether particular issues should or should not be left to the jury. Thus, in a murder case, the defendant might put forward the defence of diminished responsibility under s.2 of the Homicide Act 1957, which places a persuasive burden on the accused. A judge might well refuse to leave this issue to the jury if the defence had produced so little evidence that a reasonable jury, properly directed, could not find on the balance of probabilities that the accused acted under diminished responsibility.

The narrow limits allowed by *Galbraith* for judicial intervention have been criticised,[70] not least because there is a wider power to stop unmeritorious prosecutions in the magistrates' court. A Practice Direction from 1962[71] directs

---

[68] *Alexander v Rayson* [1935] 1 All E.R. R. 185; *Benham Ltd v Kythira Investments Ltd* [2003] EWCA Civ 1794 although *Mullan v Birmingham City Council* [2000] C.P. Rep. 61 indicates that the judge has discretion as to whether to put the defendant to election in such cases.

[69] *Young v Rank* [1950] 2 All E.R. 166.

[70] R. Pattenden, "The Submission of No Case—Some Recent Developments". [1982] Crim.L.R. 558.

[71] [1962] 1 All E.R. 448.

justices to uphold a submission where "..the evidence adduced by the prosecution has been so discredited as a result of cross-examination or is so manifestly unreliable that no reasonable tribunal could safely convict on it . . ." There is little justification to distinguish between summary trial and trial on indictment.

R. Pattenden. "The Submission of No Case—Some Recent Developments" [1982] Crim.L.R. 558 at 564–5:

The object of a submission of no case on a trial on indictment is two-fold. To avoid the risk of a perverse jury verdict and to protect the accused against a prosecutor who has failed to make out a prima facie case and hopes to make good the deficiency by cross-examining the witnesses for the defence. The accused needs this sort of protection as much in a case where the prosecution evidence is so unsound that no reasonable jury could believe the evidence against him as in a case where the prosecution has not mustered sufficient evidence, even if all the evidence is believed, for a lawful conviction. There is no good reason to trust the jury more in the first than in the second case and no inherent reason why a judge should be better equipped to deal with the second than the first matter. In some ways the judge is in a better position to decide the first point than an appellate court to whom the accused may eventually appeal. He sees the witnesses in person, though unlike the appellate court when it considers whether a conviction is unsatisfactory he has only the prosecution evidence to go on—the appellate court reviews all the evidence presented at the trial. An accused may feel genuinely aggrieved if an appellate court upholds a conviction where the trial judge has indicated that he considers a conviction unsupportable.[72]

The Royal Commission on Criminal Justice accepted this position and recommended that the *Galbraith* rule be overturned.[73] However the Privy Council in *Daley*[74] rejected the opportunity to broaden the base for judicial intervention. In that case, the prosecution rested upon identification evidence considered by the judge to have serious weaknesses. Under the *Turnbull* rule,[75] a judge should warn the jury about the dangers of convicting on unsupported evidence of identification but, further, should withdraw the case from the jury altogether where that evidence is poor. This latter rule appears to clash with the *Galbraith* rule that the honesty and reliability of witnesses is a matter for the jury. Lord Mustill resolves this dilemma.

Daley [1993] 4 All E.R. 86 at 94g–j, *per* Lord Mustill:

A reading of the judgment in *R v Galbraith* as a whole shows that the practice which the court was primarily concerned to proscribe was one whereby a judge who

---

[72] Pattenden, above at 564–565.
[73] Royal Commission on Criminal Justice: *op.cit.*, para.4.42.
[74] [1993] 4 All E.R. 86.
[75] *Turnbull* [1976] 3 All E.R. 549—see Ch.9.

considered the prosecution evidence as unworthy of credit would make sure that the jury did not have an opportunity to give effect to a different opinion. By following this practice the judge was doing something which . . . was not his job. By contrast, in the kind of identification case dealt with by *R v Turnbull* the case is withdrawn from the jury not because the judge considers that the witness is lying, but because the evidence even if taken to be honest has a base which is so slender that it is unreliable and therefore not sufficient to found a conviction: and indeed as *R v Turnbull* itself emphasised, the fact that an honest witness may be mistaken on identification is a particular source of risk. When assessing the 'quality' of the evidence, under the Turnbull doctrine, the jury is protected from acting upon the type of evidence which, even if believed, experience has shown to be a possible source of injustice. Reading the two cases in this way, their Lordships see no conflict between them . . .

A successful submission of "no case to answer" terminates the case. The Law Commission proposed[76] that the prosecution should, in some circumstances, be able to appeal rulings such "terminating rulings". The government welcomed these recommendations and introduced a limited right of prosecution appeal against pre-trial rulings, admissibility rulings during the course of the Crown case as well as "no case" submissions in Pt 9 of the Criminal Justice Act 2003.[77]

C. *Summing up—Directing the Jury*

After the parties have presented their evidence and made their closing speeches, the judge will sum up the case for the jury. This is also known as directing the jury. The summing up will consist of several aspects. The judge will remind the jury of the different functions played by the judge and jury with the jury's responsibility to weigh the evidence and decide the facts. The jury will be told about the burden and standard of proof, as a failure to say that the prosecution bears the burden of proof beyond reasonable doubt can lead to any conviction being overturned.[78] The judge will caution jurors to treat both the individual defendants and the different counts in the indictment separately.

As the final arbiter of the law, the judge must explain all the elements of the offence charged. In *McVey*,[79] the accused was an employee suspected of stealing from his employer. A trap was set by marking all the bank notes at the accused's place of work and he was later found in possession of two marked £10 notes. His defence was that he had changed a £20 note. The judge told the jury that there was only one issue for them to consider, namely whether the accused was dishonest when he took the notes. The conviction was quashed as the jury had not been directed as to all the ingredients of the offence of theft. Obviously judges must mention all such ingredients even if

[76] Law Commission Report No. 267, *Double Jeopardy and Prosecution Appeals* (2001).
[77] Home Office, *Criminal Justice: The Way Ahead* (2001) Cm 5074 paras 3.53–3.56; also see the Auld Report *op. cit.*, Ch. 12 paras 47–65.
[78] *Donoghue* (1987) 86 Cr.App.R 267; *Edwards* (1983) 77 Cr.App.R.5.
[79] [1988] Crim.L.R. 127.

they place emphasis on those aspects that are related to the facts of the particular case. Judges must also refer to any defences raised expressly by the accused or disclosed by the evidence, whether that evidence was led by the prosecution or the defence.

The judge will also mention any necessary aspects of evidence: for example, the nature of circumstantial evidence and the need to distinguish between arriving at conclusions based on reliable circumstantial evidence[80] and mere speculation; the need to look for supportive evidence in certain situations, such as accomplice's evidence; the dangers of convicting on identification evidence; the accused's right of silence and any inferences that may be drawn from a failure to testify; how to deal with evidence of good and bad character. Misdirections on points of law or evidence are frequently the basis of any appeal.

The second aspect of the judge's direction will be an abbreviated version of the evidence that the jury have heard. The judge considered this otiose in *Wilson*[81] and told the jury, after a short case, that it was unnecessary for him to review the facts which must still be fresh in their minds. In that case, the Court of Appeal did not interfere but disapproved of this course in *Gregory*,[82] saying that the jury must be reminded by the judge of the facts in all cases. The difficulty is that any summary of the facts cannot be wholly neutral and must inevitably transmit the judge's opinions. "It is not unknown for judges, while emphasising that matters of fact are for the jury and not for the judge, to comment on the facts in such a way as to attempt to influence the jury in one direction or another".[83] The Royal Commission on Criminal Justice considered the possibility of introducing written jury charges, such as those used in New York State, which are in effect a string of explanatory notes by the judge. This was supported by the Auld Report.

Lord Justice Auld, A Review of the Criminal Courts of England and Wales (2001), Ch.10, para.209:

. . . I am strongly of the view that the time has come for the judge to give the jury at the start of all cases a fuller introduction to their task as jurors than is presently conventional, including: the structure and practical features of a trial as it may affect them, a word or two about their own manner of working, for example note-taking, early selection of a foreman and his role, asking questions, time and manner of deliberation etc. He should also give them an objective summary of the case and the questions they are there to decide, supported with a written aide-memoire . . . The parties' advocates should prepare and agree the summary in draft before the trial (and be paid for doing so) for the judge's approval and use by him, them and the jury throughout the trial. The summary should identify:

---

[80] *McGreevy v DPP* [1973] 1 All E.R. 503—there is no special rule for directing juries on cases based wholly on circumstantial evidence.
[81] [1991] Crim.L.R. 838.
[82] [1993] Crim.L.R. 623.
[83] Royal Commission on Criminal Justice, *op.cit.*, para.8.21.

- the nature of the charges;
- as part of a brief narrative, the evidence agreed, reflecting the admissions of either side at the appropriate point in the story (not leaving them to be read or provided in written form to the jury then or at some later stage simply as a list of admissions);
- also as part of the narrative, the matters of fact in issue; and
- with no, or minimal, reference to the law, a list of the likely questions for their decision.

There is little new in the proposal of a short introduction by the judge to the jury of the case and the issues they are there to decide. Some judges in England and Wales do it. Scottish judges often do it by reference to the narrative indictment which is customary in their jurisdiction. And the practice is well established in the United States. As I have seen, it serves as an impressive and effective objective introduction to the jury of the task ahead of them. If and to the extent that the issues narrow or widen in the course of the trial, the case and issues summary should be amended and fresh copies provided to the judge and jury as an update of the matters on which they have to focus. At the end of the trial, it should also serve as a common point of reference for the judge and advocates when considering any matters of difficulty before speeches, and also for the jury during speeches and the summing-up. Now that most judges and practitioners use word processors as a normal working tool, creating and maintaining such a running and useful aide-memoire is not the burden it might have been only a few years ago.

A corollary to succinct directions is the need for a judge to be wholly neutral in any comment on the credibility of the evidence.

It is appropriate for judges to identify for a jury, questions, which are for them to decide, of a witness's credibility; it is inappropriate for judges to intrude their own views of whether or not a witness is to be believed. This is consistent with the need in some cases, for example where there is identification or confession evidence, for special guidance to be given as to its reliability. The precise balance between law and fact in a judge's summing up will be a matter for the judge to decide in the light of the facts of each case. We are well aware that summing up is an extremely difficult task, often calling for the exercise of great skill and judgment.[84]

Judges cannot direct the jury to accept their version of any disputed facts. In *Marr*,[85] a conviction for indecent assault was quashed after the judge ridiculed the defence that the accused had stumbled and accidentally put his hand between the woman's legs. ". . . however distasteful the offence, however repulsive the defendant, however laughable his defence, he is nevertheless entitled to have his case fairly presented to the jury both by counsel and by the judge".[86] Nor can the judge direct the jury to bring in a verdict of guilty, although the direction to acquit, when the judge concludes that there is insufficient evidence for the jury to convict, is possible. There can be a directed acquittal after a defence submission of 'no case to answer' at the close of the prosecution case.

The "directed conviction" was discounted in *DPP v Stonehouse*. A prominent politician who was in financial difficulties arranged life insurance in

---

[84] *ibid.*, para.8.23.
[85] (1989) 90 Cr.App.R 154.
[86] *ibid.*, at 156 *per* Lord Lane C.J.

favour of his wife and then faked his own death by drowning in Miami. No claims were made on the policies and, after the defendant was discovered in Australia and extradited, he was charged with attempting to obtain property by deception. At the trial the judge directed the jury to bring in a verdict of guilty if they were satisfied that he staged the death with a dishonest intention. By such a direction, the judge effectively withdrew from the jury another fundamental element of the offence, namely whether the act was sufficiently proximate to constitute an attempt.

D.P.P. v Stonehouse [1977] 2 All E.R. 909 at 927f–928c, *per* Lord Salmon:

Whilst there is no doubt that, if a judge is satisfied that there is no evidence before the jury which could justify them in convicting the accused and that it would be perverse for them to do so, it is the judge's duty to direct them to acquit.

This rule, which has long been established, is to protect the accused against being wrongly convicted. But there is no converse rule, although there may be some who think that there should be. If the judge is satisfied that, on the evidence, the jury would not be justified in acquitting the accused and indeed that it would be perverse of them to do so, he has no power to pre-empt the jury's verdict by directing them to convict. the jury alone have the right to decide that the accused is guilty. In an appropriate case (and this was certainly such a case) the judge may sum up in such a way as to make it plain that he considers that the accused is guilty and should be convicted. I doubt however whether the most effective way of doing so would be for the judge to tell the jury that it would be perverse for them to acquit. Such a course might well be counter-productive.[87]

The "directed" conviction is a response to the spectre of the "uncontrolled" jury. This could be seen in 1996 when women who broke into a British Aerospace factory caused an estimated £1.5 million damage to a Hawk fighter jet. They were acquitted after claiming that their actions were justified on political grounds—a jury accepted the women's claim that they had a lawful excuse to damage the aircraft because they were using reasonable force to prevent a crime. The jet was to be sold to Indonesia and the accused feared that it would be used by the government there against the people of East Timor.[88]

The judge in *Hill*[89] did not allow a similar case to proceed so far. The defendant caused criminal damage to the fence of a US naval base fence. The defence was that she had lawful cause in that by forcing the Americans to withdraw, she would be protecting her own property from the threat of nuclear attack. The trial court held that this was not lawful cause and thus directed the jury to convict. The Court of Appeal distinguished *Stonehouse* and did not interfere. But *Hill* was doubted in *Kelleher*[90] where the accused entered an art gallery and decapitated a statue of Baroness Thatcher. The

---

[87] Lord Diplock and Viscount Dilhorne dissented.
[88] *The Times* July 31, 1996.
[89] [1989] Crim.L.R. 136.
[90] [2003] EWCA Crim 2846.

judge directed the jury. "Therefore, in the light of what this defendant admits he did, I must direct you that there can only be one verdict in this case and that is one of guilty." On appeal, this was held to be wrong although the conviction was upheld. The *Stonehouse* position has been reaffirmed by the House of Lords in *Wang*.

Wang [2005] 1 All E.R. 782:

. . . in England and Wales it has been possible to assume, in the light of experience and with a large measure of confidence, that jurors will almost invariably approach their important task with a degree of conscientiousness commensurate with what is at stake and a ready willingness to do their best to follow the trial judge's directions. If there were to be a significant problem, no doubt the role of the jury would call for legislative scrutiny. As it is, however, the acquittals of such high profile defendants as Ponting,[91] *Randle and Pottle*[92] have been quite as much welcomed as resented by the public, which over many centuries has adhered tenaciously to its historic choice that decisions on the guilt of defendants charged with serious crime should rest with a jury of lay people, randomly selected, and not with professional judges.

Before the jury retire to consider their verdict, the judge will also instruct them to select a foreman to speak. Judges will also counsel jurors that they should reach a unanimous verdict, although they will mention the possibility of a later direction on majority verdicts.

III FUNCTIONS OF JURIES

In a narrow sense, the jury is not a democratic part of the trial as they are not elected or representative. In a broader sense, they are the essence of democracy as they are randomly selected, untrained and unpaid[93] amateurs from all sections of the population and are, in theory, the least controlled aspect of criminal justice.[94] Jury trial is largely confined to criminal proceedings in the Crown Court—there are very few jury trials in civil actions. Trial by jury has been regarded as a paradigm of English criminal law, described as a bulwark against oppression, a safeguard of our liberties since the common sense of the ordinary person prevails when all else fails.[95]

The functions of the jury are to listen to testimony and other evidence; to listen to judge's direction; to assess the weight to be given to evidence in relation to standard of proof; to determine what happened and thus the existence of the relevant facts in issue and, of course, to arrive at a verdict.

[91] [1985] Crim.L.R. 318.
[92] [1992] 1 All E.R. 370.
[93] Although there is a financial loss allowance, wholly inadequate for the self-employed—Royal Commission on Criminal Justice: *op.cit.*, para.8.56.
[94] Lord Justice Auld: op.cit., Ch.5 provides a review of the jury system.
[95] P. Devlin: *Trial By Jury* (Stevens, 1956).

But how far can the jury go in ignoring the law or acquitting in disregard of the evidence that has been put in front of them? Such jury "nullification" is known in the USA[96] and cases such as the acquittal of Clive Ponting indicates that juries may still regard "justice" as separate from the technicalities of the law. Ponting was a senior civil servant who had sent documents to an opposition MP, which related to the sinking of the Argentinean battleship, the Belgrano, during the course of the Falklands conflict. Prosecuted under the Official Secrets Act 1911, he admitted passing the documents. There was no defence known to law, as the judge pointed out to the jury, yet they still acquitted.[97] Similarly in 1966, disarmament campaigners Michael Randle and Pat Pottle assisted in the escape from Wormwood Scrubs of the double agent, George Blake, serving a 42-year-sentence. In 1991 they stood trial for their part in the escape. They conducted their own defence, arguing that although they did not approve of Blake's espionage activities, the sentence he received was inhumane. The judge again directed the jury that there was no defence to the charges but the jury acquitted them on all counts.[98]

Jury nullification was considered but rejected by Auld who described it as:

Lord Justice Auld, A Review of the Criminal Courts of England and Wales (2001), Ch.5, para.99ff:

'. . . a blatant affront to the legal process and the main purpose of the criminal justice system—the control of crime—of which they are so important a part. With respect to Lord Devlin, I think it unreal to regard the random selection, not election, of 12 jurors from one small area as an exercise in democracy, 'a little parliament', to set against the national will. Their role is to find the facts and, applying the law to those facts, to determine guilt or no. They are not there to substitute their view of the propriety of the law for that of Parliament'.[99]

The Report recommended that juries should have no right to acquit in defiance of the law or in disregard of the evidence. However this recommendation was not pursued in the Criminal Justice Act 2003, although there are provisions for trials without juries and for increased avenues for prosecution appeals.

Perverse verdicts by juries in the face of state pressure are part of the idealised image of the jury. Whether they often live up to that ideal is moot.[1] Jackson wrote that the only cure for admiration of juries is to read *Howell's State Trials*. One place to start is the account of the conviction by a jury in 1792, of Thomas Paine for writing *The Rights of Man*. He was charged at Guildhall, London, that he "being a person of a wicked, malicious and

[96] M. Freeman, "Why not a Jury Nullification Statute Here?" (1981) 131 N.L.J. 304.
[97] *The Times*, February 12, 1985; [1985] Crim.L.R. 318.
[98] [1992] 1 All E.R. 370.
[99] Lord Justice Auld: *op.cit.*, Ch.5 para.99ff.
[1] See discussion in J. Spencer, *Jackson's Machinery of Justice* (8th ed., CUP 1989) p.390ff.

seditious disposition . . . did publish that the crown of this kingdom was contrary to the rights of the inhabitants . . .". Despite the efforts of Thomas Erskine who defended Paine, the carefully selected jury, which received two guineas each and a free dinner for a conviction, returned a verdict of guilty. What is undoubted that it is "the most ancient relic in any modern legal system",[2] dating from Anglo–Saxon and Anglo–Norman times. While the continental legal systems devised complex systems of logical proof, the English used the jury.[3]

T. Arnold Symbols of Government (Harbinger, 1962), pp.144–145:

In addition to the notion of fair hearing, the ceremonial trial must dramatize the impersonal application of logical rules to facts. Here we have the contradiction between the ideal of a permanent unyielding law which must be enforced without respect to persons, and the ideal of justice, which can never ignore persons. This conflict is resolved as most conflicts are resolved, by inventing a devil who can be blamed for the inconsistencies of the system. In the American trial the part of the devil is taken by the jury. We are constantly defending the jury as the best device for securing 'Justice' ever invented, and at the same time attacking it and seeking to limit its functions. The defense always refers to juries in general as an institution protecting our liberties, etc. The attack always centers about juries in particular types of cases, considered as an unpredictable body, moved by emotional considerations, and not careful of the fundamental principles of law because of ignorance, prejudice, etc. Yet the jury continues as the great symbol of justice, in spite of constant proof of its inadequacy in particular cases.

Actually, of course, the reason for the existence of the jury is to absorb the criticism of the numerous unsatisfactory results in the trial of cases, and thus to deflect it against the judicial system itself. When [a notorious criminal] is acquitted, we blame the jury if we do not like the result. We cannot blame the law, because according to the law there was a question of fact to be left to the jury which the law had no right to decide.

Apart from its role as a simple and understandable symbol, the jury has to listen to the testimony and other evidence provided by the prosecution or defence. It is their function to assess the credibility of a witness, to measure the weight that should be given to any piece of evidence and to determine the existence or non-existence of the facts in the case. They must determine the facts on the evidence presented to them in court. A juror cannot conduct independent investigation—for example, on an overnight adjournment, researching on the Internet and bringing downloaded material into the jury room the next day.[4] Having determined the facts on the evidence, the jury must apply those facts to the legal issues in the case, as explained to them by the judge, and, by applying the burden and standard of proof, come to a conclusion.

Often this process can require considerable clarity of thought on the part of jurors who may be told that they are entitled to use an accused's confession

---

[2] S. Milsom, *Historical Foundations of the Common Law* (Butterworths, 1981) p.413.
[3] *ibid.*, 410.
[4] See Ch.21.

as evidence against that defendant but not as evidence against a co-accused; that the previous convictions which have been put to the defendant in cross-examination are not evidence of guilt but simply go to the defendant's credibility; that a previous statement consistent with present testimony is not evidence of the facts but can merely enhance the weight the jury might give to that witness's evidence. The extent to which the jury understand and implement the judge's directions remains unclear.[5]

There is an apparently clear demarcation between the judicial function as final arbiter of substantive and evidential law and the juror as the trier of fact. But this distinction often becomes clouded as the definitions of many offences include legal concepts which masquerade as "facts". Although there is a general rule that the construction of ordinary words in a statute is a question of fact for the trier of fact, these concepts are relatively imprecise in their definition. The key elements of theft, for example, are legal concepts of appropriation, property belonging to another and intent to deprive, all of which may need explanation and definition by the judge because the law uses the terms in a manner which is outside any common usage of the terms themselves. But theft also requires "dishonesty" and this can be left, more or less straightforwardly,[6] as a matter of fact for the jury.

Gilks [1972] 3 All E.R. 280:

> Well, it is a matter for you to consider, members of the jury, but try to place yourselves in [the appellant's] position and answer the question whether in your view he thought he was acting honestly or dishonestly?[7]

While some terms have acquired a special meaning as a result of statute and of authority and the judge can direct the jury as to their meaning, others remain ordinary word which should be left to the jury to construe. How do we tell which terms fall into which category? In *Brutus v Cozens*,[8] the defendant, an anti-apartheid demonstrator, had interrupted Wimbledon by blowing whistles and distributing leaflets. He was charged under section 5 of the Public Order Act 1936 with using insulting behaviour in a public place. The justices (who, in summary trials, are the tribunal of fact and equivalent to the jury) held that the behaviour was not insulting and dismissed the information. The Divisional Court held that conduct which evinced disrespect for the rights of others so as to cause resentment was insulting within the meaning of the Act. The House of Lords reversed this approach, holding that the construction of the term was not a matter of law for the judge but for the trier of fact.

---

[5] Not least because empirical research into the way juries function would be contempt of court under Contempt of Court Act 1981, s.8.

[6] *Feely* [1973] 3 All E.R. 341 but matters have become more complex with *Ghosh* [1982] 2 All E.R. 689.

[7] Trial judge's direction to the jury in *Gilks* [1972] 3 All E.R. 280 at 283.

[8] [1972] 2 All E.R. 1297.

Brutus v Cozens [1972] 2 All E.R.: 1297, *per* Lord Reid:

The meaning of an ordinary word of the English language is not a question of law. The proper construction of a statute is a question of law. If the context shows that a word is used in an unusual sense the court will determine in other words what that unusual sense is. But here there is in my opinion no question of the word 'insulting' being used in an unusual sense. It appears to me . . . to be intended to have its ordinary meaning. It is for the tribunal which decides the case to consider, not as law but as fact, whether in the whole circumstances the words of the statute do or do not as a matter of ordinary usage of the English language cover or apply to the facts which have been proved . . .[9]

In *Stonehouse*[10], the issue was whether the defendant's acts (faking his own suicide) were "sufficiently proximate" to his wife's obtaining the insurance money to form the *actus reus* of the offence of an attempt to obtain that money by deception. This idea of "proximity" was in itself is a fact which needed to be proved and decided by the jury.

D.P.P. v Stonehouse [1977] 2 All E.R. 909, *per* Lord Diplock:

There are some crimes whose definition incorporates as a constituent element a concept which is imprecise in that it involves some matter of degree on which opinions of reasonable men may differ and as to which the legal training and experience of a judge does not make his opinion on the matter more likely to be right than that of a non-lawyer. Under our system of trial by jury the question whether the facts proved conform to such a concept is one for the jury despite its involving interpretation of the definition of a crime; because, it being a matter on which opinions may reasonably differ, an opinion shared by at least ten jurors is thought to be more reliable than that of a single judge.[11]

Stonehouse and *Brutus v Cozens* are both authority for the proposition that it is for the jury to decide upon and apply the meaning of ordinary English words. This remains the approach–in *Evans*,[12] the defendant had been convicted of harassing her neighbours and a restraining order was made against her. The order prohibited her from, inter alia, using abusive words or actions towards her neighbours. Her neighbour called a plumber, who parked his van in the street. Shortly after his arrival, the defendant drove her car, which was already parked in the street, forward a short distance so that the plumber's van was blocked in. She was convicted for breaching her restraining order. On appeal, it was held that it is for the jury to decide what constitutes abusive behaviour contrary to s.5(5) of the Protection from Harassment Act 1997.

---

[9] *ibid.* at 1299a-d *per* Lord Reid.
[10] [1977] 2 All E.R. 909.
[11] *Stonehouse*, above at 918g-j *per* Lord Diplock.
[12] [2004] EWCA Crim 31; *Hammond v DPP* [2004] EWHC 69.

In theory the jury interpret the meaning of words in legislation but it only takes a cursory glance around the criminal law to see that these common sense concepts are frequently circumscribed by quite detailed definitions: in murder cases such *Nedrick*[13] and *Woollin*,[14] the appellate courts address the issue of when the accused "intentionally" kills. It is difficult to see why a court should interpret "intentional" for a jury but not the term "insulting". *Brutus v Cozens* is often honoured more in its breach than in its observance.

---

[13] [1986] 3 All E.R. 1.
[14] [1998] 4 All E.R. 103.

3

THE BURDEN AND STANDARD OF PROOF

I. What is Proof?

In both the everyday and the legal world, the term "proof" is used quite loosely. When we wish to test an assertion, we often say, "Have you any proof of that?" For the lawyer, such a question can have two basic meanings. The first is, "Do you have any evidence of what you say?"—asking for information on which we might make a decision. As such, 'proof' is simply the evidence which has been given in a particular case. The second sense takes this further, not merely asking for information but demanding of a party "Can you demonstrate the correctness of what you say?" Is that information or evidence sufficient to establish a fact or to produce belief in the certainty of something?

This chapter uses the term in the latter sense: to prove an assertion is to demonstrate that the assertion is correct. In a court, the range of assertions that can be made is wide—from a simple factual issue of identification of a criminal to the proper interpretation of a contractual term to a qualitative judgment as to what may be in the best interests of a child. The court needs to reach an authoritative determination of each of these issues, establishing the truth. In daily life, we work on the assumption that there is a truth and that we can and do know things, especially matters that we perceived through our senses of sight, hearing, taste, touch and smell; we remember those sensory perceptions and can recall them when required. But we also know things intellectually that have been demonstrated to us by scientific evidence—that $\sqrt{4}$ is 2 or that the earth is round. A third, less valid, sense is when we talk of "knowing" things which at best are a matter of ethical or aesthetic judgment or simple belief such as religious faith.

Investigation and trial are posited on the idea that through the process of evidence and rational decision making, it is possible to know things, in the dictionary sense—"to hold for true or real with assurance and on (what is held to be) an adequate objective foundation". In particular the legal process aims to recreate the past and discover what happened and in what circumstances at a particular time and place. But at the same time we know that there are significant difficulties here for the law.

First is the realistic point: courts and juries are practical reasoners, operating in a "cognitive economy" of acquiring information and making decisions.[1]

---

[1] I draw here on unpublished material by Professor Gabbay from King's College, London.

They need to be practical because they deal with scarce resources, in terms of time and available raw material; lawyers have modest cognitive expectations, in terms of outcome. The court focuses on the issues that it needs to decide, listens only to relevant data about those issues and settles on the "best truth" even if that truth is not perfect. Timeliness, constraints on information, or the "computational capacity" of fact finders (protecting juries from complex issues) are all aspects of this economy. The strictness of cognitive standards should also be part of this and the law parades the concept of "beyond reasonable doubt" as its banner of certainty in criminal cases. But when compared to scientific standards of certainty, legal standards seem woeful. Lawyers and juries do their best but moral certainty does not compare with scientific certainty.

A second difficulty is a philosophical issue about the possibility of knowing with certainty what happened and how people acted. We might aim for truths in life and through legal process but in both we usually have to be satisfied with less. But when do we regard ourselves as satisfied that we "know" something? Neither life nor law operates as a mathematical proof which, given certain assumptions and the operation of mathematical functions, always produces the correct answer. In contrast, the inferential, common sense logic of the courtroom requires that we must test, as best we can, the strength and validity of our assumptions and the inferences that are drawn from them. How strong must that inference be before we regard it as correct? How confident must we be in our conclusions?

In normal life, we do not lay down formal standards of "proof". If a person alleges that they "know" something or "believe" it, we test such statements by differing techniques. First, we may compare the assertion against other information available to us; secondly, we may question them on why they know or believe; thirdly we may accept their word, presuming it to be true until there is other information which might confirm or refute the original statement; and finally we may disbelieve, presuming it to be untrue until other information becomes available. Parents may use these techniques when they listen to an account of a child's fight with another child—they will compare, contrast, question, trust or suspect. Often the parent will invoke a moral language of "truth" or "honesty" and exhort their child to tell the 'truth' and give as accurate an account as possible. Police officers have been known to employ the same techniques—"get it off your chest", "it'll be for the best". But neither parent nor officer will 'know' whether the account they have heard is "true". Who was the aggressor? Who was the victim? Necessarily we come to decisions based on what probably happened, mediated perhaps through other factors such as a parent's desire to trust their child or a police officer's need to bring an investigation to a successful conclusion.

In an adversarial trial in a court of law, the trier of fact listens to conflicting narratives and must turn probabilities into certainties and come to a conclusion—a verdict of guilty or not guilty or, in civil proceedings, a finding for one of the parties involved. The court must direct the trier of fact as to what level of confidence must be made explicit as one of the law jobs is to resolve and define what is real.[2] The mere production of evidence is not proof and at the end of a trial, the trier of fact must decide whether the facts in issue have been satisfactorily established. This involves a two stage process of reasoning.

1. *Burden of proof.* The first stage is to establish which party has the task of proving a fact? At its most basic level we might ask, in civil proceedings, if no evidence at all were presented, which party would succeed? In a criminal trial, must the accused satisfy the jury of their innocence or must the prosecution convince the jury of their guilt? As soon as such questions are asked, there are, in general terms, straightforward answers. The person who mobilises the legal machinery has the obligation to demonstrate the correctness of any assertions. Thus it is normally accurate to say that the prosecution bear the burden of proof in criminal cases while the claimant bears that burden in civil actions.

But legal actions, civil and criminal, often involve a plethora of issues. The burden of proof on any particular issue is not necessarily on the claimant or prosecution. For example, in a murder trial, the defendant might raise the defence of diminished responsibility under s.2 of the Homicide Act 1957 and proof of that condition lies with the accused. In a civil action for negligence, the defendant may well claim contributory negligence on the part of the claimant as a partial defence and again the proof of that would rest on the defendant.[3] But knowing who bears the burden of proving a fact does not tell us what proof consists of. That is a question of how a party can discharge any burden of proof cast upon them, *i.e.* the standard of proof.

2. *Standard of proof.* For the lay person, it is important that the decision of a court should be right and that, as a result of the trial, we can be sure as to what happened. We express ourselves in certainties and hesitate to do so in mere probabilities. Yet in court, what is provable must be expressed in terms of what is probable. In a criminal trial when an individual's liberty is at stake, proof of guilt requires that a jury is "sure" or is satisfied "beyond reasonable doubt". In civil cases, the standard of proof is expressed in terms of the "balance of probabilities". Despite the language of probability, judges are reluctant to express such concepts of proof in mathematical terms and prefer more subjective language—indeed in France, that 'subjective probability' is expressed in the idea of *intime conviction* which a judge should possess before any finding of guilt. However there is an increasing use (and abuse) of statistics in the courtroom as well as a complex literature on the extent to which probability theories have a part to play in the factual problems confronting courts.[4]

For the lawyer, the standard of proof is merely the designation of a certain level of probability that a specific fact or state of affairs exists.

---

[2] W. Mansell, B. Meteyard and A. Thomson, *A Critical Introduction to Law* (3rd ed., Cavendish, 2004), p.20ff.

[3] Contributory negligence was a full defence until Law Reform (Contributory Negligence) Act 1945, s.1, but the old common law which casts burden of proof on the defendant still applies—*Caswell v Powell Duffryn Collieries* [1940] A.C. 152.

[4] Discussed later in this chapter.

R. Eggleston, Evidence, Proof and Probability (2nd ed., Weidenfeld. 1983), pp.8–9:

The word 'probable', from which the term 'probability' is derived, originally meant 'provable' or 'capable of being tested'. In the course of time, however, it acquired the secondary meaning of 'likely to happen', so that when we speak of an event as being 'probable', we mean that we think the chances of its happening are at least better than even. We also mean that it is less than certain . . .

While we ordinarily use the term 'probability theory' as if it were a single thing, there are in fact several theories of probability . . . In 'classical' probability theory, probability is the ratio of favourable outcomes to all possible outcomes, where all outcomes have an equal likelihood of happening; the probability of throwing a six with a 'fair' die is one-sixth, since the die has six faces, and if the die is fair, each face has an equal chance of being uppermost.

For the statistician, probability refers to the frequency of occurrences of an event which happens a number of times. Thus, if a statistician is asked to estimate the probability of a person living to a certain age, he will refer to life tables that tell him what proportion of people of the same age as the subject have, in past experience, survived to the specified age.

There is a third concept of probability which is often referred to as a 'degree of belief' but which I would prefer to call a 'degree of likelihood' or 'degree of persuasion'. This is often called 'subjective probability' or 'psychological probability'. While probabilities of the first and second kind can be given mathematical equivalents, any attempt to put a figure on subjective probabilities is likely to meet with the criticism that it is incapable of quantification . . . the kind of probabilities that lawyers are mainly concerned with are of the subjective kind. They sometimes relate to the past and sometimes to the future, but except in rare cases they are not susceptible of verification. By contrast, if the assumptions of classical probability theory are accepted . . . the conclusions follow from the premises; and for probabilities based on frequency, past experience offers a measure of frequency that can be applied to the case in hand . . .

In England and Wales, in civil cases, the standard of proof is expressed in terms of the "balance of probabilities". In a criminal trial when an individual's liberty is at stake, proof of guilt requires a similar high standard and that occurs when the jury is 'sure' or is satisfied 'beyond reasonable doubt'. A judge should possess this before any finding of guilt. Occasionally we can see that standard move—for example, fingerprints are commonly used in court to prove the presence of the accused at the scene of the crime. The lay person often assumes that such evidence is conclusive proof on the assumption that every individual's fingerprints are unique.[5] However even here we are dealing with probabilities—the expert will testify that fingerprint impressions were taken from the scene and compared with those taken from the suspect and give an opinion as to whether there is a match. In the 1990s, a match could only be declared if there was a very high degree of probability with the witness being able to point to at least 16 points of similarity with no points of disagreement. After a Home Office review,[6] that standard has been changed

---

[5] The reliability of this claim has been questioned: J. Randerson, and A. Coghlan, "Forensic Evidence Stands Accused" New Scientist, January 31, 2004, p.6.

[6] I. Evett, and A. Williams, "A Review of the Sixteen Point Fingerprint Standard in England and Wales" Journal of Forensic Identification, 46 (1), January/February, 1996.

and in *Buckley*,[7] the Court of Appeal held that the admission of such evidence was a matter for the discretion of the judge and that where there are eight or more similar points, a judge may exercise their discretion to admit, bearing in mind the expert witness's experience in the field, consideration of the number of matching points, whether there were any dissimilar characteristics to the fingerprint and the quality and clarity of the print upon the item relied. The judge will warn the jury that the witness's opinion is not conclusive but juries will often base their decision that the accused was present at the scene on evidence of a lower quality than previously.

II. THE BURDEN OF PROOF

The burden of proof has been described as 'Whose task is it to establish a fact?' but there are preceding questions, namely, 'What fact?' and 'Why does that fact have to be established?' For example, in criminal law, the summons or indictment will specify an offence which has particular elements as part of its definition: murder involves causing death with intent to kill or cause serious harm. It is the prosecution's task to prove those elements which are, so to speak, already on the court's agenda. But in response to the charge, the accused may wish to raise a legally recognised defence such as self-defence, duress or provocation. It is not part of the prosecution's task in presenting its evidence-in-chief to disprove all possible defences. These issues are not on the agenda until the defendant has produced some evidence that a particular defence applies in this case.

An example of this can be seen in *Hill v Baxter* where the defendant was charged with a road traffic offence. His explanation was that he had blacked out just before the incident. This raised a possible defence of non-insane automatism,

Hill v Baxter [1958] 1 Q.B. 277 at 284–5, *per* Devlin J.:

I am satisfied that even in a case in which liability depended upon full proof of mens rea, it would not be open to the defence to rely upon automatism without providing some evidence of it. If it amounted to insanity in the legal sense, it is well established that the burden of proof would start with and remain throughout upon the defence. But there is also recognised in the criminal law a lighter burden which the accused discharges by producing some evidence, but which does not relieve the prosecution from having to prove in the end all the facts necessary to establish guilt . . . It would be quite unreasonable to allow the defence to submit at the end of the prosecution's case that the Crown had not proved affirmatively and beyond a reasonable doubt that the accused was at the time of the crime sober, or not sleepwalking or not in a trance or black-out. I am satisfied that such matters ought not to be considered at all until the defence has produced at least prima facie evidence . . .[8]

By the end of the prosecution case, they will have adduced evidence relating to all definitional elements of the offence. But by that stage there is no

[7] [1999] EWCA Crim 1191.
[8] [1958] 1 Q.B. 277.

requirement to disprove all possible defences. If the defence wishes the court to consider a defence, normally they will have to adduce some evidence relating to it. If they persuade the judge that they have produced enough evidence, at the end of the case the prosecution normally must satisfy the court that not only did the defendant commit the offence but also they had no viable defence.

Hill v Baxter demonstrates that the term "burden of proof" is used in two different ways—in Devlin's terms, a lighter and a heavier version.

1. *Evidential burden.* The lighter process may be described as agenda-setting. This is the burden a party bears to adduce enough evidence for the judge to be satisfied that the issue should be left to the trier of fact. All issues in an action must be established in this way. This is known as imposing an evidential burden and might be referred to as the problem of "passing the judge" because any failure to satisfy the evidential burden means that the issue will never reach the jury. The issue is bound up with that of the judge's role in withdrawing issues from the jury, discussed earlier.[9]

2. *Legal burden.* Simply adducing enough evidence to raise an issue must be distinguished from the burden placed on a party to persuade the trier of fact to find for them on any particular issue. This latter stage is the burden of proof in a strict sense and is also known as the persuasive or probative burden.

J. Thayer, Preliminary Treatise on Evidence at Common Law:

. . . the peculiar duty of him who has the risk of any given proposition on which the parties are at issue—who will lose the case if he does not make this proposition out, when all has been said and done.[10]

Certain preliminary points follow from this and should be emphasised.

a) Burdens relate not to the action as a whole but to particular issues within a case.
b) In general, the evidential burden and the legal burden on any issue will both be borne by the same party but, as *Hill v Baxter* shows, even in the criminal law, the burdens can rest on different parties. In that case, the accused had the evidential burden to adduce enough evidence to raise the issue of automatism but the prosecution bore the legal burden of disproving this defence.
c) Deciding who has the burden is separate from discharging that burden—the standard of proof. A party must adduce sufficient evidence to discharge an evidential or a legal burden. But what is

---

[9] See Ch.2.
[10] J. Thayer, *Preliminary Treatise on Evidence at Common Law* 355 (although the substitution of "issue" for "case" would be wise).

"sufficient" will vary. The test of evidential sufficiency to raise the defence of automatism and thus require the prosecution to disprove it is clearly very different to that required to prove the guilt of an accused. This is discussed later.

Does the burden of proof shift in the course of a trial? The evidential burden and the legal burden attach themselves to parties at the beginning of a trial as a matter of law, allocated either at common law or by statute. These burdens do not shift. What does change in the course of a trial is the tactical balance between the parties. For example, in a rape case, the prosecution will produce evidence in chief that the accused had intercourse with the victim without her consent. If this remained unchallenged, it may (but not necessarily will) prove sufficient for the jury to convict. The defendant is at a tactical disadvantage and at serious risk of conviction unless he produces some evidence which challenges the prosecution case, either by cross-examining the prosecution witnesses or by adducing evidence of his own that there was consent or that he believed on reasonable grounds that there was consent. But there has been no shifting of the legal burden of proof.

D.P.P. v Morgan [1975] 2 All E.R. 347, *per* Lord Cross:

If [the prosecution] adduces evidence to show that intercourse took place and that the woman did not consent to it, then in the absence of any evidence from the defendant the jury will certainly draw the inference that he was aware that she was not consenting. So as a practical matter he is bound—if he wishes to raise the point—to give evidence to the effect that he believed that she was consenting and as to his reason for that belief; and the weaker those reasons are, the more likely the jury are to conclude that he had no such belief. But the issue as to the accused's belief in the woman's consent is before the jury from the beginning, and is an issue in respect of which the evidential burden is on the Crown from the first to the last. There is never any question of any evidential burden with regard to it being on the accused or of the judge withdrawing it from the jury.[11]

The only situation when the legal burden may be said to shift is where there is the operation of another rule of law, such as the impact of a rebuttable presumption. For example, under s.75 of the Sexual Offences Act 1975, where the prosecution prove that, *inter alia*, a rape victim was asleep or unconscious, then ". . . the complainant is to be taken not to have consented to the relevant act unless sufficient evidence is adduced to raise an issue as to whether he consented, and the defendant is to be taken not to have reasonably believed that the complainant consented unless sufficient evidence is adduced to raise an issue as to whether he reasonably believed it." If there is proof that the victim was asleep, a new evidential burden is placed on the defendant to show some evidence that she was consenting.

[11] Submission of appellant in *DPP v Morgan* [1975] 2 All E.R. 347 at 349j–350b, *per* Lord Cross.

In civil proceedings, where a litigant bears the burden of showing that a third party is dead, they may adduce proof that the third party has been seven years absent without being heard from. This raises a rebuttable presumption of death and the burden of proving that the third party is still alive now rests on the other party to the action.[12]

A. *Allocation of the Legal Burden*

The allocation of the legal burden is determined by the rules of substantive law.[13] It is straightforwardly the allocation of risk which means that the party shouldering the burden loses if there is no evidence at all or if the evidence does not satisfy the finder of fact. It is often called the probative or persuasive burden and it has various effects:

a) in specifying the right to start calling evidence
b) in dictating who can make submissions of "no case to answer"
c) in settling doubts for the trier of fact

The common law principle is that "he who asserts must prove", namely that the burden of proof falls on the party making the positive assertion. In *Wakelin v London and South Western Railway*,[14] a man was killed on a railway level crossing. The widow sued. The defendant railway admitted that he had been run over by a train and also that they had neglected certain warnings. But they called no evidence and submitted that there was no case to answer, since there was no proof as to whether the man had been killed because of their fault or because he had thrown himself against the train.

Wakelin v London and South Western Railway [1887] 12 A.C. 41, *per* Lord Halsbury L.C.:

My Lords, it is incumbent upon the plaintiff in this case to establish by proof that the husband's death had been caused by some negligence of the defendants . . . That is the fact to be proved. If the fact is not proved, the plaintiff fails, and if in the absence of direct proof the circumstances which are established are equally consistent with the allegation of the plaintiff as with the denial of the defendant, the plaintiff fails for the very simple reason that the plaintiff is bound to establish the affirmative of the proposition . . .[15]

The claimant had to prove that her husband died on the railway and that his death was caused by the defendant's negligence. Simply proving his death did not put any burden on the defendant to disprove their negligence.

---

[12] See section on presumptions in Ch.21.
[13] For a discussion of such rules, see A. Kiralfy, *The Burden of Proof* (Professional Books, 1987).
[14] [1887] 12 A.C. 41.
[15] *ibid*, at 44–45 *per* Lord Halsbury L.C.

1. The legal burden in criminal cases

The prosecution will bear the burden of proof in relation to most issues in any criminal trial. However, on occasion, there is a reversal of this position so that the defendant bears the burden. There are a few examples at common law—if the accused is seeking a verdict of "not guilty through reason of insanity", the burden of proving that the accused is mad is on the defence and must be shown on the balance of probabilities.[16] This reversal of the burden of proof is more likely under statute—for example, if the accused has pleaded "not guilty" to murder but is arguing for a conviction for manslaughter on the grounds of diminished responsibility, s.2(2) of the Homicide Act 1957 places the legal burden of proof on that issue on the accused, again on the preponderance of probabilities.

The basic common law rule in criminal cases is that the prosecution bear the legal burden of proof. This was laid down by Lord Sankey in *Woolmington v DPP*.[17] The accused was charged with murdering his wife from whom he was separated. He called at her mother's house and shot her dead. His story was that he decided to take a gun, show it to his wife and threaten to shoot himself if she did not return. He attached the gun to himself with wire flex under his coat and, as he brought it out, it somehow went off. The trial judge directed the jury as follows.

> The Crown has got to satisfy you that this woman . . . died at the prisoner's hands. They must satisfy you of that beyond any reasonable doubt. If they satisfy you of that, then he has to show that there are circumstances to be found in the evidence which has been given from the witness box in this case which alleviate the crime so that it is only manslaughter, or which excuse the homicide altogether by showing that it was a pure accident.

This direction placed the burden of proving that the incident was an accident on the accused. In the House of Lords, the conviction was quashed.

Woolmington v D.P.P. [1935] A.C. 462 at 473–481, *per* Lord Sankey:

It is true, as stated by the Court of Criminal Appeal, that there is apparent authority for the law as laid down by the learned judge . . . Rather would I invite your Lordships to begin by considering the proposition of law which is contained in *Foster's Crown Law*, written in 1762 . . .

> In every charge of murder, the fact of killing being first proved, all the circumstances of accident, necessity, or infirmity, are to be satisfactorily proved by the prisoner, unless they arise out of the evidence produced against him; for the law presumeth the fact to have been founded in malice until the contrary appeareth.

---

[16] There is a presumption of sanity—the defendant must prove on the balance of probabilities that he or she is insane within the meaning of the M'Naghten Rules (1843) 10 Cl. & F. 200.

[17] [1935] A.C. 462.

And very right it is, that the law should so presume. The defendant in this instance standeth upon just the same foot that every other defendant doth; the matters tending to justify, excuse, or alleviate must appear in evidence before he can avail himself of them.

. . . The question arises: Is that statement correct law? . . . If at any period of a trial it was permissible for the judge to rule that the prosecution had established its case and that the onus was shifted on the prisoner to prove that he was not guilty, and that, unless he discharged that onus, the prosecution was entitled to succeed, it would be enabling the judge in such a case to say that the jury must in law find the prisoner guilty and so make the judge decide the case and not the jury, which is not the common law . . .

. . . Throughout the web of English criminal law one golden thread is always to be seen—that it is the duty of the prosecution to prove the prisoner's guilt subject to what I have already said as to the defence on insanity and subject also to any statutory exception. If, at the end of and on the whole of the case, there is a reasonable doubt, created by the evidence given by either the prosecution or the prisoner, as to whether the prisoner killed the deceased with a malicious intention, the prosecution has not made out the case and the prisoner is entitled to an acquittal. No matter what the charge or where the trial, the principle that the prosecution must prove the guilt of the prisoner is part of the common law of England and no attempt to whittle it down can be entertained.

Lord Sankey's "golden thread" is that, in criminal proceedings, the Crown must prove the facts in issue beyond reasonable doubt. In *Woolmington*, those facts were that the defendant caused the victim's death and that he intended to cause her death. The accused bears neither a legal burden nor an evidential burden on these issues—he does not have to prove that it was an accident. Accident is not an additional issue, e.g. such as self-defence, but is merely a denial of intention, proof of which is the function of the prosecution. It was for the prosecution to prove beyond reasonable doubt that the defendant had intended to fire the gun and to kill his wife.

The dynamics of the trial are, of course, different: having proved the shooting, the prosecution is entitled to rely on an inference that the defendant intended to kill. In these circumstances, if he chose not to testify, he would take a considerable risk. But silence would not mean inevitable conviction because the jury must still be directed by the judge that the prosecution must prove malice aforethought beyond reasonable doubt and the jury might not have been convinced by the prosecution witnesses. There is without doubt a tactical reason why the accused should testify in order to implant a doubt in the jury's mind about whether the shooting was intentional or accidental. But such tactical decisions must be distinguished from legal or evidential burdens.

In *Woolmington*, Lord Sankey mentions specifically two exceptions to this "golden thread", namely the defence of insanity and statutory exceptions. These reverse the burden of proof and place it on the accused. This raises two questions, first in what circumstances does the criminal law allow such reversals and secondly the issue whether a reverse onus can be compliant with the guarantees of as fair trial under Art.6?

(i) *Reversing the burden in criminal proceedings*
The burden of proof can be placed upon the defendant in three situations.

1. *At common law.* As a result of *M'Naghten's Case*[18] the accused who raises the defence of insane automatism bears the burden of proof. That burden is discharged by proof on the balance of probabilities.[19]

2. *By express statutory provision.* There are many statutes which expressly place the burden of proof on the defendant. An example is section 2 of the Prevention of Corruption Act 1916 which requires that a public servant, charged with corruption, would have to prove that any money or gift was not received corruptly,

Prevention of Corruption Act, s.2:

2.—Where in any proceedings against a person for an offence under the Prevention of Corruption Act 1906, . . . it is proved that any money, gift, or other consideration has been paid or given to or received by a person in the employment of Her Majesty . . . by or from a person, or an agent of a person, holding or seeking to obtain a contract from Her Majesty . . ., the money, gift, or consideration shall be deemed to have been paid or given and received corruptly as such inducement or reward as is mentioned in such Act unless the contrary is proved.

Similarly under s.1(1) of the Prevention of Crimes Act 1953, it is for the accused to show that they have a lawful excuse for carrying offensive weapon;[20] under s.5(2) of the Road Traffic Act 1988, where the defendant is charged with being in charge of a motor vehicle with excess alcohol, the defendant has the burden of proving that there was no likelihood of his driving the vehicle while over the limit; and under s.2(2) of the Homicide Act 1957, it is for the accused to prove that they are suffering from diminished responsibility.

The extent to which such reversals of the burden are compliant with Article 6 and the guarantee of a fair trial is discussed below.

3. *By implied statutory provision.* More controversially, there is also a third category, the "implied" exception. The principle that the prosecution must prove the guilt of the accused has been 'whittled away' by an acceptance that Lord Sankey's statutory exceptions were not limited to those statutes which expressly cast the burden of proof on the accused but extended to those which did it by implication. An early example of this is *Turner*[21] where the defendant was charged with having pheasants in his possession without the

---

[18] above.
[19] *Podola* [1959] 3 All E.R. 418.
[20] This is also the case with analogous offences created by Offensive Weapons Act 1996, ss.4 and 6.
[21] (1816) 5 M. & S. 206.

necessary authorisation. The statute creating the offence also provided a list of situations where an accused might be authorised to possess the pheasants and Bayley J. said,

Turner (1816) 5 M.&S. 206:

If a negative averment be made by one party, which is peculiarly within the knowledge of the other, the party within whose knowledge it lies and who asserts the affirmative, is to prove it and not he who asserts the negative.[22]

This asserts a limited principle behind the reversal of the burden of proof in statutory offences—a court can require a defendant to prove a fact where the defendant alone has the necessary information. The modern statement of this 'implied statutory exception' to the normal allocation of the burden of proof can be found in the Magistrates' Courts Act 1980.

Magistrates' Courts Act 1980, s. 101:

101.—Where the defendant to an information or complaint relies for his defence on any exception, exemption, proviso, excuse or qualification, whether or not it accompanies the description of the offence or matter of complaint in the enactment creating the offence or on which the complaint is founded, the burden of proving the exception, exemption, proviso, excuse or qualification shall be on him; and this notwithstanding that the information or complaint contains an allegation negativing the exception, exemption, proviso, excuse or qualification.

This allows a magistrates' court, when interpreting a statute, to place the burden of proof on the defendant in certain circumstances. Section 101 could have been interpreted with the *Turner* restrictions in mind. However in *Edwards*[23] the defendant was convicted under s.160 of the Licensing Act 1964 of selling alcohol without a justices' licence. The prosecution did not call evidence that the appellant did not hold a justices' licence, leaving the appellant to show, if he could, that he did possess one. The conviction was upheld by the Divisional Court. Two issues emerge.

The first was whether the principle behind s.101 applied only to summary trials. *Edwards* held it to be an expression of a common law rule and therefore applicable to trials on indictment. The argument runs: the origins of this section are to be found in the establishment of a new system of summary jurisdiction in the Summary Jurisdiction Act 1848. In passing the 1848 legislation, Parliament was applying the common law rules as to proof as

---

[22] *ibid.* at 211.
[23] [1974] 2 All E.R. 1085.

then applied by the judges hearing trials on indictment. If that was the case, those common law rules must be applicable to modern trials on indictment. Although s.101 (and thus the common law) is limited to offences created by enactments, this is scarcely restrictive since the majority of criminal offences are contained in statute.

The second issue was the scope of this principle. At first glance, the result accords with common sense, since in the circumstances of the case, it would have been no hardship for the defendant to produce a justices' licence, if such existed. On the other hand, it would have been easy for the prosecution to conduct a search of the relevant register and adduced evidence that no record could be found.[24] This was not information peculiarly within the knowledge of the defendant nor where it would have been particularly difficult for the prosecution to acquire the information and prove a negative. Restricting any reversal of the burden of proof on such lines would have been both practical and also corresponded with principles of fairness: the statute would have been narrowly interpreted[25] and the ratio would have accorded with the principle of ease of proof.[26] Unfortunately the ratio is much broader than common sense requires since, unlike *Turner*, the court held that the transfer of the burden of proof is not limited to those cases and instead the decision was based on the linguistic structure of the statute.

Edwards was approved by the House of Lords in *Hunt*,[27] where the accused was charged with possession of morphine. Possession is only illegal where the preparation contained more than 0.2 per cent morphine. The defendant argued that the prosecution had not adduced any evidence as to the strength of the preparation but was still convicted on the basis that the burden of proving that the concentration of the preparation was less than this lay on the defence. The House of Lords (while allowing the appeal) accepted that statutes could by implication cast the burden of proof on the accused even in indictable offences.

Hunt [1987] 1 All E.R. 1 at 10e–12a, *per* Lord Griffiths:

I would summarise the position . . . by saying that *Woolmington v DPP* did not lay down a rule that the burden of proving a statutory defence lay only on the defendant if the statute specifically so provided, that a statute can, on its true construction, place a burden of proof on the defendant although it does not do so expressly and that if a burden of proof is placed on the defendant it is the same burden whether the case be tried summarily or on indictment, namely a burden that has to be discharged on the balance of probabilities.

The real difficulty in these cases lies in determining on whom Parliament intended to place the burden of proof when the statute has not expressly so provided. It

---

[24] Probably such testimony was hearsay at that time: *Patel* [1981] 3 All E.R. 94; now such records would be admissible under Criminal Justice Act 2003, s. 117.

[25] This should be the fundamental approach with any penal statute—A. Ashworth, *Principles of Criminal Law* (4th ed., Oxford OUP, 2003), p.80.

[26] Ashworth A., *ibid.* p.85.

[27] [1987] 1 All E.R. 1.

presents particularly difficult problems of construction when what might be regarded as a matter of defence appears in a clause creating the offence rather than in some subsequent proviso from which it may more readily be inferred that it was intended to provide for a separate defence which a defendant must set up and prove if he wishes to avail himself of it . . .

My Lords, I am, of course, well aware of the body of distinguished academic opinion that urges wherever a burden of proof is placed on a defendant by statute the burden should be an evidential burden and not a persuasive burden, and that has the support of the distinguished signatories to the 11th Report of the Criminal Law Revision Committee . . .[28] My Lords, such a fundamental change is, in my view, a matter for Parliament and not a decision of your Lordships' House . . .

The problem is treated here, not as one involving the erosion of the presumption of innocence, but as one of statutory construction. The worst effects of *Edwards* are avoided as Lord Griffiths states that the fact that a statute employs the language of exceptions or provisos does not automatically place the burden of proof on the accused. Indeed he placed stress on practical considerations such as the ease or difficulty that a defendant might have in discharging this burden. In a drugs case, the prosecution would have the substance analysed and the defendant does not have any right to a sample for their own analysis. The House also made it clear that in any serious criminal offence, it was right to resolve any ambiguity in favour of the defendant.

Hunt accepts that statutes can impliedly reverse the burden of proof and is relatively relaxed about the situations in which this can occur. The potential scope of interpreting statutes in this fashion is enormous as a multitude of statutes use the language of 'excuse, proviso, exemption or qualification'. It is an approach that undermines the presumption of innocence expressed in *Woolmington*.[29] Courts continue to apply *Hunt*, albeit in the context of the Art.6 concerns discussed below. *R. (Grundy and Co Excavations Ltd) v Halstead Magistrates Court*[30] involved felling trees without a licence contrary to s.17 of the Forestry Act 1967. Grundy's employees cut down 86 trees on the instructions of a landowner on the landowner's land in order to make a hard standing. A felling licence under s.9(1) of the Act had not been obtained. Grundy's defence was that he was not aware that a licence was required. The trial judge held that the only burden of proof on the prosecutor was to prove that the accused felled the trees and that it was then for the accused to prove on the balance of probabilities either that he had a licence or that a licence was not required because the Act provided for a number of exceptions. Grundy accepted that there was an evidential burden on the accused to show that one of the exceptions applied but the Divisional Court interpreted the Act as imposing a legal burden on the defendant.

[28] (1972) Cmnd 4991.
[29] P. Mirfield "The Legacy of Hunt" [1988] Crim.L.R. 19 at 29. See the reply by D. Birch, "Hunting the Snark: the Elusive Statutory Exception" [1988] Crim.L.R. 221.
[30] [2003] EWHC Admin 272; N. Parpworth, "Unlicensed Tree Felling. . ." [2003] J.P.L. 1234.

(ii) *Reverse onus and human rights*

The debate about the legitimacy of a reverse onus now centres on the European Convention. Art.6(2) embodies the presumption of innocence—that is, the defendant is to be treated as not having committed any offence until the state through the prosecuting authorities adduces sufficient evidence to satisfy an independent and impartial tribunal that they are guilty as charged. This leads to the proposition that the burden of proving the accused's guilt rests on the state[31] at all times and that any doubt should benefit the accused.

Strict liability offences are an obvious exception as the Crown is simply put to proof of the *actus reus* of the offence without being required to prove that the defendant either intended to act in that way or to produce that result. This is not a reversal of the burden of proof but is an exemption for the state from being required to adduce proof of what ought to be an integral part of any offence. In *Salabiaku v France*,[32] the European Court of Human Rights held that states may, under certain conditions, penalise a simple or objective fact as such, irrespective of whether it results from criminal intent or from negligence. Strict liability offences are not in themselves contrary to the Convention.

More germane to the study of evidence is the reversal of the burden of proof, which frequently occurs where the defendant has to prove some defence. Does this infringe the presumption of innocence?[33] In *Salabiaku*, the applicant was charged not only with the strict liability customs offence of smuggling prohibited goods but also with the criminal offence of unlawful importation of narcotics. For this latter crime, there was a defence under French law but he would have to prove that it was impossible for him to have known about the narcotics. The Court held that presumptions of fact or of law which affect the burden of proof operate in every legal system and that the Convention does not prohibit such presumptions in principle. It does, however, require the States to remain within certain limits which take into account the importance of what is at stake and maintain the rights of the defence. The Court drew a clear distinction between the criminal offence of unlawful importation of narcotics and the customs offence of smuggling prohibited goods. For the more serious offence, the prosecution must shoulder the burden of proof whereas for the less serious offence, a reversal of that burden is acceptable.[34]

There are many UK statutes which expressly or impliedly reverse the burden of proof. To what extent are these compliant with Art.6 requirements under the Human Rights Act 1998?[35] The common law showed a principled approach to the interpretation of such instruments in *AG of Hong Kong v Lee Kwong-kut*[36] where the Privy Council held that the obligation on the accused

---

[31] *Barbera, Messegue and Jabardo v Spain* Application, No. 10590/83, A 146, (1988) 11 E.H.R.R. 360.

[32] Application No. 10519/83, (1988) 13 E.H.R.R. 379.

[33] Ashworth and Blake discovered 219 examples amongst 540 offences triable in the Crown Court of legal burden or presumptions operating against the defendant (see [1996] Crim.L.R. 314).

[34] It is acceptable to place the burden on the accused to show that he was not living off the earnings of a prostitute who was living with him—*X v UK*, Application No. 5124/71, 42 CD 135 (1972).

[35] I. Dennis, "Reverse Onuses and the Presumption of Innocence" [2005] Crim.L.R. 901.

[36] [1993] A.C. 951.

to prove that money in his possession had not been stolen breached the Hong Kong Bill of Rights. It was for the prosecution to prove a definitional element of the crime. The issue was confronted by the House of Lords in *Lambert*.[37] The defendant was charged under the Misuse of Drugs Act 1971 with possession of cocaine with intent to supply. Under s.28, ". . . it shall be a defence for the accused to prove that he neither knew of nor suspected nor had reason to suspect the existence of some fact alleged by the prosecution . . ." On its face, this provision places the legal burden of proof on the defendant and was not compliant with Art.6 requirements. Lord Steyn said that,

Lambert [2001] 3 All E.R. 577:

34. . . It is nevertheless right to say that in a constitutional democracy limited inroads on the presumption of innocence may be justified. The approach to be adopted was stated by the European Court of Human Rights in *Salabiaku v France.*

> Presumptions of fact or of law operate in every legal system. Clearly, the Convention does not prohibit such presumptions in principle. It does, however, require the contracting states to remain within certain limits in this respect as regards criminal law . . . Article 6(2) does not therefore regard presumptions of fact or of law provided for in the criminal law with indifference. It requires states to confine them within reasonable limits which take into account the importance of what is at stake and maintain the rights of the defence.

This test depends upon the circumstances of the individual case. It follows that a legislative interference with the presumption of innocence requires justification and must not be greater than is necessary. The principle of proportionality must be observed.

35 . . . In the present case the defence under section 28 is one directly bearing on the moral blameworthiness of the accused. It is this factor alone which could justify a maximum sentence of life imprisonment. In my view there is an inroad on the presumption even if an issue under section 28 is in strict law regarded as a pure defence.

36 It is now necessary to consider the question of justification for the legislative interference with the presumption of innocence. I am satisfied that there is an objective justification for some interference with the burden of proof in prosecutions under section 5 of the 1971 Act. The basis for this justification is that sophisticated drug smugglers, dealers and couriers typically secrete drugs in some container, thereby enabling the person in possession of the container to say that he was unaware of the contents. Such defences are commonplace and they pose real difficulties for the police and prosecuting authorities.

37 That is, however, not the end of the matter. The burden is on the state to show that the legislative means adopted were not greater than necessary. Where there is objective justification for some inroad on the presumption of innocence the legislature has a choice. The first is to impose a legal burden of proof on the accused. If such a burden is created the matter in question must be taken as proved against the accused unless he satisfies the jury on a balance of probabilities to the contrary . . . The second is to impose an evidential burden only on the accused. If this technique is adopted the matter must be taken as proved against the accused unless there is sufficient evidence

37 [2001] 3 All E.R. 577.

to raise an issue on the matter but, if there is sufficient evidence, then the prosecution have the burden of satisfying the jury as to the matter beyond reasonable doubt in the ordinary way . . . It is important to bear in mind that it is not enough for the defence merely to allege the fact in question: the court decides whether there is a real issue on the matter . . . A transfer of a legal burden amounts to a far more drastic interference with the presumption of innocence than the creation of an evidential burden on the accused. The former requires the accused to establish his innocence. It necessarily involves the risk that, if the jury are faithful to the judge's direction, they may convict where the accused has not discharged the legal burden resting on him but left them unsure on the point. This risk is not present if only an evidential burden is created.

The House held that the phrase". .a defence for the accused to prove" in s.28 placed an evidential rather than a persuasive burden on the defendant. Such an interpretation was possible without doing undue violence to the text. Where the prosecution had produced evidence that the defendant was in possession of the proscribed drug, the defence had to adduce some evidence that they were unaware of the nature of the substance. If they succeeded in doing this, the legal burden of proof was on the prosecution to persuade the jury beyond reasonable doubt that the accused in fact did know the true nature of the substance. If the defence failed to adduce any evidence which countered the presumption of knowledge, then the judge could direct the jury that they could presume guilty knowledge on the part of the accused.

The judgment provides little guidance on principle—for the House of Lords, this was a case by case issue. The House returned to the problem in *Johnstone*[38] which involved making bootleg recordings of performances by well-known artists. There was a defence under s.92(5) of the Trade Marks Act 1994, for the accused to ". . . show that he believed on reasonable grounds that the use of the sign in the manner in which it was used, or was to be used, was not an infringement of the registered trade mark . . ." Lord Nicholls considered this reversal of proof and concluded the following.

Johnstone [2003] 3 All E.R. 884, *per* Lord Nicholls

[51] In evaluating these factors the court's role is one of review. Parliament, not the court, is charged with the primary responsibility for deciding, as a matter of policy, what should be the constituent elements of a criminal offence. I echo the words of Lord Woolf in *A-G of Hong Kong v Lee Kwong-kut.* . .

> In order to maintain the balance between the individual and the society as a whole, rigid and inflexible standards should not be imposed on the legislature's attempts to resolve the difficult and intransigent problems with which society is faced when seeking to deal with serious crime.

The court will reach a different conclusion from the legislature only when it is apparent the legislature has attached insufficient importance to the fundamental right of an individual to be presumed innocent until proved guilty.

[52] I turn to s 92. (1) Counterfeiting is fraudulent trading. It is a serious contemporary problem. Counterfeiting has adverse economic effects on genuine trade. It also has

---

[38] [2003] 3 All E.R. 884.

adverse effects on consumers, in terms of quality of goods and, sometimes, on the health or safety of consumers. The Commission of the European Communities has noted the scale of this 'widespread phenomenon with a global impact'. Urgent steps are needed to combat counterfeiting and piracy ... Protection of consumers and honest manufacturers and traders from counterfeiting is an important policy consideration. (2) The offences created by s 92 have rightly been described as offences of 'near absolute liability'. The prosecution is not required to prove intent to infringe a registered trade mark. (3) The offences attract a serious level of punishment: a maximum penalty on indictment of an unlimited fine or imprisonment for up to ten years or both, together with the possibility of confiscation and deprivation orders. (4) Those who trade in brand products are aware of the need to be on guard against counterfeit goods. They are aware of the need to deal with reputable suppliers and keep records and of the risks they take if they do not. (5) The s 92(5) defence relates to facts within the accused person's own knowledge: his state of mind, and the reasons why he held the belief in question. His sources of supply are known to him. (6) Conversely, by and large it is to be expected that those who supply traders with counterfeit products, if traceable at all by outside investigators, are unlikely to be co-operative. So, in practice, if the prosecution must prove that a trader acted dishonestly, fewer investigations will be undertaken and fewer prosecutions will take place.
[53] In my view factors (4) and (6) constitute compelling reasons why the s 92(5) defence should place a persuasive burden on the accused person ...

A similar view was taken by Lord Bingham in *Sheldrake v D.P.P.*[39] where the defendant was charged before the justices with being in charge of a motor vehicle with excess alcohol. He argued that the defence under s.5(2) of the Road Traffic Act 1988 which cast upon the defendant the burden of proving that there was no likelihood of his driving the vehicle while over the limit, was not compliant with the presumption of innocence guaranteed by Art.6(2),

Sheldrake v D.P.P. [2005] 1 All E.R. 237, *per* Lord Bingham

41 It may not be very profitable to debate whether section 5(2) infringes the presumption of innocence. It may be assumed that it does. Plainly the provision is directed to a legitimate object: the prevention of death, injury and damage caused by unfit drivers. Does the provision meet the tests of acceptability identified in the Strasbourg jurisprudence? In my view, it plainly does. I do not regard the burden placed on the defendant as beyond reasonable limits or in any way arbitrary. It is not objectionable to criminalise a defendant's conduct in these circumstances without requiring a prosecutor to prove criminal intent. The defendant has a full opportunity to show that there was no likelihood of his driving, a matter so closely conditioned by his own knowledge and state of mind at the material time as to make it much more appropriate for him to prove on the balance of probabilities that he would not have been likely to drive than for the prosecutor to prove, beyond reasonable doubt, that he would. I do not think that imposition of a legal burden went beyond what was necessary. If a driver tries and fails to establish a defence under section 5(2), I would not regard the resulting conviction as unfair, as the House held that it might or would be in *R v Lambert*. I find no reason to conclude that the conviction of Mr Sheldrake was tainted by any hint of unfairness.

The House of Lords has found the provisions of s.11 of the Terrorism Act 2000 more difficult to interpret. This section makes it an offence to belong to a

[39] [2005] 1 All E.R. 237.

proscribed organisation but provides a defence under s.11(2) for the accused to show that the organisation was not proscribed when he joined and that he had not taken part in the activities of the organisation since it was proscribed. It was clear that Parliament had intended this to impose a legal burden on the defendant, since s.118 of the Act lists a number of sections which are to be understood as imposing an evidential burden only, and s.11(2) is not among those listed. In *Attorney-General's Reference (No. 4 of 2002)*,[40] the majority felt that the section could be *read down* to impose merely an evidential burden. Dissenting, Lord Carswell points out that the offence is belonging to a proscribed organisation whereas the defence raises the issue, not merely of when the defendant joined but of taking part in activities. He takes the point that these issues are peculiarly within the defendant's knowledge.

Attorney-General's Reference (No.4 of 2002) [2005] 1 All E.R. 237:

91. . . (a) It is not easy to determine what is to be proved and by whom in respect of the date when the defendant joined the organisation. If he raises the issue, it would hardly be appropriate for the prosecution to have to prove that he became a member before the date on which it was proscribed. The only sensible answer must be that the defendant has to establish this fact, but it would be a strange procedure if the onus then reverted to the prosecution to prove that he had taken part in the activities of the organisation.

The balancing test for reversing the burden of proof is assessing the justification and the proportionality. This is easier said than done—there is a persuasive burden upon the defendant charged with murder to prove that they were acting under diminished responsibility[41] or on the defendant in a road traffic offence to prove that he consumed alcohol after the offence but before providing a specimen.[42] For offences under the Insolvency Act 1986, in *Carass*,[43] the Court of Appeal held that s.206(4) of that Act created an evidential burden only. This string of decisions demonstrates no clear guidance as to how to interpret statutes which appear to impose the burden of proof on the defendant.

N. Padfield. "The Burden of Proof Unresolved" [2005] Cambridge L.J. 17:

The time has come for a category of "administrative regulations" which would carry little stigma and no possibility of imprisonment. Only for such "non-crimes" should strict liability or reverse burdens be acceptable. Meanwhile, we will continue to have a

---

[40] [2005] 1 All E.R. 237 at 263.
[41] *Ali* [2001] 1 All E.R. 1014 (CA—heard with Lambert).
[42] *Drummond* [2002] 2 Cr.App.R. 25.
[43] [2002] 2 Cr.App.R. 4.

"blizzard of single instances" . . . until the courts shout loudly that whenever an accused is required to prove some fact to avoid conviction, the provision violates the presumption of innocence.[44]

Ian Dennis has sought to impose some order on this process,

I. Dennis; "Reverse Onuses and the Presumption of Innocence" [2005] Crim.L.R. 901 at 937

The imposition by statute of an onus on the defendant in relation to a criminal charge raises a potential issue of compatibility of the onus with the presumption of innocence in Art.6(2) of the ECHR. The issue is resolved by a three-stage process of decision-making.

The first stage of the decision-making process deals with the question whether a statute imposes a burden of any kind on the defendant, and, if so, whether it is a legal or an evidential burden. This question is settled by ordinary principles of statutory construction. These include the effect of s.101 of the Magistrates' Courts Act 1980, as explained and expanded by Edwards and Hunt. If the burden is an evidential one no problem of compatibility with Art.6 arises. If the burden is a legal one, the issue of compatibility must be considered.

The second stage of decision-making requires a court to decide the issue of compatibility according to whether the reverse onus (legal burden) is justified as a proportionate measure in pursuance of a legitimate aim. It is at this stage that the main problems and uncertainties arise. The debate is almost entirely about proportionality, but analysis of the case law shows considerable disagreement and inconsistency about the use of one or more of six relevant factors in determining this question. If no broader principles for applying the relevant factors can be identified, the decisions as to the justifiability of particular reverse onuses will continue to resemble a forensic lottery. A search for principle suggests that issues of moral blameworthiness should be proved by the prosecution. These issues will include, in addition to the relevant prohibited acts, any requisite culpable mental states, any objective fault such as negligence, and the unavailability of any common law defences raised by the defendant . . .

If the reverse onus is justified as proportionate to a legitimate aim no further decision is necessary. If it is not justified according to these criteria the third stage of decision-making requires the court to read down the legal burden to an evidential burden if it is possible to do this using s.3 of the HRA. On the basis of Sheldrake it seems that it will almost always be possible to do this; it is hard to envisage a case that would not come within the scope of Lord Bingham's reasoning. Accordingly a declaration of incompatibility of a reverse onus will almost never be necessary.

2. The legal burden in civil cases

In civil cases, the general rule is that the party who makes an assertion must prove the truth of that assertion. On its face, this suggests that the burden is borne by the party who makes the positive assertion. This does not mean that a party cannot bear the onus of proving a negative. Thus it is probably better expressed that a party who wishes the court to take action on

---

[44] N. Padfield, "The Burden of Proof Unresolved", [2005], C.L.J. 17.

a particular issue should bear the responsibility of showing why action should be taken. In *Soward v Leggatt*,[45] the claimant was the landlord of the defendant and his claim was that the latter had not properly repaired and maintained the premises in question. The defendant in the pleadings positively stated that he had done so. Even though linguistically the defence case was a positive assertion, the burden of proof still rested on the claimant.

Soward v Leggatt (1836) 7 C.&P. 613 at 615, *per* Lord Abinger C.B.:

Looking at these things according to common sense, we should consider what is the substantive fact to be made out, and on whom it lies to make it out. It is not so much the form of the issue which ought to be considered, as the substance and effect of it. In many cases, a party, by a little difference in the drawing of his pleadings might make it either affirmative or negative, as he pleased. The plaintiff here says, 'You did not repair'; he might have said, 'You let the house become dilapidated.' I shall endeavour by my own view to arrive at the substance of the issue, and I think in the present case that the plaintiff's counsel should begin.

A similar point arose in *Abrath v North Eastern Railway*[46] which involved an action for malicious prosecution. In such a case, it is necessary for the claimant to prove not only the fact of prosecution but also the lack of reasonable and probable cause for the prosecution.

Abrath v North Eastern Railway [1883] 11 Q.B.D. 440 at 457–458, *per* Bowen L.J.:

Now in an action for malicious prosecution the plaintiff has the burden throughout of establishing that the circumstances of the prosecution were such that a judge can see no reasonable or probable cause for instituting it. In one sense this is the assertion of a negative, and we have been pressed with the proposition that when a negative is to be made out the onus of proof shifts. That is not so. If the assertion of a negative is an essential part of the plaintiff's case, the proof of the assertion still rests upon the plaintiff. The terms 'negative' and 'affirmative' are after all relative and not absolute. In dealing with a question of negligence that term may be considered either as negative or affirmative according to the definition adopted in measuring the duty which is neglected. Wherever a person asserts affirmatively as part of his case that a certain state of facts is present or is absent, or that a particular thing is insufficient for a particular purpose, that is an averment that he is bound to prove positively. It has been said that an exception exists in those cases where the facts lie peculiarly within the knowledge of the opposite party. The counsel for the plaintiff have not gone the length of contending that in all those cases the onus shifts, and that the person within whose knowledge the truth peculiarly lies is bound to prove or disprove the matter in dispute. I think a proposition of that kind cannot be maintained, and that the

---

[45] (1836) 7 C. & P. 613.
[46] [1883] 11 Q.B.D. 440.

exceptions supposed to be found amongst cases relating to the game laws may be explained on special grounds . . .

In civil actions generally, the legal burden rests on the claimant: in a negligence action, the claimant would bear the burden of proving the existence and the breach of the duty of care as well as the extent of the injuries and damage. In *Bonnington Castings Ltd v Wardlaw*,[47] an employee contracted an industrial disease in the course of work in a factory owned by the defendants. The employers were in breach of certain safety regulations although it was unclear that these breaches caused the harm.

Bonnington Castings Ltd v Wardlaw [1956] A.C. 613, *per* Lord Reid:

It would seem obvious in principle that a plaintiff must prove not only the negligence or breach of duty but also that such fault caused or materially contributed to his injury, and there is ample authority for that proposition. I can find neither reason nor authority for the rule being different when there is a breach of a statutory duty . . . In my judgment the employee must in all cases prove his case by the ordinary standard of proof in civil actions: he must make it appear that at least on a balance of probabilities the breach of duty caused or materially contributed to his injury.[48]

The defendant in a negligence action may bear the burden of proof where the defence goes beyond mere denial. For example, where questions of *volenti* or contributory negligence arise, the burden of proving those issues rests upon the defendant. Thus the defence of contributory negligence has been raised in a number of cases where a motorist was not wearing a seat belt and suffered more serious injuries than would otherwise have been the case. In such cases, the onus of proving negligence on the part of the claimant rests on the defendant.[49] In contract litigation, likewise, the claimant must bear the burden of proving the existence of the contract, its breach and the extent of any damages.

In civil proceedings, the incidence of the burden of proof is rarely decisive, although it proved to be in *Rhesa Shipping Co. SA v Edmunds*.[50] The claimant ship-owners sought to recover from the underwriters under a policy of insurance for the total loss of their ship. The claimants argued that the cause was a collision with a submarine and thus came under the 'perils of the sea' clause while the underwriters argued that it was prolonged wear and tear over many years. There was no direct evidence of either contention.

---

[47] [1956] A.C. 613.

[48] *ibid.* at 620 *per* Lord Reid; *McTear v Imperial Tobacco*, The Times, June 14, 2005—claimant had not demonstrated individual link between smoking and her husband's lung cancer; but courts will draw obvious inferences that breach of statutory duty caused harm—*Otaegui v Gledhill* (unreported QBD (Liverpool–Elias J.) June 2, 2003) where employee had fallen down stairs for which employers failed to provide handrail.

[49] *e.g. Froom v Butcher* [1976] Q.B. 286.

[50] [1985] 2 All E.R. 712; *Stone and Rolls Ltd v Micro Communication* [2005] EWHC 1052 (Ch).

Rhesa Shipping Co. SA v Edmunds [1985]2 All E.R. 712 at 718; *per* Lord Brandon:

My Lords, the late Sir Arthur Conan Doyle in his book, *The Sign of Four*, describes his hero, Mr Sherlock Homes, as saying to the latter's friend, Dr Watson: 'How often have I said to you that, when you have eliminated the impossible, whatever remains, however improbable, must be the truth?' It is, no doubt, on the basis of this well-known but unjudicial dictum that [the trial judge] decided to accept the shipowners' submarine theory, even though he regarded it . . . as extremely improbable.

In my view there are three reasons why it is inappropriate to apply the dictum of Mr Sherlock Holmes . . . to the process of fact-finding which a judge of first instance has to perform at the conclusion of a case of the kind here concerned.

The first reason is one which I have already sought to emphasise as being of great importance, namely that the judge is not always bound to make a finding one way or the other with regard to the facts averred by the parties. He has open to him the third alternative of saying that the party on whom the burden of proof lies in relation to any averment made by him has failed to discharge that burden. No judge likes to decide cases on burden of proof if he can legitimately avoid having to do so. There are cases, however, in which, owing to the unsatisfactory state of the evidence or otherwise, deciding on the burden of proof is the only just course for him to take.

The second reason is that the dictum can only apply when all the relevant facts are known, so that all possible explanations, except a single extremely improbable one, can properly be eliminated. That state of affairs does not exist in the present case: to take but one example, the ship sank in such deep water that a diver's examination of the nature of the aperture, which might well have thrown light on its cause, could not be carried out.

The third reason is that the legal concept of proof of a case on a balance of probabilities must be applied with common sense. It requires a judge of first instance, before he finds that a particular event occurred, to be satisfied on the evidence that it is more likely to have occurred than not. If such a judge concludes. .. that the occurrence of an event is extremely improbable, a finding by him that it is nevertheless more likely to have occurred than not, does not accord with common sense. This is especially so when it is open to the judge to say simply that the evidence leaves him in doubt whether the event occurred or not, and that the party on whom the burden of proving that the event occurred lies has therefore failed to discharge such burden.

This was a case where the judge should have relied on the burden of proof to settle the case but did not. In *Stephens v Cannon*,[51] the master was faced with two conflicting valuations of a property and relied on the burden of proof. The Court of Appeal felt that this should be a last resort. Wilson J. reviewed the authorities.

Stephens v Cannon [2005] EWCA Civ 222:

[46] From these authorities I derive the following propositions:
(a) The situation in which the court finds itself before it can despatch a disputed issue by resort to the burden of proof has to be exceptional.

---

[51] [2005] EWCA Civ 222.

(b) Nevertheless the issue does not have to be of any particular type. A legitimate state of agnosticism can logically arise following enquiry into any type of disputed issue. It may be more likely to arise following an enquiry into, for example, the identity of the aggressor in an unwitnessed fight; but it can arise even after an enquiry, aided by good experts, into, for example, the cause of the sinking of a ship.

(c) The exceptional situation which entitles the court to resort to the burden of proof is that, notwithstanding that it has striven to do so, it cannot reasonably make a finding in relation to a disputed issue.

(d) A court which resorts to the burden of proof must ensure that others can discern that it has striven to make a finding in relation to a disputed issue and can understand the reasons why it has concluded that it cannot do so. The parties must be able to discern the court's endeavour and to understand its reasons in order to be able to perceive why they have won and lost. An appellate court must also be able to do so because otherwise it will not be able to accept that the court below was in the exceptional situation of being entitled to resort to the burden of proof.

(e) In a few cases the fact of the endeavour and the reasons for the conclusion will readily be inferred from the circumstances and so there will be no need for the court to demonstrate the endeavour and to explain the reasons in any detail in its judgment. In most cases, however, a more detailed demonstration and explanation in judgment will be necessary.

This approach can be seen in *Datec Electronic Holdings v United Parcels*[52] which involved the loss of packages carried by the defendant company. The Court of Appeal considered *Rhesa Shipping* but held that there was sufficient evidence about the three packages and the surrounding circumstances to enable the court to engage in an informed analysis of the possible causes of the loss and to reach a reasoned conclusion as to the probable cause. In this case, the packages had reached the defendant's warehouse and disappeared. The Court of Appeal held that the possibilities of accidental loss referred to by the trial judge were in fact improbable, and employee theft was much more probable than the judge had found it to be.

The defendant might carry a burden on a particular issue in a breach of contract action. This might be the case with affirmative defences, for example, an assertion that there was a material non-disclosure on the part of the claimant.[53] In *Joseph Constantine Steamship Line Ltd v Imperial Smelting Corp Ltd*,[54] a ship on charter was destroyed in an explosion, the cause of which was unknown. The claimant charterers claimed damages from the owner for failure to load. The owners' defence was that the charter party had been frustrated by the explosion. The House of Lords decided that, where the defendant establishes a frustrating event, the burden rested on the claimant charterers to show that event had occurred and the contract had been broken as a result of the owners' fault.

---

[52] [2006] 1 Lloyd's Rep. 279.
[53] *Everett v Hogg, Robinson and Gardner Mountain (Insurance) Ltd* [1973] 2 Lloyds Rep. 217.
[54] [1941] 2 All E.R. 165.

Joseph Constantine Steamship Line Ltd v Imperial Smelting Corp Ltd [1941] 2 All E.R. 165 at 179–180, *per* Viscount Maugham:

I think the burden of proof in any particular case depends on the circumstances under which the claim arises. In general, the rule which applies is 'Ei qui affirmat non ei qui negat incumbit probatio'. It is an ancient rule founded on considerations of good sense and it should not be departed from without strong reasons. The position as to proof of non-responsibility for the event in such a case as the present is not very different from the position of a plaintiff in an action for negligence where contributory negligence on his part is alleged. In such a case the plaintiff must prove that there was some negligent act or omission on the part of the defendant which caused or materially contributed to the injury, but it is for the defendant to prove affirmatively, if he so contends, that there was contributory negligence on the part of the person injured, though here again the onus may easily be shifted . . .

If, however, I am right in the opinion above expressed that the onus of establishing absence of default did not rest on the appellants, the mere possibility of default on their part is not sufficient to disentitle them to rely on the principle of frustration . . .[55]

Is this as straightforward as it seems? The charterers had shown breach of contract. It may be as legitimately argued that it should have been for the owners pleading frustration to show that that breach was beyond their control? The House placed some stress on the difficulty of proving a negative but it has been suggested that the decision was one of policy since most frustrating events occur without fault on the part of the defendant. Less injustice is likely to be caused by placing the burden of proving fault on the claimant.[56] But this situation might be contrasted with that in bailment: where there is a contract of bailment and the goods are lost, the bailor merely has to show the bailment and the failure to restore the goods. The legal burden is on the bailee to show lack of fault on his part.[57]

Contracts can expressly or impliedly vary the incidence of the burden of proof. With insurance contracts, insurers sometimes seek to show that a loss falls within an exception to the contract: the policy may expressly put the burden on the insured to prove that the loss falls outside the exception. Even where this is not done expressly, the courts have sometimes held that the insured bears the burden of proof in showing that it falls outside any proviso.[58] But in *Munro, Brice & Co v War Risks Association*,[59] a policy of marine insurance covered loss of a ship through perils of the sea but with an exception in the case of loss by enemy action. The ship had simply disappeared and the court held that the insurers bore the burden of proof of showing that the ship had been lost through enemy action.

In *The Glendarroch*,[60] a ship was lost when it struck a rock and the claimant sued for non-delivery of the sacks of cement it was carrying. The contract expressly provided that the shipowners were not liable in respect of loss

[55] See *BHP Billiton Petroleum v Dalmine* [2003] EWCA Civ 170.
[56] J. Stone, "Burden of proof and the judicial process. . .." [1944] 60 L.Q.R. 262.
[57] *Coldman v Hill* [1919] 1 K.B. 443; *Levison v Patent Steam Carpet Cleaning Co. Ltd* [1978] Q.B. 69.
[58] *Hurst v Evans* [1917] 1 K.B. 352.
[59] [1918] 2 K.B. 78.
[60] [1894] P. 226.

caused by perils of the sea, provided that the owners were not negligent. If the claimant proved the contract and breach, the burden was on the owners to show that it was "peril of the sea". However once it had been shown that the ship had sunk because of a "peril of the sea", it was for the claimants to show negligence, if they were to rely upon the proviso.

The Glendarroch [1894] P. 226, *per* Lord Esher:

The plaintiffs would have to prove the contract and the non-delivery. If they leave that in doubt, of course they fail. The defendants' answer is 'Yes; but the case was brought within the exception—within its ordinary meaning'. That lies upon them. Then the plaintiffs have a right to say there are exceptional circumstances, viz, that the damage was brought about by the negligence of the defendants' servants, and it seems to me that it is for the plaintiffs to make out the second exception.

In civil cases, as in criminal, statutes can affect the burden of proof.[61] This does not create the same problems as does the reversal of proof with criminal proceedings where Art.6(2) guarantees the presumption of innocence in criminal trials and has no application to civil proceedings. But statutes can expressly allocate the burden or indeed effectively refuse to allocate—for example, in unfair dismissal cases, after proof of dismissal, historically the burden of proving that it was objectively fair lay on the employer.[62] This requirement was removed in 1980[63] and the issue is now governed by s.98 of the Employment Rights Act 1996.

Employment Rights Act 1996, s.98:

98.—(1) In determining for the purposes of this Part whether the dismissal of an employee is fair or unfair, it is for the employer to show—
(a) the reason (or, if more than one, the principal reason) for the dismissal, . . .
(4) Where the employer has fulfilled the requirements of subs.(1), the determination of the question whether the dismissal is fair or unfair (having regard to the reason shown by the employer) . . .
(b) shall be determined in accordance with equity and the substantial merits of the case.

The employer has to adduce a reason for dismissal under subs.(1) but under subs.(4)(b), the issue is to be decided in accordance with equity and substantial merits. The Employment Appeal Tribunal has indicated the discretion that this permits the tribunal, ". . . s.98 does not lay out an obstacle

---

[61] *ibid.* at 231, *per* Lord Esher
[62] Examples include Factories Act 1961, s.29; Consumer Credit Act 1974, s.171(7); Bills of Exchange Act 1882, s.30(2).
[63] Trade Union and Labour Relations Act, Sch.1, para.6(8).

course which employers have to negotiate. It enshrines within it a requirement that fundamental criteria of fairness are satisfied; it gives discretion to the tribunal to decide the cure, having regard to those fundamental criteria."[64] This has been described as 'highly unsatisfactory'[65] but has caused few practical problems.

B. *Allocation of the Evidential Burden*

The allocation of the legal burden normally determines the incidence of the evidential burden. The party shouldering the evidential burden on a particular issue carries the risk that, if there is no evidence on that issue or if the evidence does not satisfy the judge, the issue will be withdrawn from the trier of fact.

1. The evidential burden in criminal cases

It is a significantly lesser hurdle to adduce enough evidence to satisfy the judge to leave an issue to the jury than it is to convince the jury. Simply clearing the hurdle of the evidential burden does not mean that the party will therefore succeed in that issue. The general rule is that whosoever carries the legal burden also bears the evidential burden. The prosecution in a criminal case will bear both burdens in relation to most issues: in other words, the Crown must adduce enough evidence in relation to each and every element of the offence that a defence submission of no case to answer at the end of the prosecution case would be unsuccessful and the judge would consider that there was evidence on which a reasonable jury, properly directed, could convict.[66]

The defence would bear the evidential burden, on such issues as insanity or diminished responsibility where they also bear the legal burden. But there are issues on which the defence will bear the evidential burden, although the legal burden of disproof will rest on the prosecution. This occurs when the defendant raises certain positive defences, over and above a denial of a definitional element of the offence. Examples are defences such as self-defence, provocation or duress. The defendant bears an evidential burden if that defence is to be left to the jury. In *Bratty v Attorney-General for Northern Ireland*,[67] the accused was charged with murder, having strangled a young girl. His defences, based on some evidence of psychomotor epilepsy, were twofold: first there was the plea of insanity which was an issue that the judge left to the jury who rejected it; secondly there was the defence of non-insane automatism. The latter was not left to the jury. Bratty appealed on the grounds that the judge should have directed the jury on the issue of non-insane automatism. The appeal was rejected by the House of Lords,

---

[64] Employment Act, s.6.
[65] *Palmer v Post Office* (1998) (Transcript EAT/472/98).
[66] C. Tapper, *Cross and Tapper on Evidence* (10th ed., 2004) Butterworths, p.153.
[67] *Galbraith* [1981] 2 All E.R. 1060; see Ch.2 for further discussion.

Bratty v Attorney-General for Northern Ireland [1961] 3 All E.R. 523 at 527, *per* Viscount Kilmuir L.C.:

. . . 'Automatism' was defined by the Court of Criminal Appeal in this case 'as connoting the state of a person who, though capable of action, is not conscious of what he is doing . . . It means unconscious involuntary action, and it is a defence because the mind does not go with what is being done'

. . . The first portion of the argument before them that 'automatism' should have been left to the jury was summarised by the Court of Criminal Appeal as being that the whole of the evidence on the issue of insanity was relevant on the issue whether automatism itself existed, however it was caused; in view of the onus being on the defence to show on a preponderance of probabilities that the necessary constituents of the M'Naghten formula were present, it was therefore submitted that, although the evidence might have failed to prove some constituent of insanity, the lack of consciousness itself might have seemed a genuine possibility to the jury, and the jury might at least have had a reasonable doubt as to whether the appellant was conscious of his acts so as to be guilty of murder . . .

The Court of Criminal Appeal rejected that 'first portion of the argument' on the ground that the learned judge was right in not leaving to the jury the defence of automatism, in so far as it purported to be founded on a defect of reason from disease of the mind within the M'Naghten Rules. In this I think they were right . . .

What I have said does not mean that, if a defence of insanity is raised unsuccessfully, there can never, in any conceivable circumstances, be room for an alternative defence based on automatism. For example, it may be alleged that the accused had a blow on the head, after which he acted without being conscious of what he was doing or was a sleepwalker. There might be a divergence of view as to whether there was a defect of reason from disease of the mind . . . The jury might not accept the evidence of a defect of reason from disease of the mind, but at the same time accept the evidence that the prisoner did not know what he was doing. If the jury should take that view of the facts they would find him not guilty. But it should be noted that the defence would only have succeeded because the necessary foundation has been laid by positive evidence which, properly considered, was evidence of something other than a defect of reason from disease of the mind. In my opinion, this analysis of the two defences (insanity and automatism) shows that where the only cause alleged for the unconsciousness is a defect of reason from disease of the mind, and that cause is rejected by the jury, there can be no room for an alternative defence of automatism. Like the Court of Criminal Appeal, I cannot therefore accept the submission that the whole of the evidence directed to the issue of insanity should have been left to the jury to consider whether there was automatism due to another cause. It was conceded . . . that there was nothing to show or suggest that there was any other pathological cause for automatism . . .

It is necessary that a proper foundation be laid before a judge can leave 'automatism' to the jury. That foundation, in my view, is not forthcoming merely from an unaccepted evidence of a defect of reason from disease of the mind. There would need to be other evidence on which a jury could find non-insane automatism . . .

In *Bratty*, the accused bore first the legal burden of proving insanity. He adduced evidence of psychomotor epilepsy that satisfied the evidential burden cast on him so that the issue was left to the jury who, on the preponderance of probabilities, decided that he was, in fact, sane. Secondly, the defendant bore the evidential burden of raising the issue of non-insane automatism: the only evidence of a possible cause of his (allegedly) involuntary conduct was psychomotor epilepsy. As a matter of law, the trial judge had already ruled that this condition was a disease of the mind and therefore evidentially could only form the foundation for a defence of insane automatism. As no other possible cause had been put forward, the judge was correct in withdrawing the issue from the jury.

This requirement to lay an evidential foundation applies to other defences, whether common law such as self-defence or duress or statutory defences such as provocation. The accused has to produce enough cogent evidence to satisfy the judge that the issue should be left to the jury. Only when the defence has laid such a foundation, does the prosecution have to disprove it beyond reasonable doubt.

There is a difficult distinction to be drawn here. Where the defence is based on a denial of one of the constituent elements of the offence, the prosecution bear both burdens and the jury must be directed on the requirement for proof beyond reasonable doubt on each and every element. The accused in *Woolmington* was entitled to a direction on the lack of intention, regardless of the quality of his own evidence or indeed of whether he had testified at all. But where the defence raises issues other than those expressly or impliedly contained in the offence itself, it is for the accused to raise the issue and to surmount an evidential burden. Such was the case in *Hill v Baxter*[68] and yet it might be argued that the defendant in that case was simply pleading lack of volition as opposed to Woolmington's lack of intention?

The difficulty is that the criminal law provides no satisfactory analytical distinction between offence and defence. The fine line that needs to be drawn can be seen in relation to the question of consent in rape. What constitutes the elements of an offence is a question of substantive law and the Crown obviously bear the onus of showing intercourse and the lack of the victim's consent. But *D.P.P. v Morgan*[69] decided that the mental ingredient of the offence was an intention to have non-consensual intercourse with the victim. The House of Lords held that the accused's belief in consent was not a separate defence in itself but was simply a denial of the requisite *mens rea*. As a result, there was no evidential burden on the defendant in a rape case to raise the issue of his belief in consent. This remains the case under s.1 of the Sexual Offences Act 2003 as the Crown must prove penetration, lack of consent and lack of reasonable belief in consent. The jury will still be directed that the prosecution must satisfy then that the defendant had no reasonable basis for believing that the victim had consented. It would have been a minor but valuable reform if that issue did not have to be considered by the jury unless the defendant had adduced some evidence that first he had believed that the victim was consenting and secondly that he had reasonable grounds for that belief.

2. Evidential burden in civil cases
In civil proceedings, the allocation of the evidential burden runs with that of the legal burden. Normally defences aimed at defeating a claim need to be proved by the party asserting them. For example, where a party to a contract

[68] [1961] 3 All E.R. 523.
[69] [1958] 1 Q.B. 277.

alleges it is voidable for duress or undue influence, the burden of proving the necessary facts falls on the party alleging them. However there are some cases where equity will presume undue influence from the fact of the relationship and, although there is an evidential burden on the party alleging the undue influence, the legal burden falls on the party seeking to show that no such influence was exerted.[70]

III. The Standard of Proof

A court is concerned with the problem of reconstructing the past and attempting to discover the truth. Such an exercise is at best an approximation and any conclusions are not certainties but exist only at varying levels of likelihood. For the benefit of the trier of fact, courts need to specify the level of probability that constitutes proof and this is referred to as the standard of proof. There are two levels: proof beyond reasonable doubt or proof on the balance of probabilities. Although formally there are only two standards of proof, judges and scholars have pointed out that some acts are inherently less likely than others and the consequences of some decisions are more serious than others. Thus the prosecutor in a murder case should have a higher hurdle to surmount than one on a less serious change, since people are less likely to kill and the consequences is life imprisonment. But such reasoning has not led the appellate courts to develop flexible standards and we are left with standard formulae.

A. *Discharge of Evidential Burden in Criminal Cases*

As has been explained, the first stage of "proof" is to overcome the evidential burden, to "pass the judge". If the judge does not believe that sufficient evidence has been adduced by the prosecution on each element of the offence so that a reasonable jury, properly directed, might convict, he or she might direct the jury to acquit. This often happens at the end of the prosecution case on a submission by the defence of "no case to answer". This is a common occurrence—in Crown Court approximately 40% of all acquittals are the result of the prosecution offering no evidence or the judge directing the jury to return a verdict of "not guilty" at the conclusion of the Crown case. This can be the result of such matters as prosecution witnesses not turning up to testify or failing to testify as effectively as had been expected or simply bad preparation of the case.[71]

The evidential burden is discharged if the judge feels that there is sufficient evidence. But what is "sufficient"? The leading authority is *Galbraith*.[72]

---

[70] [1975] 2 All E.R. 347—now regulated by Sexual Offences Act 2003, s.1.

[71] *Allcard v Skinner* (1887) 36 Ch. D 145; explained by Lord Scarman in *National Westminster Bank PLC v Morgan* [1985] 1 All E.R. 821; *Royal Bank of Scotland v Etridge* [2001] 4 All E.R. 449.

[72] S. Uglow, *Criminal Justice* (2nd ed., Sweet and Maxwell, London, 2002) p.200ff.

Galbraith [1981] 2 All E.R 1060 at 1062; *per* Lord Lane CJ.:

How then should the judge approach a submission of 'no case'? (1) If there is no evidence that the crime alleged has been committed by the defendant, there is no difficulty. The judge will of course stop the case. (2) The difficulty arises where there is some evidence but it is of a tenuous character, for example, because of inherent weakness or vagueness or because it is inconsistent with other evidence. (a) Where the judge comes to the conclusion that the prosecution evidence, taken at its highest, is such that a jury properly directed could not properly convict upon it, it is his duty, upon a submission being made, to stop the case. (b) Where, however, the prosecution evidence is such that its strength or weakness depends on the view to be taken of a witness's reliability, or other matters which are generally speaking within the province of the jury and where on one possible view of the facts there is evidence upon which a jury could properly come to the conclusion that the defendant is guilty, then the judge should allow the matter to be tried by the jury . . .

Lord Devlin in *Jayasena*[73] put it simply: "such evidence as, if believed, and if left uncontradicted and unexplained, could be accepted by the jury as proof".The judge should assume that the jury will accept the evidence and should draw any inferences which favour the prosecution. At the end of the day, of course, the jury do not have to accept it and might still acquit. The test for the discharge of the evidential burden is whether the judge considers that there is evidence which is capable of sustaining a verdict beyond reasonable doubt. *Sharman v North London Coroner*[74] involved the quashing of a verdict of unlawful killing by a coroner's jury after police officers had shot and killed a man whom they believed was armed but was in fact carrying a chair leg in a black bag. The issue was, before the jury could reach the verdict of unlawful killing, whether they had to come to the conclusion that the defence of self-defence had been disproved beyond reasonable doubt. The coroner had not applied the *Galbraith* test to this particular issue: namely was there sufficient evidence upon which a reasonable jury could conclude beyond reasonable doubt that the officers were not acting in self defence? As a result the Court of Appeal held that it had not been safe for the jury to come to that verdict.

Discharging the evidential burden, when it rests on the defendant, is not onerous, merely needing to produce enough evidence to leave a jury in a reasonable doubt on the issue. If the judge does not believe that sufficient evidence has been adduced by the defendant and that a reasonable jury, properly directed, could not find a reasonable doubt, the judge can withdraw that issue from the jury. This was discussed in *Hill v Baxter*[75] where the Court of Appeal held that, in spite of the justices accepting the defendant's evidence that he became unconscious while driving, this did not constitute evidence which was a proper foundation for a defence of non-insane automatism. Devlin J. said,

Hill v Baxter [1975] 2 All E.R. 347; *per* Devlin J.:

. . . In my judgment there is not to be found in the case stated evidence of automatism of a character which would be fit to leave to a jury . . . he was not saying

---

[73] [1981] 2 All ER 1060; *AS* [2004] EWCA Crim 2019; *Jeneson* [2005] EWCA Crim 1984.
[74] [1970] 1 All E.R. 219 at 221g-h.
[75] [2005] EWCA Civ 967.

that he was a victim of a disease of the mind. Unless there was evidence that this irrationality was due to some cause other than disease of the mind, the justices were not entitled simply to acquit . . .

While the principle applied here is correct, Devlin's interpretation of the facts seems flawed. Why was it necessary for the defendant to show the cause of the blackout? The defendant gave sworn testimony, believed by the justices, that he suffered a blackout. If the blackout occurred, regardless of its cause, that should satisfy the evidential burden on the accused—a reasonable bench of magistrates, properly directed, could reasonably have concluded that there was a reasonable doubt that the defendant had been in a state of automatism?

B. *Discharge of Evidential Burden in Civil Cases*

In civil cases, an analogous procedure might occur. At the end of the claimant's case, the defence, might make a 'no case' submission. The judge would regard the evidential burden as discharged if sufficient evidence has been adduced that would justify the trier of fact in concluding that the legal burden (on the preponderance of probabilities) on that issue has been discharged. This is supported by *Coys Ltd v Autocherish Ltd*,[76] a defamation action where the claimant sought an interlocutory injunction. This would only be issued if there were no grounds for holding that the statement was true or there was no other defence such as justification, fair comment or qualified privilege that might succeed. Tugendhat J. decided that there was no basis on which these issues could be withdrawn from the jury and that therefore the application for an injunction failed.

Coys Ltd v Autocherish Ltd [2004] EWHC 1334, *per* Tugendhat J.:

46 So far as concerns the defences of qualified privilege and fair comment, I remind myself that while a judge does have the right to withdraw such defences from a jury in an appropriate case, the test is very high. Because this is a libel action where the parties both have a right to trial by jury, the test I must apply on this application to these proposed defences is closely analogous to the test used in criminal trials in the light of *R v Galbraith*. This is re-emphasised by May L.J. in *Alexander v Arts Council of Wales*.[77] Unless I can make a ruling here and now on meaning and on each of the proposed defences that pass this high test, namely that I can properly withdraw the case from the jury, then the case must go forward to a jury unless or until some other judge reaches a different conclusion at a later stage in the circumstances prevailing at that time.

C. *Discharge of Legal Burden in Criminal Cases*

At the close of a criminal trial, the party with the legal burden must persuade the trier of fact of the 'truth' of the assertions. There are two levels: for the

---

[76] [1958] 1 Q.B. 277 at 298.
[77] [2004] E.M.L.R. 25; [2004] EWHC 1334.

prosecution, that level of persuasion is that proof must be beyond reasonable doubt; for the defence, that standard is proof on the balance of probabilities.[78] The standard of proof of 'beyond reasonable doubt' is seen as one of the cornerstones of the presumption of innocence.

Fitzjames Stephen, History of the Criminal Law, Vol. 1 354:

If it be asked why an accused person is presumed to be innocent, I think the true answer is, not that the presumption is probably true, but that society in the present day is so much stronger that the individual, and is capable of inflicting so very much more harm on the individual than the individual as a rule can inflict upon society, that it can afford to be generous. It is, however, a question of degree, varying according to time and place, how far this generosity can or ought to be carried . . .

This strict requirement of the standard of proof in criminal proceedings is linked closely to the presumption of innocence in criminal law, underpinned by Art.6(2).

The Judicial Studies Board[79] gives the following direction as guidance.

How does the prosecution succeed in proving the defendant's guilt? The answer is—by making you sure of it. Nothing less than that will do. If after considering all the evidence you are sure that the defendant is guilty, you must return a verdict of 'Guilty'. If you are not sure, your verdict must be 'Not Guilty'.

The Board suggests that it is not necessary to use the phrase "beyond reasonable doubt". But the phrase is often mentioned and the judge should ensure that the jury realise that being "sure of guilt" is the same as proving the case beyond reasonable doubt. The Court of Appeal cautioned against any attempt at a more elaborate definition of "being sure" or "beyond reasonable doubt" and that it is unhelpful to seek to distinguish between being 'sure' and 'certain'.

The two standards of proof, namely "beyond reasonable doubt" and "balance of probabilities", were discussed in *Miller v Ministry of Pensions*.[80] The widow of an army officer was appealing from the decision of a pensions tribunal that she was not entitled to the higher pension awarded to widows of soldiers who had died in war service.

Miller v Ministry of Pensions [1947] 2 All E.R. 372 at 373–374, *per* Denning J.:

The first point of law in the present appeal is whether the tribunal properly directed itself as to the burden of proof. The proper direction is covered by decisions of this court. It is as follows,

[78] [2001] 1 W.L.R. 1840 at paras [37]–[38].
[79] *Carr-Briant* [1943] 2 All E.R. 156.
[80] Available at *www.jsboard.co.uk/criminal_law/cbb/index.htm* (accessed April 1, 2006).

1. In cases falling under art 4(2) and art 4(3) of the Royal Warrant Concerning Pay, Pensions etc, 1943 (which are generally cases where the man was passed fit at the commencement of his service, but is later afflicted by a disease which leads to his death or discharge) there is a compelling presumption in the man's favour which must prevail unless the evidence proves beyond reasonable doubt that the disease was not attributable to or aggravated by war service, and for that purpose the evidence must reach the same degree of cogency as is required in a criminal case before an accused person is found guilty. That degree is well settled. It need not reach certainty, but it must carry a high degree of probability. Proof beyond reasonable doubt does not mean proof beyond the shadow of a doubt. The law would fail to protect the community if it admitted fanciful possibilities to deflect the course of justice. If the evidence is so strong against a man as to leave only a remote possibility in his favour which can be dismissed with the sentence 'of course it is possible, but not in the least probable,' the case is proved beyond reasonable doubt, but nothing short of that will suffice.

2. In cases falling under art 4(2) and art 4(4) (which are generally cases where the man was fit on his discharge, but incapacitated later by a disease) there is no compelling presumption in his favour, and the case must be decided according to the preponderance of probability. If at the end of the case the evidence turns the scale definitely one way or the other, the tribunal must decide accordingly, but if the evidence is so evenly balanced that the tribunal is unable to come to a determinate conclusion one way or the other, then the man must be given the benefit of the doubt. This means that the case must be decided in favour of the man unless the evidence against him reaches the same degree of cogency as is required to discharge a burden in a civil case. That degree is well settled. it must carry a reasonable degree of probability, but not so high as is required in a criminal case. If the evidence is such that the tribunal can say: 'We think it more probable than not,' the burden is discharged, but, if the probabilities are equal, it is not . . .

In *Hepworth*,[81] Lord Goddard C.J. expressed his misgivings about 'reasonable doubt'.

Hepworth [1955] 2 All E.R. 918 at 919–920, *per* Lord Goddard C.J.:

. . . it is very difficult to tell a jury what is a reasonable doubt. To tell a jury that it must not be a fanciful doubt is something that is without real guidance. To tell them that a reasonable doubt is such a doubt as to cause them to hesitate in their own affairs never seems to me to convey any particular standard . . . It may be that in some cases the word 'satisfied' is enough. Then, it is said that the jury in a civil case has to be satisfied and, therefore, one is only laying down the same standard of proof as in a civil case. I confess that I have had some difficulty in understanding how there is or there can be two standards; therefore one would be on safe ground if one said in a criminal case to a jury: 'You must be satisfied beyond reasonable doubt' and one could also say: 'You, the jury, must be completely satisfied,' or better still: 'You must feel sure of the prisoner's guilt.' But I desire to repeat what I said in *R v Kritz*[82]: 'It is not the formula that matters: it is the effect of the summing up. If the jury are made to understand that they have to be satisfied and must not return a verdict against a defendant unless they feel sure, and that the onus is all the time on the prosecution and not on the defence, that is enough.

---

[81] [1947] 2 All E.R. 372.
[82] [1955] 2 All E.R. 918.

This difficulty was shown in *Yap Chuan Ching*,[83] where the jury had difficulty in reaching a verdict and asked for help. They were told the following by the trial judge.

Yap Chuan Ching (1976) 63 Cr.App.R. 7 at 9–10, *per* Lawton L.J.:

'. . . a reasonable doubt, it has been said, is a doubt to which you can give a reason as opposed to a mere fanciful sort of speculation such as 'Well, nothing in this world is certain, nothing in this world can be proved.' As I say, that is the definition of a reasonable doubt—something to which you can assign a reason. It is sometimes said the sort of matter which might influence you if you were to consider some business matter. A matter, for example, of a mortgage concerning your house, or something of that nature . . .'

The Court of Appeal accepted this but felt that judges should not seek to define further 'sure' or 'beyond reasonable doubt'.

[The appellant] attacked the final direction on three grounds. He said that it was unsatisfactory for a judge to define a 'reasonable doubt' as one for which a reason could be given: he pointed to a criticism of that phrase which was made by Edmund Davies LJ . . . in *Stafford and Luvaglio*[84] [who] said: 'We do not, however, ourselves agree with the trial judge when directing the jury upon the standard of proof, he told them to 'Remember that a reasonable doubt is one for which you could give reasons if you were asked,' and we dislike such a description or definition.' So do we. It does not help juries. But that is not the problem in this case. The problem is whether its use made this conviction unsafe. The next ground of complaint was that by using the mortgage of a house analogy, the learned judge was doing something which had been condemned a number of times in this Court . . . In the past this Court has criticised trial judges for using that kind of analogy. The use of any analogy is to be avoided whenever possible. The final criticism was that when giving the direction of which complaint is made, the judge did not emphasise once again that the jury had to be sure. But we have no doubt that by the time the jury had retired for the last time, they must have appreciated that they had to be sure before they could return a verdict of guilty. Nevertheless, in most cases . . . judges would be well advised not to attempt any gloss upon what is meant by 'sure' or what is meant by 'reasonable doubt'.[85]

It is easy for judges to stray in trying to be helpful to juries. In *Stephens*,[86] the jury, after retiring, asked the judge what constituted reasonable doubt and how certain did they have to be? The trial judge replied,

Stephens [2002] EWCA Crim 1529:

'The first of your questions I read to remind you, and to read into the record is this: what constitutes reasonable doubt? My answer to the question is this: a reasonable

---

[83] [1949] 2 All E.R. 406.
[84] (1976) 63 Cr.App.R 7.
[85] [1968] 3 All E.R. 752.
[86] [2002] EWCA Crim 1529.

doubt is the sort of doubt that might affect the mind of a person dealing with matters of importance in his own affairs. Your second question is this: how certain do you have to be? And my answer to that question is that you do not have to be certain. You have to be sure. Which is less than being certain.'

The Court of Appeal was happy with the first answer but did not approve of judges drawing a distinction between "sure" and "certain". It is very well-established that the jury should be told that they have to be satisfied so that they are sure of guilt. There is a more limited point that the jury is not concerned with scientific certainty, a degree of certainty such that an expert witness could exclude any other possibility at all.[87]

Where the legal burden is on the accused, that burden is discharged by proof on the balance of probabilities. *Carr-Briant*[88] involved a charge under the Prevention of Corruption Acts 1906 and 1916 which placed the legal burden on the accused to show that a gift to him or her as a public servant was in fact not made corruptly. The trial judge directed the jury that the defendant had to discharge this burden on the same standard as that resting on the prosecution.

Carr-Briant [1943] 2 All E.R. 156 at 158, *per* Humphreys J.:

We see no reason why the rebuttable presumption created by the section should not be construed in the same manner as similar words in other statutes or similar presumptions at common law, for instance, the presumption of sanity in the case of an accused person who is setting up the defence of insanity. .. In our judgment, in any case where, either by statute or at common law, some matter is presumed against an accused person 'unless the contrary is proved', the jury should be directed that it is for them to decide whether the contrary is proved, that the burden of proof required is less than that required at the hands of the prosecution in proving the case beyond a reasonable doubt, and that the burden may be discharged by evidence satisfying the jury of the probability of that which the accused is called upon to establish.

Statistics and proof

Directing the jury to be sure of guilt or to make up their minds on the balance of probabilities, brings into focus the fact that in trials, legal proof is merely the designation of a certain level of probability that a specific fact or state of affairs exists. But advances in DNA technology and a series of decisions involving Sudden Infant Death Syndrome (SIDS) or cot deaths have demonstrated the distinction between making a general statement of proba-bility and a specific finding that an individual is guilty. There is an increasing use (and abuse) of statistics in the courtroom as well as a complex literature on the extent to which probability theories have a part to play in the factual problems confronting courts.[89]

---

[87] *Bracewell* 68 Cr.App.R. 44.
[88] [1943] 2 All E.R. 156.
[89] Eggleston, *op.cit.* Ch.3; J. Cohen, *The Probable and the Provable* (Oxford, 1977); Glanville Williams, "The Mathematics of Proof" [1979] Crim.L.R. 297 and 340; J. Cohen, "The Logic of Proof" [1980] Crim.L.R. 91; T. Anderson and W. Twining, *Analysis of Evidence* (Weidenfeld 1991), p.385ff; B. Robertson and G. Vignaux, *Interpreting Evidence: Evaluating Forensic Science in the Courtroom* (Wiley, 1995).

In *Clark*[90] and *Cannings*[91], mothers were convicted of murdering their children. There was no conclusive evidence as to the cause of death and considerable reliance on expert testimony. The convictions in both cases were quashed. The court in *Clark* was concerned in particular with the non-disclosure of pertinent medical evidence but also with misleading testimony about statistical probabilities. The expert stated that the likelihood of two natural cot deaths in one family was 1 in 73 million. That figure was derived by squaring 1 in 8,543 which was the risk of a single SIDS within such a family. The President of the Royal Statistical Society pointed out the following.

Quoted in C. Wells, "The Impact of Feminist Thinking on Criminal Law and Justice" [2004] Crim.L.R. (Anniversary Edition) 88:

The calculation leading to 1 in 73 million is invalid. It would only be valid if SIDS cases arose independently within families, an assumption that would need to be justified empirically. Not only was no such empirical justification provided in the case, but there are very strong reasons for supposing that the assumption is false. There may well be unknown genetic or environmental factors that predispose families to SIDS, so that a second case within the family becomes much more likely than would be a case in another, apparently similar, family. A separate concern is that the characteristics used to classify the Clark family were chosen on the basis of the same data as was used to evaluate the frequency for that classification. This double use of data is well recognised by statisticians as perilous, since it can lead to subtle yet important biases . . . The Court of Appeal [in her first appeal] recognised flaws in its calculation, but seemed to accept I it as establishing '. . . a very broad point, namely the rarity of double SIDS'. However, not only is the error in the 1 in 73 million figure likely to be very large, it is almost certainly in one particular direction—against the defendant. Moreover, following from the 1 in 73 million figure at the original trial, the expert used a figure of about 700,000 UK births per year to conclude that '. . . by chance that happening will occur every 100 years'. This conclusion is fallacious, not only because of the invalidity of the 1 in 73 million figure, but also because the 1 in 73 million figure relates only to families having some characteristics matching that of the defendant. This error seems not to have been recognised by the Appeal Court, who cited it without critical comment.[92]

In *Cannings* there was little direct evidence but although three unexplained deaths in the same family were rare, this improbability did not establish that the deaths resulted from the deliberate infliction of harm. The Court of Appeal held that the case should have proceeded on the basis that if there was nothing to explain the deaths, they remained unexplained and still possible natural deaths despite the known fact that some parents did smother their infant children. [93]

---

[90] [2003] EWCA Crim 1020.
[91] [2004] 2 Cr.App.R. 7.
[92] Quoted in C. Wells, "The Impact of Feminist Thinking on Criminal Law and Justice" [2004] Crim.L.R. (Anniversary Edition) 88.
[93] Distinguished in *Kai-Whitewind* [2002] 2 Cr.App.R. 31; *Anthony* [2005] EWCA Crim 952.

The problems surrounding the use of statistical probability as evidence have emerged particularly in the context of DNA evidence. The National DNA Database (NDNAD) was set up under s.64 of the Police and Criminal Evidence Act 1984. [94] It already contains some 3 million samples which can be checked against samples found at the scene of the crime. [95] If a match is found, it may link the suspect to the crime scene. In court, this may be expressed, somewhat crudely, as ". . . reduced the possibility of it being anyone but [the defendant] to one in four million of the male population".[96] The Court of Appeal addressed the problems of how such evidence should be presented in *Doheny*.[97] The defendant was appealing against conviction for rape and buggery based largely on DNA evidence.

Doheny [1997] 1 Cr.App.R. 369: at 372–375, *per* Phillips L.J.

We shall take a match probability, or random occurrence ratio, of one in a million as an example to demonstrate the conclusions that can properly be drawn from such data and those which cannot. We shall start with the latter.

"The Prosecutor's Fallacy"

It is easy, if one eschews rigorous analysis, to draw the following conclusion:
1) Only one person in a million will have a DNA profile which matches that of the crime stain.
2) The Defendant has a DNA profile which matches the crime stain.
3) Ergo there is a million to one probability that the Defendant left the crime stain and is guilty of the crime.

Such reasoning has been commended to juries in a number of cases by Prosecuting Counsel, by judges and sometimes by expert witnesses. It is fallacious and it has earned the title of "The Prosecutor's Fallacy". The propounding of the Prosecutor's Fallacy in the course of the summing up was the reason, or at least one of the reasons, why the appeal against conviction was allowed in *Deen*. [98] The nature of that fallacy was elegantly exposed by Balding and Donnelly.[99] . . .

Taking our example, the Prosecutor's Fallacy can be simply demonstrated. If one person in a million has a DNA profile which matches that obtained from the crime stain, then the suspect will be one of perhaps 26 men in the United Kingdom who share that characteristic. If no fact is known about the Defendant, other than that he was in the United Kingdom at the time of the crime the DNA evidence tells us no more than that there is a statistical probability that he was the criminal of 1 in 26.

---

[94] Amended by Criminal Justice and Public Order Act 1994, the Criminal Justice and Police Act 2001 and Criminal Justice Act 2003 s.10.

[95] See NDNAD Report for 2003–2004 at *www.forensic.gov.uk/forensic_t/inside/about/docs/NDNAD_AR_3_4.pdf*

[96] *Melias, The Times,* November 14, 1987.

[97] [1997] 1 Cr.App.R. 369; *Jessie Smith; Lashley* (both February 8, 2000 (CA) unreported); *Pringle* [2003] UKPC 9; M. Redmayne, 'Appeals to Reason' (2002) 65 M.L.R. 19.

[98] *The Times* January 10, 1994.

[99] D. Balding and P. Donnelly, "The Prosecutor's Fallacy and DNA Evidence" [1994] Crim.L.R. 711.

The significance of the DNA evidence will depend critically upon what else is known about the suspect. If he has a convincing alibi at the other end of England at the time of the crime, it will appear highly improbable that he can have been responsible for the crime, despite his matching DNA profile. If, however, he was near the scene of the crime when it was committed, or has been identified as a suspect because of other evidence which suggests that he may have been responsible for the crime, the DNA evidence becomes very significant. The possibility that two of the only 26 men in the United Kingdom with the matching DNA should have been in the vicinity of the crime will seem almost incredible and a comparatively slight nexus between the Defendant and the crime, independent of the DNA, is likely to suffice to present an overall picture to the jury that satisfies them of the Defendant's guilt.

The reality is that, provided there is no reason to doubt either the matching data or the statistical conclusion based upon it, the random occurrence ratio deduced from the DNA evidence, when combined with sufficient additional evidence to give it significance, is highly probative. As the art of analysis progresses, it is likely to become more so, and the stage may be reached where a match will be so comprehensive that it will be possible to construct a DNA profile that is unique and which proves the guilt of the Defendant without any other evidence. So far as we are aware that stage has not yet been reached.

The cogency of DNA evidence makes it particularly important that DNA testing is rigorously conducted so as to obviate the risk of error in the laboratory, that the method of DNA analysis and the basis of subsequent statistical calculation should—so far as possible—be transparent to the Defence and that the true import of the resultant conclusion is accurately and fairly explained to the jury.

The Court went on to discuss the role of the expert in such cases.

He will properly explain to the Jury the nature of the match ("the matching DNA characteristics") between the DNA in the crime stain and the DNA in the blood sample taken from the Defendant. He will properly, on the basis of empirical statistical data, give the Jury the random occurrence ratio—the frequency with which the matching DNA characteristics are likely to be found in the population at large. Provided that he has the necessary data, and the statistical expertise, it may be appropriate for him then to say how many people with the matching characteristics are likely to be found in the United Kingdom—or perhaps in a more limited relevant sub group, such as, for instance, the Caucasian sexually active males in the Manchester area. This will often be the limit of the evidence which he can properly and usefully give. It will then be for the Jury to decide, having regard to all the relevant evidence, whether they are sure that it was the Defendant who left the crime stain, or whether it is possible that it was left by someone else with the same matching DNA characteristics.

The scientist should not be asked his opinion on the likelihood that it was the Defendant who left the crime stain, nor when giving evidence should he use terminology which may lead the Jury to believe that he is expressing such an opinion.

Finally the Court suggested the following direction.

Members of the Jury, if you accept the scientific evidence called by the Crown, this indicates that there are probably only four or five white males in the United Kingdom from whom that semen stain could have come. The Defendant is one of them. If that is the position, the decision you have to reach, on all the evidence, is whether you are sure that it was the Defendant who left that stain or whether it is possible that it was one of that other small group of men who share the same DNA characteristics.

Doheny raises many issues about the use of statistical evidence in court. [1] This can reach beyond DNA cases and Redmayne gives the following example.

M., Redmayne, "Science, Evidence and Logic" [1996] 59 M.L.R. 747:

Modern debates about the role of mathematical models in adjudicative fact-finding are commonly traced back to People v Collins.[2] The Collinses were accused of robbery, the case against them being largely that they fitted eyewitness descriptions of the robbers. The prosecutor identified several characteristics of the defendants, such as that the man had a moustache and that they drove a yellow car, which matched the eyewitness descriptions. The prosecutor assigned probabilities to the occurrence of each of the characteristics and, relying on the testimony of a mathematics instructor who had described the prudct rule, multiplied these probabilities together. He claimed that the resulting figure of 1/12,000,000 represented the probability of any couple possessing all of the characteristics of the defendants. The jury convicted.

While the newspapers triumphantly announced that 'Law of Probability Foils 2 Robbers in Tough Case,' the Collinses appealed and their convictions were overturned by the Supreme Court of California. There were two main problems with the prosecutor's strategy. First the figures he used seemed to have been plucked out of thin air: they lacked any objective grounding, while some of the characteristics chosen were not independent, making use of the product rule for independent events untenable. Secondly, even if the prosecutor could have proved the validity of the calculations underlying the 1/12,000,000 figure, it was not obvious what the figure meant: it does not necessarily follow that there was only a 1/12,000,000 probability that the Collinses were innocent.

The Court of Appeal has rejected this use of expert evidence from statisticians. In *Adams*,[3] the prosecution in a rape case was based on DNA evidence which suggested that the probability of the defendant being innocent was 200 million to one. The defence were permitted to introduce expert evidence from a statistician to evaluate the relative probabilities of the non-DNA evidence and to incorporate that with the DNA evidence. This involved the use of Bayes Theorem which gives each separate piece of evidence a numerical percentage representing the ratio between the proba-bility of circumstance A and the probability of circumstance B granted the existence of that evidence. The testimony looked at the probabilities of the culprit being a local man in the light of the alibi provided by the accused's girlfriend and the weakness of the identification evidence. The witness was even permitted to speculate as to the odds on the defendant being guilty.

Although their Lordships expressed no concluded view on the matter, they had very grave doubts as to whether that evidence was properly admissible, because it trespassed on an area peculiarly and exclusively within the jury's

[1] I. Evett, L. Foreman, G. Jackson and J. Lambert, "DNA Profiling: A discussion of the Issues Relating to the Reporting of Very Small Match Probabilities" [2000] Crim.L.R. 341; M. Redmayne, 'Appeals to Reason' (2002) 65 M.L.R. 19.
[2] (1968) 68 Cal 2d 319.
[3] (1996) 2 Cr.App.R. 467.

province, namely the way in which they evaluated the relationship between one piece of evidence and another.

Quashing the conviction, Rose L.J. said.

Adams [1996] 2 Cr.App.R. 467 at 481, *per* Rose L.J.:

The Bayes Theorem might be an appropriate and useful tool for statisticians . . . it is not appropriate for use in jury trials or as a means to assist the jury in their task. In the first place, the theorem's methodology required that items of evidence be assessed separately according to their bearing on the guilt of the accused, before being combined in the overall formula. That in our view is far too rigid an approach to evidence of the nature which a jury characteristically had to assess. More fundamentally, the attempt to determine guilt or innocence on the basis of a mathematical formula, applied to each separate piece of evidence, is simply inappropriate to the jury's task. Jurors evaluate evidence and reach conclusions not by means of a formula, mathematical or otherwise, but by the joint application of their individual common sense and knowledge of the world to the evidence before them.

It was common for juries to evaluate scientific evidence but their Lordships had never heard it suggested that a jury should consider the relationship between such scientific evidence and other evidence by reference to probability formulae. In *Doheny*, the Court strongly endorsed the comment that to introduce Bayes Theorem, or any similar method, into a criminal trial plunges the jury into inappropriate and unnecessary realms of theory and complexity deflecting them from their proper task. However in *Hookway*,[4] a robbery case, the main evidence was that of a "facial mapping" expert who compared photos of the robber with photos of Hookway and concluded that they were one and the same. Redmayne[5] suggests that the case employed a *Doheny*-style statistical mode—how many males in the robbery area might match this facial map? But this question was unanswerable as there was no DNA-type database for facial features. There may have been two or three such males or alternatively several dozen. Despite this, Hookway's conviction was upheld.

While statistical evidence can have great probative value, there are limits to such reasoning.

M. Redmayne, "Appeals to Reason", [2002] 65 M.L.R. 19:

Recently Piers Rawling[6] has used a statistical argument to suggest that criminal proof is almost impossible. His argument is simple. If the presumption of innocence

---

[4] [1999] Crim.L.R. 751.
[5] Redmayne (2002) *op.cit*. pp. 23–24.
[6] P. Rawling, "Reasonable Doubt and the Presumption of Innocence: the Case of the Bayesian Juror" (1999) 18 Topoi 117.

requires a fact-finder to approach a case on the assumption that, before hearing any evidence, there is no more reason to suspect the accused than any other person in a large population, then the prosecution will rarely be able to muster sufficient evidence to justify conviction. For example, if the criminal standard of proof is set at a probability of 0.95 and the suspect population (s) is 1 million, the prosecution will need to present evidence with a combined likelihood ratio[7] of around 1.9×10^7. In terms of DNA evidence, a match probability of about 1 in 20,000,000 would be needed before there is a case for the defendant to answer. Take s to be the population of the United Kingdom, and a match probability of 1 in 200,000,000 is called for. DNA evidence of this power is now available but it is unlikely other evidence types— confessions, eyewitness identifications—come anywhere close. Even if the prosecution is able to produce several pieces of evidence, the threshold will be very difficult to meet.

Redmayne responds that juries are practical reasoners who, even when the evidence is not compelling, work on other assumptions, especially the idea of trust in the police and that there is likely to be other evidence which drew the defendant to police attention, usually assuming the defendant is of previous bad character. Such unarticulated assumptions will continue, although some are no longer necessary. Under section 101 of the Criminal Justice Act 2003, bad character evidence will be increasingly available to the prosecution.

D. *Discharge Of Legal Burden in Civil Cases*

In *Miller*, Denning J. said.

Miller [1947] 2 All E.R. 372, *per* Denning J.:

. . . the case must be decided according to the preponderance of probability. If at the end of the case the evidence turns the scale definitely one way or the other, the tribunal must decide accordingly, but if the evidence is so evenly balanced that the tribunal is unable to come to a determinate conclusion one way or the other, then the man must be given the benefit of the doubt.[8]

It is settled that in civil cases the burden of proof is discharged on proof on the preponderance of probabilities. This is not a matter of the relative quantity of evidence adduced by the parties but whether the party bearing the burden has shown in absolute terms that their proposition is more likely than not. The burden is not successfully discharged by merely showing that your account of the events is more likely than that of your opponent.

Rhesa Shipping Co SA v Edmunds [1985] 2 All E.R. 712 at 718f, *per* Lord Brandon:

. . . the legal concept of proof of a case on a balance of probabilities must be applied with common sense. It requires a judge of first instance, before he finds that a

---

[7] A likelihood ratio is a means of conceptualising the probative value of a piece of evidence. Rawling's ratio means that the evidence is 1.9×10^7 times more likely to occur if the defendant is guilty than if he is innocent.
[8] *Miller* above at 374a.

particular event occurred, to be satisfied on the evidence that it is more likely to have occurred than not. If such a judge concludes . . . that the occurrence of an event is extremely improbable, a finding by him that it is nevertheless more likely to have occurred than not, does not accord with common sense. This is especially so when it is open to the judge to say simply that the evidence leaves him in doubt whether the event occurred or not, and that the party on whom the burden of proving that the event occurred lies has therefore failed to discharge such burden.

However the civil standard is often described as flexible—although adhering to the basic formula, the court needs to consider the seriousness of the allegations and the nature of the proceedings. In *Re H (Minors)*,[9] the local authority applied to take a mother's three children into care under s.32(2) of the Children Act 1989. Their grounds were that a fourth child in the same household had accused the stepfather of sexually abusing her. He had been acquitted of rape. The House of Lords considered what the requisite standard of proof should be.

Re H (Minors) [1996] 1 All E.R. 1 at 16–17, *per* Lord Nicholls:

Where the matters in issue are facts the standard of proof required in non-criminal proceedings is the preponderance of probability, usually referred to as the balance of probability. This is the established general principle. There are exceptions such as contempt of court applications, but I can see no reason for thinking that family proceedings are, or should be, an exception. By family proceedings I mean proceedings so described in the Act of 1989, sections 105 and 8(3). Despite their special features, family proceedings remain essentially a form of civil proceedings. Family proceedings often raise very serious issues, but so do other forms of civil proceedings.

The balance of probability standard means that a court is satisfied an event occurred if the court considers that, on the evidence, the occurrence of the event was more likely than not. When assessing the probabilities the court will have in mind as a factor, to whatever extent is appropriate in the particular case, that the more serious the allegation the less likely it is that the event occurred and, hence, the stronger should be the evidence before the court concludes that the allegation is established on the balance of probability. Fraud is usually less likely than negligence. Deliberate physical injury is usually less likely than accidental physical injury. A step-father is usually less likely to have repeatedly raped and had non-consensual oral sex with his under age stepdaughter than on some occasion to have lost his temper and slapped her. Built into the preponderance of probability standard is a generous degree of flexibility in respect of the seriousness of the allegation. Although the result is much the same, this does not mean that where a serious allegation is in issue the standard of proof required is higher. It means only that the inherent probability or improbability of an event is itself a matter to be taken into account when weighing the probabilities and deciding whether, on balance, the event occurred. The more improbable the event, the stronger must be the evidence that it did occur before, on the balance of probability, its occurrence will be established. Ungoed-Thomas J. expressed this neatly in *Re Dellow's Will Trusts*. . .:

The more serious the allegation the more cogent is the evidence required to overcome the unlikelihood of what is alleged and thus to prove it.

[9] [1996] 1 All E.R. 1.

This substantially accords with the approach adopted in authorities such as the well known judgment of Morris L.J. in *Hornal v. Neuberger Products Ltd*. This approach also provides a means by which the balance of probability standard can accommodate one's instinctive feeling that even in civil proceedings a court should be more sure before finding serious allegations proved than when deciding less serious or trivial matters.

Where allegations of crime are made in civil proceedings, the standard of proof is the preponderance of probabilities. In *Hornal v Neuberger Products Ltd*,[10] the claimant claimed damages for breach of warranty or, alternatively, for fraudulent misrepresentation after the defendant had sold the claimant a lathe on the representation that it had been reconditioned by certain tool-makers. The judge awarded damages on the basis of a fraudulent misrepresentation, stating that he had been satisfied on the balance of probabilities that fraud had occurred but had not been satisfied beyond reasonable doubt. Should he have been satisfied beyond reasonable doubt? The Court of Appeal held that in civil proceedings, proof of an allegation of crime need only be on the basis of the balance of probabilities.

Hornal. Neuberger Products Ltd [1956] 3 All E.R. 970 at 973, *per* Denning L.J.:

I must say that, if I was sitting as a judge alone, and I was satisfied that the statement was made, that would be enough for me, whether the claim was put in warranty or on fraud. I think it would bring the law into contempt if a judge were to say that on the issue of warranty he finds the statement was made and that on the issue of fraud he finds it was not made.

Nevertheless, the judge having set the problem to himself, he answered it, I think, correctly; he reviewed all the cases and held rightly that the standard of proof depends on the nature of the issue. The more serious the allegation the higher the degree of probability that is required: but it need not, in a civil case, reach the very high standard required by the criminal law.

Although the decision establishes that allegations of crime in civil proceedings need only be established on the balance of probabilities, where that allegation is very serious, different considerations come into play. In *Re Dellow's Will Trusts*,[11] the issue was whether a wife had murdered her husband before killing herself.

Re Dellow's Will Trusts [1964] 1 All E.R. 771, *per* Ungoed-Thomas J.:

It seems to me that in civil cases it is not so much that a different standard of proof is required in different circumstances varying according to the gravity of the issue, but

[10] [1956] 3 All E.R. 970.
[11] [1964] 1 All E.R. 771 at 773 per Ungoed—Thomas J.

... the gravity of the issue becomes part of the circumstances which the court has to take into consideration in deciding whether or not the burden of proof has been discharged. The more serious the allegation the more cogent is the evidence required to overcome the unlikelihood of what is alleged and thus to prove it ...

Furthermore, the standard of proof in contempt of court cases, whether occurring in a criminal or civil court, is the criminal standard beyond reasonable doubt. In a passing off case, *Comet Products UK Ltd v Hawkex Plastic Ltd*,[12] the claimants applied to the court for the committal of the defendants for contempt of court. The question arose whether the defendant could be cross-examined.

Comet Products UK Ltd v Hawkex Plastic Ltd [1971] 1 All E.R. 1141 at 1143, *per* Lord Denning M.R.:

... A criminal contempt is one which takes place in the face of the court, or which prejudices a fair trial and so forth. A civil contempt is different. A typical case is disobedience to an order made by the court in a civil action ... Although this is a civil contempt, it partakes of the nature of a criminal charge. The defendant is liable to be punished for it. He may be sent to prison. The rules as to criminal charges have always been applied to such a proceeding ... we ourselves in this court, in *Re Bramblevale Ltd*,[13] said that it must be proved with the same degree of satisfaction as in a criminal charge. It follows that the accused is not bound to give evidence unless he chooses to do so ...

E. *Discharge of the Legal Burden in Voir Dire*

At the *voir dire*, the burden of proving that the conditions of admissibility have been met must lie on the party wishing to adduce the evidence. Sometimes, that burden will be allocated by statute.[14] Proof must be by admissible evidence.[15] In criminal proceedings, where the prosecution bear the onus of proof, the evidence will not be admissible unless the conditions for admissibility are proved beyond reasonable doubt. In *Yacoob*,[16] the competence and compellability of a prosecution witness depended on whether or not she was married to the defendant. She had been through a ceremony of marriage with him in 1971 but there was also a certificate of another marriage in 1968. The judge held that the presumption of validity of

---

[12] [1971] 1 All E.R. 1141; C. Miller, "Proof of Civil Contempt" [1996] 112 L.Q.R. 539; M. Redmayne, "Standards of Proof in Civil Litigation" (1999) 62 Mod. 167.

[13] [1969] 3 All E.R. 1062.

[14] Police and Criminal Evidence Act 1984, s.76.

[15] *O'Loughlin* [1988] 3 All E.R. 431—in construing s.13(3) Criminal Justice Act 1925, police officers' evidence that the witnesses were frightened was direct evidence and admissible but their statements as to what the witnesses had said about the specific threats was hearsay.

[16] (1981) 72 Cr.App.R 313.

the 1971 marriage was rebutted by the evidence relating to the 1968 ceremony and the burden was on the defence to prove that the witness was incompetent.

Yacoob (1981) 72 Cr.App.R. 313, *per* Watkins L.J.:

As to the burden of proof in this context, it is for the prosecution, once the issue of competence of one of its witnesses is raised, to prove that that person is competent to testify . . . The burden will be discharged if the trial judge is satisfied beyond a reasonable doubt upon admissible and sufficient evidence of competence.[17]

Ewing[18] involved expert comparison of handwriting under section 8 of the Criminal Procedure Act 1865.

Criminal Procedure Act 1865, s.8:

8.—Comparison of a disputed writing with any writing proved to the satisfaction of the judge to be genuine shall be permitted to be made by witnesses; and such writings, and the evidence of witnesses respecting the same, may be submitted to the court and jury as evidence of the genuineness or otherwise of the writing in dispute.

Under the section, the judge has to be satisfied that the writing alleged to be by the accused was in fact by the accused before expert comparison can take place. Was the standard one of balance of probabilities or did the judge have to be satisfied beyond reasonable doubt?

Ewing [1983] 2 All E.R. 645 at 652–653, *per* O'Connor L.J.

In our judgment, the words in s.8 of the 1865 Act, 'any writing proved to the satisfaction of the judge to be genuine', do not say anything about the standard of proof to be used, but direct that it is the judge, and not the jury, who is to decide, and the standard of proof is to be governed by common law . . . It follows that when the section is applied in civil cases, the civil standard of proof is used, and when it is applied in criminal cases, the criminal standard should be used. Were it otherwise, the situation created would be unacceptable, where conviction depends on proof that disputed handwriting is that of the accused person and where that proof depends on comparison of the disputed writing with samples alleged to be genuine writings of the accused; we cannot see how this case can be said to be proved beyond reasonable doubt, if the Crown only has to satisfy the judge on a balance of probabilities, that the

[17] *ibid.* at 317 *per* Watkins L.J.
[18] [1983] 2 All E.R. 645.

allegedly genuine samples were in fact genuine. The jury may be satisfied beyond reasonable doubt that the crucial handwriting is by the same hand as the allegedly genuine writings, but if there is a reasonable doubt about the genuineness of such writings, then that must remain a reasonable doubt about the fact the disputed writing was that of the accused and the case is not proved . . .[19]

When the issue is one of the preconditions for admissibility of evidence tendered by the defendant or of evidence tendered in civil proceedings, the test is one of the balance of probabilities. In *Mattey and Queeley*,[20] the defence sought to rely on the written statements of witnesses now in France and unable to be present for the trial. This would now come under the provisions of s.116 of the Criminal Justice Act 2003. It is for the defence to show that the witnesses were abroad and that it was not reasonably practicable for them to attend court. There should be independent and admissible evidence on this issue. This probably requires more evidence than statements by the absent witnesses contained in the document in question. But the evidence, of whatever nature, when proffered by the defence, merely has to satisfy the judge on the balance of probabilities.

---

[19] Not following *Angeli* [1978] 3 All ER 950 and following the reasoning of the House of Lords in *Blyth v Blyth* [1966] 1 All E.R. 524.
[20] [1995] Crim.L.R. 308.

4

DISCRETION TO EXCLUDE EVIDENCE: JUDICIAL OVERSIGHT OVER POLICE INVESTIGATIONS

I. Judicial Discretion and Exclusion of Evidence

One of the key judicial functions in the course of a trial will be the exercise of discretion in relation to the admissibility of evidence. Evidence may satisfy the legal criteria for admissibility but the judge may still exclude that evidence. This discretion arises as part of a general supervisory function over the trial and an obligation to ensure a fair trial. It is normally exercised on the grounds that the admission of the evidence would adversely affect the fairness of the proceedings. This chapter deals with the principles under which the judge may exercise that exclusionary discretion. The use of the discretion is most often to be found in a contested criminal trial in which many of the evidential issues will concern the police conduct of the investigation.

The defence may question the admissibility of items of evidence that have been gathered in the course of the investigation—examples might include material found in the course of a search of the defendant or the defendant's home; covert recording of the defendant's conversation or other information gathered in the course of undercover surveillance; forensic evidence gathered from intimate samples from the defendant; or, most importantly, the record of any interview between the defendant and investigating officers which often contain incriminating statements. The normal defence argument is that the material should not be admitted because it has been obtained by the police in an improper or illegal fashion. The nature and extent of police powers therefore form the backdrop of this discussion and, although detailed knowledge is not necessary here, an outline of basic ideas and sources will be useful.[1]

A. *Police Powers*

Effective investigation was much more of a problem for the 19th century police officer than their modern counterpart. There were few powers which

---

[1] S. Uglow, *Criminal Justice* (2nd ed., Sweet and Maxwell 2002) London, pp. 114–176; L. Jason-Lloyd *Introduction to Policing and Police Powers* (Cavendish, 2005).

permitted preliminary work in gathering evidence through searching prem-ises or people, through questioning or by detaining suspects. The core power was that of arrest, namely the detention of a person. The common law required that there had to be reasonable suspicion that a serious offence had been committed by the suspect. Once arrested, you could search suspects and any premises belonging to them. But the accused had to be taken before magistrates as soon as possible, normally within 24 hours. These formal powers occurred at a late stage in any investigation and there were few powers which facilitated the investigation itself. There was no power to stop, search or detain people outside of arrest; searches, outside of arrest, required a judicial warrant; there was no obligation to answer questions put to you by police officers. Questioning suspects was not seen as police job but as a matter for magistrates. However in the 20th century, interviewing became a normal police function and the questioning and treatment of suspects was regulated by the Judges' Rules 1912, which remained influential guidelines until 1984.

These restricted common law powers of the police were added to in a piecemeal fashion but there are now three general statutes which by and large govern police investigative procedures and pre-trial process. These are the Police and Criminal Evidence Act 1984 (PACE), the Criminal Procedure and Investigations Act 1996 (CPIA) and the Regulation of Investigatory Powers Act 2000 (RIPA). The statutory powers under the Acts are regularly amended by enactments such as the Criminal Justice Act 2003 or the Serious Organised Crime and Police Act 2005. The statues are also supplemented by Codes of Practice. For example, there are codes under PACE which cover areas such as stop and search, road blocks, detention and questioning of suspects, identi-fication procedures, tape recording of interviews and the exercise of powers of arrest. Under RIPA there is a code of practice governing covert sur-veillance. These codes are secondary legislation but are codes of *practice* and not of *law*. A breach of a provision in the code is not an offence, nor will it necessarily lead to disciplinary action. It may provide the basis to argue that evidence obtained as a result should be excluded.

Since the 1970s, police powers have developed extensively.

1. *Stop and search.* Prior to 1984, over most of the country, the police had no power to stop pedestrians in order to question them or to search them. Section 1 of PACE provided a general power that the police could, on reasonable suspicion that any person or vehicle was carrying stolen goods or other prohibited items, stop that person or vehicle and conduct a desultory search, such as checking pockets or looking in bags. It is now regulated by Code A under PACE. There are also such powers under 19 other statutes such as the Sporting Events Act 1985.[2] Where a search is carried out in breach of the Code, it is possible that evidence can be excluded.[3]

2. *Road blocks.* There are some common law powers for constables to control traffic.[4] Section 4 of PACE provides much greater powers than

---

[2] For a full list, see Code of Practice A Annexe.
[3] *McCarthy* [1996] Crim.L.R. 818—although in this case the argument was rejected.
[4] e.g. where an officer apprehends a breach of the peace: *Moss v McLachlan* 1985 149 J.P. 167; *R. (Laporte) v Chief Constable of Gloucestershire* [2005] Q.B. 678.

previously existed for the police to mount roadblocks authorised by senior officers. There are similar powers in s.60 of the Criminal Justice and Public Order Act 1994 and s.44 of the Terrorism Act 2000.

3. *Searching premises.* The police have no general power to enter and search private premises in order to investigate criminal acts. They may do so under Part II of PACE, which provides the police with statutory powers to enter and search premises for evidence. These powers can either be executed with or without a warrant: only a small proportion of searches are carried out under magisterial warrant. Under s.32, an officer making an arrest can search the premises without warrant where the suspect was immediately before the arrest. Under s.18 after a suspect has been arrested and taken to the station, a senior officer can authorise a search of premises occupied or controlled by them where it is suspected that there is evidence which relates to the offence. Searches of premises are governed by Code B which states that searches should be made at a reasonable time, that only reasonable force should be used and that due consideration for the property and privacy of the occupier should be shown.

4. *Interception of communications.* The interception of communications can take place through phone taps or by the cloning of mobile phones or pagers as well as through the opening of mail. The practice of intercepting letters under the Home Secretary's warrant is of very long standing although the authority for doing so is obscure.[5] Statutory authority arrived with the Interception of Communications Act 1985, which has now been replaced by Pt I of the Regulation of Investigatory Powers Act 2000. Authorisation at the level of the Secretary of State is necessary for the police to conduct such intercepts of post or telecommunications. It is now a criminal offence for a person intentionally to intercept a communication except under a warrant issued by the Secretary of State or where there were reasonable grounds to believe that the sender or recipient of the communication consented.[6] The Secretary of State can issue a warrant in the interests of national security; for the purpose of preventing or detecting serious crime or for the purpose of safeguarding the economic well being of the UK.[7] Despite the evidential value of such intercepts, s.17 imposes a prohibition on revealing in evidence the existence of such intercepts.

5. *Other forms of covert surveillance.* These are regulated under s.92 of the Police Act 1997 (for surveillance involving unlawful conduct such as trespass to property) or Pt II of the Regulation of Investigatory Powers Act 2000. This latter Act applies to directed surveillance, intrusive surveillance and the use of covert human intelligence sources. This latter category will include informants, agents provocateurs and entrapment.[8] In all these cases, the

---

[5] The issue was considered by the Birkett Committee appointed in 1957—Report of the Committee of Privy Councillors (Cmnd. 283).
[6] Regulation of Investigatory Powers Act 2000, s.1.
[7] *ibid.*, s.5(3).
[8] For these definitions, see Regulation of Investigatory Powers Act 2000, s.26.

surveillance is regarded as lawful if an authorisation under the Acts is obtained and subsequent actions are in accordance with that authorisation. There is national oversight by a surveillance commissioner.

6. *Arrest.* The power of arrest, and the consequent deprivation of liberty is the most coercive of police powers. There are powers of arrest under judicial warrant but arrest without warrant by police officers is governed by s.24 of PACE. This has been completely rewritten by s.110 of Serious Organised Crime and Police Act 2005 which allows a constable to arrest for any offence whatsoever where there are reasonable grounds for suspecting that the defendant is responsible and it is necessary for one of the reasons given in s.110(5). It is now regulated by Code G under PACE. A lawful arrest normally involves a physical touching and a statement to the person that they are under arrest and an explanation of the grounds for arrest.

7. *Searching persons.* Apart from s.1 stops, other provisions for searching suspects occur after arrest:

(1) Under s.32, a constable may conduct a limited search of an arrested person at a place other than a police station if there are reasonable grounds for believing there might be evidence or anything that might assist escape or present a danger. The search is limited to the extent that is reasonably required for by s.32(4).

(2) Under s.53, once the suspect is at the police station, the arresting officer no longer has the power to search. Searches of detained persons, including a strip search if deemed necessary, must be carried out by an officer of the same sex, supervised by the custody officer under s.54. Code C regulates this procedure.

(3) Under s.55, the police have the power to conduct intimate searches without the consent of the suspect. An intimate search is one of body orifices, other than the mouth. It requires the authorisation of a superintendent who must have reasonable grounds for believing that a weapon or Class A drug is concealed. Section 5 of the Drugs Act 2005 now allows an inspector to authorise an X-ray or ultrasound scan of a suspect.

Even if there is a lawful stop or arrest, searches must not violate the guarantees against degrading treatment under Art.3 or the right to privacy under Art.8.

8. *Detention.* The custody officer is initially responsible for the length of time that an arrested person is detained in a police station. That detention must be periodically reviewed. Prior to the Act, the police probably had to bring a suspect before a court within 24 hours. Now, with some safeguards, they can hold people without charge for up to four days. Although s.41 of PACE lays down the principle that a person should not be held without charge for more than 24 hours, this can be derogated from in certain circumstances. Continued detention for a further 12 hours can be authorised

by a senior officer (superintendent or above) if the detention is necessary to secure or preserve evidence, if the offence is a serious arrestable offence[9] and if the investigation is being conducted "diligently and expeditiously".[10] Further periods of continued detention up to 96 hours are possible with approval from the magistrates' court.[11]

9. *Questioning.* Conditions of the interview are regulated by Code C. There is still no obligation to answer police questions, either inside or outside the police station but a failure to mention salient facts may now prejudice one's defence in court as a result of s.34, 36 and 37 of the Criminal Justice and Public Order Act 1994. These issues are discussed later in this chapter.

10. *Fingerprints.* Section 61 of PACE enables the police to fingerprint a person without consent if the person has been charged with a recordable offence or if the fingerprinting is authorised by an officer of at least the rank of superintendent—this is undertaken in order to confirm or disprove involvement of the person. Section 27 of PACE empowers the police to take fingerprints from those who had been convicted of recordable offences but had never been in custody—s.78 of the Criminal Justice and Police Act 2001 now extends that to enable fingerprints to be taken from those cautioned (or given a reprimand or final warning in the case of young offenders). Fingerprints are now kept in perpetuity—under s.82(2) of the Criminal Justice and Police Act 2001, the police will be permitted to retain fingerprints of suspects taken in the course of an investigation even if the individual is not subsequently prosecuted or is acquitted. Further, s.82(4) allows for the retention of volunteer fingerprints given for elimination purposes. These cannot be used in connection with the investigation of another offence unless there is written consent but in that case, the prints can be used for the investigation of an offence and the conduct of a prosecution. Once given, that consent cannot be withdrawn.

11. *Intimate and non-intimate samples.* Section 62 of PACE confers the right to take intimate samples from a suspect but only with consent in writing under the provisions of s.62.[12] A refusal to consent allows a court or jury to draw inferences, which may be used as evidence against that person and the suspect must be cautioned to that effect. Non-intimate samples such as mouth swabs, hair or nail clippings can be taken from a suspect compulsorily under s.63 although again it must be authorised by a superintendent in writing and recorded on the custody record.[13]

Many jurisdictions require that any state agency may only act on the basis of identifiable powers established in law. In the UK, officers were always able

[9] Police and Criminal Evidence Act 1984, Sch.3.
[10] *ibid.*, s.42.
[11] *ibid.*, s.43.
[12] The procedure is detailed in Code D.
[13] Police and Criminal Evidence Act 1984, s.65 as amended by Criminal Justice and Public Order Act 1994.

to act in any manner not prohibited by the civil or criminal law without possessing positive legal authority to act. The authorities developed their systems and protocols of aural and visual surveillance based on this principle. The impact of the Human Rights Act 1998 and the incorporation of the Strasbourg jurisprudence[14] have meant that states must demonstrate a legal foundation for police powers. As a result in the last decade the government have developed a broad statutory base of police powers, broadly compliant with the European Convention on Human Rights.[15]

This preceding sketch of police powers, both ancient and modern, is necessary as it is through the exercise of these powers that investigators acquire evidence. Misuse of powers can result in evidence being presented which is either unreliable or which the Crown should not have obtained. *Prima facie* admissible as relevant and probative, should such evidence be excluded by the exercise of the judge's discretion?

B. *Discretion at Common Law*

Admissibility of evidence depends on both general criteria (such as relevance and reliability) and specific criteria for particular categories. An item of evidence may well satisfy both the general and specific criteria and yet its admissibility may still be questioned on the basis that it has been obtained by questionable methods. The common law had two options—the courts could develop a general principle of exclusion wherever the admission of the evidence would mean that the defendant would not have a fair trial or the courts might concern themselves only with the quality of the evidence (are the general and specific criteria met?) and not consider extraneous issues concerning the provenance of the evidence at all.

The common law tradition embraced this latter approach. Although judges often condemned such police tactics, this concern rarely led to the exclusion of evidence. In *Jeffery v Black*,[16] two drugs squad officers arrested the accused for the theft of a sandwich in a pub. Having charged him with that offence, they took him to his rooms which they searched without his consent and without a warrant, discovering cannabis. The magistrates refused to allow the evidence of the finding of the drugs. The Divisional Court allowed the appeal by the prosecutor, considering that the evidence of finding the drugs was admissible despite the officers lacking the appropriate authority.[17] But Lord Widgery qualified this: there was judicial discretion to exclude evidence, albeit an exclusionary discretion to be used rarely where there had been trickery, oppression or unfairness.

---

[14] e.g. *Malone v UK* [1984] 7 E.H.R.R. 14; *Sultan Khan v UK*. Application No. 35394/97, [2000] Crim.L.R. 684, [2002] 31 E.H.R.R. 45.
[15] Interception of Communications Act 1984. Police Act 1997 and Regulation of Investigatory Powers Act 2000 were all responses to decisions by the European Court of Human Rights.
[16] [1978] 1 All E.R. 555.
[17] See Privy Council decision in *Kuruma Son of Kaniu v R.* [1955] 1 All E.R. 236.

Jeffery v Black [1978] 1 All E.R. 555 at 558j–559g, *per* Lord Widgery C.J.:

But ... the magistrates sitting in this case, like any other criminal tribunal in England sitting under English law, have a general discretion to decline to allow any evidence to be called by the prosecution if they think it would be unfair or oppressive to allow that to be done .... It is a discretion which every criminal judge has all the time in respect of all the evidence which is tendered by the prosecution. It would probably give magistrates some idea of the extent to which this discretion is used if one asks them whether they are appreciative of the fact that they have the discretion anyway, and it may well be that a number of experienced magistrates would be quite ignorant of the possession of this discretion. That gives them, I hope, some idea of how relatively rarely it is exercised in our courts. But if the case is exceptional, if the case is such that not only have the police officers entered without authority, but they have been guilty of trickery or they have misled someone, or they have been oppressive or they have been unfair, or in other respects they have behaved in a manner which is morally reprehensible, then it is open to the justices to apply their discretion and decline to allow the particular evidence to be let in as part of the trial.

This approach resonates today—there is no automatic exclusion of evidence because the police have acted outside their powers or in breach of the relevant Code of Practice. A court must consider whether the admission of the evidence would affect the overall fairness of the proceedings. Lord Widgery is clear that, if evidence was relevant, it would normally be admissible notwithstanding its provenance. The discretion to exclude the evidence was only to be used very rarely.

Shortly afterwards, in *Sang*,[18] the House of Lords reduced the scope of this discretion still further. This time their Lordships were considering entrapment and the use of an agent provocateur, a situation whereby a police agent participates in or incites the commission of an offence. In substantive criminal law, there is no defence of entrapment although the courts have consistently expressed strong disapproval of such police methods.[19] But can the same result be reached through the rules of evidence, whereby the court exclude evidence obtained by such means? In the case, the accused had been in Brixton prison where he met a fellow inmate, alleged to be a police informer. Shortly before the accused was about to be released, the informer who was aware that the accused's business was dealing in forged banknotes, told the accused that he knew of a safe buyer who would get in touch with the accused by telephone. After the accused left prison, he was telephoned by a man who inquired whether the accused would sell him any forged banknotes. A rendezvous was arranged but the accused had no idea that the man was a sergeant in the police force. The accused and some of his associates went to the rendezvous carrying with them a large number of forged American dollars and walked straight into a police trap. The appellant argued that, where the judge was satisfied at *voir dire* that the offence was instigated by an agent provocateur acting on the instructions of the police, the judge had discretion to refuse to allow the prosecution to prove its case by such

---

[18] [1979] 2 All E.R. 1222.
[19] *Brannan v Peek* [1947] 2 All E.R. 572.

evidence. Does the judge have common law discretion to exclude evidence which was both relevant and of more than minimal probative value but which had been unfairly obtained?

The House of Lords concluded that the authorities revealed discretion to exclude evidence which was limited to confessions and to the exclusion of bad character evidence where the prejudicial impact was greater than the true evidential value. Did this discretion extend further?

Sang [1979] 2 All E.R. 1222 at 1231, *per* Lord Diplock:

What [this submission] really involves is a claim to a judicial discretion to acquit an accused of any offences in connection with which the conduct of the police incurs the disapproval of the judge. The conduct of the police where it has involved the use of an agent provocateur may well be a matter to be taken into consideration in mitigation of sentence; but under the English system of criminal justice it does not give rise to any discretion on the part of the judge himself to acquit the accused or to direct the jury to do so, notwithstanding that he is guilty of the offence.

Ought your Lordships to go further and to hold that the discretion extends more widely than this, as the comparatively recent dicta . . . suggest? [*Kuruma Son of Kaniu v R*[20]] was a case in which the evidence of unlawful possession of ammunition by the accused was obtained as a result of an illegal search of his person. The Board held that this evidence was admissible and had rightly been admitted; but Lord Goddard CJ, although he had earlier said that if evidence was admissible 'the court is not concerned with how the evidence was obtained', nevertheless went on to say:
> No doubt in a criminal case the judge always has a discretion to disallow evidence if the strict rules of admissibility would operate unfairly against the accused . . . . If, for instance, some admission of some piece of evidence, eg, a document, had been obtained from the defendant by a trick, no doubt the judge might properly rule it out.[21]
> . . . That statement was not, in my view, ever intended to acknowledge the existence of any wider discretion than to exclude (1) admissible evidence which would probably have a prejudicial influence on the minds of the jury that would be out of proportion to its true evidential value and (2) evidence tantamount to a self-incriminatory admission which was obtained from the defendant, after the offence had been committed, by means which would justify a judge in excluding an actual confession which had the like self-incriminating effect.[22] . . .
> Outside this limited field in which for historical reasons the function of the trial judge extending to imposing sanctions for improper conduct on the part of the prosecution before the commencement of the proceedings in inducing the accused by threats, favour or trickery to provide evidence against himself, your Lordships should, I think, make it clear that the function of a judge at a criminal trial as respects the admission of evidence is to ensure that the accused has a fair trial according to law. It is no part of a judge's function to exercise disciplinary powers over the police or prosecution as respects the way in which evidence to be used at the trial is obtained by them.

[20] [1955] 1 All E.R. 236.
[21] *ibid.* at 239.
[22] *e.g. Payne* [1963] 1 All E.R. 848.

I would accordingly answer the question certified . . . (1) A trial judge in a criminal trial has always a discretion to refuse to admit evidence if in his opinion its prejudicial effect outweighs its probative value. (2) Save with regard to admissions and confessions and generally with regard to evidence obtained from the accused after commission of the offence, he has no discretion to refuse to admit relevant admissible evidence on the ground that it was obtained by improper or unfair means. The court is not concerned with how it was obtained. It is no ground for the exercise of discretion to exclude that the evidence was obtained as the result of the activities of an agent provocateur.

Sang limits discretion at common law to exclude evidence to cases where:

a) the prejudicial effect of the evidence outweighs probative value[23];
b) confessions (and analogous evidence) have been obtained unfairly.

The function of the judge is to ensure the accused has a fair trial and it is no part of that function to exercise disciplinary powers over police or prosecution as the defendant has available civil and disciplinary remedies. But the House of Lords draw a distinction between the streets and the police station. They are willing to exercise discipline over unfair methods employed in the interview room and to exclude unfairly obtained confessions but not over illegal or unethical tactics of investigation. The justification is that the rules on confessions are there to protect the accused's right to silence. They were not willing to exclude the product of illegal searches in order to protect an accused's right to privacy.

American decisions show no such reluctance. The Supreme Court has on several occasions excluded evidence which has been illegally obtained acting under the Fourth Amendment to the Constitution which forbids unreasonable searches and seizures. The key case is *Mapp v Ohio*.[24]

W. Stuntz, 'The American Exclusionary Rule and Defendants' Changing Rights' [1989] Crim.L.R. 117 at 118–119:

Police officers broke into Dollree Mapp's boarding house, in search of both gambling paraphernalia and a fugitive. When Ms. Mapp asked to see a warrant (it was clear that a warrantless search was not authorised under the circumstances), one of the officers produced a piece of paper but would not let Ms Mapp read it; in subsequent proceedings the state all but conceded that the 'warrant' was fraudulent. The police proceeded to ransack the whole house, examining, among other things, all of Ms Mapp's books and papers. During this process, they found four books that under then-governing state law were deemed obscene, though today they would probably be protected by the First Amendment. Ms Mapp was prosecuted for possession of

---

[23] It is this element in the ratio in *Sang* that is retained by s.82(3) of the Police and Criminal Evidence Act 1984, 'Nothing in this Part of this Act shall prejudice any power of a court to exclude evidence (whether by preventing questions from being put or otherwise) at its discretion.'

[24] 367 U.S. 643, (1961).

obscene materials, an offence that the Supreme Court has since invalidated as infringing constitutionally protected freedom of thought (no matter how obscene the materials).[25]

The Court chose this combination of a questionable offence and egregious police misconduct to hold that the states are bound not only by the Fourth Amendment but by its exclusionary remedy as well. The majority opinion gave a host of reasons for this conclusion, but three stand out as particularly important. The first, and most obvious, is deterrence: exclusion removes the incentive for police to conduct illegal searches. The second is 'the imperative of judicial integrity', the notion being that it is dishonest and hypocritical for courts to admit illegally obtained evidence. The third ground is one that permeates the entire *Mapp* opinion: that exclusion of illegally obtained evidence is in some normative sense the defendant's entitlement that it does no more than right the wrong the police have done. Though not framed in these terms, the argument is that the exclusionary rule serves a necessary compensatory purpose . . .

The legal structure *Mapp* created endures, at least in its basic outline, today. As a precaution against police overreaching, the Fourth Amendment requires a police officer to obtain a warrant from a neutral and detached magistrate before undertaking any major search, unless doing so is plainly infeasible. Violation of this requirement leads automatically to the suppression of evidence obtained as a result of the search . . .

Recent US decisions have restricted this exclusionary rule to criminal proceedings[26] and treated the primary rationale as that of deterring illegal police conduct. In *US v Leon*,[27] the warrant was technically improperly issued by the magistrate but on its face was valid. Evidence resulting from a search by police officers relying in good faith on the warrant was not excluded. The rationale of such a limitation is that magistrates do not need to be forced to apply the proper standards of 'probable cause' in issuing warrants. While police officers do need policing by the courts, the deterrent force of the exclusionary rule only operates where the police officer can do something to prevent the illegality. In *Leon* the only error was by the issuing magistrate which could not be detected by the officers involved.[28]

The divergence between the English and American courts shows the conflict of differing public interests involved: on the one hand, the proper determination of cases which requires that all relevant and reliable evidence is before the courts whereas, on the other, the due process of law which states that the proper administration of justice requires respect for the rights of the accused (with the corollary that state officials must be deterred from committing illegal acts).

C. *Discretion Under Statute*

The common law basis for discretionary exclusion was challenged in the 1970s as concerns about the criminal justice system were growing. In 1977 the

---

[25] *Stanley v Georgia* 394 U.S. 557, (1969).

[26] *US v Janis*, 428 U.S. 433, (1976) where the rule was inapplicable in civil tax proceedings.

[27] 468 U.S. 897, (1984).

[28] *United States v. Koerth*, 312 F.3d 862 (7th Cir. 2002); Z. Bray, "Appellate Review and the Exclusionary Rule" [2004] 113 Yale L.J. 1143.

Confait case saw three boys arrested, interrogated and, as a result of their confessions, convicted of murder. Three years later, they were all released after the Fisher Report[29] concluded that they had nothing to do with the killing. The Labour government set up the Royal Commission on Criminal Procedure to examine police procedures. The Commission's Report[30] led to the passage of the Police and Criminal Evidence Act 1984, seen by many at the time as unjustifiably extending police powers and, in hindsight, by the police as imposing an unnecessary bureaucratic regime.

What was clear was that the appellate courts had done nothing to prevent a series of significant miscarriages of justice and in the course of parliamentary debate on the Act, Lord Scarman introduced an amendment to broaden the powers of judges to exclude evidence obtained by improper means. This was based on his dissenting judgment in *Sang* where he had argued for a wider discretion to the judge to exclude evidence on the basis of the judicial duty to ensure a fair trial,

Sang [1979] 2 All E.R. 1222 at 1247d–1248c *per* Lord Scarman:

If an accused is misled or tricked into providing evidence (whether it be an admission or the provision of fingerprints or medical evidence or some other evidence), the rule against self-incrimination, nemo tenetur se ipsum prodere, is likely to be infringed. Each case must, of course, depend on its circumstances. All I would say is that the principle of fairness, though concerned exclusively with the use of evidence at trial, is not susceptible to categorisation or classification, and is wide enough in some circumstances to embrace the way in which, after the crime, evidence is obtained from the accused . . .

In reaching my conclusion that the discretion is a general one designed to ensure the accused a fair trial, I am encouraged by what I understand to be the Scots law. Such research as I have been able to make makes clear that the Scots judges recognise such a discretion. Indeed, I think they go further than the English law, the Scots principle being that evidence illegally or unfairly obtained is inadmissible unless in the exercise of its discretion the court allows it to be given . . .[31]

. . . How far the Scots judges have extended 'the discretionary principle of fairness to the accused' I am not qualified to say. It is, however, plain that by the law of Scotland it may be invoked in a case where, after the commission of a crime, illegal or irregular methods have been used to obtain evidence from the accused . . . Though differences of emphasis and scope are acceptable, it would be, I think, unfortunate if 'the discretionary principle of fairness to the accused' was not recognised in all the criminal jurisdictions of the United Kingdom. Indeed, it must be a fundamental principle in all British criminal jurisdictions that the court is under the duty to ensure the accused a fair trial, and I do not believe that a judge can effectually discharge his duty without, at the very least, the availability of the discretion I have endeavoured to describe.

The Scarman amendment was not passed but the government accepted that there was a need for such an exclusionary clause and introduced the rather obscure text of s.78.

---

[29] Sir H. Fisher: *The Confait Case: Report* HCP 1977/78 90.
[30] Royal Commission on Criminal Procedure: Report (1981) Cmnd. 8092.
[31] *Lawrie v Muir* 1950 J.C. 19 at 27.

PACE 1984, s.78:

78.– (1) In any proceedings the court may refuse to allow evidence on which the prosecution proposes to rely to be given if it appears to the court that, having regard to all the circumstances, including the circumstances in which the evidence was obtained, the admission of the evidence would have such an adverse effect on the fairness of the proceedings that the court ought not to admit it.

(2) Nothing in this section shall prejudice any rule of law requiring a court to exclude evidence.

It reflects the spirit of the Scarman amendment and perhaps goes wider—in his judgment, he was clearly concerned with illegalities and irregularities after the commission of a crime. The final wording allows the court to consider whether police conduct prior to the offence, whether perhaps by illegal bugging or by entrapment, affects the overall fairness of the proceedings. It has been invoked to challenge the admissibility of a wide range of material.

Section 78 does not expressly overturn the ruling in *Sang* but that decision has been overtaken by the application of s.78 and the common law doctrine of abuse of process. This chapter will now discuss the interpretation of s.78 both generally and in relation to particular categories of evidence, namely evidence obtained by entrapment, by tricks and by covert surveillance. The chapter then considers police interviews—statements made by the suspect in the police station and the criteria for their admissibility as evidence. But s.78 has a wide remit whenever the admissibility of evidence is considered. For example, it may become an important counterweight to the increased availability of hearsay evidence; furthermore s.78 caselaw is relevant to s.101(3) of the Criminal Justice Act 2003 which uses almost identical wording in delineating judicial discretion to exclude evidence of the bad character of the accused.

1. General characteristics

The defence will normally raise the question of exclusion of evidence under s.78. They bear an evidential burden to satisfy the judge that there is an issue to be decided. There is no clear authority on whether either party has the persuasive burden.

(i) *Significant and Substantial*

If the defence are to succeed, they will need to show that any illegality or breach was significant and substantial. In *Walsh*[32] the defendant was convicted of robbery. He was arrested and held in custody at a police station. He requested a solicitor, but was denied access to one for no proper reason. In breach of Code C, the police conducted the interview with a person who had asked for but not received legal advice, failed to make contemporaneous notes, failed to record in the officers' pocket books the reasons for not keeping

---

[32] (1990) 91 Cr.App.R. 161.

a record in the course of the interview, failed to give the appellant a chance to read and sign an interview record and conducted the interview in a cell rather than in an interview room. The trial judge admitted the statement, holding that the police had not acted in bad faith and that the presence of a lawyer would not have affected the course of the interview. Saville J. quashed the conviction.

Walsh (1990) 91 Cr.App.R. 161 at 163, *per* Saville J.

The main object of s.58 of the Act and indeed of the Codes of Practice is to achieve fairness—to an accused or suspected person so as, among other things, to preserve and protect his legal rights; but also fairness for the Crown and its officers so that again, among other things, there might be reduced the incidence or effectiveness of unfounded allegations of malpractice. To our minds it follows that if there are significant and substantial breaches of s.58 or the provisions of the Code, then prima facie at least the standards of fairness set by Parliament have not been met. So far as a defendant is concerned, it seems to us also to follow that to admit evidence against him which has been obtained in circumstances where these standards have not been met, cannot but have an adverse effect on the fairness of the proceedings. This does not mean, of course, that in every case of a significant or substantial breach of s.58 or the Code of Practice the evidence concerned will automatically be excluded. Section 78 does not so provide. The task of the court is not merely to consider whether there would be an adverse effect on the fairness of the proceedings, but such an adverse effect that justice requires the evidence to be excluded. In the present case, we have no material which would lead us to suppose that the judge erred in concluding that the police officers were acting in good faith. However, although bad faith may make substantial or significant that which might not otherwise be so, the contrary does not follow. Breaches which are in themselves significant and substantial are not rendered otherwise by the good faith of the officers concerned.

The opposite result was reached in *McCarthy*,[33] where the defendant was charged with supply of drugs. The police surveillance team stopped the car in which she was travelling, pretending that it was simply a routine inquiry and not involving an investigation into drugs. This was a breach of Code A as the police had failed to tell the defendant of the real reason for stopping the car. The police found a substantial sum of money which was later introduced into evidence. An application to exclude it was rejected as this breach was neither significant nor substantial.

(ii) *Bad faith by the police*
It is not relevant whether the police are acting in good faith. In *Brine*,[34] the police officers failed to recognise that the accused was suffering from a mild form of paranoid psychosis. There was no bad faith involved and he was properly interviewed but the interview was still excluded after medical

[33] above.
[34] [1992] Crim.L.R. 122

evidence. Bad faith on the part of the investigators may make a breach of the Code serious and significant.[35]

(iii) *Intervention in trial judge's ruling*

It is clear that the discretion of the trial judge is central with regard to the admissibility of evidence in criminal proceedings. There are few "rules" as such and the judge works on a case–to–case basis using concepts (such as "fairness", "justice" or even "significant") which have no concrete definitions. But as long as the judge addresses the correct issues and the correct principles, the Court of Appeal will not interfere with the exercise of the discretion, usually quoting *Wednesbury* reasonableness as the limits of discretion.

Associated Provincial Picture Houses Ltd v Wednesbury Corporation [1948] 1 K.B. 223 at 229 *per* Lord Greene M.R.:

It is true the discretion must be exercised reasonably. Now what does that mean? Lawyers familiar with the phraseology commonly used in relation to exercise of statutory discretions often use the word "unreasonable" in a rather comprehensive sense. It has frequently been used and is frequently used as a general description of the things that must not be done. For instance, a person entrusted with a discretion must, so to speak, direct himself properly in law. He must call his own attention to the matters which he is bound to consider. He must exclude from his consideration matters which are irrelevant to what he has to consider. If he does not obey those rules, he may truly be said, and often is said, to be acting "unreasonably". Similarly, there may be something so absurd that no sensible person could ever dream that it lay within the powers of the authority. Warrington L.J. in *Short v. Poole Corporation*[36] gave the example of the red-haired teacher, dismissed because she had red hair. That is unreasonable in one sense. In another sense it is taking into consideration extraneous matters. It is so unreasonable that it might almost be described as being done in bad faith; and, in fact, all these things run into one another.

Where a judge comes to a conclusion about the fairness of the proceedings that no reasonable judge could have reached, this is *Wednesbury* unreasonableness. Further, excluding relevant matters or including irrelevant matters can lead to the Court of Appeal quashing the conviction. As *Walsh* shows, the judge paid undue attention to the fact of the 'good faith' of the police officers.

(iv) *Reform*

Section 78 in one sense is not a true discretion—where the judge finds that the admission of the evidence would have an adverse effect on the fairness of the

---

[35] *Walsh* above.
[36] [1926] Ch. 66, 90, 91.

proceedings, it is mandatory that the evidence should be excluded. Although the section says that the judge 'may' exclude, there is no choice here. But as long as judges address their minds to the correct principle involved, the Court of Appeal will not interfere. But is there a need for reform?

D. Ormerod and D. Birch, "The Evolution of the Discretionary Exclusion of Evidence" [2004] Crim.L.R. 767 at 786–787:

The calls for rationalisation of the section in favour of a more structured approach have been made with increasing vigour by eminent commentators. Thus, Auld L.J.'s Review of the Criminal Courts of England and Wales advocates clarification of the applicability of s.78 to cases of improperly obtained evidence "where the evidence, despite the impropriety, is potentially reliable and cogent."[37] Although Auld is inclined to view the discretion as reliability-based, he concedes the cogency of two arguments against this narrow view: first, that a rights-based discretion specifically enables the courts to exclude evidence which should never have been adduced, because it violates Art.6, and second that it would be incongruous to stay proceedings for abuse of process—say in entrapment cases—in circumstances where an individual item of reliable evidence could not be excluded. The potency of such reservations has led other critics to argue that the potential to use s.78 to deprive the prosecutor of an unfair advantage should be rendered more explicit.

The obvious advantages to structuring s.78 include the opportunity to identify for the judiciary (including of course the lay benches of the magistrates' courts who hear the overwhelming majority of criminal cases) the significant factors to which they should attach importance in exercising their discretion. This should ease the burden on the trier of law by unpacking the concept of unfairness. In addition, the cataloguing of significant factors would have an important value in providing clarity and transparency in the decision making process. It would also render the appeal courts' task in reviewing the exercise of discretion far easier. Arguably, nearly twenty years of unstructured discretion should yield more specific guidelines for its future exercise.

There are also perceived advantages in a more radical reform, adopting not only a structure to the section by providing a catalogue of relevant criteria to be evaluated, but also to guide the judge further by providing a presumption of exclusion for breach of specified rights. This would reflect the need for a discretion that better reflects the rights-based era in which the criminal justice system now operates.

2. Excluding evidence obtained by entrapment

Entrapment still does not exist as a defence in criminal law and the appellate courts have remained reluctant to allow such a defence through the backdoor of the rules of evidence. To a large extent the courts adhere to the position laid down by Lord Salmon in *Sang*.

Sang [1979] 2 All E.R. 1222:

I would now refer to what is, I believe, and hope, the unusual case, in which a dishonest policeman, anxious to improve his detection record, tries very hard with the

---

[37] Lord Justice Auld, *A Review of the Criminal Courts* (2001) Ch.11 para.108.

help of an agent provocateur to induce a young man with no criminal tendencies to commit a serious crime; and ultimately the young man reluctantly succumbs to the inducement. In such a case, the judge has no discretion to exclude the evidence which proves that the young man has committed the offence.[38]

American law permits a substantive defence of entrapment,[39] so that, although "artifice and stratagem may be employed to catch those engaged in criminal enterprises", government agents may not originate a criminal design. If the state does this, the defendant is entitled to an acquittal. In English common law, control over operations involving the participation of the police is exercised by the indirect (and less satisfactory) means of exclusion of evidence through section 78 of PACE or by staying the proceedings as an abuse of process.[40]

(i) *The application of section 78*[41]

The criteria for excluding evidence obtained by entrapment under section 78 have been considered in two decisions by the Court of Appeal, *Christou*[42] and *Smurthwaite and Gill*.[43] In the former, an undercover police operation in London set up a shop to buy and sell jewellery commercially. It was staffed solely by undercover officers purporting to be shady jewellers willing to buy stolen property. Discreetly-sited cameras and sound equipment recorded all that occurred over the counter. The object was to recover stolen property for the owners and obtain evidence against persons who had either stolen or dishonestly handled it. The cameras clearly identified the property on the counter and the vendors who produced it. There were conversations between the officers and the vendors bartering about price. To maintain their cover, the officers asked questions such as the area of London in which it would be unwise to resell the goods. They also required the signing of receipts recording the money paid for specified goods. The appellants, who each made repeated sales at the shop, pleaded not guilty to indictments charging burglary and handling stolen goods and challenged the admissibility of the evidence resulting from the undercover operation on the grounds that it should be excluded under section 78.[44] The evidence was admitted and the appeal was dismissed. On a preliminary point, Lord Taylor held that such police operations were not contrary to public policy. The operation allowed the offenders to commit further offences which may have been obviated had they been arrested earlier and could be said to facilitate crime. The court felt that the balance between arresting an individual offender and the desirability

---

[38] *ibid.* at 1236c-e.

[39] *Jacobson v US*, 503 U.S. 540, (1992); *Sorrells v US*, 287 U.S. 435, (1932); *US v Russell*, 411 U.S. 423 (1973).

[40] A. Choo, *Abuse of Process and Judicial Stays of Criminal Proceedings* (1993).

[41] D. Ormerod and D. Birch, *op.cit.*

[42] [1992] 4 All E.R. 559; *DPP v Marshall* [1988] 3 All E.R. 683.

[43] [1994] 1 All E.R. 898.

[44] An alternative ground of appeal was that the police had infringed the Code of Practice on the conduct of interviews. The court held that what occurred was not an interview. Were police officers to use an undercover pose to ask questions about an offence with the effect of circumventing the Code, the interview would be inadmissible—*Bryce* [1992] 4 All E.R. 567.

of apprehending a larger number of offenders and recovering property was an operational decision for the police.[45] On the question of the scope of s.78, he said,

Christou [1992] 4 All E.R. 559 at 564e-j, *per* Lord Taylor C.J.:

The learned judge held that discretion under s.78 may be wider than the common law discretion identified in *R v Sang*, the latter relating solely to evidence obtained from the defendant after the offence is complete, the statutory discretion not being so restricted. However he held that the criteria of unfairness are the same whether the trial judge is exercising his discretion at common law or under the statute. We agree. What is unfair cannot sensibly be subject to different standards depending on the source of the discretion to exclude it.

In the result the learned judge concluded that to admit the challenged evidence would not have an adverse effect on the fairness of the trial. He said:

Nobody was forcing the defendants to do what they did. They were not persuaded or encouraged to do what they did. They were doing in that shop exactly what they intended to do and, in all probability, what they intended to do from the moment they got up that morning. They were dishonestly disposing of dishonest goods. If the police had never set up the jewellers shop, they would, in my judgment, have been doing the same thing, though of course they would not have been doing it in that shop, at that time. They were not tricked into doing what they would not otherwise have done; they were tricked into doing what they wanted to do in that place and before witnesses and devices who can now speak of what happened. I do not think that is unfair or leads to an unfairness in the trial.

Putting it in different words, the trick was not applied to the appellants; they voluntarily applied themselves to the trick. It is not every trick producing evidence against an accused which results in unfairness. There are, in criminal investigations, a number of situations in which the police adopt ruses or tricks in the public interest to obtain evidence. For example, to trap a blackmailer the victim may be used as an agent of the police to arrange an appointment and false or marked money may be laid as a bait to catch the offender. A trick, certainly; in a sense too, a trick which results in a form of self-incrimination; but not one which could reasonably be thought to involve unfairness.

Smurthwaite involved allegations that the defendant had solicited another to murder his wife. An undercover police officer was introduced to the defendant by a third party and pretended to be a contract killer. Conversations incriminating the defendant were then recorded by a tape recorder concealed by the police officer. Evidence of the conversations was admitted. The Court of Appeal held that s.78 had not altered the substantive rule that entrapment or use of an agent provocateur did not afford a substantive defence in law to a criminal charge. However, that was not to say that the use of such methods was irrelevant to the application of s.78. If obtaining evidence in that way would have an adverse effect on the fairness of the proceedings, the court may exclude it.

Smurthwaite [1994] 1 All E.R. 898 at 903a-d, *per* Lord Taylor C.J.:

In exercising his discretion whether to admit evidence of an undercover officer, some, but not an exhaustive list, of the factors that the judge may take into account are

---

[45] *ibid.* at 567c.

as follows. Was the officer acting as an agent provocateur in the sense that he was enticing the defendant to commit an offence he would not have otherwise committed? What was the nature of any entrapment? Does the evidence consist of admissions to a completed offence, or does it consist of the actual commission of an offence? How active or passive was the officer's role in obtaining the evidence? Is there an unassailable record of what occurred, or is it strongly corroborated? In *R v Christou* this court held that discussions between suspects and undercover officers, not overtly acting as police officers, were not in the ambit of the codes under the 1984 Act. However, officers should not use their undercover pose to question suspects so as to circumvent the code. In *R v Bryce* the court held that the undercover officer had done just that. Accordingly a further consideration for the judge in deciding to admit an undercover officer's evidence is whether he has abused his role to ask questions which ought properly to have been asked as a police officer and in accordance with the codes.

The Court of Appeal is using its exclusionary power to develop an investigative model of pre-trial process, laying down guidelines so that traps will only yield admissible evidence when the police operate within specified limits (now requiring authorisation through the Regulation of Investigatory Powers Act 2000) and where there is a clear chain of reliable evidence so that phone calls are recorded and crucial meetings taped. It is a pragmatic approach, preferable to the "anything goes" approach of *Sang* but one which lacks guiding principle. It has been argued that society has a real interest in limiting the use of entrapment techniques.

Mack v The Queen (1988) 44 C.C.C. 3d 513 at 541:

One reason is that the State does not have unlimited power to intrude into our personal lives or to randomly test the virtue of individuals. Another is the concern that entrapment techniques may result in the commission of crimes by people who would not otherwise become involved in criminal conduct . . . Ultimately we may be saying that there are inherent limits on the power of the State to manipulate people and events for the purpose of attaining the specific objective of obtaining convictions.[46]

In applying current criteria, English courts need to take into account Art.6 requirements. An entrapment operation must be necessary, its extent proportional and it must be properly managed and supervised. These issues were raised in *Ludi v Switzerland*[47] and in *Teixeira de Castro v Portugal*,[48] in both of which undercover police officers made sample purchases of drugs. The issue was whether the admission of the testimony of the officers was in breach of the accused's right to a fair trial under Art.6. The outcomes were different. In *Ludi*, the operation was part of a judicial investigation and the drugs deal was already under way when the undercover officers arrived. The operation was not seen as a violation. In *Teixeira de Castro*, there was no real judicial

---

[46] Cited in G. Robertson, "Entrapment Evidence: Manna from Heaven or Fruit of the Poisoned Tree?" [1994] Crim.L.R. 805.
[47] Application No. 12433/86, [1992] 15 E.H.R.R. 173.
[48] Application No. 25829/94, [1998] 28 E.H.R.R. 101; [1998] Crim.L.R. 751.

supervision of the operation nor was there any pre-existing evidence to implicate the defendant. This latter point suggests that a covert operation is only fair when there is a reason for the operation.

One of the primary problems in the interpretation of s.78 has been the lack of a clear rationale. Are the courts excluding improperly obtained evidence because it is not reliable? Is the primary aim disciplining the police? Are they seeking to protect the integrity of the criminal process? Or is the issue the protection of the rights of the accused? Exclusion of evidence is only an indirect means of achieving those latter three objectives, which would be better achieved by a stay of proceedings for abuse of process.

(ii) *Abuse of process*

In Canada and Australia, courts have the power to exclude evidence or to stay proceedings for abuse of process. English courts have now also gone down this road. Entrapment was the issue in *Looseley*.[49] The accused was telephoned by an undercover police officer who asked him if he could obtain "a couple of bags" for him. The accused did so on various occasions. At his trial he submitted by way of a preliminary issue that the indictment should be stayed as an abuse of process on the ground of entrapment. The House of Lords reaffirmed that entrapment was not a substantive defence but the common law had remedies in respect of entrapment: first (and preferably) the court could stay the proceedings as an abuse of process and secondly the court could exclude evidence under s.78 as the admission of the evidence would adversely affect the fairness of the proceedings. A judge should consider whether the defendant would have committed the offence but for the police? Did the police officer cause the commission of the offence or merely provide an opportunity?[50] They should consider the nature of the offence—drug dealing and bribery are examples where such tactics are justified.[51] What is the nature of the entrapment—whether the police had grounds for suspicion as it is not the role of the police to tempt people in order to expose their bad characters. The court must consider how passive or active the police's role had been and whether the officer was acting as part of a proper, supervised operation. The defendant's predisposition to commit the offence and his criminal record should rarely be factors. The limits of acceptable police behaviour include whether the police had done no more than present the defendant with an unexceptional opportunity to commit a crime and whether the police conduct was no more than might have been expected from members of the public in the circumstances. Ultimately the overall consideration was always whether the conduct of the police or other law enforcement agency was so seriously improper that it brought the administration of justice into disrepute.

---

[49] [2001] 4 All E.R. 897.

[50] *Moon* [2004] EWCA Crim 2872—no evidence, with the exception of supply to the undercover officer, that M would have been prepared to supply any would-be purchaser.

[51] Criminal Justice and Police Act 2001, s.31 allows young persons under 18 to make sample purchases of alcohol to ensure that landlords are carrying out age checks.

Williams v D.P.P. was a case which would now raise issues of abuse of process.[52] The police left a Transit van apparently loaded with cigarettes in public view, arresting the appellants when they attempted to take some of the cartons. The court held that they had not acted as agents provocateurs and admitted the evidence but it is clear that the police procured the commission of an offence which would not otherwise have been committed.

3. Excluding incriminating statements obtained by tricks

Police deception which leads to the accused making an incriminating statement is certainly envisaged in the judgments in *Sang*. The example given is *Payne*[53] where the defendant, charged with drunk driving, was induced to see a doctor on the understanding that the doctor would not examine him for the purpose of seeing whether he was fit to drive. The doctor later testified in court that he was in fact unfit to drive. Lord Diplock treated this as analogous to unfairly inducing the defendant to confess.[54] Section 78 does not change this position. In *Mason*,[55] the police falsely told the defendant, accused of arson of a car, in the presence of his solicitor that they had the defendant's fingerprints on a fragment of glass. As a result he made a confession. The conviction was quashed and the Court of Appeal stressed the need to balance the gravity of the charge, the public interest, the position of the defendant and the nature of the police illegality. This was a significant deception on a minor charge, not only of the defendant but also of his lawyer.

Another trick leading to self-incriminating statements was perpetrated in *Bailey and Smith*,[56] when the police put the two suspects into the same cell and then staged a pantomime to convince the men that this was being forced on them by an uncooperative custody officer. The men made damaging admissions which were recorded, despite having been warned by their solicitor that the police were likely to act in exactly this fashion. The balance of fairness is harder to assess: the court felt that it was a serious charge and suspects in police stations can have no justified expectation of privacy and this was reinforced by their solicitor's warning. There was also no illegality on the part of the police. However there is an expectation that within the police station, officers will behave not only in strict accordance with the Codes but perhaps in a "proper" fashion. An express deception (for example, telling the suspects that they could consult together without fear of eavesdropping) would surely rule out the admissibility of any damaging statements. On the facts there is an intentional, implied, deception to lure the suspects into a false sense of security. Should the fact that the deception is implied rather than express make a difference? In *Wood v UK*,[57] on similar facts, the European Court of Human Rights found that the

---

[52] [1993] 3 All E.R. 365.See comment by John Smith in [1993] Crim. L.R. 775.
[53] [1963] 1 All E.R. 848.
[54] *Sang*, above at 1229 c-d.
[55] [1987] 3 All E.R. 481.
[56] [1993] 3 All E.R. 513.
[57] Application No. 00023414/02.

applicant's Art.8 rights had been breached and awarded damages. In *Allan v UK*,[58] a long-standing police informer had been placed by police in the cell in order to obtain evidence against the defendant after he had indicated to police that he was not prepared to answer police questions. The informer's testimony formed the principal prosecution evidence at the defendant's trial and the European Court held that this was a breach of his right against self-incrimination and of the requirements of Art.6.

Police deception, resulting in acquisition of incriminating evidence, will not normally trigger the exclusionary discretion. In *Maclean and Kosten*[59] the customs had arrested a drugs courier with a carload of cannabis but wished to implicate the real importer. The police created a story that the courier was in hospital after a car crash and this was used to trap the importer into making arrangements regarding the car in order to recover the cannabis, and into making various tape-recorded statements which were used in evidence against him. He appealed against conviction on the grounds that the evidence should not have been admissible as it had been unfairly obtained by trickery. Unlike *Mason* and similar cases, outside the police station, there can be no expectation of privacy nor that the people with whom you are dealing are honest, especially if you are engaged in illegal activity. Although the police officer became involved in an ongoing offence, his role was relatively passive and an accurate record was provided. It is difficult to argue that the fairness of the proceedings has been affected.

4. Evidence obtained by covert surveillance

Covert surveillance[60] of one form or another is undertaken in order to obtain evidence of offences. In the UK, until 1998, such surveillance was carried out under Home Office guidelines published in 1984 which required the personal authority of the Chief Constable for such an operation. Prior to 1997, this system was clearly not adequate for the purposes of Art.8 of the European Convention on Human Rights.

European Convention on Human Rights, Art.8:

1. Everyone has the right to respect for his private and family life, his home and his correspondence.
2. There shall be no interference by a public authority with the exercise of this right except such as is in accordance with the law and is necessary in a democratic society in the interests of national security, public safety or the economic well-being of the country, for the prevention of disorder or crime, for the protection of health or morals, or for the protection of the rights and freedoms of others.[61]

---

[58] Application No.: 00048539/99; [2003] 36 E.H.R.R. 12.
[59] [1993] Crim.L.R. 687.
[60] Evidentiary issues arising from the interception of communications under Pt I of the Regulation of Investigatory Powers Act 2000 are discussed in Ch.7.
[61] See C. Joubert, "Undercover Policing—A Comparative Study" [1994] European Journal of Crime, Criminal Law and Criminal Justice 18.

Interceptions of communications as well as other methods of surveillance are *prima facie* violations of the right to 'respect for private life'. In *Klass v Germany*,[62] the European Court acknowledged the significance of the technical advances made in surveillance as well as the development of terrorism. That the state must be entitled to counter terrorism with secret surveillance of mail, post and telecommunications under exceptional circumstances does not however give it the right to adopt whatever measures it thinks appropriate in the name of counteracting espionage and terrorism. The Court provided the following general guidance as to the application of Art.8 to legislation authorising surveillance.

a) the legislation must be designed to ensure that surveillance is not ordered haphazardly, irregularly or without due and proper care;
b) surveillance must be reviewed and must be accompanied by procedures which guarantee individual rights;
c) it is in principle desirable to entrust the supervisory control to a judge in accordance with the rule of law, but other safeguards might suffice if they are independent and vested with sufficient powers to exercise an effective and continuous control;
d) if the surveillance is justified under Art.8(2) the failure to inform the individual under surveillance of this fact afterwards is, in principle, justified.[63]

Insufficient safeguards against possible abuses can violate Art.8 even where the surveillance is carried out on the instructions and under the supervision of investigating judges. The legislation should make it clear the categories of people liable to have their telephones tapped and the nature of the offence which might give rise to such an order; there must be proper time limits and procedures for dealing with the material as well as rules for the destruction of recordings.[64] Any system must be lawful, necessary, proportionate and with proper systems of accountability. In *Leander v Sweden*,[65] the European Court held that the gathering of information in a secret police register and its release to the public service had the legitimate aim of protecting national security and that it was "in accordance with the law." The Swedish system also had significant controls with the involvement of parliamentarians, the Parliamentary Ombudsman and the Parliamentary Committee on Justice.

Today many jurisdictions possess statutory schemes and most require a judicial warrant before listening devices can be used to intercept private conversations. This is the norm in Australia, New Zealand, United States, Canada, France and the Netherlands. In the UK, the government responded to the promptings of the European Court of Human Rights and covert surveillance now has a basis in law with oversight provided by the Office of Surveillance Commissioners.[66] There are Codes of Practice for interception

---

[62] [1978] 2 E.H.R.R. 214.
[63] *ibid.* at 232–6.
[64] *Huvig v France* [1990] 12 E.H.R.R. 528; *Kruslin v France* [1990] 12 E.H.R.R. 547.
[65] [1987] 9 E.H.R.R. 433.
[66] *www.surveillancecommissioners.gov.uk*

of communications, for surveillance and for the use of covert human intelligence.[67] However there is no general requirement for judicial warrant.[68] The statutes involved are:

1. Part III of the Police Act 1997 deals with a limited, but very important, area of police activity: namely those forms of police surveillance which involves some form of unlawful conduct on the part of the police. Normally the unlawfulness will involve civil trespass. Section 92 makes such conduct lawful under certain conditions and states: *No entry on or interference with property or with wireless telegraphy shall be unlawful if it is authorised by an authorisation having effect under this Act.*

This section is very broadly drawn—it makes lawful any entry or interference with property where the necessary authorisation has been given under ss.93 or 94. There are, however, many constraints:

   a) authorisation will normally be given by the chief officer of the force;
   b) the criteria for interference with property are reasonably specific;
   c) all authorisations will be scrutinised by the commissioners;
   d) there are channels for complaint.

It does not provide a general scheme to regulate covert surveillance generally. The aims were more limited, namely to protect the police from civil actions on the grounds of civil trespass.

2. The Regulation of Investigatory Powers Act 2000 creates a parallel system of authorisations for undercover investigations which are not unlawful but although the police would not face domestic civil action, they may be acting in breach of the suspect's right of privacy. To that end, authorisation is needed for "directed surveillance", "intrusive surveillance" and the "use of covert human intelligence sources".[69]

   a) directed surveillance is undertaken for the purposes of a specific investigation, is likely to result in obtaining private information about a person. It does not include situations where the surveillance is an immediate response to events;
   b) intrusive surveillance is carried out on residential premises or in private vehicles and which either involves an investigator on the premises or in the vehicle or the use of a

---

[67] As of April 2006, these can be accessed at *security.homeoffice.gov.uk/surveillance/*.

[68] Authorisation is normally by law enforcement officers although there are cases where it is necessary to get authorisation from a surveillance commissioner.

[69] There are about 950 public authorities (including local authorities and health trusts) which are entitled to conduct covert surveillance under the provisions of the 2000 Act.

surveillance device. This includes interception of communications where one party consents and there is no
interception warrant[70];

c) the use of a covert human intelligence source involves
agents who establish a personal relationship to obtain
information which is then covertly disclosed. This will
cover undercover officers and other informants.[71]

In all these cases, the surveillance is regarded as lawful if there is
authorisation from a designated officer and the operation is in the interests
of national security, the prevention and detection of crime and disorder, the
economic well-being of the state, public safety, public health or tax collection.[72] The defendant is not entitled to see the underlying material placed
before the surveillance commissioners for the purpose of obtaining
approval.[73] Non-police surveillance, for example by neighbours filming the
defendant's does not come under RIPA regulations as long as the police are
not complicit.[74]

These statutory schemes must be read alongside the requirements of s.78
and Arts 6 and 8. In *Khan v UK*,[75] the appellant was suspected of importing
drugs. He visited the house of another man where, unknown to both of
them, the police had installed a listening device from which they subsequently obtained a tape recording of a conversation that clearly showed the
accused's involvement. There were no statutory provisions that authorised
such an action, which was both a civil trespass and also a *prima facie* breach
of the right to respect for private and family life protected by Art.8. The
Home Office guidelines, however, had been complied with. Domestic courts
held that the trial judge had been entitled to hold that the circumstances did
not require the exclusion of the evidence.[76] This was reviewed by the
Strasbourg Court which unanimously held that there was a breach of Art.8.
The key issue was whether the surveillance was "in accordance with law".
The Court said that this phrase required not just compliance with domestic
law but also relates to the quality of that law, requiring it to be compatible
with the rule of law. Domestic law must provide protection against arbitrary
interference. The Home Office guidelines that existed were not adequate
and the surveillance could not be considered to be in accordance with law.
Similar conclusions were reached in relation to a cloned pager in *Taylor-
Sabori v UK*.[77]

More surprisingly the Court went on to rule that, despite the admission of
the evidence obtained by the breach of Art.8 and despite the fact that this

---

[70] The device can be outside the premises where it provides information of the same quality as a
device on the premises.
[71] For these definitions, see Regulation of Investigatory Powers Act 2000, s.26.
[72] For intrusive surveillance, the purposes are national security, the prevention and detection of
serious crime or disorder, the economic well-being of the state.
[73] *GS* [2005] EWCA Crim 887.
[74] *Rosenberg* [2006] EWCA Crim 6.
[75] [2001] Application No. 35394/97, [2002] 31 E.H.R.R. 45; *Lewis v UK* Application No.:
0001303/02; [2004] 39 E.H.R.R. 9.
[76] *Khan* [1996] 3 All E.R. 289.
[77] Application No.: 00047114/99; [2003] 36 E.H.R.R. 17.

was the main evidence against the accused, there was no violation of the right to a fair trial.[78] The applicant did not suggest that there was an "automatic exclusion" rule where a Convention right had been breached but argued that there must be an effective procedure to challenge admissibility of evidence, that the trial court must have regard to the nature of the violation and that conviction should not be based solely on evidence obtained by a breach of a Convention right. The Court reiterated the general principle that the essential issue was the overall fairness of the proceedings. The applicant had the opportunity to challenge the validity of the evidence (under s.78) at each stage and the Court gave weight to the fact that the domestic courts did not feel that the admissibility of the evidence had given rise to substantive unfairness. The weaknesses of this judgment are brought out by the one dissentient, Judge Loucaides, who defined "fairness" as implying observance of the rule of law and suggested that, although there was no breach of domestic law, the UK courts ought not to admit evidence obtained in breach of the Convention. Effective enforcement of the Convention is hindered, because the police would not be deterred from repeating the conduct.

For the Court of Appeal, the issue is complicated by s.2 of the Criminal Appeal Act 1995, which directs their attention to whether the conviction is "safe", which sits alongside the question of the overall fairness of the proceedings. The concept of "safety of the conviction" can pull in an opposite direction to fairness and, as in *Khan*, a court may be reluctant to exclude relevant and reliable evidence. Earlier European Court cases such as *Schenk v Switzerland*[79] held that the key issue was whether the impugned evidence was the main or sole item against the accused—if so, it should be excluded but if not, it may be admitted without violating the overall fairness of the proceedings. Presumably fairness is the primary value—the state has a dominant position which it must be prevented from abusing by ensuring that its agents observe the rule of law. This is an aspect of the doctrine of equality of arms and where the disputed evidence is the only evidence, the state, by its breach of the Convention, has irredeemably altered that balance. Parity and fairness can only be achieved by refusing to allow the state to rely on evidence obtained by abuse of power, however compelling that evidence may be. But where the disputed evidence merely forms part of the prosecution case and is accompanied by other (lawfully obtained) items of incriminating evidence, the admission of the disputed evidence becomes a minor unfairness and it is possible to conclude that as a whole the proceedings are fair. This is not a balancing act between fairness and safety—in the sense that the more probative and reliable the evidence, the less we need to concern ourselves with fairness. Instead *Schenk* suggests that a court should put the disputed evidence on one side and consider the

---

[78] A similar conclusion was reached in *PG and JH v UK* Application No. 00044787/98; [2002] Crim. L.R. 308.

[79] *Schenk v Switzerland*, Application No. 10862/8; [1988] 13 E.H.R.R. 242, compare *Doorson v Netherlands*, Application No. 20524/92; [1996] 22 E.H.R.R. 330 where other evidence existed with *Unterpertinger v Austria*, Application No. 9120/80; [1986] 13 EHRR 175 where it did not.

strength and reliability of the surrounding evidence—if this supports the prosecution case, the admission of the impugned evidence need not be unfair.

The exclusionary discretion vested in judges by s.78 has been used to monitor the legitimacy of police investigative techniques. Allied to the European caselaw, it has led to the creation of a framework for police action. But the courts have developed no single rationale—whether it is to protect the accused's rights, to discipline law enforcement agencies or to maintain an image of "moral integrity" for the criminal justice system.

II. THE ADMISSIBILITY OF CONFESSIONS

The focus of many criminal trials is the interview in the police station. Police questioning of the accused will often lead to incriminating statements and interrogation designed to obtain such admissions has always been a major investigative technique for the police. Despite developments in police crime strategies, emphasising the targeting of offences and offenders, which should lead to the gathering of more tangible forms of evidence, interviewing remains an essential police task. Compared to other forms of acquiring evidence, it is cheap and the end result, a confession, is evidence that is seen as reliable and convincing. The rate of those detained for questioning in England who make complete or partial, verbal or written admissions of guilt has remained around 60 per cent for 25 years.[80]

The use of confessions as evidence for the prosecution at first sight infringes the rule against hearsay. The hearsay rule prohibits a witness repeating an out–of–court oral or written statement in order that the court should rely on the truth of that statement. This is exactly what police officers do when they testify to a defendant's confession, whether that confession has been taped, written down or merely remembered by the officer. Confessions are admissible because they form the most important exception[81] to the hearsay rule: an incriminating statement is admissible evidence against the person who made that statement. This is so whether it is a full confession or simply a partial admission.[82]

Indeed all incriminating statements made by a suspect to the police, even where the statement is partly exculpatory, are accepted into evidence.[83] Once admitted, such statements are very harmful to the defendant's case since a juror will often, not unreasonably, place greater weight on the confession and less attention being paid to the extent to which any other independent evidence supports or undermines that confession.

Confession is an exception to the hearsay rule, perhaps because the rationales for excluding hearsay do not apply. The first reason for exclusion

---

[80] B. Mitchell, "Confessions and Police Interrogation of Suspects" [1983] Crim.L.R. 596; G.H. Gudjonsson, *The Psychology of Interrogations and Confessions: A Handbook* (2003).

[81] J. Langbein, *The Origins of Adversary Criminal Trial* (OUP Oxford, 2003), 218 ff.

[82] Now preserved in criminal proceedings by s.118 (5) Criminal Justice Act 2003.

[83] *Sharp* [1988] 1 All E.R. 65.

is that repetition of what another person may have said is regarded as unreliable and consequently of less probative value. The second is that it is unfair to admit such evidence as the real witness is absent and the defendant is denied the opportunity to confront and/or cross-examine that person. Both carry less weight when considering confessions: confessions are inherently more reliable since people are unlikely to admit a state of affairs which is contrary to their own interests; furthermore there is normally written or taped evidence of the confession; finally all the relevant people are in court so defendants are able both to confront the officer who took the statement and, should they choose to do so, can testify on their own behalf, either to deny making the statement or to explain the contents.

A. *The Reliability of Confessions and Police Interviews*

Confessions may be reliable evidence but in practice over-reliance on them can be dangerous. The young, as in the Confait Case,[84] the disturbed,[85] the mentally ill or those with learning disabilities,[86] let alone those subject to brutality and intimidation,[87] are obviously vulnerable. But under hostile interrogation in the psychologically intimidating environment of a police station, even non-vulnerable people are also likely to make admissions which are not true,[88] not realising that once a statement had been made, there is great difficulty in retracting it.

S. Kassin and G. Gudjonsson, "The Psychology of Confessions: A Review of the Literature and Issues" (2004) 5(2) Psychological Science in the Public Interest 33–67:

Kassin and Wrightsman[89] proposed a taxonomy of alse confessions. Reviewing case reports that have stained the pages of legal history, and drawing on social-psychological theories of attitude change, they distinguished among three types of false confessions: voluntary, coerced-compliant, and coerced-internalized . . ..

Voluntary False Confessions
    Sometimes innocent people offer confessions without much prompting or pressure from police. When Charles Lindbergh's baby was kidnapped in 1932, some 200

---

[84] *Lattimore* (1976) 62 Cr.App. R. 53.
[85] *Ward* [1993] 2 All E.R. 577.
[86] Timothy Evans confessed to killings of his wife and child committed by John Christie—L. Kennedy: *Ten Rillington Place* (1961).
[87] The Birmingham Six were seriously assaulted before they made any statements—C. Mullin: *Trial and Error* (1986); other disturbing cases are documented on *www.innocent.org.uk*
[88] Generally Sanders and Young, *Criminal Justice* (2nd ed., 2001), Ch.5; G. Gudjonsson: *Persons at Risk during Interviews in Police Custody* (Royal Commission on Criminal Justice Research Study No.12 1992); M. McConville et al (1991): The Case For the Prosecution (Routledge, 1991), p.56.
[89] S.M. Kassin, & L.S. Wrightsman, "Confession evidence" in S.M. Kassin & L.S. Wrightsman (Eds.), *The Psychology of Evidence and Trial Procedure* pp. 67–94 (Sage, 1985).

people stepped forward to confess. In the 1980s, Henry Lee Lucas falsely confessed to hundreds of unsolved murders, making him the most prolific serial confessor in history. There are several possible reasons why people might voluntarily give a false confession, including a pathological desire for notoriety, especially in high-profile cases reported in the news media; a conscious or unconscious need for self-punishment to expiate feelings of guilt over prior transgressions; an inability to distinguish fact from fantasy due to a breakdown in reality monitoring, a common feature of major mental illness; and a desire to aid and protect the real criminal. The possible motives for voluntary false confessions are limited only by the imagination. Radelet[90] for example, described one case in which an innocent man confessed to murder to impress his girlfriend and another in which a woman pled guilty to provide an alibi for her whereabouts while having extramarital sex. Gudjonsson[91] described the case of a man who confessed to murder because he was angry at having been arrested while drinking at a party and wanted to mislead police in an act of revenge.

Compliant False Confessions

In contrast to voluntary false confessions are those in which suspects are induced through police interrogation to confess to a crime they did not commit. In these cases, the suspect acquiesces to the demand for a confession for instrumental purposes: to escape an aversive situation, to avoid an explicit or implied threat, or to gain a promised or implied reward. Demonstrating the form of influence observed in studies of conformity, research on obedience to authority, studies of compliance, and social impact theory, this type of confession is a mere act of public compliance by a suspect who comes to believe that the short-term benefits of confession relative to denial outweigh the long-term costs.

The pages of legal history are filled with stories of this type of confession—as in the Salem witch trials of 1692, during which roughly 50 women confessed to being witches, some, in the words of one observer, after being "tyed . . . Neck and Heels till the Blood was ready to come out of their Noses", and as in *Brown v. Mississippi* (1936), a case in which three Black tenant farmers confessed to murder after they were whipped with a steel-studded leather belt. This type of false confession is also illustrated in the Central Park jogger case, in which each of the boys retracted his confession immediately upon arrest and said he had confessed because he had expected to be allowed to go home. From a review of other cases, identified some very specific incentives for this type of compliance—such as being allowed to sleep, eat, make a phone call, go home, or, in the case of drug addicts, feed a drug habit. The desire to bring the interview to an end and avoid additional confinement may be particularly pressing for people who are young, desperate, socially dependent, or phobic of being locked up in a police station.

Internalized False Confessions

Internalized false confessions are those in which innocent but vulnerable suspects, under the influence of highly suggestive interrogation tactics, come not only to capitulate in their behavior, but also to believe that they committed the crime in question, sometimes confabulating false memories in the process.

. . . this kind of false confession results from "memory distrust syndrome," a condition in which people develop a profound distrust of their memory, which renders them vulnerable to influence from external cues and suggestions. Kassin[92] likened this process of influence during interrogation to the creation of false memories sometimes seen in psychotherapy patients. In both situations, an authority

---

[90] M.L., Radelet, H.A., Bedau, & C.E. Putnam, *In spite of innocence: Erroneous convictions in capital cases* (1992).

[91] G.H. Gudjonsson, (2003) *op.cit.*

[92] S.M. Kassin, "False memories against the self" [1997] 8 Psychological Inquiry, 300–302.

figure claims to have privileged insight into the individual's past, the individual is in a heightened state of malleability, all interactions between the expert and individual occur in a private and socially isolated setting devoid of external reality cues, and the expert ultimately convinces the individual to accept a negative and painful self-insight by invoking concepts like dissociation or repression. Linking this phenomenon to research on the biasing effects on autobiographical memory of photographs, imagination exercises, reports of co-witnesses, and dream interpretation, all of which lead people to become confused about the source of a memory, Henkel and Coffman[93] argued that the reality-distorting processes of interrogation provide fertile ground for internalized false confessions.

A number of cases illustrate this phenomenon. The case of 18-year-old Peter Reilly, mentioned earlier, provides a classic example. Reilly immediately called the police when he found that his mother had been murdered, but he was suspected of matricide. After gaining his trust, the police told Reilly that he failed a lie-detector test, which was not true, and that the test indicated he was guilty despite his lack of a conscious recollection of committing the crime. After hours of relentless interrogation, Reilly underwent a chilling transformation from adamant denial through confusion, self-doubt, conversion ("Well, it really looks like I did it"), and eventual utterance of a full confession ("I remember slashing once at my mother's throat with a straight razor I used for model airplanes . . . I also remember jumping on my mother's legs"). Two years later, independent evidence revealed that Reilly could not have committed the murder, and that the confession he came to believe was false . . .[94]

Models of police interviewing

The interrogation model still holds sway in the US where the most influential manual recommends an interrogative, guilt presumptive, aggressive approach to questioning.[95] The officers should interview in rooms which are small, with little furniture, away from normal sounds. Isolated and removed from familiar surroundings, this increases a suspect's anxiety and stress. It recommends nine psychological techniques to 'effective' interrogation, starting from a presumption of guilt, developing themes, building up rapport and finding moral excuses for the incident. The accused is to be interrupted if there are denials or defences. Any factual, moral, and emotional objections are to be overcome and the passive subject is not to be allowed to withdraw. The attention of the suspect is retained by moving closer, maintaining eye contact, touching and is urged to cooperate. Opportunities to confess which offer the chance to present excuses or explanation is followed by the suspect recounting the details orally and then in writing. It is a procedure ". . . designed to get suspects to incriminate themselves by increasing the anxiety associated with denial, plunging them into a state of despair, and minimizing the perceived consequences of confession."[96] There is interplay of three processes: custody and isolation, confrontation, and minimisation. Confession is the only way out.

---

[93] L.A., Henkel, & K.J. Coffman, "Memory distortions in coerced false confessions" [2004] 18 Applied Cognitive Psychology 567–588.

[94] S. Kassin, and G. Gudjonsson, "The Psychology of Confessions: A Review of the Literature and Issues" [2004] 5(2) Psychological Science in the Public Interest 33–67 [some references have been removed].

[95] F.E. Inbau, J.E. Reid, J.P. Buckley, & B.C. Jayne, *Criminal interrogation and confessions* (2001 4th ed.).

[96] S. Kassin, and G. Gudjonsson, (2004) *op.cit.*

The UK experience has been different. Baldwin's study[97] of 600 interviews found that over one third were not of an acceptable standard, grouping his criticisms in four ways—the officers were inept, there was an assumption of guilt, interviewing skills were poor or the officers were unprofessional. Building on such research and on cognitive psychology, UK forces have developed an ethical interviewing framework, using the mnemonic PEACE.

a) preparation and planning so that the officer is cognisant of all the details of the offender and offence;
b) engagement of the interviewee;
c) allow them to present their accunt;
d) the officer should clarify and challenge information;
e) there should be an evaluation, post-interview, of what the officer has learned.

An evaluation of this has found that the quality of interviews had not markedly improved and that interviewers still used a closed-questioning style, with leading questions and little opportunity for the interviewee to present their account.[98]

The doubts of the reliability of police interviews and the lack of any proper judicial supervision lead to the issue of what safeguards should be imposed by the court before such material is permitted in evidence. A central question for the Royal Commission on Criminal Justice in 1993 was whether independent corroborative evidence should be required for all confession cases. An independent study suggested that 95 per cent of such cases had such supporting evidence[99] which indicated that a rule requiring corroboration would lead to few additional acquittals. Although three members of the Commission felt that there should never be a conviction based solely on a confession, the majority were satisfied with a recommendation that the judge in all cases should give a strong warning that care was needed before convicting on the basis of the confession alone,[1] explicitly referring to reasons why people might confess to crimes that they did not commit.[2] Such a provision already exists in regard to a confession made by a mentally handicapped person under s.77 of PACE but this has not been made a general rule for all confession evidence. The issue of supportive evidence and of jury warnings is discussed further in Ch.7.

---

[97] J. Baldwin, *Video Taping Police Interviews with Suspects—an Evaluation* (Home Office, Police Research Series, Paper 1) (1992).

[98] C. Clarke and R. Milne, *National Evaluation of the PEACE Investigative Interviewing Course* (Home Office 2001).

[99] M. McConville: *Corroboration and Confessions: The Impact of a Rule Requiring that no Conviction be sustained on the Basis of Confession Evidence Alone* (Royal Commission on Criminal Justice Research Study No.13, HMSO 1993). Corroboration is not a panacea against wrongful conviction—in the Birmingham Six case, there were confessions to the pub bombings and there was independent forensic evidence, later proved fatally flawed, that the defendants had handled explosives.

[1] Such a development does not need legislation and a similar warning was implemented in the case of identification evidence by the Court of Appeal in *Turnbull* [1977] Q.B. 224.

[2] Royal Commission on Criminal Justice: Report Cm. 2263 (HMSO 1993) paras 4.56–4.87.

B. *The Development of Safeguards*

At common law, the judge had the discretion to exclude a confession if it was involuntary.

Ibrahim [1914] A.C. 599 at 610, *per* Lord Sumner:

It has long been established as a positive rule of English law that no statement by an accused is admissible in evidence against him unless it is shown by the prosecution to have been a voluntary statement, in the sense that it has not been obtained from him by fear of prejudice or hope of advantage exercised or held out by a person in authority.

The considerable uncertainty, not to say hostility, with which 19th—century judges regarded police powers to detain and to question suspects led to divergent attitudes towards statements made to the police while in police custody, with some judges happy to admit such statements as evidence while others excluded them.[3] Generally, arrest signalled the end of police interrogation. The courts sought to limit the police powers of interrogation and insisted that a suspect should be taken before a magistrate with all speed, normally within 24 hours. Eventually it was the judges themselves who took the initiative to resolve this uncertainty by issuing the Judges' Rules in 1912 to regulate police procedure over the treatment of detained persons. These Rules remained as influential guidelines until 1984 although they had neither the authority of common law nor of statute. They acted as a basis for the courts to decide on whether to admit incriminating statements into evidence. Originally they prohibited police questioning after arrest, still reflecting the 19th century distrust of the "new" policing arrangements. It was not until the revision of the Rules in 1964 that the police power to question while the suspect was in custody was recognised. But by the 1960s, the judicial attitude towards breaches of the Rules had become very permissive and rarely did police misconduct lead to the exclusion of the evidence. By the 1970s, although police powers appeared quite restricted as a matter of law, in practice they were relatively wide: the power to stop, search and question on the streets was exercised *de facto*; premises were often searched without the "technicality" of a warrant; people "assisted the police with their enquiries" at police stations (although the courts did not recognise the legal concept of "detention for question-ing"); suspects were held for extended periods without access to legal advice. The Judges' Rules provided no barrier to miscarriages of justice and many of the most notorious cases date from this period.

The modern law is contained in the Police and Criminal Evidence Act 1984 which codifies pre-trial procedures including the powers of the police

---

[3] *Knight and Thayre* (1905) 20 Cox 711.

to stop people, search them, arrest them, hold them in police custody and interrogate them. It also lays down the suspect's privileges. The statute's history was discussed earlier.[4] It arose from the Report of the Royal Commission on Criminal Procedure.[5] Its recommendations were presented as balancing the "interests of the community" (sufficient police powers to tackle the crime problem) with the "liberties of the individual" (providing safeguards for suspects in the police station). This balance is shown in the statute itself which extended police powers, especially in the areas of stop and search, arrest and detention at the police station but provided a more rigorous regime once the suspect was in custody. There were new controls especially the role of the custody officer, the documentation procedures, tape-recording of interviews, access to legal advice, a duty solicitor scheme and, in 1985, an independent prosecution service.[6] The 1984 Act has been constantly amended and added to in the past twenty years but its basic structure remains.

(i) *Section 76*

Where the accused challenges the admissibility of a confession which the prosecution seek to adduce as evidence, there is a two stage process:

a) the basic criteria for admissibility are laid down under s.76—where a confession is challenged, the court should firstly consider s.76(2), namely, whether the prosecution has proved beyond reasonable doubt that a confession was not obtained by oppression or in circumstances which might render it unreliable;

b) if the prosecution is able to satisfy the court that the s.76 requirements have been met, it is still open to the defendant to argue that the confession should be excluded under the provisions of s.78, namely that the admission of the statement would have such an adverse affect on the fairness of the proceedings, that it ought not to be admitted.

The first stage is governed by s.76 which states,

PACE 1984. s.76:

76.– (1) In any proceedings a confession made by an accused person may be given in evidence against him in so far as it is relevant to any matter in issue in the proceedings and is not excluded by the court in pursuance of this section

(2) If, in any proceedings where the prosecution proposes to give in evidence a confession made by an accused person, it is represented to the court that the confession was or may have been obtained—

---

[4] K. de Gama: "Police Process and Public Prosecutions: Winning by appearing to Lose?" (1988) 16 Int.J.Soc.L. 339.

[5] Royal Commission on Criminal Procedure: Report (HMSO 1981) Cmnd. 8092.

[6] Prosecution of Offences Act 1985.

(a) by oppression of the person who made it; or
(b) in consequence of anything said or done which was likely, in the circum-
     stances existing at the time, to render unreliable any confession which might
     be made by him in consequence thereof,
the court shall not allow the confession to be given in evidence against him except
in so far as the prosecution proves to the court beyond reasonable doubt that the
confession (notwithstanding that it may be true) was not obtained as aforesaid

(ii) *Defining "confession"*

A confession is defined in s.82(1) as including ". . . any statement wholly or
partly adverse to the person who made it, whether made to a person in
authority or not and whether made in words or otherwise". Statements can
include representations by words or conduct, express or implied.[7] A lie by
the accused could be seen as a ". . . statement adverse to the person who
made it" but is not necessarily indicative of guilt. In *Broadhurst*,[8] Lord
Devlin pointed out that there were many powerful motives for lying, both
in and out of court, such as shame or terror.[9]

More difficult are incriminating inferences which are drawn from silence
or from a party's reactions when taxed outside the court with an allegation
of some sort. The statements and the response are both admissible as is
shown in *Christie*,[10] where the defendant was charged with the indecent
assault of a small boy. The boy testified and identified the defendant.
However the boy's mother was also allowed to testify that she and the boy
went up to the accused and the boy had said "That is the man" and
described the assault. Christie had said "I am innocent". The House of
Lords admitted the mother's testimony as to the allegation and Christie's
response.

Christie [1914] A.C. 545 at 554, *per* Lord Atkinson:

. . . the rule of law undoubtedly is that a statement made in the presence of an
accused person, even upon an occasion which would be expected reasonably to call
for some explanation or denial from him, is not evidence against him of the facts
stated save so far as he accepts the statement, so as to make it, in effect, his own. If
he accepts the statement in part only, then to that extent alone does it become his
statement. He may accept the statement by word or conduct, action or demeanour,
and it is the function of the jury that tries the case to determine whether his words,
action, conduct or demeanour at the time when a statement was made amounts to an
acceptance of it in whole or in part. It by no means follows, I think, that a mere
denial by the accused of the facts mentioned in the statement necessarily renders the
statement inadmissible, because he may deny the statement in such a manner and
under such circumstances as may lead a jury to disbelieve him, and constitute
evidence from which an acknowledgement may be inferred by them.

[7] *Moriarty v London Chatham and Dover Railway* (1870) L.R. 5 [1870] Q.B. 314.
[8] [1964] A.C. 441.
[9] *Lucas* [1981] 2 All E.R. 1008—for discussion of the Lucas direction, see Ch.11.
[10] [1914] A.C. 545.

Admissions can come in many shapes and sizes but the common law rule in *Ibrahim* only dealt with incriminating statements made to persons in authority. Section 76 now covers all incriminating statements, however and to whomever made. In *Elleray*,[11] the defendant confessed to a series of rapes in the course of an interview on another matter with a probation officer. There was no right to the safeguards that would apply in a police interview but whether it was fair to rely on the statement depended on the facts of the case.

Elleray [2003] 2 Cr.App.R. 11, *per* Lord Woolf C.J.:

11 . . . .In deciding whether to exclude the evidence it is perfectly appropriate for the court to have in mind the contrast between the position that exists where an offender is interviewed by the police and that which exists when the offender is interviewed by a probation officer. The court should bear in mind the need for frankness between the offender and the probation officer; the fact that there may not be a reliable record of what was said; that the offender has not been cautioned; and that the offender has not had the benefit of legal representation. The protection which the court can provide under s.78 in the majority of cases should be sufficient to ensure that no unfairness occurs to an offender.

12. Reference has already been made to the steps which were taken by the probation officers in this particular case. A course which in some cases may be appropriate if an offender starts making a confession is to stop him and ask him whether he would like to see his solicitor before he makes any further remarks.

A neutral or exculpatory statement is not a confession within the meaning of s.76—in *Hasan*,[12] the defendant was charged with burglary and claimed a defence of duress, namely that he and his family would be harmed if he did not carry out the burglary. At trial, the judge allowed the Crown to rely on a confidential statement made by the accused in an "off the record" interview with the police investigating a different offence, on the basis that it was not a confession. The report of the interview contained nothing adverse to the defendant in respect of the burglary and was in that respect entirely neutral. But there were differences between what he said during the interview and what he said at trial and the Crown relied on the statement to show that he was a dishonest witness. The House of Lords relied on the decision in *Sat-Bhambra*.

Sat-Bhambra (1989) 88 Cr.App.R. 55 at 61, *per* Lord Lane:

First, were the answers given by the appellant upon the interviews properly to be described as a confession or confessions? S.82(1) of the Act defines confession as

---

[11] [2003] 2 Cr.App.R 11; N [2003] EWCA Crim 3239—confession by young girl to social worker; *Taylor* (unreported March 16, 2000)—statement to prison officers.

[12] [2005] 4 All E.R. 685.

follows: "confession" includes any statement wholly or partly adverse to the person who made it, whether made to a person in authority or not and whether made in words or otherwise.' His answers upon the interviews, the tapes of which the jury heard, were, as his counsel described, exculpatory. Their principal damaging effect was to demonstrate that the appellant was evasive and prevaricating and that many of the statements which he made proved eventually to be false. The question therefore arises: can a statement be described as wholly or partly adverse to the person making it, when it is intended by the maker to be wholly exculpatory and appears to be so on its face, but becomes damaging at the trial because, for example, its contents can by then be shown to be evasive or false or inconsistent with the maker's evidence on oath?

. . . The words of the section do seem prima facie to be speaking of statements adverse on the face of them. The section is aimed at excluding confessions obtained by words or deeds likely to render them unreliable, i.e. admissions or partial admissions contrary to the interests of the defendant and welcome to the interrogator. They can hardly have been aimed at statements containing nothing which the interrogator wished the defendant to say and nothing apparently adverse to the defendant's interests. If the contentions of the appellant in the present case are correct, it would mean that the statement ' I had nothing to do with it' might in due course become a 'confession', which would be surprising, with or without s.82(1). We are inclined to the view that purely exculpatory statements are not within the meaning of s.82(1).

Such off-the-record interviews can lead the investigators to potentially incriminating evidence and yet the interview may well be oppressive or have other undesirable features. The House of Lords appears to jettison the safeguards of PACE by this decision but in *Hasan*, Lord Steyn concluded that this interpretation of s.82 was compatible with the requirements of the Human Rights Act 1998, particularly because of ". . . the unrestricted capability of s.78 to avoid injustice by excluding any evidence obtained by unfairness (including wholly exculpatory or neutral statements obtained by oppression).."[13]

(iii) *Burden of proof*

Confession evidence is highly regarded and is admissible as relevant and reliable. Yet it is to be excluded unless the prosecution meets the strict conditions for admissibility. There is a burden on the Crown to prove beyond reasonable doubt that that the statement was not obtained by oppression (defined by s.76(8) as including torture, inhuman or degrading treatment or the use or threat of violence) or in circumstances that would make the statement unreliable. There are different rationales to explain this.

1. The state possesses overwhelming power and resources in the criminal justice process and this power must not be abused. The Crown must not be allowed to use these advantages to obtain evidence by illegal or immoral behaviour. The role of the court is to place constitutional constraints upon the state so that, regardless of the relevance and reliability of the confession, wherever there is improper conduct, the confession should be excluded.

---

[13] *Hasan, op.cit.* para.62 *per* Lord Steyn.

Wong Kam-Ming [1979] 1 All E.R. 939 at 946g, *per* Lord Hailsham:

... Any civilised system of criminal jurisprudence must accord to the judiciary some means of excluding confessions or admissions obtained by improper methods. This is not only because of the potential unreliability of such statements, but also, and perhaps mainly, because in a civilised society it is vital that persons in custody or charged with offences should not be subjected to ill treatment or improper pressure in order to extract confessions.

2. Morally, a society should never compel a person to incriminate themselves since within a liberal society, the autonomy of the individual must always be given precedence over the power of the collective. But if there is no compulsion and the statement is genuinely voluntary, there is no reason to exclude it.
3. There must be proper adjudication of disputes and this requires that standards of fairness be met. Although this incorporates elements of the two preceding points (abuse of a dominant position and the right of silence), it also stands by itself,

Sang [1979] 2 All E.R. 1222 at 1248b-c, *per* Lord Scarman:

Though differences of emphasis and scope are acceptable, it would be, I think, unfortunate if the 'the discretionary principle of fairness to the accused' was not recognised in all the criminal jurisdictions of the United Kingdom. Indeed, it must be a fundamental principle in all British criminal jurisdictions that the court is under the duty to ensure the accused a fair trial, and I do not believe that a judge can effectually discharge his duty without, at the very least, the availability of the discretion I have endeavoured to describe.

(iv) *Section 78 and the Codes*

Even if the s.76 requirements are met, these are not the only criteria by which the court can rule a confession inadmissible. The court's power to exclude evidence at its discretion is expressly preserved by s.82(3) which states that "Nothing in this Part of this Act shall prejudice any power of a court to exclude evidence (whether by preventing questions from being put or otherwise) at its discretion." That discretion, as we have seen, exists to a limited extent at common law but has been radically extended by s.78 so that, even where there is neither oppression nor circumstances likely to render the confession unreliable under s.76, it may still be that the admission of the evidence would have an adverse effect on the fairness of the proceedings.

These statutory provisions must be read with the Code C which governs the detention, treatment and questioning of suspects. A breach of the Code's procedures may lead to the exclusion of an incriminating statements allegedly made by the accused. Adherence to the procedure laid down in the Code is generally necessary before any transcript of a police interview becomes admissible evidence. This had been the concern of the Royal Commission in 1981 to ensure that the transcript was valid evidence both in terms of reliability and in terms of fairness.[14] While many other countries use an intermediary judicial official[15] to compile this record, the Royal Commission were unwilling to take this step towards a more inquisitorial role for the courts. Instead it is the police who have been placed in a quasi-judicial role in interrogating suspects inside the police station.

This combination of the Codes of Practice and s.76 and 78 has brought a sea-change in appellate courts' attitudes. The previous strategy was a "crime-control" model: the objective for the court was to convict the guilty by accepting any relevant evidence regardless of its provenance and subordinating the protection of a defendant's rights to that end. There is now a limited 'due-process' model in the English courts whereby violation of the defendant's rights will frequently lead to the exclusion of the evidence, even where that evidence is highly relevant. The courts have been driven in particular by the fairness criterion contained in s.78 and by the Strasbourg jurisprudence. But there is still considerable pragmatism about the Court of Appeal's approach: as we have seen any breach of the Act or of the Code must be serious and substantial.[16] The court has demonstrated that it is not the primary function to discipline the police and that there is neither automatic exclusion nor a presumption of exclusion where there has been a breach of the accused's rights. There is recognition that the investigative and prosecution process must have a moral integrity which must be protected by the courts. The courts need to perform a difficult balancing act, on the one hand ensuring that an ill-defined right to a fair trial is not put in jeopardy while, on the other, not bringing the courts into disrepute by excluding what the public would see as relevant and convincing evidence.

Many of the problems of the last twenty years have been eased by the improved reliability of the record of what occurs during interview. Tape-recording of interviews under s.60 is now mandatory for all indictable and either way cases. The recording of interviews is governed by Code E. Designated police stations[17] have equipped interview rooms in which everything said will be recorded. A master tape is made which is signed and sealed by all parties and will normally remain unopened. There will be copies for the prosecution and defence. It must be remembered that the recording is only part of the interaction between suspect and police officer and conversations take place outside the interview room. The recording is never wholly satisfactory.[18] Under s.76 of the Criminal Justice and Police Act

---

[14] Royal Commission on Criminal Procedure, *op.cit.* paras 4.2ff.

[15] Such as the juge d'instruction in France—see the Royal Commission on Criminal Procedure, *op.cit.* para.6.25ff; any move to an inquisitorial system was also rejected by the Royal Commission on Criminal Justice, *op.cit.* paras 1.11–1.15.

[16] *Walsh* (1989) 91 Cr.App.R 161—denying access to a solicitor would usually mean denial of a fair trial (cf. *Oliphant* [1992] Crim.L.R. 40) but a technical breach of detention rules would not.

[17] Under Police and Criminal Evidence Act 1984 s.35, certain police stations are designated for the purpose of detention and questioning of arrested suspects.

[18] S. Moston and G. Stephenson, *The Questioning and Interviewing of Suspects Outside the Police Station* (Royal Commission on Criminal Justice Research Study No.22 HMSO 1993).

2001, there is also provision for visual recording of interviews. This is regulated by Code F and, although used in investigations for serious crimes, is not mandatory.

Reliability can still be an issue—statements are made outside the station, perhaps on arrest or in the patrol car as it takes the scenic route to the station.[19] Sometimes there may be an informal interview[20] prior to the recorded version. Even in the interview room, the police still use oppressive questioning with the recorder switched on and with a solicitor present.[21] These issues will be discussed later. A preliminary but vital question relates to the obligation on the defendant to answer police questions.

C. The Right to Silence

Fundamental to any discussion of interviewing is the concept of the right to silence. At common law, this right had many different facets.[22]

1. *A caution must be given.* The police must warn suspects that they need not say anything and that, if they do say anything, any statement might be used in evidence. Proceedings can only be fair if suspects are fully aware of the circumstances in which they find themselves and of the likely consequences of their decisions. This must apply at all stages and a caution has to be given when the investigating officer has grounds for suspecting that that person has committed an offence and the purpose of the questions is to obtain evidence to use in court.[23] A caution has to be given on arrest[24] and at the start of an interview and after every break. The caution is repeated at formal charge. The terms of the modern caution are;

You do not have to say anything. But it may harm your defence if you do not mention when questioned something which you later rely on in Court. Anything you do say may be given in evidence.

2. *The burden of proof is on the Crown.* In criminal proceedings, the prosecution must prove the defendant's guilt beyond reasonable doubt.[25] Art.6(2) reinforces this by guaranteeing a presumption of innocence. Such

[19] M. Maguire and C. Norris, *The Conduct and Supervision of Criminal Investigations* (Royal Commission on Criminal Justice Research Study No.5 HMSO 1992).

[20] McConville et al.(1991), op.cit.60.

[21] *Paris* (1993) 97 Cr.App.R. 99—Royal Commission on Criminal Justice, *op.cit.* para.1.22 were concerned at the endless repetitive questioning that the tapes revealed.

[22] These have been affected by the Criminal Justice and Public Order Act 1994 and the Criminal Procedure and Investigations Act 1996 and the Criminal Justice Act 2003.

[23] Code C 10.1—there is no need to caution a person if questions are being put prior to a search and in exercise of stop and search powers under PACE, s.1.

[24] Code C 10.4—unless it is impracticable or if the person has been cautioned immediately before.

[2] *Woolmington v D.P.P.* [1935] A.C. 462.

provisions mean that there should be no obligation on the accused to produce evidence by answering police questions or to testify in court. The extent to which this has been affected by statutory change is discussed below.

3. *The defendant is not a compellable witness for the prosecution.*   This is a corollary to the previous point. It would be convenient for the prosecution to be able to call defendants and examine them on their involvement. Defendants only became competent witnesses for the first time under the Criminal Evidence Act 1898[26] but that was as a witness on their own behalf and they could not be compelled to testify for the Crown.

4. *The prosecution could not comment on silence.*   At trial the prosecution were not permitted to comment either on the defendant's decision to remain silent in the police station[27] or not to testify.[28] There were some limited exceptions—the prosecution could adduce evidence of silence when accusation was made by victim[29] or parent[30] or where the accused was on 'level terms' with the police.[31] The extent to which this has been affected by statutory change is discussed below.

5. *The judge could only make limited comment on silence.*   The judge is entitled to comment on the accused's silence[32] but must do so in measured terms and must warn the jury that they must not assume guilt from the defendant's silence. This is now governed primary by the provisions of the Criminal Justice and Public Order Act 1994 and is discussed below.

6. *There is a privilege against self-incrimination.*   There also exists a general maxim and a more technical privilege against self-incrimination.[33]

There has been a constant debate about using defendants' silence as evidence against them. Attempts at reform started with the Criminal Law Revision Committee in 1972[34] whose arguments were rejected by the Royal Commission on Criminal Procedure in 1981.[35] The police have argued that the PACE safeguards, especially the suspect's access to legal advice, tipped the balance too much in favour of suspects and that prosecutions for serious offences were either being discontinued or were ending in acquittals.

---

[26] Now contained in s.53(4) Youth Justice and Criminal Evidence Act 1999.

[27] *Hall* [1971] 1 All E.R. 322.

[28] s.1(b) Criminal Evidence Act 1898—the failure of any person charged with an offence to give evidence shall not be made the subject of any comment by the prosecution.

[29] *Horne* [1990] Crim.L.R.188.

[30] *Parkes* [1976] 3 All E.R. 380.

[31] *Chandler* [1976] 3 All E.R. 105.

[32] *Bathurst* [1968] 1 All E.R. 1175; *Sparrow* [1973] 2 All E.R. 129; *Martinez-Tobon* [1994] 2 All E.R. 90, although see Rupert Cross's forthright comments on gibberish – "The Evidence Report: Sense or Nonsense. . ." [1973] Crim.L.R. 329 at 333.

[33] see Ch.8.

[34] 11th Report (HMSO 1972) Cmnd. 4991 paras 28–52.

[35] Royal Commission on Criminal Procedure: *op.cit.* paras 4.33.

"Ambush" defences were singled out for criticism—this meant that at trial the defence relied on significant facts which had not been mentioned to the police at the time of the investigation, which had not been disclosed to the prosecution and which they were in no position to rebut. A Home Office Working Group[36] again favoured the idea of reform, only for its arguments to be rejected in their turn by the Royal Commission on Criminal Justice in 1993 which commissioned two separate reports.[37] The empirical evidence[38] put forward did not suggest that there was either an unacceptable acquittal rate or 'no further action' rate for those few defendants, charged with serious crimes, who choose to remain silent.[39] Nor did the research studies consider that there was any serious problem of "ambush" defences. The Royal Commission Report did suggest that the defence should be under an obligation to disclose aspects of its case but stood firm against the wholesale abolition of the right to silence. Despite this, the Criminal Justice and Public Order Act 1994 introduced sweeping changes to allow juries to use silence as evidence against the accused. This was similar to the reforms which had already been introduced in Northern Ireland.[40]

The extent to which the jury should be expressly allowed to use the defendants' silence as evidence has many issues of ethics, policy and practice.[41] The ethical question centres on the idea of "self-incrimination", namely the idea that nobody should be required to be their own betrayer. It is unfair to offer defendants a choice between speaking and convicting themselves out of their own mouths, or not speaking and being convicted by default. The European Court of Human Rights has held this to be a contravention of Art.6. *Saunders v UK*[42] involved sec.2 of the Criminal Justice Act 1987 which requires any person under investigation by the Serious Fraud Office to answer questions, produce documents and furnish information. Failure to do so was itself an offence. The defendant was convicted of fraud on the basis of answers that he had been compelled to give in the course of investigations by inspectors from the Department of Trade. The Court concluded that this infringed his freedom from self-incrimination and was in breach of the presumption of innocence and Art.6(2). Both *Saunders* and *Funke v France*[43] establish that coercion to co-operate with the authorities in the pre-trial process may infringe the privilege against self-incrimination and jeopardise the fairness of any subsequent hearing, were the prosecution to use the product of that coercion as evidence. The British government

---

[36] A. Zuckerman: "Trial By Unfair Means" [1989] Crim.L.R. 855.

[37] R. Leng: *The Right to Silence in Police Interrogation* (Royal Commission on Criminal Justice Research Study 10 HMSO 1993); M. McConville and J. Hodgson: *Custodial Legal Advice and the Right to Silence* (Royal Commission on Criminal Justice Research Study 16 HMSO 1993).

[38] This is summarised in Leng: *op.cit.* Ch.2.

[39] M. Zander: "The investigation of crime: a study of cases tried at the Old Bailey" [1979] Crim.L.R. 203.

[40] Criminal Evidence Order (No. 1987 of 1988); for its impact, see J. Jackson: "Curtailing the Right of Silence: Lessons from N. Ireland" [1991] Crim.L.R. 404.

[41] A. Ashworth and M. Redmayne, *The Criminal Process* (4th ed., 2005) Ch.4; D. Galligan "The Right to Silence Reconsidered" [1988] C.L.P. 69 at 88.

[42] Application No. 19187/91; [1996], 23 E.H.R.R. 313.

[43] Application No. 10828/84; [1993], 16 E.H.R.R. 297.

response has been to restrict the use in evidence of answers given under such circumstances.[44]

The ethical approach of "fairness" to silence is reinforced by certain policy considerations. The power and resources of the state which are available to investigate and prosecute far outweigh those available to the defendant. Equality of arms would suggest either that equal resources be provided for the defence or that the risks of miscarriages are redressed by imposing very high standards on the prosecution: thus the state should only use evidence obtained through proper means; the quality of evidence produced should be scrutinised; or a heavy burden of proof should be required. Silence, at best, is ambiguous and weak. Logically, it can be suspicious but, like lying,[45] there can be many possible reasons. This is especially the case immediately after arrest, when being questioned in a police station, after limited discussion with a legal adviser. This position is reinforced by our increasing understanding of the psychology of the interview, discussed above. It is hard to justify using silence in the face of police questions as evidence in a trial. It becomes less of problem when defendants have had full disclosure of the case against them, access to a lawyer and time to draft a statement of defence prior to the trial. A jury should be able to assume that both parties have had prior notice of the other side's case and the opportunity to develop arguments in rebuttal.

The right of silence, as it existed at common law, has been considerably modified as a result of s.34–37 of the Criminal Justice and Public Order Act 1994.[46] The accused must also now disclose aspects of the defence case prior to the trial—this is discussed in Ch. 6.

1. Ambush defences

A judge is empowered to direct the jury that they may "draw such inferences as appear proper" from a failure to mention a relevant fact relied on in the defence when it might reasonably have been mentioned during police questioning. The objective is to force the accused into early disclosure of the defence. Such inferences can only be drawn where the prosecution have supplied substantial evidence linking the accused with the offence and on which a reasonable jury could convict. A jury would thus be told to attach less weight to a defence which has only been revealed at the trial and which logically is less credible.

Criminal Justice and Public Order Act 1994. s.34:

34.– (1) Where, in any proceedings against a person for an offence, evidence is given that the accused—

---

[44] Youth Justice and Criminal Evidence Act 1999, s.59 and Sch.3 for a list of relevant statutes.
[45] *Lucas* [1981] 2 All E.R. 1008.
[46] I. Dennis, "The Criminal Justice and Public Order Act 1994. . ." [1995] Crim.L.R. 4.

(a) at any time before he was charged with the offence, on being questioned under caution by a constable trying to discover whether or by whom the offence had been committed, failed to mention any fact relied on in his defence in those proceedings; or

(b) on being charged with the offence or officially informed that he might be prosecuted for it, failed to mention any such fact,

being a fact which in the circumstances existing at the time the accused could reasonably have been expected to mention when so questioned, charged or informed, as the case may be, subsection (2) below applies.

(2) Where this subsection applies— . . .

(c) the court, in determining whether there is a case to answer; and

(d) the court or jury, in determining whether the accused is guilty of the offence charged,

may draw such inferences from the failure as appear proper.

This has been amended by s.58 of the Youth Justice and Criminal Evidence Act 1999 which prevents a court from drawing adverse inferences where the suspect has not had the opportunity to consult a solicitor.

Section 38(3) prevents a court from convicting a person solely on the basis of an inference drawn from this failure. In principle, such inferences should only be drawn where the prosecution have supplied substantial evidence linking the accused with the offence and on which a reasonable jury could convict. The judge must direct the jury specifically to those facts which have been relied on at the trial but which were not mentioned at the time of interview.[47] The prosecution is also entitled to comment on any such failure.[48] In these circumstances, a jury may be told in effect to attach less weight to issues and evidence raised by the defence when these have only been revealed at the trial and where they have little, if any, supporting evidence. The failure to mention these at the police interview allows the jury to treat them as less credible.

Since 1994, there have been new provisions for disclosure of the defence case prior to the trial. The objective was early guilty pleas by the defence or more discontinuances by the prosecution. Defence disclosure means that genuine "ambush" defences are so infrequent that they no longer provide justification for s.34. Dissentients have further pointed out that likely defences are usually apparent on the face of the witness statements.[49] Despite seeming redundancy, s.34 has not been repealed. The impact has been to make the jury aware in many more cases that a "no comment" interview was conducted—that is, where the suspect is advised by the legal adviser not to answer police questions.

Is a s.34 direction in violation of Art.6? The European Court of Human Rights held that such an analogous Northern Ireland provision was not—in *Murray v UK* (1996),[50] a terrorist case, the court held that, although the right to silence was a core value which lay at the heart of fair procedure, the

---

[47] *Chenia* [2002] EWCA Crim 2345.

[48] The prohibition on such comment in s.1(b) Criminal Evidence Act 1898 has been repealed by s.168(3) and Sch.11 of the Act.

[49] These are often ignored by the police—"It is routine police work not to follow up evidence raised by an accused which may support a defence." McConville et al. (1991): *op.cit.* p.77.

[50] Application No.: 00018731/91; 22 EHRR 29.

requirement placed on the defendant to answer questions or to testify was not incompatible with the Convention, although it would be if the conviction were based solely or mainly on any refusal to answer questions or to give evidence.

However, in a normal criminal prosecution, *Condron v UK*,[51] the applicants had been tried on counts of possession of heroin with intent to supply. Their solicitor had considered that the applicants were not fit to give interviews because they were suffering from heroin withdrawal. A police doctor however found that the applicants were fit for interview. The applicants remained silent during the interviews on the advice of their solicitor but, at trial, they testified. The judge directed the jury in accordance with s.34. The European Court distinguished *Murray*, especially because the accused had testified and the trial was before a jury. The Court held that the right to silence was not absolute but that "particular caution" was required by domestic courts before drawing adverse inferences. In all the circumstances of this case, the jury should have been directed that silence could be taken into account but only if they were satisfied that the applicants' silence could not be sensibly attributed to their having no answer or none that would stand up to cross-examination.

The English courts have applied this approach in a series of decisions. In *Beckles*,[52] the defendant was convicted of robbery and attempted murder. The victim had fallen from a window of a flat where the robbery had taken place. On arrest, the defendant said that the victim "wasn't pushed, he jumped". At interview, he refused to answer any questions when interviewed. At trial, he indicated that he was willing to waive privilege and disclose his conversations with his solicitor to explain why he had remained silent. The trial judge directed the jury that they might draw such inferences as they thought fit from the appellant's silence at interview. The judge failed to mention the defendant's statement to the police (the basis of his defence) and emphasised to the jury that there was "no independent evidence" of the solicitor's advice. There was a finding by the European Court[53] that there had been a violation of Art.6. The Court of Appeal quashed the conviction and ordered a retrial—the judge must allow the jury to consider fully whether the reason for silence was genuine or whether, on the contrary, silence was consistent only with having no answer to the allegations and was merely a convenient excuse. Lord Woolf approved *Beckles* in *Hoare and Pierce*.[54]

Hoare and Pierce (2005) 1 Cr.App.R. 355, *per* Lord Woolf C.J.

45 . . . "It is not the purpose of s.34 to exclude a jury from drawing an adverse inference against a defendant because he genuinely or reasonably believes that,

---

[51] Application No.: 00035718/97; 31 EHRR 1.
[52] (2005) 1 All E.R. 705.
[53] *Beckles v United Kingdom* (2002) 36 E.H.R.R. 13.
[54] [2005] 1 Cr.App.R. 355 at paras 54 and 55.

regardless of his guilt or innocence, he is entitled to take advantage of that advice to impede the prosecution case against him. In such a case the advice is not truly the reason for not mentioning the facts. The section 34 inference is concerned with flushing out innocence at an early stage or supporting other evidence of guilt at a later stage, not simply with whether a guilty defendant is entitled, or genuinely or reasonably believes that he is entitled, to rely on legal rights of which his solicitor has advised him. Legal entitlement is one thing. An accused's reason for exercising it is another. His belief in his entitlement may be genuine, but it does not follow that his reason for exercising it is. . .

The question in the end, which is for the jury, is whether regardless of advice, genuinely given and genuinely accepted, an accused has remained silent not because of that advice but because he had no or no satisfactory explanation to give. For this purpose, but only for this purpose, s.34 in its provision for the drawing of an adverse inference, qualifies a defendant's right to silence. However, it is still for the prosecution to prove its case, s.38(3) of the 1994 Act ensures that a finding of a case to answer or a conviction shall not be based solely on such an inference."

46 In our judgment, in a case where a solicitor's advice is relied upon by the defendant, the ultimate question for the jury remains under s.34 whether the facts relied on at the trial were facts which the defendant could reasonably have been expected to mention at interview. If they were not, that is the end of the matter. If the jury consider that the defendant genuinely relied on the advice, that is not necessarily the end of the matter. It may still not have been reasonable for him to rely on the advice, or the advice may not have been the true explanation for his silence. In *Betts & Hall*,[55] Kay L.J. was particularly concerned at para.54, with "whether or not the advice was truly the reason for not mentioning the facts." In the same paragraph he also says "A person, who is anxious not to answer questions because he has no or no adequate explanation to offer, gains no protection from his lawyer's advice because that advice is no more than a convenient way of disguising his true motivation for not mentioning facts". If, in the last situation, it is possible to say that the defendant genuinely acted upon the advice, the fact that he did so because it suited his purpose may mean he was not acting reasonably in not mentioning the facts. His reasonableness in not mentioning the facts remains to be determined by the jury. If they conclude he was acting unreasonably they can draw an adverse inference from the failure to mention the facts.

The outcome of these authorities is that the jury must be directed that:

    a) there were facts which defendant could reasonably have been expected to mention in the interview;

    b) if defendants did not mention those facts, as a result of legal advice, were they genuinely relying on such advice or was their silence because any answer would stand up to scrutiny? and

    c) if the defendant was genuinely relying on the advice, was that reasonable? If the jury conclude it was unreasonable, they can draw an adverse inference.

The police interview is in essence an inquisitorial procedure imposed upon the culture and rules of adversarialism within the criminal justice system. This creates a structural tension within contemporary criminal justice—s.34 undermines the work of the defence lawyer, who must be capable of acting robustly in their client's interests. The very purpose and utility of legal

---

[55] [2001] 2 Cr.App.R. 257.

advice is called into question as the courts expand their power to draw adverse inferences.[56]

2. Failure to testify

S.35 applies where the prosecution have satisfied the court that there is a case to answer and a defendant declines to testify in his or her own defence. The judge, in the presence of the jury, is empowered to tell defendants that the stage has been reached at which they can give evidence and to issue a warning that if they remain silent, that it will be permissible for the jury to draw whatever inferences appear to be proper.

Criminal Justice and Public Order Act 1994, s.35:

35.– (1) At the trial of any person who has attained the age of fourteen years for an offence, subsections (2) and (3) below apply unless –
(a) the accused's guilt is not in issue; or
(b) it appears to the court that the physical or mental condition of the accused makes it undesirable for him to give evidence;
but subsection (2) below does not apply if, at the conclusion of the evidence for the prosecution, his legal representative informs the court that the accused will give evidence or, where he is unrepresented, the court ascertains from him that he will give evidence.
(2) Where this subsection applies, the court shall, at the conclusion of the evidence for the prosecution, satisfy itself (in the case of proceedings on indictment, in the presence of the jury) that the accused is aware that the stage has been reached at which evidence can be given for the defence and that he can, if he wishes, give evidence and that, if he chooses not to give evidence, or having been sworn, without good cause refuses to answer any question, it will be permissible for the court or jury to draw such inferences as appear proper from his failure to give evidence or his refusal, without good cause, to answer any question.
(3) Where this subsection applies, the court or jury, in determining whether the accused is guilty of the offence charged, may draw such inferences as appear proper from the failure of the accused to give evidence or his refusal, without good cause, to answer any question.

As a result of s.38(3), a person should not be convicted solely on the basis of an inference drawn from this failure.

To use a failure to testify as an element in the prosecution case is, in an evidential and logical sense, suspect, even though this section can only come into play once the prosecution have supplied substantial evidence. There is some basis in logic for the changes introduced in s.34, 36 and 37. A defence raised late in the proceedings and without notice may be less credible. A refusal to account for one's presence in a particular place or one's possession of articles may justifiably lead to an inference of guilty knowledge. These sections focus on specific facts in issue whereas, under

---

[56] See comment on *Beckles* [2005] Crim.L.R. 560.

s.35, there is no requirement that the accused's failure to testify strengthens any particular element of the prosecution case and thereby justifies a specific inference, the strength and validity of which can be identified. The main result of a refusal to testify, in most cases, would be a general presumption of guilt.

There are other concerns about any legislation where the state pressures individuals into answering questions, let alone testifying. Briefly these can be framed first, as constitutional arguments since the right to silence is the final guarantee of the autonomy of the individual, in itself a central concept of a liberal society. Such arguments underlie the principle of the rule of law that the prosecution should prove guilt and thereby of the presumption of innocence. Secondly, there are ethical considerations whether the state should ever use evidence obtained in such a manner as the basis of a conviction. S.35 is a major breach of the privilege against self-incrimination: accused persons are damned if they answer and damned if they don't. Thirdly, s.35 sits uneasily alongside the old common law rule in *Sang* that if the prejudicial effect of a piece of evidence outweighs its probative value, it should be excluded. Here the prejudicial effect on the jury of the failure to testify must far outweigh any probative weight. To an extent this has been recognised by the caution shown in Northern Ireland where failure to testify has been taken into account only where the prosecution case just rests on the brink of the necessary standard of proof.[57]

The impact of s.35 was considered by the Court of Appeal in *Cowan*.

Cowan [1995] 4 All E.R. 939 at 942f–945d *per* Lord Taylor C.J.:

The issues raised are: (1) whether the discretion to draw inferences from silence under s.35(3) should be open in the generality of cases or only exceptionally, and (2) if it is to apply in a jury trial, what directions should the judge give?

. . . the judge has a discretion as to whether and in what terms he should advise a jury for or against drawing inferences. In what circumstances, then, should the court or jury be prepared to draw an adverse inference? [Counsel for the appellant's] answer is: 'only exceptionally where there is no reasonable possibility of an innocent explanation for the defendant's silence'. He suggested a number of possible reasons for silence at trial which may be consistent with innocence. They were: (1) a weak case barely surviving a submission of no case; (2) other defence evidence contradicting prosecution evidence; (3) if the defendant is nervous, inarticulate or unlikely to perform well; (4) if the defendant's medical condition is abnormal although not within s.35(1); (5) fear, duress or the protection of others; (6) previous convictions of the defendant where he is liable to be cross-examined on them; . . ..

If any of these reasons or excuses exists or may do so, it is submitted the court should not draw, or the jury should be directed not to draw, an adverse inference. Moreover [counsel for the appellant] suggests such reasons or excuses could properly be advanced by defending counsel without the need for evidence.

The breadth of these propositions is patently inconsistent with the scheme and plain words of s.35. To use the inevitable cliché, they would drive a coach and horses through the statutory provisions . . . . We cannot agree.

[57] Jackson, *op.cit.* pp.410–412.

. . . the general proposition that a previous criminal record upon which a defendant could be cross-examined (if he has attacked prosecution witnesses) is a good reason for directing a jury that they should not hold his silence against him, would lead to a bizarre result. A defendant with convictions would be in a more privileged position than one with a clean record. The former could avoid submitting himself to cross-examination with impunity; the latter could not. We reject that proposition.[58]

We accept that, apart from the mandatory exceptions in s.35(1), it will be open to a court to decline to draw an adverse inference from silence at trial and for a judge to direct or advise a jury against drawing such inference if the circumstances of the case justify such a course. But in our view there would need either to be some evidential basis for doing so or some exceptional factors in the case making that a fair course to take. It must be stressed that the inferences permitted by the section are only such 'as appear proper'. The use of that phrase was no doubt intended to leave a broad discretion to a trial judge to decide in all the circumstances whether any proper inference is capable of being drawn by the jury. If not, he should tell them so; otherwise it is for the jury to decide whether in fact an inference should properly be drawn.

. . . there are certain essentials which we would highlight.
(1) The judge will have told the jury that the burden of proof remains upon the prosecution throughout and what the required standard is.
(2) It is necessary for the judge to make clear to the jury that the defendant is entitled to remain silent. That is his right and choice. The right of silence remains.
(3) An inference from failure to give evidence cannot on its own prove guilt . . ..
(4) Therefore, the jury must be satisfied that the prosecution have established a case to answer before drawing any inferences from silence. Of course, the judge must have thought so or the question whether the defendant was to give evidence would not have arisen. But the jury may not believe the witnesses whose evidence the judge considered sufficient to raise a prima facie case. It must therefore be made clear to them that they must find there to be a case to answer on the prosecution evidence before drawing an adverse inference from the defendant's silence.
(5) If, despite the evidence relied upon to explain his silence or on the absence of any such evidence, the jury conclude the silence can only sensibly be attributed to the defendant's having no answer or none that would stand up to cross-examination, they may draw an adverse inference.

The Court of Appeal rejected any attempt to restrict the operation of s.35 but stressed that the nature, extent and degree of inferences to be drawn from silence lay within the discretion of the trial judge. *Cowan* requires the jury to be directed accordingly.

a) No adverse inference from the defendant's failure to give evidence should be drawn until the prosecution case is sufficiently compelling to call for an answer.
b) If there is a sufficiently compelling case to call for an answer and the only sensible reason for the decision not to give evidence is that there is no explanation or answer to give, or none that would stand up to cross-examination, then it is open to the jury to hold a failure to give evidence against the defendant.

---

[58] Upheld by the House of Lords in *Becouarn* [2005] 4 All E.R. 673—although this issue is no longer relevant as a result of the passage of Criminal Justice Act 2003 s.101.

c) The jury is not bound to do so and it is a matter for them to decide.

In *Becouarn*,[59] the House of Lords approved such a direction and did not accept that the operation of s.35 was unfair so as to require legislation. *Cowan* probably stands up in terms of Art.6. *Murray v UK*[60] considered that, where a *prima facie* case was established and the burden of proof remained on the prosecution, adverse inferences may be drawn from a failure to testify. As discussed earlier in relation to s.34, in *Condron*, the Court held that the right to silence was not absolute but that 'particular caution' was required by domestic courts before drawing adverse inferences. In all the circumstances of this case, the jury should have been directed that silence could be taken into account but only if they were satisfied that the applicants' silence could not be sensibly attributed to their having no answer or none that would stand up to cross-examination.

3. Failure to account for objects, substances or marks

Section 36 applies where the suspect gives no explanation to police about certain specific facts such as objects, substances or marks on clothing which tend to suggest the accused's participation in the offence. This section only comes into play after arrest and thus the suspect will have been cautioned and told in ordinary language what the consequences were of any failure to give an explanation.[61]

Criminal Justice and Public Order Act 1994, s.36:

36.– (1) Where—
- (a) a person is arrested by a constable, and there is –
  - (i) on his person; or
  - (ii) in or on his clothing or footwear; or
  - (iii) otherwise in his possession; or
  - (iv) in any place in which he is at the time of his arrest,

  any object, substance or mark, or there is any mark on any such object; and
- (b) that or another constable investigating the case reasonably believes that the presence of the object, substance or mark may be attributable to the participation of the person arrested in the commission of an offence specified by the constable; and
- (c) the constable informs the person arrested that he so believes, and requests him to account for the presence of the object, substance or mark; and
- (d) the person fails or refuses to do so,

then if, in any proceedings against the person for the offence so specified, evidence of those matters is given, subsection (2) below applies
- (2) [This is in identical terms to s.34 (2) supra]

One of the possible inferences that the prosecution will be seeking to draw in these circumstances (and in those envisaged in s.37) will be that of

---

[59] above at para.23 *per* Lord Carswell.
[60] [1994] 18 E.H.R.R. CD 1.
[61] s.36(4).

guilty knowledge:—that the accused knew what the substance was or that the article was stolen. In many offences this is a central fact in issue and the failure to give an explanation will be relied on by the prosecution as evidence of that fact. In this way, it is similar to the common law rule that allows inferences to be drawn from silence on an accusation.[62] But this section (and s.37) differs from the preceding sections in the sense that a fact in issue can be proved solely on the basis of the failure to explain: where the charge is handling stolen goods, a jury might reasonably convict on proof of possession of the stolen goods and a refusal to account for that possession. Although s.38(3) states that a person should not be convicted solely on the basis of an inference drawn from such a failure, there would be other evidence, namely of the possession, and the inference could be used to remedy the lack of evidence on the question of knowledge. In any case the prosecution is entitled to comment on this failure.[63]

The test to be applied here, laid down in *Benn*,[64] is similar to that applied with s.34 and 35—that the judge must make it clear to the jury that before any adverse inference may be drawn, there has to be a case for that defendant to answer. Silence or a refusal to answer questions is not enough. That can never be a proper foundation for a conviction. Secondly the judge must direct the jury that they could only draw an adverse inference if satisfied that silence meant that they had no explanation or no explanation that would survive questioning.

4. Failure to account for presence

Section 37 applies where suspects give no explanation to police about their presence at a particular place and this refusal tends to suggest participation in an offence. This section only comes into play after arrest and thus the suspect will have been cautioned and told in ordinary language what the consequences were of any failure to give an explanation.[65]

Criminal Justice and Public Order Act 1994. s.37:

37.– (1) Where –
(a) a person arrested by a constable was found by him at a place at or about the time the offence for which he was arrested is alleged to have been committed; and
(b) that or another constable investigating the case reasonably believes that the presence of the person at that place and at that time may be attributable to the participation of the person arrested in the commission of the offence; and
(c) the constable informs the person that he so believes, and requests him to account for that presence; and

---

[62] *Cramp* (1880) 14 Cox. 390.
[63] The prohibition on such comment in s.1(b) Criminal Evidence Act 1898 has been repealed by s.168(3) and Sch.11 this Act.
[64] [2004] EWCA Crim 2100; *Compton* [2002] EWCA Crim 2835.
[65] s.37(3).

(d) the person fails or refuses to do so,
then if, in any proceedings against the person for the offence, evidence of those matters is given, subsection (2) below applies
(2) [This is in identical terms to s. 34(2) supra]

Obviously this is very similar in structure to s.36. There may be different inferences which the prosecution will be seeking to draw: perhaps the silence might be used, on a charge of burglary, to suggest that the accused, without any lawful reason to be on the premises, had an intent to steal; perhaps where drugs have been abandoned nearby, the proper inference is that the accused had just abandoned them. The silence will be used to prove a fact in issue and the failure to give an explanation will be relied on by the prosecution as evidence of that fact. If this is correct, a fact in issue can be proved solely on the basis of the failure to explain. Again, s.38(3) does not apply because there is other evidence, although not necessarily relating to that particular element of the offence. In any case the prosecution is entitled to comment on this failure to account for presence in a particular place.

Section 34, 36 and 37 require the accused to have been arrested and to have been warned about the consequences of a failure to answer. Although this indicates that the objective threshold of 'reasonable grounds' for arrest should have been satisfied, the police often have a lot of suspicion and perhaps little hard evidence. They already use arrest as a technique to gain that evidence by putting pressure on a suspect, through interrogation.[66] These sections will encourage this practice, putting even greater pressure on the suspect since a refusal can be part of the prosecution's case, contributing to proof beyond reasonable doubt. While silence in answer to questions has some weight, it is very far from conclusive. There are defendants who are confused and vulnerable, defendants who wish to protect others, as well as those who are just unwilling to co-operate. Can a jury ever regard silence as sufficient to quash a reasonable doubt they might harbour about the prosecution case?

These changes will increase the pressure brought on people detained in police stations to answer questions. Bentham wrote, "*Innocence claims the right of speaking as guilt invokes the privilege of silence*".[67] He bears the burden of suggesting that the right to silence only protects the guilty and the criminally sophisticated. But he did so at a time when the right to silence as we know it did not exist, when the defendant was not permitted to testify in his own defence and when police interrogation did not exist. The pressure to answer police questions necessarily bears on the innocent as well as the guilty. The controversy surrounding the right to silence encompasses empirical questions and evidential problems but ultimately it should be a decision based on concepts of due process of law and proper constitutional

---

[66] This practice has been approved by the House of Lords in *Mohammed-Holgate v Duke* [1984] A.C. 437—it was not unreasonable to arrest someone against whom there were reasonable grounds for suspicion but with the predominant motive that they were more likely to confess in the police station than if interviewed elsewhere.

[67] J. Bentham, *Rationale of Judicial Evidence*. (Garland reprint, New York, 1978 (orig. 1825)).

principles. It is another of those important markers which define the relationship of state and citizen, delineating constraints on the state and underlining our moral choice that prosecution and punishment should not be based on evidence from the accused.

D. *Interviews in the Police Station—Access to Legal Advice*[68]

When a person is brought to a police station under arrest, they have various rights under PACE and Code C.

- a) Section 56 provides for a right for a person to be informed of the fact of your arrest.
- b) Section 58 gives a right to legal advice—namely that "A person arrested and held in custody in a police station or other premises shall be entitled, if he so requests, to consult a solicitor privately at any time".[69]
- c) Section 59 provides for a duty solicitor scheme.
- d) Section 57 provides additional rights for young persons.

Detained persons will be given a written notice stating these rights. They also have the opportunity to consult the Codes of Practice and to be given a copy of the Custody Record.[70] They will be asked if they wish to consult a solicitor and if they do not, they will sign the custody record to that effect. Additionally, vulnerable suspects will be protected by the presence of an "appropriate adult"[71] who must be present in the case of a juvenile and in the case of a person who is mentally disordered or mentally handicapped, an important safeguard in the light of alleged confessions by such suspects.

The right to legal advice was previously enshrined in the Judges Rules and has recently been acknowledged as a right in common law.[72] More recently the Human Rights Act ensures that a right to legal assistance is seen as a fundamental human right. It is implied in Art.5(4) which requires that a person is entitled to: "take proceedings by which the lawfulness of his detention shall be decided speedily by a court". This inference is reinforced by Art.6(3)(b) which provides that persons charged with a criminal offence should be provided with adequate time and facilities for the preparation of

---

[68] Royal Commission on Criminal Justice: *op.cit.* paras 3.46–3.64; J. Baldwin: *The Role of Legal Representatives at the Police Station* (Royal Commission on Criminal Justice Research Study No. 3, HMSO, 1992); M. McConville and J. Hodgson: *Custodial Legal Advice and the Right to Silence* (Royal Commission on Criminal Justice Research Study No. 16 HMSO 1993).

[69] Access can be delayed (but never refused altogether) under s.58(6) and (8) if the person is suspected of a serious arrestable offence and access might lead to interference with evidence, alerting of accomplices or hindering recovery of property. Similar provisions apply for s.56.

[70] Code C paras 3.1–3.2.

[71] defined at Code C:1.7(a).

[72] *R. v Chief Constable of South Wales Ex p. Merrick* [1994] 2 All E.R. 560—s.58 does not apply to a prison held on remand in police cells but there is a common law right to legal advice which must be allowed by the police if reasonably practicable.

their defence and Art.6(3)(c) which provides a specific guarantee of the right to defend oneself or be legally represented and to be granted legal aid where appropriate. A failure to allow an accused legal advice in detention will be seen as a breach of a right to a fair hearing under Art.6.[73]

In the 1970s, that common law right was more honoured in the breach than the observance.[74] Today the defendant, isolated in the police station, is recognised as vulnerable and capable of being manipulated by interviewers even without malpractice on their part.[75] The police remain very hostile to a solicitor's intervention which is seen as increasing a suspect's resistance to questioning.[76] Despite proper communication of these rights by custody officers[77] and more robust monitoring by the Court of Appeal, there is a low take-up rate of legal advice of between 25–30 per cent. The Royal Commission's recommendations included the video-recording of events in a custody suite and interviewers both reminding suspects of their rights to advice at the beginning of an interview and asking for their reasons for waiving those rights, reasons which would be recorded on tape.[78]

The protection of suspects' rights also depends on the quality of the advice received. Doubts have been raised[79] about the quality of the legal work, with solicitors or their representatives failing to obtain information from the investigating officers, often failing to acquire important facts from their own client and intervening in the interview on the client's behalf in less than one third of cases. However legal representatives in police stations now have to be accredited by the Law Society.[80]

Questions about the take up of these rights and about the quality of defence advice do not disguise the fact that the right to legal advice has become a substantial safeguard. Failure to observe the correct procedure in the Code of Practice, especially in relation to the provision of legal advice before interviews start, can lead to the evidence obtained from the subsequent interview being excluded. In *Absolam*,[81] the accused was arrested for threatening behaviour and taken to a police station. He emptied his pockets but the custody officer, knowing that the defendant had previously been arrested for possession of cannabis, said "Put the drugs on the table". The accused took a packet from inside his trousers and also admitted selling the

[73] B. Emmerson, "Crime and Human Rights" [2000] 150 New L.J. 13.
[74] M. Zander: "Access to a Solicitor in the Police Station" [1972] Crim.L.R. 342; J. Baldwin and M. McConville: "Police Interrogation and the Right to See a Solicitor" [1979] Crim.L.R.145.
[75] P. Softley: *Police Interrogation* (Royal Commission on Criminal Procedure Research Study No. 4, HMSO, 1980); G. Gudjonsson, *The Psychology of Interrogation, Confessions and Testimony* (Wiley, 1992).
[76] M. McConville et al.(1991): *op.cit.* 47–54.
[77] B. Irving and I. McKenzie: *Police Interrogation* (Police Foundation, 1989): A. Sanders et al. *Advice and Assistance at Police Stations* (Lord Chancellor's Dept., 1989).
[78] Royal Commission on Criminal Justice: *op.cit.* Para.3.47. But in a recent study of visually recorded interviews, Kent police are seen spending a considerable amount of time on this at the start of every interview.
[79] Royal Commission on Criminal Justice: op.cit. paras 3.56ff. J., Baldwin *Preparing the Record of Taped Interview* (Royal Commission on Criminal Justice Research Study No. 2 1992 HMSO); M. McConville and J. Hodgson (1993): *op.cit.*
[80] *www.lawsociety.org.uk/professional/accreditationpanels/policestation.law* (accessed April 2006).
[81] [1988] Crim.L.R. 748.

drugs. Only then was he reminded of the caution and of his rights to legal advice under s.58. Bingham L.J. agreed that the answers should be excluded.

Absolam [1988] Crim.L.R. 748:

Everything proceeded unobjectionably until the moment when, in answer to the custody officer's inspired question, the drugs were produced and put on the table. It then became apparent to the officer, as he acknowledged, that an offence had been committed. At that stage the appellant had not been advised of his right to legal advice, but the situation had arisen in which it was plainly necessary that he should be advised of his right to legal advice and, in particular, it was necessary that he should not in the light of his apparent guilt be further questioned until he had been offered that opportunity and, if he sought legal advice, had had the opportunity of receiving it.

The Code specifies the sequence of events which should not be overridden. In *Absolam*, the Court of Appeal considered the officer's questions to be a 'serious and substantial breach' and considered the evidence, although not obtained by oppression or in circumstances which question its reliability, ought to have been excluded under s.78.[82]

Not every breach of the Code necessarily leads to the exclusion of the evidence obtained—as has been seen in the benchmark decision in *Walsh*.[83] There was an interview in the cell which was not contemporaneously recorded and there had been no legal advice. The Court of Appeal held that the main objective of s.58 was to achieve fairness to the suspect and to the Crown. Where there were significant and substantial breaches, *prima facie* those standards of fairness have not been met and to admit evidence obtained in such circumstances meant that there would be an adverse effect on the fairness of the proceedings. But a breach of s.58 does not lead to the automatic exclusion of the statements and the breach must be shown to affect fairness to an extent that justice required that the evidence should not be admitted. In this case the breach had made a difference and the good faith or otherwise of the officers did not affect this.

Any refusal of the right of access to a solicitor is closely scrutinised by the Court of Appeal. The police cannot refuse to allow a suspect access to legal advice on the grounds that legal advice will be to remain silent but under the provisions of s.58(8) delay can be authorised where the person is suspected of a serious arrestable offence and access might lead to interference with evidence, alerting of accomplices or hindering recovery of property. In *Samuel*,[84] the police relied on these provisions. Hodgson J. pointed out that relying on these provisions required that the police believe that an individual solicitor would interfere with evidence, alert other

---

[82] See also *Williams* [1989] Crim.L.R. 66 and *Sanusi* [1992] Crim.L.R. 43.
[83] above.
[84] [1988] 2 All E.R. 135; see also *Parris* [1989] Crim.L.R. 214.

suspects or hinder the recovery of evidence, albeit inadvertently.[85] Such a belief could only be rarely held.

Samuel [1988] 2 All E.R. 135 at 147, *per* Hodgen J.

Therefore, inadvertent or unwitting conduct apart, the officer must believe that a solicitor will, if allowed to consult with a detained person, thereafter commit a criminal offence. Solicitors are officers of the court. We think that the number of times that a police officer could genuinely be in that state of belief will be rare. Moreover it is our view that, to sustain such a basis for refusal, the grounds put forward would have to have reference to a specific solicitor. We do not think they could ever be successfully advanced in relation to solicitors generally.

Legal advice was characterised as, "one of the most important and fundamental rights of the citizen". This was illustrated in *Vernon*[86] where the accused nominated a solicitor who was unavailable since it was late at night. She agreed to be interviewed without legal advice but was not told of the availability of the duty solicitor. The record of the interview was deemed inadmissible under s.78 as she would not have consented to be interviewed but for this breach.

These authorities have not led to the position that any refusal of access to legal advice has led to the exclusion of any statement made at interview. The "serious and substantial" approach brought a different result in *Alladice*,[87] again an armed robbery case. Although there was a clear breach of s.58, Lord Lane C.J. held that the admission of the interview statement did not adversely affect the overall fairness of the proceedings.

Alladice [1988] Crim.L.R. 608 *per* Lord Lane:

What the appellant himself said in evidence was that he was well able to cope with the interviews; that he had been given the appropriate caution before each of them; that he had understood the caution and was aware of his rights. Indeed he asserted that he had said nothing at all after the first four (innocuous) questions, and what had been written down by the interviewing officer was nothing that he said but had been invented by the writer. His reason for wanting a solicitor was to have some sort of check on the conduct of the police during the interview.

The judge rejected the allegations that the police had invented the admissions. He found as a fact that the interviews had been conducted properly. He concluded that the only difference the presence of a solicitor would have made would have been to

---

[85] Where an officer believes that a lawyer may inadvertently or otherwise act which will have one of the consequences mentioned in s.58(8), the officer should refuse to all the lawyer access but allow the suspect to make other arrangements —Code C, Annex B a–3.

[86] [1988] Crim.L.R. 445.

[87] [1988] Crim.L.R. 608.

provide additional advice as to the appellant's right to say nothing, a right which he knew and understood and indeed at times during the interview exercised. It may seldom happen that a defendant is so forthcoming about his attitude towards the presence of a legal adviser. That candour does however simplify the task of deciding whether the admission of the evidence "would have such an adverse effect on the fairness of the proceedings" that it should not have been admitted. Had the solicitor been present, his advice would have added nothing to the knowledge of his rights which the appellant already had. The police, as the judge found, had acted with propriety at the interviews and therefore the solicitor's presence would not have improved the appellant's case in that respect.

In *Dunford*,[88] the judge was said to be entitled to take account of the accused's criminal record and his awareness of the arrest and detention procedures, so that the absence of the solicitor did not affect the fairness of the proceedings so adversely so as to require the exclusion of the evidence. It is useful to compare *Chahal*[89] and *Franklin*.[90] In both cases, the accused initially chose not to see a solicitor and in both cases, the family arranged for one to be present. However the police did not inform the accused until the interviews were concluded. The conviction was upheld in *Chahal* where the defendant was a mature businessman who knew the position and suffered no prejudice. However in *Franklin*, the defendant was a young unemployed man who had never been in a police station before and the Court of Appeal held that the judge had exercised his discretion wrongly and should have excluded the admissions.

Samuel adopts a "rights" approach, protecting the rights of defendants by putting them into the position that they would have been in had their rights had been observed. *Alladice* displays a harder line, looking at the nature of the right interfered with and the causal link between that interference and the evidence obtained as factors to be taken into account under s.78 in reaching a solution which reflects "justice". Such cases suggest that the Court of Appeal is weaving a rather uneasy road between the two rationales for excluding evidence. They have turned their backs on the strict 'reliability' approach which would merely test the quality of the statement regardless of the infringement of the defendant's rights. But they find it hard to embrace the full American "fairness" model which would lead to exclusion whenever the suspects' rights are infringed. The pragmatic approach in *Walsh* allows the judge discretion to measure the significance of the breach with the adverse affect on the fairness of the proceedings created. But does it create uncertainty for prosecution and defence? Inevitably there are inconsistencies: in *Alladice*, the appellant was aged only 18 although accustomed to police interviews—would a modern court allow the police to interview a youth without allowing him first to be advised by a lawyer?

E. *Interviews in the Police Station—Other Matters*

A refusal to allow access to legal advice is often a serious breach of Code C. Other breaches might also lead to the exclusion of evidence. When taken to

---

[88] [1991] Crim.L.R. 370; also *Oliphant* [1992] Crim.L.R. 40.
[89] [1992] Crim.L.R. 124.
[90] *The Times*, June 16, 1994.

a police station, the arrested person is taken before the custody officer,[91] who must decide whether sufficient evidence exists either to charge the person or to warrant further detention for the purpose of obtaining evidence through interview.[92] The custody officer must ensure that the person is aware of their rights to legal advice, to notify someone of the fact of their arrest and to see that the Codes of Practice are not necessarily observed by monitoring the conditions of the custody: how long and how often a person is interviewed; whether medical advice is required and whether proper sleep and refreshment has been provided. Custody officers must be aware of the special provisions regarding the mentally handicapped, those with sight or speech impediments, the ill, foreigners, those needing interpreters and juveniles. All of this should be recorded on the custody record,[93] an essential source of information for the defendant and the court in the event of, say, a disputed confession. Proper documentation was seen by the Royal Commission to be a critical safeguard for both police and suspect, not just the custody record but also a proper interview record. From the trial perspective, reliable records prevent disputes over what was said or done.

1. Conditions and Length of Detention

The periods during which people can be held in detention are specified in statute. The custody officer is responsible for the length of time that a person is detained in a police station and that detention must be periodically reviewed.[94] Prior to the Act, the police probably had to bring a suspect before a court within 24 hours. Now, with certain safeguards, it is possible to hold people without charge for up to four days. Although s.41 lays down the principle that a person should not be held without charge for more than 24 hours, this can be derogated from in certain circumstances. Continued detention for a further 12 hours can be authorised by a senior officer (a superintendent or above) if the detention is necessary to secure or preserve evidence, if the offence is a serious arrestable offence[95] and if the investigation is being conducted "diligently and expeditiously".[96] Further periods of continued detention up to 96 hours are possible with approval from the magistrates' court.[97]

Where reasonable grounds for arrest exist, detention for interviewing is not a breach of Art.5 (3) which guarantees the right of a suspect to be

---

[91] s.36 outlines the role of the custody officer; s.37 defines the custody officer's duties before charge; s.38 defines the custody officer's duties after charge and s.39 outlines the custody officer's responsibilities to the arrested person. The custody officer will not be involved in the investigation.

[92] In practice, detention is almost never refused—I. McKenzie et al: "Helping the Police with their inquiries" [1990] Crim.L.R. 22; figures from police force in SE England in 2000 show that, of 50,000 arrests, detention was refused in 1.25% of cases.

[93] s.37 (4)—typically there are 5 copies: for the station record, for the suspect, for case papers, a transit copy and finally for the local intelligence unit.

[94] s.40—the extent to which such reviews are carried out is doubtful—D. Dixon et al.: "Safeguarding the rights of the accused. . ." (1990) 1 Policing and Society p.115.

[95] These are listed in, Sch.3, Police and Criminal Evidence Act 1984.

[96] s.42.

[97] s.43.

brought before a court "promptly".[98] Unlawfully extended detention would provide grounds for exclusion of evidence but not minor delays—in *Taylor*[99] there was a breach of length of detention regulations as a result of delay in organising an identification process. A short delay or a technical infraction would not lead to the exclusion of the identification evidence.

The basic rights[1] of a suspect being interviewed include properly heated, ventilated and lit interview rooms, with no requirement to stand and with proper breaks for refreshment at recognised mealtimes. The Code designates a minimum 8-hour continuous period of rest without interrogation in any 24-hour period. In *Trussler*,[2] the suspect was a drug addict who was arrested at 9 a.m. and eventually made a statement 18 hours later with no proper period of rest. A doctor had been provided and the suspect had talked to his lawyer on the phone but there were long periods of questioning without adequate rest periods and the statements were eventually excluded as potentially unreliable by the Court of Appeal.

Any serious infringement of these conditions will be characterised as oppressive—in *Ireland v UK*,[3] the Court found a violation of Article 3 when the evidence disclosed severe beatings of four detainees by Northern Ireland security forces. They designated five interrogation techniques in use in Northern Ireland as inhuman treatment, namely wall-standing for long periods, hooding, subjection to noise, sleep deprivation and deprivation of food and drink. Under English law, coercive interviewing can lead to confessions being excluded under s.78 of the Police and Criminal Evidence Act 1984. General oppressive conduct can lead to exclusion as in *Beales*,[4] where the officer 'hectored and bullied' and fabricated evidence. In *Paris*, the Court of Appeal quashed the convictions on listening to the tapes of the interview. The suspect denied involvement on more than 300 occasions.

Paris (1993) 97 Cr.App.R. 99 at 103 *per* Taylor L.C.J.:

. . . each member of this Court was horrified. Miller was bullied and hectored. The officers . . . were not questioning him so much as shouting at him what they wanted him to say. Short of physical violence, it is hard to conceive of a more hostile and intimidating approach by officers to a suspect. It is impossible to convey on the printed page the pace, force and menace of the officer's delivery.

The House of Lords recently reviewed the use of evidence obtained by torture in *A and others v Secretary of State for the Home Department*.[5] The government sought a ruling which would allow the Special Immigrations

---

[98] *Brogan v UK* [1988] 13 E.H.R.R. 439.
[99] [1991] Crim.L.R. 541.
[1] Code C 12.2, 12.7, 12.8 inter alia.
[2] [1988] Crim.L.R. 446.
[3] (1978) 2 E.H.R.R. 25.
[4] [1991] Crim.L.R. 118.
[5] [2006] 1 All E.R. 575.

Appeal Tribunal to rely on evidence obtained by governments abroad using torture. The House of Lords held that the principles of common law, standing alone, compelled the exclusion of evidence obtained by torture by a third party as unreliable, unfair, offensive to ordinary standards of humanity and decency, and incompatible with the principles that should animate a tribunal seeking to administer justice. However a majority held that such evidence should only be excluded when it was *established* that the information relied on was obtained by torture. This is in contrast to s.76 where the burden of proof is on the prosecution to show that the confession was not obtained by oppression. Dissenting, Lord Nicholls said,

A v Secretary of State for the Home Department [2006] 1 All E.R. 575, *per* Lord Nocholl:

80 . . . I associate myself with the observations of Lord Bingham of Cornhill on the burden of proof where the admissibility of evidence is challenged before SIAC on the ground it may have been procured by torture. The contrary approach would place on the detainee a burden of proof which, for reasons beyond his control, he can seldom discharge. In practice that would largely nullify the principle, vigorously supported on all sides, that courts will not admit evidence procured by torture. That would be to pay lip-service to the principle. That is not good enough.

2. Proper recording

Many of the miscarriage of justice cases in the 1970s involved failures to make a proper record of interview, particularly to contemporaneously make a written note. This is now unnecessary as interviews are tape-recorded. *Paris* shows the importance of a reliable record of interviews but also demonstrates that all safeguards are not necessarily observed when the suspect is in the police station with a legal adviser. Another example is informal interviews. These are a substantial breach of the Code and yet statements are still sometimes admitted. In *Matthews*,[6] the accused was remanded in police cells as the remand centre was full. She was alleged to have made incriminating statements. These were neither contemporaneously recorded, shown on the custody sheet nor was any note shown to the defendant. It is a matter for the trial judge's discretion whether such unverified accounts should be admitted, and as long as the judge addresses the correct issues under s.78, the appellate court will not interfere with the decision although other trial judges might well have considered the breaches in this case substantial and significant. However the accused's statement led directly to the discovery of the victim's clothes and it is hard to resist the conclusion that the judge must have considered that this confirmed the reliability of the statement, although its reliability should not be a relevant issue for the purposes of s.78. In later cases, statements resulting from such informal interviews were excluded as evidence in *Sparks*[7] and in *Hunt*.[8]

6 [1990] Crim.L.R. 190.
7 [1991] Crim.L.R. 128.
8 [1992] Crim.L.R. 582.

Cell confessions

Weak prosecution cases often are boosted by the evidence of other prisoners, either in the police station or in prison, who claim to have heard confessions by the defendant.[9] There is normally no record or independent verification of this. In *Allan v UK*,[10] a long-standing police informer had been placed by police in the cell in order to obtain evidence against the defendant after he had indicated to police that he was not prepared to answer police questions. The informer's testimony formed the principal prosecution evidence at the defendant's trial and the European Court held that this was a breach of his right against self-incrimination and of the requirements of Art.6. The Privy Council have also reviewed this area in *Benedetto*,[11] where the defendant was alleged to have confessed to another prisoner who had a long record of dishonesty and had testified to nothing that was not available in the newspapers. In addition, on a previous occasion he had testified to a cell confession and had obtained favourable parole treatment.

Benedetto [2003] Crim.L.R. 880 at 882—comment by D.Ormerod:

The Privy Council underlined by its conclusion in the present case that the judge must inform the jury of two equally important matters: (1) the indicators which suggest that the witness's evidence might be unreliable (i.e. an explanation as to why the witness might lie) and (2) the significance those factors have in assessing the weight of the evidence they heard. Beyond that the Board has left the matter of how to formulate the warning to the discretion of the trial judge who must respond to the needs of the individual case. In an appropriate case, it is submitted that the jury might also need to be told that if they do accept that the cell confession occurred, they should have regard to the possible motives the accused might have had for fabricating such a confession in the prison environment.

. . . A number of commentators have questioned whether a formal rule of admissibility or at least one of corroboration for cell confessions needs to be developed. Further support for such a rule might derive from the increasing use of informers in cells, on which see Allan v UK. Although an exclusionary rule has obvious attractions when viewed in the context of cases such as the instant one and Pringle, a number of problems arise. First, there is an assumption that a workable definition of cell confession could be created. Secondly, it prompts the question by what criteria cell confessions are to be treated as sufficiently reliable to become admissible? Clearly there are none of the safeguards of reliability comparable to a police confession. An admissibility test based merely on the status of the witness as a prisoner would be overbroad, and there is a danger that the inquiry could become divorced from the underlying principle applicable in any scenario—that caution is needed because the witness has a motive for lying. In addition, any exclusionary rule would create technicality and complexity in the law and would run contrary to the trend in recent years away from rules with exceptions to broader admissibility subject to discretion. Finally, if the evidence is deemed admissible, there will still be a need for an appropriate warning.

---

[9] *Stone* [2005] EWCA Crim 105.
[10] Application No.: 00048539/99; [2003] 36 E.H.R.R. 12.
[11] [2003] 2 Cr.App.R. 25; *Pringle v R.* [2003] UKPC 9.

Alternatively, judges could be required to withdraw cases from the jury if the prosecution was based wholly on cell confession evidence that lacked sufficient indicia of reliability. Advocates of such an approach might draw comparisons with the Turnbull rule requiring judges to perform a filtering process with weak identification evidence. Arguably the cell confession is distinguishable and presents a less compelling case for terminating a prosecution. With identification evidence, the problem is of mistaken but honest witnesses, and the jury needs special protection from such evidence because of that latent but dangerous dimension. With cell confessions the dangers are patent, and judicial warnings can more readily safeguard against the jury assigning undue weight to the evidence.

3. Tricks

Investigators do on occasion act unethically. In *Blake*,[12] the interviewer told the defendant that his voice had been recognised—this was untrue and the record of interview excluded. In *Kirk*,[13] the defendant was arrested for an assault and theft of a handbag. The victim died the day after the offence. The police interviewed him on the basis of the minor assault and theft without revealing that he faced more serious charges of robbery or manslaughter. The defendant declined legal representation. The record of interviews was excluded. But in *Fulling*,[14] the police told the defendant that her lover had been unfaithful to her with another woman (being held in the next cell). The accused made a statement which was not excluded since this was not 'oppressive' behaviour under s.76. Lord Taylor defined "oppression".

Fulling (1987) 85 Cr.App.R. 136 at 142 *per* Lord Taylor:

... "oppression" in section 76(2)(a) should be given its ordinary dictionary meaning. The Oxford English Dictionary as its third definition of the word runs as follows: "exercise of authority or power in a burdensome, harsh, or wrongful manner; unjust or cruel treatment of subjects, inferiors, etc., or the imposition of unreasonable or unjust burdens." One of the quotations given under that paragraph runs as follows: "There is not a word in our language which expresses more detestable wickedness than oppression."
We find it hard to envisage any circumstances in which such oppression would not entail some impropriety on the part of the interrogator. We do not think that the judge was wrong in using that test. What however is abundantly clear is that a confession may be invalidated under section 76(2)(b) where there is no suspicion of impropriety. No reliance was placed on the words of section 76(2)(b) either before the judge at trial or before this Court. Even if there has been such reliance, we do not consider that the policeman's remark was likely to make unreliable any confession of the appellant's own criminal activities

The conviction was upheld but questions remain. Could the statement be said to be "reliable" in such circumstances for the purpose of section 76? Or

[12] [1991] Crim.L.R. 119.
[13] [2000] 1 W.L.R. 567.
[14] [1987] 85 Cr.App.R. 136 at 142.

could it be said that deliberately (but not illegally) undermining the willpower of a suspect (already held for two days) in this manner does not have an "adverse effect on the fairness of the proceedings"? *Fulling* can be contrasted with the exclusion of the evidence in *Mason*[15] which involved a deception not only of the defendant but also of his solicitor. The conviction was quashed with the Court of Appeal stressing the need to balance the gravity of the charge, the public interest, the position of the defendant and the nature of the police illegality.

If the facts which are equivalent to a confession are discovered as a result of a trick, they are not admissible. In *Payne*[16] the defendant, charged with drunk driving, was induced to see a doctor on the understanding that the doctor would not examine him for the purpose of seeing whether he was fit to drive. The doctor later testified that he was in fact unfit to drive. This can also be seen in *Barker*,[17] where the defendant was charged with tax fraud. He had been impliedly promised immunity from prosecution and as a result, produced papers and documents which disclosed tax irregularities. The Court of Appeal quashed the conviction as the documents stood on exactly the same footing as an oral or written confession which was brought about as a result of a promise or a threat.[18]

4. Vulnerable suspects

The custody officer needs to be aware of the particular needs of vulnerable suspects[19]—the discretion to exclude evidence is exercised freely with regard to vulnerable defendants. In *Lamont*,[20] the interrogation was of a mentally retarded suspect with an IQ of 73 and acting under s.77 PACE, the Court of Appeal excluded evidence of a confession which provided the only evidence of intention in an attempted murder case. Exclusion of evidence is not predicated on proof of police misconduct as could be seen in *Brine*,[21] where the suspect was properly interviewed but the interview was excluded after medical evidence that the accused was suffering from a mild form of paranoid psychosis. But in *Clarke*,[22] the accused admitted attempted theft while being taken to the police station. A record of the conversation was made and signed but at trial the defendant alleged that he was deaf and thus there had been a breach of the Codes.[23] On appeal, this argument was rejected. There was no breach of the Codes if the officer had been unaware

---

[15] [1987] Crim.L.R. 757; but compare *Bailey* [1993] Crim.L.R. 681 where play-acting by the police convinced the suspects that their cell had not been bugged and they made incriminating statements.

[16] [1963] 1 All E.R. 848.

[17] [1941] 2 K.B. 381.

[18] The decision itself was negatived by s.105 Taxes Management Act 1970.

[19] *Utip* (unreported, April 11, 2003, CA) shows value of the appropriate adult for both the suspect and the prosecution.

[20] [1989] Crim.L.R. 813.

[21] [1992] Crim.L.R. 122.

[22] [1989] Crim.L.R. 892.

[23] Code C 13.5 which specifies that if a person appears to be deaf, he must not be interviewed in the absence of an interpreter.

that the suspect was deaf but if shown as fact that the defendant was deaf, it could still be excluded under s.78.

The failure to provide an appropriate adult as required by the Code for juveniles and those with mental difficulties will often lead to the exclusion of any incriminating statements. In *DPP v Stratford Youth Court*,[24] the defendant was 17, had not been in a police station before and had been in police custody for some 24 hours before interview commenced. A 17-year-old is dealt with in Youth Court but Code C only refers to suspects who are under 17. The Court of Appeal approved of the decision of the district judge to exclude the confession as a 17-year-old suspect should be provided with the assistance of an appropriate adult. A suspect has to be able to deal with questioning properly and after 24 hours in custody, the judge could not be satisfied that the defendant was able to make a balanced judgment about the interview.

5. Inadmissible Statement followed by Proper Interview

If a statement is excluded because of a breach of the Codes, this does not automatically lead to exclusion of a second statement occurring in course of a properly conducted interview.[25] But if the grounds for impugning the first statement still exist, then the second statement suffers the same fate. In *Canale*,[26] the officers deliberately broke the rules and the court refused to permit the prosecution from gaining advantage. This was followed in *Conway*,[27] where an informal and unrecorded cell interview was followed 20 minutes later by a "proper" interview. In *McGovern*,[28] the suspect had an IQ of 73 and it was felt that the impact of the first statement could not be excluded from affecting reliability of the second statement even though this latter was in the presence of his solicitor.

F. *Interviews Outside the Station*

The Codes of Practice were intended to eliminate the damning unrecorded verbal admission[29] by focusing on the interview in a designated police station where there were the central safeguards of the caution, notification of the right to legal advice and the recording of interviews. The interview is defined in Code C 11A:

An interview is the questioning of a person regarding their involvement or suspected involvement in a criminal offence or offences which . . . must be carried out under caution. Whenever a person is interviewed they must be informed of the nature of the offence...

---

[24] [2001] EWHC Admin 615.
[25] *Y v DPP* [1991] Crim.L.R. 917.
[26] [1990] Crim.L.R. 329.
[27] [1994] Crim.L.R. 838.
[28] [1991] Crim.L.R. 124.
[29] *Pattinson* (1973) 58 Cr.App.R. 417 at 425 where Lawton L.J. stigmatised this practice.

Interviews should take place at the station and the arrested person should be taken there as soon as practicable.[30] But, under s.30(10) of PACE, an officer may delay taking the suspect to the police station in order to carry out investigations which reasonably can be carried out. Going to a shop to check whether the suspect had bought the goods or to their home to inspect papers or assess an alibi would all be reasonable courses of action for the constable. But any interview should not happen at this point, unless any delay would lead to interference with evidence, the alerting of other suspects, or hinder the recovery of property.[31]

If there are answers to preliminary questions or the suspect makes a spontaneous statement, these may well be admissible. In *Parchment*,[32] the suspect was discovered naked in the cupboard in his flat. Arrested and cautioned over some burglaries, he made spontaneous admissions, allegedly repeated in the police car. There was no record made at the time and the officers later wrote up a joint note which was neither shown to nor signed by the defendant. By the time of the formal interview, he was denying the offences. The Crown Court admitted the statements arguing that, while the police were operating within the Codes, they could not be said to be acting unfairly under s.78. But at that time, there was no obligation under Code C to show the accused the joint note. The Code has been amended so that interviews outside the police station are subject to safeguards similar to those applying to interviews inside the station.[33] Significant statements or silences, whether in an interview or not, that occur before arrival at the police station must be put to the suspect at the beginning of the formal interview.[34] Failure to do this may well lead to such previous statements, however spontaneous, being excluded by s.78. The rationale would be that the accused, even where cautioned at the scene, will have had no notification of any right to see a solicitor nor will the record have been taped or been noted contemporaneously. It will simply be an unverified police account.

Parchment shows that spontaneous statements by a suspect will only be excluded by section 78 if there are circumstances that would suggest that the statement was unreliable. But the police cannot evade the Code's requirements by questioning at the scene and argue that such questions do not constitute an interview (as defined above). If it is an interview, the Code applies. Interviews can, under Code C 11.1, take place away from a police station. Initially the courts took a restrictive view of when an interview occurred. In *Maguire*,[35] the police officer arrested the suspect for attempted burglary. In the police car, the officer advised him to "tell the truth" and the accused said that ". . . we were only going in to have a look around . . . for anything, for money, whatever". The Court of Appeal held that though Code did not apply only to interviews in police stations, in this case, this questioning did not constitute an 'interview' since there were no questions

---

[30] Police and Criminal Evidence Act 1984, s.30(1).
[31] Code C 11.1
[32] [1989] Crim.L.R. 290.
[33] Code C 11.7ff.
[34] Code C 11.4
[35] [1989] Crim.L.R. 815.

asked. But this was post-arrest questioning and the suspect was prompted for an explanation about his involvement. Were courts to permit such statements to be admitted into evidence, the Police and Criminal Evidence Act safeguards would be largely by-passed as 'verbals' would move from the police station to the scene of crime and police car, before the Code of Practice started to run.[36]

A preferable and broader approach was taken in *Hunt*,[37] where police officers saw the defendant in a garden with a flick knife. He was searched and asked, without caution, what it was for. He replied that it was his but ran off. He was arrested and in the police car, he was again asked why he had the knife and made certain admissions. The Court of Appeal held that even at the time of the original search, the officer had ample grounds for suspecting that he had committed an offence and should have cautioned at that point. Certainly in the car, the single question and answer constituted an interview and the statements should have been excluded under s.78. A similar approach is taken in *Goddard*,[38] where the appellant was arrested and cautioned and then questioned about three polythene wraps that he had thrown away. He admitted that these contained heroin. The Court of Appeal quashed the convictions, holding that the questions were an interview designed to obtain admissions and that the appellant had been denied the protection of the Code.

An investigating officer must be able to ask questions which do not comprise an "interview". At an early stage of any investigation, the police are endeavouring to discover whether an offence has been committed and whether the suspect is involved. Once they are satisfied about these, a caution must be administered and any further questions must be an interview within the meaning of Code C. But questioning only to obtain information or an explanation or in the ordinary course of an officer's duties does not constitute an interview.[39] Nor do questions which are confined to the proper conduct of a search.[40] In *Park*,[41] the appellant was convicted of burglary. The car he was driving (with the stolen goods in it) had been stopped because of a defective rear light. The appellant told the police officer that the car belonged to his father, that the electrical goods on the rear seat were his and that he was moving home. The police officer cautioned and arrested him. The answers given at the roadside were not to be excluded by s.78 and could be put to the appellant in cross-examination as statements inconsistent with his testimony. The officer had asked some exploratory questions which were merely an inquiry. That stopped when the officer felt that there was evidence on which the appellant could be arrested and cautioned. However a record must still be

---

[36] Royal Commission on Criminal Justice: *op.cit.* paras 3.7ff.; S. Moston and G. Stephenson: *The Questioning and Interviewing of Suspects Outside the Police Station* (Royal Commission on Criminal Justice Research Study No.22 HMSO, 1993); McConville et al. (1991) 83ff.

[37] [1992] Crim.L.R. 582.

[38] [1994] Crim.L.R. 46.

[39] But seeking information in the course of duties might well be questioning about a person's involvement in an offence—*Cox* [1993] Crim.L.R. 382; *Marsh* [1991] Crim.L.R. 455.

[40] *Langiert* [1991] Crim.L.R.777; *White* [1991] Crim.L.R. 779; *Chung* [1991] Crim.L.R. 622.

[41] [1994] Crim.L.R. 285.

made, even if not contemporaneously, and the suspect given the opportunity to check the record.

The Royal Commission found that about 30 per cent of suspects report being questioned prior to arrest and there was evidence that negotiations took place off-record inside the police station as to what was to be said on the record.[42] Despite the dangers involved in the use of such informal interviewing, the Royal Commission did not consider recommending the exclusion of all except formal, recorded interviews, but instead contented themselves merely with discussing the possibilities of extending tape-recording to all transactions between officer and suspect.

G. *Evidence Found in Consequence of Inadmissible Confession*

At common law, the inadmissibility of the confession made no difference to the admissibility of any evidence which was discovered as a consequence of that confession. In *Warickshall*,[43] the accused was charged as an accessory after the fact, with having received stolen property. As a result of her confession, the stolen property was recovered having been hidden in her bedroom. But the confession had been obtained as a result of inducements and was held to be inadmissible. Was evidence of the finding of the property also inadmissible?

Warickshall (1783) 1 Leach 263 at 264 *per* Nares J.:

A free and voluntary confession is deserving of the highest credit, because it is presumed to flow from the strongest sense of guilt, and therefore it is admitted as proof of the crime to which it refers; but a confession forced from the mind by the flattery of hope, or by the torture of fear, comes in so questionable a shape when it is to be considered as evidence of guilt, that no credit ought to be given to it; and therefore it is rejected. This principle respecting confessions has no application whatever as to the admission or rejection of facts, whether the knowledge of them be obtained in consequence of an extorted confession, or whether it arises from some other source; for a fact, if it exists at all, must exist invariably in the same manner, whether the confession from which it is derived be in other respects true or false. Facts thus obtained, however, must be fully and satisfactorily proved, without calling in aid of any part of the confession from which they have been derived...

This rule is preserved in the Police and Criminal Evidence Act 1984.

Police and Criminal Evidence Act 1984, s.76:

76.– (4) The fact that a confession is wholly or partly excluded in pursuance of this section shall not affect the admissibility in evidence—

[42] S. Moston and G., Stephenson *op.cit.*, B. Irving and C. Dunnighan: *Human Factors in the Quality Control of CID Investigations* (Royal Commission on Criminal Justice Research Study No.21, HMSO, 1993).

[43] (1783) 1 Leach 263.

(a) of any facts discovered as a result of the confession;
(b) where the confession is relevant as showing that the accused speaks, writes or expresses himself in a particular way, of so much of the confession as is necessary to show that he does so.[44]

In *Warickshall*, the discovery of the property in the accused's bedroom necessarily linked her with the crime without reference to the confession. In *Chalmers v HM Advocate*,[45] the accused made an inadmissible confession to murder and then accompanied police officers to a cornfield where he pointed out the victim's purse. The High Court of Justiciary held that evidence of the defendant pointing to the purse was inadmissible since it was part of the same transaction as the interrogation itself and that if that confession was unfairly obtained, so was the visit to the cornfield. But the purse itself was admissible, although of little probative value. It would be necessary to find another link to the accused, such as his fingerprints been found on the object.

---

[44] subs.(b) preserves the common law as demonstrated by the facts in *Voisin* [1918] 1 K.B. 531.
[45] 1954 S.L.T. 177.

5

DOCUMENTARY AND REAL EVIDENCE

I. Documentary Evidence

Evidence which is placed in front of a court can take three basic forms, namely documentary evidence, real evidence or the testimony of witnesses. Real evidence is considered at the end of this chapter and oral testimony is discussed later. But documentary evidence is of considerable importance in both civil and criminal proceedings. The document may be the issue itself, a will or contract or deeds to land or it may contain information which a party wishes to put before the court as evidence of an issue in the case—correspondence, an expert's report or a record of an interview.

Reliance on documentary evidence is often worthwhile as it is regarded as having greater weight. Often the information has been compiled closer to the events and, unlike a witness, a document will not be shaken by cross-examination. A document is subject to the general criteria of admissibility, namely relevance, probative weight and avoidance of prejudice as well as subject to the exclusionary rules such as hearsay, public interest or opinion.

But there are criteria specific to documents. Just as a witness must be identified and shown to be competent in order to give oral testimony, a document must be shown to be what it purports to be. This involves two additional conditions which must be met before the document will be admitted as evidence.

    a) The first of these is known historically as "proof of contents". At common law, a document was only evidence of its contents if it was the original document, although in certain circumstances, copies or oral testimony of the contents was permitted.

    b) the second requirement is "proof of due execution". This means proof that the document was signed or written by the person by whom it purports to have been signed or written.

These conditions need to be met with regard to any document—the original document duly executed is undoubtedly the "best evidence". But, as is discussed later, these conditions have been significantly changed by statute.[1] A preliminary issue is what comes within the definition of a "document"?

---

[1] In particular, Criminal Justice Act 2003, s.133 and Civil Evidence Act 1995, s.8.

II. WHAT IS A DOCUMENT?

Everyday language would confine the term "documentary evidence" to statements recorded on some form of paper but in *Daye*,[2] Darling J. talked of a document as any "written thing capable of being evidence" and pointed out that paper has been preceded by parchment, stone, marble, clay and metal. Nowadays even the adjective "written" is too restrictive and there is an even wider meaning: *"'document' means anything in which information of any description is recorded."*[3]

For both criminal and civil proceedings, the legal definition of the term no longer bears much resemblance to its everyday meaning. Photographs,[4] audio tape,[5] microfilm,[6] all are capable of being documents as well as video tape, computer disks or a fax. In *Senior v Holdsworth Ex p. Independent Television News*,[7] the claimants sought damages against the police for assault and sought to make ITN produce film of a pop festival which had been held in Windsor Great Park. The county court rules allowed a witness to be summonsed to attend court and produce a document. The Court of Appeal held that the film was a document within those rules[8] and that a witness could be compelled to produce it in court.

Parties to a civil action must disclose all relevant documents in their possession—in *Derby & Co Ltd v Weldon (No. 9)*,[9] the court was asked to decide whether a computer database was a document for these purposes.

Derby & Co [1991] 2 All E.R. 901 at 905h–906d, *per* Vinelott J.:

The first question raised by this application is whether the database of a computer's on-line system which is recorded in back-up files is a document within the meaning of RSC Ord 24.[10] An analogous question came before Walton J in *Grant v Southwestern and County Properties Ltd*.[11] The question there was whether a tape recording of a telephone conversation was a document. In *Beneficial Finance Corp Co v Conway*[12] McInerney J had held that it was not, on the ground that, although a tape recording records information and serves a function corresponding to that of a document, it is not a document because the information is not capable of being visually inspected. Walton J took the opposite view and pointed to the absurdity of the conclusion that if two parties to

---

[2] [1908] 2 K.B. 333.
[3] Criminal Justice Act 2003, s.134(1) Civil Procedure Rules, r.31.4; cf Civil Evidence Act 1995, s.13 implementing the recommendations of the Law Commission, *The Hearsay Rule in Civil Proceedings* (1993 Law Comm No. 216). Compare these with the cumbersome approach in s.5 and s.10(1) Civil Evidence Act 1968.
[4] *Lyell v Kennedy* (No. 3) (1884) 27 Ch. D 1.
[5] *Wallace Smith Trust Co. Ltd (in liquidation) v Deloitte Haskins & Sells* [1996] 4 All E.R. 403.
[6] *Grant v Southwestern and County Properties Ltd* [1974] 2 All E.R. 465.
[7] [1975] 2 All E.R. 1009.
[8] Now Civil Procedure Rules, r.34.2.
[9] [1991] 2 All E.R. 901.
[10] Now Civil Procedure Rules, r.31.
[11] [1974] 2 All E.R. 465.
[12] [1970] V.R. 321.

litigation recorded a conversation, one on a tape recorder and one in shorthand, the one record would and the other record would not be discoverable, though both were ways of recording the same conversation and although, if the second was written in a private shorthand system, both would need a key before the message could be read. He said:

> ... the mere interposition of necessity of an instrument for decyphering the information cannot make any difference in principle. A litigant who keeps all his documents in microdot form could not avoid discovery because in order to read the information extremely powerful microscopes or other sophisticated instruments would be required. Nor again, if he kept them by means of microfilm which could not be read without the aid of a projector.

I respectfully adopt that statement of principle. It must, I think, apply a fortiori to the tape or discretionary on which material fed into a simple word processor is stored. In most businesses, that takes the place of the carbon copy of outgoing letters which used to be retained in files.

Hearsay Documents and Documents Admissible in their own Right

A party will normally introduce a document into evidence in order to rely upon the contents of that document. The document may record a state of affairs in words, whether spoken or written, or in numbers; it may do so by means of a chart or a graph; it may do so pictorially by film or photo; it may be a map or even an artist's representation. A litigant may seek to demonstrate the truth or falsity of those contents. In considering the conditions under which such documents become admissible, we must distinguish:

a) documents admissible in their own right;
b) documents containing admissible hearsay.

The requirements relating to the proof of the contents and to the proof of the proper execution of the document apply to both categories. But if the document contains hearsay, before it is admissible, it must also satisfy the conditions laid down by the Civil Evidence Act 1995 or by the Criminal Justice Act 2003 or by some other statutory exception to hearsay.

The classic statement of the rule was formulated by Cross; "an assertion other than one made by a person while giving oral evidence in the proceedings is inadmissible as evidence of any fact stated."[13] The rule against hearsay is discussed later[14] but as a general rule, documents containing a person's writing (letters, memos etc) or speech (such as a tape recording) are likely to be hearsay. But courts are increasingly faced with documents produced by mechanical devices, such as cameras, speed guns, devices that test alcohol levels in the blood, etc. These do not purport to be statements by a person but a machine recording a state of affairs. Again as a rule of thumb, they are original rather than hearsay evidence. For example, the videotape on

---

[13] Now to be found in C. Tapper, *Cross and Tapper on Evidence* (Butterworths 10th ed., 2004) at p. 578. This formula was approved by the House of Lords in *Sharp* [1988] 1 All E.R. 65 at 68b-c.
[14] see Ch.16.

which there is a visual record of an event is original evidence of that incident; a printout which details a computer's analysis of a substance is evidence of the constituent elements of that compound.[15] If the evidence is original, the jury can draw inferences from the thing itself, although they will normally be assisted by expert testimony.

In *The Statue of Liberty*,[16] a film record of a radar screen showing two ships' courses before a collision in the Thames. This was admitted as real evidence.

The Statue of Liberty [1968] 2 All E.R. 195 at 196g–h
per Sir Jocelyn Simon P.:

If tape-recordings are admissible, it seems that a photograph of radar reception is equally admissible—or indeed any other type of photograph. It would be an absurd distinction that a photograph should be admissible if the camera were operated manually by a photographer, but not if it were operated by a trip or clock mechanism. Similarly, if evidence of weather conditions were relevant, the law would affront common sense if it were to say that those could be proved by a person who looked at a barometer from time to time, but not by producing a barograph record. So, too, with other types of mechanical recordings. Again, cards from clocking-in-and-out machines are frequently admitted in accident cases. The law is now bound to take cognizance of the fact that mechanical means replace human effort.

If the radar map can be termed an "assertion" or a "statement", it is a statement by a machine automatically tracking the ships and is not a hearsay statement which must be by a person. Where a machine is being used to collect, process and output information without any human input (apart from the original building and programming of the machine), the output is original evidence.[17]

In *Wood*, the question was the origin of certain metals—were those found in the possession of the appellant the same as those which had been stolen? The chemical composition of the metals was achieved by computer calculation and the printout was adduced in evidence. Was it hearsay? The court held,[18]

Wood (1983) 76 Cr.App. R.23 at 26, *per* Lord Lane C.J.

The computer in the present case was being used as a calculator. Its programming and its use were both covered by oral evidence. But, it was argued, because the

---

[15] *Wood* (1983) 76 Cr.App.R. 23.

[16] [1968] 2 All E.R. 195—the case was decided before the Civil Evidence Act 1968 allowed the admission of much hearsay evidence in civil proceedings.

[17] This formulation might well cast doubt on the example of the 'clocking-in-and-out machine' given by Sir Jocelyn Simon P.—this is surely no different to the worker writing down the times of arrival and departure on a card. This in turn must be distinguished from machines that can recognise a palm print or thumbprint!

[18] above at 26.

computer was interposed in the course of the production of the final figures, those figures are hearsay. In our judgment this argument cannot be accepted. Witnesses, and especially expert witnesses, frequently and properly give factual evidence of the results of a physical exercise which involves the use of some equipment, device or machine. Take a weighing machine; the witness steps on to the machine and reads a weight off the dial, receives a ticket printed with the weight or, even, hears a recorded voice saying it. None of this involves hearsay evidence. The witness may have to be cross-examined as to whether he kept one foot on the ground; the accuracy of the machine may have to be investigated. But this does not alter the character of the evidence which has been given.

In *Castle v Cross*,[19] the defendant breathed several times into an Intoximeter, a machine for measuring the alcohol level in blood. It produced a printout which stated that the machine had not received a sufficient sample in order to carry out an analysis. It was held by the Divisional Court that this printout was admissible evidence against the accused on a charge of failing to supply a breath specimen. In *Sophocleous v Ringer*,[20] a scientist gave evidence of analyses of a blood sample by gas chromatography to decide on blood alcohol level, again carried out by computer. The Divisional Court held that the scientist was merely using the computer as a tool and was entitled to refresh her memory from the computer figures.

A visual recording is also non-hearsay documentary evidence—in *Taylor v Chief Constable of Cheshire*,[21] a video was made of a shoplifter. Policemen were able to identify the accused from the video. Later the recording was erased by accident. The officers gave evidence of what they had seen on the video and Taylor was convicted. The video itself was direct evidence and the witnesses testified as to what they had seen on the video with their own eyes.

Taylor v Chief Constable of Cheshire [1987]1 All E.R. 225 at 230b *per* Ralph Gibson L.J.:

. . . [the respondent prosecutor] submitted that once it was proved that a video recording was a recording of what a machine detected and reproduced at the time and place in question, evidence for witnesses of what they say they saw on the recording is not different in law in point of principle from evidence of witnesses who claim to have seen the events by direct vision. She contended that all the arguments advanced on behalf of this appellant are in truth arguments properly directed at weight and not at admissibility. I think she adds that they were present to the mind of the justices, and that they were fully taken into account. She has referred the court to no further authority.

In substance I accept the contention made for the respondent. For my part I can see no effective distinction so far as concerns admissibility between a direct view of the action of an alleged shoplifter by a security officer and a view of those activities by the officer on the video display unit of a camera, or a view of those activities on a recording of what the camera recorded. He who saw may describe what he saw

---

[19] [1985] 1 All E.R. 87.
[20] [1987] Crim.L.R. 422.
[21] [1987] 1 All E.R. 225.

because . . . it is relevant evidence provided that that which is seen on the camera or recording is connected by sufficient evidence to the alleged actions of the accused at the time and place in question. As with the witness who saw directly, so with him who viewed a display or recording, the weight and reliability of his evidence will depend upon assessment of all relevant considerations, including the clarity of the recording, its length, and, where identification is in issue, the witness's prior knowledge of the person said to be identified, in accordance with well established principles . . .

In *Neville*,[22] the evidence adduced was the itemised record by a phone company of the calls made from a mobile phone which the court accepted as original evidence and this was confirmed by the House of Lords judgment in *Shephard*,[23] where the evidence involved the use of computerised checkouts using bar codes to identify the item being bought. The till roll showed no trace of the unique barcode on the items alleged to have been stolen by the accused. This was original evidence that the item had not been paid for.[24]

In all of these cases, the information is generated by the machine. This must be distinguished from information originally coming from a person but being stored in the machine. The printout from a word-processing programme remains hearsay as do statements on audio-tape or a videotaped re-enactment of the crime as in *Li Shu-ling*.[25] Such an enactment by the accused was clearly hearsay by conduct[26] but it was also an admission and as such is admissible. The Privy Council held that a re-enactment in words during interrogation was admissible and there was no reason in principle why re-enactment on film was not equally admissible.[27]

III. PROOF OF CONTENTS

Before discussing the current position in civil and criminal proceedings, it is necessary to outline briefly the common law rules. The brevity is justified as these are now simply residual—for example, where a document and any copies have been lost, it may be necessary to prove the contents by oral evidence from a witness who has seen the document.

A. *The Common Law—the Primary Evidence Rule and its Exceptions*

The basic rule is that where a party wishes to rely on the contents of a document as direct evidence, they must adduce primary evidence of the

[22] [1991] Crim.L.R. 288; *Spiby* [1991] Crim.L.R. 199.
[23] [1993] 1 All E.R. 225.
[24] The other problem faced by the courts in these cases was whether the conditions laid down by s.69 Police and Criminal Evidence Act 1984 for the admissibility of computer-generated documents applied. This section was repealed by s.60 Youth Justice and Criminal Evidence Act 1999—see Ch.18.
[25] [1988] 3 All E.R. 138.
[26] As it was in *Quinn, Bloom* [1961] 3 All E.R. 88.
[27] Such re-enactments are admissible in Australia (*R. v Lowery and King* [1972] V.L.R. 554), Canada (*R. v Tookey and Stephenson* (1981)) 58 C.C.C. 2d 421) and in the USA (*People v Dabb* (1948) 32 Cal. 2d 491).

contents of that document. It was a rule that arose when documents were mainly handwritten and there was a greater risk of fraud and forgery, let alone of the potential inaccuracy of the copy.

In *MacDonnell v Evans*,[28] the defence produced a letter purporting to have been written by a witness called by the claimant. That witness was asked in cross-examination whether he had written that letter in response to another letter accusing the witness of forgery. The prior letter was not produced and defence counsel was thus seeking to prove its contents by secondary evidence, namely the oral testimony of the witness. The question was disallowed since that letter had to be proved by production of the original.

MacDonnell v Evans (1852) 11 CB 930 at 943, *per* Maule J.:

It is a general rule . . . that, if you want to get at the contents of a written document, the proper way is to produce it, if you can. That is a rule in which the common sense of mankind concurs. If the paper is in the possession of the party who seeks to have the jury infer something from its contents, he should let them see it. That is the general and ordinary rule; the contents can only be proved by the writing itself. If the document does not exist, or the party seeking to show its contents cannot get at it, he is at liberty to give secondary evidence, because in that case no better is to be had . . . Here the very form of the question, 'Did you not write that letter in answer to a letter containing so and so?' assumes that there is another letter in existence, the production of which would be the best proof of its contents. There was nothing to show why that letter was not forthcoming . . .

In common law, the original of a document can be in different forms.

a) *Signed duplicates and signed copies.* These are equivalent to originals.[29] Unsigned versions or photocopies would not be treated as originals where the issue is the contents of the signed copy. Thus in *Regan*,[30] the original of a telegram was the written message handed in at the Post Office and not the message as delivered. However, if the issue is, for example, the contents of a pamphlet handed out in the street, any of the copies could be treated as the original.

b) *Enrolled documents.* If the original document has to be enrolled by being filed in a court or other public office, an official copy is sufficient as primary evidence of its contents.

c) *Admission of contents.* Where there is an admission (whether formal or informal, oral or written) made by a party about the contents of a private document, this admission is primary evidence of the contents of that document. In *Slatterie v Pooley*,[31] the claimant sued on a covenant which

---

[28] (1852) 11 C.B. 930.
[29] *Forbes v Samuel* [1913] 3 K.B. 706.
[30] (1887) 16 Cox 203.
[31] (1840) 6 M. & W. 664.

created an indemnity in respect of certain debts, covered in a schedule to the deed. The schedule was inadmissible but there was an oral admission by the defendant that a particular debt was included in that schedule and that admission was binding on the defendant.

At common law, there are exceptions to the primary evidence rule which allow secondary evidence of the contents of a document to be given, by producing a copy or giving oral evidence. These are as follows:

a) *Failure to produce by other party.* Where the opponent is given notice and fails to produce the original document, a party is entitled to rely on secondary evidence. A party cannot prevent an opponent from using a document by withholding the original nor can they later rely on the original if secondary evidence proves to be at variance with original document. In criminal proceedings, an accused cannot be compelled to produce a document as any failure would be excused because of the privilege against self-incrimination. But a refusal to produce after notice can lead to secondary evidence being given. In *Collins*,[32] the accused was charged with deception offences, having cashed a cheque on an account that he knew to be closed. He was called on to produce the letter closing the account but refused. As a result a carbon copy would have been admissible on behalf of the Crown, although the conviction was quashed since the witness had not proved that it was a true copy. This has now to be read in the light of s.133 of the Criminal Justice Act 2003 which would permit the admission of the copy. But if no copy were in existence, the bank manager would be permitted at common law to give oral evidence that such a letter was in fact written.

b) *Lawful refusal to produce by a stranger.* Strangers to the proceedings may be served with a witness summons, ordering them to produce a document. That person may lawfully refuse to produce such documents: for example, where the documents are privileged through legal professional privilege or public interest immunity; where diplomatic immunity exists or where the person is outside the jurisdiction.[33] If the refusal is lawful, secondary evidence of the contents of the document is admissible.

c) *Lost documents.* Where a party is seeking to introduce secondary evidence of the contents of a document because that document has been lost, it is necessary to show that all reasonable steps to search for that document have been taken. In *Brewster v Sewell*,[34] there had been a fire at the claimant's premises in 1813 and the insurance company had paid out on the policy. Afterwards a new policy was taken out. The claimant had reason to testify about the original policy but could not produce the original. He gave evidence that he had searched but had been unable to find it. Secondary evidence of the contents was permitted.

---

[32] (1960) 44 Cr.App.R. 170.
[33] *Kilgour v Owen* (1889) 88 L.T.J. 7.
[34] (1820) 3 B.&Ald. 297.

Brewster v Sewel (1820) 3 B.&Ald. 297 at 299 *per* Abbott C.J.:

All evidence is to be considered with regard to the matter with respect to which it is produced. Now it appears to be a very different thing, whether the subject of inquiry be a useless paper, which may reasonably be supposed to be lost, or whether it be an important document which the party might have an interest in keeping, and for the non-production of which no satisfactory reason is assigned. This is the case of a policy of insurance by which a company undertook to indemnify the plaintiff against losses by fire. A fire took place, and a loss was paid. That having taken place, the original policy became mere waste paper. There was no reason to suppose that the policy could, at any future time, be called for, to answer any reasonable purpose whatever . . . This being a case, therefore, where the loss or destruction of the paper may almost be presumed, very slight evidence of its loss or destruction is sufficient . . .

However, as a result of *Masquerade Music v Springsteen*,[35] the limits of this common law exception may no longer have relevance and the question of introducing secondary evidence of lost documents may now be a matter of weight rather than of admissibility. In that case, Parker L.J. reviewed the common law and concluded,

Masquerade Music v Springsteen [2001] E.M.L.R 25, *per* Jonathan Parker L.J.:

'..Where the party seeking to adduce the secondary evidence could readily produce the document, it may be expected that (absent some special circumstances) the court will decline to admit the secondary evidence on the ground that it is worthless. At the other extreme, where the party seeking to adduce the secondary evidence genuinely cannot produce the document, it may be expected that (absent some special circumstances) the court will admit the secondary evidence and attach such weight to it as it considers appropriate in all the circumstances.'

d) *Production of the original is impractical.* In *Owner v Bee Hive Spinning*,[36] there was a notice giving the times of meal breaks which was affixed to the wall of a factory. Statute required that it remained fixed there at all times and secondary evidence of its contents was admissible. Another example might be photographic evidence of the "tags" of graffiti artists facing criminal damage charges. Such tags might well be on walls, bridges or even tube trains.

e) *Proof of public and judicial documents.*[37] At common law, a range of public documents can be proved by copies under this principle.[38] However there are also many statutes which regulate the proof of public documents.

---

[35] [2001] E.M.L.R. 25.
[36] [1914] 1 K.B. 105.
[37] Often such documents are also hearsay but come under s.118 Criminal Justice Act 2003 as well as forming an exception to the primary evidence rule—see Ch.17.
[38] *Mortimer v M'Callan* (1840) 6 M.&W. 58.

(i) *Legislation*: private and local and personal Acts of Parliament are proved by the Queen's Printer's or Stationery Office copies.[39] Judicial notice is taken of all public Acts under s.3 of the Interpretation Act 1978. As a general rule, the content of foreign law cannot be proved by the production of the record but has to be proved by oral testimony of an expert witness.[40]

(ii) *Statutory instruments*: these are proved by Queen's Printer's or Stationery Office copies.[41]

(iii) *By-laws*: these are proved by certified printed copies. That is, a copy signed and certified as correct by officials having custody of the originals.[42] This method is also used in the case of entries in registers[43] or company proceedings.

(iv) *Judicial proceedings*: in the superior court, these may be proved by office copies, that is, copies made by officials having custody of the documents and sealed with the seal of the court[44]; in the county court, records can be proved by certified copies[45]; in the magistrates' court, r.6.4 of the Criminal Procedure Rules provides that the register of a magistrates' court or any document purporting to be an extract from the register and to be certified by the clerk as a true extract, shall be admissible as evidence of the proceedings of the court.

(v) *Convictions and acquittals*: these are proved under s.73 of the Police and Criminal Evidence Act 1984.

PACE 1984, s.73:

73—(1) Where in any proceedings the fact that a person has in the United Kingdom been convicted or acquitted of any offence otherwise than by a Service court is admissible in evidence, it may be proved by producing a certificate of conviction or, as the case may be, of acquittal relating to that offence, and proving that the person named in the certificate as having been convicted or acquitted of the offence is the person whose conviction or acquittal is to be proved.

(vi) *Public records*: records in the Public Record Office are proved by copies certified by the Keeper of the Public Records.[46]

Two further provisions are of importance. First, s.1 of the Evidence Act 1845 provides that, where a document may be proved by a certified, signed or

---

[39] Evidence Act 1845, s.3; Documentary Evidence Act 1882, s.2.
[40] *Sussex Peerage Case* (1844) 11 Cl. and Finn. 85.
[41] Documentary Evidence Act 1868, s.2; Documentary Evidence Act 1882, s.2; Statutory Instruments Act 1946, s.3.
[42] Local Government Act 1972, s.238.
[43] For example, births, deaths and marriages under Births and Deaths Registration Act 1953, s.34.
[44] See also Supreme Court Act 1981, s.132.
[45] County Courts Act 1984, s.12.
[46] Public Records Act 1958, s.9.

sealed copy, any copy bearing the signature, seal or stamp should be admissible without any further proof. In other words the copy is presumed to be authentic. Secondly, under s.14 of the Evidence Act 1851, where there is a public document not covered by a statutory provision, a certified or examined copy will be admissible evidence.

Evidence Act 1851. s.14:

14. Whenever any book or other document is of such a public nature as to be admissible in evidence on its mere production from proper custody, and no statute exists which renders its contents provable by means of a copy, any copy thereof or extract therefrom shall be admissible in evidence in any court of justice, or before any person now or hereafter having by law or by consent of parties authority to hear, receive, and examine evidence, provided it be proved to be an examined copy or extract, or provided it purport to be signed and certified as a true copy or extract by the officer to whose custody the original is entrusted, and which officer is hereby required to furnish such certified copy or extract to any person applying at a reasonable time for the same, upon payment of a reasonable sum for the same.

The Death of "Best Evidence"?

Whether secondary evidence of a document can ever be excluded on the grounds that it is not the best evidence must be doubted. The policy of the courts appears to be that secondary evidence of originals will always be admissible and that it is simply a matter of weight.

Masquerade Music v Springsteen [2001] E.M.L.R. 25, *per* Jonathan Parker L.J.:

85. In my judgment, the time has now come when it can be said with confidence that the best evidence rule, long on its deathbed, has finally expired. In every case where a party seeks to adduce secondary evidence of the contents of a document, it is a matter for the court to decide, in the light of all the circumstances of the case, what (if any) weight to attach to that evidence. Where the party seeking to adduce the secondary evidence could readily produce the document, it may be expected that (absent some special circumstances) the court will decline to admit the secondary evidence on the ground that it is worthless. At the other extreme, where the party seeking to adduce the secondary evidence genuinely cannot produce the document, it may be expected that (absent some special circumstances) the court will admit the secondary evidence and attach such weight to it as it considers appropriate in all the circumstances. In cases falling between those two extremes, it is for the court to make a judgment as to whether in all the circumstances any weight should be attached to the secondary evidence. Thus, the "admissibility" of secondary evidence of the contents of documents is, in my judgment, entirely dependent upon whether or not any weight is to be attached to that evidence. And whether or not any weight is to be attached to such secondary evidence is a matter for the court to decide, taking into account all the circumstances of the particular case.

B. *Criminal Proceedings*

The primary evidence rule and its exceptions are no longer of much relevance in criminal proceedings. The facts in *Kajala v Noble*[47] show how the issue used to intrude—the defendant was charged with using threatening behaviour likely to cause a breach of the peace. A prosecution witness who was familiar with the accused testified that he had recognised him on a BBC television news programme. The BBC supplied a video cassette recording of the incident but not the original footage. The normal rule at that time was that a party seeking to rely upon the contents of a document must adduce primary evidence of that document, generally the original document itself. Was the video cassette copy good enough? Here the copy was admitted into evidence. Ackner L.J. avoided the "best evidence" rule by holding that it was confined to written documents in the strict sense and did not apply to tapes or films. This was not a narrower definition of "document" for the general purposes of the common law but simply for the purpose of the "best evidence" rule in criminal proceedings.

Kajala v Noble might have provided significant problems with the developments in IT storage systems. But now this issue is governed by statute—where a party seeks to rely on a document, a copy will be sufficient under the provisions of s.133 of the Criminal Justice Act 2003.

Criminal Justice Act 2003. s.133:

133 Where a statement in a document is admissible as evidence in criminal proceedings, the statement may be proved by producing either—
a) the document; or
b) (whether or not that document exists) a copy of that document, or of the material part of it,
authenticated in whatever way the court may approve.

The predecessor of s.133[48] in effect abolished the common law rule. As a result, a party is now entitled to introduce a copy of the document, regardless of whether the original exists, as long as that copy is properly authenticated by the court. Furthermore the section does not allow the argument that it is not a direct copy as it is immaterial how many removes there are between the copy and the original. On its wording, the section applies to all documents, whether the document could be characterised as original evidence or hearsay. In *Kajala*, the "document", *i.e.* the film, was original evidence and, had s.133 been in force, a videotape copy would have been admissible. If these provisions apply in all cases where documentary evidence (be it hearsay or not) is adduced, this leaves no scope in criminal proceedings for the operation of a 'primary evidence' rule.

---

[47] (1982) 75 Cr.App.R. 149.
[48] Criminal Justice Act 1988, s.27.

But the section might be interpreted in a narrower manner. S.133 is contained within ch.2 of Pt 11 of the Criminal Justice Act 2003. This chapter is clearly labelled hearsay and it might be legitimately argued that s.133 should be read as applying only to the proof of documents containing hearsay and not to the proof of documents containing original evidence. Such authority as exists suggests a broader approach. In *Foxley*,[49] copies of credit notes were advanced as evidence of certain corrupt payments. These notes were not hearsay statements but original evidence of the payments themselves and yet copies were permitted to be adduced in evidence. Commenting, Professor Smith argues that the section is concerned, not with hearsay, but with the best evidence rule, allowing admission of copies authenticated in such manner as the court may approve. He suggests persuasively that the question of authenticity is substantially the same whether the document is tendered as hearsay or as direct evidence.

The general thrust has been one of liberalisation so that copies of documents are admissible without accounting for the absence of the original document. This includes copies of copies. The 1988 Act stated that it was immaterial how many removes there were between the copy produced in court and the original. This provision is missing in the 2003 Act but presumably because it was thought unnecessary. Now copies are freely admitted and they can be authenticated in any way acceptable to the court. Authentification itself can be through written statements and these do not have to be by the maker of the copy, as is required in Scotland.[50]

Even where s.133 applies, it does not override certain common law or statutory provisions.

a) At common law, the contents of a document may be proved not merely by copies of the document but by other forms of secondary evidence, including oral evidence. Where the original document and any copies are lost or are otherwise unavailable, s.133 does not apply. The common law comes into its own as it allows other secondary evidence to be admissible. In *Nazeer*,[51] there was a complex fraud carried out by a postmaster. Part of the evidence was contained on computerised records, held on a computer which could not provide a printout. Witnesses testified as to what was shown on the computer screen.

Nazeer [1998] Crim.L.R. 750, *per* Beldam L.J.:

..[the appellant] in reply drew on s 27 of the Criminal Justice Act 1988, a section intended to make provision for the case where in complicated fraud cases, photocopies

---

[49] [1995] Crim.L.R. 636.
[50] Civil Evidence Act (Scotland) 1988, s.6.
[51] [1998] Crim.L.R. 750 *per* Beldam L.J.

of documents had been put in evidence, and it had been argued that they were inadmissible. It provides that the statement contained in a document admissible in criminal proceedings can be proved either by the production of a document or any copy of the document, and that it is immaterial how many removes there are between the copy and the original. The wording of that section, is in our view, permissive; it is not exclusive and in a case such as the present, where the production of the 'document' itself or indeed a copy of the document is wholly impracticable, if not to say impossible, the Court should fall back on the common law rule that there are no degrees of secondary evidence. If secondary evidence is admissible, as in our view it is, it may be given in a number of ways. In this case, the evidence of [the witnesses] was in our view admissible, and that ground of appeal fails.[52]

The conditions for the admission of such evidence are the same in criminal and in civil proceedings, as outlined in *Brewster v Sewell*, discussed above.

b) There are a range of statutory as well as common law exceptions to the general rule, mainly relating to public and judicial documents, including bankers' books. These permit proof of contents by copies but such copies normally have to be in a specific form. Such specificity is unnecessary under s.133 but is not overridden by that section.

C. *Civil Proceedings*

As with criminal proceedings, the primary evidence rule has now limited application in civil proceedings as a result of section of the Civil Evidence Act 1995.

Civil Evidence Act 1995. s.8:

8.—(1) Where a statement contained in a document is admissible as evidence in civil proceedings, it may be proved–
a) by the production of that document; or
b) (whether or not that document is still in existence) by the production of a copy of that document, or of the material part of it,
authenticated in such manner as the court may approve.
(2) It is immaterial for this purpose how many removes there are between a copy and the original.[53]

This section applies to all documents, whether original or containing hearsay statements, although commentators have treated its predecessor, s.6(1) of the Civil Evidence Act 1968,[54] as restricted to the proof of documents

---

[52] Lawtel transcript, *per* Bedlam L.J.
[53] "Document" and "copy" are defined in Civil Evidence Act 1995, s.13.
[54] Law Commission, *op.cit.* para.4.37.

containing hearsay statements. But to restrict s.8 in this fashion would be absurd: the 1995 Act abolishes the hearsay rule in civil proceedings and there will be virtually no difference between the admissibility of hearsay and non-hearsay statements. It would be counter- productive to have different conditions for the proof of the contents of documents admissible in their own right as opposed to the conditions for the proof of contents of documents which contain hearsay statements. Moreover the argument that s.8 is applicable to all documents gains weight from the fact that it is obviously modelled on s.27 of the Criminal Justice Act 1988 which, as has been argued above, is of general application.

A document, whether containing original or hearsay evidence, can be proved by producing a copy, no matter at how many removes from the original that copy is. This resolves some doubts as to whether a copy of a copy was admissible.[55] Nor is the definition of "copy" limited as the extended interpretation of 'copy' is to be found in s.13 of the Civil Evidence Act 1995, ". . . 'copy', in relation to a document, means anything onto which information recorded in the document has been copied, by whatever means and whether directly or indirectly".

The conclusion from this is that the primary evidence rule in civil proceedings has been as undermined as in criminal proceedings. But, even if s.8 is given this broad interpretation, it does not override certain common law or statutory provisions.

a) At common law, the contents of a document may be proved not merely by copies of the document but by other forms of secondary evidence, including oral evidence. As was seen with regard to criminal proceedings, where the document and any copies are lost, other secondary evidence might be admissible. But, as was seen in *Masquerade Music v Springsteen*,[56] the limits of these common law exceptions may no longer have relevance and the question of secondary evidence may now be a matter of weight rather than of admissibility.

b) There are a range of statutory exceptions to the general rule, mainly relating to public and judicial documents, including bankers' books, which lay down criteria for admissibility of such documents.

D. *Bankers' Books*

With the exception of the records of the Bank of England, the records of banks are private documents. Production in court of the original books in the 19th century would have been at the very least inconvenient to the everyday business of banks. By s.3 of the Bankers Books Evidence Act 1879, copies were permitted.

---

[55] *Everingham v Roundell* (1838) 2 Mood. & R. 138.
[56] (2001) E.M.L.R. 25.

3. Subject to the provisions of this Act, a copy of any entry in a banker's book shall in all legal proceedings be received as prima facie evidence of such entry, and of the matters, transactions, and accounts therein recorded.[57]

Under s.5, copies of entries are admissible as long as they are examined copies. An officer of the bank would need to prove the copy but would not have to prove the particular entry.

Under s.4, the 'book' must be one of the ordinary books in the control and custody of the bank and the entry must be made in the usual course of business. This has been developed with technological change—in *Barker v Wilson*,[58] it was held that microfilmed records (and presumably computerised databases) were sufficient and this is now incorporated in s.9 of the 1879 Act by the Banking Act 1979. But this relaxation of the primary evidence rule only applies to 'bankers' books' and does not apply to other banking business. This is seen in *Dadson*,[59] where the defendant was charged with offences relating to the misuse of a cheque card. It was necessary to prove the accused's knowledge about the state of his account and copies of the bank's letters to the defendant about the state of his account were admitted in reliance on the 1879 Act. The fact that such letters were sent would be admissible evidence of the defendant's mens rea[60] but they were not admissible under s.3 as these were not 'books' even under the broad interpretation employed in *Barker v Wilson*. Nowadays, under ss.117 and 133 of the Criminal Justice Act 2003, notice to the defendant to produce the originals would be necessary and, if that failed to produce the letters, production of copies from the bank would be possible.

In civil proceedings, a similar result was reached in *Williams v Williams*,[61] where a wife sought inspection of her husband's bank account under s.7 of the Act, including bundles of paid cheques and paying-in slips as these would reveal more information than a bank statement. The Court of Appeal held that the 1879 Act did not extend to paid cheques and paying-in slips. Such documents should be admissible in evidence under s.1 of the Civil Evidence Act 1995.

Documents are covered by the 1879 Act are also admissible under the provisions of the Civil Evidence Act 1995 and the Criminal Justice Act 2003 but the copies of bankers' books must conform with the slightly more rigorous conditions of the 1879 Act. But the scope of the Act is particularly interesting because of the extremely wide power of inspection of bankers' books contained in s.7.

Bankers Books Evidence Act 1879. s.7:

7. On the application of any party to a legal proceedings a court or judge may order that such party be at liberty to inspect and take copies of any entries in a banker's

---

[57] This section also creates an exception to hearsay as the entry is prima facie admissible evidence of the matters it records.
[58] [1980] 2 All E.R. 81.
[59] (1983) 77 Cr.App.R. 91.
[60] *Collins* (1960) 44 Cr.App.R. 170.
[61] [1987] 3 All E.R. 257; Howglen Ltd (2001) 1 All E.R. 376.

book for any of the purposes of such proceedings. An order under this section may be made either with or without summoning the bank or any other party, and shall be served on the bank three clear days before the same is to be obeyed, unless the court or judge otherwise directs.

Any party to criminal or civil proceedings can inspect and take copies of any relevant entry in a banker's book. This power can be exercised *ex parte* and does not even require notice to the bank or any other party affected. The account to be inspected may be that of a person not party to the case. In *R. v Andover Justices Ex p. Rhodes*,[62] the accused was charged with theft and told the police that the money was in her husband's bank account. The Divisional Court upheld a s.7 order in respect of that account, noting in addition that the husband was not a competent witness against his wife. However s.7 orders should only be made in exceptional circumstances where the public interest outweighs the interest in the confidentiality of banking transactions. *Grossman*,[63] limits it to inspecting bankers' books within the jurisdiction.

Williams v Summerfield [1972] 2 All E.R. 1334 at 1337g–1338g
per Lord Widgery C.J.:

So far as civil proceedings are concerned a working rule has long since been established, and it is conveniently expressed in *Re Bankers' Books Evidence Act 1879, R v Bono*[64] . . . The effect of the judgment in Bono's case and other authorities is that the courts have set their face against s.7 being used as a kind of searching enquiry or fishing expedition beyond the ordinary rules of discovery.

In civil proceedings the normal approach to the use of s.7 is that documents which would not be discoverable under the ordinary rules are not to be disclosed by a side wind, as it were, by the application of s.7. It is quite clear that the section applies to ordinary criminal proceedings . . .

On the other hand, one must I think recognise that an order under s.7 can be a very serious interference with the liberty of the subject. It can be a gross invasion of privacy; it is an order which clearly must only be made after the most careful thought and on the clearest grounds . . .

I think that in criminal proceedings, justices should warn themselves of the importance of the step which they are taking in making an order under s.7; should always recognise the care with which the jurisdiction should be exercised; should take into account amongst other things whether there is other evidence in the possession of the prosecution to support the charge; or whether the application under s.7 is a fishing expedition in the hope of finding some material on which the charge can be hung.

. . . if [justices] are always alive to the requirement of not making the order extend beyond the true purposes of the charge before them, and if in consequence they limit the period of the disclosure of the bank account to a period which is strictly relevant to the charge before them; and if finally they recognise the importance of considering whether there is other evidence in the possession of the prosecution before they provide the bank account as perhaps the only evidence, I feel . . . they will in fact produce a situation in which the section is used properly, wisely and in support of the interests of justice, and will not allow it to be used as an instrument of oppression . . .

---

[62] [1980] Crim.L.R. 644.
[63] (1981) 73 Cr.App.R. 302.
[64] (1913) 29 T.L.R. 635.

Courts should only make an order under s.7 under 'careful consideration' and only when it is to strengthen an existing case. In *R. v Nottingham Justices Ex p. Lynn*,[65] it was stated that applications under s.7 should not be used as fishing expeditions to create a case.

IV. PROOF OF DUE EXECUTION

Producing the document itself (or secondary evidence of it) is one matter. It is also necessary to prove that it was made at the time and in the manner alleged by the person adducing the document as evidence. In other words, a proper foundation must be laid.

Demonstrating authenticity, showing that the document is what it purports to be, becomes increasingly difficult with advances in technology—false documents and records can be created or photographs can be digitally altered. While computer-generated information should be treated similarly to other records, its weight depends on its reliability and parties might need to provide information as to the security of their computer system. Initially, in both criminal and civil proceedings, the proper functioning of the machine had to be proved to the court under the provisions of s.69 of the Police and Criminal Evidence Act 1984[66] and s.5 of the Civil Evidence Act 1968. The former was repealed and not replaced by s.60 of the Youth Justice and Criminal Evidence Act 1999 and a similar fate befell s.5 under the Civil Evidence Act 1995.[67] These provisions were not to be resolved by creating new and inevitably complex conditions of admissibility. Computerised records are now admissible in the same manner as other records.

The common law had survived without guidelines for verifying these, non-written, forms of document, although a witness should testify to the circumstances in which a security video was recorded, a photo was taken or news film produced.

Law Commission Report The Hearsay Rule in Civil Proceedings
(1993 Law Comm No.216)

It is interesting to compare the technical manner in which the admissibility of computer-generated records has developed, compared with cases concerning other forms of sophisticated technologically produced evidence, for example, radar records.[68] In the *Statue of Liberty* case radar records, produced without human involvement and reproduced in photographic form, were held to be admissible to establish how a collision of two ships occurred. It was held that this was 'real' evidence, no different in kind from a monitored tape recording of a conversation.

[65] (1984) 79 Cr.App.R. 238.
[66] See its operation in *Shephard* [1993] 1 All E.R. 225.
[67] See the arguments for abolition in Law Commission, 1993 *op.cit.* paras 3.14–3.21.
[68] Statue of Liberty, above.

Furthermore, in these cases, no extra tests of reliability need to be met and the common law rebuttable presumption is applied, that the machine was in order at the material time. The same presumption[69] has been applied to intoximeter printouts.

In this, the Law Commission suggests that there is a rebuttable presumption[70] that machinery is in proper working order. There is authority supporting such a presumption—that traffic lights and speedometers[71] were working properly at the time. Indeed this is reinforced by s.129(2) of the Criminal Justice Act 2003 which talks of "... the presumption that a mechanical device has been properly set or calibrated."

The authenticity can be admitted by opponent: in civil proceedings "..a party shall be deemed to admit the authenticity of a document disclosed to him under Part 31 (disclosure and inspection of documents) unless he serves notice that he wishes the document to be proved at trial";[72] and in criminal proceedings under s.10 of the Criminal Justice Act 1967.

Where the document is a more traditional, written document, the common law has more specific, positive, demands in relation to proof of handwriting or proof of attestation.

a) *Evidence of handwriting.* It is necessary to prove that a letter, a contract or a lease was written or signed by the person that purported to write or sign it. This can be done:

    (i) by direct evidence by the signatory, witnesses or someone who saw the execution of the document;
    (ii) by the opinion of a non-expert who is familiar with the handwriting in question. In *Doe d. Mudd v Suckermore*;[73]

    He did not see him sign it; nor has he ever seen him write; but this is professedly immaterial, if he has had other adequate means of obtaining a knowledge of his hand . . . The clerk who constantly read the letters, the broker who has ever consulted upon them, is as competent to judge whether another signature is that of the writer of the letters, as the merchant to whom they were addressed. The servant who has habitually carried letters addressed by me to others has an opportunity of obtaining a knowledge of my writing though he never saw me write, or received a letter from me . . .[74]

    (iii) by means of the Criminal Procedure Act 1865;

    8. Comparison of a disputed writing with any writing proved to the satisfaction of the judge to be genuine shall be permitted to be made by witnesses; and such writings, and the evidence of witnesses respecting the same, may be submitted to the court and jury as evidence of the genuineness or otherwise of the writing in dispute.

[69] *Castle v Cross* [1985] 1 All E.R. 87.
[70] This could only place an evidential burden on the opposing party.
[71] *Nicholas v Penny* [1950] 2 All E.R. 89.
[72] Civil Procedure Rules r.32.19(1).
[73] (1837) 5 Ad. & El. 703.
[74] *ibid.* at 739 *per* Lord Denman C.J.

This is applicable in civil or criminal proceedings. In *Ewing*,[75] the Court of Appeal had to decide on the meaning of the phrase "satisfaction of the judge".

Ewing [1983] 2 All E.R. 645, *per* O'Connor L.J. at 652j–653d:

In our judgment, the words in s.8 of the 1865 Act, 'any writing proved to the satisfaction of the judge to be genuine', do not say anything about the standard of proof to be used, but direct that it is the judge, and not the jury, who is to decide, and the standard of proof is governed by common law . . . It follows that when the section is applied in civil cases, the civil standard of proof is used, and when it is applied in criminal cases, the criminal standard should be used . . .

. . . We hold that in a criminal trial, where handwriting is to be used for comparison under s.8, it should be proved to the satisfaction of the judge to be genuine, and the standard of proof should be the ordinary criminal standard, namely proof beyond reasonable doubt.

'. . . with any writing, proved . . . to be genuine' includes photocopies.[76] Expert witnesses are permitted to state opinion on authorship and juries should not be invited to make comparison without expert assistance—as in *Tilley*[77] where jurors were supplied with photographs and a magnifying glass! But jurors should also not be directed to accept inevitably the evidence of an expert witness, even where that is uncontradicted, although there is a fine line for the judge to draw and they must not invite juries to disregard such testimony in favour of their own unaided lay opinion.

b) *Proof of attestation.* Due execution sometimes requires witnesses to the signatures on the document. At common law, one of the attesting witnesses should be called to prove attestation but this rigorous condition disappeared with s.3 of the Evidence Act 1938 which now allows such documents to be proved by other means.

Evidence Act 1938, s.3:

3. Subject as hereinafter provided, in any proceedings, whether civil or criminal, an instrument to the validity of which attestation is requisite may, instead of being proved by an attesting witness, be proved in the manner in which it may be proved if no attesting witness were alive;

Provided that nothing in this section shall apply to proof of wills or other testamentary documents.

Wills remain an exception. To prove the due execution of a will at common law still requires one of the attesting witnesses to testify. An attesting witness is a witness of the court and can be cross-examined or contradicted even by the party seeking to rely on the will. Such a witness cannot claim legal

---

[75] [1983] 2 All E.R. 645 overruling *Angeli* [1978] 3 All E.R. 950.
[76] *Lockheed-Arabia v Owen* [1993] 3 All E.R. 641.
[77] [1961] 3 All E.R. 406.

privilege. Only if the attesting witnesses are dead, mad, beyond jurisdiction or untraceable can the document be proved by other means such as proof of handwriting of one of the witnesses or testimony by someone who saw the will signed, although not an attesting witness themselves. Once the will contains the signatures of the deceased and the witness, the presumption of due execution would prevail.[78]

In contrast to these positive requirements for authentification, there are some exceptions:

c) *Presumptions:*

(i) *Public documents:* it is necessary to distinguish public from private documents. For public documents, mere production of an admissible copy is normally sufficient as the statutes, such as those mentioned above, which provide for the admissibility of the copy, often dispense with the need to prove due execution. This reflects a common law rebuttable presumption that official documents which *prima facie* are properly executed are assumed to be in fact properly executed in the absence of the party adversely affected by such a document producing evidence to the contrary.

(ii) *Ancient private documents:* for private documents, a presumption that they have been properly executed only arises when the document is shown to over 20 years old[79] and has been in proper custody for that period. Proper custody does not require proof that the document was in the best and most proper place, as long as the custody was reasonable and natural in the circumstances. In *Meath (Bishop) v Winchester (Marquis)*,[80] documents which had belonged to a dead bishop and which should have gone to his successor were found amongst his private papers held by his family. Was this "proper custody"?

Meath (Bishop) v Winchester (Marquis) (1836) 3 Bing. N.C. 183 at 201 *per* Tindal C.J.:

These documents were found in a place in which, and under the care of persons with whom, papers of Bishop Dopping might naturally and reasonably be expected to be found; and that is precisely the custody which gives authenticity to documents found within it; for it is not necessary that they should be found in the best and most proper place of deposit. If documents continue in such custody there never would be

---

[78] *Sherrington v Sherrington* [2005] EWCA Civ 326; The Times, March 24, 2005.
[79] At common law, the period was 30 years but 20 years was substituted by the Evidence Act 1938.
[80] (1836) 3 Bing. N.C. 183.

any question as to their authenticity; but it is when documents are found other than in their proper place of deposit that investigation commences, whether it was reasonable and natural under the circumstances in the particular case, to expect that they should have been in the place where they are actually found; for it is obvious that whilst there can only be one place of deposit strictly and absolutely proper, there may be various and many that are reasonable and probable . . .

(iii) There are other presumptions relating to all (not necessarily ancient) documents: a document is presumed to have been executed on [the] date it bears[81] and that any alterations to the document were made before the execution of that document. However this latter presumption does not apply to wills where it is presumed that any alterations are made after execution.[82] Where such presumptions apply, it normally changes the legal burden of proof on that issue so that burden falls on the party adversely affected to adduce evidence and prove that the document was executed on a different date or was altered after execution.

V. Electronic Signatures

Electronic documents are documents in UK law. According to s.13 of the Civil Evidence Act 1995 "document" means anything onto which information of any description has recorded, and "copy", in relation to a document, means anything onto which information has been recorded in the document has been copied, by whatever means and whether directly or indirectly. Thus electronic documents in whatever form including diskettes, CD-ROMS and printouts thereof may be admissible in evidence as long as they are certified or authenticated in such manner as the court may approve.

The verification of the authenticity of electronic documents will become an important issue in litigation and one in which digital signatures have an important role to play. Organisations are relying more and more on electronic records to replace paper records. These often require signatures. This is occurring in both the private sphere and in the public sector. For example, there are a large number of transactions in banks and building societies such as authorisations and receipts that have signatures attached to identify the person and acknowledge their agreement to the contents. Further examples are public agencies such as government departments or the police—the latter require signatures from the public for documents such as witness statements or from officers themselves for, say, the authorisation of the continued detention of a suspect.

To what extent can electronic signatures replace the manuscript signature? First, it must be recognised that there are statutes which require a "signature"—an electronically signed document in such cases is not an alternative to a manually signed document.[83] This is the situation at common

---

[81] *Anderson v Weston* (1840) 6 Bing. N.C. 296.
[82] *Doe d. Tatum v Catomore* [1851] 16 Q.B. 745.
[83] C. Reed, "What is a Signature?" (2000) Journal of Information, Law and Technology.

law and is not altered by the Electronic Communications Act 2000. That this was not the intention is shown by s.8 of that Act which gives the Secretary of State the power to amend legislation "in such manner as he may think fit for the purpose of authorising or facilitating the use of electronic communications or electronic storage". This provision would not be necessary if an electronic signature were to be equivalent to a manuscript signature. The past three years have seen statutory instruments using this power in the areas of income tax, prescriptions and town and country planning so that, for example, a person can now submit a tax return online.

However for most documents, a signature is not required as a matter of law. This is the case with most bank and building society documents, with police station records or in government departments. What is the admissibility and weight of electronic signatures in these circumstances? In general terms, a signature attached to a document is accepted by courts as identifying the signatory, his or her intention to be bound by the contents of the document and its authenticity. Where the authenticity of a document is challenged, is an electronic signature admissible evidence as proof of these issues?

Where digital signatures are attached to electronic communications, admissibility is governed by s.7 of the Electronic Communications Act 2000.[84] This establishes the legal validity and admissibility of electronic records, including signatures, in all private documents. It provides that in any legal proceeding, an electronic signature incorporated into or logically associated with a particular electronic communication or particular electronic data, and the certification by any person of such a signature, will be admissible in evidence in relation to any question as to the authenticity of the communication or data or as to the integrity of the communication or data. Further provision is made in relation to electronic signatures by secondary legislation.[85]

VI. REAL EVIDENCE

As has been explained, information can be presented to the court in different forms: through the oral evidence of a physically present witness; through documents or through real evidence such as material objects produced in court. With the latter, the jury is invited to draw conclusions from the object's nature and condition. But real evidence is not restricted to physical objects but also encompasses facts such as the demeanour of witnesses or visits to the site of an occurrence. There is an overlap with documentary evidence—some documentary evidence such as CCTV footage can be evidence which the jury can watch and draw their own conclusions.

A. *Material Objects*

The trier of fact can draw conclusions from the object itself. For example, under s.1(4) of the Prevention of Crime Act 1953, an offensive weapon includes

---

[84] This implements certain provisions of the EU Directive on Electronic Signatures.
[85] Electronic Signatures Regulations 2002/318.

items that have been adapted to cause injury. If the prosecution produce as evidence a nail–studded baseball bat, the jury can draw their conclusions as to whether the item has been "adapted". In *Line v Taylor*,[86] there was an action for keeping a fierce and mischievous dog. The judge allowed the dog to be brought into court and told the jury that they might assess whether it was vicious from their own experience of dogs and from their observations of this particular animal. However a jury will often need expert assistance on the inferences that can be properly drawn from the object.

An object is admissible under general conditions of admissibility, that is, if it is relevant, possesses sufficient probative weight and its admission would not be unduly prejudicial. A proper foundation would need to be laid to establish that relevance. No further criteria need to be satisfied. Thus the boundary between real evidence and documents must be properly demarcated. In *Hunt*, the charge was one of seditious meeting and riot. Part of the prosecution case was that there were various banners with inflammatory slogans. Oral evidence was admitted of the wording on the banners.

Hunt (1820) 3 B. & Ald. 566 at 574, *per* Abbott C.J.:

. . . I think it was not necessary either to produce the flags or to give notice to the defendants to produce them. The cases requiring the production of a writing itself will be found to apply to writings of a very different character. There is no authority to show that in a criminal case ensigns, banners, or other things exhibited to public view, and of which the effect depends upon such public exhibition, must be produced or accounted for on the part either of the prosecutor or of the defendants. And in many instances the proof of such matters from eyewitnesses, speaking to what they saw on the occasion, has been received, and its competency was never, to my knowledge, called in question until the present time. Inscriptions used on such occasions are the public expression of the sentiments of those who bear and adopt them, and have rather the character of speeches than of writings. If we were to hold that words inscribed on a banner so exhibited could not be proved without the production of the banner, I know not upon what reason a witness should be allowed to mention the colour of the banner or even to say that he saw a banner displayed, for the banner itself may be said to be the best possible evidence of its existence and its colour. And if such parol proof may be received generally, the proof at this trial was properly received . . .

It is difficult not to see the banner as a document which should nowadays require the prosecution to produce primary evidence, *i.e.* the banner itself.[87] However although that part of the decision can be criticised, *Hunt* is some authority for the proposition that the best evidence rule does not apply to material objects and there is no requirement to produce the thing itself. Secondary and oral evidence is admissible.[88]

B. *Appearance of Persons or Animals*

The height, weight, colour of eyes or hair or other personal characteristics of a person, such as poor hearing or sight can be important items of information

---

[86] (1862) 3 F.&F. 731.
[87] Under Criminal Justice Act 2003, s.133, a copy would suffice—would a photograph of the banner be a copy?
[88] *Francis* (1874) 12 Cox 612.

as can a particular local accent. Frequently juries might view security videos and draw their own conclusions by comparing them with their observation of the defendant in court.

C. *Demeanour of Witness*

Courts have always accepted that the demeanour of witnesses (their frankness, anxiety, evasiveness or attitude to the court) is an element of information that can be used to give greater or lesser weight to the credibility of the testimony. Appeal courts have often refused to interfere with jury verdicts on the ground that the jurors had the opportunity to see and assess the witnesses. Yet this common sense that jurors are able to differentiate between the truthful and untruthful witness is increasingly being doubted.[89]

M. Stone, "Instant Lie Detection? Demeanour and Credibility in Criminal Trials" [1991] Crim.L.R. 821 at 829:

There is no sound basis for assessing credibility from demeanour. There is no known physiological connection between the brain processes of a lying person and any bodily or vocal signs. Also, psychological research confirms that there are no specific physical signs of lying, although there are physical expressions of emotions, including anxiety. Bodily or vocal emotional clues to sincerity in normal relationships tend to be neutralised in court. Witnesses are strangers. They are controlled, can only answer questions and give edited testimony. Witnesses tend to be inhibited and to lose their spontaneity. The demeanour of witnesses tends to be flattened and sterilised so that it has minimal, if any, value for assessing credibility.

Anxiety or relaxation, even if detected correctly, cannot be relied on to indicate veracity. Truthful witnesses may be anxious, and liars may be, or seem to be, relaxed.

Evidence is evaluated holistically by integrating all of it from every angle. This includes assessing witnesses' personalities, characters and motives as well as objective analysis of evidence, i.e. its consistency and probability.

Any significance of demeanour for veracity, would, at best, be relatively minor in this context. Courts should refrain from practising 'instant lie detection; from the demeanour of a single witness. This should never be the basis of crucial decisions, particularly convictions.

D. *Views*

This is an inspection by the court of a relevant physical location or of an object that it is too inconvenient to bring to court.[90] What is the evidential status of this?

---

[89] P. Ekman, *Telling Lies* (Berkley Books, New York, 1986).
[90] In *London General Omnibus Co. Ltd v Lavell* [1901] 1 Ch. 135, the item was a bus.

D. Ormerod, "A Prejudicial View?" [2000] Crim.L.R. 452:

The evidential status of views, demonstrations and reconstructions: There is no express definition of any of these terms. It seems to be generally accepted that a view is an inspection of a scene or object without seeing it in operation or witnesses providing further explanation of the events. A demonstration is a view incorporating an explanation by a witness of the incident in question or a demonstration of the machine or other object in operation. A reconstruction goes further still and is an attempt to recreate the incident (whether in full or part) with witnesses and testimony. [These]. . . are properly regarded as testimony, and involve quite separate problems such as the possible infringement of the hearsay rule . . .

Views and demonstrations present more difficulty, with confusion in the case law as to the precise evidential status of each. Historically, a mere view was regarded as something less than evidence. In *London General Omnibus Co. v. Lavell*,[91] Lord Alverstone C.J. observed that a view was "for the purpose of enabling the tribunal to understand the questions that are being raised, to follow the evidence and to apply the evidence." His Lordship rejected the idea that it could constitute evidence in its own right: "I have never heard it said, and speaking for myself, I should be very sorry to endorse the idea that the judge is entitled to put a view in the place of evidence. ". . . In contrast, the demonstration, involving the explanation of the incident by witnesses, has always been treated as an item of real evidence . . .

More recent decisions might seem to cast doubt on this distinction between a view and a demonstration . . . In *Goold v. Evans and Co.*[92] Lord Denning stated that "I think that a view is part of the evidence just as much as an exhibit. It is real evidence. The tribunal sees the real thing instead of having a drawing or a photograph of it. But even if a view is not evidence, the same principles apply. ". . . It seems that there is no explicit judicial authority that views per se are real evidence and that the concern of the courts has been limited to ensuring procedural property.

It is submitted that the better approach is to regard the view as a species of evidence . . . Cases in other jurisdictions provide clear illustrations of the illogicality of any such distinction. For example, Henshaw J. had no doubt that a door with a bullet-hole could be brought to court and admitted as evidence, and asked rhetorically what difference it would make if the door were too big to transport?[93] . . .

A further strand of argument which has also been convincingly rejected suggests that a view is not evidence because it cannot be transmitted to the appellate court should the need arise. This ignores the fact that a great deal of evidence which is influential in the jury's deliberations cannot be recorded in the transcript to go before appellate courts, as for example with the tone and demeanour of a witness. The significance of the conclusion that views, like demonstrations, ought to be treated as an item of real evidence is that, as with any item of evidence adduced at trial, they are susceptible not just to the procedural rules governing their reception—who should attend and when—but more fundamental rules relating to the legitimacy of their reception and the uses to which they may be put.

Many of the authorities have involved issues of the proper procedures to be followed rather than discussing the more abstruse notions of evidential status of views. All interested parties, legal representatives and jurors (if involved) should attend. In *Gurney*,[94] the conviction was quashed when one juror was deputed to view and to report back to the other jurors. It was said in *Hunter*,[95]

---

[91] [1901] 1 Ch. 135.
[92] [1951] 2 T.L.R. 1189.
[93] *People v Milner*, 122 Cal. 171.
[94] [1976] Crim.L.R. 567.
[95] [1985] 2 All E.R. 173.

that the judge should always be present at a view. In that case, the accused was charged with importing cannabis through Newport docks and the judge sent the jury to see the docks but did not accompany them.

In *Buckingham v Daily News Ltd*, the claimant was injured while cleaning a machine at his place of work. He sued his employers. The court inspected the machine and watched a demonstration of the operation. Judgment was given for the defendants.

Buckingham v Daily News Ltd [1956] 2 Q.B. 534 at 539–543, *per* Birkett L.J.:

[The] substantial submission that [counsel] makes is that what the judge did in this case was something forbidden by law, according to the authorities; namely, that he cast to the winds the evidence that was given for the plaintiff in this case and substituted for that evidence the impression which he had gained when he made the view . . .

..In a case which I tried it was alleged that an accident had been caused by a defective stairway. The parties said: We would like you to see it; you can form your own view by seeing the stairway. I went to see the stairway. I had in mind what was said upon the one side and the other, and could make up my own mind whether, in my view, every relevant fact being before me, it was a reasonable thing to say it was a dangerous stairway or a dangerous floor, a too-highly polished floor, and matters of that kind. As a judge of first instance, I visited factories, workshops, shops, cinemas— all for the purpose of seeing for myself the nature of the place where the accident occurred—the very material upon which the accident was itself founded.

Then, in addition to that, there are the exhibits that are brought into court. I have seen the model of the side of a house, with all the elaborate modern scaffolding, in order to save me and the parties making a journey to where the house was, the parties having agreed that that model was a faithful representation of the scaffolding and the house. I have seen models of aeroplanes in which it was alleged that accidents had occurred, such models being brought into court by the wish of the parties, so that I could see for myself and form my own opinion . . .

. . . when a judge goes to see machinery, and sees it in operation when the parties are present and everything is done regularly and in order, it is just the same as though the machinery were brought into court and the demonstration made in the well of the court . . .

Demonstrations can also include reconstructions of a crime. In *Li Shu-ling*,[96] the appellant reconstructed the crime on video. The Privy Council accepted the video as admissible evidence of the accused's confession. In *Thomas*,[97] the police made a video of the route of a car chase as evidence of the defendant's reckless driving. As such it was no different in principle from the use of maps and photographs to illustrate the events to the jury. However this has to be distinguished from *Quinn*,[98] where the prosecution sought to introduce a film purporting to be a reconstruction of the actual events of the night in question. This was held to be inadmissible as such a film could never be sufficiently accurate.

[96] [1988] 3 All E.R. 138.
[97] [1986] Crim.L.R. 682.
[98] [1961] 3 All E.R. 88.

6

DISCLOSURE OF EVIDENCE: PROVIDING INFORMATION BEFORE THE TRIAL

I. Providing Information

The centrepiece of adversarial trial is the day in court. But it is counter-productive for parties to conceal the information on which they intend to rely until the trial itself. Increasingly, the efficiency and effectiveness of the courts depends upon parties revealing their hands to a greater or lesser extent before the issues come to trial.

A. Zuckerman, "Privilege and public interest" in C.Tapper (ed), Crime, Proof and Punishment (Butterworths, 1981), p.248 at 248–249:

It is a fundamental principle in the administration of justice that parties to litigation have a right to bring before the court all evidence relevant to their case and to call on others to produce such evidence as they may have. This right is derivative from the right to equal and just trial. Without it the efficacy of substantive rights would be much reduced and rendered uncertain. This principle—which may for convenience be termed the principle of unimpeded access to evidence—is therefore of cardinal constitutional significance and bears close relation to the constitutional right of unimpeded access to the courts of law generally. Although these two principles have much in common, both on account of their goals and their supremacy over other, lesser, principles, the courts have not been nearly as zealous in upholding the former as they have been in relation to the latter. The principle of access is particularly important in an adversary system of adjudication where litigants have to rely on their own efforts to find and present evidence. More specifically, this principle serves two basic goals: securing the correctness of legal decisions on question of fact and promoting procedural fairness. Although partially overlapping, these two goals are somewhat distinct. The first goal has to do with ensuring that the correctness of the actual result of litigation is not distorted by the absence of a relevant piece of evidence, as would be the case if access to the only evidence in support of an allegation was barred. The cogency of an inference of fact is a function of two factors: first, the logical correctness of the conclusion on the evidence presented to the court and, secondly, the extent to which such evidence as was presented was complete. The conclusion may well be logically flawless on the evidence presented, but if there is further relevant evidence which was not presented, this logically correct conclusion may be in fact unreliable, and at least the weight of the conclusion is reduced; it is therefore less certain that justice will be done. The second goal is that of promoting confidence in the machinery of justice as a just and efficient means of resolving disputes. When a litigant is denied access to relevant evidence he may understandably feel aggrieved, whether or not such evidence would have affected the actual result of the litigation; whether or not justice has been done, it would not appear to have been done.

Such obligations in civil actions are to an extent mirrored in criminal proceedings where there are increasing duties of disclosure on both the prosecution and defence. In all actions, the parties' ability to surprise their opponents by not revealing the evidence on which they seek to rely or by concealing other material facts has become increasingly circumscribed. In *Rowe and Davis v UK*,[1] without notifying the trial judge, the prosecution withheld certain evidence from the defence on grounds of public interest.

Rowe and Davis v UK [2000] 30 E.H.R.R. 1:

60. It is a fundamental aspect of the right to a fair trial that criminal proceedings, including the elements of such proceedings which relate to procedure, should be adversarial and that there should be equality of arms between the prosecution and defence. The right to an adversarial trial means, in a criminal case, that both prosecution and defence must be given the opportunity to have knowledge of and comment on the observations filed and the evidence adduced by the other party. In addition Article 6(1) requires, as indeed does English law, that the prosecution authorities should disclose to the defence all material evidence in their possession for or against the accused.

61. However, as the applicants recognised, the entitlement to disclosure of relevant evidence is not an absolute right. In any criminal proceedings there may be competing interests, such as national security or the need to protect witnesses at risk of reprisals or keep secret police methods of investigation of crime, which must be weighed against the rights of the accused. In some cases it may be necessary to withhold certain evidence from the defence so as to preserve the fundamental rights of another individual or to safeguard an important public interest. However, only such measures restricting the rights of the defence which are strictly necessary are permissible under Article 6(1). Moreover, in order to ensure that the accused receives a fair trial, any difficulties caused to the defence by a limitation on its rights must be sufficiently counterbalanced by the procedures followed by the judicial authorities.

. . . 63. During the applicants' trial at first instance the prosecution decided, without notifying the judge, to withhold certain relevant evidence on grounds of public interest. Such a procedure, whereby the prosecution itself attempts to assess the importance of concealed information to the defence and weigh this against the public interest in keeping the information secret, cannot comply with the above-mentioned requirements of Article 6(1).

The concept of "a fair trial" embodied in Art.6 suggests not only that all parties know the basis of the action (the civil claim or the criminal charge) but also that the parties are aware of what evidence will be produced, what issues raised and what arguments put forward. A pragmatist might argue that this will lead to more efficient decision-making as parties will be aware of the relative strengths and weaknesses and will be more likely to make realistic

[1] [2000] 30 E.H.R.R. 1.

assessments of outcomes. The idealist might suggest that fairness requires equality of arms so that all parties are in possession of all relevant information; further, as parties are able to prepare an informed response to the opposing position, the decisions made by the court itself will be of a higher quality.

This chapter explores the extent to which disclosure of relevant information to the other side is required and the role of pre-trial hearings in achieving these aims.

II. Disclosure of Evidence in Civil Cases

In civil proceedings, access to evidence is mainly facilitated by what the common law termed "discovery".

A. Zuckerman, "Privilege and public interest" in C.Tapper (ed). Crime, Proof and Punishment (Butterworths, 1981), p.248 at 248–249:

In relation to a litigant's right of access to evidence the law draws a distinction between rights *inter partes* and rights as against third parties. As between the parties to pending proceedings the law provides machinery whereby the parties may, before the trial has begun, obtain from each other disclosure of information which is in each other's possession relating to the dispute. The main device is discovery whereby one party may obtain access to documents relating to matters in dispute which are in the other party's possession. The right to discovery of documents is not confined to documents which are admissible; it extends to documents containing information which may directly or indirectly enable the party to advance his own case or challenge that of his adversary, or which may lead to a train of inquiry which may have these consequences. This and other processes, such as interrogatories, are intended to enable the parties to appraise the strength of their respective cases and facilitate a good preparation for the trial. English law has recognised from an early time the importance of *inter partes* discovery for the promotion of just determination of disputes.

In addition to these pre-trial rights the parties may call on each other to give evidence and produce documents at the trial. As against third parties, ('mere witnesses'), the parties have a limited right of access to evidence. Their right extends only to the freedom to call on third parties . . . to give evidence or produce documents admissible and relevant to matters in dispute.

Civil pre-trial process has always involved written pleadings. Pleadings reduce trial length by concentrating on those matters in dispute and this can be achieved by preliminary hearings. The finder of fact, whether judge or jury, is entitled to a proper definition of the issues and clear exposition of the evidence. In civil proceedings, there is considerable scope for full disclosure as well as pre-trial review.

This is now regulated by the Civil Procedure Rules. In the early 1990s, civil procedure was governed by two separate codes—the Rules of the Supreme Court 1965 (RSC) and the County Court Rules 1981 (CCR). There was considerable dissatisfaction with the system of managing civil litigation which was seen as involving too high a level of expense, complexity and delay. Lord Woolf's review of civil justice[2] sought to make civil litigation more efficient. The reforms that were introduced had the following aims:

- Litigation should be avoided wherever possible: court proceedings to resolve disputes should be used only as a last resort with information on sources of alternative dispute resolution (ADR) will be provided at all civil courts.
- Litigation should be less adversarial and more co-operative: there should be an expectation of openness and co-operation between parties from the outset, supported by pre-litigation protocols on disclosure and experts. The courts will be able to give effect to their disapproval of a lack of co-operation prior to litigation.
- Litigation should be less complex: there will be a single set of simpler rules applying to the High Court and the county courts with fewer technical documents. There would be active judicial case management.
- The timescale of litigation should be shorter and more certain: all cases will progress to trial in accordance with a timetable set and monitored by the court.
- The cost of litigation would be more affordable, more predictable, and more proportionate to the value and complexity of individual cases. Parties of limited financial means will be able to conduct litigation on a more equal footing.
- The structure of the courts and the deployment of judges will be designed to meet the needs of litigants: heavier and more complex civil cases would be concentrated at trial centres which have the resources needed, including specialist judges, to ensure that the work is dealt with effectively. Smaller local courts will continue to play a vital role in providing easy access to the civil justice system. Housing claims, small claims, debt cases and cases allocated to the fast track will be dealt with there, as well as case management of the less complex multi-track cases.
- Judges should be deployed effectively so that they can manage litigation in accordance with the new rules and protocols.[3]

The Civil Procedure Rules allows for much more proactive case management by the court with pre-trial hearings to ensure this.[4] The disclosure of relevant information is achieved through two basic methods which are explained below.

A. *Exchange of Statements*

In civil proceedings, the issues in a case are revealed by the initial pleadings but further information is obtained by exchange of witness statements. In

[2] Lord Woolf, *Access to Justice* (HMSO, 1996).
[3] For further explanation of these aims, see Lord Woolf, above "Overview" para.8.
[4] *e.g.* Civil Procedure Rules, r.3.1 or r.29.3.

Mercer v Chief Constable of Lancashire,[5] where the Chief Constable appealed against an order that witness statements be exchanged. It was held that the exchange of witness statements before trial was an important and appropriate procedure and the normal rule is that there should be a simultaneous exchange of witness statements. No exceptions applied as a class to jury trials involving claims for wrongful arrest and false imprisonment. However a general order that the statements should stand as examinations-in-chief depended upon the circumstances of each case and was a matter for the judge.

Mercer v Chief Constable of Lancashire [1991] 2 All E.R. 504 at 508–509, *per* Lord Donaldson MR.:

Over the last quarter of a century there has been a sea change in legislative and judicial attitude towards the conduct of litigation, taking the form of increased positive case management by the judiciary and the adoption of procedures designed (a) to identify the real issues in dispute and (b) to enable each party to assess the relative strengths and weaknesses of his own and his opponent's case at the earliest possible moment and well before any trial. Not only does this make for shorter trials and save costs, even more important it facilitates and encourages settlements. The most important change has been the requirement that, save in exceptional cases witness statements be exchanged prior to the trial.

This approach of 'cards on the table' is nowadays achieved by the r.32.4 and 32.5 of the Civil Procedure Rules.

Civil Procedure Rules. rr.32.4 and 32.5:

32.4 (1) A witness statement is a written statement signed by a person which contains the evidence which that person would be allowed to give orally.
(2) The court will order a party to serve on the other parties any witness statement of the oral evidence which the party serving the statement intends to rely on in relation to any issues of fact to be decided at the trial.

Having served a witness statement, a party must either call that witness or put the statement in as hearsay evidence. If the witness is called, the statement serves as evidence-in-chief.[6] If a party chooses not to use the statement at all, any other party may call the witness or put the statement in as hearsay evidence.[7]

A more proactive approach by the judiciary to case-management was one of Woolf's major themes and he has suggested that there should be a

---

[5] [1991] 2 All E.R. 504.
[6] Civil Procedure Rules r.32.5(2). Previously witness statements are often elaborately over-drafted—see Woolf, *op.cit.*, Ch.12 para.54ff.
[7] Civil Procedure Rules, r.32.5(5).

fundamental transfer in the responsibility for the management of civil litigation from litigants and their advisors to the courts.[8]

B. *Disclosure and Inspection of Documents*

The old common law phrase was "discovery of documents" but nowadays this is simply referred to as disclosure. Lord Woolf's review of civil justice recommended curtailing the categories for discovery of documents to those which are more directly significant and making extra disclosure dependent on a court order.[9] The Civil Procedure Rules have changed the culture of disclosure.[10] Before the new rules, "discovery" was a process where solicitors took pride of place, visiting clients and taking responsibility for all possible documents to be revealed. Now it is the responsibility of the client who needs only to make a proportionate and reasonable search.

Disclosure is no longer automatic—a court in a civil case will make an order for disclosure which may be dispensed with or limited, either by agreement or by the court. When an order is made under r.31 of the Civil Procedure Rules, parties to civil proceedings are liable to disclose the fact that a relevant document exists or has existed. Each party must make and serve on the other party a list of relevant documents in an orderly and concise form. Once the existence of a document has been disclosed, the opposing party has the right to inspect it. The disclosing party need not make it available if they have a right or duty not to disclose (for example under public interest immunity), if it is no longer within their control or if inspection would be disproportionate to the issues in the case. Usually they must disclose whether any relevant documents are being withheld.

By r.31.4, a document is anything in which information of any description is recorded. Standard disclosure is defined by r.31.6.

Civil Procedure Rules, r.31.6.:

31.6 Standard disclosure requires a party to disclose only—
(a) the documents on which he relies; and
(b) the documents which—
    (i) adversely affect his own case;
    (ii) adversely affect another party's case; or
    (iii) support another party's case; and
(c) the documents which he is required to disclose by a relevant practice direction.

A party need only disclose a document which is disclosable within these rules. The earlier common law incorporated a broad test, contained in *Compagnie Financière et Commerciale du Pacifique v Peruvian Guano Co.*[11]

---

[8] Woolf, *op.cit.* Section II generally and recommendation 1 at 299.
[9] *ibid.*, Ch.12 para.37ff; continental systems dispense with disclosure entirely.
[10] V. Rylatt, "Train of Inquiry" [2005] 155 New L.J. 1015.
[11] [1882] 11 Q.B.D. 55 at 63 *per* Brett L.J.

Compagnie Financière et Commerciale du Pacifique v Peruvian Guano Co (1882) 11 QBD 55 at 63, *per* Brett L.J.:

It seems to me that every document relates to the matters in question in the action, which not only would be evidence upon any issue, but also which, it is reasonable to suppose, contains information which may not which must—either directly or indirectly enable the party requiring the affidavit either to advance his own case or to damage the case of his adversary. I have put in the words "either directly or indirectly," because, as it seems to me, a document can properly be said to contain information which may enable the party requiring the affidavit either to advance his own case or to damage the case of his adversary, if it is a document which may fairly lead him to a train of inquiry.

More recently, in *Air Canada v Secretary of State for Trade (No. 2)*, Lord Edmund-Davies said,

Air Canada v Secretary of State for Trade (No.2) [1983] 1 All E.R. 910 at 921–922, *per* Lord Edmund-Davies:

My Lords, I proceed to state the obvious. Under our Supreme Court practice, discovery of documents between parties to an action with pleadings . . . is restricted to documents 'relating to the matters in question in the action' and no order for their inspection by the other party or to the court may be made 'unless the Court is of the opinion that the order is necessary either for disposing fairly of the cause or matter or for saving costs'. It is common sense that the litigant seeking an order for discovery is interested, not in abstract justice, but in gaining support for the case he is presenting, and the sole task of the court is to decide whether he should get it. Applying that test, any document which, it is reasonable to suppose, contains information which may enable the party applying for discovery either to advance his own case or to damage that of his adversary, if it is a document which may fairly lead him to a train of inquiry which may have either of those two consequences, must be disclosed[12] . . . It is accordingly insufficient for a litigant to urge that the documents he seeks to inspect are relevant to the proceedings. For, although relevant, they may be of merely vestigial importance, or they may be of importance (great or small) only to his opponent's case. And to urge that, on principle, justice is most likely to be done if free access is had to all relevant documents is pointless, for it carries no weight in our adversarial system of law.

Can a party disclose only part of a document by blanking out irrelevant material? In *GE Capital Corporate Finance Group Ltd v Bankers Trust*,[13] the claimant had blanked out certain irrelevant passages in some documents. The defendants sought to inspect the complete documents and submitted that the test was not whether the concealed part was relevant but whether it dealt with a separate subject matter. This was analogous with the test for the

---

[12] *Compagnie Financière et Commerciale du Pacifique v Peruvian Guano Co. op.cit.*
[13] [1995] 2 All E.R. 993.

waiver of privilege, on the authority of *Great Atlantic Insurance*.[14] Hoffman L.J. disapproved of dicta in that case that it might be dangerous to allow disclosure of part of a document and assertion of privilege over the remainder and that this was only possible where the document could be seen to deal with two different subject matters.

GE Capital Corporate Finance Group Ltd v Bankers Trust [1995] 2 All E.R 993 at 997d–998d, *per* Hoffman L.J.:

If this test is confined to the context in which it was applied, namely the case of a party who puts in evidence part of a privileged document, I would not in any way differ. But if (as certain dicta in the case suggest) it is extended to the discovery of parts of documents, I do not think that it can be reconciled with well-established principle. In my view, the test for whether on discovery part of a document can be withheld on grounds of irrelevance is simply whether that part is irrelevant. The test for whether part can be withheld on grounds of privilege is simply whether that part is privileged. There is no additional requirement that the part must deal with an entirely different subject matter from the rest.

. . . In the case of documents partly privileged, the dicta in the *Great Atlantic* case have caused some practical difficulty in the preparation of lists. Parties have been reluctant to disclose part of a document . . . and claim privilege for the rest . . . in case it should be said that because they relate to the same subject matter, privilege has been waived as to the whole . . . I think that Seville J was right in *Bank of Nova Scotia v Hellenic Mutual War Risks Association (Bermuda) Ltd, The Good Luck*[15] when he held that the disclosure of an unprivileged part of a document was not a waiver of privilege for the rest, even though both dealt with the same subject matter . . .

Discovery depends on the honesty and diligence of the parties because withholding documents cannot necessarily be detected. Parties are expected to undertake a reasonable search for relevant documents—this duty is detailed under r.31.7. The factors involved in deciding the reasonableness of a search will include the number and significance of the documents, the nature and complexity of the proceedings and the expenses involved in retrieval. If a party has not searched for a particular category of document on the grounds that it would be unreasonable, this fact must be disclosed. Where a party fails to disclose a particular document, they cannot rely on it at any stage of the proceedings and a false disclosure statement can leave one open to contempt of court proceedings.[16]

Disclosure from third parties

Obtaining information before the action starts is also possible against those likely to be party to any subsequent proceedings under rule 31.16 although any order will be for specified documents or classes of document. This is also

---

[14] [1981] 2 All E.R. 485—on legal professional privilege, see Ch.8.
[15] [1992] 2 Lloyd's Rep. 540.
[16] Civil Procedure Rules r.31.23.

possible against third parties who are not going to be parties in the litigation. In *Norwich Pharmacal Co. v Customs and Excise Commissioners*,[17] the applicants owned the patent of a chemical compound 'furazolidone'. This chemical was being imported into the country in breach of the patent and before the substantive action started, the applicants sought the names of the importers from the Customs and Excise Commissioners. There were two issues—the extent to which disclosure could be ordered against third parties and secondly whether the information was subject to public interest immunity. The House of Lords ordered that the Commissioners disclose the information. The principle of access to information is not confined to the parties in the case but litigants are able to demand the identity of a wrongdoer from a third party.[18]

Norwich Pharmacal Co. v Customs and Excise Commissioners [1973] 2 All E.R. 943 at 973c, *per* Lord Kilbrandon:

This may be the place to dispose of the "mere witness" rule. It is settled, rightly or wrongly, that you cannot get discovery against someone who has no connection with the litigious matters other than that he might be called as a witness either to testify or to produce documents at the trial. We are not here in that territory. The defendant is not a mere witness, or any kind of witness, because the whole basis of the application is that, until the defendant has disclosed what he knows, there can be no litigation in which he could give evidence. Furthermore, if he were to disclose, either voluntarily or under compulsion, the names of the third parties whom the plaintiff desires to pursue, even then he might well not be a witness in the ensuing litigation. He might have no evidence to give . . .

The most attractive way to state an acceptable principle, intellectually at least, may be as follows. The dispute between the plaintiff and the defendants is of a peculiar character. The plaintiff is demanding what he conceives to be his right, but that right in so far as it has patrimonial substance is not truly opposed to any interest of the defendants; he is demanding access to a court of law, in order that he may establish that third parties are unlawfully causing him damage. If he is successful, the defendants will not be the losers, except in so far as they may have been put to a little clerical trouble. If it be objected that their disclosures under pressure may discourage future customers, the answer is that they should be having no business with wrongdoers. Nor is their position easily distinguishable from that of the recipient of a subpoena, which, in total disregard of his probable loss of time and money, forces him to attend the court for the very same purpose as that for which discovery is ordered, namely, to assist a private citizen to justify a claim in law. The policy of the administration of justice demands this service from him.

But it is not necessary, in such a case as is being figured, to go as far as this. The defendants are not mere bystanders—although even if they be such they could in due time be called on to give oral evidence. The position in which they find themselves has been described in several ways; . . . the case of *Post v. Toledo, Cincinnati and St. Louis Railroad Co.*, in which the Supreme Judicial Court of Massachusetts reviewed all the earlier English authorities, was concerned to state

. . . the principles declared in the few cases where the plaintiff does not know the names of the persons against whom he intends to bring a suit, and brings a bill

[17] [1973] 2 All E.R. 943.
[18] See also *Bankers Trust Co v Shapira* [1980] 3 All E.R. 353.

against persons who stand in some relation to them, or to their property, in order to discover who the persons are against whom he may proceed for relief.[19]

These words appear to me to provide an apt, and by no means too wide, classification of those against whom discovery may in such circumstances be obtained . . .

As a general rule, no independent action for disclosure would lie against a third party against whom no cause of action was going to be alleged, or who was simply likely to be a mere witness in the case. This did not apply where the action could not be begun against the wrongdoer without discovery of the information, and where the third party had, albeit through no fault of their own, been involved in those wrongful acts. In such circumstances, that third party is under a duty to assist the claimant by giving full information and disclosing the identity of the wrongdoer.[20]

The issue of discovery is discussed further in relation to claims of privilege and public interest immunity.[21]

III. Disclosure of Evidence in Criminal Cases

The "cards on the table" and full disclosure aspects of Art.6 has had more significance in criminal cases in the past twenty years, mainly because of cases involving the failure of the prosecution to disclose important informa-tion. There is, of course, a general duty on the court to ensure a fair trial which would require the prosecution to produce all the material evidence.[22] Disclosure by the prosecution of the evidence against the accused contributes to the efficiency of the pre-trial and trial process but it is also a major element of a fair hearing.[23] Several notorious cases in England involving miscarriages of justice have emphasised the need for the accused to have access to information necessary for the proper preparation of the defence. An example came in *Taylor*,[24] where the main witness identified the defendants as the two white girls he had seen running from the scene. A senior policeman withheld information from the prosecution that the witness had made an earlier statement inconsistent with that testimony, in which he said that one of the girls he had seen was black and did not mention them running. Nor was it disclosed that he had claimed a reward. The officer withheld the information fearing that it would be disclosed to the defence. The conviction was quashed as this was a material irregularity which would have led to a very different cross-examination of the witness.

---

[19] (1887) 11 N.E.Rep. 540 at 547.
[20] For limits to this procedure, see *Mitsui & Co. Ltd v Nexen Petroleum UK Ltd* [2005] 3 All E.R. 511; *Rylatt* (2005), above.
[21] See Chs 7 and 8.
[22] *R. v Liverpool Crown Court Ex p. Robinson* [1986] Crim.L.R. 622.
[23] European Convention on Human Rights, Art. 6; International Covenant on Civil and Political Rights, Art. 14.
[24] (1993) 98 Cr.App.R. 361; see *Murphy* [2002] EWCA Crim 120 where police material that victim had a gun was not disclosed to the defence.

Unlike civil proceedings, criminal procedure traditionally never involved the forms of civil pre-trial process such written pleadings.[25] Pre-trial hearings have also not been the norm in criminal cases[26] but the opportunities for holding these have multiplied over recent years—these have been discussed in Ch. 2.

A. *Disclosure: pre-1996—the Common Law*

1. Prosecution

Precedent and statute have significantly altered the regulation of prosecution and defence disclosure in recent years. Prior to these reforms, in magistrates' courts:

- with summary offences, there was no obligation on the prosecution even to disclose the evidence on which their case was based. This did not occur until guidelines by the Attorney-General in 2000[27] which require advance notice to the defence of all proposed prosecution evidence in 'sufficient time' to allow proper consideration. Prior to 1996 there was no advance disclosure of unused material;
- with triable-either-way offences being tried summarily, there was a statutory obligation[28] on the prosecution to disclose their case. Prior to 1996 there was no advance disclosure of unused material.

In trials on indictment, the defendant was entitled to:

- advance disclosure of the evidence on which the prosecution were intending to rely;
- from the early 1990s, all unused material gathered in the course of the investigation.

It was the interpretation of "unused material" that was controversial. This was originally the subject of guidelines by the Attorney-General.[29] "Unused" material was information which had some bearing on the offence and the surrounding circumstances such as witness statements not included in the committal bundles. Its importance was illustrated in *Taylor*.[30] The boundaries of "unused material" became the subject of active judicial debate. In 1991 Henry J., at the trial of Ernest Saunders,[31] ruled that 'unused material' applied

---

[25] One reason for this is that the plea of not guilty puts the entire prosecution case in issue. Criminal Justice Act 1967, s.10 provides for formal admissions but is rarely used.

[26] See Court of Appeal dicta in *Thorn* (1977) 66 Cr.App.R. 6.

[27] Attorney-General's Guidelines on Prosecution Disclosure (November 29, 2000).

[28] Criminal Law Act 1977 and Magistrates Courts (Advance Information) Rules 1985 (SI 1985/601), s.48.

[29] Reported in (1982) 74 Cr.App.R. 302.

[30] above.

[31] A Serious Fraud Office prosecution arising out of the Guinness affair—see Royal Commission on Criminal Justice: Report Cm. 2263 (HMSO, 1993) para.6.38ff.

to almost all material collected during the course of an investigation and that whether it was "relevant" was not a matter for the prosecution. This ruling was upheld in *Maguire*[32] and *Ward*.[33] The prosecution had also to disclose any matters which might be held against prosecution witnesses, for example, police disciplinary hearings.[34] These developments were bitterly resented by the police and prosecution. It was not simply the quantity and inconvenience of the procedures but the nature of the information that they were being required to disclose. The argument was that they were faced with the dilemma of either having to disclose sensitive and confidential material, especially in relation to informants, or having to discontinue prosecution.

Before discussing recent developments in relation to prosecution disclosure, it is necessary to consider the position of the defence.

2. Defence

There was never a common law obligation on the defendant to disclose the nature of the defence. It has been introduced in some circumstances by statute.

a. *Alibi defences by the Criminal Justice Act 1967*. The provisions of alibi or defences are now contained in s.11 of the Criminal Procedure and Investigations Act 1996.

Criminal Procedure and Investigations Act 1996:

11.—(1) On a trial on indictment the defendant shall not without the leave of the court adduce evidence in support of an alibi unless, before the end of the prescribed period, he gives notice of particulars of the alibi.[35]

This is amended by s.33(2) of the Criminal Justice Act 2003 so that the defence statement of alibi must give the name, address and date of birth of any alibi witness and any information in the accused's possession which might be of material assistance in identifying any such witness.

b. *Expert evidence under PACE 1984, s.81*. This makes provision for the Crown Court Rules to specify conditions for the admission of expert evidence and under subs.(2) may specify the kind of evidence to which the rules apply.[36] These provisions are now contained in the Criminal Procedure and Investigations Act 1996.[37]

---

[32] (1992) 94 Cr.App.R. 133.
[33] (1993) 96 Cr.App.R. 1.
[34] *Edwards* [1991] 2 All E.R. 266—see *Edwards v UK* [1992] 15 E.H.R.R. 417.
[35] The prescribed period is 7 days after the end of any preliminary proceedings in magistrates' court.
[36] Criminal Procedure Rules, r.24.
[37] As amended by Criminal Justice Act 2003, s.34.

c. *Preparatory hearings in serious fraud cases under the Criminal Justice Act 1987*. The judge may order the defendant to give the court and the prosecution a statement setting out in general terms the nature of the defence, indicating the principal matters on which issue is taken with the prosecution.[38]

B. *The Case for Reform*

Obviously the shorter the notice that the prosecution have of a defence witness or item of evidence, the less able they are to counter the impact of such evidence. One argument for defence disclosure is that the principal function of the court and a jury is to determine the truth and they should be entitled both to an indictment which lays out an agenda of the issues to be decided and also to both parties putting forward their own evidence as to those issues and how they intend to answer the other's evidence. Concealment of evidence until a late stage by either side necessarily leads to the jury unable to assess the weight or probative quality of such evidence. Such principles of proof argue for joint disclosure and Scotland has operated such a practice for several years with little dissent.[39]

The Runciman Commission,[40] while maintaining the defendant's right of silence at police station or trial, recommended that in all contested trials, the defence would have to indicate the substance of the defence or the fact that no evidence would be called.

Royal Commission on Criminal Justice, Report (Cm 2763 1993) paras 6.59–6.60:

. . . we believe that there are powerful reasons for extending the obligations on the defence to provide advance disclosure. If all the parties had in advance an indication of what the defence would be, this would not only encourage earlier and better preparation of cases but might well result in the prosecution being dropped in the light of the defence disclosure, an earlier resolution through a plea of guilty, or the fixing of an earlier trial date. The length of the trial could also be more readily estimated, leading to a better use of the time both of the court and of those involved in the trial; and there would be kept to a minimum those cases where the defendant withholds his or her defence until the last possible moment in the hope of confusing the jury or evading investigation of a fabricated defence.

We do not, as we have said, believe that a requirement on the defence to disclose the substance of their case sooner rather than later infringes the right of defendants not to incriminate themselves. Where defendants advance a defence at trial it does not

---

[38] s.9.
[39] J. Glynn: "Disclosure" [1993] Crim.L.R. 841 at 842.
[40] Royal Commission on Criminal Justice: *op.cit.*, para.6.57ff (note of dissent by Professor Zander, pp.221–223); J. Glynn "Disclosure" [1993] Crim.L.R. 841.

amount to an infringement of their privilege not to incriminate themselves if advance warning of the substance of such a defence has to be given. The matter is simply one of timing. We emphasise that under our proposals defendants may, if they so choose, still stay silent throughout the trial.

The arguments employed were pragmatic: defence disclosure would prevent the 'ambush' defence; it would encourage better preparation as well as guilty pleas or prosecution discontinuances where appropriate; it would facilitate better estimates of length of trial and thus more efficient use of resources. Opposition to the proposal points to the lack of any evidence either of the widespread use of defence 'ambushes'[41] or of the effectiveness of defence disclosure.[42] However there are also issues of principle.

Royal Commission on Criminal Justice, *op.cit.*, p.221—Note of Dissent by Professor M. Zander, para.2:

The fundamental issue at stake is that the burden of proof lies throughout on the prosecution. Defence disclosure is designed to be helpful to the prosecution and, more generally, to the system. But it is not the job of the defendant to be helpful either to the prosecution or to the system. His task, if he chooses to put the prosecution to the proof, is simply to defend himself. Rules requiring advance disclosure of alibis and expert evidence are reasonably exceptions to this general principle. But, in my view, it is wrong to require the defendant to be helpful by giving advance notice of his defence and to penalise him by adverse comment if he fails to do so.

Runciman[43] felt that the common law in England had swung too far in the direction of the defence. The Report saw practical problems in the sheer volume of material especially since many major investigations nowadays will use computerised databases. But there were also issues of principle. Should confidential and sensitive information contained in the material be so readily disclosed? This was seen as particularly acute where informants or undercover police officers were involved and the Attorney-General's guidelines left considerable discretion to the prosecution. As far as the defence were concerned, the Report recommended that in all contested trials, the defence would have to indicate the substance of the defence or the fact that no evidence would be called.

C. *Disclosure under the Criminal Procedure and Investigations Act 1996*

The Criminal Procedure and Investigations Act 1996 put the recommendations on a statutory basis.[44] There is a three-stage process: first there is

---

[41] M. Zander and P. Henderson: *Crown Court Study* (Royal Commission on Criminal Justice: Research Study No.19) (HMSO, 1993) suggests that prosecution counsel see such ambushes in 7% of case whereas for the CPS and the police, the figures are 10% and 23% respectively. Counsel only considered them a serious problem in 3% of cases.

[42] In serious fraud cases under s.9 Criminal Justice Act 1987, one study has shown that the system requiring a statement from the accused setting out the defence has proved largely ineffectual— M. Levi, *The Investigation, Prosecution and Trial of Serious Fraud* (Royal Commission on Criminal Justice: Research Study No.14) (HMSO, 1993).

[43] Royal Commission on Criminal Justice: op.cit. para.6.41ff.

[44] S. Sharpe "Article 6 and the Disclosure of Evidence" [1999] Crim L.R. 273.

primary disclosure by the prosecution which is automatic. A police officer known as a disclosure officer records all information gathered in the investigation, prepares a schedule of the material for the prosecutor. There is a revised code of practice setting out the manner in which police officers are to record, retain and reveal to the prosecutor material obtained in a criminal investigation.[45]

The prosecution would be under a duty to supply the defence with copies of all material relevant to the offence, the offender and the circumstances of the case. This would include material which may undermine the credibility of defence witnesses as well as those appearing for the prosecution.[46] Schedules of other information held by the police or other key participants such as expert scientific witnesses would be supplied at this point. The only potential problem here is the lack of formal judicial scrutiny over this procedure.

1. Primary prosecution disclosure

Primary disclosure by the prosecution is ensured by s.3 of the Criminal Procedure and Investigations Act 1996.

Criminal Procedure and Investigations Act 1996, s.3:

3.—(1) The prosecutor must—
(a) disclose to the accused any prosecution material which has not previously been disclosed to the accused and which might reasonably be considered capable of undermining the case for the prosecution against the accused, or[47]
(b) give to the accused a written statement that there is no material of a description mentioned in paragraph (a).

The prosecution must provide a copy of the material to the defence or allow the defence to inspect it at a reasonable time and in a reasonable place.

Prosecution material does not include material held by a third party—in *Wood*,[48] the charge was drunk driving. The defence statement alleged that the breathalyser device was no longer of a type approved as it had been changed without the prior consent of the secretary of state and they sought to get disclosure about the device. The Divisional Court held that manufacturer was a third party and did not become part of the prosecution because it had supplied the device to the police. The provisions under the 1996 Act were not directed to creating duties for third parties to follow. The disclosure duties were created in respect of material that the prosecution or the police had and which the prosecution had inspected. Material was not prosecution material

---

[45] Criminal Procedure and Investigations Act 1996 (Code of Practice) Order 2005 (S.I. 2005 No. 985).
[46] *Brown* [1997] 3 All E.R. 780.
[47] S.3(1)(a) was amended by s.32 of the Criminal Justice Act 2003—". . .might reasonably be considered capable of undermining' replaced '..in the prosecutor's opinion might undermine".
[48] [2006] EWHC 32.

under the Act unless it was held by the investigator or by the disclosure officer. The Attorney-General's Guidelines require a prosecutor to pursue third party disclosure if there was a suspicion that documents would be detrimental to the prosecution or of assistance to the defence. However in such circumstances, the prosecutor enjoyed a margin of consideration as to what steps were appropriate.[49]

2. Defence disclosure

Following primary disclosure by the prosecution, there will be a statement by the defence setting out the material lines of their case. The contents of such a statement is regulated by s.6A.[50]

Criminal Procedure and Investigations Act 1996, s.6:

6A Contents of defence statement
(1) For the purposes of this Part a defence statement is a written statement—
(a) setting out the nature of the accused's defence, including any particular defences on which he intends to rely,
(b) indicating the matters of fact on which he takes issue with the prosecution,
(c) setting out, in the case of each such matter, why he takes issue with the prosecution, and
(d) indicating any point of law (including any point as to the admissibility of evidence or an abuse of process) which he wishes to take, and any authority on which he intends to rely for that purpose.

The 2003 Criminal Justice Act tightened up the rules for defence procedures. Sections 33–36 introduced a new s.6A which provided for enhanced contents of any general statement; a s.6B which puts a duty of updating the defence statement, and a s.6C which requires that a defendant should provide details of defence witnesses. Whether the disclosure is compulsory or voluntary, flaws in the defence statement can lead to adverse consequences for the accused as the jury may draw such inferences as they think proper from a failure to give a defence statement or where the defence in court differs from the one set out in the statement.[51]

In the case of proceedings in the Crown Court, disclosure is mandatory as a result of s.5. It is not compulsory in the magistrates' court but the accused may give a defence statement to the prosecution and to the court on a voluntary basis.[52] If the defendant fails to submit a statement or puts forward a different defence at trial, the judge can direct the jury that they can draw an adverse inference under s.11.

Criminal Procedure and Investigations Act 1996, s.6:

11(3) Where this section applies—

[49] *Alibhai* [2004] EWCA Crim 681.
[50] As inserted by Criminal Justice Act 2003, s.33.
[51] Now under ss.36 and 39 Criminal Justice Act 2003.
[52] Criminal Procedure and Investigations Act 1996, s.6.

(a) the court or, with the leave of the court, any other party may make such comment as appears appropriate;

(b) the court or jury may draw such inferences as appear proper in deciding whether the accused is guilty of the offence concerned.

However there are no provisions for ensuring that a statement is signed by and attributable to the accused. Where this is not done and the accused departs from that statement, it becomes difficult to use it against him.[53]

The analogy must be drawn with the adverse inferences that can be drawn under the ss.34–37 of the Criminal Justice and Public Order Act 1994.[54] In *Condron v UK*,[55] the European Court of Human Rights held that the right to silence at the police station or in court was not absolute but that 'particular caution' was required by domestic courts before drawing adverse inferences. With defence statements, where there has been a failure to submit, in all the circumstances of this case, the jury should have been directed that the failure could be taken into account but only if they were satisfied that it could not be sensibly attributed to the defendant having no answer or none that would stand up to sensible analysis.

3. Secondary prosecution disclosure

The third stage of disclosure comes under s.7. Where the accused has given a defence statement to the prosecution, the prosecutor is under a duty to make any additional disclosures that become necessary. An example is *Lewisham LBC v Marylebone Magistrates*[56] which involved a noise abatement order served the defendant. The defence statement argued that the noise did not come from the defendant's premises but from the pub next door. The prosecution failed to disclose that a previous abatement order had been served on the pub's landlady.

Under these provisions (but reinforced by s.37 of the Criminal Justice Act 2003), the prosecutor remains under a continuing duty to keep under review the question whether there is prosecution material which might undermine the prosecution case and which has not been disclosed to the accused and, should such material exist, it should be disclosed to the accused as soon as reasonably practicable.[57] The defence would be obliged to establish the relevance of the material sought, relating it to their disclosed case. Where the parties disagree on this aspect, the court could rule, after weighing the potential importance of the material to the defence.

The statutory scheme has been amended by the Criminal Justice Act 2003. Redmayne describes the changes.

---

[53] *V* [2005] EWCA Crim 581.
[54] See Ch.4.
[55] Application No.: 00035718/97; 31 EHRR 1.
[56] [2004] Env. L.R. 14.
[57] Criminal Procedure and Investigations Act 1996, s.9.

M. Redmayne, "Disclosure and its Discontents" [2004] Crim.L.R. 441:

Prosecution disclosure: clarification

The Criminal Justice Act 2003 does not radically change the prosecution disclosure scheme introduced by the CPIA. It does, however, improve it slightly. The distinction between primary and secondary disclosure, with different tests applied at each stage, is no longer significant. The Act changes the wording of the primary test: the prosecution must disclose material which "might reasonably be considered capable of undermining the case for the prosecution or of assisting the case for the accused." The improvement here is that the new test is objective, and specifically includes helpfulness to the defence case as a criterion for disclosure. The original CPIA only included material assisting the defence case at the secondary stage, and then only in the terms set by the defence statement . . .

Under the new law—by means of a new s.7A inserted in the CPIA—the prosecution has to keep the primary test under review, in particular, "following the giving of a defence statement." This effectively gets rid of the primary/secondary disclosure distinction, and makes it difficult to read the Act as making prosecution disclosure conditional on the service of a defence statement . . .

These changes, then, introduce improvements to prosecution disclosure requirements. They make the prosecution's obligations clearer and simpler. But their significance should not be overstated. The problems that afflict prosecution disclosure are too deep-rooted to be cured by legislative tweaking. They stem from the fact that the police are naturally reluctant to reveal information which may damage the prosecution case, and that they know that undisclosed material will often not be discovered. Because the police are the ones with the key obligations here—to draw up accurate schedules which contain sufficient detail for judgments to be made by prosecutors, and for challenges to be made by the defence—failings on their part are difficult to remedy later in the process. The Criminal Justice Act does nothing to address these problems . . .

Defence disclosure: expansion

Prior to 1996, with minor exceptions, the defence did not have to disclose its case prior to trial. The CPIA introduced a general disclosure requirement: compulsory in the Crown Court, and voluntary in the magistrates' court. A failure to disclose a case statement before trial, or departure from the statement at trial, can now be sanctioned with adverse inferences. It seems, however, that these provisions work poorly. Many defence statements lack the required degree of detail, yet judges are reluctant to sanction defendants with adverse inferences. A telling fact is this: while the provisions in the Criminal Justice and Public Order Act 1994 allowing adverse inferences to be drawn from silence have generated a huge amount of case law, there seems to be only one reported case dealing directly with the conditions under which an adverse inference can be drawn from non-disclosure.[58] . . .

Defence statements will need to be somewhat more detailed. The central requirement of the original scheme remains: defendants must set out the nature of their defence, indicating the matters on which they take issue with the prosecution as well as why they do so. To this is added disclosing details of "any particular defences" and any points of law on which they intend to rely. The defence statement will need to be updated if the time between its issue and the trial exceeds the specified period. A court will also be able to order disclosure of defence statements to co-defendants. In addition to these general requirements are two more specific ones. The defence must give names, addresses and dates of birth of any witnesses it proposes to call. It must also give notification of the names and addresses of any experts consulted, whether or not it intends to call them at trial.

---

[58] *Tibbs* [2000] 2 Cr.App.R. 309.

As well as these extended obligations, the Criminal Justice Act amendments of the CPIA give sharper teeth to the enforcement of defence disclosure. One reason why judges may feel reluctant to give an adverse inferences direction for faults in defence disclosure is that the fault may lie with the defence lawyer more than with his client. A new s.6E of the CPIA provides that, unless the contrary is proved, defence statements will be deemed to have been given with the authority of the accused . . .

While these changes certainly indicate that the Government is determined to get defendants disclosing case details before trial, it is not obvious how workable they are. In many circumstances, inferences from failures in disclosure are artificial. What is meant by this is best brought out by comparing s.34 of the Criminal Justice and Public Order Act 1994. Where a defendant relies on a fact at trial which he did not mention during police interview there is, ceteris paribus, a common sense inference that the failure is suspicious. Even though there is no duty to give an account to the police at interview, silence raises questions. The defence failure to disclose its case before trial is not immediately suspicious in the same way: an adverse inference depends on the creation of a duty to disclose. Perhaps in some cases this duty means that failures in disclosure are suspicious: a complete failure to reveal that the defence intend to rely on self-defence is an example; the situation in Tibbs, where the facts relied on at trial differed from those disclosed is another (though even in these situations it is not obvious that jurors will be persuaded to make much of the failing). Things are not so obvious where the claim is that disclosure was insufficiently detailed, or was made late. In these situations, the precise nature of the appropriate inference is a delicate matter, and despite the gateway to independent comment opened by the amendments, prosecutors will surely be well advised to run proposed comments past the judge before making them. Where co-defendants are concerned, however, the ability to comment without leave may cause significant problems.

The 1996 framework for disclosure has worked reasonably well. There have been some examples of flagrant abuse as in *Early*,[59] where Customs and Excise failed to disclose that prosecution witnesses were participating informants who had, moreover, lied in evidence. The effectiveness and efficiency of the statutory scheme has come under scrutiny.[60] The studies suggest that disclosure officers are junior and inadequately trained, that there is insufficient time for prosecutors to review the material or to make sound decisions. This should improve with the CPS and police working together in co-located criminal justice units. The requirements for defence disclosure are seen as either unfair and a breach of the accused's right of silence or inadequate in that there is no obligation to reveal proposed evidence or to state how he or she intends to controvert the prosecution case. The Crown Prosecution Service Inspectorate[61] found that the Act did not command the confidence of criminal practitioners and highlighted:

- the failure of police disclosure officers to prepare full and reliable schedules of unused material;
- undue reliance by the prosecutors on disclosure officers' schedules and assessment of what should be disclosed;

[59] [2002] EWCA Crim 1904, [2003] 1 Cr.App.R. 19.
[60] J. Plotnikoff and R. Woolfson, *A Fair Balance? Evaluation of the Operation of Disclosure Law* (Home Office, RDS Occasional Paper No.76) (2001); Auld Report, *op.cit.* Ch.10 para.115ff; D. Ormerod, "Improving the Disclosure Regime" [2003] 7 E.&P. 102; N. Butterfield, *"Review of the Prosecutions conducted by HM Customs and Excise"* (HM Treasury July 2003).
[61] CPS Inspectorate, *Report on the Thematic Review of the Disclosure of Unused Material* (2000).

- the awkward split of responsibilities, in particular between the police and the CPS in the task of determining what should be disclosed.

Both the Inspectorate and the Auld Report recommend greater involvement of prosecutors, if not in the collation process, in identifying disclosable unused material. There should be more involvement of counsel in the prosecution's duty of continuing review of unused material and the Inspectorate would like to see firmer reaction by prosecutors to no or inadequate defence statements. But Auld suggests that the requirements for the defence statement should remain as they are.

Under the Convention, Art.6(3)(a) requires that the accused is entitled to more detailed and specific information than notification of the charge itself. This must be given before the trial in order to permit a reasonable period for the preparation of the defence. The amount of detail required remains unclear—the Court has suggested that a judicial notification did not identify "in detail . . . the nature and cause of the accusation".[62] Such phrasing does not necessarily include the evidence against the accused let alone all material uncovered during an investigation. But *Rowe and Davis v UK*[63] suggests a broader obligation to disclose any material which may "assist the accused in exonerating himself",[64] to ensure equality of arms. The margin of appreciation accorded to States means that the 1996 Act in all probability satisfies such criteria in respect of time scale and detail. The issues concerning disclosure, confidential material and public interest immunity are discussed in the following chapter.

---

[62] *Brozicek v Italy*, Application No. 10964/84, A 167, [1989] 12 EHRR 371.
[63] [2000] 30 E.H.R.R. 1.
[64] *Jespers v Belgium* (1981) 27 DR. 61.

7

IMMUNITIES FROM TESTIFYING: PUBLIC INTEREST IMMUNITY

I. Access to Evidence

Article 6(3)(a) of the European Convention on Human Rights states that everyone charged with a criminal offence has to be informed promptly and in detail of the nature of the accusation. As was discussed in the preceding chapter, full information is a key element of a fair trial.

A. Zuckerman, "Privilege and public interest" in C.Tapper, (ed.) Crime, Proof and Punishment (Butterworths, 1981), p.248:

It is a fundamental principle in the administration of justice that parties to litigation have a right to bring before the court all evidence relevant to their case and to call on others to produce such evidence as they may have. This right is derivative from the right to equal and just trial. Without it the efficacy of substantive rights would be much reduced and rendered uncertain. This principle—which may for convenience be termed the principle of unimpeded access to evidence—is therefore of cardinal constitutional significance and bears close relation to the constitutional right of unimpeded access to the courts of law generally . . .

The goals of correct decision-making and of procedural fairness underpin this principle of access to evidence. This in turn is secured by the fact that all witnesses to the facts who are competent to testify can be compelled to testify through subpoena or witness summons. But there are exceptions to this.

1. There are certain competent witnesses who cannot be compelled to give evidence, especially the accused and the accused's spouse.[1]
2. There are other witnesses who, although competent and compellable, are able to claim immunity from testifying about certain matters. If, as is often the case, those matters are contained in a document, that document also cannot be received into evidence. In this group are:

   a) the privilege against self-incrimination;

---

[1] See Ch.9.

      b) the privilege that attaches to legal advice and to litigation;

      c) public interest immunity;

      d) a limited concept of confidentiality.

Immunity is an issue which emerges in advance of trial, in relation to the disclosure and discovery, especially of documents.[2] It is a question which can arise in the context of both criminal and civil proceedings. Legal professional privilege tends to be of more significance in civil work. Public interest immunity has become of greater importance in criminal proceedings as a result of the increase in the proactive and intelligence-based side of police work which means that the police are less willing to release information about informants or covert surveillance procedures. The enhanced duty of the prosecution to disclose unused material[3] has meant more claims by the police for immunity and non-disclosure.

II. Public Immunity versus Private Privilege: Preliminary Issues

A major principle of litigation is that parties should disclose all relevant information for inspection. This is based on the public interest involved in the proper administration of justice but the principle can be overridden by countervailing public interests or by certain private interests, principally legal professional privilege, the privilege against self-incrimination and a limited press privilege. There are differences between the public and the private.

A. *Waiver of Privilege*

When a privilege not to disclose information is based upon a private interest, the party to whom the privilege attaches has to assert it but they can also waive it.[4] Waiver can be express or it can be implied through disclosure. This is not the case with public interest immunity. First, anyone, including the court and those not party to the proceedings, can object to disclosure on the ground of public interest immunity. Secondly, if public interest immunity applies, it cannot be waived by the Crown, senior police officers or anyone else.[5]

There have been dicta to the contrary—in *Hehir v Metropolitan Police Commissioner*,[6] the claimant was suing the police for false imprisonment. He had previously and unsuccessfully complained about his treatment and there had been an inquiry under the provisions of the Police Act 1964. At the

---

[2] See Ch.6.

[3] Initially at common law but now regulated by the Criminal Procedure and Investigations Act 1996.

[4] Discussed further in Ch.8.

[5] *Rogers v Secretary of State for the Home Department* [1972] 2 All E.R. 1057 at 1066d-e *per* Lord Simon.

[6] [1982] 2 All E.R. 335.

hearing, the police sought to cross-examine him on his statement to the inquiry. At that time, such material was in a category immune from disclosure yet the Court of Appeal considered thatit was arguable that public interest immunity might cease to apply if the maker of the statement wished disclosure to be made.[7] There are other dicta suggesting that public interest immunity could be waived where the maker of the statement is willing for the information to be disclosed. In *Campbell v Tameside Metropolitan Borough Council*,[8] a teacher had been assaulted by a pupil and sought disclosure of the local education authority's reports on that pupil to show that he should not have been allowed to be educated in an ordinary school.

Campbell v Tameside Metropolitan Borough Council [1982] 2 All E.R. 791 at 795, *per* Lord Denning M.R.:

I know that in the days of the old Crown privilege it was often said that it could not be waived. That is still correct when the documents are in the vital category spoken of by Lord Reid in *Conway v Rimmer*.[9] This category includes all those documents which must be kept top secret because the disclosure of them would be injurious to national defence or to diplomatic relations or the detection of crime (as the names of informers). But not where the documents come within Lord Reid's lower category. This category includes those documents which are kept confidential in order that subordinates should be frank and candid in their reports, or for any other good reason. In those cases the privilege can be waived by the maker and recipients of the confidential document.[10]

Lord Denning's suggested that there were two categories of documents, namely secret documents which were wholly immune and confidential documents where public interest immunity might be waived. This has fallen on stony ground. In essence, this argument put the cart before the horse. The decision for the court is not whether public interest immunity should be waived but whether it applies at all. This decision, as we shall see, involves the court performing a balancing act between, on the one hand, the public interest in the proper administration of justice (that is, putting all relevant information before the court) and, on the other, the specific public interest in not disclosing this specific item of information. Many factors are involved in this balancing process, not least the nature of the document, its significance to the case and, not least, whether the information is in the public domain or whether the makers or recipients of the statements object to disclosure. There is little point in keeping information secret where "owners" of that information are willing for it to be revealed. In other words, the fact of the maker's

---

[7] This argument also found favour with Lord Cross in *Alfred Crompton Amusement Machines Ltd v Customs and Excise Commissioners (No. 2)* [1973] 2 All E.R. 1169 at 1185e.

[8] [1982] 2 All E.R. 791.

[9] [1968] 1 All E.R. 874.

[10] *Campbell* above at 795e-g—the old term of "Crown Privilege" has long since been superseded by the phrase "public interest immunity".

willingness to give evidence or to reveal the information goes to the question of the weight of the public interest involved and not to the issue of whether that public interest should be waived.

The better view is that, once such an interest does exist, it cannot be waived.

Makanjuola v Commissioner of Police of the Metropolis [1992] 3 All E.R. 617 at 623e–j, *per* Bingham L.J.:

. . . Where a litigant asserts that documents are immune from production or disclosure on public interest grounds he is not (if the claim is well founded) claiming a right but observing a duty. Public interest immunity is not a trump card vouchsafed to certain privileged players to play when and as they wish. It is an exclusionary rule, imposed on parties in certain circumstances, even where it is to their disadvantage in the litigation. This does not mean that in any case where a party holds a document in a class prima facie immune he is bound to persist in an assertion of immunity even where it is held that, on any weighing of the public interest, in withholding the document against the public interest in disclosure for the purpose of furthering the administration of justice, there is a clear balance in favour of the latter. But it does, I think, mean: (1) that public interest immunity cannot in any ordinary sense be waived, since, although one can waive rights, one cannot waive duties; (2) that, where a litigant holds documents in a class prima facie immune, he should (save perhaps in a very exceptional case) assert that the documents are immune and decline to disclose them, since the ultimate judge of where the balance of public interest lies is not him but the court; and (3) that, where a document is, or held to be, in an immune class, it may not be used for any purpose whatever in the proceedings to which the immunity applies, and certainly cannot (for instance) be used for the purposes of cross-examination.

The argument is that public interest immunity involves the observation of a duty which cannot be waived. This raises the question as to the extent to which a person asserting the immunity, whether they are a senior police officer or a minister of the Crown, should inquire into the weight of the public interest factors involved. This is discussed below.

B. *The Use of Secondary Evidence*

When a document (or testimony) is excluded, is it just that document itself that is the subject of that exclusion or can the contents be proved by some other means? With regard to private privilege, documents must be guarded carefully since if their contents become known, secondary evidence may be admissible,[11] such as a copy of a letter from lawyer to client or oral testimony as to its contents.

Where public interest immunity applies, a party cannot use secondary evidence. Looking at the facts of *Rogers*,[12] the applicant had requested a

---

[11] See Ch.8.
[12] above.

gaming licence from the responsible public body, the Gaming Board. The Board had taken advice from the police and refused to grant the licence. The applicant obtained, by improper means, a copy of the letter from the police to the Board which he considered libellous and brought a private prosecution for criminal libel. He sought to call the secretary of the Gaming Board as a witness in order that he might produce the letter. The House of Lords held that the letter was covered by public interest immunity. As a result its contents could not be proved either by the oral testimony of the secretary or by production of the purloined copy. Where facts are excluded on grounds of public policy, they cannot be proved by secondary evidence.

Sometimes it is clearly against the public interest to disclose the facts that are contained in the document. The sinking of the submarine Thetis was the subject of the action in *Duncan v Cammell Laird & Co. Ltd.*[13] No wartime court would have permitted proof of the method of construction of the submarine to enter the public domain, whether by production of the plans or by the testimony of workmen who built it. But such a blanket ban is inappropriate in many other cases. In *Makanjuola*,[14] the claimant alleged that she had been assaulted by a police officer. She complained and there was an investigation, leading to a disciplinary tribunal and further to a disciplinary appeals tribunal. The claimant sought, inter alia, the witness statements taken in the course of the investigation and the evidence given before the tribunals. The Court of Appeal held that these documents were covered by public interest immunity.[15] Yet in any actual trial of the action for assault, the claimant (and any other witness) would be able to testify as to her recollection of the assault even though these facts would have been covered in her witness statement and in any evidence to the disciplinary tribunal. Presumably no witness could be cross-examined on any previous inconsistent statement made in a witness statement or given in evidence before the tribunal. There is obviously a distinction between such cases and the Thetis situation where public interest immunity applies not only to the discovery of the documents but also to the information itself.

Information already in the hands of the parties, although replicated in the document, can be reproduced. In *Air Canada v Secretary of State for Trade (No. 2)*,[16] airlines using Heathrow challenged increased landing charges and brought an action against the Trade Secretary and the British Airports Authority arguing that he had forced the BAA into this action and had taken irrelevant considerations into account. They sought discovery of ministerial documents which related to the formulation of the policy. The House of Lords rejected an argument that Cabinet minutes were automatically immune from disclosure but considered that the information contained in the minutes added little to the claimants' case.

---

[13] [1942] 1 All E.R. 587.
[14] above.
[15] Although now see the House of Lords' decision in *R v Chief Constable of the West Midlands Ex p. Wiley* [1994] 3 All E.R. 420.
[16] [1983] 1 All E.R. 910.

Air Canada v Secretary of State for Trade (No.2) [1983] 1 All E.R. 910 at 920f-j, *per* Lord Wilberforce:

There is . . . the allegation that the Secretary of State took 'irrelevant' considerations into account in that his dominant purpose was to contain the public sector borrowing requirement and to implement government policy in accordance with a White Paper. As to this allegation, there is available the White Paper on *The Nationalised Industries* (Cmnd 7131), there is also available the text of the statement made by the Secretary of State in the House Of Commons on 26 February 1980, and a letter dated 13 December 1979 from the Department of Trade to the managing director of BAA. These documents are direct and primary evidence as to the policy in fact followed by the Secretary of State in relation to the matters complained of and the appellants' case . . . for good or ill, must primarily depend on them. By contrast, the documents of which inspection is sought relate to the formulation of this policy . . . As compared with the pronouncements I have referred to, they are of a wholly secondary character. I am unable to see that any case, still less any convincing case, can be made for saying that, even assuming that they are admissible at all, they would add, in any material way to the first hand evidence which has been provided.

III. Public Interest Immunity

Once known as "Crown privilege",[17] public interest immunity encompasses the important idea that information should not be publicly revealed in court that is injurious to the public interest. Where it applies, it displaces the principle that all relevant information should be disclosed to the court. As already discussed, this principle cannot be waived and, if neither party to the proceedings claims the immunity, the court or another person such as a government minister may assert it.

A. *A Brief History—Ministerial Certificates*

In its incarnation as "Crown privilege", public interest immunity had far reaching effects. It is now more circumscribed. There are two themes in this development, the first being the substantive issue as to how wide the net of immunity should be cast and what categories of information should attract it. The second is more procedural, namely who should decide whether a particular document is covered by public interest immunity: is this the province of the trial court or of the government minister? This is not merely procedural as it contains an important principle of transparency of government. These two questions were linked until the 1960s and there was a clear rule that where public interest immunity was claimed by the requisite certificate from a minister, that certificate would be accepted by the courts at face value. This was normally claimed, not on the basis of the contents of the particular document, but on the class to which the document belonged.

---

[17] Albeit inaptly as it is not a privilege nor does it attach solely to the Crown.

Consequently this meant that public interest immunity covered a broad range of public service records that had little to do with national defence or vital state interests.

Documents with a genuine sensitivity can be seen in early cases such as *Asiatic Petroleum Co. Ltd v Anglo-Persian Oil Co. Ltd*,[18] where the court refused to permit disclosure of documents which would reveal military plans. Similarly in *Duncan v Cammell Laird*, there was an action for damages for personal injury and the claimants sought discovery of documents including contracts with the Admiralty which would reveal the design of a new submarine.

Duncan v Cammell Laird [1942] 1 All E.R. 587 at 592, *per* Lord Simon:

The rule that the interest of the State must not be put in jeopardy by producing documents which would injure it is a principle to be observed in administering justice, quite unconnected with the interests or claims of the particular parties in litigation . . .

It is suggested that this case is early authority that judges may inspect and decide upon a claim of privilege but Lord Simon did say that a minister,

. . . ought not to take the responsibility of withholding production except in cases where the public interest would otherwise be damnified, for example, where disclosure would be injurious to national defence, or to good diplomatic relations, or where the practice of keeping a class of documents secret is necessary for the proper functioning of the public service.[19]

The practice developed that the minister's decision was conclusive and that public interest immunity covered defence, diplomatic relations and the proper functioning of public service. If Lord Simon intended all three to be of a similar level of importance, it is doubtful whether he ever meant for routine, low-level, administrative communications to be included in this latter category. However he talked of,

. . . the view that the public interest requires a particular class of communications with, or within, a public department to be protected from production on the ground that the candour and completeness of such communications might be prejudiced if they were ever liable to be disclosed in subsequent litigation rather than upon the contents of the particular document itself.[20]

The result was that the contents of the document itself were not considered and instead whole classes of innocuous records were protected by ministerial fiat. The rationale was that civil servants would not communicate fully and candidly with each other unless they had the shield of immunity from

---

[18] [1916–1917] All E.R. 637.
[19] *ibid.* at 595g.
[20] *ibid.* at 592b.

disclosure. In *Ellis v Home Office*,[21] the claimant sued the Home Office when he was assaulted by another prisoner. He sought but was refused medical reports on the attacker's mental state. Similarly in a divorce action, *Broome v Broome*,[22] reconciliation reports, written by the social welfare service for the armed services, were treated as subject to Crown privilege.

Broome v Broome [1955] P. 190:

. . . experience suggests that if public interest immunity class claims are sanctioned, Whitehall departments will inevitably seek to bring within the recognised classes an increasing range of documents. I do not believe that the instinctive Whitehall reaction to seek to withhold Government documents from public inspection is likely to change.[23]

The civil service's desire for secrecy and such decisions as *Ellis* raised the question whether the judge should have the discretionary power to go behind the ministerial certificate, to inspect the document and to decide whether the public interest in the administration of justice outweigh any injurious effects of disclosure on the State. Were judges to inspect and review the contents of documents, they would necessarily need to review which substantive areas ought to attract public interest immunity.

B. *Modern Times—The Right to Inspect*

The starting point in modern law is *Conway v Rimmer*[24] where a probationer police officer was charged and acquitted of theft. Shortly afterwards he was sacked by his police authority. He brought an action for malicious prosecution against his former superintendent. Both parties wished for various documents to be produced, including the internal reports on the claimant's performance as a probationary constable. The Home Secretary certified that he had personally inspected the documents and regarded them as belonging to a class of documents, the production of which would be injurious to the public interest. In the House of Lords, Lord Reid began to loosen the stranglehold of the ministerial certificate.

Conway v Rimmer [1968] 1 All E.R. 874 at 880f–889a, *per* Lord Reid:

It is universally recognised that here there are two kinds of public interest which may clash. There is the public interest that harm shall not be done to the nation or the

---

[21] [1953] 2 Q.B. 135.
[22] [1955] P. 190.
[23] Sir Richard Scott, Report of the Inquiry into the Export of Defence Equipment and Dual Use Goods to Iraq and Related Prosecutions (HCP 1995–96 115), para.K6.16 at 1789.
[24] [1968] 1 All E.R. 874.

public service by disclosure of certain documents, and there is the public interest that the administration of justice shall not be frustrated by the withholding of documents which must be produced if justice is to be done. There are many cases where the nature of the injury which would or might be done to the nation, or the public service is of so grave a character that no other interest, public or private, can be allowed to prevail over it. With regard to such cases it would be proper to say, as Lord Simon did, that to order production of the document in question would put the interest of the state in jeopardy; but there are many other cases where the possible injury to the public service is much less and there one would think that it would be proper to balance the public interests involved. I do not believe that Lord Simon really meant that the smallest probability of injury to the public service must always outweigh the gravest frustration of the administration of justice.

It is to be observed that . . . Lord Simon referred to the practice of keeping a class of documents secret being 'necessary for the proper functioning of the public service'. But the certificate of the Home Secretary in the present case does not go nearly so far as that. It merely says that the production of a document of the classes to which it refers would be 'injurious to the public service': it does not say what degree of injury is to be apprehended. It may be advantageous to the functioning of the public service that reports of this kind should be kept secret—that is the view of the Home Secretary—but I would be very surprised if anyone said that was necessary . . .

Two questions will arise: first, whether the court is to have any right to question the finality of a Minister's certificate and secondly, if it has such a right, how and in what circumstances that right is to be exercised and made effective.

A Minister's certificate may be given on one or other of two grounds: either because it would be against the public interest to disclose the contents of the particular document or documents in question, or because the document belongs to a class of documents which ought to be withheld whether or not there is anything in the particular document in question disclosure of which would be against the public interest. It does not appear that any serious difficulties have arisen or are likely to arise with regard to the first class. However wide the power of the court may be held to be, cases would be very rare in which it could be proper to question the view of the responsible Minister that it would be contrary to the public interest to make public the contents of a particular document . . . In the present case your lordships are directly concerned with the second class of documents . . .

. . . In this field, however, it is more than ever necessary that in a doubtful case the alleged public interest in concealment should be balanced against the public interest that the administration of justice should not be frustrated. If the Minister, who has no duty to balance these conflicting public interests, says no more than that in his opinion the public interest requires concealment, and if that is to be accepted as conclusive in this field as well as with regards to documents in his possession, it seems to me that not only very serious injustice may be done to the parties, but also that the due administration of justice may be gravely impaired for quite inadequate reasons.

. . . I would therefore propose that the House ought now to decide that the courts have and are entitled to exercise a power and duty to hold a balance between the public interest, as expressed by a Minister, to withhold certain documents or other evidence, and the public interest in ensuring the proper administration of justice. That does not mean that a court would reject a Minister's view: full weight must be given to it in every case, and if the Minister's reasons are of a character which judicial experience is not competent to weigh then the Minister's view must prevail; but experience has shown that reasons given for withholding whole classes of documents are often not of that character . . .

I do not doubt that there are certain classes of documents which ought not to be disclosed whatever their content may be. Virtually everyone agrees that cabinet minutes and the like ought not to be disclosed until such time as they are only of historical interest; but I do not think that many people would give as the reason that premature disclosure would prevent candour in the cabinet . . .

It appears to me that, if the Minister's reasons are such that a judge can properly weigh them, he must on the other hand consider what is the probable importance in the case before him of the documents or other evidence to be withheld. If he decides that on the balance the documents probably ought to be produced, I think it would generally be best that he should see them before ordering production and, if he thinks that the Minister's reasons are not clearly expressed, he will have to see the documents before ordering production. I can see nothing wrong in the judge seeing documents without their being shown to the parties . . .

The House of Lords unanimously agreed that the judges had to regain their control over such issues. They held that the minister's certificate was no longer conclusive and that the trial judge has a residual power to inspect and to balance the state interest against the public interest in the proper admin-istration of justice. The House considered the consequences of the *Conway* decision in *Rogers*,[25] concluding that the Gaming Board needed full informa-tion in order to identify persons of dubious character and to prevent them from obtaining a gaming licence. Consequently there was a public interest that required that documents of this kind should not be disclosed. But again, as in *Conway v Rimmer*, there were dicta which suggested that there were certain classes of document that ought never to be disclosed.

Rogers v Secretary of State for the Home Department [1972] 2 All E.R. 1057 at 1066d–e, *per* Lord Salmon:

There are also classes of documents and information which for years have been recognised by the law as entitled in the public interest to be immune from disclosure. In such cases the affidavit or certificate of a Minister is hardly necessary. I refer to such documents as Cabinet minutes, minutes of discussions between heads of government departments and despatches from ambassadors abroad. Although different in nature, any evidence as to the sources from which the police obtain their information has always been recognised by the courts as entitled to the same immunity.

Despite such dicta, modern courts have been reluctant to countenance the view that there are any classes of documents that are automatically immune from disclosure, perhaps reflecting a modern public wish to see more openness and transparency in government. In *Burmah Oil Co Ltd v Bank of England*,[26] an agreement was made between Burmah Oil and the Bank of England. The Bank was acting under the direction of the government with a view to rescuing the company from financial difficulties. One part of the agreement was the sale in 1975 of shares in British Petroleum to the Bank at a price below the current market valuation. As BP shares continued to rise, the company sought to set aside the sale. The Bank's list of documents disclosed the part played by the government in the transaction. These included Bank memos of high level meetings attended by government ministers as well as others of meetings at which government officials but not ministers were present. Ought these to be disclosed? The trial judge refused the company's

[25] above.
[26] [1979] 3 All E.R. 700.

application for discovery and this was upheld by the House of Lords but only *after* they had inspected the documents in question.

Burmah Oil Co Ltd v Bank of England [1979] 3 All E.R. 700 at 727f–735g, *per* Lord Scannan:

The truth is that the appeal raises a question of law of great importance. Your Lordships are asked to determine the respective spheres of the executive and the judiciary where the issue is whether documents for which 'public interest immunity' is claimed are to be withheld from disclosure in litigation to which they are relevant. More specifically, the House has to decide whether *Conway v Rimmer* is definitive of the law, i.e. sets limits statute-wise to the power of the court, or is an illustration on its particular facts of a broader principle of judicial review.

. . . It is said, and this view commended itself to the majority of the Court of Appeal, that the Bank has given very full discovery of the documents directly relevant to the critical issue in the action, namely the conduct by the Bank of the negotiations with Burmah, that Burmah knows as much about this issue as does the Bank, and that it can be fully investigated and decided on the documents disclosed and the evidence available to Burmah without recourse to documents noting or recording the private discussions between the Bank and the government. On this view, Burmah's attempt to see these documents is no more than a fishing expedition.

I totally reject this view of the case. First, as a matter of law, the documents for which immunity is claimed, relate to the issues in the action and, according to the *Peruvian Guano*[27] formulation, may well assist towards a fair disposal of the case. It is unthinkable that in the absence of a public immunity objection and without a judicial inspection of the documents disclosure would have been refused. Secondly, common sense must be allowed to creep into the picture. Burmah's case is not merely that the Bank exerted pressure: it is that the Bank acted unreasonably, abusing its power and taking an unconscionable advantage of the weakness of Burmah. On these questions the withheld documents may be very revealing. This is not 'pure speculation'.

.. the advance made in the law by *Conway v Rimmer* was that the certificate was not final. I think, therefore, that it would now be inconsistent with principle to hold that the court may not, even in a case like the present, review the certificate and balance the public interest of government to which it alone refers, against the public interest of justice, which is the concern of the court.

I do not therefore accept that there are any classes of documents which, however harmless their contents and however strong the requirement of justice, may never be disclosed until they are only of historical interest. In this respect I think there may well be a difference between a 'class' objection and a 'contents' objection, though the residual power to inspect and to order disclosure must remain in both instances. A Cabinet minute, it is said, must be withheld from production. Documents relating to the formulation of policy at a high level are also to be withheld. But is the secrecy of the 'inner workings of the government machine' so vital a public interest that it must prevail over even the most imperative demands of justice? If the contents of a document concern the national safety, affect diplomatic relations or relate to some sort of state secret of high importance, I can understand an affirmative answer. But if they do not (and it is not claimed in this case that they do), what is so important about secret government that it must be protected even at the price of injustice in our courts?

The reasons given for protecting the secrecy of government at the level of policy-making are two. The first is the need for candour in the advice offered to Ministers; the

[27] *Compagnie Financière Commerciale du Pacifique v Peruvian Guano Co.* [1882] 11 Q.B.D. 55.

second is that disclosure 'would create or fan ill-informed or captious public or political criticism'. Lord Reid in *Conway v Rimmer* thought the second 'the most important reason'. Indeed he was inclined to discount the candour argument.

I think both reasons are factors legitimately to be put into the balance which has to be struck between the public interest in the proper functioning of the public service (i.e. the executive arm of government) and the public interest in the administration of justice. Sometimes the public service reasons will be decisive of the issue; but they should never prevent the court from weighing them against the injury which would be suffered in the administration of justice if the document was not to be disclosed. And the likely injury to the cause of justice must also be assessed and weighed. Its weight will vary according to the nature of the proceedings in which disclosure is sought, the relevance of the documents and the degree of likelihood that the document will be of importance in the litigation. In striking the balance, the court may always, if it thinks necessary, itself inspect the documents.

Inspection by the court is, I accept, a power to be exercised only if the court is in doubt, after considering the certificate, the issues in the case and the relevance of the documents whose disclosure is sought. Where documents are relevant (as in this case they are), I would think a pure 'class' objection would by itself seldom quieten judicial doubts, particularly if, as here, a substantial case can be made for saying that disclosure is needed in the interest of justice.

I am fortified in the opinion which I have expressed by the trend towards inspection and disclosure to be found both in the United States and in Commonwealth countries. [His Lordship considered *Nixon v USA*[28] and *Sankey v Whitlam*[29]]

For these reasons I was one of a majority of your Lordships who thought it necessary to inspect the ten documents. Having done so, I have no doubt that they are relevant and, but for the immunity claim, would have to be disclosed, but their significance is not such as to override the public service objections to their production . . .

Lord Scarman suggests that there is no class which is automatically excluded from inspection, "I do not accept that there are any classes of document which . . . may never be disclosed". This argument applies even with regard to cabinet minutes, ". . . what is so important about secret government that it must be protected even at the price of injustice in our courts?" The majority of the House agreed that the documents could be inspected but having done so, refused to order disclosure. Lord Wilberforce dissented on the issue of inspection, feeling that the need for 'candour' was still relevant and underestimated.

The modern authorities are clear that a court can question a claim to withhold disclosure of a document and that a court will inspect the document and decide on the balance between the public interest in full disclosure and the administration of justice as opposed to the public interest which may be damaged by revealing the document. In *Air Canada v Secretary of State for Trade (No. 2)*,[30] the House of Lords was quite prepared to inspect ministerial papers on the formulation of government policy. Lord Fraser said that ". . . even Cabinet minutes are [not] completely immune from disclosure in a case where, for example, the issue in litigation involves serious misconduct by a Cabinet Minister."[31]

[28] 418 U.S. 683, (1975).
[29] 21 A.L.R. 505, (1978).
[30] [1983] 1 All E.R. 910.
[31] *ibid.* at 915c.

However, in *Balfour v Foreign and Commonwealth Office*,[32] the claimant sought damages for unfair dismissal by the Foreign and Commonwealth Office for having accepted £5,000 from a foreign citizen, to whom he issued a visa in 1989, which he paid to a numbered bank account. When he sought to obtain material from the Foreign Office concerning his claim, the Secretary of State for the Home Department issued three public interest immunity certificates in relation to the documents. The burden of proof is on the claimant to show reason why the documents would assist the case and the Court of Appeal was unconvinced that he had discharged that burden. But they reverted to a different era when they said,

Balfour v Foreign and Commonwealth Office [1994] 2 All E.R. 588:

In this case the Court has not abdicated its responsibility, but it has recognised the constraints placed upon it by the terms of the certificates issued by the executive. There must always be vigilance by the courts to ensure that public interest immunity of whatever kind is raised only in appropriate circumstances and with appropriate particularity, but once there is an actual or potential risk to national security demonstrated by an appropriate certificate the Court should not exercise its right to inspect.

On the contrary, the history demonstrates that the key issue is that there needs to be judicial scrutiny of documents for which public interest immunity is claimed. As the Scott inquiry into the Matrix Churchill affair showed,[33] public interest immunity certificates can be used to conceal the errors and illegalities of the executive. Claims of a "potential risk to national security" can be all too easily made. However well drafted the "appropriate certificate" may be, the courts must inspect the material itself.

Balfour goes against the trend of decisions—the history also shows that the 'class claim' has received its quietus and there is no category of document which is exempt in all circumstances. The final category of documents where there was a presumption of exclusion was that related to inquiries into police misconduct.[34] This exemption was originally based on the long-recognised refusal to disclose the names of informants to crime.[35] But immunity from disclosure had become automatic and there have been many actions when the court has needed to decide whether to make the documentation from the complaints procedure available to civil litigants suing the police.[36] The general view of the authorities was that adopted by the Court of Appeal in *Makanjuola*.[37]

---

[32] [1994] 2 All E.R. 588.

[33] Sir Richard Scott, *op.cit.*

[34] Police Act 1996, ss. 65–88.

[35] *Marks v Beyfus* [1890] 25 Q.B.D. 494; *D v National Society for the Prevention of Cruelty to Children* [1977] 1 All E.R. 589.

[36] *e.g. Neilson v Laugharne* [1981] 1 All E.R. 829; *Hehir v Metropolitan Police Commissioner* [1982] 2 All E.R. 335; *Peach v Metropolitan Police Commissioner* [1986] 2 All E.R. 129; *Ex p. Coventry Newspapers Ltd* [1993] 1 All E.R. 86.

[37] above.

Makanjuola v Commissioner of Police of the Metropolis [1992] 3 All E.R. 617 at 622a–e, *per* Bingham L.J.:

The claim [to public interest immunity] raised an issue on which this court might have taken either one or other of two views. One view, urged by the claimant in that action, was that any statement made for the purposes of a s.49 investigation[38] might be used either in disciplinary proceedings or in a criminal prosecution against a police officer and so its contents might become known to the police officer, other witnesses and members of the public at large in the ordinary course of events. Since these consequences would be foreseeable from the outset such statements could not be regarded as confidential and would not be appropriate subjects for public interest immunity.

The competing view was that, in the public interest, statements made for the purposes of a s.49 investigation should be available for use to further those purposes (whether disciplinary and private, or criminal and public) but no other. The underlying public interest asserted was (one infers) in the maintenance of an honourable, disciplined, law-abiding and uncorrupt police force. The protection of that public interest required that allegations of improper or criminal conduct by police officers should be investigated and appropriate action taken. To that end it was necessary that members of the public or other police officers should be encouraged to give any relevant information they had to the appropriate authority without fear of harassment, intimidation or use of any statement in any other proceedings. It was therefore desirable in the public interest that statements made to the appropriate authority investigating a complaint against a police officer should not be liable to be produced or disclosed or referred to in any proceedings save disciplinary or criminal proceedings officially brought against the police officer in question. To hold otherwise would frustrate the statutory purpose of any investigation under this Act.

This view was that immunity was required to uphold the public interest in ". . . an honourable, disciplined, law-abiding and uncorrupt police force". It was reconsidered by the House of Lords in *R. v Chief Constable of the West Midlands Police Ex p. Wiley*[39] in rather different circumstances. The applicant had made complaints against the police which were being investigated by the Police Complaints Authority. The applicant requested that the chief constable give an undertaking not to use the documents arising out of the investigations or to rely on any information in those documents in civil proceedings by the applicant. The applicant sought judicial review of this refusal to give an undertaking. The House of Lords held that a class claim to public interest immunity did not attach generally to all documents coming into existence in consequence of an investigation into a complaint against a police officer.

R. v Chief Constable of the West Midlands Police Ex p. Wiley [1994] 3 All E.R. 420 at 445j–446j, *per* Lord Woolf:

. . . the [Police Complaints] authority has accepted that in general the class immunity created by the *Neilson* decision can no longer be justified. However, in my

---

[38] This refers to Police Act 1964, s.49 which governed investigations of complaints into the police until replaced by Pt IX Police and Criminal Evidence Act 1984 and subsequently by the Police Act 1996.

[39] [1994] 3 All E.R. 420.

opinion, this is the case, not because of any change in the balance of public interest or change in attitudes since the *Neilson* decision, but because establishing a class of public interest immunity of this nature was never justified. This lack of justification is part of the explanation for the problems which the courts have since had in finding a logical limit to the application of the class and creating a sensible balance between the interest of those involved in subsequent legal proceedings and the interest of those responsible for conducting the investigations into police complaints.

The recognition of a new class-based public interest immunity requires clear and compelling evidence that it is necessary. Yet as the present case has demonstrated, the existence of this class tends to defeat the very object it was designed to achieve. The respondents to the present appeal only launched their proceedings for judicial review to avoid the existence of a situation where their position would be prejudiced as a result of their not being given access to material to which the police had access. Their non-co-operation was brought about because of the existence of the immunity . . . While I agree with Lord Hailsham . . . in *D v National Society for the Prevention of Cruelty to Children*[40] that, "The categories of public interest are not closed, and must alter from time to time whether by restriction or extension as social conditions and social legislation develop", in my opinion no sufficient case has ever been made out to justify the class of public interest immunity recognised in *Neilson*.

The *Neilson* case and the cases in which it was subsequently applied should therefore be regarded as being wrongly decided. This does not, however, mean that public interest immunity can never apply to documents that come into existence in consequence of a police investigation into a complaint. There may be other reasons why because of the contents of a particular document it would be appropriate to extend immunity to that document . . .

This finally cleared away the absurdity of this particular blanket immunity, allowing the trial court to inspect the documents, consider the competing interests and determine whether a claim to public interest immunity should be upheld. The following year, it was one of the recommendations of the Scott Report on the Matrix Churchill case[41] that public interest immunity claims should never be made on a class basis.

C. *Judicial Determination of Claim*

The trial judge must determine any claim to public interest immunity. There must, of course, be an objection to disclosure, identifying the documents and the grounds for withholding them. An initial question is, where material exists which is potentially within public interest immunity, does the holder of the material have a duty to lodge an objection and to resist disclosure? This issue arose in the context of the Matrix Churchill case in which company directors were prosecuted for exporting defence equipment to Iraq. Ministers signed public interest immunity certificates for various documents. These documents showed that the Government, in granting licences to the company, were aware of the use to which the equipment would be put. However the Attorney-General's advice to ministers[42] was that they were obliged to resist

---

[40] [1977] 1 All E.R. 589 at 605.
[41] Sir Richard Scott, *op.cit.*, para.K6.18 at 1790.
[42] see Written Answer by the Attorney-General on 15th December 1993: HC Deb Vol c.636–7 15.12.1993.

disclosure even where the documents might prove the innocence of the defendants.[43] In the case itself, the trial judge rejected the claim and the prosecution collapsed. Should the ministers have automatically claimed immunity, as suggested by Bingham L.J. in *Makanjuola*?

Makanjuola v Commissioner of Police of the Metropolis [1992] 3 All E.R. 617 at 623e–j, *per* Bingham L.J.:

. . . Where a litigant asserts that documents are immune from production or disclosure on public interest grounds he is not (if the claim is well founded) claiming a right but observing a duty . . . This does not mean that in any case where a party holds a document in a class prima facie immune he is bound to persist in an assertion of immunity even where it is held that, on any weighing of the public interest, in withholding the document against the public interest in disclosure for the purpose of furthering the administration of justice, there is a clear balance in favour of the latter. But it does, I think, mean: (1) that public interest immunity cannot in any ordinary sense be waived, since, although one can waive rights, one cannot waive duties; (2) that, where a litigant holds documents in a class prima facie immune, he should (save perhaps in a very exceptional case) assert that the documents are immune and decline to disclose them, since the ultimate judge of where the balance of public interest lies is not him but the court . . .

The House of Lords took issue with this position in ex parte Wiley.

R. v Chief Constable of the West Midlands Police Ex p. Wiley [1994] 3 All E.R. 420 at 424e–f, *per* Lord Templeman:

It has been said that the holder of a confidential document for which public interest immunity may be claimed is under a duty to assert the claim, leaving the court to decide whether the claim is well founded. For my part I consider that when a document is known to be relevant and material, the holder of the document should voluntarily disclose it unless he is satisfied that disclosure will cause substantial harm. If the holder is in doubt he may refer the matter to the court. If the holder decides that a document should not be disclosed then that decision can be upheld or set aside by the judge. A rubber stamp approach to public interest immunity by the holder of a document is neither necessary nor appropriate.

Although *obiter*, this position would require the holders of sensitive material to come to an initial decision on the contents of a document as to whether to disclose it. But they should never adopt a blanket policy of, for example, never disclosing child care records in the absence of a court order.[44]

---

[43] T. Allan, "Public Interest Immunity and Ministers' Responsibilities" [1993] Crim.L.R. 600; A. Zuckerman, "Public Interest Immunity—A Matter of Prime Judicial Responsibility" [1994] 57 M.L.R. 703; R. Webb "Public Interest Immunity: The Demise of the Duty to Assert" [1995] Crim.L.R. 556.

[44] But see [1994] Family Law 513 at 515.

It also allows prosecution authorities more latitude in the disclosure of unused material. It was a position mirrored in the report on the Matrix Churchill affair in which Scott V.C. recommended[45] that no claim should be put forward by a minister or other person unless they had reflected on the weight of the public interest factors involved and formed the opinion that disclosure would cause substantial harm.

1. Civil proceedings

By the Civil Procedure Rules, a person can apply to withhold disclosure of a document on the ground that disclosure would damage the public interest.[46] This can be *without notice* to the other party—the process is governed by r.31.19 of the Civil Procedure Rules. The person must support the application with evidence and the court can inspect the document.

A claim to withhold *with notice* does not require an application to the court. Where such a claim has been made, three stages occur,

1. *Proving materiality.* Parties who wish to challenge non-disclosure must apply to the court and demonstrate that it is 'very likely' that the documents will support their case. Neither the party seeking disclosure nor the judge[47] sees the documents at this point. In *Air Canada*, Lord Fraser laid down this strict test before judicial inspection,

> . . . in order to persuade the court even to inspect documents for which public interest immunity is claimed, the party seeking disclosure ought at least to satisfy the court that the documents are very likely to contain material which would give substantial support to his contention on an issue which arises in the case, and that without them he might be 'deprived of the means of . . . proper presentation' of his case.[48]

The airlines in *Air Canada* failed this test since they were unable to show any fact or motive which might be in the privileged documents, which might be significant in the proceedings, and which were not revealed in other material. The rationale for imposing this burden of proof on the party seeking disclosure is to prevent fishing expeditions but the party will have already shown from the pleadings that there is substance to the cause of action.[49] Furthermore, where documents appear on the list for discovery, this shows that the party resisting disclosure considers them "related to a matter in the case" under the *Peruvian Guano* rule. Litigants seeking to show that these documents are very likely to assist their case have a significant burden which they are ill-equipped to discharge. On the other hand it would be relatively simple task for the party resisting disclosure to show that the documents

---

[45] Sir Richard Scott, *op.cit*, Vol. IV para.K6.18 at 1790.
[46] Civil Procedure Rules, Practice Direction 31, para 6.1.
[47] The "judicial peep" suggested by Lord Edmund-Davies in *Burmah Oil*, above at 721g is disapproved of by Lord Fraser in *Air Canada*, above at 917j.
[48] *Air Canada*, above at 917d-f.
[49] *Laurence v Metropolitan Police Commissioner* (unreported CA Civ February 13, 2006) for a good example of trying to use the disclosure rules to provide a basis for a claim.

would not be of assistance to the other party. The danger is that such a restrictive rule will neutralise the benefits of *Conway v Rimmer*.

2. *Judicial inspection.* If this initial burden is satisfied, it is for the judge to inspect the documents privately, to ensure that they are of a nature which *prima facie* attracts public interest immunity, that proper consideration has been given by the person taking the objection and to determine whether the documents are in fact necessary for the disposition of the case.

3. *Balancing interests.* The final stage of this process is for the judge to decide whether the public interest in non-disclosure set out in the certificate outweighs the public interest in the efficacy and fairness of the proper administration of justice. But this balancing process should only take place after a proper case for disclosure has been made out. In *Burmah Oil*, Lord Wilberforce said,

Burmah Oil Co Ltd v Bank of England [1979] 3 All E.R.700:

A claim for public interest immunity having been made, on manifestly solid grounds, it is necessary for those who seek to overcome it to demonstrate the existence of a counter-interest calling for disclosure of particular documents. When this is demonstrated, but only then, may the court proceed to a balancing process.[50]

The House agreed that the court should be persuaded that the documents contained material evidence before inspection. But after inspection, the court must engage in a balancing exercise.

. . . the balance which has to be struck between the public interest in the proper functioning of the public service (i.e. the executive arm of government) and the public interest in the administration of justice. Sometimes the public service reasons will be decisive of the issue; but they should never prevent the court from weighing them against the injury which would be suffered in the administration of justice if the document was not to be disclosed. And the likely injury to the cause of justice must also be assessed and weighed. Its weight will vary according to the nature of the proceedings in which disclosure is sought, the relevance of the documents and the degree of likelihood that the document will be of importance in the litigation. In striking the balance, the court may always, if it thinks necessary, itself inspect the documents.[51]

Certainly the judge must consider the weight that the documents are likely to carry in the litigation is an important criterion, whether their absence would mean a complete or partial denial of justice to the party concerned and the significance of the proceedings themselves must be considered. In *Campbell v Tameside Metropolitan Borough Council*,[52] a teacher sought disclosure of school reports on a pupil, who had assaulted him.

---

[50] *Burmah Oil*, above at 708f-g.
[51] *ibid.* at 734a-b *per* Lord Scarman.
[52] [1982] 2 All E.R. 791.

**Campbell v Tameside Metropolitan Borough Council [1982] 2 All E.R. 791
at 797f,** *per* **Ackner L.J.:**

A judge conducting the balancing exercise needs to know whether the documents in question are of much or of little weight in the litigation, whether their absence will result in a complete or partial denial of justice to one or the other of the parties or perhaps to both, and what is the importance of the particular litigation to the parties and the public. All these are matters which should be considered if the court is to decide where the public interest lies . . .

The objection to disclosure of a document might not be to the contents on which the litigant wishes to rely but to the publication of sensitive but subsidiary details such as the sources of the information which are not material. Partial disclosure with names and other sensitive but irrelevant matters covered up is acceptable.[53]

2. Criminal proceedings

The police and prosecution resist extensive disclosure, not simply because of the inconvenience of the procedures but because of the nature of the information. They will often characterise material gained in the course of an investigation as sensitive and confidential, especially the identity of informants. They may be faced with the dilemma of either having to disclose that material, or having to discontinue the prosecution. But the prosecution are entitled to seek immunity from disclosure on the grounds of public interest immunity because the information would, for example, reveal the identity of informants or details of police operational practices.

Public interest immunity issues emerge as a result an application by the Crown not to disclose information which would normally be required under the regime of the Criminal Procedure and Investigations Act 1996. Such issues may also arise as the result of the accused issuing a summons to a third party to produce documents for which public interest immunity is claimed. The following course should be followed:

1. the application would normally be made to the court for hearing. This can be of three types:

   a) full notice would be given to the defendant of the application and the nature of the material and there would be an *inter partes* hearing with all sides represented;
   b) limited notice would be given to the defendant of the application but not of the nature of the material. Where ". . . the prosecutor has reason to believe that to reveal to the accused the nature of the material to which the application relates would have the effect of disclosing that which the

---

[53] *Science Research Council v Nasse* [1979] 3 All E.R. 673.

prosecutor contends should not in the public interest be disclosed,"[54] there would be an *Ex parte* hearing in the absence of the defence;

c) no notice would be given to the defendant of the application. The prosecution can make an application without informing the defence where "... the prosecutor has reason to believe that to reveal to the accused the fact that an application is being made would have the effect of disclosing that which the prosecutor contends should not in the public interest be disclosed .."[55] There would be again be an *ex parte* hearing but without the defence even aware of the fact of the hearing.

2. where there is an *inter partes* hearing, both prosecution, defence and third parties can make representations. Where the Crown has applied not to disclose documents under the statutory regime, there is an implied acknowledgement that these are relevant to the case. However where a third party is summonsed to produce documents, the defendant clearly has a burden of proving materiality—that the documents contain information which is of support to the defence case. In *Reading Justices*,[56] the issue was whether local authority files on children who had been in care, should be produced.

R v Reading Justices Ex p. Berkshire County Council [1996] 1 Cr.App.R. 239 at 246, *per* Simon Brown L.J.:

Before any issue of public interest immunity arises, however, and before, therefore, the Local Authority is properly troubled in that way, an important initial test has to be satisfied by whoever seeks the production of documents from a third party. He must satisfy the Justices that the documents are "likely to be material evidence" within the meaning of section 97(1) of the Magistrates' Courts Act 1980 . . .

The central principles to be derived from those authorities are as follows:

a. to be material evidence documents must be not only relevant to the issues arising in the criminal proceedings, but also documents admissible as such in evidence;

b. documents which are desired merely for the purpose of possible cross examination are not admissible in evidence and, thus, are not material for the purposes of section 97;

c. Whoever seeks production of documents must satisfy the Justices with some material that the documents are "likely to be material" in the sense indicated, likelihood for this purpose involving a real possibility, although not necessarily a probability;

---

[54] Criminal Procedure Rules, r.25.1(4).

[55] *ibid.*, r.25.1(5).

[56] *R. v Reading Justices Ex p. Berkshire County Council* [1996] 1 Cr.App.R. 239; *Brushett* [2001] Crim.L.R. 471.

Where the material is shown to be relevant, the judge should inspect the documents to ensure that they are of a nature which *prima facie* attracts public interest immunity, that proper consideration has been given by the person taking the objection and to determine whether the documents are in fact necessary for the disposition of the case. The final stage, as set out above, is for the judge to decide whether the public interest in non-disclosure set out in the certificate out-weighs the public interest in the efficacy and fairness of the proper administration of justice. When public interest immunity is claimed in criminal proceedings "...touching or concerning liberty or con-ceivably on occasion life, the weight to be attached to the interests of justice is plainly very great indeed".[57]

Where material is excluded from a criminal trial on the grounds of public interest immunity, do these procedures satisfy the "fair trial" guarantees under Art.6 of the European Convention? Defendants must have "equality of arms" so that their defence is not substantially disadvantaged in comparison to the prosecution and the state.[58] Public interest immunity may involve depriving a defendant of access to information in circumstances where the prosecution invariably had such access. In *Edwards v UK*,[59] the European Court of Human Rights held that the withholding of information may have affected the conditions under which cross-examination took place and may have been relevant to credibility. This position holds even more weight where the information is material to an issue in the case. But where there is an adversarial procedure, with both the prosecution and defence given the opportunity to comment on the process, the entitlement of disclosure of relevant evidence is not an absolute right. Where measures restricting that right are strictly necessary and incorporate adequate safeguards to protect the interests of the accused, this is probably still compliant with the Convention. Legitimate restrictions can be placed upon the defendant's right to disclosure in the public interest.

Different considerations come into play when the application for public interest immunity is an *Ex parte* application without any representations from the defence. Such decisions as *Keane*[60] and *Davis*[61] approved the procedure by which material could be placed before the court for a ruling on whether it should be disclosed without compromising its confidentiality. The prosecu-tion can approach the court for an order for immunity from disclosure without informing the defence at all. The Criminal Procedure and Investiga-tions Act 1996 did not significantly affect these procedures. Section 3(6) allows the prosecutor, on application to the trial court, not to disclose information where it would not be in the public interest to do so. Where the trial is in the Crown Court, there is a duty on the judge to keep the issue under review at all times without the need for an application.[62]

---

[57] *R. v Governor of Brixton Prison Ex p. Osman* (No. 1) [1992] 1 All E.R. 108 at 116d *per* Mann L.J.
[58] *Kaufman v Belgium* 50 D.&R. 98 at 115, para.2.
[59] [1992] 15 E.H.R.R. 417.
[60] [1994] 2 All E.R. 478.
[61] [1993] 2 All E.R. 643.
[62] Criminal Procedure and Investigations Act 1996, ss.14 and 15.

This position is at odds with requirements of the Convention. The caselaw takes the position that if material is relevant, it should be disclosed and cases in which a domestic court can derogate from this will be carefully scrutinised.[63] Most significantly, it is normally a violation for a court to hear the prosecution in the absence of the accused.[64] If this is the case, the common law rules relating to public interest immunity infringe Art.6. In *Rowe and Davis v UK*, the defendants were charged with robbery and murder. The police investigation had centred on a south London house which was divided into two flats. There was considerable evidence linking the crimes to the occupants of both flats but only the occupants of one flat were prosecuted and the prosecution relied heavily on the testimony of the occupants of the other flat, one of whom was a police informant who had received a substantial reward for testifying. The prosecution failed to disclose this information. They sought to remedy this on appeal with an *Ex parte* hearing in front of the Court of Appeal which accepted that public interest immunity applied. The European Court held that the procedures had breached Art.6 guarantees.

Rowe and Davis v UK [1993] 2 All E.R. 643:

. . . it is a fundamental aspect of the right to a fair trial that criminal proceedings, including the elements of such proceedings which relate to procedure, should be adversarial and that there should be equality of arms between the prosecution and defence. The right to an adversarial trial means, in a criminal case, that both prosecution and defence must be given the opportunity to have knowledge of and comment on the observations filed and the evidence adduced by the other party. In addition Art.6(1) requires, as indeed does English law that the prosecution authorities should disclose to the defence all material evidence in their possession for or against the accused. However . . . the entitlement to disclosure of relevant evidence is not an absolute right . . . Only such measures restricting the rights of the defence which are strictly necessary are permissible.

At the trial stage, the prosecution attempted to assess the importance of the information and weigh this against the public interest. Such a procedure, without notifying the judge, cannot comply with Art.6. The Court of Appeal review of the undisclosed evidence (again in *Ex parte* hearings) was not sufficient to remedy the unfairness caused at the trial by the absence of any scrutiny of the withheld information by the trial judge. A different result was reached in *Fitt and Jasper v UK*,[65] where the European Court distinguished *Rowe and Davis*. In *Fitt*, the defence were kept informed and permitted to make submissions and participate in the above decision-making process as far as was possible without revealing to them the material which the prosecution sought to keep secret on public interest grounds. Furthermore, the non-disclosed material played no further role in the case.

[63] *Jespers v Belgium*, Application No.8403/78; (1981) 27 D.&R. 61.
[64] *Neumeister v Austria (No.1)*, Application No.1936/631, [1968] E.H.R.R. 91.
[65] Application No.27052/95 (2000) and Application No. 29777/95 (2000).

These decisions should clarify the role of the judge. Art.6(3) (a) is intended to ensure that defendants have sufficient information to prepare their defence[66] but not necessarily full disclosure of all the material gathered. Where information has not been disclosed, the 1996 Act requires the judge to keep this decision under review in the light of the nature of the defence. It is unlikely that these procedures infringe the right to a fair hearing. As has been noted, the rights guaranteed in Art.6(1) may be derogated from in the interests of public order and national security. The Court has recognised that a police informer need not be called as a witness as such a system is necessary to the administration of justice and to require such people to testify would undermine that system.[67] However there still remains the need to protect the interests of the accused in *Ex parte* hearings and Auld recommends the use of independent counsel for this purpose.

Lord Justice Auld: A Review of the Criminal Courts of England and Wales (2001) Ch.10 para. 193:

But there is widespread concern in the legal professions about lack of representation of the defendant's interest . . . and anecdotal and reported instances of resultant unfairness to the defence. This concern has been fuelled by the clear unease of the European Court of Justice as to whether, in the absence of the defence, hearings for such purpose are Article 6 compliant. A suggestion, argued on behalf of applicants in Strasbourg and widely supported in the Review, is that the exclusion of the defendant from the procedure should be counterbalanced by the introduction of a "special independent counsel". He would represent the interest of the defendant at first instance and, where necessary, on appeal on a number of issues: first, as to the relevance of the undisclosed material if and to the extent that it has not already been resolved in favour of disclosure but for a public interest immunity claim; second, on the strength of the claim to public interest immunity; third, on how helpful the material might be to the defence; and fourth, generally to safeguard against the risk of judicial error or bias.

This was carried further in *Edwards and Lewis v UK*,[68] where the defendant was convicted of possessing a Class A drug with intent to supply. There had been an entrapment operation by the police and the defendant had been arrested in the company of people he believed to be either undercover police officers or police informers. Their identities had been withheld on grounds of public interest immunity. The European court found that the right to a fair trial precluded the use of evidence obtained by entrapment. However, the entitlement to disclosure was not an absolute right, and there may be competing interests, such as national security or the need to protect witnesses, which must be weighed against the rights of the accused. But the rights of the defendant should only be restricted only as far as is strictly necessary. The

---

[66] *Bricmont v Belgium*, Application No. 10857/84; (1986) D.&R. 106.
[67] *Kostovski v Netherlands*, Application No.11454/85, A 166; [1989] 12 E.H.R.R. 434.
[68] Application No.00039647/98; [2005] 40 E.H.R.R. 240.

European court did not consider that the *Ex parte* procedures employed (especially the lack of special counsel to represent the interests of the accused) to determine the issues of disclosure of evidence and entrapment complied with the requirements to provide adversarial proceedings and equality of arms and did not incorporate adequate safeguard to protect the interests of the accused.

The impact of this was considered by the House of Lords in *H and C*,[69] where the defendants were convicted of conspiracy to supply heroin and where the prosecution case rested on police surveillance evidence. The defence made far-reaching requests for disclosure which were resisted by the prosecution. The trial judge refused to consider the public interest immunity requests unless special counsel was appointed to safeguard the interests of the defence. The Crown challenged this ruling.

H and C (2004) 1 All E.R. 1269, *per* Lord Bingham:

18. Circumstances may arise in which material held by the prosecution and tending to undermine the prosecution or assist the defence cannot be disclosed to the defence, fully or even at all, without the risk of serious prejudice to an important public interest. The public interest most regularly engaged is that in the effective investigation and prosecution of serious crime, which may involve resort to informers and under-cover agents, or the use of scientific or operational techniques (such as surveillance) which cannot be disclosed without exposing individuals to the risk of personal injury or jeopardising the success of future operations. In such circumstances some deroga-tion from the golden rule of full disclosure may be justified but such derogation must always be the minimum derogation necessary to protect the public interest in question and must never imperil the overall fairness of the trial . . .

22. There is as yet little express sanction in domestic legislation or domestic legal authority for the appointment of a special advocate or special counsel to represent, as an advocate in PII matters, a defendant in an ordinary criminal trial, as distinct from proceedings of the kind just considered. But novelty is not of itself an objection, and cases will arise in which the appointment of an approved advocate as special counsel is necessary, in the interests of justice, to secure protection of a criminal defendant's right to a fair trial. Such an appointment does however raise ethical problems, since a lawyer who cannot take full instructions from his client, nor report to his client, who is not responsible to his client and whose relationship with the client lacks the quality of confidence inherent in any ordinary lawyer-client relationship, is acting in a way hitherto unknown to the legal profession. While not insuperable, these problems should not be ignored, since neither the defendant nor the public will be fully aware of what is being done. The appointment is also likely to cause practical problems: of delay, while the special counsel familiarises himself with the detail of what is likely to be a complex case; of expense, since the introduction of an additional, high-quality advocate must add significantly to the cost of the case; and of continuing review, since it will not be easy for a special counsel to assist the court in its continuing duty to review disclosure, unless the special counsel is present throughout or is instructed from time to time when need arises. Defendants facing serious charges frequently have little inclination to co-operate in a process likely to culminate in their conviction, and any new procedure can offer opportunities capable of exploitation to obstruct and

---

[69] (2004) 1 All E.R. 1269.

delay. None of these problems should deter the court from appointing special counsel where the interests of justice are shown to require it. But the need must be shown. Such an appointment will always be exceptional, never automatic; a course of last and never first resort. It should not be ordered unless and until the trial judge is satisfied that no other course will adequately meet the overriding requirement of fairness to the defendant . . .

The House of Lords supported the argument that special counsel should be appointed where the need arose. This should be on a case by case basis. There is no rule that requires the appointment of special counsel in any particular kind of case, such as entrapment. It was a matter for the judge, seized of the facts and issues in the case, to determine whether circumstances were such as to require in the interests of justice the appointment of special counsel.[70] However the Court of Appeal will review the material themselves.[71]

D. *Matters Commonly Covered by Public Interest Immunity*

Public interest immunity does not only cover the workings of central government but also local government, executive agencies, charities, professional organisations, and the police. This is not to imply that particular organisations attract immunity. It is the nature of the information which they hold which attracts protection. The mere fact that that information is confidential is insufficient in itself and there has to be a more substantial public interest. Matters of national defence or economic policy are obvious examples. Information about the welfare of children is another area where disclosure would be limited. A further pervasive theme is the whole field of crime detection when it concerns matters which, if public, would assist criminals or deter people from helping the police. Such information will be subject to public interest immunity. But the scope of public interest immunity is not constrained by precedent.

In *D v National Society for the Prevention of Cruelty to Children*,[72] the claimant claimed damages after an officer of the NSPCC had falsely alleged that she had mistreated her child. The society acted on information given to it in confidence and the claimant sought discovery of documents which would disclose the identity of the informant. Although the decision not to disclose the identity rested on the well-established analogy with police informants, Lord Hailsham felt that ". . . the categories of the public interest are not closed and must alter from time to time whether by restriction or extension as social conditions and social legislation develop." Lord Edmund-Davies summarised the position.

D v National Society for the Prevention of Cruelty to Children [1977] 1 All E.R. 589, *per* Lord Edmund-Davies:

i. In civil proceedings a judge has no discretion, simply because what is contemplated is the disclosure of information which had passed between persons in a

---

[70] *Ebcin* [2005] EWCA Crim 2006.
[71] *McDonald* [2004] EWCA Crim 2614.
[72] [1977] 1 All E.R. 589.

confidential relationship (other than that of lawyer and client), to direct a party to that relationship that he need not disclose that information even though its disclosure is (a) relevant to, and (b) necessary for the attainment of justice in the particular case. If (a) and (b) are established, the doctor or the priest must be directed to answer if, despite the strong dissuasion of the judge, the advocate persists in seeking disclosure. This is also true of all other confidential relationships . . .

ii. But where (i) a confidential relationship exists (other than that of lawyer and client) and (ii) disclosure would be in breach of some ethical or social value involving the public interest, the court has a discretion to uphold a refusal to disclose relevant evidence provided it considers that, on balance, the public interest would be better served by excluding such evidence.

iii. In conducting the necessary balancing operation between competing aspects of public interest, the presence (or absence) of involvement of the central government in the matter of disclosure is *not* conclusive either way, though in practice it may affect the cogency of the argument against disclosure . . .

iv. The sole touchstone is the public interest, and not whether the party from whom disclosure is sought was acting under a 'duty'—as opposed to merely exercising 'powers'. A party who acted under some duty may find it easier to establish that public interest was involved than one merely exercising powers, but that is another matter.

v. The mere fact that relevant information was communicated in confidence does not necessarily mean that it need not be disclosed. But where the subject-matter is clearly of public interest, the *additional* fact (if such it be) that to break the seal of confidentiality would endanger that interest will in most (if not all) cases probably lead to the conclusion that disclosure should be withheld. And it is difficult to conceive of any judicial discretion to exclude relevant and necessary evidence save in respect of confidential information communicated in a confidential relationship.

vi. The disclosure of all evidence relevant to the trial of an issue being at all times a matter of considerable public interest, the question to be determined is whether it is clearly demonstrated that in the particular case the public interest would nevertheless be better served by excluding evidence despite its relevance. If, on balance, the matter is left in doubt, disclosure should be ordered.

The categories of the public interest may not be closed but there established areas which attract public interest immunity.

1. State interests

Where national defence[73] or diplomatic relations[74] are involved, the judges consider that ministers of the crown are in a better position to evaluate the overall public interest. 'National' means the public interest of the UK (and possibly those of the European Union) but those requirements may be met if compelling disclosure of confidential information held by or concerning other states would affect relations between the UK and the other state. Another state, however, cannot claim public interest immunity on its own behalf.[75]

The court remains the final arbiter even in balancing vital state interests with the requirements of the proper administration of justice. Where the guilt or innocence of defendants is at stake, the court will often inspect documents

---

[73] *Duncan v Cammell Laird*, above.
[74] *R. v Governor of Brixton Prison Ex p. Osman (No. 1)* [1992] 1 All E.R. 108 at 115 b where disclosure is resisted because of the prejudicial effect on the UK's relations with Malaysia.
[75] *Buttes Gas & Oil Co. v Hammer (No. 3)* [1980] 3 All E.R. 475.

which appear to deal with important economic and military matters, as was seen in the *Matrix Churchill*[76] affair. Other governmental interests arise such as the formulation or execution of government policy at high level—both *Burmah Oil* and *Canada Air* involved economic and fiscal policy—which *prima facie* attract claims to public interest immunity but are not immune from judicial inspection.

2. Administrative practices

The history of public interest immunity has seen non-disclosure of more routine administrative information, both governmental and non-governmental. This was justified on the grounds that the proper functioning of public service required candour and openness form officials and from those who supplied information. Disclosure would inhibit this. The candour argument has been attacked but remains a factor, although the court would perhaps look at the specifics of the relationship and not accept (or at least give much weight) to the rationale as a general principle.

Burmah Oil Co Ltd v Bank of England [1979] 3 All E.R. 700 at 733, *per* Lord Scarman:

The reasons given for protecting the secrecy of government at the level of policy-making are two. The first is the need for candour in the advice offered to Ministers; the second is that disclosure 'would create or fan ill-informed or captious public or political criticism'. Lord Reid in *Conway v Rimmer* thought the second 'the most important reason'. Indeed he was inclined to discount the candour argument.

I think both reasons are factors legitimately to be put into the balance which has to be struck between the public interest in the proper functioning of the public service (i.e. the executive arm of government) and the public interest in the administration of justice.

All public interest does not have the same strength or importance. In *Campbell v Tameside*, the claim was on the 'candour' basis to which the Court of Appeal gave little weight in contrast to the significance of the reports on the violent disposition of the pupil involved. There is a useful contrast of approach when the courts deal with private information held by public bodies. In *Norwich Pharmacal Co. v Customs and Excise Commissioners*,[77] the applicants owned the patent of a chemical compound 'furazolidone'. This chemical was being imported into the country in breach of the patent and the applicants sought the names of the importers from the commissioners who claimed that the information was subject to public interest immunity. The House of Lords rejected this claim, feeling that disclosure would not impair the commissioners' functions and that the documents demanded were

---

[76] Sir Richard Scott, *op.cit.*
[77] [1973] 2 All E.R. 943.

ordinary commercial records which were scarcely confidential and over which it was difficult to assert a right of privacy. The protection given to confidential information is further discussed in the next chapter but as shown in *Ashworth Hospital Authority v MGN Ltd*,[78] the issue is subject to a similar balancing act as public interest immunity.

In *Alfred Crompton Amusement Machine Ltd v Customs and Excise Commissioners*,[79] the company were in dispute with the commissioners over the company's liability for purchase tax. The commissioners objected to disclosure of a range of documents, both internal and with third parties, which had been used as a basis of the assessment. The House of Lords confirmed that confidentiality itself was not a basis for upholding a claim to public interest immunity.

Alfred Crompton Amusement Machine Ltd v Customs and Excise Commissioners [1973] 2 All E.R. 1169 at 1184f–1 185d, *per* Lord Cross:

'Confidentiality' is not a separate head of privilege, but it may be a very material consideration to bear in mind when privilege is claimed on the ground of public interest. What the court has to do is to weigh on the one hand the considerations which suggest that it is in the public interest that the documents in question should be disclosed and on the other hand those which suggest that it is in the public interest that they should not be disclosed and to balance one against the other. Plainly there is much to be said in favour of disclosure. The documents in question constitute an important part of the material on which the commissioners based their conclusion . . . On the other hand, there is much to be said against disclosure. The case is not, indeed, as strong as the case against disclosing the name of an informer . . . Nevertheless, the case against disclosure is, to my mind, far stronger than it was in the *Norwich Pharmacal* case. There it was probable that all the importers whose names were disclosed were wrongdoers and the disclosure of the names of any, if there were any, who were innocent would not be likely to do them any harm at all. Here, on the other hand, one can well see that the third parties who have supplied this information to the commissioners because of the existence of their statutory powers would very much resent its disclosure by the commissioners to the appellants and that it is not at all fanciful . . . to say that the knowledge that the commissioners cannot keep such information secret may be harmful to the efficient working of the Act . . .

It is not the court's function to protect private information which is held in public hands—were such information still to reside with the individual, it would be obtainable by a litigant. The court must address the extent to which disclosure will impair the functioning of the public body. This would not be affected in the *Norwich Pharmacal* case where it appears the commissioners were merely recording everyday commercial documents and the third party documents emanated from wrongdoers whereas in *Alfred Crompton*, the third parties were innocent members of the public who would expect the information to be kept secret. But Lord Cross only felt that disclosure "may be

---

[78] [2002] 4 All E.R. 193.
[79] [1973] 2 All E.R. 1169.

harmful" and suggested, probably incorrectly, that where the competing interests were evenly balanced, the courts should uphold a claim to public interest immunity.

This seems a slender argument on which to base the suppression of information which is relevant to the fair disposition of the case. Elsewhere the courts have been more robust. In *Williams v Home Office*,[80] a prisoner challenged the Home Office's experimental "control units" for the long-term isolation and segregation of troublesome inmates. The department resisted disclosure for some 23 documents on the grounds of "candour" which McNeill J. rejected although he felt that he should take into account the factor that. ". . . such disclosure would create or fan, ill-informed or captious public or political criticism".[81] Despite this opinion, he inspected the documents after treating the "rights of the citizen and the liberty of a prisoner" as the prevailing interest.

Non-disclosure is more likely when the public interest claimed is analogous to an established head. The non-disclosure of the identity of informers is often used as in *D v National Society for the Prevention of Cruelty to Children*[82] where claimant was denied disclosure of the name of the person who had accused her of mistreating her children. This approach can also be seen in *Buckley v Law Society (No. 2)*,[83] where the claimant unsuccessfully sought names of complainants whose complaints had led to an inquiry into a solicitor's conduct. The claim to immunity was upheld.

3. Information given for the detection of crime

It has long been a rule that no question may be asked nor answer given which would reveal the identity of a person who has given information for the detection of crime. In *Marks v Beyfus*[84] the claimants sought damages for malicious prosecution and called upon the Director of Public Prosecutions to give the names of informants on whose information he had acted in bringing the prosecution.

Marks v Beyfus (1890) 25 QBD 494 at 498, *per* Lord Esher M.R.:

In the case of *Attorney-General v Briant*,[85] Pollock CB . . . says '. . . that in a public prosecution a witness cannot be asked such questions as will disclose the informer, if he be a third person . . . and we think the principle of the rule applies where a witness is asked if he himself is the informer.' Now this rule . . . was founded on grounds of public policy, and if this prosecution was a public prosecution the rule attaches; I think it was a public prosecution and that the rule applies. I do not say it is a rule which can

[80] [1981] 1 All E.R. 1151.
[81] *Conway v Rimmer* above at 888 *per* Lord Reid.
[82] [1977] 1 All E.R. 589.
[83] [1984] 1 W.L.R. 1101.
[84] [1890] 25 Q.B.D. 494.
[85] (1846) 15 M.&W. 169.

never be departed from; if . . . the disclosure of the name of the informant is necessary or right in order to show the prisoner's innocence, then one public policy is in conflict with another public policy, and that which says that an innocent man is not to be condemned when his innocence can be proved is the policy that must prevail. But, except in that case, this rule . . . is not a matter of discretion; it is a rule of law . . .

In civil cases, the anonymity of informants also tends to be protected—the interest of a civil litigant suing for money, although significant, is not as strong as the interest of an accused.[86] In criminal proceedings, as discussed earlier, the trial judge will decide whether a claim to public interest immunity succeeds in these circumstances. It is hard to designate modern practice as a 'rule'—in balancing the different public interests, the judge is exercising a difficult discretion between the need for effective criminal investigation and the importance of disclosing any information that might demonstrate innocence. The balance of interests will normally be exercised in favour of the accused[87] unless the documents are of extreme sensitivity.

But in many cases, the Court of Appeal holds that revealing identity has no evidential value—in *Mulayim Dervish*,[88] the court explained that the public interest in protecting the identification of an informant had to be balanced against the right of the defendant to a fair trial. Only if there was material that might assist the defence, would the necessity for the defendant to have a fair trial outweigh the other interests in the case so that the material would have to be disclosed or the prosecution discontinued. *Keane* makes it clear that, even in relation to the identity of informants, the court must balance the public interest in protecting the informant against the need to avoid miscarriages of justice. If the information may prove the defendant's innocence, "the balance comes down resoundingly in favour of disclosing it". The test is whether disclosure is necessary for the proper presentation of the defence case.[89] The court must continually review any decision in the light of developments during the case.[90]

The police may not wish to disclose to the defence such matters as the identity of informants, the location of surveillance posts, the fact of interception of communications, whether by telephone taps or other bugging devices, the development of new forensic techniques or computer files which may disclose trends in an investigation. But non-disclosure can go wider—in *Rankine*,[91] at the start of the trial, the prosecution asked for a ruling that police witnesses should not be asked questions as to the location of their observation post. The public interest was the need for the police to solicit co-operation of this nature which would be put at risk if members of the public realised that their identities would be revealed and that they might be at risk of reprisals. The Court of Appeal held that the reasons for the suppression of the names of informants applied with equal force to the identification of the premises used for surveillance and to the identification of the owner.

---

[86] *Powell v Chief Constable of North Wales, The Times*, February 11, 2000.
[87] *Ex p. Osman*, above; *Keane* (1994) 2 All E.R. 478 at 483g–484e *per* Lord Taylor C.J.
[88] [2002] 2 Cr.App.R. 6.
[89] *Williams and Bellinfantie* [1988] Crim.L.R. 113.
[90] *Keane*, above, at 484e–485c *per* Lord Taylor C.J.
[91] [1986] 2 All E.R. 566.

These rules have not been extended to prevent evidence being given of all police methods and techniques. In *Brown and Daley*,[92] surveillance was from an unmarked car. The officer in charge refused to disclose any information about the vehicles used. The judge allowed this information to be withheld but the convictions were quashed. Evidence of police methods was not necessarily covered by public interest immunity although the Court of Appeal conceded that sophisticated methods of investigation might lead to such claims being successfully invoked.

With the identity of informants, the court presumes that a public interest exists. In other cases, the prosecution should provide an evidential basis. For example, if it is possible to show the difficulty faced by the police in getting co-operation for observation posts and link that to the fear for the safety of occupiers and of informants, immunity from disclosure should be routine unless the defence are able to show that the identity of the informant is necessary for the proper presentation of the defence. In *Johnson*,[93] it was held that a senior officer should ascertain the attitude of the occupiers towards the disclosure of their address. If the occupiers wished to remain anonymous and were in fear of harassment, if not of physical violence, even where non-disclosure will restrict the defence, their identity should attract public interest immunity. *Blake v DPP*[94] suggests that this protection is available even where the offence is minor (indecency in a churchyard) and where there was no substantial evidential basis for the occupier's apprehension.

Covert surveillance, including the use of covert human intelligence sources, has to be now authorised under the provisions of the Police Act 1997 or Regulation of Investigatory Powers Act 2000. Information which has been used to obtain the authorisation is disclosable but only where it is relevant to the defence or might weaken the prosecution case.[95]

4. Interception of communications

The interception of communications can take place through phone taps or by the cloning of mobile phones or pagers as well as through the opening of mail. The practice of intercepting letters under the Home Secretary's warrant is of very long standing although the original authority for this is obscure. The practices were considered by the European Court of Human Rights in *Malone v UK*[96] and they held that such practices were not compliant with the convention, largely because of the lack of any basis in law. Authority arrived with the Interception of Communications Act 1985, which has now been replaced by Part I of the Regulation of Investigatory Powers Act 2000.

These statutory procedures for intercepting communications are now in conformity with the convention. The court has accepted that such intercepts may be justified in order to counter threats from espionage, terrorism or

[92] [1988] Crim.L.R. 239.
[93] [1989] 1 All E.R. 121; *Grimes* [1994] Crim.L.R. 213; *Hewitt and Davies* [1992] Crim.L.R. 650.
[94] [1993] Crim.L.R. 283.
[95] *Templar* [2003] EWCA Crim 3186.
[96] [1985] 7 E.H.R.R. 14.

serious crime. In *Klass v Germany*,[97] German legislation permitted the state to open and inspect mail and listen to telephone conversations in order to protect against, inter alia, "imminent dangers" threatening the "free democratic constitutional orde" and "the existence or the security" of the State. Intercepts were convention compliant where there was a lawful basis, the surveillance was necessary and proportionate and there was proper machinery for supervision. The machinery under the 1985 Act (replicated in 2000) was considered adequate in *Christie v UK*.[98]

Under the 2000 Act, intercepts of communications by post or by means of a public telecommunication system may be authorised by an interception warrant. Such warrants may be issued for the purpose of preventing and detecting serious crime but not for prosecuting crime. Despite the evidential value of such intercepts, s.17 imposes a prohibition on revealing in evidence the existence of such intercepts, whether authorised or not.

Regulation of Investigatory Powers Act 2000, s.17:

17.—(1) Subject to section 18, no evidence shall be adduced, question asked, assertion or disclosure made or other thing done in, for the purposes of or in connection with any legal proceedings which (in any manner)-

(a) discloses, in circumstances from which its origin in anything falling within subsection (2) may be inferred, any of the contents of an intercepted communication or any related communications data; or

(b) tends (apart from any such disclosure) to suggest that anything falling within subsection (2) has or may have occurred or be going to occur.

The Act was plainly drafted to prevent any inquiry in a courtroom as to the procedure for obtaining or giving effect to warrants. In essence, the accused is unable to ask questions in any circumstances as to whether the intercepts were authorised and who carried them out. It protects the Home Secretary's sources of knowledge and the methods of surveillance employed by the police (or other agency).[99] It also extends to unauthorised intercepts—in *Sargent*,[1] the car and home of a telephone engineer were damaged by fire. He suspected his former wife and her lover and illegally monitored an incriminating telephone conversation between them. The tape was played to the defendant in the police station and as a result he made a confession. At trial the engineer testified as to the intercept and a transcript was made available. The House of Lords held that the Act did not prevent the use of the tape at the police station. But the Act prevented evidence of the fact of the

---

[97] Application No.5029/71; [1978] 2 E.H.R.R. 214.
[98] Application No.21482/93, 78A D.&R.
[99] A Home Office review of communications intercept as evidence ordered in 2003 recommended no change—the Home Secretary announced this to the House of Commons on January 26, 2005; see Hansard HC col. 1232 ff February 7, 2005; R. Ford, "Phone Tap Evidence is Bad for Security" *The Times*, November 4, 2005.
[1] [2002] 1 All E.R. 161.

intercept and any tape or transcript of the recorded conversation being given in court.

The absurdity of such relevant and cogent evidence being excluded has been the subject of some controversy. The genesis of the provision is explored by Lord Bingham in *Attorney-General's Reference (No. 5 of 2002)*,[2] who makes the point that the refusal to accept intercept evidence is a political choice,

Attorney-General's Reference (No.5 of 2002) [2004] 4 All E.R 901, *per* Lord Bingham:

14 . . . the United Kingdom practice has been to exclude the product of warranted interception from the public domain and thus to preclude its use as evidence. But this has been a policy choice, not a requirement compelled by the Convention, and other countries have made a different policy choice. Article 8(2) of the European Convention permits necessary and proportionate interference with the right guaranteed in article 8(1) if in accordance with the law and if in the interests of national security, public safety, the economic well-being of the country, the prevention of disorder or crime, the protection of health or morals or the protection of the rights and freedoms of others. Save where necessary to preserve the security of warranted interception, there is no reason why it should have been sought to exclude the product of any lawful interception where relevant as evidence in any case whether civil or criminal.

The prosecution are under no duty to disclose the fact of such intercepts or to reveal their contents. In *Preston*,[3] the defence sought to know the contents of the intercepted calls in the belief either that these would support the defence of duress or that nothing had been said in such calls to suggest that the defendant was party to the alleged conspiracy. Although the prosecution cannot be compelled to disclose the fact of an intercept, there may be occasions when the interests of justice demand that this should be done. However the contents should never be disclosed.[4]

Covert surveillance is not just about interception of mail and telephone calls. The Police Act 1997 and the 2000 Act permit the use of other covert listening devices. Section 17 does not apply to the product of such intercepts —indeed in *E*,[5] the investigators bugged the defendant's car and then relied upon the recording of what went on in the car as evidence. This included the defendant speaking on his mobile phone—the defence argued that evidence of this conversation was excluded by s.17 but as this interception was not regulated by Pt I of the 2000 Act, it was admissible. Normally, the police and security services will be unwilling to disclose the existence and product of such covert surveillance and will often claim public interest immunity, frequently using an *Ex parte* procedure. The general principles regarding disclosure and public interest immunity apply.

---

[2] [2004] 4 All E.R. 901.
[3] [1993] 4 All E.R. 638.
[4] *ibid.* at 672e *per* Lord Mustill (but see headnote at 641e).
[5] [2004] 2 Cr.App.R. 29.

8

IMMUNITIES FROM TESTIFYING: PRIVATE PRIVILEGES AND CONFIDENTIAL INFORMATION

Private privilege, like public interest immunity, bars the court from access to certain kinds of information. This chapter discusses legal professional privilege, without prejudice communications, confidential information and the privilege against self–incrimination. Such privileges protect private interests and, unlike public interest immunity, can be waived by the person to whom the privilege attaches. In addition the privilege can be lost and the matter proved by secondary evidence.

I. LEGAL PROFESSIONAL PRIVILEGE

Lawyers, clients and, in some circumstances, third parties may validly claim not to answer questions or to supply information when those questions or that information relates to a lawyer–client relationship. The privilege may arise under two heads.

1. *Legal advice privilege.* Communications between a lawyer and the client which have the purpose of seeking or giving legal advice.

2. *Litigation privilege.* Communications between a lawyer and third parties or between the client and third parties which are made for the purposes of existing or contemplated legal proceedings.

The rationale for this privilege is grounded in the principle of a fair trial.

A. Zuckerman, "Privilege and public interest" in C. Tapper, Crime, Proof and Punishment. (Butterworths, 1981) 248 at 262–263:

Legal professional privilege is now well established and governed by fairly clear rules. It is not necessary for the present purposes to examine these rules, except to remark on the relation between this privilege and the principle of access to evidence. This privilege ... exists, broadly speaking, in order to enable a party to legal proceedings to prepare his case adequately and to facilitate uninhibited access to legal advice. In an adversary system free and uninhibited access to professional legal advice is an essential corollary of the right to just and equal trial. In this sense both this privilege and the principle of access to evidence have the same basic goal: promoting the efficacy of the legal procedure as a means of just determination of disputes. The conflict between the privilege and the principle is, therefore, confined within the basic goal of equal and just trial . . . Since the conflict . . . takes place within the confines of the administration of justice, a correct compromise of the conflict will promote the ends of the administration of justice rather than detract from them. It may be doubted whether the balance was correctly struck when extending legal professional privilege to communications made to the legal adviser for the purpose of obtaining advice on matters unconnected with pending or contemplated litigation, but the most recent trend in relation to this privilege is more cautious.

The justification for litigation privilege is straightforward—parties to legal actions need to have confidential discussions with their advisers. This justification is less obvious in relation to legal advice privilege. This was considered by the Court of Appeal in *Three Rivers*, a case concerning the adequacy of the supervision exercised by the Bank of England prior to the collapse of a bank, BCCI. The Court of Appeal, while accepting the justification for litigation privilege, questioned why communications with a solicitor should be privileged where litigation was not anticipated and argued that the two privileges should be merged into a single litigation privilege. The House of Lords upheld the old order.

Three Rivers District Council v Bank of England [2005] 1 A.C. 610, *per* Lord Scott:

28. So I must now come to policy. Why is it that the law has afforded this special privilege to communications between lawyers and their clients that it has denied to all other confidential communications? In relation to all other confidential communications, whether between doctor and patient, accountant and client, husband and wife, parent and child, priest and penitent, the common law recognises the confidentiality of the communication, will protect the confidentiality up to a point, but declines to allow the communication the absolute protection allowed to communications between lawyer and client giving or seeking legal advice. In relation to all these other confidential communications the law requires the public interest in the preservation of confidences and the private interest of the parties in maintaining the confidentiality of their communications to be balanced against the administration of justice reasons for requiring disclosure of the confidential material . . . [There] are the administration of justice reasons to be placed in the balance. They will usually prevail . . .

30. [The Court of Appeal] questions the justification for legal advice privilege where the legal advice has no connection with adversarial litigation. A number of cases in our own jurisdiction and in other common law jurisdictions have sought to answer the question. In *R v Derby Magistrates' Court ex parte B*,[1] Lord Taylor of Gosforth CJ said this—"In *Balabel v Air India*[2] the basic principle justifying legal professional privilege was again said to be that a client should be able to obtain legal advice in confidence.

---

[1] [1996] 1 A.C. 487 at 507.
[2] [1988] Ch.317.

The principle which runs through all these cases . . . is that a man must be able to consult his lawyer in confidence, since otherwise he might hold back half the truth. The client must be sure that what he tells his lawyer in confidence will never be revealed without his consent" and that ". . . once any exception to the general rule is allowed, the client's confidence is necessarily lost". In *R (Morgan Grenfell Ltd) v Special Commissioner of Income Tax*[3] Lord Hoffmann referred to legal professional privilege as "a necessary corollary of the right of any person to obtain skilled advice about the law" and continued—"Such advice cannot be effectively obtained unless the client is able to put all the facts before the adviser without fear that they may afterwards be disclosed and used to his prejudice." And in *B v Auckland District Law Society*[4] Lord Millett justified legal professional privilege on the ground that ". . . a lawyer must be able to give his client an absolute and unqualified assurance that whatever the client tells him in confidence will never be disclosed without his consent." . . .

34. None of these judicial dicta tie the justification for legal advice privilege to the conduct of litigation. They recognise that in the complex world in which we live there are a multitude of reasons why individuals, whether humble or powerful, or corporations, whether large or small, may need to seek the advice or assistance of lawyers in connection with their affairs; they recognise that the seeking and giving of this advice so that the clients may achieve an orderly arrangement of their affairs is strongly in the public interest; they recognise that in order for the advice to bring about that desirable result it is essential that the full and complete facts are placed before the lawyers who are to give it; and they recognise that unless the clients can be assured that what they tell their lawyers will not be disclosed by the lawyers without their (the clients') consent, there will be cases in which the requisite candour will be absent. It is obviously true that in very many cases clients would have no inhibitions in providing their lawyers with all the facts and information the lawyers might need whether or not there were the absolute assurance of non-disclosure that the present law of privilege provides. But the dicta to which I have referred all have in common the idea that it is necessary in our society, a society in which the restraining and controlling framework is built upon a belief in the rule of law, that communications between clients and lawyers, whereby the clients are hoping for the assistance of the lawyers' legal skills in the management of their (the clients') affairs, should be secure against the possibility of any scrutiny from others, whether the police, the executive, business competitors, inquisitive busy-bodies or anyone else . . .

This ringing endorsement is based on the rationale that the lawyer must have full knowledge in order to give appropriate legal advice. The client is promised absolute confidentiality and this is seen as in the public interest, "The whole community benefits when lawyers give their clients sound advice, accurate as to the law and sensible as to their conduct".[5] Legal advice privilege has been said to be a cornerstone of the rule of law. It is, however, in a non–contentious context, difficult to differentiate the arguments from confidentiality and privacy which apply to the lawyer-client relationship from those which would apply to, say, the doctor-patient relationship.

A statutory declaration of the common law is to be found in s.10 of the Police and Criminal Evidence Act 1984 which was said by the House of Lords in *Francis and Francis v Central Criminal Court*[6] to be consistent with the common law position.

---

[3] [2003] 1 A.C. 563.
[4] [2003] 2 A.C. 736 at 757.
[5] *ibid.* at para.61 *per* Baroness Hale.
[6] [1988] 3 All E.R. 775 at 796g *per* Lord Goff.

PACE 1984, s.10:

10.—(1) Subject to subsection (2) below, in this Act 'items subject to legal privilege' means—

(a) communications between a professional legal adviser and his client or any person representing his client made in connection with the giving of legal advice to the client;

(b) communications between a professional legal adviser and his client or any person representing his client or between such an adviser or his client or any such representative and any other person made in connection with or in contemplation of legal proceedings and for the purpose of such proceedings; and

(c) items enclosed with or referred to in such communications and made—

(i) in connection with the giving of legal advice; or

(ii) in connection with or in contemplation of legal proceedings and for the purposes of such proceedings,

when they are in the possession of a person who is entitled to possession of them.

Most jurisdictions have significant protection for professional secrecy, although in recent years, there has been a trend towards limiting that secrecy with tougher statutory restrictions in order to overcome organised crime, drugs and terrorism.[7]

A. *An "Absolute" Privilege*

The judicial "balancing of conflicting interests" which characterises public interest immunity has no place with legal professional privilege. It is not for the judge to decide if the client's interest in maintaining confidentiality is outweighed by the interests of the administration of justice. Until recently it was considered that the public interest in the accused's right to prove their innocence overrode the need for candour between lawyer and client. For example, in *Barton*,[8] a defendant who was employed by a firm of solicitors was charged with fraud. He sought various documents which had come into existence as a result of the firm's probate work for clients. The firm alerted the clients and a claim to legal professional privilege was made and rejected.

Barton [1972] 2 All E.R.I 192 at 1194d-f, *per* Caulfield J.:

I think the correct principle is this, and I think that it must be restricted to these particular facts in a criminal trial, and the principle I am going to enunciate is not supported by any authority that has been cited to me; I am just working on what I

---

[7] D. Edward, "The Professional Secret:, Confidentiality and Legal Professional Privilege in Europe" (CCBE 2003) – accessed at *www.ccbe.org/doc/En/update_edwards_report_en.pdf* (April 2006).

[8] [1972] 2 All E.R. 1192.

conceive to be the rules of natural justice. If there are documents in the possession or control of a solicitor which, on production, help to further the defence of an accused man, then in my judgment no privilege attaches. I cannot conceive that our law would permit a solicitor or other person to screen from a jury information which, if disclosed to the jury, would perhaps enable a man either to establish his innocence or to resist an allegation made by the Crown.

This sweeping approach was modified in *Ataou*,[9] where there were co-accused who shared the same solicitor. The other defendant, H, made a statement to the solicitor that the appellant was not involved but later changed his mind, pleaded guilty and gave prosecution evidence implicating the appellant. The appellant's counsel sought to examine H on this incon-sistent statement but the trial judge held that the statement was privileged. The Court of Appeal held that there was a balancing act to be performed and held that it would be for the accused to show on the balance of probabilities that the accused's interest in seeking to breach the privilege outweighed that of the client in seeking to maintain it. The co-accused had been convicted and no longer had an interest. As a result the conviction was quashed.

Ataou [1988] 2 All E.R. 321 at 326g–h, *per* French J.:

When a communication was originally privileged and in criminal proceedings privilege is claimed against the defendant by the client concerned or his solicitor, it should be for the defendant to show on the balance of probabilities that the claim cannot be sustained. That might be done by demonstrating that there is no ground on which the client could any longer be regarded as having a recognisable interest in asserting the privilege. The judge must then decide whether the legitimate interest of the defendant in seeking to breach the privilege outweighs that of the client in seeking to maintain it.

But both *Barton* and *Ataou* were overruled by the House of Lords in *R. v Derby Magistrates' Court Ex p. B.*[10] In 1978 the applicant was acquitted of murder, having made various statements admitting the killing but later retracting these and instead accusing his stepfather of the murder. In 1992 the stepfather was charged with murder and at the committal proceedings, the applicant was called as a witness for the Crown. Counsel for the stepfather sought to cross-examine him about instructions he had given to his solicitors in 1978 which were inconsistent with his statements implicating his step-father. The applicant declined to waive his privilege and counsel applied under ss.4 and 5 Criminal Procedure Act 1865 to the magistrates for those instructions to be produced. The magistrates issued a witness summons under s.97 of the Magistrates' Court Act 1980 ordering the applicant to produce these documents on the grounds that they were likely to be material evidence and that the public interest in securing that all relevant information

---

[9] [1988] 2 All E.R. 321.
[10] [1995] 4 All E.R. 526.

was before the court outweighed any interest protecting confidential communications between solicitor and client. Lord Taylor C.J. held that s.97 had not been affected by the expansion of the prosecution's duty of disclosure in such cases as *Keane*.[11] If an order to produce a document was a condition of a s.97 witness summons, that document must be admissible evidence in its own right and not simply to secure discovery of the document for use in cross-examination.[12] Lord Taylor reviewed the history of legal professional privilege and made important points as to its status.

R v Derby Magistrates' Court Ex p. B [1995] 4 All E.R. 526 at 540–542, *per* Lord Taylor:

The principle which runs through all these cases, and many other cases which were cited, is that a man must be able to consult his lawyer in confidence, since otherwise he might hold back half the truth. The client must be sure that what he tells his lawyer in confidence will never be revealed without his consent. Legal professional privilege is thus much more than an ordinary rule of evidence, limited in its application to the facts of a particular case. It is a fundamental condition on which the administration of justice as a whole rests.

. . . [Counsel for the respondent] submitted that in other related areas of the law, privilege is less sacrosanct than it was. He points to the restrictions recently imposed on the right to silence, and the statutory exceptions to the privilege against self-incrimination in the fields of revenue and bankruptcy. But these examples only serve to illustrate the flaw in [counsel's] thesis. Nobody doubts that legal professional privilege could be modified, or even abrogated by statute, subject always to the objections that legal professional privilege is a fundamental human right protected by the European Convention for the Protection of Human Rights and Fundamental Freedoms[13] as to which we did not hear any argument. [Counsel's] difficulty is this: whatever inroads may have been made by Parliament in other areas, legal professional privilege is a field which Parliament has so far left untouched.

[The amicus curiae] acknowledged the importance of maintaining legal professional privilege as the general rule. But he submitted that the rule should not be absolute. There might be occasions, if only by way of rare exception, in which the rule should yield to some other consideration of even greater importance. He referred by analogy to the balancing exercise which is called for where documents are withheld on the ground of public interest immunity . . . But the drawback to that approach is that once any exception to the general rule is allowed, the client's confidence is necessarily lost. The solicitor, instead of being able to tell his client that anything which the client might say would never in any circumstances be revealed without his consent, would have to qualify his assurance. He would have to tell the client that his confidence might be broken if in some future case the court were to hold that he no longer had 'any recognisable interest' in asserting his privilege. One can see at once that the purpose of the privilege would thereby be undermined.

As for the analogy with public interest immunity, I accept that the various classes of case in which relevant evidence is excluded may . . . be regarded as forming part of a continuous spectrum. But it by no means follows that because a balancing exercise is called for in one class of case, it may also be allowed in another. Legal professional

[11] [1994] 2 All E.R. 478.
[12] *R. v Cheltenham Justices Ex p. Secretary of State for Trade* [1977] 1 All E.R. 460.
[13] Rome, November 4, 1950; TS 71 (1953) (Cmnd. 8969).

privilege and public interest immunity are as different in their origins as they are in their scope. Putting it another way, if a balancing exercise was ever required in the case of legal professional privilege, it was performed once and for all in the sixteenth century, and since then has applied across the board in every case, irrespective of the client's individual merits.

. . . it is not for the sake of the appellant alone that the privilege must be upheld. It is in the wider interests of all those hereafter who might otherwise be deterred from telling the whole truth to their solicitors. For this reason I am of the opinion that no exception should be allowed to the absolute nature of legal professional privilege, once established.

The width of this judgment is extraordinary. To hold that the court is never justified in undertaking a balancing exercise in these circumstances is to give unwarranted priority to the public interest in the lawyer–client relationship. The public interest in, for example, the liberty of an individual is as (if not more) important. Lord Taylor called in aid the European Convention to justify the assertion that legal professional privilege is a fundamental condition on which the administration of justice rests. But Art.5 of the same convention asserts the right to liberty which is an equally fundamental concept. If a person's liberty is dependent upon the disclosure of communications between a third party and their lawyer, it seems bizarre to state that legal professional privilege must in all circumstances outweigh the injury that would occur if an innocent person received a lengthy prison sentence. The public's confidence in the rule of law and in the criminal justice system would surely be severely dented.

The European Court of Justice's position would appear to differ.

AM&S Europe Ltd v EC Commission [1983] 1 All E.R. 705 at 721d–f, *per* Advocate-General Warner:

[The applicant] submitted that the right to confidential communication between lawyer and client was a fundamental human right. I do not think it is. There is no mention of it, as such, in the European Convention . . . or, seemingly, in the constitution of any member state; and your Lordships have already seen that, in England and France at least, it is acknowledged to be a right that can be overridden or modified by an appropriately worded statute . . . In my opinion it is a right that the laws of civilised countries generally recognise, a right not lightly to be denied, but not one so entrenched that, in the Community, the Council could never legislate to override or modify it.

This emphasises the importance of legal professional privilege but not as an absolute right. The European Court of Human Rights has taken a similar position in *Foxley v UK*.[14] The court was considering the extent to which a bankrupt's correspondence could be interfered with. Here the issue was the concealment of a bankrupt's assets to the detriment of his creditors in which circumstances the state may consider it necessary to have recourse to the

---

[14] [2001] 31 E.H.R.R. 25.

interception of a bankrupt's correspondence in order to identify and trace the sources of his income. The notion of necessity implies that the interference corresponds to a pressing social need and, in particular, that it is proportionate to the legitimate aim pursued. Nevertheless, the implementation of the measures must be accompanied by adequate and effective safeguards which ensure minimum impairment of the right to respect for his correspondence. This is particularly so where, as in the case at issue, correspondence with the bankrupt's legal advisers may be intercepted. The Court stressed that the lawyer–client relationship is, in principle, privileged and should be invaded only in exceptional circumstances.

The House of Lords has continued to emphasise the importance of legal professional privilege. In *Ex p. Daly*,[15] they struck down the Home Office policy that allowed prison officers to examine a prisoner's legal correspondence in the absence of the prisoner. In *Ex p. Morgan Grenfell*,[16] the inspector of taxes was not permitted to see legal advice on which Morgan Grenfell based a new tax avoidance scheme. Legal professional privilege could be removed only by express language or necessary implication.[17]

The absolute nature of the privilege was considered by the House of Lords in *Three Rivers*.

Three Rivers District Council v Bank of England [2005] 1 A.C. 610, *per* Lord Scott:

25 . . . if a communication or document qualifies for legal professional privilege, the privilege is absolute. It cannot be overridden by some supposedly greater public interest. It can be waived by the person, the client, entitled to it and it can be overridden by statute (*c/f R (Morgan Grenfell Ltd) v Special Commissioner of Income Tax*), but it is otherwise absolute. There is no balancing exercise that has to be carried out (see *B v Auckland District Law Society*[18]). The Supreme Court of Canada has held that legal professional privilege although of great importance is not absolute and can be set aside if a sufficiently compelling public interest for doing so, such as public safety, can be shown (see *Jones v Smith*[19]). But no other common law jurisdiction has, so far as I am aware, developed the law of privilege in this way. Certainly in this country legal professional privilege, if it is attracted by a particular communication between lawyer and client or attaches to a particular document, cannot be set aside on the ground that some other higher public interest requires that to be done.

The European Court of Human Rights has not yet had occasion to consider whether, in criminal proceedings, an absolute privilege is compatible with the defendant's Art.6 right to a fair trial.

B. *Legal Advice Privilege*

The first head of legal professional privilege concerns confidential communications passing between a client and his legal adviser. Such communications

---

[15] *R. v Secretary of State for the Home Department Ex p. Daly* [2001] 3 All E.R. 433.
[16] *R. v Special Commissioner of Income Tax Ex p. Morgan Grenfell* [2002] 3 All E.R. 1.
[17] Also applied in context of the Civil Procedure Rules—*General Mediterranean Holdings v Patel* [2000] 1 W.L.R. 272.
[18] [2003] 2 A.C. 736 paras 46 to 54.
[19] [1999] 1 S.C.R. 455.

need not be given in evidence by the client nor can they be given in evidence by the client's legal adviser without the client's consent, as long as the communication was made in order to enable the adviser to give legal advice and the client to obtain it.

Alfred Crompton Amusement Machines Ltd v Commissioners of Customs and Excise (No.2) [1972] 2 All E.R 353 at 376e–h, *per* Lord Denning M.R.:

The law relating to discovery was developed by the Chancery courts in the first half of the 19th century. At that time nearly all legal advisers were in independent practice on their own account. Nowadays it is very different. Many barristers and solicitors are employed as legal advisers, whole time, by a single employer. Sometimes the employer is a great commercial concern. At other times it is a government department or local authority. It may even be the government itself, like the Treasury Solicitor and his staff. In every case these legal advisers do legal work for their employer and for no one else. They are paid, not by fees for each piece of work, but by a fixed annual salary . . . They are regarded by the law as in every respect in the same position as those who practice on their own account. . . They must uphold the same standards of honour and of etiquette. They are subject to the same duties to their client and to the court. They must respect the same confidences. They and their clients have the same privileges.

Whether independent practitioners or salaried employees, it is only qualified lawyers[20] who are covered by the privilege. This includes lawyers qualified in other jurisdictions.[21] Those not qualified, for example, workers in a Citizens' Advice Bureau, would not be able to claim privilege, no matter how experienced or capable they were.[22]

Salaried lawyers, whether working for companies or government, are in the same position as the independent solicitor or barrister. A decision of the Australian Capital Territory Supreme Court in *Vance v McCormack*[23] raises the question whether more restrictive conditions may be attached in the future. It was held that communications with lawyers in the Australian Defence Force were not privileged because the lawyers did not have a current practising certificate, important because of the professional standards enforced by disciplinary proceedings. Furthermore they were employed under rules and in a culture where they were not sufficiently independent and which was not necessarily conducive with the ethical and professional standards of an independent lawyer. Within the forces, there is an authoritarian structure in which obedience may be enforced by penal sanctions as well as a strong culture of obedience and loyalty. In the UK, legal privilege attaches without such conditions but such reasoning may have future significance for both government and corporate employers of in-house lawyers.

---

[20] The privilege can be extended by statute as it is, for example, to patent and trademark agents by sections 280 and 284 of the Copyright, Designs and Patents Act 1988.

[21] *Great Atlantic Insurance Co. v Home Insurance Co* [1981] 2 All E.R. 485—a memorandum from American legal advisers was undoubtedly privileged.

[22] The privilege did not cover communications to a legal aid officer working within in a prison—*Umoh* [1987] Crim.L.R. 258.

[23] [2004] A.C.T.S.C. 78.

The extension of the privilege to legal advice was recognised in *Greenough v Gaskell*,[24] which recognised that the privilege applied to communications where litigation was not contemplated.

Greenough v Gaskell (1833) [1824–31] All E.R. Rep 767 at 770d–e, *per* Lord Brougham:

If it were confined to proceedings begun or in contemplation, then every communication would be unprotected which a party makes with a view to his general defence against attacks which he apprehends, although at the time no one may have resolved to assail him. But were it allowed to extend over such communications, the protection would be insufficient, if it only included communications more or less connected with judicial proceedings; for a person oftentimes requires the aid of professional advice upon the subject of his rights and his liabilities, with no references to any particular litigation, and without any other reference to litigation generally than all human affairs have, in so far as every transaction may, by possibility, become the subject of judicial inquiry. 'It would be most mischievous,' said the learned Judges in the Common Pleas, 'if it could be doubted whether or not an attorney, consulted upon a man's title to an estate, was at liberty to divulge a flaw'.

Later decisions narrow the scope of the privilege to the giving and taking of advice.

Minter v Priest [1930] All E.R. 431 at 440, *per* Lord Atkin:

As to this it is necessary to avoid misapprehension lest the protection be too limited. It is, I think, apparent that if the communication passes for the purpose of getting legal advice, it must be deemed confidential. The protection, of course, attaches to the communications made by the solicitor as well as the client. If there the phrase is expanded to professional communications passing for the purpose of getting or giving professional advice, and it is understood that the profession is the legal profession, the nature of the protection is, I think, correctly defined.

Recent authorities are broader and suggest that the privilege is not limited to those communications that specifically give or seek advice but applies to the wide range of documents (letters, memoranda, emails, notes) that are created in the course of lawyers' relationship with their clients. But it is not all documents that are privileged—a client account ledger maintained in relation to the client's money; conveyancing documents; an appointment's diary time recording or attendance notes; notes of open court proceedings or conversations; correspondence or attendance notes of meetings with opposing lawyers; and a lawyer's records of a client's telephone numbers and of dates

---

[24] [1824–31] All E.R. 767.

when the client telephoned the lawyer. All these have been held not to be privileged.

The scope of the privilege was considered in *Balabel v Air India*.[25] An action was brought claiming specific performance of an agreement to grant a lease. The claimants sought documents requested were all communications between the defendants and their solicitors, other than those seeking or giving legal advice, all working documents relating to the lease as well as internal communications of the defendants.

Balabel v Air India [1988] 2 All E.R. 246 at 247g–255j, *per* Taylor L.J.:

This case raises an important point concerning legal professional privilege. Broadly, the issue is whether such privilege extends only to communications seeking or conveying legal advice or to all that passes between solicitor and client on matters within the ordinary business of a solicitor . . .

It is common ground that the basic principle justifying legal professional privilege arises from the public interest requiring full and frank exchange of confidence between solicitor and client to enable the latter to receive necessary legal advice. Originally it related only to communications where legal proceedings were in being or in contemplation. This was the rationale which distinguished the solicitor and client relationship from that between any other professional man and his client. There is no doubt that legal professional privilege now extends beyond legal advice in regard to litigation. But how far?

. . . Although originally confined to advice regarding litigation, the privilege was extended to non-litigious business. Nevertheless, despite that extension, the purpose and scope of the privilege is still to enable legal advice to be sought and given in confidence. In my judgment, therefore, the test is whether the communication or other document was made confidentially for the purpose of legal advice. Those purposes have to be construed broadly. Privilege obviously attaches to a document conveying legal advice from solicitor to client and to a specific request from the client for such advice. But it does not follow that all other communications lack privilege. In most solicitor and client relationships, especially where a transaction involves protracted dealings, advice may be required or appropriate on matters great or small at various stages. There will be a continuum of communications and meetings between the solicitor and client. The negotiations for a lease such as occurred in the present case are only one example. Where information is passed by the solicitor or client to the other as part of the continuum aimed at keeping both informed so that advice may be sought and given as required, privilege will attach. A letter from the client containing information may end with such words as 'please advise me what I should do'. But, even if it does not, there will usually be implied in the relationship an overall expectation that the solicitor will at each stage, whether asked specifically or not, tender appropriate advice. Moreover, legal advice is not confined to telling the client the law; it must include advice as to what should prudently and sensibly be done in the relevant legal context.

. . . It follows from this analysis that those dicta in the decided cases which appear to extend privilege without limit to all solicitor and client communication on matters within the ordinary business of a solicitor and referable to that relationship are too wide. It may be that the broad terms used in the earlier cases reflect the restricted range of solicitor's activities at the time. Their role then would have been confined for

---

[25] [1988] 2 All E.R. 246.

the most part to that of lawyer and would not have extended to business adviser or man of affairs. To speak therefore of matters 'within the ordinary business of a solicitor' would in practice usually have meant the giving of advice and assistance of a specifically legal nature. But the range of assistance given by solicitors to their clients and of activities carried out on their behalf has greatly broadened in recent times and is still developing. Hence the need to re-examine the scope of legal professional privilege and keep it within justifiable bounds.

Those bounds were further considered in *Nederlandse Reassurantie Groep Holding NV v Bacon and Woodrow*[26] in which the claimants, a Dutch company, after consulting accountants, its banking and corporate finance advisers and its lawyers, took over other insurance companies. These companies proved to be over-exposed in the reinsurance market and the claimants sought to recover damages from their non-legal advisers. The defendants argued that the lawyers gave advice of a general nature going to the commercial viability of the agreement and sought discovery of communications between the claimants and their lawyers. The court held that *Balabel* had laid down that a solicitor' professional duty was not confined to giving advice on matters of law but could also relate to the commercial wisdom of entering into a given transaction in respect of which legal advice was also sought. In such a situation, all communications between the solicitor and the client relating to the transaction would be privileged, even though they did not give advice on matters of law or construction, provided that they were directly related to the performance by the solicitors of their professional duty as legal advisers.

The question of what was covered by legal advice privilege was thrown into disarray by the Court of Appeal decisions in *Three Rivers*.[27] These decisions created considerable uncertainty on the scope of legal advice privilege, particularly for corporations and other organisations, first by adopting a restrictive definition of 'the client' and secondly by confining the privilege to advice about legal rights and liabilities. This series of cases were against the Bank of England and a consequence of the collapse of the Bank of Credit and Commerce International (BCCI) in 1991. As a result, the government set up an inquiry, known as the Bingham Inquiry, to investigate the Bank of England's supervision of BCCI. The bank created a small team to liaise with the inquiry—the Bingham Inquiry Unit (BIU). A firm of solicitors advised the BIU on all communications with the Inquiry. Once the Inquiry Report was published, the BCCI liquidator and BCCI depositors sued the bank and sought disclosure both of communications between the solicitors and bank employees not belonging to the BIU and also disclosure of communications between the solicitors and the BIU. The Court of Appeal decided that only the BIU was to be regarded the 'client' and therefore documents from other Bank employees were not privileged. Such documents were in the same position as third party documents—namely that they would only be protected by litigation privilege if made for the dominant purpose of being used in adversarial litigation (but the proceedings of the Inquiry were

[26] [1995] 1 All E.R. 976.
[27] *Three Rivers District Council v Bank of England (No.5)* ([2003] Q.B. 1556 (2003) 7 E. & P. 198); *Three Rivers District Council v Bank of England (No.6)* ([2004] Q.B. 916 (2004) 8 E. & P. 191).

not adversarial). Later the Court of Appeal also ordered disclosure of the BIU's communications with the layers because the dominant purpose of these communications was to obtain advice about the presentation of the bank's evidence to the Bingham Inquiry rather than advice about the bank's legal rights and obligations.

This latter decision was reversed by the House of Lords,[28] endorsing Taylor L.J.'s description of legal advice in *Balabal*[29]. Lord Scott said that legal rights and obligations must include advice about public law rights, liabilities and obligations.

Three Rivers District Council v Bank of England [2005] 1 A.C. 610, *per* Lord Scott:

35. Legal advice privilege should, in my opinion, be given a scope that reflects the policy reasons that justify its presence in our law . . . The Court of Appeal has restricted the scope of legal advice privilege to material constituting or recording communications between clients and lawyers seeking or giving advice about the clients' legal rights and obligations. It has excluded legal advice sought or given for presentational purposes. The particular issue . . . was whether advice that related to the presentation of material to the Inquiry qualified for legal advice privilege. In holding that it did not, the Court of Appeal distinguished between a lawyer-client relationship "formed for the purpose of obtaining advice or assistance in relation to rights and liabilities" and a lawyer-client relationship where "the dominant purpose is not the obtaining of advice and assistance in relation to legal rights and obligations". In relation to the former, "broad protection will be given to communications passing between solicitor and client in the course of that relationship"; in relation to the latter, a similar broad protection could not be claimed . . .

36. The authorities on which the Court of Appeal founded their approach were all concerned with private law rights and obligations . . . It is clear, however, that whatever view may be taken of the presentational advice point, legal advice privilege must cover also advice and assistance in relation to public law rights, liabilities and obligations . . .

37. In my opinion, the impossibility of a principled exclusion from legal advice privilege of communications between lawyer and client relating to the client's public law rights, liabilities and obligations is conclusive of the narrow issue in this appeal. One of the main purposes of the Inquiry was to examine whether in relation to BCCI the Bank had properly discharged its public law duties of supervision imposed by the Banking Acts. The Bank was naturally anxious that the Inquiry's conclusions should be as favourable as possible or, to put the point in reverse, that the Inquiry's criticisms of the Bank should be as limited as possible. Every public inquiry conducts its proceedings and expresses its conclusions under the shadow of potential judicial review. The inquiry's procedures may be judicially reviewed if they are perceived to be unfair. The inquiry's conclusions may be judicially reviewed if they are thought to be unsustainable in the light of the evidence the inquiry has received. Presentational advice or assistance given by lawyers to parties whose conduct may be the subject of criticism by the inquiry is advice or assistance that may serve to avoid the need to invoke public law remedies. It would be—or should be—readily accepted that, once an

---

[28] *Three Rivers District Council v Bank of England* [2005] 1 A.C. 610: [2004] 3 W.L.R. 1274.
[29] above.

inquiry's conclusions have been reached and communicated to the sponsors of the inquiry, advice from lawyers to someone criticised as to whether a public law remedy might be available to quash the critical conclusions would be advice that qualified for legal advice privilege. It makes no sense at all, in my opinion, to withhold the protection of that privilege from presentational advice given by the lawyers for the purpose of preventing that criticism from being made in the first place.

38. In *Balabel v Air India*, Taylor LJ . . . said that for the purposes of attracting legal advice privilege—". . . legal advice is not confined to telling the client the law; it must include advice as to what should prudently and sensibly be done in the relevant legal context". I would venture to draw attention to Taylor LJ's reference to "the relevant legal context". That there must be a "relevant legal context" in order for the advice to attract legal professional privilege should not be in doubt. Taylor LJ said that—". . . to extend privilege without limit to all solicitor and client communication upon matters within the ordinary business of a solicitor and referable to that relationship [would be] too wide." This remark is, in my respectful opinion, plainly correct. If a solicitor becomes the client's "man of business", and some solicitors do, responsible for advising the client on all matters of business, including investment policy, finance policy and other business matters, the advice may lack a relevant legal context. There is, in my opinion, no way of avoiding difficulty in deciding in marginal cases whether the seeking of advice from or the giving of advice by lawyers does or does not take place in a relevant legal context so as to attract legal advice privilege. In cases of doubt the judge called upon to make the decision should ask whether the advice relates to the rights, liabilities, obligations or remedies of the client either under private law or under public law. If it does not, then, in my opinion, legal advice privilege would not apply. If it does so relate then, in my opinion, the judge should ask himself whether the communication falls within the policy underlying the justification for legal advice privilege in our law. Is the occasion on which the communication takes place and is the purpose for which it takes place such as to make it reasonable to expect the privilege to apply? The criterion must, in my opinion, be an objective one . . .

43. There may, as I have said, be marginal cases where the answer is not easy. But, in my opinion, the present case is not in the least marginal. The preparation of the evidence to be submitted and the submissions to be made to the Inquiry on behalf of the Bank were for the purpose of enhancing the Bank's prospects of persuading the Inquiry that its discharge of its public law obligations under the Banking Acts in relation to BCCI was not deserving of criticism and had been reasonable in the circumstances. The presentational advice given by Freshfields and counsel for that purpose was advice "as to what should prudently and sensibly be done in the relevant legal context" . . .

The House of Lords declined to consider whether the Court of Appeal had been right in adopting a restrictive view of "client" although it was made it clear that this refusal should not be taken as endorsement of the Court of Appeal's position. There is a dearth of domestic authority[30] and any opinions expressed by the House would be *obiter dicta*. The guiding precedent remains the Court of Appeal judgment in *Three Rivers (No.5)*.[31] This position will cause practical difficulties for lawyers working with companies, government departments and large organisations generally.

C. *Litigation Privilege*

The second head of legal professional privilege has, in one sense, a narrower scope as it comes into existence only where the communications are made

[30] But see *Upjohn Co. v United States* (1981) 449 U.S. 383.
[31] [2003] 3 W.L.R. 667.

with reference to litigation that is actually taking place or in contemplation. It cannot exist in the context of non-adversarial proceedings such as the Bingham Inquiry. In another sense, it is a much broader privilege —the "legal advice" head of privilege only encompasses communications between the lawyer and client but the "litigation" head also encompasses communications between the client and third parties or between the legal adviser and third parties. It also applies to "without prejudice" correspondence between opposing parties.

This broad scope, embracing third parties, can be seen in the leading case of *Wheeler v Le Marchant*.[32] The Court of Appeal ordered the defendants to produce letters which had passed between the defendants' solicitors and a surveyor with regard to property, except for those which had been prepared after the conflict over the property had arisen.

Wheeler v Le Marchant (1881) 50 L.J. Ch. 793 at 795–796, *per* Lord Jessel M.R.:

. . . the principle is of a very limited character. It does not protect all confidential communications which a man must necessarily make in order to obtain advice, even when necessary for the protection of his life or of his honour, to say nothing of his fortune. There are many communications which must be made, because without them the ordinary business of life cannot be carried on, and yet they are not protected. As I have said in the course of argument, the communication made to a medical man, whose advice is sought by a patient . . . is not protected. Communications made to the priest in the confessional, on matters perhaps considered by the penitent to be more important even than the care of his life or his fortune, are not protected. Communications made to a friend with respect to matters of the most delicate nature, on which advice is sought with respect to a man's honour or reputation, are not protected. Therefore it must not be supposed that there is any principle which says that every confidential communication which in order to carry on the ordinary business of life, must necessarily be made, is protected. The protection is of a very limited character. It is a protection in this country restricted to the obtaining of assistance of lawyers, as regards the conduct of litigation or the rights of property. It has never gone beyond the obtaining of legal advice and assistance; and all things reasonably necessary in the shape of communication to the legal advisers are protected from production or discovery, in order that that legal advice may be obtained safely and sufficiently . . .

The actual communication to the solicitor by the client is, of course, protected, and it is equally protected whether that communication is made by the client in person or by an agent on behalf of the client, and whether made to the solicitor in person or to a clerk or subordinate of the solicitor, who acts in his place and under his direction. Again, with the same view, the evidence obtained by the solicitor, or by his direction, or at his instance, even if obtained by the client, is protected if obtained after litigation has commenced or threatened, or with a view to the defence or prosecution of such litigation. So, again, it does not matter whether the advice is obtained from the solicitor as to a dealing which is not the subject of litigation. What is protected is the communication necessary to obtain legal advice. It must be a communication made to the solicitor in that character or for that purpose.

---

[32] (1881) 50 L.J. Ch.793.

But what we are asked to protect here is this: the solicitor being consulted in a matter as to which no dispute has arisen, thinks he would like to know some further facts before giving his advice, and applies to a surveyor to tell him what the state of a given property is, or information of that character, and it is said that information given in answer to such application ought to be protected because it is desired or required by the solicitor in order to enable him the better to give legal advice. It appears to me that it is not only extending the rule beyond what has been previously laid down, but beyond what necessity warrants . . .

Litigation must be definitely in the contemplation of the parties. *United States of America v BAT*[33] involved US litigation against tobacco companies alleging that the companies had engaged in an unlawful enterprise to deceive and defraud the American public about the health risks of smoking. It was an important part of that case that the companies had destroyed or suppressed documents which they believed might damage them in any litigation. The US government wished to take a deposition from a London solicitor who had acted for BAT. BAT argued that the lawyer would be examined on communications which were the subject of, inter alia, litigation privilege. The judge directed himself that the issue was whether litigation was reasonably in prospect—on appeal it was held that this was correct and that a mere possibility of litigation was not sufficient to invoke privilege. He was also correct to conclude that the fact that there was a distinct possibility that someone might make a claim was insufficient. That view was reinforced by the fact that BAT hired the solicitor's firm for other reasons entirely. The appropriate test was that litigation must have been reasonably in prospect.

In *Alfred Crompton Amusement Machines Ltd v Commissioners of Customs and Excise (No.2)*,[34] the company were in dispute with the commissioners over their liability for purchase tax for gambling machines. The commissioners objected to disclosure of communications, both internal and with third parties, which had been used as a basis for the assessment. The commissioners were entitled to claim legal professional privilege for the communications with their own salaried legal advisers. But there were also documents received from third parties used to assess the market value of the machines in question.

Alfred Crompton Amusement Machines Ltd v Commissioners of Customs and Excise (No.2) [1973] 2 All E.R. 1169 at 1183f–1184c, *per* Lord Cross:

Here the two purposes for which the documents in question were obtained or came into existence were parts of a single wider purpose—namely, the ascertainment of the wholesale value in the manner prescribed by the Act. The first, and the sole immediate, purpose was to help the commissioners to fix what in their opinion was the true value; the second purpose was to help the solicitor, if the commissioners' opinion was challenged, to prepare their case for arbitration. It was not—and hardly

---

[33] [2004] EWCA Civ.330.
[34] [1973] 2 All E.R. 1169.

could have been—suggested that the mere fact that the commissioners would know in every case that their opinion might be challenged would itself enable them to claim that such documents as are in question here would be the subject of legal professional privilege whenever in fact their opinion was challenged. What is said to make them privileged in this case is the fact that the commissioners happened to expect that there would be an arbitration and called in the solicitor to 'hold their hands' in the early stages. But, even so, in this case just as much in cases in which no arbitration was in fact anticipated the commissioners had to form their own opinion as to value on the evidence available to them, including these documents, before any arbitration could take place. This feature of the case appears to me to . . . make it analogous to *Jones v Great Central Railway Co. Ltd.*[35] There a member of a trade union who thought that he had been unjustly dismissed by his employers furnished the union authorities (as required by the rules) with information in writing as to the facts of the case as he saw them in order to satisfy them that it was proper for them to sanction the employment of a solicitor to conduct the case and also for use by the solicitor in the conduct of the action if the employment of a solicitor was sanctioned. This House held that the letters in question were not the subject of legal professional privilege because the union authorities had themselves to consider them and act on them before the solicitor was employed to conduct the case. So here the commissioners had to form their own opinion as to value before the solicitor would use the documents for the purpose of defending their opinion in the anticipated arbitration.

Here the documents in question came into existence because the commissioners were seeking to inform themselves about the value of the machines. There was an incidental purpose that the documents might be used by lawyers in later litigation. This secondary purpose was insufficient to attract legal professional privilege. Where litigation is the only purpose of the communication, there is no problem but where there are other objectives, *Alfred Crompton* shows a restrictive approach to the privilege.

This was considered further by the House of Lords in *Waugh v British Rail.*[36] The widow of a train driver, killed in an accident, sued his employers and sought internal reports on the accident, made two days after the accident by two officers of British Rail. The early authorities such as *Ogden v London Electric Railway Co.*[37] suggested that such reports need not be disclosed if one of their purposes (even if that were subsidiary) was to inform the solicitor with a view to possible litigation. But *Ogden* was distinguished in *Alfred Crompton* and by the Australian High Court in *Grant v Downs.*[38] The latter adopted a very restrictive policy, allowing privilege to be claimed only where the document was produced *wholly* for the purpose of furthering the litigation. But in that case, Barwick C.J. dissented and preferred a test which allowed legal professional privilege to be asserted whenever the "dominant purpose" of creating the document was to further the litigation. Other subsidiary objectives need not destroy that privilege. It was this latter approach that the House of Lords adopted, although on the facts they held that the dominant purpose of the accident report was not to assist in possible litigation but to inform British Rail about the cause of the accident with the aim of preventing any recurrence. As a result the reports were not privileged.

[35] [1910] A.C. 4.
[36] [1979] 2 All E.R. 1169.
[37] [1933] All E.R. 896.
[38] (1976) 135 C.L.R. 674.

Waugh v British Rail [1979] 2 All E.R. 1169 at 1181c–l 183d, *per* Lord Edmund-Davies:

It is for the party refusing disclosure to establish his right to refuse. It may well be that in some cases where that right has in the past been upheld the courts have failed to keep clear the distinction between (a) communications between client and legal adviser, and (b) communications between the client and third parties, made . . . 'for the purpose of obtaining information to be submitted to the client's professional legal advisers for the purpose of obtaining advice upon pending or contemplated litigation'. In cases falling within (a), privilege from disclosure attaches to communications for the purpose of obtaining legal advice and it is immaterial whether or not the possibility of litigation were even contemplated . . . But in cases falling within (b) the position is quite otherwise/ Litigation, apprehended or actual, is its hallmark . . .

Preparation with a view to litigation, pending or anticipated, being thus the essential purpose which protects a communication from disclosure in such cases as the present, what in the last resort is the touchstone of the privilege? Is it sufficient that the prospect of litigation be merely one of the several purposes leading to the communication coming into being? And is that sufficient . . . despite the fact that there is also 'another and even more important purpose'? Is an appreciable purpose sufficient? Or does it have to be the main purpose? Or one of its main purposes . . .? Ought your Lordships to declare that privilege attaches only to material which . . . 'comes within the words "wholly or mainly" for the purpose of litigation'? Or should this House adopt the majority decision of the High Court of Australia in Grant v Downs that legal professional privilege must be confined to documents brought into existence for the sole purpose of submission to legal advisers for advice or for use in legal proceedings?

. . . Justice is better served by candour than by suppression. For, as it was put in the *Grant v Downs* majority judgment, 'privilege . . . detracts from the fairness of the trial by denying a party access to relevant documents or at least subjecting him to surprise'.

Adopting that approach, I would certainly deny a claim to privilege when litigation was merely one of several purposes of equal or similar importance intended to be served by the material sought to be withheld from disclosure, and a fortiori where it was merely a minor purpose. On the other hand, I consider that it would be going too far to adopt the '*sole* purpose' test applied by the majority in *Grant v Downs*, which has been adopted in no United Kingdom decision nor, as far as we are aware, elsewhere in the Commonwealth. Its adoption would deny privilege even to material whose outstanding purpose is to serve litigation, simply because another and very minor purpose was also being served. But, inasmuch as the only basis of the claim to privilege in such cases as the present one is that the material in question was brought into existence for use in legal proceedings, it is surely right to insist that, before the claim is conceded or upheld, such a purpose must be shown to have played a paramount part. Which phrase or epithet should be selected to designate this is a matter of individual judgment . . . I have finally come down in favour of the test propounded by Barwick CJ in *Grant v Downs* in the following words:

. . . a document which was produced or brought into existence either with the dominant purpose of its author, or of the person or authority under whose direction, whether particular or general, it was produced or brought into existence, of using it or its contents in order to obtain legal advice or to conduct or aid in the conduct of litigation, at the time of its production in reasonable prospect, should be privileged and excluded from inspection.

Dominant purpose, then, in my judgment, should now be declared by this House to be the touchstone . . .

This test was applied in *Guinness Peat Properties Ltd v Fitzroy Robinson*.[39] The claimants, who were building developers, sued the architects of an office

[39] [1987] 2 All E.R. 716.

building which had developed a fault. The architects wrote to their insurers, enclosing a copy of the claim, other relevant memoranda and asking the insurers' opinion. Were these communications privileged? Even though the architects might have regarded the matter as 'insurance', litigation was the underlying and dominant purpose of the insurers. The court quoted Brightman L.J. in *Buttes Gas and Oil Co. v Hammer (No.3)*.

Buttes Gas and Oil Co v Hammer (No.3) [1980] 3 All E.R. 475 at 502:

. . . if two parties with a common interest and a common solicitor exchange information for the dominant purpose of informing each other of the facts, or the issues, or advice received, or of obtaining legal advice in respect of contemplated or pending litigation, the documents or copies containing that information are privileged from production in the hands of each

The documents were therefore privileged.

D. *Legal Professional Privilege—General Issues*

1. Ownership and Waiver

Legal professional privilege is a privilege of the client who is able in certain circumstances to prevent the lawyer or a third party from revealing confidential communications. The objective is to encourage candour between the lawyer and the client so as to enable the lawyer to represent the client effectively. As the privilege is based upon a private interest, the party to whom the privilege attaches has to assert it but also can waive it. Waiver can be express or it can be implied through disclosure. Those purporting to waive privilege must be acting within their powers.[40] Once the privilege has been waived by the client, the lawyer cannot refuse to disclose the information. In contrast, in France, the obligation is considered to be *d'ordre publique* so that, even where the client waives the privilege, the lawyer retains a discretion whether or not to disclose the contents of the communication.[41]

In criminal proceedings, the issue of waiver has come up recently in the context of s.34 of the Criminal Justice and Police Act 1994 where the defendant gives a 'no comment' interview at the police station. Often this is on the basis of legal advice. At trial, the defendant often seeks to negate any adverse inferences that may be drawn from this silence by explaining the reasons behind this advice. By revealing part of the discussion with their lawyer, does the defendant waive privilege? In *Bowden*,[42] the accused, charged with robbery, stayed silent in interview on legal advice but his solicitor made

---

[40] *GE Capital Corporate Finance Group Ltd v Sutton* [2004] EWCA Civ.315 (receivers of a company).
[41] *AM&S Europe Ltd v EC Commission* [1983] 1 All E.R. 705 at 718c *per* Advocate-General Warner.
[42] (1999) 4 All E.R. 43; *Condron* (1997) 1 W.L.R. 827; *Wishart* [2005] EWCA Crim 1337.

a statement to the interviewing officer as to why he had given that advice. At trial, the officer was asked about that statement by defence counsel. The trial judge held that the accused had waived his privilege and allowed the prosecution to question the defendant on what he had told his solicitor. On appeal, the court held, on a preliminary point, that where defendants testified to facts not previously mentioned and the Crown alleged that these were a fabrication, the accused could certainly mention prior consistent statements to their solicitor without waiving privilege. Further if they merely stated that they remained silent on legal advice, this did not constitute a waiver of privilege but if they went beyond that to testify the grounds on which that advice was given, the privilege would be waived.

Bowden (1999) 4 All E.R. 43 at 50b–f, *per* Lord Bingham C.J.:

If, at trial, the defendant or his solicitor gives evidence not merely of the defendant's refusal to answer pre-trial questions on legal advice but also of the grounds on which such advice was given, or if (as here) the defence elicit evidence at trial of a statement made by a defendant or his solicitor pre-trial of the grounds on which legal advice had been given to answer no questions, the defendant voluntarily withdraws the veil of privilege which would otherwise protect confidential communications between his legal adviser and himself, and having done so he cannot resist questioning directed to the nature of that advice and the factual premises on which it had been based. This approach is, we consider, consistent with that taken by this court in previous cases. In *R v Condron*, the court said

"If an accused person gives as a reason for not answering questions, that he has been advised by his solicitor not to do so, that advice, in our judgment, does not amount to a waiver of privilege. But, equally, for reasons which we have already given, that bare assertion is unlikely by itself to be regarded as a sufficient reason for not mentioning matters relevant to the defence. So it will be necessary, if the accused wishes to invite the court not to draw an adverse inference, to go further and state the basis or reason for the advice. Although the matter was not fully argued, it seems to us that once this is done that it may well amount to a waiver of privilege so that the accused, or if his solicitor is also called, the solicitor, can be asked whether there were any other reasons for the advice, and the nature of the advice given, so as to explore whether the advice may also have been given for tactical reasons".

Parties need to exercise caution since, if privilege is waived for part of an otherwise privileged document, it is waived for the whole. In *Great Atlantic Insurance v Home Insurance*[43] the claimants received a memorandum from their US attorneys relating to the litigation. The first two paragraphs of the memo related to discussions between the attorneys and third parties. In the course of discovery, the claimants disclosed the first two paragraphs. Their solicitor intended to claim privilege for the remainder of the memo but failed to do so. At the trial, the claimants' counsel read the first two paragraphs under the impression that it was complete as it stood. The defence asked for disclosure of the whole document and this was granted.

[43] [1981] 2 All E.R. 485.

Great Atlantic Insurance v Home Insurance [1981] 2 All E.R. 485 at 488j–492a, *per* Templeman L.J.:

In my judgment, the whole of the memorandum was privileged because it was a communicatiOn by the plaintiffs' American attorneys to the plaintiffs relating to a matter . . . on which the American attorneys were instructed to act as legal advisers to the plaintiffs. The fact that the memorandum included an account of a conversation . . . which conversation was not privileged, does not alter the confidentiality attaching to the memorandum as a whole by virtue of the relationship between the American attorneys in their capacity as legal advisers and the plaintiffs in their capacity as clients of those legal advisers.

. . . The second question is whether, the whole of the memorandum being a privileged communication between legal adviser and client, the plaintiff may waive the privilege with regard to the first two paragraphs of the memorandum but assert privilege over the additional matter. In my judgment severance would be possible if the memorandum dealt with entirely different subject matters or different incidents and could in effect be divided into two separate memoranda each dealing with a separate subject matter . . .

Counsel for the plaintiffs argued that severance is permissible where the part disclosed is only an account of a discussion which in itself is not privileged. But, once it is decided that the memorandum deals with only one subject matter, it seems to me that it might be or appear dangerous or misleading to allow the plaintiffs to disclose part of the memorandum and assert privilege over the remainder. . . In my judgment, the simplest, safest and most straightforward rule is that if a document is privileged then privilege must be asserted, if at all, to the whole document unless the document deals with separate subject matters so that the document can in effect be divided into two separate and distinct documents, each of which is complete.

. . . in my judgment the plaintiffs deliberately chose to read part of a document which dealt with one subject matter to the trial judge, and must disclose the whole. The deliberate introduction by the plaintiffs of part of the memorandum into the trial record as a result of a mistake by the plaintiffs waives privilege with regard to the whole document. I can see no principle whereby the court could claim to exercise or could fairly and effectively exercise any discretion designed to put the clock back and to undo what has been done.

2. The use of secondary evidence

When legal professional privilege is claimed, does it cover just the document or the conversation that is the subject of that exclusion or can the contents be proved by some other means? Unlike public interest immunity, when private privilege is in issue, documents must be guarded carefully since if their contents become known, secondary evidence of those contents may be admissible.

In *Calcraft v Guest*,[44] an action for trespass to a fishery, some documents about a previous action but involving the same rights, fell into the hands of the opposite party by accident. His lawyers took copies and returned the originals but sought to use the copies as evidence. The originals were still subject to privilege.

Calcraft v Guest [1898] 1 Q.B. 759 at 761–762, *per* Lindley M.R.:

I take it that, as a general rule, one may say once privileged always privileged. I do not mean to say that privilege cannot be waived, but that the mere fact that documents

[44] [1898] 1 Q.B. 759.

used in previous litigation are held and have not been destroyed, does not amount to a waiver of the privilege . . . It appears that the appellant has obtained copies of some of these documents, and is in a position to give secondary evidence of them; and the question is whether he is entitled to do that. That appears to me to be covered by the authority of *Lloyd v Mostyn*,[45] (where) Parke B. said, 'Where an attorney intrusted confidentially with a document communicates the contents or suffers another to take a copy, surely the secondary evidence so obtained may be produced. Suppose the instrument were even stolen, and a correct copy taken, would it not be reasonable to admit it?' The matter dropped there; but the other members of the court all concurred in that, which I take to be a distinct authority that secondary evidence in a case of this kind may be received.

There was a similar situation in *Tompkins*[46] when the defendant wrote a note to his counsel. This was accidentally dropped on the floor and was handed over to the prosecution who had not acted improperly and were allowed to cross–examine the accused on the note's contents. Nowadays, before any cross-examination, the trial judge must consider the issue of fairness—in *Cottrill*,[47] the accused's lawyers passed on an otherwise privi-leged statement by the accused to the prosecution who questioned him on its contents. In the absence of impropriety by the prosecution, the privilege had been lost and the judge was within the limits of his discretion in deciding that the admission of the evidence would not have an adverse effect on the fairness of the proceedings.[48]

Cottrill is authority that s.78 would restrain the prosecution from using the material if they had acted improperly. In civil proceedings, it is also possible to protect the privilege where there has been some impropriety. In *Lord Ashburton v Pape*,[49] the defendant, an undischarged bankrupt, improperly obtained letters written by the claimant to his solicitor. He intended to use these in pending bankruptcy proceedings but the claimant was able to obtain an injunction to prevent this.

Lord Ashburton v Pape [1913] 2 Ch 469 at 473, *per* Cozens-Hardy M.R.:

. . . The rule of evidence as explained in *Calcraft v Guest*, merely amounts to this, that if a litigant wants to prove a particular document which by reason of privilege or some circumstance he cannot furnish by the production of the original, he may produce a copy as secondary evidence although that copy has been obtained by improper means, and even, it may be, by criminal means. The Court in such an action is not really trying the circumstances under which the document was produced. That is not an issue in the case and the Court simply says 'Here is a copy of a document which cannot be produced; it may have been stolen, it may have been picked up in the street, it may have improperly got into the possession of the person who proposes to produce it, but that is not a matter which the Court in the trial of the action can go into.' But that does

---

[45] (1842) 10 M.&W. 478.
[46] (1977) 67 Cr.App.R. 181.
[47] [1997] Crim.L.R. 56.
[48] Police and Criminal Evidence Act 1984, s.78.
[49] [1913] 2 Ch.469.

not seem to me to have any bearing upon a case where the whole subject-matter of the action is the right to retain the originals or copies of certain documents which are privileged. It seems to me that, although Pape has had the good luck to obtain a copy of these documents which he can produce without a breach of this injunction, there is no ground whatever in principle why we should decline to give the plaintiff the protection which in my view is his right as between him and Pape . . .

If the party claiming privilege acts quickly, they can obtain an injunction to prevent the use in the trial itself of copies of the privileged originals. In *ITC Film Distributors v Video Exchange Ltd*,[50] one party brought into court documents which were the subject of legal privilege. The other party obtained them by underhand means and was prevented from using them. This suggests that a party is able to restrain an opponent making use of copies which have been wrongfully obtained. *Butler v Board of Trade* appears to extend this,

. . . In the present case there was no impropriety on the part of the defendants in the way in which they received the copy, but that, in my judgment, is irrelevant because an innocent recipient of information conveyed in breach of confidence is liable to be restrained.[51]

It is principles of equity (rather than rules of privilege) that govern whether a litigant is able to make use of any secondary evidence of one's opponent's documents. In *Goddard v Nationwide Building Society*,[52] a solicitor had acted for both house buyers and building society in a house purchase. The buyers sought to sue the building society for its surveyor's negligence. The defendants obtained a note of a conversation between one of the claimants and the solicitor. Were the claimants entitled to an injunction preventing use of this material?

Goddard v Nationwide Building Society [1986] 3 All E.R. 264 270f–h, *per* May L.J.:

I confess that I do not find the decision in *Lord Ashburton v Pape* logically satisfactory, depending as it does on the order in which applications are made in litigation. Nevertheless I think that it and *Calcraft v Guest* are good authority for the following proposition. If a litigant has in his possession copies of documents to which legal professional privilege attaches, he may nevertheless use such copies as secondary evidence in his litigation; however, if he has not yet used the documents in that way, the mere fact that he intends to do so is no answer to a claim against him by the person in whom the privilege is vested for delivery up of the copies or to restrain him from disclosing or making use of any information contained in them.

The rule in *Calcraft v Guest* was "guard it or lose it" but equitable injunctions limit the ambit of this. But the jurisdiction cannot prevail over

[50] [1982] 2 All E.R. 241.
[51] [1971] Ch. 680 at 690 *per* Goff J.
[52] [1986] 3 All E.R. 264.

evidentiary rules generally. The law of evidence does not privilege confidential communications between a doctor and a patient and if a litigant
sought to use these in some unauthorised fashion, equity would not restrain
him or her.

Calcraft v Guest [1898] 1 Q.B. 759 at 270h–j, *per* Nourse L.J.:

The equitable jurisdiction is well able to extend, for example, to the grant of an
injunction to restrain the unauthorised disclosure of confidential communications
between priest and penitent or doctor and patient. But those communications are not
privileged in legal proceedings and I do not believe that equity would restrain a
litigant who already had a record of such a communication in his possession from
using it for the purposes of his litigation. It cannot be the function of equity to accord a
de facto privilege to communications in respect of which no privilege can be claimed.
Equity follows the law.

The *Goddard* approach was followed and extended in *Guinness Peat Properties v Fitzroy Robinson Partnership*,[53] where the developers of a building sued
the architects after the building had developed faults. The defendant architects wrote to their insurers about the claim and expressing views on its
merits. This letter was inadvertently disclosed to the claimants who inspected
it and took a copy. Usually the rule is that, once inspected, it is too late to
claim privilege for a document. But the court has equitable powers to
intervene since there had been an obvious error which the claimants' solicitor
must have realised and the defendant had acted promptly to seek relief.

Guinness Peat Properties v Fitzroy Robinson Partnership [1987] 2 All E.R. 716 at 730–731, *per* Slade L.J.:

In my judgment the relevant principles may be stated broadly as follows. (1) where
solicitors for one party to litigation have, on discovery, mistakenly included a
document for which they could properly have claimed privilege . . . to a list of
documents without claiming privilege, the court will ordinarily permit them to amend
the list . . . at any time before inspection of the document has taken place . . . (2)
However, once in such circumstances the other party has inspected the document . . .
the general rule is that it is too late for the party who seeks to claim privilege to
attempt to correct the mistake by applying for injunctive relief . . . (3) If, however, in
such a last-mentioned case the other party or his solicitor either (a) has procured
inspection of the relevant document by fraud, or (b) on inspection, realises that he has
been permitted to see the document only by reason of an obvious mistake, the court
has the power to intervene for the protection of the mistaken party by the grant of an
injunction in exercise of the equitable jurisdiction . . . Furthermore, in my view, it
should ordinarily intervene in such cases . . .[54]

---

[53] [1987] 2 All E.R. 716.
[54] See *IBM Corp v Phoenix International Computers Ltd* [1995] 1 All E.R. 413.

This leaves open the question as to how the court should exercise its discretion. This was considered in *Webster v James Chapman & Co.*[55]

Webster v James Chapman & Co. [1989] 3 All E.R. 939 at 946h–947d, *per* Scott J.:

If a document has been disclosed, be it by trickery, accident or otherwise, the benefit and protection of legal privilege will have been lost. Secondary evidence of the document will have come into the possession of the other side to the litigation. The question then will be what protection the court should provide given that the document which will have come into the possession of the other side will be confidential and that use of it will be unauthorised. If a document was obviously confidential and had been obtained by a trick or by fraud, it is not difficult to see that the balance would be struck in favour of the party entitled to the confidential document. If the document had come into the possession of the other side not through trick or fraud but due to a mistake or carelessness on the part of the party entitled to the document or by his advisers, the balance will be very different from the balance in a fraud case.

. . . I do not think that this branch of the law is one where any firm rules as to how the balance should come down should be stated. It must be highly relevant to consider the manner in which the privileged document has come into the possession of the other side. It must be highly relevant to consider the issues in the action and the relevance of the document to those issues. It must be highly relevant to consider whether, under the Rules of the Supreme Court, the document ought in one way or another to have been disclosed anyway. All circumstances will have to be taken into account, as it seems to me, in deciding how the balance is to be struck.

Whatever the intrusion of equitable principles may be in civil proceedings to restrain the use of secondary evidence relating to privileged information, in criminal proceedings, it seems likely that the accused has no such rights.

Butler v Board of Trade [1971] Ch. 680 at 690, *per* Goff J.:

In my judgment it would not be a right or permissible exercise of the equitable jurisdiction in confidence to make a declaration at the suit of the accused in a public prosecution in effect restraining the Crown from adducing admissible evidence relevant to the crime with which he is charged. It is not necessary for me to decide whether the same result would obtain in the case of a private prosecution, and I expressly leave that point open.

3. Ownership and duration of the privilege

The term "legal professional privilege" is often judicially denounced as unfortunate since it is not a privilege that attaches to the legal profession but

---

[55] [1989] 3 All E.R. 939—see *Istil Group v Mohammed Zahoor* [2003] EWHC 165 (Ch)—no injunction lies to restrain where the claimant has acted improperly.

to the client. In *Wilson v Rastall*,[56] a witness wished to testify as to what he had learned whilst acting as the defendant's attorney. He was rebuked by Buller J.

Wilson v Rastall (1792) [1775–1802] All E.R. Rep 597:

... I strongly animadverted on his conduct, and would not suffer him to be examined; he had acquired his information during the time that he acted as attorney; and I thought that the privilege of not being examined to such points was the privilege of the party, ... and not of the attorney: and that the privilege never ceased at any period of time. In such a case it is not sufficient to say that the cause is at an end; the mouth of such a person is shut for ever.

The privilege belongs to the client and is everlasting—'once privileged, always privileged' was the maxim that decided the issue in *Derby Magistrates' Court Ex p. B*[57] and affirmed by the House of Lords in *Three Rivers*,[58] as was discussed earlier. But another problem emerges when a third party, not the client entitled to the privilege, seeks to rely on that privilege. In *Schneider v Leigh*,[59] the claimant originally sued a company, Pedigree Stock, for personal injuries. The company arranged for the defendant doctor to examine him and report. This report was privileged but certain paragraphs of it were revealed to the claimant. As a result the claimant decided to sue the doctor for libel and claimed disclosure of the full report. The defendant claimed it was subject to legal professional privilege.

Schneider v Leigh [1955] 2 All E.R.173 at 177c–g, *per* Hodson L.J.:

It is conceded by the defendant that the medical reports which form the basis of the libel action were brought into existence in contemplation of the action brought by the plaintiff against the company, and that privilege from production accordingly attaches to the company in the proceedings taken by the plaintiff against it. The question is whether the privilege from production extends beyond the company, so as to protect the defendant in separate proceedings brought against him, although the privilege is not his, but that of the company.

It is essential to bear in mind that the privilege is the privilege of the litigant, accorded to him in order that he may be protected in preparing his case, and not the privilege of his witnesses as such. The litigant can waive the privilege if he chooses, and if he does so the proofs of his witnesses can be shown to the opposing party without the witnesses having any ground for complaint. What is being sought here is, in effect, to extend the umbrella of the protection which the privilege gives the company to the defendant, who is, on the hypothesis that he is the author of the libel, to be looked at for the purpose of this application as a proposed witness on behalf of

---

[56] (1792) [1775–1802] All E.R. Rep 597.
[57] above.
[58] above.
[59] [1955] 2 All E.R. 173.

the company. In this capacity not only has he no privilege of his own, but he is under no duty to assert the rights of the company to resist the production of any documents.

I have emphasised that the privilege is the privilege of the company. This statement is subject to the qualification that the privilege enures for the benefit of successors in title to the party to an action, at any rate, where the relevant interest subsists . . .

The privilege attaches to the client who is entitled to play it as the ace of trumps at their discretion, even when the original litigation is at an end. In a New Zealand case, *Craig*,[60] the third party was the defendant who was accused of giving perjured evidence on behalf of a claimant in earlier proceedings. The prosecution sought to call the claimant's solicitor who had taken notes of Craig's evidence for the original hearing. The claimant in that case instructed his solicitor to claim privilege and the New Zealand Supreme Court held that the privilege did not last only for the original litigation. The court felt that there were limits to privilege but that the onus was on the prosecution to show that the client no longer had any reasonable interest in asserting the privilege.

In *Schneider*, the doctor being sued for defamation could not rely on another's privilege. But privilege can be claimed by third parties but only where there is a clear congruence of interest between themselves and any client to whom the privilege attaches. In *Lee v South West Thames Regional Health Authority*,[61] a small boy suffered brain damage while being transferred to and from hospitals in London. Three health authorities were involved as defendants, in particular Hillingdon where one of the hospitals was located and South West Thames who were responsible for the transfer by ambulance. Before any case had started, the child's mother sought pre-action disclosure— Hillingdon revealed many documents but not a report that they had obtained from the ambulance crew employed by South West Thames. They claimed that it was obtained for the purpose of getting legal advice on their liability. The child's mother now turned her attention to South West Thames as they had a copy of that report and sought to compel the authority to disclose it. Hillingdon "owned" the privilege—could South West Thames take advantage of the existence of this privilege to resist disclosure? An analogy is where a litigant writes to a particular engineer and asks for a report and the engineer delivers his report and keeps a copy. That copy is plainly in the same position as far as privilege is concerned as the original document in the hands of the client. The privilege attaches to the litigant and the engineer would have no right to waive such privilege until there was authority from 'the true owners'. The Court of Appeal held that a third party was not generally entitled to rely on a defendant's privilege unless there was some common interest between them. In this case there was no common interest because, if the mother sued both authorities, their defences were likely to be of the "cut-throat" variety. But on the other hand, any actions against them arose out of the same incident and were likely to be tried together. If there was disclosure, the claim could not be tried in a way that would allow the document to be used against one defendant and not the other and thus there was no way of protecting the

[60] [1975] 1 N.Z.L.R. 597.
[61] [1985] 2 All E.R. 385.

rights of Hillingdon as potential defendants if disclosure was ordered against South West Thames.

(4) The subject matter of the privilege

The privilege is about communications. It is not about facts. In *Brown v Foster*,[62] a lawyer attended a hearing on behalf of his client who was charged with embezzlement. The prosecution produced an accounts book in which the defendant was supposed to record money received. There was no entry for one particular transaction. Subsequently the book was again produced and miraculously an entry recording that transaction in the accused's handwriting was found. The defendant brought an action for malicious prosecution. The issue was whether the lawyer could be called as a witness to testify that, on the first production of the book, there was no entry.

Brown v Foster (1857) 1 H.&N. 736, *per* Pollock C.B.:

The counsel was called to state, not what he learned from his client, but whether a certain entry was then in that book. There is no breach of professional confidence in answering those questions. I agree that what passes between counsel and client ought not to be communicated and is not admissible in evidence, but with respect of matter which counsel sees with his eyes, he cannot refuse to answer.[63]

From this principle, where a defendant possesses documents which may be open to seizure by the police, these cannot be handed over to a solicitor for safekeeping and to secure immunity through privilege. In *Justices of the Peace for Peterborough Ex p. Hicks*[64] the clients sent their solicitor a document, a forged power of attorney, to seek advice. A warrant was issued to search the solicitor's premises and seize the document under s.16 of the Forgery Act 1916.

Justices of the Peace for Peterborough Ex p. Hicks [1978] 1 All E.R.225 at 228d–e, *per* Eveleigh J.:

. . . the solicitor who holds the document in the right of his client and can assert in respect of its seizure no greater authority than the client himself or herself possesses. The client in this case would have possessed no lawful authority or excuse that would prevent the document's seizure. In my view the solicitor himself can be in no better position. The solicitor's authority or excuse in a case like this is the authority or excuse of the client.

---

[62] (1857) 1 H.&N. 736.
[63] *cf. Bursill v Tanner* (1885) 16 Q.B.D. 1—a solicitor can be obliged to disclose the identity of his client.
[64] [1978] 1 All E.R. 225.

Similarly in *King*,[65] the defendant forged an invoice which he hoped would support a possible defence and would throw the blame on a third party. This document was handed to the solicitor and then was forwarded to a handwriting expert to be compared with other documents which had been in possession of the Crown. The prosecution called the expert to produce the document which became an exhibit in the case.

King [1983] 1 All E.R. 929 at 931c–e, *per* Dunn L.J.:

. . . the rule is that in the case of expert witnesses legal professional privilege attaches to confidential communications between the solicitor and the expert, but it does not attach to the chattels or documents on which the expert based his opinion, or to the independent opinion of the expert himself: see *Harmony Shipping Co v Davis*.[66] The reasons for that are that there is no property in an expert witness any more than in any other witness and the court is entitled, in order to ascertain the truth, to have the actual facts which the expert has observed adduced before it in considering his opinion.

Such a document was not privileged because it had not been produced for the purpose of the lawyer–client relationship. However the instructions to the expert and his report remained privileged. This can be distinguished from *R v R*,[67] where the accused was charged with rape and incest. A scientist carried out DNA tests on a sample of the defendant's blood at the request of the defence. At the trial, the scientist was called as a witness for the prosecution. The dispute centred on the fact that the scientist's evidence was based on a blood sample which had been taken by the appellant's doctor. That sample was not produced in evidence and in all likelihood had been used up in the tests. But at common law and under s.10 of the Police and Criminal Evidence Act 1984, the sample was an item which could be subject to legal privilege because it was brought into existence (unlike the document in *King*) for the purposes of obtaining the expert's advice. Thus the sample was privileged as was any opinion which the expert had formed as a result of her tests on that sample.

In *Ex p. Howe*,[68] in 2003 the defendant was charged with driving having been disqualified in 2000. He denied that he was the person involved in the earlier proceedings—his solicitor (who had also been the solicitor in 2000) was called to identify his client as the person who had been disqualified. While he could not testify to anything that his 2003 client might have said to him about the 2000 proceedings, there were permissible questions which did not infringe legal professional privilege. They are questions solely as to the identity of the person disqualified from driving in 2000 and as to the

---

[65] [1983] 1 All E.R. 929.
[66] [1979] 3 All E.R. 177.
[67] [1994] 4 All E.R. 260.
[68] *R. (On the application of Howe) and Law Society (Interested Party) v South Durham Magistrates' Court and Crown Prosecution Service (Interested Party)* [2004] EWHC 362 (Admin).

identification of this claimant as being the same person. The question was whether, when the solicitor saw the claimant in 2003, he remembered him. What he could not be asked was anything about what he was told by his client. A similar situation arose in *Ex p. Rogers*[69] where a solicitor was asked to produce documents which recorded information about the time the client arrived at the solicitor's officer and the duration of the interview. Attendance notes on a time sheet or fee records are not communications between lawyer and client and do not attract privilege.

5. Pre-existing documents

Legal professional privilege protects documents and other items which are brought into existence for the purpose of instructing a lawyer and obtaining advice. Where a document existed before the litigation was contemplated but was obtained by the solicitor for the purposes of the litigation, this is not privileged. In *Ventouris v Mountain*,[70] the claimant claimed against the underwriters for the loss of a ship in an explosion. The defendants believed that the claimant had caused or connived at the loss of the ship and, as a result of information supplied by the claimant's cousin, refused to pay. The claimant sought discovery of documents obtained by the defendants from the cousin.

Ventouris v Mountain [1991] 3 All E.R. 472 at 475g–477f, *per* Bingham L.J.:

The doctrine of legal professional privilege is rooted in the public interest, which requires that hopeless and exaggerated claims and unsound and spurious defences be so far as possible discouraged, and civil disputes so far as possible settled without resort to judicial decision. To this end it is necessary that actual and potential litigants, be they claimants or respondents, should be free to unburden themselves without reserve to their legal advisers, and their legal advisers be free to give honest and candid advice on a sound factual basis, without fear that these communications may be relied on by an opposing party if the dispute comes before the court for decision. It is the protection of confidential communications between client and legal adviser which lies at the heart of legal professional privilege . . .

Even confining oneself to the litigious field, it is however plain that legal professional privilege does not end there. Confidential communications between a party to litigation or his legal adviser and third parties for the purposes of the litigation are without doubt protected from production to the other party. So are documents prepared for the dominant purpose of submission to a legal adviser in connection with actual or anticipated litigation . . . The issue is how much further the privilege extends. The plaintiff argues that it does not extend to cover any original document, even if obtained by a party to litigation or his legal adviser for the purposes of the litigation, if the document did not come into existence for purposes of the litigation. The defendant argues that the privilege covers any original document obtained by a party to litigation or his legal adviser for purposes of the litigation whether or not the document came

[69] *R. v Manchester Crown Court Ex p. Rogers* (1999) 4 All E.R. 35.
[70] [1991] 3 All E.R. 472.

into existence for purposes of the litigation and (therefore) whether or not the document existed before the litigation was contemplated or commenced.

I begin with *Anderson v Bank of British Columbia*[71] . . . James LJ did, however, formulate the principle, much quoted since, 'that as you have no right to see your adversary's brief, you have no right to see that which comes into existence merely as materials for the brief'. The words I have emphasised make clear that he did not contemplate the extension of privilege to documents which were in existence before any question of litigation arose . . .

In *Southwark and Vauxhall Water Co v Quick*[72] the plaintiff company sued its former engineer. Before the action documents were prepared to be laid before the company's solicitor for his advice, although there was some doubt whether all the documents were laid before him. The Court of Appeal held that if the documents came into existence merely for the purpose of being laid before the solicitor for his advice it made no difference whether they were prepared at his request or not and that if the documents were brought into existence for that purpose it made no difference whether they were in fact laid before him or not. While pre-existing documents (by which I mean documents in existence before there was any question of litigation) were not in issue, the rules as formulated would plainly not have covered them.

Pre-existing documents can not be subject to legal professional privilege. But it was suggested in *Inland Revenue Ex p. Goldberg*[73] that where a copy of an existing document was made for the purpose of obtaining legal advice, that copy might be privileged even where the original document was not privileged. This was based on *The Palermo*[74] which was a collision action between two ships, the British–owned Rivoli and the foreign-owned Palermo. The Board of Trade took depositions from the crew of the Rivoli and allowed the solicitors for the Rivoli owners to take copies. They refused to allow the same latitude to the solicitors for the owners of the Palermo, the defendants, since no similar depositions had been made by that ship's crew. The defendants sought discovery of the claimants' copies. This was refused.

The Palermo (1884) 9 P.D. 6 at 7–8, *per* Cotton L.J.:

Here discovery is sought of copies of certain depositions and these were obtained for the purposes of this action, and as the phrase is, 'to form part of the brief'. Therefore I think that they are privileged, and I shall not inquire for what purpose the original depositions were taken, since it is the copies of which discovery is sought, and which were obtained for the purposes I have stated.

But this was doubted in *Chadwick v Bowman*[75] in which Denman J. said,

The originals of these documents would have been admissible in evidence against the defendant, and it seems to me that there is nothing in the circumstances under which the copies came into existence to render them privileged against inspection.

[71] [1876] 2 Ch. D 644.
[72] (1878) 3 Q.B.D. 315.
[73] [1988] 3 All E.R. 248.
[74] (1884) 9 P.D. 6.
[75] (1886) 16 Q.B.D. 561.

This approach was certainly approved in *Ventouris v Mountain*, when Bingham L.J. said that non–privileged documents do not, without more, acquire privilege simply because they are copied by a solicitor for purposes of an action. A non-privileged original document handed to a solicitor for purposes of an action and not copied would seem to be even more remote from any sustainable claim to privilege.[76] Translations of non–privileged documents, prepared to assist lawyers, are not privileged.[77]

Legal professional privilege may be available if there is a selection of pre-existing documents, not themselves privileged, but which have been copied or assembled by a solicitor and which, if disclosed, would be likely to betray the trend of legal advice. In *Lyell v Kennedy (No.3)*,[78] the defendant successfully objected to producing (*inter alia*) copies of entries in registers and public records and photographs of tombstones and houses on the grounds that these documents had been made by his solicitor for the purpose of the defence. This selection issue was addressed in *Sumitomo Corporation v Credit Lyonnais Rouse Ltd*.

Sumitomo Corporation v Credit Lyonnais Rouse Ltd (2002) 4 All E.R. 68, *per* Parker L.J.:

71. In addressing the selection issue, a distinction has in our judgment to be made between a selection made from unprivileged documents which are disclosable by the party claiming privilege ("own client documents"), and a selection made from documents which are not so disclosable ("third party documents").

72. *Lyell v Kennedy* concerned a selection made from third party documents, and the judgments in that case must, in our judgment, be read in that context. *Lyell v Kennedy* is undoubtedly authority for the proposition that where a solicitor has copied or assembled a selection of third party documents, the selection will be privileged if its production would "betray the trend of the advice which he is giving the client" . . . but in our judgment it is not authority for the proposition that a selection made from own client documents may similarly attract privilege.

73. In *Dubai Bank Ltd v Galadari (No 7)*,[79] Morritt J rejected a submission that the *Lyell v Kennedy* principle could not apply to a selection made from own client documents, saying this,

At one stage the plaintiffs submitted that [the *Lyell v Kennedy* principle] could not apply to copies made by a solicitor of his own client's pre-existing documents which were not themselves privileged, but it seems to me that, as the plaintiff's counsel ultimately accepted, there is no warrant for such a distinction. There is no authority to support it. As a matter of principle the selection of own client documents is just as likely to betray the trend of advice as a selection of third party documents, if not more so. And if I am right that the photocopies are discoverable there is every reason to uphold the application of the principle in respect of own client documents . . .

76. We think that the question can be tested in this way. Imagine that a solicitor made a selection from his client's disclosable documents in order to obtain the advice

---

[76] above at 480e–f.
[77] *Sumitomo Corporation v Credit Lyonnais Rouse Ltd* (2002) 4 All E.R. 68.
[78] (1884) [1881–5] All E.R. Rep 814.
[79] [1992] 1 All E.R. 658.

of counsel on a point of particular concern. And imagine that the remainder of the disclosable documents were destroyed in a fire. We do not believe that it would be right to extend the principle in *Lyell v. Kennedy* to cloak with privilege the remaining documents. What if the selection was effected by copying the original documents and then all the originals were destroyed by fire? Should the principle in *Lyell v. Kennedy* be extended to cloak with privilege the copies which, as Morritt J. recognised, would otherwise be disclosable? We do not believe that it should. A gloss on the principle that a lawyer's advice is privileged from discovery should not result in the right of a party to refuse discovery of documentary evidence that was in the possession of that party before the selection was made, or copies or translations of such evidence.

77. In our judgment, therefore, the *Lyell v. Kennedy* principle does not and should not extend to copies—or translations—which represent the fruits of a selection made for litigious purposes from own client documents, and *Dubai Bank Ltd v. Galadari* (No 7) was wrongly decided on this point.

The Court of Appeal disapproved of *Dubai Bank Ltd* holding that professional privilege does cover selections of third party documents but does not extend to copies of client's pre-existing documents if these are not in themselves privileged, even if the selection tends to betray the advice given by the solicitor to the client. But the court suggested that there is a residual discretion, emphasised by Bingham L.J. at the conclusion of his judgment in *Ventouris v Mountain*.

Ventouris v Mountain [1991] 3 All E.R. 472 at 485c, *per* Lord Bingham:

I end on a point which may possibly give the defendant some comfort. [Counsel for the defendant] suggested that, the nature of the present case being what it is, there was a risk that production of those documents could lead to violence, intimidation, interference with witnesses and destruction of evidence. We are not, I must emphasise, in a position to assess the merit, if any, of these contentions. But his argument appeared to assume that there was no choice between a finding of legal professional privilege and an order for immediate disclosure and inspection. In my judgment, that is not so. The process of discovery is not an un controllable juggernaut . . . In *Science Research Council v. Nasse*[80] and *Dolling-Baker v. Merrett*[81] . . ., the Court of Appeal made plain that production and inspection are not automatic once relevance and the absence of entitlement to privilege are established. While the court's ultimate concern must always be to ensure the fair disposal of the cause or matter, it need not be unmindful of other legitimate concerns nor is it powerless to control the terms upon which production and inspection may be ordered. I would not wish it thought that because, as I conclude, production and inspection may be ordered therefore they must at once be ordered unconditionally.

6. No "ambushing"

In civil proceedings, while legal professional privilege enables a party to keep, for example, witness statements or reports from expert witnesses secret, it does not enable that party to "ambush" the opposition with them. In civil

[80] [1980] A.C. 1028.
[81] [1991] 1 W.L.R. 1205.

proceedings, r.32.4 of the Civil Procedure Rules empowers the court to order a party to give written statements of the oral evidence on which that party is going to rely.

The court will order a party to serve on the other parties any witness statement of the oral evidence which the party serving the statement intends to rely on in relation to any issues of fact to be decided at the trial.

If any party fails to disclose evidence on which they intend to rely, albeit on the basis of privilege, they can only adduce such evidence with the leave of the court.

32.10 If a witness statement or a witness summary for use at trial is not served in respect of an intended witness within the time specified by the court, then the witness may not be called to give oral evidence unless the court gives permission.

31.21 A party may not rely on any document which he fails to disclose or in respect of which he fails to permit inspection unless the court gives permission.

Even where the party does produce witness statements, under r.32.5(3) and (4), when the witness testifies, they must confine themselves to the matters in the written statement. A witness cannot amplify this or give evidence in relation to new matters unless there is the consent of the other parties or the leave of the court. While there is no compulsory disclosure of privileged material, if parties wish to rely on the material, they have no choice.

In criminal cases, there is mutual disclosure under the provisions of the Criminal Procedure and Investigations Act 1996. If the prosecution sought to adduce evidence in court where there had been no advance notice, the judge has the power to exclude such evidence under s.78 of the Police and Criminal Evidence Act 1984. If the defence were to introduce new matters or witnesses not mentioned in the defence statement, then the evidence would not be excluded. But under s.39(5) of the Criminal Justice Act 2003, the judge and prosecution can comment on that failure and the jury may be invited to draw "such inferences as appear proper"—in other words, may be invited to disbelieve the new evidence.

E. *Exceptions to Legal Professional Privilege*

There are only a few exceptions where the circumstances are such that any claim to privilege fails.

1. Proof of innocence

As discussed earlier, legal professional privilege is absolute and there is no balancing act to be performed, even where the innocence of the accused is at stake. This was established by the House of Lords in *Derby Magistrates' Court Ex p. B*[82] but may need to be reconsidered in the light of the passage of the

---

[82] [1995] 4 All E.R. 526.

Human Rights Act 1998. The Strasbourg jurisprudence emphasises the importance of legal professional privilege but not as an absolute right. In a non-criminal case, *Foxley v UK*,[83] the European Court of Human Rights considered the extent to which a bankrupt's privileged correspondence could be interfered with. Interference was justifiable where that interference corresponded to a pressing social need and was proportionate to the legitimate aim pursued. The aim in *Foxley* was to prevent a bankrupt from concealing assets to the detriment of his creditors. Let us assume a case arose where information was required to prove innocence but could not be put before the court because of legal professional privilege and as a result the accused was convicted. The European Court would undoubtedly regard failure to put the information before the trial court as a breach of Art.6 rights and moreover would point to the fact that, although the privilege was *prima facie* justified under Art.8, that article allows for interference where it is in accordance with law and ". . . is necessary in a democratic society . . . for the protection of the rights and freedoms of others."

2. Communications to facilitate fraud

Communications between lawyer and client are not privileged if their purpose was to guide the commission of a crime. In *Cox and Railton*[84] the defendants sought the advice of a solicitor with reference to drawing up a bill of sale which was alleged to be fraudulent. The solicitor was compelled to disclose what had passed in the meeting.

Cox and Railton (1884) 15 Cox CC 611 at 613j. 620–621, *per* Stephen J.:

The conduct of . . . the solicitor appears to have been unobjectionable. He was consulted in the common course of business, and gave a proper opinion in good faith. The question therefore is, whether, if a client applies to a legal adviser for advice intended to facilitate or to guide the client in the commission of a crime or fraud, the legal adviser being ignorant of the purpose for which his advice is wanted, the communication between the two is privileged. We expressed our opinion at the end of the argument that no such privilege existed. If it did, the result would be that a man intending to commit treason or murder might safely take legal advice for the purpose of enabling himself to do so with impunity, and that the solicitor to whom the application was made would not be at liberty to give information against his client for the purpose of frustrating his criminal purpose . . .

We are greatly pressed with the argument that, speaking practically, the admission of any such exception to the privilege of legal advisers as that it is not to extend to communications made in furtherance of any criminal or fraudulent purpose would greatly diminish the value of that privilege. The privilege must, it was argued, be violated in order to ascertain whether it exists. The secret must be told in order to see whether it ought to be kept . . .

In each particular case the court must determine upon the facts actually given in evidence, or proposed to be given in evidence, whether it seems probable that the

---

[83] [2001] 31 E.H.R.R. 25.
[84] (1884) 15 Cox 611.

accused person may have consulted his legal adviser, not after the commission of the crime for the legitimate purpose of being defended, but before the commission of the crime, for the purpose of being guided or helped in committing it. We are far from saying that the question whether the advice was taken before or after the offence will always be decisive as to the admissibility of such evidence. Courts must in every instance judge for themselves on the special facts of each particular case, just as they must judge whether a witness deserves to be examined on the supposition that he is hostile or whether a dying declaration was made in the immediate prospect of death . . . Of course, the power in question ought to be used with the greatest care not to hamper prisoners in making their defence, and not to enable unscrupulous persons to acquire knowledge to which they have no right, and every precaution should be taken against compelling unnecessary disclosures.

A modern example is where a borrower deceives a building society into lending money in circumstances where, if no deception had been practised, no loan might well have been forthcoming. While the borrower is entitled at first glance to claim privilege over the conveyancing file in such circumstances, the iniquitous behaviour is sufficiently exceptional for the privilege to be lost.[85]

The limits of this rule can be seen in civil proceedings in *Crescent Farm (Sidcup) Sports Ltd v Sterling Offices Ltd*.[86] The claimants had originally sold land to the first defendants but with a right to buy it back if the defendants sold it within 20 years. The first defendants wished to sell it to the second defendants and, while appearing to negotiate a re-sale with the claimants, sought counsel's opinion as to the validity of the pre-emption clause and in fact conveyed the land to the second defendants. The claimants sought discovery of the relevant documents, including instructions to the defendants' solicitors. Goff J. held that the wide submission of the claimants would endanger the whole basis of legal professional privilege. 'Fraud' did not extend to every act or scheme which could give rise to a civil claim. Parties were entitled to seek legal advice as to their liability in contract and tort if they followed a particular course of action.

Where fraud is alleged, the party seeking disclosure must show a strong evidential basis for the allegation and a court will be slow to deprive a party of the protection of legal professional privilege on an interlocutory application.[87]

Kuwait Airway Corporation v Iraqi Airways Co. unreported, February 16, 2005, QBD (Comm), *per* Steel J.:

7. Legal professional privilege does not however attach to a communication between a client and his legal advisor which is intended to facilitate or guide the client

---

[85] *Nationwide Building Society v Various Solicitors* [1999] P.N.L.R. 52; *Abbey National PLC v Prosser*, unreported September 11, 2000 Ch. D; *R. (on the application of Hallinan Blackburn Gittings and Nott) v Middlesex Guildhall Crown Court* (2005) 1 W.L.R. 766.

[86] [1971] 3 All E.R. 1192.

[87] *Derby & Co. Ltd v Weldon (No. 7)* [1990] 3 All E.R. 161.

in the commission of a crime or fraud (whether or not the legal advisor is a party to the fraud) . . .

8. The application of this exception to cases where the privilege claimed is one of litigation privilege is likely to be rare. It will of course not be enough that a solicitor has simply been the conduit of untruthful evidence . . . But it cannot be part of the professional duty of a solicitor to assist in the presentation of a bogus defence particularly with the assistance of manufactured documents and the deliberate suppression of others . . .

9. But strong evidence of fraud in the conduct of the proceedings will seldom become available until the relevant proceedings have been determined. The risk of injustice of requiring earlier disclosure on the basis of merely a prima facie case of fraud will be high . . . But the present case is unusual since it has been divided up into a sequence of hearings on the major issues and the fraud on the Court in obtaining an order extending Iraqi Airways' entitlement to sovereign immunity (and otherwise pursuing its claim in the main action) has in the present instance been unearthed and established during the course of the litigation.

10. It is true that the allegation of deliberate concealment of documents has yet to be established. But for present purposes, I accept that there is a remarkably strong prima facie case that such concealment has taken place . . .[88]

In criminal proceedings, the limits on legal professional privilege have been tested in relation to police search warrants issued under Pt II Police and Criminal Evidence Act 1984. Under section 8 warrants should not be issued to seize items subject to legal professional privilege, as defined in s.10. However under s.10(2) "Items held with the intention of furthering a criminal purpose are not items subject to legal privilege."

This subsection was interpreted in *Francis & Francis v Central Criminal Court*,[89] in which the police were investigating the affairs of a suspected drug trafficker. They believed that he was laundering the proceeds of the trafficking by purchasing property for various members of his family. The police applied for a warrant requiring the solicitor acting for one of the family to produce all files in their possession relating to a particular conveyance. Were these documents privileged? The question arose as to whether s.10(2) refers the intention of the person holding the items (*i.e.* the solicitor) or whether it included the intention of any other person (*i.e.* the client or the alleged trafficker) irrespective of whether the solicitors holding the documents were party to that intention. The solicitors were ignorant of the source of the money and argued that the documents could not be "held with the intention of furthering a criminal purpose" as they did not have such an intention. On a subsidiary issue, the House agreed that a "criminal purpose" was not limited to "criminal offence." The bank robber salting away the proceeds of the robbery does not have "the intention of furthering a criminal offence" but does so with the intention of furthering his criminal purpose.[90]

On the central question, a minority, Lords Bridge and Oliver, adopted a literal interpretation of the statute and held that s.10(2) means that it is the holder of the documents (*i.e.* the solicitor) who must have the criminal purpose.

[88] Appeal dismissed [2005] EWCA Civ 286.
[89] [1988] 3 All E.R. 775.
[90] *ibid.* at 797j–798a *per* Lord Goff.

Francis & Francis v Central Criminal Court [1988] 3 All E.R. 775 at 780d-f, *per* Lord Bridge:

My noble and learned friend Lord Griffiths gives the example: 'Ammunition held in the armoury with the intention of firing it at Bisley must be inspected'. Here the context is designed to demonstrate that the phrase 'held with the intention' cannot refer to the intention of the holder. But all this shows, with respect, is that the sentence is expressed in slipshod and ungrammatical English. To convey the writer's evident meaning accurately and grammatically it must read: 'Ammunition held in the armoury and intended to be fired at Bisley must be inspected'. This analysis may sound pedantic, but it is a basic rule of statutory construction that the draftsman is presumed to use the English language accurately and grammatically.

But the issue is not the construction of this subsection and thus the limits of police powers of search and seizure. The House of Lords is defining the scope of legal professional privilege, not simply for the purposes of s.10(2) but generally. The dissentients felt that their restrictive attitude was narrower than the common law expounded by Stephen J in *Cox and Railton* when he talked of the privilege being overridden only where the client has conspired with the lawyer or deceived him. Even this latter ground requires the judge to exercise his discretion on the "special facts of each particular case" and seemingly does not encompass every straightforward situation of the client lying to his lawyer. Lord Bridge's concern was that the majority went beyond Stephen's statement of the common law, treating otherwise privileged communications between an innocent solicitor and an innocent client as losing their privilege by reference to the intention of some third party who has a criminal purpose to further.

The majority rejected this and felt that the subsection reflected the common law.

Francis & Francis v Central Criminal Court [1988] 3 All E.R. 775 at 797a-h, *per* Lord Goff:

... does the relevant intention have to be the intention of the person (*i.e.* in this example the solicitor) who has the items in his possession at the time when production of them is called for?

When one looks at the full meaning of the words, there is no compelling reason why the words should be so read. If documents are said to have come into the possession of a solicitor with the intention of furthering a criminal purpose, that intention could just as well be the intention of some person other than the solicitor, and in particular, the intention of his client. Furthermore, there are overwhelming reasons which favour that interpretation. First, the interpretation would reflect the common law position; and since in my opinion subsection (1) is intended to reflect the common law position, it would be most surprising if subsection (2) was not likewise intended to do so ... Second, it would be equally surprising if, in the context of Pt II of the 1984 Act, and its evident purpose, the legislature should have intended to restrict the effect of subsection (2), and therefore the power of the police in their efforts to detect crime, by confining subsection (2) (which is expressly directed towards a case where there is an intention to further a criminal purpose) only to those cases where the solicitor has an intention, and so extending legal privilege to protect the criminal. It is not to be forgotten that the privilege is the privilege of the client, not of the solicitor; and so it is to be expected that the privilege should be negatived where the client has the intention to further a criminal purpose, whether or not his intention is shared with his solicitor. Indeed, one of the most important points established in the leading case of *R v Cox and Railton* was that legal professional privilege does not exist where the client has such an intention, even though his intention is unknown to his solicitor; and it would surely be most extraordinary if s.10(2) was drafted with the intention of excluding that principle, thereby substantially extending the scope of the privilege to protect the dishonest client. Furthermore, the opposite conclusion would not merely lead to the remarkable result that two different versions of legal privilege would have to coexist, the common law version, which has long been entrenched in our law, and the statutory version encapsulated in s.10; but also that, in consequence, the extraordinary position would be reached that in certain circumstances the police would be prevented by legal privilege from calling for the production of certain documents although such documents, if obtained, would not be protected by legal privilege when placed in evidence before the court.

The majority's willingness to interpret the subsection broadly and treat it as reflecting the common law is defensible. But the criminal purpose in the case appears to be that of the drug trafficker and the House proceeded on the basis that both solicitor and client were innocent parties. It seems a dubious suggestion that the criminal intention of a third party, neither solicitor nor client, might defeat legal professional privilege. Lord Oliver commented on the proposition that the interpretation reflected the common law.

But this is, with respect, pure speculation. There is no, so far as I am aware, any authority in the common law dealing with the question whether a criminal intent on the part of a stranger to the relationship of solicitor and client destroys the privilege of the client. If, therefore, the subsection does indeed bear the meaning now sought to be ascribed to it by the respondent, it is breaking new ground and the legislative intent has to be gathered not from some supposed logical extension of the common law rule but from the words which Parliament has chosen to use.[91]

3. Statutory exclusion

Legal professional privilege may be expressly or impliedly excluded by statute. One example may be proceedings where the welfare of the child is the court's paramount consideration. In *Barking and Dagenham London Borough Council v O*,[92] care proceedings were commenced by the local authority under the Children Act 1989. The mother was permitted not to disclose medical reports obtained by her solicitors. Although there was authority[93] that in wardship proceedings, legal professional privilege could be overridden, Douglas Brown J. held that the particular nature of the wardship jurisdiction had not been inherited by the Children Act jurisdiction. However in *Re R*[94] Thorpe J. declined to follow this lead.

---

[91] *ibid.* at 793g-h *per* Lord Oliver.
[92] [1993] 4 All E.R. 59.
[93] *Re A* [1991] 2 F.L.R. 473.
[94] [1993] 4 All E.R. 702.

Re R [1993] 4 All E.R. 702 at 704j–705a, *per* Thorpe J.:

Legal professional privilege is a creature of case law and, where limitations by exception have seemed necessary, those limitations have equally been developed by case law. In my judgment, where the court considers the welfare of a child, the power that it holds, allied to its responsibility, enables it to override a legal professional privilege which is set up to preserve or enhance the adversarial position of one of the parties.

For my part, I would wish to see case law go yet further and to make it plain that the legal representatives in possession of such material relevant to determination but contrary to the interests of their client, not only are unable to resist disclosure by reliance on legal professional privilege, but have a positive duty to disclose to the other parties and to the court.

This position was strengthened by the decision of the House of Lords in *Re L (A Minor)(Police Investigation: Privilege)*.[95] Care proceedings were instituted in relation to a two-year-old baby of parents addicted to heroin. The baby had ingested some methadone and had been taken to hospital. The court permitted the mother access to court papers so that a consultant chemical pathologist could give her an independent opinion as to whether the child's medical condition when admitted to hospital was consistent with the mother's account. The report was adverse to the mother. Could it be used in the care proceedings? The mother claimed that it was privileged as it was drawn up in contemplation of litigation. The Lords held that a distinction was to be drawn between legal advice privilege, which attached to all communications between legal advisers and their clients and which was absolute, and litigation privilege which was a component of the courts' adversarial procedure. The majority argument was that, since proceedings under Part IV of the Children Act 1989 were investigative and non-adversarial in nature and placed the welfare of the child as the primary consideration, litigation privilege was by necessary implication excluded from the terms and overall purpose of the Act and did not extend to reports obtained by a party to care proceedings which could not have been prepared without the leave of the court. Lord Nicholls, dissenting, firstly saw family proceedings as having both inquisitorial and adversarial features. He also refused to draw the distinction between legal advice privilege and litigation privilege which he described as integral parts of a single privilege.

II. Statements Without Prejudice

In civil actions, negotiation and settlement by the parties is encouraged in preference to contested trial. Lawyers talk and write to opposing lawyers, often making concessions and offers which would be damaging to their clients if they were revealed in court. Such communications do not in themselves attract legal professional privilege since they are between the

---

[95] [1997] A.C. 16.

parties or, more realistically, between their lawyers. But the risk of such statements being held against them is removed by treating them as "without prejudice" statements to which privilege attaches. Even a letter not marked "without prejudice" can nevertheless be treated as such impliedly, if it bears all the required hallmarks and formed part of a negotiation.[96]

In *Walker v Wilsher*,[97] after the conclusion of an action, an application was made by the losing defendant to deprive the claimant of his costs on the grounds that the defendant had offered to settle the case before trial for the amount of damages finally accepted. This was proved by letters marked "without prejudice" which had been exchanged by the parties before the trial. The Court of Appeal held that these letters should not have been admitted.

Walker v Wilsher (1889) 23 QBD 335 at 337, *per* Lord Esher M.R.:

It is, I think, a good rule to say that nothing which is written or said without prejudice should be looked at without the consent of both parties, otherwise the whole object of the limitation would be destroyed. I am therefore of opinion that the learned judge should not have taken these matters into consideration in determining whether there was good cause, and as that was all that was before him on the point, if that is excluded, it follows that there was no good cause, and that the plaintiff should not have been deprived of his costs.

As Lord Esher makes clear, the privilege is a joint privilege which can only be waived with the consent of both parties. It is a privilege that attaches to all forms of communication, oral as well as written. The term "without prejudice" need not be expressly used as the court will often infer that negotiations are without prejudice. The rule was explained in *Rush and Tompkins Ltd v Greater London Council*.

Rush and Tompkins Ltd v Greater London Council [1988] 3 All E.R. 737 at 739h–740j, *per* Lord Griffiths:

The 'without prejudice' rule is a rule governing the admissibility of evidence and is founded upon the public policy of encouraging litigants to settle their differences rather than litigate them to a finish. It is nowhere more clearly expressed than in the judgment of Oliver LJ in *Cutts v Head*[98]

That the rule rests, at least in part, upon public policy is clear from many authorities, and the convenient starting point of the inquiry is the nature of the underlying policy. It is that parties should be encouraged so far as possible to settle their disputes without resort to litigation and should not be discouraged by the knowledge that anything that

---

[96] *Cadle Co v Hearley* [2002] 1 Lloyd's Rep. 143.
[97] (1889) 23 QBD 335; *Reed Executive PLC v Reed Business Information Ltd* [2004] 4 All E.R. 942.
[98] [1984] Ch.290 at 306.

is said in the course of such negotiations (and that includes, of course, as much the failure to reply to an offer as an actual reply) may be used to their prejudice in the course of the proceedings . . . The public policy justification, in truth, essentially rests on the desirability of preventing statements or offers made in the course of negotiations for settlement being brought before the court of trial as admissions on the question of liability.

The rule applies to exclude all negotiations genuinely aimed at settlement whether oral or in writing from being given in evidence. A competent solicitor will always head any negotiating correspondence 'without prejudice' to make clear beyond doubt that in the event of the negotiations being unsuccessful they are not to be referred to at the subsequent trial. However, the application of the rule is not dependent upon the use of the phrase 'without prejudice' and if it is clear from the surrounding circumstances that the parties were seeking to compromise the action, evidence of the content of those negotiations will, as a general rule, not be admissible at the trial and cannot be used to establish an admission or partial admission. I cannot therefore agree with the Court of Appeal that the problem in the present case should be resolved by a linguistic approach to the meaning of the phrase ' without prejudice'. I believe that the question has to be looked at more broadly and resolved by balancing two different public interests namely the public interest in promoting settlements and the public interest in full discovery between parties to litigation.

Nearly all the cases in which the scope of the 'without prejudice' rule has been considered, concern the admissibility of evidence at trial after negotiations have failed. In such circumstances no question of discovery arises because the parties are well aware of what passed between them in the negotiations. These cases show that the rule is not absolute and resort may be had to the 'without prejudice' material for a variety of reasons when the justice of the case requires it. It is unnecessary to make any deep examination of these authorities to resolve the present appeal but they all illustrate the underlying purpose of the rule which is to protect a litigant from being embarrassed by any admission made purely in an attempt to achieve a settlement.

III. Confidential Communications

Many communications may be regarded by those making them as confidential. That confidentiality is protected by the law of evidence whenever the concepts of public interest immunity and legal professional privilege can be invoked. But there are other significant confidential relationships such as those with one's doctor, priest, therapist or investigative journalist. In evidential terms, the law does not recognise any privilege for confidential communications outside the sphere of legal professional privilege. In *Alfred Crompton Amusement Machine Ltd v Customs and Excise Commissioners*, the House of Lords confirmed that confidentiality itself was not a basis for upholding a claim to public interest immunity,

'Confidentiality' is not a separate head of privilege, but it may be a very material consideration to bear in mind when privilege is claimed on the ground of public interest.[99]

Confidentiality is not a basis for an assertion of a private privilege. Doctors and priests can be compelled to disclose communications received in the course of their work in court. But to a certain extent such confidentiality is

---

[99] [1973] 2 All E.R. 1169 at 1184f–1185d *per* Lord Cross.

respected and protected, if not by the law of evidence then by other legal mechanisms. Such protection remains patchy.

A. *Search and Seizure*

There is some immunity from search and seizure by the police. This immunity is provided under ss.9 and 11 of the Police and Criminal Evidence Act 1984 and relates to certain kinds of material such as personal records held in confidence, human tissue or tissue fluid or journalistic material. But such "special material" is not completely protected as the police may obtain access to such material by application to a circuit judge under Sch.1 of the Act.[1]

B. *Disclosure*

As we have seen, the doctrine of public interest immunity can be used to prevent sensitive information being disclosed in both civil and criminal proceedings. But elsewhere common law will compel disclosure of all relevant information, whether this is held by the parties to the action or by third parties. In *Norwich Pharmacal Co v Customs and Excise Commissioners*,[2] the applicants owned the patent of a chemical compound "furazolidone". This chemical was being imported into the country in breach of the patent and the applicants sought the names of the importers from the commissioners. The House of Lords decision to order disclosure means that litigants are able to demand the identity of a wrongdoer from a third party even where that party is not involved in the wrong.[3]

Of particular interest is the disclosure of a journalist's sources. In *British Steel Corp v Granada Television Ltd*,[4] a television company received copies of secret documents from British Steel's files. These were then used in making a programme about a nationwide steel strike. British Steel applied for an order that Granada reveal the identity of their informant. The House of Lords held that journalists do not enjoy any immunity from the obligation to disclose. However it was recognised that there is a public interest in the free flow of information and in the protection of a source. Confidences given in good faith should not be breached unless it was necessary in the interests of justice.

British Steel Corp v Granada Television Ltd [1981] 1 All E.R. 417 at 459j–460a, *per* Lord Wilberforce:

Although, as I have said, the media, and journalists, have no immunity, it remains true that there may be an element of public interest in protecting the revelation of the

---

[1] For an example, see *R. (on the application of Hallinan Blackburn Gittings and Nott) v Middlesex Guildhall Crown Court* [2005] 1 W.L.R. 766.

[2] [1973] 2 All E.R. 943- discussed in Ch.6.

[3] For limits to this procedure, see *Mitsui & Co Ltd v Nexen Petroleum UK Ltd* [2005] 3 All E.R. 511.

[4] [1981] 1 All E.R. 417.

source. This appears from the speeches in *Norwich Pharmacal* . . . The court ought not to compel confidences bona fide given to be breached unless necessary in the interests of justice . . . There is a public interest in the free flow of information, the strength of which will vary from case to case. In some cases it may be very weak; on others it may be very strong. The court must take this into account. How ought the discretion which the court undoubtedly has to be exercised? [The trial judge] considered this and exercised it in favour of BSC. I would, for myself, give somewhat greater weight to the public interest element involved in preserving, qua the relevant information, the confidence under which it was obtained than he did. But I think that even so the balance was strongly in BSC's favour. They suffered a grievous wrong, in which Granada themselves became involved, not innocently, but with active participation. To confine BSC to its remedy against Granada and to deny them the opportunity of a remedy against the source would be a significant denial of justice. Granada had on their side, and I recognise this, the public interest that people should be informed about the steel strike, of the attitude of BSC, and perhaps that of the government towards settling the strike. But there is no 'iniquity' here, no misconduct to be revealed. The courts . . . had to form their opinion whether the strong public interest in favour of doing justice and against denying it was outweighed by the perfectly real considerations that Granada put forward. I have reached the conclusion that it was not.

This common law position was given more shape by the statutory privilege provided under the Contempt of Court Act 1981:

10. No court may require a person to disclose, nor is any person guilty of contempt of court for refusing to disclose, the source of information contained in a publication for which he is responsible, unless it be established to the satisfaction of the court that disclosure is necessary in the interests of justice or national security or for the prevention of disorder or crime

In *Secretary of State for Defence v Guardian Newspapers*,[5] a copy of a classified document about the arrival of cruise missiles at RAF Greenham Common was leaked to the *Guardian* who published it. The Crown sought recovery of the photocopy in order to discover the identity of the informant. The House of Lords held that the protection afforded by s.10 applied in such circumstances and that the burden of proof of showing that disclosure was necessary (and not merely expedient) rested on the party seeking that disclosure.

Secretary of State for Defence v Guardian Newspapers [1984] 3 All E.R. 601 at 606e–607g, *per* Lord Diplock:

The nature of the protection is the removal of compulsion to disclose in judicial proceedings the identity or nature of the source of any information contained in the publication, even though the disclosure would be relevant to the determination by the court of an issue in those particular proceedings; and the only reasonable inference is that the purpose of the protection is the same as that which underlay the discretion

[5] [1984] 3 All E.R. 601.

vested in the judge at common law to refuse to compel disclosure of sources of information, viz unless informers could be confident that their identity would not be revealed sources of information would dry up.

The words with which the section starts, before it comes to specifying any exceptions, impose a prohibition on the court itself that is perfectly general in its terms . . . This prohibition is in no way qualified by the nature of the judicial proceedings . . .

Again, what the court is prohibited from requiring is not described by reference to the form the requirement takes but by reference to its consequences, viz disclosure of the source of information. If compliance with the requirement, whatever form it takes, will, or is sought in order to enable, another party to the proceedings to identify the source by adding to the pieces already in the possession of that party the last piece to a jigsaw puzzle in which the identity of the source of information would remain concealed unless that last piece became available to put into position, the requirement will fall foul of the ban imposed by the general words with which the section starts . . .

So I turn next to the exceptions that the latter part of s.10 provides to the general ban on the court requiring disclosure of sources of information that is imposed by the opening words. There are only four interests, and each of these is specific, that are singled out for protection, viz, (a) justice, (b) national security, (c) prevention of disorder and (d) the prevention of crime . . .

The onus of proving that an order of the court which has or may have the consequences of disclosing the sources of information falls within any of the exceptions lies on the party by whom the order is sought. The words 'unless it be established to the satisfaction of the court' make it explicit and so serve to emphasise what otherwise might have been left to be inferred from the application of the general rule of statutory construction: the onus of establishing that he falls within an exception lies on the party who is seeking to rely on it.[6]

The issue came to the House of Lords again in *Ashworth Hospital Authority v MGN Ltd*,[7] where a newspaper published the medical records of a notorious child murderer, Ian Brady. Could the claimants use the *Norwich Pharmacal* ruling to compel the newspaper to disclose the name of the source? Lord Woolf C.J. makes it clear that, although there has to be a wrongdoer (the original source) a *Norwich Pharmacal* order for disclosure extends beyond situations where there are existing or contemplated proceedings. For example, the hospital here is seeking to identify the source in order that he could be dismissed. The order also lies against innocent third parties.

Ashworth Hospital Authority v MGN Ltd [2002] 4 All E.R. 193:

30. Similar statements can be found in the Norwich Pharmacal case in the other speeches of their Lordships. They make it clear that what is required is involvement or participation in the wrongdoing and that if there is the necessary involvement, it does not matter that the person from whom discovery is sought was innocent and in ignorance of the wrongdoing by the person whose identity it is hoped to establish.

A subsequent question is whether the hospital was entitled to disclosure under the "interests of justice" of s.10. Since the passage of the 1981 Act, there

---

[6] See also *Re an inquiry under Companies Securities (Insider Dealing) Act 1985* [1988] 1 All E.R. 203; *Maxwell v Pressdram Ltd* [1987] 1 All E.R. 656.
[7] [2002] 4 All E.R. 193.

had been the Human Rights Act 1998. Article 10 provides a right to freedom of expression—did a *Norwich Pharmacal* order against the newspaper infringe that right or was such order a necessary and proportionate interference in that right of expression?

Ashworth Hospital Authority v MGN Ltd [2002] 4 All E.R. 193, *per* Lord Wolf:

61. It is contended that the order for disclosure was not proportionate or necessary on the facts of this case. This argument is not based on technicalities and it raises considerations of considerable importance as to how section 10 and article 10 in practice protect journalist's sources. Any disclosure of a journalist's sources does have a chilling effect on the freedom of the press. The court when considering making an order for disclosure in exercise of the Norwich Pharmacal jurisdiction must have this well in mind. The position is analogous to the long recognised position of informers under the criminal law. In *D v NSPCC*[8] their Lordships applied the approach of the courts to police informants to those who provided information to the NSPCC. Having referred, at p 218, to *Marks v Beyfus*[9] Lord Diplock explained the rationale of the rule as being plain, if the identity of informers were too readily liable to be disclosed in a court of law the sources of information would dry up and the police would be hindered in their duty of preventing and detecting crime. Ordering journalists to disclose their sources can have similar consequences. The fact is that information which should be placed in the public domain is frequently made available to the press by individuals who would lack the courage to provide the information if they thought there was a risk of their identity being disclosed. The fact that journalists' sources can be reasonably confident that their identity will not be disclosed makes a significant contribution to the ability of the press to perform their role in society of making information available to the public. It is for this reason that it is well established now that the courts will normally protect journalists' sources from identification. However, the protection is not unqualified. Both section 10 and article 10 recognise this. This leads to the difficult issue at the heart of this appeal, namely whether the disclosure ordered was necessary and not disproportionate. The requirements of necessity and proportionality are here separate concepts which substantially cover the same area. [Counsel for the respondents] relied correctly on the decision of the European Court in *Goodwin v United Kingdom*.[10] I find no difficulty in accepting the approach that the European Court emphasised, in paragraph 40 of its judgment, that: (i) "As a matter of general principle, the 'necessity' for any restriction of freedom of expression must be convincingly established" and (ii) "limitations on the confidentiality of journalistic sources call for the most careful scrutiny by the court."

On the facts, the House found that the requirement to disclose was sufficient and proportionate.[11]

---

[8] [1978] A.C. 171.

[9] (1890) 25 Q.B.D. 494.

[10] In *Goodwin v UK* [1996] 22 E.H.R.R. 123, the European Court held, on the facts of the case, that the UK had acted disproportionately in compelling a journalist to disclose the identity of an informant.

[11] In *Mersey Care NHS Trust v Ackroyd* [2006] EWHC 107 (QB), the court found that the balance was on the side of non-disclosure of a journalist's source.

C. *Substance*

In substantive terms, the law will protect confidential relationships and intervene to protect by injunction the voluntary disclosure of confidential matters. In *Goddard v Nationwide Building Society*,[12] it was said,

> The equitable jurisdiction is well able to extend, for example, to the grant of an injunction to restrain the unauthorised disclosure of confidential communications between priest and penitent or doctor and patient.

Equity will prevent general disclosure of such confidential information but it cannot prevent otherwise admissible evidence being used in court. If a party to litigation already has a record of the information, they cannot be prevented from using it.

IV. THE PRIVILEGE AGAINST SELF-INCRIMINATION

Witnesses may, if they wish, decline to answer a question where such answers might expose them[13] to subsequent criminal proceedings. In the USA, this is commonly called, "Taking the Fifth"—this is a reference to the 5th Amendment to the Constitution which states that no person ". . . shall be compelled in any criminal case to be a witness against himself". You may refuse to answer a question because the response could be incriminating evidence. A witness's refusal, on the advice of a solicitor, to answer questions on the grounds of self-incrimination amounted to an assertion of legal professional privilege.[14] A court cannot accept such an assertion without investigating it and could not simply adopt the conclusion of the solicitor. Rather, it should satisfy itself that there were reasonable grounds to apprehend a real and appreciable risk of prosecution.

In *Blunt v Park Lane Hotel Ltd*,[15] the claimant sued for slander based on an allegation that she had been guilty of adultery. The defendants were allowed to administer interrogatories to her to support their plea of justification as there was no likelihood of any criminal proceedings. Because the old sanctions of church courts over sexual misconduct were now obsolete and adultery was not a criminal offence, the witness could not claim the shelter of the privilege. Goddard L.J. explained the scope of the privilege.

> . . . the rule is that no one is bound to answer any question if the answer thereto would, in the opinion of the judge, have a tendency to expose the deponent to any criminal charge, penalty or forfeiture which the judge regards as reasonably likely to be preferred or sued for.

---

[12] [1986] 3 All E.R. 264.
[13] Or spouse when the privilege is claimed in civil proceedings—Civil Evidence Act 1968, s.14(1)(b).
[14] *R. (on application of the Crown Prosecution Service) v Bolton Magistrates' Court* [2005] 2 All E.R. 848.
[15] [1942] 2 All E.R. 187.

There must be reasonable grounds on which to apprehend a risk of such proceedings. In *Boyes*,[16] the witness was handed a written pardon after declining to answer a question. He still declined to answer on the grounds that he might still be impeached by Parliament which was a process to which the pardon provided no bar. The court rejected the claim as there must be a real and appreciable risk. It is a privilege that applies in any legal proceedings and relates not only to oral testimony but also would permit a witness to refuse to produce documentary and real evidence.

The principle of access to evidence is displaced by the need for fairness to the accused and to minimise the risk that he or she will be convicted out of their own mouth. The instinct is that it is contrary to fairness to put witnesses in a position that they may be prosecuted if they answer or punished in different ways if they refuse to answer. This was accepted by the House of Lords in *AT & T Istel Ltd v Tully*, who nevertheless would restrict the scope of the privilege.

AT & T Istel Ltd v Tully [1992] 3 All E.R. 523 at 530, *per* Lord Templeman:

..in my opinion, the privilege can only be justified on two grounds, first that it discourages the ill–treatment of a suspect and secondly that it discourages the production of dubious confessions. Neither of these considerations applies to the present appeal. It is difficult to see any reason why in civil proceedings the privilege against self-incrimination should be exercisable so as to enable a litigant to refuse relevant and even vital documents which are in his possession or power and which speak for themselves. And it is fanciful to suggest that an order on Mr Tully to say whether he has received Abbey's money and so what has happened to that money could result in his ill-treatment or in a dubious confession. I regard the privilege against self-incrimination exercisable in civil proceedings as an archaic and unjustifiable survival from the past when the court directs the production of relevant documents and requires the defendant to specify his dealings with the plaintiff's property or money.

Such a restrictive judicial attitude is mirrored in the numerous statutory exceptions which require persons to provide information which may be used as the basis for a criminal prosecution.[17] Examples are ss.434 and 436 of the Companies Act 1985 which require company officers to answer questions put by Board of Trade inspectors appointed to investigate fraud within the company; environmental legislation which requires compulsory provision of water quality information by self-monitoring which can provide evidence for subsequent prosecutions; s.2 of the Criminal Justice Act 1987 which requires any person under investigation by the Serious Fraud Office to answer questions, produce documents and furnish information.

---

[16] (1861) 30 L.J.Q.B. 301.

[17] There are other statutes which compel the provision of information but where any statements made are inadmissible as evidence: Theft Act 1968 s.31(1); Criminal Damage Act 1971 s.9; Children Act 1989, s.98.

The approach of the European Court of Human Rights in decisions such as *Funke v France*[18] has been to hold that any legal compulsion to produce incriminating evidence infringed the right of silence. The compatibility of such legislation with Art.6 was questioned in *Saunders v UK*.[19] The defendant was convicted of fraud on the basis of answers that he had been compelled to give in the course of investigations by inspectors from the Department of Trade. The Court concluded that this infringed his freedom from self-incrimination and was in breach of the presumption of innocence and Art.6(2). Both *Saunders* and *Funke* establish that coercion to co-operate with the authorities in the pre-trial process may infringe the privilege against self-incrimination and jeopardise the fairness of any subsequent hearing, were the prosecution to use the product of that coercion as evidence. The British government response has been to restrict the use in evidence of answers given under such circumstances.[20]

But is this privilege absolute? The power of the state to compel disclosure of information under threat of criminal prosecution can be seen in many forms: it is an offence to refuse to provide a sample to test for blood alcohol levels. If a court were to hold that driver were entitled to withhold such a sample on the grounds that to do so would be to incriminate themselves, the legislation on drunk driving would be made completely ineffective. In *Brown v Stott*, [21] the issue concerned s.172(2) of the Road Traffic Act 1988 which made it an offence, when a driver of a vehicle has been involved in a traffic offence, for the owner of that vehicle not to identify who was driving at that particular time. The Privy Council held that the admission of evidence obtained under s.172 did not infringe Art.6 rights. Limited qualification of those rights, such as the privilege against self-incrimination, was acceptable if it was directed towards proper public objectives and if the qualification was proportionate. On *Saunders* Lord Steyn said,

Brown v Scott [2001] 2 All E.R. 97 at 122, *per* Lord Steyn:

The court emphasised the rationale of improper compulsion. It does not hold that anything said under compulsion of law is inadmissible. Admittedly, the court also observed:

The right not to incriminate oneself, in particular, presupposes that the prosecution in a criminal case seek to prove their case against the accused without resort to evidence obtained through methods of coercion or oppression in defiance of the will of the accused. In this sense the right is closely linked to the presumption of innocence contained in art 6(2) of the convention.

Again one finds the link with the non-absolute right of silence. In any event 'methods of coercion or oppression in defiance of the will of the accused' is probably

---

[18] [1993] 16 E.H.R.R. 297.
[19] Application No.19187/91, [1996] 23 E.H.R.R. 313.
[20] See Youth Justice and Criminal Evidence Act 1999, s.59 and Sch.3 for a list of relevant statutes.
[21] [2001] All E.R. 97.

another way of referring to improper compulsion. This is consistent with the following passage

In the present case the Court is only called upon to decide whether the use made by the prosecution of the statements obtained from the applicant by the inspectors amounted to an unjustifiable infringement of the right. This question must be examined by the Court in the light of all the circumstances of the case. In particular, it must be determined whether the applicant has been subject to compulsion to give evidence and whether the use made of the resulting testimony at his trial offended the basic principles of a fair procedure inherent in art 6(1) of which the right not to incriminate oneself is a constituent element.

The expression 'unjustifiable infringement of the right' implies that some infringements may be justified. In my view the observations in *Saunders v UK* do not support an absolutist view of the privilege against self incrimination.

Lord Steyn felt that the right was plainly not absolute and from that premise it followed that an interference with the right may be justified if the particular legislative provision was enacted in pursuance of a legitimate aim and if the scope of the legislative provision is necessary and proportionate to the achievement of the aim. Whether it was or not depended on the policy pursued. Having reviewed the number of fatal and serious traffic accidents, he continued,

The real question is whether the legislative remedy in fact adopted is necessary and proportionate to the aim sought to be achieved. There were legislative choices to be made. The legislature could have decided to do no more than to exhort the police and prosecuting authorities to redouble their efforts. It may, however, be that such a policy would have been regarded as inadequate. Secondly, the legislature could have introduced a reverse burden of proof clause which placed the burden on the registered owner to prove that he was not the driver of the vehicle at a given time when it is alleged that an offence was committed. Thirdly, and this was the course actually adopted, there was the possibility of requiring information about the identity of the driver to be revealed by the registered owner and others. As between the second and third techniques it may be said that the latter involves the securing of an admission of a constituent element of the offence. On the other hand, such an admission, if wrongly made, is not conclusive. And it must be measured against the alternative of a reverse burden clause which could without further investigation of the identity of the driver lead to a prosecution. In their impact on the citizen the two techniques are not widely different. And it is rightly conceded that a properly drafted reverse burden of proof provision would have been lawful.

It is also important to keep in mind the narrowness of the interference. Section 172(2) is directed at obtaining information in one category, namely the identity of the driver at the time when an offence was allegedly committed . . .[22]

This approach has also been followed in bankruptcy cases—in *Kearns*,[23] the accused bankrupt failed to account various moneys as required under the Insolvency Act 1986. It was held by the Court of Appeal that the implied rights in Art.6 to remain silent and not to incriminate oneself were not rights of an absolute character and could be qualified or restricted by statutory provisions. Where a person was compelled to give information that could be used in a criminal trial, the right not to incriminate oneself could be infringed,

[22] *ibid.* at 120F.
[23] [2002] Crim.L.R. 653.

dependent on the circumstances of the case and whether the statutory response to the particular social or economic issue was proportionate. The demand for information by the official receiver under s.354(3)(a) of the 1986 Insolvency Act was made in the course of an extra-judicial procedure in accordance with the official receiver's statutory duty to investigate on the estate of a bankrupt. The demand had not been made in order to provide evidence to prove a case against the appellant by means of "coercion or oppression in defiance of the will of the accused".

9

RELIABILITY, COMPETENCE AND COMPELLABILITY

I. The Primacy of Oral Evidence and Modes of Proof

The trial system in England and Wales is adversarial, centring on the day in court.[1] That in turn relies on the oral testimony of witnesses, physically present in the courtroom. Despite statutory inroads into this principle,[2] it is assumed that the evidence given by a witness present in court is superior to other forms of evidence. But the history of the use of evidence in our courts reveals no such early tradition.

A. Harding, A Social History of English Law (Pelican, 1966), pp. 126–128:

The findings of the jury were the seeds of the trial as we know it today . . . The jury listened to no evidence in court, for it was called in only when pleading had arrived at a special issue of fact or the defendant asked for a decision on the general issue; and then it was expected to know the facts in dispute, rather than to decide upon them. The very simplicity of the jury as a method of settling cases often caused to be left to it both the functions of a group of witnesses providing facts and of a judge deciding questions of law. A number of different institutions seem to merge into each other: the twelve Anglo-Saxon oath-helpers, the 'jury' (its very name means 'sworn') which in some early instances seems to have been nominated jointly by the parties from their supporters, the 'suit' of supporters necessary in every claim, and sworn witnesses of the modern type. An early jury was sometimes composed of sworn groups from a number of villages, which provided the court with material for its decision: 'The eight men of Wormley being sworn say . . .

In practice the jury would usually not know the facts directly and would have to go to a man's house and ask him what he knew . . . But coroners, as part of their duty of recording the preliminaries of accusations, examined persons who could give information. A statute of 1554[3] made examination of criminals and the recording of it incumbent on coroners and JPs. A contemporary description of an Elizabethan criminal trial shows that the preliminary depositions were already being used as evidence in the trial, and that sworn witnesses for the prosecution carried on an altercation with the prisoner till the judges had heard enough.

---

[1] The origins and nature of adversarial trial are discussed in Ch.1.
[2] Notably the admissibility of documentary hearsay under Civil Evidence Act 1995 and Criminal Justice Acts 1988 and 2003.
[3] 1 and 2 Philip and Mary c.13; see J. Langbein, *Prosecuting Crime in the Renaissance* (Harvard University Press, 1974).

The treatment of evidence was rudimentary: the criminal had no notice of those witnesses who would appear against him, and he was not allowed to arrange for any on his own behalf. The last condition was slowly modified in Elizabeth's reign, but at first the prisoner's witnesses could not be sworn . . . In any event, criminal trial was essentially still by jury and not by witnesses, as Chief Justice Coke often said, perhaps in dislike of the Crown's use of examination and bullied witnesses in political trials.

The chancellor's subpoena was the only way of enforcing the appearance of civil witnesses before 1563. Nevertheless throughout the middle ages witnesses to deeds and commercial transactions had appeared to sit with the jury when those deeds were in dispute. Here the witnesses were taking over some of the jury's original functions and forcing the jury into something like its modern position. Counsel became interested towards the end of the Middle Ages in assembling evidence to convince the jurymen: that is the modern way of presenting a case.[4] The change began in Chancery, for the chancellor, like the Roman Law judge, worked in his court without a jury, deciding issues on the evidence of deeds and witnesses. So, unlike his Common Law brethren, he had to evolve 'rules of evidence', to decide the relative weight of the different sorts of evidence and assess the reliability of witnesses. Only at this point, when it begins to be weighed in the balance, does a statement cease to be a verdict and becomes a piece of evidence at all.

Seventeeth century criminal trials were largely lawyer-free, an altercation between victim and the accused, with the trial itself an instructional proceeding for the jury, which had by now lost its earlier characteristic of being self-informing.[5] The change to the form of adversarial trial that we recognise was to come in the 18th century.

J Langbein., The Origins of Adversary Criminal Trial (OUP, Oxford. 2003), pp.274–275:

The Trial of Treason Act (1696) was a turning point in the just regulation of criminal trials. The man accused of treason was to be given a copy of the indictment at least five days before arraignment; he was to have free access to counsel (whom the court would assign at the prisoner's request); And processes were allowed him to summon witnesses on his behalf, who would be sworn. He was not, however, to know the names of the witnesses against him; ordinary felons were not allowed counsel till 1837; and there were still few rules on the admissibility of evidence. The verbatim reports of the trial of John Donellan for murder, before Mr Justice Buller at Warwick assizes in 1781, shows well-developed methods of cross-examination, with objections to leading questions; but also a willingness to allow expert witnesses (physicians—it was a case of poisoning) to give decisive opinions on the whole question of guilt. The judge's summing up of the merely circumstantial evidence was weighted against the prisoner. Before the trial, the accused submitted a written defence which was read in court, for he could still not give evidence on oath—a grave disadvantage for a poor and ignorant man, unable to afford an elaborate defence.

Treason trials were governed by their own procedural rules and John Langbein sees the change to adversarial trial as a result of cases such as the

---

[4] M. Hastings, *The Court of Common Pleas in Fifteenth-Century England* (1971).
[5] For a fuller account, J. Langbein, *The Origins of Adversary Criminal Trial* (OUP Oxford, 2003), Ch.1.

Rye House Plot in the late 17th century. The miscarriages of justice in these trials led to legislation regulating such trials.[6] The 18th century saw both the emergence of prosecution and defence lawyers in felony trials and the development of the central concepts of the law of evidence. It is a history that has led to jury trial as the dominant form of legal proceedings with the emphasis placed upon the single self-contained hearing at which the facts are established and the issues are decided.

In that earlier, less literate, world, it was not surprising to find the requirement that witnesses attend that hearing and testify orally. But the principle of orality has stubbornly remained—everything that will inform the decision has to be said in court. Oral evidence is assumed to be the best type of evidence because of traditional assumptions regarding cross-examination as the optimum method for testing witnesses, the reliability ensured by the oath, the importance of the fact-finder observing the demeanour of the witness, the exposure of the witness to public scrutiny and the formality and solemnity of the courtroom setting. All of these factors mean that, with very few exceptions, witnesses in English criminal trials must deliver their evidence in oral form, live in the courtroom.[7]

It has been argued[8] that this preference for oral testimony is a purely cultural one in the English-speaking world. The civil law systems in continental Europe display a marked preference for documentary evidence. As a German jurist puts it,

> Owing to the deficiencies of human observation and memory, and in view of the conscious or unconscious prejudice of the witnesses involves, a greater or lesser attitude of reserve [towards testimonial evidence] is called for. Testimonial evidence is therefore—apart from statements of the parties—the *least certain* means of proof. Generally speaking expert evidence, and above all documentary evidence, is to be preferred to it.[9]

Courts in civil law systems make extensive use of documents: in criminal proceedings, the system is under the direction of an examining magistrate and there will be pre-trial interviews with the suspect and witnesses, whose written depositions will be their testimony at the trial proper.

J. Cooper, "Criminal Investigations in France" [1991] 141 N.L.J. 381:

. . . All civil law systems are grounded in a philosophy of state responsibility and the French system is no exception. Thus, with an infallible Cartesian logic, it is

---

[6] Langbein (2003), *op.cit.* Ch.2.

[7] K. Quinn, [2003] "Justice for Vulnerable and Intimidated Witnesses in Adversarial Proceedings?" M.L.R. 66 (1), 139.

[8] J. Spencer and J. Flin, *The Evidence of Children—The Law and the Psychology* (2nd edn., Blackstones, 1993) Ch. 10; J. Spencer, *"Orality and the Evidence of Absent Witnesses"* [1994] Crim.L.R. 628.

[9] Stein-Jonas, *Zivilprozessordnanz* (19th ed) Vol. II 1572 cited in T. Honore, "The Primacy of Oral Evidence?" in C. Tapper (ed) *Crime, Proof and Punishment* (details 1981) 172 at 173.

axiomatic to the French system that the juge d'instruction, who is charged by the State with establishing the truth, should suffer no procedural or technical hindrance in investigating any matter that may be relevant to establishing guilt or innocence . . .

A list of the powers of the juge d'instruction illustrates this point. They are very substantial. They include the power to interrogate the defendant anywhere, at any time; to interrogate any witness; to visit the scene of the crime with the defendant and any witness; to arrange identifications, or confrontations between accused and victim; to set up reconstructions of the crime to test evidence; and to investigate the social, economic and—if relevant—criminal background of the defendant and witnesses, and to draw inferences from such evidence. The investigation is not limited by time. And most significant of all, if the juge thinks there is a case to answer, he or she is obliged to pass on to the subsequent trial court a dossier which will contain all the relevant evidence on which the belief is grounded.

After such an investigation, the trial itself is a much shorter affair, dealing with the dossier prepared by the juge d'instruction, using witness depositions in a manner which would undoubtedly shorten common law trials but also revealing much information that would be inadmissible in a common law trial. The Western Australian Law Commission has also reviewed the civil law approach.

Law Reform Commission of Western Australia (1999):

Before the trial takes place the evidence has largely been identified and gathered, in a statutorily determined documentary format, in the form in which it is to be heard (or more correctly seen) at the trial. In some cases, the evidence has been received prior to the trial in an adversarial format (before the investigating magistrate, acting in his judicial capacity), but generally speaking the pre-trial stage (the information) is secret and not contradictoire. Nonetheless the accused has a limited right of access to the dossier at a given moment prior to the trial.

Exclusionary rules of evidence are said to originate in the predominance of jury trials in the common law system, dependent as they are on oral and continuous presentation of evidence. However they also result from professionalisation of representation of accused persons in adversarial trial. Be that as it may, it is better accepted in civilian jurisdictions, where juries are very rare that a professional judge (specialised in criminal matters to boot) will not be swayed by unreliable, unfairly prejudicial evidence. Nor are there strict rules excluding evidence about the previous conduct of the accused. Again a professional judge is thought capable of avoiding the trap of determining guilt by disposition, and to give full weight to the right to silence, and the presumption of innocence, of the accused. Conversely there is not, in inquisitorial systems, the kind of adversarial pressure that results in partisan presentation of evidence in an adversarial trial.

The civil law system is thus said to be simpler, without the rules of evidence that are such an unpredictable factor in criminal prosecutions in adversarial jurisdictions.[10]

In civil proceedings, the preference for documentary evidence is even clearer. The French make documentary evidence a requirement in any matter involving €800 or above[11] and also make oral evidence inadmissible to

---

[10] Law Reform Commission of Western Australia (1999) Review of the Criminal and Civil Justice System: Consultation Drafts Vol 1 Section 1.3 'Advantages and Disadvantages of the Adversarial System in Criminal Proceedings', pp. 74–75.

[11] Art. 1341 Code Civil, discussed in Honoré, op.cit. 172 at 181.

contradict such a document.[12] This contrast between common law and civil law, between oral and written traditions in evidence, can be exaggerated as the practices of differing systems often converge. But the distinction can be useful since, as Honoré argues, it demonstrates that a key characteristic of systems of evidence is the extent to which they control the mode of proof—namely restricting how a matter may be proved in court. To give greater priority to either oral or to documentary evidence is such a controlling feature.[13] An ideal system of evidence would require a free system of proof so that all relevant evidence is admissible, leaving the probative value of the evidence, the weight, to be determined by the trier of fact. The traditional role of the jury, especially in the common law criminal trial, has made such an open-ended approach impossible.

II. Evaluating Witness Testimony

The commitment to the oral tradition in the common law system is deep rooted. But how justified is it? There are said to be many advantages for the triers of fact themselves to listen to a witness:

- oral evidence is heard directly with no errors of transmission;
- evidence is given on oath and in a formal and public setting, enhancing the likelihood that the witness will tell the truth;
- the demeanour of the witness is in itself evidence from which the trier is able to assess the witness's credibility and therefore the weight to be given to the testimony; and
- that demeanour will be tested in cross-examination.

However this presumes rationality behind a trial, in the presentation of evidence and in the decision-making. Is this the case? In a contested trial, rational decision-making can take a backseat to the high level of ritual in a trial. This is present in the formal procedures, the wigs and gowns, and the language. On one level, ritual is functional, symbolising the court's authority to the parties and to the outside world. It contributes to establishing the authoritative version of the events. But ritualism is also an appeal to the irrational, reinforcing a view of the courtroom as a reified rather than a human process. For example, one American sociologist[14] has suggested that the trial is a process of recasting the defendant, away from his own identity and into a stereotyped social role (as mugger, hooligan, drunk, or vagrant). The criminal trial becomes a degradation ceremony which reduces defendants to a lower status and through them personifies broader patterns of social authority. Witnesses, jurors, lawyers and judges collude, voluntarily or not, in such a process.

---

[12] Art. 1344 – comparable to the "parol evidence" rule in common law.
[13] Honoré, *op.cit.* 172 at 181.
[14] H. Garfinkel: "The Trial as a Degradation Ceremony" (1956) 66 American Journal of Sociology 420.

Witnesses experience the courtroom as an imposed and imposing "world of authority"[15] with dominance and subordination clearly signposted. There is the deference shown by all the personnel towards the bench as well as those elements of "majesty": the elevated bench, private access to judge's "chambers" and the judge's throne-like chair. The geography of the court carries this on: in the dock, the defendant is raised but on a lesser level; there is a rail surround, not to stop an escape attempt but representative of captivity. The public are well to the back of the court, segregated so that we are allowed to observe but not to participate. Carlen suggests that the organisation of space is such as to impede communication, especially for those who are not part of the routine cast and who are unfamiliar with a courtroom. Distances are much greater than one would normally use for disclosure of private or traumatic incidents or indeed for effective intervention. Communication is through the lawyers and there is also the sense of a play being carefully stage-managed, again maintaining the sense of domination, of the inexorability of the law.

The language employed, with its technical vocabulary and flowery and archaic forms of address again put the uninitiated at a disadvantage. The court insists upon precise technical words,[16] and any involvement by witnesses or the defendant is essentially passive, responding to questions. Indeed the mode of discourse in the courtroom involves either interrogation or monologue, both of which are extraordinary (and resented) when they occur in day-to-day conversation.[17] Even the intelligent and articulate witness is ill-equipped to deal on an equal basis. Defendants feel confused, alienated and by-passed so that even the practice of asking the defendant if he has anything to say before sentence is now delegated to the lawyer.

Through the ritual, the geography and the language, there is a high level of situational control by the court and the lawyers. "After all, they're near enough mates in the same play. They're the cast of the play, you're just the casual one-day actor. It's just another day's work to them."[18] This control is experienced by witnesses, defendants and jurors alike. The very context of the trial challenges a witness's capacity to provide clear, reliable and objective information for a court and a jury's ability to make rational and just decisions.

A. *Testimony and Story-Telling*

Do we over-estimate the quality of evidence put before juries and their ability to assess that evidence? Is too much weight placed on identification, confession or eye-witness testimony? Witnesses' ability to assess the passage of time or speed or to recall colours, events or statements varies considerably.

---

[15] P. Carlen: "Remedial Routines for the Maintenance of Control in Magistrates Courts" 1 Brit. Jour. of Law and Society (1974) 101.
[16] Carlen, *ibid.* 107.
[17] J.M. Atkinson and P. Drew *Order in Court* (Macmillan, 1979).
[18] J. Baldwin and M. McConville *Negotiated Justice* (Blackwell, 1977), p. 85.

Good powers of perception and recall are not related to the coherence and demeanour with which they present their testimony which are major factors in a jury's assessment of the reliability of a witness. Whether we believe or disbelieve what people tell us has as much to do with their abilities as story-tellers as with the truth of their story. We might think about the trial as story-telling. Narrative plays an important part in imposing order on our lives.[19] We see our own selves in terms of a biographical narrative, with the events of our lives moving in a connected flow, linked to some central theme. Similarly, narrative helps us to impose order on the external world. This can be done through imaginative fiction (and police and courtroom dramas are one of the most popular forms of these) as well through media in the non-fiction world, such as newspapers. Stories, of course, are the stuff of real courtroom interaction and it is the party that puts together the most credible narrative that often wins.

It is the lawyer who is responsible for the construction of a story, summoning witnesses to support the client's case and seeking to undermine the coherence of the opposition story by the cross-examination of their witnesses. Being called as a witness is an ordeal in itself,[20] with the stress of testifying in addition to lost time from work and inadequate expenses. Once in the witness box, witnesses discover that they are not allowed to tell their own story or even to have an ordinary conversation. The techniques of witness's examination are divorced from discourse in ordinary life which revolves around "turn-taking"

A central property of conversation appears to be that it is organised into single-speaker turns, with regular transitions between speakers. Participants take turns to talk, with one party at a time occupying a turn, then a next, then a next (though a 'next' can include a prior speaker) and so on until the end of the conversation.[21]

The order of speaking, the length of turns and what is said in a turn: all vary in everyday life and are not specified in advance. The more formal the situation, the more structured becomes the dialogue. Even in ordinary conversation, there are still unarticulated rules since we criticise those who dominate conversations, who withdraw from them or who seek to interrogate ("I'm not here to be cross-examined!"). Compared to everyday life, the courtroom plays by a wholly different set of rules.

J. M. Atkinson and P. Drew, Order in Court (Macmillan, 1979), p.61–62:

. . . examination differs markedly from conversation in two major respects: in examination *turn order is fixed,* as is the *type of turn* which each speaker's talk constitutes. These features both arise from the fact that the talk in examination is restricted to two parties only, whose turns are pre-allocated (although a caveat to the

---

[19] W. Bennett and M. Feldman, *Reconstructing Reality in the Courtroom* (Tavistock, 1981).
[20] D. McBarnett, *Conviction* (Macmillan, 1983), p.90ff.
[21] J.M. Atkinson and P. Drew, *Order in Court* (Macmillian, 1979), p.36.

term 'parties' will be mentioned in a moment). The way in which turn order and types of turn are fixed, can be summarised as follows:

1. The talk in examination is organised into series of 'question' and 'answer' pairs. Whatever else these utterances may be heard to do, and however else they might be characterised . . . speaker turns should be designed at least minimally as either questions or answers. This is in clear contrast to conversation, in which there is no guarantee that utterances can be treated as questions or answers, and in which even an utterance's interrogative syntactic structure does not assure its status as a question . . .

2. But these two types of speaker turns are not randomly distributed between the participants. Crucially, only one party—the one conducting the examination, generally the counsel—has the right to ask questions. A consequence of that is that the other (examined) party's utterances are always produced in the sequential position of post-question, and should therefore be answers; this means that persons who are being examined may not exercise the option of selecting by, for instance, themselves asking the other party (i.e. the examiner) a question.

Such a move away from everyday conversation occurs in many situations: in the doctor's examining room, the conversation is likely to comprise questions and answers but the good doctor will allow patients to tell the story in their own way. This raises the issue as to which method of eliciting information from a witness is the most effective.

D. Greer, "Anything but the Truth? The Reliability of Testimony in Criminal Trials" (1971) 11 BJC 131:

[This question] was the basis for a well-known experiment in 1924.[22] The usual sort of dramatic incident was staged during a lecture on legal psychology. The persons attending the lecture were all qualified lawyers and the incident contained a large number of details (over 100) of possible legal significance. None of those present had any intimation that an experiment was to be performed, and none was aware that a test was in progress until the incident had been concluded and the lecturer began to issue instructions for the recording of testimony . . .

The conclusions drawn [on the different methods of eliciting testimony] . . . were that

1. Free narration is less complete but more accurate than the other two methods: i.e. on free narration a witness will not give as many details, but those he does give are most likely to be correct.

2. Direct examination is both more complete and more accurate than cross-examination: i.e. on direct examination a witness will give more details than on cross-examination and these are also more likely to be correct.

3. Cross-examination shows greater caution than direct examination without any corresponding gain in either completeness or accuracy. It would appear to follow that added caution does an important, though hidden, work in redeeming cross-examination from a degree of inaccuracy which would render it almost wholly worthless: i.e. when a witness does not know the answer on cross-examination, he is as likely to answer erroneously as 'I don't know', but on direct examination he is more likely to answer erroneously than 'I don't know'.

---

[22] W. Marston, "Studies in Testimony" 15 (1924) J.C.L.C. 5.

These conclusions again are confirmed by later experiments . . .

Far from Wigmore's assertion that cross-examination is the "greatest legal engine ever invented for the discovery of truth", witnesses are confronted by techniques which both alienate them and restrict the information that is elicited. The witness responds to questions which frame the acceptable answer. Witnesses who transgress and seek to give unasked for information are quickly put in their place. Questions are ring-fenced, raising single points so that the lawyer can transform a mass of information into 'the facts of the case'.

D. McBarnett, *Conviction* (Macmillan, 1983), p.23:

Interrogation means not just filtering potential information but imposing order and meaning upon it by the sequence and context of questions asked—whatever meaning it may have had to the witness, control by questioning can impose the meaning of the questioner. The case thus takes on its own logic within the framework of the 'facts of the case', and any other issues mentioned, hinted at or unknown, lose any relevance to the meaning of the case that they may have had to the meaning of the incident. What is more the order and logic of a controlled case is much more visible than that in the welter of social reality, and therefore, arguably, the more persuasive in carrying its evidence along.[23]

But witnesses are not mere pawns. They and the lawyer co-operate to seek to convince the trier of fact of the truth of their story but the truth of the story does not guarantee belief or acceptance.

G. Stephenson, *The Psychology of Criminal Justice* (Blackwell, 1992), pp.137–138:

Essentially this is because stories in court are a technique for ordering and presenting evidence, an activity that can be performed more or less skilfully, and which is dependent for its success on the quality of available evidence, something over which the story teller (defence or prosecution lawyer) may have little control. In addition, the hearers of the story may be overly impressed by who tells the story and how, rather than its effectiveness in accounting for the available evidence.

The importance of story structure to its acceptance by hearers was demonstrated in an experiment by Bennett and Feldman[24] in which student subjects were asked to tell true or false stories to the group of students. The listeners were asked to vote privately on the status of the stories as 'true' or 'false', and it was discovered that these

---

[23] The process of translation of the social into the legal is a central law job—W. Mansell, B. Meteyard and A. Thomson, *A Critical Introduction to Law* (3rd edn Cavendish, 2004), Ch.5.
[24] *op.cit.*

judgements were totally unrelated to the actual truth value of the stories; a true story was as likely to receive a 'false' as a 'true' vote, and vice versa. Story length in words, and the number of actions it contained—straightforward measures of complexity— were also unrelated to truth judgements, as were the number and length of pauses—a measure of uncertainty. The important feature of the story to which listeners appeared to respond was the coherence of the story, as assessed by a measure that Bennett and Feldman termed 'structural ambiguity'. To be coherent, a story should have a central action to which various characters, objects and events ('elements') in the story should be clearly connected, either directly, or indirectly by virtue of their clear relation to other elements. The key feature here is the clarity of the relationships between elements and their linking to the central action. Bennett and Feldman found that the larger the proportion of ambiguous links in the story, the less likely it was to be believed. Structural ambiguity was the only measure which successfully predicted how listeners would vote: the less ambiguous a story, the more believers it would attract.

The relevance of this study to courtroom interaction is clear. Judges and juries will be impressed by, and tend to believe, that version of events and explanation of evidence whose elements are the more unambiguously related one to another and to the 'central action' which accounts for the known or alleged harm that has been done. In the adversarial system, it is in each side's interests so to distort its presentation of the evidence that its own story or version of events has the greater clarity and is therefore to be believed. Of course, structural ambiguity may be perceived in stories that are true, leading those whose stories may lack clarity through no fault of their own to become embittered and angry. Members of minority groups, for example, may find that their accounts of events are ill-received because the conventions of their social group which serve to clarify the actions in a story are not shared by the minority who sit in judgement upon them.

Thus we do not believe poor story-tellers since their narrative is often internally inconsistent, jumps from one point to another and does not link to central action. But whether we believe or disbelieve what people tell us is more related to their abilities as story-tellers than it is to the truth or otherwise of their story. Those who testify regularly probably acquire such skills in contrast to the "one-off" witness. The demeanour and coherence of a police officer or expert witness can lead the trier of fact to infer that they are more credible and that their accounts deserve greater weight. Similarly Stephenson suggests that class and gender are factors going to the "weight" of the evidence, as working class defendants and witnesses were more ill-at-ease than middle class defendants. The latter's plausible stories were gener-ally believed, and they received sympathetic treatment.[25]

B. *The Reliability of Witnesses*

The coherence and consistency of the narrative is important. But it is eye-witness testimony that is most highly regarded, perhaps mistakenly. In the USA, there have been cases where convictions have been quashed as the result of DNA evidence. One study examined 62 cases (including 8 individuals who had been sentenced to death). Of these, 52 contained identifications

---

[25] *ibid.* at 150.

from 77 confident but mistaken eyewitnesses.[26] Witnesses, especially in criminal cases, are often liable to be under pressure—from friends and relatives, lawyers, police or defendants. The frankness and quality of their testimony can always be affected. But how reliable is the neutral, honest and unpressured observer of an incident? There is an immense psychological research literature on this area.[27]

D. Greer, "Anything but the Truth? The Reliability of Testimony in Criminal Trials" (1971) 11 BJC 131:

The first common lawyer to take an interest in these developments appears to have been Wigmore. In 1905 he had conducted . . . a series of 'Testimonial and Verdict Experiments' which carried the 'reality experiment' a couple of stages further in legal relevance. The details of the dramatic incident—a quarrel between four of the students in his class—were agreed on beforehand and written down. The 'row' was then enacted during a lecture. An immediate adjournment took place to the law school courtroom. There, a jury of law students who had not witnessed the row was empanelled. Thirteen witnesses of the incident were arbitrarily selected and each was asked a series of nine questions about what had happened. The jurors then retired to consider the evidence and returned with their verdict—i.e. their version of the row. This version was then compared with the pre-arranged version and the following are some of the differences discovered:

1. The person found by the 'jury' to have made the first move did not in fact make it.
2. Several relevant 'facts' were not mentioned in the jury's version—e.g. that one of the participants had shouted 'That is an insult and I shall here resent it.'
3. The jury's version of another statement uttered during the incident differed from that actually made
. . . On the whole, it seems, psychological theory in the field of perception is fairly well advanced. It is now generally recognised that there is an important distinction between 'actual' and 'perceived' characteristics of the environment . . . What a witness cognises perceptually is not necessarily an exact reproduction of the data presented and for legal purposes at any rate the most important finding in this area is that there can be a very considerable discrepancy between the two.
Many of the causes of this discrepancy are already well-known, e.g. the adverse effect on accuracy of testimony of poor lighting, long distance, short duration of exposure, etc. Less well-known factors influencing perception include emotion, interest, bias, prejudice or expectancy, on the part of the perceive . . .

Research of this nature shows us that the accuracy of the honest witness cannot be assumed. Poor lighting, long distance and short duration are obviously factors that the trier of fact is likely to take into account. But there are many others which can run counter to the instincts of the lay person and the judge:

---

[26] B. Scheck, P. Neufeld, & J. Dwyer, *Actual innocence: Five days to execution and other dispatches from the wrongly convicted.* (Doubleday, New York, 2000).
[27] E. Loftus, Eyewitness Testimony (Harvard UP – republished 1996); S. Lloyd-Bostock and B. Clifford (eds), *Evaluating Witness Evidence* (Wiley, 1983).

1. The heightened level of arousal experienced by a victim or witness to, for instance, a violent crime does not lead to any improved ability to perceive and recall details.[28]

Stephenson G., The Psychology of Criminal Justice (Blackwell, 1992), p. 169:

. . . subjects viewing a film will focus on a gun held by a customer in a restaurant, rather than (in the alternative version of the film) on a cheque in his hand. Identification of the suspect in a line-up, and the answers to a number of specific questions, were more accurate in the 'cheque' than in the 'gun' condition. In an ingenious and realistic simulation of the 'weapon effect', [researchers] enrolled students to participate in an experiment on sport-related activity and psychological well-being. The investigators demonstrated that having been approached by a white-coated female experimenter with a syringe, who then talked to them for 20 seconds before leaving, a student subject was very much more likely to misidentify foils[29] in a live identification parade than when the similarly white-coated female had approached them with a pen in her hand. The distraction caused by the syringe is similar . . . to the distraction that witnesses to a crime may experience by the weapon in the hand of the assailant.[30]

2. Police officers are probably no better than civilians at recalling details, especially in identifying faces. Studies suggest that it is difficult to train people to become better at recognising faces.
3. Perception and recall is related to age: children improve steadily up to the age of 14 and people deteriorate from late middle age onwards. The young perform less well, perhaps because of their inexperience. The old can rely too much on stereotypes, although they are more cautious than the young.[31]
4. Much of the literature has stressed that the criminal justice system needs guidance with regard to the limitations of identification evidence.[32] In particular it has concluded that cross-race eyewitness identifications are less accurate than same-race eyewitness identifications.[33]

The problems surrounding witness reliability are exacerbated by the "law's delays". A witness may have made a statement relatively contemporaneously with the incident. But the trial may be many months, if not years, after the event. The common law's preference for oral testimony means that the truth

[28] There is a review of research in Stephenson (1992) *op.cit.* at 168.
[29] *i.e.* persons who are generally similar to the suspect.
[30] This raises interesting questions about the assumptions behind the *res gestae* rule—see Ch.17.
[31] Stephenson (1992), *op.cit.* pp.165–166.
[32] Loftus (1996), *op.cit.*; B. Clifford and R. Bull, *The Psychology of Person Identification* (Routledge, 1978).
[33] R. Lindsay and G. Wells, "What do we really know about cross-race eyewitness identification?" in Lloyd-Bostock (1983) *op.cit.* p.219.

of a person's testimony is assessed on the quality of their memory and on the performance in the witness box. Memory inevitably fades, although the decline is minimised when witnesses know that they are to be tested.[34] An equally important point is that we are all suggestible and information received after the event can interfere with accurate recall.

E. Loftus and K. Ketcham, "The Malleability of Eyewitness Accounts" in Lloyd-Bostock (1983), Evaluating Witness Testimony (1983), pp. 159–160:

This extraordinary malleability of memory has been recently demonstrated . . . Consider a typical experiment in which college students were presented with a film of an automobile accident and immediately afterwards were asked a series of questions about the accident. Some of the questions were designed to present misleading information—that is, to suggest the existence of an object that did not in fact exist. Half the subjects were asked 'How fast was the white sports car going when it passed the barn while travelling along the country road?' In fact no barn existed. The remaining subjects were asked, 'How fast was the white sports car going while travelling along the country road?' Later all subjects were asked if they had seen a barn. When questioned again about the accident a week later, more than 17% of those exposed to the false information about the barn said they had seen one. Apparently the assumption of a barn in the initial questioning caused many subjects to incorporate the non-existent barn into their recollections of the event.

It has been said that ". . . human memory is a fragile and elusive creature. It can be supplemented, partially restructured, or even completely altered by post-event inputs. It is susceptible to the power of a single word."[35]

1. Testing reliability in court

Courts have not sought expert assistance in assessing the reliability of witnesses.[36] In criminal cases, the function of expert witnesses is regulated by the *Turner* rule,[37] that such witnesses should not express opinions on those matters which are within the competence of the jury.[38] The jurors are representatives of the community and are expected to understand how 'normal' people behave and react. Expert evidence by psychologists is not admissible as to whether a witness is reliable or not. It only becomes admissible in dealing with the "abnormal" witness or abnormal circumstances which lie outside the experience of the jury.[39] In *Robinson*,[40] the

---

[34] D. Egan, M. Pittner and A. Goldstein, "Eyewitness Identification—photographs v live models" (1977) 1 Law and Human Behaviour 199.

[35] *ibid.* at p.168.

[36] Psychologists frequently give expert testimony on this issue in the USA—S. Kassin, V. A. Tubb, H. Hosch, and A. Memon, "On the "General Acceptance" of Eyewitness Testimony Research : A New Survey of the Experts" American Psychologist. Vol. 56(5(2001) 405.

[37] *Turner* [1975] 1 All E.R. 70.

[38] This does not apply in civil proceedings since under s.3(1) of the Civil Evidence Act 1972, '. . . where a person is called as a witness. . . his opinion on any relevant matter on which he is qualified to give expert evidence shall be admissible in evidence.'

[39] *Toohey v Metropolitan Police Comm* [1965] A.C. 595.

[40] [1994] 3 All E.R. 346.

defendant was accused of indecent assault on a mentally retarded young woman. At the trial the judge admitted the evidence of an educational psychologist to the effect that the victim was a credible witness, not being suggestible or imaginative. On appeal Lord Taylor C.J. reviewed the state of the law.

Robinson [1994] 3 All E.R. 346 at 350–352, *per* Taylor C.J.:

But . . . there is no case in which psychiatric or psychological evidence has been admitted to boost, bolster or enhance the evidence of a witness for the Crown or indeed of any witness. [Counsel for the appellant] submits that it is for the jury to assess the reliability and persuasiveness of witnesses and it cannot be right to allow evidence, however expert, to suggest to the jury that they should believe a witness of fact. [Counsel for the appellant] drew our attention to a Canadian case, *R v Kyselka*[41] The headnote reads:

In a rape trial, where the complainant was mentally retarded, the Crown called a psychiatrist who testified that a person of her mental classification, which was a mental age of 10–11 years, was likely to be a truthful witness because such a person would lack the imagination to fabricate. Held, that such evidence was inadmissible. While the credit of a witness may be impeached by the opposite party, a party cannot call witnesses to testify to the credibility or truth of his own witnesses

. . . In our view the Crown cannot call a witness of fact and then, without more, call a psychologist or psychiatrist to give reasons why the jury should regard that witness as reliable.

Neither the prosecution nor defence can engage in "oath helping", bolstering the credibility of a witness and in the light of such decisions, the prospects for the admissibility of psychological evidence on the general reliability of an eyewitness's account seem remote, especially when compared with the more liberal position in the USA.[42] Recently there has been greater willingness to accept medical expert evidence on the issue of the credibility of a witness. In *MacKenney*[43] there were considerable doubts about the psychological state of the chief prosecution witness. The defence were prevented from calling an expert witness to testify that the witness suffered from a personality disorder and his behaviour was psychopathic. The defendants served over 20 years in prison before the appeal court quashed the convictions. Where the witness's evidence is of major importance in the trial, the admission of expert evidence is more likely even where there has been no examination of that witness. However this was a case in which the psychologist's opinion was that ". . . severely psychopathic individuals . . . may deliver statements in a bizarre and

---

[41] (1962) 133 C.C.C. 103.
[42] Under Federal Rules of Evidence, r. 702, expert testimony is admissible where it will assist the finder of fact. However the leading appellate decision (*US v Amaral* (1973) 488 F.2d 1148) stresses the discretion of the trial judge in deciding whether to admit such testimony—see E. Loftus "Expert testimony on the eyewitness" in E. Loftus and G. Wells (eds) *Eyewitness Testimony* (CUP, Cambridge, 1984), p.273.
[43] The initial appeals are (1981) 72 Cr.App.R. 78; affirmed (1983) 76 Cr.App.R. 271; conviction quashed [2004] 2 Cr.App.R. 5.

eccentric fashion, but they do not exhibit the signs of lying which allow detection from the manner in which evidence is given. The lack of coherent physiological response to fabrication affects not only the mechanical lie-detector, it is also bound to confuse the naive human observer." In no way does this open the door to the use of expert witnesses to comment on the general reliability of eyewitness testimony.

2. Using witness statements

Question marks surround the reliability of the oral testimony of eyewitnesses. Yet their earlier, potentially more reliable, witness statements are inadmissible to supplement the oral testimony,[44] as these were regarded as hearsay. The best evidence was the oral evidence of the witness. The common law's technique for avoiding the worst effects of this was to allow witnesses in the witness box to "refresh their memory" from contemporaneous statements.[45] But before taking the oath, witnesses are permitted to consult their statements prior to going into the witness box, even if this leads to the rather disreputable spectacle of witnesses frantically "learning their lines" before entering the court.

Testimony in the witness box becomes more a test of memory than of truthfulness if witnesses are deprived of the opportunity of checking their recollection beforehand by reference to statements or notes made at a time closer to the events in question . . . Refusal of access to statements would tend to create difficulties for honest witnesses but be likely to do little to hamper dishonest witnesses.[46]

This statement was approved in *Richardson*,[47] in which prosecution witnesses in a burglary case were shown statements that had been made to the police 18 months earlier and a few weeks after the offences in question.

Richardson [1971] 2 All E.R. 773 at 777, *per* Sachs L.J.:

Obviously it would be wrong if several witnesses were handed statements in circumstances which enabled one to compare with another what each had said. But there can be no general rule (which incidentally would be unenforceable, unlike the rule as to what can be done in the witness box) that witnesses may not before trial see the statements that they had made at some period reasonably close to the time of the event which is the subject of the trial. Indeed one can imagine many cases particularly those of a complex nature, where such a rule would militate very greatly against the interests of justice.[48]

---

[44] At least in criminal proceedings—in civil proceedings, this is common practice under the proviso to Civil Evidence Act 1995, s. 6(2); even in criminal cases, children's depositions can act as their evidence in chief in certain cases under Criminal Justice Act 1988, s.32A.

[45] See Ch.12.

[46] *Lau Pak Ngam v R* [1966] Crim.L.R. 443.

[47] [1971] 2 All E.R. 773.

[48] The sharp distinction between the 'contemporaneous' statement (used in the witness box to refresh the memory) and the 'not-so-contemporaneous' statement which is not permitted to be used in this way was significantly reduced in *Da Silva* [1990] 1 All E.R. 29.

The rules allowing witnesses to 'refresh their memory' have been expanded by section 139 of the Criminal Justice Act 2003. Section 120 also allows the earlier statements of various categories of witness to be used as the primary evidence, including that of the 'forgetful' witness.[49] However these reforms rejected the straightforward solution of allowing the witness statement to be introduced as the evidence in chief and on which they can be examined by both parties. A good memory (or at least the appearance of one) remains an important attribute for a witness at a criminal trial.

III. WHO CAN TESTIFY? WHO MUST TESTIFY?

The general rule is that everyone is competent to give evidence; everyone can be compelled to attend court; everyone is under an obligation to disclose the truth.

1. Competence refers to a person's ability to testify. The law presumes that ordinary individuals are competent. When a person is not competent, they are barred from testifying. This happens mainly in cases of the very young or where the prospective witness is mentally handicapped. A witness will testify either on oath or (in some cases[50]) unsworn

2. A person who is competent to testify can be compelled to testify. Where a person is reluctant to testify:

    a) in civil cases, under the provisions of r.34 of the Civil Procedure Rules, a party may summons a person to attend court, produce documents and testify. To refuse to attend court would put that person in contempt of court and liable to imprisonment;

    b) In trials on indictment, a party may summons a person to attend court, produce documents and testify by a witness summons under s.2 of the Criminal Procedure (Attendance of Witnesses) Act 1965.[51]

Criminal Procedure (Attendance of Witnesses) Act 1965, s.2:

2.—(1) This section applies where the Crown Court is satisfied that,

---

[49] s.120(6).

[50] Basically children under 14 and those over that age but unable to appreciate the solemnity of the occasion testify unsworn in criminal cases under Youth Justice and Criminal Evidence Act 1999, s.55; in civil cases, children can testify unsworn under Children Act 1989, s.96. For many years (from the passage of s.1(h) Criminal Evidence Act 1898) the defendant could make an unsworn statement from the dock but that right was removed by Criminal Justice Act 1982, s.72.

[51] s.2 was substituted, together with s.2A–2E, by the Criminal Procedure and Investigations Act 1996 s.66(1) and (2). Section 2 was amended by the Crime and Disorder Act 1998 Sch.8, para.8 and the Courts Act 2003 Sch.8, para.126(a). It is further amended by the Criminal Justice Act 2003 Sch.3, Pt 2, para.42(a), with effect from a date to be appointed.

(a) a person is likely to be able to give evidence likely to be material evidence, or produce any document or thing likely to be material evidence, for the purpose of any criminal proceedings before the Crown Court, and

(b) the person will not voluntarily attend as a witness or will not voluntarily produce the document or thing.

(2) In such a case the Crown Court shall . . . issue a summons (a witness summons) directed to the person concerned and requiring him to-

(a) attend before the Crown Court at the time and place stated in the summons, and

(b) give the evidence or produce the document or thing.

Under the old procedure the summons was issued automatically. Now a summons requires an application that is timely, specific and with the grounds given for believing why the third party is able to give the evidence or produce the document.[52] Under s.3 of the Act, disobedience is an offence, punishable by a maximum of three months' imprisonment.

> c) For trials in magistrates' courts, witness summonses can be issued under the Magistrates' Courts Act 1980 and under rule 28.1 of the Criminal Procedure Rules.

97.—(1) Where a justice of the peace . . . is satisfied that any person in England or Wales is likely to be able to give material evidence, or produce any document or thing likely to be material evidence, at the summary trial of an information or hearing of a complaint by a magistrates' court for that commission area and that person will not voluntarily attend as a witness or will not voluntarily produce the document or thing, the justice shall issue a summons directed to that person requiring him to attend before the court . . . to give evidence or to produce the document or thing . . .[53]

There remain similar provisions for witnesses in committal proceedings, although such proceedings will be abolished as a result of the Criminal Justice Act 2003. A witness order can be set aside if the evidence likely to be given is not material or inadmissible.[54]

3. a person who is competent and compellable is under an obligation to disclose "the truth, the whole truth and nothing but the truth". They must answer honestly all questions put to them in the witness box under pain of committing perjury or being in contempt of court. The principle is that the proper administration of justice requires that priority be given to securing information for the court over other interests of citizens. As we have seen in the preceding chapter, some classes of witness may have a limited privilege not to answer certain questions: examples would be public interest immunity, legal professional privilege or the right against self-incrimination.

---

[52] Criminal Procedure Rules, 28.3.

[53] As amended by Criminal Procedure and Investigations Act 1996, s.51 and Sch.1, para.7.

[54] *Derby Magistrates' Court* [1995] 4 All E.R. 526; cricketers will appreciate the decision in *Marylebone Justices Ex p. Gatting and Emburey* [1990] Crim.L.R. 578.

A. *Competence: Some History*

By the end of the 18th century, the categories of incompetent and disqualified witnesses were numerous. The rationale behind such exclusions has been expressed in two ways:

a) the fear of manufactured evidence arising form the self-interests of the witness. This originally excluded the parties themselves, their spouses or people with other interests in the outcome of the proceedings and

b) the fear of evidence being unreliable due to the moral or other characteristics of the person giving evidence. Thus heathens, atheists, convicts, the mentally ill and children were treated as incompetent to testify.

Although initially there were a considerable number of categories of incompetent witnesses, these rapidly diminished in the 19th century.

- Non-Christians were permitted to give evidence from the 18th century. In *Omychund v Barker*,[55] the witness held a belief in the 'Governor of the Universe' and his evidence was receivable, having sworn an oath reflecting that belief. Atheists however had to wait until the Evidence (Further Amendment) Act 1869 before they became entitled to testify.
- Convicts finally became competent by the Evidence Act 1843.
- Those with an interest in the outcome of the proceedings were also made competent by the Evidence Act 1843.
- The parties in civil cases were recognised as competent witnesses by the Evidence Act 1851 (except for adultery and breach of promise cases where the parties were made competent by the Evidence (Further Amendment) Act 1869. The plaintiff or defendant could give evidence and also subpoena the other side (if that was tactically advisable!). Through this legislation, the spouses of parties also became competent and compellable.
- The defendants (and their spouses) in criminal cases have provided a longer lasting problem. At common law, the accused was incompetent as a witness as there was the fear that he or she might perjure himself or herself as a result of the personal interest in the proceedings but also the fear that the judiciary might compel the accused to incriminate themselves. A defendant could always make an unsworn statement from the dock. It was only with s.1 of the Criminal Evidence Act in 1898 that the accused became a competent witness for the defence in all criminal proceedings. The position of the accused as a witness is discussed below.

---

[55] (1745) 1 Atk. 21.

- For the accused's spouse, the situation remained unclear after 1898. There was great reluctance to allow husbands or wives to give evidence against their spouse. The 1898 legislation permitted spouses to testify for the defence but whether a spouse was a competent witness for the prosecution remained obscure. At common law, the spouse was a competent witness in cases of personal violence or treason but even then was probably not a compellable witness. But this was resolved by s.80 of the Police and Criminal Evidence Act 1984 which made the spouse a competent witness in all criminal proceedings and a compellable witness in some cases. The position of the accused's spouse or civil partner as a witness is discussed below.

B. *Competence:—The Modern Law*

In the late 20th century, the issue of competency was brought into sharp focus around the problems of the physical and sexual abuse of children. Many evidentiary rules hindered the prosecution of the assailants, particularly in the area of corroboration and competence. There were limited reforms aimed solely at children, with a specific test of competence for children so that "A child's evidence shall be received unless it appears to the court that the child is incapable of intelligible testimony."[56] In addition, those under the age of fourteen were allowed to testify unsworn.[57] In 1999, the Youth Justice and Criminal Evidence Act introduced more general reforms.

1. A test of competence for all witnesses
2. A further test to decide whether a witness should be sworn or give unsworn testimony.

The test for competence comes under s.53 of the Youth Justice & Criminal Evidence Act 1999.

53.—(1) At every stage in criminal proceedings all persons are (whatever their age) competent to give evidence . . .
(3) A person is not competent to give evidence in criminal proceedings if it appears to the court that he is not a person who is able to-
(a) understand questions put to him as a witness, and
(b) give answers to them which can be understood.

This establishes the presumption that everyone is capable of testifying. If there is any doubt about this, there is a straightforward cognitive test—can the witness understand the question and give an understandable answer? If

---

[56] Criminal Justice Act 1988, s. 33A(2A), as inserted by Criminal Justice and Public Order Act 1994, Sch.9, (repealed in 1999).
[57] Criminal Justice Act 1988, s.33A, as inserted by s.52(1) of the Criminal Justice Act 1991(repealed in 1999).

there is an objection on the grounds of competence, this should be made in a preparatory hearing or at least before the witness starts to give evidence—although there are examples where the incompetency only emerges after the witness has started.[58] The procedure is governed by s.54 of the Youth Justice & Criminal Evidence Act 1999.

> 54.—(1) Any question whether a witness in criminal proceedings is competent to give evidence in the proceedings, whether raised-
> (a) by a party to the proceedings, or
> (b) by the court of its own motion,
> shall be determined by the court in accordance with this section.
> (2) It is for the party calling the witness to satisfy the court that, on a balance of probabilities, the witness is competent to give evidence in the proceedings.
> (3) In determining the question mentioned in subsection (1) the court shall treat the witness as having the benefit of any directions under section 19 which the court has given, or proposes to give, in relation to the witness.
> (4) Any proceedings held for the determination of the question shall take place in the absence of the jury (if there is one).
> (5) Expert evidence may be received on the question.
> (6) Any questioning of the witness (where the court considers that necessary) shall be conducted by the court in the presence of the parties.

It is an investigative hearing in the absence of the jury—this clarifies the position reached by the common law in *Deakin*,[59] where the victim was a woman with Downs' Syndrome, indecently assaulted by a care assistant. At the competency hearing, the judge heard from the victim and also took expert testimony from two psychologists whose opinion was that she was capable of telling the truth. The appellant contended that this evidence should not have been heard in front of the jury who might well have been influenced by the experts' acceptance of the complainant's story. The Court of Appeal agreed on the point of law but dismissed the appeal. The court drew a sharp line between the question of competence which is a matter of admissibility for the judge and the question of weight which is within the competence of the jury. The problem was that the expert testimony that the complainant was capable of telling the truth was admissible on the first question but trespassed on the jury's preserve on the second point.

In a competency hearing, the judge will listen to evidence from the witness and possibly from others, including expert witnesses. For example, in *D*[60] the charge was attempted rape of a woman who was 81 years old, had long-standing delusional problems and had recently been diagnosed with early Alzheimer's disease. The contested evidence was a video interview which the prosecution sought to rely on under s.23 of the Criminal Justice Act 1988.[61] The judge listened to medical evidence from both sides and declared that he was satisfied that the witness was competent. It was accepted that the judge had to be persuaded on the criminal standard of proof.

In such cases, the initial decision must be kept under review during the trial. In *P*,[62] the defendant was accused of indecent assault on a three-and-

---

[58] *Jacobs v Layborn* (1843) 11 M.&W. 685.
[59] [1994] 4 All E.R. 769.
[60] [2002] 2 Cr.App.R. 36; followed in *Ali Sed* [2005] 1 Cr.App.R. 4.
[61] This would now be introduced under Criminal Justice Act 2003, s.116.
[62] [2006] EWCA Crim 3.

a-half-year-old girl who was allowed to give evidence in chief by video. The judge should have been reviewed the situation after the girl was cross-examined by the defence. The answers given on cross-examination were not intelligible and indicated that she was not competent. The test relates to the whole of the witness's evidence and not just to part of it.

Having crossed the competency hurdle, the issue arises as to whether the witness is to give sworn testimony. Originally, at common law, it was only those prepared to take an oath on the Bible who were allowed to testify, although that was sometimes relaxed.

J. Spencer and J. Flin. The Evidence of Children—The Law and the Psychology (2nd edn. Blackstones 1993). p.47:

Originally there were rules forbidding certain persons to take oaths but no blanket rule against the acceptance of unsworn evidence and the courts would listen to unsworn evidence from those who were ineligible to be sworn. Thus defence witnesses were barred from taking oaths until 1702 and the defendant himself until the Criminal Evidence Act 1898: but both were permitted to make unsworn statements— an option the defendant retained until the Criminal Justice Act 1982. Similarly it seems that the courts would formerly listen to unsworn evidence from children who failed the competency examination. In his *History of the Pleas of the Crown*, Sir Matthew Hale (1609–76) wrote this:

> If the rape be committed upon a child under twelve years old, whether or how she may be admitted to give evidence may be considerable. It seems to me, that if it appear to the court, that she hath the sense and understanding that she knows and considers the obligation of an oath, tho she be under twelve years, she may be sworn . . . But if it be an infant of such tender years, that in point of discretion the court sees it unfit to swear her, yet I think she ought to be heard without oath to give the court information, tho singly of itself it ought not to move the jury to convict the offender . . .[63]

This was a restrictive test that stressed the theological side of understanding the nature of the oath.[64] This was the case both for the mentally handicapped[65] and for children. A more secular approach emerged in *Hayes*[66] which emphasised the ". . . appreciation of the solemnity of the occasion and the added responsibility to tell the truth". That remained the common law test of competency to take the oath until 1999, although by then children under the age of fourteen testified unsworn.[67] The issue is now governed by s.55, of the Youth Justice Criminal Evidence Act 1999.

55.—(1) Any question whether a witness in criminal proceedings may be sworn for the purpose of giving evidence on oath, whether raised-

---

[63] The move to more restrictive practices, requiring testimony to be heard on oath began with *Brasier* (1779) 1 Leach 199.

[64] For some entertaining accounts of the examination of child witnesses, J. Spencer and J. Flin, *op.cit.*, Ch.4.

[65] *Hill* (1851) 2 Den. 254.

[66] [1977] 2 All E.R. 288.

[67] Criminal Justice Act 1988, s.33A, as inserted by Criminal Justice Act 1991, s.52(1)

(a) by a party to the proceedings, or
(b) by the court of its own motion,
shall be determined by the court in accordance with this section.
(2) The witness may not be sworn for that purpose unless-
(a) he has attained the age of 14, and
(b) he has a sufficient appreciation of the solemnity of the occasion and of the particular responsibility to tell the truth which is involved in taking an oath.
(3) The witness shall, if he is able to give intelligible testimony, be presumed to have a sufficient appreciation of those matters if no evidence tending to show the contrary is adduced (by any party).
(4) If any such evidence is adduced, it is for the party seeking to have the witness sworn to satisfy the court that, on a balance of probabilities, the witness has attained the age of 14 and has a sufficient appreciation of the matters mentioned in subsection (2)(b).

The process is similar to that to decide competency—the jury are sent away and the judge will hold a hearing, listening to evidence from the witness and possibly from others, including expert witnesses. The judge must be satisfied that the witness has attained the age of 14, and has a sufficient appreciation of the solemnity of the occasion. Thus the old common law, expressed in *Hayes*, remains not as a test of competency but as a criterion for whether a witness is to be sworn.

whether the child has a sufficient appreciation of the solemnity of the occasion and the added responsibility to tell the truth, which is involved in taking an oath, over and above the duty to tell the truth which is an ordinary duty of normal social conduct.[68]

The requirement for witnesses to take an oath has historically affected the competence of both children and those with learning disabilities but the 1999 reforms mean that this has less impact. Where a witness is competent to take the oath, this is administered according to s.1 of the Oaths Act 1978, which permits an oath to be administered ". . . in any lawful manner" allowing a witness of any religious faith to take the oath. Section 5 permits agnostics and atheists to make a solemn affirmation. The primary purpose of the ceremony is to make the person aware of the solemnity of the occasion, of the legal requirement to tell the truth and of the possible penalties for perjury—thus under s.4(2) if an oath has been administered, the fact that the person has no religious belief does not affect the validity of the oath. However, in *Mehrban*,[69] a Moslem witness chose to affirm where it might be expected that they would take the religious oath. Normally, where a witness affirmed, a party was not entitled to cross-examine on the reason why they had done so. But there might be cases at the discretion of the judge where the reason why a person had not taken the holy oath could be explored in a sensitive manner. Lord Auld's view was that the oath should be replaced.

Lord Auld, Report: A Review of the Criminal Courts (2001) Ch.11, para.196:

In my view, there is a need to mark the beginning of a witness's evidence with a solemn reminder of the importance of telling the truth and to require him expressly

---

[68] *Hayes* above at 290–291, *per* Bridge L.J.
[69] [2002] 1 Cr.App.R. 40.

and publicly to commit himself to do so. However, for many -both witnesses and those observing them—the combination of archaic words invoking God as the guarantor of the proposed evidence and the perfunctory manner in which they are usually uttered detracts from, rather than underlines, the solemnity of the undertaking. I consider that it should now be enough to mark the beginning of a witness's evidence and to acknowledge the great diversity of religious or non-religious beliefs, by requiring him simply to promise to tell the truth. If greater solemnity or emphasis is thought necessary, the oath could be administered by the judge.

I recommend that the witness's oath and affirmation should be replaced by a solemn promise to tell the truth

Failure to take an oath when it is necessary can render the evidence inadmissible—in *Sharman*[70] a girl of 14 years was not sworn. On appeal, the court said that the failure to administer the oath was not a mere technicality and the court could not assume that it would have made no difference to the witness's answers if she had been sworn. To do so would be to diminish the requirement that evidence be sworn or affirmed to the point where the procedure became meaningless.

C. *The Defendant as Witness*

The defendant was not a competent witness until the passage of s.1 of the Criminal Evidence Act 1898. But, in a criminal trial, when can the accused be called as a witness for the prosecution, for the defence or for a co-accused?

1. As a witness for the prosecution

The common law rule is that defendants in a criminal case are not competent witnesses for the prosecution, even if they should wish to testify. This is only likely in a case where there are co-accused—one defendant cannot be called from the dock to give evidence on behalf of the prosecution against another defendant.[71] Once the defendant has ceased to be a co-accused, they become an ordinary person and may be competent and compellable for any party. This is now regulated by s.53(4) of the Youth Justice and Criminal Evidence Act 1999.

53.—(4) A person charged in criminal proceedings is not competent to give evidence in the proceedings for the prosecution (whether he is the only person, or is one of two or more persons, charged in the proceedings).

(5) In subsection (4) the reference to a person charged in criminal proceedings does not include a person who is not, or is no longer, liable to be convicted of any offence in the proceedings (whether as a result of pleading guilty or for any other reason).

Subsection (5) raises the possibility of the accused testifying for the prosecution where he or she, "is not, or is no longer, liable to be convicted of any offence in the proceedings".

[70] [1998] 1 Cr.App.R. 406.
[71] *Grant* [1944] 2 All E.R. 311.

(i) *Pleading guilty*

Where defendants plead guilty, the subsection expressly permits them to testify. The accused has either pleaded guilty to all charges or has pleaded guilty to some charges and a plea of not guilty to the other charges has been accepted by the prosecution. At this stage, the accused is competent and compellable not only for the prosecution but for a co-defendant. A question which arises is whether the defendant should normally be sentenced after giving evidence. The position put forward in *Payne*[72] was that accomplices should be sentenced before giving evidence against their partners in crime. The obvious rationale is that the witness will no longer have any incentive to tailor evidence in favour of the prosecution in the hope of receiving a lighter sentence. This was reconsidered in *Palmer*[73] in which the accomplice was committed for trial separately and pleaded guilty. The accused opted for an old-style committal at which the accomplice testified. On appeal, it was argued that it was improper for the Crown to have called the accomplice without their first having been sentenced. The Court of Appeal upheld the conviction, on the basis that modern sentencing practice had generally been not to sentence an accomplice until all the facts of the case had been heard, although it remained a matter of discretion for the trial judge

(ii) *Where the accused has been omitted from indictment*

Where the accomplice will not be tried in these proceedings but in some future proceedings, they can testify. In *Pipe*,[74] the defendant was being prosecuted for theft and an accomplice who was to be tried separately for handling stolen goods, was called to testify. The court said that, as a rule of practice, in such circumstances, accomplices should not be called to testify unless the prosecution has agreed to discontinue the case against them. In *Turner*,[75] Lawton L.J. held that the fact that the accomplice might be influenced by continuing inducements was not a bar to testifying, although whether an accomplice should be permitted to testify is a matter of discretion for the trial judge. This was reviewed and supported in *Ex p. Schneider*.[76] Obviously courts should be wary of witnesses with an interest in the outcome of the proceedings and the judge should ensure that the jury were aware of the self-interest and potential fallibility of an accomplice's evidence.[77]

(iii) *Where proceedings against the accused have ended*

The accused can testify where they have been acquitted through the prosecution offering no evidence or through the submission of a successful "no case

---

[72] [1950] 1 All E.R. 102.
[73] (1993) 99 Cr.App.R. 83; [1994] Crim.L.R. 122; see also *Weekes* (1982) 74 Cr.App.R 161.
[74] (1966) 51 Cr.App.R. 17.
[75] (1975) 61 Cr.App.R. 67.
[76] *R. v Pentonville Prison Governor Ex p. Schneider* (1981) 73 Cr.App.R. 200; see also *Tillett* (unreported—June 28, 1999, Privy).
[77] Especially since the mandatory corroboration warning in the case of accomplices is no longer necessary—see Ch.11; for the new sentencing procedure for accomplices assisting the prosecution pursuant to a written agreement, Serious Organised Crime and Police Act 2005, s.73.

to answer" plea at the close of the prosecution case or through a *nolle prosequi* being entered by the Attorney-General.

2. As a witness for the defence

The accused became a competent witness for the defence as a result of the Criminal Evidence Act 1898.[78]

> 1.(1) person charged in criminal proceedings shall not be called as a witness the proceedings except on his own application . . .

An accused is competent to testify at every stage of the proceedings which includes committal, trial or *voir dire* or at the sentencing stage. Having decided to testify, the accused should give evidence before other defence witnesses in order to prevent testimony being tailored to fit that of those witnesses. This is provided for under s.79 of the Police and Criminal Evidence Act 1984, although the court has an unfettered discretion to depart from this procedure.

The free choice provided by "except on his own application" as to whether to testify or to remain silent has been undermined by s.35 of the Criminal Justice and Public Order Act 1994. This section (discussed earlier) applies where the prosecution have satisfied the court that there is a case to answer[79] and a defendant declines to testify in their own defence. The judge, in the presence of the jury, is empowered to tell the defendant that the stage has been reached at which they can give evidence and to issue a warning that if they remain silent, that it will be permissible for the jury to draw whatever inferences appear to be proper.[80] It is not only the judge who can comment on such a failure—at common law, counsel for a co-accused at common law was permitted to do so.[81] Under the 1994 Act, the prosecution also has that right.

Having elected, willingly or not, to testify, the accused's position is analogous to any other witness. Once the accused has entered the witness box, they must answer all questions, even though they might incriminate themselves. This is made explicit under s.1(2)[82] of the Criminal Evidence Act 1898.

> Subject to s.101 of the Criminal Justice Act 2003, a person charged in criminal proceedings who is called as a witness in the proceedings may be asked any question in cross-examination notwithstanding that it would tend to criminate him as to the offence with which he is charged in the proceedings

A failure to answer any specific question may be the subject of comment and adverse inferences, in the same manner as does a failure to testify at all.

---

[78] As amended by the Police and Criminal Evidence Act 1984, Criminal Justice and Public Order Act 1994 and the Youth Justice and Criminal Evidence Act 1999.

[79] *Birchall* (1999) Crim.L.R. 311.

[80] *Cowan* [1995] 4 All E.R. 939; *Becouarn* [2005] UKHL 55; the issue of the right of silence is discussed further in Ch.4.

[81] *Wickham* (1971) 55 Cr.App.R. 199.

[82] As amended by the Youth Justice and Criminal Evidence Act 1999 and Criminal Justice Act 2003.

The defendant is subject to cross-examination and can be questioned about involvement in the offence. Such cross-examination is not limited to matters dealt with in the examination in chief. In *Paul*,[83] the accused limited himself to a statement admitting his own involvement but was cross-examined about his co-defendants' involvement. On appeal this was accepted as proper but it has been argued that this circumvents the policy which prevents the prosecution from calling co-accused to testify against each other.[84] The trial judge does have discretion to prevent such cross-examination.[85]

The evidential impact of a defendant's testimony is the same as any other witness. When a defendant testifies, his evidence might well implicate a co-accused. In such circumstances, the testimony is evidence for all purposes.

..while a statement made in the absence of the accused person by one of his co-defendants cannot be evidence against him, if the co-defendant goes into the witness box and gives evidence in the course of a joint trial, then what he says becomes evidence for all the purposes of the case including the purpose of being evidence against a co-defendant.[86]

During cross-examination, the defendant is most at risk from questions about previous convictions and bad character generally. Under the common law, bolstered by the Criminal Evidence Act 1898, the prosecution were by and large prevented from asking such questions. However under s.101 of the Criminal Justice Act 2003, these barriers have been significantly reduced. This is discussed later.[87]

3. As a witness for a co-defendant

The accused is a competent but not compellable witness for a co-accused. Defendants are unlikely to give evidence for a co-accused where they have not given evidence on their own behalf, since they would open themselves up to cross-examination on their own involvement. However they might wish to do this in a *voir dire*, for example, where a co-accused is seeking a ruling on the admissibility of a confession. If a defendant has ceased to be a defendant, (for example, by pleading guilty or where there has been a directed acquittal[88]), they become a competent and compellable witness.

D. *The Spouse of the Defendant*

At common law, the spouse of a party was not a competent witness. After 1853,[89] this was no longer the case with civil proceedings but remained so in

---

[83] [1920] 2 K.B. 183.
[84] *Grant* [1944] 2 All E.R. 311.
[85] *Young v HM Advocate* [1932] J.C. 63.
[86] *Rudd* (1948) 32 Cr.App.R. 138 at 140 *per* Humphreys J.
[87] see Ch.15.
[88] *Conti* (1973) 58 Cr.App.R. 387.
[89] Evidence (Further Amendment) Act 1853.

criminal proceedings until 1898 when the spouse became a competent and compellable witness for the defence as a result of s.1 of the Criminal Evidence Act. But the spouse was still generally not a competent witness for the prosecution,[90] subject to a range of common law[91] and statutory exceptions. The unsatisfactory state of the law was compounded by decisions such as *Hoskyn v Metropolitan Police Commissioner*[92] in which the House of Lords held that, even where the husband was charged with an offence of violence against her, the wife, while a competent witness against the husband, was still not compellable.

Significant changes were brought about by s.80 of the Police and Criminal Evidence Act 1984. Husbands and wives are now like other witnesses, competent for the prosecution in any case and compellable in some. From 2005, the s.80 rules do apply to same sex couples who have entered into civil partnerships under the Civil Partnership Act 2004. By s.84(1),

(1) Any enactment or rule of law relating to the giving of evidence by a spouse applies in relation to a civil partner as it applies in relation to the spouse.

These provisions do not apply to former spouses or former civil partners. It is necessary to note that "husband or wife" is narrowly interpreted and limited to those who are *de jure* married to (or have been through a ceremony of civil partnership with) the defendant. In *Khan*,[93] the witness, a woman, had gone through a Moslem ceremony of marriage with the accused who was already married to another woman under English law. The marriage was bigamous and void and the witness was not a spouse for the purposes of s.80. This applies equally to long term partners—in *Pearce*,[94] the appellant's partner of 19 years was called to testify against him and was treated as a hostile witness. Had they been married, she would have been a witness who was competent but not compellable. One ground of appeal was that the possession of a marriage certificate should not be the touchstone of compellability. A wife was not compellable in order to protect relationships within the family and the court should look at the substance of the relationship, supported as it is by Art.8 of the European Convention on Human Rights which talks of a 'right to respect for private and family life'. Kennedy L.J. did not accept this argument.

Pearce [2002] 1 Cr.App.R 39, *per* Kennedy L.J.:

12 . . . We do not accept the proposition . . . namely that proper respect for family life as envisaged by Article 8 requires that a co-habitee of a defendant, whether or not

---

[90] *Deacon* [1973] 2 All E.R. 1145.
[91] Especially with cases of personal violence.
[92] [1979] A.C. 474.
[93] (1986) 84 Cr.App.R. 44.
[94] [2002]1 Cr.App.R. 39.

married to him, should not be required to give evidence or to answer questions about a statement which he has already made. This is plainly . . . an area where the interests of the family must be weighed against those of the community at large, and it is precisely the sort of area in which the European Court defers to the judgment of states in relation to their domestic courts. There may be much to be said for the view that with very limited exceptions all witnesses who are competent should also be compellable, and certainly the material before us does not enable us to conclude that because a concession has been made to husbands and wives proper respect for family life requires that a similar concession be made to those in the position of a husband or a wife . . . if the concession were to be widened it is not easy to see where logically the widening should end. That objection may not be insuperable but the possibility of serious limitations being placed upon society's power to enforce the criminal law is obvious . . . at one level the requirement that Loveina Pearce give evidence can be regarded as an interference with her rights under Art.8(1) but, she further submits, the situation is clearly within the ambit of Art.8(2). The interference is in accordance with the law and it is properly regarded as necessary in a democratic society for the prevention of crime.

The relevant legislation is s.80 of the Police and Criminal Evidence Act 1984.

80.—(2) In any proceedings the spouse or civil partner of a person charged in the proceedings shall, subject to subsection (4) below, be compellable to give evidence on behalf of that person.

(2A) In any proceedings the spouse or civil partner of a person charged in the proceedings shall, subject to subsection (4) below, be compellable—

(a) to give evidence on behalf of any other person charged in the proceedings but only in respect of any specified offence with which that other person is charged; or

(b) to give evidence for the prosecution but only in respect of any specified offence with which any person is charged in the proceedings.

(3) In relation to the spouse or civil partner of a person charged in any proceedings, an offence is a specified offence for the purposes of subsection (2A) above if-

(a) it involves an assault on, or injury or a threat of injury to, the spouse or civil partner or a person who was at the material time under the age of 16;

(b) it is a sexual offence alleged to have been committed in respect of a person who was at the material time under that age; or

(c) it consists of attempting or conspiring to commit, or of aiding, abetting, counselling, procuring or inciting the commission of, an offence falling within paragraph (a) or (b) above.

(4) No person who is charged in any proceedings shall be compellable by virtue of subsection (2) or (2A) above to give evidence in the proceedings.

(4A) References in this section to a person charged in any proceedings do not include a person who is not, or is no longer, liable to be convicted of any offence in the proceedings (whether as a result of pleading guilty or for any other reason).[95]

The 1984 reforms were largely the result of the proposals of the Criminal Law Revision Committee.[96] The policy to treat a spouse, wherever possible, as any other witness was obvious as was the principle that the spouse should always be compellable on behalf of the accused. But the issues surrounding compellability for the prosecution were more complex.

---

[95] As amended by the Youth Justice and Criminal Evidence Act 1999, the Sexual Offences Act 2003 and the Civil Partnership Act 2004.

[96] Eleventh Report, Evidence (General) Cmnd. 4991 paras 143–157.

P. Creighton, "Spouse Competence and Compellability" [1990] Crim.L.R. 34 at 35:

In general, the Committee accepted that a wife ought not to be compelled to testify against her husband. Compulsion could unnecessarily disrupt marital harmony and place the wife in the invidious position of having to incriminate her spouse. It was concluded, however, that, for certain offences against the person of the wife or children (aged under 16 years) of the household, the wife should be compellable, for otherwise these crimes would go unpunished, as in most cases there would be no other adult witnesses. Further, in offences against children of the household, the wife, although not charged, might have been guilty of some complicity and this might be reluctant to testify. These two factors, when combined with the serious nature of the offences, justified compellability; the seriousness of the offences was not in itself sufficient: 'The law has never made the seriousness of an offence by itself a ground for compellability, and we do not favour doing so now'.

The growing concern about sexual and physical abuse within the home was a motivating force behind the enactment of s.80. In such cases, there are several strategies open to the prosecution where a spouse is unwilling to testify—reliance on formal evidential rules on compellability is not necessarily the most effective.

1. Under s.80(3), the spouse may be compelled to testify under the threat of being held in contempt of court. Traditionally, the Crown Prosecution Service has tended to discontinue prosecutions where the spouse is reluctant to testify and the Code still acknowledges that some victims may not wish the criminal route to be engaged at all, preferring to make use of other safety and support mechanisms.[97] However other jurisdictions have pursued a pro-arrest and pro-prosecution policy for offenders and some studies suggest that policies which pursue a prosecution regardless of the witness's reluctance to testify reduce the number of reported domestic assaults.[98] Other studies take a different view and suggest that victims coerced into reluctant co-operation with prosecution may be less likely to involve the police if they are abused again and that victims were significantly less likely to report further offences if they felt they had no voice or rights in the original prosecution.[99] The UK adopts a policy of victim choice—there have been few UK studies but one at least reinforced this approach.

M. Barnish, "Domestic Violence—A Literature Review" (HM Inspectorate of Probation, 2004) para. 12.2:

In their small qualitative study of victim responses to domestic violence in the Thames Valley area, Hoyle and Sanders[1] found that most of the women for

---

[97] CPS: *Policy for Prosecuting Victims of Domestic Violence* (2005) para.1.5; S. Edwards, "Compelling a Reluctant Spouse" (1989) 139 New L.J. 691.

[98] S. Torgbor, "Police Intervention in Domestic Violence—A Comparative View" (1989) 19 Family Law 195.

[99] M. Barnish, *Domestic Violence—A Literature Review* (HM Inspectorate of Probation 2004) para.12.2.

[1] C. Hoyle and A. Sanders, "Police Response to Domestic Violence" (2000) 40 B.J.C. 14.

whom all violence had ceased had supported successful prosecutions of their abusers. By not withdrawing statements as they had in the past, women felt they had sent powerful symbolic statements through prosecution. However the deterrent effect of prosecution was most likely when accompanied by other action by the woman to end the relationship. In some cases, the process of arrest and prosecution had given women the confidence to take such action. Emotional and practical support from specialist domestic violence police officers had been a key factor for almost all the women who had managed to leave violent relationships and/or who had proceeded with prosecution of their abusers . . .

2. Where the spouse is intimidated, under s.116(2)(e) of the Criminal Justice Act 2003,[2] a written witness statement may be admissible if the spouse-witness does not give evidence through fear. The prosecution of the abuser still proceeds and the victim, although protected from giving oral evidence, may be less likely to involve the criminal justice system again if they felt they had no choice in the issue of prosecution.

3. Where the spouse is called as a witness by the Crown and refuses to answer questions, she can be treated as a hostile witness[3] under s.3 of the Criminal Procedure Act 1865. This can occur either when the spouse is a compellable witness under s.80(3) or where the offence is not a 'compellable' offence but the spouse has chosen to take the oath but then has changed their mind. In *Pitt*,[4] the husband was accused of violence to his baby daughter. His wife initially chose to testify but in the course of testimony, gave answers that led the prosecution to apply to treat her as a hostile witness. She was then cross-examined and her prior statements to the police, inconsistent with her evidence, were put to her. The appeal was on the basis that it was not correct to treat the wife, who was not a compellable witness, as hostile,

Pitt [1982] 3 All E.R. 63at 66b-d, *per* Peter Pain J.:

Up to the point where she goes into the witness box, the wife has a choice: she may refuse to give evidence or waive her right of refusal. The waiver is effective only if made with full knowledge of her right to refuse. If she waives her right of refusal, she becomes an ordinary witness. She is by analogy in the same position as a witness who waives privilege, which would entitled him to refuse to answer questions on a certain topic.

In our view, in these circumstances, once the wife has started on her evidence, she must complete it. It is not open to her to retreat behind the barrier of non-compellability if she is asked questions that she does not wish to answer. Justice should not allow her to give evidence which might assist, or injure, her husband and then to escape from normal investigation.

[2] Ch.18.
[3] See Ch.13.
[4] [1982] 3 All E.R. 63.

It follows that if the nature of her evidence justifies it, an application may be made to treat her as a hostile witness . . .

The right to refuse to testify is not lost because a statement is made to the police or evidence is given at committal proceedings. The key point is taking the oath at trial but the Court of Appeal made it clear that it would be desirable for a judge to make it clear to a spouse that there is a right to refuse to testify and that a verdict may be upset if a spouse gives evidence without fully appreciating that there is such a right.

In enacting s.80, Parliament did not limit compellability to cases of domestic violence but extended the list of offences to include offences against children outside the family as well. This was on the grounds of the seriousness of the offences included but is open to the criticism, 'Why these offences and not others?' Offences involving violence to people aged over sixteen are as serious and yet are not included. This is especially the case with crimes against the elderly. The principles involved in weighing 'offence seriousness' against the significance of the spouse's evidence and the impact on the marriage mean that any approach involving listing offences is inevitably flawed.

P. Creighton, "Spouse Competence and Compellability" [1990] Crim.L.R. 34 at 36:

Considerations of this kind led to the enactment in the Australian State of Victoria of a provision[5] making the wife compellable against her husband in all cases, but conferring on the trial judge a discretion to exempt the wife from giving evidence, generally or in part, where the interest in obtaining the wife's evidence is outweighed by either or both the likely damage to the marital relationship and the harshness of compelling her to testify. The factors to be considered by the judge in exercising the discretion include the nature of the offence charged, the likely significance of the wife's evidence in the case, the state of the relationship between the spouses and the likely impact upon it of compelling her to testify.

In England at this time, the spouse is always competent for the prosecution but has a choice whether to testify or not, unless the offence falls under s.80(3).

A. Zuckerman, The Principles of Criminal Evidence (OUP, Oxford, 1989). pp.290–292:

When marriage was indissoluble, the souring of relations between spouses would have condemned them to living together in enmity for the rest of their lives or,

---

[5] Crimes Act 1958, s.400.

alternatively, to separation without the prospect of establishing another family. However matrimonial morality and matrimonial policy have undergone radical transformation. If marital relations have deteriorated, the marriage can be brought to an end. Indeed, a very considerable proportion of marriages do in fact end in divorce. It is difficult to imagine that granting spouses immunity from having to testify against each other makes an appreciable contribution to the general stability of marriage in our community.

There are further considerations that weaken the justification based on marital harmony. If the wife is accorded a freedom to choose whether or not to testify, her accused husband will in many cases bring pressure to bear on her to refuse to testify when invited to do so by the prosecution . . .

Even where a spouse freely chooses to decline the prosecution's call to testify, the moral position of withholding information that may lead to the accused's conviction is highly ambivalent. One may perhaps be able to defend a failure to initiate a complaint but it could hardly be maintained that withholding incriminating evidence from the court, once the accused has been charged, is morally acceptable, especially where the offence is a grave one.

Zuckerman argues that there is a basic flaw in the rationale behind spousal privilege which has meant that the definition of its scope in s.80, although clear, is essentially haphazard. This point is supported by the fact that if it is repugnant to see a wife being compelled to testify against her husband, there are other levels of relationship to which the same argument would apply—a mother against her son, for example or unmarried couples. In Victoria, the Crimes Act 1958 gives discretion to the judge to exempt the parents or children of the accused from testifying.[6]

In summary, the current situation regarding the competence and compellability of the spouse (or civil partner) of the accused is:

(i) *For the prosecution*

    a) The spouse (or civil partner) is always competent but only compellable in the small range of offences under s.80(3).

    b) The spouse (or civil partner) is not competent where the husband and wife are jointly charged with the same offence under s.80(4). However this excludes those cases where they are being tried for related but different offences in the same proceedings.

    c) Where the accused is charged with multiple offences and the spouse (or civil partner) is a compellable witness with regard to one of these, the better view would be that the spouse (or civil partner) could only be compelled to answer questions in relation to that offence

(ii) *For the defence*

    a) The spouse (or civil partner) is always competent and compellable[7] save for the situation under s.80(4) where they are jointly charged with the same offence. In such cases the spouse is still competent.

---

[6] Also see Israel Evidence Ordinance (New Version) 1971, cl.4.

[7] Prior to s.80 Police and Criminal Evidence Act 1984, the spouse was not a compellable witness for the accused—*Boal* [1964] 3 All E.R. 269.

(iii) *For the co-accused*

    a) The spouse (or civil partner) is always competent under s.80(1)(b) but is only compellable in the circumstances of s.80(3), even where this is necessary to prove the innocence of an accused. However this restrictive interpretation was dented in *Woolgar*,[8] where the defendants, M and W, were charged in the same indictment but with different offences. M was convicted of assault and W of criminal damage. W had sought to call M's wife as to testify on his behalf but the trial judge held that the accused were 'jointly charged' within s.80(1)(b) and, since neither was charged with an offence under s.80(3), the wife was not compellable. The Court of Appeal quashed the conviction, holding that M and W were not jointly charged with any single offence and as a result the wife was compellable—this would have been the outcome if there had been separate trials.[9]

(iv) *Failure to testify*

    a) Where the spouse (or civil partner) has the choice whether to testify or not, any failure to testify cannot be made the subject of comment by the prosecution under s.80(8).

> The failure of the wife or husband of the accused to give evidence shall not be made the subject of any comment by the prosecution

This restriction applies to the prosecution and not to the judge or any co-accused. In *Whitton*,[10] the accused's husband had been present at the scene but was not called as a defence witness. Prosecuting counsel commented on this fact in his closing speech, in breach of s.80(8). The judge also commented on the husband's silence. The judge should have stopped the prosecutor but was himself entitled to make such a comment.

This mirrored the position of the accused under the Criminal Evidence Act 1898 until its repeal by s.35 of the Criminal Justice and Public Order Act 1994. But the 1994 Act did not change the position with regard to the spouse's (or civil partner's) "right to silence". The rationale for this restriction is ambiguous since marital harmony is not under threat from a spouse's refusal to testify and if it is possible to draw legitimate inferences from that refusal, there is little reason not to do so.

E. *Former Spouse or Civil Partner*

Fortunately the old common law rules have now been superseded, at least in criminal proceedings. The problems can be seen in *Algar*[11] in which the

---

[8] [1991] Crim.L.R. 545.

[9] Commentators have stressed that precedent would interpret "jointly charged" as "jointly indicted"—Creighton (1991) op.cit.; Smith J.C. in the commentary on *Woolgar*, above.

[10] [1998] Crim.L.R. 494 distinguishing *Naudeer*[1984] 3 All E.R. 1036.

[11] [1954] 1 Q.B. 279.

defendant was charged with the forgery of his wife's signature on certain cheques. The cheques were drawn in 1947/48 and the marriage was annulled on the ground of the defendant's impotence in 1949. Despite the length of time since the annulment and the absence of any need to maintain 'marital harmony', the wife was held to be incompetent to testify against the defendant since the marriage had been subsisting at the time of the offences.

By s.80(5) and (5A), the old rules have been abolished with relation to former spouses and former civil partners,

> (5) In any proceedings, a person who has been but is no longer married to the accused shall be competent and compellable to give evidence as if that person and the accused had never been married.

This refers only to criminal proceedings. "... no longer married" means divorce or annulment or dissolution for civil partnerships. It does not encompass judicial separation or just non-cohabiting.[12] In these latter situations, these would be spouses and civil partners and not former spouses or civil partners. Once the marriage or partnership is over, the spouse or civil partner is competent to testify about matters which occurred in the course of that relationship.[13]

But in civil proceedings, the old common law made both spouses and former spouses incompetent witnesses—former spouses were only incompetent witnesses with regard to matters that happened during the course of the marriage. The reforms of the 19th century[14] made the spouses competent but said nothing about former spouses. Therefore, however incongruously, *Monroe v Twistleton*[15] remains good law. In that case, the plaintiff sought to call the divorced wife of the defendant to prove a contract but as the matter at issue occurred in the course of the marriage, she was an incompetent witness. This position has not been changed by statute or by common law since that time.

---

[12] *Moss v Moss* [1963] 2 All E.R. 829; *Mathias* [1989] Crim.L.R. 64.
[13] *Cruttenden* (1991) 3 All E.R. 242.
[14] Evidence Amendment Act 1853 and Evidence (Further Amendment) Act 1869.
[15] (1802) Peake Add. Cas. 219.

10

VULNERABLE AND INTIMIDATED WITNESSES

I. Taking Care of Witnesses

This chapter concentrates on criminal proceedings. Witnessing crime is common—the British Crime Survey in 1998 showed that a third of adults had witnessed at least one of three different types of incident in the last five years. Willingness to testify is another matter. There have been long-standing concerns about the impact of the adversarial process on witnesses. The culture of the adversarial trial, the requirement that witnesses are physically present in court to give oral evidence and their exposure to challenging, if not aggressive, cross examination have all contributed to a perception that the criminal justice system fails to strike an appropriate balance between the rights of the defendant and the needs of the victims and witnesses.[1]

Royal Commission on Criminal Justice: Report Cm.2263 (1993) para.5.44:

The evidence of victims and other witnesses is crucial to the criminal justice process because prosecutions will founder, and guilty people thus escape justice, if victims and other witnesses are not prepared to make statements to the police and thereafter to give evidence. It is important therefore that everything possible is done to support and, where necessary, protect witnesses in what is often and unenviable role. We received a great deal of evidence that for witnesses to give evidence in a criminal trial is a daunting (and sometimes even dangerous) task and one that many come to regret having undertaken.

While cross examination by barristers may be daunting, testifying itself can be dangerous. Witness intimidation remains a problem: a Home Office study[2] suggested that according to the 1998 figures the risk of intimidation is about 8 per cent for all victims covered by the survey but increases to 15 per cent for victims who may be considered to be in a potentially intimidating situation.[3]

---

[1] L. Ellison, *The Adversarial Process and the Vulnerable Witness* (OUP, Oxford, 2002); J. Doak, "Victims' Rights in Criminal Trials" [2005] 32 Journal of Law and Society 294.

[2] R. Tarling, L. Dowds, T. Budd, *Tackling Witness Intimidation: Findings from the British Crime Survey* (HO Occasional Paper 2000); M. Maynard, *Witness Intimidation: Strategies for Prevention* (Police Research Group, Crime Detection and Prevention Series, Paper 55) (1994).

[3] But see B. Hamlyn, A. Phelps, J. Turtle and G. Sattar, *Are Special Measures Working?* (2004) (Home Office Research Study 283).

But the intimidation is less to deter a witness from giving evidence—intimidation is inextricably bound up with the phenomenon of 'multiple' or 'repeat' victimisation and much of the intimidation arises in the course of domestic violence.

A second area of concern has been that the experience of testifying has led to witness disenchantment with the criminal justice system (CJS) as a whole. Satisfaction surveys are relatively comforting—in 2002 nearly 80 per cent were satisfied overall with the experience.[4] These studies have cast their net widely, questioning victim-witnesses, prosecution and defence witnesses and child witnesses. But they only surveyed people attending court who were willing to participate and where a court verdict has been reached. Therefore, it sampled a small percentage of all victims and witnesses who engage with the CJS, and an even smaller percentage of all people who experience crime and disorder. As such, the survey misses a whole range of people who drop out of the system along the way and the results do not reflect the views of all victims and witnesses.

The rights of victims and vulnerable and intimidated witnesses to be treated fairly and with respect have been ignored by government and the criminal justice system for centuries but the last 25 years has seen increasing focus on such issues. In 1980s, the scandals surrounding physical and sexual abuse of children led to some improvements relating to the rules of competence and corroboration for child witnesses, introduced in the Criminal Justice Act 1988. At this point, the pace of change quickened—in the1990s John Spencer and Rhona Flin published a resounding academic critique of the law's treatment of child witnesses but which had obvious implications for witness testimony generally.[5] Furthermore, the Home Office had looked at the possibility of children testifying through video and the Pigot Report[6] came to the conclusion that,

> . . . children who came within the ambit of our proposals, ... ought never to be required to appear in public as witnesses in the Crown Court, whether in open court or protected by screens or closed circuit television, unless they wish to do so.[7]

Such radical reform has not been enacted and there was continuing piecemeal reform in the Criminal Justice Act 1991 which allowed the child's evidence in chief to be given by video recording but the child had to be available for cross-examination.[8]

In 1993, the Royal Commission on Criminal Justice took a broader view and saw manifold defects in the system of witness care. Their recommendations are still being implemented.[9]

---

[4] H. Angle, S. Malam, and C. Carey, *Witness Satisfaction: Findings from the Witness Satisfaction Survey 2003* (Home Office Online Report 19/03).

[5] J. Spencer and J. Flin, *The Evidence of Children—The Law and the Psychology* (2nd ed., 1993).

[6] Report of the Advisory Group on Video Evidence (Home Office December 1989).

[7] *ibid.*, para.2.26.

[8] Criminal Justice Act 1988, S.32A.

[9] *op.cit.*, paras 5.44–5.52; 8.36–8.47.

(i) *Improved communication and support.*
Victims were to be kept informed of progress and this was allied to the development of witness support schemes in all Crown Court centres to prevent witness intimidation. For a decade after 1993, witnesses have continued to fall between several stools with neither the police, nor the CPS nor the courts taking responsibility. No specific national funding stream was attached to victim and witness care apart from that allocated to Victim Support which ran witness support programmes which provided pre-court familiarisation visits and supporters in court.[10] It was not until 2003 that national witness care units were introduced, bringing police and the Crown Prosecution Service together to meet the individual needs of victims and witnesses. Pilot schemes saw witness attendance improve, a decline in adjourned and cracked trials and greater use of victim personal statements. There are expected to be 165 such units in 2006.[11]

(ii) *Taking the views of the victim into account.*
The CPS should ascertain the views of the victim as to issues such as the decision to prosecute. This is now addressed specifically in the CPS Code,[12] especially in relation to bail decisions.[13] Cases where women have been the victims of violence or rape need particular care.

(iii) *Meetings with victims and key witnesses before the trial.*
There has been a long–established rule of practice prohibiting counsel from interviewing witnesses (other than their own client or an expert witness) before the trial. The abolition of this rule is being tested in pilot studies involving prosecution lawyers interviewing witnesses. These were to start in January 2006.[14]

(iv) *Adequate facilities at the court.*
There was a lack of waiting areas which segregated victims and prosecution witnesses from the defendant and defence witnesses. By 2003, a study found an improvement and that the majority of witnesses (86 per cent) had a separate room to wait in before the trial started.[15] But the prospect of appointment systems so as not to waste witnesses' time is still a long way off. There is still a major problem about 'ineffective' cases—where a case is scheduled for trial but collapses on the day due perhaps to a late plea of

---

[10] Approximately £29m in 2003.

[11] Cabinet Office, *No Witness, No Justice* (2004).

[12] Crown Prosecution Service, *Code for Crown Prosecutors* (2004) paras 5.12–5.13; also see A. Ashworth and M. Redmayne, *The Criminal Process* (3rd ed., OUP, Oxford, 2005), p.199ff.

[13] Ashworth, *ibid.*; p.224 ff.

[14] C. Dyer, "Criminal justice revolution to secure more convictions" *Guardian*, November 11, 2005.

[15] Victim Support, *Evaluation of the Street Crime Initiative: supporting victims and witnesses of street crime* (2003) para.5.2; H. Fenwick, "Rights of Victims in the Criminal Justice System: Rhetoric or Reality?" [1995] Crim.L.R. 843 at 849.

guilty, a prosecution decision to present no evidence or other witnesses failing to turn up. In Kent in 2005, approaching 50 per cent of trials with anticipated not guilty pleas were ineffective with witnesses sent home without testifying. In another study, 37 per cent of witnesses were not heard on the scheduled day.[16]

(v) *Restrictions on publicity.*
The recommendation was that the witness should be allowed to hand over their address rather than having it read out in court. Part IV of the Youth Justice and Criminal Evidence Act 1999 now provides for a wider range of reporting restrictions.

(vi) *Greater use of witness written statements.*
Such statements may replace the oral evidence of witnesses who are too frightened to testify. Originally introduced under the Criminal Justice Act 1988, these provisions have now been replaced by s.116(2)(e) of the Criminal Justice Act 2003. Particularly important is subs.(3) which provides that "fear" is to be interpreted widely.

(vii) *Greater vigilance by judges to prevent unfair and intimidatory cross-examination.*
This can include allegations made about the victim in mitigation pleas. This has been addressed by s.100 of the Criminal Justice Act 2003 whereby questions about the "bad character" of a witness can only be undertaken in limited circumstances and with the leave of the court. The judge also has powers to prohibit reporting of unsupported slurs.[17]

As this review shows, a decade later the concerns of the Royal Commission are still being addressed. The importance of witnesses engaging with the criminal justice system, reporting crime, co-operating with the police and testifying, was emphasised in a report by the Audit Commission.[18] For successive governments, the issue has been formulated as one of the balance between the rights of the accused and the needs of witnesses. This is regarded as a key element in re-establishing public confidence in the criminal justice system[19] and such matters were central to the 2003 White Paper, *Justice for All*.[20] There has been a plethora of government strategy documents, legislation and policy initiatives at grass roots level to achieve this and this chapter will look at the reform of the laws protecting witnesses and at two categories of vulnerable witness, namely the child and the victim of sexual assault.

---

[16] Fenwick, above at 850.
[17] A judge can now prevent the reporting of derogatory assertions under ss.58–61 Criminal Procedure and Investigations Act 1996.
[18] Audit Commission, *Victims and Witnesses* (2003); S. Spencer, and B. Stern, (2001) *Reluctant Witness*, London: Institute of Public Policy Research.
[19] Home Office, *Speaking Up for Justice* (1998).
[20] Cm. 5563 (2003); Home Office, *A New Deal for Victims and Witnesses* (2003); J. Jackson, "Justice for All: Putting Victims at the Heart of Criminal Justice?" [2003] 30 Journal of Law and Society 309.

II. THE YOUTH JUSTICE AND CRIMINAL EVIDENCE ACT 1999 AND BEYOND

The 1999 legislation had a clear brief to protect the vulnerable or intimidated witness. Its structure involves three stages:

1. establishing whether a witness is within the criteria of 'eligible witness';
2. in such cases, allowing the judge to make a special measures direction; and
3. providing the judge with a variety of measures to assist the witness and to improve the quality of the testimony.

A. *Eligible Witnesses*

There are three categories of witness who may be eligible for a special measures direction coming either under s.16 or 17 of the 1999 Act.

1. Children under the age of 17.

16.—(1) For the purposes of this Chapter a witness in criminal proceedings (other than the accused) is eligible for assistance by virtue of this section—
(a) if under the age of 17 at the time of the hearing

There is no further condition attached. The party calling the child does not have to show that the quality of the evidence would be diminished because of age or that the special measures would enhance that quality.

2. Those who have a physical or mental disorder or impairment.

16.—(2) The circumstances falling within this subsection are-
(a) that the witness-
    (i) suffers from mental disorder within the meaning of the Mental Health Act 1983, or
    (ii) otherwise has a significant impairment of intelligence and social functioning;
(b) that the witness has a physical disability or is suffering from a physical disorder.

In such cases, the court must also determine whether the disability will affect the quality of the testimony.

16(1)(b) . . . if the court considers that the quality of evidence given by the witness is likely to be diminished by reason of any circumstances falling within subsection (2).

The references to the quality of a witness's evidence are to its quality in terms of completeness, coherence and accuracy.[21]

3. Those in fear.

This is broadly construed by s.17 and, in the case of victims of sexual assault, is presumed.

---

[21] s.16(5).

Youth Justice and Criminal Evidence Act 1999, s.16(5):

17.—(1) For the purposes of this Chapter a witness in criminal proceedings (other than the accused) is eligible for assistance by virtue of this subsection if the court is satisfied that the quality of evidence given by the witness is likely to be diminished by reason of fear or distress on the part of the witness in connection with testifying in the proceedings.

(2) In determining whether a witness falls within subsection (1) the court must take into account, in particular—

(a) the nature and alleged circumstances of the offence to which the proceedings relate;

(b) the age of the witness;

(c) such of the following matters as appear to the court to be relevant, namely,

    (i) the social and cultural background and ethnic origins of the witness,

    (ii) the domestic and employment circumstances of the witness, and

    (iii) any religious beliefs or political opinions of the witness;

(d) any behaviour towards the witness on the part of—

    (i) the accused,

    (ii) members of the family or associates of the accused, or

    (iii) any other person who is likely to be an accused or a witness in the proceedings.

(3) In determining that question the court must in addition consider any views expressed by the witness.

Under neither s.16 or 17, can the defendant be an eligible witness. This may well raise human rights issues in youth courts where both witnesses and defendants may be juveniles and yet only the former be entitled to special measures. There is an argument here surrounding "equality of arms" denying defendants the same opportunity to give their evidence under the conditions which are presumed to produce the best evidence from other child witnesses.[22] In *R (D) v Camberwell Youth Court*,[23] Baroness Hale addressed the issue as to whether the statutory scheme was therefore not compliant with Art.6.

R. (D) v Camberwell Youth Court [2005] 1 All E.R. 999, *per* Baroness Hale:

56. . . . we should understand the realities of life in the Youth Court. The child defendants appearing there are often amongst the most disadvantaged and the least able to give a good account of themselves. They lack the support and guidance of responsible parents. They lack the support of the local social services authority. They lack basic educational and literacy skills. They lack emotional and social maturity. They often have the experience of violence or other abuse within the home. Increasing numbers are being committed for trial in the Crown Court where these disadvantages will be even more disabling.

57. These are very real problems. But the answer to them cannot be to deprive the court of the best evidence available from other child witnesses merely because the 1999

---

[22] L. Hoyano, "Striking the Balance between the Rights of the Defendants and Vulnerable Witnesses" [2001] Crim. L.R. 948.

[23] [2005] 1 All E.R. 999.

Act scheme does not apply to the accused. That would be to have the worst of all possible worlds. Rather, the question is what, if anything, the court needs to do to ensure that the defendant is not at a substantial disadvantage compared with the prosecution and any other defendants (see *Delcourt v Belgium*[24]). That can only be judged on a case by case basis at trial and on appeal.

The defendant is excluded from the statutory scheme because it is clearly inappropriate to apply the whole scheme to him. But the court has wide and flexible inherent powers to ensure that the accused receives a fair trial, and this includes a fair opportunity of giving the best evidence. While video-recorded testimony in chief is a problem,[25] Baroness Hale felt that the court could allow the defendant the equivalent of an interpreter to assist with communication, might permit a detailed written statement to be read to the jury so that they knew what they wanted to say, with leading questions based upon that document, and possibly arrange for the defendant to testify through a live TV link.[26]

The aim is to enable the defendant to give a proper and coherent account and to accord to the principles laid down in *V v United Kingdom*[27] where the court said,

> . . . it is essential that a child charged with an offence is dealt with in a manner which takes full account of his age, level of maturity and intellectual and emotional capacities, and that steps are taken to promote his ability to understand and participate in the proceedings.

B. *Special Measures Directions*

A judge will determine whether a witness falls into any of these categories and whether making special measures available to an eligible witness is likely to improve the quality of the evidence given by the witness. Children under 17 and, under s.17(4), victims of sexual assault will be presumed to need assistance in giving evidence. Both the prosecution and defence will be able to apply, normally before the trial, for the court to make a special measures direction authorising the use of special measures.[28] The court may also decide to make a direction even though no such application has been made. The special measures can include:[29]

1. Screening to ensure that a witness does not see the defendant

23.—(1) A special measures direction may provide for the witness, while giving testimony or being sworn in court, to be prevented by means of a screen or other arrangement from seeing the accused.

---

[24] [1970] 1 E.H.R.R. 355, para.28.

[25] *R. v H* [2003] EWCA Crim 1208.

[26] *Camberwell Youth Court, op.cit.* at para.63, Baroness Hale doubts the decision in *R. v Waltham Forest Youth Court* [2004] 2 Cr.App.R. 21.

[27] [1999] 30 E.H.R.R. 121.

[28] See Criminal Procedure Rules, r.29 for detailed regulations.

[29] Not all special measures are available in all courts—for the state of implementation in January 2006, see M. Burton, R. Evans and A. Sanders, *Are Special Measures Working?* (Home Office Online Report 01/06) Appendix 1, p.73.

(2) But the screen or other arrangement must not prevent the witness from being able to see, and to be seen by—
(a) the judge or justices (or both) and the jury (if there is one);
(b) legal representatives acting in the proceedings; and
(c) any interpreter or other person appointed (in pursuance of the direction or otherwise) to assist the witness.

Prior to the Act, in *Lynch*[30] the 18-year-old victim of an indecent assault was sufficiently distressed for the judge to allow her to testify behind a screen and with a representative of Victim Support with her in the witness box. The Court of Appeal rejected the appellant's submission that this would have prejudiced the defendant in the eyes of the jury. The judge must warn the jury not to read anything into the use of the screens but the court saw little in the argument that screens were *per se* prejudicial to the accused.[31] That screens do not prejudice a fair trial was accepted by the Privy Council in *AG for Sovereign Base Areas of Akrotiri and Dhekelia v Steinhof*.[32] The witness could only be seen by counsel either for the prosecution or for the defence. They accordingly moved position so that whoever was questioning the witness could see her. Section 23(2)(b) required that both should see and hear her throughout her testimony. The Privy Council held that, despite the irregularity, it had not led to a substantial miscarriage of justice or in any way prejudiced the conduct of the defence or compromised the requirements of a fair trial.

2. Allowing a witness to give evidence from outside the courtroom by live television link

24.—(1) A special measures direction may provide for the witness to give evidence by means of a live link.
(2) Where a direction provides for the witness to give evidence by means of a live link, the witness may not give evidence in any other way without the permission of the court.
(3) The court may give permission for the purposes of subsection (2) if it appears to the court to be in the interests of justice to do so, and may do so either—
(a) on an application by a party to the proceedings, if there has been a material change of circumstances since the relevant time, or
(b) of its own motion.

For child witnesses, there is a presumption under s.21(3) that their evidence in chief will be given through a video-recorded interview and that the rest of their testimony will be given by live link.[33]

Section 24 provisions have now been widened to include all witnesses, whether eligible or not. Section 51 of the Criminal Justice Act 2003 allows the judge to consider circumstances such as the availability of the witness, the need to attend in person, the importance of the testimony, the views of the witness, the suitability of the facilities and whether a direction might inhibit a

[30] [1993] Crim.L.R. 868.
[31] *Foster* [1995] Crim.L.R. 333.
[32] [2005] UKPC 31—the statute was in force in Cypriot military bases.
[33] *Coleman* (2001) EWCA Crim 1054.

party from effectively testing the witness's evidence. If satisfied, the judge may make a direction for evidence to be given by video link if it is in the interests of the efficient or effective administration of justice.

Does this infringe the basic human rights principle that all evidence should be produced in the presence of the accused at a public hearing and with a view to adversarial argument? In *R (D) v Camberwell Youth Court*,[34] Baroness Hale addressed this question.

R. (D) v Camberwell Youth Court [2005] 1 All E.R. 999, *per* Baroness Hale:

50. Our attention has been drawn to only two cases in which measures similar to those in question here were considered. One was a live link transmission where both counsel were in the room with the witness while the judge and accused remained in the courtroom. The application was declared inadmissible—see *Hols v Netherlands*.[35] Another was a video-recording of an interview conducted by a police officer with the child complainant, and an audio-recording of a second interview conducted by the same police officer, putting questions which he had been asked by the accused's counsel to put. Despite the fact that counsel had had no opportunity to question the child directly, no violation of article 6(3)(d) was found—see *S.N. v Sweden*.[36] The Court reiterated "that evidence obtained from a witness under conditions in which the rights of the defence cannot be secured to the extent normally required by the Convention should be treated with extreme care"; but it was satisfied that the national court had done just that . . .

51. The measures with which we are concerned do give the accused the opportunity of challenging the witness directly at the time when the trial is taking place. The court also has the opportunity to scrutinise the video-recorded interview at the outset and exclude all or part of it. At the trial, it has the fall-back of allowing the witness to give evidence in the court room or to expand upon the video recording if the interests of justice require this. There is nothing in the case law cited to suggest that this procedure violates the rights of the accused under article 6.

3. Giving evidence in private

This measure allows a judge to clear the press (except for a nominated representative) and public from the court. This section envisages two situations—first where the charge is a sexual offence and the witness can be spared from disclosing intimate details in public and secondly where the very presence of people associated with the defendant is likely to intimidate the witness.

25.—(1) A special measures direction may provide for the exclusion from the court, during the giving of the witness's evidence, of persons of any description specified in the direction.

(2) The persons who may be so excluded do not include—

(a) the accused,

(b) legal representatives acting in the proceedings . . .

---

[34] above.

[35] Application No. 25206/94, Commission decision, October 19, 1995.

[36] Application No. 34209/96, Judgment, July 2, 2002.

(3) A special measures direction providing for representatives of news gathering or reporting organisations to be so excluded shall be expressed not to apply to one named person who—

(a) is a representative of such an organisation, and

(b) has been nominated for the purpose by one or more such organisations,

unless it appears to the court that no such nomination has been made.

(4) A special measures direction may only provide for the exclusion of persons under this section where—

(a) the proceedings relate to a sexual offence; or

(b) it appears to the court that there are reasonable grounds for believing that any person other than the accused has sought, or will seek, to intimidate the witness in connection with testifying in the proceedings.

4. Informality

Under s.26, a special measures direction may provide for the wearing of wigs or gowns to be dispensed with during the giving of the witness's evidence.

5. Video-recorded evidence in chief

This allows an interview with a witness which has been video-recorded before the trial to be shown at trial as the witness's evidence in chief. For child witnesses, there is a presumption under s.21(3) that their evidence in chief will be given through a video-recorded interview and that the rest of their testimony will be given by live link.

27.—(1) A special measures direction may provide for a video recording of an interview of the witness to be admitted as evidence in chief of the witness.

(2) A special measures direction may, however, not provide for a video recording, or a part of such a recording, to be admitted under this section if the court is of the opinion, having regard to all the circumstances of the case, that in the interests of justice the recording, or that part of it, should not be so admitted.

(3) In considering for the purposes of subsection (2) whether any part of a recording should not be admitted under this section, the court must consider whether any prejudice to the accused which might result from that part being so admitted is outweighed by the desirability of showing the whole, or substantially the whole, of the recorded interview . . .

This section permits video taping of a witness's direct testimony for any eligible witness of whatever age. The detailed regulations are under r.29.7 of the Criminal Procedure Rules. It is based upon a recommendation of the Pigot Report[37] in relation to children. It was envisaged that video-recorded preliminary hearing should be held in informal surroundings, as soon as practicable after the video interview had been admitted as evidence.[38] The child witness would be shown the video and asked to adopt the account which it contains and expand upon any aspects which the prosecution wishes to explore. The defence should then have the opportunity to cross-examine

---

[37] *op.cit.*

[38] There is good practice guidance on the CPS website; *G v D.P.P.* [1997] 2 Cr.App.R. 78; *D and S,* 166 J.P. 792.

the child, but with the accused observing only by CCTV. The advantages[39] of videoed pre-trial evidence in chief would enable the questioning of the victim to take place at an early stage, while the evidence is still fresh in their mind and reduce the stress of waiting for a court appearance. This measure reduces the need for the witness to appear in court.

Another advantage for the prosecution is that the tape is available to be reviewed by the jury—in *Mullen*[40] it was emphasised that the replaying of video evidence is a departure from the normal method of conducting a criminal trial, that it disturbs the traditional balance of a trial and may be seen as giving the prosecution a second bite at the "evidential cherry". This should only take place where there are exceptional reasons. But when a jury has requested to review the evidence of a complainant for the purpose of seeing *how* they gave their evidence, as opposed simply to being reminded of the *content* of that evidence, any potential for prejudice as a result is something which may fairly be guarded against by an appropriate "balancing" direction.

The discretion under s.27 is wide. In *P*,[41] a three and a half year-old-child gave evidence by video recording. The issue was whether the judge had misused her discretion in admitting the tape under s.27(2) which provides for the video to be excluded: ". . . . if the court is of the opinion, having regard to all the circumstances of the case, that it is in the interests of justice the recording . . . should not be admitted." The interviewing procedure had been deficient, being poorly planned and conducted, resulting in improvised and incomplete evidence, undertaken in an environment ill-suited for the purpose, and with substantial delay between the incident and the interview. The Court of Appeal recognised the validity of these points but considered that they did not make the whole process fundamentally unfair. The discretion under s.27(2) is a wide one; it requires the judge to look at the whole of the circumstances of the case and apply a test on the interests of justice which did not include the interests of the defendant alone.

These provisions have now been widened to include all witnesses, regardless of age, disability or vulnerability, by s.137 of the Criminal Justice Act 2003. The criteria are that the person is a witness to the offence or events closely connected to the offence. They have given a video-recorded account of those events. In such circumstances, the video-recording can stand as evidence in chief where the witness testifies that the recording was made at a time when the events were fresh in their mind, that their recollection is likely to have been significantly better and that they represent the truth.

6. Video-recorded cross-examination

This will allow an interview with a witness which has been video-recorded before the trial to be shown at trial as the witness's cross examination.[42]

---

[39] A. Sanders, J. Creaton, S. Bird, and L. Weber, *Witnesses with Learning Disabilities* (Home Office Research Findings No.44)(1996).
[40] [2004] 2 Cr.App.R. 18.
[41] [2006] EWCA Crim 3.
[42] This section has not yet been implemented.

28.—(1) Where a special measures direction provides for a video recording to be admitted under section 27 as evidence in chief of the witness, the direction may also provide—

(a) for any cross-examination of the witness, and any re-examination, to be recorded by means of a video recording; and

(b) for such a recording to be admitted, so far as it relates to any such cross-examination or re-examination, as evidence of the witness under cross-examination or on re-examination, as the case may be.

(2) Such a recording must be made in the presence of such persons as rules of court or the direction may provide and in the absence of the accused, but in circumstances in which—

(a) the judge or justices (or both) and legal representatives acting in the proceedings are able to see and hear the examination of the witness and to communicate with the persons in whose presence the recording is being made, and

(b) the accused is able to see and hear any such examination and to communicate with any legal representative acting for him.

This section permits video taping of a witness's cross-examination for any eligible witness of whatever age. The detailed regulations are under r.29.7 of the Criminal Procedure Rules. The advantages[43] are that the witness, particularly the young, those with learning disabilities or those in fear, can avoid the often humiliating process of being cross-examined in open court. There is the possibility of recall for further cross-examination but under subs.(5), once a recording has been made of any examination of the witness, the witness may not be subsequently cross-examined or re-examined in respect of any evidence given by the witness in the proceedings unless the court makes a further special measures direction. Routine cross examination in person has been ruled out.

7. Questioning of a witness through an intermediary

This is of value for witnesses with learning disabilities or other particular problems.

29.—(1) A special measures direction may provide for any examination of the witness (however and wherever conducted) to be conducted through an interpreter or other person approved by the court for the purposes of this section ("an intermediary").

(2) The function of an intermediary is to communicate—

(a) to the witness, questions put to the witness, and

(b) to any person asking such questions, the answers given by the witness in reply to them,

and to explain such questions or answers so far as necessary to enable them to be understood by the witness or person in question.

8. Special devices

Further, under s.30, a special measures direction may provide for the witness to be provided with such device as the court considers appropriate with a view to enabling questions or answers to be communicated to or by

---

[43] A. Sanders, above.

the witness despite any disability or disorder or other impairment which the witness has or suffers from.

Where a special measures direction has been made and implemented, at the close of the trial, the judge must, under s.32, warn the jury that they should not draw any prejudicial inference from the fact that such a direction was made in relation to a witness.

The effectiveness of these measures has been recently studied.[44] One of the central findings was that, on a conservative estimate, 24 per cent of witnesses are probably within the category of 'vulnerable or intimidated'. Identifying such witnesses is difficult and they are often first identified by the Witness Service when they arrived at court. This makes it extremely difficult to arrange for special measures if they are needed. Court familiarisation visits are potentially the most useful of the non-statutory measures available in the pre-trial phase but were rarely offered. Video-recorded evidence and the live television link are highly regarded but are made use of for only a minority of VIW interviews. Screens are less regarded by the agencies but have advantages for witnesses. Informal dress is rarely used.[45] Vulnerable and intimidated witnesses have become more satisfied, especially with the witness service, the court staff and judges. Such witnesses find the live link and recorded evidence in chief particularly helpful, often saying that they would not have been able to testify without these.[46]

C. *Cross-Examination by the Defendant*

Generally the law respects the right of defendants to conduct their own defence and undertake the cross examination of witnesses but it presents difficulties for trial judges. At common law, the inherent power of judges to control proceedings gave them the weapons to restrain such cross-examination when it went beyond the bounds of relevance. In 1993, the Runciman Commission[47] revealed some concern about the treatment of witnesses and recommended that, in keeping with their wish to see judges take a more interventionist approach where necessary, judges should be particularly vigilant to check unfair and intimidatory cross-examination by counsel of witnesses who in the nature of the case are likely to be distressed or vulnerable. An example of this was seen in the case of Ralston Edwards who subjected his adult rape victim to a series of very detailed and intimate questions over three days. At that time, only child victims of violence and sexual violence were protected from such examination. This case led to pressure to change the law.

[44] Burton et al., above; B. Hamlyn, A. Phelps, J. Turtle and G. Sattar, *Are Special Measures Working?* (2004) (Home Office Research Study 283).
[45] For a summary see M. Burton, R. Evans, and A. Sanders, *An Evaluation of the Use of Special Measures* (2006) (Home Office Findings 270).
[46] Hamlyn et al., above xii–xiv.
[47] Royal Commission on Criminal Justice: *Report* Cm. 2263 (HMSO, 1993) para.8.43.

The Times, Leader comment, August 23,1996:

Care must be taken, however, not to alter procedure in such a way as to deprive defendants of their historic and legitimate rights. The right of an accused man to speak in his own defence is entrenched in our legal tradition as indeed, until recently, was his right to remain silent and have no inference drawn. Debate in the past had concerned the right to representation. . . . The idea that professional representation should move from being a right to a mandatory requirement in certain cases is a relatively recent innovation . . .

It would be tempting, but probably wrong, to move quickly to change the law. There are other safeguards for victims which might wisely be deployed first, from screens in court to prevent eye-contact and more vigorous intervention from the judge to prevent questions which are gratuitous or irrelevant. It is already the case that the victim's previous sexual history should not be admitted as evidence. Judges should not feel they have to give those who defend themselves greater leeway because of their lack of legal knowledge if that freedom is abused to pursue a line of inquiry which is unnecessarily offensive or intimidatory.

Eroding the rights of defendants to choose how, and whom, to conduct their own defence, no matter how compelling the circumstances of any one case, could tilt the careful balance of the scales of justice. It is wrong in principle and could lead to unforeseen consequences in practice. . .

There are strong regulatory powers in the common law itself—the judge is the master in court. In *Milton Brown*,[48] the Court of Appeal emphasised that the trial judge was obliged to have regard not only to the need to ensure a fair trial for the defendant but also to the reasonable interests of witnesses. The trial judge should do everything, consistent with giving the defendant a fair trial, to minimise the trauma suffered by witnesses. Judges did not lack the power to protect witnesses and control questioning. The trial judge should discuss the course of the proceedings with the defendant in order to elicit the general nature of the defence and to identify the specific points in the evidence in dispute. Despite such exhortations, cases such as Ralston Edwards demonstrated that judges did not protect witnesses and supportive legislation was needed. Under the provisions of the Youth Justice and Criminal Evidence Act 1999,[49] a defendant can be prevented from cross-examining a witness.

There are three circumstances where this is possible.

1. Section 34 now provides protection to all complainants of sexual assault, adults and children.

   34. No person charged with a sexual offence may in any criminal proceedings cross-examine in person a witness who is the complainant, either—

   (a) in connection with that offence, or
   (b) in connection with any other offence (of whatever nature) with which that person is charged in the proceedings.

2. Section 35 widens that protection in the case of children—the defendant cannot cross-examine a child witness where the offence involves a sexual offence, kidnapping, false imprisonment or any

[48] [1998] 2 Cr.App.R. 364.
[49] Replacing Criminal Justice Act 1988, s.34A. itself inserted by Criminal Justice Act 1991 s.55(7).

offence which involves an assault on, or injury or a threat of injury to, any person.

3. Where neither s.34 nor 35 operates to prevent an accused in any criminal proceedings from cross-examining a witness in person, s.36 provides a safety net. Where cross examination by the defendant in person would diminish the quality of evidence, the judge can intervene to prevent such cross examination.

36(2) If it appears to the court—
    (a) that the quality of evidence given by the witness on cross-examination—
        (i) is likely to be diminished if the cross-examination (or further cross-examination) is conducted by the accused in person, and
        (ii) would be likely to be improved if a direction were given under this section, and
    (b) that it would not be contrary to the interests of justice to give such a direction,

In cases where the defendant is prevented from cross-examining a witness in person and refuses to seek a legal representative, the court may appoint a lawyer to conduct the examination and furthermore should warn the jury not to be prejudiced against the accused because of these events.[50]

D. *Anonymity and Reporting Restrictions*

Under Art.6 of the European Convention on Human Rights, "everyone is entitled to a fair and public hearing within a reasonable time by an independent and impartial tribunal established by law". The administration of justice should take place in open court and the accused had the right to see and know their accusers, that is, the witnesses testifying against them. Witnesses normally testify in the full glare of press publicity. Such publicity may be avoided in three situations: where the proceedings themselves are in secret; where the proceedings are public but the witness's name is not revealed; and where the proceedings are public but there are restrictions on press reporting.

1. Trials in camera

The first of these is the trial heard *in camera*.[51] Dame Butler-Sloss in *Clibbery v Allan*[52] discusses the use of terms such as "in camera", "in chambers" and "private".

Clibbery v Allan [2002] 1 All E.R. 865, *per* Dame Butler-Sloss:

16. The starting point must be the importance of the principle of open justice. This has been a thread to be discerned throughout the common law systems:

[50] Youth Justice and Criminal Evidence Act 1999, ss.38 and 39; also see Part 31 Criminal Procedure Rules.
[51] One example is under Official Secrets Act 1920, s.8(4).
[52] [2002] 1 All E.R. 865.

"Publicity is the very soul of justice. It is the keenest spur to exertion and the surest of all guards against improbity. It keeps the judge himself while trying under trial." (Bentham)

. . . the exclusion of the public from proceedings has objectively to be justified. It is not good enough for it to be said that we have always done it this way so it has to be right. That principle of open justice applies to all courts and in principle the family courts are not excluded from it . . .

17. Proceedings in the courts are either held in open court, where the public is entitled to enter and listen or in circumstances in which the public is largely excluded either by rule of court or by practice. This exclusion does not, of itself, have the consequence of a ban on later publication . . .

20. I would therefore suggest that there are three categories of case, those heard in open court, those heard in private and those heard in secret where the information disclosed to the court and the proceedings remain confidential.

Civil and criminal procedure rules allow for hearings to be *in camera*[53] but there must be legal basis for exclusion of the public. This can be statutory such as under s.8(4) of the Official Secrets Act 1920 but a court also has a common law power and may order the exclusion of the public. This was accepted by the House of Lords in *Scott v Scott*.[54]

Scott v Scott [1913] A.C. 417 at 446, *per* Lord Loreburn:

I cannot think that the High Court has an unqualified power in its discretion to hear civil proceedings with closed doors. The inveterate rule is that justice shall be administered in open court. . . To this rule of publicity there are exceptions, and we must see whether any principle can be deduced from the cases in which the exception has been allowed. . . It would be impossible to enumerate or anticipate all possible contingencies, but in all cases where the public has been excluded with admitted propriety, the underlying principle, as it seems to me, is that the administration of justice would be rendered impracticable by their presence, whether because the case could not be effectively tried, or because the parties entitled to justice would be reasonably deterred from seeking it at the hands of the court.

This power is used protect matters relating to national security,[55] to safeguard confidential information (including information relating to personal financial matters); to look after the interests of a child or patient; or to prevent disclosure of a witness's identity. That basis must be objectively established but in such circumstances, it need not be in breach of Art.6 protection.[56]

2. Witness anonymity

The second situation is more restricted. The proceedings may be public but judges at common law do have the power to grant anonymity to witnesses.[57]

---

[53] Criminal Procedure Rules, r.16.10; Civil Procedure Rules r.39.2.

[54] [1913] A.C. 417 at 446.

[55] *Shayler* [2003] EWCA Crim 2218.

[56] *R. v Central Criminal Court Ex p. Times Newspapers* [2006] EWCA Crim 04.

[57] For a general look at this topic, see R. Munday "Name Suppression" [1991] Crim.L.R. 680 and 753.

Examples can be found in cases of blackmail victims, national security, police informants[58] or those who permit their premises to be used as police observation posts.[59] In many cases, the defendant will know the identity of the witness but in certain cases, the witness may also conceal their identity from the accused and testify from behind a screen. In *Attorney-General v Leveller Magazine Ltd*,[60] magistrates had allowed an army officer to be called 'Colonel B' while testifying in committal proceedings for offences under the Official Secrets Acts. The defendant magazine published his name and was prosecuted for contempt of court.

Attorney-General v Leveller Magazine Ltd [1979] 1 All E.R. 745 at 761a–c, *per* Lord Edmund-Davies:

It is beyond doubt that a court has a wide inherent jurisdiction to control its own procedure. In certain circumstances it may decide to sit wholly or in part in camera. Or witnesses may be ordered to withdraw, 'lest they trim their evidence by hearing the evidence of others' (as Earl Loreburn put it in *Scott v Scott*). Or part of a criminal trial may be ordered to take place in the absence of the jury, such as during the hearing of legal submissions or during a 'trial within a trial' regarding the admissibility of an alleged confession. Or the court may direct that throughout the hearing in open court certain witnesses are to be referred to by letter or number only.[61]

This discretion applies in different contexts. In *Watford Magistrates' Court Ex p. Lenman*,[62] a group of youths rampaged through a city centre, violently attacking people. The identities of the witnesses who identified the accused were withheld and at trial they were referred to by the names of colours, gave evidence behind screens and had their voices disguised. There is some risk of prejudice to the defence who were handicapped since they were restricted in cross-examination, unable to question the credibility of the witnesses, especially as to whether they had any personal animosity against the accused. In this case, this risk was minimised since there was ample supportive evidence.

This common law power to grant anonymity was reviewed by the House of Lords in *Re Al-Fawwz*,[63] an extradition case where the appellants submitted that the magistrate was wrong in law and/or acted irrationally in admitting the evidence of an anonymous source. Lord Hutton discussed at length the decision in *Taylor*,[64] where the appellant had been convicted of perverting the course of justice by being involved in the disposal of the body of a murder victim. In *Taylor*, the trial judge had permitted a witness to give evidence behind the screen without revealing her name and address. The defendant

[58] *Rogers v Home Secretary* [1973] A.C. 388.
[59] *Rankine* [1986] 2 All E.R. 566.
[60] [1979] 1 All E.R. 745.
[61] The appeal was allowed on other grounds.
[62] [1993] Crim L.R. 388.
[63] [2002] 1 All E.R. 545.
[64] [1995] Crim. L.R. 253.

appealed on the ground that he had a fundamental right to see and hear the identity of the witness called against him except in rare or exceptional circumstances. The appeal in *Taylor* was rejected. Lord Hutton approved the judgment of Evans L.J. in that case and the factors that he enunciated.

Re Al-Fawwz [2002] 1 All E.R. 545 per Lord Hutton:

82. . . . In delivering the judgment of the court Evans LJ stated:

In so far as counsel for the appellant submitted that it was a fundamental right of a defendant to see and know the identity of his accusers, including witnesses for the Crown, which should only be denied in rare and exceptional circumstances, their Lordships agreed with him. The matter was pre-eminently one for the exercise of the judge's discretion, and the following factors were relevant to the exercise of that discretion:

1. There must be real grounds for fear of the consequences if the evidence were given and the identity of the witness revealed. In practical terms it might well be sufficient to draw a parallel with section 23(3)(b) of the Criminal Justice Act 1988,[65] which concerned the admissibility of statements where the witness did not wish to give oral evidence through fear, but in principle it might not be necessary for the witness himself to be fearful or to be fearful for himself alone. There could be cases where concern was expressed by other persons, or where the witness was concerned for his family rather than for himself.

2. The evidence must be sufficiently relevant and important to make it unfair to make the Crown proceed without it. A distinction could be drawn between cases where the creditworthiness of the witness was in question rather than his accuracy.

3. The Crown must satisfy the court that the creditworthiness of the witness had been fully investigated and disclosed.

4. The court must be satisfied that there would be no undue prejudice to the accused, although some prejudice was inevitable, even if it was only the qualification placed on the right to confront a witness as accuser. There might also be factors pointing the other way, for example as in the present case where the defendants could see the witness on a video screen.

5. The court could balance the need for protection of the witness, including the extent of that protection, against unfairness or the appearance of unfairness.

It seemed to their Lordships that there was no reason in principle why the same considerations should not apply to a witness for the defence. The judge's ruling in the present case was detailed and referred to the factors listed above. The law gave the trial judge the power to make an order that a witness remain anonymous in the exercise of his discretion, and the present case was not one where there were any grounds for supposing that the witness was not impartial or had an axe to grind. In their Lordships' view the judge was entitled to conclude that the witness be allowed to give her evidence anonymously . . .

86. I would add that there is a degree of inconsistency between the statement of the Court of Appeal in *R v Taylor* . . . that the accused has a fundamental right to see and know the identity of his accusers save in rare and exceptional circumstances and its statement of the factors which the judge should balance in the exercise of his discretion, some of which point to the preservation of the anonymity of a witness. The later judgments in *R v D J*[66] and *Ex p. Lenman*[67] lay emphasis on the magistrate or judge

---

[65] Now under Criminal Justice Act 2003, s.116.
[66] (1989) 91 Cr.App.R. 36.
[67] above.

having to strike a balance of fairness between the prosecution and the accused, in which process the importance of the accused knowing the identity of his accuser is a factor of great weight, but I think that in some cases the balance of fairness may come down in favour of the prosecution notwithstanding that the circumstances could not be described as rare and exceptional.

Such anonymity for witnesses is exercised only exceptionally. The trial judge has a duty to see that justice was done, in the sense that the system operated fairly not only to the defendant but also to the prosecution and witnesses. Where the court felt there was a real risk to the administration of justice because, for example, witnesses feared for their safety if their identity were revealed, it was within the court's power not to disclose the identity. This balancing act has been affected by the legislation which allows a court to admit the witness statement of a witness who is too frightened to give oral testimony.[68] In such cases the defence would have no cross-examination at all and allowing witnesses to testify behind a screen and/or to withhold their identity is a sensible compromise.

3. Restricting press reporting

The third exception to the custom of identifying witnesses is a corollary to the above—where a witness has not been identified in court, the court can reinforce this by giving directions under s.11 of the Contempt of Court Act 1981 prohibiting the publication of that name. Other restrictions on the press which may provide a measure of anonymity for a witness come under s.4(2) of the Contempt of Court Act 1981,

42(2) In any such proceedings the court may, where it appears to be necessary for avoiding a substantial risk of prejudice to the administration of justice in those proceedings, or in any other proceedings pending or imminent, order that the publication of any report of the proceedings, or any part of the proceedings, be postponed for such period as the court thinks necessary for that purpose.[69]

There has to be a substantial risk. Lord Denning in *Horsham Justices Ex p. Farquharson* put it rather optimistically.

Horsham Justices Ex p. Farquharson (1983) 76 Cr.App.R. 87 at 98, *per* Lord Denning:

In considering whether to make an order under s.4(2), the sole consideration is the risk of prejudice to the administration of justice. Whoever has to consider it should remember that at a trial judges are not influenced by what they may have read in the newspapers. Nor are the ordinary folk who sit on juries. They are good, sensible

---

[68] Criminal Justice Act 2003, s.116.
[69] See also Practice Direction (Criminal Proceedings: Consolidation) para.1.3, [2002] 1 W.L.R. 2870.

people. They go by the evidence that is adduced before them and not by what they may have read in the newspapers. The risk of their being influenced is so slight that it can usually be disregarded as insubstantial—and therefore not the subject of an order under s.4 (2).

There is a further and more general restriction on what can be reported in the press. For eligible adult witnesses, it is possible to make a reporting direction under s.46 of the Youth Justice and Criminal Evidence Act 1999.[70] To be eligible, the court must find that the quality of evidence given by the witness, or the level of co-operation given by the witness is likely to be diminished by reason of the witness's fear or distress in connection with being identified by members of the public as a witness. The fear does not need to be associated with the defendant. In such cases, no matter shall be published during the witness's lifetime if it is likely to lead members of the public to identify them as being a witness.

This chapter will now consider two categories of vulnerable witnesses, namely victims of sexual assault and children.

III. Victims of Sexual Offences

In 2004–2005, there were 60,946 sexual offences recorded by the police of which 20,761 (34 per cent) were cleared up. Of this figure, there were 14,002 rapes, of which 4029 (29 per cent) were cleared up. In the same year, 1,725 defendants accused of rape were tried at Crown Court. 82 per cent pleaded not guilty and 31 per cent of those not guilty pleas were convicted. Including those pleading guilty, these figures mean that just 750 defendants were convicted of rape. This amounts to merely 5.7 per cent of the offences of rape recorded by the police ending in a conviction.[71]

These statistics paint a picture of the gap between the number of offences reported to the police and the number of prosecutions and convictions in court. Trial procedure and the rules of evidence are frequently cited as one of the major reasons for this. The focus falls on the treatment of the victim, especially when testifying as a witness in court. Women's experience suggests that many victims are deterred from reporting offences. The physical and mental suffering of the victim of rape or other sexual assault is extreme. It is an experience which needs to be understood by the court when assessing aspects of their evidence, especially when considering the inferences that may properly be drawn from the timing of the complaint, their ability to confront their alleged attacker and the law's apparent willingness to disbelieve the victim of rape to an extent that occurs nowhere else.

J. Waddle and M. Parts, "Rape Trauma Syndrome" (1989) Univ of Chicago Legal Forum 399:

Researchers have divided Rape Trauma Syndrome (RTS) into two phases. The first phase of RTS is known as the acute phase. It is marked by extreme fear. The victim

---

[70] Criminal Procedure Rules, r.16.1.

[71] These figures are generated from *Crime in England and Wales 2004–05* (Home Office Statistical Bulletin 11/05); L. Kelly, J. Lovett and L. Regan, *A Gap or a Chasm: Attrition in reported rape cases* (Home Office Research Study 293) (2005).

sometimes openly expresses this fear and sometimes controls her observable reactions and appears calm. Physical symptoms can include skeletal muscle tensions, sleep disturbances, and gastrointestinal and genitourinary problems. The second phase of RTS often begins two to three weeks after the attack. This is the period when the victim attempts to reorganise her life. Women during this phase often develop specific fears connected with the events of the rape. For example, women who were raped in open spaces may develop a fear of the outdoors while those raped at home may develop a fear of indoors. These phobia are often accompanied by nightmares involving specific incidents of the rape. Many women move during this phase, change telephone numbers or take other steps to hide their identity. During the second phase of RTS, many women change their sexual behavior and attitudes.

. . . RTS can only be induced through a non-consensual sexual incident. There is, however, a related syndrome, Post-traumatic Stress Disorder (PTSD), which can be provoked by a number of traumatic incidents. Rare, traumatic incidents which can trigger the disorder include earthquakes, airplane crashes or torture.

. . . . . In *Pittsburgh Action Against Rape*[72] Judge Larsen described the unique nature of the trauma suffered by rape victims:

> The depth and range of emotional and psychological disturbance is not felt by the victims of most other crimes. Trauma is the natural consequence of any violent crime. However, many of the symptoms of RTS will not be experienced with any degree of regularity by victims of non-rape crimes. Little anguish over the role the non-rape victim might have played is likely (except, perhaps, for a feeling that one might have been careless or gullible). Rarely is a robbery, or even assault, victim traumatized over possible contributory behavior. Certainly no social rebuke is forthcoming for the usual non-rape victim—society will not look askance at that victim . . .

Rape is an experience that ". . . shakes the foundations of the lives of the victims. For many its effect is a long-term one, impairing their capacity for personal relationships, altering their behaviour and values and generating fear."[73] Probably the best the legal system can aim for is not to make things worse. The criminal justice system has failed too often to meet even this modest target: the investigation of the offence by the police has all too frequently turned into an investigation of the victim; in the courtroom, victims have had to confront their assailants, be subjected to cross-examination into the most intimate details of their lives and (until 1994) listen to the judge warn the jury that their word was not to be believed without independent supporting evidence.

Many of the general reforms discussed earlier apply to victims of sexual assault, especially the special measures direction which can allow the witness to testify by live link. Equally important are the provisions which prevent the defendant from cross examining in person. Other, more specific, protections have also been introduced.

A. *Anonymity and the Media*

This common law power to grant anonymity is discussed above. This privilege was rarely, if ever, extended to complainants of rape. The particular

---

[72] (1981) 428 A2d 126.
[73] W. Young, *Rape Study—A Discussion of Law and Practice* (Dept. of Justice, Wellington, New Zealand, 1983) cited in J. Temkin, *Rape and the Legal Process* (2nd ed., OUP, Oxford, 2002) p.3.

problem is not one of anonymity in court but of restrictions on press coverage. The insatiable desire of the press to report rape cases in full accentuated the problems for victims who might be subject to cross-examination on their past sexual history and find that this was blazoned across the tabloid press. This was considered by the Heilbron Committee in 1975[74] and their recommendations were partially implemented in s.4 of the Sexual Offences (Amendment) Act 1976. This provided anonymity for the victim but only after a person had been accused of rape. The structure set up by the 1976 Act was severely flawed.[75] The victim's anonymity only became protected from the moment of accusation: in 1986, in the Vicarage rape case,[76] prior to any arrests, the press reported the site of the assault and photos of the victim which scarcely masked her identity. In 1988, s.158 of the Criminal Justice Act sought to improve this by protecting the victim's anonymity from the moment of allegation rather than accusation. Once the victim has reported the matter to the police, her identity should no longer be disclosed. Section 158(6) also met another criticism levelled at the 1976 legislation and removed the anonymity of the rape defendant. A further weakness was that the legislation excluded a whole range of forcible sexual acts which the law does not define as rape. In such cases, the victim's reluctance to report is often as great as in rape itself and the arguments for the victim's privacy are equally irresistible.[77] The Sexual Offences (Amendment) Act 1992 now extends the statutory anonymity of rape victims to other sexual offences.[78] There are sound pragmatic grounds for this policy as it will encourage victims to report serious offences to the police. The policy also ensures that the harm suffered as a result of the assault is not accentuated by further publicity. But should victims of sexual assault be treated, as a matter of principle, any differently from victims of non-sexual assault? If not, should the policy be extended to cover all witnesses who request that their name and address remain confidential?

B. *Supportive Testimony*

English law does not normally require evidence from more than one source but historically victims of sexual offences constituted an exception.[79] Juries were permitted to convict solely on the testimony of the victim but they were warned of the dangers of that course of conduct since such evidence could be unreliable. This mandatory warning was finally removed by the Criminal Justice and Public Order Act 1994.

---

[74] Advisory Group on the Law of Rape: *Report* Cmnd. 6352 (1975).

[75] The problems preceding the Criminal Justice Act 1988 and the Sexual Offences Act 1992 are cogently discussed in Temkin J. *op.cit.*

[76] J. Saward and W. Green, *Rape: My Story* (Pan, 1991).

[77] The Criminal Law Revision Committee argued against the extension of anonymity to such offences—Criminal Law Revision Committee 15th Report, *Sexual Offences* (Cmnd. 9213 1984) para.2.92.

[78] As amended by Youth Justice and Criminal Evidence Act 1999, s.4 and Sch.2; *O'Riordan v DPP* [2005] EWHC 1240 (Admin).

[79] J. Temkin *op.cit.* p.255ff.

32—(1) Any requirement whereby at a trial on indictment it is obligatory for a court to give the jury a warning about convicting the accused on the uncorroborated evidence of a person merely because that person is—
  (b) where the offence charged is a sexual offence, the person in respect of whom it is
        alleged to have been committed
is hereby abrogated.

This abolished the need, as a matter of law, for a warning to be given to the jury. But judges have discretion to warn juries about the testimony of witnesses whose reliability or motivation is suspect. In *Makanjuola*,[80] Lord Taylor put it,

Makanjuola [1995] 3 All E.R. 730 at 732g-j, *per* Lord Taylor:

. . . The circumstances and evidence in criminal cases are infinitely variable and it is impossible to categorise how a judge should deal with them. But it is clear that to carry on giving 'discretionary' warnings generally and in the same terms as were previously obligatory would be contrary to the policy and purpose of the 1994 Act. Whether, as a matter of discretion, a judge should give any warning and if so its strength and terms must depend upon the content and manner of the witness's evidence, the circumstances of the case and the issues raised. The judge will often consider that no special warning is required at all. Where, however, the witness has been shown to be unreliable, he or she may consider it necessary to urge caution. In a more extreme case, if the witness is shown to have lied, to have made previous false complaints, or to bear the defendant some grudge, a stronger warning may be thought appropriate and the judge may suggest it would be wise to look for some supporting material before acting on the impugned witness's evidence. We stress that these observations are merely illustrative of some, not all, of the factors which judges may take into account in measuring where a witness stands in the scale of reliability and what response they should make at that level in their directions to the jury. We also stress that judges are not required to conform to any formula . . .

Makanjuola rejects any notion that warnings that were, before 1994, a matter of law should now routinely become a matter of practice. The fact that the witness falls into a particular category (child, victim of sexual assault or accomplice) will not necessarily trigger a warning. Only where there is an evidential basis showing that an individual witness in whatever sort of case may be unreliable, the trial judge may warn the jury. This will not be in terms of corroboration but may be a simple caution or may be stronger in that the judge may suggest that it would be wise to look for some supportive evidence.

Such warnings will not automatically be delivered just because the trial involves a sexual offence but defendants will argue that such warnings be given. It is not possible to assess the extent to which warnings are given as a matter of practice at trial. Where warnings are not given, the Court of Appeal shows no signs of treating victims of sexual assault as a special case and is reluctant to interfere with the exercise of the trial judge's discretion.[81] The complainant in *L*[82] was a child and the court held that whether a direction would be needed depended entirely upon the judge's view of the circumstances of the case, the issues raised and the content and quality of the witness's evidence. In *L* the judge had merely stated that there was a "need for care" when dealing with evidence from children and gone on to say that children were "too unsophisticated" to make up a story and sustain it from beginning to end, as the victim had done. The court has stressed that *Makanjuola* envisaged a more extreme case before warnings would be given— previous false complaints, grudges against the defendant or retraction of a complaint.[83] Judges may intervene where the witness is inconsistent in testifying or inconsistent with other witnesses.

C. *Hearsay*

Victims of crime may make complaints to family, friends and neighbours. More formally they make witness statements to the police. The hearsay rule traditionally excludes such statements as evidence. This means that, however traumatised or intimidated, the victim of sexual assault has physically to attend court to give oral evidence. The formal statement to the police is not admissible as evidence on the grounds that it is hearsay.

There are two avenues by which the victim is able to avoid part or all of this.

a) As explained above, the victim will be able to rely on accounts of events given earlier as a result of s.137 of the 2003 Act. Video-recordings will be able to be played as evidence in chief. However the witness would still have to attend court for cross examination.

b) There is one possibility to avoid a court appearance under the Criminal Justice Act 2003.[84] Under s.116(2)(e), the victim's statement can be used in evidence if the victim does not give evidence through fear. Under subs.(3) ". . . 'fear' is to be widely construed and (for example) includes fear of the death or injury of another person or of financial loss." Witness statements to the police are normally not admissible evidence, if the witness is available to testify. But even though the rape victim is physically available to testify, if still intimidated by the events, this provision creates the possibility that their witness statement, although hearsay, can be used.

Obviously significant considerations of the balance of fairness arise here as the defendant is denied the right to cross-examine the victim. Equally the

---

[81] *Ely* [2005] EWCA Crim 3248.
[82] [1999] Crim.L.R. 48; *L&N* [2004] EWCA Crim 1414.
[83] *MJW* (unreported February 17, 2000, CA).
[84] Originally under Criminal Justice Act 1925, s.13(3) subsequently Criminal Justice Act 1988, s.23.

prosecution will be reluctant to lose the impact on the jury of the victim giving oral evidence. The Court of Appeal have been robust in rejecting appeals of unfairness—in a murder case, *Sellick*,[85] the defendants appealed on the basis that their Art.6 rights had been infringed by the admission of a hearsay document, relying on *Luca v Italy*[86] to argue that as the statements were the decisive evidence against them, permission should not have been granted. The Court of Appeal held that it was the defendant who had denied himself the opportunity to examine the witness and so could not complain of an infringement of Art.6(3)(d). Although these provisions have attracted criticism,[87] they can also been seen as protection for the vulnerable witness, such as victims of sexual violence.

D. *Previous Consistent Statements*

Informal complaints and witness statements are excluded by the hearsay rule as evidence of the facts stated in them. Nor did the common law in general allow the statements to be admitted to show that the victim has been consistent throughout the case—the rule against narrative bans witnesses being asked about earlier oral or written statements that they have made which are consistent with current testimony. One major exception to this rule has been that complaints made by the victim of a sexual assault soon after the attack are admissible in support of the victim's testimony.[88] The justification for this exception was that, without evidence of a contemporaneous complaint, it might be assumed that there was a failure to complain and an inference of consent might be drawn. The complaint can be adduced to rebut any such an inference. The logic was always flawed—modern knowledge about rape trauma syndrome explains why many rape victims fail to report rape to a third party, either immediately or at all.

The position of the victim has been significantly changed. As explained above, the victim will now be able to rely to a greater extent on accounts of events given earlier. Under s.120(7), a previous statement by a victim becomes admissible evidence of the matters contained,

120 (7) The. . . condition is that-
(a) the witness claims to be a person against whom an offence has been committed,
(b) the offence is one to which the proceedings relate,
(c) the statement consists of a complaint made by the witness (whether to a person in authority or not) about conduct which would, if proved, constitute the offence or part of the offence,
(d) the complaint was made as soon as could reasonably be expected after the alleged conduct,
(e) the complaint was not made as a result of a threat or a promise, and
(f) before the statement is adduced the witness gives oral evidence in connection with its subject matter.

---

[85] [2005] EWCA Crim 651.
[86] [2003] 36 E.H.R.R. 46.
[87] D. Wolchover "Keeping Witnesses Out of the Way" (1988) 138 N.L.J. 461.
[88] J. Temkin *op.cit.* p.187ff.

This provision provides for all victims of crime and not just victims of sexual assault. The victim must enter the witness box, testify that the statement was made and that it represents the truth and be subject to cross-examination. The admission of this statement is no longer just to enhance the credibility of the victim.[89] For the rape victim, the complaint in itself is evidence of lack of consent and any details given in the complaint are evidence of the facts.

The key common law conditions for the complaint to be admitted were that it must be spontaneous and contemporaneous. The requirement of spontaneity, once so central,[90] is now of less importance—the complaint is only inadmissible if it has been obtained as the result of a threat or a promise. However s.120(7)(d) still requires that *"the complaint was made as soon as could reasonably be expected after the alleged conduct."* The common law tells us that a victim need not complain to the first person encountered: in *Cummings,*[91] the victim did not complain to a male supervisor in the camp but waited to speak to a woman friend the next morning. Although flexible, the criterion is still there to be applied.

E. *Credibility and Sexual History*

The Criminal Justice Act 2003 brought in strict statutory limits as to how far witnesses can be cross-examined on their credibility. At common law, credibility did not refer solely to the witness's knowledge of the facts, their disinterestedness or integrity. Counsel were allowed to probe many aspects of the witness's character and prior conduct.[92] Section 100 now prohibits questions about a witness's bad character unless the answers will be *"important explanatory material"*[93] or else possess *". . . substantive probative value."*[94]

Particular problems have arisen in the past within rape and sexual assault cases where victims have been freely cross-examined about their past sexual behaviour. Protection of the witness from intrusive and humiliating questioning has led to the creation of rape shield laws. These have not been wholly effective.[95]

1. The common law

The common law rule was that evidence that a woman was a prostitute,[96] had a bad sexual reputation or had had sex previously with the defendant

---

[89] This was the case under pre-2003 law: *Wallwork* (1958) 42 Cr.App.R. 153.
[90] *Osborne* [1905] 1 K.B. 551.
[91] [1948] 1 All E.R. 551.
[92] Within certain limits—*Hobbs v C T Tinling & Co. Ltd* [1929] 2 K.B. 1; see Ch.13.
[93] *Sawoniuk* [2000] 2 Cr.App.R. 220.
[94] *Osbourne* [2005] EWCA Crim 2826.
[95] J. Temkin: *op.cit.,* p.196ff.; J. Temkin: "Sexual History Evidence—the Ravishment of Section 2" [1993] Crim.L.R. 3.
[96] *Barker* (1829) 3 C.&P. 589.

was considered relevant to credibility and to the issue of consent. Alongside such questions, the victim might be asked about any sexual relationships with other men but that once an answer has been given, counsel had to accept it. This is the normal rule of finality of answers to collateral questions. In *Holmes*,[97] the charge was indecent assault. The victim was asked whether she had had 'connection' with another man. She denied it and the defence sought to call the man to rebut this. The judge disallowed the evidence and this was upheld in the Court for Crown Cases Reserved.

Holmes (1871) 12 Cox CC 137 at 143, *per* Kelly C.B.:

On the trial of an indictment for rape, or an attempt to commit a rape, or for an indecent assault, which in effect may amount to an attempt to commit a rape, if the prosecutrix is asked whether she has not had connection with some other man named, and she denies it, we are clearly of the opinion that that man cannot be called to contradict her. The general principle is, that when a witness is cross-examined as to a collateral fact, the answer must be taken for better or worse, and the witness cannot be contradicted as to that by a third person. If the proposed evidence were receivable, the prosecutrix might be cross-examined as to the whole history of her life. . . There is no doubt the prosecutrix may be asked as to connection with the prisoner on a prosecution for rape . . .

As Kelly C.B. says, if the victim denies earlier sex with the defendant, this can be rebutted. There the fact has a direct bearing on the question before the court, which involves the fact of consent or non-consent on the part of the prosecutrix. In *Riley*[98] the victim denied ". . . previous voluntary connection . . ." and the trial judge rejected the prisoner's evidence in rebuttal.

Riley (1887) 16 Cox CC 191 at 194, *per* Lord Coleridge C.J.:

It appears to me clear that that such evidence was admissible. Now, it has been held over and over again, that where evidence is denied by the prosecutrix with regard to acts of connection committed by her with persons other than the prisoner, she cannot be contradicted. The rejection of such evidence is founded on good common sense, not only because it would put very cruel hardship on a prosecutrix; but also on the ground that the evidence does not go to the point in issue . . .
. . . but to reject evidence as to the particular person is another matter. Because not only does it render it more likely that she would or would not have consented, but it is evidence which goes to the very point in issue.

Discussion in open court of a victim's past sexual behaviour can prejudice the jury, in the sense that they will morally judge the victim as much, if not

---

[97] (1871) 12 Cox 137.
[98] (1887) 16 Cox 191.

more so, that the defendant. It can distract from the real issue of whether she was consenting on this specific occasion. The prospect of cross-examination on this inevitably will make the victim think carefully as to whether to report it to the police or proceed with the prosecution.

2. The Facts in Issue

The basic question remains whether past sexual conduct is relevant to any issue at a sexual assault trial? To ask whether evidence is relevant always requires knowledge of the legal facts in issue in the case. One problem was the definition of rape. As a result of the House of Lords' decision in *DPP v Morgan*,[99] the prosecution had to prove that the victim did not in fact consent but also that the accused did not believe that his victim was consenting. The objective unreasonableness of that belief was irrelevant and the defendant was entitled to a direction from the judge to the jury that they must be sure that he possessed such an intention to have non-consensual sex. By defining the legal fact in issue in that way, the victim's prior sexual history could provide a basis for those beliefs. For example, in *Bashir*,[1] the defence was that the victim was a prostitute and, if the defendant knew this, there was a greater possibility that he believed that the victim was consenting.

But the border between relevance to the issues and a question of credibility is very fine. *Morgan* made it difficult to maintain the distinction between questions which go to a fact in issue as opposed to those which go merely to credibility. If the only issue is the defendant's belief in consent and the only witnesses are the defendant and the complainant, the conclusion that the complainant is not worthy of credit must be decisive of the issue.

The impact of the Sexual Offences Act 2003 has been to change the fact in issue—s.1 requires the Crown to prove that the victim did not consent and that the defendant had no reasonable grounds for believing that she was consenting. The defendants in *Morgan* would now be convicted. Furthermore ss.75 and 76 introduce certain presumptions about consent.

1. Under s.75, consent is *rebuttably presumed* not to exist where the person was using violence against complainant, where the complainant was unlawfully detained, where the complainant was asleep, where the complainant's physical disability meant [she] could not communicate on consent, or where a stupefying substance had been administered to the complainant. Where the prosecution proves any of these circumstances, this casts an evidential burden on the defendant to show some evidence that, despite appearances, the victim was consenting.

2. Under s.76, where the defendant is shown to have deceived the complainant as to the nature or purpose of act or where the defendant has induced the complainant to consent by impersonating person known personally to complainant, the victim is conclusively presumed not to have consented—this is an *irrebuttable presumption*.

[99] [1976] A.C. 182.
[1] [1969] 3 All E.R. 692.

These reforms put additional pressure on the accused to testify as he needs some testimony which would establish reasonable grounds for belief or which would rebut a s.75 presumption. Without such testimony, he runs a serious risk of conviction. Sections 34 and 35 of the Criminal Justice and Public Order Act 1994 strengthen this—if the defendant relies on the defence of consent but has failed to mention this when questioned by the police or later fails to testify at the trial, the jury can be invited to draw the inference that the accused did not believe that any such consent existed.

3. Rape shield legislation

The fact in issue may have changed but how far does the victim of sexual assault still face intrusive and humiliating questioning? To subject any witness, let alone the victim of a serious assault, to questioning about intimate details of their private lives is at the very least humiliating for them and a major blemish on any legal system. The importance of legislation which shields witnesses from this was recognised in the recommendations of the Heilbron Committee which recognised that sexual experiences ". . . are neither indicative of untruthfulness nor of a general willingness to consent."[2] The report led to the passage of s.2 of the Sexual Offences (Amendment) Act 1976 which required the leave of the court before any question could be asked of a rape victim about their sexual experience with people other than the defendant. This permitted such cross-examination only with the leave of the judge and this should only be permitted if not to do so would otherwise be 'unfair' on the defendant. The section had a sorry history as the breadth of judicial interpretation removed protection from the very witnesses that it was designed for.[3] In case after case, the Court of Appeal quashed convictions when defendants argued that they should have been permitted to cross-examine the victim on her sexual history.[4]

The key issue is relevance: if the evidence is of negligible probative value, the cross-examination is unfair in compelling a vulnerable witness to submit intimate details to public gaze. If the evidence is directly relevant to an issue, it would be unfair on the defendant not to have this brought to the attention of the jury.[5]

J. Temkin, Rape and the Legal Process (2nd edn, OUP, Oxford, 2002) 3:

That a woman has had consensual sexual relations with some or many men in the near or distant past is a reflection of current sexual mores and can shed no light on

[2] *op.cit.*, para.131.
[3] Temkin *op.cit.* p.198ff; Z. Adler, "Rape—The Intention of Parliament and the Practice of the Courts" [1982] 45 M.L.R. 664.
[4] *Viola* [1982] 3 All E.R. 73; *Cleland* [1995] Crim.L.R. 742; *Brown* (1989) 89 Cr.App.R. 97; *Bogie* [1992] Crim.L.R. 301; *SMS* [1992] Crim.L.R. 310; *Said* [1992] Crim.L.R. 433.
[5] e.g. *Funderburk* [1990] 2 All E.R. 482 at 487e.

whether she consented to this particular defendant on the occasion in question. Relevance is in the mind of the beholder and all too often it can be swayed by stereotypical assumptions, myth and prejudice. As L'Heureux-Dube J. stated in the Supreme Court of Canada's decision in *Seaboyer*:[6]

> Regardless of the definition used, the content of any relevancy decision will be filled by the particular judge's experience, common sense and/or logic. . . There are certain areas of enquiry where experience, common sense and logic are informed by stereotype and myth. . . This area of the law [i.e. sexual history evidence] has been particularly prone to the utilization of stereotype in determinations of relevance.[7]

Notably lacking in the Court of Appeal judgments on s.2 was any discussion as to the degree of relevance needed to qualify for admissibility. It has been pointed out that evidence,

'. . . must not merely be remotely relevant, but proximately so. Again it must not unnecessarily complicate the case, or too much tend to confuse, mislead or tire. . . the jury, or withdraw their attention too much from the real issues of the case.'[8]

These issues are very pertinent where sexual history is concerned and merited greater judicial consideration.[9] Section 2 had proved inadequate to the task and reform[10] came with the passage of s.41 of the Youth Justice and Criminal Evidence Act 1999.

Youth Justice and Criminal Evidence Act 1999. s.41:

41.—(1) If at a trial a person is charged with a sexual offence, then, except with the leave of the court—
 (a) no evidence may be adduced, and
 (b) no question may be asked in cross-examination,
 by or on behalf of any accused at the trial, about any sexual behaviour of the complainant.
 (2) The court may give leave in relation to any evidence or question only on an application made by or on behalf of an accused, and may not give such leave unless it is satisfied—
 (a) that subsection (3) or (5) applies, and
 (b) that a refusal of leave might have the result of rendering unsafe a conclusion of the jury or (as the case may be) the court on any relevant issue in the case.
 (3) This subsection applies if the evidence or question relates to a relevant issue in the case and either—
 (a) that issue is not an issue of consent; or
 (b) it is an issue of consent and the sexual behaviour of the complainant to which the evidence or question relates is alleged to have taken place at or about the same time as the event which is the subject matter of the charge against the accused; or

---

[6] *Seaboyer*; Gayme. 83 D.L.R. (4th) 193.
[7] *Temkin, op.cit.* 199.
[8] Thayer, *A Preliminary Treatise on Evidence at Common Law* (1898) p.516.
[9] J. Temkin, "Sexual history Evidence—the Ravishment of Section 2" [1993] Crim.L.R. 3 at 5–6; see also Z. Adler, "The Relevance of Sexual History Evidence in Rape: Problems of Subjective Interpretation" [1985] Crim.L.R. 769.
[10] Home Office, *Speaking Up for Justice* (1998).

(c) it is an issue of consent and the sexual behaviour of the complainant to which the evidence or question relates is alleged to have been, in any respect, so similar—

    (i) to any sexual behaviour of the complainant which (according to evidence adduced or to be adduced by or on behalf of the accused) took place as part of the event which is the subject matter of the charge against the accused, or

    (ii) to any other sexual behaviour of the complainant which (according to such evidence) took place at or about the same time as that event,

that the similarity cannot reasonably be explained as a coincidence.

(4) For the purposes of subsection (3) no evidence or question shall be regarded as relating to a relevant issue in the case if it appears to the court to be reasonable to assume that the purpose (or main purpose) for which it would be adduced or asked is to establish or elicit material for impugning the credibility of the complainant as a witness.

(5) This subsection applies if the evidence or question—

(a) relates to any evidence adduced by the prosecution about any sexual behaviour of the complainant; and

(b) in the opinion of the court, would go no further than is necessary to enable the evidence adduced by the prosecution to be rebutted or explained by or on behalf of the accused.

(6) For the purposes of subsections (3) and (5) the evidence or question must relate to a specific instance (or specific instances) of alleged sexual behaviour on the part of the complainant (and accordingly nothing in those subsections is capable of applying in relation to the evidence or question to the extent that it does not so relate).

This section provides a shield to all victims of sexual offences as leave to question the witness about prior sexual conduct will only be given in the following circumstances.

1. When it is not an issue of consent: in *Garaxo*,[11] the prosecution disclosed that the victim had made similar allegations on two previous occasions. The conviction was quashed as the defendant had not been allowed to cross-examine the witness on these prior allegations in order to demonstrate their falsity. It was not examination on sexual behaviour—s.41(3)(a)

2. Where issue is consent, questioning on sexual behaviour is only permitted.

    a) if the questions relate to activity at or about the same time—s.41(3)(b) or

    b) if the questions relate to very similar behaviour on part of witness—s.41(3)(c); or

    c) if the evidence has been adduced by the prosecution and the cross examination goes no further than rebutting or explaining that evidence s.41(5).

But even when these conditions are met, the judge might still reject such a line of questioning.

1. if the refusal would not render any conviction 'unsafe'—s.41(2)(b); or

---

[11] [2005] EWCA Crim 1170.

2. if the main purpose is to impugn credibility—s.41(4).

Is s.41 in conflict with Art.6 (3)(d) of the European Convention on Human Rights which provides a right to examine witnesses? This was raised in *A*,[12] where the defence sought to question the witness on an alleged affair between herself and the defendant—s.41 applies not only to the victim's experience with people other than the defendant but also with the defendant. Denying the defendant the right to cross-examine would infringe his right to a fair trial but could the cross-examination come within any of the gateways detailed above? The issue was one of consent and Lord Steyn held the gateways under s.41(3)(c) or (5) were excluded by the facts.

A [2001] 3 All E.R. 1, *per* Lord Steyn:

42. The third gateway is section 41(3)(c). . . . This gateway is only available where the issue is whether the complainant consented and the evidence or questioning relates to behaviour that is so similar to the defence's version of the complainant's behaviour at the time of the alleged offence that it cannot reasonably be explained as a coincidence. An example would be the case where the complainant says that the accused raped her; the accused says that the complainant consented and then after the act of intercourse tried to blackmail him by alleging rape; and the defence now wishes to ask the complainant whether on a previous occasion she similarly tried to blackmail the accused.

43. Rightly none of the counsel appearing before the House were prepared to argue that on ordinary methods of interpretation section 41(3)(c) can be interpreted to cover, for example, cases similar to the one before the House where it is alleged that there was a previous sexual experience between the complainant and the accused on several occasions during a three week period before the occasion in question. Let me consider ordinary methods of interpretation in a little more detail. One could say that section 41(3)(c) is a statutory adoption of the striking similarity test enunciated in *R v Boardman*.[13] So interpreted section 41(3)(c) is a narrow gateway, which will only be available in rare cases. Alternatively, one could argue that section 41(3)(c) involves the test of high probative force of the evidence, which makes it just to admit it, in accordance with the principle stated in *Director of Public Prosecutions v P*.[14] Even if this approach was consistent with the language of section 41, the threshold requirement would be too high: often the evidence will be relevant but not capable of being described as having "high probative value". These ways of interpreting section 41(3)(c) cannot solve the problem of the prima facie excessive inroad on the right to a fair trial. It is important to concentrate in the first place on the language of section 41. Making due allowance for the words "in any respect" in section 41(3)(c), the test "that the similarity cannot reasonably be explained as a coincidence" is inapt to allow evidence to be admitted or questioning to take place that, for example, (i) the complainant invited the accused at an office party on a Friday to come to her flat on the Sunday to make love to her or (2) that the complainant and the accused had sexual relations on several occasions in the previous month. While common sense may rebel against the idea that such evidence is never relevant to the issue of consent, that is the

[12] [2001] 3 All E.R. 1.
[13] [1975] A.C. 421.
[14] [1991] 2 A.C. 447.

effect of the statute. In my view ordinary methods of purposive construction of section 41(3)(c) cannot cure the problem of the excessive breadth of the section 41, read as a whole, so far as it relates to previous sexual experience between a complainant and the accused. Whilst the statute pursued desirable goals, the methods adopted amounted to legislative overkill.

44. On the other hand, the interpretative obligation under section 3 of the [Human Rights Act 1998] is a strong one. It applies even if there is no ambiguity in the language in the sense of the language being capable of two different meanings. It is an emphatic adjuration by the legislature. . . The White Paper made clear that the obligation goes far beyond the rule which enabled the courts to take the Convention into account in resolving any ambiguity in a legislative provision . . .

45. In my view section 3 requires the court to subordinate the niceties of the language of section 41(3)(c), and in particular the touchstone of coincidence, to broader considerations of relevance judged by logical and common sense criteria of time and circumstances. After all, it is realistic to proceed on the basis that the legislature would not, if alerted to the problem, have wished to deny the right to an accused to put forward a full and complete defence by advancing truly probative material. It is therefore possible under section 3 to read section 41, and in particular section 41(3)(c), as subject to the implied provision that evidence or questioning which is required to ensure a fair trial under article 6 of the Convention should not be treated as inadmissible. The result of such a reading would be that sometimes logically relevant sexual experiences between a complainant and an accused may be admitted under section 41(3)(c). On the other hand, there will be cases where previous sexual experience between a complainant and an accused will be irrelevant, eg an isolated episode distant in time and circumstances. Where the line is to be drawn must be left to the judgment of trial judges. On this basis a declaration of incompatibility can be avoided. If this approach is adopted, section 41 will have achieved a major part of its objective but its excessive reach will have been attenuated in accordance with the will of Parliament as reflected in section 3 of the 1998 Act. That is the approach which I would adopt.

46. It is of supreme importance that the effect of the speeches today should be clear to trial judges who have to deal with problems of the admissibility of questioning and evidence on alleged prior sexual experience between an accused and a complainant. The effect of the decision today is that under section 41(3)(c) of the 1999 Act, construed where necessary by applying the interpretative obligation under section 3 of the Human Rights Act 1998, and due regard always being paid to the importance of seeking to protect the complainant from indignity and from humiliating questions, the test of admissibility is whether the evidence (and questioning in relation to it) is nevertheless so relevant to the issue of consent that to exclude it would endanger the fairness of the trial under article 6 of the convention. If this test is satisfied the evidence should not be excluded.

Lord Steyn's test is that the line of questioning must be so relevant that to reject it would risk being in breach of Art.6. The Court of Appeal has policed this line strictly, especially when compared to its record on appeals under the 1976 Act. In the first five years, the court considered 21 cases relating to s.41.[15] In two thirds of cases, the appeal was dismissed. The primary issue remains one of relevance.

1. *Prior sexual experience with the defendant.*

As Lord Steyn in *A* suggests, there is a distinct line between questioning the victim about isolated sex sometime in the past as opposed to an examination

---

[15] This is based on a Lawtel search (March 2006) and excludes the decision in *A*, above.

about a recent and relatively steady relationship. The victim's experiences with accused have some relevance, as they can form the basis of his belief on reasonable grounds that the victim was consenting. There is, of course, a weakness in this argument: the removal of spousal immunity in rape[16] recognises that a husband can rape his wife and it becomes apparent that consent to sex at one period in a woman's life does not imply consent at the time of the alleged rape. Nor, by itself, should previous consent be sufficient to found a belief that the victim is consenting at that time. However the courts remain wedded to the belief that a fair trial is not possible if cross-examination on this is not permitted. In *Richardson*,[17] the conviction was quashed as the defendant was not given leave to cross-examine the victim about sex with the defendant four months before the attack and again eleven months later. The court held that, although a strict reading of section 41 would lead to the exclusion of this evidence, following *A*, it should be permitted under s.41(3)(c). Perhaps, had only the earlier episode occurred, the cross-examination would not have been permitted. It is the renewal of relations that creates the problem.

2. *Prior sexual experience generally.*
The policy of the 1999 Act was to prevent intrusive cross examination. Questioning has not been allowed on whether the victim was a virgin before the incident,[18] had behaved lewdly at that time[19] or had prior partners.[20] In *M*, the defendant was not permitted to question the victim on whether she had sex with the defendant's brother (and flatmate) two hours before the incident.[21]

3. *Previous allegations of rape.*
If the victim has made previous allegations of rape which cross examination may show to be false, it would be wrong to prevent the defendant from suggesting to the jury that the current allegation is false. In *Garaxo*,[22] the prosecution disclosed that the victim had made similar allegations on two previous occasions. The conviction was quashed as the defendant had not been allowed to cross-examine but there has to be a proper evidential basis that the previous allegations were untrue. In *Abdelrahman*,[23] the defence sought to question the victim about prior allegations but without introducing any evidence that they had been untrue.

4. *Other relevant issues.*
In *T*,[24] the defendant had arranged to meet the victim in the park. They went inside a triangular climbing frame where various sexual acts had taken place.

[16] *R. v R* [1992] 4 All E.R. 481.
[17] [2003] EWCA Crim 2754.
[18] *McKendrick* [2004] EWCA Crim 1393.
[19] *Bahador* (unreported 2005, February 15, CA)—questions on the victims' behaviour in a club immediately preceding the rape.
[20] *TW* [2004] EWCA Crim 3103.
[21] [2002] 1 Crim.App.R. 20.
[22] above; *MH* [2001] EWCA Crim 1877.
[23] [2005] EWCA Crim 1367.
[24] [2004] 2 Cr.App.R. 32.

The issue at trial had been whether there was consent. An application for leave to question the victim on the fact that three weeks earlier they had had consensual sex in the climbing frame in a similar position was refused by the trial judge. The Court of Appeal quashed the conviction on the basis that this line of questioning could be pursued under (3)(c).

In other successful appeals, the sexual conduct has been peripheral. In *RT*,[25] the victim had made a complaint about sexual abuse by others at a time when she would have been expected to also detail the abuse by the defendant. This omission could only be seen as highly material to whether the abuse in fact occurred. In *Lloyd*,[26] the witness testified that the indecent assault had occurred on a particular day and referred to a diary entry. The next entry in the diary, deleted but readable, referred to a sex act that the witness had apparently performed. The questioning went to the accuracy and veracity of the diary and was relevant. In *F*,[27] the defendant was charged with the sexual abuse of a step-daughter some time in the past. The defendant denied that the abuse had taken place. It was acknowledged that they had had an adult relationship over six years and the defendant sought to establish that the breakdown of this later relationship was the motive behind the victim's accusations. The fact of the relationship was put to the victim who testified that she only participated out of fear. The defendant was refused leave to play tapes which showed the victim happily participating. The Act did not compel the exclusion of this evidence—the issue was whether the abuse ever took place and the nature of the later relationship was material to the existence of the victim's motive.

The law and procedure have changed but perhaps the central problem is perhaps not a legal one, it is the law's disbelief in women's testimony.

K. Mack, "Continuing Barriers to Women's Credibility: A Feminist Perspective on the Proof Process" (1993) 4 Crim.Law Forum 327:

In the area of sexual assault, the dominant story in the law has been that propounded by Hale more than two and a half centuries ago. Rape is 'an accusation easy to be made and hard to be proved, and harder to be defended by the party accused, tho' never so innocent'.[28] This commitment to women's lack of credibility when testifying about rape, based on no evidence and indeed in the face of contrary evidence, has consistently been expressed in legal rules, in jury instructions, in appellate opinions, and in law treatises. This dominant legal story appears in many forms, but at its heart lies the assumption that women lie when talking about rape. One commentator[29] has noted that the myth of the lying woman is the most powerful myth in the tradition of rape law.

---

[25] [2001] EWCA Crim 1877.
[26] [2005] EWCA Crim 1111.
[27] [2005] 2 Cr.App.R. 13.
[28] Sir Matthew Hale, *The History of the Pleas of the Crown*, (1736), p.634.
[29] S. Estrich, "Palm Beach Stories" 11 Law & Phil. 5 at 11 (1992).

Mack surveys general problems facing women as witnesses: many features of women's language are associated with powerlessness such as superlatives, intensifiers, fillers, hedges and politeness markers; women tend to be more hesitant even when certain, unlike men who are more likely to speak confidently even when unsure or wrong. The trier of fact gives greater weight to those who use a more powerful style of speech. But when women testify about sexual assault, other features emerge.

K. Mack, "Continuing Barriers to Women's Credibility: A Feminist Perspective on the Proof Process" (1993) 4 Crim. Law Forum 327, pp. 332–335:

In fact, the common law developed a set of rules specifically to attack the credibility of women testifying in rape cases; these rules related to the expectation of a recent complaint, the relevance of sexual history, the requirement (mainly in the United States) of force or other forms of resistance, and the need for corroboration. The corroboration rules pertaining to women alleging rape contrasted sharply with the usual common law rule that the jury were entitled to convict on the unsupported testimony of one witness. The corroboration rules in rape cases ranged from a demand for corroboration of every material fact essential to constitute the crime to a judicial warning that it was unsafe to convict on the basis of a woman's uncorroborated testimony about rape (the usual rule in the United Kingdom and Australia).

The explicit basis of such rules was a belief in the untrustworthiness of women in general and their allegations of rape in particular. The Law Commission, summarizing the law of England and Wales in 1991, stated that the judge must explain to the jury why it was dangerous to convict only on the uncorroborated evidence of the complainant. The reason commonly given related to the putative nature of women and girls. Perhaps the most widely quoted version of this view was that articulated by Lord Justice Salmon:

> [H]uman experience has shown that . . . girls and women [in these courts] do sometimes tell an entirely false story which is very easy to fabricate, but extremely difficult to refute. Such stories are fabricated for all sorts of reasons, which I need not now enumerate, and sometimes for no reason at all.[30]

Besides reasons related to the likelihood of falseness in the woman's story, including the alleged ease of making unfounded allegations (and the ease of fabricating corroboration!), judicial explanations for requiring corroboration outlined the difficulty for a man to refute a false charge of rape, the likelihood of jury sympathy for the victim, and more detailed observations about qualities alleged to be significant in female psychology—neurosis, jealousy, spite, fantasy, and shame.

But the law's bias toward women went deeper than merely assuming that they are malicious and mendacious. It also regarded women as particularly adept at concealing these qualities, thus the need to warn jurors, based on some notion of the 'law's vast experience' or 'history'.

Some commentators took their distrust of women to fantastic extremes. John Henry Wigmore recommended that no rape case should go forward unless the victim had a psychiatric examination. . . .

4. The Accused's Sexual History

At common law, we witnessed "the double standard of sexual morality in its most virulent form". The jury was told about the victim's sexual past but

---

[30] *Henry* (1968) 53 Cr.App.R. 150.

the same jurors were prevented from learning whether the defendant had previously committed crimes of sexual assault. The 1999 legislation has significantly affected the protection given to the victim in these cases. Furthermore s.101 of the Criminal Justice Act 2003 opens up the prospect of the accused's sexual "bad character"[31] being put before the court.

1. Under s.101(1)(c), that bad character may be "important explanatory evidence". In *Campbell*,[32] the defendant was convicted of kidnapping and murdering his 15-year-old niece. The prosecution advanced evidence of the accused's Internet activity involving access to teenage sex sites and downloading of material from those sites as well of his attempts to photograph other teenage girls. The Court of Appeal held that, without this evidence, the jury would have been left with an incomplete and distorted account of the relationship between the appellant and the victim.

2. Under s.101(1)(d), the propensity of the defendant to commit offences of this nature is admissible in certain circumstances and with the leave of the court. The prosecution will inevitably seek to reinforce their case by introduction of such evidence. In *Weir*, the defendant was charged with indecent assault and the prosecution were permitted to introduce a caution, received in 2000, for taking an indecent photograph of a child.[33]

3. Under s.101(1)(f), if the defence introduces evidence of the accused's own good character, the prosecution would be permitted to adduce evidence in rebuttal.[34]

4. Under s.101(1)(g), if the defendant makes an attack on another's character, at any stage of the proceedings, evidence of the accused's own bad character can be introduced. At first glance this provision provides further protection for the victim of sexual assault from being questioned about past sexual experience. Having overcome the obstacles presented by s.41, the defendant must make a tactical decision whether to risk having his own previous convictions being placed in front of the jury. An attack on character would seem to include allegations of promiscuity or inchastity. Such a line of questioning is central to the defendant's case but the law has always taken the position that, where the defendant attacks the character of a witness, the defendant's own convictions should be revealed. This was the case even where the imputation is a necessary part of the defence.[35] In *Selvey v D.P.P.*[36] the accused was charged with buggery. There was medical evidence which supported the victim's complaint. Selvey's defence was that the complainant had already

---

[31] This is discussed in more detail in Ch.15.
[32] [2005] EWCA Crim 248.
[33] [2005] EWCA Crim 2866; *Smith* [2005] EWCA Crim 3244.
[34] *Rowton* (1865) Le. & Ca. 520; see Ch.13.
[35] The common law cases were decided under the repealed provisions of the Criminal Evidence Act 1898.
[36] [1970] A.C. 304.

committed buggery with another man on the same day which accounted for the doctor's evidence. The accused testified that the complainant had offered himself to the accused and when he refused, he had planted indecent photographs on him. The trial judge allowed the prosecution to question the accused on previous convictions for soliciting for a lewd and immoral purpose. The House of Lords held that the prosecution could adduce prior convictions even where the casting of such imputations is necessary to establish the defence.

The analogy between *Selvey* and the cross-examination of the victim in a rape trial seems compelling. Bizarrely there is a special interpretation of the statute for rape cases. In *Selvey*, Viscount Dilhorne said,

'In rape cases the accused can allege consent without placing himself in peril of such cross-examination (*R v Sheean*[37]; *R v Turner*[38]). This may be because such cases are *sui generics* (per Devlin J in *R v Cook*[39]), or on the ground that the issue is one raised by the prosecution.'

Lord Pearce distinguished rape cases as follows,

Selvey v D.P.P. [1970] A.C. 304 at 353c–354f, *per* Lord Pearce:

The other view would limit the literal meaning of the words. For it cannot, it is said, have been intended by Parliament to make a man liable to have his previous convictions revealed whenever the essence of his defence necessitates imputations on the character of the prosecutor. This revelation is always damaging and often fatal to a defence. The high-water mark of this argument is the ordinary case of rape. In this the vital issue (as a rule) is whether the woman consented. Consent (as a rule) involves imputations on her character. Therefore, in the ordinary case of rape, the accused cannot defend himself without letting in his previous convictions. The same argument extends in varying lesser degrees to many cases.

. . . The second part of the argument in favour of a construction more liberal to the accused is concerned with the words 'the conduct or nature of the defence'. One should, it can be argued, read conduct or nature as something superimposed on the essence of the defence itself. . . . This argument has obvious force, particularly in a case of rape, where the allegation of consent is in truth no more than a mere traverse of the essential ingredient which the Crown have to prove, namely, want of consent. But the argument does not, and I think cannot, fairly stop short of contending that all matters which are relevant to the crime, that is, of rebutting evidence could be proved, are excluded from the words 'conduct or nature of the defence'.

This exception is established beyond doubt by decisions such as *Turner*.[40] Where a rape victim is questioned about prior sexual activity,

---

[37] (1908) 21 Cox 561.
[38] [1944] K.B. 463.
[39] [1959] 2 Q.B. 340 at 347.
[40] [1944] K.B. 463.

this did not open up the defendant's own prior convictions to scrutiny. This rule was not affected by the rape shield introduced in 1976. Nowadays that shield is stronger as a result of s.41. But where leave to cross-examine rape victims is given, it is probably still the case that the accused does not risk having his prior convictions revealed under s.101(1)(g). To treat rape as *sui generis* is no longer tolerable. The accused in rape cases should be treated by the same standards as defendants accused of other crimes.

IV. Child Witnesses[41]

The imperatives of the adversarial trial (the formality of the trial, testifying in person, the hearsay rule, cross-examination) have their greatest impact on children. This became a matter of public concern in the 1980s as public awareness of the sexual and physical abuse of children increased, especially in the wake of the Cleveland scandal.[42] As a result there was considerable debate about legislation about the treatment of child witnesses and significant legislative improvements.

A. *Quality of Children's Testimony*

Historically there was considerable suspicion of the quality of children's evidence. Heydon summarised the perceived problems.

D. Heydon. Evidence (1st edn. Butterworths, 1984), p.84:

First, a child's powers of observation and memory are less reliable than an adult's. Secondly, children are prone to live in a make-believe world, so that they magnify incidents which happen to them or invent them completely. Thirdly, they are also very egocentric, so that details seemingly unrelated to their own world are quickly forgotten by them. Fourthly, because of their immaturity they are very suggestible and can be easily be influenced by adults and other children. One lying child may influence others to lie; anxious parents may take a child through a story again and again so that it becomes drilled in untruths. Most dangerously, a policeman taking a statement from a child may without ill will use leading questions so that the child tends to confuse what actually happened with the answer suggested implicitly by the question. A fifth danger is that children often have little notion of the duty to speak the truth, and they may fail to realise how important their evidence is in a case and how important it is for it to be accurate. Finally, children sometimes behave in a way evil

---

[41] A critique of the law's treatment of child witnesses is to be found in J. Spencer and J. Flin, *The Evidence of Children—The Law and the Psychology* (2nd ed.-1993); H.L.Westcott, G.M. Davies and R.H.C. Bull *Children's testimony. A handbook of psychological research and forensic practice* (John Wiley, 2002).

[42] Department of Health and Social Security, *Report of the Inquiry into Child Abuse in Cleveland* Cm. 412 (HMSO, 1987) [the Butler-Sloss report].

beyond their years. They may consent to sexual offences against themselves and then deny consent. They may completely invent sexual offences. Some children know that the adult world regards such matters in a serious and peculiar way, and they enjoy investigating this mystery or revenging themselves by making false accusations

This litany of the weaknesses of children's testimony has come under critical scrutiny and children's abilities to provide accurate accounts of their experienced have been studied extensively.[43]

1. A child's memory is different from that of an adult but not necessarily less reliable. Even infants and toddlers can encode, store and retrieve a great deal of information about their experiences. Children over two years old have the narrative skills to report the central components of events, even after significant delays. There appear to be age differences in terms of the quantity of information freely recalled but not in the terms of the quality—older children provide more information through free recall, requiring fewer prompts and forgetting less than younger children.

B. Gordon, L. Baker-Ward and P. Ornstein. "Children's Testimony: A Review of Research on Memory for Past Experiences" (2001) 4 Clinical Child and Family Psychology Review 292:

There are cases where a child's descriptive information has proved crucial for the apprehension of an assailant. A ten-year-old girl who had been abducted and sexually assaulted while walking home from school in Banff was abandoned in a desolate moorland culvert where her head was smashed with a boulder until, as she told the police, 'she fell asleep'. From hospital and with the help of a female detective, she was not only able to describe the man but provided precise details of an oil rig motif printed on his sweatshirt which was immediately published. She also gave an accurate description of the vinyl on the rear seat of the man's car which proved to be the vital clue. The police were amazed at the quality of the information she supplied and her attacker (who had no previous convictions) was arrested on a North Sea oil rig within a week of the assault.

The reliability of children's evidence depends crucially on how they are questioned but that if that is done properly, their evidence should be evaluated like that of any other witness.

2. The egocentricity of children can be looked at in two ways: as a moral weakness and as a cognitive weakness. Research suggests that the ability to make simple inferences about how other people think and feel develops in children who are about four or five. It is unclear

---

[43] B. Gordon, L. Baker-Ward and P. Ornstein, "Children's Testimony: A Review of Research on Memory for Past Experiences" 4 *Clinical Child and Family Psychology Review* (2001) 157; J. Spencer and J. Flin, *op.cit.* Ch.11.

whether this affects their ability to be truthful about events. Cognitively, it is suggested that children do not take account of events unconnected with their own world and this may limit the quantity of peripheral information about an incident that a young child may remember. But we all pay more attention to events that affect us!

B. Gordon, L. Baker-Ward and P. Ornstein. "Children's Testimony: A Review of Research on Memory for Past Experiences" (2001) 4 Clinical Child and Family Psychology Review 292:

. . . what is memorable to any individual child, regardless of age, and hence most likely to be encoded, is anything that is personally significant to that child. Events or actions that affect a child's sense of well-being, safety, or social acceptance are considered to be personally significant and thus, more likely to be remembered. . . Similarly, [other researchers] indicate that aspects of an event are more likely to be encoded if they are "interesting" or "distinctive," either because they are unexpected or emotionally arousing, to the child. Very traumatic experiences, for example, may be remembered very clearly despite a lack of prior knowledge because of their distinctiveness. It has also been noted, however, that high arousal, such as might occur during a traumatic experience, results in a narrowing of attention. Thus, many details of such an experience may not be encoded because the child focuses on only a few highly salient features. . . . In this regard, it is not surprising that children remember central features of even neutral events better than more peripheral features. What is central for a specific child depends on what is most relevant to that child, including the most threatening or most feared aspect of a traumatic experience.

3. One perennial theme is that children are suggestible and can easily be led.

J. Spencer and J. Flin., The Evidence of Children—The Law and the Psychology (2nd ed., Blackwells, 1993):

In certain circumstances it appears that young children are susceptible to leading questions because the child bows to the superior social status of the adult and submissively complies with any suggestions that the interviewer appears to make. This can happen because the child is unfamiliar with the social rules of a formal interview and, in an attempt to make sense of the situation, is very sensitive to the cues given by the adult (including the adult's non-verbal behaviour). The child's aim may be to please the adult or to terminate the interview as quickly as possible, or the children may simply believe that the adult has superior knowledge and therefore must be correct. In our society, children are taught that adults know best, not to contradict adults, to be polite to strangers and that it is wiser to hazard a guess rather than to admit ignorance. This powerful constellation of social rules can make children compliant in all but the most carefully conducted interviews.

There are some indications that children are more resistant to (mis)leading questions when the events have personal significance for them. There is some evidence that young children, especially those of pre-school age, are more vulnerable to suggestions than older children and adults. Improvements in the protocols for interviewing children are the key to guarding against this.[44]

4. Tradition has it that a child's imagination is so intense that there is an inability to tell the difference between fact and fantasy. Fantasy plays an important part in children's lives but they grasp the distinction between imagination and reality.

J. Spencer and J. Flin, The Evidence of Children—The Law and the Psychology (2nd ed., 1993) pp.317–318:

There is certainly no psychological research or medical case study material which suggests that children are in the habit of fantasising about the sort of incidents that might result in court proceedings: for example, observing road accidents or being indecently assaulted. Children's fantasies and play are characterised by their daily experience and personal knowledge, and unusual fantasies are seen by psychiatrists as highly suspicious: 'The cognitive and imaginative capacities of three-year-olds do not enable them to describe anal intercourse and spitting out ejaculate, for instance. Such detailed descriptions from small children, in the absence of other factors, should be seen as stemming from the reality of the past abuse rather than from the imagination'.[45] As a rule, young children have a very limited knowledge of sexual behaviour.

5. As with women accusation's of rape, much energy has been spent to prove that children also falsely accuse men of sexual assault. The proportion of false allegations is probably very low and frequently the accusations originate with other adults. False allegations in sexual offences are probably no more than false allegations of burglary, car theft or criminal damage. It would be futile to try to compare the truthfulness of children with that of adults but as the Pigot Committee said,

We understand, however, that contrary to the traditional view, recent research shows that untruthful child witnesses are comparatively uncommon and that, like their adult counterparts, they act out of identifiable motives.[46]

Many of these myths are beginning to be seen as myths. Memory research suggests that even very young children remember past experiences over long periods of time. Children older than three can provide accurate and relatively complete accounts, although it is important that proper interview techniques are used. There are differences in children's abilities to provide eyewitness

---

[44] Gordon, *op.cit.* p.158.
[45] E. Vizard et al., "Interviewing Sexually Abused Children" (1987) 11 Adoption and Fostering 20 at 24.
[46] Pigot Committee, above, para.2.24.

testimony—school-age children provide more accurate information, are more consistent, and require fewer specific prompts in recall when compared with younger children. Moreover, older children are less vulnerable to the effects of misinformation than are their younger peers. But false memory syndrome exists and it is not peculiar to children as adults can also be influenced to provide elaborate narratives about experiences that did not occur. Overall the research confirms that there is little need to construct elaborate rules for children's evidence. Where there is an evidential basis that a child witness may be unreliable, the *Makanjuola* warning should suffice.

B. *Competence and Oaths*

The common law took a restricted view of the competence of children as witnesses and historically distinguished between:

1. *Sworn testimony*.
The old common law test of competence was based on a child's capacity to take the oath. Initially the test stressed the theological but by the 1970s was more secular. The issue was whether the child had an ". . . appreciation of the solemnity of the occasion and the added responsibility to tell the truth".[47] This remains the common law test of competency to take the oath and has been put in statutory form by s.55 of the Youth Justice and Criminal Evidence Act 1999.

2. *Unsworn testimony*.
In criminal proceedings, children were allowed under section 38(1) of the Children and Young Persons Act 1933 to testify unsworn provided that they understood "the duty of speaking the truth".

The modern test for children's competence is now on the same basis as adults:

1. *Criminal proceedings*.
The test of competence for all witnesses is now regulated by s.53 of the Youth Justice and Criminal Evidence Act 1999. The competence of the very youngest children is now tested by whether they are to understand the questions and give understandable answers. The presumption is that they are and the court is under no obligation to inquire into a witness's competence unless there is some reason to doubt it. When the judge does consider it necessary to investigate a child's competence, this is done under the procedure established by s.54 in the absence of the jury.[48]

---

[47] *Hayes* [1977] 2 All E.R. 288.
[48] See Ch.9.

There is no minimum age at which a child is assumed not to be able to understand questions and give intelligible answers. Previously it has been asserted that children under six were not competent even to give unsworn evidence. This was based on *Wallwork*,[49] when Lord Goddard suggested that the jury could not attach any value to the evidence of a child aged five. This was overturned in *R v Z*,[50] which involved a six-year-old giving evidence of sexual abuse by her father. Lord Lane C.J. put it:

R v Z [1990] 2 All E.R. 971 at 973d–f, *per* Lord Lane C.J.:

Those criteria will inevitably vary widely from child to child, and may indeed vary according the circumstances of the case, the nature of the case, and the nature of the evidence which the child is called on to give. Obviously the younger the child the more care the judge must take before he allows the evidence to be received. But the statute lays down no minimum age, and the matter accordingly remains in the discretion of the judge in each case. It may be very rarely that a five-year-old will satisfy the requirements of [the statute].[51] But nevertheless the discretion remains to be exercised judicially by the judge according to the well-known criteria for the exercise of judicial discretion.

The issue of taking the oath is also simplified—children under the age of fourteen now testify unsworn and there is no discretion in the court to allow them to take the oath. For children over 14, there is a presumption that they will be sworn, providing that they satisfy the criteria laid down by s.55 of the 1999 Act.[52]

2. Civil proceedings.
Prior to 1989, there were no provisions for allowing children to testify unsworn. In 1989, the position in the civil courts was brought into line with the (as then) existing position in criminal proceedings so that children could testify unsworn provided they met the criteria for competence of children laid down by the Children Act 1989:

96.—(1) Subsection (2) applies where a child who is called as a witness in any civil proceedings does not, in the opinion of the court, understand the nature of an oath.
(2) The child's evidence may be heard by the court if, in its opinion—
(a) he understands that it is his duty to speak the truth; and
(b) he has sufficient understanding to justify his evidence being heard.

C. *Compellability*

A competent witness is a compellable witness. A child's attendance can be ensured by a formal order—a subpoena or witness summons. Failure to

---

[49] (1958) 42 Cr.App.R. 153.
[50] [1990] 2 All E.R. 971.
[51] Lord Lane was alluding to Children and Young Persons Act 1933, s.38(1) but his comments apply equally to Youth Justice and Criminal Evidence Act 1999, s.53.
[52] see Ch.9.

attend or to testify once sworn may be punishable as contempt of court. Other, less reputable, tactics may be used: in *Thompson*,[53] the father was charged with incest and one daughter was treated as a hostile witness while the other was detained overnight so that the next morning she agreed to testify!

But the court has a residual discretion at common law to permit a child not to give evidence. This is reinforced by s.44 of the Children and Young Persons Act 1933 which reads:

> Every court in dealing with a child or young person who is brought before it, either as. . . . an offender or otherwise, shall have regard to the welfare of the child or young person.

A child witness must be also given the protection of this section. The whole issue was considered by the Court of Appeal in *R v B County Council Ex p. P.*[54] A father had been accused but not convicted of sexual abuse of his stepchildren and children. Care proceedings were brought by the local council and contested. The council sought to compel the eldest stepdaughter to attend to testify. Under s.97 of the Magistrates' Court Act 1980 magistrates have to issue a witness summons when the person is likely to be able to give material evidence. Although the stepdaughter clearly would give such evidence, the magistrates rejected the father's request for a witness summons and relied on her hearsay statement.[55] Butler-Sloss L.J. supported this approach.

R v B County Council Ex p. P. [1991] 2 All E.R. 65 at 71d–g:

> Research has shown the adverse effects upon some children of the requirement to give evidence in cases of sexual abuse. In cases of young children, such harm may well be inferred. . . The introduction of the 1990 order[56] clearly envisages an alternative to oral evidence and cross-examination and to make it possible for children making allegations of, inter alia, sexual abuse to do so without the additional stress of a court hearing. The philosophy behind the Children Act would be thwarted by the ability of the alleged abuser himself being able to require the attendance of the child at court. A court should be very cautious in requiring the attendance of a child in these cases, reinforced as it must be by considerations as to how to deal with a refusal to give evidence after the issue of the summons.
>
> In my view, reading s.97 as a whole, if the juvenile court considers at the time of the application for a summons that, for reasons of welfare of the child, the child should not be called as a witness, then it would be inappropriate to issue the summons.

This decision cannot necessarily be limited to youth or family courts.[57] Lord Donaldson M.R. argued that the applicant for a witness summons under s.97 has a prima facie right for the summons to be issued but,

---

[53] (1977) 64 Cr.App.R. 96.
[54] [1991] 2 All E.R. 65.
[55] Under the Children (Admissibility of Hearsay) Order 1990 (SI 1990/143).
[56] *ibid.*
[57] *R. v Highbury Corner Magistrates Ex p. D* [1997] 1 F.L.R. 693—defendant wished to call 9-year-old son as witness of fact to assault.

. . . a summons should not be issued under the section requiring a child or young person to attend court with a view to giving evidence, if the magistrate is satisfied that service of such a summons would itself be so inimical to the welfare of that child or young person as to outweigh the legitimate interest of the person seeking the summons to secure that the child or young person does so attend court. This is the consequence of the obligation to have regard to the welfare of the child or young person which is imposed upon every court by s.44(1) Children and Young Persons Act 1933. . . .[58]

In *Ex p. P*, although there was a subsidiary reason not to issue the summons (namely that the father had no real intent to call the stepdaughter to testify), the dicta on the court's residual discretion are clear. Such reasoning based on s.44 must apply to any hearing in front of any court. A child will not be a compellable witness if testifying would have adverse effects on the child which would outweigh any legitimate interest of the party seeking to call the child to testify. The impact of such a conclusion on that party is softened by the admission of hearsay evidence in civil proceedings under Civil Evidence Act 1995. In criminal cases, a child's witness statement may be admissible under section 116 of the Criminal Justice Act 2003 but only if the child's mental condition meant that they were unable to attend as a witness or were too frightened to do so.

D. Hearsay—Videotaping Evidence-in-Chief and Cross-Examination

Taking the evidence of children in advance of the trial itself has been another objective of reformers. The stress experienced by all witnesses is particularly acute for children, remembering the often lengthy periods between the incident and trial, the strain of re-living the events, confrontation with the defendant and the ordeal of cross-examination.

J. Spencer and J. Flin, The Evidence of Children—The Law and the Psychology (2nd ed., 1993), 371–375:

First the formality of the questioning procedure is likely to be unusual and potentially threatening for the child who may never have been interviewed in this way before. Barristers are skilled at projecting their voices and may stand some distance from the child when speaking, thus requiring the child to raise her voice in reply. The child may not fully understand the purpose of the trial[59] and having told her story several times already, the point of repeating it yet again may be far from clear. The aim of the cross-examination may be even more obscure, particularly if the child is directly accused of dishonesty, by statements such as 'I put it to you that you are not telling the truth.' It is interesting to note that 'Telling the truth but no one believing me' is regarded by children as one of life's most stressful occurrences. Yet in child

---

[58] *Ex p. P*, above at 75c–e.
[59] Lack of knowledge is a stress-inducing factor at all stages of the criminal justice process.

sexual abuse prosecutions this is likely to be the principal line of attack during cross-examination. . . .

Secondly, both the semantics and syntax of the language used in the court are likely to be at best unfamiliar to a child and at worst totally incomprehensible. Legal terminology (your lordship, objection, learned friend, recess, adjourn etc.) has the effect of accentuating formality but may also serve to baffle a child witness . . .

This highly structured interrogation is often accompanied by repeated requests to amplify certain answers, which can prevent the child recounting a series of events in what she remembers as their natural order. . . . these interviewing techniques are not only difficult for children to comprehend, but they also maximise the chances of contaminating the child's memory. The various linguistic and behavioural tactics which can be used to constrain a witness's evidence, particularly during cross-examination, are obviously of enormous advantage to the defence in their attempt to discredit a hostile witness. American lawyers actually advise a comprehensive range of strategies for the deliberate manipulation of children's testimony during cross-examination.

Thirdly, irrespective of the child's level of comprehension, the experience of being examined in court can cause stress and be physically exhausting . . .

For many witnesses, the experience of being cross-examined is traumatic and adult witnesses have described it as a frustrating, humiliating and distressing ordeal. . . If mature and socially experienced adults who comprehend the meaning and purpose of the judicial process, can find their experience in the witness box to be distressing, one can only conjecture what it might feel like for a small child to be interviewed in this fashion..[60]

The Pigot Committee[61] argued that children should not be required to appear in court and that their testimony should consist of a videotape of an out-of-court hearing with an initial interview by a trained examiner and the opportunity for the defence to cross-examine. The videotapes would replace both examination-in-chief and cross-examination at the trial.

In the 1980s video-recordings of diagnostic interviews with neglected, ill-treated or abused children were being increasingly used in the 1980s especially in Great Ormond Street Hospital. These recordings became used in multi-agency teams, involving not only police officers but also local social services departments, which were established to investigate complaints of child sexual abuse. In 1988, a Home Office circular[62] recommended the spread of such schemes and the increased use of taped interviews. The potential of these tapes as evidence was obvious and the Criminal Justice Act 1988 made video recordings of child witnesses receivable as evidence in certain circumstances. These provisions have been broadened by the 1999 legislation.

Children are eligible witnesses within the provisions of section 16 of the Youth Justice and Criminal Evidence Act 1999—as such a special measures direction may cover the measures discussed earlier in the chapter. These include video-taping of both evidence in chief and cross examination under ss.27 and 28, although facilities for recording cross-examination are still not available in 2006. The child is still liable to cross-examination with all its attendant distress.

---

[60] See J. Morgan and L. Zedner *Child Victims* (Clarendon, 1992), Ch.6.
[61] Pigot Committee, above; J. McEwan "In the Box or on the Box? The Pigot Report and Child Witnesses" [1990] Crim.L.R. 363.
[62] Home Office Circular No.52 of 1988.

One of the major advantages of taping an interview is that it can be done soon after any incident is reported. The court will be presented with an accurate and full account of the child's statements before time and repetition distorts them. The tape itself will speak to whether coaching or manipulation of the witness has taken place. Before any trial, the accused can be confronted with the tape which could not occur with the child. There is some evidence that this generates more guilty pleas. The key disadvantage is that the interview can be unfairly conducted and will have a prejudicial effect on the jury. The Home Office and CPS have issued guidelines for good practice. Breach of these is not automatically a ground for quashing a conviction.[63] Section 27(2) provides that a recording should not be excluded if it is not in the interests of justice that it should not be admitted. In *Hanton*,[64] the test that the judge must apply is whether a reasonable jury properly directed could be sure that the witness had given a credible and accurate account on the video tape. If the answer is yes, the recording is admissible and the weight to be attached is a matter for the jury.

In civil proceedings, s.96(3) of the Children Act 1989 empowered the Lord Chancellor to make provision for the reception of hearsay from children. This has now been done[65] but is redundant as videotaped interviews became freely admissible as evidence in civil proceedings as a result of section 1 of the Civil Evidence Act 1995. The weight which is to be attached to such evidence was considered by the Court of Appeal in *R v B County Council Ex p. P*.[66] The magistrates had relied on a child's hearsay statement but how was that statement, untested by cross-examination, to be regarded? In *Ex p. P*, Butler-Sloss approved the observations of Neill L.J. in *Re W*.[67]

R v B County Council Ex p. P 1991 2 All E.R. 65 at 72h–j, *per* Butler-Sloss L.J.:

. . . hearsay evidence is admissible as a matter of law, but . . . this evidence and the use to which it is put has to be handled with the greatest care and in such a way that, unless the interests of the child make it necessary, the rules of natural justice and the rights of the parents are fully and properly observed.

A court presented with hearsay evidence has to look at it anxiously and consider carefully the extent to which it can properly be relied upon. It is clear from the passage from the judgment of the stipendiary magistrate . . . he has that consideration well in mind

E. *Protection in Cross-Examination and Video-Links*

Protection for the child on cross-examination is limited. As with victims of sexual assault, a child witness is allowed to have someone sitting beside him

---

[63] *Dunphy* (1994) 98 Cr.App.R. 393; *G v DPP*, above.
[64] [2005] EWCA Crim 2009; *K* [2006] EWCA Crim 472.
[65] Children (Admissibility of Hearsay) Order 1993 (S.I. 1993/621).
[66] above.
[67] [1990] 1 F.L.R. 203 at 227.

or her in the witness box. In *Smith*,[68] a social worker consoled the complainant, who was aged 12, when she broke down in tears during her testimony in a rape case. Such assistance is not a material irregularity, although the person should talk as little as possible. The judge should reduce the strain on child witnesses without prejudicing the interests of the defendant. In addition the defendant should never cross-examine the child himself. As discussed above, under the provisions of the Youth Justice and Criminal Evidence Act 1999, a defendant can be prevented from cross-examining a child witness.

Further stress factors for the child witness are the layout, formality and ceremony of the courtroom as well as the confrontation with the accused. The use of screens and live video links[69] has been discussed earlier. These provisions take away much of the distress from being physically in the courtroom while enabling the jury to judge the child's demeanour while giving evidence. A child no longer need be confronted by the alleged assailant. From 1999, these measures are no longer restricted to violent and sexual offences.

F. *Supportive Evidence*

This issue is now of historical interest. Until the late 1980s, there were technical corroboration requirements surrounding children's testimony in criminal[70] proceedings.

1. If the child gave evidence unsworn, corroboration was needed in the form of other independent evidence implicating the accused in a material particular. Without this corroborative evidence, there could be no conviction. If the accusation related to sexual abuse of a very young child, such evidence would rarely be available.
2. If the child gave sworn testimony, corroborative evidence itself was not required but there had to be a corroboration warning. The jury had to be told of the dangers of convicting on the basis of uncorroborated evidence and would be pointed in the direction of any potentially corroborating material. Confusingly they were also told that, even if no corroboration was present, they could still convict.

Nowadays a child under 14 testifies unsworn and there is no need to draw any distinction between two different categories of evidence. Furthermore, the statutory requirement for corroboration of unsworn testimony has been repealed and the common law requirement for a corroboration warning for children was removed by the Criminal Justice Act 1988. Finally it was often

---

[68] [1994] Crim.L.R. 458.
[69] For an evaluation of video links, see J. Spencer and J. Flin, *op.cit.*, p.101ff; G. Davies and E. Noon, *An Evaluation of the Live Link for Child Witnesses* (Home Office 1991).
[70] There are no requirements for civil proceedings.

the case that juries were still warned, not because the witness was a child, but because the child was the victim of a sexual assault. The need for such warnings was dispensed with by s.32 of the Criminal Justice and Public Order Act 1994.

As a result of these changes, corroboration warnings are unlikely to be given in the case of a child witness. But judges will need to warn juries about the testimony of unreliable witnesses and these may include young children. The fact that the witness was a young child would not automatically mean that a warning would be given. There must be an evidential basis for believing the child to be unreliable. In addition any warning will be couched in non-technical terms, inviting the jury to look for 'supportive evidence' and not 'corroboration'. The Court of Appeal has discussed these issues in relation to victims of sexual assault in *Makanjuola*.[71] Similar considerations will apply in relation to child witnesses.

---

[71] [1995] 3 All E.R. 730.

11

REINFORCING SUSPECT EVIDENCE

I. Suspect Evidence and Miscarriages of Justice

The preceding chapters have examined the primacy that the common law gives to oral testimony despite its shortcomings, the rules regarding witness competence and the need to protect witnesses from the excesses of the adversarial trial. This chapter changes track to look at how the law deals with suspect and unreliable evidence, examining the development of the guidelines for judges as to when they should warn the jury about these matters. It also looks at some specific categories of evidence where such warnings are given, such as the defendant's lies and identification evidence.

One of the fundamental principles of justice is that the innocent must be protected from conviction and punishment. Miscarriages of justice in recent years have highlighted this. Following the release of the Guildford Four in October 1989, the Court of Appeal has quashed convictions in a number of highly publicised cases. Miscarriages of justice are not new and throughout its history, the criminal justice system has seen its fair share of disasters. At least Adolf Beck survived his imprisonment for fraud in 1907, having been wrongly identified by several victims. On release he was imprisoned a further time, again through misidentification. Analysis of such miscarriages has revealed no single cause but shows that different elements of the system itself have at times been at fault. The rules of evidence at trial should be central to preventing unjust convictions. In the courtroom, the protection of the innocent necessarily involves rules for all defendants, innocent or not. These are the rules regarding not only the allocation of the burden of proof, which carries with it the presumption of innocence and the principles enunciated in *Woolmington v DPP*,[1] but also the requirement for a sufficiency of reliable, relevant and admissible evidence.

The formal guarantees of that sufficiency are the rules on the standard of proof in criminal proceedings, *i.e.* that the weight of the evidence is such that the prosecution have proved their case beyond reasonable doubt. But the existence of miscarriages of justice show that judges and juries in serious cases involving murder and terrorist offences can wrongly evaluate the weight of the evidence. This can come about for various causes.

---

[1] [1935] A.C. 462.

S. Greer, "Miscarriages of Criminal Justice Reconsidered" [1994] 57 M.L.R. 58 at 72–73:

A 'mistaken' conviction occurs when the tribunal of fact honestly, and without impropriety, believes the prosecution evidence, either through misunderstanding the issues or because a defence which is in fact true seems to lack credibility. There are various sources of such convictions: vital evidence simply not coming to light, outside interference with vital witnesses resulting in either their failure to testify or perjured evidence at trial, mistaken or misleading directions by otherwise unbiased judges, joint trials in which an innocent defendant may be tarnished with the guilt of a co-defendant, mistaken identity, false confessions volunteered without police pressure, poor defence tactics, mistaken or deliberately false evidence by accomplices or other witnesses, and a failure on the part of jurors to understand the legal burden of proof or the issues involved in the trial. A jury or magistrate may be inclined to convict, for example, if presented with an entirely innocent but unconvincing defendant, who has had the opportunity to commit the offence, has been wrongly identified as the offender by a mistaken or dishonest witness, has no alibi and whose defence may amount to no more than a blank denial of the charge.

These risks have been recognised for many years and a variety of procedures have been developed in an attempt to deal with them, for example, the offence of perjury, the reliability tests which confessions must pass before being admitted in evidence, opportunities for the severance of trials, and the development of warnings about the dangers of relying upon uncorroborated accomplice evidence and about the care which must be taken with eyewitness testimony. But the adequacy of these arrangements needs constantly to be reviewed.

One of the key checks on the quality of evidence has been the common law rules on the corroboration of certain categories of evidence. Any decision based on information from a single source must always be open to question and this is especially so in criminal proceedings where any verdict of guilty must be 'beyond reasonable doubt'. Logically it is difficult to exclude doubt by relying on a single witness and procedurally, fairness to a suspect demands more than accusation from one person.

Fitzjames Stephen, General View of the Criminal Law (1st ed., Macmillan, 1863), p.249:

The circumstances may be such that there is no check on the witness and no power to obtain any further evidence on the subject. Under these circumstances juries may, and often do, acquit. They may very reasonably say we do not attach such credit to the oath of a single person of whom we know nothing, as to be willing to destroy another person on the strength of it.

Despite this, the rules requiring supporting evidence in English law are now few in number and the testimony of a single witness is sufficient to base a conviction or acquittal in criminal cases or a finding in a civil matter. There is no general rule that requires supporting evidence: that is, if there is evidence from Source A as to some fact in issue, there does not need to be further evidence from Source B that tends to confirm that fact. This can be contrasted to civil systems of law based on Roman law where there is a general requirement of corroboration, although perhaps in practice, there is less difference.[2]

C. Tapper, Cross on Evidence (7th edn, Butterworths, 1990), pp.224–225:

The history of this subject is not without interest, for one of the great differences between the modern English law of evidence and that prescribed by the canon or civil law, which usually applied the maxim 'testis unus testis nullus', consists in the absence of any general requirement of a plurality of witnesses. More than one oath helper was required when compurgation was among the standard methods of trial, so English law started with something like the requirements of a number of witnesses such as were demanded by the canon law under the influence of Roman law, although the compurgators were of course quite unlike the modern witness. The two systems diverged more or less completely when English jury trial began to assume its present form in the seventeenth century. Before that period, the jurors were themselves witnesses, rather than triers, of fact, so there was a sense in which it could be said that more than one witness was always necessary at a common law trial. It is of some significance that Coke maintained that more than one witness was necessary in proceedings without a jury as where the validity of challenges fell to be determined. When the jurors ceased to resemble the modern witness, some efforts to impose rules requiring two or more witnesses were made by statute; but provisions of this nature were never generalised, and they are now of no importance.

This chapter first examines the position with regard to supportive evidence in general and then considers the particular cases of the *Lucas* direction which is required where the prosecution rely on lies from the accused; the *Turnbull* direction and other safeguards in relation to identification evidence; and the puzzling lack of any analogous safeguards with regard to confessions.

II. CORROBORATION AND SUPPORTIVE EVIDENCE

The common law never developed a general rule requiring supporting evidence but it did recognise that there were situations where the evidence of a single witness was not sufficient. This may be because of the characteristics of the witness (where there is a motive for lying or the court distrusts their intellectual faculties); the nature of the evidence (such as identification evidence); the gravity of the complaint (such as rape). But there was no coherent principle and the courts and the legislature evolved an ad hoc series of common law and statutory rules that required the judge and jury to consider whether an item of evidence was supported by any other evidence. Formal rules developed as to what constituted sufficient supporting evidence which became technically known as *corroboration*. The rules about when and how corroboration was used were complex.[3] The basics were:

---

[2] I. MacPhail, "Safeguards in the Scottish Criminal Justice System" [1992] Crim.L.R. 144; J. Langbein, *Torture and the Law of Proof* (University of Chicago, 1977).

[3] Law Commission, *Corroboration of Evidence in Criminal Trials* Cm. 1620 (HMSO, 1991); Birch D., "Corroboration: Goodbye to all that?" [1995] Crim.L.R. 524.

1. The issue of corroboration was never put to the jury in common
    sense terms as "supportive evidence". The common law required
    that the corroborating evidence verified a material part of the
    testimony in need of corroboration and that it implicated the
    defendant. This was laid down in *Baskerville*,[4] where Lord Reading
    said that corroborative evidence is evidence ". . . which confirms in
    some material particulars not only the evidence that the crime has
    been committed but also that the prisoner committed it." Thus in a
    rape case, medical evidence confirming that the victim had had sex
    at the time of the alleged rape would not corroborate her testimony
    alleging rape because, in itself and in the absence of DNA, it does
    not confirm the identity of the man involved.
2. Corroborative evidence had to be independent. This meant that the
    evidence should emanate from a source other than the original
    witness. Thus under the corroboration rules, the evidence could not
    be, for example, a recent complaint of a victim in a sexual assault
    case[5] although the visible distress of the victim, independently
    observed might be.[6] Explaining such technicalities to the jury was
    never a simple task.
3. Corroboration could not come from the testimony of a witness
    whose evidence also required corroboration. A child could not
    corroborate another child. This was an equally complex rule.
4. Corroboration should be looked at in aggregate. Where there were
    several pieces of potentially corroborative evidence but the cor-
    roborative value of any single piece might be nil, the jury could be
    directed that the cumulative effect might be seen as constituting
    corroboration.[7]

Corroboration rules appear to embody substantial safeguards but a confused
jury will rarely come to a just result. In *Hester*,[8] Lord Diplock observed that
the ". . . complicated formulae about the concept of corroboration and the
respective functions of judge and jury are . . . unintelligible to the ordinary
laymen".[9] But there are underlying principles here that are of value—
evidence must be relevant to the particular issue to provide support; an item
of evidence from an independent source has enhanced probative value; triers
of fact should look at all the evidence in aggregate. These remain of
importance in analysing the facts.

Fortunately the technical rules about corroboration have been largely
eroded but some still have limited relevance. These can be illustrated by
examining the different categories of corroboration requirements.

[4] [1916–17] All E.R. Rep. 38.
[5] *Whitehead* [1929] 1 K.B. 99.
[6] *Chauhan* (1981) 73 Cr.App.R. 232; *Redpath* (1962) 46 Cr.App.R. 319.
[7] *Hills* (1987) 86 Cr.App.R. 26.
[8] [1972] 2 All E.R. 1020.
[9] See also Law Commission, *op.cit.*, para.2.9.

A. *Corroboration as a matter of law*

This is the situation where corroboration in the form of independent evidence is required as a matter of law. In other words, if there is no supporting evidence, the judge must direct an acquittal. These situations are all statutory crimes and in recent years the number has been steadily eroded by repeal.[10] The offences which still require the prosecution to adduce corroborative evidence are:

1. Speeding offences, under the Road Traffic Regulations Act 1984,

89.—(2) A person prosecuted for such an offence shall not be liable to be convicted solely on the evidence of one witness to the effect that, in the opinion of the witness, the person prosecuted was driving the vehicle at a speed exceeding the specified limit.

These conditions are met, for example, by the police officer's observation of the car and a contemporaneous reading of a speedometer or other measuring device or indeed by the opinions of two eyewitnesses.[11] In *Nicholas v Penny*,[12] it was held that the section did not require testimony from two witnesses nor did it require evidence that the speedometer was accurate. Incidentally, this latter point is another example of the rebuttable presumption that, in the absence of contrary evidence, mechanical devices are assumed to be operating properly.[13] In *Crossland v DPP*,[14] the opinion of an expert witness who bases his opinion of speed on the indications at the scene of the accident such as skid marks and damage to the vehicle, does not require corroboration under section 89.

2. Perjury under the Perjury Act 1911,

13. A person shall not be liable to be convicted of any offence against this Act, or of any offence declared by any other Act to be perjury or subornation of perjury, or to be punishable as perjury or subornation of perjury solely upon the evidence of one witness as to the falsity of any statement alleged to be false.

Perjury was originally an offence tried in Star Chamber, itself influenced by civil law methods of proof. In 1972, the Criminal Law Revision Committee recommended the retention of the corroboration requirement on the ground that if convictions for perjury were too easy, this might discourage witnesses from testifying.[15] However courts have put no great obstacles in the way of prosecutions for the offence:

---

[10] e.g. Family Law Reform Act 1987, s.17, removed the requirement of corroboration of the mother's testimony in affiliation cases; Criminal Justice Act 1988, s.34(1), removed the requirement of corroboration of unsworn evidence of children; Criminal Justice and Public Order Act 1994, s.33, removed the requirement of corroboration of offences of procuring women for sex.

[11] *Brighty v Pearson* [1938] 4 All E.R. 127.

[12] [1950] 2 All E.R. 89.

[13] But see *D.P.P. v Underwood, The Independent* June 23, 1997; see Ch.21 for further discussion of presumptions.

[14] [1988] 3 All E.R. 712.

[15] 11th Report (1972) Cmnd. 4991, paras 178 and 190.

Threlfall (1914) 10 Cr.App.R. 112 at 114:

The meaning is this: it used sometimes to be said that there must be two witnesses; this was a delusion; the evidence of one witness and a confession may be enough, and the section has been drafted so as to make this clear. One witness can prove that the person charged swore to certain statements, but more than the evidence of one witness is required to prove that the statements were false.

The accused's confession that the statement was false is evidence of its falsity. In *Peach*,[16] the defendant made a sworn statement to a treasure trove inquest that he had found Celtic torques under the floorboards but subsequently admitted to archaeologists he had found them at a farm. Although the appellant had confessed on only one occasion, there were two witnesses who testified to it and the Court of Appeal held that the requirements of s.13 were satisfied.

B. *Corroboration warnings as a matter of law*

Corroboration usually meant independent evidence but where that was not itself required, a lesser safeguard could apply, namely a corroboration warning. There were situations where this was required as a matter of law so that the trier of fact had to be warned of the dangers of convicting on uncorroborated evidence. In such cases, if no corroboration existed, the jury was still entitled to convict as long as they did so with full awareness of the risks of the course of action and presumably having concluded that the witness whose testimony needed corroboration could be relied on. But if a warning was not given, this would be good grounds for a successful appeal.

There were three situations where the common law required a corroboration warning to be given, the sworn testimony of children (removed by s.34 of the Criminal Justice Act 1988); the testimony of victims of sexual offences (removed by s.32(1)(b) of the Criminal Justice and Public Order Act 1994); and accomplices to the offence who were testifying on behalf of the prosecution (removed by s.32(1)(a) of the Criminal Justice and Public Order Act 1994). It is hard to argue for a mandatory warning for the testimony of a child or a rape victim but there is a strong argument that accomplice evidence is presumptively unreliable.

I.Dennis, "Corroboration Requirements Reconsidered" [1984] Crim.L.R. 316 at 322:

It is argued that an accomplice may lie for a number of reasons. He may try to exculpate himself or minimise his own part in an offence by exaggerating or

---

[16] [1990] 2 All E.R. 966.

fabricating the role of the accused. He may act out of spite or revenge, as where he believes himself to have been informed against by the accused. He may be suspected of purchasing immunity from prosecution or a lesser charge or more favourable prospects of early release by ensuring the conviction of others. It is also argued that the risk of the accused being convicted on perjured evidence is increased by the accomplice's apparent plausibility. The latter will usually be familiar with at least some details of the offence and will be able to report them accurately.

A counter argument is that accomplices who incriminate themselves at the same time as incriminating the defendant are presumably more to be trusted. But the rule had degenerated into a legalistic squabble about who was an accomplice.[17] The policy of the legislature was that there were many categories of potentially unreliable witnesses and identifying one or more as requiring mandatory warning was indiscriminate and illogical. The substantive question that the court should be asking is about the witness's motives in giving evidence and whether those motives are such as to make the testimony unreliable and in need of supporting evidence. Even with accomplices, the trier of fact is dealing essentially with credibility. Are lies by accomplices any more difficult to detect than false allegations by other witnesses? The approach needed was one that gave more discretion to the trial judge who was in a position to assess potential unreliability on a case by case basis.[18]

C. *Corroboration warnings as a matter of practice*

There are now no situations where the jury must be warned as a matter of law. But the judge still retains an inherent discretion to caution the jury. This is a matter of practice—on the facts of the particular case, it may be appropriate to warn the trier of fact of the dangers of convicting on the basis of evidence which is the main or sole evidence against the defendant and is potentially unreliable. If such a warning was not given, the Court of Appeal would not necessarily quash a conviction but might do so. Historically such warnings had to be considered in relation to accomplices who testify in their own defence but who implicate a co-accused, the uncorroborated evidence of a spouse especially where sexual misconduct was alleged, claims against a dead person's estate and children's testimony.

Furthermore, decisions such as *Beck*,[19] and *Spencer*,[20] led the courts firmly away from corroboration warnings. In *Spencer*, the defendants were nurses, charged under section 126 of the Mental Health Act 1959 with assaulting the witness–patients who were detained in Rampton, suffering from mental disorders and having committed serious offences themselves. The trial judge had warned the jury to approach the complainants' evidence with great caution but had not specifically directed them as to the dangers of convicting

---

[17] *Davies v D.P.P.* [1954] 1 All E.R. 507.
[18] This was the approach favoured by the Criminal Law Revision Committee, Eleventh Report, *op.cit.*, para.183.
[19] [1982] 1 All E.R. 807; also see *Prater* [1960] 1 All E.R. 298.
[20] [1986] 2 All E.R. 928.

without corroboration. The House of Lords held that even if mental patients were analogous to the established categories for corroboration warnings, these categories were not to be extended.

D. A Fresh Start

Parliament began the retreat from mandatory corroboration requirements. The Court of Appeal have not sought to fill the vacuum by developing discretionary warnings as a matter of practice in those areas formerly covered by the rules. Instead warnings about the reliability of certain witnesses will be given when the case demands them but couched in non-technical terms, without a mention of "corroboration" nor even necessarily a reference to supportive evidence. In *Makanjuola*,[21] the defendant was convicted of an indecent assault on a young female fellow worker. On appeal it was argued that the trial judge should in his discretion have given a full direction in accordance with established corroboration rules regardless of s.32 of the Criminal Justice and Public Order Act 1994. The appellant suggested that the rationale for the old common law was that complainants in sexual offences may lie or fantasise for unascertainable reasons or for no reason at all, that this rationale had not evaporated overnight and the traditional warning should continue.

Makanjuola [1995] 3 All E.R. 730 at 731j—733g, *per* Lord Taylor C.J.:

If that were right, Parliament would have enacted s.32(1) in vain; practice would continue unchanged. It is clear that the judge does have a discretion to warn the jury if he thinks it necessary, but the use of the word 'merely' in the subsection shows that Parliament does not envisage such a warning being given just because a witness complains of a sexual offence or is an alleged accomplice.

It is further submitted that if the judge does decide a warning is necessary, he should give the jury the full old-style direction on corroboration. That means using the phrase 'dangerous to convict on uncorroborated evidence', explaining the meaning of corroboration, identifying what evidence under the old rules is capable of being corroboration, what evidence is not so capable, and the respective roles of the judge and jury in this bipartite quest . . . It was, in our judgment, partly to escape from this tortuous exercise, which juries must have found more bewildering than illuminating, that Parliament enacted s.32.

Given that the requirement of a corroboration direction is abrogated in the terms of s.32(1), we have been invited to give guidance as to the circumstances in which, as a matter of discretion, a judge ought in summing up to a jury to urge caution in regard to a particular witness and the terms in which that should be done. The circumstances and evidence in criminal cases are infinitely variable and it is impossible to categorise how a judge should deal with them. But it is clear that to carry on giving 'discretionary' warnings generally and in the same terms as were previously obligatory would be contrary to the policy and purpose of the 1994 Act. Whether, as a matter

[21] [1995] 3 All E.R. 730.

of discretion, a judge should give any warning and if so its strength and terms must depend upon the content and manner of the witness's evidence, the circumstances of the case and the issues raised. The judge will often consider that no special warning is required at all. Where, however, the witness has been shown to be unreliable, he or she may consider it necessary to urge caution. In a more extreme case, if the witness is shown to have lied, to have made previous false complaints, or to bear the defendant some grudge, a stronger warning may be thought appropriate and the judge may suggest it would be wise to look for some supporting material before acting on the impugned witness's evidence. We stress that these observations are merely illustrative of some, not all, of the factors which judges may take into account in measuring where a witness stands in the scale of reliability and what response they should make at that level in their directions to the jury. We also stress that judges are not required to conform to any formula and this court would be slow to interfere with the exercise of discretion by a trial judge who has the advantage of assessing the manner of a witness's evidence as well as its content.

To summarise:

1. Section 32(1) abrogates the requirement to give a corroboration direction in respect of an alleged accomplice or a complainant of a sexual offence simply because the witness falls into one of those categories.

2. It is a matter for the judge's discretion what, if any, warning he considers appropriate in respect of such a witness, as indeed in respect of any other witness in whatever type of case. Whether he chooses to give a warning and in what terms will depend on the circumstances of the case, the issues raised and the content and quality of the witness's evidence.

3. In some cases, it may be appropriate for the judge to warn the jury to exercise caution before acting upon the unsupported evidence of a witness. This will not be so simply because the witness is a complainant of a sexual offence nor will it necessarily be so because a witness is alleged to be an accomplice. There will need to be an evidential basis for suggesting that the evidence of the witness may be unreliable. An evidential basis does not include mere suggestions by cross-examining counsel.

4. If any question arises as to whether the judge should give a special warning in respect of a witness, it is desirable that the question be resolved by discussion with counsel in the absence of the jury before final speeches.

5. Where a judge does decide to give some warning in respect of a witness, it will be appropriate to do so as part of the judge's review of the evidence and his comments as to how the jury should evaluate it rather than as a set-piece legal direction.

6. Where some warning is required, it will be for the judge to decide the strength and terms of the warning. It does not have to be invested with the whole florid regime of the old corroboration rules.

7. . . . . Attempts to re-impose the straitjacket of the old corroboration rules are strongly to be deprecated.

8. Finally, this court is disinclined to interfere with a trial judge's exercise of his discretion save in a case where that exercise is unreasonable in the *Wednesbury*[22] sense.

Makanjuola rejects any notion that warnings that were, before 1994, a matter of law should now routinely become a matter of practice. Where there is an evidential basis showing that any witness in whatever sort of case may be unreliable, the trial judge has a discretion to remind the jury of that fact and advise caution. Such a direction will not use terms such as corroboration. There is a continuum of warnings reflecting the degree of robustness that is required in the circumstances of the case. A simple word of caution may suffice or stronger terms may be needed: the judge may suggest that the jury would be wise to look for some supportive evidence. In *Jobe*,[23] the victim had

---

[22] *Associated Provincial Picture Houses Ltd v Wednesbury Corp.* [1947] 2 All E.R. 680.
[23] [2004] EWCA Crim 3155.

clearly lied in the witness box. The judge directed the jury, "It is all a matter for you, but if you were to conclude that she was lying . . ., then it would be wise for you to look for some supporting material before acting on her evidence . . ."

Under the *Makanjuola* judgment, both the judge's task in directing the jury and the jury's own consideration should be simpler. Where the judge gives a relatively robust direction, the jury might well be advised to look for material which would not be dissimilar to corroboration in earlier days. But the direction would be shorn of complexities. For example, a jury would not be prevented from concluding that a victim's credibility might be bolstered by a prompt complaint. Under the old rules, they would be told to ignore this as it is not an independent source—the testimony of the victim in court is supported by the victim's own words outside the court and did not amount to corroboration Under *Makanjuola*, the jury would be entitled to give the term 'supportive evidence' a wider compass.

The Court of Appeal has embraced this approach and recent caselaw shows that the problems surrounding corroboration belong in the past. The court has emphasised that there has to be an evidential foundation for believing that a witness is unreliable. The court is not to draw an inference of unreliability from the category of the witness but there must be evidence which relates to this individual. Lord Taylor envisaged an extreme case before warnings would be given—previous false complaints, grudges against the defendant or retraction of a complaint.[24] There has been intervention on appeal where the witness is inconsistent when testifying and is also inconsistent with testimony of other witnesses.[25]

Overall, the caselaw demonstrates that convictions are rarely quashed on the grounds of the lack of a *Makanjuola* direction. In *L and N*,[26] the accused were convicted of sexual abuse of a young family member, aged four at the start of the abuse which lasted nearly ten years. The age of the witness and the fact that it was a sex crime would have demanded a corroboration warning prior to 1994 but the trial judge did not give a *Makanjuola* direction and this was supported by the Court of Appeal who did not see this as the kind of case envisaged by Lord Taylor. There were issues relating to the reliability of the victim, but such issues almost invariably occur in these cases. There was no particular feature of this case that took the matter into a category to demand special attention and to demand that a warning should be given to the jury.

The Court of Appeal is very reluctant to interfere with the discretion of the trial judge—an illustration is *Gregory*,[27] a burglary case where the witness had been motivated to give evidence by the police in return for escaping with a caution for his participation in the crime. The decision not to warn the jury was a matter for judicial discretion and this had not been exercised unreasonably. In *Ely*,[28] the defendant was convicted of serial sexual abuse while

---

[24] *MJW* (unreported, February 17, 2000, CA).
[25] *Bradley* (unreported, December 20, 1995, CA); *Hempton* (unreported, January 24, 2000, CA).
[26] [2004] EWCA Crim 1414.
[27] Unreported, February 28, 2000, CA.
[28] [2005] EWCA Crim 3248.

working in a children's home. The accused was 77 years old and the acts had occurred over twenty years previously. The complainants in the most part had criminal records and were unreliable. The judge gave a very limited *Makanjuola* direction and again the Court of Appeal supported this, commenting that it was a matter for the judge's discretion what, if any, warning he considered appropriate, and that the trial judge's discretion had been properly exercised

Although the dismantling of the corroboration rules is in the main welcome, it should be emphasised that convictions which are based wholly or mainly on evidence from a single source should normally remain questionable. The 'single source' was not a factor mentioned by the Court of Appeal in *Makanjuola* as a reason for a warning to the jury. This was possibly because this might be construed as an invitation to trial judges to reintroduce the 'sexual complainants' rule by the backdoor since, all too often, such offences rely wholly or mainly on the victim.

To summarise the current position:

(a) corroborative evidence is still required for a few statutory offences as perjury and speeding;
(b) corroboration warnings are no longer required as a matter of law for any offence; and
(c) where corroboration warnings were routinely considered as a matter of practice will now be subsumed under the *Makanjuola* judgment. Where there is an evidence showing that a witness may be unreliable, the trial judge has a discretion to remind the jury of that fact and advise caution

There are two categories of evidence which require specific directions: where the prosecution rely on lies made by the defendant and where they rely on identification evidence.

III. Lies by the Defendant: the *Lucas* Direction

The actions and statements of the defendant are frequently used by the prosecution as a means of strengthening the Crown case. This includes incriminating statements made by the accused; the inferences that are allowed to be drawn from the defendant's silence at interview or in court[29]; failures to supply intimate samples[30]; or failure to submit a defence statement.[31] These are discussed elsewhere. There are also the situations where the defendant is shown to have lied to the police or while testifying.

The defendant's lies can strengthen the prosecution case but lies are not necessarily indicative of guilt. In *Broadhurst*,[32] Lord Devlin pointed out that

[29] Criminal Justice and Public Order Act 1994. ss.34–37 see Ch.4.
[30] Police and Criminal Evidence Act 1984, s.62(10) see Ch.4.
[31] Criminal Procedure and Investigations Act 1996, s.5 as amended by the Criminal Justice Act 2003—see Ch.6.
[32] [1964] A.C. 441.

there were many powerful motives for lying, both in and out of court, such as shame or terror. In *Richens*,[33] the accused alleged that he had lied to the police to ensure both that his girlfriend had left the country and also that his parents had a happy Christmas before he confessed. The courts have sought to warn the jury from leaping to the 'natural' conclusion that lying means guilt. In *Lucas*,[34] an accomplice testified against the accused charged with importing drugs. The defendant gave evidence which was challenged as untrue. The trial judge suggested to the jury that corroboration could be found in the evidence of the defendant and that if the jury concluded that she had lied to them, that in itself could be corroborative of the accomplice's evidence. The Court of Appeal held that merely preferring the accomplice's testimony to that of the accused was not sufficient.

Lucas [1981] 2 All E.R. 1008 at 1011 e.g., *per* Lord Lane C.J.:

To be capable of amounting to corroboration the lie told out of court must first of all be deliberate. Secondly it must relate to a material issue. Thirdly the motive for the lie must be a realisation of guilt and a fear of the truth. The jury should in appropriate cases be reminded that people sometimes lie, for example, in an attempt to bolster up a just cause, or out of shame or out of a wish to conceal disgraceful behaviour from their family. Fourthly the statement must be clearly shown to be a lie by evidence other than that of the accomplice who is to be corroborated, that is to say by admission or by evidence from an independent witness.

As a matter of good sense it is difficult to see why, subject to the same safeguards, lies proved to have been told in court by a defendant should not equally be capable of providing corroboration.

The issue in *Lucas* was about using the lie as corroboration. As discussed earlier, this is no longer a relevant issue. But the judgment demonstrates, first, that the lies themselves can be relied on as prosecution evidence. Secondly, the judge must caution the jury about the dangers of placing too much probative weight on such lies. This approach was approved by the Court of Appeal in *Goodway*[35] and *Burge*.[36]

Burge [1996] Cr.App.R. 163 at 173–174, *per* Kennedy L.J.:

. . . it may be helpful if we conclude by summarising the circumstances in which, in our judgment, a Lucas direction is usually required. There are four such circumstances but they may overlap:
1. Where the defence relies on an alibi.

---

[33] [1993] 4 All E.R. 877.
[34] [1981] 2 All E.R. 1008.
[35] [1993] 4 All E.R. 894.
[36] [1996] Cr.App.R. 163.

2. Where the judge considers it desirable or necessary to suggest that the jury should look for support or corroboration of one piece of evidence from other evidence in the case, and amongst that other evidence draws attention to lies told, or allegedly told, by the defendant.

3. Where the prosecution seek to show that something said, either in or out of the court, in relation to a separate and distinct issue was a lie, and to rely on that lie as evidence of guilt in relation to the charge which is sought to be proved.

4. Where although the prosecution have not adopted the approach to which we have just referred, the judge reasonably envisages that there is a real danger that the jury may do so.

If a Lucas direction is given where there is no need for such a direction (as in the normal case where there is a straight conflict of evidence), it will add complexity and do more harm than good. Therefore, in our judgement, a judge would be wise always, before speeches and summing up in circumstance number 4, and perhaps also in other circumstances, to consider with counsel whether, in the instant case, such a direction is in fact required, and, if, so how it should be formulated. If the matter is dealt with in that way, this Court will be very slow to interfere with the exercise of the judge's discretion. Further, the judge should, of course, be assisted by counsel in identifying cases where a direction is called for. In particular, this Court is unlikely to be persuaded, in cases allegedly falling under number 4 above, that there was a real danger that the jury would treat a particular lie as evidence of guilt if defence counsel at the trial has not alerted the judge to that danger and asked him to consider whether a direction should be given to meet it. The direction should, if given, so far as possible, be tailored to the circumstances of the case, but it will normally be sufficient if it makes the two basic points:

1. that the lie must be admitted or proved beyond reasonable doubt, and
2. that the mere fact that the defendant lied is not in itself evidence of guilt since defendants may lie for innocent reasons, so only if the jury is sure that the defendant did not lie for an innocent reason can a lie support the prosecution case.

A *Lucas* direction should be given whenever there are clear lies made by the accused which are relied upon by the prosecution or which may be used by the jury. The jury must be made aware that they must not automatically conclude that 'telling lies equals guilt'. If the prosecution relies on the lie[37] or makes much of trivial untruths, a *Lucas* direction is plainly called for.[38] But if the prosecution do not rely on the lies, this may be unnecessary unless there is the prospect of the jury focusing on the issue.[39] The *Lucas* warning is unnecessary where the purpose of proving the lie is merely to undermine the defendant's credibility.[40]

There has to be a specific lie which the prosecution rely on. Defendants often deny their guilt in the witness box. The Crown often alleges that the defendant has lied. But this does not call for a *Lucas* direction. In *Edwards*,[41] Potter L.J. explained this.

Edwards [2004] EWCA Crim 2102, *per* Potter L.J.:

60 . . . It seems to us that this is a case where there was essentially no distinction between the issue of guilt and the issue of lies, in the sense that it was a case where

[37] *Nash* [2004] EWCA Crim 164.
[38] *Benedetto* [2003] UKPC 27.
[39] *Rahming* [2002] UKPC 23.
[40] *Josephine Smith* [1995] Crim.L.R. 305.
[41] [2004] EWCA Crim 2102.

evidence of witnesses for the Crown on essential matters had to be established as true in order to justify a finding of guilt, such evidence being in direct and irreconcilable conflict with the evidence for the defence. As made clear in *Harron*[42] . . . , in such a case the jury, as a matter of logic and common sense, have to decide whether the witnesses for the Crown are telling the truth and a conclusion that they are will necessarily involve a conclusion that the accused is lying. Thus the issue of lies is not a matter which the jury have to take into account separately from the central issue in the case. This was not a case where, on some collateral matter, there had been some change in evidence or the account of the defendant.

Sometimes the lie can be irrelevant to any issue in the case and the judge should make this clear—in *Gordon*,[43] the defence on a homicide charge was self-defence and the prosecution sought to undermine that by showing that the accused had originally lied about the possession of the murder weapon. While the denial was obviously a lie, it had no relevance to the subsequent plea of self-defence.

IV Eyewitness Identification and the *Turnbull* direction

In this chapter, it has been suggested that judges should take great care when a conviction would be based wholly or mainly upon evidence from a single source. This is particularly the case with evidence from a single eyewitness: the reliability of this has been discussed earlier.[44] The police interview suspects, search persons, vehicles and places for evidence of crime but a major source is the eyewitness and one of the most common aspects of eyewitness testimony is the identification of suspects. Evidence of identification is direct evidence rather than circumstantial evidence and is treated in court as possessing considerable probative weight, although, as with the confession, its probative value can be over-estimated. The opinion of a juror whether an eyewitness has made an accurate identification is critical and often is sufficient to decide the case since, if the witness is correct, the defendant is guilty. It is important to know how good people are at perception and recall, how good we are at assessing the accuracy of our own memory and what criteria we use in assessing others' eyewitness accounts.

A. *Reliability of identification evidence*

Identification evidence can be very strong, especially when it is recognition evidence of a person already known to the witness. This is commonly the case with offences of personal violence. But the identification of strangers, perhaps glimpsed for a moment at the scene of a crime can be much weaker, depending upon a range of factors which may not be taken into account at

---

[42] [1996] 2 Cr.App.R. 457.
[43] [1995] Crim.L.R. 306.
[44] Ch.9.

trial.[45] Unfortunately the jury's and the judge's perception of the weight of identification evidence is less likely to be affected by "scientific" factors (duration, range, visibility) than by the credence that is given to the witness (the witness's demeanour, the coherence of the testimony). The prejudicial effect of such testimony is strong since it is hard to doubt the impartial witness who clearly identifies the accused. Yet as psychological research has suggested, the odds on the witness being right are at best evens, odds which are difficult to square with proof "beyond reasonable doubt". In the notorious Sacco and Vanzetti case in the USA,[46] a prosecution witness claimed to have seen Sacco riding in a car which passed by her at a distance no closer than 60 feet and which she had in view for no more than the time it took for the car to travel fifty or sixty feet. Yet her identification was positive and detailed.

P.M. Wall. Eyewitness Identification of Criminal Cases (Springfield, 1965), p.20:

Q. Can you describe him to these gentlemen here?

A. Yes sir. He was a man that I should say was slightly taller than I am. He weighed possibly from 140 to 150 pounds. he was muscular— he was an active looking man. I noticed particularly the left hand was a good-sized hand, a hand that denoted strength or a shoulder that . . .

Q. So that the hand you said you saw where?

A. The left hand, that was placed..on the back of the front seat. He had a gray, what I thought was a shirt—had a grayish, like navy color, and the face was what we would call clear-cut, clean-cut face. Through here [indicating] was a little narrow, just a little narrow. The forehead was high. The hair was brushed back and it was between, I should think, two inches and two-and-one-half inches in length and had dark eyebrows, but the complexion was a white, a peculiar white that looked greenish.[47]

Whether this feat of perception and recall was possible is dubious. Witnesses have differential abilities of perception, retention and recall. These abilities are affected by event factors such as the amount of time available, the proximity to the event as well as stress experienced by the witness. The accuracy of recall will depend on the environment in which a witness is interviewed, on what questions are asked and how they are asked.

E.Loftus Eyewitness Testimory (Harvard, 1996), pp.108–109:

The conditions prevailing at the time information is retrieved from memory are critically important in determining the accuracy and completeness of an eyewitness

---

[45] B. Clifford: "The Relevance of Psychological Investigation to Legal Issues in Testimony and Identification" [1979] Crim.L.R. 153; J. Jackson: "The Insufficiency of Identification Evidence Based on Personal Impression" [1986] Crim.L.R. 203; G. Wells and E. Loftus (eds.), *Eyewitness Testimony* (Cambridge, 1984).

[46] There is a summary in E. Loftus, *Eyewitness Testimony* (Harvard, 1996), Ch.1.

[47] P.M. Wall *Eyewitness Identification of Criminal Cases* (Springfield, 1965) cited in Loftus E., above, p.18.

account. Some of the more important factors that operate during this stage are whether the retrieval environment is changed, what types of question are used to obtain information, how these questions are worded and who is asking them. Confidence in one's memory and the accuracy of that memory do not always go hand in hand; people are often confident and right, but they can also be confident and wrong . . . .

Most people, including eyewitnesses, are motivated by a desire to be correct, to be observant, and to avoid looking foolish. People want to give an answer, to be helpful, and many will do this at the risk of being incorrect. People want to see crimes solved and justice done, and this desire may motivate them to volunteer more than is warranted by their meager memory. The line between valid retrieval and unconscious fabrication is easily crossed.

Furthermore a juror's assessment of a witness is often related to factors, such as confidence and demeanour, that do not necessarily predict accuracy.

There is less concern when identification evidence is part of a broader prosecution case, where other items of evidence implicate the accused. But convictions are often based wholly or mainly on identification evidence. Figures in this area are hard to come by. The Devlin Report[48] suggested that in 1973, there were 2,116 identity parades, resulting in identifications in 45 per cent. 850 people were prosecuted, of whom 82 per cent were convicted. But 347 people were prosecuted and 258 convicted *solely or mainly* on identification evidence. Convictions on such evidence still occur today and there remains a risk of a miscarriage of justice in such cases, despite the safeguards discussed below.

There have been many notorious cases of miscarriages of justice as a result of misidentification—the most famous of these was in the early years of the 20th century when 12 women wrongly identified Adolf Beck.[49] The Devlin Committee itself was set up after the release of Luke Dougherty who was convicted of shoplifting.[50] Although Dougherty had been on a coach trip at the time and had a cast-iron alibi, he had only called two witnesses at his trial, his girlfriend and another friend who had previous convictions. The jury did not believe them and convicted. The initial appeal was rejected and it was only on a referral back to the Court of Appeal by the Home Secretary that additional alibi witnesses were heard. More recently John McGranaghan was sentenced to life imprisonment for rape after three women identified him. Routine scientific analysis of the semen stains would have proved that he could not possibly have committed those offences but he served ten years' imprisonment before the conviction was quashed.[51]

More sophisticated safeguards have developed over the past twenty years—these can exist either at the point of investigation (regulating the manner in which the police gather identification evidence) or at the point of trial (regulating the admissibility of identification evidence).

[48] Report to the Secretary of State for the Home Department of the Departmental Committee on Evidence of Identification in Criminal Cases, HC 338(1976).
[49] Glanville Williams: "Evidence of Identification" [1976] Crim.L.R. 407 gives several other examples as does the organisation: www.innocent.org.uk.
[50] Devlin Report, above, Ch.2—also discussed is the case of Laszlo Virag was convicted of stealing from parking meters and using a firearm while trying to escape police officers. Despite his alibi and other contradictions, he was wrongly identified by eight witnesses.
[51] B. Woffinden, *Hanratty: The Final Verdict* (1997) at App.A.

B. *Safeguards at point of investigation*

Properly regulated identification procedures provide both substantial safeguards for the suspect and also persuasive evidence for the Crown. Initially there were few controls at the point of investigation but the Home Office issued a 1978 circular to police forces tightening up procedures in identification parades. In 1981, the Report of the Royal Commission called for such procedures to be made statutory[52] but instead Code of Practice D was promulgated under the Police and Criminal Evidence Act 1984. Although not mandatory, the courts have taken a robust line with police improprieties in obtaining identification evidence. The Court of Appeal has excluded identification evidence in such circumstances and held that the Code was to be observed and not varied at the will of the police.[53] The current Code was brought into effect in December 2005.

A record of the initial description given by the witness must be made before any other means of identification under the Code takes place.[54] This description is disclosable to the defence prior to any subsequent trial.[55] No officer involved in the investigation may take part in these procedures, although they can consult with the identification officer as to the most appropriate procedure. The Code then provides for the following cases.

1. Where the suspect's identity is not known. Witnesses may be taken to neighbourhoods to attempt to identify suspects. Some basic safeguards include ensuring that the witness's attention is not directed to any individual as well as keeping witnesses apart. Further, witnesses can be shown photographs and composites but not where the suspect is known to the police.[56] In *Gornall*,[57] the householder disturbed burglars who fled to a nearby house. The police found twin brothers there and brought them to the witness who identified one of them. There was no breach of the Code—until the witness identified the defendant, there was no suspect.

2. Where the suspect is known and available. An identification procedure is mandatory where there is a witness who has identified a suspect or who feels that they are able to identify a suspect.[58] The Code reflects the approach taken by the House of Lords in *Forbes*[59] that there is a mandatory duty on the police to hold a parade wherever the suspect disputed the identification. This was the case even where there has been an unequivocal identification or

---

[52] Royal Commission on Criminal Procedure: Report (1981) Cmnd. 8092. para.3.138.
[53] *Quinn* [1995] Crim.L.R. 56.
[54] Code D. para.3.1.
[55] *Fergus* (1993) 98 Cr.App.R. 313.
[56] Code D. paras 3.2, 3.3 and Annex E.
[57] Unreported, March 3, 2005, CA.
[58] *ibid.* para.3.12.
[59] [2001] 1 All E.R. 686 overruling *Popat* [2000] 2 Cr.App.R. 208.

where there was difficulty in arranging a parade.[60] The police could not circumvent the requirements. The court also stressed that breaches of Code D does not lead to automatic exclusion of the identification evidence—the trial court had to consider the fairness of the proceedings as a whole.

At the time of *Forbes*, the main technique was the identification parade. Under the current Code D, the police have a range of identification procedures. The methods that may be used are:

    (a) a video identification;
    (b) an identification parade;
    (c) a group identification; or
    (d) a confrontation.

The video identification should be initially offered to the suspect unless it is more practicable and suitable to use a parade or group identification. The suspect can object and argue that another procedure should be used. The identification officer can arrange an alternative but can insist on the initial procedure being used. Reasons for this must be recorded but there is no requirement for the suspect to consent. The suspect is warned that if they do not take part in the procedure, that procedure may still go ahead and the police may also use covert video identification or covert group identification.[61]

There is some discretion on the police not to hold a procedure where it would serve no useful purpose, for example where the suspect is well known to a witness who saw them commit the crime.[62] In *R v D.P.P.*,[63] measures were taken to hold a video identification but some of the accused were unable to attend by which time the trial date had arrived. The witness was allowed to testify that the defendants were known to him by name and that he had seen them committing the offence. The trial court acted within its discretion, despite the lack of formal identification procedures. The fact that this was evidence of recognition rather than identification was significant.

But this qualification is limited—normally a prior identification by a witness does not mean that the police are exempted from holding a subsequent identification procedure. In *Brown*,[64] the victim of a robbery toured the area in a police car immediately after the attack and picked out the defendant. No parade was held but the Court of Appeal felt that the Code was mandatory and that a parade was not necessarily otiose. Once a suspect is in a police station, Code D applies and the police cannot decide simply to dispense with an identification procedure. In *Harris*,[65] the evidence was alleged to be recognition but that was disputed by the defendant. Potter L.J. emphasised the role of formal identification procedures.

---

[60] *Jamel* [1993] Crim.L.R. 52; *Campbell and Marshall* [1993] Crim.L.R. 47; *Ladlow* [1989] Crim.L.R. 21; *Gaynor* [1988] Crim.L.R. 242.

[61] Code D, para.3.17.

[62] *ibid.*, para.3.12; *Rogers* [1993] Crim.L.R. 386.

[63] [2003] EWHC 3074 (Admin).

[64] *Davies* [2004] EWCA Crim 252; *Hassan* [2004] EWCA Crim 1478—no parade necessary where identification was by clothing rather than facial features.

[65] [1991] Crim.L.R. 368.

Harris [1992] R.T.R. 270, *per* Potter L.J.:

26. It seems to us that, prima facie at least, the modified Code did require the holding of an identification parade. . . . The holding of an identification parade (if practicable) is mandatory where the suspect is known and available to the police and the suspect disputes identification unless in all the circumstances it would serve no useful purpose in proving or disproving whether the suspect was involved in committing the offence . . . Although the decision in Forbes applied to the unmodified Code and identity parades, its reasoning is equally applicable to mandatory identification procedures. An identification procedure must be held if (a) the police have sufficient information to justify the arrest of a particular person for suspected involvement in an offence and (b) an eye witness has identified or may be able to identify that person and (c) the suspect disputes his identification as a person involved in the commission of that offence.

3. Where the suspect is known but is not available.   If images are available, the identification officer can make arrangements to carry out a video identification—this can also be done using still images. There might be the possibility of group identification but covert activity should be strictly limited to that necessary to test the witness's ability to identify the suspect. Confrontation is also an option.[67]

4. Identification procedures

(i) *Video identification*

Where the police propose to arrange an identification procedure, the suspect is served with a written notice explaining the procedure and his rights and entitlements. With a video identification, a moving image of the suspect will be taken. A still image will also be made and stored. A computer search will provide other images that resemble the suspect and the identification officer will select eight other people who, as far as possible, resemble the suspect. These images are placed on a CD which should be shown to the suspect and lawyer before it is shown to any witness and any objections, if reasonable, should be addressed. However in *Middleton*,[68] the judge admitted the identification evidence even though neither the defendant nor his solicitor had seen the video before the witness viewed it. The court held that the images complied with the Code and that there was no unfettered right to object. The suspect's lawyer should be present when it is shown to the witness. Best practice is for the viewing procedure, of the witness viewing the images and the images themselves, to be video–taped and for the identification officer to record key events in the process such as the date of viewing, the service of first descriptions and whether the witness, prior to viewing, has seen any press releases about the case. These conditions are outlined in

---

[67] Code D, paras 3.21–23.
[68] Unreported, March 11, 2005, CA.

Annex A to Code D—a breach may result in the evidence being excluded. In *Marcus*,[69] the officer arranged for a video with masked faces as there were too few images resembling the defendant. Unknown to the defendant, he also arranged a video with the masks removed which were shown to the witness. This extraordinary process was condemned as a deliberate device to evade the provisions of Code D.

(ii) *Identity parades*

Where identification is disputed[70] or where the police feel it would be useful, the suspect shall initially be offered a video identification. Where this is not practicable or suitable, a parade may be offered. This in turn may not be practicable because of the unusual appearance of the suspect or for some other reason, such as the suspect's refusal to participate.

Identity parades have been in common use throughout this century. It was and remains a voluntary system and if the suspect chooses not to take part or to disrupt it (perhaps by refusing to wear some item of clothing or to speak certain words), there are no sanctions.[71] An identification procedure must be conducted by a uniformed officer, inspector or above, not concerned with the case.[72] Suspects must be told of their rights, for example to legal advice or not to participate.[73] Under Annex B, the process must be documented—the parade has to be photographed or videoed. Everything said or done should take place in the presence or hearing of the accused but where the witness is behind a screen, a representative of the suspect must be able to see and hear everything. If there is no such representative, everything relevant should be recorded on video.

There should be a minimum of eight others on the parade.[74] The Code requires that these resemble the suspect as far as possible.[75] There may be a discrepancy between the suspect's appearance and the eyewitness's initial description—in such cases, should the other members of the parade resemble that description rather than the suspect? The places are numbered and if the witness makes a positive identification, it is by number. Suspects are able to make objections to the arrangements and such objections should be met, if practicable. They are allowed to stand where they like and to change position. The triers of fact will be in a position to assess the fairness of the composition of the parade for themselves because of the requirement that the line-up be photographed or videoed.

---

[69] [2004] EWCA Crim 3387.

[70] Even where the witnesses claims to be acquainted with the suspect and thus to recognise rather than to identify—*Conway* [1990] Crim.L.R. 402.

[71] Although there is some authority that the judge can comment on the fact that the suspect has refused to take part in a parade, drawing on analogy from *Robert William Smith* (1985) 81 Cr. App. R 286. It would appear that in the USA, the suspect can be forced to do this—*US v Wade* (1967) 388 U.S. 218.

[72] Code D, para.3.11 although under para.2.21 this can be delegated to lower ranks or civilians as long as there is effective supervision.

[73] *ibid.* 3.17.

[74] Code D, Annex B, para.9—a minimum of 12 is required if there are 2 suspects of similar appearance. Normally separate parades should be held for each suspect.

[75] B. Clifford, "The Relevance of Psychological Investigation to Legal Issues in Testimony and Identification" [1979] Crim.L.R. 153.

Witnesses should not be shown or reminded of their initial written description or shown photos or other descriptions prior to the parade and should be isolated from other witnesses.[76] A further source of error might be news coverage and after the procedure, witnesses are asked whether they have seen any video films or photographs that might have been released to the news media by the police. Witnesses should be encouraged to look at each member of the parade at least twice and to identify by number. The witness can ask for particular clothing to be worn, gestures to be made or words to be spoken.

A failure to hold a parade or breaches of the Code of Practice can lead to the identification evidence being excluded under s.78 of the Police and Criminal Evidence Act 1984 on the grounds that its inclusion will have an adverse effect on the fairness of the proceedings. The Code is not to be varied at the will of the police.[77] In *Graham*,[78] the accused agreed to attend a parade but none was arranged although it was practicable to do so. Since the jury should have been warned that the identification had taken place without a parade, the appeal was allowed. But the court must consider whether the alleged defects in the identification process are sufficiently established to cause the fairness of the process and therefore of the trial itself to be in doubt.[79]

Even where the difficulties of holding parades are considerable, they may still be required. In *Gaynor*,[80] the suspect asked for a parade to be held but the police decided (wrongly in the court's opinion) that it was impracticable. Difficulty in finding volunteers for a parade does not make it impracticable unless the suspect's appearance is the reason for that difficulty.[81]

(iii) *Group identifications*

These may take place with the suspect's consent or covertly. It is a form of identification that is seen as subordinate to a parade or video identification. Those forms may be impracticable or the group method may be more satisfactory than a parade, perhaps because of the witness's fear. Group identification takes place where the suspect is viewed by a witness amongst an informal group of people.[82] Many of the conditions under which group identification takes place replicate the safeguards for identity parades so that the officer in charge must give notice to suspects, *inter alia*, of its purpose, how it will be carried out, of their rights as well as warning then that a refusal to take part or any significant alteration of appearance can be given in evidence at trial. Similarly any initial description by a witness must be recorded and officers who escort witnesses to the identification scene must not discuss the case or reveal whether any other witness has made an

---

[76] Code D, Annex B, para.14.
[77] *Quinn* above.
[78] [1994] Crim.L.R. 212; *Conway* [1990] Crim.L.R. 402.
[79] *Ebanks* [2006] UKPC 6.
[80] [1988] Crim.L.R. 242.
[81] *Jamel* above.
[82] Code D, Annex C.

identification. Again witnesses are asked whether they have seen any video films or photographs that might have been released to the news media by the police.

The scene itself should be photographed or videoed where possible. The place where the group identification is held should be one where other people are passing by or waiting around informally so that the suspect can join them. The place for the identification should not be in a police station unless this is dictated by reasons of safety or security. Annex C gives examples of escalators, shopping centres or railway or bus stations. Such groups might be mobile (walking through a shopping mall) or stationary (in a bus queue). In either situation the suspect is allowed flexibility in joining the group or taking up position although unreasonable delay might be regarded as a refusal to co-operate. Anything done or said to or by the witness should be in the presence or hearing of the suspect's solicitor or friend. Witnesses should point out any person they think they saw at the earlier, relevant, occasion. If practicable, the officer in charge should arrange for a closer look and ask the witness if they can make a positive identification.

It is possible for group identifications to be held covertly, without the suspect's consent. In such situations the identification necessarily takes place without the knowledge of the suspect who thus has no right to have a solicitor or friend present. The other provisions of Annex C should be adhered to.

(iv) *Confrontation*

As a last resort, when no other method of identification is practicable, the suspect can be confronted by the witness.[83] Before the confrontation, the suspect and their lawyer is provided with details of the first description given by the witness to the police. Any material released to the media by the police should also be provided, if this is practicable. The confrontation will be in a police station, possibly in a room equipped with a screen although this may only be used when a representative of the suspect is present or where the confrontation is recorded on video. The suspect shall be confronted by the witness who is asked 'Is this the person?' Identification evidence obtained from a confrontation in the precincts of the trial court should not be admitted even when this takes place at the behest of the accused.[84]

(v) *Dock Identification*

In 1976, the Devlin Report recommended[85] that the discretion of the trial judge to admit dock identification evidence should be regulated by statute. This has not happened but dock identification, that is, identification at the trial itself without any preceding method of identification, is normally not admissible.[86] However there are exceptions—in *Lydiate*,[87] the co-defendant

---

[83] The procedures are detailed in Annex D to Code D.
[84] *Joseph* [1994] Crim.L.R. 48.
[85] Ch.8.7.
[86] *Eatough* [1989] Crim.L.R. 289; *R. v Horsham Justices Ex p. Bukhari* (1982) 74 Cr.App.R. 291.
[87] [2004] EWCA Crim 245.

testified to the accused's presence at the scene. Where the case is one of recognition of someone well known to the eyewitness, dock identification is not necessarily unfair. In *Holland v HM Advocate*,[88] the Privy Council considered whether it was necessarily in breach of Art.6 requirements. The dock identification can be criticised because it lacks the safeguards that are offered by an identification process and also puts the accused in a position in the dock which increases the risk of a wrong identification. Certainly it casts doubts upon the fairness and accuracy of the identification. But it was not inadmissible per se: the trial court should consider whether admitting the evidence would result in the accused not having a fair trial. This involved reviewing all the circumstances of the particular case, considering such matters as the ability to challenge the evidence and any directions given by the judge to the jury.

C. *Safeguards at the trial*

The safeguards at trial are the conditions imposed before identification evidence is admissible. The Devlin Committee considered a range of possible approaches:

a) that there should be no conviction based solely or mainly on identification evidence; supporting evidence, emanating from an independent source and linking the accused to the crime, should be a requirement; or

b) that the jury should be warned that conviction based solely or mainly on identification evidence is dangerous and that they should look for supporting evidence. It would not be a bar to conviction if none were found; or

c) the Devlin Report's preferred option was that there should be legislation for a special warning which explained to the jury that identification alone did not comprise probable cause for a conviction unless there were special circumstances, for instance, familiarity, where the accused was a member of a small group, one of whom had committed the crime or where the defendant had failed to counter evidence with his own story.

There was no legislation as a result of the Devlin Report. Instead the significant controls at the point of trial were introduced by the Court of Appeal's decision in *Turnbull*.[89] The court was against any rule which prevented convictions from being based on identification alone and argued that the crucial element was the quality of that identification.

Turnbull [1976] 3 All E.R. 549 at 551j–552e, *per* Lord Widgery C.J.:

First, whenever the case against an accused depends wholly or substantially on the correctness of one or more identifications of the accused which the defence allege to be

---

[88] (2005) H.R.L.R. 25.
[89] [1976] 3 All E.R. 549.

mistaken, the judge should warn the jury of the special need for caution before convicting the accused in reliance on the correctness of the identification or identifications. In addition he should instruct them as to the reason for the need for such a warning and should make some reference to the possibility that a mistaken witness can be a convincing one and that a number of such witnesses can all be mistaken. Provided this is done in clear terms the judge need not use any particular form of words.

Secondly, the judge should direct the jury to examine closely the circumstances in which the identification by each witness came to be made. How long did the witness have the accused under observation? At what distance? In what light? Was the observation impeded in any way, as for example by passing traffic or a press of people? Had the witness ever seen the accused before? How often? If only occasionally, had he any special reason for remembering the act? How long elapsed between the original observation and the subsequent identification to the police? Was there any material discrepancy between the description of the accused given to the police by the witness when first seen by them and his actual appearance? If in any case, whether it is being dealt with summarily or on indictment, the prosecution have reason to believe that there is such a material discrepancy they should supply the accused or his legal advisers with particulars of the description the police were first given. In all cases if the accused asks to be given particulars of such descriptions, the prosecution should supply them. Finally, he should remind the jury of any specific weaknesses which had appeared in the identification evidence. Recognition may be more reliable than identification of a stranger; but, even when the witness is purporting to recognise someone whom he knows, the jury should be reminded that mistakes in recognition of close relatives and friends are sometimes made.

All these matters go to the quality of the identification evidence. If the quality is good and remains good at the close of the accused's case, the danger of a mistaken identification is lessened; but the poorer the quality, the greater the danger . . .

This judgment was one of the first nails in the coffin of corroboration. Cases such as Luke Dougherty had demonstrated that miscarriages of justice might result from mis-identification and yet Lord Widgery considered that the jury could be left to assess the value of the evidence with a warning on the hazards of convicting wholly or mainly on identification evidence accompanied by instructions to consider in detail the circumstances of the identification. His opinion was that to require corroboration would be an 'affront to justice' in situations such as a kidnapping where the only significant evidence was the identification of the kidnapper by the victim.

But a *Turnbull* direction is not merely a general admonition, mentioning the general circumstances mentioned in the judgment. The full force of the *Turnbull* direction must be conveyed stressing that the need for special caution is rooted in the courts' actual experience of miscarriages of justice.[90] It requires specific attention to the facts, tailoring the summing up so that the strengths and weaknesses of the identification could be clearly appreciated. The trial judge must draw to the jury's attention any feature that might undermine the identification.[91] The Privy Council in *Langford v State*[92] approved the comments of Ibrahim J. in *Fuller v State*.[93]

---

[90] *Nash* [2004] EWCA Crim 2696, para.8 *per* Hedley J. The judgment also criticises the Judicial Studies Board specimen direction as the 'briefest permissible summary' of the dangers.
[91] *Stanton* [2004] EWCA Crim 490.
[92] [2005] UKPC 20.
[93] [1995] 52 W.I.R. 424 at 433: Court of Appeal of Trinidad and Tobago.

Fuller v State (1995) 52 WIR 424 at 433, *per* Lord Ibrahim J.A.:

We are concerned about the repeated failures of trial judges to instruct juries properly on the Turnbull principles when they deal with the issue of identification. Great care should be taken in identifying to the jury all the relevant criteria. Each factor or question should be separately identified and when a factor is identified all the evidence in relation thereto should be drawn to the jury's attention to enable them not only to understand the evidence properly but also to make a true and proper determination of the issues in question. This must be done before the trial judge goes on to deal with another factor. It is not sufficient merely to read to them the factors set out in Turnbull's case and at a later time to read to them the evidence of the witnesses. That is not a proper summing-up. The jury have heard all the evidence in the case when the witnesses testified. It will not assist them if the evidence is merely repeated to them. What they require from the judge in the final round is his assistance in identifying, applying and assessing the evidence in relation to each direction of law which the trial judge is required to give to them and also in relation to the issues that arise for their determination.

The impact of *Turnbull* has been considerable. Where this warning is not given, the conviction will normally be quashed. A full direction is necessary where the witness makes a visual identification. This can be in cases where the witness is testifying to recognising rather than identifying the defendant. In *Collins*,[94] a police officer testified that the perpetrator looked like a person he had known for 20 years—a *Turnbull* direction was still required. Furthermore it is necessary even where there is considerable other evidence: in *Andrews*,[95] three white men attacked a black youth. The police witnessed the assault, two were arrested and the accused was found nearby after the incident acting in an aggressive fashion. The evidence against the accused, alleged to be the third man, was from the police who described the third man as 'extremely well-built' and dressed in jeans and a grey T-shirt. No identification direction was given by the trial judge and the conviction quashed by the Court of Appeal. But was this a *Turnbull* case? The Crown case was almost wholly circumstantial based on his association with the other two convicted men with whom he had been drinking that evening. Furthermore, one of those was his brother and all three had had an altercation with a black youth in the pub. Even without the testimony about identification, there was substantial evidence to link the accused to the assault.[96]

As mentioned, the *Turnbull* direction is necessary when the witness makes a visual identification of the facial features of a particular person—it is not required for the identification of a car number plate.[97] Nor is it required where the witness testifies as to the clothes being worn—in *Hassan*,[98] the witness testified as to the clothes that the suspect had been wearing and the general appearance of the defendant. Neither an identification parade nor a *Turnbull* direction was necessary.[99]

---

[94] [2004] 2 Cr.App.R. 11; *Aurelio Pop* [2003] UKPC 40.
[95] [1993] Crim.L.R. 590.
[96] *ibid.*—commentary by Birch.
[97] *Hampton* (unreported, July 30, 2004, CA).
[98] [2004] EWCA Crim 1478.
[99] *Gayle* [1999] 2 Cr.App.R. 131; *Doldur* [2000] Crim.L.R. 178.

Less caution is required when the issue is not the accused's presence at the scene but whether it was the accused or another who committed the act.[1] In *Slater*,[2] there was an assault in a nightclub. The accused admitted to being present in the club and aware of the affray but denied being involved. The witness said that she had seen the man earlier and in the club witnessed him punch the victim. The judge did not give the full *Turnbull* direction but the Court of Appeal held that this was not a direction for all cases but only one where there is the possibility of mistaken identification, especially where the issue is whether the accused was present or not. The direction is not automatic when this was not in issue. It would be contrary to common sense to require a direction of this nature where the accused admits to being present and it is the conduct that is being disputed. In this particular case the defendant was of wholly unusual size, being very tall and large, and his companion (whom the witnesses distinguished) was shorter.

Slater [1995] Crim.L.R. 244, commentary by Prof Birch at 245:

[The judge] drew the jury's attention, at length and in the clearest terms, to all the factors pointing to the possibility that the prosecution witness had not seen what she claimed to have seen. Of these, by far the most potent was that she was giddy with drink and claimed the rest of the events that evening were 'a blur', although she claimed a clear recollection of the assault. There is a risk that, if the full *Turnbull* warning is given where it is not appropriate, the jury's attention will be distracted from such relevant considerations. Distraction is not in the interests of justice neither is it necessarily in the interests of the accused. A similar problem arose in relation to the corroboration of sexual complaints in *Chance*[3] where it was held to be distracting and potentially disadvantageous to the defence to give a warning geared to alerting the jury to the risk that a complaint has been fabricated in circumstances where it is common ground that an offence has occurred, and the only issue is whether the complainant has made a bona fide mistake in identifying the culprit.

Away from *Turnbull*, where there are a number of identification witnesses to a single incident, none of whose testimony would be sufficient to base a conviction, the standard of proof might be satisfied by cumulative identification.[4] A more problematic situation arises where the defendant is charged with several offences, to each of which there might be a single eye-witness. If there was evidence which suggested that all the offences were the work of one person and that evidence relating to one charge was admissible on the other charges under the similar fact rules, testimony by one identification witness (not sufficient in itself) could be used to support the evidence of identification provided by another witness. Although in *McGranaghan*,[5] the Court of Appeal suggested that ". . . an identification about which the jury

---

[1] *Oakwell* [1978] 1 All E.R. 1223.
[2] [1995] Crim.L.R. 244.
[3] [1988] 3 All E.R. 225.
[4] Analogous to the idea of "cumulative corroboration" in *Hills* (1988) 86 Cr.App.R. 26.
[5] [1995] 1 Cr.App.R. 559 at 572 *per* Glidewell L.J.

are not sure cannot support another identification of which they are also not sure however similar the facts of the two offences may be", in *Downey*,[6] the court pointed out that this proscribed using doubtful but cumulative identification evidence to establish that the offences had been committed by the same person. Once other evidence revealed that all the offences had been committed by one person, the identifications of that person might be used cumulatively.[7]

D. *Identification and Hearsay*

Where a witness testifies that another person has identified the defendant as the perpetrator, such testimony is hearsay, inadmissible at common law. The absent witness is in effect making an identification of the culprit. Recent authorities tend to suggest that such identifications can operate as an exception to hearsay. In *Osborne and Virtue*,[8] two witnesses to an armed robbery picked out the accused in an identification parade but were unable to do so at the trial proper. A police officer was permitted to testify as to the conduct of the parade and as to whom the witnesses had identified on that parade. Lawton L.J. treated it as a question whether the officer was contradicting the evidence of the witnesses and did not mention the difficult hearsay issue.

Osborne and Virtue [1973] 1 All E.R. 649 at 657a–e, *per* Lawton L.J.:

It was submitted that the admission of that evidence was contrary to a decision of the House of Lords in *R v Christie*.[9] This case has long been regarded as a difficult one to understand because the speeches of their Lordships were not directed to the same points; but this can be got from the speeches—evidence of identification other than identification in the witness box is admissible.

All that the Crown were seeking to do was to establish the fact of identification at the identity parade . . . . This court can see no reason why that evidence should not have been admitted.

In *McCay*,[10] the identification parade took place behind a two-way mirror, preventing those on the parade from seeing the witnesses. The witness picked out the accused by number but at the trial, having testified that he had made a positive identity, was unable to recall the number of the person he had identified. The officer in charge of the parade was permitted to testify to the fact of the identification. Russell L.J. approved of this, regarding the statement as one that accompanied and explained a relevant act.

---

[6] [1995] 1 Cr.App.R. 547.
[7] *Barnes* [1996] Crim.L.R. 39; *Black* [1995] Crim.L.R. 640.
[8] [1973] 1 All E.R. 649.
[9] [1914] A.C. 545.
[10] [1991] 1 All E.R. 232.

McCay [1991] 1 All E.R. 232 at 234g-235c, *per* Russell L.J.:

We are satisfied, however that the admissibility of the words 'It is number 8' can be fully justified, albeit spoken by the witness in the absence of the appellant, because the contemporary statement accompanied a relevant act and was necessary to explain that relevant act. The statement was not relevant as to the identity of the assailant, but it was relevant as to the identification of the suspect by the witness. Whether that identification assisted the jury was a matter for them. In asserting that the man whom the witness thought was the assailant was numbered 8 on the parade, Mr Beach was doing no more and no less than explaining his physical and intellectual activity in making the identification at the material time . . .

In our view, whether the true analysis of the statement is that it was original evidence or whether it was admissible as an exception to the hearsay rule, the judge came to a proper decision.

The identification is seen as an aspect of the *res gestae* exception to hearsay as a statement accompanying a relevant act,[11] but an aspect that has previously only been applied when the words accompany an ambiguous act. It is an interpretation which is "at odds with some respected authority".[12] Other jurisdictions have specifically legislated for this situation. In the USA.

A statement is not hearsay if—
(1) Prior statement by witness. The declarant testifies at the trial or hearing and is subject to cross-examination concerning the statement, and the statement is . . .
. . . (c) one of identification of a person made after perceiving the person;[13]

Any residual questions have been made redundant by s.120(4) and (5) of the Criminal Justice Act 2003.

120 Other previous statements of witnesses
. . . (4) A previous statement by the witness is admissible as evidence of any matter stated of which oral evidence by him would be admissible, if—
(a) any of the following three conditions is satisfied, and
(b) while giving evidence the witness indicates that to the best of his belief he made the statement, and that to the best of his belief it states the truth.
(5) The first condition is that the statement identifies or describes a person, object or place.

The officer conducting the identification process can testify as to the fact of the identification, where witnesses have difficulty remembering and do not testify to the fact of the identification. But they must testify that there was in fact an initial identification and that to the best of their belief, the identification was accurate. Further, where a witness does testify as to the identification and doubt is cast upon that evidence, the prior statement can be introduced not only as evidence that the witness has been consistent but as evidence of the facts.

The hearsay issue also arises with any drawing or construction of the likeness of a suspect made according to the instructions of the witness.

---

[11] *Howe v Malkin* (1878) 40 L.T. 196.
[12] Comment on *McCay* by Birch in [1990] Crim.L.R. 338 at 341.
[13] Federal Rules of Evidence, r. 801.

Nowadays this is likely to be produced using a computer graphics package. In *Cook*,[14] the photofit itself was permitted in evidence. But why? If a witness had made a written or oral statement describing the characteristics of, say, an assailant, such a statement would have been admissible in evidence neither of its facts (since it is hearsay) nor as a prior consistent statement. Similarly a sketch produced by an artist following the directions of a witness is merely transforming words into images and must still be inadmissible. Watkins L.J. in *Cook* disagrees with this.

Cook [1987] 1 All E.R. 1049 at 1054c–j, *per* Watkins L.J.:

The [hearsay] rule is said to apply not only to assertions made orally but to those made in writing or in conduct. Never so far as we know has it been held to apply to this comparatively modern form of evidence, namely the sketch made by the police officer to accord with the witness's recollection of a suspect's physical characteristics and mode of dress and the even more modern photofit compiled from an identical source. Both are manifestations of the seeing eye, translations of vision onto paper through the medium of a police officer's skill of drawing and composing which a witness does not possess. The police officer is merely doing what the witness could do if possessing the requisite skill. When drawing or composing he is akin to a camera, without, of course, being able to match in clarity the photograph of a person or scene which the camera automatically produces.

There is no doubt that a photograph taken, for example, of a suspect during the commission of an offence is admissible . . .

The court treated a photofit as direct evidence and thus admissible even if the eyewitness is unable to attend court. However the judgment conflates two different situations:

a) photographs or video–tapes taken at the scene of a crime by, say, a news cameraman or automatically by a security video are not hearsay evidence and admissible[15];

b) an image generated by an eye witness, whether they draw it themselves or through the medium of a police artist or a computer screen, is an assertion by a person and is not automatically created. As such, it is caught by the hearsay rule.

This objection to *Cook* has been overcome—clearly the graphic representation of the suspect is a previous statement by a witness describing a person and is thus admissible under s.120.

The jury themselves can identify a defendant using a photograph or security video, although they may be warned of the perils of identification on such a basis. Furthermore, a witness who knows the identity of the person on the video can testify to this effect. This is illustrated in *Taylor v Chief Constable*

[14] [1987] 1 All E.R. 1049.
[15] *The Statue of Liberty* [1968] 2 All E.R. 195.

of Cheshire,[16] in which a video was made of a shoplifter. Policemen were able to identify the accused from the video. Later the recording was erased by accident. The officers gave evidence of what they had seen on the video and Taylor was convicted. The video itself was direct evidence[17] and the court accepted the argument that there is no difference in principle between the evidence of witnesses who viewed the recording and those witnesses who claim to have seen the events directly. Code D does not apply but there must be a *Turnbull* direction.

In *Attorney-General's Reference (No. 2 of 2002)*,[18] the Court of Appeal considered how such material could be used.

Attorney General's Reference (No.2 of 2000) 1 Cr.App.R. 21, *per* Rose L.J.:

19. In our judgment, on the authorities, there are, as it seems to us at least four circumstances in which . . . a jury can be invited to conclude, that the defendant committed the offence on the basis of a photographic image from the scene of the crime:

    (i)   where the photographic image is sufficiently clear, the jury can compare it with the defendant sitting in the dock (*Dodson & Williams*[19]);

    (ii) where a witness knows the defendant sufficiently well to recognise him as the offender depicted in the photographic image, he can give evidence of this (. . . *Caldwell & Dixon*[20]); and this may be so even if the photographic image is no longer available for the jury (*Taylor v The Chief Constable of Cheshire*[21]);

    (iii) where a witness who does not know the defendant spends substantial time viewing and analysing photographic images from the scene, thereby acquiring special knowledge which the jury does not have, he can give evidence of identification based on a comparison between those images and a reasonably contemporary photograph of the defendant, provided that the images and the photograph are available to the jury . . .;

    (iv) a suitably qualified expert with facial mapping skills can give opinion evidence of identification based on a comparison between images from the scene, (whether expertly enhanced or not and a reasonably contemporary photograph of the defendant, provided the images and the photograph are available for the jury.[22]

V Confessions and Supporting Evidence

A confession by the defendant is direct evidence of guilt and common sense suggests that the trier of fact can rely upon it since people do not make

---

[16] [1987] 1 All E.R. 225.
[17] *Kajala v Noble* (1982) 75 Cr.App.R. 149.
[18] [2003] Crim. L.R. 192.
[19] [1984] 79 Cr.App.R. 220.
[20] [1993] Crim.L.R. 862.
[21] above.
[22] *Stockwell*, 97 Cr.App.R. 260, *Clarke* [1995] 2 Cr.App.R. 425 and *Hookway* [1999] Crim. L.R. 750.

statements against their own interests unless those statements are true. However experience over the past decades has shown that common sense is an unreliable guide. Under police interrogation, people have confessed to offences that they have not committed. Such admissions may be a result of police malpractice[23] or occur without any impropriety on the part of the questioners.[24] Not only has experience revealed the risks of relying on unsupported admissions. Research has also begun to explore the reasons for this phenomenon.

Royal Commission on Criminal Justice, Report (Cm 2263, 1993) para.4.32:

There is no way of establishing the frequency of false confessions: a retracted confession may nevertheless be true, and defendants who have made false confessions may have reasons of their own for adhering to them. However there is now a substantial body of research[25] which shows that there are four distinct categories of false confession:
  i. people who make confessions entirely voluntarily as a result of a morbid desire for publicity or notoriety; or to relieve feelings of guilt about a real or imagined previous transgression; or because they cannot distinguish between reality and fantasy;
  ii. a suspect may confess from a desire to protect someone else from interrogation and prosecution;
  iii. people may see a prospect of immediate advantage from confessing (for example,, an end to questioning or release from the police station), even though the long-term consequences are far worse (the resulting confessions are termed 'coerced-compliant' confessions); and
  iv. people may be persuaded temporarily by the interrogators that they really have done the act in question (the resulting confessions are termed 'coerced-internalised' confessions).
It is important therefore that the criminal justice system should contain effective safeguards against false confessions being believed.

A central question for the Runciman Commission[26] was whether existing safeguards were adequate. As with identification evidence, such safeguards can be built in at the point of investigation or at the point of trial. At trial, the key issue is whether independent supporting evidence should be required for all cases resting solely or substantially on the defendant's confession. Some jurisdictions[27] use corroboration as that safeguard.[28]

Royal Commission on Criminal Justice, Report (Cm 2263) paras 4.57–4.59

4.57. In Scotland, there is a general rule of evidence (to which there are a few minor statutory exceptions) that the accused's guilt cannot be established by the evidence of

---

[23] *Paris* [1994] Crim.L.R. 361.
[24] *Ward* [1993] 2 All E.R. 577.
[25] G. Gudjonsson, *The Psychology of Interrogations, Confessions and Testimony* (Wiley, 1992).
[26] Royal Commission on Criminal Justice, *Report* (HMSO, 1993) Cm. 2263, paras 4.56–4.87.
[27] A. Choo: 'Confessions and Corroboration: a Comparative Perspective' [1991] Crim.L.R. 867.
[28] Royal Commission on Criminal Justice, *op.cit.*, paras 4.57–4.59.

only one witness. There must be testimony incriminating the accused from two separate sources. This rule applies to all cases and not just those involving confession evidence. Applied to confession evidence, it means that no one who confesses to a crime, unless by a formal plea of guilty, can be convicted solely on his or her own confession. There must be evidence from some other source which supports the confession and incriminates the accused.

4.58. What amounts to corroboration of a confession varies from case to case. Something more than the confession itself is needed but what is required must depend on the circumstances of the case. As the Lord Justice-General said in the recent case of *Meredith and Lees*.[29]

> In some cases there may be ample evidence from other sources that the crime libelled has been committed. The remaining question will then be whether the accused committed it. A clear and unequivocal confession of guilt on his part may then require little more by way of evidence to corroborate it, if the admission is in terms which leave no room for doubt on this point and there is no reason to suspect that it was not freely made.

4.59. A further aspect of the Scottish rules of corroboration which was raised by many witnesses to the Commission was the 'special knowledge principle'. Confession evidence may be corroborated by facts which were mentioned by the accused in the course of the confession, which the accused would not have known if he or she had not been the perpetrator of the crime. For example, in *Manuel v HMA*[30] the accused confessed to murdering a young woman and offered to point out to the police the separate places in a field where he had buried the victim and one of her shoes. His ability to do this was held to be corroborative. Doubts have, however, arisen about the width of this principle because the courts have held that 'special knowledge' does not necessarily mean 'sole knowledge'. It is, in other words, possible that facts mentioned in a confession may be held to corroborate that confession even though they were known to other people before the confession had been made. The passage of time between the date of the crime and the date of the confession is, however, relevant since the longer the delay the more likely it is 'that an accused person had acquired his knowledge of the detail not as a perpetrator of the crime or offence but as a recipient of the information from other sources'.[31]

Confessions can be contrasted with identification evidence as the courts have not felt the need to develop safeguards by analogy with the *Turnbull* direction. Why should this be? The reforms brought in by Police and Criminal Evidence Act 1984 established many safeguards at the point of investigation, surrounding the conditions under which an interview can take place.[32] Admissibility of confessions was tightened up by sections 76 and 78. But these also related to the conditions of the interview and did not address the research findings that people confess for other reasons.

Should there be a rule requiring corroboration as in Scotland? The practical impact of this might be less dramatic than supposed—an independent study suggested that 95 per cent of confession case in fact had such supporting evidence.

Royal Commission on Criminal Justice, *op.cit.* paras 4.69:

In order to assess how many cases might be affected by a requirement for supporting evidence, the Home Office Research and Planning Unit examined at our

---

[29] [1992] S.C.C.R. 459.
[30] [1958] J.C. 41.
[31] McAvoy v HMA (1983) SLT 16.
[32] see Ch.4.

request 2,210 recent cases from 13 CPS branch offices in 7 CPS areas. These were all magistrates' court cases. 30 (or less than 1.4 per cent) relied on confession evidence alone or on admissions that fell short of a confession. A more detailed study, also carried out at our request, by Michael McConville[33] examined the evidence available to the police in a sample of 524 cases. In 305 of these there was a confession. The study found that there were very few confession cases in which the police did not have other supporting evidence. In fact, the police and prosecution files showed that even the stricter *Baskerville* test of corroboration could have been satisfied in 87 per cent of such cases. In the remaining 13 per cent, corroborative evidence of this nature was not brought before the court but in close to half of these the police probably could, in McConville's view, have produced corroboration if the rule had required it. There were 15 confession cases (5 per cent) in which the author estimated that the *Baskerville* test could not have been satisfied, but in some of these the different Scottish rules might have been satisfied. McConville estimated that 14 convictions (5 per cent of confession cases) would probably have become acquittals because of the apparent lack of supporting evidence of any kind.

It is unlikely that any rule requiring corroboration or a cautionary direction would lead to a higher acquittal (or non-prosecution) rate of people who should be properly convicted on the basis of a confession. The arguments for reform centre on fairness—a jury should be fully aware of the weaknesses of certain categories of evidence, whether identification or confessions.

Pragmatically, the Runciman Commission recognised that legislative policy was to move away from corroboration requirements. The majority of the Commission recommended that the judge should give a strong warning that care was needed before convicting on the basis of the confession alone.[34] The judge should explicitly refer to reasons why people might confess to crimes that they did not commit and, in suitable cases, refer to cases where persons were known to have confessed to crimes that they had not committed. The judge should direct them to the facts of the confession, so that the strengths and weaknesses of the evidence could be clearly appreciated. The jury's attention should be drawn to any feature that might undermine the identification. The judge may also draw attention to any supporting evidence or lack of it but explain that, having given full weight to the warning, the jury could convict even in the absence of supporting evidence. As yet Parliament has not legislated for such a warning nor has the Court of Appeal developed the common law, acting on analogy with *Turnbull*.

---

[33] M. McConville: *Corroboration and Confessions: The Impact of a Rule Requiring that no Conviction be sustained on the Basis of Confession Evidence Alone* (Royal Commission on Criminal Justice Research Study, No.13, HMSO, 1993). Corroboration is not a panacea against wrongful conviction—in the Birmingham Six case, there were confessions to the pub bombings and there was independent forensic evidence, later proved fatally flawed, that the defendants had handled explosives.

[34] *ibid.*, para.4.77—such a development does not need legislation.

12

ORAL TESTIMONY: EVIDENCE IN CHIEF

I. Oral Testimony

Adversarial trial allows parties to determine what issues to litigate and what evidence to call. In contested cases, especially in criminal cases, adversarial trial still relies heavily upon oral testimony, from a witness physically present in court. Furthermore, in criminal trials, every element of the prosecution case needs to be proved by admissible evidence. This means that oral testimony needs to given even where there is no dispute. The witness will first be questioned by the party calling the witness—this is known as direct examination or evidence in chief. Following this, the witness will be subject to critical scrutiny by the opposing party—this is known as cross-examination. By observing and listening to a witness, the assumption is that the trier of fact is more able to assess the weight to be attached to the witness's evidence than by reading a written statement.

In civil proceedings, there is less emphasis on oral testimony as only those matters in dispute need to be proved. There is greater reliance on documentary evidence and, under the Civil Evidence Act 1995, hearsay evidence has become generally admissible so that the witness need not be present in court, unless required to be there for cross examination. Furthermore, even where the witness is in court, a witness statement can be adopted as that witness's evidence in chief.[1]

In criminal proceedings, there are more circumstances where written statements or recordings are becoming admissible.[2]

- Evidence in magistrates' and Crown courts can be given through the medium of agreed statements under s.9 of the Criminal Justice Act 1967.[3]
- Formal admissions can also be adduced in any proceedings under s.10 of the 1967 Act—for example, proof where a defendant is charged with driving while disqualified, proof of that disqualification may be provided by a formal admission by the defendant.[4]

---

[1] Civil Evidence Act 1995, s.6.
[2] These do not include specific provisions for the protection of child and other vulnerable witnesses, for example, under Part II Youth Justice and Criminal Evidence Act 1999.
[3] Criminal Procedure Rules, r. 27.1; see Ch.18.
[4] *Moran v DPP* (2000) 164 J.P. 562 (Divisional Court).

- Under the Criminal Justice Act 2003, especially under ss.116 and 117, documentary hearsay may be admitted without the need for the original declarant to be present under certain conditions

The primacy of oral testimony and the principle of confronting one's accusers have both been chipped away at in recent years. But the adversarial nature of the trial remains. Is it true or a myth that the oral testimony of a physically-present witness, recollecting the relevant events, is the most reliable form of evidence? Whether the 'fight' theory is the best technique for a court to discover the facts in a case has been subject to critical analysis.

J. Frank: Courts on Trial (Princeton. 1949), pp.80–82:

. . . to have each side strive as hard as it can, in a keenly partisan spirit, to bring to the court's attention the evidence favorable to that side. Macaulay said that we obtain the fairest decision 'when two men argue, as unfairly as possible, on opposite side,' for then 'it is certain that no important consideration will altogether escape notice'

Unquestionably that view contains a core of good sense . . . . But frequently the partisanship of the opposing lawyers blocks the uncovering of vital evidence or leads to a presentation of vital testimony in a way that distorts it.

This is perhaps most obvious in the handling of witnesses. Suppose a trial were fundamentally a truth-inquiry. Then, recognising the inherent fallibilities of witnesses, we would do all we could to remove the cause of their errors when testifying. Recognising also the importance of witnesses' demeanour as clues to their reliability, we would do our best to make sure that they testify in circumstances most conclusive to a revealing observation of that demeanour by the trial judge or jury. In our contentious trial practice, we do almost the exact opposite.

No business man, before deciding to build a new plant, no general before launching an attack, would think of obtaining information on which to base his judgment by putting his informants through the bewildering experience of witnesses at a trial . . .

In a book by Henry Taft (brother of Chief Justice Taft, and himself a distinguished lawyer) we are told: 'Counsel and court find it necessary through examination and instruction to induce a witness to abandon for an hour or two his habitual method of thought and expression, and conform to the rigid ceremonialism of court procedure. It is not strange that frequently truthful witnesses are . . . misunderstood, that they nervously react in such a way as to create the impression that they are either evading or intentionally falsifying. It is interesting to account for some of the things that witnesses do under such circumstances. An honest witness testifies on direct examination. He answers questions promptly and candidly and makes a good impression. On cross-examination, his attitude changes. He suspects that traps are being laid for him. He hesitates; he ponders the answer to a simple question; he seems to 'spar' for time by asking that questions be repeated; perhaps he protests that counsel is not fair; he may even appeal to the court for protection. Altogether the contrast with his attitude on direct examination is obvious; and he creates the impression that he is evading or withholding'. Yet on testimony thus elicited courts every day reach decisions affecting the lives and fortunes of citizens.

Frank's concerns remain valid today. As has been discussed in earlier chapters, there is an increasing body of research that casts doubt on the accuracy and reliability of eyewitnesses, especially in relation to identification evidence.[5] Studies also shows that the structure of the trial and the questioning strategies employed ensure that witnesses are constrained in what they can say and are provided with little, of any, opportunity to give a complete account of the matter.

M. Kebbell. S. Deprez and G. Wagstaff, "Direct and Cross Examination" Psychology, Crime & Law, 2003, Vol. 9, pp.49–59:

An extensive literature shows that that 'leading', 'open', 'closed', 'yes =no' questions, questions with a 'negative' and a 'double negative' and 'multiple questions' can influence witnesses' accuracy. Leading questions are those that suggest or imply the response required. For instance, an example of a leading question is, "was his shirt red?" and a more heavily leading question is, "his shirt was red wasn't it?" Both suggest that the man wore a red shirt. The accuracy of answers provided can be adversely affected by leading questions if the suggestion is incorrect because of the tendency to provide the answer believed to be required by the questioner. This form of questioning can also distort witness answers through an apparent change in the representation of an event in memory and also through compliance to the questioner's wishes.

Similarly, open questions (e.g., "describe your attacker"), closed questions (e.g., "what colour was his shirt?"), and yes = no questions (e.g. "was the colour of his shirt red?") can have a dramatic influence on the accuracy of witness answers. The kinds of questions to which people tend to provide the most accurate answers (i.e., where the proportion of correct to incorrect information is greatest) are open questions. The more closed questioning strategies mentioned above can reduce the accuracy although they can add detail. As a general proposition, as questions become more and more specific responses become less accurate. Consequently, police officers are recommended to use more open forms of questioning.

The influence of these questions can be understood in terms of the relative demands of the questions. For more open questions, the task is to tell the questioner what the witness can remember. For more specific, closed questions, however, the task changes to one of providing the interviewer with what he or she wants the witness to remember. One result of this is that witnesses tend to provide less accurate answers to specific questions because they replace memory gaps with distorted or inaccurate material. In other words, they may become suggestible to the demands of the interviewer. Answers to yes = no questions may be particularly inaccurate because of acquiescence. Acquiescence is the tendency of an individual to answer questions with a 'yes' irrespective of the content.

Problems may also occur if witnesses are asked questions involving negatives, double negatives, and multiple questions. Negatives are questions involving the word 'not' (e.g. "Did the man not tell you to be quiet?"). Double negatives are questions involving using the word 'not' twice (e.g. "did John not say that he would not go to the shops?"). These may cause problems because witnesses may have difficulty understanding the question. For instance, evidence from child witness studies shows that with respect to children, "don't know" responses are often given to questions that are not understood. However, if the question is put to them in a simplified form they often know the answer. Alternatively, and additionally, instead of saying "I don't know" witnesses may be tempted to 'guess' the right answer.

---

[5] For a more positive view of eyewitnesses, see John C. Yuille, and Judith L., Cutshall, "A case study of eyewitness memory of a crime" Journal of Applied Psychology. 1986 May Vol 71(2) 291–301

Multiple questions are questions involving two or more parts that have different answers (e.g. "At eleven o'clock were you in the bar? Was John at the garage?"). Again, in experimental simulations these kinds of questions cause eyewitnesses problems because they may fail to understand the question and usually only give one answer rather than an answer to both questions.[6]

This study showed that open questions were comparatively rare, closed questions more frequent and yes/no questions were most frequent. Constraints on the witness account result not only from the nature of advocacy but also from the rules which surround the examination of witnesses. The impact of such questioning strategies on witness reliability was discussed further in Ch.9.

II. Examination in Chief

Examination in chief is the questioning of a witness by the party calling that witness. Its objective is to elicit testimony which is favourable to that party's cause. A witness will be called into the witness box and must normally be identified.[7] After a witness has taken the oath or affirmed, they will then be examined by the party calling them about matters which are relevant to the facts in issue in the case. They answer from memory, without the benefit of any written statements that they may have given to police or lawyers— however there is a practice which allows witnesses to "refresh their memories", if they become forgetful. There are also some restrictions on what counsel may ask—they cannot ask leading questions nor ask the witness to narrate prior consistent statements.

A. *Leading Questions*

It is dangerous to assume that a trial lawyer's examination strategy is to elicit a complete and accurate account from their witness. They ask questions which constrain the witness to reply in a certain way and which allow the lawyer to present a particular narrative of events to the court. They are trained to believe that an accurate and complete account of events might damage their case and even in direct examination lawyers exhibit an over abundance of caution.

Leading questions would be a powerful tool in such a strategy but the first "rule" for examining in chief aims to ensure that witnesses should present an account of events based on their own perceptions and recall. Counsel must not ask questions which either prompt the witness by suggesting the answer or which assume the existence of certain facts. These are known as "leading questions". This is not a cast-iron rule and it is possible to lead the witness on formal and introductory matters and where there is no dispute between the

---

[6] References have been omitted.
[7] Witness anonymity is discussed at greater length in Ch.10.

parties. It is a rule often ignored—the Kebbell study suggested that 20% of questions asked on direct examination were leading or heavily leading.[8] Where one witness has testified to a particular fact, another witness may be asked, directly, whether that fact took place.[9]

The absurdity is that the witness will normally have given a statement within a relatively short time of the events in question. The conditions under which these are generally taken are far from ideal: a statement made by a witness to the police is not regulated in the same manner, for example, as an interview with a suspect. Despite this, any statement is more likely to be reliable as evidence of the facts than the witness seeking to remember those events months, if not years, later. Counsel will be aware of the contents of the statement and there is great temptation to ensure that all the necessary facts emerge by leading questions rather than allowing the witness to recollect them freely. The "leading question" rule prevents this.

B. *Refreshing the Memory*

This insistence on oral testimony can reduce a criminal trial[10] to a test of memory. Only the expert witness is spared this as their report is admissible as that evidence in chief.[11] Vulnerable witnesses may also be spared an initial examination in chief—this is the result of the Youth Justice and Criminal Evidence Act 1999 whereby a special measures direction may be made to allow a videotape of the direct examination (or cross examination) of a vulnerable witness or child's testimony[12] to stand as the evidence in chief of that witness.

For most witnesses, it is wise to read through their statements *before* they go into court to refresh the memory.[13] Counsel would recommend this, always remembering a lawyer should not coach a witness nor should witnesses discuss their testimony at this point. Rule 705 of the Bar's Code of Conduct, specifies what a barrister must not do, namely "rehearse, practise or coach a witness in relation to his evidence". Despite this, in the future, CPS lawyers will be permitted to interview witnesses in advance of trial.[14]

1. Before entering the witness box

Reading a statement before testifying to refresh one's memory of the events is permitted. In *Richardson*,[15] shortly before testifying, the prosecution wit-

---

[8] M. Kebbell, (2003). *op.cit.* Table 1 on p.53—this was a small study of rape trials.
[9] *Courteen v Touse* (1807) 1 Camp. 43.
[10] In civil proceedings, witness statements can be admissible as evidence in chief under Civil Evidence Act 1995, s.6.
[11] Criminal Justice Act 1988, s.30.
[12] Youth Justice and Criminal Evidence Act 1999, s.27.
[13] In some other jurisdictions, witnesses have been hypnotised to improve their memory—L. Wrightman, C. Willis and K. Saul, *On the Witness Stand: Controversies in the Courtroom* (1987), Section II.
[14] The Attorney General's Report on this can be seen at www.lslo.gov.uk/pretrial.htm (accessed January 11, 2006); advice on legitimate witness preparation can be found in P. Cooper, "A Stitch in Time Saves Nine" Counsel Magazine (July 2003).
[15] [1971] 2 All E.R. 773.

nesses were given their statements to read although they were not allowed to take these into the witness box. These statements had been made to the police some weeks after the commission of the offences.

Richardson [1971] 2 All E.R. 773 at 776j–777f, *per* Sachs L.J.:

. . . it is however necessary to consider what should be the general approach of the court to there being shown in this way to witnesses their statements—which were not 'contemporaneous' within the meaning of that word as normally applied to documents used to refresh memory. First, it is to be observed that it is the practice of the courts not to allow a witness to refresh his memory in the witness box by reference to written statements unless made contemporaneously. Secondly . . . witnesses for the prosecution in criminal cases are normally (though not in all circumstances) entitled, if they so request, to copies of any statements taken from them by police officers. Thirdly, it is to be noted that witnesses for the defence are normally, as is known to be the practice, allowed to have copies of their statements and refresh their memories from them at any time up to the moment they go into the witness box—indeed counsel for the appellant was careful not to submit that there was anything wrong about that. Fourthly, no one has ever suggested that in civil proceedings witnesses may not see their statements up to the moment they go into the witness box. One has only to think for a moment of witnesses going into the box to deal with accidents which took place five or six years previously to conclude that it would be highly unreasonable if they were not allowed to see them. Is there then anything wrong in the witnesses in this case being offered an opportunity to see that which they were entitled to ask for and to be shown on request? In a case such as the present is justice more likely to be done if a witness may not see a statement made by him at a time very much closer to that of the incident?

The rationale is that, were this prohibited, testimony in the witness box becomes little more than a test of memory rather than of truthfulness. It would be impossible to police and this would create difficulties for honest witnesses but do little to hamper dishonest witnesses. Where a witness looks at a document outside the courtroom, if the prosecution is aware of that, they have a duty to disclose this fact to the defence and must allow the defence to see the document, if it has not already been disclosed.

2. Leaving the witness box

Prior to 1990, a line was drawn at the moment the witness entered the box —a witness could read the statement before taking the oath but could not interrupt testimony in order to leave the witness box, refresh memory and then resume testifying. But in *Da Silva*,[16] the witness had already begun to give evidence but faltered. The judge permitted him to leave the box to refresh his memory from a statement. The appellant submitted that the witness could either have read his statement before he entered the box or, if it were made contemporaneously, have refreshed his memory while testifying.

[16] [1990] 1 All E.R. 29.

However, having started to testify, there was no third way, namely, a pause for reviewing a statement that was not made contemporaneously. The Court of Appeal disagreed.

Da Silva [1990] 1 All E.R. 29 at 33c–e, *per* Stuart-Smith L.J.:

In our judgment, therefore, it should be open to the judge, in the exercise of his discretion and in the interests of justice, to permit a witness who has begun to give evidence to refresh his memory from a statement made near to the time of events in question, even though it does not come within the definition of contemporaneous, provided he is satisfied (1) that the witness indicates that he cannot now recall the details of events because of the lapse of time since they took place, (2) that he made a statement much nearer the time of the events and that the contents of the statement represented his recollection at the time he made it, (3) that he had not read the statement before coming into the witness box and (4) that he wished to have an opportunity to read the statement before he continued to give evidence.

We do not think that it matters whether the witness withdraws from the witness box and reads his statement, as he would do if he had had the opportunity before entering the witness box, or whether he reads it in the witness box. What is important is that, if the former course is adopted, no communication must be had with the witness, other than to see that he can read the statement in peace. Moreover, if either course is adopted, the statement must be removed from him when he comes to give his evidence and he should not be permitted to refer to it again, unlike a contemporaneous statement which may be used to refresh memory while giving evidence.

The key limitation in *Da Silva* was that the witness had not previously refreshed the memory by reading the statement. This was not the case in *South Ribble Magistrates Ex p. Cochcrane*,[17] where the witness was permitted to leave the witness box to re-read a statement which he had read 15 minutes earlier. The Divisional Court distinguished *Da Silva.* and Henry L.J. said,

South Ribble Magistrates Ex p. Cochcrane [1996] 2 Cr.App.R. 544, *per* Henry L.J.:

. . . in relation to the relevance as to whether a witness has taken the opportunity to read their statement before going into the witness box, there can be no logical difference between someone who has read the statement and for some reason not taken it in properly and one who has never read it at all. It seems to me that the judge has a real discretion as to whether to permit a witness to refresh his memory from a non-contemporaneous document. By "real discretion" I mean a strong discretion, a choice of alternatives free of binding criteria.

This discretion of the judge was reinforced in *Gordon*,[18] which stressed that there were no fixed and immutable rules in this matter. This process has now

---

[17] [1996] 2 Cr.App.R. 544.
[18] [2002] EWCA Crim 1.

been simplified by section 139 of the Criminal Justice Act 2003, discussed below, which merely requires any document to have been made at an earlier time rather than contemporaneously.

3. In the witness box

Once in the witness box, there is a further means for witnesses to remind themselves of the events to which they will be testifying. Without leaving the witness box, a witness is allowed to refer to any document, made at the time of the events by that witness. This is known as 'refreshing the memory.

M. Newark and A. Samuels, "Refreshing Memory" [1978] Crim.L.R. 408:

Human memory is probably not as good as we believe. Generally contemporaneous notes made by a witness are likely to be fuller and more accurate than his memory at a trial many months after the incident. Moreover, contemporaneous notes, if referred to, may help to stimulate the memory to recall further facts not contained in the notes which would not otherwise have been recalled. It is therefore desirable that a court should allow use to be made of such notes. However, there are dangers involved. The notes may create a spurious impression of a vivid recollection. Inaccuracies in perception and memory become crystallised. The witness believes he remembers the incident but in truth only remembers his record of it. The testimony of an untruthful witness is given enhanced credibility and he is able to tailor his evidence to fit in with his notes.

This practice was most commonly seen with police officers who, once sworn, produce and proceed to read from their notebooks, which contain the information about the events that they wrote down at the time. The problem is that notebooks and other such documents are hearsay and not admissible as evidence in their own right. Police witnesses are permitted to do this, not because they are constables, but because, as part of their duties, they have written up the notes at the time of the incident. As a result of this "contemporaneous recording", they can review the document in order to jog the memory. They then testify and it is this oral testimony which is evidence and not the notebook.

This bizarre process is a "hearsay fiddle": an avoidance of the consequences of the hearsay rule more than an aid to recollection. This is illustrated in cases where the document does not stimulate the witness's present recollection at all but where the witness accepts that his past recollection must have been as recorded in the document. In *Maugham v Hubbard*,[19] a witness was called to prove the receipt of money and was shown an unstamped acknowledgement of the receipt signed by him. He had no recollection whatsoever of the transaction but swore that the receipt must be accurate and that he had received the money.

---

[19] Also *Topham v McGregor* (1844) 1 Car. & Kir. 320 where the witness, having refreshed his memory, deposed to the state of the weather 14 years previously.

Maugham v Hubbard (1828) 8 B. & C. 14 at 16, *per* Lord Tenterden C.J.:

In order to make the paper itself evidence of the receipt of the money it ought to have been stamped. The consequence of its not having been stamped might be that the party who paid the money, in event of the death of the person who received it, would lose his evidence of such payment. Here the witness, on seeing the entry signed by himself, said that he had no doubt that he had received the money. The paper itself was not used as evidence of the receipt of the money, but only to enable the witness to refresh his memory; and when he said that he had no doubt that he had received the money there was sufficient parol evidence to prove the payment.

In *Kelsey*,[20] the witness had dictated a car number plate to a police constable who wrote it down and repeated it back to the witness. The officer gave evidence that the note produced was the note the witness saw him make and as a result the witness was allowed to look at the notebook to "refresh his memory". In fact as the witness has no present recollection of the registration number, the notebook is the evidence, introduced through the medium of the witness.

Other jurisdictions cut through this tangle, *e.g.* the Federal Rules of Evidence, r. 80(3)(5).

Federal Rules of Evidence, r.803(5):

A memorandum or record concerning a matter about which a witness had knowledge but now has insufficient recollection to enable the witness to testify fully and accurately, shown to have been made or adopted by the witness when the matter was fresh in the witness's memory and to reflect that knowledge correctly. If admitted, the memorandum or record may be read into evidence but may not itself be received as an exhibit unless offered by an adverse party.

In civil proceedings, these contortions are unnecessary as the note would be admissible evidence under the Civil Evidence Act 1995. In criminal proceedings, this is now governed by s.139 of the Criminal Justice Act 2003 which states:

139(1) A person giving oral evidence in criminal proceedings about any matter may, at any stage in the course of doing so, refresh his memory of it from a document made or verified by him at an earlier time if—
  (a) he states in his oral evidence that the document records his recollection of the matter at that earlier time, and
  (b) his recollection of the matter is likely to have been significantly better at that time than it is at the time of his oral evidence.[21]

This provision does not replace the common law but it does affect the conditions that have to be met before the witness can use the document as an *aide-memoire* while testifying.

---

[20] (1982) 74 Cr.App.R. 213.

[21] This came into force in April 2004—by subs. (2), this also applies to transcripts made from oral recordings.

1. It is not necessary to show neither that the witness's memory is impaired nor that they have any independent recollection of the facts.[22] The request to refresh the memory can come from counsel or the judge.[23] Nor is it too late to make such a request after a witness has departed from their statement.

2. The chief common law condition, before a witness could 'refresh the memory', was contemporaneity. The document must have been made by the witness (or at least verified by them) at the time of the incident or soon after.

M. Newark and A. Samuels, "Refreshing Memory" [1978] Crim.L.R. 409:

. . . Wigmore believed that in the case of a present recollection revived it was an unnecessary requirement which had spilled over from cases of past recollection recorded. His point was that if the memory is truly revived it does not matter what triggers it off. But although the witness may genuinely believe that his memory is revived there is always the danger that he is deceiving himself. On the whole it seems better to insist on some degree of contemporaneity. However contemporaneity must be a flexible concept, a matter of fact and degree in the circumstances of each case.

The common law requirement was not strict but, despite its justifications, it has been jettisoned by s.139 which merely requires that the statement was made or verified "at an earlier time". The police officer who observes an incident and a short time later in the station writes up the observations in a notebook will always be allowed refer to them. Previously, a gap of a month led the trial judge to pause before giving leave for the witness to refresh his memory[24] but that would no longer be a problem. In the future, the most extreme scenario is where a witness, in the days or weeks preceding the hearing, writes an account of events which they later seek to refer to while testifying. The literal interpretation of the section permits this.

3. The document does not have to be written by the witness but it must be verified by him or her. Section 139 does not affect this requirement. Thus ships' logs kept by the mate but later checked by the captain, can be used to refresh the captain's memory.[25] If a witness dictates a car number plate to a police constable who writes this down and repeats it back to the witness, the witness can look at the notebook to refresh his memory, even though he did not look at it at the time.

Kelsey (1982) 74 Cr.App.R. 213 at 217, *per* Taylor J.:

The question we have to decide is, therefore, whether witness A can verify a note he dictates to B only by reading it himself, or whether it is sufficient if the note is read

---

[22] *Bryant and Dickson* [1946] 31 Cr.App.R. 146.
[23] *Tyagi, The Times,* July 21, 1986.
[24] *Graham* [1973] Crim.L.R. 628.
[25] *Burrough v Martin* (1809) 2 Camp.112.

back by B to A at the time of confirmation. In most cases we would expect the note to be read by A if it is made in his presence. But what of the instant case, or cases involving the blind or the illiterate? In our view, there is no magic in verifying by seeing as opposed to verifying by hearing . . . . What must be shown is that witness A has verified in the sense of satisfying himself whilst matters are fresh in his mind (1) that a record has been made and (2) that it is accurate. If A makes a 'contemporaneous' note himself or if A reads and adopts at the time a 'contemporaneous' note made by B, A may refresh his memory from it without need of another witness.[26]

But there must be some form of verification. In *Eleftheriou*,[27] customs officers investigating a VAT fraud were keeping observation on a fish and chip shop. One officer kept watch and said what was happening while the second officer wrote this down. Although both signed the document at the end of their shift, the observer did not read it through. The convictions were quashed as the observer should not have been permitted to use the record to refresh his mmeory. In *Sekhon*,[28] one officer maintained an observation log, based on his own observations and on those of fellow officers. Those latter entries were verified by the other officers. Officers were permitted to refresh their memories from the entire log and the court rejected the argument that sought to distinguish notes made by an individual witness from record such as this observation log.

4. The note can be a result of collaboration. In *Bass*,[29] the constables who interviewed the defendant denied making a joint note. But the Court of Appeal held that, even if they had collaborated, both could refresh their memory from it.

Bass [1953] 1 All E.R. 1064 at 1067, *per* Byrne J.:

With regard to the second ground of appeal, the matter stood in this way. The officers' notes were almost identical. One officer made his notes after the appellant had been charged, and the other made his an hour later. Counsel for the appellant suggested to the officers in cross-examination that they had collaborated. They denied that suggestion. This court has observed that police officers nearly always deny that they have collaborated in the making of notes, and we cannot help wondering why they are the only class of society who do not collaborate in such a matter. It seems to us that nothing could be more natural prosecution proper, when two persons have been present in an interview with a third person, that they should afterwards make sure that they have a correct version of what was said. Collaboration would appear to be a better explanation of almost identical notes than the possession of a superhuman memory.[30]

---

[26] Compare *McLean*, 52 Cr.App.R. 80 where the witness dictated the number but failed to verify it and was not able to refer to the document.
[27] [1993] Crim.L.R. 947.
[28] (1986) 85 Cr.App.R. 19.
[29] [1953] 1 All E.R. 1064.
[30] *ibid.* at 1067 *per* J. Byrne, cited in G. Stephenson, 'Should collaborative testimony be permitted in courts of law?' [1990] Crim.L.R. 302.

Collaborative testimony increases accuracy and completeness as well as being administratively convenient. But it might also camouflage differences between witnesses, lead to the suppression of evidence and prevent effective cross-examination. This has been shown in experimental studies.

G. Stephenson. "Should collaborative testimony be permitted in courts of law?" [1990] Crim.L.R. 313:

The cost of these benefits is high. Much straightforward evidence that would have surfaced is excluded from group accounts. Group accounts are selective, conventional and devoid of descriptive and interpretative evidence. Moreover, groups are more or less unable to distinguish at all between answers which are correct and those about which individuals would express some doubt. Taking the formal objections one by one, it is clear that disagreement will, indeed, be camouflaged, and maybe just as importantly, individuals' recollections are not fully represented in a combined account. Evidence of all kinds—facts and wider-ranging observations- are excluded as groups compile a partial, conventional version of events. The extent to which hearsay is willingly included in collaborative accounts is unclear, especially since groups tend to be indiscriminately confident about all their answers. It appears that one person's confidence serves to generate confidence in others, or at least provides an excuse for belief in the veracity of the group decision.

5. The document need not be the original and a copy of the original notes can be used. In *Topham v Mcgregor*,[31] the witness, a journalist, no longer had his article but was entitled to refresh his memory from the 14-year-old newspaper in which that article was printed. This will continue to be the case—the 2003 Act clearly intends to extend those situations where a witness is permitted to refresh their memory and it is inconceivable that section 139 would be restricted to original documents.

The documents used for refreshing the memory must be made available for inspection by other parties. It may also be appropriate for the jury to inspect those parts of the document relied on.[32] This assists the jury in following the cross-examination and in assessing the witness's credibility. The opposition is allowed to cross-examine the witness on the relevant parts of the document, without making the document part of the evidence but if counsel chooses to examine on other parts of the document, the party calling the witness is entitled to require the cross-examiner to make the document evidence.[33]

M. Newark and A. Samuels, "Refreshing Memory" [1978] Crim.L.R. 411:

At first sight this looks like one of those rules that gets the law of evidence a bad name . . . . The justification for the rule would seem to be this: When a cross-examiner

---

[31] above.
[32] *Sekhon* above.
[33] *Britton* [1987] 2 All E.R. 412—the defendant had made a note of the events, following his arrest for public order offences.

confines his cross-examination to the part of the document used by the witness to refresh his memory he is merely testing the genuine nature of the refreshment of the witness's memory or challenging the accuracy of the past recollection recorded and deposed to by the witness. But when he cross-examines on other parts of the document he is attempting to elicit testimony from the witness, or to discredit him by means of a document that is not before the jury as evidence in the case. The argument is that it would be wrong to allow the cross-examiner to make use of the document in a way quite unrelated to the testing of the refreshment of memory, and then to complain about being required to put the document in evidence.

At common law, where the document became an exhibit, the jury could not use it as evidence of the facts but merely as evidence of the credibility of the witness. In *Virgo*,[34] the witness in a police corruption trial was Humphries, a man whose business interests involved Soho sex shops. He was permitted to use his diaries to 'refresh his memory' as to dates of payments made to Virgo and was cross-examined extensively by the defence on other aspects of his diaries which unsurprisingly revealed his character to be far from unblemished. The diaries were admitted into evidence. Humphries was an accomplice to the corruption—at that time, the law required that an accomplice's testimony be corroborated[35] whose evidence at that time required corroboration. The diaries could not be used for that purpose and could only go towards Humphries' credibility as a witness, as the diary entries were consistent with his sworn testimony.

Section 120(3) of the Criminal Justice Act 2003 does not alter the common law as to the circumstances in which a document becomes an exhibit. However it does alter the impact.

120: Other previous statements of witnesses
(3) A statement made by the witness in a document-
(a) which is used by him to refresh his memory while giving evidence,
(b) on which he is cross-examined, and
(c) which as a consequence is received in evidence in the proceedings,
is admissible as evidence of any matter stated of which oral evidence by him would be admissible

This provision now allows jurors to treat the document as evidence of the facts that it contains as opposed simply to confirming the witness's consistency.

C. *The Rule Against Narrative—Previous Consistent Statements*[36]

There is a well-settled rule that a party cannot ask their own witness about earlier oral or written statements made by the witness which are consistent with current testimony. In *Roberts*,[37] the defendant was charged with murder.

---

[34] (1978) 67 Cr.App.R. 323.
[35] This requirement was removed by Criminal Justice and Public Order Act 1994, s.32.
[36] For historical background, see R. Gooderson, "Previous Consistent Statements" (1968) 26 Cambridge L.J. 64.
[37] [1942] 1 All E.R. 187.

In his evidence, he wished to testify that it had been an accident and that, two days after the killing, he told his father that it had been an accident. He was not entitled to retail his statement to his father.

Roberts [1942] 1 All E.R 187 at 191e–f, *per* Humphreys J.:

It is because it does not assist the elucidation of the matters in dispute that the evidence is said to be inadmissible on the ground that it is irrelevant. It would not help the jury in this case in the least to be told that the appellant said to a number of persons, whom he saw while he was awaiting his trial, or on bail if he was on bail; that his defence was this, that or the other. The evidence asked to be admitted was tat the father had been told by his son that it was an accident. We think the evidence was properly refused.

This rule is also rigorously applied in the USA—in *Tome v US*,[38] a father was accused of sexually abusing his daughter. The Government presented six witnesses who recounted out of court statements that she had made about the alleged assault while she was living with her mother. These were excluded under the Federal Rule of Evidence 801(d) (1)(B) as hearsay, *i.e.* as proof of the fact that the father abused his daughter. But the statements are also powerful evidence of the victim's consistency and credibility—in other words, when the daughter testifies that her father abused her, those statements show that she is more likely to be telling the truth. Prior consistent statements are admitted for a different purpose than hearsay statements but despite this, such statements are still excluded.

There is a logical reason to admit a prior consistent statement but the courts view such evidence as a distraction. In *Corke v Corke and Cooke*,[39] the husband in a divorce action had gone to his wife's house at midnight and accused his wife and the lodger of having recently committed adultery. The wife telephoned the doctor, asking him to examine both herself and the lodger to show that there had been no recent intercourse. The doctor refused but at trial the court admitted evidence of the telephone conversation. On appeal, this evidence was treated as inadmissible.

Corke v Corke and Cooke [1958] 1 All E.R. 224 at 235g–i, *per* Sellers L.J. :

In my view, not only is the evidence of what the wife did and said valueless and might indeed be misleading to the court, but it is not admissible. To what issue, it should be asked, does it go? It does nothing to prove the condition of either the female or male organ respectively of the parties alleged to be involved. It does nothing to

---

[38] 513 U.S. 150 (1995); R. Burns, "Bright Lines and Hard Edges" [1995] Journal of Criminal Law and Criminology, Vol. 85 843.
[39] [1958] 1 All E.R. 224.

disprove the intercourse the husband had alleged. The most that could be said is that the wife was showing a belief in her own story and adding some reason why the court should believe her. In this case I do not think the conduct and statement of the wife have that effect, but it is clear that a skilful witness might well embark on circumstantial matters to bolster up his or her story. Neville J.'s statement in *Jones v South Eastern & Chatham Railway Co*[40] cited by my Lord, 'that you are not entitled to give evidence of statements on other occasions by the witness in confirmation of her testimony' neatly and accurately, in my opinion, states the law which is applicable to the question raised by the husband.

Whether or not this rule is strictly logical, it is one which keeps the evidence to the main issues in dispute and tends to avoid deception of the court by a resourceful witness . . . .

The rationale for this exclusion takes various forms:

a) there is a danger of manufactured evidence to bolster the credibility of a witness;
b) such statements add little weight to a witness's testimony and are superfluous; or
c) there is a danger of irrelevant side issues as to whether this prior statement was actually made.

But, as long ago as 1961, Cross was dismissive of the need for such a rule.

R. Cross, "Some Proposals for Reform in the Law of Evidence" [1961] 24 M.L.R. 32:

The justification of the rule under consideration is usually said to be the risk that the evidence may be fabricated. In the oft-quoted and cynical words of Eyre C.B. "the presumption is that no man would declare anything against himself unless it were true; but every man, if he was in a difficulty, or in the view to any difficulty, would make declarations for himself."[41] Like so much of the reasoning on which our law of evidence is based, this may well be thought to belong to a bygone age, an age when the parties could not give evidence and when it was perfectly reasonable to hold that there was no such guarantee of the trustworthiness of a self-serving statement as would justify its reception as evidence of the facts stated under what would now be described as an exception to the rule against hearsay. The situation is entirely different when the party is before the court, as he is today, ready to be cross-.examined with regard to his previous statement and the circumstances in which it was made. Even if the reasoning of Eyre C.B. remains valid at all, it can, and always could, only apply so as to exclude the previous consistent statements of a party, whereas the rule under consideration applies to all witnesses.

A sounder and less cynical justification of the rule is that the confirmatory evidence is insufficiently relevant to warrant its reception having regard to the collateral issues which might be raised concerning such matters as the precise terms of the previous statement and the circumstances in which it was made. Once it is realised that the whole question is one of relevancy, it is easy to see how the rule against the reception

---

[40] (1918) 87 L.J.K.B. 775.
[41] *Hardy* (1794) 4 St.Tr. 1065 at p.1093.

of prior consistent statements should be formulated. The proof of such statements ought to be prohibited if, and only if, the sole reason why they are relevant is that they tend to prove some degree of consistency on the part of the witness. Unfortunately the courts tend to treat the rule as something independent of the general requirement that, in order to be admissible, an item of evidence must possess a reasonably high degree of probative value. The result is that evidence which undoubtedly complies with this requirement is sometimes excluded.

For example, while everyone would agree that the fact that a wife denied a charge of adultery in telephone conversations two days after it was made is at most only remotely relevant as tending to confirm her testimony to the same effect, most people would take a very different view of a telephone conversation with a doctor immediately after the adultery was alleged to have taken place in which the wife denied the charge and asked the doctor to examine her. Yet evidence of this nature was excluded under the rule prohibiting the proof of prior consistent statements in Corke v. Corke and Cook.

A further reason for the abolition of this rule as a separate rule of evidence may be found in the difficulty of enumerating the exceptions to it. Statements forming part of the res gestae, statements made at such a time as rebut the cross-examiner's suggestion that the maker's testimony is a recent invention and complaints in sexual cases are obvious instances, but there may well be others. For example, it is the common practice at a criminal trial to admit everything said by the accused when charged, including assertions favourable to his case which he repeats in his evidence. How is this eminently sensible and fair procedure to be justified as a matter of strict legal theory? As it has never been discussed, it is perhaps pointless to pursue the question.

In terms of logic and theory, there is little to be said for this rule but the opportunity to abolish it altogether in 2003 was missed. Section 120 of the Criminal Justice Act 2003 has, to a limited extent, modified it.[42] Abolition would have been a boon to those who have to testify in the criminal justice system and the problems of manufactured evidence and alleged lack of probative weight could easily have been overcome by using the judge's discretion to exclude irrelevant evidence.[43]

Exceptions

It is said that there are three common law exceptions to this rule against narrative, namely recent complaint by a victim of sexual assault, allegation of recent fabrication by the witness or where the statement was part of the *res gestae*. To that list, one might also add statements made on accusation or on finding incriminating items or statements made on identification. Although based in the common law, the exceptions have all been affected by recent statutory reform. But there is no general exception that, where a witness has been subject to cross-examination to show inconsistencies, that witness can be re-examined to show consistency.[44] This was supported in *Ali*,[45] although Potter L.J. did suggest that there is.

---

[42] D. Birch, "Same Old Story, Same Old Song" [2004] Crim. L.R. 556 at 570; G. Durston, "Previous (In) Consistent Statements After the Criminal Justice Act 2003" [2005] Crim L.R. 206.

[43] This discretion has been given added weight by the Criminal Justice Act 2003, s.126.

[44] *Beattie*(1989) 89 Cr.App.R. 302.

[45] [2004] 1 Cr.App.R. 39.

Ali [2004] 1 Cr.App.R. 39, *per* Potter L.J.:

... residual discretion, necessary in the interests of justice, which permits, and indeed requires, close examination of the position in relation to a suggestion of recent fabrication, as well as the need in all cases to ensure that, as a result of a question put in cross-examination, the jury is not positively misled as to the existence of some fact or the terms of an earlier statement.[46]

(i) *Allegation of "recent fabrication"*

In criminal proceedings, the prior consistent statement may be used to rebut an allegation of "recent fabrication". This does not permit a witness to retail previous occasions on which the same story was told just because they have been attacked on cross-examination but only where counsel has accused the witness of recently inventing the story. In *Oyesiku*,[47] the defendant was charged with assault on a police officer and his wife testified that it was the officer who was the aggressor. It was put to her that she had colluded with the defendant, to make up this story. The conviction was quashed after the judge did not allow the defence to show that the wife had made such a statement to the solicitor before she had even visited the defendant at the police station.

Oyesiku (1971) 56 Cr.App.R. 240 at 246, *per* Karminski L.J.:

If the credit of a witness is impugned as to some material fact to which he deposes upon the ground that his account is a late invention or has been lately devised or reconstructed, even though not with conscious dishonesty, that makes admissible a statement to the same effect as the account he gave as a witness, if it was made by the witness contemporaneously with the event or at a time sufficiently early to be inconsistent with the suggestion that his account is a late invention or reconstruction.[48]

Sekhon[49] also illustrates this—police officers kept observation on the defendant who was suspected of supplying drugs. They maintained an observation log. The defence cross-examination of the officers involved a suggestion that the police had concocted the record and the observation log was admissible to rebut this suggestion. The American courts allow this as one of the only exceptions to this rule and it is interpreted restrictively. In *Tome v US*,[50] the statements of the victim were excluded, although they were made well before any allegation of fabrication had arisen. However they had been made after her alleged motive to fabricate arose, a rationale that, if applied in England, would have excluded the witness's statement in *Oyesiku*.

---

[46] *ibid.* at para.31.
[47] (1971) 56 Cr.App.R. 240.
[48] at 246 *per* Karminski L.J. citing Dixon C.J. in *Nominal Defendant v Clements* (1961) 104 C.L.R. 476.
[49] (1986) Cr.App.R. 19.
[50] 513 U.S. 150 (1995); R. Burns, "Bright Lines and Hard Edges" [1995] Journal of Criminal Law and Criminology, Vol. 85, 843.

At common law, the impact of admitting such a prior consistent statement was simply to show the consistency of the witness's sworn testimony. Section 120 of the Criminal Justice Act 2003 does not alter the common law as to the circumstances in which a prior statement becomes admissible. However it does alter the impact.

120: Other previous statements of witnesses
(2) If a previous statement by the witness is admitted as evidence to rebut a suggestion that his oral evidence has been fabricated, that statement is admissible as evidence of any matter stated of which oral evidence by the witness would be admissible.

This provision now allows jurors to treat the document as evidence of the facts that it contains as opposed simply to confirming the witness's consistency.

(ii) *Complaints made by victims*

In sexual assault cases, the common law admitted into evidence complaints made soon after the attack in support of the victim's testimony.[51] This exception is a relic from the rule that a woman should raise the hue and cry directly after an attack as a preliminary to an appeal of rape. Otherwise a strong inference could be drawn from a failure to complain and the bare fact of the complaint could be given to rebut any such inference. Section 120 of the Criminal Justice Act 2003 has now broadened this exception to include victims of any offence.

120 Other previous statements of witnesses
(4) A previous statement by the witness is admissible as evidence of any matter stated of which oral evidence by him would be admissible, if—
(a) any of the following three conditions is satisfied, and
(b) while giving evidence the witness indicates that to the best of his belief he made the statement, and that to the best of his belief it states the truth . . .
(7) The third condition is that—
(a) the witness claims to be a person against whom an offence has been committed,
(b) the offence is one to which the proceedings relate,
(c) the statement consists of a complaint made by the witness (whether to a person in authority or not) about conduct which would, if proved, constitute the offence or part of the offence,
(d) the complaint was made as soon as could reasonably be expected after the alleged conduct,
(e) the complaint was not made as a result of a threat or a promise, and
(f) before the statement is adduced the witness gives oral evidence in connection with its subject matter.
(8) For the purposes of subsection (7) the fact that the complaint was elicited (for example, by a leading question) is irrelevant unless a threat or a promise was involved.

The common law had evolved rules which laid down the circumstances in which such statements could be admitted which will still be relevant to the

[51] J. Temkin, *Rape and Legal Process* (2nd ed., OUP, 2002), Ch.4.

interpretation of s.120(7). First, the prior statement must be about the offence to which the proceedings relate. It is admissible evidence not merely of the fact of the crime but also the substance. In *Lillyman*,[52] the employer of the victim was allowed to testify as to details of the attempted rape that the prosecutrix had narrated to her.

Lillyman [1896] 2 Q.B. 167 at 170–177, *per* Hawkins J.:

After very careful consideration we have arrived at the conclusion that we are bound by no authority to support the existing usage of limiting evidence of the complaint to the bare fact that a complaint was made . . . .

Those details are now evidence of the facts (s.120(4)) rather than mere reinforcement of the victim's consistency and credibility. In *Xhabri*,[53] the Latvian victim was abducted and forced to work as a prostitute. Statements from her parents about phone calls from her were admitted under these provisions.

The key common law conditions for the complaint to be admitted were that it must be spontaneous and contemporaneous. The requirement of spontaneity, once so central,[54] is now of less importance—the complaint is only inadmissible if it has been obtained as the result of a threat or a promise. However s.120(7)(d) still requires that "the complaint was made as soon as could reasonably be expected after the alleged conduct". The common law tells us that a victim need not complain to the first person encountered: in *Cummings*,[55] the victim did not complain to a male supervisor in the camp but waited to speak to a woman friend the next morning. Although flexible, the criterion is still there to be applied.

D. Birch, "Same Old Story, Same Old Song" [2004] Crim.L.R. 556 at 571:

. . . in *Birks*[56] the Court of Appeal questioned the basis of the common law rule allowing only prompt complaints of sexual assault to be adduced to confirm a complainant's testimony. In that case the complainant was an adult giving evidence about what had happened to her when a small child. Although she had told her mother about it not long after it happened, she had been too frightened to do as so as promptly as required by the rule, and the complaint, though very compelling, was therefore inadmissible. It is hard not to sympathise with the view of the Court that the evidence ought to have been admissible, in fact it would be a sound rule if the

---

[52] [1896] 2 Q.B. 167.
[53] [2006] 1 All E.R. 776.
[54] *Osborne* [1905] 1 K.B. 551.
[55] [1948] 1 All E.R. 551.
[56] [2003] EWCA Crim 3091; [2003] Crim.L.R. 401.

evidence of a first complaint was always admissible, but the CJA 2003 does no more than substitute a slightly more open-ended form of words ("as soon as can reasonably be expected") for the promptness requirement. Thus the statement in *Birks* could still not be received, unless either the court is prepared to take a very creative approach to the wording (which was not intended to bring about dramatic change) or (which would be most encouraging) to take up the safety valve as a "flexible weapon to achieve justice" by admitting a compelling but late complaint.

Whether the complaint was made expeditiously is a matter of fact for the judge. Delay in complaining, even where the complaint is admitted, may still tell against the consistency of the account and accordingly affect a jury's assessment of credibility.

(iii) *Statements made as part of the res gestae*

Another common law exception, unaffected by the 2003 Act, is that involving self-serving statements which are made as part of the *res gestae*.[57] Everything which is part of and contemporaneous with the event itself can be rehearsed in court. In *Fowkes*,[58] the accused was charged with murder. The son of the dead man was sitting in the room with his father and a policeman when a face appeared at a window and the fatal shot was fired. The son testified that he thought that the face was that of the accused but also that on seeing the face at the window, he shouted "There's Butcher". The policeman also testified as to what was said. Such statements have always been admitted as evidence of the facts contained.

(iv) *Statements made on accusation*

At some point in a criminal investigation, an accusation will be put to the defendant, normally by a police officer to the suspect. Often the result of the accusation is an admission of some kind and this is admissible as evidence of the facts it contains, although procedurally it must conform to ss.76 and 78 of the Police and Criminal Evidence Act 1984.[59] But generally any witness can testify to the accused's response to accusation, be it by conduct, verbally or by demeanour. This response can consist of a denial or admission of guilt, or a mixture where an admission is accompanied by a justification or excuse for the conduct. The accused can also, of course, lie and such lies can be used in evidence.[60] There may be no statement at all but where the suspect remains silent upon accusation, where a response may reasonably be expected, at common law that silence can be admissible and supportive evidence.[61]

---

[57] This is discussed further in Ch.17.
[58] The Times, March 8, 1856.
[59] Confessions are discussed in Ch.4.
[60] *Lucas* [1981] 2 All E.R. 1008—but not against a co-accused: *Collins and Keep* [2004] 2 Cr.App.R. 11.
[61] *Cramp* (1880) 14 Cox 390; *Horne* [1990] Crim. L.R. 188; the situation where the prosecution may seek to draw an adverse inference from silence under ss.34, 36 or 37 of the Criminal Justice and Public Order Act 1994 are discussed in Ch.4.

The traditional authority for this is *Christie*,[62] where the defendant was accused of indecently assaulting a young boy. With his mother and a police officer, the boy went up to Christie and said "That's the man". Christie denied his guilt.

Christie [1914] A.C. 545 at 554, *per* Lord Atkinson:

The rule of law undoubtedly is that a statement made in the presence of an accused person even upon an occasion which should be expected reasonably to call for some explanation or denial from him, is not evidence against him of the facts stated save so far as he accepts the statement so as to make it in effect his own. If he accepts the statement in part only, then to that extent alone does it become his statement. He may accept the statement by word or conduct, action or demeanour, and it is the function of the jury which tries the case to determine whether his words, action, conduct or demeanour at the time when the statement was made amounts to an acceptance of it in whole or in part. It by no means follows, I think, that a mere denial by the accused of the facts mentioned in the statement necessarily renders the statement inadmissible, because he may deny his statement in such a manner and under such circumstances as may lead a jury to disbelieve him, and constitute evidence from which an acknowledgement can be inferred by them.

An accusation may be met with a verbal admission or a reaction from which a jury might infer guilt. Both are admissible at common law. But suspects might seek to deny or justify their actions—the statement is a mixed statement rather than simply an incriminating one. Everything said to the police is in practice admissible evidence[63] and this includes not only inculpatory and exculpatory statements but statements that include both elements. In *Duncan*,[64] the defendant, accused of strangling a woman, told the police that he had lost his temper when the victim teased him. There was thereby both an admission and perhaps some evidence of provocation. At trial, the accused testifies about the conduct of the victim and seeks to use the statement made to the police in support of this. That statement is a prior statement consistent with present testimony but is admissible as an exception to the rule.

The confession itself is treated as evidence of the facts contained and the question arises whether the self-serving statement is to be treated in the same way or merely as supportive of the accused's credibility? In *Duncan*, the trial judge said that the exculpatory part of the statement was not evidence of facts but this was disapproved of by the Court of Appeal. This approach was supported by the House of Lords in *Sharp*[65] so that a mixed statement to the police is admissible as evidence of the facts it contains whether the statement is an admission or is self-serving.

Sharp [1988] 1 All E.R. 65 at 71e–g, *per* Lord Havers:

My Lords, the weight of authority and common sense lead me to prefer the direction to the jury formulated in *R v Duncan* to an attempt to deal differently with the

[62] [1914] A.C. 545.
[63] *Pearce* (1979) 69 Cr.App.R. 365.
[64] (1981) 73 Cr.App.R. 359; *Aziz* [1996] A.C. 41.
[65] [1988] 1 All E.R. 65.

different parts of a mixed statement. How can a jury fairly evaluate the facts in the admission unless they can evaluate the facts in the excuse or explanation? It is only if the jury think the facts set out by way of excuse or explanation might be true that any doubt is cast on the admission and it is surely only because the excuse or explanation might be true that it is thought fair that it should be considered by the jury. I agree . . . that a jury will make little of a direction that attempts to draw a distinction between evidence which is evidence of facts and evidence in the same statement which whilst not being evidence of facts is nevertheless evidentiary material of which they may make use in evaluating evidence which is evidence of facts. One only has to write out the foregoing sentence to see the confusion it engenders.

Even where the suspect's statement to the police is simply exculpatory, it is still admissible. In *Storey*,[66] the accused told the police that the cannabis found in her flat had been brought there by another against her will.

Storey (1968) 52 Cr.App.R. 334 at 337–338, *per* Widgery L.J.:

The question which arises in this case is whether the fact that she gave shortly afterwards an explanation which, if true, would provide a completely innocent explanation is enough to produce a situation in which the learned judge's duty was to say that there was no case to answer . . . We think it right to recognise that a statement made by the accused to the police, although it always forms evidence in the case against him, is not in itself evidence of the truth of the facts stated. A statement made voluntarily by an accused person to the police is evidence in the trial because of its vital relevance as showing the reaction of the accused when first taxed with the incriminating facts. If, of course, the accused admits the offence, then as a matter of shorthand one says that the admission is proof of guilt, and, indeed, in the end it is. But the accused makes a statement which does not amount to an admission, the statement is not strictly evidence of the truth of what was said but is evidence of the reaction of the accused which forms part of the general picture to be considered by the jury at the trial.[67]

Where the statement is wholly self-serving, especially if it is made after long consideration and after legal advice, it may not be admissible.

Pearce (1979) 69 Cr.App.R. 370:

Although in practice, most statements are given in evidence even when they are largely self serving, there may be a rare occasion when an accused produces a carefully prepared written statement to the police, with a view to its being made part of the prosecution evidence. The trial judge would plainly exclude such a statement as inadmissible.[68]

---

[66] (1968) 52 Cr.App.R. 334.
[67] *ibid.* at 337–338 *per* Widgery L.J.; followed in *Pearce* (1979) above.
[68] *Pearce*, above at 370; *Newsome* (1980) 71 Cr.App.R. 325.

(v) *Statements made on discovery of recently stolen or otherwise incriminating articles*

Police officers often seek explanations for a suspect's possession of various articles. Suspects often give an account which can be incriminating or may be justificatory. Witnesses can testify as to what suspects say when found in possession of, for example, recently stolen or otherwise incriminating articles. Where the only evidence is possession and the defendant offers no proper explanation, the jury is entitled to infer guilty knowledge.[69] Any statement on discovery, whether self-serving or not, is admissible as evidence.[70] There is authority that this applies even in a case of murder, where, for example, the defendant is discovered in possession of the murder weapon or of items taken from the scene.[71]

(vi) *Statements made at identification*

Identification evidence[72] is often treated exceptionally and so it is with previous consistent statements. When a witness identifies an accused in the course of the trial, evidence of a previous identification, normally at an identity parade, is admissible. This is not simply to add weight to the witness's consistency but the evidence of the previous identification is evidence in its own right. Where the identifying witness is unable to confirm the previous identification on oath, evidence of that identification can be given. In *Osbourne*,[73] the witness could not identify the defendant or remember that she had identified him previously at a parade. The police officer who had been in charge of the parade was permitted to testify to the fact of the identification. This was admitted despite a strong argument that such testimony was hearsay. Any such questions have been made redundant by s.120(4) and (5) of the Criminal Justice Act 2003 which permits the prior statements of witnesses to be admitted as evidence of their facts where those statements concern identification.[74]

(vii) *Statements of the forgetful witness*

At common law, if a witness does not remember matters well enough to give oral evidence of those matters, they would not be called as a witness. Any previous statement, oral or written, about those matters was hearsay and the 1988 reforms did not help, straightforwardly because the witness was available to give evidence. A more far-reaching reform has been introduced by s.120(6) of the Criminal Justice Act 2003 which now allows the previous statements of forgetful witnesses to be admitted.

This is not an exception to the rule against prior consistent statements, although it is convenient to deal with it at this point. What it represents is an exception to the hearsay rule and would be better placed under s.116.

---

[69] *Schama and Abramovitch* (1914) 11 Cr.App.R. 45.
[70] *Abraham* (1848) 3 Cox 430.
[71] *Muller* (1865) 4 F.&F. 383n—the defendant was in possession of the victim's hat. See comment by L. Blake *Estates Gazette* October 14, 1995; Gooderson, *op.cit.* at 71.
[72] This will normally be subject to the regime of Code D, Police and Criminal Evidence Act 1984.
[73] [1973] Q.B. 678; *Christie* [1914] A.C. 545; *McCay* [1991] 1 All E.R. 232.
[74] This is discussed in Ch.11.

120 Other previous statements of witnesses

(4) A previous statement by the witness is admissible as evidence of any matter stated of which oral evidence by him would be admissible, if-

(a) any of the following three conditions is satisfied, and

(b) while giving evidence the witness indicates that to the best of his belief he made the statement, and that to the best of his belief it states the truth.

(6) The second condition is that the statement was made by the witness when the matters stated were fresh in his memory but he does not remember them, and cannot reasonably be expected to remember them, well enough to give oral evidence of them in the proceedings.

Witnesses must be sworn and testify that they recall making the statement —this can be a written witness statement or an informal oral statement. They must state that at that time the matters were fresh in their memory and that the statement is true. Witnesses must also explain that they do not remember the matters contained in the statement. There must be reasonable grounds for not remembering—presumably those grounds would include the detailed nature of the information that was given, the passage of time or maybe the fact that the information did not seem significant at that time.

(viii) *Civil proceedings*

Prior consistent statements are admissible in civil proceedings under s.6 of the Civil Evidence Act 1995,

6.—(1) Subject as follows, the provisions of this Act as to hearsay evidence in civil proceedings apply equally (but with any necessary modifications) in relation to a previous statement made by a person called as a witness in the proceedings.

(2) A party who has called or intends to call a person as a witness in civil proceedings may not in those proceedings adduce evidence of a previous statement made by that person, except—

(a) with the leave of the court, or

(b) for the purpose of rebutting a suggestion that his evidence has been fabricated.

A previous statement of a witness is only admissible as of right to rebut the suggestion that the witness's testimony has been fabricated under s.6(2)(b) and in all other cases, the leave of the court must be obtained before a previous statement is advanced in evidence.

13

THE HOSTILE WITNESS AND CROSS-EXAMINATION

I. INTRODUCTION

Examination in chief is designed to lead a party's own witnesses through their testimony in a facilitative manner, eliciting an account which is favourable to the party calling them. It is witness-friendly. But there are two stages of a trial where counsel will be more aggressive. The first of these is cross-examination where counsel examines the witnesses presented by the other side. The second is that where a party has called a witness who gives unexpected, often unfavourable, evidence that deviates from that contained in a witness statement. In such circumstances, counsel might well seek to ask more forceful questions than are generally allowed in direct examination. It is appropriate to discuss the position of such 'hostile' witnesses alongside issues surrounding cross-examination. The basic techniques involve suggesting that:

a) the specific facts retailed by the witness to the court are incorrect and that the witness's powers of perception, memory and recall were faulty. Counsel can put leading questions, suggesting a contradictory account to that of the witness;[1]

b) the witness has made contradictory statements in the past. Counsel can put previous inconsistent statements to the witness and, if necessary, prove them;

c) the witness's general character means they are not to be believed. This might be general discreditable conduct or involve putting specific criminal convictions to the witness.

All three are used in cross-examination but the last, that of impugning character, cannot be employed against your own witness.

II. IMPEACHING WITNESSES

Where a party is confronted with a witness who has given unfavourable evidence, they should first offer the witness the opportunity to refresh their memory from the witness statement. Where the witness refuses to do so or

---

[1] Always remembering that counsel's questions are not evidence.

adheres to the testimony already given, can a party challenge that witness, whether by questioning the accuracy of the witness's account or by putting previous inconsistent statements to the witness? Such tactics, suggesting that the witness that you have presented to the court is not worthy of belief, are usually prohibited and parties find themselves bound by the rule which prohibits impeaching one's own witness.

M. Newark "The Hostile Witness and the Adversary System" [1986] Crim.L.R.441:

It is clear that the origin of the rule against impeaching one's own witness lies in the development of the adversary system of trial. Certain rules follow from the notion of party responsibility for the collection and presentation of evidence. Others flow from the requirements of a well regulated contest under such conditions. The latter group includes rules designed as a corrective to the wayward operation of such a system. But there is a difference between those rules that interfere with the free choice of the parties merely to preserve the true adversary character of the contest, and rules that are designed to subvert the system in some respect. Into the former character fall the rule against leading one's own witness, the rule against narrative, the regulation of refreshing memory. These rules are designed to preserve the oral character of the trial so as to make it a test of witness performance rather than a regurgitating of rehearsed statements. But the rule that prevents a party from discrediting his own witness seems to be part of the basic philosophy of the adversary trial and any exception to the rule must have the effect of undermining the adversary principle. The various rationale of the non-impeachment rule, that a party is bound by his own witness, that he guarantees his credibility, that he should not be allowed to blow hot and cold with his witness, while they emphasise adversarial responsibility in evidence presentation, seem to leave no room for the hostile witness exception. Nevertheless, attempts have been made to force the hostile witness exception into an adversary mould. So long as the treatment of the hostile witness was confined to a cross-examination to persuade the witness to tell the truth it was possible to accommodate the exception within adversary theory. The hostile witness is not open to the dangers of suggestion, so some of the ordinary rules of examination-in-chief can be relaxed. However, in criminal cases after 1865 when the impeachment of the hostile witness becomes possible, an adversary justification for such treatment must be sought in remedying some more serious dysfunctioning of the system. This is achieved by regarding testimony hostile witness as in reality the opponent's witness so that he may be treated much as though he were a witness for the other side.[2]

In the USA, this rule has been abolished so that "The credibility of a witness may be attacked by any party, including the party calling the witness."[3]

The rationale for the American position is that the traditional rule against impeaching one's own witness is based on false premises. Litigants are not responsible for the presentation of evidence and thus do not hold out their witnesses as worthy of belief, since there is rarely a free choice in selecting

[2] Newark also gives a useful account of the historical origins of the hostile witness rule.
[3] Federal Rules of Evidence r.607.

them. Denial of the right to impeach leaves the party at the mercy of the witness and the adversary. If the impeachment is by prior statement, it is free from the dangers of hearsay. Despite this persuasive position, the English courts have eschewed this *laissez-faire* mentality and still regulate those situations where you may impeach your own witness. We should distinguish two situations—first, where the witness simply testifies in an unforeseen and unfavourable manner and secondly, where the witness is hostile.

A. *The Unfavourable Witness*

A witness may not give the testimony anticipated by the party who calls him or her. It may be actively hostile or just less favourable than was hoped for. But, while the general rule is that counsel cannot question their own witness's character or credibility, this does not stop a litigant from calling other witnesses to contradict the unfavourable testimony. In *Ewer v Ambrose*,[4] a defence witness called to prove the existence of a partnership, proved the contrary.

Ewer v Ambrose [1825] 3 B. & C. 746, *per* Littledale J.:

Where a witness is called by a party to prove his case and he disproves that case, I think the party is still at liberty to prove his case by other witnesses. It would be great hardship if the rule were otherwise, for if a party had four witnesses upon whom he relied to prove his case, it would be very hard that, by calling first the one who happened to disprove it, he should be deprived of the testimony of the other three . . . The order in which witnesses happen to be called ought not, therefore, to make any difference . . .

In civil proceedings, the witness statement frequently stands as the evidence in chief which makes it unlikely that unexpected and unfavourable testimony will be given. Where this does happen (but the witness is not deemed hostile), a party may ask the leave of the court to introduce the witness's previous inconsistent statement under s.6(2)(a) of the Civil Evidence Act 1995.

6.—(1) Subject as follows, the provisions of this Act as to hearsay evidence in civil proceedings apply equally (but with any necessary modifications) in relation to a previous statement made by a person called as a witness in the proceedings.
(2) A party who has called or intends to call a person as a witness in civil proceedings may not in those proceedings adduce evidence of a previous statement made by that person, except—
(a) with the leave of the court . . .

This would certainly be possible where the witness has become senile.[5]

---

[4] (1825) 3 B. & C. 746.
[5] *Harvey v Smith-Wood* [1963] 2 All E.R. 127.

In criminal proceedings, there is no general rule which would allow a witness's statement to be introduced as their evidence in chief.[6] However there are some possibilities, particularly where the quality of the witness's testimony is likely to be affected by age, illness, forgetfulness or fear—for example, a witness might turn up but prove to have been intimidated. In such cases, a prior witness statement may be admissible under the Criminal Justice Act 2003. Such statements might be inconsistent with what testimony has been given, might be a complete substitute because no testimony has been given or might simply fill in the gaps. There are several possibilities.

a) The first arises where the witness gives unexpected testimony through physical or mental illness—s.116(2)(b) refers to the witness being "unfit to attend as a witness". This does not refer solely to the physical act of getting to court. In *Setz–Dempsey*,[7] the witness came to court but, because of mental illness, was unable to recall the events. *Prima facie* the statement that he had previously made to the police was admissible.[8]

b) The second possibility arises where the witness is intimidated— section 116(2)(e) envisages the situation where the witness "does not continue to give" oral evidence through fear. This clearly applies not only where the intimidated witness refuses to testify but also where a witness attends court, is sworn but testifies in a hostile or simply unfavourable manner. The prosecution[9] can rely on a previous statement.[10]

c) A third avenue has emerged for the forgetful witness. At common law, if a witness did not remember matters well enough to give oral evidence, they did not testify nor was any previous statement was admissible—it was hearsay. But now, where counsel finds themselves not with an ill or intimidated witness but a merely forgetful one, a previous witness statement may be admitted under s.120(6) of the Criminal Justice Act 2003 as long as the witness could not reasonably be expected to remember the relevant matters.[11]

B. *The Hostile Witness*

A witness may be not simply unfavourable but actively hostile to the party calling them and fail to reproduce their pre-trial accounts. In these circum-

---

[6] There are possibilities for young and vulnerable witnesses under the Youth Justice and Criminal Evidence Act 1999.

[7] [1994] Crim.L.R. 123.

[8] See Ch.19—under the 2003 Act, it is admissible as of right but the judge could exclude if the admission of the evidence would infringe Police and Criminal Evidence Act 1984, s.78.

[9] More rarely, the defence might rely on these provision—see the facts in *Parkinson* [2004] EWCA Crim 3195.

[10] see Ch.19.

[11] see Ch.12.

stances, it becomes possible to impeach your own witness. Witnesses can be treated as hostile in both civil and criminal proceedings. The authority for treating a witness as hostile lies in both common law and statute.

1. At common law, the judge has discretion, if the attitude and demeanour of the witness is hostile, to allow leading questions and to put any prior inconsistent statements to the witness.[12] Prior to s.22 of the Common Law Procedure Act 1854,[13] it was undecided at common law whether these previous inconsistent statements could be proved as opposed merely to being put to the witness in cross-examination.

2. By statute under s.3 of the Criminal Procedure Act 1865, if in the opinion of the judge the witness's "present testimony" should prove adverse, counsel can contradict by proving prior inconsistent statements, providing that these have first been put to the witness.

> 3.—A party producing a witness shall not be allowed to impeach his credit by general evidence of bad character, but he may, in case the witness shall, in the opinion of the judge, prove adverse, contradict him by other evidence, or, by leave of the judge, prove that he has made at other times a statement inconsistent with his present testimony; but before such last-mentioned proof can be given the circumstances of the supposed statement, sufficient to designate the particular occasion must be mentioned to the witness, and he must be asked whether or not he has made such statement.

Neither common law nor statute exposes the hostile witness to the full panoply of the discrediting techniques used in cross-examination: in particular, counsel is not permitted to produce evidence of the witness's general bad character. Essentially a judge's ruling that a witness is hostile entitles counsel to ask leading questions and put previous inconsistent statements to that witness. The importance of this can be seen from the study that showed that potential jurors perceived that the most salient indicator of witness inaccuracy was a statement that was inconsistent with a previous statement made by that same witness.[14]

The statute does not nullify the common law which gives discretion to the judge over the issue of mode of examination. In *Thompson*,[15] the defendant was accused of incest with his daughter. She had earlier given a statement to the police but at the trial, having been sworn, refused to answer questions. The judge gave permission for her to be treated as a hostile witness and eventually she agreed that her previous statements were true. It was argued on appeal that, since she had stayed silent, there was no "present testimony" to be inconsistent with these earlier statements and therefore s.3 could not apply. The Court of Appeal held, regardless of s.3, that the common law gave the judge discretion as to what questions could be put to the witness.[16]

---

[12] *Clarke v Saffery* (1824) Ry. & M. 126.

[13] Superseded by s.3 of the Criminal Procedure Act 1865—see *Newark, op.cit.* 443–445.

[14] N. Brewer, R. Potter et al. "Beliefs and Data on the Relationship between Consistency and Accuracy of Eyewitness Testimony" Appl. Cognit. Psychol. 13: 297 (1999)—the study also concluded that the most consistent witness is not necessarily the most accurate.

[15] (1976) 64 Cr.App.R. 96.

[16] Had the witness denied making these earlier statements, they certainly could be proved under s.3. But it is a moot question whether they could have been proved at common law—see the authorities cited in R. Pattenden, "The Hostile Witness" (1992) 56 Jour.Crim. Law 414, fn5.

Thompson (1976) 64 Cr.App.R.96 at 98–99, *per* Lord Parker C.J.:

We do not find it necessary to express any view upon the section as applied to cases where there is an inconsistent statement. We think this matter must be dealt with by the provisions of the common law in regard to recalcitrant witnesses. Quite apart from what is said in section 3, the common law did recognise that pressure could be brought to bear upon witnesses who refused to co-operate and perform their duties. We have had the advantage of looking at one or two of the earlier cases . . . . The first is *Clarke v Saffery*[17] . . . . Best CJ said 'there is no fixed rule which binds the counsel calling a witness to a particular mode of examining him. If a witness, by his conduct in the box, shows himself decidedly adverse, it is always in the discretion of the judge to allow a cross-examination'.[18]

The key point is the definition of "hostile"? The 1865 Act uses the word "adverse" but it is the same test for common law and statute. Prior to 1847, the prosecution was responsible for calling all necessary witnesses, whether for the Crown or for the defence and thus the threshold at which they could be treated as equivalent to defence witnesses was relatively low.

M. Newark. "The Hostile Witness and the Adversary System" [1986] Crim.L.R. 445–446:

The phrase 'hostile' was not universally applied prior to the Common Law Procedure Act 1854 to the kind of witness that might be cross-examined by the party calling him. Indeed section 22 refers to a witness proving 'adverse' and it is not until *Greenough v Eccles*[19] that it is clearly established that this means something more than merely unfavourable. In *Greenough v Eccles* we see the origin of the idea that it is manifest antipathy that is the hall-mark of the hostile witness. The trial judge, Cockburn CJ, had refused leave under section 22 on the basis that the witness had not proved adverse 'in the sense of showing a mind hostile to the party calling him'. On appeal Williams J. said that 'the Judge's discretion must be principally, if not wholly, guided by the witness's behaviour and language in the witness box (for the Judge can know nothing, judicially, of his earlier conduct)' . . . . This shifting of focus from treachery and surprise to manifest antipathy seems to be due to a number of reasons. A need is felt to distinguish sharply between the hostile and the merely unfavourable witness. The test must be applicable with the minimum of fuss, leaving a substantial discretion to the trial judge so that appellate courts will not be burdened with appeals on this issue.

If the witness is not a compellable witness, it must be explained to them at the start and in the absence of the jury, that they have the right to refuse to testify but that if they choose to give evidence, they will be treated as any

---

[17] (1824) Ry. & M. 126.

[18] The comments about "recalcitrant" witnesses who "refuse to co-operate and perform their duties" scarcely seem apposite in talking about a 16 year old girl, sexually abused by her father, no doubt interviewed in embarrassing detail and at length by the police and now called to testify to these matters in a public court.

[19] (1859) 5 C.B.N.S. 786.

other witness and can be cross-examined as a hostile witness. In particular this might apply to the wife of the accused.[20] Before any application, counsel should ensure that the answers received have not been the result of a mistake and will perhaps invite the witness to refresh their memory but should not browbeat.[21] If there is no error, there should be an application to the judge in the absence of the jury. Procedurally it is for the judge to determine whether a witness is hostile. If the judge agrees that the application has merit and chooses to examine the witness, this should be in the presence of the jury since it will give them a yardstick to assess what credit is, ultimately, to be given to the testimony.[22] It is generally agreed that the judge can look at any previous inconsistent statement.

The test of "hostility" that the judge has to apply is whether the witness is ". . . desirous of telling the truth to the Court at the instance of the party calling him . . ."

Stephen's Digest on the Law of Evidence Art.147:

If a witness called by a party to prove a particular fact in issue or relevant to the issue fails to prove such fact or proves an opposite fact the party calling him may contradict him by calling other evidence and is not thereby precluded from relying on those parts of such witness's evidence as he does not contradict.

If a witness appears to the judge to be hostile to the party calling him, that is to say, nor desirous of telling the truth to the Court at the instance of the party calling him, the judge may in his discretion permit his examination by such party to be conducted in the manner of cross-examination to the extent to which the judge considers necessary for the purpose of doing justice

Such a witness may be leave of the judge be cross-examined as to (1) facts in issue or relevant or deemed to be relevant to the issue; (2) matters affecting his accuracy, veracity, or credibility in the particular circumstances of the case; and as to (3) whether he has made any former statement, oral of written, relative to the subject-matter of the proceeding and inconsistent with his present testimony . . .

In the case of a witness who is treated as hostile, proof of former statement, oral or written made by him inconsistent with his present testimony may by leave of the judge be given . . .[23]

This was accepted in *Jobe*.[24] The facts here demonstrate the low threshold at which a witness can be treated as hostile. The Crown witness in a rape case had not referred in his witness statement to any sexual remarks or overtures by the victim towards the defendant but had clearly stated that she had been quiet in the appellant's company, and that he had not seen her doing anything to him. But his evidence in cross-examination was that victim had been behaving in a flirtatious manner and had been touching the appellant.

[20] *Pitt* [1982] 3 All E.R. 63.
[21] The procedure is discussed in *Maw* [1994] Crim.L.R. 841.
[22] *Darby* [1989] Crim.L.R. 817.
[23] Approved by Lane L.C.J. in *Prefas and Pryce* (1987) 86 Cr.App.R. 111.
[24] [2004] EWCA Crim 3155.

This was plainly inconsistent with his prior statements, and was seen by the trial judge as evidence of critical importance which suggested collusion between the defendant and the witness. That rendered him liable to be treated as a hostile witness.

Of course pressure can be put on witnesses in other ways—perhaps McBarnet's example from a Scottish court is, procedurally, more typical.

D. McBarnet Conviction (Macmillan, 1983). p.98:

In another case where a victim of assault failed at first to identify the knife then to give clear evidence on what had been said during the attack, both prosecutor and judge made it clear they had ways and means of eliciting the information required:

Prosecutor:	Did he say anything?
Witness:	He might have. I couldn't make it out exactly.
Prosecutor:	Have you always said that?
Witness:	Yes.
Prosecutor:	What did you say to the police?
Witness:	Oh aye, he said he was going to get me or something.
Prosecutor:	Was it not more specific? I'm going to be talking to the policeman you spoke to that night you know, so let us be clear on what you are telling the court.
Judge:	Now, Mr S., you have at the moment made two contradictory statements. [Reading] 'I couldn't make it out' and 'he was going to get me or something'. If I think you are prevaricating—do you know what prevaricating means?
Witness:	It means, eh, saying something . . .
Judge:	[interrupting] It means avoiding a question. Now if I get the impression you are prevaricating then, believe me, I have powers to use. If you are going to answer, answer truthfully.

The prosecutor resumes with the now largely intimidated witness:

Prosecutor:	Did you tell the policeman you were not 100% sure or did you give him two clear sentences?
Witness:	(pause) Yes. He said he had a knife for me. He said he'd use it through my heart.

Informal pressure such as this will not always be successful and witnesses may be assessed by the judge as hostile. The result of this is that, under s.3 of the Criminal Procedure Act 1865, the party affected can ". . . by leave of the judge, prove that he has made at other times a statement inconsistent with his present testimony". The practice is to put that previous inconsistent statement to the witness. The witness can adopt it as their sworn testimony. If they refuse to do this, these prior statements can still be admitted into evidence.

The witness, however, might still adhere to the original testimony—for example, the witness in *Jobe* might well admit that he had failed to mention the victim's flirtatious behaviour in his original statement. He might justify that omission by saying that it had not seemed significant at the time but he now realised his error and his sworn oral testimony represented the truth. The prosecution are allowed to adduce those original witness statements as evidence. But what is their evidential status?

In civil proceedings, such statements are evidence of the facts they contain. But at common law in criminal cases, they merely reduce the credibility of the witness who made them. For example, in *White*,[25] the witness gave statements to the police implicating the accused in a public order offence but gave different testimony in court. Confronted with the prior statement, the witness insisted the sworn evidence was the correct version. The judge admitted the previous inconsistent statements and told the jury that they had to decide which story to believe. The conviction was quashed since the prior statement could only be introduced as casting doubt on the witness' credibility. It was not evidence of the accused's guilt.

This position has now been changed. The Law Commission[26] recommended that a previous inconsistent statement, where admitted, should be admissible as evidence of the truth of its contents. It was too subtle to ask a jury to distinguish between adducing a statement for the truth of the matters stated and adducing it merely to undermine the credibility of the declarant Contradictory statements by the same person should confront one another on the same evidential footing. The result of this has been s.119(1) of the Criminal Justice Act 2003.

119 (1) If in criminal proceedings a person gives oral evidence and—
(a) he admits making a previous inconsistent statement, or
(b) a previous inconsistent statement made by him is proved by virtue of section 3, 4 or 5 of the Criminal Procedure Act 1865 (c. 18),
the statement is admissible as evidence of any matter stated of which oral evidence by him would be admissible.

Where a witness has been declared hostile but has declared that the testimony in court is the truth and that the previous statement is not, the trier of fact can now choose which (or neither) of these accounts to believe. But they should weigh these two accounts with care, with regard to the circumstances in which the prior statement was made, the witness's explanation for the discrepancies and the extent to which the statements tie in with the other evidence in the case.

III. Cross-Examination

Cross-examination is that stage in the trial which involves the questioning of the witnesses called by the other party "to complete and correct the witness's story". It is one of the central techniques of adversarial advocacy.[27] The objectives of cross-examination are:

- to elicit facts favourable to your case which have not emerged; and
- to challenge and undermine adverse evidence given by the witness on behalf of your opponent.

---

[25] (1922) 17 Cr.App.R. 59.
[26] Law Commission Report 245: *Evidence in Criminal Proceedings: Hearsay and Related Topics* (1997) para.10.91.
[27] M. Stone, *Cross-Examination in Criminal Trials* (Butterworths, 1997).

A. *Supporters and critics*

Criticisms of cross-examination techniques and their effects in recent years have centred on the position of the child witness who has been sexually or physically abused.[28] But challenges to our system of questioning witnesses have a long history.

Anthony Trollope quoted in J. Frank, Courts on Trial (Princeton, 1973), p.83:

One would naturally imagine that an undisturbed thread of clear evidence would be best obtained from a man whose position was made easy and whose mind was not harassed; but this is not the fact; to turn a witness to good account, he must be badgered this way and that till he is nearly mad; he must be made a laughing stock for the court; his very truths must be turned into falsehoods, so that he may be falsely shamed; he must be accused of all manner of villainy, threatened with all manner of punishment; he must be made to feel that he has no friend near him, that the world is all against him; he must be confounded till he forget his right hand from his left, till his mind is turned into chaos, and his heart into water; and then let him give his evidence. What will fall from his lips when in this wretched collapse must be of special value, for the best talents of practised forensic heroes are daily used to bring it about; and no member of the Humane Society interferes to protect the wretch. Some sorts of torture are as it were tacitly allowed even among humane people. Eels are skinned alive, and witnesses are sacrificed, and no one's blood curdles at the sight, no soft heart is sickened at the cruelty.

But cross-examination has powerful support. Indeed recently at least one civil law system has moved to a more adversarial system of trial,[29] trusting in Wigmore's view.

J. Wigmore, Evidence (revised ed., Little Brown, 1974), para.1367:

Not even the abuses, the mishandlings, and the puerilities which are so often associated with cross-examination have availed to nullify its value . . . . It is beyond any doubt the greatest legal engine ever invented for the discovery of truth. However difficult it may be for the layman, the scientist, or the foreign jurist to appreciate its

---

[28] J. Spencer and J. Flin, *The Evidence of Children—The Law and Psychology* (2nd ed., Blackstones, 1993).

[29] M. Zander, "From Inquisitorial to Adversarial—the Italian Experiment" (1991) 141 New L.J. 67; but see Illuminati, Giulio, "The Frustrated Turn to Adversarial Procedure in Italy" (Italian Criminal Procedure Code of 1988) Washington University Global Studies Law Review, (forthcoming); J. Jackson, "The Effect of Human Rights on Criminal Evidentiary Processes: Towards Convergence, Divergence or Realignment?" [2005] 68 M.L.R. 737.

wonderful power, there has probably never been a moment's doubt upon this point in the mind of a lawyer of experience. He may, it is true, do more than he ought to do; he may 'make the worse appear the better reason to perplex and dash maturest counsels'—may make the truth appear like falsehood. But this abuse of its power is able to be remedied by proper control. The fact of this unique and irresistible power remains, and is the reason for our faith in its merits . . . . Cross-examination, not trial by jury, is the great and permanent contribution of the Anglo-American system of law to improved methods of trial procedure.

The "greatest legal engine ever invented for the discovery of truth" or a torture chamber—novelists and lawyers, psychologists and linguists all argue about the efficacy of the adversarial trial. But the ethical foundation is to be found in the notion of fairness—an accused person should have the right to confront the evidence against them. This is within the notion of a fair trial and is to be found in Art.6 3(d) of the European Convention, by which the accused has a right to examine, or to have examined, witnesses who are used against him. According to the wording, the provision implies no possibilities of exception to that right to cross-examine witnesses.[30]

The importance of the right of confrontation as the foundation of a fair trial cannot be overstated. But there remain major criticisms of cross-examination as a technique.[31]

a) Compared to other methods of eliciting testimony, cross-examination produces the largest number of errors, inducing greater caution[32] without any gain in completeness.[33] Questions are not open-ended to enable witnesses to construct their own account, are frequently narrowly defined and take the witness along in small steps, permitting no deviation. Such deviation can be countered by warnings, repeating the question and demanding a proper answer. An alternative tactic is to present a comprehensive account ("I suggest to you that . . . .") which obtains a blanket denial but provides little scope for countering on points of detail.

b) Distortion is also produced by putting leading questions to witnesses about peripheral matters ("What colour were his shoes?") and similarly confusion is induced by asking unconnected questions.

Brennan M. and R., Strange Language (Wagga Wagga, 1988):

In everyday interactions the unspoken conventions for changing topics of conversation are accepted. There is generally an obvious link between what has

---

[30] M. Holdgaard, "The Right to Cross-Examine Witnesses—Case Law under the European Convention on Human Rights" (2002) 71 Nordic Journal of International Law 83.

[31] See J. Spencer and J. Flin, *op.cit.* p.270ff.

[32] Witness accounts under cross-examination are much more defensive than under direct examination, giving justifications for their conduct before they have been asked—see M. Atkinson and P. Drew, *Order in Court* (Macmillan), 1979 esp. Ch.5 'Justifications and Excuses in Cross-examination'.

[33] D. Greer, "Anything but the Truth? The Reliability of Testimony in Criminal Trials" (1971) 11 Brit. Jour. Crim. 131; E. Luus and G. Wells, "The Perceived Credibility of Child Eyewitnesses" in H. Dent and R. Flin (eds), *Children as Eyewitnesses* (Wiley, 1992).

just been discussed and the new item of conversation on the agenda. It is common to hear people say ". . . speaking of such and such . . . did you read about . . . . have you seen . . ." If these cues are left out communication becomes disjointed and frustrated. Someone is inevitably left stranded by the privacy.

In court there is no provision within the language to establish these linkages. The cross-examiner jumps from topic to topic and the child witness is expected to keep pace. The juxtaposition of questions seems inexplicable as topics are jostled randomly. The effects of this are most critical when intimate details of the child's alleged sexual assault are questioned, and juxtaposed with general and more objective questions.

The technique of juxtaposing unrelated topics excludes the possibility of any transition time. Without this accommodation time, it is likely that the child will become disorientated, confused and unclear about the general line of questioning. The greater the frequency of these shifts from the personal to the objective, the greater the cumulative effect of the confusion will be.[34]

c) Cross-examination is designed to put the witness in a state of stress, especially when in the course of testing the witness's sincerity, counsel is allowed to suggest that the witness is lying. This causes anger in adults and considerable distress in children. Witnesses who were cross-examined were less likely to feel satisfied overall and less likely to feel satisfied with prosecution and defence lawyers than those who were not cross examined.

A Home Office study[35] on witness satisfaction showed that three in five witnesses felt they were treated courteously by the lawyer acting for the other side. Male witnesses and older witnesses are more likely to think they were treated courteously. Female witnesses and younger witnesses, especially victims thought that they were not treated courteously. Nearly two-thirds of witnesses were given the opportunity to say everything they wanted to by the other side's lawyer, although again victims, women and the young were less likely to think this.[36]

It has been argued that cross-examination and confrontation is not a means of getting to the truth.

J. Spencer and J. Flin, The Evidence of Children—The Law and Psychology (2nd ed., Blackstones, 1993), pp.278–279:

. . . when child witnesses are confronted with the defendant at a trial, quite often the effect is literally to scare them speechless. Of those who do succeed in giving evidence, many will be to some extent afraid, and . . . . psychological research makes it plain that stress beyond a certain point makes it harder for witnesses to order their thoughts and produce accurate information from memory. Studies by Dent and Stephenson[37]

[34] Cited in J. Spencer and J. Flin, *op.cit.* p.274.
[35] H. Angle, S. Malam and C. Carey *Findings From the Witness Satisfaction Survey 2002* (Home Office Online Report 19/03).
[36] H. Angle, S. Malam and C. Carey, *op.cit.* at 32.
[37] H. Dent and G. Stephenson, "Identification Evidence: Experimental Investigation of Factors Affecting the Reliability of Juvenile and Adult Witnesses" in D. Farrington, K. Hawkins and S. Lloyd-Bostock (eds), *Psychology, Law and Legal Process* (Macmillan, 1979).

shed some interesting light on the likely effect of confrontation on the accuracy of honest children's evidence. Children who had seen a workman enter their classroom were later asked to identify the man, some from a live parade, and others from slides. The children did significantly better from the slides than from the live parades, where a number showed significant signs of nervousness, and some refused to participate at all. Dent and Stephenson found a similar effect when the experiment was repeated using adults, but the effect of the suspect's presence was less marked . . . .

If it is clear that confrontation makes it harder for honest witnesses to tell the truth, is there any validity in the common belief that it makes it more difficult for dishonest ones to lie? This could be so, at least in some cases. If a false accuser's conscience is already pricking, it is possible that the sight of the person he has wronged may give him the necessary psychological shove to return him to the path of righteousness. However we are unaware of any psychological research that suggests it is generally harder to tell unpleasant lies about someone in their presence than unpleasant truths. It may be that the notion that confrontation generally causes liars to retract is false; and if it is, psychology provides a possible explanation for the unfounded belief. Studies with mock juries have shown that people tend to think that confidence in a witness is a sure sign of truthfulness—although in fact it is anything but this. Confrontation will make many witnesses feel uncomfortable, and in this state they will seem unconfident. If lawyers and lay people are inclined to confuse confidence with truthfulness, the fact that confrontation makes some witnesses more unconfident than others might give rise to a false belief that confrontation enables the court to tell which witnesses are telling lies.

Such criticisms must be placed alongside the importance of putting the defence version of events to witnesses and to the court. That importance lies in procedural justice, the right of confrontation, and in preventing the evils that would follow from anonymous accusation. The place of cross-examination in achieving this is firmly rooted in the adversarial system. Lord Justice Auld's review of the criminal courts in 2001 made sweeping recommendations for the reform of law and procedure but still fell short of a root and branch review of the adversarial style of the common law trial.

Lord Justice Auld: A Review of the Criminal Courts of England and Wales (2001) Ch.11, paras 79–80:

A common justification for our system of orality of evidence, including the rule against hearsay, is that seeing the demeanour and hearing the evidence of a witness in the witness box is the best means of getting at the truth. But there is much judicial, academic and psychological scepticism about the weight that even seasoned observers of witnesses should attach to the impressions they form of them in the witness box. It may be a factor, depending on the witness and what he has to say and on the experience and good judgment of the fact finder. But it is only one factor and I respectfully agree with the Law Commission that it is not of such significance, on its own, as to justify the exclusion of hearsay. I would go further and join Lord Bingham and a growing band of other distinguished jurists who, on the whole, doubt the demeanour of a witness as a reliable pointer to his honesty.[38]

Nevertheless, I can see no well-founded argument for a general move away from orality of evidence in criminal proceedings where there is an issue of the reliability or

---

[38] Lord Bingham of Cornhill, *The Business of Judging*, (OUP, Oxford, 2000), "The Judge as Juror: The Judicial Determination of Factual Issues", at pp.7–13.

credibility of a witness's account on a material matter. For there are features other than the demeanour of the witness which make it a convenient way of testing the truthfulness of his evidence, in particular its external and internal consistency, consistency with what he has said previously, and matters going to credit. And, in issues not turning on truthfulness, but accuracy or reliability of memory, there is clear advantage in an oral process, at least for the purpose of testing the strength of the evidence in cross examination. The witness box (or by way of video-tape or video-link) is the place for such critical evidence to be tested and, if necessary, challenged.

In 2003, the Criminal Justice Act made sweeping reforms of the double jeopardy rule, prosecution appeal, trials without jury as well the evidence rules relating to hearsay and bad character but the tradition of cross-examination emerged unscathed.

B. *Basics of cross examination*

All witnesses are liable to cross-examination unless they have been called either by mistake or merely to produce a document. Cross-examination is normally by counsel but can be taken over by the judge. Generally judges should exercise their right to ask questions sparingly and courteously, to elicit information and to clear up ambiguities. Excessive intervention is often a basis for an appeal.[39] A more unusual circumstance is for the judge to take over the examination—in *Cameron*,[40] the judge took over the cross-examination of the 14-year-old victim in a rape trial after she had refused to answer any further questions from the defence counsel.

Cameron [2001] EWCA 562, *per* Potter L.J.:

22 . . . . the joint industry of counsel before us has failed to reveal any reported decision dealing directly with the problem which arose in this case. We approach the matter on the basis that it is the overall duty of the judge to ensure that a fair trial takes place before him. It goes without saying that such a trial is normally to be conducted in the traditional manner adopted under our adversarial system, namely the examination and cross-examination of witnesses by the advocates for the prosecution and defence or, in default of representation, by the defendant himself, save insofar as alternative procedures are provided by statute. Nonetheless, we do not think that necessarily precludes a judge from dealing with a matter of this kind arising *ex improviso* within the spirit, rather than by the letter, of the system. The solution adopted by the judge in this case would not ordinarily be appropriate to the situation of an adult witness who, without good excuse, refuses to answer questions put in cross-examination, though we do not necessarily, for example, exclude such a procedure in the case of a witness who is labouring under a mental handicap or a frightened or traumatised witness in the case of a sexual complaint.

---

[39] *Hulusi* (1973) 58 Cr.App.R. 378; *Shaw* (Lexis 18/3/1999 CA) where trial judge had interrupted counsel on 164 occasions, although often to make a note of the answer.
[40] [2001] Crim.L.R. 587.

In addition, the judge is under a duty to regulate cross-examination, intervening when the examination becomes unnecessary, perhaps prolix or repetitious or infringing the Bar's Code of Conduct.[41] Counsel face judicial disapproval and strong comment in the summing up where their conduct in cross-examination is challenged. For example, in *O'Neill*,[42] instructions were to challenge the police account of how the confessions came about, alleging assault on the defendants. In the event, the defendants exercised their right not to testify and thus the prosecution were not able to put their previous convictions to them as the law then stood. Lord Goddard commented,

O'Neill (1950) 34 Cr.App.R.108 at 111, *per* Lord Goddard C.J.:

In this case a violent attack was made on the police. It was suggested that they had done improper things . . . . The applicants had the opportunity of going into the box at the trial and explaining and supporting what they had instructed their counsel to say. They did not dare to go into the box and therefore counsel, who knew that they were not going into the box, ought not to have made these suggestions against the police . . . It is . . . entirely wrong to make such suggestions as were made in this case, namely that the police beat the prisoners until they made confessions, and then, when there is a chance for the prisoners to substantiate what has been said by going into the box, for counsel not to call them . . .[43]

Further problems can arise where defendants represent themselves. It is the judge's duty to restrain unnecessary cross-examination. As was discussed earlier, judges failed to take a more proactive stance and restrain cross examination of witnesses who in the nature of the case are likely to be distressed or vulnerable. As a result, the provisions of the Youth Justice and Criminal Evidence Act 1999[44] prevent a defendant from cross-examining a witness in person in certain circumstances.

1. Section 34 provides that the defendant cannot cross-examine in person the victims of sexual assault, whether adults or children.
2. Section 35 widens that protection in the case of children—the defendant cannot cross examine a child witness where the offence involves a sexual offence, kidnapping, false imprisonment or any offence which involves an assault on, or injury or a threat of injury to, any person.
3. Section 36 provides a safety net—where neither s.34 nor 35 operates to prevent an accused in any criminal proceedings from cross-examining a witness in person, the judge can prevent such cross-

---

[41] Especially r. 708 Code of Conduct for Bar of England and Wales; for the duty of defence counsel, see *McFadden*, 62 Cr.App.R. 187 at 193.

[42] (1950) 34 Cr.App.R. 108 at 111, *per* Lord Goddard C.J.

[43] With the benefit of forward vision and our knowledge of police conduct over the next 30 years, the court might have been more sympathetic to the defendants' dilemma.

[44] These provisions are discussed in Ch.10.

examination where the quality of the evidence would thereby be improved.

All witnesses are liable to cross-examination by any party to the case or their counsel. In *Hilton*,[45] the accused gave evidence in his own defence which did not adversely affect the position of his co-accused. The judge refused permission for the counsel for the co-accused to cross-examine him. A fair trial requires that an accused person is at liberty to cross examine any witness.

Hilton [1971] 3 All E.R. 541 at 543f–544f, *per* Fenton Atkinson L.J.:

. . . counsel for one of two or more co-accused has for many years past invariably been allowed to cross-examine a co-accused who has given evidence whether or not such evidence was in any way adverse to his client . . . We are all quite satisfied that the practice to allow such cross-examination is well established in our courts and that it is necessary for justice to be done. This can be illustrated as follows. A and B are charged with an offence and are separately represented. A gives evidence in his own defence, making no mention of B. B's counsel knows that there is in fact important evidence that A can give in B's favour. If he cannot elicit the matter in cross-examination, he has no right to call A to give evidence a second time as A is not a compellable witness and may be unwilling for a number of reasons to give evidence for a second time. Clear though we believe the established practice to be, it is true . . . that the only authority supporting the right to cross-examine in such cases consists of dicta in the House of Lords in *Murdoch v Taylor*[46] . . . . We agree entirely with the statement of the South African judge, Harcourt J., in the case of *The State v Langa*[47] . . . when he said: 'An accused ought, if a fair trial is what is aimed at, to be at liberty to cross-examine a co-accused or any witness (not called by him) who may not have inculpted him in any way in order to establish facts which may tend to support the alibi'

Where a witness gives evidence-in-chief but becomes unavailable for cross-examination, for example, through illness, the judge has discretion as to whether to order a new trial. In *Stretton*,[48] the trial was allowed to continue after the witness had collapsed in the witness box after 3 and-a-half hours of cross-examination. There was medical evidence that the witness would not be available for a new trial and the judge gave a clear warning about how they were to approach their task. The Court of Appeal upheld the conviction. Similarly in *Wyatt*,[49] a seven-year-old girl became distressed and it was not possible to continue the cross-examination. The conviction was upheld as the jury had been properly directed as to how to approach the girl's evidence.

In cross-examining, counsel may ask leading questions but this should not consist of questions such as "I suggest to you that . . .", "Do you ask the jury

---

[45] [1971] 3 All E.R. 541.
[46] [1965] 1 All E.R. 406.
[47] 1963 (4) SA 941 at 945.
[48] (1986) 86 Cr.App.R. 7.
[49] [1990] Crim.L.R. 343.

to believe that . . ." which are more in the nature of an invitation to argument than seeking answers to matters of fact. The true purpose of cross-examination is to obtain "answers to questions of fact".[50] Counsel are not restricted to matters that have been covered in examination in chief but is constrained by relevance, whether to the facts in issue or the witness's credit. The questioner is also limited by the rules of evidence: questions cannot be put to a witness which would elicit inadmissible evidence. In *Treacy*,[51] the prosecution sought to introduce a confession allegedly made by the accused as part of their evidence in chief. The confession was deemed inadmissible. When the accused testified, the prosecution sought to cross-examine him on the contents of the confession as a statement inconsistent with the defendant's oral testimony under s.4 of the Criminal Procedure Act 1865.

Treacy [1944] 2 All E.R. 229 at 236, *per* Humphreys J.:

In our view, a statement made by a prisoner is either admissible or it is not admissible. If it is admissible, the proper course for the prosecution is to prove it, give it in evidence, let the statement if it is in writing be made an exhibit, so that everybody knows what it is and everybody can inquire into it and do what they think right about it. If it is not admissible, nothing more ought to be heard of it, and it is quite a mistake to think that a document can be made admissible in evidence which is otherwise inadmissible simply because it is put to a person in cross-examination

This is not a rule that binds a co-accused. In *Myers*,[52] the accused and her boyfriend were convicted of the killing of a mini-cab driver. She made statements to the police after her arrest in which she had at first admitted stabbing the victim but then asserted it was her co-accused. The prosecution were not allowed to introduce these statements because of breaches of Code C of PACE 1984. The House of Lords held that this fact did not preclude the co-accused from raising the confession when cross-examining her on her assertion that he had murdered the cab driver. Her original statement was clearly relevant to his defence that she was the killer. Obviously one or the other had killed the driver and justice required that he should be allowed to bring out the earlier confession. Judicial discretion should not be allowed to fetter a defendant in seeking to extract, by cross-examination, evidence of assistance to his own defence. But at common law, such examination goes to the defendant–witness's credibility and the jury must be warned from placing weight on it in considering the prosecution case.

This has been overtaken by s.128(1) of the Criminal Justice Act 2003.[53]

128 (1) In any proceedings a confession made by an accused person may be given in evidence for another person charged in the same proceedings (a co-accused) in so far

---

[50] *Baldwin* (1925) 18 Cr.App.R. 175, *per* Lord Hewart at 178.
[51] [1944] 2 All E.R. 229.
[52] [1998] A.C. 124.
[53] This is now Police and Criminal Evidence Act 1984, s.76A.

as it is relevant to any matter in issue in the proceedings and is not excluded by the court in pursuance of this section.

However subs.(2) imposes a condition that a defendant can only rely on a confession by a co-accused where the defendant can prove on the balance of probabilities that it was not obtained by oppression or in circumstances that may make it unreliable.[54]

In cross-examination, counsel is under a duty to challenge every part of the witness's testimony which runs counter to instructions, to put to the witness any allegations and any relevant matters. A failure to cross-examine any witness on any part of the testimony may be taken as an acceptance of that evidence.[55] In *Browne v Dunn*,[56] witnesses in a libel matter were not cross-examined on a relevant issue and it was held by the House of Lords that the jury could not be asked to disbelieve those witnesses.

Browne v Dunn (1894) 6 R. 67, *per* Lord Herschell L.C.:

It seems to be absolutely essential to the proper conduct of a cause, that where it is intended to suggest that a witness is not speaking the truth on a particular point, to direct his attention to the fact by some questions put in cross-examination showing that the imputation is intended to be made, and not to take his evidence and pass it by as a matter altogether unchallenged, and then, when it is impossible for him to explain, as perhaps he might have been able to do if such questions had been put to him, the circumstances which it is suggested indicate that the story he tells ought not to be believed, to argue that he is a witness unworthy of credit . . . .

C. *Previous Inconsistent Statements*

Witnesses can be cross-examined on any relevant matter which either goes to the issue in front of the court or to the credibility of the witness. In particular counsel will question the witness about any prior statements made by the witness and which are inconsistent with the present testimony in chief can be put to the witness. Under the Criminal Procedure Act 1865,

4.—If a witness, upon cross-examination as to a former statement made by him relative to the subject matter of the indictment or proceeding, and inconsistent with his present testimony, does not distinctly admit that he has made such a statement, proof may be given that he did in fact make it; but before such proof can be given, the circumstances of the supposed statement, sufficient to designate the particular occasion, must be mentioned to the witness, and he must be asked whether or not he has made such statement.

---

[54] Where the Crown wish to rely on a confession, they must prove *beyond reasonable doubt* that it was not obtained by oppression or in circumstances that might render it unreliable.

[55] *Bircham* [1972] Crim.L.R. 430.

[56] (1894) 6 R. 67.

Despite the name of the statute, this section applies to both criminal and civil proceedings. At trial, counsel would ask the witness whether they made the earlier statement—it can be any statement, however made and whether on oath or not.[57] Counsel must supply sufficient details about the circumstances in which it was made to make it possible to recall it. If the witness denies making the statement or cannot recall making the statement, evidence can be led that it was made.

The way in which section 4 is worded is clearly more apposite to oral statements. When the particular prior inconsistent statement is in writing, s.5 applies.

5.—A witness, may be cross-examined as to previous statements made by him in writing or reduced into writing relative to the subject matter of the indictment or proceeding, without such writing being shown to him; but if it is intended to contradict such witness by the writing, his attention must, before such contradictory proof can be given, be called to those parts of the writing which are to be used for the purpose of so contradicting him; provided always, that it shall be competent for the judge, at any time during the trial, to require the production of the writing for his inspection, and he may thereupon make such use of it for the purposes of the trial as he may think fit.

The writing does not initially need to be shown to the witness. If it is shown, it does not need to be put into evidence unless counsel wishes to use it to contradict a statement by the witness who by then will have had an opportunity to explain any contradiction. Counsel cannot state that the document does contradict the witness unless the document is put into evidence.[58]

It has been argued that section 4 applies only to oral statements and s.5 only to written statements.[59] But in *Derby Magistrates Ex p. B*,[60] Lord Lane C.J. disagreed.

Derby Magistrates Ex p. B [1995] 4 All E.R. 526 at 533b–c, *per* Lord Lane C.J.:

Although section 5 clearly refers only to written statements, we see no reason to confine section 4 to oral statements. Its wording does not so confine it and its content is apt to cover statements both oral and written . . . . Section 4 allows proof that a previous inconsistent statement was made if that is not distinctly admitted. Section 5 additionally permits (a) cross examination of a witness as to a previous inconsistent written statement without showing him or her the statement and (b) contradiction of the witness's testimony by putting the previous statement to him. If he denies making it, the statement can be proved: section 4. Even if he admits making the statement but adheres to evidence inconsistent with it, the statement, or such part of it as the judge thinks proper, may be put before the jury: section 5, and see *Reg. v Beattie*[61]

[57] *Hart* (1957) 42 Cr.App.R. 47.
[58] *Riley* (1866) 4 F.&F. 964.
[59] *Archbolds* (2006) 8–124.
[60] [1995] 4 All E.R. 526 at 533b–c.
[61] (1989) 89 Cr.App.R. 302.

The witness can admit the truth of that earlier statement or stick to the testimony given in the witness box. In those circumstances, at common law, the trier of fact could only use that earlier statement as casting doubt on the credibility of the witness. It was not evidence of the facts contained. But, as has been seen with hostile witnesses, s.119(1) of the Criminal Justice Act 2003 now allows the trier of fact to treat the prior statement as evidence of the truth of what it contains. In civil cases, previous inconsistent statements are admissible under s.1 of the Civil Evidence Act 1995 as evidence of their facts.[62]

Where a witness's character is being questioned and the witness denies some discreditable act, do these provisions enable counsel to put to the witness a previous inconsistent statement admitting that act? Is character a matter "relative to the subject-matter of the indictment or proceeding"? The correct test of questions going only to credit was discussed in *Funderburk*,[63] where the accused was charged with unlawful sexual intercourse with a 13-year-old girl. The girl and her mother had been lodgers with the defendant but had left after arguments. The defence was that the complainant was lying in support of her mother who bore the accused a grudge. The girl gave detailed accounts of sex with the defendant, which strongly suggested that she was a virgin at that time. The defendant sought to put to her in cross-examination conversations about sex with two other men. These conversations were prior to the first incident with the defendant. The defence suggested that she was transposing those experiences to the appellant. The trial judge held that this was not material to the issue of whether she had had sex with the appellant. The Court of Appeal explored the relationship between questions in cross-examination which went to the witness's credibility and the function of s.4.

Funderburk [1990] 2 All E.R. 482 at 485h–491h, *per* Henry J.:

When one comes to cross-examination, questions in cross-examination equally have to be relevant to the issues before the court, and those issues of course include the credibility of the witness giving evidence as to those issues. But a practical distinction must be drawn between questions going to an issue before the court and questions merely going either to the credibility of the witness or to facts that are merely collateral. Where questions go solely to the credibility of the witness or to collateral facts the general rule is that answers given to such questions are final and cannot be contradicted by rebutting evidence. This is because of the requirement to avoid multiplicity of issues in the overall interests of justice . . . .

As far as the general test as to the limits of cross-examination as to credit, the locus classicus of that is to be found in Lawton J.'s judgment in *R v Sweet-Escott*.[64] There the

---

[62] However in civil proceedings, if such statements are adduced to attack the credibility of the witness, the provisions of Criminal Procedure Act 1865 must be observed—s.6(3)(b) Civil Evidence Act 1995, s.4.

[63] [1990] 2 All E.R. 482.

[64] (1971) 55 Cr.App.R. 316 at 320.

witness was cross-examined as to his credit in relation to conviction 20 years ago. As a general test Lawton J, having found that the question should not have been allowed, said:

> What, then, is the principle upon which the judge should draw the line? It seems to me that it is this. Since the purpose of cross-examination as to credit is to show that the witness ought not to be believed on oath, the matters about which he is questioned must relate to his likely standing after cross-examination with the tribunal which is trying him or listening to his evidence.

> . . . Was the trial judge right to apply the test set out in s.4 . . . instead of the ordinary test set out in *R v Sweet-Escott* relating to questions going to the credibility of a witness? We see nothing in s.4 which would prevent a witness's previous statement inconsistent with his testimony before the judge being put to him to challenge his credibility even where the section did not allow the evidence of the making of the inconsistent statement to be given . . .

> [Having considered the nature of the girl's evidence-in-chief] . . . it is submitted that this is not a challenge which goes merely to credit but that the disputed questions go directly to the issue and not merely to a collateral fact or, alternatively at least, in the words of s.4 of the 1865 Act, that her accounts of having lost her virginity on a previous occasion were statements 'inconsistent with [her] present testimony' made by her 'relative to the subject matter of the indictment'.

At this time, questions on the victim's sexual history were not prohibited by the provisions of s.2 of the Sexual Offences (Amendment) Act 1976 which applied only in rape cases. In *Funderburk*, the offence was unlawful sexual intercourse. Such questions about a complainant's sexual history are now regulated by s.41 of the Youth Justice and Criminal Evidence Act 1999 which applies to all sexual offences and significantly restricts the accused's right to explore the victim's previous sexual conduct. However these restrictions come into play when the accused raises the defence of consent. The court is able to give leave for such questions where the issue is not a matter of consent.[65] In *Funderburk*, the defendant is denying that the event took place at all and is alleging that the witness is lying. Her evidence strongly suggested that she had no previous sexual experience and her previous statement to her friend is admissible under s.4 to suggest to the jury that on that particular point, she was lying.

D. *Use of documents in cross-examination*

There are two situations where documents may be used in cross-examination. The first is where the document emanates from the cross-examiner but has not been put into evidence. Where there is such a document, not made by the witness, and not admissible in evidence, counsel can ask the witness to look at it and whether they wish to amend their answer.[66] If they accept the contents of the document, that becomes evidence. But the witness who refuses to accept those contents cannot be asked to read the document into evidence. In *Gillespie and Simpson*, the accused were charged with theft from

---

[65] Youth Justice and Criminal Evidence Act 1999, s.41(3)—discussed in Ch.10.
[66] *Yousry* (1914) 11 Cr.App.R. 13 at 18, *per* Lord Coleridge.

the store of which they were employees and that they had falsified the accounts to conceal this. In cross-examining the accused, the prosecution handed them bills prepared by shop girls which, if true, would have suggested that the defendants had failed to account for the full amount. The accused dissented from the contents but were still required to read them aloud and the judge referred to the documents in his summing-up. The Court of Appeal regarded the documents as hearsay and their inadmissibility could not be avoided by putting them to the accused in cross-examination.

Gillespie and Simpson (1967) 51 Cr.App.R. 172 at 177, *per* Winn L.J.:

. . . if a document is produced to a witness and the witness is asked, 'Do you see what that document purports to record?' the witness may say 'I see it, I accept it as true' in which case the contents of the document become evidence; or he may say, 'I see what is there written, I do not accept it as true', whereupon that which is purported to be recorded in the document is not evidence against that person who has rejected the contents; it becomes what one might call non-evidence, the document itself being nothing but hearsay.

The second situation is where the document does not emanate from the cross-examiner who calls on his adversary to produce it. The common law rule is that the cross-examiner is bound to put the document into evidence if required, even if it is otherwise inadmissible. In the divorce case of *Stroud v Stroud*,[67] the husband's counsel was cross-examining a doctor who was a witness for the wife. Counsel inspected medical reports by other doctors which were in the hands of the witness but which were inadmissible hearsay. The court held that documents were able to be put into evidence at the option of the wife. In civil proceedings, this rule is now obsolete as a result of the modern rules on discovery and the Civil Evidence Act 1995. There is no authority that it has ever been applied in a criminal case.

E. *Cross-examination as to credit*

The common law drew a clear distinction between questioning witnesses about the issues in the case and collateral issues, such as their credibility. Credibility could be explored through questions on the witness's knowledge of the facts, their disinterestedness, integrity and veracity. Counsel could explore their powers of perception and opportunities for observation, their reasons for remembering the incident and their quality of memory as well as any prior inconsistent statements. The cross-examiner was also allowed to probe a witness's prejudices, prior disreputable conduct or criminal record and physical and mental disabilities. At all times counsel are expected to

---

[67] [1963] 3 All E.R. 539.

remain within the limits laid down by the Bar Council. The key source was Sankey L.J.'s judgment in *Hobbs v C T Tinling & Co. Ltd*.

Hobbs v C T Tinling & Co. Ltd [1929] 2 K.B. 1 at 50–51, *per* Lord Sankey:

The Court can always exercise its discretion to decide whether a question as to credit is one which the witness should be compelled to answer . . . In the exercise of its discretion the Court should have regard to the following considerations: (1) Such questions are proper if they are of such a nature that the truth of the imputation conveyed by them would seriously affect the opinion of the Court as to the credibility of the witness on the matter to which he testifies. (2) Such questions are improper if the imputation which they convey relates to matters so remote in time, or of such a character, that the truth of the imputation would not affect, or would affect in a slight degree, the opinion of the Court as to the credibility of the witness on the matter to which he testifies. (3) Such questions are improper if there is a great disproportion between the importance of the imputation made against the witness's character and the importance of his evidence.

1. The Criminal Justice Act 2003

The common law has now been supplanted by section 100 of the Criminal Justice Act 2003 which was designed to limit questioning about previous misconduct of witnesses, be they the victim or other persons. "Bad character" is very broadly defined by s.98.

98. References in this Chapter to evidence of a person's "bad character" are to evidence of, or of a disposition towards, misconduct on his part

This encompasses much more than criminal convictions—perhaps any behaviour that might lower a person's reputation in the eyes of a reasonable person.

Where the parties cannot agree, such questioning will only be allowed with the leave of the court. This will be given where it is demonstrated that such questioning is likely to provide important explanatory evidence or that has substantial probative value.

Criminal Justice Act 2003, s.100:

100(1) In criminal proceedings evidence of the bad character of a person other than the defendant is admissible if and only if—
(a) it is important explanatory evidence,
(b) it has substantial probative value in relation to a matter which—
    (i) is a matter in issue in the proceedings, and
    (ii) is of substantial importance in the context of the case as a whole,
  or

(c) all parties to the proceedings agree to the evidence being admissible.

(2) For the purposes of subsection (1)(a) evidence is important explanatory evidence if—

(a) without it, the court or jury would find it impossible or difficult properly to understand other evidence in the case, and

(b) its value for understanding the case as a whole is substantial.

(3) In assessing the probative value of evidence for the purposes of subsection (1)(b) the court must have regard to the following factors (and to any others it considers relevant)—

(a) the nature and number of the events, or other things, to which the evidence relates;

(b) when those events or things are alleged to have happened or existed;

(c) where—

(i) the evidence is evidence of a person's misconduct, and

(ii) it is suggested that the evidence has probative value by reason of similarity between that misconduct and other alleged misconduct,

the nature and extent of the similarities and the dissimilarities between each of the alleged instances of misconduct;

(d) where—

(i) the evidence is evidence of a person's misconduct,

(ii) it is suggested that that person is also responsible for the misconduct charged, and

(iii) the identity of the person responsible for the misconduct charged is disputed,

the extent to which the evidence shows or tends to show that the same person was responsible each time.

(4) Except where subsection (1)(c) applies, evidence of the bad character of a person other than the defendant must not be given without leave of the court.

Section 100 protects witnesses who can be the victim or any other witness, including those who do not give oral testimony but whose statements are admissible through, for example, the hearsay exceptions in the 2003 Act.[68] But the section goes further and also limits the extent to which the bad character of non-witnesses can be introduced in evidence: for example, in a murder trial the defence may well wish to raise the issue of the victim's violent nature as a foundation for a defence of self defence.

Questions can be asked about the bad character of a witness or other person when,

- it is important explanatory evidence or
- it has substantial probative value in relation to a matter in issue.

(i) *Important explanatory evidence*

This permits the prosecution or defence to introduce essentially background evidence which has no immediate relevance to any fact in issue but without which the trier of fact would be left in the dark—for example, it would be difficult to properly adjudicate on an assault case involving two young men without the knowledge that this took place in a boxing ring in a youth club in a competition conducted under the rules of the Amateur Boxing Association.

---

[68] s.100 is applicable to such witnesses through the operation of s.124.

In such a case, the background information reveals nothing disreputable and is uncontentious. Usually this is not the case as such background evidence often reveals the disclosure of prior criminal actions by the accused but also by others. The principles to be applied are the same in relation to defendants and non-defendants.

In *Sawoniuk*,[69] the defendant was charged with crimes by virtue of the War Crimes Act 1991, in particular the murders of two Jewish women in Belorussia where he was a police officer. The Crown called expert evidence to describe Nazi policy towards the Jews in that locality and that a large number of Jewish victims, 2,900 according to German records, were shot with the assistance of the local police. This evidence was not disputed, although it was not formally admitted. On appeal it was argued that the judge should not have admitted this evidence.

Sawoniuk [2000] 2 Cr.App.R. 220 at 235–236, *per* Lord Bingham C.J.:

. . . we incline to the view that the admission of this evidence could be upheld on a broader basis. Criminal charges cannot be fairly judged in a factual vacuum. In order to make a rational assessment of evidence directly relating to a charge it may often be necessary for a jury to receive evidence describing, perhaps in some detail, the context and circumstances in which the offences are said to have been committed. This, as we understand, is the approach indicated by this court[70] . . .

> Where it is necessary to place before the jury evidence of part of a continual background of history relevant to the offence charged in the indictment and without the totality of which the account placed before the jury would be incomplete or incomprehensible, then the fact that the whole account involves including evidence establishing the commission of an offence with which the accused is not charged is not of itself a ground for excluding the evidence.[71]

This approach seems to us of particular significance in an exceptional case such as the present, in which a London jury was asked to assess the significance of evidence relating to events in a country quite unlike our own, taking place a very long time ago in the extra-ordinary conditions prevailing in 1941 to 1942. It was necessary and appropriate for the Crown to prove that it was the policy of Nazi Germany first to oppress and then to exterminate the Jewish population of its conquered territories in Eastern Europe. This was done by expert evidence, which was very largely unchallenged. No objection was taken to this evidence. But it was not the subject of any formal admission. It was next necessary and appropriate for the Crown to establish that locally-recruited police in areas which included Belorussia and Domachevo played a significant part in enforcing the Nazi policy against the Jewish population. This was proved, partly by expert evidence and partly by the oral evidence of eye-witnesses . . .

It seems to us that evidence relevant to all these matters was probative and admissible, even if it disclosed the commission of criminal offences, other than those charged, by the appellant and his colleagues. It has not been suggested that the jury

---

[69] [2000] 2 Cr.App.R. 220.

[70] *Pettman* (unreported, May 2, 1985), approved in *Sidhu* (1994) 98 Cr.App.R. 59 and *Fulcher* [1995] 2 Cr.App.R. 251.

[71] *Fulcher op.cit.* at 258.

should have been invited to reach a verdict on counts one and three having heard no more than the evidence of a single eye-witness on each; had these gruesome events not been set in their factual context, the jury would have been understandably bewildered.

Section 100(1)(a) puts the common law on a statutory footing. Section 100(2) expands the idea.

For the purposes of subsection (1)(a) evidence is important explanatory evidence if—

(a) without it, the court or jury would find it impossible or difficult properly to understand other evidence in the case, and

(b) its value for understanding the case as a whole is substantial

An illustrative example[72] might be a case involving the abuse by one person of another over a long period of time. For the jury to properly understand the victim's account of the offending and why they did not seek help from, for example, a parent or other guardian, it might be necessary for evidence to be given of a wider pattern of abuse involving that other person. But such background information must possess substantial value for the court in understanding the case as a whole. In other words, it will not be enough for the evidence to assist the court to understand some trivial piece of evidence, without which the trier of fact would find it impossible or difficult to understand other evidence in the case. Another illustration can be seen in *Akram*,[73] where the judge permitted questions about prior incidents which put the witness in a bad light to demonstrate animosity between the witness and the defendant.

(ii) *Substantial probative value in relation to a matter in issue*

The issues surrounding cross-examination of a witness as to their credibility rests on the validity of the distinction between questions which go to the issue and questions which are collateral. The common law failed to regulate this robustly and allowed wide ranging questioning. As a Home Office study[74] showed, this was resented by witnesses who felt that they were badly treated by the other side's lawyer. This was particularly the case with complainants in sexual offences.

Section 100(1)(b) will undoubtedly restrict counsel's ability to cross-examine on matters of credit, adducing evidence of bad character of the witness where it has,

. . . (b) it has substantial probative value in relation to a matter which—

(i) is a matter in issue in the proceedings, and

(ii) is of substantial importance in the context of the case as a whole.

If all questions have to be related to a "matter in issue", does this mean that counsel can never question on issues of bad character where the sole purpose is to cast doubt on the credibility of the witness? This cannot be the case—

[72] Explanatory Notes to the Criminal Justice Act 2003, para.360.
[73] [2005] EWCA Crim 2826.
[74] H. Angle, S. Malam and C. Carey (2003), *op.cit.*

creditworthiness is frequently a "matter in issue" and often one that is of "substantial importance in the context of the case as a whole".

The objective of testimony is to elicit an item of information which is to be put before the trier of fact who must decide whether to accept or reject this. Their decision will inevitably rely on a judgment about the creditworthiness of the person providing that information. You cannot evaluate testimony without such information. An analogy would be with documentary evidence where a party wishes to rely on statements in that document—any court would need to know when, where, how and by whom that document was produced before being in a position of deciding whether to rely on its contents. So it is with witnesses. Zuckerman would also argue that matters in issue and matters of credit are intertwined.

A. Zuckerman, The Principles of Criminal Evidence (OUP, 1989), p.94ff:

Let us take the case in which the only issue is the offender's identity and the only evidence for the prosecution is W's testimony who claims to have observed the accused from thirty yards. The accused adduces evidence to show that W cannot see beyond ten yards. According to the rule we are discussing this evidence is inadmissible because it is only relevant to credit of the witness and to the issue of the commission of the offence. By contrast, if the accused calls evidence to show that he was a close friend of the victim, this evidence will be admissible because it is relevant to the issue; it makes it less probable that the accused would harm his friend. Yet the evidence of motive is far less significant in this case than W's ten-yard eyesight. It would not be irrational for the trier of fact both to believe that the accused was the victim's friend and to conclude that the accused committed an offence against the friend. But if the trier of fact believes that W could not have observed the offence, a conviction could not properly take place. It can hardly be maintained that evidence affecting credibility is as a general rule less important than evidence which impinges directly on the issue.

If our object is to arrive economically at factually correct conclusions, admissibility should depend on the degree to which evidence contributes towards this end. Since the distinction between relevance to credibility and relevance to issue does not reflect a divergence in probative force we should not allow it to govern admissibility.

The validity of the distinction between relevance to credibility and relevance to issue may be questioned at a more fundamental level. One fact is relevant to another when it renders the existence of the other more probable. The fact that the witness says: 'The man who committed the offence was the accused' is relevant because it renders more probable that the accused was the offender. However, W's testimony could have this effect only if it has some credibility. If the testimony has no credibility at all, for example, because it is the blabber of a madman, it is irrelevant. It follows that the connecting link between W's testimony and the conclusion based on it is credibility. In other words, the relevance of a witness's testimony is embedded in his credibility, actual or potential. Credibility is not something separate (a separate issue) which is somehow suspended between the witness's statement and the fact asserted therein. W's ten-yard eyesight does not pertain to something that is different from the relevance of W's testimony to the issue . . . .

It is the probative weight of these collateral matters that is important. To what extent does our assessment of the messenger affect our reliance on the message? In some cases, the information may be of marginal importance which can be disregarded—whether a rape victim had prior sexual experience should normally never affect our judgement as to whether she is telling the truth and is to be relied upon. But in *Funderburk*, this is the key question. The complainant had given a detailed account of events, which strongly suggested that she was a virgin at that time. Information about her prior sexual experience would substantially affect the jury's assessment of that testimony.

Funderburk [1990] 2 All E.R. 482 at 491d-j, *per* Henry J.:

. . . . where the disputed issue is a sexual one between two persons in private the difference between questions going to credit and questions going to the issue is reduced to vanishing point . . . . The difficulty we have in applying that celebrated test (in *A-G v Hitchcock*) is that it seems to us to be circular. If a fact is not collateral then clearly you can call evidence to contradict it, but the so-called test is silent on how you decide whether that fact is collateral. The utility of the test may lie in the fact that the answer is an instinctive one based on the prosecutor's and the court's sense of fair play rather than any philosophic or analytic process. Applying the test in argument before us, Morland J put to counsel for the Crown the hypothetical question 'If the defence had medical evidence that this child was not a virgin before the date on which she gave her account of losing her virginity, would the defence be allowed to call such evidence?' On reflection, counsel accepted that they would be allowed to call such evidence, and we think that answer to the question not only right but inevitable. Otherwise there would be the danger that the jury would make their decision as to credit on an account of the original incident in which the most emotive, memorable and potentially persuasive fact was, to the knowledge of all in the case, false.

In *Funderburk*, the issue was whether sex took place or whether the witness was lying. Her account of the offence could only be true if she were a virgin at that time. Her previous experience speaks directly to that issue and would be treated nowadays as having substantial probative value—it illustrates Zuckerman's point that credibility is not a separate issue from relevance. An example of irrelevance can be seen in *Yaxley-Lennon*,[75] where the defendant was convicted of assault—his girlfriend was questioned about her caution for possession of cocaine. The first point of the appeal was that s.100 does not encompass matters of credibility—the Court of Appeal held that credibility could be a matter in issue for the purposes of the section and that to find otherwise would leave a significant lacuna in the legislation. The second point was that, if credibility can be a matter in issue, evidence of credibility was only admissible if it passed a significant threshold, namely that it possessed substantial probative value and was of substantial importance in the context of the case as a whole. On these facts, the judge had erred in permitting questioning on the caution as it had no substantial probative value in relation to the witness's credibility.[76]

---

[75] [2005] EWCA Crim 2866.
[76] *op.cit.* paras 73–74, *per* Kennedy L.J.

Such decisions demonstrate that this section will considerably reduce the extent to which such marginal questioning will be permitted in the future. The court will have to assess firstly the extent to which the information about the witness is sufficiently probative in relation to the witness's creditworthiness and secondly whether that information is of importance to the case as a whole. Such an approach can be seen in the pre–2003 case of *Edwards*,[77] a case involving the behaviour of police officers attached to the West Midlands Serious Crimes Squad.[78] The Court of Appeal held a police witness could be cross-examined on any relevant convictions or disciplinary charges found against him. Under the new law, such convictions must be shown not merely to be relevant but also be of substantial importance to the case—in *Edwards*, the witness's prior conduct was relevant as the defence was that the witness was lying and the prior events showed a disposition to lie.

The distinction between relevant and irrelevant bad character can be seen in *Osbourne*,[79] where the defendant was charged with robbery of a pub. The defence was that the landlord had invented the robbery in order to conceal his own financial mismanagement. The defence were permitted to question the landlord about these issues but were not permitted to question him about allegations of drug misuse at the premises. Similarly in *Bovell*,[80] the defendant was charged with wounding with intent and sought leave under section 100 to show that the victim had been convicted ten years previously of robbery. The trial judge rejected the submission and this was upheld on appeal. The appeal court also heard fresh evidence of allegations against the witness of assault which occurred in 2001.

Bovell [2005] 2 Cr.App.R. 27, *per* Rose L.J.:

21. . . . we entertain considerable doubt as to whether the mere making of an allegation is capable of being evidence within section 100(1). As the allegation was, in the circumstances which we have identified, withdrawn, our doubt on this aspect is increased.

22. It is apparent from the circumstances, as we have summarised them, that if there was to be any question of the [assault] allegation being admitted before the jury, it would necessarily have given rise to investigation of the other subsequent matters, including the aspersions on the credibility of the victim, the want of independent confirmation of his account, and the fact that he had withdrawn the allegation. An excursion into those satellite matters is, as it seems to us, precisely the sort of excursion which . . . a trial judge should be discouraged from embarking upon.[81]

The court in *Edwards*[82] also considered the issue of allegations and whether questions should be permitted about complaints by members of the public,

---

[77] [1991] 2 All E.R. 266.

[78] T. Kaye, *Unsafe and Unsatisfactory* (Civil Liberties Trust 1991).

[79] [2005] EWCA Crim 2826.

[80] [2005] 2 Cr.App.R. 27.

[81] But while mere allegations should not be put to witnesses under s.100, they may be admissible evidence against the accused under the bad character provisions of s.101—*Edwards* [2005] EWCA Crim 3244 at para.81 *per* Scott-Baker L.J.

[82] *op.cit.*

which had not yet been adjudicated by the Police Complaints Authority, on discreditable conduct by officers of the same squad? Alternatively should questions be permitted on other cases in which the witness had given evidence which had resulted either in the acquittal of the defendant or where the conviction was quashed on appeal? Lord Lane C.J. decided that it would not be proper to put questions to the witness on the subject of any outstanding criminal charges or complaints. Nor could the witness be questioned about the allegedly discreditable conduct by other officers. But where previous acquittals or quashed convictions could be demonstrated to be based on disbelief in the police officer's testimony, it was proper that the jury were made aware of this fact. If those prior decisions meant no more than the previous court or jury disbelieved some part of the prosecution case, it would not be proper to cross-examine the officer on this issue.[83]

2. Finality of answers to collateral issues

Prior to the Criminal Justice Act 2003, the common law developed a rule that was a necessary adjunct to the distinction drawn between cross-examining on those matters pertaining to credit and those which were relevant to issues which need to be decided in the case. These former matters are known as collateral issues. This distinction became important when counsel wants to introduce evidence in rebuttal of a witness's testimony. If the answers given concern the issues which the court has to decide, rebuttal is possible. But if they concerned a collateral issue, such as the credit of a witness, counsel is bound by the answer given by the witness and cannot call independent evidence to contradict. The rule is ". . . necessary to confine the ambit of the trial within its proper limits and to prevent the true issue from becoming submerged in a welter of detail."[84]

The classic decision is *Attorney-General v Hitchcock*,[85] where the defendant was charged with unlawful use of a cistern. A witness testified that the cistern had been used. In cross-examination, the witness was asked and denied that he had been offered £20 by the Excise officers to testify to this effect. Was the witness bribed? Although this seems a central question, the defence were not permitted to contradict his denial by other independent evidence.

Attorney-General v Hitchcock (1847) 1 Exch. 91 at 99–101, *per* Pollock C.B.:

. . . the test, whether an inquiry is collateral or not, is this: if the answer of a witness is a matter which you would be allowed on your part to prove in evidence—if it have such a connection with the issue, that you would be allowed to give it in evidence—then it is a matter on which you may contradict him. Or it may be as well put, or perhaps better, in the language of my Brother Alderson this morning, that, If you ask a

[83] *Thorne* (1977) 66 Cr.App.R.6; cf *Cooke* (1984) 84 Cr.App.R. 286.
[84] *Edwards* above at 274c *per* Lord Lane C.J.
[85] (1847) 1 Exch. 91.

witness whether he has not said so and so, and the matter he is supposed to have said would, if he had said it, contradict any other part of his testimony, then you may then call another witness to prove that he had said so . . . . It must be connected with the issue as a matter capable of being distinctly given in evidence, or it must be so far connected with it as to be a matter which, if answered in a particular way, would contradict part of the witness's testimony; and if it is neither the one or the other of these, it is collateral to, though in some sense it may be considered as connected with, the subject of the inquiry. A distinction should be observed between those matters which may be given in evidence by way of contradiction, as directly affecting the story of a witness touching the issue before the jury, and those matters which affect the motives, temper, character of the witness . . . It is certainly allowable to ask a witness in what manner he stands affected towards the opposite party in the cause, and whether he does not stand in such a relation to that person as is likely to affect him and prevent him from having an unprejudiced state of mind, and whether he has not used expressions importing that he would be revenged on some one, or that he would give such evidence as might dispose of the cause in one way or the other. If he denies that, you may give evidence as to what he has said, not with a view of having a direct effect on the issue, but to show what is the state of mind of that witness. But those cases, where you may show the condition of a witness, or his connection with either of the parties, are not to be confounded with other cases, where it is proposed to contradict a witness on some matter unconnected with the question at issue . . .

In this case it is admitted, that, with reference to the offering of a bribe, it could not originally have been proved that the offer of the bribe had been made to the witness to make a particular statement, the bribe not have been accepted by him. And the reason is, that it is totally irrelevant to the matter in issue, that some person should have thought fit to offer a bribe to the witness to give an untrue account of a transaction, and it is of no importance whatever, if that bribe was not accepted. It is no disparagement to a man that a bribe is offered to him . . . .

Thus the common law allowed questions to be put to a witness which suggested that they may have been guilty of some discreditable behaviour. However, where those questions are irrelevant to any issue in the case, you cannot call other witnesses to contradict the answer given. This was known as the rule of the finality of answers to collateral issues. The significance of this rule post–2003 can be doubted, largely because such collateral issues concerned the bad character of the witness. The legislative policy behind section 100 is to prevent those questions being put to the witness in the first place, which pre-empts any question as to when rebuttal is permitted. Such questions can only be put to a witness under section 100 where they are of "substantial probative value in relation to a matter in issue" and "of substantial importance to the case as a whole". Where the trial judge has given leave in such circumstances and where the witness has denied the matter, it would be impossible to treat it as a mere collateral issue and not permit rebuttal.

The test now is one that stresses the probative weight of the evidence and it allows the judge initially to decide whether the bad character of the witness will significantly affect the trier of fact's assessment of the testimony. If the "collateral" fact materially affects those probabilities, not only should the question be asked but the party asking it should be permitted to adduce evidence in rebuttal.

However there are "collateral" issues other than bad character where the old artificial distinction between relevance to an issue and relevance to credibility will still hold sway. In these cases, the rule against finality still survives, as do the exceptions to the rule. These exceptions permit evidence in rebuttal to be brought even on matters of credit.

(i) *Prior statement inconsistent with present testimony*:   as has been discussed earlier, these can be proved under s.4 and 5 of the Criminal Procedure Act 1865.

(ii) *Denial of previous convictions*:   these can be proved under section 6 of the Criminal Procedure Act 1865.

6. If, upon a witness being lawfully as to whether he has been convicted of any felony or misdemeanour . . . he either denies or does not admit the fact or refuses to answer, it shall be lawful for the cross-examining party to prove such convictions. . . .[86]

Convictions are normally proved under the provisions of s.73 of the Police and Criminal Evidence Act 1984. Generally any conviction, relevant under section 100, can be put to a witness, even those which are spent under the Rehabilitation of Offenders Act 1974.[87]

(iii) *Denial of bias*:   in *Thomas v David*,[88] the witness denied that she was the mistress of the party calling her and it was held that evidence in rebuttal could be adduced. Usually when the witness is related to the party, it is unnecessary to bring out the potential bias but in *Mendy*,[89] the wife was charged with assault and the husband was due to give evidence on her behalf. As witnesses in criminal cases are kept out of court before testifying, the husband got a man to take notes of other testimony before he himself went into the box. He denied this but, despite the fact that no-one seriously disputed that it was a wholly collateral matter, the prosecution were permitted to introduce witnesses in rebuttal. Similarly in *Phillips*,[90] a father was accused of sexual abuse of his young daughters. His defence was that they had been schooled by their mother, repeating what she had told them to say. The girls denied this and the father was denied the opportunity of calling witnesses who were to testify that the daughters had admitted lying in previous criminal proceedings against their father for indecent assault. Although, on appeal, these questions were said to go, not to the credibility of the daughters but to the foundation of the defence, they do reveal animosity against a particular defendant.

Bias can be more insidious—in *Busby*,[91] defence counsel cross-examined police officers with a view to showing that the accused had not made certain

---

[86] Convicted persons only became competent to testify after 1843 Evidence Act; s.6 was amended by s.331 and Sch.36, para.79 of the Criminal Justice Act 2003.
[87] s.7(2)(a).
[88] (1836) 7 C.&P. 350.
[89] (1976) 64 Cr.App.R. 4.
[90] (1936) 26 Cr.App.R. 17.
[91] (1982) 75 Cr.App.R. 79.

incriminating remarks and that one of the officers had threatened a potential defence witness. The officers denied this and the defence were not permitted to question this witness whether he had been threatened by the police officer. The Court of Appeal quashed the conviction, agreeing on the difficulty of deciding whether a question relates to facts that are collateral only but suggesting that here, if the evidence were true, it would indicate that the policeman was prepared to go to improper lengths to secure a conviction. In *Edwards*,[92] it was held that *Busby* was an example of witnesses who were biased against a particular defendant in a particular case and that the decision did not create a broader exception in relation to the police misconduct generally. In *Edwards* itself, for example, the officers were questioned about other trials in which they had testified and which had ended in acquittals or convictions being quashed because of doubts about the officers' veracity. Such questions were permitted as they went to the officers' credibility but,

Edwards [1991] 2 All E.R. 266 at 278g–h, *per* Lord Lane C.J.:

. . . There was in each case a sufficient connection between the evidence given by the police officers and the eventual outcome of the trial to entitle the defence to cross-examine the officers concerned about these matters upon the question of their credibility in the instant case.

That leaves the second question, namely whether it would have been proper to allow the defence to call evidence to contradict any answers given by the police officers in cross-examination, in the unlikely event of those officers giving answers unfavourable to the defence. In our judgment this questioning would have been as to credit alone, that is to say on a collateral issue. It would not have fallen within any exception to the general rule.

Cross-examination of the officers about the outcomes of previous trials was to be permitted but once the officers had answered those questions, evidence in rebuttal of that testimony was not permitted.

(iv) *Denial by witnesses that they are suffering from a mental or physical disability.* In *Toohey v Commissioner of Metropolitan Police*.[93] The defendants were charged with assault with intent to rob. The defendants argued that the victim had been drinking and that they were trying to get him home when he became hysterical, alleging the accused were attacking him. A doctor examined the victim soon afterwards but, although he was allowed to testify whether the victim was drunk or hysterical, he was not allowed to give evidence as to whether drink would exacerbate hysteria or whether the victim was more prone than normal to hysteria. The House of Lords held that this had been wrongly excluded.

[92] above at 274d–j, *per* Lord Lane C.J.
[93] [1965] A.C. 595.

Toohey v Commissioner of the Metropolitan Police [1965] A.C. 595 at 608b–e, *per* Lord Pearce

Human evidence shares the frailties of those who give it. It is subject to many cross-currents such as partiality, prejudice, self-interest and, above all, imagination and inaccuracy. Those are matters with which the jury, helped by cross-examination and common sense, must do their best. But when a witness through physical (in which I include mental) disease or abnormality is not capable of giving a true or reliable account to the jury, it must surely be allowable for medical science to reveal this vital hidden fact to them. If a witness purported to give evidence of something which he believed that he had seen at a distance of 50 yards, it must surely be possible to call the evidence of an oculist to the effect that the witness could not possibly see anything at a greater distance than 20 yards, or the evidence of a surgeon who had removed a cataract from which the witness was suffering at the material time and which prevented him from seeing what he thought he saw. So, too, must it be allowable to call medical evidence of mental illness which makes a witness incapable of giving reliable evidence, whether through the existence of delusions or otherwise.

This decision demonstrates that a party can introduce medical evidence which casts doubt upon a witness's credibility where that evidence goes to an issue which is beyond the knowledge and competence of the jury.[94] On this point it may be compared with *MacKenney*,[95] where there were considerable doubts about the psychological state of the chief prosecution witness. The defence were prevented from communicating to the jury the fact that the witness suffered from a personality disorder and his behaviour was psychopathic. They relied on a psychologist one whose credentials were academic rather than clinical and the trial judge and the Court of Appeal declined to regard that witness as an expert. The defendants served over 20 years in prison before the appeal court quashed the convictions accepting that the psychologist should have been permitted to testify.[96]

(v) *Denial that witness has a reputation for untruthfulness*: in *Brown and Hedley*,[97] the defence sought to call evidence to prove that the court should not believe the prosecution witnesses. The Court for Crown Cases Reserved held that this evidence should have been received and that it had been the practice for centuries to show that the general reputation of a witness was such that they could not be believed on oath. In *Richardson and Longman*,[98] the trial judge permitted a witness to testify about the veracity of a prosecution witness but in a restricted fashion, limiting questions to whether the witness was aware of the prosecution witness's reputation for truthfulness and whether he would believe her on oath.

---

[94] *Turner* [1975] 1 All E.R. 70; see Ch.20.
[95] (1981) 72 Cr.App.R. 78; affirmed (1983) 76 Cr.App.R. 271.
[96] [2004] 2 Cr.App.R. 5.
[97] (1867) 36 L.J.M.C. 59.
[98] (1968) 52 Cr.App.R. 317.

Richardson and Longman (1968) 52 Cr.App.R. 317 at 323, *per* Edmund Davies L.J.

1. A witness may be asked whether he has knowledge of the impugned witness's general reputation for veracity and whether (from such knowledge) he would believe the impugned witness's sworn testimony.

2. The witness called to impeach the credibility of another witness may also express his individual opinion (based upon personal knowledge) as to whether the latter is to be believed upon his oath, and is not confined to giving an opinion based merely on general reputation.

3. But whether his opinion as to the impugned witness's credibility be based simply upon the latter's general reputation for veracity or upon his personal knowledge, the witness cannot be permitted to indicate during his examination-in-chief the particular facts, circumstances or incidents which formed the basis of his opinion, although he may be cross-examined as to them . . .

The impeaching witness cannot, in evidence in chief, give detailed reasons for the belief, although these may be brought out in cross-examination.

These exceptions are not a closed list. An example of this is perhaps the issue of the good character of a prosecution witness. As we have seen, a witness's reputation for untruthfulness can be explored. But generally a party cannot bolster the testimony of witnesses by advancing evidence of the good character of those witnesses.[99] Such testimony had no probative value regarding any issue. This is not a hard and fast rule—in *Tobin*,[1] the charge was indecent assault on a drunken 16-year-old-girl as the defendant drove her home. There was no suggestion that the victim had a reputation for untruthfulness but the victim's mother gave evidence at trial about aspects of the victim's background, her attitude to alcohol and her reaction to the incident. By these means, the prosecution had sought to boost the victim's credibility by adducing collateral evidence. Pill L.J. accepted that there were cases when this was acceptable.

Tobin [2002] EWCA Crim 190; *per* Pill L.J.:

31. . . . [The Crown's] extreme position was that evidence is admissible which goes to establish that the complainant is not the type of person who would conduct herself in the manner alleged by the defendant. As a general proposition, that is not acceptable. It could amount to oath-helping. The approach could lead to evidence of a lack of propensity being admissible whenever allegations of unacceptable behaviour are made against a prosecution witness. Moreover, in this case, the complainant was plainly seriously under the influence of drink, a disinhibitor, and the possibility of behaviour in drink which may be out of character is not excluded by evidence of normal behaviour when sober.

32. We do however, respectfully, recognise the force of the observation of Henry J in Funderburk . . . that in sexual cases such as these much is likely to depend on the balance of credibility between the parties and that the difference between questions

---

[99] *Hamilton, The Times*, July 25, 1998.
[1] [2002] EWCA Crim 190.

going to credit and questions going to the issue may be reduced to vanishing point. Moreover, in such a situation . . . the answer to the question whether evidence of the type to which objection is taken in the present case is admissible is "an instinctive one based on the prosecutor's and the Court's sense of fair play".

33. In *Amado-Taylor*[2] evidence of the complainant's opinions was admissible as relevant to the issue whether intercourse was consensual. The present case is different, on its facts and the offence alleged, and, secondly, the disputed evidence does not involve the complainant's opinions but what may be described as her attitude to other people. However, the approach of the Court in *Amado-Taylor*, as in *Funderburk*, points clearly in the direction that, in sexual cases, prosecution evidence of the complainant's background and characteristics is not inevitably excluded.

The court suggests that the issue of the comparative credibility is of particular importance in sexual cases but allowing supportive evidence opens difficult issues, particularly where a witness suggests that a victim has limited or no sexual experience. In *Tobin*, it emerged that the girl had missed an appointment for a contraceptive injection on the day of the incident. It would be patently unfair for the "good character" evidence not to be rebuttable but to do so opens up many issues, not least in relation to s.41 of the Youth Justice and Criminal Evidence Act 1999, which protects complainants in sexual cases from being questioned on their sexual experience. This potential conflict is discussed elsewhere.[3]

IV RE-EXAMINATION

After cross-examination, a witness may be re-examined by the party initially calling him or her. The witness can be asked to explain any part of the cross-examination or about any new facts which may have emerged.

Queen Caroline's Case (1820) 2 Brod.Bing. 284 at 297, *per* Lord Tenterden:

I think counsel has a right, on re-examination, to ask all questions which may be proper to draw forth an explanation of the sense and meaning of the expressions used by the witness on cross-examination, if they be in themselves doubtful and also of the motive by which the witness was induced to use those expressions; but I think he has no right to go further, and to introduce new matters not suited to the purpose of explaining either the expressions or the motives of the witness.[4]

The purpose of re-examination is to limit any damage done during cross-examination: it is not the repetition of the evidence given originally. Counsel can only raise new matters with the leave of the judge. Leading questions cannot be asked and documents only used to the same extent that they could be in examination in chief. However inadmissible evidence may have become admissible: for example, a previous consistent statement by a witness may have been rendered admissible by an allegation of recent fabrication.

---

[2] [2001] EWCA Crim 1898.
[3] Ch.10.
[4] See *Prince v Samo* (1838) 7 L.J.Q.B. 123.

14

CHARACTER EVIDENCE

I. The Relevance of Character in Civil Proceedings

Issues of character would appear to have no place in a civil action. Whether a party is of unblemished reputation or has a criminal record would on first glance have no relevance to any issue that might arise. But such issues can emerge in three ways in the course of civil proceedings:

1. Character as a fact in issue. Defamation is the most obvious example where the character of the claimant is a fact in issue. If the claimant is suing as a result of being accused of being a fraud, evidence of convictions for dishonesty would be admissible. Equally in *Cornwell v Myskow*,[1] the claimant, an actress, sued over newspaper comment about her ability and the quality of her performance in a show. Evidence of her ability and reputation at the time of the publication may be adduced by the claimant. Such evidence can also go to the quantum of damages. In *Scott v Sampson*,[2] the claimant, a *Daily Telegraph* journalist, sued after the defendant alleged that he had obtained money by threatening to publish damaging stories and had abused his position as a drama critic and journalist to extort money. The trial judge, Lord Coleridge, refused to receive evidence first of the claimant's character, secondly of rumours to the same effect as the alleged libel and thirdly of specific acts of misconduct. The Divisional Court held that evidence of the claimant's character was admissible but this was evidence of reputation and not rumours or specific acts.

Scott v Sampson (1882) 8 QBD 491 at 503–505, *per* Cave J.:

. . . it seems most material that the jury who have to award damages should know, if the fact is so, that he is a man of no reputation . . . To enable the jury to estimate the probable quantum of injury sustained, a knowledge of the party's previous character is not only material, but seems to be absolutely essential . . .

---

[1] [1987] 2 All E.R. 504.
[2] (1882) 8 Q.B.D. 491.

As to the second head of evidence, or evidence of rumours and suspicions to the same effect as the defamatory matter complained of, it would seem that upon principle such evidence is not admissible, as only indirectly tending to affect the plaintiff's reputation. If these rumours and suspicions have, in fact, affected the plaintiff's reputation, that may be proved by general evidence of reputation. If they have not affected it, they are not relevant to the issue . . . . Unlike evidence of general reputation, it is particularly difficult for the plaintiff to meet and rebut such evidence; for all those who know him best can say is that they have not heard anything of these rumours. Moreover, it may be that it is the defendant who himself has started them. . .

As to the third head, or evidence of facts and circumstances tending to show the disposition of the plaintiff, both principle and authority seem equally against its admission. At the most it tends to prove not that the plaintiff has not, but that he ought not to have, a good reputation, and to admit evidence of this kind is, in effect, to throw upon the plaintiff the difficulty of showing a uniform propriety of conduct during his whole life . . .[3]

2. Character as relevant to a fact in issue. Normally evidence of the character of the parties in civil proceedings is irrelevant. In *Attorney-General v Bowman*,[4] there was a civil suit for keeping false weights. The defendant sought to adduce evidence of good character but this was deemed inadmissible as it was not relevant to the issue as to whether he had used false weights on this occasion. In *Secretary of State for Trade and Industry v Coulthard*,[5] the respondents were facing disqualification as company directors and filed affidavits as to their honesty and capability. Insofar as the affidavits contained evidence of general good character they were inadmissible: unless character in the sense of general reputation were in issue, evidence of character is inadmissible in civil proceedings because it was not probative of any issue.

But where the prior acts are of such a nature that those acts possess some probative weight and tend to show that the defendant is more likely to have committed the act complained of, such evidence may be admissible under the similar fact rules. This doctrine has a significant role in criminal proceedings[6]—the basic elements were that the bad character has first to be relevant to an issue before the court and secondly has to be sufficiently probative in relation to that issue to be able to discount any unfairness.[7]

Similar principles apply to the admission of similar fact evidence in civil cases, although there is not the emphasis on the protection of the defendant from prejudice or unfairness that is found in criminal cases. The key factors are again the relevance and the probative force. In *Mood Music Publishing v De Wolfe Publishing Ltd*,[8] the claimants owned the copyright of a musical work. The defendants supplied a musical work for use in a television play. The claimants complained that the work infringed their copyright. The defendants conceded that the works were similar but argued that this was coincidence. The claimants adduced evidence, some of which was obtained by a trap

---

[3] Confirmed *Plato Films Ltd v Speidel* [1961] A.C. 1090.
[4] (1791) 2 Bos. & P. 532n.
[5] (1997) 1 B.C.L.C. 329.
[6] Now governed by Criminal Justice Act 2003, s.101(1)(d).
[7] *Makin v Attorney-General for New South Wales* [1894] A.C. 57; *R. v P* [1991] 3 All E.R. 337.
[8] [1976] 1 All E.R. 763.

engineered by the claimant, that the defendants had reproduced other musical works that were subject to copyright. The Court of Appeal upheld the decision to admit this evidence.

Mood Music Publishing v De Wolfe Publishing Ltd [1976] 1 All E.R. 763 at 766c–h, *per* Lord Denning M.R.:

The admissibility of evidence as to 'similar facts' has been much considered in the criminal law. Some of them have reached the highest tribunal . . . The criminal courts have been very careful not to admit such evidence unless its probative value is so strong that it should be received in the interests of justice: and its admission will not operate unfairly to the accused. In civil cases the courts will admit evidence of similar facts if it is logically probative, that is it is logically relevant in determining the matter which is in issue; provided that it is not oppressive or unfair to the other side; and also that the other side has fair notice of it and is able to deal with it.

The matter in issue in the present case is whether the resemblances . . . are mere coincidences or are due to copying. on that issue it is very relevant to know that there are these other cases of musical works which are undoubtedly the subject of copyright, but yet the defendants have produced musical works bearing a close resemblance to them. Whereas it might be due to mere coincidence in one case, it is very unlikely that there would be coincidences in four cases. It is rather like *R v Sims* where it was said 'The probative force of all the acts together is much greater than one alone'. So the probative force of four resemblances together is much better than one alone. It seems to me the judge was right . . . I would dismiss the appeal.

The place of similar fact evidence was reviewed by the House of Lords in *O'Brien v Chief Constable of the South Wales Police.*[9] The claimant had been convicted of murder but the conviction had eventually been quashed. He sought damages on grounds of misfeasance in a public office and malicious prosecution by officers of the police force and sought to adduce evidence of other murder investigations which demonstrated the investigating police officers had behaved with similar impropriety. Lord Carswell rejected the submission that similar fact evidence is only admissible in a civil suit if it is likely to be reasonably conclusive of a primary issue in the proceedings or alternatively if it has enhanced relevance so as to have substantial probative value.

O'Brien v Chief Constable of the South Wales Police [2005] 2 A.C. 534, *per* Lord Caswell:

75. The limitation which [counsel for the police] propounded with most vigour was his third, that the similar fact evidence must have enhanced relevance, that is to say, it must be strongly probative. Again he called in aid statements . . . in *R v Boardman.*[10]

---

[9] [2005] 2 A.C. 534; *Thorpe v Greater Manchester CC* [1989] 2 All E.R. 827; *West Midlands Passenger Executive v Singh* [1988] 2 All E.R. 873.
[10] [1975] A.C. 421.

Again, however, it has to be borne in mind that they were considering the test in criminal cases . . . . There is no good reason in principle to require that evidence of similar facts in civil cases must, to be admissible, be strongly probative or have enhanced relevance. Nor is there in my opinion any authority which supports such a proposition, for the cases cited on behalf of the appellant, when properly analysed, do not bear it out. On the contrary, the clear statement of Lord Denning MR in the Mood Music case is firmly against it. I accordingly agree with the conclusion expressed by Lord Bingham . . . that in the first stage of the enquiry admissibility turns only on whether the evidence proposed to be adduced is probative. In a criminal trial . . . it may be necessary to look for enhanced relevance or substantial probative value, for that may be necessary to offset the degree of prejudice caused, but that is a matter for the second stage.

3. Character as to credit.   Any witness in civil proceedings, whether a party to the proceedings or not, is liable to cross-examination as to credit.

Hobbs v Tinling & Co. Ltd [1929] 2 K.B. 1 at 18–19, *per* Scrutton L.J.:

. . . When a witness has given evidence material to the issues . . . you can cross-examine him on matters not directly material to the case in order to ask the jury to infer from his answers that he is not worthy of belief, not a credible person, and therefore that they should not accept his answers on questions material to the case as true. This is cross-examination as to his credibility, commonly called cross-examination to credit. But as it is on matters not directly material to the case, the party cross-examining is not allowed to call evidence-in-chief to contradict his answers. To permit this would involve the court in an interminable series of controversies not directly material to the case on alleged facts of which the witness had no notice when he came into court, and which he or the party calling him might not be prepared without notice to meet. This rule, which has been established by cases in which the party cross-examining has desired to call rebutting evidence-in-chief, has been expressed in various ways . . . . But this does not go to the extent contended for by the appellant's counsel that the jury must believe the answers given by the witness. No case has been found where such a contention has been put forward, and if the jury, hearing the answers given by the witness, do not believe him they are entitled to do so, and to use the view thus obtained as to his credibility in rejecting answers given by him on matters material to the case. But rejecting his denials, does not prove the fact he denies, of which there is, and can be, no other evidence. It only destroys his credibility in respect of other evidence . . .

The common law drew a clear distinction between questioning witnesses about the issues in the case and collateral issues, such as their credibility. The party asking the question will normally be bound by the answer received as the rule about the finality of answers to collateral questions applies, as do the exceptions to the rule.[11] Credibility can be explored through questions on the witness's knowledge of the facts, their disinterestedness, integrity and veracity. At all times counsel are expected to remain within the limits laid down by the Bar Council.

[11] see Ch.13.

II. The Relevance of Character in Criminal Proceedings

Does the character of the defendant, whether churchgoer or sinner, provide help in deciding whether they committed an offence? At first sight, such information seems irrelevant. It is often said that the fact that the accused has committed several previous burglaries does not make it more probable that he has committed the specific burglary with which he is now charged. On reflection, this is wrong as such information does have relevance: a defendant with such a record is more likely to have committed this offence than another person with no such background. But that is a statement about probabilities and not whether this particular defendant committed this particular burglary. The question is how we use such information: if there is little evidence to link the defendant to the offence except bad character, such evidence should be excluded; if there is substantial linking evidence, the bad character evidence can be legitimately used to rebut any lingering doubts about possible defences.

While evidence of previous convictions can be relevant, it can also be grossly unfair—magistrates and juries might rush to judgment, failing to properly assess the hard evidence in the case and pre-judging the defendant on their record. Recognising this, the common law firmly drew the line on excluding information about prior convictions and prior bad character. The rationale was based less on irrelevance, but on the prejudicial effect on the trier of fact of such a revelation before conviction. Recent statutory reforms have shifted the balance in favour of revealing past record[12] but the rule remains in place in many common law jurisdictions. After sentence, of course, prior convictions are relevant to the issue of sentence.

If the rationale is one of fairness and not of irrelevance, this helps to acquit the common law of a charge of inconsistency. If prior bad character is irrelevant, prior good character should also be. But the vicar charged with misappropriating the Sunday collection is allowed to introduce character witnesses as part of the defence and is entitled to a direction from the judge that this is not simply relevant to credibility but also to the likelihood that they committed the offence.[13] The truth is that character has relevance in a criminal trial: it is not feasible to treat the biography of the accused as a blank sheet. This and the following chapters explore the use of good and bad character. It is perhaps helpful to provide a summary of the different contexts in which evidence relating to the accused's character can be admitted.

1. As part of the prosecution case.

   a) bad character evidence which needs to be proved by the prosecution as an element of the offence;
   b) bad character evidence which is admissible under one of the seven gateways provided by s.101 of the Criminal Justice Act 2003. This can be where:

---

[12] see Ch.15.
[13] *Vye* [1993] 2 All E.R. 241.

(i)   the parties agree to admitting the evidence;
(ii) the defendant introduces the evidence;
(iii) the evidence provides important explanatory background to the case;
(iv) the evidence is relevant to an issue between the prows and the defence;
(v)   the evidence is very relevant to an issue between co-accused;
(vi) the evidence rebuts a false impression created by the defendant; or
(vii) the evidence is admissible because the defendant has attacked another person's character.

As long as the bad character evidence satisfies one of these gateways, the prosecution may introduce it as part of their evidence in chief or it may be the subject of a question in cross-examination of the accused or of a defence witness. These will be discussed fully later in the following chapters.

2. As part of the defence case. Normally the defence is only likely to introduce evidence of the defendant's good character, suggesting that the accused is not the sort of person likely to commit such an offence. There may be situations where the defendant is charged with one category of offence and wishes to show that they have no previous similar offences. To do this, it may be necessary to own up to convictions or cautions for other unrelated offences.

III. The Accused's Good Character

1. What evidence can be advanced?

Defendants can adduce evidence of their own good character, either by testifying themselves or through witnesses. In *Rowton*, the defendant was charged with indecent assault and was permitted to introduce such evidence of good reputation.

Rowton (1865) 34 L.J.M.C. 57 at 60–61, *per* Cockburn C.J.:

. . . Now, in determining this, it becomes necessary in the first instance, to consider what is the meaning of evidence of character. It is laid down in the books that a prisoner is entitled to give evidence as to his general character. What does that mean? Does it mean evidence as to his reputation amongst those to whom his conduct and position are known, or does it mean evidence of disposition? I think it means evidence of reputation only . . . . No one ever heard of a question put deliberately to a witness called on behalf of a prisoner as to the prisoner's disposition of mind; the way, and the only way the law allows of your getting at the disposition and tendency of his mind, is by evidence as to his general character found upon the knowledge of those who know anything about him and his general conduct. Now, that is the sense in which I find the word "character" used and applied in all the books of the text-writers of authority upon the subject of evidence . . .

No one pretends that, according to the present practice, examination can be made as to a specific fact, though every one would agree that evidence of one fact of honesty or dishonesty, as the case might be, would weigh infinitely more than the opinions of a man's friends or neighbours as to his general character. The truth is, this part of our law is an anomaly. Although, logically speaking, it is quite clear that an antecedent bad character would form quite as reasonable a ground for the presumption and probability of guilt, as previous good character lays the foundation for the presumption of innocence, yet the prosecution cannot go into evidence as to the prisoner's bad character. The allowing evidence of a prisoner's good character to be given has grown from a desire to administer the law with mercy, as far as possible . . .

When we come to consider the question of what, in the strict interpretation of the law, is the limit of such evidence, I must say that, In my judgment, it must be restrained to this: the evidence must be of the man's general reputation, and not the individual opinion of the witness . . . . The witness who acknowledged that he knew nothing of the general character, and had no opportunity of knowing it in the sense of reputation, would not be allowed to give an opinion as to a man's character in the more limited sense of his disposition.

The law still insists that a witness may only speak to general reputation. Yet opinions about individuals vary widely and there is no realistic way of assessing any generality of opinion. In other words, witnesses are often generalising from their own opinions and are unable to testify in detail about specific creditable acts which at least would give some credibility to such an opinion. Nor can a witness be asked as to the accused's disposition, for example, whether or not they were a violent person who might be likely to commit the offence charged. But a character witness can be cross-examined about particular matters.[14]

In *Redgrave*,[15] the appellant was charged with persistently importuning for an immoral purpose contrary to s.32 of the Sexual Offences Act 1956. He sought to tender detailed evidence of documents and photos of his heterosexual relationships in order to rebut the inference from his conduct, as observed by police officers, that he had been making homosexual approaches. The judge ruled the evidence inadmissible and this was upheld on appeal. The accused can call evidence to show that they did not commit the acts alleged against them but (save in special circumstances) they could not, by reference to particular facts, call evidence that they were of a particular disposition that made it unlikely that they had committed the offence. Although disposition to commit the kind of offence was relevant, in *Redgrave*, the accused could go no further than to call evidence of general reputation that suggests that he was not the kind of young man who would behave in the way charged. It might seem hard that he could not call other evidence but the Court of Appeal considered it was in the public interest generally that evidence should be so limited.

---

[14] *Winfield* [1939] 4 All E.R. 164.
[15] (1981) 74 Cr.App.R. 10.

In *Rowton*, Cockburn C.J. talked of ".... a desire to administer the law with mercy, as far as possible. . .", suggesting that evidence of character and disposition are, at best, evidence going to the credibility of the accused's denials. Such evidence is seen as collateral, a side-issue to the focus of the court on the direct questions as to whether the accused committed the acts alleged. But how valid is this distinction between testimony going to the issues and testimony merely going to credibility?

A. Zuckerman, The Principles of Criminal Evidence (OUP, Oxford, 1989), pp.94–95:

. . . the justification of the present rule rests on the supposition that evidence which merely tends to discredit a witness makes, on the whole, insufficient probative contribution to warrant its reception . . . If our object is to arrive economically at factually correct conclusions, admissibility should depend on the degree to which evidence contributes towards this end. Since the distinction between relevance to credibility and relevance to issue does not reflect a divergence in probative force we should not allow it to govern admissibility.

The validity of the distinction between relevance to credibility and relevance to issue may also be questioned at a more fundamental level. One fact is relevant to another when it renders the existence of the other more probable. The fact that the witness says: 'The man who committed the offence was the accused' is relevant because it renders it more probable that the accused was the offender. However, W's testimony could have this effect only if it has some credibility. If the testimony has no credibility at all, for example, because it is the blabber of a madman, it is irrelevant. It follows that the connecting link between W's testimony and the conclusion based on it is credibility. In other words, the relevance of a witness's testimony is embedded in his credibility, actual or potential.

Such an analysis also goes to good character—specific acts and disposition such as Redgrave's sexual orientation can have probative force. Furthermore,

J. McEwan, Evidence and the Adversarial Process (2nd ed., Hart, 1998), p.183:

. . . it is nonsense to argue that evidence of heterosexuality, however established, has something to do with credibility on oath. Redgrave was not asking the court to believe what he said in the witness-box because he was really a heterosexual. He was suggesting that his sexual proclivities made it unlikely that he would approach men in a public lavatory. The fact is that 'character' evidence is a broad category, at times relating to honesty and at others to very different attributes. A defendant might suggest that he has a gentle disposition incompatible with the violent offences alleged. He might wish to establish lifelong patriotism in order to suggest that he would not betray his country. He might even argue that as a committed homosexual he is an unlikely rapist. None of these arguments has anything to do with credibility as a witness; whether or not he gives evidence has absolutely no effect on its relevance. The proper direction to the jury must therefore depend on the purpose for which the evidence is admitted, rather than some *ex post facto* categorization by the judge. It would be absurd . . . to demand that if the accused gives evidence of these matters he or she should do so by way of establishing his or her own reputation, and he or she should not be dependent on the generosity of judges to get it in. It would be better simply to acknowledge, as Continental courts do, that it is irrational to try an individual without knowing what sort of person is before the court.

2. The impact of good character evidence—the Vye direction

Not only is the accused permitted to introduce evidence of good character, they are also entitled to a direction as to the effect of that evidence.[16] The purpose of such testimony appears primarily to go to the credibility of the defendants who have testified, giving their denials more weight.[17] However, whether or not the defendant has testified, they are entitled to a direction that good character is an indicator of innocence, a 'propensity' direction. In *Vye*,[18] the defendant appealed against a rape conviction on the grounds that the direction to the jury was inadequate.

Vye [1993] 3 All E.R 241 at 243h–248g, *per* Lord Taylor:

. . . At one time these issues would not have been regarded even as arguable in this court. The trial judge was understood to have a broad discretion to comment on the defendant's good character or not as he thought fit. The principle applied by this court was that the judge had no obligation to give directions on good character or even to remind the jury of it.[19] Since about 1989, however, there has been a dramatic change. This court has been inundated with appeals based upon the judge's alleged misdirection or failure to give any direction to the jury about good character . . .
. . . in *R v Berrada*[20] this court considered, amongst other grounds, an alleged misdirection about good character. The defendant had given evidence. Waterhouse J. giving the judgment of the court, said:

> In the judgment of this Court, the appellant was entitled to have put to the jury from the judge herself a correct direction about the relevance of his previous good character to his credibility. This is a conventional direction and it is regrettable that it did not appear in the summing-up in this case. It would have been proper also (but was not obligatory) for the judge to refer to the fact that the previous good character of the appellant might be thought by them to be one relevant factor when they were considering whether he was the kind of man who was likely to have behaved in the way that the prosecution alleged . . . We have no doubt, however, that the modern practice is that, if good character is raised by a defendant, it should be dealt with in the summing-up. Moreover, when it is dealt with, the direction should be fair and balanced, stressing its relevance primarily to a defendant's credibility.[21]

---

[16] *Berrada* (1989) 91 Cr.App.R. 131.
[17] In medieval England the accused could escape liability by such means through compurgation—producing sufficient neighbours to swear to your honesty and credibility.
[18] [1993] 3 All E.R. 241.
[19] *Aberg* [1948] 1 All E.R. 601; *Smith* [1971] Crim.L.R. 531.
[20] (1989) 91 Cr.App.R. 131.
[21] *ibid.* at 134.

That decision, therefore, confirmed that, whatever the position may have been previously it is now an established principle that, where the defendant of good character has given evidence, it is no longer sufficient for the judge to comment in general terms. He is required to direct the jury about the relevance of good character to the credibility of the defendant. Conventionally this has come to be described as the 'first limb' of a character direction. The passage quoted also stated that the judge was entitled, but not obliged, to refer to the possible relevance of good character to the question whether the defendant was likely to have behaved as alleged by the Crown. That . . . is the 'second limb'.

. . . Accordingly, we turn to the three problems which seem presently to be unresolved on the authorities. They are (a) whether a 'first limb' direction needs to be given in a case where the defendant does not give evidence but has made statements to the police or others, (b) whether the 'second limb' direction should now be regarded as discretionary or obligatory and (c) what course the judge should take in a joint trial where one defendant is of good character but another is not.

(a) Defendant of good character not giving evidence

. . . In our judgment, when the defendant has not given evidence at trial but relies on exculpatory statements made to the police or others, the judge should direct the jury to have regard to the defendant's good character when considering the credibility of those statements. He will, of course, be entitled to make observations about the way the jury should approach such exculpatory statements in contrast to evidence given on oath (see *R v Duncan*[22]), but when the jury is considering the truthfulness of any such statements, it would be logical for them to take good character into account, just as they would in regard to a defendant's evidence.

Clearly if a defendant of good character does not give evidence and has given no pre-trial answers or statements, no issue as to his credibility arises and a first limb direction is not required.

(b) The 'second limb' direction

The relevant authorities as to the judge's duty with regard to the 'second limb' are confusing. On a number of occasions it has been said that the second limb direction is 'discretionary' or 'not obligatory' . . . . we have been unable to discern any principle or consistent pattern as to when a second limb direction should be given and when it need not. Neither the nature of the crime, its gravity, the age of the defendant, whether he is merely of no previous convictions or of positively good character nor the nature of the defence would seem to have provided clear guidance . . .

. . . At one extreme there is the case of an employee who has been entrusted with large sums of money over many years by his employer and, having carried out his duties impeccably, is finally charged with stealing from the till. There a second limb direction is obviously relevant and necessary. At the other extreme is a case such as *R v Richens*[23] where the defendant, charged with murder, admits manslaughter. It might be thought that in such a case a second limb direction would be little help to the jury

. . . .

. . . It cannot be satisfactory for uncertainty to persist so that judges do not known whether this court, proceeding on a case by case basis, will hold that a 'second limb' direction should or should not have been given. Our conclusion is that such a direction should be given where the defendant is of good character. Does the need for a second limb direction still exist when the defendant has not given evidence . . . We can see no logical ground for distinguishing . . . between cases where the defendant has given evidence and cases where he has not.

c) Two or more defendants of good and bad character

This situation clearly creates difficulties for the trial judge in summing up. Lord Lane CJ in *R v Gibson*[24] put the matter thus:

> There may be very difficult problems facing a judge in dealing with cases of character where one of the participants in this sort of offence is of good character

---

[22] (1981) 73 Cr.App.R. 359.

[23] [1993] 4 All E.R. 877.

[24] (1991) 93 Cr.App.R. 9 at 1 1–12.

and the other is not, because by stressing the good character of the one he may be doing two things: first of all highlighting the bad character of the other and secondly, by reason of highlighting the bad character of the other, reflecting that bad character on to the good character of the first offender.

It may be that when there are two defendants, one of good character and the other not of good character, it will be advisable for the judge to say very little, if anything, about the character of the defendant who has no previous convictions. If that is the judge's view, it will be prudent for him, in the absence of the jury, to indicate to counsel that that is what is in his mind, namely to make no reference about character at all, and to explain to counsel the reasons for it. That will enable counsel not only to address the judge on the point but also, if necessary, to make such reference to character as counsel may think fit in the case of his individual client in the course of his speech to the jury. It seems to us that that is the proper way in circumstances such as these, which may provide very great difficulty for the judge to balance fairness in respect of each of the defendants

... [this] suggestion ... involves a number of undesirable features and possible results. First the defendant is entitled ... to a direction from the judge in regard to his good character. For the direction to be left to counsel without indorsement by the judge would be to devalue that factor ... Secondly, it cannot be desirable for the content of the summing up to be determined by whether counsel insists on a particular direction or not. It should be for the judge to decide what directions to give. Further should the jury seek directions ... the judge could not abstain from assisting them ... Again it would seem undesirable that there should be negotiations ... over the content of the summing up ...

... we conclude that the solution suggested in *Gibson* is not satisfactory ... In our judgment a defendant of good character is entitled to have the judge direct the jury even if he is jointly tried with a defendant B of bad character. This leaves the question as to what, if anything, the judge should say about the latter. In some cases the judge may think it best to grasp the nettle in his summing up and tell the jury that they must try the case on the evidence, that there has been no evidence about B's character, that they must not speculate and must not take the absence of information as to B's character as evidence against B. In other cases the judge may, however, think it best to say nothing ...

A *Vye* direction is required whenever issues of good character emerge:

1. *The first limb.* Where a defendant has testified or given a statement to the police, the judge must direct the jury that good character is relevant to credibility. This does not need to be given where there has been no pre-trial statements or testimony

2. *The second limb.* Where there is evidence of good character, the judge should direct the jury that that evidence is relevant to the likelihood of the defendant having committed the offence. This does not depend on whether the defendant has testified or answered questions in police interviews.

3. *The codicil.* Where one defendant is of good character and another is of bad character, the judge should still direct the jury along the lines of the first and second limbs as far as the defendant of good character is concerned. The judge should normally warn the jury not to speculate about any co-accused.

A failure to give direction on either or both of the limbs of credibility or propensity is a material irregularity and may well be the basis for a successful appeal against conviction.[25]

---

[25] *Gray* [2004] 2 Cr.App.R. 30.

When does a defendant put his character into issue? What constitutes 'good character'? *Vye* is concerned with the scope of a judge's directions to the jury, not only when there is positive evidence of good character but also the usual case of the defendant with no previous convictions. The question remains of the threshold required before a direction is given. In *Teeluck*,[26] the defendant appealed on his conviction for murder on the grounds that the judge had failed to give a good character direction to the jury. The defendant had testified (incidentally, falsely) that he had never been arrested or charged—the Privy Council held that this had not raised the issue distinctly enough for the purposes of a *Vye* direction. This is contrary to earlier authority—in *West*,[27] cross-examining a prosecution witness about the lack of previous convictions was held to be sufficient to cross the threshold.

When are the *Vye* limbs not applicable? In *Clarius*,[28] the defendant had only one previous conviction for shoplifting as a 14-year-old. The judge gave a *Vye* direction on credibility but not on propensity. The conviction was quashed as the defendant's claim to be of good character, could not be described as spurious and did not defy common sense. The propensity limb of the direction had not been damaged by his caution for shoplifting and should not have been omitted.

The difficulty of applying these principles where there is positive evidence of misconduct is shown in *Aziz*,[29] the respondents were charged with evasion of income tax and VAT. At the trial the first defendant did not testify but relied on statements given to the investigating officers, in the course of which he made significant admissions but also exculpatory claims. The second and third defendants did testify, denying the offences charged but admitting previously making false mortgage applications, false tax returns and lying in interview. All three relied on their lack of previous convictions. The Court of Appeal certified the following question for the consideration of the House of Lords, ". . . whether directions in accordance with *R v Vye* must be given in all cases in which a defendant has adduced evidence of previous good character, and if not, in what circumstances must such directions be given?"

Aziz [1995] 3 All E.R. 149 at 157j–158g, *per* Lord Steyn:

The certified question, although phrased in very general terms, was intended to raise the problem whether a defendant without any previous convictions may 'lose' his good character by reason of other criminal behaviour. It is a question which was not directly before the Court of Appeal in *R v Vye*. It is a complex problem. It is also an area in which generalisations are hazardous. Acknowledging that a wide spectrum of cases must be kept in mind, the problem can be illustrated with a commonplace

---

[26] [2005] UKPC 14.
[27] (1890) 112 C.C.C. Sess. Pap. 724.
[28] Unreported July 10, 2000, CA.
[29] [1995] 3 All E.R. 149.

example. A middle-aged man is charged with theft from his employers. He has no previous convictions. But during the trial it emerges, through cross-examination on behalf of a co-defendant, that the defendant has made dishonest claims on insurance companies over a number of years. What directions about good character, if any, must the judge give?

. . . A good starting point is that a judge should never be compelled to give meaningless or absurd directions. And cases occur from time to time where a defendant, who has no previous convictions, is shown beyond doubt to have been guilty of serious criminal behaviour similar to the offence charged in the indictment. A sensible criminal justice system should not compel a judge to go through the charade of giving directions in accordance with *R v Vye* in a case where the defendant's claim to good character is spurious. I would therefore hold that a trial judge has a residual discretion to decline to give any character directions in the case of a defendant without previous convictions if the judge considers it an insult to common sense to give directions in accordance with *R v Vye*. I am reinforced in thinking that this is the right conclusion by the fact that after *R v Vye* the Court of Appeal . . . ruled that such a residual discretion exists: see *R v H*[30] and *R v Zoppola-Barraza*.[31]

That brings me to the nature of the discretion. Discretions range from open-textured discretionary powers to narrowly circumscribed discretionary powers. The residual discretion of a trial judge to dispense with character directions in respect of a defendant of good character is of the more limited variety. Prima facie the directions must be given. And the judge will often be able to place a fair and balanced picture before the jury by giving directions in accordance with *R v Vye* and then adding words of qualification concerning other proved or possible criminal conduct of the defendant which emerged during the trial. On the other hand, if it would make no sense to give character directions in accordance with *R v Vye*, the judge may in his discretion dispense with them . . .[32]

That discretion is shown in *Young*,[33] where the appellant was convicted of murder and had no previous convictions. The trial judge refused to give a *Vye* direction. The Court of Appeal upheld the conviction. Although on the face of it, the defendant was entitled to a full good character direction, the circumstances of the particular case were that he had relentlessly lied during the investigation. Further, a search of his home had revealed at least two illicit firearms that had been modified in such a way that he could not have had a legitimate reason for owning them. It would have been absurd to give a direction that he was a person of good character and that the jury should therefore give credibility to his denials.

---

[30] [1994] Crim.L.R. 205.
[31] [1994] Crim.L.R. 833.
[32] *Aziz*, above, at 157j–158g.
[33] [2004] EWCA Crim 3520; *Howell* [2001] EWCA Crim 286; *Normandale*, unreported November 4, 1999—earlier lies by the defendant meant that no *Vye* direction was given.

15

BAD CHARACTER

I. Bad Character at Common Law

At common law, the prosecution were generally prohibited from mentioning the accused's bad character or prior convictions.[1]

Makin v Attorney-General for New South Wales [1894] A.C. 57 at 65, *per* Lord Herschell:

It is undoubtedly not competent for the prosecution to adduce evidence tending to show that the accused has been guilty of criminal acts other than those covered by the indictment, for the purpose of leading to the conclusion that the accused is a person likely from his criminal conduct or character to have committed the offence for which he is being tried.

The argument has always been that there is considerable risk that bad character is accorded much more weight than that relevance warrants. As such its prejudicial effect may well outweigh its probative value and the jury, with little experience in assessing such matters, should be prevented from hearing about previous convictions.[2] That was supported when the Law Commission[3] commissioned research which showed that knowledge of previous convictions may prejudice a jury or magistrates unfairly against the defendant. Redmayne's study considered the usual justifications for the exclusionary rule, namely irrelevance or the disproportionate and prejudicial impact on the jury. The conclusion was after reviewing the psychological research on character and statistical data on recidivism, that those with previous convictions are much more likely to offend than are those without a criminal record, which implies that evidence of bad character will usually be sufficiently probative to justify its admission as proof of guilt.[4] There are no simple conclusions from this—probative value and potential prejudice both

---

[1] It can emerge by accident—R. Munday, "Irregular Disclosure of Evidence of Bad Character" [1990] Crim.L.R. 92.

[2] C. Tapper, "The Criminal Justice Act 2003: Evidence of Bad Character" [2004] Crim. L.R. 533 for a review of the flaws in the common law and the reform movement.

[3] Law Commission, *Evidence of Bad Character in Criminal Proceedings*, Law Comm. No.273 (2001).

[4] M. Redmayne, "The Relevance of Bad Character" 61 Cambridge L.J. (2002) 684.

exist when the prosecution introduces the accused's criminal record. Policing that line in the interests of a fair trial for the defendant and for the community at large was never going to be easy.

The common law adopted a default policy of exclusion of such evidence, although previous convictions are used at trials in the rest of Europe where many jurisdictions permit the judge to have access to the record of the defendant's prior convictions. In many countries, they are said to be relevant only to determining sentence but in Belgium, the prosecution can refer to them and in France, all the facts, the background and life history of the accused is known before the court reaches its judgment.[5] Other jurisdictions use such information more freely not merely because they employ an investigative mode of trial but also because they place more emphasis on the professionally trained judge rather than on a lay jury. The latter are assumed to be more likely to pre-judge a case on the basis of an accused's prior convictions than the former.

The common law restrictions on the use of previous convictions have come under considerable scrutiny, from the Law Commission and from the Auld Report on criminal courts. The Report came down strongly on increasing the scope of bad character evidence.

Lord Auld, Review of the Criminal Courts: Report (2001) paras 11.119–11.120:

119. . . . Professor Spencer and others have advanced the following arguments:

1. it is illogical for the law to allow a defendant to put in his good character to indicate lack of propensity but to deny the prosecution the opportunity to establish the converse when he has a bad one;
2. jurors rapidly learn and magistrates and judges know that if there is no mention of a defendant's good character, he probably has a bad one, and so it permits the tribunal of fact to guess what it is not officially allowed to know;
3. magistrates, in any event, soon recognise the regular offenders in their court;
4. in the case of the exception where a defendant's character goes in because he has wrongly sought to establish his own good character or attacked a prosecution witness, the requirement on the judge to tell a jury that it goes only to credibility, not to propensity, is confusing and unreal;
5. evidence showing that a defendant has committed offences of a similar type before statistically and logically suggests that he is more likely than those without such a record to commit such offences again, and should for that reason be regarded as relevant evidence—and some propensities can be more significant than others;
6. though studies have shown that juries would be influenced to some extent by knowledge that the defendant has a criminal record, they do not show that juries would be unduly influenced by it;
7. to remove the scope for possibly prejudicial speculation, fact-finders should be informed at the start of the trial whether the defendant has a criminal record and, if so, what it is;

---

[5] Extracted from N. Osner, A. Quinn and G. Crown: *Criminal Justice Systems in Other Jurisdictions* (Royal Commission on Criminal Justice (HMSO, 1993).

8. we should substitute weight for admissibility, confining the prosecutor to making active use of the criminal record or bad tendencies where they appear to be relevant to some disputed element in the case, and we should trust jurors and other fact finders to give it the weight it deserves;

9. adequate safeguards against juries and other fact finders giving unduly prejudicial weight to such evidence would be to prevent prosecutors inflating its importance and to prohibit a conviction when there is no other prosecution evidence of substance; and

10. such a system would be simpler and more honest.

120. Those are powerful pointers to the futility of a rule, whatever its form, for rendering inadmissible prejudicial matter inferential knowledge of which cannot and arguably need not be kept from fact finders. As I have said, magistrates will know, and so will most jurors—if not the first time they sit on a jury, the second time—that silence about a defendant's character probably means he has a criminal record. They may not know what it is, but they can speculate about it. Professional judges, sitting as fact finders in the magistrates' courts or on appeal in the Crown Court usually cannot avoid knowing the full details if an issue arises before them as to character. Prominent among the reasons for retaining a lay element in the administration of criminal justice is a belief in their worldly judgment and common sense. Magistrates and jurors are seemingly trusted now, where as a result of the conduct of a defendant's case his previous bad character goes in, to distinguish between its relevance to his credibility but not to his propensity, a distinction which must be incomprehensible to most jurors and, possibly to many magistrates. Yet they are not to be trusted as a generality to assess such evidence for themselves. In my view, there is much to be said for a more radical view than has so far found favour with the Law Commission, for placing more trust in the fact finders and for introducing some reality into this complex corner of the law.

The radical proposal of reading out convictions as a matter of routine was not supported in the Government's White Paper on criminal justice.[6] The legislative policy has been one of extending the use of bad character evidence but to a more limited extent.

II. The Criminal Justice Act 2003

The common law position has been changed by the 2003 reforms, although the Act remains conventional in its approach to evidence of bad character. Section 99 clears the undergrowth by the sweeping away of the common law. There follows a three part structure—definition of the category (s.98), statement of the rule (implicit in s.101(1)) and listing of the exceptions (s.101(1)(a)-(g)). The outcome is that the prosecution has been given greater scope to adduce such evidence under the seven gateways of s.101.[7]

A. Definition

"Bad character" is broadly defined under s.98, of the Criminal Justice Act 2003.

---

[6] Home Office: *Justice For All* Cm. 5563 (HMSO, 2002) 79.

[7] R. Munday, "What constitutes reprehensible behaviour?" [2005] Crim. L.R. 24; R. Munday, "Bad Character Rules and Riddles" [2005] Crim. L.R. 337; R. Munday, "Cut Throat Defences and the Propensity to be Untruthful" [2005] Crim. L.R. 624.

References in this Chapter to evidence of a person's "bad character" are to evidence of, or of a disposition towards, misconduct on his part, other than evidence which—
(a) has to do with the alleged facts of the offence with which the defendant is charged, or
(b) is evidence of misconduct in connection with the investigation or prosecution of that offence.

The term clearly encompasses prior conduct which goes beyond convictions or cautions for criminal offences. It would include responsibility for crimes for which the accused has not been charged or prosecuted, or for actions which are not offences but people would regard as reprehensible.

Bad Character as an Element of the Offence

The definition excludes prior disreputable conduct, especially convictions and cautions, which are integral to the immediate charge. Under s.98(a), the prosecution can adduce evidence that "has to do with the alleged facts of the offence." Bad character, in the shape of a previous conviction, can be an element of another offence. In such circumstances, this conviction can be proved. Obvious examples are the offence of driving while disqualified under s.103 of the Road Traffic Act 1988 or that of possessing firearms being a person sentenced to three years or more imprisonment contrary to s.21 of the Firearms Act 1968.

It may be the conviction of another person that needs to be proved—when the charge is, for example, acting as a secondary party to a crime committed by a principal. The commission of the offence by a third person, normally prohibited by the provisions of s.100, has to be proved. The defence may also have reason to bring up the prior conviction, for example in pleas of *autrefois convict*.[8]

B. *The Seven Gateways*

It is implicit within s.101 of the CJA 2003 that there is a rule that makes bad character evidence inadmissible. That rule is immediately qualified by exceptions—bad character can be adduced by the Crown if it can be brought within one of the seven gateways of s.101.

Criminal Justice Act 2003, s.101:

101(1) In criminal proceedings evidence of the defendant's bad character is admissible if, but only if—
(a) all parties to the proceedings agree to the evidence being admissible,

---

[8] These issues are discussed in Ch.21.

(b) the evidence is adduced by the defendant himself or is given in answer to a question asked by him in cross-examination and intended to elicit it,

(c) it is important explanatory evidence,

(d) it is relevant to an important matter in issue between the defendant and the prosecution,

(e) it has substantial probative value in relation to an important matter in issue between the defendant and a co-defendant,

(f) it is evidence to correct a false impression given by the defendant, or

(g) the defendant has made an attack on another person's character.

(2) Sections 102 to 106 contain provision supplementing subsection (1).

(3) The court must not admit evidence under subsection (1)(d) or (g) if, on an application by the defendant to exclude it, it appears to the court that the admission of the evidence would have such an adverse effect on the fairness of the proceedings that the court ought not to admit it.

(4) On an application to exclude evidence under subsection (3) the court must have regard, in particular, to the length of time between the matters to which that evidence relates and the matters which form the subject of the offence charged.

Where the prosecution wish to rely on an accused's bad character, they must satisfy the court that the criteria for one of these gateways have been satisfied. Section 101(3) imposes a further condition for gateways (1)(d) or (1)(g), namely that the admission of the evidence will not have an adverse effect on the fairness of the proceedings. This appears to put a burden on the Crown to show that there would be no such effect.

There is no such further condition with the other gateways, although the defence may choose to make an application to exclude the evidence under s.78 of PACE. In these circumstances, the burden would be on the defence to show that such an issue arose.

Impact of bad character evidence

The issue arises as to the way in which the evidence may be put, once it has been admitted in evidence. For example, the evidence may be admitted to rebut evidence of the accused's good character under *(f)* or because there has been an attack on a prosecution witness under *(g)*. In both cases, it might be argued that the prior bad character should only be used to cast doubt on the credibility of the defendant and not as evidence of a propensity to commit such crimes. The Court of Appeal has held, however, that the use to which the evidence could be put depended upon the matters to which it was relevant rather than upon the gateway through which it was admitted. In *Highton*,[9] the accused attacked the prosecution witnesses, accusing them of fabricating the story of kidnapping and robbery. Under *(g)*, the accused's prior convictions for robbery and theft were introduced. These were clearly relevant to propensity and the judge invited the jury to consider this. Lord Woolf C.J. upheld the conviction,

Highton [2005] 1 W.L.R. 3472, *per* Lord Woolf C.J.:

10. We therefore conclude that a distinction must be drawn between the admissibility of evidence of bad character, which depends upon it getting through one

---

[9] [2005] 1 W.L.R. 3472.

of the gateways, and the use to which it may be put once it is admitted. The use to which it may be put depends upon the matters to which it is relevant rather than upon the gateway through which it was admitted. It is true that the reasoning that leads to the admission of evidence under gateway (d) may also determine the matters to which the evidence is relevant or primarily relevant once admitted. That is not true, however, of all the gateways. In the case of gateway (g), for example, admissibility depends on the defendant having made an attack on another person's character, but once the evidence is admitted, it may, depending on the particular facts, be relevant not only to credibility but also to propensity to commit offences of the kind with which the defendant is charged.

Once the evidence is in front of the jury, it may be used as proof of any matter to which it is relevant regardless of the gateway by which it was admitted.

Gateway 1: all parties to the proceedings agree to the evidence being admissible
This requires no further explanation.

Gateway 2: the evidence is adduced by the defendant himself
Although it seems unlikely that the defendant would wish to allude to previous convictions, there may be good tactical reason. For example, the prior record might provide some supporting evidence to the defence story ("I was on probation so I wasn't likely to have done this . . .") or the charge relates to one category of offence (sexual assault, for example) and the defendant wishes to demonstrate to the jury that they have no prior convictions for such acts. In such cases it might be necessary to admit to other offences in a different category. This would come under s.101(1)(b).

Gateway 3: important explanatory evidence
This has been discussed in relation to the cross-examination of witnesses.[10] Sections 100(1)(a) and 101(1)(c) both allow prosecution or defence to introduce essentially background evidence which has no immediate relevance to any fact in issue but without which the trier of fact would be left in the dark. Often this is uncontentious but such background evidence may well reveal the disclosure of prior criminal actions by witnesses, third parties or by the accused.

In *Sidhu*,[11] the defendant was charged with a conspiracy to possess explosives. Following an undercover police investigation, the appellant and his two co-defendants were arrested in connection with a suspected plot to further the cause of setting up an independent Sikh state, Khalistan, in India. The appellant had gone to the house of his co-defendants, taking Semtex explosive, which had been supplied to them by an undercover police officer.

[10] see Ch.14.
[11] (1993) 98 Cr.App.R. 59.

During the course of interviews with the police, the appellant refused to account for his presence at the house and maintained that he was a law-abiding citizen. He denied any involvement with a terrorist organisation. He did not give evidence. The disputed evidence admitted by the trial judge involved a video recording, made in Pakistan, of him as one of a group of heavily armed people practising the use of various weapons and singing in support of the Khalistan Liberation Force. The Court of Appeal held that the recording was not admissible to rebut his statement in the police interview that he was a law-abiding citizen[12] and was not involved with a terrorist organisation. But the appellant's association with those preparing to advance the cause of Khalistan by violent means was plainly relevant.

This decision supports the *Pettman*[13] principle which states that evidence is admissible, even where it indicates prior disreputable conduct by the accused.

> . . . where it is necessary to place before the jury evidence of part of a continual background or history relevant to the offence charged in the indictment, and without the totality of which the account placed before the jury would be incomplete or incomprehensible.

This was applied in *Sawoniuk*,[14] a war crimes case where expert evidence of the Nazi policy of genocide towards the Jews was admitted.

Sawoniuk [2000] 2 Cr.App.R. 220 at 234, *per* Lord Bingham C.J.:

> . . . we incline to the view that the admission of this evidence could be upheld on a broader basis. Criminal charges cannot be fairly judged in a factual vacuum. In order to make a rational assessment of evidence directly relating to a charge it may often be necessary for a jury to receive evidence describing, perhaps in some detail, the context and circumstances in which the offences are said to have been committed. This, as we understand, is the approach indicated by this court . . .

Section 101(1)(c) puts these common law principles on a statutory footing, supplementing (1)(c) in s.102 which provides a definition of "important explanatory evidence".

> s.102 For the purposes of section 101(1)(c) evidence is important explanatory evidence if—
> (a) without it, the court or jury would find it impossible or difficult properly to understand other evidence in the case, and
> (b) its value for understanding the case as a whole is substantial.

In *Campbell*,[15] the defendant was convicted of kidnapping and murdering his 15-year-old niece. The prosecution advanced evidence of the accused's

---

[12] But now see s.105(2)(a) Criminal Justice Act 2003.
[13] *Pettman* (unreported, May 2, 1985), approved in *Sidhu* (1994) 98 Cr.App.R. 59 and *Fulcher* [1995] 2 Cr.App.R. 251.
[14] [2000] 2 Cr.App.R. 220.
[15] [2005] EWCA Crim 248.

Internet activity involving access to teenage sex sites and downloading of material from those sites as well of his attempts to photograph other teenage girls. The Court of Appeal held that, without this evidence, the jury would have been left with an incomplete and distorted account of the relationship between the appellant and the victim.

Gateway 4: relevant to an important matter in issue between the defendant and the prosecution

Section 101(1)(d) will be the key gateway, allowing bad character evidence where, "it is relevant to an important matter in issue between the defendant and the prosecution." There is a significant restriction under subs.(3) that the court "must not admit evidence under subs.(1)(d) or (g) if, on an application by the defendant to exclude it, it appears to the court that the admission of the evidence would have such an adverse effect on the fairness of the proceedings that the court ought not to admit it."

(i) *Introduction*

There are three stages to consider when proposing adducing bad character evidence as proof of a crime.

   a) To what issue that the court needs to decide is this evidence relevant?
   b) Does it have sufficient probative force to make it just to admit it?
   c) Would the admission of such evidence make the proceedings unfair whether as a result of prejudice or for any other reason?

These issues have been debated by the common law for a century under the category of "similar fact" evidence. Although these common law rules on bad character have been abolished by s.99, the jurisprudence will inevitably affect the interpretation of s.100.

   a) To what issue that the court needs to decide is this evidence relevant?

An important preliminary step is to identify the "matters in issue between the defendant and prosecution" to which the bad character evidence is relevant. These matters encompass the facts in issue revealed in the offence charged— whether the accused did the act with the necessary mental element and whether any defence applied? The common law always, albeit reluctantly, recognised that the defendant's prior convictions or other bad conduct could be relevant to and probative of such matters. The classic example of this is *Makin v Attorney-General for New South Wales*,[16] in which the defendants were tried for the murder of a baby. The couple had accepted a child from its mother, alleging that they would adopt and care for it on payment of a small

---

[16] [1894] A.C. 57.

sum of money. A baby's body was found buried in the garden and the accused were charged with the murder. The prosecution sought to adduce evidence from other mothers that the couple had received their children on the same basis. They also were allowed to show that thirteen other such bodies had been found in gardens of three other houses occupied by the defendants. The evidence showed that the Makins had probably committed murders other than the one with which they were charged. The prosecution had to prove that the accused intentionally caused the death of the child. The relevance of the finding of the other bodies was that this tended to rebut any defence of accident or natural causes. Lord Herschell delivered the judgment of the Privy Council.

Makin v Attorney-General for New South Wales [1894] A.C. 57 at 65, *per* Lord Herschell:

In their Lordships' opinion the principles which must govern the decision of the case are clear, though the application of them is by no means free from difficulty. It is undoubtedly not competent for the prosecution to adduce evidence tending to show that the accused has been guilty of criminal acts other than those covered by the indictment for the purpose of leading to the conclusion that the accused is a person likely from his criminal conduct or character to have committed the offence for which he is being tried. On the other hand, the mere fact that the evidence adduced tends to show the commission of other crimes does not render it inadmissible if it be relevant to an issue before the jury and it may be so relevant if it bears upon the question whether the acts alleged to constitute the crime charged in the indictment were designed or accidental or to rebut a defence which would have been otherwise open to the accused.

Makin established the common law rule is that evidence of the accused's disposition is normally inadmissible: in *Brown*,[17] the defendants were charged with shopbreaking and the prosecution sought to show that one of the accused had broken into another shop five days previously, during the lunch-hour and using a skeleton key. All of these were also characteristics of the immediate charge but the evidence was excluded. Simply being a shop-breaker is not evidence of committing the particular offence with which they were charged.

Lord Herschell then qualifies the general rule by accepting that evidence of the commission of crimes other than the one charged can be admissible if it is probative with regard to an issue in this particular case. In other words, it has a purpose other than persuading the jury that the defendant is a disreputable character and shows that the defendant did the act charged with the requisite mental element or that it rebutted a possible defence. The wording of section 101 reflects the same approach—the evidence is relevant to an important matter in issue. Unless the issue is clearly identified, the relevance of the evidence cannot be demonstrated. We will now look at four issues where bad character evidence may be relevant.

[17] (1963) 47 Cr.App.R. 204.

1. *Causing the actus reus.* A fundamental fact in issue is to demonstrate to the satisfaction of the jury that the accused was responsible for the act charged. Prior convictions can have such probative value where they show a particular *modus operandi* or abnormal propensity. In *Straffen*,[18] the accused had been committed to Broadmoor after being found unfit to plead to a charge of manually strangling two small girls. He escaped and was at large for four hours. During that time, another young girl, Linda Bowyer, was strangled. The defendant admitted being in the neighbourhood and that he had seen her. On trial for the third killing, evidence of the other murders was admitted.

Straffen [1952] 2 Q.B. 911 at 916–917, *per* Slade J.:

Abnormal propensity is a means of identification . . . It is an abnormal propensity to strangle young girls and to do so without any apparent motive, without any attempt at sexual interference, and to leave their bodies where they can be seen and where, presumably, their deaths would be detected. In the judgment of the court, that evidence was admissible because it tended to identify the person who murdered Linda Bowyer with the person who confessed in his statements to having murdered the other two girls a year before, in exactly similar circumstances

The circumstances of murders 1 and 2 were such that the murderer in those killings was also responsible for murder 3.

Another issue may be that of identity—that it was the accused who committed the crime, for example, by showing the accused to be a member of a particular class or group. In *Thompson*,[19] the defendant was accused of gross indecency with two boys. He did not deny that the offences had taken place but denied that he was the person involved. However the offender, whoever he was, had made a second rendezvous with the boys and they had taken the police to the place. On that occasion, the defendant met the boys and gave them money. He was arrested without any further offence taking place. The prosecution were allowed to use evidence that the accused had two powder puffs on him on arrest and that he had indecent photographs of boys in his flat. The House of Lords upheld the conviction on the basis that the accused's sexuality could be seen as confirming the boys' identification of him as the offender.

2. *Mental element.* Equally fundamental for the prosecution is to demonstrate to the satisfaction of the jury that the accused possessed the necessary mental element for the crime. Prior convictions can have considerable relevance where, for example, the defence is that of accident or lack of intent. Prior acquittals may have similar probative value.[20] But there need

---

[18] [1952] 2 Q.B. 911.
[19] [1918] A.C. 221.
[20] *R. v Z* [2000] 3 All E.R. 385 discussed later as illustrative of rebutting a defence.

not have been previous proceedings—evidence of previous similar acts will suffice. In *Smith*,[21] the defendant was tried, in 1915, for the murder in July 1912 of Beatrice Mundy by drowning her in the bath. He had been through a bigamous form of marriage with her in 1910 and she believed herself to be his wife. After her death, Smith 'married' Alice Burnham in November 1913. She died in the same manner in December that year. On December 17, 1914, he 'married' Margaret Lofty—she died, also in her bath, on December 18! Although only charged with one murder, the prosecution were allowed to advance evidence that the second and third 'wives' had died in identical circumstances: all the 'brides' were in the bath, had apparently slipped backwards, hit their heads on the taps and died through drowning. Smith had benefited from all three wills. Smith's unlucky marital history is clearly relevant to the offence charged because the defence claimed that Beatrice's death was an accident. The evidence of the fate of Alice and of Margaret made that claim look not just less likely but incredible.

Smith [1915] 11 Cr.App.R 229 at 233, *per* Scrutton J.:

And then comes in the purpose and the only purpose for which you are allowed to consider the evidence as to the other deaths. If you find an accident which benefits a person and you find that the person has been sufficiently fortunate to have that accident happen to him a number of times, benefiting him each time, you draw a very strong, frequently irresistible inference, that the occurrence of so many accidents benefiting him is such a coincidence that it cannot have happened unless it was design.[22]

3. *Guilty knowledge.* The Crown may well need to address subsidiary issues around the circumstances of an offence such as 'guilty knowledge'. Did the accused 'know' a particular fact or circumstance: were the goods stolen? was the substance an illegal drug? Previous convictions are obviously relevant to the issue of what the accused knew. This is reflected in section 27 of the Theft Act 1968. Where a person is charged with handling stolen goods, evidence of other dishonest handling is admissible.

27.—(3) Where a person is being proceeded against for handling stolen goods . . . the following evidence shall be admissible for the purpose of proving that he knew or believed the goods to be stolen goods:—
  a) evidence that he has had in his possession, or has undertaken or assisted in the retention, removal, disposal or realisation of, stolen goods from any theft taking place not earlier than twelve months before the offence charged; and

---

[21] (1915) 11 Cr.App.R. 229; Sir Travers Humphreys, A *Book of Trials* (Pan, 1955), pp.82–86.
[22] The words of the trial judge, Scrutton J. to the jury quoted at the appeal.

b) . . . evidence that he has within the five years preceding the date of the offence charged been convicted of theft or of handling stolen goods.[22a]

A previous conviction is relevant to whether the accused "knows or believes" the goods to be stolen. The jury are also entitled to know the details of the conviction—in *Hacker*,[23] the accused was charged with handling a stolen car, namely a Ford Escort RS Turbo. The prosecution sought to prove guilty knowledge under s.27(3) by adducing evidence of a previous handling conviction. The problem was that the prosecution wished not merely to show the fact of conviction but also that the previous offence was also for handling a Ford Escort RS Turbo. The House of Lords held that s.27 must be read alongside s.73(2) of the Police and Criminal Evidence Act 1984 which states that where a conviction is admissible in evidence, the certificate shall give "the substance and effect (omitting the formal parts) of the indictment and of the conviction". Lord Slynn held that the particulars of the motor car were "of the substance of the indictment". He quoted the judgment of the Court of Appeal.

Hacker [1995] 1 All E.R. 45 at 51h–j, *per* Lord Slynn:

If the only evidence that can go in is the bare evidence of handling stolen goods, then what will happen if the jury indicate that they wish to know what goods were stolen? They might, quite sensibly, take the point that if it was a handling of a stolen motor car it might be very different from handling of half a pound of sugar. However, that is a matter on the authorities as they presently stand either for the legislator or for a higher court than this.[24]

Where the previous misconduct is directly relevant to a specific element of the prosecution case, the evidence is admissible even though it reveals the accused's bad character. In *Ollis*,[25] the defendant was acquitted of obtaining by false pretences when a cheque he gave the victim was dishonoured, his defence being that he thought the cheque would be honoured. The accused was then tried on another indictment on similar counts of obtaining money on cheques which were dishonoured. The prosecution called the first victim to prove guilty knowledge and the admission of this evidence was upheld on appeal. A recent example is *Caceres-Moreira*,[26] where the accused was charged with importation of cocaine and a previous incident was admitted as going to the issue of the defendant's knowledge that the parcel contained drugs.

4. *Rebutting defences.* Further issues can arise around the establishment of a defence. In *Jones v DPP*,[27] the accused was charged with murder and rape

---

[22a] R. Munday, "Handling the Evidential Exception" [1988] Crim.L.R. 345.
[23] [1995] 1 All E.R. 45.
[24] *ibid.* at 51h–j.
[25] [1900] 2 Q.B. 758.
[26] [1995] Crim.L.R. 489.
[27] [1962] A.C. 635.

of a young girl guide. Previously he had been convicted of the rape of another young girl. In the course of that trial, he put forward a defence of alibi and narrated a long conversation with his wife in which he admitted that he had been with a prostitute. At his trial for murder, the Crown chose not to introduce the earlier rape conviction as part of the prosecution case. The accused testified and gave an account of his movements which again involved his being with a prostitute and having had a long conversation with his wife when he returned home. The two conversations corresponded almost word for word. The disclosure that he had been tried previously in circumstances that required him to produce an alibi would normally be excluded but the truth or falsity of the alibi in the murder trial is clearly an "important issue" and cross-examination would now be permitted under s.101(1)(d).[28] Another example would be where the evidence is used to rebut a defence of innocent association. In *Ball*,[29] the accused were brother and sister charged with incest. The House of Lords held that evidence that the sister had a child by the brother before the passage of the Incest Act was admissible.

In *R v Z*,[30] the defence to a charge of rape was that the accused believed the victim consented. He had been tried for rape on four previous occasions. In three of the trials the defendant was acquitted and in the fourth, he was convicted. In each of the four trials the defendant raised the same defence. The Crown wished to call the four previous complainants to rebut the defence of belief as to consent. Had the earlier cases all ended in convictions, they would have satisfied the criteria required for them to be admitted under common law as similar fact evidence. The House of Lords held that the acquittals were also admissible—this would remain the case under (1)(d).

These four categories are not exclusive and overlap but they would clearly come within s.101(1)(d) as 'important matters in issue' and the evidence adduced is generally highly probative in relation to the issue. To this extent, the new legislation reflects the common law, except with regard to the expanded propensity provisions under s.101(3).

b) Does the bad character evidence have sufficient probative force to make its admission justifiable?

Identifying the issue to which the bad character evidence is relevant is straightforward. It is much more difficult to address the question whether it possesses sufficient probative force to justify its admission. Lord Herschell in *Makin* did not address this problem—the evidence of the babies' bodies was

---

[28] The facts in this case are illustrative—the argument is no longer relevant as it centred around the relationship of s.1(e) and s.1(f) of the Criminal Evidence Act 1898.

[29] (1911) A.C. 47.

[30] above.

damning. But subsequently courts needed to consider how they framed this particular question. The common law first approached this through enumerating formal categories where relevance and probative value were assumed to exist. If the evidence did not fit the category, it could be neither relevant nor sufficiently probative. Those categories were:

- where the previous acts revealed a propensity to commit acts in a specific manner, a *modus operandi*, as in *Straffen*;
- where the evidence supported evidence of identity as in *Thompson*;
- where the evidence would rebut a defence of innocent association as in *Ball*; or
- where evidence of previous similar acts would rebut a defence of accident as in *Smith*.[31]

Such formal categories were restrictive as to the issues that could be addressed through such evidence and were a means of sidestepping the question of whether the evidence was sufficiently probative. For example, excluded from such categories would have been the question of "guilty knowledge". Did the accused "know" a particular fact or circumstance? Did the accused believe the goods were stolen? Prior misconduct was obviously relevant.

The House of Lords in *D.P.P. v Boardman*[32] threw off the shackles of the earlier category approach and their judgments seemed to herald a return to a simpler approach, based on a judicial discretion which required the judge to consider the probative value of the evidence but to balance that against the prejudicial effects. In the case, the accused was a headmaster of a boarding school for boys charged with sexual offences on separate occasions on two pupils. The similarities in the accounts by the two pupils were striking but the defence was that the boys were lying and that the incidents never occurred. Were the accounts given by each boy admissible on the charge relating to the other boy? The House of Lords upheld the trial judge's decision to admit the evidence. Evidence of similar facts may be admitted if the judge views its probative force in relation to an issue in the trial as outweighing its prejudicial effect. The strength of the probative force lies in its striking similarity and where that similarity is inexplicable on the basis of coincidence or concoction.

D.P.P. v Boardman [1974] 3 All E.R. 887 at 897c ff, *per* Lord Wilberforce:

If the evidence was to be received, then it must be on some general principle not confined to sexual offences. There are obvious difficulties in the way of formulating any such rule in such a manner as, on the one hand, to enable clear guidance to be

---

[31] (1915) 11 Cr.App.R. 229; Sir Travers, Humphreys, *A Book of Trials* (Pan, 1955) pp.82–86.
[32] [1974] 3 All E.R. 887.

given to juries, and, on the other hand, to avoid undue rigidity. The prevailing formulation is to be found in the judgment of the Court of Criminal Appeal in *R v Sims* where it was said,

> The evidence of each man was that the accused invited him into the house and there committed the acts charged. The acts they describe bear a striking similarity. That is a special feature sufficient in itself to justify the admissibility of the evidence . . . The probative force of all the acts together is much greater than one alone; for, whereas the jury might think that one man might be telling an untruth, three or four are hardly likely to tell the same untruth unless they were conspiring together. If there is nothing to suggest a conspiracy their evidence would seem to be overwhelming.

Sims has not received universal approbation or uniform commentary, but I think that it must be taken that this passage has received at least the general approval of this House in *R v Kilbourne*.[33] For my part, since the statement is evidently related to the facts of that particular case, I should deprecate its literal use in other cases. It is certainly neither clear nor comprehensive. A suitable adaptation, and, if necessary, expansion, should be allowed to judges in order to suit the facts involved. The basic principle must be that the admission of similar fact evidence (of the kind now in question) is exceptional and requires a strong degree of probative force. This probative force is derived, if at all, from the circumstance that the facts testified to by several witnesses bear to each other such a striking similarity that they must, when judged by experience and common sense, either all be true, or have arisen from a cause common to the witnesses or from pure coincidence. The jury may, therefore, properly be asked to judge whether the right conclusion is that all are true, so that each story is supported by the other(s).

The result of *Boardman* was that bad character evidence could be relevant to a broader range of issues than previously. But when was it sufficiently relevant? There has to be significant probative weight and a common theme from the judgments in *Boardman* was that the similar fact evidence should possess a "unique or striking similarity" to the offence charged. Bad character evidence should not be introduced just because it has some marginal relevance to an issue but because it has real probative value. But the outcome of the decision was that the old formal categories were replaced by a sound bite—trial courts looked for that probative value only through the test of "striking similarity". This criterion proved to be as much a distraction as the older category-based approach to relevance. Courts became fixated by the phrase, "striking similarity", seeing it as the only test for the necessary probative weight whereas similar fact evidence may be not at all striking and yet highly probative. This can be seen in cases such as *Roy*,[34] where a doctor was accused of indecent assault on a number of patients. There was nothing "striking" about the accounts nor were there any bizarre elements. But aggregated, the stories had considerable probative weight, rebutting any suggestion that these assaults might have been bona fide medical examinations. Pragmatically the test proved less than easy to apply.[35]

The modern common law, reflected in the 2003 Act, is to address the issue of "probative weight" directly. The House of Lords addressed these issues in

---

[33] [1973] A.C. 529.

[34] [1992] Crim.L.R. 185; *Laidman and Agnew* [1992] Crim.L.R. 428.

[35] *Novac* (1976) 65 Cr.App.R. 107; *Johannsen* (1977) 65 Cr.App.R. 101; *Tricoglus* (1976) 65 Cr.App.R. 16; *Barrington* [1981] 1 W.L.R. 419.

R v P,[36] where the defendant was accused of incest with and rape of his two daughters. There was evidence that he had engaged in incest over a long period, using force and threatening both girls unless they kept silent. He had paid for abortions for both. At trial, he applied for the counts relating to each daughter to be tried separately. The judge refused, holding that the testimony of one daughter was admissible evidence on charges involving the other. The Court of Appeal quashed the conviction on the grounds that there was no feature of striking similarity. The House of Lords restored the conviction and held that the test of admissibility was whether the evidence was relevant and had probative value which outweighed its prejudicial effect. It was not necessary to single out "striking similarity" as an essential element, though in some cases where identity was in issue a "signature" might be looked for.

R v P [1991] 3 All E.R. 337 at 346e–34df, *per* Lord Mackay:

From all that was said by the House in *Boardman* I would deduce the essential features of evidence which is to be admitted is that its probative force in support of the allegation that an accused person committed a crime is sufficiently great to make it just to admit the evidence, notwithstanding that it is prejudicial to the accused in tending to show that he was guilty of another crime. Such probative force may be derived from striking similarities in the evidence about the manner in which the crime was committed and the authorities provide illustrations of that, of which *Straffen* and *Smith* provide notable examples. But restricting the circumstances in which there is sufficient probative force to overcome prejudice of evidence relating to another crime to cases in which there is some striking similarity between them is to restrict the operation of the principle in a way which gives too much effect to a particular manner of stating it, and is not justified in principle. Hume in his work *Commentaries on the Law of Scotland Respecting Crimes*,[37] said long ago:

> . . . the aptitude and coherence of the several circumstances often as fully confirm the truth of the story, as if all the witnesses were deponing to the same facts.

Once the principle is recognised, that what has to be assessed is the probative force of the evidence in question, the infinite variety of circumstances in which the question arises demonstrates that there is no single manner in which this can be achieved. Whether the evidence has sufficient probative value to outweigh its prejudicial effect must in each case be a question of degree.

. . . In the present case the evidence of both girls describes a prolonged course of conduct in relation to each of them. In relation to each of them force was used. There was a general domination of the girls with threats against them unless they observed silence and a domination of the wife which inhibited her intervention. The accused seemed to have an obsession for keeping the girls to himself, for himself. The younger took on the role of the elder daughter when the elder daughter left home. There was also evidence that the accused was involved in regard to payment for the abortions in respect of both girls. In my view these circumstances taken together gave strong probative force to the evidence of each of the girls in relation to the incidents involving the other, and was certainly sufficient to make it just to admit that evidence, notwithstanding its prejudicial effect. This was clearly the view taken by the Court of Appeal and they would have given effect to it were it not for the line of authority in the Court of Appeal to which I have referred.

---

[36] [1991] 3 All E.R. 337.
[37] (4th edn. 1844), Vol. 2, p.384.

. . . When a question of the kind raised in this case arises I consider that the judge must first decide whether there is material upon which the jury would be entitled to conclude that the evidence of one victim, about what occurred to that victim, is so related to the evidence given by another victim, about what happened to that other victim, that the evidence of the first victim provides strong enough support for the evidence of the second victim to make it just to admit it, notwithstanding the prejudicial effect of admitting the evidence. This relationship, from which support is derived, may take many forms and while these forms may include 'striking similarity' in the manner in which the crime is committed, consisting of unusual characteristics in its execution the necessary relationship is by no means confined to such circumstances. Relationships in time and circumstances other than these may well be important relationships in this connection. Where the identity of the perpetrator is in issue, and evidence of this kind is important in that connection, obviously something in the nature of what has been called in the course of argument a signature or other special feature will be necessary. To transpose this requirement to other situations where the question is whether a crime has been committed, rather than who did commit it, is to impose an unnecessary and improper restriction upon the application of the principle.

For the reasons which I have given, I am of the opinion that there was sufficient connection between the circumstances spoken of by the two girls in the present case for their evidence mutually to support each other, that the appeal should be allowed, and the conviction restored.

Lord Mackay is clear that it is "not appropriate" to single out "striking similarity" as an essential element. Just as relevance to an issue can be found in a wide array of situations so can probative weight be discovered in different factual situations. This judgment reflects the principles propounded by Lord Wilberforce in *Boardman* while at the same time casting off the strait-jacket of "striking similarity". Relevance depends on the issue which needs to be decided. The degree of relevance of one victim's account to that of the other is provided by the circumstances and relationships. This may take many forms. But the probative force must be of such a degree that it is 'just to admit the evidence' despite the prejudicial effect. Under (1)(d), the absence of such probative force would mean that the evidence should be excluded as it adversely affect the fairness of the proceedings.

c) Would the admission of such evidence make the proceedings unfair whether as a result of prejudice or for any other reason?

Unfairness and prejudice inevitably surrounds the admission of bad character evidence. This can be seen in *Thompson* where the boys identify Thompson as the man who assaulted them. There were two items of evidence in dispute, the first being the possession of powder puffs, items which were used in the course of the initial offence. These are unusual items for males to carry and their existence tends strongly to support the boys' identification of Thompson: an analogy might be where a police man were looking for a suspected burglary, stopped someone and discovered that they were carrying lock-picking equipment. This corroboration of the boys' identification has considerable probative value but it has to be set alongside the prejudice which is engendered. Prejudice comes in because the powder puffs also suggest that Thompson is homosexual, a dominant and damning characteristic in the eyes of an all-male, middle class, Edwardian jury. Does the admission of the evidence tip the balance of the trial unfairly towards the prosecution? The House of Lords felt it did not but their own judgments are not free from prejudice, with Lord Sumner talking of ". . . the habitual gratification of a particular perverted lust . . ."

Until the 2003 reforms, the common law engaged in this balancing act between the probative weight of the evidence and its prejudicial effect. But, in both *Boardman* and *P*, their Lordships give considerable attention to the issue of relevance but the nature of the prejudice generated gets short shrift, apart from the need to balance the probative value and the prejudicial effect. The 2003 Act now talks, under s.101(3) in terms of the evidence having, ". . . such an adverse effect on the fairness of the proceedings that the court ought not to admit it." The issue of balance remains the same but while relevance can be logically demonstrated, there are no objective criteria for unfairness or the prejudicial effect. Without guiding criteria, the admission of similar fact evidence becomes a lottery and abrogates the principle is that it is unfair that an accused should be answerable at a trial for anything other than the offence charged. The admission of such evidence also infringes the concept of treating like cases alike because an accused with a criminal record will be treated differently from an accused without a record. As long as the trial judge addresses their mind to the issue of unfairness, the appellate court will rarely interfere. The need is for the courts take a less relaxed attitude to identifying and combating unfairness and prejudice.

Lloyd-Bostock conducted a study on the impact on juries of discovering that the accused had a criminal record.

Lloyd Bostock S., "The effects on juries of hearing about the defendant's previous criminal record: a simulation study" [2000] Crim.L.R. 734:

The results clearly confirm that evidence of previous convictions can have a prejudicial effect, especially where there is a recent previous conviction for a similar offence. Significant effects were found even though no information about the previous conviction other than the offence was provided, and where there was only one previous conviction. It may well be that greater effects would be found for a longer criminal record, especially one including several similar previous convictions. The findings concerning the effects of a previous conviction for indecent assault on a child in particular show the potential for such convictions to be highly prejudicial. It appears that, in addition to any effect of similarity to the current charge, the nature of the offence produces a more general negative evaluation, including a perceived propensity to commit a range of other offences.

The effects of dissimilar as compared with similar previous convictions are particularly interesting for what they tell us about the decision processes underlying the effects of information about previous convictions. Participants appear to be drawing on beliefs about typical offenders and patterns of offending which include not only beliefs about the likelihood that offenders will commit similar offences in future, but also beliefs that offenders who commit certain types of crime typically do not commit certain others. Defence counsel may be right occasionally to reveal old or dissimilar previous convictions to a jury, although we do not know how the effect may vary according to the particular combination of previous and current offences.

The study throws yet further doubt on the usefulness of the common law rule . . . , whereby a direct inference of guilt from propensity is forbidden, but an indirect inference mediated by an assessment of likely truthfulness is permitted. The results for similarity and dissimilarity of previous convictions strongly suggest that the effects of previous conviction evidence are mediated by stereotypes of typical criminality. On the other hand, there was nothing to suggest that the participants thought of honesty or truthfulness as a trait that could help them decide whether the defendant's evidence could be believed: indeed, perceived likelihood that the defendant would lie in court was unrelated to a previous conviction for dishonesty. It seems that the standard judicial instruction is not only hard to understand, but also asks jurors to confine their reasoning to a form that does not come at all naturally. It is doubtful that a jury could be relied on to avoid the compelling effects of similarity to the current charge.

Of course, the study has limitations, and could only address a limited set of questions. In particular, the defendant's prior record consisted of only one conviction: many questions remain about how the effects of similarity and recency could operate where there is a mixed record of multiple convictions. Some of the results may be specific to particular combinations of offences studied: the man who handles stolen goods may have a particular image that contrasts him with the man who commits a violent assault or indecently assaults a woman. The study does not even touch on the likely effects of a defendant's race on the way previous convictions are interpreted. These are all questions that require further research. In addition, as mentioned earlier, the simulation method has inherent limitations as well as advantages. Research of the kind reported here does not provide the basis for deciding whether any particular defendant has been wrongly convicted, nor what the effect of revealing convictions will be in a particular case. Nonetheless, the central findings of this and already existing research are consistent and make theoretical sense. Very thin information about a previous conviction (the name of the offence) is evidently sufficient to evoke a quite rich stereotype, so that a similar recent conviction (especially for sexual abuse of a child) is potentially damaging for no reason that the law permits.

Section 101(3) requires that the admission of the evidence should not have an adverse effect on the fairness of the proceedings—if the impact of previous conviction evidence is to create stereotypes of typical criminality in the minds of the jury, under what conditions can this be considered fair? The answer must be that it can only be fair where the probative weight of the evidence is very significant or, if the probative weight is less, the prosecution case as a whole is strong.

There is a subsidiary issue of fairness especially where witnesses tell similar stories about acts by the defendant on other occasions. The prosecution advance such testimony on the basis that these stories all derive from a common cause and that the witnesses are all telling the truth. But the witnesses may have agreed together to tell those stories or the incidents may all have happened purely coincidentally. Fairness requires that a court is able to rule out collusion or coincidence. This led to the exclusion of the evidence in *Ananthanarayanan*,[38] which held that bad character evidence should be excluded where there was the possibility of collusion. This carried a serious risk of rendering the ruling in *P* ineffective since in cases of sexual abuse there must always be a real risk of contamination between siblings living under the same roof or attending the same school or club. It was reconsidered by the House of Lords in *R v H*,[39] which involved a defendant accused of

---

[38] [1994] 2 All E.R. 847; applied in *Ryder* [1994] 2 All E.R. 859.
[39] [1994] 2 All E.R. 881.

sexual offences carried out against his adopted daughter and stepdaughter between 1987 and 1989. The complaints were made in 1992, after confiding in the appellant's wife. Russell L.J. reviewed the decision of Laws J. in *Ananthanarayanan*.

R v H [1994] 2 All E.R. 881 at 886b–887a, *per* Russell J.:

For our part we pause and venture to suggest that in the passage cited from *Ananthanarayanan* the court was confusing the admissibility of evidence with the quality of evidence, that is, the role that the evidence, once admitted, plays in the jury's deliberations. If there is a risk of contamination the evidence cannot be used as corroboration. it does not necessarily follow that the evidence becomes wholly inadmissible as is the case when the judge excludes evidence because of breaches of the code made under the provisions of the Police and Criminal Evidence Act 1984. In our judgment the two situations are quite different and the one is not an analogy of the other.

In our judgment and experience, in almost every case where two or more daughters are living under the same roof and complain of molestation by their father it is virtually inevitable that at some stage the daughters will have talked between themselves and usually with their mother. Whether this contaminates their evidence is very much a fact-finding process. Active collaboration will invariably be denied. there may be extreme cases where the judge concludes, having seen and heard the witnesses, that collaboration has taken place, and in such a case he may exercise his powers to stop the trial and direct an acquittal on *Galbraith* principles[40] or abort the trial and sever the indictment. But these exceptional cases apart, we take the view that a jury, having seen and heard the witnesses, should form its own assessment of the dangers and, provided it receives the warnings and directions to be found in the summing up of Tucker J. in the instant case, the jury can properly decide whether the evidence of one complainant corroborates the evidence of another. In our view, to deny the jury the responsibility of this fact-finding exercise is to usurp the function of the jury and we do not believe that the long line of authority to which reference was made in *Ananthanarayanan* was ever intended to assert the contrary . . . .

. . . The judge is not deciding a question of admissibility when he considers whether evidence can be used as corroboration. The evidence of the individual complainant remains admissible even if it is contaminated. Contamination goes not to admissibility but to the part to be played by the evidence after it is admitted. The proper role of the evidence, once admitted, can be left to the jury, who will receive appropriate directions from the judge. It must depend, in our judgment, upon the degree of contamination . . .

Bad character evidence will be admitted under (1)(d) and any evidence of collusion or other contamination goes to weight. The impact of this is somewhat mitigated by s.107 which provides for the case to be stopped if the evidence is found to be contaminated—under subs.(5) contamination includes cases where the evidence is false or misleading as a result of collusion.

---

[40] *Galbraith* [1981] 1 W.L.R. 1039.

(ii) *Propensity as a matter in issue under section 103 of the Criminal Justice Act 2003*
In addition to the general matters in issue between the prosecution and the
defence discussed above, there is now another category under section 103—
that a propensity to commit the offence or to be untruthful can be matters in
issue between the defendant and the prosecution.

Criminal Justice Act 2003, s.103:

s.103(1) For the purposes of section 101(1)(d) the matters include—

(a) the question whether the defendant has a propensity to commit offences of the
kind with which he is charged, except where his having such a propensity
makes it no more likely that he is guilty of the offence;

(b) the question whether the defendant has a propensity to be untruthful, except
where it is not suggested that the defendant's case is untruthful in any respect.

(2) Where subsection (1)(a) applies, a defendant's propensity to commit offences of
the kind with which he is charged may (without prejudice to any other way of doing
so) be established by evidence that he has been convicted of—

(a) an offence of the same description as the one with which he is charged, or

(b) an offence of the same category as the one with which he is charged.

(3) Subsection (2) does not apply in the case of a particular defendant if the court is
satisfied, by reason of the length of time since the conviction or for any other reason,
that it would be unjust for it to apply in his case.

(4) For the purposes of subsection (2)—

(a) two offences are of the same description as each other if the statement of the
offence in a written charge or indictment would, in each case, be in the same
terms;

(b) two offences are of the same category as each other if they belong to the same
category of offences prescribed for the purposes of this section by an order made
by the Secretary of State.

(5) A category prescribed by an order under subsection (4)(b) must consist of
offences of the same type

(6) Only prosecution evidence is admissible under section 101(1)(d).

The primary purpose is to encourage courts to make greater use of previous
convictions. In the White Paper, *Justice for All*,[41] it was stated that the aim was
not routine introduction of the defendant's previous convictions but, where
these are relevant to an issue in the case, then unless the court considers that
the information will have a disproportionate effect, the jury should be
allowed to know about it. It will be for the judge to decide whether the
probative value of introducing this information is outweighed by its prejudicial effect. This text sounded very close to the common law position but the
impact has been to encourage the prosecution to apply for leave to adduce
such evidence in many more cases.

Under the general part of s.101(1)(d), the prosecution can rely on bad
character revealed by evidence that the accused had committed such crimes
before, although never charged or prosecuted. The prosecution must show
that the evidence is relevant to a specific matter in issue. But under section

---

[41] *op.cit.* para.4.57.

103, propensity to commit offences can be such a matter in issue. When the prosecution seek to rely on simple propensity, only prior convictions can be used as evidence of that propensity. Those convictions can be of the same description or of the same category as the offence charged. Secondary legislation has been introduced to define "offences of the same category".[42]

Is simple propensity just the routine parading of the defendant's criminal record before the court? There are constraints—the propensity must be an "important matter in issue" and make it more likely that the defendant is guilty (s.103(1)(a)). This suggests that there must be other evidence linking the defendant to the offence. But, significantly, s.101(1)(d) does not make it necessary to show that the bad character evidence has substantial probative value—clearly the intent of the legislature is to allow such evidence to be adduced more easily.[43] Section 103(3) also suggests that ancient spent convictions should not be adduced where it would be unjust to do so. This seems to echo s.101(3) that a court should not admit evidence under s.101(1)(d) where this would have an adverse effect on the fairness of the proceedings.

The implications of the section were considered in *Hanson*.[44] Rose L.J. laid down the following guidelines.

Hanson (2005) 2 Cr.App.R. 21, *per* Rose L.J.:

7. Where propensity to commit the offence is relied upon there are thus essentially three questions to be considered;
    1. Does the history of conviction(s) establish a propensity to commit offences of the kind charged?
    2. Does that propensity make it more likely that the defendant committed the offence charged?
    3. Is it unjust to rely on the conviction(s) of the same description or category; and, in any event, will the proceedings be unfair if they are admitted?

8. In referring to offences of the same description or category, section 103(2) is not exhaustive of the types of conviction which might be relied upon to show evidence of propensity to commit offences of the kind charged. Nor, however, is it necessarily sufficient, in order to show such propensity, that a conviction should be of the same description or category as that charged.

9. There is no minimum number of events necessary to demonstrate such a propensity. The fewer the number of convictions the weaker is likely to be the evidence of propensity. A single previous conviction for an offence of the same description or category will often not show propensity. But it may do so where, for

---

[42] *e.g.* Criminal Justice Act 2003 (Categories of Offences) Order 2004, s.1. 2004 No. 3346, prescribes offences in the categories of theft and sexual offences against persons under the age of 16.

[43] Contrast this to s.101(1)(e) where it is necessary to show that the evidence has substantive probative value; also to s.100(1)(b) which permits questioning a witness about bad character but only where the evidence has substantive probative value to a matter in issue and that issue is of substantial importance.

[44] [2005] 2 Cr.App.R. 21—considered in *Edwards* [2005] EWCA Crim 3244, *Highton* [2005] 1 W.L.R. 3472, *Bovell* [2005] 2 Cr.App.R. 27.

example, it shows a tendency to unusual behaviour or where its circumstances demonstrate probative force in relation to the offence charged . . . Child sexual abuse or fire setting are comparatively clear examples of such unusual behaviour but we attempt no exhaustive list. Circumstances demonstrating probative force are not confined to those sharing striking similarity. So, a single conviction for shoplifting, will not, without more, be admissible to show propensity to steal. But if the modus operandi has significant features shared by the offence charged it may show propensity.

10. In a conviction case, the decisions required of the trial judge under section 101(3) and section 103(3), though not identical, are closely related. It so to be noted that wording of section 101(3)—"must not admit"—is stronger than the comparable provision in section 78 of the Police and Criminal Evidence Act 1984—"may refuse to allow". When considering what is just under section 103(3), and the fairness of the proceedings under section 101(3), the judge may, among other factors, take into consideration the degree of similarity between the previous conviction and the offence charged, albeit they are both within the same description or prescribed category. For example, theft and assault occasioning actual bodily harm may each embrace a wide spectrum of conduct. This does not however mean that what used to be referred as striking similarity must be shown before convictions become admissible. The judge may also take into consideration the respective gravity of the past and present offences. He or she must always consider the strength of the prosecution case. If there is no or very little other evidence against a defendant, it is unlikely to be just to admit his previous convictions, whatever they are.

11. In principle, if there is a substantial gap between the dates of commission of and conviction for the earlier offences, we would regard the date of commission as generally being of more significance than the date of conviction when assessing admissibility. Old convictions, with no special feature shared with the offence charged, are likely seriously to affect the fairness of proceedings adversely, unless, despite their age, it can properly be said that they show a continuing propensity.

12. It will often be necessary, before determining admissibility and even when considering offences of the same description or category, to examine each individual conviction rather than merely to look at the name of the offence or at the defendant's record as a whole. The sentence passed will not normally be probative or admissible at the behest of the Crown, though it may be at the behest of the defence. Where past events are disputed the judge must take care not to permit the trial unreasonably to be diverted into an investigation of matters not charged on the indictment . . .

15. If a judge has directed himself or herself correctly, this Court will be very slow to interfere with a ruling either as to admissibility or as to the consequences of non-compliance with the regulations for the giving of notice of intention to rely on bad character evidence. It will not interfere unless the judge's judgment as to the capacity of prior events to establish propensity is plainly wrong or discretion has been exercised unreasonably in the *Wednesbury* sense . . .

18. Our final general observation is that, in any case in which evidence of bad character is admitted to show propensity, whether to commit offences or to be untruthful the judge in summing-up should warn the jury clearly against placing undue reliance on previous convictions. Evidence of bad character cannot be used simply to bolster a weak case, or to prejudice the minds of a jury against a defendant. In particular, the jury should be directed that they should not conclude that the defendant is guilty or untruthful merely because he has these convictions; that, although the convictions may show a propensity, this does not mean that he has committed this offence or been untruthful in this case; that whether they in fact show a propensity is for them to decide; that they must take into account what the defendant has said about his previous convictions; and that, although they are entitled, if they find propensity as shown, to take this into account when determining guilt, propensity is only one relevant factor and they must assess its significance in the light of all the other evidence in the case . . . .

If this judgment sets the standard for subsequent cases, it is a conservative standard, which echoes the language of the old common law and often cites the authorities. It is emphasised that it is necessary for the prosecution to demonstrate why the convictions have probative value and that there is a strong and clear warning to the jury. However, in *Hanson*, one of the linked appeals is from Gilmore who has been convicted of theft from a garden shed. The trial judge admits three recent convictions for shoplifting and the Court of Appeal upheld the conviction saying, "The Recorder was fully entitled to conclude that the offences showed a recent persistent propensity to steal." It is unlikely that the court would have decided that way under the old law. But the court also mentioned that there was substantial other evidence against the defendant and in that context the conviction was not unsafe.

Section 103(1)(b) also allows bad character evidence to be adduced to demonstrate a propensity to be untruthful. Does this mean that prior convictions can always be adduced to show that the defendant is not a credible witness? This appears not to have been the intent of Parliament.

Criminal Justice Act 2003—Explanatory Notes, para.374:

Section 103(1)(b) makes it clear that evidence relating to whether the defendant has a propensity to be untruthful (in other words, is not to be regarded as a credible witness) can be admitted. This is intended to enable the admission of a limited range of evidence such as convictions for perjury or other offences involving deception (for example, obtaining property by deception), as opposed to the wider range of evidence that will be admissible where the defendant puts his character in issue by for example, attacking the character of another person. Evidence will not be admissible under this head where it is not suggested that the defendant's case is untruthful in any respect, for example, where the defendant and prosecution are agreed on the facts of the alleged offence and the question is whether all the elements of the offence have been made out.[45]

This was discussed by Rose L.J. in Hanson.[46]

Hanson [2005] 2 Cr.App.R. 21, *per* Rose L.J.:

13. As to propensity to untruthfulness, this, as it seems to us, is not the same as propensity to dishonesty. It is to be assumed, bearing in mind the frequency with which the words honest and dishonest appear in the criminal law, that Parliament deliberately chose the word "untruthful" to convey a different meaning, reflecting a defendant's account of his behaviour, or lies told when committing an offence. Previous convictions, whether for offences of dishonesty or otherwise, are therefore

---

[45] Criminal Justice Act 2003—Explanatory Notes, para.374; see R. Munday "Cut Throat Defences" *op.cit.* at 625ff.
[46] *op.cit.*

only likely to be capable of showing a propensity to be untruthful where, in the present case, truthfulness is an issue and, in the earlier case, either there was a plea of not guilty and the defendant gave an account, on arrest, in interview, or in evidence, which the jury must have disbelieved, or the way in which the offence was committed shows a propensity for untruthfulness, for example, by the making of false representations.

This is far from clear. Evidence introduced under s.103(1)(b) does not need to show that the propensity to be untruthful makes it more likely that the defendant is guilty, unlike a propensity to commit the offence in (1)(a). But the prosecution must demonstrate for the purposes of s.101(1)(d) that the propensity to be untruthful is relevant to an "important matter in issue". It can only be relevant if it has probative value with regard to that matter. Creditworthiness is undoubtedly a matter in issue and often, for the jury, an important issue. There is scope for a broad interpretation of this provision but it is necessary to echo s.101(3) that a court should not admit evidence under s.101(1)(d) where this would have an adverse effect on the fairness of the proceedings. A court will always approach, if not cross, the borderline of fairness where it admits previous convictions for the purpose not of demonstrating that the accused is guilty of the offence but only that he is untruthful

Gateway 5: substantial probative value in relation to an important matter in issue between the defendant and a co-defendant

Criminal trials will frequently involve more than one defendant. In such cases, it is often the case that one accused will seek to deny or underplay their involvement in the crime and place responsibility at the door of their co-accused. Adducing the co-accused's prior criminal convictions may well be an element of such a "cut throat" defence. The common law was always permissive about this:

R. Pattenden, "Character of Victims and Third Parties in Criminal Proceedings" [1986] Crim.L.R. 367 at 370:

Cut-throat defences which involve laying sole responsibility for a crime at the door of an accomplice are a commonplace in joint trials. The Privy Council in *Lowery v R*[47] treated evidence from a psychologist of the sadistic and aggressive disposition of a co-accused as admissible at the instance of an accused, even though such evidence could not have been introduced by the Crown. Victorian courts have said that a judge can exclude character evidence tendered by an accused which has little probative force and is prejudicial to a co-accused.[48] Such an exercise of discretion will, it has been said, be rare. Indeed the existence of such a discretion runs directly counter to statements in numerous English cases[49] which have stressed the right of an accused to establish his innocence by relevant evidence regardless of the impact on other defendants.

---

[47] [1974] A.C. 85.
[48] *Darrington* (1980) 1 A.Crim.R 124, 162 (Vic.F.C.).
[49] *Allen* [1965] 2 Q.B. 295; *Neale* (1977) 65 Cr.App.R. 304; *Bracewell* (1978) 68 Cr.App.R. 44; *Rowson* [1985] 2 All E.R. 539.

At common law, an accused could only lead evidence in chief on a co-accused's general bad character where the line of questioning was relevant to an issue. An accused could cross examine a co-accused but such questions went to credibility and opened up the accused to questions about their own criminal record.[50] This area is now regulated by s.101(1)(e), of the CJA 2003.

> 101(1) In criminal proceedings evidence of the defendant's bad character is admissible if, but only if—
> (e) it has substantial probative value in relation to an important matter in issue between the defendant and a co-defendant.

Section 104 supplements this provision,[51]

> 104(1) Evidence which is relevant to the question whether the defendant has a propensity to be untruthful is admissible on that basis under section 101(1)(e) only if the nature or conduct of his defence is such as to undermine the co-defendant's defence.
> (2) Only evidence—
> (a) which is to be (or has been) adduced by the co-defendant, or
> (b) which a witness is to be invited to give (or has given) in cross-examination by the co-defendant,
> is admissible under section 101(1)(e).

An accused might wish to adduce evidence (although not necessarily bad character evidence) against a co-defendant in three situations where the evidence could be said to have substantial probative value in relation to an important matter in issue between the co-accused:

1. where the co-accused has made an incriminating statement to the police that the prosecution cannot or do not rely upon;
2. where the co-accused has displayed a particular propensity that makes it more likely that he or she committed the offence charged; or
3. where the co-accused has a disposition to untruthfulness.

The defence may introduce such evidence either by evidence-in-chief or through cross-examination.

(i) *Incriminating Statements*
An incriminating statement by a co-accused is not bad character evidence but it is sensible to consider in this context. But if the admission is inadmissible for the prosecution, is it also inadmissible for the defence? A statement may be ruled inadmissible, for example, where the prosecution are unable to satisfy the court that a confession by a co-accused conforms to the requirements of s.76 of PACE.

But even where the co-accused's confession is inadmissible as far as the prosecution is concerned, can another defendant cross-examine the co-

---

[50] This was under the [now repealed] s.1(f) Criminal Evidence Act 1898.
[51] R. Munday, "Cut Throat Defences and the Propensity to be Untruthful" [2005] Crim. L.R. 624.

accused on that statement? The general rule is that questions cannot be put to a witness which would elicit inadmissible evidence. In *Treacy*,[52] the prosecution sought to introduce a confession allegedly made by the accused as part of their evidence in chief. The confession was deemed inadmissible. When the accused testified, the prosecution sought to cross-examine him on the contents of the confession as a statement inconsistent with present testimony under s.4 of the Criminal Procedure Act 1865.

Treacy [1944] 2 All E.R. 229 at 236, *per* Humphreys J.:

In our view, a statement made by a prisoner is either admissible or it is not admissible. If it is admissible, the proper course for the prosecution is to prove it, give it in evidence, let the statement if it is in writing be made an exhibit, so that everybody knows what it is and everybody can inquire into it and do what they think right about it. If it is not admissible, nothing more ought to be heard of it, and it is quite a mistake to think that a document can be made admissible in evidence which is otherwise inadmissible simply because it is put to a person in cross-examination.

This is not a rule that binds a co-accused. In *Myers*,[53] the accused and her boyfriend were convicted of the killing of a mini-cab driver. She made statements to the police after her arrest in which she had at first admitted stabbing the victim but then asserted it was her co-accused. The House of Lords held that the fact that the prosecution was not able to introduce the evidence because of breaches of Code C of PACE did not preclude the co-accused from raising the confession when cross-examining her on her assertion that it was her boyfriend who had murdered the cab driver. Her confession was clearly relevant to his defence that it was not he who had killed. Obviously either one or the other had killed the driver and justice required that he should be allowed to bring out the earlier confession. Judicial discretion should not be allowed to fetter a defendant in seeking to extract, by cross-examination, evidence of assistance to their own defence. But under *Myers*, such examination goes to the defendant-witness's credibility and the jury had to be warned from placing weight on it in considering the prosecution case.

This has been overtaken by s.128(1) of the Criminal Justice Act 2003[54]

(1) In any proceedings a confession made by an accused person may be given in evidence for another person charged in the same proceedings (a co-accused) in so far as it is relevant to any matter in issue in the proceedings and is not excluded by the court in pursuance of this section.

However subs.(2) imposes a condition that it must be shown that the confession was not obtained by oppression or in circumstances that may

---

[52] [1944] 2 All E.R. 229.
[53] (1998) A.C. 124.
[54] This is now Police and Criminal Evidence Act 1984, s.76A.

make it unreliable. A defendant can only rely on a confession by a co-accused where the defendant can prove on the balance of probabilities that it was not obtained through these means.[55]

Is this a wholly satisfactory solution? The Crown benefits as they are now able to use as evidence a statement which failings in the investigation process had rendered inadmissible. But this is the necessary cost of ensuring fairness to the defendant, who is entitled to emphasise the co-accused's inconsistency even at the cost of considerable prejudice to the co-accused's case.

(ii) *Particular Propensity*

Another tactic of the 'cut-throat' defence is to suggest that one's co-accused possesses a particular trait of character that makes it more likely that he or she committed the offence. In *Miller*,[56] one defendant alleged that the offences had been committed by a co-accused and to that end sought to ask a prosecution witness whether or not it was true that the offences stopped when that accused had been in prison and re-started after his release. Although the prosecution would be barred from such a line of questioning, Devlin J. held that questioning by a co-accused was only limited by considerations of relevance.

In *Lowery*,[57] the two accused, L and K, attacked and sadistically killed a 15-year-old girl. K's defence was that the killing was the work of L, that he (K) had been under the influence of drugs and that, although he had seen L strangling the girl, he had been helpless to stop him. He wished to introduce testimony from a psychologist who had examined both defendants. The psychologist's expert opinion was that L possessed a sadistic and aggressive disposition. L's defence was that K had committed the killing. He (L) had driven to the spot as he believed that K wished to have sex with the victim. Only later did he follow them and found K assaulting the girl. L also called evidence as to his own reputation with a view to showing that his disposition made him unlikely to have committed such a crime. In this context the Privy Council agreed that the psychologist's testimony was admissible.

Lowery [1973] 3 All E.R. 662 at 668–671, *per* Lord Morris:

. . . It was said that the evidence was not relevant to any issue and was of no probative value in considering the guilt of the accused; that evidence of the psychological condition of an accused person as tending to prove his guilt ought never to be introduced either by the prosecution or by the defence of a co-accused person; that the evidence whether adduced by prosecution or by defence ought to have been excluded as a matter of law because its introduction would merely show disposition; that the

---

[55] Where the Crown wish to rely on a confession, they must prove *beyond reasonable doubt* that it was not obtained by oppression or in circumstances that might render it unreliable.
[56] (1952) 36 Cr.App.R. 169.
[57] [1973] 3 All E.R. 662.

evidence did not fall within any of the exceptions denoted in *Makin v Attorney-General for New South Wales* . . .

. . . The questions arise whether the evidence was (a) relevant and (b) admissible: not all evidence that is relevant is admissible because its prejudicial effect heavily overbalances its probative value and as a matter of fairness or of public policy a court will not allow the prosecution to call such evidence . . . . [Lord Morris summarises the psychologist's conclusions on the psychological make-up of L and K] .

In all these circumstances it was necessary on behalf of K to call all relevant and admissible evidence which would exonerate K and throw responsibility entirely on L. If in imaginary circumstances similar to those of this case it was apparent that one of the accused was a man of great physical strength whereas the other was a weakling it could hardly be doubted that in forming an opinion as to the probabilities it would be relevant to have the disparity between the two in mind. Physical characteristics may often be of considerable relevance: see *Toohey v Metropolitan Police Commissioner.*[58] The scientific evidence . . . was not related to crime or criminal tendencies: it was scientific evidence as to the respective personalities of the two accused . . . .

These authorities have now been supported by the House of Lords in *Randall.*[59] The two accused put forward differing accounts of the fatal assault. They both adduced evidence of the other's prior convictions—the appellant had been convicted of relatively minor offences whereas his co-accused, who was acquitted, had a bad record and at the time of the assault, was on the run from the police in connection with an armed robbery. The trial judge directed the jury that the record was only relevant to credibility and irrelevant to the likelihood of him having been the person who attacked the victim. It was argued on appeal that the evidence was relevant to the issue as to which of the co-accused was more likely to have attacked the victim. The Court of Appeal agreed and ordered a re-trial. The House of Lords rejected an appeal from the Crown.

Randall (2004) 1 All E.R. 467, *per* Lord Steyn:

18. . . . the discretionary power to exclude relevant evidence which is tendered by the prosecution, if its prejudicial effect outweighs its probative value, does not apply to the position as between co-accused. In a joint criminal trial a judge has no discretionary power at the request of one accused to exclude relevant evidence tending to support the defence of another accused . . .

19. It is therefore common ground that in the present case the only issue is whether the evidence of [the co-accused's] propensity to use and threaten violence, which was placed before the jury, was relevant to the issue whether it was Randall who committed the attack on the deceased.

20. The theme that ran through the Crown's case and oral argument was that evidence of [the co-accused's] propensity to violence "proves nothing". Taken in isolation that is right. But relevance in cases such as the one under consideration is a more subtle concept: Article 1 of Stephen's Digest of the Law of Evidence[60] explains relevance as follows:

[58] [1965] 1 All E.R. 506.
[59] [2004] 1 All E.R. 467.
[60] 12th ed., (1936).

"any two facts to which it is applied are so related to each other that according to the common course of events one either taken by itself or in connection with other facts proves or renders probable the past, present or future existence or non-existence of the other."

In *R v Kilbourne*,[61] Lord Simon of Glaisdale put the position more simply:

"Evidence is relevant if it is logically probative or disprobative of some matter which requires proof . . . Relevant . . . evidence is evidence which makes the matter which requires proof more or less probable."

A judge ruling on a point of admissibility involving an issue of relevance has to decide whether the evidence is capable of increasing or diminishing the probability of the existence of a fact in issue. The question of relevance is typically a matter of degree to be determined, for the most part, by common sense and experience . . .

22. It is difficult to support a proposition that evidence of propensity can never be relevant to the issues. Postulate a joint trial involving two accused arising from an assault committed in a pub. Assume it to be clear that one of the two men committed the assault. The one man has a long list of previous convictions involving assaults in pubs. It shows him to be prone to fighting when he had consumed alcohol. The other man has an unblemished record. Relying on experience and common sense one may rhetorically ask why the propensity to violence of one man should not be deployed by the other man as part of his defence that he did not commit the assault. Surely such evidence is capable, depending on the jury's assessment of all the evidence, of making it more probable that the man with the violent disposition when he had consumed alcohol committed the assault. To rule that the jury may use the convictions in regard to his credibility but that convictions revealing his propensity to violence must otherwise be ignored is to ask the jury to put to one side their common sense and experience. It would be curious if the law compelled such an unrealistic result.

These authorities, decided prior to the implementation of the Criminal Justice Act 2003, suggest that a defendant can introduce evidence of a co-accused's disposition when that evidence is clearly relevant to the defendant's case. This is what is envisaged in s.101(1)(e)—the defendant can lead evidence or cross-examine on the issue without waiting for the co-accused to put character into issue. In *Murell*,[62] co-defendants on a drug importation charge were permitted to cross-examine the police officer on the appellant's previous conviction for the importation of cocaine and on the evidence of the firearm and ammunition found at the appellant's house. The only limit is that of relevance and the trial court should not use its discretion to balance the probative weight against the prejudicial effect.

(iii) *Disposition to Untruthfulness*
Under s.104,

'Evidence which is relevant to the question whether the defendant has a propensity to be untruthful is admissible on that basis under section 101(1)(e) only if the nature or conduct of his defence is such as to undermine the co-defendant's defence.'

There is a similar provision under s.103(1)(b). The Explanatory Notes suggest that this restricts the admissibility of bad character evidence that shows a propensity to be untruthful to circumstances in which a defendant

---

[61] [1973] A.C. 729 at 756 d–e.
[62] [2005] EWCA 382.

has undermined a co-accused's defence. But the co-accused must demonstrate for the purposes of s.101(1)(e) that the propensity to be untruthful is relevant to an "important matter in issue" and has substantial probative value with regard to that matter. Credit-worthiness is undoubtedly a matter in issue and where there is a cut-throat defence, it is clearly an important issue and evidence of a propensity to untruthfulness on its face might be highly probative. Once this threshold is crossed, there is no scope for judicial discretion, as Lord Steyn pointed out in *Randall*:

Randall (2004) 1 All E.R. 467, *per* Lord Steyn:

18 . . . the discretionary power to exclude relevant evidence which is tendered by the prosecution, if its prejudicial effect outweighs its probative value, does not apply to the position as between co-accused. In a joint criminal trial a judge has no discretionary power at the request of one accused to exclude relevant evidence tending to support the defence of another accused . . .

When does a defendant undermine a co-accused's defence? The leading case is *Murdoch v Taylor*,[63] where Murdoch, who had a criminal record, was tried for handling stolen goods jointly with Lynch, who had no previous convictions. Lynch testified, implicating Murdoch. Murdoch testified under cross-examination that the box containing the stolen property had been in Lynch's possession. Counsel for Lynch then cross-examined Murdoch on his previous convictions. This was upheld on appeal where Lord Donovan stressed that it does not matter whether the evidence is given in chief or under cross-examination. The issue is the effect on the jury. It does not require hostile intent on part of the co-accused.

Testifying and perhaps denying something said by the co-accused is not sufficient. The subsection is not triggered unless there is either support of the prosecution case or the undermining of the co-accused's defence: in *Bruce*,[64] the two accused were charged with robbery. The first admitted the plan to rob but denied taking part in its execution. The second denied any plan to rob at all. The first defendant cross-examined the second on his previous convictions. The second defendant's conviction was quashed. Although he had contradicted his co-defendant's evidence, he had not given evidence against him. In *Varley*,[65] the court took a different view—the appellant was jointly charged with Dibble with offences of robbery and possession of a firearm. The appellant initially admitted his part in the robbery but at trial denied that he had participated at all. Dibble's defence was that he had been forced to take part by Varley and he testified to this.

Varley [1982] 2 All E.R. 519 at 521 –522, *per* Kilner Brown J.:

. . . What was the nature of the guidance in *R v Stannard*[66]? It was this, approved by Lord Donovan in *Murdoch's* case '. . . 'evidence against' means evidence which

---

[63] [1965] A.C. 574.
[64] [1975] 3 All E.R. 277.
[65] [1982] 2 All E.R. 519.
[66] [1964] 1 All E.R. 34.

supports the prosecution in a material respect or which undermines the defence of the co-accused.' There are three reported cases in the Court of Appeal, Criminal Division, in which this interpretation has been considered and to which we were referred. They are *R v Davis*,[67] *R v Bruce*[68] and *R v Hatton*.[69] Now putting all the reported cases together, are there established principles which might serve as guidance . . . .?

(1) If it is established that a person jointly charged has given evidence against the co-defendant that defendant has a right to cross-examine the other as to previous convictions and the trial judge has no discretion to refuse an application.

(2) Such evidence may be given either in chief or during cross-examination.

(3) It has to be objectively decided whether the evidence either supports the prosecution in a material respect or which undermines the defence of the co-accused. A hostile intent is irrelevant.

(4) If consideration has to be given to the undermining of the other's defence care must be taken to see that the evidence clearly undermines the defence. Inconvenience to or inconsistency with the other's defence is not of itself sufficient.

(5) Mere denial of participation in a joint venture is not of itself sufficient to rank as evidence against a co-defendant. For the proviso to apply, such denial must lead to the conclusion that if the witness did not participate then it must have been the other who did.

(6) Where the one defendant asserts or in due course would assert one view of the joint venture which is directly contradicted by the other such contradiction may be evidence against the co-defendant.

In *Crawford*,[70] Lord Bingham C.J. stated that the evidence of one defendant is evidence against a co-defendant if it supports the prosecution case against the co-defendant in a material respect or undermines the defence of the co-defendant. Lord Bingham saw this as a matter of common sense and that a clear and simple rule was propounded in *Murdoch*. The essential question put is this: Does the evidence given by the defendant in the witness box, if accepted, damage in a significant way the defence of the co-defendant? It is suggested that these principles, although decided under the provisions of the 1898 Criminal Evidence Act, will apply to the new Act.

Gateway 6: evidence to correct a false impression given by the defendant

At common law, there were just two opportunities for the prosecution to adduce evidence of the accused's bad character, firstly under the similar fact rules and secondly in order to rebut evidence advanced of the accused's good character. In *Rowton*, after the accused had put his own character into issue, the prosecution were able to call witnesses as to his reputation, one of which, when asked as to the defendant's general reputation for decency and morality of conduct, answered,

I know nothing of the neighbourhood's opinion, because I was only a boy at school when I knew him; but my opinion, and the opinion of my brothers, who were also

[67] [1975] 1 All E.R. 233.
[68] [1975] 3 All E.R. 277.
[69] (1976) 64 Cr.App.R. 88.
[70] (1998) 1 Cr.App.R. 338.

pupils of his, is that his character is that of a man capable of the grossest indecency and the most flagrant immorality.

Was this admissible? Such evidence is restricted to reputation and not to specific discreditable acts. Cockburn C.J. is quite clear that this has to be the reputation of the neighbourhood and not an individual's opinion,

Rowton (1865) 34 L.J.MC 57 at 62, *per* Cockburn C.:

. . . within what limits must the evidence be confined which is adduced in rebutting evidence to meet the evidence which the prisoner has brought forward? I think that that evidence must be of the same character and kept within the same limits: that while the prisoner can give evidence of general good character, so the evidence called to rebut it must be evidence of the same general description, showing that the evidence which has been given to establish a good reputation is not true, because the man's general reputation is bad.

Although testimony in chief was restricted to general good reputation, it was permissible to cross-examine about specific acts (including previous convictions). A further oddity of the common law was that, once the accused's character was in issue,[71] every aspect of that character is included. In *Winfield*,[72] the charge was indecent assault and the accused led evidence of his sexual propriety. But the prosecution were permitted to counter this by cross-examining on the defendant's previous convictions for dishonesty. But questions on simple allegations were not permitted—in *Stirland*,[73] the defendant was accused of forgery and testified as to his own good character and good employment record. He was cross-examined as to suspicions about forgery that had been voiced by that previous employer, questioning that was deemed inadmissible by the House of Lords.

Stirland [1944] A.C. 315 at 327 per Viscount Simon:

It is no disproof of good character that a man has been suspected or accused of a previous crime. Such questions as 'Were you suspected?' or 'Were you accused?' are inadmissible because they are irrelevant to the issue of character and can only be asked if the accused has sworn expressly to the contrary.

A simple assertion of innocence did not put your character into issue at common law, as that required adducing positive evidence of good character.

---

[71] Character cannot be put into issue "accidentally" by witnesses blurting out their good opinion of the accused—*Gadbury* (1838) 8 C.&P. 676; *Redd* [1923] 1 K.B. 104.
[72] [1939] 4 All E.R. 164.
[73] [1944] A.C. 315.

Where the accused was questioned about prior bad conduct on disproof of assertions of good character, this went solely to the credibility.

How have these provisions survived the 2003 reforms?

101(1) In criminal proceedings evidence of the defendant's bad character is admissible if, but only if—

    (f) it is evidence to correct a false impression given by the defendant

This is supplemented by s.105,

(1) For the purposes of section 101(1)(f)—

(a) the defendant gives a false impression if he is responsible for the making of an express or implied assertion which is apt to give the court or jury a false or misleading impression about the defendant;

(b) evidence to correct such an impression is evidence which has probative value in correcting it.

(2) A defendant is treated as being responsible for the making of an assertion if—

(a) the assertion is made by the defendant in the proceedings (whether or not in evidence given by him),

(b) the assertion was made by the defendant—

    (i) on being questioned under caution, before charge, about the offence with which he is charged, or

    (ii) on being charged with the offence or officially informed that he might be prosecuted for it,

and evidence of the assertion is given in the proceedings,

(c) the assertion is made by a witness called by the defendant,

(d) the assertion is made by any witness in cross-examination in response to a question asked by the defendant that is intended to elicit it, or is likely to do so, or

(e) the assertion was made by any person out of court, and the defendant adduces evidence of it in the proceedings.

(3) A defendant who would otherwise be treated as responsible for the making of an assertion shall not be so treated if, or to the extent that, he withdraws it or disassociates himself from it.

(4) Where it appears to the court that a defendant, by means of his conduct (other than the giving of evidence) in the proceedings, is seeking to give the court or jury an impression about himself that is false or misleading, the court may if it appears just to do so treat the defendant as being responsible for the making of an assertion which is apt to give that impression.

(5) In subsection (4) "conduct" includes appearance or dress.

(6) Evidence is admissible under section 101(1)(f) only if it goes no further than is necessary to correct the false impression.

What is a false impression? There is probably little change to the common law. It is clearly intended that this should cover express, albeit bland, assertions of good character—in *Coulman*[74] the defendant testified that he was married with children and in regular employment and was then questioned on his previous convictions. Non-verbal behaviour can also amount to an assertion—dressing as a priest, for example. But in *Robinson*,[75] the accused testified holding a small bible. Henry L.J. did not feel that this warranted a loss of protection from being questioned about his previous convictions,

[74] 20 Cr.App.Rep. 106.

[75] [2001] Crim.L.R. 478.

Robinson [2001] EWCA Crim 214, *per* Henry L.J.:

17. The judge clearly did not believe that the defendant was a believer, or that he was genuinely looking to God for guidance as he had said. But, to take it in stages, a defendant does not put his character in just by taking the oath, even though that might arguably cloak him with an apparent respectability which his record belied. Nor does that situation change if, as often happens, in the course of his evidence, he reminds the court and the jury that he has sworn on the Bible to tell the truth. Nor does taking up of the Bible for whatever reason amount to an assertion that the defendant is putting himself forward as being of good character. While the court will want to discourage disruptive or exhibitionist behaviour, the penalty for potentially offensive behaviour should not be loss of the protection.

It is possible that the wording of s.105(4) would cause the court to rethink this. However one definite change is that the defendant is held responsible for a misleading assertion at any stage of the proceedings, not simply in the trial. This can be seen in subs.(2)—assertions made under caution or at charge may be rebutted by the prosecution at trial. However subs.(3) does allow for the defence to disassociate themselves from such assertions, whether made by the accused or another.

There is a very significant change from the common law. This is the abrogation of the rule in cases such as *Winfield* and *Stirland* that once the accused raises the issue of good character, all aspects of that character can be examined. Under subs.(6), only that evidence can be adduced that is necessary to correct the false impression. Thus in *Winfield*, evidence to correct his claim of sexual propriety might be introduced but not evidence of dishonesty. This is supported by subs.(1)(b) that says that evidence to correct the impression must have "probative value in correcting it."

Gateway 7: the defendant has made an attack on another person's character

The final gateway is under s.101(1)(g),

(1) In criminal proceedings evidence of the defendant's bad character is admissible if, but only if—
(g) the defendant has made an attack on another person's character.

This is supplemented by s.106,

106 "Attack on another person's character"
(1) For the purposes of section 101(1)(g) a defendant makes an attack on another person's character if—
(a) he adduces evidence attacking the other person's character,
(b) he . . . asks questions in cross-examination that are intended to elicit such evidence, or are likely to do so, or
(c) evidence is given of an imputation about the other person made by the defendant—
(i) on being questioned under caution, before charge, about the offence with which he is charged, or
(ii) on being charged with the offence or officially informed that he might be prosecuted for it.

(2) In subsection (1) "evidence attacking the other person's character" means evidence to the effect that the other person—

(a) has committed an offence (whether a different offence from the one with which the defendant is charged or the same one), or

(b) has behaved, or is disposed to behave, in a reprehensible way;

and "imputation about the other person" means an assertion to that effect.

At common law there was no power to retaliate if the accused attacked the reputation of Crown witnesses. The prosecution were not permitted to lead evidence in chief and, at that time, the defendant was not a competent witness. After 1898, the defendant could choose to testify and the Criminal Evidence Act regulated the questions that could be asked in cross-examination. Thus there was a significant gap—if the accused attacked Crown witnesses and chose not to testify, the prosecution could not introduce evidence in chief.[76]

Under the 2003 provisions, the position has been clarified and broadened. First the prosecution can retaliate whenever the defence involves an attack on another person's character and not merely on the character of prosecution witnesses. Secondly, the prosecution are entitled adduce evidence in chief or to cross-examine the accused in these circumstances.

When does the defendant attack another's character? Usually this person will be the prosecution witness but not necessarily—for example, assertions made about police officers who are not testifying or about the victim in a homicide case. In *Bovell*,[77] the defendant asserted that, on the day before burglary charged, his co-accused had committed another burglary. However there must be some association between the 'other person' and the case —this can be policed by the use of the exclusionary discretion of the judge under s.101(3).

Nor are 'attacks' limited to questions or assertions made in court. Section 106(1)(c) covers the situation where such imputations are made at caution or charge and evidence to that effect is given in court. A key issue is the nature of an attack—the imputation must be that the person has committed a crime or otherwise behaved in a reprehensible fashion. The jurisprudence on this issue interpreting the provisions of the1898 Act will still be relevant.[78]

The problems lie in deciding what is an attack on another's character? Mere denials of guilt are not enough although these may imply that the prosecution witnesses are lying. Sometimes it is clear—the nature or character of the defence will involve making allegations about the conduct or character of the prosecutor or the prosecution witnesses or those associated with the investigation and prosecution. Clear examples might include the defence putting prior convictions, sexual peccadilloes or other character defects to the witness. In sexual abuse and rape cases, it is often alleged that the complainant is fabricating the account.[79] In a murder case, the allegation that the victim struck the first blow went beyond mere denial.[80] A frequent scenario will be

---

[76] *Butterwasser* [1948] 1 K.B. 4.

[77] [2005] 2 Cr.App.R. 2 at para.30.

[78] *Hanson, op.cit. per* Rose L.J .at para.14.

[79] *Pickstone* (reported in *Hanson op.cit.*) per Rose L.J. at paras 48–51.

[80] *Blackford* (unreported November 7, 2005, CA).

an attack on the police in charge of the investigation or interrogation, suggesting violent or manipulative conduct or simply that the police witnesses are lying. It is this latter category where the boundary between the proper and improper presentation of a defence has proved difficult.[81]

In *Jones*,[82] Lord Hewart said that it was one thing for the defendant merely to deny making a confession but quite another matter to allege that it was a deliberate and elaborate police concoction. In *Britzman*,[83] the Court of Appeal were considering a burglary conviction. The accused had been arrested on May 29, denying guilt and refusing to make statement. He remained in custody during May 30, still asserting innocence. However on June 1, (pre-Police and Criminal Evidence Act 1984) the police officers said that there had been a long interview, recorded in their notebooks which contained comments from the accused from which the jury might infer guilt. One officer testified that he had heard the accused shouting to one another whilst in their cells, again making statements that were highly suggestive of guilt ('Look, we've only got to sweat this out. They can't keep us here forever. That old bird won't pick us out. Just keep your mouth shut. We'll be OK'). The accused denied that the June 1 interview or the shouting between the cells had taken place. They were cross-examined on their previous convictions and the Court of Appeal upheld this decision.

Britzman [1983] 1 All E.R. 369 at 372a–374c, *per* Lawton L.J.:

In our judgment the nature and conduct of the defence did involve imputations on the characters of the three officers . . . This opinion is in accord with two decisions of this court, namely *R v Tanner*[84] and *R v McGee and Cassidy*[85]. In *Tanner*, . . . Browne L.J. said:

> In some cases the distinction may be a very narrow one, but that it exists in principle is clear. the decision whether a case is on one side of the line or the other must depend on the facts of each particular case. In our judgment, the nature and conduct of the defence in the present case did involve imputations on the character of the police officers. This was not a case of a denial of a single answer, nor was there any suggestion or possibility of mistake or misunderstanding. The appellant was denying not only his admission, nut in the case of each interview a series of subsequent important answers attributed to him by the police . . . .

We hope that it will be helpful for both judges and counsel if we set out some guidelines for the exercise of discretion in favour of defendants. First, it should be used if there is nothing more than a denial, however emphatic or offensively made, of an act or even a short series of acts amounting to one incident or in what was said to have been a short interview . . . The position would be different however if there were a denial of evidence of a long period of detailed observation extending over hours and just as in this case and in *Tanner*, where there were denials of long conversations.

Second, cross-examination should only be allowed if the judge is sure that there is no possibility of mistake, misunderstanding or confusion and that the jury will

[81] *Tanner* (1977) 66 Cr.App.R. 56; *Nelson* (1978) 68 Cr.App.R. 12.
[82] (1923) 17 Cr.App.R. 117.
[83] [1983] 1 All E.R. 369.
[84] (1977) 66 Cr.App.R. 56.
[85] (1979) 70 Cr.App.R. 247.

inevitably have to decide whether the prosecution witnesses have fabricated evidence. Defendants sometimes make wild allegations when giving evidence. Allowance should be made for the strain of being in the witness box and the exaggerated use of language which sometimes results from such strain or lack of education or mental instability. Particularly care should be used when a defendant is led into making allegations during cross-examination. The defendant who, during cross-examination, is driven to explaining away the evidence by saying it has been made up or planted on him usually convicts himself without having his previous convictions brought out . . .

The specific facts of *Britzman* are less likely to occur because of the PACE safeguards. But the general approach is useful: where there is a denial of a short interview, the presumption will be in favour of the defendant but if the accused denies a long conversation, makes wild allegations or uses unrestrained language and the judge was sure that there is no possibility of mistake or confusion, cross-examination under s.101(1)(g) is permissible. Prosecutors should not rely on s.101(1)(g) where the other evidence was overwhelming.

The fact that any attack on another's character or imputation is a necessary part of the defence will not protect the defendant from the revelation of prior misconduct, despite the dicta of Viscount Simon in *Stirland*,

An accused is not to be regarded as depriving himself of the protection of the section because the proper conduct of his defence necessitates the making of injurious reflections on the prosecutor or his witnesses.[86]

But in *Selvey v DPP*,[87] the accused was charged with buggery. There was medical evidence which supported the victim's complaint. Selvey's defence was that the complainant had already committed buggery with another man on the same day and that this accounted for the doctor's evidence. The complainant had offered himself to Selvey who had refused and the complainant had planted indecent photographs on him. The trial judge allowed the prosecution to question the accused on previous convictions for soliciting for a lewd and immoral purpose. The House of Lords held that the accused could be cross-examined on his previous convictions under the provisions of the 1898 Criminal Evidence Act which were applicable even where the casting of such imputations is necessary to establish the defence. Lord Pearce considered two views of these provisions.

Selvey v D.P.P. [1968] 2 All E.R. 497 at 521a–522h, *per* Lord Pearce:

Two main views have been put forward. One view adopts the literal meaning of the words. The prosecutor is cross-examined to show that he has fabricated the charge for improper reasons. That involves imputations on his character. Therefore, it lets in the previous convictions of the accused. The practical justification for this view is the 'tit

---

[86] *Stirland* above at 327.
[87] [1968] 2 All E.R. 497.

for tat' argument. If the accused is seeking to cast discredit on the prosecution, then the prosecution should be allowed to do likewise. If the accused is seeking to persuade the jury that the prosecutor behaved like a knave, then the jury should know the character of the man who makes these accusations, so that it may judge fairly between them instead of being in the dark as to one of them.

The other view would limit the literal meaning of the words. For it cannot, it is said, have been intended by Parliament to make a man liable to have his previous convictions revealed whenever the essence of his defence necessitates imputations on the character of the prosecutor. This revelation is always damaging and often fatal to a defence. The high-water mark of this argument is the ordinary case of rape. In this the vital issue (as a rule) is whether the woman consented. Consent (as a rule) involves imputations on her character. Therefore, in the ordinary case of rape, the accused cannot defend himself without letting in his previous convictions. The same argument extends in varying lesser degrees to many cases . . .

So large a gloss upon the words is not easy to justify, even if one were convinced that it necessarily produced a fair and proper result which Parliament intended. But there are two sides to the matter. So liberal a shield for an accused is in many cases unfair to a prosecution.

Lord Pearce suggested that it cannot be a fair trial if the jury is kept in ignorance of the defendant's character even where the line of questioning is a necessary part of the defence. This is well–illustrated in *Bishop*[88] where the accused had been the tenant of a room in a house belonging to Mr Price. He only stayed there for 12 days before leaving and Mr Price complained that his bedroom door had been forced and after-shave and money taken. Bishop was charged with burglary. Not only had he left precipitously, the after-shave was found in his room. Worse, Bishop's fingerprints were found in Price's bedroom. Bishop's explanation was that, during his brief stay, he had had a homosexual affair with Price. Price vehemently denied this. The prosecution sought and were allowed to cross-examine about his previous convictions. The conviction was upheld since the allegation of homosexual relations between Mr Price and the appellant was an imputation on Mr Price's character and it was not material that the imputation had been made, not to blacken the name of the witness but to explain the presence of the accused's fingerprints at the scene of the crime. Had the occupant been a woman and the allegation one of a heterosexual affair, would the result have been different?

One major exception to this rule lies in the area of rape to which the logic of *Selvey* and *Bishop* would seem to apply. Where the defence is that the victim consented and the victim is questioned as to past sexual conduct, this should theoretically mean that the accused opens himself to cross-examination on his own record. Yet the House of Lords in *Selvey* held that the accused in rape cases can allege consent without risking such cross-examination, either because rape is *sui generis*[89] or on the ground that the issue is one raised by the prosecution.

Selvey v D.P.P. [1968] 2 All E.R. 497 at 522c–f, *per* Lord Pearce:

The second part of the argument in favour of a construction more liberal to the accused is concerned with the words 'the conduct or nature of the defence'. One

---

[88] [1975] Q.B. 274.
[89] *Cook* [1959] 2 Q.B .340 at 347 *per* Devlin J.

should, it can be argued, read conduct or nature as something superimposed on the essence of the defence itself . . . . This argument has obvious force, particularly in a case of rape, where the allegation of consent is in truth no more than a mere traverse of the essential ingredient which the Crown have to prove, namely, want of consent. But the argument does not, and I think cannot, fairly stop short of contending that all matters which are relevant to the crime, that is, of which rebutting evidence could be proved, are excluded from the words 'conduct or nature of the defence.'

This exception was established beyond doubt[90] under the 1898 Act but there was little justification for treating rape as a special case. Nowadays, questioning a complainant about their sexual history in any sexual offence case is governed by s.41 of the Youth Justice and Criminal Evidence Act 1999.[91] Such questioning is constrained and leave must be given by the court. The factual circumstances will vary—questioning may simply be about the victim's past relationship with the accused and be relatively uncontroversial. In other cases, the victim may be questioned about sexual behaviour that could easily be seen as "reprehensible" within s.106(2)(b). It is open to a court to treat such questioning as an attack on the victim's character. It may be necessary for a fair trial to allow the defendant to pursue this line of questioning under s.41 but, to use Lord Pearce's argument, the trial cannot be fair if the jury is kept in ignorance of the defendant's own character.

To what extent are the prosecution entitled to adduce evidence of the details of such a prior conviction? When bad character evidence was introduced to undermine the accused's credibility, such details were not introduced. In *Khan*,[92] the charge was assault on a police officer. He alleged that the police had lied and the prosecution cross-examined on a previous conviction for assault, eliciting details with obvious similarities to the present case. The conviction was quashed because these details should not be referred to as a matter of course but only where they are relevant to issues of credit. Details such as *modus operandi* should only be admitted where they would be admissible as similar fact evidence.[93] Where there was a risk that the jury might believe that the cross-examination went to the probability that the accused committed the offence, the judge might disallow the examination. In *Watts*,[94] the charge was indecent assault and the accused alleged that the admission had been fabricated. The prosecution were allowed to cross-examine on previous convictions for indecent assault on young girls. The conviction was quashed since the risk of prejudice was too great.

These authorities were reviewed in *McLeod* in which the defendant was charged with armed robbery of a Securicor van and was cross-examined about details of his convictions for previous robberies. Stuart-Smith L.J. laid down these principles:

---

[90] *Turner* [1944] K.B. 463.
[91] see Ch.10.
[92] [1991] Crim.L.R. 51.
[93] *Duncalf* [1979] 2 All E.R. 1116.
[94] [1983] 3 All E.R. 101; reviewed in *Powell* [1986] 1 All E.R. 193 and *Owen*, 83 Cr.App.R. 100.

McLeod [1994] 3 All E.R. 254 at 267, *per* Stuart-Smith L.J.:

As to the nature of the questions that may properly be put, we consider that the following propositions should be borne in mind.

1. The primary purpose of the cross-examination as to previous convictions and bad character of the accused is to show that he is not worthy of belief. It is not, and should not be, to show that he has a disposition to commit the type of offence with which he is charged . . . . But the mere fact that the offences are of a similar type to that charged or because of their number and type have the incidental effect of suggesting a tendency or disposition to commit the offence charged will not make them improper: Powell, Owen and Selvey.

2. It is undesirable that there should be prolonged or extensive cross-examination in relation to previous offences. This is because it will divert the jury from the principal issues in the case, which is the guilt of the accused on the instance offence, and not the details of earlier ones. Unless the earlier ones are admissible as similar fact evidence, prosecuting counsel should not seek to probe or emphasise similarities between the underlying facts of previous offences and the instant offence.

3. Similarities of defences which have been rejected by juries on previous occasions, for example false alibis or the defence that the incriminating substance has been planted and whether or not the accused pleaded guilty or was disbelieved having given evidence on oath, may be a legitimate matter for questions. These matters do not show a disposition to commit the offence in question; but they are clearly relevant to credibility.

4. Underlying facts that show particularly bad character over and above the bare facts of the case are not necessarily to be excluded. But the judge should be careful to balance the gravity of the attack on the prosecution with the degree of prejudice to the defendant which will result from the disclosure of the facts in question. Details of sexual offences against children are likely to be regarded by the jury as particularly prejudicial to an accused and may well be the reason why in Watts the Court thought the questions impermissible.

5. If objection is to be taken to a particular line of cross-examination about the underlying facts of a previous offence, it should be taken as soon as it is apparent to defence counsel that it is in danger of going too far. There is little point in taking it subsequently, since it will not normally be a ground for discharging the jury.

6. While it is the duty of the Judge to keep cross examination within proper bounds, if no objection is taken at the time it will be difficult thereafter to contend that the Judge has wrongly exercised his discretion. In any event, this Court will not interfere with the exercise of the Judge's discretion save on well-established principles.

7. In every case where the accused has been cross-examined as to his character and previous offences, the judge must in the summing-up tell the jury that the purpose of the questioning goes only to credit and they should not consider that it shows a propensity to commit the offence they are considering.

To what extent are these principles still valid post–2003?

1. The law in *McLeod*, under the 1898 Act, only dealt with the cross-examination of the accused's character in these circumstances[95] and such questioning went only to the credibility of the accused. But the number and type of past offences which might be put to the accused might well lead the jury to conclude that the accused had tendency to commit such

---

[95] Under the 2003 Act, an attack on another's character can lead to the Crown adducing character evidence as part of their case as well as through cross examining the accused.

offences and was more likely to have committed the offence charged. As *McLeod* suggests, this did not make such questions improper, even under the pre–2003 law. Now, the Court of Appeal has held that evidence admitted under section 101(1)(g) can go to the likelihood of the accused having committed the offence. The use depended upon the matters to which it was relevant rather than upon the gateway through which it was admitted. In *Highton*,[96] the accused alleged that the prosecution witnesses had fabricated their robbery story. The accused's prior convictions for robbery and theft were introduced under pathway (g). These were clearly relevant to propensity and the judge invited the jury to consider this. The convictions were upheld.

2. As *McLeod* suggests, extensive cross-examination on the facts of earlier convictions is undesirable, unless those facts were admissible under the similar fact rules. This remains the case—the primary purpose of adducing evidence under section 101(1)(g) is to demonstrate to the jury what kind of person the accused is. The details are not relevant and, unless the earlier convictions are admissible under (1)(d), counsel should not seek to "emphasise similarities" between the previous and the current offences.

3. The court in *McLeod* stressed that "similarities of defences which have been rejected by juries on previous occasions, for example false alibis or the defence that the incriminating substance has been planted . . . may be a legitimate matter for questions" An example, discussed earlier, was the exploration of the false alibi in *Jones v DPP*. Under the 2003 Act, such questions of detail are clearly admissible but would need to be brought under subs.(1)(d) as probative of an important matter in issue between the defendant and prosecution.

4. Where evidence of bad character is introduced, the issue of excluding highly prejudicial evidence is raised. Under the 1898 Act, that discretion was exercised in cases such as *Watts*.[97] Now evidence may not be admissible under gateway (d) but be adduced under gateway (g) to show the jury the "true" nature of the defendant. The details may well be prejudicial and the court retains the discretion to restrict questions on those details or even to exclude evidence of past convictions under s.101(3)—if such questions would have an adverse effect on the fairness of the proceedings. The Court of Appeal is unlikely to interfere with this discretion unless there is an error in principle.

---

[96] above.
[97] above.

16

HEARSAY—ITS SCOPE AND RATIONALE

I. Hearsay and the exclusionary rule

A major concept in the study of evidence is hearsay and its associated rule which prevents adducing hearsay statements as evidence. In simple terms, this is a rule aimed at preventing a court from using second-hand evidence—a witness should not be permitted to narrate matters which the court should hear from other people. It is those "other people" who are the "proper" witnesses and who should be called to the court to testify and be cross-examined. Lord Normand's comments in *Teper* remain appropriate.

Teper [1952] 2 All E.R. 447 at 449:

The rule against admission of hearsay evidence is fundamental. It is not the best evidence and it is not delivered on oath. The truthfulness and accuracy of the person whose words are spoken to by another witness cannot be tested by cross-examination and the light which his demeanour would throw on his testimony is lost.[1]

The classic statement of the rule was formulated by Cross.

an assertion other than one made by a person while giving oral evidence in the proceedings is inadmissible as evidence of any fact stated.[2]

This is echoed by s.1 of the Civil Evidence Act 1995.

1. (1) In civil proceedings evidence shall not be excluded on the ground that it is hearsay.
(2) In this Act—
    a) 'hearsay' means a statement otherwise than by a person while giving oral evidence in the proceedings which is tendered as evidence of the matters stated

This defines the concept of hearsay—generally it is hearsay when a witness narrates to a court a statement made by another person in order that the court

---

[1] [1952] 2 All E.R. 447 at 449.
[2] Now to be found in C. Tapper, *Cross and Tapper on Evidence* 10th ed., (Butterworths 2004), p.578. This formula was approved by the House of Lords in *Sharp* [1988] 1 All E.R. 65 at 68b–c.

may rely on the truth of the contents of that statement. In *Sparks*,[3] the white defendant was accused of indecently assaulting a young girl who was too young to testify. She had told her mother that her attacker was "a coloured boy". The mother cannot go into the witness box in place of her daughter and testify as to what her daughter had said.

The common law rule was that hearsay was inadmissible, although there were a large number of exceptions which permitted the reception of hearsay evidence in particular circumstances. However the rule itself was abolished in civil proceedings by the 1995 Act so that evidence cannot now be excluded on the ground that it is hearsay. However there are certain procedural considerations, even in civil proceedings, when hearsay evidence is adduced.[4]

The rule still makes a considerable impact on criminal proceedings where the admissibility of hearsay evidence is now governed by the Criminal Justice Act 2003. This statute broadened the scope of the exceptions to hearsay but maintained the exclusionary rule. There is a conventional structure to any exclusionary rule: the definition of the concept, the statement of the rule and the listing of any exceptions.

i) The 2003 act does not define the concept of hearsay although it echoes Cross's definition of hearsay when, in s.114, it talks of ". . . a statement not made in oral evidence in the proceedings is admissible as evidence of the matter stated if, but only if, . . ." The definition is still to be found in common law. This can be contrasted with the Act's treatment of bad character evidence where 'bad character' is specifically defined in s.98.

ii) The Act clearly reaffirms the rule against the admissibility of hearsay evidence in criminal proceedings. Section 114 states that hearsay statements are only admissible under certain conditions.

iii) The only exceptions to the inadmissibility of hearsay are through the gateways established by the 2003 Act. These exceptions are significantly broader than previously.

The Civil Evidence Acts of 1968 and 1995 have significantly reduced the impact of the hearsay rule in civil proceedings but, despite considerable criticism from judges, academics[5] and other sources,[6] in criminal proceedings[7] the appellate courts have maintained the operative boundaries of the concept

---

[3] [1964] A.C. 964.

[4] see Ch.19.

[5] S. Guest, "The Scope of the Hearsay Rule" (1985) 101 L.Q.R. 355; A. Ashworth and R. Pattenden, "Reliability. Hearsay Evidence and the English Criminal Trial" (1986) 102 L.Q.R. 292; D. Birch, "Hearsay-logic and Hearsay-fiddles: Blastland revisited" in P. Smith (Ed.), *Essays in Honour of J.C.Smith* (Sweet and Maxwell, London, 1987) 24; R. Pattenden, "Conceptual Versus Pragmatic Approaches to Hearsay" [1993] 56 M.L.R. 138.

[6] Law Commission: *Evidence in Criminal Proceedings: Hearsay and Related Topics* (Report No. 245, Cm. 3670 1997).

[7] The rule does not apply in certain non-criminal proceedings such as breach of bail hearings (*R. v Havering Magistrates ex p. D.P.P.* [2001] 3 All E.R. 99) or extradition (*Khalid Al Fawwaz v Governor HM Prison Brixton* (2001) 4 All E.R. 14; but compare *R. v West Sussex County Council Ex p. K* (2001) E.L.R. 311 where a school headmaster and exclusion panel should not rely on the opinions of an absent witness.

of hearsay.[8] Even the 2003 legislation, with its new exceptions, accepts the traditional exclusionary rule. We must first consider why such evidence should be excluded.

II. The rationale for excluding hearsay

At common law, we were dealing with a *rule* of exclusion—if the evidence was characterised as hearsay, previously the judge had no discretion to admit it simply on the grounds that, as evidence, it is relevant, reliable and probative. Even where the evidence can be shown to be necessary for the defence,[9] it is still excluded. It is a rule that can produce results that are wholly contrary to common sense. As we have seen in *Sparks*, the mother was not permitted to say what the child had said, despite its importance for the defendant. On appeal to the Privy Council, Lord Morris said,

Sparks [1964] A.C. 964 at 978, *per* Lord Morris:

The mother would clearly be giving hearsay evidence if she were permitted to state what her girl had said to her. It becomes necessary, therefore, to examine the contentions which have been advanced in support of the admissibility of the evidence. It was said that 'it was manifestly unjust for the jury to be left throughout the whole trial with the impression that the child could not give any clue to the identity of her assailant'. The cause of justice is, however, best served by adherence to rules which have long been recognised and settled. If the girl made a remark to her mother (not in the presence of the appellant) to the effect that it was the appellant who had assaulted her and if the girl was not to be a witness at the trial, evidence as to what she said would be the merest hearsay. In such circumstances it would be the defence who would wish to challenge a contention, if advanced, that it would be 'manifestly unjust' for the jury not to know that the girl had given a clue to the identity of her assailant.

The conviction in *Sparks* was overturned on other grounds but what can justify a rule of evidence that would have produced such palpable injustice? Its very status as a rule provides part of the answer, as explained by Lord Morris in *Sparks*,

Sparks [1964] A.C. 964 at 978, *per* Lord Morris:

If it is said that hearsay evidence should freely be admitted and that there should be concentration in any particular case upon deciding as to its value or weight it is sufficient to say that our law has not been evolved upon such lines but is firmly based

---

[8] *Kearley* [1992] 2 All E.R. 345.
[9] *Harry* (1988) 86 Cr.App.R. 105.

upon the view that it is wiser and better that hearsay should be excluded save in certain well-defined and rather exceptional circumstances.

However, recently, the position has changed—the rule itself has been abolished in civil proceedings and in criminal cases, discretion has been introduced by s.114(1)(d) of the Criminal Justice Act 2003 whereby hearsay evidence can be admissible if, "the court is satisfied that it is in the interests of justice for it to be admissible". But what is the rationale for maintaining even a limited exclusionary rule? This centres around two ideas: that hearsay is unreliable or its admission is unfair.

1. Unreliability

A traditional plank for the rule's proponents is the unreliability of hearsay. This can take a number of forms

a) The probative value of a hearsay statement is evidentially inferior as it is not the "best evidence".[10] But often hearsay is not only the best evidence, it is the only evidence and yet is excluded because of the hearsay rule: a witness to a traffic accident repeats a car number to a constable, who writes it down but does not get the witness to inspect it. That constable cannot testify to that number in the absence of the witness.[11]

b) Admitting hearsay evidence encourages parties to manufacture evidence.[12]

c) The trier of fact is denied the opportunity to judge the demeanour (and thus the reliability) of the witness especially under cross-examination.

A. Zuckerman, The Principles of Criminal Evidence (OUP, Oxford, 1989) 180–181:

A hearsay statement may be flawed in four principal respects. First, the person whose statement is reported, the declarant, may have wrongly perceived the event in question. This can occur because of some defect in the declarant's sense of perception or for some other reason. Secondly, the declarant's memory may have been faulty or inaccurate when he made the statement. Thirdly, he may have lied or deliberately distorted the event. Fourthly the declarant's statement may have been misunderstood by the witness now reporting it. Since meaning is so dependent on context, nuance and shared cultural background, the scope for misunderstanding is substantial.

---

[10] This is related to but is not the same as the "best evidence" rule in relation to documents which states that there is ". . . but one general rule of evidence, the best that the nature of the case will admit" *Omychund v Barker*, (1744) 1 Atk. 2; Law Commission, *op.cit.* para.3.1.

[11] *Jones v Metcalfe* [1967] 3 All E.R. 205 but see s.116 Criminal Justice Act 2003.

[12] Criminal Law Revision Committee, *Evidence* (11th Report) (1972) Cmnd. 4991 para.229; Law Commission, *op.cit.*, para.3.5.

All of these risks, save the fourth, are also present when the person who observed the facts testifies in court. There is, however, one fundamental difference: when a witness is in court, the opponent is able to cross-examine him in order to investigate his powers of perception, test his memory, and appraise his veracity, thus enabling the trier of fact to determine the probative value of the testimony according to the witness's performance in the witness-box. It is the unavailability of a hearsay declarant for cross-examination which constitutes the central reason for the exclusion of hearsay statements. It is said that in the absence of cross-examination of the declarant jurors are likely to overestimate the probative significance of his hearsay statement. This argument cannot be dismissed altogether. On introspection most of us will admit to undue susceptibility to hearsay especially when the hearsay appears to confirm a belief we already hold or a prejudice to which we are predisposed.

But psychological research suggests that our ability to judge character or to spot the liar is less than we would suppose.[13] The Law Commission concluded:

Law Commission: Evidence in Criminal Proceedings: Hearsay and Related Topics (Report No.245, Cm.3670 1997), para.3.11:

Psychological evidence suggests that it is the doubters who are right. Studies indicate that if observers are familiar with a speaker they might be better able to tell when he or she is lying; but this point is of little value in the case of factfinders, because they will not know the witness. After reviewing the available psychological literature, J R Spencer and Rhona Flin[14] conclude: The most that can be said for the value of the demeanour of a witness as an indicator of the truth is that it is one factor, which must be weighed up together with everything else. It would be quite wrong to promote it to the level where we use it to accept or reject the oral testimony of a witness in the face of other weighty matters all of which point the other way . . . . Our provisional conclusion was that, insofar as a witness's demeanour does help the fact-finder to reach an accurate verdict, it is not so significant a fact in itself as to justify the exclusion of hearsay evidence.

Attitudes vary widely as to the value of cross-examination as a mechanism for discovering truth. For Wigmore, it was the ". . . greatest legal engine ever invented for the discovery of truth." whereas others see it as a means for making an honest witness seem at best confused and at worst a liar.[15]

d) Juries are unqualified in assessing the probative value of hearsay evidence as opposed to direct evidence. But already in criminal cases, juries follow complex directions on issues of doctrine, for

---

[13] O.G. Wellborn, "Demeanor" (1991) Cornell L.R. 1075; J.A. Blumenthal, "A Wipe of the Hands, A Lick of the Lips: The Validity of Deameanor Evidence in Assessing Witness Credibility" (1993) 72 Neb L.R. 1157; Law Commission, above para.6.22 ff.

[14] J. Spencer and R. Flin, *The Evidence of Children: The Law and the Psychology* (2nd ed., 1993). 280–281.

[15] see Ch.13.

example, the relationship between foresight and intention[16] or the concept of dishonesty.[17] Assessing the relative weight of items of evidence is no more complex.

Little weight is now attached to these arguments—in civil proceedings and, increasingly, in criminal cases, hearsay is now admissible. The triers of fact are directed to its weight relative to non-hearsay testimony. Jurors would not be required to undertake any different intellectual exercise, if oral hearsay were to become generally admissible evidence.

Was reliability ever a satisfactory rationale for the hearsay rule? If there were no reason to doubt the reliability of the evidence and therefore no reason to exclude, at common law the evidence would still be excluded. If "reliability" were the true rationale for the exclusion of hearsay, there would not have been a rule of exclusion, but judicial discretion. It is not the unreliability but the fact that the declarant is not available for cross examination which is the fundamental reason for the exclusion of hearsay statements.

2. Unfairness

Hearsay evidence is unsatisfactory not because of its unreliability but because the declarant is not subject to cross-examination and this means that the trial itself can be stigmatised as unfair and an abuse of due process. One of the hallmarks of totalitarian societies is the anonymous accusation based on rumour.[18] While medieval England might have been content to hang a man who "everyone knows" was a "notorious thief", modern legal values require specificity both as to what acts of theft have been committed and as to those who witnessed it. The latter must be identified and not anonymous and must be confronted publicly with their accusation. It is this notion of fairness which lies behind the hearsay rule and is expressed in several human rights documents, such as the Sixth Amendment to the US Consitution:

> In all criminal prosecutions, the accused shall enjoy the right to a speedy and public trial, by an impartial jury of the state and district wherein the crime shall have been committed, which district shall have been previously ascertained by law, and to be informed of the nature and cause of the accusation; to be confronted with the witnesses against him; to have compulsory process for obtaining witnesses in his favour, and to have the assistance of counsel for his defence.

The right to confront one's accusers is linked to the rule excluding hearsay. Testifying in public is regarded as a key component of justice and evidence which is given anonymously, secretly or at one remove is inevitably tainted with suspicion.[19] In England, there is a lack of an entrenched constitutional right to publicly confront one's accusers. This right is camouflaged in other

---

[16] *Woollin* (1999) 1 A.C. 82.

[17] *Ghosh* [1982] 2 All E.R. 689.

[18] However this practice is still to be found in Western European jurisdictions where police officers are able to testify that X, who is not named, saw the accused commit the offence. Such testimony is admitted—J. Andersen, "The Anonymity of Witnesses—a Danish Development" [1985] Crim.L.R. 363.

[19] see Ch.10.

concepts, especially that of hearsay. Hearsay is thus an aspect of procedural due process and this is reflected in Art.6 of the European Convention on Human Rights and Fundamental Freedoms.

6(3). Everyone charged with a criminal offence has the following minimum rights
. . .
(d) to examine or have examined witnesses against him and to obtain the attendance and examination of witnesses on his behalf under the same conditions as witnesses against him;

It is this paragraph which impinges on the operation of the hearsay rule and which underlines an accused's right to be protected from anonymous accusation.

C. Osborne, "Hearsay and the Court of Human Rights" [1993] Crim.L.R. 255 at 261–263:

Prima facie Article 6(3)(d) imposes a strict rule against the use of hearsay evidence by the prosecution. This is because if one has the right to 'examine or have examined' witnesses against one, then that on the face of it requires the witness to be present in court for cross-examination. Three matters need to be considered to arrive at a full understanding of the Article, namely:
1. What is meant by 'witness against' and does that phrase apply to absent persons whose statements are tendered in evidence?
2. What is meant by 'examine or have examined' and would it, for example, suffice that the 'examination should be by the judge rather than one's own counsel?
3. Is it sufficient if that examination of witnesses takes place at some preliminary stage rather than in the 'public hearing' which is guaranteed by Article 6(1)?

The strongest view is that Article 6(3)(d) prohibits the prosecution from adducing hearsay evidence. Unsurprisingly, the Commission and Court have lately tended to shrink from so strict an interpretation, although the reasoning in the relevant cases must be scrutinised carefully. The two leading cases are those of *Unterpertinger* and *Kostovski*. In *Unterpertinger v. Austria*[20] the issue concerned the admissibility of hearsay statements admitted at Unterpertinger's trial. He was charged with causing actual bodily harm to his stepdaughter and wife. His defence was in part self-defence, and in part exaggeration of the incident. A report was prepared by the Austrian police including statements by the accused, two victims and a doctor. Under Article 152 of the Austrian Code of Criminal Procedure members of an accused's family are not compellable. The accused's wife attended a preliminary investigation and gave evidence of the assaults to a judge. However at the trial proper both victims refused to testify. The Court thereupon caused the record of Frau Unterpertinger's interview with the investigating judge to be read out. Further, under the Austrian Code of Criminal Procedure the investigation file was read out in court and this included, amongst other things, police reports of the incident, the accused's criminal record and various witness statements. Thereafter the accused was convicted and his subsequent appeal dismissed. Unterpertinger then applied to the European Commission on the grounds that the acceptance of written evidence of interviews with the judge and the police infringed Article (1) and Article (6)(3)(d), contending that his inability to have the

[20] Case 1985/87/134.

alleged victims cross-examined was in breach of the Convention. The Court concluded that whilst there were other documents which the Court had before it to assist it to arrive at the truth, including the accused's criminal record and the accused's own testimony, the conviction must have been substantially based on the statements made by the victims to the police and therefore that there was a breach of the Article. Somewhat mysteriously the Court added that 'in itself the reading out of statements in this way cannot be regarded as being inconsistent with Article 6 . . . but the use made of the statements as evidence must nevertheless comply with the rights of the defence.' The meaning of this additional phrase is opaque unless it simply means that the reading out of the evidence is in order (i.e. that examination-in-chief may be dispensed with) providing there is also an opportunity for cross-examination, i.e. that the witness must be present.

A similar result occurred in *Kostovski v. Netherlands.*[21] The accused was convicted of armed robbery, the conviction being based to a decisive extent on reports of statements by two anonymous witnesses interviewed in the absence of the accused and counsel for the accused by police, and in one case by an examining magistrate at an earlier stage. The Court stressed that it was not its task to express a view on whether statements were correctly admitted and assessed by the court of trial but to ascertain whether the proceedings as a whole, including the way in which evidence was taken and the defence rights were honoured, was fair. The Court held that in principle all the evidence had to be produced in the presence of the accused at a public hearing with a view to cross-examination, although statements obtained at a pre-trial stage could be used as evidence 'provided the rights of the defence were respected'. As a rule, however, those rights would require that the accused have at some stage a proper opportunity to challenge and question a witness against him. In the present case that opportunity had not been provided and the witnesses therefore had at no stage been cross-examined, directly or indirectly. There were further difficulties in that the prosecution witnesses' identity had been withheld, thus rendering it difficult for the accused to demonstrate prejudice, hostility or unreliability. Notwithstanding the possibility of intimidation of witnesses in serious cases, there was a need to balance the use of anonymous statements with the interests of the accused and the present conviction was held to be irreconcilable with the guarantee in Article 6.

The Commission considered the relationship between the provisions of the Act's predecessor, the Criminal Justice Act 1988, and Art.6 in *Trivedi v UK*,[22] where a doctor was charged with false accounting by claiming for more night visits to a patient than had in fact occurred. The prosecution relied on written statements by the patient who was elderly and infirm. The Commission declared the application inadmissible as the statements were not the only evidence, the judge had conducted an inquiry into the patient's condition and evidence on the patient's reliability had been admitted. The jury had been specifically warned against attaching undue weight to the patient's evidence.

Under Art.6, the precise rules of evidence are a matter for domestic law, although they must conform to the need for a fair trial. Anonymous and hearsay evidence are not automatically in violation of the Convention but the provisions for admitting such evidence must be laid down by law and the exceptions to the rule need to be necessary and proportional. The Strasbourg cases suggest that the safeguards built into English law, particularly with the Criminal Justice Act 2003, backed up by s.78, are adequate to ensure a fair trial.

---

[21] Case 10/1988/154/208.
[22] [1997] E.H.R.L.R. 520.

3. Inclusionary discretion

Before 2003, there was an argument that the concept of a fair hearing requires an inclusionary discretion to admit hearsay statements on behalf of the accused. Third party confessions illustrate this issue as historically, the appeal court judges has been unwilling to accept such evidence—in 1946, Walter Rowland was convicted of the murder of a Manchester prostitute, Olive Balchin, by hitting her over the head with a hammer. Asked if he had anything to say before the inevitable death sentence was passed, Rowland replied: "I am going to face what lies before me with the fortitude and calm that only a clear conscience can give. Somewhere there is a person who knows that I stand here today an innocent man." David Ware read about Rowland and made a full confession to Balchin's murder to the police. But the appeal court decided it was outside their powers to hear the new confession evidence from Ware, and Rowland was executed. Four years later, Ware was found guilty of the attempted murder of another woman. "I don't know what is the matter with me," he said. "I keep having an urge to hit women over the head." He was committed to an asylum. A further example was in 1977—the IRA unit, captured following a siege in Balcombe Street, confessed to the bombings for which the Guildford Four had been convicted. It took another 12 years before they were released.[23]

Blastland[24] was a murder case in which a third party made a statement which strongly suggested that person's involvement in the killing. This statement was held inadmissible by the House of Lords. The result of the exclusion of the items of evidence involved—the third party's confession and his knowledge of the crime—was to deprive the jury of information which might have left them with a reasonable doubt about the defendant's guilt. The common law rule means that a third party's confession is often excluded. But fairness cannot be ensured without a power to admit such evidence in an appropriate case and where the context and circumstances of a third party's confession can be fully related, it should sometimes be brought to the attention of the jury. But when this decision was tested in Europe, in *Blastland v UK*,[25] the Commission held the application inadmissible and that the statements could be excluded provided that the accused could call the third party as a witness. Commonwealth authorities tend to support the admissibility of the evidence.[26]

If the principle of a "fair trial" is accepted as the rationale for excluding hearsay evidence adduced by the prosecution, the impact of Art.6 may require amendment to the rigid application of the rule as far as defendants are concerned. An inclusionary discretion on behalf of the defence was seen as a way of avoiding the apparent injustices in *Sparks* and *Blastland*.

---

[23] Other examples can be seen in R. Woffinden, "An Appeal to Hypocrisy" *Guardian*, August 4, 2005.

[24] [1985] 2 All E.R. 1095—a confession to the murder by a third party was excluded; *Turner* [1975] 1 All E.R. 70; *Harry* (1986) 86 Cr.App.R. 105; *Beckford and Daley* [1991] Crim.L.R. 833.

[25] Application No.12045/86, 52 D.R. 273 (1987).

[26] G. Taylor, "Two English Hearsay Heresies" [2005] 9 E.&P. 110.

T. Allen, "Implied Assertions as Hearsay" [1992] 142 N.L.J. 1194:

While the judges' reluctance to modify the formal rules of evidence may be understood, it is however important to stress that there should be no barrier to wider exercise of the court's discretion. Exercise of an inclusionary discretion may reasonably be thought to be an integral feature of the principal constitutional function of the trial judge—to ensure the defendant receives a fair trial. In that context, the distinction between exclusionary and inclusionary discretions is somewhat arbitrary. In *Sang*,[27] Lord Scarman concluded that the various forms of the exclusionary discretion were all instances of a general discretion founded on the right to a fair trial; and also that the demands of fairness inevitably depended on all the circumstances of particular cases.

Lord Scarman's denial that the 'principle of fairness' was 'susceptible to categorisation and classification'—even in the context of exclusionary discretion—reflected the importance of allowing the judge to depart from the rules when their application would cause injustice in particular cases. There is an ineradicable tension between formal legality and substantive equity—between legal rule and judicial discretion—which we cannot finally (or safely) resolve except in the circumstances of particular cases. Even if the rules of evidence should generally be altered by formal legislation alone, the judge's discretion should be invoked at common law whenever it is necessary to prevent injustice. All relevant evidence—even hearsay, express or implied—should be admitted in support of the defence where the interests of justice plainly support it.

The US Supreme Court has held that the exclusion of evidence of confessions made by a third party, in accordance with ordinary rules of evidence, deprived the defendant of a fair trial.[28] . . . It cannot be accepted that the right to a fair trial is any less fundamental in Britain than in the US—could Parliament abolish the right to a fair trial?—and similar consequences must surely follow. As the Supreme Court said, '. . . where constitutional rights directly affecting the ascertainment of guilt are implicated, the hearsay rule may not be applied mechanically to defeat the ends of justice'.

If the principle of fairness underlies the rule against hearsay, the rule's primary objective must be the protection of the defendant who is most at risk from anonymous accusation by the state. But this does not mean that the defence must also be prevented from adducing hearsay evidence. The prosecution (and the community they represent) should be protected from "dirty tricks" by the accused but as long as there is due notice, the state possess the resources to ensure that the prosecution will not be improperly prejudiced by hearsay introduced on behalf of the defence.

The Law Commission argued for a limited inclusionary discretion.[29] The reasoning was that such a discretion would prevent unsafe convictions. But the Commission also felt that this should be available for the prosecution and that there was no danger of hearsay evidence of poor quality being admitted against a defendant. In the 2003 Act, s.114(1)(d) provides that hearsay evidence can be admissible if, 'the court is satisfied that it is in the interests of justice for it to be admissible'. In exercising this discretion, the judge must consider the factors detailed in s.114(2).[30] The impact of the 2003 legislation on third party confession cases such as *Blastland* will be limited—where the third

---

[27] [1980] A.C. 402 at 453–457.
[28] *Chambers v Mississippi*, (1973) 410 U.S. 295.
[29] Law Commission, *op.cit.* para.8.133ff.
[30] see Ch.18.

party is available to testify, section 116 cannot be called into aid by the defendant. But the development of an inclusionary discretion under s.114(1)(d) will now allow judges to admit such evidence where they feel that it is in the interests of justice for the jury to hear the statement.

In the US, policy has moved away from such discretion. In 1980, in *Ohio v Roberts*,[31] the Supreme Court argued that the underlying goal of the Sixth Amendment was to safeguard against the use of unreliable evidence. As a result, the court held that a prosecutor could introduce a hearsay statement so long as there were sufficient "indicia of reliability". Reliability could be established either by a "firmly rooted" hearsay exception or else a prosecutor could demonstrate reliability by making a "showing of particularized guarantees of trustworthiness". This thinking underlies the provisions of s.114(2) which centre on the notion of reliability. But the US experience was that it was difficult assessing circumstances for trustworthiness and "the only constant in this area of the law was confusion".[32]

As we have seen, the other reason for excluding hearsay is fairness and the right of the accused persons to confront the evidence against them. Under this rationale, a more rigid exclusionary rule can be justified. The US Supreme Court swung towards this rationale in *Crawford v Washington*.[33] Justice Scalia was particularly scathing of the move towards judicial discretion, speaking of reliability as an "amorphous, if not entirely subjective, concept".

Crawford v Washington (2004)541 US 36, *per* Scalia J.:

Where testimonial statements are involved, we do not think the Framers meant to leave the Sixth Amendment's protection to the vagaries of the rules of evidence, much less to amorphous notions of "reliability." Certainly none of the authorities discussed above acknowledges any general reliability exception to the common-law rule. Admitting statements deemed reliable by a judge is fundamentally at odds with the right of confrontation. To be sure, the Clause's ultimate goal is to ensure reliability of evidence, but it is a procedural rather than a substantive guarantee. It commands, not that evidence be reliable, but that reliability be assessed in a particular manner: by testing in the crucible of cross-examination. The Clause thus reflects a judgment, not only about the entertainment': if a witness testified as to hearing someone singing, it idissent), but about how reliability can best be determined . . . .

The Roberts test allows a jury to hear evidence, untested by the process, based on a mere judicial determination of reliability. It thus replaces the constitutionally prescribed method of assessing reliability with a wholly foreign one. In this respect, it is very different from exceptions to the Confrontation Clause that make no claim to be a surrogate means of assessing reliability. For example, the rule of forfeiture by wrongdoing (which we accept) extinguishes confrontation claims on essentially equitable grounds; it does not purport to be an alternative means of determining reliability.

---

[31] 448 U.S. 56 (1980).
[32] C. Fishman '*Crawford v Washington*. . .' 8 E.&P. 240.
[33] 541 US 36 (2004).

III. Definition of hearsay

Witnesses should provide information for the court based on their own knowledge; they should not provide information based on statements made by other people as to what those people knew. Witnesses thus give evidence of what they themselves perceived: what they saw, heard, felt, tasted or heard. A witness cannot testify about another's perceptions. For example, were the court seeking to establish the accused's presence at the scene of the crime, a witness can testify that they were present at the scene and saw the accused. The court, through the prosecution and defence counsel, are in a position to investigate the probative value of that identification. But if a witness were permitted to say, "My husband told me that he saw the defendant at the scene", in the absence of the husband as a witness, there is no way to test the strength of the evidence. The witness is limited to saying, 'Well, that's what he said' and the court would be able to inquire whether the husband spoke those actual words because that alone is within the wife's own perceptions. But the court could not explore other factors such as the circumstances (lighting, distance) in which the identification was made or the husband's credibility as a witness. To that extent the court cannot assess whether the contents of the statement ("the accused was there") are likely to be true. Thus the wife's testimony is hearsay and is not admissible evidence to prove the fact that the defendant was at the scene. If the prosecution wishes to prove that, they have to call the husband (the declarant[34]) to testify to that effect.

It is precisely because the husband is not available that the prosecution is seeking to rely on the wife's evidence. The hearsay rule is mainly about excluding the evidence of absent witnesses.

But the rule does not only apply to repeating other people's statements. Witnesses cannot testify as to what they themselves said prior to the court proceedings. In the example above, if the husband were to testify and to state that "I told my wife that I saw the defendant at the scene", this would also not be admissible as evidence that the defendant was there. The fact that the witness told his wife does not prove anything about the defendant's whereabouts. If the witness has already testified that he saw the accused at the place, it is possible to argue that the statement is not being introduced for its truth but just to show the witness's consistency but there are considerable limitations on introducing such prior consistent statements.[35]

The rule against hearsay prevents a witness from retailing to the court, any out-of-court statement:

- whether it is sworn or unsworn;
- whether the person making the statement is a witness or not;
- whether the statement is oral or in writing (or in any kind of document) or by conduct; or

---

[34] "Declarant"—the absent witness who made the original statement which one of the parties seeks to adduce in evidence.
[35] see Ch.12.

- whether the statement expressly asserts a fact or does so only by implication.

As this chapter will show, the scope of the common law rule against hearsay is very broad, its rationale is seemingly unclear to the judiciary and its boundaries indefinite.[36] Understanding the scope is only the first step, as there are a range of exceptions, some based in common law, others more recent statutory reforms.

A. *The form of a hearsay statement*

The hearsay rule is mainly about preventing witnesses from telling the court about assertions as to the facts of the case made by others, not present in court—in other words, excluding the evidence of absent witnesses. We often think of this in terms of a witness testifying, 'Well, X told me that he saw the defendant'. While repeating another's words is the most common and obvious form of hearsay, there are different forms in which such assertions can be communicated to the court.

1. Oral statements

The oral statement is the most common example of hearsay. In *Sparks*,[37] the mother was not permitted to narrate what her young daughter had told her about the identity of the assailant.

Sparks [1964] A.C. 964 at 978, *per* Lord Morris:

In fact the girl neither gave evidence nor did she say anything in the presence of the appellant. Their lordships can see no basis on which evidence concerning a remark made by her to her mother could be admitted. Even if any basis for its admission could be found the evidence of the making of the remark would not be any evidence of the truth of the remark. Evidence of the making of the remark could not in any event possess a higher probative value than would attach to evidence of the making of a complaint in a case where the complainant gives evidence or to evidence of an accusation made to or in the presence of an accused. Nor can the principle of the matter vary according as to whether a remark is helpful to or hurtful to an accused person.

In *Jones v Metcalfe*,[38] the witness reported a lorry number involved in an incident to a police officer. The witness could not later recollect that number nor could the officer testify in the witness's place as to what he had said. In

---

[36] *Woodhouse v Hall* (1980) 72 Cr.App.R. 39; *Kearley op.cit.*
[37] above.
[38] [1967] 3 All E.R. 205.

both cases, the witness (mother or police officer) was retailing to the court a statement by another person as proof of the contents of the statement—that is, that the assailant was black or that the registration number was ABC 123. The testimony is hearsay and the exclusionary rule operates unless an exception applies.

2. Written statements

It would make no difference if the mother or police officer had produced a written statement by the child or the witness to the traffic incident which detailed the ethnicity of the assailant or the number of the car. The written document speaks to the court in place of the absent witness in the same way as the mother or the police officer. The *written* document need not be written—the same principle applies to a video or audio recording of the absent witness. A document can be any medium on which information is recorded, including computer discs. A document can contain hearsay but not all documents contain hearsay.[39]

The classic case here is *Myers v DPP*[40] where the defendant bought wrecked cars for their registration certificates. He would then steal a similar car and alter it to fit the details in the document. He would sell the disguised stolen car along with the genuine log book of the wrecked car. The prosecution sought to show that the cars and registration documents did not match up by reference to the engine block numbers and introduced microfilm evidence kept by the manufacturer, showing that this block number did not belong in a car of this registration date. The microfilm was prepared from cards which were themselves prepared by workers on the assembly line. Lord Reid in the House of Lords held that the microfilm was inadmissible since it contained the out-of-court assertions by unidentified workers.

Myers v D.P.P. [1964] 2 All E.R. 877 at 886b–887h, *per* Lord Reid:

It is not disputed before your Lordships that to admit these records is to admit hearsay. They only tend to prove that a particular car bore a particular number when it was assembled if the jury were entitled to infer that the entries were accurate, at least in the main; and the entries on the cards were assertions by the unidentifiable men who made them that they had entered numbers which they had seen on the cars. Counsel for the respondents were unable to adduce any reported case or any textbook as direct authority for their submission. Only four reasons for their submission were put forward. It was said that evidence of this kind is in practice admitted at least at the Central Criminal Court. Then it was argued that a judge has a discretion to admit such evidence. Then the reasons given in the Court of Criminal Appeal were relied on. And lastly it was said with truth that common sense rebels against the rejection of this evidence.

At the trial counsel for the prosecution sought to support the existing practice of admitting such records, if produced by the persons in charge of them, by arguing that

[39] see Ch.5.
[40] [1964] 2 All E.R. 877.

they were not adduced to prove the truth of the recorded particulars but only to prove that they were records kept in the normal course of business. Counsel for the accused then asked the very pertinent question—if they were not intended to prove the truth of the entries, what were they intended to prove? I ask what the jury would infer from them: obviously that they were probably true records. If they were not capable of supporting an inference that they were probably true records, then I do not see what probative value they could have, and their admission was bound to mislead the jury.

The first reason given by the Court of Criminal Appeal for sustaining the admission of the records was that, although the records might not be evidence standing by themselves, they could be used to corroborate the evidence of other witnesses. I regret to say that I have great difficulty in understanding that . . . . Unless the jury were entitled to regard them as probably true records they afforded no corroboration at all. If the jury were entitled so to regard them, I can see no reason why they should only become admissible evidence after some witnesses have identified the cars for different reasons . . .

At the end of their judgment, the Court of Criminal Appeal gave a different reason. 'In our view the admission of such evidence does not infringe the hearsay rule because its probative value does not depend upon the credit of an unidentified person but rather on the circumstances in which the record is maintained and the inherent probability that it will be correct rather than incorrect.' That, if I may say so, is undeniable as a matter of common sense. But can it be reconciled with the existing law? I need not discuss the question on general lines because I think that this ground is quite inconsistent with the established rule regarding public records. Public records are prima facie evidence of the fact which they contain but it is quite clear that a record is not a public record within the scope of that rule unless it is open to inspection by at least a section of the public. Unless we are to alter that rule how can we possibly say that a private record not open to public inspection can be prima facie evidence of the truth of its contents? I would agree that it is quite unreasonable to refuse to accept as prima facie evidence a record obviously well kept by public officers and proved never to have been discovered to contain a wrong entry though frequently consulted by officials, merely because it is not open to inspection. But that is settled law. This seems to me to be a good example of the wide repercussions which would follow if we accepted the judgment of the Court of Criminal Appeal. I must therefore regretfully decline to accept this reason as correct in law.

In argument, the Solicitor-General maintained that, although the general rule may be against the admission of private records to prove the truth of entries in them, the trial judge has a discretion to admit a record in a particular case if satisfied that it is trustworthy and that justice requires its admission. That appears to me to be contrary to the whole framework of the existing law. It is true that a judge has a discretion to exclude legally admissible evidence if justice so requires, but it is a very different thing to say that he has a discretion to admit legally inadmissible evidence. The whole development of the exceptions to the hearsay rule is based on the determination of certain classes of evidence as admissible or inadmissible and not on the apparent credibility of particular evidence tendered. No matter how cogent particular evidence may seem to be, unless it comes within a class which is admissible, it is excluded. Half a dozen witnesses may offer to prove that they heard two men of high character who cannot now be found discuss in detail the fact now in issue and agree on a credible account of it, but that evidence would not be admitted although it might be by far the best evidence available.

It was admitted in argument before your Lordships that not every private record would be admissible. If challenged it would be necessary to prove in some way that it had proved to be reliable, before the judge would allow it to be put before the jury. And I think that some such limitation must be implicit in the last reason given by the Court of Criminal Appeal. I see no objection to a judge having a discretion of this kind though it might be awkward in a civil case; but it appears to me to be an innovation on the existing law which decides inadmissibility by categories and not by apparent trustworthiness . . . .

Highly probative and reliable information was not put before the court because it fell within the category of hearsay and no common law exception applied. The House of Lords recognised the absurdity of their position but felt strongly that it was for the legislature to reform the law and create new exceptions. Such documents in criminal proceedings would now be dealt with under s.117 of the Criminal Justice Act 2003.[41] In civil proceedings they would be admissible under the Civil Evidence Act 1995.[42]

Myers has been overtaken by legislative reform but the decision remains good authority for the core issue of what constitutes hearsay. It was regularly followed in such cases as *Patel v Comptroller of Customs*,[43] where the appellant was convicted of making a false declaration to customs, having stated that the bags of seed were originally from India. The prosecution sought to prove that the seed originated in Morocco and adduced evidence that the bags were stamped with "Produce of Morocco". The Privy Council, following *Myers* held that these words were hearsay and inadmissible. Unlike *Myers*, there was no evidence that the writing was at all reliable, there being no testimony as to how or by whom the bags were marked.

3. Statements by conduct

Actions speak louder than words and statements can also be made by the actions of a declarant. In *Chandrasekera*,[44] the victim had her throat cut. At the trial, evidence was admitted that she was unable to speak as a result of her injuries but had indicated that it was the defendant who had committed the act. This was an intentional assertion on the victim's part and as such was hearsay.[45] A similar situation arose in *Gibson*,[46] where the victim was injured by a stone. The victim testified that, shortly after the attack, an unidentified woman had pointed to a house and said that the assailant had gone in there— it was the accused's home. As Lord Coleridge said "It is admitted that the statement was not made in the prisoner's hearing, and therefore could not legally be given in evidence against him." The testimony was excluded and the conviction was quashed.

4. Implied assertions

In *Chandrasekera*, the declarant intentionally sought to communicate information—she answered a direct question: "Was it Alisandiri?" (the name by which the accused was ordinarily known) and she nodded her head. Implying a fact from a person's behaviour is one form of implied assertion.

---

[41] Previous attempts to deal with the problem of documentary hearsay were the Criminal Evidence Act 1965, s.68, Police and Criminal Evidence Act 1984 and ss.23 and 24 of the Criminal Justice Act 1988.

[42] The original reforms were under the Civil Evidence Act 1968.

[43] [1965] 3 All E.R. 593.

[44] [1936] 3 All E.R. 865.

[45] Although hearsay, it was admissible under an exception provided by s.32 of the Ceylon Evidence Ordinance, No.14 of 1895.

[46] (1887) 18 Q.B.D. 537.

We can also imply facts from speech, although the declarant is not asserting that fact expressly. The classic case,[47] *Wright v Tatham*,[48] concerned a will in which the testator, John Marsden, had left a substantial amount of property to his steward, Wright. Tatham, heir-at-law and entitled on intestacy, challenged the will, asserting the mental incompetence of the testator. Those parties seeking to uphold the will and asserting John Marsden's competence, sought to introduce evidence of letters written to the testator. Had the writers of these letters been called as witnesses, they could have testified as to their opinion of Marsden's sanity. In their place, the court had the letters which did not expressly state that the testator was sane and would clearly have been inadmissible hearsay had they done so. But the inference that could be drawn from reading the letters was that the letter writers regarded the testator as in full possession of his mental faculties. Was such an implied assertion admissible?

Wright v Tatham (1837) 7 Ad. & El. 313 at 384–389, *per* Parke B.:

. . . Each of the three letters, no doubt, indicates that in the opinion of the writer the testator was a rational person. He is spoken of in respectful terms in all. Mr Ellershaw describes him as possessing hospitality and benevolent politeness; and Mr Marton addresses him as competent to do business to the limited extent to which his letter calls upon him to act; and there is no question but that, if any one of those writers had been living, his evidence, founded on personal observation, that the testator possessed the qualities would be admissible on this issue. But the point to be determined is, whether these letters are admissible as proof that he did possess these qualities? I am of the opinion that, according to the established principles of the law of evidence, the letters are all inadmissible for such a purpose . . . .

But the question is, whether the contents of these letters are evidence of the fact to be proved upon this issue—that is, the actual existence of the qualities which the testator is, in those letters, by implication, stated to possess; and those letters may be considered in this respect to be on the same footing as if they had contained a direct and positive statement that he was competent. For this purpose they are mere hearsay evidence, statements of the writers, not on oath, of the truth of the matter in question, with this addition, that they have acted upon the statements on the faith of their being true, by their sending the letters to the testator. That the so acting cannot give a sufficient sanction for the truth of the statement is perfectly plain; for it is clear that, if the same statements had been made by parol or in writing to a third person, that would have been insufficient; and this is conceded by the learned counsel for the plaintiff in error . . . .

Many other instances of a similar nature, by way of illustration were suggested by the learned counsel for the defendant in error . . . [the testator's] election, in his absence, to some high and responsible office; the conduct of a physician who permitted a will to be executed by a sick testator; the conduct of a deceased captain on a vessel, embarked in it with his family; all these, when deliberately considered are, with reference to the matter in issue in each case, mere instances of hearsay evidence, mere statements, not on oath, but implied in or vouched by the actual conduct of persons by whose acts the litigant parties are not to be bound. The conclusion at which

---

[47] Although described by the editor of Cross as "old and unsatisfactory".
[48] (1837) 7 Ad. & El. 313.

I have arrived is, that proof of a particular fact, which is not itself a matter in issue, but which is relevant only as implying a statement or opinion of a third person on the matter in issue, is inadmissible in all cases where such a statement or opinion not on oath would itself be inadmissible; and, therefore, in this case the letters which are offered only to prove the competence of the testator, that is the truth of the implied statements therein contained, were properly rejected, as the mere statements or opinions of the writer would certainly have been inadmissible . . . .

The letters were excluded as hearsay. Parke B. gave the example of the ship's captain who is seen to examine a ship thoroughly before embarking on it with his family and setting off on a voyage. The ship disappears, presumably sunk and litigation follows on the cause of the disappearance. Was the captain's conduct a statement that in his opinion the ship was seaworthy? Obviously this was the case and perhaps it was the more reliable because it was unintentional and thus there was less likelihood that it was manufactured. But Parke B. still treated it as hearsay. The party adversely affected by the captain's assertion could never cross-examine him on what facts or perceptions led him to the conclusion that the ship was seaworthy. That inability to question exists whether the witness expressly states an opinion or simply implies it through conduct. The hearsay rule certainly covers assertions implied from conduct or speech.[49]

The old common law embodied a strict rule of exclusion, both for express and implied assertions. If a court were to rely on a witness's perceptions, no matter through what medium they were expressed, that witness had to be present in court for that information to be admissible, unless there was an applicable exception.

B. *The Scope of Hearsay*

So far this chapter has looked at an outline definition of hearsay, the rationales behind the exclusionary rule and the different forms which hearsay statements might adopt. It has deliberately avoided the substance of the concept—when is a statement hearsay? The common law and statutory formulations agree that "an assertion other than one made by a person while giving oral evidence in the proceedings is inadmissible as evidence of any fact asserted". Establishing whether an assertion is hearsay is the critical first step—if it is not hearsay but original evidence, the assertion is admissible (unless another exclusionary rule applies); if it is hearsay, we must consider in civil proceedings what pre-trial procedural steps must be taken or in criminal cases whether any exception applies.

There are two central conceptual issues:

> i) not all out-of-court assertions are hearsay statements: they are only hearsay if the statements are adduced as evidence of any fact asserted. This suggests that a statement may be introduced for a

---

[49] This is now affected by s.115(3) of the Criminal Justice Act 2003, discussed below.

purpose other than that of proving the truth of the facts contained in it. For example, where a witness's truthfulness has been doubted, evidence that, before the trial, the witness made a statement which was consistent with current testimony may be introduced. It is an out-of-court statement but it is being introduced, not as evidence of the facts that the statement contains but as evidence that the witness has been consistent and therefore more likely to be truthful and credible.[50] Another example would be where the fact in issue was whether a person was drunk or deranged. A witness can testify that the defendant had stated that there were pink elephants in the road. Although the witness is repeating another's words, such a statement is not hearsay because it is introduced, not as evidence that the elephants existed but that the defendant was drunk or mad.[51] This is what may be termed the "purpose rule" and requires us to identify the purpose for which the statement is being introduced.

ii) the second issue centres around the word 'assertion'. Does the hearsay rule only exclude those statements in which the declarant expressly and intentionally asserted a fact, whether orally, in writing or by conduct? Or does it also strike out those statements where the fact is asserted unintentionally and by implication? In *Kearley*,[52] the police raided a house searching for drugs. Drugs were found but not in sufficient quantities that any trier of fact would be justified in concluding that there was any intent to supply. Whilst the police were searching the flat, ten telephone calls were made to the flat in which the caller asked for the appellant and asked for drugs. In addition to this seven people called at the flat asking for the appellant and offering to buy drugs for cash. The prosecution did not call any of these people but instead sought to rely on the testimony of police officers as to what had been said on these occasions. These callers had spoken in terms which suggested that the accused was their drug supplier, although they had not expressly stated that he was a dealer. The House of Lords ruled that such "implied assertions" were also excluded by the hearsay rule. This ruling must now be considered in the light of s.115(3) of the Criminal Justice Act.

These two issues define the boundaries of hearsay and will be examined in more detail.

1. The Purpose Rule

The definition of hearsay is that any assertion other than one made by a person while giving oral evidence in the proceedings was inadmissible as evidence of any fact asserted. A statement will only be treated as hearsay if the party adducing it intends to rely on the truth of its contents.

---

[50] *Oyesiku* (1971) 56 Cr.App.R. 240—see Ch.12.
[51] *Ratten* [1971] 3 All E.R. 801.
[52] [1992] 2 All E.R. 345.

It is essential to isolate the fact in issue that you are seeking to prove by adducing the statement. Only then is it possible to identify the purpose of introducing the statement. For example, the accused is charged with driving away from the scene of an accident. The prosecution must show, *inter alia*, that it was the accused's car. A police officer interviewed a witness at the scene who saw the registration number. That witness has now disappeared. Can the officer testify as to what was said? For the prosecution, the purpose is to demonstrate that it was the accused's car that was involved—in other words, the court should rely on the truth of the absent witness's assertion. As such the officer's testimony would be hearsay.[53]

But if the witness had deliberately given a false registration number to mislead the officer and is now charged with obstruction of a police officer, the officer could quite properly recount the statement. In these circumstances, the prosecution would not be relying on the truth of the statement. The court would not be interested in the perceptions of the declarant but only in whether these words were in fact spoken and the police officer's testimony is admitted for that purpose. This is illustrated in *Chapman*,[54] when the defendant was charged under the Road Safety Act 1967 with drunk driving. Section 2(2)(b) of the Act provided that a hospital patient should not provide a breath specimen if the doctor objected. A breath test had been administered to the defendant while in hospital. The constable gave evidence that the doctor had not objected. On appeal, the appellant contended that the prosecution should have called the doctor to prove that there was no objection. The conviction was affirmed as this was not a hearsay statement—the fact which needed to be proved was that no objection to a breath test had been made. If there had been no objection, the proper procedure was followed and the appellant had no grounds for appeal. The constable testified that there had been no objection. Whether the doctor spoke the truth or not was immaterial.

It is a very fine line between statements which contravene the hearsay rule and those statements which courts regard as original evidence. Although fine, it is a distinct line which the courts neglect at their peril.[55] To illustrate this, we might consider two categories.

(1) *Existence of a statement may be a fact in issue in a case*

In these examples, it is the fact that the statement was made, rather than the truth of the contents, that needs to be proved:

- where the accused is charged with obtaining property by deception,[56] the prosecution must prove that a false representation was made. It is not hearsay because the prosecution are not relying on the statement's truth. Indeed they must prove its falsity;

---

[53] It may be admissible under s.116 of the Criminal Justice Act 2003.

[54] [1969] 2 All E.R. 321.

[55] In *Kearley*, the majority in the House of Lords focus solely upon the category of implied assertions and fail to recognise the argument that the statements may be admissible to prove the use of the premises, a fact which is itself of circumstantial relevance to proving the accused's intent to supply.

[56] Under Theft Act 1968, s.15.

- in an action for defamation, the claimant must prove that the defamatory words were uttered. The publication in which the words appear may be proved or a witness can testify that the defendant spoke the words. The claimant is not relying on their truth but simply the fact that the words were spoken or written. Often the claimant is seeking to show that the words are untrue;
- in breach of contract, the claimant might well wish to rely on the words of acceptance spoken by the defendant. They must show that the words were uttered and that a reasonable person would have understood them to mean the acceptance of the offer.

This important point is illustrated by *Subramaniam v Public Prosecutor*.[57] The defendant was accused of being in unlawful possession of ammunition. His defence was that he was acting under duress and he sought to testify that he had been threatened by terrorists. The trial judge excluded the evidence of the threats as hearsay but the conviction was quashed on appeal. The fact in issue before the court was the defence of duress which required the defendant to show that he believed that he would be killed if he refused to carry out the terrorists' orders. To establish that belief and thus the defence of duress, there must be evidence that threatening words were spoken. It was not relevant whether those words were true or not—the issue was whether the defendant believed them.

Subramaniam v Public Prosecutor [1956] 1 W.L.R. 965 at 970, *per* Mr L.M.D. De Silva:

In ruling out peremptorily the evidence of conversation between the terrorist and the appellant the trial judge was in error. Evidence of a statement made to a witness by a person who is not himself called as a witness may or may not be hearsay. It is hearsay and inadmissible when the object of the evidence is to establish the truth of what is contained in the statement. It is not hearsay and is admissible when it is proposed to establish by the evidence, not the truth of the statement, but the fact that it was made. The fact that the statement was made, quite apart from its truth, is frequently relevant in considering the mental state and conduct thereafter of the witness or of some other person in whose presence the statement was made. In the case before their Lordships statements could have been made to the appellant by the terrorists, which, whether true or not, if they had been believed by the appellant, might reasonably have induced in him an apprehension of instant death if he failed to conform to their wishes.

In the rest of the evidence given by the appellant statements made to him by the terrorists appear now and again to have been permitted, probably inadvertently, to go in. But, a complete, or substantially complete, version according to the appellant of what was said to him by the terrorists and by him to them has been shut out. This version, if believed, could and might have afforded cogent evidence of duress brought to bear upon the appellant. Its admission would also have meant that the complete story of the appellant would have been before the trial judge and assessors and

[57] [1956] 1 W.L.R. 965.

enabled them more effectively to have come to a correct conclusion as to the truth or otherwise of the appellant's story . . . .

In *Subramaniam* the court is not interested in perceptions of the terrorists but in the mental processes of the witness in the courtroom. Did he believe the words spoken to him? Often the question is whether the court has the right witness in the witness box—in other words, the witness who it is most appropriate to examine and cross examine. Is a party being denied the right to confront the evidence against them? Here the accused can testify whether a threat was made and whether he believed that it would be carried out. The prosecution are able to cross-examine and thus the testimony is original evidence and not hearsay.

(ii) *The statement itself might be relevant to a legally constitutive fact*
In *Woodhouse v Hall*,[58] the defendant was charged with managing a brothel contrary to s.33 of the Sexual Offences Act 1956. Plainclothes officers kept observation on the building and also entered as customers for a massage. They alleged that they had been offered masturbation by the masseuses working there. Could the officers testify what had been said to them and that these offers had been made? The justices excluded the evidence as hearsay but the Divisional Court held these statements were operative words. Why? The prosecution had to prove that the use of the premises amounted to a brothel. The officers could not testify to statements made by customers or by the employees that "This is a brothel" as this relies on the perceptions and beliefs of those persons. But they could testify as to any sexual activity that they themselves observed. Furthermore the fact in issue that the prosecution must prove is that the premises were being used as a brothel. This is a place where offers of sexual services are made and accepted. Regardless of truth, the very existence of such offers tends to prove the fact in issue, namely the use to which the premises are being put.

A similar answer is to be found in cases such as *Davidson v Quirke*,[59] in which the accused was charged with using premises for the purposes of betting. Evidence was given by police officers of a number of phone calls to the premises from people seeking to place bets.

Davidson v Quirke [1923] N.Z.L.R. 552 at 555–557, *per* **Salmond J.:**

If the testimony of the police officers was limited to the mere fact that on the day in question a large number of persons rang up the appellant's house within the space of an hour and twenty-five minutes, all evidence as to the contents of the communications being excluded, such testimony would prove merely that the premises were being used for a business of some kind, but would fall short of proving that they were

---

[58] (1980) 72 Cr.App.R. 39.
[59] [1923] N.Z.L.R. 552.

being used for the business of betting. I am of opinion that, notwithstanding the general rule which excludes evidence of statements, the contents of those telephone messages as received and testified to by the police officers are legally admissible in evidence. This is an illustration of the principle that, notwithstanding the rule against hearsay, where the purpose or meaning of an act done is relevant, evidence of contemporaneous declarations accompanying and explaining the act is admissible in proof of such purpose or meaning . . . since the act of numerous strangers in using the appellant's telephone for the purpose of betting is relevant to the issue, the statements made by them at the same time are admissible as explaining their actions and showing the purpose of them.

The judgment here over-complicates the issue—it suggests that the statements are admissible under the common law *res gestae* exception, discussed later. "Explanations" of the acts of the callers or what they believed or purposed is not in issue. There is no need to use an exception to the hearsay rule as the testimony is not hearsay at all. The fact in issue for the court is the "use of the premises"—were they being used for gambling? To show this, a witness can testify that bets were being made. Compare this to the imaginary crime of "involved in the management of premises for the purpose of entertainment"—evidence that singing was heard would surely be admissible evidence of "entertainment" and nobody would suggest that it was necessary to call the singer as a witness. Similarly the witness can testify to hearing a statement such as "£5 on Fighting Scot on the nose" neither because of its truth or falsity (it has none) nor because of the implied belief of the declarant that the receiver of the call is a bookmaker. The statement is admitted as evidence which tends to prove that these are premises where bets are made.

Is the admission into evidence of these statements fair in terms of the accused's "right of confrontation"? Are the accused in all these cases being convicted on the testimony of absent witnesses? To take the example of the imaginary crime of "using premises for the purpose of entertainment": if a witness testified as to hearing someone singing, it is the correct witness who is testifying and who can be cross-examined on their perceptions. The singer, were they to testify, would merely add more or less weight. This is the situation with the phone calls in *Davidson v Quirke* and *Woodhouse v Hall* as the accused is able to cross-examine the witness as to the content of these statements—did the masseuse say "hand relief", did the phone caller say '£5 each way'? We are interested in whether the statement, an offer of a sexual service or a bet, was in fact made. This is the same question that would be put to the declarant, were they to testify. It is not the declarant's perceptions that are in issue but whether a particular form of words were used.[60]

Many commentators would argue that such an analysis is simply an artificial technique from escaping from the logical consequences of the hearsay rule, another "hearsay fiddle".

---

[60] Although I argue that admission of such statements is within the principles of a fair trial, there are other policy considerations. PACE and its Codes of Practice sought to remove police "verbals" from the courtroom—*i.e.* unverified police accounts of what the accused said. The argument above might well be attacked on the grounds that it would encourage a new species of verbals—*i.e.* unverified police accounts of what unidentified witnesses said. In my defence, I might say that a police officer would have to be well-versed in the intricacies of hearsay versus original evidence to succeed in such manoeuvres.

A. Zuckerman, The Principles of Criminal Evidence (OUP, Oxford 1989) 197:

The methodology just described illustrates a fairly common tendency in this area. A certain type of statement is taken to be reliable. To avoid exclusion the court searches for a convenient tag which may be given to this type of evidence so that it may pass for something other than hearsay. To fulfil its function the tag or label must be associated with admissible evidence. Hence the usefulness of notions such as 'operative words' and 'circumstantial evidence directly relevant to the issue'. Once the label is attached to a piece of evidence, the inhibiting effect of the hearsay rule disappears as if by magic.

Zuckerman places emphasis not on the express words but on the implications that can be drawn from the women's statements. The obvious inference to be drawn was their knowledge that the establishment operated as a brothel. This might be countered by the argument that it is essential to identify the fact in issue to which the statements are relevant. Once that fact is identified as the use of the premises, as in *Woodhouse v Hall*, it becomes a question of whether offers of sexual services were or were not being made. What the women may or may not have intended or what their implicit beliefs are, on this argument, irrelevant.

Our problem with the purpose rule now appears: the same statement can be said to perform two different functions:

i) testifying to the fact that these types of statement are being made is admissible and relevant evidence, on which the trier of fact can rely as proof of the use to which the premises are put; and

ii) the statements also reveal the women's knowledge about the function of the establishment and relying on the truth of that knowledge is hearsay and inadmissible.

Is it justifiable for a court to direct a jury that the words spoken are admissible but that the beliefs of the witness are not? In *Kearley*,[61] Lord Browne-Wilkinson says

Kearley [1992] 2 All E.R. 345 at 384h, *per* Lord Browne-Wilkinson:

. . . But the fact that his action (viz asking for drugs or queuing for coffee) is capable of raising an inadmissible inference of irrelevant fact does not mean that evidence of that action cannot be admitted with a view to proving a relevant fact.[62]

However in the Court of Appeal in the same case, Lloyd L.J. observed,

We have been assuming that the words had a dual purpose, first, to show the commercial supply of drugs from the premises, and, secondly, to show that the

---

[61] [1992] 2 All E.R. 345.
[62] *ibid.* at 384h.

appellant was the supplier. But in truth there is no distinction. It was all part and parcel of the same purpose. If the evidence was admissible to prove the first purpose, it was admissible to prove the second. Any attempt to draw a line between the two would, we think, be indefensible.[63]

Far from "indefensible", the recognition of the distinction seems essential. Another example of such a dual statement is in *Ratten*.[64] The defendant was convicted of murdering his wife. She was shot at about 1:20 p.m. The defence was that the accused was cleaning his gun and it went off accidentally. The central issue was the "accidental" nature of the shooting. The defendant testified and the prosecution sought to introduce evidence in rebuttal that in the minutes before the shooting, the telephonist at the local exchange had taken a call from that number and from a woman who sobbed and whose voice had sounded hysterical and that the caller had said, "Get me the police, please." Was this evidence hearsay?

Ratten [1971] 3 All E.R. 801 at 805–806, *per* Lord Wilberforce:

The mere fact that evidence of a witness includes evidence as to words spoken by another person who is not called is no objection to its admissibility. Words spoken are facts just as much as any other action by a human being. If the speaking of the words is a relevant fact, a witness may give evidence that they were spoken. A question of hearsay only arises when the words spoken are relied on 'testimonially', i.e. as establishing some fact narrated by the words. Authority is hardly needed for this proposition . . .

The evidence, relating to the act of telephoning by the deceased was, in their Lordships' view, factual and relevant. It can be analysed into the following elements.

(1) At about 1.15 pm the number Echuca 1494 rang. I plugged into that number.
(2) I opened the speak key and said number please.
(3) A female voice answered.
(4) That voice was hysterical and sobbed.
(5) The voice said 'Get me the police, please'.

The factual items numbered (1)-(3) were relevant in order to show that, contrary to the evidence of the appellant, a call was made, only some three to five minutes before the fatal shooting, by a woman. It not being suggested that there was anybody in the house other than the appellant, his wife and small children, this woman, the caller, could only have been the deceased. Items (4) and (5) were relevant as possibly showing (if the jury thought fit to draw the inference) that the deceased woman was at this time in a state of emotion or fear . . . They were relevant and necessary evidence in order to explain and complete the fact of the call being made. A telephone call is a composite act, made up of manual operations together with the utterance of words . . . To confine the evidence to the first would be to deprive the act of most of its significance. The act had content when it was known that the call was made in a state of emotion. The knowledge that the caller desired the police to be called, helped to indicate the nature of the emotion—anxiety or fear at an existing or impending emergency. It was a matter for the jury to decide what light (if any) this evidence, in the absence of any explanation from the appellant, who was in the house, threw on what situation was occurring or developing at the time.

---

[63] *ibid.* at 377–378 quoted by Lord Oliver.
[64] [1971] 3 All E.R. 801.

If, then, this evidence had been presented in this way, as evidence purely of relevant facts, its admissibility could hardly have been plausibly challenged. But the appellant submits that in fact this was not so. It is said that the evidence was tendered and admitted as evidence by the deceased that she was being attacked by the appellant, and that it was, so far, hearsay evidence, being put forward as evidence of the truth of facts asserted by his statement. It is claimed that the learned chief justice so presented the evidence to the jury and that, therefore, its admissibility, as hearsay, may be challenged.

Their Lordships, as already stated, do not consider that there is any hearsay element in the evidence . . . .

In order to conclude that there is no hearsay element in the evidence, Lord Wilberforce needs to pursue a particular line of reasoning:

- the ultimate fact in issue is whether Ratten intended to kill his wife or whether the gun went off by accident;
- the victim's state of mind just before the shooting is relevant to that ultimate issue. If she were calm and composed, it is more likely that the shooting was accidental; if she was in fear and hysterical, it tends to make the defence of accident less credible;
- a witness may give an opinion on another's state of mind, usually supporting this by reference to perceived factors such as tone of voice, appearance, mannerisms. The operator's opinion of Mrs Ratten's state of mind, based on non-verbal indications such as the caller sobbing or sounding panicky, is clearly admissible;[65]
- But is the operator allowed to repeat the words used? Can a witness testify that the victim shouted "Help me!"? The evidence is being adduced to support the witness's perception as to the victim's state of mind, not for the truth of the victim's statement. The witness is answering the question "In your opinion, was she upset?" and she may refer to the words she heard as evidence of that.

An alternative analysis to Lord Wilberforce's is to concentrate on the implications of the victim's statement. It does not merely reveal her state of mind but impliedly asserts a fact, as in *Woodhouse v Hall*. In this analysis, the victim is heard to say, "I need protection (from my husband)—get me the police". If so, this is hearsay since the court is being asked to rely on the truth of the statement and it is only admissible if an exception such as *res gestae* applies.[66] Thus *Ratten* is an example of how the facts can be analysed in two, equally valid, ways:

- the purpose of adducing the statement is to establish the wife's state of mind. From that fact it is permissible to infer that all was not well in the Ratten household that night and therefore that it was less likely that the gun went off by accident. The wife's state of mind is simply circumstantial evidence of the accused's *mens rea*; or

[65] If it is an opinion, it is one which does not call for specialist knowledge and where the non-expert witness would find it difficult to separate fact from inference; see Ch.20.
[66] see Ch.17.

- alternatively, the purpose is to establish the accused's *mens* rea directly from the assertion implied in the wife's statement, "He's trying to kill me!". This infringes the hearsay rule.

Where there are competing analyses of this sort, directing the jury to use the testimony as evidence of her state of mind and to draw the necessary inferences from that fact seems both practical and logically justified. The important question to ask is whether this is unfair? Has the defendant been denied his right to confront the relevant witness? In *Ratten*, the key testimony is the telephone operator's perception that Mrs Ratten was frightened and upset. She is present in court and can be examined as to the validity of this opinion.

2. Implied Assertions

The facts of *Ratten* and *Woodhouse v Hall* both contain out-of-court statements by the murder victim and by the masseuses which can be analysed to show an implied assertion, different from the words themselves—"This is a brothel" or "My husband's trying to kill me". Another example is that given in *Wright v Tatham* of the ship's captain who is seen to examine a ship thoroughly and then embarking on it with his family. The captain's conduct clearly expresses an opinion that the ship was seaworthy. It is not only an implied assertion—it is also unintentional. In none of the examples do the declarants intend to assert those facts. Is the common law definition of hearsay wide enough to cover such unintentional implied assertions?

The old common law, demonstrated in *Wright v Tatham*, embodied a strict rule of exclusion, both for express and implied assertions. If a court were to rely on a witness's perceptions, no matter through what medium they were expressed, that witness had to be present in court for that information to be admissible. How is this to be distinguished from *Ratten*?

- In *Ratten*, the evidence goes to establish the victim's emotional state, that of high anxiety, which tends to rebut the accused's testimony that the shooting was accidental. As long as the court treats the caller's mental state as the relevant fact and not any assertion by the caller, it is the telephone operator's perceptions and testimony that need to be tested.
- In *Wright v Tatham*, the evidence goes to establish a belief of the absent witness and it is the content of that belief that is relied upon to establish the fact of Marsden's sanity. In this case it is the assertion of the letter-writer that is in issue and this cannot be tested in court.

In the 1990s, the strict rule seemed destined for the rubbish bin. Authorities such as *Ratten* and *Woodhouse v Hall* suggested that a more relaxed attitude was emerging to the admission of hearsay. There was also strong academic support: the editor of Cross[67] argued that the rationale for hearsay only

[67] C. Tapper, *Cross and Tapper on Evidence* (8th edn, Butterworths, 1995), pp.583ff.

covered the intentional direct assertion of fact and that there was neither doctrinal nor policy reasons to include the implied assertion. There was support also from other jurisdictions, especially the USA where implied assertions are excluded from the scope of the hearsay rule.

A statement is (1) an oral or written assertion or (2) nonverbal conduct of a person if it is intended by the person as an assertion.[68]

This is also the case under the Evidence Act 1995 in Australia,

59.—(1) Evidence of a previous representation made by a person is not admissible to prove the existence of a fact that the person intended to assert by the representation.

In the US, District Judge Bertelsman outlined the criticisms of the old rule in *US v Zenni*, another prosecution for illegal bookmaking.

US v Zenni [1980] 492 F. Supp. 464, *per* Bertelsman J.

The common law rule that implied assertions were subject to hearsay treatment was criticised by respected commentators for several reasons. A leading work on the Federal Rules of Evidence, referring to the hotly debated question whether an implied assertion stands on better ground with respect to the hearsay rule than an express assertion, states: "By the time the federal rules were drafted, a number of eminent scholars and revisers had concluded that it does. Two principal arguments were usually expressed for removing implied assertions from the scope of the hearsay rule. First, when a person acts in a way consistent with a belief but without intending by his act to communicate that belief, one of the principal reasons for the hearsay rule—to exclude declarations whose veracity cannot be tested by cross-examination—does not apply, because the defendant's sincerity is not then involved. In the second place, the underlying belief is in some cases self-verifying: 'There is frequently a guarantee of trustworthiness of the inference to be drawn . . . because the actor has based his actions on the correctness of his belief, i.e. his actions speak louder than words.'"[69]

The "implied" assertion is seen as less vulnerable as an express assertion: passers-by had their umbrellas up for the sake of keeping dry, not for the purpose of telling anyone it was raining. If someone has no intention of asserting a fact, we are more able to rely on their trustworthiness. The argument being advanced for the exclusion of implied assertions from the operation of the hearsay rule is one based on the lack of any need to question the witness's sincerity and on a corresponding reliability. But just because the witness treats a "fact" as "to be taken for granted" and acts accordingly, this is no guarantee of other forms of unreliability. It is not the witness's sincerity but their perceptions and powers of judgment that need to come under scrutiny. Moreover, as has been argued, the primary principle in support of the hearsay rule is that of the fair trial which requires that every party, let

---

[68] Federal Rules of Evidence, r. 801.
[69] Weinstein's Evidence, para.801(a)[01] at 801–55.

alone an accused person, should be able to confront every witness on whose perceptions the opposing party relies.

The tide towards excluding implied assertions from the scope of hearsay seemed unstoppable but despite the criticism, the rigidity of the old common law position was reasserted by the House of Lords decision in *Kearley*.[70] The Dorset police raided a flat occupied by the appellant, his wife and one other person. In the course of the raid they recovered a relatively small quantity of amphetamine and while on the premises the police answered the phone and encountered visitors many requesting drugs from "Chippie", the appellant's nickname. Since the actual amount of drugs and money discovered in the flat were not enough to raise an irresistible presumption that the accused was in possession of the drugs "with intent to supply", the prosecution sought to rely on the testimony of police officers who had heard these requests. The appeal raised two issues. The first of these was whether the officer's testimony was relevant to proving intent to supply and secondly, if it were relevant, was it excluded by the hearsay rule?

The majority regarded the evidence as irrelevant and inadmissible on that basis.[71] They accepted that the evidence established the caller's belief that the accused was a drug supplier but that belief did not make it any more likely that the accused possessed intent to supply. But, on the assumption that the evidence was relevant, they would have excluded it as hearsay.

Kearley [1992] 2 All E.R. 345 at 370–371, *per* Lord Oliver:

But the state of mind of the caller is not the fact in issue and is, in itself, irrelevant, for it is not probative of anything other than its own existence. It becomes relevant only if and so far as the existence of other facts can be inferred from it. So far as concerns anything in issue at the trial, what the caller said and the state of mind which that fact evinces becomes relevant and probative of the fact in issue (namely the intent of the appellant) only if, or because, (i) what was said amounts to a statement, by necessary implication, that the appellant has in the past supplied drugs to the speaker (as in two cases in which requests were made for 'the usual') or (ii) it imports the belief or opinion of the speaker that the appellant has drugs and is willing to supply them. And here, as it seems to me, we are directly up against the hearsay rule which forms one of the major established exceptions to the admissibility of relevant evidence. Clearly if, at the trial, the prosecution had sought to adduce evidence from a witness to the effect that the appellant had, in the past, supplied him with quantities of drugs, that evidence would have been both relevant and admissible; but equally clearly, if it had been sought to introduce the evidence of a police constable to the effect that a person not called as a witness had told him, in a conversation in a public house, that the appellant had supplied drugs, that would have been inadmissible hearsay evidence and so objectionable. It cannot, it is cogently argued, make any difference that exactly the same evidence is introduced in an indirect way by way of evidence from a witness that he has overheard a request by some other person for 'the usual', from which the jury is asked to infer that which cannot be proved by evidence of that

---

[70] [1992] 2 All E.R. 345—see also *Harry* (1988), above.
[71] Discussed further in Ch.1.

other person's direct assertion. Equally if, at the trial, the prosecution had sought to adduce evidence from a witness not that drugs had been supplied but that it was his opinion or belief that drugs had been or would be supplied, that evidence would be inadmissible as amounting to no more than a statement of belief or opinion unsupported by facts upon which the belief is grounded. A fortiori, it is argued, that same inadmissible belief or opinion cannot be introduced by inference from the reported statements of someone who is not even called as a witness. Thus, it is said, in seeking to introduce the evidence of the police officers of what the callers said, the Crown faces the difficulty that it has to contend that by combining two inadmissible items of evidence—that is to say, the evidence of the calls (which are, standing alone, inadmissible because irrelevant) and the evidence of what was said by the callers (which might be relevant but is inadmissible because hearsay)—it can produce a single item of admissible evidence.

The impermissibility of such a course rests upon a well-established principle expounded in the context of civil proceedings some 150 years ago in *Wright v Doe d Tatham* . . . .

The importance of *Kearley* lies in this affirmation that unintentional implied assertions come within the definition of hearsay and are therefore excluded by the hearsay rule. If the statements of the callers are adduced as evidence to prove the accused's intent and the jury are asked to draw the inference, "Chippie is a drug dealer", these statements remain out-of-court assertions by persons not called as a witness and are thus subject to the hearsay rule. The majority in *Kearley* considered the argument that the rule itself is restricted to express and intentional assertions but adopted the *Wright v Tatham* position. The hearsay rule excludes a police officer testifying that they had answered the phone and had heard the caller had said "Hey, that Kearley's dealing drugs again". Logically the rule must also exclude implied assertions to the same effect.

Kearley [1992] 2 All E.R 345 at 363–364, *per* Lord Ackner:

Such being the law, [counsel for the Crown] frankly concedes that if the inquirer had said in the course of making his request, 'I would like my usual supply of amphetamine at the price which I paid you last week' or words to that effect, then, although the inquirer could have been called to give evidence of the fact that he had in the past purchased from the appellant his requirements of amphetamine[72] and had made his call at the appellant's house for a further supply on the occasion when he met and spoke to the police, the hearsay rule prevents the prosecution from calling police officers to recount the conversation which I have described. This is for the simple reason that the request made in the form set out above contains an express assertion that the premises at which the request was being made were being used as a source of supply of drugs and the supplier was the appellant.

If, contrary to the view which I have expressed above, the simple request or requests for drugs to be supplied by the appellant, as recounted by the police, contains in substance, but only by implication, the same assertion, then I can find neither authority nor principle to suggest that the hearsay rule should not be equally applicable and

---

[72] This would be giving evidence of bad character and could presumably only be admitted on the basis that it constituted similar fact evidence.

exclude such evidence. What is sought to be done is to use the oral assertion, even though it may be an implied assertion, as evidence of the truth of the proposition asserted. That the proposition is asserted by way of necessary implication rather than expressly, cannot, to my mind, make any difference.

Although as a matter of policy, there are reasons to restrict the scope of the hearsay rule, Lord Ackner points out that reliance on an implied assertion is the same as reliance on an express assertion. The argument that the implied assertion is more reliable may well be correct but, as we have seen, reliability is not the touchstone for the exclusion of hearsay. Above all it is fairness—just as the defendant could not confront the absent witness who said expressly, "Chippie deals drugs", nor can he confront the absentee who has merely said "Chippie, let's have the usual".

But as the minority judgments point out, the activity of the callers proved a different fact—not the fact in issue of the accused's intent but a fact relevant to that issue, namely the use of the premises to sell drugs. The caller's beliefs about the accused's *mens rea* might be irrelevant and inadmissible. But the fact that a number of people resorted to those premises, asking to buy drugs is evidence from which a jury might properly infer that the premises were being used to supply drugs. The analogy drawn was with the witness who testified that she had seen a queue. Such evidence would be relevant as it indicated that there was a market for the goods or services alleged to be on offer.

Kearley [1992] 2 All E.R. 345 at 383–384, *per* Lord Browne-Wilkinson (dissenting):

On that basis, [counsel for the appellant] submitted that such belief of third parties was irrelevant and inadmissible in deciding the intent of the accused. I accept that the opinions or beliefs of the callers were irrelevant and as such inadmissible. But in my judgment the calls prove more than the opinions or beliefs of the callers.

The evidence was, in my judgment, relevant because it showed that there were people resorting to the premises for the purposes of obtaining drugs from Chippie. Although evidence of the existence of such would-be buyers is not, by itself, conclusive, the existence of a substantial body of potential customers provides some evidence which a jury could take into account in deciding whether the accused had an intent to supply. The existence of a contemporaneous potential market to buy drugs from Chippie, by itself, shows that there was an opportunity for the accused to supply drugs.

In order to eliminate, for the purpose of considering relevance only, the complication that the purpose of the callers can only be demonstrated by the words that the callers use, I will seek to demonstrate the position by reference to a case where no such recourse is necessary. Suppose a shop which has a sole proprietor and sells only coffee. Say the issue is whether the proprietor had an intent to supply coffee. On a particular day there was a long queue of persons at the door of the shop waiting for it to open. Evidence of the existence of the queue would surely be admissible towards proving an intent to supply. The presence of potential purchasers is circumstantial evidence from which a jury can draw the inference that the shopkeeper was going to supply coffee. There can be no supply without persons to whom supply is made: if the existence of such persons is shown, that provides evidence of the opportunity for supply.

[Counsel for the appellant] submitted . . . that on analysis the only effect of such evidence is to prove a belief in the minds of members of the queue that the shopkeeper will supply coffee. But although that is one of the matters which may be inferred from the existence of the queue, in my judgment it is not the only matter which can be inferred. The existence of the queue is a fact from which a jury could draw any one or more of a number of inferences, viz: (1) the existence of potential buyers of coffee on that day from the shop; (2) the belief of the members of the queue that the proprietors will sell coffee; (3) the fact that some at least of the members of the queue are running short of coffee; (4) the opinion of at least some of the members of the queue that the proprietor sells good coffee etc. Inferences (3) and (4) are wholly irrelevant to the issue. Inference (2), though bearing on the issue, is irrelevant because it is mere belief. But the existence of irrelevant inferences which could be drawn does not mean that the evidence is not probative in support of inference (1), although a judge would no doubt be careful as the judge was in this case to caution the jury against drawing the wrong inferences.

In my view [counsel for the appellant]'s analysis seeks to eliminate the probative fact (that people were seeking to buy drugs) by concentrating on the reasons why they were seeking to buy drugs. The reasons for a third party doing an act will, normally, be irrelevant and inadmissible. Any action involving human activity necessarily implies that the human being had reasons and beliefs on which his action was based. But the fact that his action (viz asking for drugs or queuing for coffee) is capable of raising an inadmissible inference of irrelevant fact does not mean that evidence of that action cannot be admitted with a view to proving a relevant fact.

In my view therefore the fact that there were a number of people seeking to buy drugs was legally relevant and admissible as showing that there was a market to which the accused could sell, even though such evidence was also capable of giving rise to an impermissible secondary inference, viz that the callers believed Chippie supplied drugs. If the callers themselves had given evidence at the trial and said only that on the relevant day they had made a call for the purpose of obtaining drugs from Chippie, I can see no ground on which such evidence could have been excluded as being irrelevant.

These dissenting arguments take the analysis of *Kearley* away from the issue of implied assertions and back to the purpose rule. For the dissentients, this case is not about hearsay at all since the purpose of introducing the statements is not to rely on the truth of their contents. For the minority in *Kearley*, the statements establish the use to which the premises are being put, namely as a market for drugs. For this purpose the statements are relevant, admissible and highly probative—the house is indeed being used to sell drugs. When introduced for that purpose, the statements are not hearsay. Establishing the existence of a market for drugs as a fact has relevance because the jury is entitled to infer from that fact that somebody on the premises is intending to supply drugs. In the light of all the evidence in the case, they may conclude that is the accused.

From the point of view of the definition of hearsay, the House of Lords decides that implied assertions are within that definition. Has that been changed by the Criminal Justice Act 2003?

3. Section 115(3) of the Criminal Justice Act 2003

Section 115(3) of the Criminal Justice Act 2003 has the avowed purpose of reversing the position established by *Kearley* and to place unintentional implied assertions outside the definition of hearsay and thus become admissible non–hearsay evidence. The explanatory notes to the Act say that the section changes the common law position and will not prevent the admission of such implied assertions on the basis of the hearsay rule. Does it achieve its object? One way to approach the interpretation is to consider the structure of the common law exclusionary rule and see how this part of the 2003 Act has amended that structure. The common law identifies the category of evidence, defines that category, applies a rule to it and specifies the exceptions. The statute:

- identifies the category of hearsay;
- does not seek to define the concept in a conventional or express sense. A definitional section might read, "Hearsay means a statement made otherwise than by a person while giving oral evidence in the proceedings which is tendered as evidence of the matter stated". Instead s.114 states "In criminal proceedings, a statement not made in oral evidence in the proceedings is admissible as evidence of the matter stated if, but only if . . ." This is not a definition of hearsay but asserts the rule excluding hearsay, followed by the exceptions. The reader is entitled to interpret this as "Hearsay (as we have always known it) is excluded unless . . .";
- Section 114 continues by specifying the exceptions to the exclusionary rule laid out in ss.116, 117 and 118 and indeed adding a new discretionary power to admit hearsay. The Act does not abolish the common law rule against the admissibility of hearsay but extends and expands the exceptions to the rule.

We might compare this approach to the statute's approach to bad character evidence where s.98 defines the category of bad character evidence, s.99 sweeps away the old rules governing the admissibility of bad character evidence and ss.100 and 101 insert a wholly new code. In contrast, the hearsay provisions have no statutory definition of hearsay and thus leave the common law definition of hearsay in place but ss.114 and 118(2) sweep away the old rules of admissibility and ss.116–118 provide a new statutory code of exceptions.

Where does this leave s.115(3)? The section reads:

115(3) A matter stated is one to which this Chapter applies if (and only if) the purpose, or one of the purposes, of the person making the statement appears to the court to have been—
a) to cause another person to believe the matter . . .

The wording is obscure but the purpose is not—its objective is to draw a line between the intentional implied assertion (still to be caught by the hearsay rule) and the unintentional implied assertion (no longer to be treated as hearsay). Chapter 2 of Pt 11 was intended only to apply to those statements where the purpose of the person making the statement was to cause their hearer to believe the matter stated which are admissible if they come within the provisions of the Chapter. The Chapter was not to apply to *unintentional* implied assertions.

So far, so good—s.114 must now be read,

'In criminal proceedings, a statement not made in oral evidence in the proceedings is admissible as evidence of the matter stated if the purpose of the person making the statement was to cause another person to believe the matter and if, but only if, [one of the following statutory exceptions applies] . . .'

The question is whether reading the two sections in this manner redefines hearsay? Crucially the wording of s.114 is not exclusive—it lays down that, if a hearsay statement is to be admissible, it must come under the provisions of the Act. What it does not say, either expressly or by necessary implication, is that there cannot be a hearsay statement outside the parameters of the chapter. The way in which the statute has been drafted means that there can still be out-of-court statements that are still hearsay. An (the only?) example of this is the *Kearley* unintentional implied assertion. The argument goes:

- only hearsay statements that come under s.114 can be admissible under the statutory exceptions;
- the wording of s.115(3) means that s.114 does not apply to those statements where the purpose of the person making the statement was not to cause their hearer to believe the matter stated;
- the unintentional implied assertion remains hearsay—s.114 states that the chapter does not apply to such assertion but this does not change their jurisprudential nature. They remain hearsay because the House of Lords in *Kearley* said they were hearsay and there is nothing in the Act which says otherwise; and
- The *Kearley* assertion not only remains hearsay—it is always inadmissible. Hearsay can be admissible under the exceptions provided by the Act. But s.115(3) specifically excludes s.114 and the rest of the Chapter applying to *Kearley* assertions.

In the future, the prosecution do have a further possibility which is to persuade the court to exercise their discretion to admit the evidence under s.114(1)(d) on the grounds that it is in the interests of justice. But when you consider the nine factors that are specified in s.114(2) that judges should take into account before reaching a decision, they are unlikely to admit (in a 21st century variant of *Kearley)* an anonymous, unverifiable statement of a potentially unreliable witness addicted to drugs. Nor of course should they!

Such considerations did not affect the Court of Appeal which considered and rejected this argument in *Singh*.[73] The facts were wholly different from *Kearley* and involved the admissibility of the memories of mobile phones.[74] Rose L.J. stated that the common law rule against the admissibility of hearsay

---

[73] Unreported, February 23, 2006, CA.

[74] The issue of hearsay should not have arisen as these memories are not assertions of a person but a mechanical record demonstrating that the handset had been used to dial a particular number—in *Neville* [1991] Crim.L.R. 288 the evidence adduced was the itemised record by a phone company of the calls made from a mobile phone which the court accepted as original evidence.

was abolished by the clear express terms to that effect in s.118(2) which, read alongside s.114, abolished the common law hearsay rules and created instead a new rule against hearsay which did not extend to implied assertions. This judgment misreads s.118(2), the purpose of which is quite limited, namely to abolish those common law exceptions to hearsay which are not expressly preserved by the section. It also displays a lack of robustness to the issue of statutory interpretation—if a new definition of hearsay is to be created, this should be by clear and express words.

Had the draftsmen been a little more radical and had s.114 defined hearsay (the policy adopted by s.1 of the Civil Evidence Act 1995), they might have achieved their ends. For example,

In this Act—
1. "hearsay" means a statement made otherwise than by a person while giving oral evidence in the proceedings which is tendered as evidence of the matter stated; and
2. here a statement made otherwise than by a person while giving oral evidence in the proceedings is tendered as evidence of the matter stated and it appears to the court that the person making the statement did not have the purpose of causing another person to believe the matter, such a statement shall not be excluded on the ground that it is hearsay
3. hearsay statements, as defined in this Act, shall be admissible in criminal proceedings as evidence of any matter stated if, but only if, it is admissible under the provisions of this Act.

Such a formulation at least makes it clear that unintentional implied assertions should not be excluded solely on the grounds that they are hearsay. It would also have the unintended consequence that hearsay had different meanings in criminal and civil proceedings.

17

SECTION 118—COMMON LAW EXCEPTIONS TO HEARSAY

I. Introduction

There is a conventional structure to any exclusionary rule: the definition of the concept, the statement of the rule and the listing of any exceptions. The previous chapter considered the definition of hearsay and the scope of the exclusionary rule. The next three chapters consider the exceptions to that rule. In the 19th and 20th century, these exceptions were based in common law but have been extended by statute. The common law exceptions themselves have either been preserved by statute or are repealed. The major exceptions at common law were matters such as statements in public documents; certain statements by deceased persons; *res gestae* statements made spontaneously as an intrinsic part of the action or event and admissions where parties made statements adverse to their own case, for example confessions made by defendants in criminal cases.

Such statements were often hearsay but at common law, they were admissible as evidence of the truth of what they contain. This position has been radically altered and the hearsay rule has been amended by statute over the past 40 years. Significant exceptions have been introduced.

1. In civil proceedings, hearsay is governed by the Civil Evidence Act 1995.[1] Evidence can no longer be excluded in civil proceedings on the basis that it is hearsay. Hearsay still has significance in civil proceedings as such evidence requires special procedures.[2]
2. In criminal proceedings inroads into hearsay started with the Criminal Evidence Act 1965, introducing a statutory exception for documentary hearsay. Hearsay is now only admissible under the gateways specified under s.114 of the Criminal Justice Act 2003 which allows first hand oral hearsay (s.116), all kinds of documentary hearsay (s.117) and also preserves many of the old common law exceptions (s.118(1)). Any other exception (for example, the category of statements by deceased persons) has been abolished by s.118(2).

---

[1] Earlier Acts such as the 1968 Civil Evidence Act were less radical, merely extending the category of exceptions.
[2] see Ch.19.

In such cases the statement will only be admissible if it can be brought within the other provisions of the Act.

3. Confessions in criminal proceedings are now wholly governed by s.76 of the Police and Criminal Evidence Act 1984.

The standard rationale for these exceptions, whether statutory or common law, is that the evidence in these categories is more reliable and probative than other types of hearsay statement. But, as has been suggested, fairness is a more important rationale than reliability as the core criterion for the exclusion of hearsay. The confusion between the different rationales for the hearsay rule perhaps explains the pragmatism which seemingly underlies the piecemeal nature of the exceptions to the rule.

First, it may be useful first to look at the definition, rule and exceptions schematically.

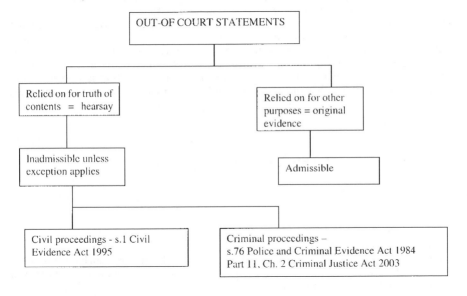

II. THE LEGISLATION

This chapter discusses those exceptions which were under the common law and which have been preserved either by s.7 of the Civil Evidence Act 1995 or s.118 of the Criminal Justice Act 2003.

Civil Evidence Act 1995, s.7

7.—(1) The common law rule effectively preserved by section 9(1) and (2)(a) of the Civil Evidence Act 1968 (admissibility of admissions adverse to a party) is superseded by the provisions of this Act.

(2) The common law rules effectively preserved by section 9(1) and (2)(b) to (d) of the [1968 c. 64.] Civil Evidence Act 1968, that is, any rule of law whereby in civil proceedings—

(a) published works dealing with matters of a public nature (for example, histories, scientific works, dictionaries and maps) are admissible as evidence of facts of a public nature stated in them,

(b) public documents (for example, public registers, and returns made under public authority with respect to matters of public interest) are admissible as evidence of facts stated in them, or

(c) records (for example, the records of certain courts, treaties, Crown grants, pardons and commissions) are admissible as evidence of facts stated in them,

shall continue to have effect.

(3) The common law rules effectively preserved by section 9(3) and (4) of the Civil Evidence Act 1968, that is, any rule of law whereby in civil proceedings—

(a) evidence of a person's reputation is admissible for the purpose of proving his good or bad character, or

(b) evidence of reputation or family tradition is admissible—

    (i) for the purpose of proving or disproving pedigree or the existence of a marriage, or

    (ii) for the purpose of proving or disproving the existence of any public or general right or of identifying any person or thing,

shall continue to have effect in so far as they authorise the court to treat such evidence as proving or disproving that matter. Where any such rule applies, reputation or family tradition shall be treated for the purposes of this Act as a fact and not as a statement or multiplicity of statements about the matter in question.

(4) The words in which a rule of law mentioned in this section is described are intended only to identify the rule and shall not be construed as altering it in any way.

Criminal Justice Act 2003, s.118

118.—(1) The following rules of law are preserved.

1 Any rule of law under which in criminal proceedings—

(a) published works dealing with matters of a public nature (such as histories, scientific works, dictionaries and maps) are admissible as evidence of facts of a public nature stated in them,

(b) public documents (such as public registers, and returns made under public authority with respect to matters of public interest) are admissible as evidence of facts stated in them,

(c) records (such as the records of certain courts, treaties, Crown grants, pardons and commissions) are admissible as evidence of facts stated in them, or

(d) evidence relating to a person's age or date or place of birth may be given by a person without personal knowledge of the matter.

2 Any rule of law under which in criminal proceedings evidence of a person's reputation is admissible for the purpose of proving his good or bad character.

Note: the rule is preserved only so far as it allows the court to treat such evidence as proving the matter concerned.

3 Any rule of law under which in criminal proceedings evidence of reputation or family tradition is admissible for the purpose of proving or disproving

(a) pedigree or the existence of a marriage,

(b) the existence of any public or general right, or

(c) the identity of any person or thing.

Note: the rule is preserved only so far as it allows the court to treat such evidence as proving or disproving the matter concerned.

4 Any rule of law under which in criminal proceedings a statement is admissible as evidence of any matter stated if—
  (a) the statement was made by a person so emotionally overpowered by an event that the possibility of concoction or distortion can be disregarded,
  (b) the statement accompanied an act which can be properly evaluated as evidence only if considered in conjunction with the statement, or
  (c) the statement relates to a physical sensation or a mental state (such as intention or emotion).
5 Any rule of law relating to the admissibility of confessions or mixed statements in criminal proceedings.
6 Any rule of law under which in criminal proceedings—
  (a) an admission made by an agent of a defendant is admissible against the defendant as evidence of any matter stated, or
  (b) a statement made by a person to whom a defendant refers a person for information is admissible against the defendant as evidence of any matter stated.
7 Any rule of law under which in criminal proceedings a statement made by a party to a common enterprise is admissible against another party to the enterprise as evidence of any matter stated.
8 Any rule of law under which in criminal proceedings an expert witness may draw on the body of expertise relevant to his field.
(2) With the exception of the rules preserved by this section, the common law rules governing the admissibility of hearsay evidence in criminal proceedings are abolished.

Section 118 is headed "Preservation of certain common law categories of admissibility" and this chapter will follow its structure. With the exception of statements by deceased persons, the Law Commissions recommended the retention of most of the common law exceptions because they fulfil useful functions and the Commission were not aware that they caused any difficulties.

III. PUBLIC INFORMATION

In civil proceedings, the common law nature of this exception to the hearsay rule was preserved by s.7(2)(a)-(c) of the Civil Evidence Act 1995. If admissible at common law, in civil proceedings, public documents are now admissible by virtue of s.7. Documents not covered by the statutory provisions will be admissible by virtue of s.1 of the Act but will need to comply with the notice and weighting provisions of the Act. In criminal cases, public information may be admissible under s.118 of the Criminal Justice Act 2003 which is in the same terms as s.7. Documents not covered this section may be admissible under ss.116 or 117.

A. *Public documents*

What constitutes a "public document"? The criteria of the common law are still relevant:

  i) made and preserved for public use;

ii) entries made promptly and by person acting under a strict duty to
inquire into the circumstances recorded; and

iii) open to public inspection.

Such a document[3] is admissible evidence of the facts contained in it. Foreign
as well as British public records are within this rule but whatever the
provenance, the conditions above must be adhered to. In *Sturla v Freccia*[4] a
report of a public committee in Genoa, a foreign state, was deemed
inadmissible.

Sturla v Freccia (1880) 5 App.Cas. 623 at 642–647, *per* Lord Blackburn:

It is an established rule of law that public documents are admitted for certain
purposes. What a public document is, within that sense, is of course the great point
which we have now to consider . . . the principle, upon which it goes is, that there
should be a public inquiry, and a public document, made by a public officer. I do not
think that 'public' there is to be taken in the sense of meaning the whole world. I think
an entry in the books of a manor is public in the sense that it concerns all the people
interested in the manor. And an entry probably in a corporation book concerning a
corporate matter, or something in which all the corporation are concerned, would be
'public' within that sense. But it must be a public document, and it must be made by a
public officer. I understand a public document there to mean a document that is made
for the purpose of the public making use of it, and being able to refer to it. It is meant
to be where there is a judicial, or quasi-judicial, duty to inquire, as might be said to be
the case with the bishop acting under the writs issued by the Crown. That may be said
to be quasi-judicial. He is acting for the public when that is done; but I think the very
object of it must be that it should be made for the purpose of being kept public, so that
the persons concerned in it may have access to it afterwards . . . . Can the document in
this case be said to come within that class of cases? I think it impossible to look at it in
this way. There is not the slightest evidence, or the least circumstance, to lead me to
the conclusion that it was ever intended that this private and confidential report
should be seen by anyone interested in it. It was meant for private information, to
guide the discretion of the Government. It was not, like the bishop's return of the first-
fruits, for public information, to be kept in the office and to be seen by all in the
diocese who might be concerned when there came to be any litigation.

In many public offices, there is a duty to record accurately but officials have
neither the time nor resources to inquire into the correctness of the information being recorded. In *Halpin*,[5] the defendant was charged with conspiracy to
defraud a local council by making false claims for work allegedly done by a
limited company. The Crown sought to prove that at the relevant time the
accused and his wife were the sole shareholders in that company by adducing
extracts from the annual returns of the company filed at the Companies
Registry. Obviously the official who received the returns had no personal
knowledge of the facts being recorded.

---

[3] There is an interesting historical note in P. Carter, *Cases on Evidence* (2nd ed., Sweet and
Maxwell, 1990) 332 with examples of public documents.

[4] [1880] 5 A.C. 623.

[5] [1975] Q.B. 907.

Halpin [1975] Q.B. 907 at 915, *per* Geoffrey Lane L.J.:

The common law as expressed in the earlier cases which have been cited were plainly designed to apply to an uncomplicated community where those charged with keeping registers would, more often than not, be personally acquainted with the people whose affairs they were recording and the vicar, as already indicated, would probably himself have officiated at the baptism, marriage or burial which he later recorded in the presence of the churchwarden on the register before putting it back in the coffers. But the common law should move with the times and should recognise the fact that the official charged with recording matters of public import can no longer in this highly complicated world, as like as not, have personal knowledge of their accuracy.

What has happened now is that the function originally performed by one man has had to be shared between two: the first having the knowledge and the statutory duty to record that knowledge and forward it to the registrar, the second having the duty to preserve that document and to show it to members of the public under proper conditions as required.

On appeal, Lane L.J. held that the judge was correct to admit the document and that the duty could be divided between the provider of the information and the officer with the statutory duty to record.

B. *Works of Reference*

At common law, authoritative works of reference were admissible to prove the facts contained in them[6] or to allow the court to take judicial notice of such facts. This is now governed by s.7(2)(a) of the Civil Evidence Act 1995 and s.118(1) of the Criminal Justice Act 2003, both of which are in the same terms. Published works dealing with matters of a public nature such as histories, scientific works, dictionaries and maps are admissible as evidence of facts of a public nature stated in them.

IV. REPUTATION AS TO CHARACTER

In criminal proceedings, evidence of the *bad character* of witnesses or other people or of the defendant is governed by ss.100 and 101 of the Criminal Justice Act 2003. Evidence of the *good character* of the defendant has always been admissible: when this is adduced in evidence in chief, the witness can only speak as to the general reputation of the defendant,[7] although a witness to character can be cross-examined as to specific events.[8] This common law exception to hearsay would have been abolished under the provisions of s.118(2)—hence it is specifically preserved by s.118(1) 2.

In civil proceedings, character evidence is less important but the common law rules are preserved, initially by the Civil Evidence Act 1968, and now by s.7(3)(a) of the 1995 Act.[9]

---

[6] That is, any facts of a public nature—*Read v Bishop of Lincoln* [1892] A.C. 644.
[7] *Rowton* (1865) 34 L.J.M.C. 57 at 60 *per* Cockburn C.J.
[8] *Winfield* (1939) 4 All E.R. 164.
[9] For a discussion of character evidence, see Chs. 14 and 15.

V. Reputation or Family Tradition

A. *Declarations as to pedigree*

In criminal proceedings, the common law exception to hearsay admitting statements pertaining to a family's pedigree was retained by s.118(1) 3. The exception is still available in criminal proceedings, although some imagination is needed to devise cases where it might be used.

In civil proceedings, these types of statement have more relevance in terms on inheritance or family law. Evidence will normally be admitted as a result of s.1 of the Civil Evidence Act 1995. Where they are not capable of being admitted under those sections, s.7(3) of that Act may be relevant so that evidence of reputation or family tradition is admissible for the purpose of proving or disproving pedigree or the existence of a marriage.

There is a proviso that ". . . reputation or family tradition shall be treated for the purposes of this Act as a fact and not as a statement or multiplicity of statements about the matter in question."

The significance of this is that strict application of the notice and weighing provisions of the 1995 Act would otherwise have been impossible.[10] The common law permits a multiplicity of hearsay handed down through the family. In *Goodright d. Stevens v Moss*,[11] the issue was a person's legitimacy. Declarations of the dead parents that the child was born before the marriage were admissible.

> An entry in a father's family Bible, an inscription on a tombstone, a pedigree hung up in the family mansion, are all good evidence. So too the declarations of parents in their lifetime . . .[12]

In such circumstances it is necessary to observe the common law preconditions:

    i) that the declaration relates to an issue of pedigree: for example, a declaration as to a date of birth would not necessarily be a question of pedigree which is the subject of family relationships[13];

    ii) that the declarant is related by blood or marriage to the person whose pedigree is in issue; and[14]

    iii) that the declaration was made before the dispute in question arose.[15]

B. *Declarations as to public and general rights*

In criminal proceedings, the common law exception to hearsay admitting evidence of reputation pertaining to public and general[16] rights was retained

---

[10] Law Commission, *The Hearsay Rule in Civil Proceedings* (Cm. 2321 HMSO, 1993) para.4.34; see Ch.19.

[11] (1777) 2 Cowp. 591.

[12] *ibid.* at 594 *per* Lord Mansfield C.J.

[13] *Haines v Guthrie* (1884) 53 L.J.Q.B. 521.

[14] *Johnson v Lawson* (1824) 2 Bing. 86.

[15] *Butler v Mountgarret (Viscount)* (1859) 7 HL Cas 633.

[16] Public rights are those common to everyone (a highway, for example) whereas general rights are those available to a considerable class—for example, all those belonging to a particular parish.

by s.118(1) 3. The exception is still available in criminal proceedings, although it can have no practical application.

In civil proceedings, these statements will normally be admissible as a consequence of s.1 of the Civil Evidence Act 1995. Where they are not capable of being admitted under those sections, s.7(3)(b)(ii) of that Act may be relevant so that evidence of reputation may be admitted to prove the existence of any public or general right or of identifying any person or thing. The preconditions at common law are that there was a declaration about the right in question and that should have been made before the dispute arose and should concern the reputed existence of the right.

VI. RES GESTAE

Alongside admissions, the major exception at common law was that which glories in the name of *res gestae*. Civil and criminal cases often concern a key event, especially in criminal law where, for example, the court can be dealing with an act of violence which takes only moments. It would be absurd for witnesses only to testify as to what they saw and not as to what they heard as such words are often the key to understanding the incident. Although the speaker might not be a witness, the evidence is seen as more reliable as the statement is made spontaneously as an intrinsic part of the action or event. In such cases, that statement is admissible as evidence of the truth of what it contains. All acts and statements which are part of the whole event are admissible and this exception overrides all other exclusionary rules. The key question is to determine what is "part of the action" as opposed to acts and statements preceding or subsequent to the event?

This is an important rule in criminal proceedings, although detested by commentators,[17] perhaps because the principles have never been comprehensively or clearly enunciated in precedent. But in civil proceedings, it was not an exception that was preserved by the Civil Evidence Acts of either 1968 or 1995 and as a result, such statements will nowadays be admitted as a result of s.1 of the 1995 Act. It is expressly preserved as a category in criminal proceedings by the 2003 legislation.

Historically the rule was strictly applied and the critical elements were that the statement had to be spontaneous and contemporaneous with the events. These elements were often seen as technical rules. *Bedingfield*[18] was a case where the defendant was charged with murder by cutting the victim's throat. The defence was one of suicide. There was evidence that the accused was in a room with the victim, who emerged with her throat cut and said, "Oh dear, Aunt, see what Bedingfield has done to me!" The evidence of that statement was held inadmissible because it occurred after the throat cutting and the '*res*' had been completed. As will be seen, such a strict approach to contemporaneity has long since disappeared.

---

[17] Heydon gives a selection of abuse—"damnably pretended doctrine" (Pollock); 'The marvellous capacity of a Latin phrase to serve as a substitute for reasoning. ..' (Morgan)—J. Heydon, *Evidence* (3rd ed., Butterworths, 1991), p.349.

[18] (1879) 14 Cox 341.

The broad scope of the exception means that all acts and statements which are part of the whole event are admissible—the *res gestae* rule overrides all exclusionary rules. In *Ellis*,[19] the defendant was charged with stealing certain marked coins from a till. Evidence was given that he was seen taking money from the till and was also caught in possession of these marked coins as well as other money, presumably also from the till. This evidence tended to show that the defendant was guilty of other crimes other than the one with which he was charged and such "bad character" evidence is normally inadmissible but as it was part of the whole event of "taking", it was admitted.

The inclusionary effect of *res gestae* has been to soften the effect of sundry exclusionary rules such as the similar fact rule. In *O'Leary*,[20] the victim was killed at the end of a day-long drunken orgy at a logging camp in Australia. The actions of the accused throughout the day, including assaults on others, were admitted as evidence since ". . . a connected series of events occurred which should be considered as one transaction".[21] Perhaps the greatest impact is on the hearsay rule as is seen in *Manchester Brewery Co. v Coombs*,[22] when a brewery sued a publican for the latter's breach of an undertaking to buy all his beer from the brewery. The defence was that the beer supplied was not of acceptable quality and part of the evidence concerned complaints from customers who had not been called as witnesses. Statements from absent customers such as "This beer is bad" were admitted to prove the poor quality of the beer were admitted to explain why the customers had abandoned their drinks after tasting it.

Such examples raise problems as to the scope of this exception. It has been suggested that the *res gestae* rule lacks "plausible logical analysis" and thus any form of classification is likely to be more expedient than principled.[23] Cross isolated four different situations where *res gestae* might apply— statements by participants or observers to events, statements accompanying a relevant act, statements concerning a physical sensation, statements concerning the maker's state of mind. These are not exclusive categories and often can cover the same territory. The draftsmen of s.118(1) 4 use basically the same concepts:

(a) the statement was made by a person so emotionally overpowered by an event that the possibility of concoction or distortion can be disregarded,

(b) the statement accompanied an act which can be properly evaluated as evidence only if considered in conjunction with the statement, or

(c) the statement relates to a physical sensation or a mental state (such as intention or emotion)

A. *Statements by a person emotionally overpowered by an event*

The phrasing of this category no longer reflects Cross's calm wording of statements by "participants or observers of events". Section 118 talks of the

---

[19] (1826) 6 B.& C. 145.

[20] (1946) 73 C.L.R. 566.

[21] *ibid.* at 577 *per* Dixon J.

[22] (1900) 82 L.T. 347.

[23] E. Morgan, "A Suggested Classification of Utterances Admissible as Res gestae" (1922) 31 Yale L.J. 229.

declarant being "emotionally overpowered" and now emphasises the declarant's response to the situation and is closer to the "excited utterance" exception to the US rules on hearsay which talks of,

statement relating to a startling event or condition made while the declarant was under the stress of excitement caused by the event or condition.[24]

The 2003 Act reflects the state of current authorities. *Teper*[25] was an early case in which the defendant was charged with the arson of a shop belonging to his wife. A police officer testified that he heard an unidentified woman say to a passing motorist, "Your place burning and you going away from the fire". The officer also testified that the driver resembled the accused. It was introduced to rebut a defence of alibi. But the alleged identification took place nearly 30 minutes after the fire started.

Teper [1952] A.C. 480 at 486–487, *per* Lord Normand:

The rule against the admission of hearsay is fundamental. It is not the best evidence and it is not delivered on oath. The truthfulness and accuracy of the person whose words are spoken to by another witness cannot be tested by cross-examination, and the light which his demeanour would throw on his testimony is lost. Nevertheless, the rule admits of certain carefully safeguarded and limited exceptions, one of which is that the words may be proved when they form part of the res gestae..[This exception] appears to rest ultimately on two propositions—that human utterance is both a fact and a means of communication, and that human action may be so interwoven with words that the significance of the action cannot be understood without the correlative words and the dissociation of the words from the action would impede the discovery of truth. But the judicial application of these two propositions, which do not always combine harmoniously, have never been precisely formulated as a general principles. Their Lordships will not attempt to arrive at a general formula, nor is it necessary to review all of the considerable number of cases cited in the argument. This, at least, may be said, that it is essential that the words sought to be proved by hearsay should be, if not absolutely contemporaneous with the action or event, at least so clearly associated with it, in time, place and circumstance, that they are part of the thing being done, and so an item of real evidence and not merely a reported statement . . . . How slight a separation of time and place may suffice to make hearsay evidence of the words spoken incompetent is well illustrated . . . . In [*O'Hara v Central Scottish Motor Traction Co Ltd*[26]], a civil action, the event was an injury to a passenger brought about by the sudden swerve of the omnibus in which she was travelling. The driver of the omnibus said in his evidence that he was forced to swerve by a pedestrian who hurried across his path. Hearsay evidence of what was said by the man on the pavement at the scene of the accident as soon as the injured party had been attended to was held to be admissible in corroboration of the driver's evidence. But what was said twelve minutes later and away from the scene by the same man was held not to be part of the res gestae . . . . In *R v Gibson*[27] the prosecutor gave evidence in a criminal

---

[24] Federal Rules of Evidence, r.804.
[25] [1952] A.C. 480.
[26] 1941 S.C. 363.
[27] (1887) 18 QBD 537.

trial that, immediately after he was struck by a stone, a woman going past, pointing to the prisoner's door, said: 'The person who threw the stone went in there.' This evidence was not objected to at the trial, but it was admitted by counsel for the prosecution in a Case Reserved that the evidence was incompetent. The conviction was quashed, and from their judgments it is clear that the learned judges who took part in the decision were far from questioning the correctness of counsel's admission. In *Gibson's* case the words were closely associated in time and place with the event, the assault. But they were not directly connected with that event itself. They were not words spontaneously forced from the woman by the sight of the assault but were prompted by the sight of a man quitting the scene of an assault and they were spoken for purpose of helping to bring him to justice . . .

These strict criteria in *Teper* were relaxed in *Ratten*,[28] in which the telephone operator took a call from the house at 1:15p.m. It was made by an hysterical woman, the accused's wife, asking for the police. By 1:20p.m, the wife was dead. As discussed in the previous chapter, Lord Wilberforce argued that the statement "Get me the police, please" could be interpreted as direct evidence of the speaker's state of mind but went on to consider whether the statement was also part of the *res gestae*. The strict *Bedingfield* approach to contemporaneity would have undoubtedly led to the exclusion of the evidence. But the Privy Council held that the statement was made under the overwhelming pressure of the situation and thus admissible as an exception to hearsay. The approach was not purely technical in the sense of lapse of time or change of venue. Although these were factors, they were not decisive. The judge must be satisfied that the statement was made in circumstances of spontaneity or of involvement so that the possibility of concoction could be disregarded.

In the first part of his judgment, Lord Wilberforce concluded that there was no hearsay element in the evidence at all but continued, in the second part, to deal with the appellant's submission on the assumption that there was. The Crown defended the admissibility of the words as part of the *res gestae*.

Ratten [1971] 3 All E.R. 801 at 806b–809e, *per* Lord Wilberforce:

The expression 'res gestae' like many Latin phrases, is often used to cover situations insufficiently analysed in clear English terms. In the context of the law of evidence it may be used in at least three different ways:

1. When a situation of fact (e.g. a killing) is being considered, the question may arise when does the situation begin and when does it end. It may be arbitrary and artificial to confine the evidence to the firing of the gun or the insertion of the knife, without knowing in a broader sense what was happening. Thus in *O'Leary v R*[29] evidence was admitted of assaults, prior to the killing, committed by the accused during what was said to be a continuous orgy. As Dixon J. said,[30]

> Without evidence of what, during that time, was done by those men who took any significant part in the matter and especially evidence of the behaviour of the prisoner, the transaction of which the alleged murder formed an integral part

---

[28] [1971] 3 All E.R. 801.
[29] (1946) 73 C.L.R. 566.
[30] *ibid.* at 577.

could not be truly understood and, isolated from it, could only be presented as an unreal and not very intelligible event.

2. The evidence may be concerned with spoken words as such (apart from the truth of what they convey). The words are then themselves the res gestae or part of the res gestae, i.e. are the relevant facts or part of them.

3. A hearsay statement is made either by the victim of an attack or by a bystander—indicating directly or indirectly the identity of the attacker. The admissibility of the statement is then said to depend on whether it was made as part of the *res gestae*. A classical instance of this is the much debated case of *R v Bedingfield* and there are other instances of its application in reported cases. These tend to apply different standards, and some of them carry less than conviction. The reason, why this is so, is that concentration tends to be focused upon the opaque or at least imprecise Latin phrase rather than upon the basic reason for excluding the type of evidence which this group of cases is concerned with. There is no doubt what this reason is: it is twofold, the first is that there may be uncertainty as to the exact words used because of their transmission through the evidence of another person than the speaker. The second is because of the risk of concoction of false evidence by persons who have been victims of assault or accident. The first matter goes to weight. The person testifying to the words used is liable to cross-examination: the accused person (as he could not at the time when earlier reported cases were decided) can give his own account if different. There is no such difference in kind or substance between evidence of what was said and evidence of what was done (for example, between evidence of what the victim said as to an attack and evidence that he (or she) was seen in a terrified state or was heard to shriek) as to require a total rejection of one and admission of the other.

The possibility of concoction, or fabrication, where it exists, is on the other hand an entirely valid reason for exclusion, and is probably the real test which judges in fact apply. In their Lordships' opinion this should be recognised and applied directly as the relevant test: the test should be not the uncertain one whether the making of the statement was in some sense part of the event or transaction. This may often be difficult to establish: such external matters as the time which elapses between the events and the speaking of the words (or vice versa), and differences in location being relevant factors but not, taken by themselves, decisive criteria. As regards statements made after the event it must be for the judge, by preliminary ruling, to satisfy himself that the statement was so clearly made in circumstances of spontaneity or involvement in the event that the possibility of concoction can be disregarded. Conversely, if he considers that the statement was made by way of narrative of a detached prior event so that the speaker was so disengaged from it as to be able to construct or adapt his account, he should exclude it. And the same must in principle be true of statements made before the event. The test should be not the uncertain one, whether the making of the statement should be regarded as part of the event or transaction. This may often be difficult to show. But if the drama, leading up to the climax, has commenced and assumed such intensity and pressure that the utterance can be safely regarded as a true reflection of what was unrolling or actually happening, it ought to be received. The expression 'res gestae' may conveniently sum up these criteria, but the reality of them must always be kept in mind: it is this that lies behind the best reasoned of the judges' rulings.

. . . The authorities show that there is ample support for the principle that hearsay evidence may be admitted if the statement providing it is made in such conditions (always being those of approximate but not exact contemporaneity) or involvement or pressure as to exclude the possibility of concoction or distortion to the advantage of the maker or the disadvantage of the accused.

. . . In the present case, in their Lordships' judgment, here was ample evidence of the close and intimate connection between the statement ascribed to the deceased and the shooting which occurred very shortly afterwards. They were closely associated in place and time. The way in which the statement came to be made (in a call for the police) and the tone of voice used, showed intrinsically that the statement was being forced from the deceased by an overwhelming pressure of contemporary event. It carried its own stamp of spontaneity and this was endorsed by the proved time sequence and the proved proximity of the deceased to the accused with his gun. Even on the assumption that there was an element of hearsay in the words used, they were safely admitted. The jury was, additionally, directed with great care as to the use to which they might be put. On all counts, therefore, their Lordships can find no error of law in the admission of the evidence . . .

Lord Wilberforce's judgment was accepted by the House of Lords in *Andrews*,[31] where the victim was attacked and stabbed in his own flat by two men. One pleaded guilty to manslaughter and testified against Andrews. As his testimony was that of an accomplice, at that time corroborating evidence was required. Andrews' possession of the victim's video, his lies to the police and the existence of forensic evidence made it a strong case. But the Crown also sought to use the victim's statements, after he had crawled to the neighbouring flat, at which point he identified his attackers. In the House of Lords, Lord Ackner quoted at length from *Ratten* and continued,

Andrews [1987] 1 All E.R. 513 at 519–521, *per* Lord Ackner:

Counsel for the appellant submitted . . . that a hearsay statement cannot be admitted under the doctrine if made after the criminal act or acts charged have ceased. He contended that the hearsay statement must form part of the criminal act for which the accused is being tried. He relied strongly on *R v Bedingfield* . . . . [That] exclamation was not admitted by Cockburn CJ because 'It was something stated by her after it was all over, whatever it was, and after the act was completed'. Counsel for the appellant submits that the decision in Ratten's case involved an extension of the existing hearsay rule and so was in conflict with the ruling of the majority in your Lordships' House in *Myers v DPP*[32] that it is now too late to add a further exception to the rule against hearsay otherwise than by legislation. This submission is not assisted by the fact that both Lord Reid and Lord Hodgson, who were party to the majority decision in the *Myers* case, were also members of the Board in the *Ratten* case.

I do not accept that the principles identified by Lord Wilberforce involved any extension to the exception to the hearsay rule. Lord Wilberforce clarified the basis of the res gestae exception and isolated the matters which the trial judge, by preliminary ruling, must satisfy himself before admitting the statement. I respectfully accept the accuracy and the value of this clarification. Thus it must, of course, follow that *R v Bedingfield* would not be so decided today. Indeed, there could, as Lord Wilberforce observed, hardly be a case where the words uttered carried more clearly the mark of spontaneity and intense involvement.

My Lords, may I therefore summarise the position which confronts the trial judge when faced in a criminal case with an application under the res gestae doctrine to admit evidence of statements, with a view to establishing the truth of some fact thus narrated, such evidence being truly categorised as 'hearsay evidence'.

1) The primary question which the judge must ask himself is: can the possibility of concoction or distortion be disregarded?

2) To answer that question the judge must first consider the circumstances in which the particular statement was made, in order to satisfy himself that the event was so

[31] [1987] 1 All E.R. 513.
[32] [1964] 2 All E.R. 881.

unusual or startling or dramatic as to dominate the thoughts of the victim, so that his utterance was an instinctive reaction to that event, thus giving no real opportunity for reasoned reflection. In such a situation the judge would be entitled to conclude that the involvement or the pressure of the event would exclude the possibility of concoction or distortion, providing that the statement was made in conditions of approximate but not exact contemporaneity.

3) In order for the statement to be sufficiently 'spontaneous' it must be so closely associated with the event which has excited the statement that it can fairly stated that the mind of the declarant was still dominated by the event. Thus the judge must be satisfied that the event which provided the trigger mechanism for the statement was still operative. The fact that the statement was made in answer to a question is but one factor to consider under this heading.

4) Quite apart from the time factor, there may be special features in the case, which relate to the possibility of concoction or distortion. In this instant appeal the defence relied on evidence to support the contention that the deceased had a motive of his own to fabricate or concoct, namely a malice which resided in him against [the accomplice] and the appellant because, so he believed, [the accomplice] had attacked and damaged his house and was accompanied by the appellant, who ran away, on a previous occasion. The judge must be satisfied that the circumstances were such that, having regard to the special feature of malice, there was no possibility of any concoction or distortion to the advantage of the maker or the disadvantage of the accused.

5) As to the possibility of error in the facts narrated in the statement, if only the ordinary fallibility of human recollection is relied on, this goes to the weight to be attached to and not the admissibility of the statement and is therefore a matter for the jury. However here again there may be special features that may give rise to the possibility of error. In the instant case there was evidence that the deceased had drunk to excess, well over double the permitted limit for driving a motor car. Another example would be where the identification was made in circumstances of particular difficulty or where the declarant suffered from defective eyesight. In such circumstances the trial judge must consider whether he can exclude the possibility of error.

. . . Where the trial judge has properly directed himself as to the correct approach to the evidence and there is material to entitle him to reach the conclusions which he did reach, then his decision is final, in the sense that it will not be interfered with on appeal . . . .

The Law Commission accepted that these authorities create a five stage test.

Law Commission: Evidence in Criminal Proceedings: Hearsay and Related Topics (Report No.245, Cm.3670 1997) para.8.117:

(1) Can the possibility of concoction or distortion be disregarded?

(2) To answer this, ask if the event was so unusual, startling or dramatic that it dominated the thoughts of the victim causing an instinctive reaction without the chance for reasoned reflection, in conditions of approximate, but not necessarily exact, contemporaneity.

(3) To be sufficiently spontaneous the statement must be closely connected with the event causing it.

(4) There must be no special features making concoction or distortion likely.

(5) There must be no special features likely to result in error, for example, drunkenness.

It is not just the common law conditions about place and time that have been relaxed. Lord Normand was clear in *Teper* that the words should be connected with the criminal act itself. The reported cases mainly deal with identification of the accused after the event is over. But the Court of Appeal decisions such as *Carnall*[33] as well as the Privy Council in *Mills*[34] treat *Andrews* as authoritative. Section 118 contains no limitations on the content of the statement.

The *res gestae* doctrine cannot be used as an excuse for failing to call a witness who should have been called. In *Tobi v Nicholas*,[35] the accused was convicted of drink-driving and failing to stop after an accident. He was identified when, 20 minutes after the accident, a police constable took the other driver to the defendant's home nearby where a damaged car was parked. When the defendant answered the door, the witness said 'That's the guy'. The police office cannot take the place of the witness and testify as to what was said.

B. *Statements accompanying relevant acts*

Where a statement is made by a person performing an act and the statement contributes to an understanding of the action, the statement is admissible to prove the truth of its contents. The brevity and simplicity of the Cross formulation has been replaced in s.118 by ''. . . the statement accompanied an act which can be properly evaluated as evidence only if considered in conjunction with the statement''. But both imply that the act itself has to be admissible evidence before the statement is admitted to clarify and explain the act. The authorities suggest that the required conditions are:

 i) that the statement relates to the act in question;
 ii) that it is more or less contemporaneous with the act—

> '. . . a contemporaneous declaration may be admissible as part of a trans-action, but an act done cannot be varied or qualified by insulated declarations made at a later time.[36]

 iii) that it is made by the person who is performing the act. In *Howe v Malkin*,[37] the issue was the position of a boundary. During the claimant's father's lifetime, work had been carried out on the land by builders and the claimant sought to prove statements made by his father at that time. Even though the builders' actions might be said to be vicariously those of the person who employed them, this evidence was rejected. Grove J. said,

Howe v Malkin (1878) 40 L.T. 196, *per* Grove L.J.:

> It appears to me that the evidence was properly rejected; no act was shown to have been done by the plaintiff's father at the time of making the alleged

---

[33] [1995] Crim.L.R. 944.
[34] [1995] Crim.L.R. 884.
[35] [1987] Crim.L.R. 774.
[36] *Peacock v Harris* (1836) 5 Ad. & El. 449 at 454, *per* Lord Denman.
[37] (1878) 40 L.T. 196.

statement, so that the declaration was by one person, and the accompanying act by another. That does not appear to me to come within the rule. The rule is that, though you cannot give in evidence a declaration per se, yet when there is an act accompanied by a statement which is so mixed up with it as to become part of the res gestae, evidence of such statements may be given. The statements here do not come fairly within that rule.

The scope of this exception is potentially very broad. What must the nature of an act be to justify the statements accompanying it being admitted as evidence? One approach would be to require that the act itself possesses sufficient probative value to be relevant and admissible evidence before the statements are introduced to enhance that probative value. But the authorities seek to expand these limits. In *Davidson v Quirke*,[38] the accused was charged with using premises for the purposes of betting and evidence was given by police officers of a number of phone calls to the premises from people seeking to place bets.

Davidson v Quirke [1923] N.Z.L.R. 552 at 556, *per* Salmond J.:

If the testimony of the police officers was limited to the mere fact that on the day in question a large number of persons rang up the appellant's house within the space of an hour and twenty-five minutes, all evidence as to the contents of the communications being excluded, such testimony would prove merely that the premises were being used for a business of some kind, but would fall short of proving that they were being used for the business of betting. I am of opinion that, notwithstanding the general rule which excludes evidence of statements, the contents of those telephone messages as received and testified to by the police officers are legally admissible in evidence. This is an illustration of the principle that, notwithstanding the rule against hearsay, where the purpose or meaning of an act done is relevant, evidence of contemporaneous declarations accompanying and explaining the act is admissible in proof of such purpose or meaning . . . since the act of numerous strangers in using the appellant's telephone for the purpose of betting is relevant to the issue, the statements made by them at the same time are admissible as explaining their actions and showing the purpose of them.

In *McGregor v Stokes*,[39] the facts were similar to *Davidson v Quirke*.

McGregor v Stokes [1952] V.L.R. 347 at 350–351, *per* Herring C.J.:

What the caller had to say in each case was an utterance that accompanied his act of calling, and also explained his purpose in calling. Without the words his act taken as a whole was incomplete. The fact that he has called on the telephone by itself tells you no more than that he has made the call and the making of the call unexplained is an

---

[38] [1923] N.Z.L.R. 552.
[39] [1952] V.L.R. 347.

equivocal act. Till you know what he has to say, you cannot tell whether he has rung up to ask the occupant about a dog or to invite him to dinner or what his purpose was. And so it is in the case of many things we do that our acts are partly conducted and partly utterance. A man walks into a shop for example, but the significance of his visit cannot be ascertained until he states his business. The learned author of Wigmore on Evidence has this to say about utterances that form a verbal part of an act:- 'A second kind of situation in which utterances are not offered testimonially arises when the utterance accompanies conduct to which it is desired to attach some legal effect. The conduct or act has intrinsically no definite significance, or only an ambiguous one, and its whole purport or tenor is to be more precisely ascertained by considering the words accompanying it. The utterance thus enters merely as a verbal part of the act, or, in common phrase, a 'verbal act' . . .'

These authorities were used by Lord Browne-Wilkinson in *Kearley*,[40] to suggest that the statements of the telephone callers were admissible as 'verbal acts',

Kearley [1992] 2 All E.R 345 at 386, *per* Lord Browne-Wilkinson:

One of the classic examples of evidence which does not fall within the hearsay rule is a statement by a third party accompanying and explaining his acts, sometimes called verbal acts. Such evidence is admitted not to prove the truth of what the third party said but to explain the acts of the third party.

Were this analysis to be accepted, the hearsay rule would cease to exist since the "acts" of making a telephone call or calling at a house would suffice to permit the statements explaining the act to be given in evidence. Yet the fact that the telephone rang is not by itself admissible evidence as it has neither relevance nor probative value to any fact in issue. The correct principle is found in the Manchester Brewery case where a brewery sued a publican for the latter's breach of an undertaking to buy all his beer from the brewery. The defence was that the beer supplied was not of acceptable quality and part of the evidence concerned complaints from customers who had not been called as witnesses. Statements from absent customers were admitted to prove the poor quality of the beer.

Manchester Brewery (1900) 82 L.T. 347 at 349, *per* Farwell J.:

. . . Counsel can certainly ask as to the facts—Did the customer order beer? Did he finish it? What did he do with it? If the matter is left there with the answer that he tasted and left it or threw it away, the judge cannot avoid drawing an inference, and the cross-examining counsel is driven to ask for some explanation. It is simpler, therefore, to allow the statement of the customer of the reason for his conduct to be given in chief.[41]

---

[40] [1992] 2 All E.R. 345.
[41] (1900) 82 L.T. 347 at 349, *per* Farwell J.

Here the landlord could testify to what he saw—the act of customers tasting their pints and then leaving them unfinished on the bar. This act (unlike a telephone call) is in itself relevant and probative. The accompanying statement ("what a dreadful pint") is admissible to clarify and explain an already admissible act.

C. *Statements concerning physical sensation*

Statements by the declarant concerning both physical sensation and mental state are admissible under s.118(1) 4(c). Where a person makes a statement about their contemporaneous physical feelings, that statement is admissible evidence of that fact—pain,[42] disgust,[43] fear[44] may all be proved under this exception. Declarations of hunger by a child may be admissible in a case involving child neglect.[45] But the admissibility is limited to the physical sensation itself and cannot be used collaterally to prove, for example, the cause of such feelings. Statements by a child to a teacher and a foster parent about sexual abuse by a close family relative may be admissible as to the fact of abuse; they have no probative weight as to the identity of the abuser.[46] In *Gloster*,[47] the deceased was the victim of an illegal abortion. The prosecution sought to introduce statements by the deceased not only as to how she was feeling but as to the fact of the abortion and as to who had performed it. Charles J. also held that the "admissible statements were to be confined to contemporaneous symptoms". The authorities show that "contemporaneous" is to be interpreted to include the recent past.

D. *Statements concerning the maker's state of mind*

Statements detailing a physical sensation are analogous to those detailing an emotion or a belief. Indeed these categories obviously overlap. Is a feeling of disgust a physical feeling or a state of mind? Where a person makes a statement that reveals a mental state, this is admissible as part of the *res gestae*. This permits statements which reveal the speaker's emotions,[48] knowledge, beliefs[49] or intentions. Lies or delusions do not come under this heading since these are provable as original, non-hearsay, evidence since the statements would not be relied on for the truth of their contents but for the reverse!

[42] *Aveson v Lord Kinnaird* (1805) 6 East 188; *Gilbey v Great Western Railway Co.* (1910) 102 L.T. 202.
[43] *Gott* (1922) 16 Cr.App.R. 87.
[44] *Vincent* (1840) 9 C. & P. 275.
[45] *Conde* (1867) 10 Cox 547.
[46] *K* (1989) 139 N.L.J. 864.
[47] (1888) 16 Cox 471.
[48] Such as fear (*Neil v North Antrim Magistrates' Court* [1992] 4 All E.R. 846 at 854) or marital affection (*Trelawney v Coleman* (1817) 1 B. & Ald. 90).
[49] See statements admitted to prove political opinion—*Tooke* (1794) 25 State Tr. 344.

Ratten again provides a useful example. Even were the wife's plea for help not spontaneous (and as such admissible under the first category of *res gestae*), her agitation and fear were in themselves relevant facts since they tend to disprove the defence argument of accident. Not only her tone of voice but also her words could be adduced as evidence of that state of mind. But are we dealing with an exception to hearsay or with original evidence here?[50] If the state of mind (or a physical sensation) is a fact relevant to a fact in issue, are statements which reveal that emotion, being relied on for their truth or because they are in themselves the manifestation of that inner state?

The statement is adduced to prove the state of mind. In handling stolen goods, the Crown must show that the goods were stolen and that the accused "knew or believed" the goods to be stolen. If the defendant were to answer the question "Where did the goods come from?" with the statement "Oh, they fell off the back of a lorry", this would be admissible to prove a belief that the goods were stolen. But it does not prove that the goods were in fact stolen and the burden of proof remains on the Crown to show this.[51] Analogously, in *Thomas v Connell*,[52] it was alleged that a bankrupt made a payment to one creditor in order to defraud others. It was necessary to show that he was aware of his financial state at that time in order to prove the fraud. While the statement he made at the time of the payment was admissible to show his knowledge, that statement could not be used to prove the fact of insolvency itself.

The issue is whether the state of mind is relevant. In *Ratten*, the fact that the victim was upset was relevant as it tended to disprove the defence of accident. In *Kearley*, the majority felt that the statements proved the state of mind of the callers which had no relevance to whether the defendant had an intent to supply—the minority felt that their state of mind did have relevance to whether the premises were being used to supply drugs. In *Blastland*, the accused was charged with the murder of a young boy. The defence was that another person, Mark, was the killer—he confessed to the killing but withdrew the confession. Mark had shown knowledge about the murder before the discovery of the body and had been in a very agitated state at that time. Under this exception, Mark's statements are admissible to prove his knowledge of the killing but the House of Lords held that Mark's state of mind was not relevant.

Blastland [1985] 2 All E.R 1095 at 1099, *per* Lord Bridge:

. . . statements made to a witness by a third party are not excluded by the hearsay rule when they are put in evidence solely to prove the state of mind either of the maker of the statement or the person to whom it was made. What a person said or

---

[50] P. Carter, "Hearsay: Whether and Whither?" (1993) L.Q.R. 573 at 585.
[51] *Hulbert* (1979) 69 Cr.App.R. 243; *Overington* [1978] Crim.L.R. 692; *McDonald* [1980] Crim.L.R. 242.
[52] (1838) 3 M. & W. 267.

heard said may well be the best and most direct evidence of that person's state of mind. This principle can only apply, however, when the state of mind evidenced by the statement is either itself directly in issue at the trial or is of direct and immediate relevance to the issues which arise at the trial.

Their Lordships felt that there were many different ways that Mark could have come by his knowledge and that admitting the statement would give rise to collateral issues. But the key fact in issue was whether Blastland caused the death of the victim. Mark's early knowledge of the killing was a circumstance which rendered that conclusion less probable and thus was relevant under normal rules.

In criminal law, the prosecution always bears the burden of proving *mens rea*. Although intent is often inferred from the offence itself, statements by the accused that they intend to commit an offence are admissible. In *Moghal*,[53] the defendant was jointly accused of murder with his lover, S. She was tried separately and acquitted. His defence was that he was a terrified spectator and it was accepted by the Court of Appeal that a tape-recorded statement made six months previously by S to the effect that she intended to kill the victim was admissible. Not only are such statements admissible but such a declaration can be used as evidence that she still possessed the intent to kill six months later.[54]

It is more controversial whether it is justifiable to infer from a declaration of intent that the intended action was in fact carried out. In *Buckley*,[55] the accused was charged with the murder of a police officer. The victim had told his superior officer that he had heard that Buckley was "at his old game of thieving again" and that "he intended to watch his movements that night". The statement was admitted as evidence, not merely of the officer's state of mind but from which the inference could be drawn that the officer in fact acted in this way and thus provided opportunity and motive for the accused. As such, the state of mind becomes relevant to an issue and furthermore any inferences possess greater weight because the statement was made by the police officer to a senior officer in the course of his duty.

No such obligation existed in *Wainwright*.[56] The statement by the victim of a killing that she was going to pay a social visit to the accused's premises was held by Cockburn C.J. to be inadmissible.

It was no part of the act of leaving, but only an incidental remark. It was only a statement of intention which may or may not have been carried out. She would have gone away under any circumstance.[57]

A similar conclusion was reached in *Thomson*.[58] The defendant was charged with procuring an abortion on a woman who had subsequently died. The defence was that the victim operated on herself and sought to introduce a

[53] (1977) 65 Cr.App.R. 56.
[54] Or indeed, a month earlier—*Re Fletcher, Reading v Fletcher* [1917] 1 Ch. 339.
[55] (1873) 13 Cox 293—a first instance case.
[56] (1875) 13 Cox 171.
[57] *ibid*, at 172.
[58] [1912] 3 K.B. 19.

witness to testify that the victim had stated that she intended to operate on herself and a later statement that she had indeed carried out the operation. The later statement was more clearly hearsay but both were excluded.

These authorities suggest, however weakly, that declarations of intention, while evidence of *mens rea*, cannot be used as evidence that the act was actually performed. The opposite is the case in Australia where in *Walton*[59], a husband was charged with the murder of his wife and a witness was permitted to testify that the victim received a phone call and announced that she was going to meet her husband in the town centre. Similarly in *Mutual Life Insurance v Hillmon*,[60] the insurance company contested a claim on a life insurance policy taken out on the life of Hillmon. A body had been found in Colorado, alleged to be Hillmon. The insurers sought to introduce letters written by one Walters which stated his intention of accompanying Hillmon on the trip. The US Supreme Court admitted the letters as evidence of Walters' intentions, from which, presumably, the jury might draw appropriate inferences.

These limitations in cases such as *Thomson* have been resolved by the passage of s.116 of the Criminal Justice Act 2003 whereby first hand oral hearsay is admissible—for example, in 2005, Michael Morton was convicted of the manslaughter of his wife, whose body had never been found. The marriage had broken down and the couple had already separated. On the day of her disappearance, his wife had told her solicitor she planned to meet her husband to discuss their child's schooling. This statement was admitted. From this, the jury could validly infer that a meeting in fact took place, an item of evidence that could then be considered in the light of the other evidence in the case.[61]

VII. Confessions

Confessions in criminal proceedings will be admissible as long as the circumstances in which the statement was made conform to the conditions in ss.76, 76A and 78 of the Police and Criminal Evidence Act 1984.[62]

VIII. Informal Admissions and Admissions by Agents

Admissions are representations of fact, made in words or by conduct, by a party or another, adverse to his or her own case. At common law such statements were generally admissible as evidence of the truth of what they contain. In English law, the whole statement is admissible as proof of its contents. The major effect of such a statement is to admit a fact which is against the interest of the declarant. But the statement might also include

---

[59] (1989) 84 A.L.R. 59.
[60] (1892) 145 U.S. 284.
[61] For a report of the trial, see *Guardian*, August 2, 2005.
[62] see Ch.4.

some material which advances the declarant's case. Under the rule in *Sharp*,[63] the whole statement is put into evidence, including the self-serving aspects.

A. *Rationale*

The rationale of this rule is that the statement is likely to be reliable as parties are unlikely to make statements against their own interests but the theoretical basis for admissions is still debated.

I. Scott, "Reception in Evidence of Unreliable Admissions" [1981] Crim.L.R. 285 at 286–287:

Professor Wigmore took the view that admissions are not hearsay because they are not affirmative proof but operate only destructively to shake the admitting party's case just as prior inconsistent statements of a witness may be introduced to shake his testimony.[64] Professor Morgan strongly advanced the view[65] that admissions could be received for the purpose of proving the truth of their contents (that is, as affirmative evidence) and this opinion has prevailed in the United States.

There is no question that, in England, evidence of relevant admissions may be received . . . . The acceptance . . . of the Morgan approach to admissions may be seen, as it operates in criminal cases, as yet another illustration of the subtle ways in which the rules of evidence may be developed in a manner which weakens the impact of rules relating to the allocation of the burdens of proof and the various manifestations of the privilege against self-incrimination.

Although the 'admissions exception' to the hearsay rule is now well-established on both sides of the Atlantic, in both civil and criminal cases, attempts to construct a satisfactory theory or doctrinal basis for it have produced considerable disagreement amongst judges and legal writers. And it seems that this controversy, together with the uncertainties which necessarily existed before the exception became universally accepted and which have tended to linger in the minds of lawyers, has created doubts about the precise legal rules which govern the circumstances in which admissions may be received and the evidential weight to be given to them. It has been said that admissions are an anomalous exception to the hearsay rule because this exception admits statements 'that do not in theory carry some special guarantee of reliability or provide some extra test of [the] declarant's credibility'. On the other hand it has been argued that, though hearsay, the reception of informal admissions is justified by the fact that the person against whom an admission is introduced, being a party to the proceedings and interested in weakening the effect of the statement, may deny it or explain it in court. Further, it has been said that admissions will usually be against the party's interest when made and therefore more likely to be true because citizens do not lightly make statements that tend to be self-disserving . . .

Professor Morgan thought it was fruitless to search for a satisfactory explanation of the admissions exception based on factors that gave special reliability to admissions sufficient to allay our usual fears about hearsay. He preferred to say that the

---

[63] [1988] 1 All E.R. 65.
[64] Wigmore on *Evidence* (1904), para.1048.
[65] E. Morgan, "Admissions as an Exception to the Hearsay Rule" (1921) 30 Yale L.J. 355.

explanation for the exception lay in 'the adversary theory of litigation' and thought it 'too obvious for comment' that a party whose statements are offered against him is in no position to object, as he may be when other forms of admissible hearsay are offered against him, that he did not have an opportunity to cross-examine the declarant or that the statement was not made on oath. Therefore admissions are free from the main objections to hearsay testimony. Professor Morgan put his point more strikingly when he wrote[66] that a party can hardly say 'that he is unworthy of credence save when speaking under sanction of oath'.[67]

B. *Formal admissions*

Informal admissions must be distinguished from formal admissions which may be made to save an opposing party time and trouble.

i) In civil cases, a fact may be formally admitted in a variety of ways—this can be done in the pleadings, in response to a notice to admit facts under CPR r.32.18 or by letter[68] There can also be formal admissions during pre-trial hearings or at the trial itself.

ii) In criminal cases, parties can make formal admissions under the conditions laid down in s.10 of the Criminal Justice Act 1967. Normally such an admission will be in writing but it can be made orally by counsel in court.[69]

The facts in a formal admission need not be proved and evidence to contradict them is not admissible

C. *Informal admissions*

In contrast, informal admissions are not conclusive and parties can lead evidence to rebut them. In criminal cases, the common law is no longer relevant as the conditions for the admissibility of confessions are laid down by s.76 of the Police and Criminal Evidence Act 1984.[70] In civil matters, the old common law rules on admissions were retained under s.9 of the Civil Evidence Act 1968. But the Law Commission considered that admissions should be treated similarly to other hearsay statements and differently from other common law exceptions.

Law Commission, The Hearsay Rule in Civil Proceedings (Cm 2321 1993) para.4.33:

So far as the notice and weighting provisions are concerned, adverse admissions are in a different category from the other exceptions and it is clearly necessary that the

---

[66] E. Morgan, *Basic Problems of Evidence* (1962) 266.
[67] I. Scott, "Reception in Evidence of Unreliable Admissions" [1981] Crim.L.R. 285 at 286–287.
[68] *Ellis v Allen* [1914] 1 Ch. 904.
[69] *Lewis* [1989] Crim.L.R. 61.
[70] see Ch.4.

same provisions need to apply to these as apply to other hearsay statements. By contrast, in the case of published works dealing with matters of a public nature, and public documents and records, it will be rare for the weight to be attached to such evidence to be a matter for debate. Moreover, we are preserving the common law rules concerning public registers, and it is not our policy to add procedural burdens where none exist at present. We have therefore concluded that the notice and weighting provisions should not apply to these cases.

As a result of s.7(1) of the 1995 Act, the common law basis of admissibility has been removed so informal admissions are now admissible only as a result of s.1(1) of the Act which provides that evidence shall not be excluded on the grounds that it is hearsay.

Whether a statement constitutes an informal admission is no longer of any relevance in civil proceedings but aspects of the common law might still be applicable in criminal proceedings where a confession is defined in s.82 of the Police and Criminal Evidence Act 1984.[71] Inferences adverse to a party's case might be drawn from their words or their conduct, express or implied.[72] Such inferences might be drawn from lies,[73] from reactions to accusation[74] or from silence.[75]

In criminal proceedings, the weight to be attached to a confession will be assessed by the trier of fact according to such factors as the circumstances in which it was made, its contents and its consistency with other evidence. In civil cases, s.4 of the 1995 Act mentions specific considerations to be taken into account. These include whether the original statement was made contemporaneously with the occurrence or existence of the matters stated, whether the evidence involves multiple hearsay, whether any person involved had any motive to conceal or misrepresent matters or whether the original statement was an edited account, or was made in collaboration with another or for a particular purpose.

D. *Non-party admissions*

At common law, admissions did not need to be made by the party to the proceedings so long as the person who makes the admission was in some form of privity with the party. In criminal proceedings, such admissions are no longer admissible unless they are expressly preserved by s.118 of the Criminal Justice Act 2003. Under s.118(1) 6, they may be admissible against the defendant:

    a) where the admission is made by an agent of the defendant, it is admissible against the defendant as evidence of any matter stated. Common law authorities suggest that there must be an existing

---

[71] see Ch.4.
[72] *Moriarty v London Chatham and Dover Railway* (1870) L.R. 5 Q.B. 314.
[73] *Lucas* [1981] 2 All E.R. 1008—for discussion of the *Lucas* direction, see Ch.11.
[74] *Christie* [1914] A.C. 545.
[75] *Bessela v Stern* (1877) 46 L.J.C.P. 467; *Wiedemann v Walpole* [1891] 60 L.J. Q.B. 762.

relationship of principal and agent,[76] the agent must be acting in the course of employment[77] and within the scope of their authority when the admission is made.[78] This can be seen to have greater probative value in evidence against the principal if the agent was authorised to make the statement and the statement was made to a third party and not to the principal.

b) where a statement is made by a person to whom a defendant refers a person for information, is admissible against the defendant as evidence of any matter stated. Here there is express or implied authority: in *Williams v Innes*,[79] the defendants were executors of an estate and referred the claimant to a third party for information concerning the estate. It was held that they were bound by the statements of the third party. "If a man refers another upon any particular business to a third person, he is bound by what this third person says or does concerning it, as much as if that had been said or done by himself".[80]

These are the only situations where such statements are admissible against a defendant in criminal proceedings. However, in civil proceedings under the 1995 legislation, many more such "non-party" admissions will be admissible, even if there is no privity or agency. The weight that is attached to such a statement may well be greater where there is agency or where express or implied authority has been given. It may also be greater where privity exists: predecessors in title, partners, and trustees might all be seen to be in "privity" with the party. There is no exhaustive definition but it requires some identity of interest in the property or obligation.

The major exception at common law to this rule about the admissibility of vicarious admissions is that there is no privity between spouses or between parents and children just because of their familial relationship. In civil cases, such statements are straightforwardly admissible under s.1 of the 1995 Act—if the wife made an admission concerning the joint ownership of the family home, that statement would be admissible against the husband and the issue would be one of weight. In criminal proceedings, if a spouse or other family member made a statement incriminating the accused, it would need to be admissible under s.114 of the 2003 Act.

IX. COMMON ENTERPRISE

Normally statements by one accused are not admissible against another. But at common law, acts done or declarations made in furtherance of a conspiracy

---

[76] *Peto v Hague* (1804) 5 Esp. 134—Lord Ellenborough said that what an agent said about former transactions (prior to his becoming an agent) would not be admissible evidence against his master.

[77] *Burr v Ware Rural District Council* [1939] 2 All E.R. 688.

[78] *Kirkstall Brewery v Furness Rly* (1874) 43 L.J.Q.B. 142.

[79] (1808) 1 Camp. 364.

[80] *ibid.* at 365 *per* Lord Ellenborough C.J.

or joint enterprise are admissible against all parties to the conspiracy, so long as the existence of the conspiracy has been proved by other evidence.[81] Thus a statement by a party to a common enterprise is admissible evidence against any other party to that enterprise, as long as the accused as charged with conspiracy or the joint commission of offences.[82] This amounts to an exception to hearsay. In *Devonport and Pirano*, the court found,

Devonport and Pirano [1996] 1 Cr.App.R. 221 at 225–226, *per* Judge J.:

Our attention was then drawn to a much more recent case *R v Donat*.[83] In that case documents were found in the possession of a co-conspirator called Slack. They were admitted before the jury as evidence against Donat. It was argued that they should not have been considered as evidence against Donat and that the jury should have been so directed. This criticism failed. The principle was expressed by Lord Lane CJ in this passage:

> The problem of to what extent documents made out in furtherance of a conspiracy and actions done in furtherance of a conspiracy by people other than a particular defendant are admissible is never an easy one to solve. The matter is dealt with in *Cross on Evidence* in a manner which seems to us to be helpful . . . and it reads as follows:
>
> > 'In determining whether there is such a common purpose as to render the acts and extra-judicial statements done or made by one party in furtherance of the common purpose evidence against the others, the judge may have regard to these matters, although their admissibility is in issue, as well as to other evidence. This doctrine is obviously liable to produce circularity in argument . . . The answer is that the agency may be proved partly by what A said in the absence of B, and partly by the other evidence of common purpose. It makes no difference which is adduced first, but A's statement will have to be excluded if it transpires that there is no other evidence of common purpose; it is another instance of conditional admissibility.'

There was in fact ample evidence apart from the documents in *Donat* . . . From these authorities we derive the principle that in the present case the document . . . was admissible against the appellants if it constituted an act or declaration by New in furtherance of the conspiracy, provided that there was some further evidence beyond the document itself that they were parties to the conspiracy alleged against them.

The Law Commission[84] considered that the exception could be justified as a pragmatic one, as it might be hard to prove a conspiracy without it and this is preserved by s.118(1) 7.

X. Expert Evidence

Section 118(1)8 preserves the rule of law whereby, in criminal proceedings, ". . . an expert witness may draw on the body of expertise relevant to his

---

[81] *R. v Governor of Pentonville Prison, Ex p. Osman* [1989] 3 All E.R. 701, 731; *Devonport and Pirano* [1996] 1 Cr.App.R. 221.

[82] *Gray* [1995] 2 Cr.App.R. 100; [1997] 2 Cr.App.R. 136.

[83] (1985) 82 Cr.App.R. 173.

[84] Law Commission: *Evidence in Criminal Proceedings: Hearsay and Related Topics, op.cit.* para.8.132.

field." This codifies the rule whereby an expert may give an opinion on the basis of facts supplied by others and of which the witness has no first-hand knowledge. An example of this is *Abadom*,[85] where the witness relied on Home Office statistics to express an opinion on the likelihood that the glass in the accused's shoe had come from the scene of the robbery. At that time, the Home Office research would have been excluded as hearsay. A witness can rely on otherwise inadmissible hearsay as the basis of an expert opinion. Of course, the impact of legislative reform, especially the Criminal Justice Acts of 1988 and 2003 makes this provision redundant as such research information will be admissible in its own right.[86]

XI. STATEMENTS BY DECEASED PERSONS

At common law only certain categories of statements by people now dead were admissible as exceptions to hearsay. These included declarations against interest, declarations in the course of a duty, dying declarations, declarations as to pedigree, declarations by testators about their wills and declarations as to public and general rights. The Law Commission felt that this motley group had no coherent rationale.[87]

- In criminal proceedings, the common law rules relating to such exceptions were abolished by s.118(2) of the 2003 legislation. Such statements will be admissible, if at all, under the first hand, often oral, hearsay provisions of s.116, the documentary provisions of s.117, under other common law exceptions preserved by s.118 (for example, where it involves an issue of pedigree or public or general rights) or through judicial discretion exercised under s.114(1)(d).
- In civil proceedings, these statements will normally be admissible under s.1 of the Civil Evidence Act 1995. Where they are not capable of being admitted under those sections and it involves an issue of pedigree or public and general rights, s.7(3) of that Act will be relevant.

A brief summary of the old categories is included, mainly for historical interest but also to consider factors that go to reliability and weight.

1. Declarations against interest

In criminal proceedings, written or oral statements made by a person now dead which, when made, were known by the declarant to be against his or her pecuniary or proprietary interests, are admissible evidence of the facts contained. The principle is that people are less likely knowingly to lie about matters that affect their pockets, although it has been said 'Men lie for so

---

[85] [1983] 1 All E.R. 364.
[86] This issue is discussed further in Ch.20.
[87] Law Commission: *Evidence in Criminal Proceedings: Hearsay and Related Topics op.cit.* para.4.51.

many reasons and some for no reason at all and some tell the truth without thinking or even in spite of thinking about their pockets'.[88] Extraordinarily this exception and its rationale does not extend to declarations against penal interest: confessions to a crime by a now dead person remain inadmissible although it would seem that (in the 18th century at least) the prospect of being hanged if one admitted one's part in a crime would seem an even more effective indicator of reliability.[89] Now, under s.116, these statements can be received into evidence where the third party is dead.

2. Declarations in course of a duty

In criminal proceedings, written or oral statements made by a person now dead but which were made under a duty to report or record his or her acts were admissible evidence of the facts which relate to that duty. The rationale rested on the enhanced reliability of such records—an employee who failed to record matters accurately was likely to be dismissed. The criteria for admissibility were that a duty had to be owed to another, the record had to relate to that duty, and it had to be made contemporaneously by the person owing the duty.

All those factors can be seen to enhance the reliability and weight to be accorded to the statement. Such statements would now be admissible under ss.116 or (more likely) under s.117, if the duty arises in the course of employment where written records are kept. In civil proceedings any such records, written or oral, will be admitted as a consequence of s.1 of the Civil Evidence Act 1995.

3. Dying Declarations

This was always a much more limited exception than this phrase implies. In *Woodcock*,[90] the defendant was tried for the murder of his wife. Before she died, she made a statement on oath to a magistrate. She said nothing about her impending death but the court was clearly satisfied that she knew she was going to die:

Woodcock (1789) 1 Leach 500 at 502–504, *per* Eyre C.B.:

. . . The general principle on which the species of evidence is admitted is, that they are declarations made in extremity, when the party is at the point of death, and when every hope of this world is gone; when every motive to falsehood is silenced, and the mind is induced by the most powerful considerations to speak the truth; a situation so solemn and so awful is considered by law as creating an obligation equal to that which is imposed by a positive oath administered in a court of justice . . .

[88] Hamilton L.J. in *Ward v H S Pitt & Co.* [1913] 2 K.B. 130 at 138.
[89] *Rogers* [1995] Crim.L.R. 148.
[90] (1789) 1 Leach 500.

The limiting conditions for admissibility were that it applied only to victims in murder or manslaughter cases, that the victim was in a settled and hopeless expectation of death and that the statement must relate to the cause of death. This was one of the most colourful anachronisms of the common law of hearsay. Its justification was assaulted on all sides, not least on the basis that a victim of a serious assault, believing that they are about to die, is likely to be in a highly emotional and probably confused state, a state, moreover, where theological concerns have less significance than in previous centuries. Indeed it has been suggested that motives such as a desire to protect relatives or close friends or to pay off old scores may be as significant. But the exception became of less practical importance nowadays, probably because of the expanded scope of the *res gestae* rule.[91] The impact of the 1995 and 2003 Acts means that it no longer has any significance.

---

[91] *Andrews* discussed above.

18

HEARSAY IN CRIMINAL PROCEEDINGS—THE CRIMINAL JUSTICE ACT 2003

I. Hearsay in Criminal Cases—A Brief History

Modern legislative reform of the hearsay rule in criminal cases begins with the House of Lords judgment in *Myers v DPP*,[1] where the Crown sought to rely on microfilm evidence kept in the Austin motor company's archives. It was hearsay because the person whose responsibility it was to keep the records invariably relied on information from other people on the shop floor. It was hearsay but it was of high quality, being both reliable and probative. But Lord Reid held that the microfilm was inadmissible since it contained the out-of-court assertions by unidentified workers. There was a need for reform but this was a matter for Parliament.

Although the Civil Evidence Act 1968 introduced a comprehensive code in relation to adducing hearsay evidence in civil proceedings, reform of the hearsay rule in criminal procedure was piecemeal until the Criminal Justice Act 2003. Initially this was through s.1 of the Criminal Evidence Act 1965 which went some way towards overturning the effect of *Myers*: documentary records compiled within a trade or a business were admissible, so long as they were based on information supplied by people with direct knowledge and those people were unavailable or could not be expected to give evidence. This was restrictively interpreted: a car's registration document was not evidence of the engine number[2] nor was a Home Office record evidence of legal immigrant status.[3]

The 11th Report of the Criminal Law Revision Committee[4] in 1972 failed to lead to wholesale revisions of criminal evidence. But the Police and Criminal Evidence Act 1984, following certain of the committee's recommendations, repealed s.1 Criminal Evidence of the 1965 and replaced and extended the exception through s.68.[5] Under s.68, the document had to form part of a

---

[1] [1965] A.C. 1001.
[2] *Sealby* [1965] 1 All E.R. 701; reversed 109 S.J. 512.
[3] *Patel* [1981] 3 All E.R. 94.
[4] Cmnd. 4991 (1972).
[5] Under of the Police and Criminal Evidence Act 1984, s.69, conditions were introduced for the admissibility of documents produced by computers. This section was repealed by Youth Justice and Criminal Evidence Act 1999, s.60. There is a presumption that a computer is working properly and it is always open to the party adversely affected by such evidence to challenge this: K. Quinn, "Computer Evidence in Criminal Proceedings" 5 E.&P. 174.

record compiled by a person under a duty to compile it and the information has been supplied directly by a person with personal knowledge or to that person by someone else with personal knowledge or to such people by others acting under a duty to record the information. The person with personal knowledge must be unavailable for one of the reasons in section 68(2).

Section 68 removed the 'business or trade' limitation, ensuring a wider range of admissible documents but still only applied to records: the limits can be seen in *Cunningham*,[6] where the accused was charged with smuggling drugs from Swaziland and sought to rely on statements taken from witnesses in Swaziland who were unable to attend the trial. But such proofs were only admissible under s.68 if they formed part of a record—single statements did not qualify and so the conviction was upheld. Section 68 was itself been repealed and replaced by ss.23 and 24 of the Criminal Justice Act 1988. Section 23 allowed the admission of a wider range of first-hand hearsay but only where the hearsay was contained in a document and that the person who made the statement was unavailable to testify. Section 24 was a rewrite of the business records exemption, admitting a broad range of business records as evidence, even when they contained multiple hearsay. Nor was there any requirement in such latter cases for the maker of the document or statement to be unavailable to attend court.

In 1997, the Law Commission published its report into hearsay in criminal proceedings. Its criticisms of the current law were summarised thus:

> There is no unifying principle behind the rule and this gives rise to anomalies and confusion. Court time is wasted because of the lack of clarity and complicated nature of the rule. Cogent evidence may be kept from the court, however much it may exonerate or incriminate the accused, because the fact-finders are not trusted to treat untested evidence with the caution it deserves, but if hearsay is admitted there is nothing to prevent them from committing on it alone. Witnesses may be put off by interruptions in the course of their oral evidence. Whether evidence will be let in or not is unpredictable because of the reliance on judicial discretion.[7]

II. THE 2003 REFORMS

The Law Commission's recommendations were introduced in the Criminal Justice Act 2003. Section 114 of the Act reads:

> 114 (1) In criminal proceedings a statement not made in oral evidence in the proceedings is admissible as evidence of any matter stated if, but only if—
>   (a) any provision of this Chapter or any other statutory provision makes it admissible,
>   (b) any rule of law preserved by section 118 makes it admissible,
>   (c) all parties to the proceedings agree to it being admissible, or
>   (d) the court is satisfied that it is in the interests of justice for it to be admissible.

This creates a basic structure for the admissibility of hearsay evidence.

---

[6] [1989] Crim.L.R. 435; *cf. Iqbal* [1990] 3 All E.R. 787.
[7] Law Commission: *Evidence in Criminal Proceedings: Hearsay and Related Topics* (Report No. 245, Cm. 3670 1997) para.4.58.

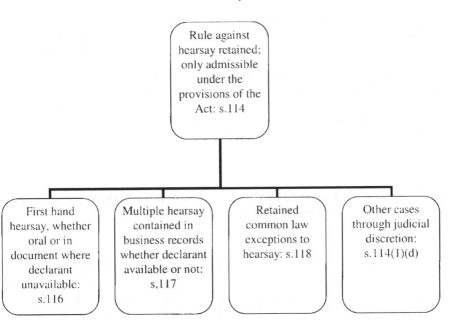

A. *Inclusionary discretion*

One of the major changes brought about by s.114(1)(d) has been the introduction of a residual discretionary power for judges to admit hearsay evidence, inadmissible under any other provision. The Law Commission argued for a limited inclusionary discretion,[8] with considerable emphasis on its advantages for the defence, reasoning that such a power would prevent unsafe convictions. However it is also be available to the prosecution but the Commission felt that there was no danger of hearsay evidence of poor quality being admitted against a defendant. The resulting legislation under s.114(1)(d) meant that hearsay evidence can be admissible if, "the court is satisfied that it is in the interests of justice for it to be admissible". In exercising this discretion, the judge must consider s.114(2):

> (2) In deciding whether a statement not made in oral evidence should be admitted under subsection (1)(d), the court must have regard to the following factors (and to any others it considers relevant)—
> (a) how much probative value the statement has (assuming it to be true) in relation to a matter in issue in the proceedings, or how valuable it is for the understanding of other evidence in the case;
> (b) what other evidence has been, or can be, given on the matter or evidence mentioned in paragraph (a);
> (c) how important the matter or evidence mentioned in paragraph (a) is in the context of the case as a whole;
> (d) the circumstances in which the statement was made;

[8] Law Commission, *op.cit.* para.8.133ff.

    (e) how reliable the maker of the statement appears to be;
    (f) how reliable the evidence of the making of the statement appears to be;
    (g) whether oral evidence of the matter stated can be given and, if not, why it
        cannot;
    (h) the amount of difficulty involved in challenging the statement;
    (i) the extent to which that difficulty would be likely to prejudice the party facing it.

The Law Commission considered how the new discretion might work in practice.

Law Commission: Evidence in Criminal Proceedings: Hearsay and Related Topics (Report No.245. Cm. 3670 1997):

8.143 A party would only need to turn to the safety-valve where none of the other exceptions could be used. By definition, therefore, the declarant must be unavailable for some reason other than death, illness, fear, disappearance, or being outside the United Kingdom. The declarant need not have been competent at the time the statement was made. The declarant need not even be identified. We do not anticipate that there would be a large number of applications to admit evidence via the safety-valve. The Crown Prosecution Service was concerned that there would be a large number of unmeritorious applications, particularly in the magistrates' courts. Our view is that all courts would regard the safety-valve as an exception to be used in very limited circumstances, and if it is too freely used, the Court of Appeal or Divisional Court will give guidance.

8.144 Where possible, an application to have evidence admitted via the safety-valve would be made at the Plea and Directions Hearing or pre-trial review. As the Judge Advocate General pointed out, if the admissibility of an item of evidence has not been resolved pre-trial, a voir dire may be necessary for the judge or magistrates to decide on the admissibility of the evidence. We believe that voir dires are best avoided if possible because, apart from the time that they take and the interruption to the flow of the trial, the evidence given at a voir dire is frequently different from that given in the trial (if the evidence is admitted), as counsel and witnesses learn from the voir dire and adapt their questions and answers accordingly. Inevitably, however, in some cases it will only become apparent that an application under the safety-valve will be needed on the day of the trial itself . . .

8.145 In theory, both section 78(1) of PACE and the common law discretion to exclude prosecution evidence will apply. In practice, these discretions will add nothing, as they are both concerned with fairness to the accused, and it would be illogical for a judge to decide that it was in the interests of justice to admit evidence but that to do so would have such an adverse effect on the fairness of the proceedings that that same evidence ought to be excluded. Similarly it is inconceivable that evidence which would otherwise have been admitted under the safety-valve might be excluded under our recommended discretion to exclude evidence which would result in undue waste of time. If evidence is sufficiently reliable to justify invoking the safety-valve, it cannot be the kind of evidence that would result in undue waste of time.

8.146 Where the evidence was admitted, a judge would warn the jury about its weaknesses, as in the case of other hearsay evidence. Any opposing party could adduce evidence to controvert the contents of the statement and to challenge the credibility of the declarant as if he or she had given oral evidence. We give some examples of cases where an application might be made at para 8.147 below.

8.147 Here are three examples of cases where an application might be made under the safety-valve:

(1) D is prosecuted for indecent assault on a child. The child is too young to testify, but she initially described her assailant as "a coloured boy". The defence is identity and the defendant is white.[9]

(2) D is prosecuted for the murder of his girlfriend. He denies that it was he who killed her. Fixing the time of the murder is an essential part of proving that D must have done it. An eight-year-old child tells the police that she saw the victim leaving her home at a time after the prosecution says she was dead. By the time the case comes to trial, the child can remember nothing about when she saw the victim.[10]

(3) D is charged with assault. X, who is not charged, admits to a friend that he, X, committed the assault. D and X are similar in appearance. X's confession is inadmissible hearsay unless the safety-valve is used.[11]

Should it be available to both the prosecution and the defence?

8.148 Three of the respondents thought that the safety-valve should only be available to the defence. They pointed out that the inspiration for the creation of a safety valve came primarily from the concern that wrongful convictions might occur if exculpatory evidence could not be admitted. In addition, it is more important for the defence to be able to predict, as early as possible, what evidence will be admissible against the defendant, and uncertainty can be eliminated by restricting the safety-valve to defence evidence.

8.149 The vast majority of respondents agreed with our provisional view that the safety valve should be available to both the prosecution and the defence. We believe that this is consistent with principle. We do not think there is any danger of hearsay evidence of poor quality being admitted against a defendant, nor of a principle which exists to protect the defendant being undermined, because the court will admit hearsay under the safety-valve only where it is in the interests of justice for it to be admitted.

The principle of fairness underlying a trial involves protecting the defendant from anonymous accusation by the state. This is the objective of the hearsay rules. But this does not mean that the defence must also be prevented from adducing hearsay evidence and the value of an inclusionary discretion has been advocated for many years.[12] But is it still needed? The Commission gives two examples which can be dealt with by other means: the child who is an incompetent witness—yet the relaxation of the rules on competency[13] is such that the child in *Sparks* may well now be treated as competent; the child who's forgotten in *Thomas* would be overcome by the use of s.117(5)(b) or s.120(6). The third example however is the third party confession and, from the defence viewpoint, the ability to introduce such a confession through this discretion is important—in *Blastland*,[14] the defendant was accused of sexual assault and murder. His defence was that he had left the victim unharmed and that another person, M, had later killed him. M made a statement confessing to the killing which was later retracted. The statement itself was held inadmissible by the House of Lords but might well be admissible under this discretion.

In *Xhabri*,[15] the Latvian victim was abducted and forced to work as a prostitute. She made phone calls to her parents and hearsay statements from

---

[9] *Sparks* [1964] A.C. 964.

[10] *Thomas* [1994] Crim.L.R. 745.

[11] *Cooper* [1969] 1 Q.B. 267.

[12] T. Allen, "Implied Assertions as Hearsay" (1992) 142 N.L.J. 1194.

[13] Youth Justice and Criminal Evidence Act 1999, s.53.

[14] [1985] 2 All E.R. 1095—consider the case of Michael Shields, imprisoned in Bulgaria for attempted despite the confession of another Liverpool football fan: *Guardian*, July, 27, 2005.

[15] [2006] 1 All E.R. 776.

her parents about these from her were admitted under s.120 but Lord Phillips suggests that there is a wide discretion under s.114 which is not in breach of Art.6.

Xhabri [2006] 1 All E.R. 776, *per* Lord Phillips:

36. Even if section 120 was not satisfied, the evidence in question plainly fell within the judge's discretion under section 114(d), always provided that admission of the evidence was in the interests of justice. We can see no basis upon which it could be suggested that the admission of this evidence was not in the interests of justice. It was probably not clear at the time that the judge made his ruling whether the Defence case would be that L never made the alleged statements or whether it would be that, when making them, she was lying. If the former, then there was every reason why the jury should hear evidence from those to whom L made the statements. If the latter, the introduction of the evidence could not unfairly prejudice the Defendant . . .

42. . . . . The discretion granted by section 114 is not restricted to the admission of a hearsay statement the maker of which is not available for cross-examination. To the extent that Article 6 would be infringed by admitting such evidence, the court has a power to exclude the evidence under section 126 and a duty so to do by virtue of the Human Rights Act. There can thus be no question of section 114 being incompatible with the Convention.

43 As to the contention that the judge, by admitting the hearsay evidence, infringed Article 6, there is no merit in this either. Article 6(3)(d) is one of the provisions designed to secure "equality of arms". The hearsay provisions of the 2003 Act apply equally to prosecution and defence, so there is no inherent inequality of arms arising out of those provisions.

44 Article 6(3)(d) does not give a defendant an absolute right to examine every witness whose testimony is adduced against him. The touchstone is whether fairness of the trial requires this. In the present case almost all the hearsay evidence derived directly, or indirectly, from L. She was available for examination. This satisfied the requirements of Article 6(3)(d).

The existence of the discretion also raises the possibility of prosecution applications to introduce hearsay evidence from unidentified persons. An illuminating civil case is *Solon South West Housing Association v James*,[16] a case where the claimant housing association sought the eviction of some tenants. There was evidence from police officers, community workers and neighbours that the tenants had behaved in a grossly anti-social manner. Some of the evidence was first-hand but a considerable amount was hearsay from people who felt intimidated by the family and did not want to be identified. In *Solon South West Housing Association*, that hearsay evidence by itself would best be characterised as 'poor quality' but it is acceptable as part of a claimant's case which involved other original evidence, consistent with the hearsay accounts. But it does not require a great leap of imagination to see a situation where the prosecution might rely on a preponderance of similar, poor quality, evidence in criminal proceedings for breach of an ASBO in a magistrates' court. Indeed, the facts of *Teper*[17] provide another lesson where an inclusionary discretion

---

[16] [2005] H.L.R. 24.
[17] [1952] 2 All E.R. 447.

might cause problems—there a police officer wished to testify that an unidentified woman had recognised the defendant at the scene of the crime. It seems foolhardy for the Law Commission to think that there is no danger of such testimony being admitted under s.114(1)(d)—and it provides an encouragement for police officers with weak cases to elaborate their stories with a few well chosen verbals from "missing" witnesses.

B. *Section 116—first-hand hearsay*

In 1986, the Roskill Committee on fraud trials recognised the need for wider admissibility of documentary evidence in such cases. This recommendation was followed in s.23 of the Criminal Justice Act 1988 which provided a general exception to the hearsay rule in criminal proceedings allowing for first-hand documentary hearsay to be admissible. In essence, the hearsay statement had to be first-hand, contained in a document (of any kind) and the maker of the statement had to be unavailable for one of the reasons specified in the section. Section 116 of the Criminal Justice Act 2003 is the successor to this and follows the same structure, although with several significant differences, discussed below. There are two key differences which separate this provision from its predecessor: the first and most important is that the first-hand hearsay need not be contained in a document but can be oral (or indeed implied through conduct) hearsay; the second is that, if the conditions in s.116 are met, there is a right[18] to have the statement admitted—no further leave is required from the court.[19]

Criminal Justice Act 2003, s.116:

116(1) In criminal proceedings a statement not made in oral evidence in the proceedings is admissible as evidence of any matter stated if—
 (a) oral evidence given in the proceedings by the person who made the statement would be admissible as evidence of that matter,
 (b) the person who made the statement (the relevant person) is identified to the court's satisfaction, and
 (c) any of the five conditions mentioned in subsection (2) is satisfied.
(2) The conditions are—
 (a) that the relevant person is dead;
 (b) that the relevant person is unfit to be a witness because of his bodily or mental condition;
 (c) that the relevant person is outside the United Kingdom and it is not reasonably practicable to secure his attendance;

---

[18] This is a qualified right—if the evidence is to be adduced under s.116(2)(e), further leave of the court is required and there is the general power of the court to exclude evidence under Police and Criminal Evidence Act, s.78.
[19] Under Criminal Justice Act 1988, ss.25 and 26, if a hearsay statement was adduced under ss.23 or 24, the court still had to consider whether its admission was in the interests of justice. This discretion has now disappeared.

(d) that the relevant person cannot be found although such steps as it is reasonably practicable to take to find him have been taken;

(e) that through fear the relevant person does not give (or does not continue to give) oral evidence in the proceedings, either at all or in connection with the subject matter of the statement, and the court gives leave for the statement to be given in evidence.

(3) For the purposes of subsection (2)(e) "fear" is to be widely construed and (for example) includes fear of the death or injury of another person or of financial loss.

(4) Leave may be given under subsection (2)(e) only if the court considers that the statement ought to be admitted in the interests of justice, having regard—

(a) to the statement's contents,

(b) to any risk that its admission or exclusion will result in unfairness to any party to the proceedings (and in particular to how difficult it will be to challenge the statement if the relevant person does not give oral evidence),

(c) in appropriate cases, to the fact that a direction under section 19 of the Youth Justice and Criminal Evidence Act 1999 (c. 23) (special measures for the giving of evidence by fearful witnesses etc) could be made in relation to the relevant person, and

(d) to any other relevant circumstances.

This is the first occasion where there has been a general exception to the hearsay rule for oral hearsay. It is not limited to a particular form that the hearsay statement may take or to any class of declarant or maker of the statement. With hearsay contained in documents, there is no restriction about documents created in the course of a trade or business and thus "document" can encompass not just records, business letters but all forms of maps, plans, discs, tapes, films, diaries, shopping lists.[20] With oral hearsay, the words need not be spoken in any specific context—even social chitchat, as long as it is relevant to the issue, can be adduced. As long as the maker of the statement is unavailable to give oral evidence in one of the ways specified in subsection (2), the statement itself can be admitted as evidence of its contents.

1. Section 116—"Statement"

(i) *Definition*

Section 116 talks of 'a statement not made in oral evidence in the proceedings'. What is a statement? Under s.115(2), there is a broad definition.

115(1) In this Chapter references to a statement or to a matter stated are to be read as follows.

(2) A statement is any representation of fact or opinion made by a person by whatever means; and it includes a representation made in a sketch, photofit or other pictorial form.

The statement must be made by a person. The absent witness will have, normally, spoken the words or written the document. There are cases where the document will have been written by another (and perhaps where the

[20] see Ch.5 for a discussion on what constitutes a document.

words would have been spoken by another) but as long as that statement has been verified by the declarant, it becomes their statement. For example, a letter dictated to and typed by a secretary, when read and signed by the boss, becomes the boss's own document. Often these authenticated statements will be made to police officers: in *McGillivray*,[21] the victim of an arson attack made a statement to the police in hospital. It was read back to him in the presence of a nurse and he agreed that it was accurate. But he was in no state to sign the document. The Court of Appeal upheld the decision to admit it under s.23.

McGillivray (1992) 97 Cr.App.R. 232 at 237, *per* Watkins L.J.:

The point is a short one and can be dealt with, with equal brevity. In our judgment where, as here, a person who has been injured and some time later, but before the trial of the defendant, dies after having made a statement to police officers which is recorded contemporaneously by one of them, and the deceased has signed the record as accurate, that is in law a statement made by that person in a document and is accordingly admissible in law. Likewise, if that person clearly indicates by speech, or otherwise, that the record of what he said made by the police officer is accurate he being at the time unable to sign the record because of some physical disability: in this instance the deceased was too badly burnt to sign, as has been said, he was heavily bandaged, his hands and arms especially.

The fact that the document was authenticated orally presents no problem. However the deceased never saw the document and it might be argued that the authentication was itself apparently based on hearsay. But the court is only interested in the words of authentication, i.e. the fact that the statement was made, and if the nurse testified that the victim agreed that the police's record was accurate, then her testimony is original evidence.[22] Of course, the facts of *McGillivray* suggest another possibility—that the victim cannot speak and the investigating officer puts statements to the victim which are answered by moving hands or eyelids. Having received non-verbal answers, the officer puts that into words, "So you're saying that, it was McGillivray who did this." The victim can again respond and agree by signs. If the victim dies before a record is written down, s.116 would allow the officer to testify as to what the victim "said".

McGillivray might be contrasted with the facts of *Re D*,[23] a civil case which involved wardship proceedings in which the maternal grandparents sought custody of a child from the father. The mother, now deceased, had had an interview with her solicitor concerning a divorce. The notes of that interview, although containing statements by the mother about violence in the family,

---

[21] (1992) 97 Cr.App.R. 232 at 237.
[22] *cf. Chapman* [1969] 2 All E.R. 321 where the repetition of the doctor's statement that he had no objection to administering a breath test was not hearsay. See a similar situation with documents used to refresh memory, see *Kelsey* (1982) 74 Cr.App.R. 213.
[23] [1986] 2 F.L.R. 189.

were not verified by her. If criminal proceedings for assault were taken against the father and the notes to be tendered as evidence, they would not be admissible as they do not constitute 'a statement by a person in a document' for the purposes of section 116. But, of course, the solicitor would now be able to testify as to what the mother had said—and use his notes to refresh his memory!

(ii) *Proof of statement*

Where a party relies on a hearsay statement, they must adduce evidence that the statement was made as proof of the statement—where the hearsay statement is spoken, it will be proved by the testimony of the witness who heard the words. Where it is a document, proof of the contents of the document comes under the provisions of s.133 which allows for a copy of the document to be produced and for it to be authenticated in whatever way the court may approve.[24]

(iii) *Contents of statements*

The statement may be tendered as evidence of any "matter stated". Under s.23, the statement had to be tendered as evidence of fact but under s.116, this has been widened. A hearsay statement which, for example, contains an opinion by an expert witness who is unavailable to testify will be admissible if the absent expert witness would have been allowed to testify in this way. However s.30 of the Criminal Justice Act 1988 already allows for expert reports to be admissible (with the leave of the court) as evidence, whether or not the person making the report attends to give oral evidence.

There are situations where non-expert opinion evidence is admissible.[25] In *Davies*,[26] the charge at a court martial was driving a vehicle while unfit through drink. The non-expert witness was allowed to testify that in his opinion the accused had been drinking. Under s.116, if that witness is unavailable to testify, hearsay evidence as to the opinion might well be admissible.

2. Section 116—conditions of admissibility

There are three general conditions of admissibility[27], both of which must be satisfied and five specific conditions, satisfying any one of which is sufficient to make the statement admissible.

(i) *General conditions*

The Act does not impose additional conditions on already admissible evidence. Section 116 and its preconditions does not prejudice the admissibility

---

[24] see Ch.5.
[25] see Ch.20.
[26] [1962] 3 All E.R. 97.
[27] Many authorities discussed here were decided under Criminal Justice Act 1988, s.23. However such precedent will still be relevant in cases arising under s.116.

of hearsay statements that might be admissible in some other way, e.g. under the common law exceptions to hearsay, confessions under s.76 of the Police and Criminal Evidence Act 1984 or documents admissible under other statutory exceptions. Similarly under s.126(2), s.116 is subject to the court's overriding power to exclude unfair evidence. The court's discretion to exclude is not fettered by these provisions.

126.—(2) Nothing in this Chapter prejudices—
(a) any power of a court to exclude evidence under section 78 of the Police and Criminal Evidence Act 1984 . . .
(b) any other power of a court to exclude evidence at its discretion (whether by preventing questions from being put or otherwise)

1. First-hand or direct hearsay

The section is limited to first-hand hearsay.

116(1) In criminal proceedings a statement not made in oral evidence in the proceedings is admissible as evidence of any matter stated if—
(a) oral evidence given in the proceedings by the person who made the statement would be admissible as evidence of that matter

The only admissible statements are those which are characterised as first—hand hearsay. The statement was either written down by the absent witness or the witness in court heard them speak the words. In other words the declarant could have given direct oral evidence of the contents of that statement.

If the declarant could not have testified about the matters contained in the statement, the hearsay evidence is also not admissible. For example, a witness cannot normally give evidence of the bad character of the accused or give their own, non-expert, opinion about relevant matters. Where the evidence the witness would have given would itself have been subject to such exclusionary rules, these cannot be circumvented through section 116. The provision only cures the vice of first hand hearsay.

However that does not affect the situation where the declarant could have testified to what another person has said. Normally this would be hearsay but an exception to that rule would apply as far as the declarant was concerned (*res gestae* would be an example) and the declarant could have testified to such matter. In such cases, Birch suggests that hearsay evidence can be adduced of any statement of which the absent witness could have given evidence, including statements made by a third party which would have been admissible under another exception to hearsay.[28]

If the declarant could not have testified at all and was not competent, this cannot be circumvented through the use of s.116. When this says, "oral evidence given in the proceedings by the person who made the statement would be admissible as evidence", a statement of an incompetent witness does not become admissible because it is written down and signed. In *H v.*

[28] See correspondence in [1989] Crim.L.R. 603 in relation to Criminal Justice Act 1988, s.23.

H,[29] the statements of a 5-year-old child to a social worker did not become admissible simply because they were written down. The Court of Appeal took a different line in *R v D*.[30] The defendant was charged with attempted rape of an 81-year-old woman suffering from Alzheimer's disease. The victim had given a video-taped interview to the police which, as she was unfit to attend trial, was shown to the jury. The court felt that the issue of competence should not be raised under s.116 but must be considered as part of the question whether the admission of the statement would have an "adverse effect on the fairness of the proceedings". However s.123 resolves this complication so that the declarant must be competent at the time of making the statement, in the sense that they must be able to understand questions and give answers that can be understood.[31]

123(1) Nothing in sections 116, 119 or 120 makes a statement admissible as evidence if it was made by a person who did not have the required capability at the time when he made the statement.

2. Identification of the declarant

The second general condition arises under s.116(1)(b).

(1) In criminal proceedings a statement not made in oral evidence in the proceed-ings is admissible as evidence of any matter stated if . . .
(b) the person who made the statement (the relevant person) is identified to the court's satisfaction

This is a new provision which was not found in the 1988 statute which merely talked of a "statement by a person". The opposing party has an opportunity of challenging the evidence if they know the source. Wherever an anonymous hearsay statement is introduced into evidence, this will raise issues under Article 6 of the European Convention on Human Rights.[32]

3. Causing unavailability

A third general condition comes under s.116(5).

(5) A condition set out in any paragraph of subsection (2) which is in fact satisfied is to be treated as not satisfied if it is shown that the circumstances described in that paragraph are caused—
(a) by the person in support of whose case it is sought to give the statement in evidence, or
(b) by a person acting on his behalf, in order to prevent the relevant person giving oral evidence in the proceedings (whether at all or in connection with the subject matter of the statement).

---

[29] [1989] 3 All E.R. 740.
[30] [2002] 3 W.L.R. 997; Ali Sed [2005] 1 Cr. App. Rep. 4.
[31] s.123(3) replicating Youth Justice and Criminal Evidence Act 1999, s.53.
[32] *Kostovski v Netherlands*, Application No. 11454/85, A 166, [1989] 12 E.H.R.R. 434.

Even if all the s.116 conditions are satisfied, the evidence will still be excluded if the party or someone acting on their behalf causes the unavailability of the witness. A court should not permit either party to benefit from wrongdoing nor indeed provide incentives for a party to use a witness's out-of-court statement rather than call them and risk subjecting them to cross-examination.

This is best illustrated in cases of witness intimidation. In *Sellick*,[33] the defendants appealed on the basis that their Article 6 rights had been infringed by the admission of a s.23 document, relying on *Luca v Italy*[34] to argue that as the statements were the decisive evidence against them, permission should not have been granted. Where the court could be sure that the identified witness, who was the sole witness and well-known to the defendant, had been deterred from attending court through fear of the defendant or persons acting for him, it could allow the witness's statement to be read by taking certain counterbalancing measures. These included taking care to ensure that the quality of the evidence was compelling, drawing the jury's attention to aspects of the witness's credibility, and giving a clear direction to the jury to exercise caution. In cases of witness intimidation, it was the defendants who had denied themselves the opportunity to examine the witness and so could not complain of an infringement of Art.6(3)(d). This position is now expressly covered in s.116(5).

(ii) *Specific conditions*

The key to admitting the hearsay statement is that the witness is unavailable to testify. Under s.116(2), there are five possibilities: that the declarant is dead, physically or mentally unfit to attend, outside the jurisdiction, cannot be found or is in fear. The party seeking to adduce the hearsay statement as evidence must satisfy the court that the conditions exist. The condition must be proved by admissible evidence—in *Eliot, Pearce and Magee*,[35] the judge was shown notes by several doctors about the health of the witnesses. The witness statements were admitted and the defence were denied the opportunity to cross-examine the doctors to ascertain the condition of the witnesses.

Eliot, Pearce and Magee [2003] EWCA 1695, *per* Royce J.:

13. The appellants' counsel wished to cross-examine those doctors to ascertain whether in reality the condition of their patients was such as to prevent them attending court. The judge came to the conclusion that that was going to be a fruitless exercise. He concluded that it was quite clear that the documents were not forgeries and he was of the view that the calling of those doctors was going to prolong the trial and was going to be an unnecessary exercise.

---

[33] [2005] EWCA Crim 651.
[34] [2003] 36 E.H.R.R. 46.
[35] [2003] EWCA 1695.

14. We are bound to say that we have some sympathy with the view that he reached. There is . . . no specification as to how the court is to be satisfied in these circumstances that a person is unfit. However, there are a number of authorities [on section 23(3) of the Criminal Justice Act 1988 which contains identical provisions] which is concerned with a person not giving evidence through fear. It is unnecessary to refer to those authorities in detail. However, in *R v Belmarsh Magistrates ex parte Gilligan*[36] Astill J. . . . said that it was necessary for the requirements under section 23(3) to be proved by admissible evidence . . .

17. Perhaps of greater importance is the approach of this Court in *R v Wood & Fitzsimmons*,[37] when this Court concluded that it was necessary, in disputed cases, for witnesses to be cross-examined about the element of fear under section 23(3).

18. By analogy in cases under section 23(2)(a), such as this, where the defence on proper grounds can point to the necessity for them to be able to cross-examine doctors, then it is, in our judgment, only right that they should be given such opportunity. There may conceivably be cases where that is not so. However, we are clear that this was not one of them.

This was supported in *Lobban*[38] where the Crown sought to rely on hearsay evidence because of the intimidation of the witnesses.

Lobban [2004] EWCA Crim 1099, *per* Fulford J.:

36. . . . [F]irst, it is necessary for the requirements to be proved by admissible evidence: *R v Belmarsh Magistrates ex parte Gilligan*,[39] and . . . it is necessary for the court to hear oral evidence as to fear. This is frequently given, for obvious reasons, not by the witness concerned but by a police officer . . .

Second, when a witness gives evidence . . . he should be sworn so that the reasons are properly before the judge: *R v Jennings and Miles*[40] . . .

Third, where the defence on proper grounds can point to the necessity for them to be able to cross examine the witness or witnesses called to give evidence about the reason for the inability of a particular witness to attend to give evidence, then, subject to the caveat we set out hereafter, they should be given such an opportunity . . . As this court observed in *R v Wood & Fitzsimmons*:

"The fact-finding process formed an integral part of (the) trial and the defence were entitled to cross-examine witnesses relied on by the Crown to establish the necessary facts."

The need to establish the condition by admissible evidence applies to all five situations under s.116. The Crown must satisfy the judge according to the criminal standard of proof.[41]

1. Where the maker of the statement is dead. This is quite straightforward. For example, *Cole*[42] was a case of assault in which the prosecution were

[36] [1998] 1 Cr.App.R. 14.
[37] [1998] Crim.L.R. 213.
[38] [2004] EWCA Crim 1099.
[39] [1998] I Cr.App.R. 14.
[40] [1995] Crim.L.R. 810.
[41] *Eliot, Pearce and Magee* above.
[42] [1990] 2 All E.R. 108.

permitted to introduce the statement of an eyewitness who had died before the trial started. In *Prussia*,[43] the victim received two stab wounds but refused hospital treatment for some 13 hours. He later made a statement identifying the accused but died some weeks later. The application to read the victim's statement was successful and the defendant was convicted of wounding with intent.

2. Where the maker of the statement is or mentally or physically unfit to attend as a witness. Usually the witness will be unable to get to court —as in *Moore*,[44] where the witness was 75 years old and in poor health and unable to attend. But this condition is not limited to physical inability to get to court but to attend *as a witness*. In *Setz-Dempsey*,[45] the witness had identified the accused but later became mentally disordered and, although physically able to attend court, he could not give coherent testimony. Section 116 will apply to the capacity of the witness to give evidence and not simply the physical act of getting to court. This can also be seen in *R. v D*[46] where the victim was an 81-year-old woman suffering from Alzheimer's disease.

3. Where the maker of the statement is outside the UK[47] and it is not reasonably practicable to secure his or her attendance. The judge must not accept too readily that the witness is outside the country and it is necessary to hold a proper inquiry to see that the threshold provisions have been reached to the criminal standard. Efforts must be made to secure attendance and the court will not assume that it is 'not reasonably practicable' from the sole fact that the witness is abroad. In *Bray*,[48] the prosecution only realised at the date of trial that the witness was in Korea and indeed had been away for seven months. They were not permitted to use the statute to cover up their incompetence. There must be evidence to show why it is not practicable to attend court—expense can be a factor.[49] It is similar for the defence: in *Mattey and Queeley*,[50] the defence wished to rely on written statements from a couple living in France. One of the accused testified that the witnesses had recently found new jobs and would find the cost of travel difficult. There was no evidence of any formal efforts to secure the witnesses' attendance. Even on the lower burden of proof for the defence (on the balance of probabilities), the application was rejected. However the subsection talks of an inability to 'secure' attendance and should the court obstruct the introduction of documentary evidence if there is evidence that witnesses outside the jurisdiction are unwilling, for good reason or not, to attend court?

---

[43] *Prussia* [2003] EWCA Crim 2402.
[44] [1992] Crim.L.R. 882; *Gent* (1989) 89 Cr.App.R. 247;
[45] [1994] Crim.L.R. 123.
[46] [2002] 3 W.L.R. 997; *Ali Sed* [2005] 1 Cr.App.R. 4.
[47] This means physically outside—it does not include a diplomat resident in the UK (*Jimenez-Paez* [1993] 98 Cr.App.R. 239.
[48] [1988] Crim.L.R. 829—this case involved one of the predecessors of s.116, namely s.68 Police and Criminal Evidence Act 1984; *De Orango* [1992] Crim.L.R. 180.
[49] *Case* [1991] Crim.L.R. 192.
[50] [1995] Crim.L.R. 308.

4. Where reasonable steps have been taken but the maker of the statement cannot be found. Not knowing the identity of the maker of the statement is not enough as under s.116(1)(b) the witness cannot be anonymous and the party seeking to rely on the hearsay must satisfy the court as to the identity of the person. As with the other criteria, the judge must inquire whether "reasonable steps" have been taken and be satisfied that there is sufficient evidence to reach the criminal standard. In *Reith*,[51] the victim in a rape case testified that after the incident she had called a French friend who was sharing her flat. The friend made a witness statement but then failed to attend trial. Her statement, which was the only evidence of "recent complaint", was admitted under the 1988 Act. The appeal was allowed on the grounds that there was no evidence of any significant attempt to trace her. It was effectively impossible to controvert the evidence without the witness being present.[52]

5. That through fear the relevant person does not give (or does not continue to give) oral evidence in the proceedings. Where the maker of the statement is available and capable of testifying, if they have been or are being intimidated, prior statements can be admitted without the witness attending court. There has always been a problem of the intimidated witness and a history of legislative attempts to deal with the issue.[53] Section 23(3) of the Criminal Justice Act 1988 was the immediate precursor but only applied to statements in a document and imposed certain conditions, namely that the statements were made to a person charged with investigating offences and where the maker of the statement was in fear or being kept "out of the way". These restrictions disappeared with s.116(2)(e)—it is simply a question whether the witness is in "fear" and that is to be interpreted widely.

116(3) For the purposes of subsection (2)(e) "fear" is to be widely construed and (for example) includes fear of the death or injury of another person or of financial loss.

The section is not limited to the prosecution but can also apply to defence witnesses. However, subs.(2)(e) differs from the other four grounds in that there is no right to adduce the hearsay statement once the conditions have been established. Once a party has satisfied the judge that there is "fear", before the evidence is admitted the judge must give leave under subs.(4).

116 (4) Leave may be given under subsection (2)(e) only if the court considers that the statement ought to be admitted in the interests of justice, having regard—
  (a) to the statement's contents,
  (b) to any risk that its admission or exclusion will result in unfairness to any party to the proceedings (and in particular to how difficult it will be to challenge the statement if the relevant person does not give oral evidence),

---

[51] Unreported—Court of Appeal 7/4/2000.
[52] *cf.* Herbert unreported—Court of Appeal 23/7/1991.
[53] Criminal Justice Act 1925, s.13(3); *O'Loughlin* [1988] 3 All E.R. 431; *Blithing* (1983) 77 Cr.App.R. 86.

(c) in appropriate cases, to the fact that a direction under section 19 of the Youth Justice and Criminal Evidence Act 1999 (c. 23) (special measures for the giving of evidence by fearful witnesses etc) could be made in relation to the relevant person, and

(d) to any other relevant circumstances.

For example, where the witness was the main or only evidence against the defendant, it would be difficult for a judge to admit hearsay evidence as the accused who would not be in a position to challenge the evidence.

The "fear" is not necessarily objective and based on reasonable grounds as long as it is genuine.[54] This must be proved by admissible evidence—in *Neil v North Antrim Magistrates' Court*,[55] a police officer could not give evidence of what he had been told by the mother of the relevant witnesses but could testify as to what those witnesses themselves told him about their state of fear.[56] In *Lobban*,[57] the accused appealed against his conviction for possession of cocaine with intent to supply on the grounds that the judge was wrong to question the witness about their fear without allowing the accused's counsel the opportunity to ask questions. Fulford J. addressed this issue.

Lobban [2004] EWCA Crim 1099, *per* Fulford J.:

37. An issue that has been debated by some of the commentators is whether the right to cross-examine in these circumstances extends to the witness who is the maker of the statement in issue and who, although not to be called before the jury, is called on the voir dire . . . This is likely only to be relevant in "fear" cases. In our judgment, bearing in mind the terms of the section and the authorities in this area, and in particular *R v James Greer*, the clear answer is that the relevant witness can be called to give evidence in relation to whether or not he is in fear. He would then be potentially liable to cross-examination, and to this possibility we now turn our attention.

38. It is trite to observe that cases vary infinitely and what is necessary to ensure fairness will differ from situation to situation. One constant is that whenever dealing with witnesses who may genuinely be frightened the court must act with sensitivity and care whilst simultaneously ensuring that the defendant's right to a fair trial is not eroded. When the relevant witness is called to give evidence of his fear, in our view the normal course of events will be for counsel on both sides to conduct the questioning in the usual way. However, there may be cases in which the court concludes, having heard submissions and having carefully considered the matter, that this is not an appropriate course. For instance, some vulnerable witnesses may insist, for reasons which the judge feels he should act on, that they are only prepared to be questioned by the judge. In those circumstances it may be appropriate to depart from the usual course, but reasonable steps, such as have been identified with the assistance of counsel, then should be taken to protect the interests of both the prosecution and the defence. The most obvious of these is that counsel should be asked to identify the questions and issues they respectively wish to have explored with the witness during the voir dire. Thereafter, it will be for the judge to determine what questions should be

---

[54] *R. v Acton Justices Ex p. McMullen* (1990) 92 Cr.App.R. 98.

[55] [1992] 4 All E.R. 846.

[56] Under the *res gestae* exception to hearsay.

[57] above.

asked, but the identification of the relevant issues in this way will significantly help to ensure the proceedings are fair. Additionally, it may be necessary, as we have already indicated, to separate the accused from the witness by means of screens or a television link.

The trial judge is encouraged to consider the particular circumstances of the case and to address the question of fairness as between the prosecution and the defendant. Although these provisions have attracted criticism,[58] they have also been seen as protection for the vulnerable witness, especially victims of domestic violence. The requirement in s.116(3) to interpret fear broadly gives statutory backing to previous calls for such an approach.

S. Edwards, "What shall we do with a frightened witness?" (1989) 139 N.L.J. 1740 at 1759:

. . . The court has the discretion to decide what constitutes fear and when a claim of 'fear' is legitimate . . . I would hope that the courts would consider seriously the vulnerable witness and in their definition of fear include a consideration of the victim's/witness's state of mind. Fear must be seen to be beyond mere fear of an appearance in court; it must relate to anticipation of subsequent action by or on behalf of the defendant following on from the giving of prejudicial evidence. Prosecution witnesses to particular offences may be more susceptible to this kind of direct intimidation or state of mind presupposing subsequent action, i.e. large scale fraud, terrorism, gang crimes, syndicate crimes, and crimes involving intimate victim/ offender 'relationships'. Whilst it is true that [the section] could be open to abuse by 'grasses' whose evidence then could not be tested, each case has to be examined in appreciating the particular pressures that are brought to bear. In domestic assault cases, allegations of previous violence in a witness statement, including previous convictions against the offender or injunctions served, and any indication of inter-ference in the pre-trial stage could be put before the judge in helping him/her to assess the reasonableness of the alleged fear.

The standard of fear should be assessed in accordance not with the reasonable man standard but rather the battered woman's perception of fear standard. This latter concept has a specific meaning and this specific meaning has been accepted in the US in cases where women pled self defence to killing violent husbands in accordance with the battered woman's perception of 'imminent danger' rather than the reasonable man standards. Many battered women live in fear and cannot make decisions in their own interests or those of their children because of fear. The meaning of fear must therefore be open to accommodate the vulnerable person and in this case the battered woman's perception of fear, even in the absence of proof of direct threats.[59]

3. Section 116—the limitations on the discretion to exclude

The 1988 legislation provided further obstacles, even when the basic conditions were satisfied. Under ss.25 and 26, the court had the power to exclude evidence, if in the interests of justice, it ought not to be admitted. The

---

[58] D. Wolchover' "Keeping Witnesses Out of the Way" (1988) 138 N.L.J. 461.
[59] J. McEwan "Documentary Hearsay Evidence—Refuge for the Vulnerable Witness" [1989] Crim.L.R. 629.

2003 legislation took a more radical approach so that for first-hand hearsay, under s.116, if the conditions are satisfied, there was a right to have that evidence admitted. There are no additional hurdles. There are just two qualifications to that statement:

    i) if the evidence is admitted under s.116(2)(e), it required leave of the court under subs.(4), as discussed above; and

    ii) there is the residual discretion under s.78 of the Police and Criminal Evidence Act 1984 which is retained under s.126. The court can refuse to admit evidence if the admission would have an adverse effect on the fairness of the proceedings.

Applications to exclude evidence will be made under these provisions to exclude the hearsay evidence of declarants who are unavailable. The difference between the 1988 and 2003 statutes lies more in the burden than in the argument. The ultimate issue is the same whether the court is considering the "interests of justice" or the "fairness of the proceedings". However the burden of persuading the court that the hearsay statement should be excluded varies.

    i) Under the intimidated witness provisions of s.116, leave may only be given if the court considers that the statement of the witness ought to be admitted in the interests of justice—this puts the burden of satisfying the court on the party, normally the prosecution, that the witness is too terrified to attend court and testify. Clearly it will be harder for the prosecution to adduce hearsay evidence in place of the intimidated witness than where witnesses are unavailable for the reasons given in subs.(2)(a) to (d). Indeed subs.(4) refers the court to the problems that the defendant might have in challenging such evidence and the potential alternative methods of testifying which are provided by the Youth Justice and Criminal Evidence Act 1999 for frightened witnesses.

    ii) Under s.78, it is more likely that the defence will be objecting to the admission of the evidence. It has been said that here the burden of proof has no part to play and that it is more accurate to speak of the burden of persuasion—the section is neutral between the prosecutor and the defence.[60]

The question is the courts' interpretation of concepts such as "interests of justice" and "fairness of proceedings". These concepts were discussed in cases arising under ss.25 and 26 under the Criminal Justice Act 1988 where power to exclude was based on an assessment of the interests of justice. These still have relevance—in *Cole*,[61] a case of assault in which the prosecution sought to introduce the statement of an eyewitness who had subsequently died. Leave was required and the appellant argued that this should have been

---

[60] *R. (Saifi) v Governor of Brixton Prison* (2000) 1 W.L.R. 1134.
[61] [1990] 2 All E.R. 108; see also *Price* [1991] Crim.L.R. 707 on the similar requirement in s.25(2)(d).

refused as the only way to controvert the statement would be for the defendant to testify or to call witnesses and this amounted to putting improper pressure on the defendant.

Cole [1990] 2 All E.R 108 at 115–117, *per* Ralph Gibson L.J.:

The first submission of counsel for the appellant was that the words 'whether it is likely to be possible to controvert the statement if the person making it does not attend' contemplate only, and should be restricted to, the possibility of controverting the statement by cross-examination directed to witnesses to be called for the prosecution.

We reject that submission. We see no reason to imply any such restriction on the plain meaning of the words. The meaning of 'controvert' includes that of 'dispute' or 'contradict'. The court is entitled, in our judgment, to have regard to such information as it has at the time that the application is made which shows 'whether it is likely to be possible to controvert the statement' in the absence of the ability to cross-examine the maker. The court cannot require to be told whether the accused intends to give evidence or to call witnesses, but the court is not required, in our judgment, to asses the possibility of controverting the statement upon the basis that the accused will not give evidence or call witnesses known to be available to him. The decision by an accused whether or not to give evidence or to call witnesses is to be made by him by reference to the admissible evidence put before the court; and the accused has no right, as we think, for the purposes of this provision, to be treated as having no possibility of controverting the statement because of his right not to give evidence or call witnesses. If Parliament had intended the question to be considered on that basis, express words would, we think, have been used to make that intention clear.

This question, however, is only one part of a complex balancing exercise which the court must perform. For example, the fact that the court concludes that it is likely to be possible for the accused to controvert the statement if the person making it cannot be cross-examined does not mean that the court will therefore necessarily be of opinion that admission of the statement will not result in unfairness to the accused or that the statement ought not to be admitted in the interests of justice.

The court must consider the contents of the statement, as explained in *R v Blithing*,[62] . . . the statement may leave relevant questions unanswered and appear to provide evidence of greater certainty than is warranted having regard to the absence of those answers. As Lord Griffiths observed in *Scott v R*,[63] after reference to a need for proper warnings when a statement is admitted:

> It is the quality of the evidence in the deposition that is the crucial factor that should determine the exercise of the discretion. By way of example, if the deposition contains evidence of identification that is so weak that a judge in the absence of corroborative evidence would withdraw the case from the jury, then, if there is no corroborative evidence, the judge should exercise his discretion to refuse to admit the deposition for it would be unsafe to allow the jury to convict on it.

Thus the weight to be attached to the inability to cross-examine and the magnitude of any consequential risk that admission of the statement will result in unfairness to the accused, will depend in part on the court's assessment of the quality of the evidence shown by the contents of the statement. Each case, as is obvious, must turn

---

[62] (1983) 77 Cr.App.R. 86.
[63] [1989] A.C. 1242 at 1529.

on its own facts. The court should, we accept, consider whether, as was the court's view in *R v Blithing*, the inability to probe a statement by cross-examination of the maker of it must be regarded as having such consequences, having regard to the terms and substance of the statement in the light of the issues in the cases, that for that reason the statement should be excluded.

In considering a submission to that effect the court is entitled, and in our view required, to consider how far any potential unfairness, arising from the inability to cross-examine on the particular statement, may be effectively counter-balanced by the sort of warning and explanation in the summing up described by Lord Griffiths and in fact given by the judge in this case. The court will also, for example, consider whether, having regard to other evidence available to the prosecution, the interests of justice will be properly served by excluding the statement.

Little assistance is found in judgments about the details of "fairness" or "the interests of justice" that are involved in this "complex balancing act". Procedural justice in criminal proceedings requires that the accused is dealt with according to established legal provisions, is made aware of the charges and evidence, is able to confront those allegations and the evidence in a neutral, public forum and to introduce witnesses, evidence and argument on their own behalf. A central element of fairness in this context is the right to confront the evidence against you—in other words, to listen to a witness's oral testimony and to challenge it. Section 116 removes that right and to that extent the statute creates an inherent unfairness—that unfairness might be mitigated where the evidence is simply a part of a large body of evidence against the accused rather than the sole or main evidence, where it is not the central item of evidence but has a more marginal quality, where the evidence is technical and little is to be gained from cross-examination or where there are other sources through which the accused can challenge or controvert the evidence.

(i) *Confronting the witness*

Simple loss of the right to cross-examine is not *per se* unfair. To hold otherwise would be to nullify these provisions. Article 6 of the European Convention on Human Rights specifies the right to a fair trial within which is contained the right to "... examine or have examined witnesses." European Court of Human Rights decisions such as *Unterpertinger v Austria*[64] and *Kostovski v Netherlands*[65] suggest that the safeguards built into the Criminal Justice Act 2003 are adequate. The Commission considered the relationship between the provisions of the Criminal Justice Act 1988 and Art.6 in *Trivedi v UK*,[66] where a doctor was charged with false accounting by claiming for more night visits to a patient than had in fact occurred. The prosecution relied on written statements by the patient who was elderly and infirm. The Commission declared the application inadmissible as the statements were not the only evidence, the judge had conducted an inquiry into the patient's condition and evidence on the patient's reliability had been

---

[64] Case 1985/87/134.
[65] Case 10/1988/154/208.
[66] [1997] E.H.R.L.R. 520.

admitted. The jury had been specifically warned against attaching undue weight to the patient's evidence.

(ii) *Forced to testify*

The admission of statements under s.116 puts pressure on the defence to testify or to call witnesses in order to controvert the statement. However this is not unfair or a breach of the defendant's right to silence. The authority for this is *Cole* but again to hold otherwise would limit the sections' effectiveness. If the defendant's actions can be demonstrated to have intimidated the witness, it is easier to conclude that it is not unfair.[67]

In *Duffy*,[68] a man and a woman were convicted of robbery and manslaughter. The woman's defence was that she took no part in the robbery or killing and was supported by a transcript of an interview between severely disabled eyewitness and a social worker. The Court of Appeal pointed out that it was important to have regard to whether it is likely to be possible to controvert the statement, and here it was possible for the man to controvert the evidence by giving evidence himself. In fact he chose not to do so.

Similarly in *Gokal*,[69] the charge was conspiracy to defraud and statements by the defendant's brother-in-law were key evidence. The brother-in-law refused to return to the UK. The defendant argued that admission of the statements would be in breach of his privilege against self-incrimination as he would have to testify to controvert these statements. Effectively, he would have to testify. The Court of Appeal stated that the statute did not abrogate the accused's rights. It made it more difficult for the accused to exercise his right to silence only in the tactical sense that the more the admissible evidence began to point to his guilt unless the case was answered, the more seriously the accused had to contemplate the need to enter the witness box. Freedom of choice whether or not to give evidence was still retained, even if the field of choice had been restricted. As there was the possibility of controverting the statement through other means, the procedure was compatible with Article 6.

(iii) *Centrality of statement*

If there is other evidence, it is easier to conclude that admission of the statement is not unfair. In *Cole*, the deceased witness had the best view of the assault but was not the only witness. Equally it is not unfair where the absent witness is required only to be cross-examined about some collateral matter.[70] But where the disputed evidence forms the hub of the prosecution case, the potential for unfairness is much greater. In *French*,[71] the judge directed the jury that the statements which had been admitted under s.23 were of material importance to the question of identification. The Court of Appeal ruled that

---

[67] *Fairfax* [1995] Crim.L.R. 949.
[68] [1998] 3 W.L.R. 1060.
[69] [1997] 2 Cr.App.R. 266.
[70] *Holman* [1995] Crim.L.R. 80 where the written evidence of Irish bank employees was accepted.
[71] (1993) 97 Cr.App.R. 421.

leave should not be given in such a case. Certainly if the evidence is inherently fragile, there may well be a foundation on which to exclude. But the centrality of the evidence is not the only issue: where the evidence is reliable and from an unimpeachable source, there is less concern. In *Phillips*,[72] a sexual assault was committed in 1998 and swabs for DNA analysis were taken from the victim. The accused was arrested some years later and the DNA profile was fundamental to the prosecution case. The person who had taken the initial swabs was now unavailable to testify but the court admitted the report. It was unclear what issues the defence might have put to the witness if they had been able to cross-examine. Further, in *Grafton*,[73] the accused and his accountant, now deceased, were the only substantial witnesses. The accused had himself referred the investigators from Customs and Excise to the accountant for information about his business affairs.[74] The accountant had made a statement which was significantly adverse to the accused. In such circumstances, the statement was admitted. The defence had themselves offered up the evidence to the Crown and it would be difficult to treat the admission of that evidence as unfair.

A contrary example is *Radak*,[75] where the prosecution sought to rely on statements from a witness in the US. May L.J. characterised the witness's evidence as an "essential link" in the prosecution's case and not a merely formal part of the case. The defendants had little or no evidence to controvert the statement except by cross-examination which reinforced the view that it would be unfair if they did not have the opportunity to test the evidence. May L.J. said, "You cannot conduct an argument with, nor ask questions of, a piece of paper." The jury had to address the issue of whether the victim had been defrauded and this is inherently difficult if the jury have never seen the victim being questioned.

(iv) *Get out of jail card*

Parties should not be permitted to use these provisions to avoid the consequences of their own incompetence. An example is *Radak*,[76] where the prosecution sought to rely on statements from a witness in the US.

Radak [1999] 1 Cr.App.R. 187, *per* May L.J.:

. . . the prosecution knew from the outset that [the witness] might not attend voluntarily. His failure to respond to letters gave no cause for optimism that he would, yet the prosecution did nothing. Time passed. The trial date was set and was

---

[72] [2004] EWCA Crim 2288.

[73] [1995] Crim.L.R. 61.

[74] At common law, such a vicarious admission where there is express authority might well be admissible—*Williams v Innes* (1808) 1 Camp. 364.

[75] (1999) 1 Cr.App.R. 187.

[76] *ibid*; *Bray* (1988) 88 Cr.App.R. 354.

approaching. The prosecution wasted a vital month between 5th May and 5th June 1998 when they did nothing to grapple with the situation when they knew that [the witness] was not going to attend. By inactivity they let slip the opportunity of obtaining cross-examined evidence on commission in time for the date fixed for the trial. In our view, the prosecution were, as the judge found, culpable in these respects and the reality was that they were seeking leave to cover their culpability by a means which, as we have held, would impose a significant unfairness on the defendants. In these circumstances, we do not consider on balance that [the witness's] first statement ought to be admitted in the interests of justice.

A further example is *French*,[77] where the original trial folded and the prosecution rejected the opportunity to sever the indictment in order to continue. In the subsequent trial, they sought to rely on statements made by the main witness who refused to attend for a second time. The Court of Appeal quashed the conviction and opined that the Crown could have been said to have brought the situation upon themselves.

(v) *Reliability*

Reliability should normally not be equated with fairness, although where the evidence was a transcript of an earlier trial at which the witness had been cross-examined,[78] admitting the evidence seems both reliable and fair. But the quality and reliability of the maker of the statement and of the information do not make it necessarily fair to admit it. This was perhaps overlooked by Lord Griffiths in *Scott*,[79] when he commented, "It is the quality of the evidence in the deposition that is the crucial factor that should determine the exercise of the discretion." Reliability is one of a number of factors that need to be addressed in this complex balancing act.

Admitting a reliable statement is not necessarily fair but the converse is more true: fairness is never served by the admission of unreliable statements. In *Patel*,[80] the accused produced an alibi statement from a witness abroad, alleging that the accused was with him at the relevant time. The Recorder termed this "very bald" and rejected the statement. However, under the more liberal approach of s.116, a court might find it more difficult to exclude such evidence, albeit while reminding the jury of its limited probative force. We see that greater willingness to admit the evidence of the mentally ill and mentally subnormal witnesses: so long as they cross the threshold of competence, their evidence is admitted. In *R. v D*,[81] the defendant was charged with attempted rape of an 81-year-old woman suffering from Alzheimer's disease. The victim had given a video-taped interview to the police which, as she was unfit to attend trial, was shown to the jury. Once such a witness has been shown to be capable of understanding and answering questions, it is difficult to argue that her illness by itself makes it unfair to admit her evidence. Other factors may come into play if, for example, the statement is the sole or main evidence against the accused.

---

[77] above.
[78] *Lockley and Corah* [1995] 2 Cr.App.R. 554; *Thomas* [1998] Crim.L.R. 887.
[79] [1989] A.C. 1242 at 1529.
[80] [1993] Crim.L.R. 291.
[81] [2002] 3 W.L.R. 997; *Ali Sed* [2005] 1 Cr.App.R. 4; Maxwell (unreported, October 25, 1999, CA).

In *Lockley and Corah*,[82] a murder case, the witness was a fellow prisoner of the accused and testified that the accused had confessed to the murder. She initially gave evidence at a first trial which was aborted but then absconded from prison before the second trial. Could a transcript of her evidence be received? There had been an opportunity to cross-examine at the original trial but the confession had been made in the absence of other witnesses. The court held that it was of the utmost importance that the jury had the opportunity of observing the manner and demeanour of the witness themselves.

(vi) Co-defendants

The court must take into account the effect on all the defendants. In *Gregory and Mott*,[83] the statement of a deceased witness would marginally have assisted one of the defendants but seriously harmed the case of the other. It was excluded and the balancing act envisaged in *Cole* here became a balance between the 'degrees of unfairness' to the two defendants. In *Duffy*,[84] a man and a woman were convicted of robbery and manslaughter. The woman's defence that she took no part in the robbery or killing was supported by an eye witness, the son of the victim. He was disabled from cerebral palsy and Parkinson's disease and suffered from severe speech difficulties and there was a transcript of his interview with a social worker had been tape recorded only because the social worker was able to "translate" what was being said. The trial judge excluded the transcript on the grounds that it would create insurmountable prejudice to the woman's co-accused. The Court of Appeal disagreed.

Duffy [1999] Q.B. 919 at 930–931, *per* Evans L.J.:

The question whether it was unfair to [the co-accused] seems to us to raise a number of issues. The fact that it was prejudicial does not mean that it was unfair to him. The question is whether leading this evidence in this form was unfair to him. What can be said is that he had no opportunity of cross-examining the witness, but that is the inevitable consequence of any order being made under section 26. The specific requirement of section 26 paragraph (ii) is that the court has to have regard to whether it is likely to be possible to controvert the statement, and here it was possible for [the co-accused] to controvert the evidence by giving evidence himself. In fact he chose not to do so. There was no doubt that the consequence of excluding the interview was unfair in the sense of being prejudicial to the appellant, because she was deprived of the effect which supporting evidence from an eye witness would have upon the jury when it came to assess her credibility.

---

[82] [1995] 2 Cr.App.R. 554.
[83] [1995] Crim.L.R. 507.
[84] [1998] 3 W.L.R. 1060.

(vii) *Jury warning*

Fairness is to be sought through the direction to the jury. The judge must stress that the evidence has not been tested by cross-examination and should point out any weaknesses or inconsistencies in the statement. In *Kennedy*,[85] the accused was a police officer accused of assaulting an alcoholic. The victim died before trial but his statements were admitted under s.23. Although the trial judge acted properly in admitting the statement and in warning the jury about the lack of cross-examination, he failed to mention how drunk the victim had been at the time of the incident and the inconsistencies between the statement and the testimony of other witnesses. In directing the jury as to the weight to be attached to the statement, the court must have regard to all the circumstances from which any inference can reasonably be drawn as to the statement's accuracy or otherwise. The sobriety of the witness was an obvious, if overlooked, factor in *Kennedy*. The speed with which the statement is made after the event or whether the supplier of the information or the creator of the document had any reason to distort the facts may be others.

An adequate warning is essential. In *Thomas*,[86] the main witness, Clee, was an accomplice with a long criminal record who had strong motives to give false evidence. The trial court allowed his statements to be read in his absence as he was afraid to testify. The Court of Appeal upheld the conviction.

Thomas [1998] Crim.L.R. 887, *per* Roch L.J.:

Clee did give evidence before the magistrates and was cross-examined although this court, as did the trial judge, recognises that the cross-examination at the Magistrates' Court was not as searching as cross-examination by counsel at a trial would have been.

The jury knew the antecedents and character of Clee. The jury could consider whether there were any significant inconsistencies between Clee's original statement and the evidence he gave to the Magistrates. The appellants had the opportunity to give evidence controverting Clee's statement and his evidence to the Magistrates and their counsel had the opportunity to address the jury and to make all the points they wished to about Clee's evidence. It was not suggested to this court that counsel did not avail themselves fully of that opportunity. Finally, and most importantly the judge, as he promised in his ruling gave the jury a careful direction with regard to the dangers of acting on Clee's evidence when they had not seen him in the witness box. In addition he reminded the jury that drug dealing could be a very dangerous activity in which people could have grudges against others for all sorts of reasons in respect of which they could resort to violence. He reminded the jury of the sharp conflict between the contents of Clee's statement and the evidence given by Flannagan and Christopher Thomas. And then he said:

> There is no doubt that Clee is a person who is capable of lying in court on his oath and indeed he has done so in his own defence and in the other case for which he has already been sentenced and as was said the jury saw through him on that occasion. In sentencing him the trial judge commented that he had plainly told lies to the jury on oath which they had little difficulty in seeing through and he got six years."

---

[85] [1994] Crim.L.R. 50.
[86] [1998] Crim.L.R. 887—transcript on Lexis.

We have looked at this aspect of this case and at the essential question which arises under Article 6 of the Convention namely whether, considering the appellants' complaints from the angle of paragraph 3(d) of Article 6 the proceedings considered as a whole were fair and the conclusion that we have reached is that the proceedings were fair.

C. *Section 117 of the Criminal Justice Act 2003—second-hand documentary hearsay*

Section 117 is the successor to s.24 of the Criminal Justice Act 1988.[87] The motivation behind this legislation was the need to admit business records into evidence.[88] There are key differences when this is compared to s.116, which emanate from the idea of a business record— first it permits multiple hearsay, recognising the realities of business life, and secondly there is no requirement that the witness is unavailable, again recognising the enhanced reliability of the business record and the likelihood that employees are unlikely to recall routine transactions. Both of these broaden the scope of s.117 as opposed to s.116 but, of course, it is more constrained as the section is limited to hearsay contained in documents created in a business or similar environment.

Criminal Justice Act 2003, s.117:

117(1) In criminal proceedings a statement contained in a document is admissible as evidence of any matter stated if—
  (a) oral evidence given in the proceedings would be admissible as evidence of that matter,
  (b) the requirements of subsection (2) are satisfied, and
  (c) the requirements of subsection (5) are satisfied, in a case where subsection (4) requires them to be.
  (2) The requirements of this subsection are satisfied if—
  (a) the document or the part containing the statement was created or received by a person in the course of a trade, business, profession or other occupation, or as the holder of a paid or unpaid office,
  (b) the person who supplied the information contained in the statement (the relevant person) had or may reasonably be supposed to have had personal knowledge of the matters dealt with, and
  (c) each person (if any) through whom the information was supplied from the relevant person to the person mentioned in paragraph (a) received the information in the course of a trade, business, profession or other occupation, or as the holder of a paid or unpaid office.
  (3) The persons mentioned in paragraphs (a) and (b) of subsection (2) may be the same person.

---

[87] This is the culmination of a chain of reforms introduced following the decision in *Myers*, namely the 1965 Criminal Evidence Act, of the Police and Criminal Evidence Act 1984, s. 68 and finally Criminal Justice Act 1988, s.24.
[88] D. McEvoy, "Police Documents as Admissible Hearsay" [1993] Crim.L.R. 480; J. Smith, "Sections 23 and 24 of the Criminal Justice Act 1988: Some Problems" [1994] Crim.L.R. 426.

(4) The additional requirements of subsection (5) must be satisfied if the statement—

(a) was prepared for the purposes of pending or contemplated criminal proceedings, or for a criminal investigation, but

(b) was not obtained pursuant to a request under section 7 of the Crime (International Co-operation) Act 2003 (c. 32) or an order under paragraph 6 of Schedule 13 to the Criminal Justice Act 1988 (c. 33) (which relate to overseas evidence).

(5) The requirements of this subsection are satisfied if—

(a) any of the five conditions mentioned in section 116(2) is satisfied (absence of relevant person etc), or

(b) the relevant person cannot reasonably be expected to have any recollection of the matters dealt with in the statement (having regard to the length of time since he supplied the information and all other circumstances).

(6) A statement is not admissible under this section if the court makes a direction to that effect under subsection (7).

(7) The court may make a direction under this subsection if satisfied that the statement's reliability as evidence for the purpose for which it is tendered is doubtful in view of—

(a) its contents,

(b) the source of the information contained in it,

(c) the way in which or the circumstances in which the information was supplied or received, or

(d) the way in which or the circumstances in which the document concerned was created or received.

1. Section 117—introductory issues

Section 117(1)[89] states "a statement contained in a document is admissible as evidence of any matter stated". What is a statement? As already mentioned, under s.115(2), there is a broad definition—"a statement is any representation of fact or opinion made by a person by whatever means." These issues have been discussed with reference to s.116.

What is a document? Everyday language would confine the term to statements recorded on paper in some form but in *Daye*,[90] Darling J. talked of a document as any "written thing capable of being evidence" and pointed out that paper has been preceded by parchment, stone, marble, clay and metal. Nowadays even the adjective "written" is too restrictive and there is an even wider meaning: "document" means anything in which information of any description is recorded.[91] The legal definition of the term no longer bears much resemblance to its everyday meaning. Films, photographs, video tape, audio tape, computer disks, and a fax—all are capable of being documents.[92]

Where a party relies on a document containing a hearsay statement, they must adduce evidence of the document as proof of the statement. This comes under the provisions of s.133 which permits copies of the document to be adduced, authenticated in whatever manner the court approves. Having done

---

[89] Many authorities discussed here were decided under Criminal Justice Act 1988, s.24. However such precedent will still be relevant in cases arising under s.117.

[90] [1908] 2 K.B. 333.

[91] Criminal Justice Act 2003, s.134(1); *cf.* Civil Evidence Act 1995, s.13 implementing the recommendations of the Law Commission Report, The Hearsay Rule in Civil Proceedings (1993 Law Comm Reports No. 216).

[92] These issues are discussed in Ch.5.

this, the statement in the document is now evidence of any "matter stated". This is broader than the 1988 provision by which the statement could only be tendered as evidence of fact. Under s.117, this has been widened to include matters of opinion.

One general condition of admissibility is that, under s.117(1)(a), "oral evidence given in the proceedings would be admissible as evidence of that matter" This is simpler than with s.116 and requires just that the initial supplier of the information could have given evidence of the information. A statement of an incompetent witness does not become admissible because it is written down and signed, even in the context of a business or profession. Section 123 lays down that the relevant person must be competent in the sense that they must be able to understand questions and give answers that can be understood.[93]

A further point is that the document cannot contain information which would be inadmissible if given in oral testimony. If the original supplier of the information is retailing hearsay, that would be inadmissible. Similarly the document cannot contain evidence of the bad character of the accused or non-expert, opinion about relevant matters. Where the evidence the witness would have given would itself have been subject to an exclusionary rule, that exclusionary rule cannot be circumvented through s.117.

2. Section 117—specific conditions

This section allows documents created in specific circumstances to be admitted, despite containing hearsay statements. The legislation conceives of a three-part process.

a) The supply of information—at some point, a person would supply information and that person had or may reasonably be supposed to have had personal knowledge of the matters dealt with. In other words, we might have expected that person to have been able to give direct oral evidence of the fact. It is unnecessary to prove by evidence that the supplier would have had personal knowledge—in *Foxley*,[94] proof that sums of money were paid to Swiss intermediary companies and Swiss numbered bank accounts in respect of certain ordnance contracts which the appellant had corruptly influenced when he was a civil servant at the Ministry of Defence, was established by documents produced by the appropriate authorities in Italy, Germany and Norway. These documents could speak for themselves without any necessity for calling the document keeper or supplier of the information.

b) The creation of the document—the document itself was created or received by a person in the course of a trade, business, profession or other occupation, or as the holder of a paid or unpaid office. Under subs.(3), the supplier of the information and the creator of the document may be one and the same person.

---

[93] s.123(3) replicating Youth Justice and Criminal Evidence Act 1999, s.53.
[94] (1995) Crim.L.R. 636.

c) The passage of the document through various stages—in business enterprises, the record containing the information may pass through several stages, from the initial recording on the shop floor, to filling out card indexes, creating a database to archiving. Thus the document can contain multiple hearsay, (*i.e.* where the information has been transferred at least twice. There is no limit to the length of the chain through which the information passes. At each stage when the information was passed on (this can be done orally and not necessarily through intermediate documents), it must be received in the course of a "trade, business, profession or other occupation . . ." However this is not a required condition in relation to the initial supplier of the information.

(i) *Business documents*

Section 117 provides considerable scope for the admissibility of business documents. This embraces not merely private business but the public sector, charities, private associations, the officers of sports clubs and so on. *Foxley*[95] suggests that the documents are allowed to speak for themselves and the court will infer the source of the documents from their contents. This is also seen in *Vehicle and Operator Service Agency v George Jenkin Transport*,[96] where the magistrates' courts held that time sheets were inadmissible as evidence under s.24 to assist the prosecution of the respondent company for offences of failures to use tachographs properly and permitting driving in excess of permitted hours. The Divisional Court reversed this as the purpose of the legislation was to enable documents to speak for themselves. It plainly envisaged that the court could draw inferences about documents without the requirement for oral evidence from the maker or keeper of them. The very look of the time sheets (weekly records showing the names of particular drivers, the mileage driven, fuel used and hours worked) was sufficient.

(ii) *Created or received*

Section 117(2)(a) allows for a document to be admissible where it is "created or received" within a business setting. "Created" provides few problems as the routine nature of the business world is some guarantee of accuracy. However the term "received" poses difficulties: an everyday document such as a diary can become admissible under s.117 if it is handed over to the police who "receive" it in the course of their business.[97] If such an interpretation were correct, the writer of the diary needs no longer to be proved to be unavailable.[98] This would give too wide a meaning to "receive". Obviously, if a letter is handed to a postman who receives it in the course of their

---

[95] [1995] Crim.L.R. 636.
[96] [2003] EWHC 2879 (Admin) QBD.
[97] M. Ockelton, "Documentary Hearsay in Criminal Cases" [1992] Crim.L.R. 15.
[98] We have to bear in mind s.117(4) and the exclusionary discretionary discretion under s.117(7) as well as under s.78 Police and Criminal Evidence Act 1984.

employment, such a transaction should not bypass the requirements of s.116. Others[99] have argued that received must mean received "qua hearsay and not merely qua physical object". A sealed letter sent to your solicitor for safekeeping must remain a s.116 document whereas a letter outlining the provisions of your will and which becomes part of your file is admissible under s.117, although even in this latter scenario, it is difficult to understand why mere receipt should have any bearing on admissibility.

This drafting provides potential problems with regard to police documents. For example, an officer's notebook might well record speculative information supplied by an informant but unseen by that informant and as such not a s.116 document. By the time of trial, the informant has died but the notebook could be admissible evidence under s.117. The courts might well need to use their exclusionary discretion under subs.(7).

(iii) *Documents prepared for criminal investigation*

In any criminal investigation, the police gather witness statements which are clearly admissible documents under s.117 so that there is no requirement that the relevant witness was not available to testify. This would be unacceptable as it would remove any opportunity for the accused to cross-examine the witnesses against them. Therefore under subss.(4) and (5) where the statement was made for the specific purpose of a criminal investigation or criminal proceedings, it is only admissible if it is shown that the witness is incapable of testifying and the requirements of s.116(2) are met.

Interestingly subs.(5) creates an additional possibility for the unavailability of the witness, namely that the person who made the statement cannot reasonably be expected to have any recollection of the matters dealt with in the statement. An example can be seen in *Farrand v Galland*,[1] the accused was charged with supplying a car with a false odometer reading. The evidence was the record cards of a previous owner, a car-hire firm. The person who had compiled the record was available but not called and it would be unreasonable to expect the person who filled out the card to have any recollection of the mileage.

What constitutes for the "purposes of pending criminal investigation" can be seen in *Meaden*,[2] where the defendant was accused of failure to comply with an enforcement notice. There had been correspondence between the local authority and the defendant's agents—this was held to have been seeking voluntary compliance with the notice and not to have been part of a criminal investigation and therefore the correspondence was admissible.

With s.116, there is no problem about whose unavailability must be shown—it is the declarant who is unavailable. The 1988 legislation drew an

---

[99] D. McEvoy, "Police Documents as Admissible Hearsay" [1993] Crim.L.R. 480; J. Smith, "Sections 23 and 24 of the Criminal Justice Act 1988: Some Problems" [1994] Crim.L.R. 426 at 429.
[1] [1989] Crim.L.R. 573 (relevant to s.117 although decided under s.68 Police and Criminal Evidence Act 1984).
[2] [2002] EWCA Crim 2740.

unhappy distinction between the supplier of the information and the maker of the statement and the confusion can be seen in *Carrington*.[3] The accused attempted to pay for goods in a supermarket using a stolen Switch card but made off when suspected. The cashier alerted the supervisors, the first of whom spotted the accused driving out of the car park and noted the registration number of the car which was reported via the telephone to a second supervisor who wrote it down on a memo pad. Was the memo pad admissible evidence of the registration number? Here the information is gathered in the course of a business but is also noted with a view to criminal investigation. The first supervisor is the supplier of the information and the "absent witness" whose absence should be justified. The first supervisor could not "reasonably be expected to have any recollection of the matters dealt with in the statement" so that the statement should be admitted.[4] A better approach was taken in *Deroda*,[5] which involved a false insurance claim for a burglary where the accused was alleged to have taken out the insurance policy after the burglary took place. The prosecution sought to prove the date of the burglary by relying on the statement of a lodger in the house (who could not be traced) who had phoned the police incident room to report the crime. The court accepted that it was the lodger who was the "maker of the statement" whose absence had to be justified as opposed to the police officer who took and recorded the call.

Section 117 makes it clear that the "relevant person" will be the initial supplier of the information and no such confusion should occur.

(iv) *Discretion to Exclude*

As discussed earlier, the1988 legislation provided further obstacles, giving the court the power to exclude such evidence as business documents, if in the interests of justice, they ought not to be admitted. The 2003 legislation took a more radical approach which establishes a defeasible right to have that documentary business records admitted under s.117. However this can be challenged under subs.(7) and, of course, the court retains a residual discretion to exclude the evidence if the admission would have an adverse effect on the fairness of the proceedings contrary to s.78. In these provisions, the ultimate issue differs—under s.117(7), it is the document's reliability as evidence; whereas for s.78 it is the "fairness of the proceedings".

It would appear that the burden of persuading the court that the hearsay statement should be excluded varies. Under the wording of s.117(7), the court "... may make a direction under this subsection if satisfied that the statement's reliability as evidence for the purpose for which it is tendered is doubtful". This puts the burden of satisfying the court on the party seeking to exclude the statement. Discharging this burden of proof will be difficult as the

---

[3] (1993) 99 Cr.App.R. 376.
[4] In the original case, the Court of Appeal held that it was the absence of B, the second supervisor, and the 'maker of the statement' which had to be justified. This confusion will not occur under the Criminal Justice Act 2003.
[5] (2001) 1 Cr.App.R. 41.

party adversely affected by the admission of the business records would have to show unreliability. This would involve some evidence that there were faults in the gathering, recording or transmission of the data or that there was some evidence of fraud or forgery in the documents.

D. *Credibility under the 2003 Act*

When a witness gives oral testimony, the jury are able to see the demeanour of the witness or assess their credibility and reliability as witnesses of truth under cross-examination, subject to the provisions of s.100 of the Criminal Justice Act 2003. When that testimony is provided not by the person but in the form of a document or another witness, that possibility of cross-examination is lost. However the party who is adversely affected by the reception of the hearsay evidence does have some means to attack the credit of the absent witness.

124(1) This section applies if in criminal proceedings—
(a) a statement not made in oral evidence in the proceedings is admitted as evidence of a matter stated, and
(b) the maker of the statement does not give oral evidence in connection with the subject matter of the statement.
(2) In such a case—
(a) any evidence which (if he had given such evidence) would have been admissible as relevant to his credibility as a witness is so admissible in the proceedings;
(b) evidence may with the court's leave be given of any matter which (if he had given such evidence) could have been put to him in cross-examination as relevant to his credibility as a witness but of which evidence could not have been adduced by the cross-examining party;
(c) evidence tending to prove that he made (at whatever time) any other statement inconsistent with the statement admitted as evidence is admissible for the purpose of showing that he contradicted himself.
(3) If as a result of evidence admitted under this section an allegation is made against the maker of a statement, the court may permit a party to lead additional evidence of such description as the court may specify for the purposes of denying or answering the allegation.
(4) In the case of a statement in a document which is admitted as evidence under section 117 each person who, in order for the statement to be admissible, must have supplied or received the information concerned or created or received the document or part concerned is to be treated as the maker of the statement for the purposes of subsections (1) to (3) above.

There are common law rules restricting the extent to which a party can cross-examine on credibility. Generally witnesses giving oral testimony can be cross-examined on collateral issues going to their credibility as a witness. However at common law there is the rule of finality of answers on collateral issues—having received an answer on a matter of credibility, a party is, with some exceptions, not entitled to pursue the matter further or adduce independent evidence to contradict the witness. There are now statutory limitations under section 100 of the Criminal Justice Act 2003 which restricts such questioning to matters which are "important explanatory evidence" or which have "substantial probative value". Section 124 must be read in that context.

There are three avenues by which the credit of the maker of the statement may be impeached.

i) Under subs.(2)(a), the party can rely, as of right, on evidence which could have been called if the maker had been called as a witness. This includes evidence which could be put to the witness under section 100 where the creditworthiness of the witness was "important explanatory evidence" or had "substantial probative value." There may also be situations where the section does not apply. Evidence on credit which is outside the bad character rules is introduced and the rule on finality does not apply—here a party could adduce evidence in rebuttal. Such exceptions include the fact that the absent witness was biased,[6] suffered from a physical or mental disability,[7] had previous convictions[8] or was reputed to be untruthful.[9]

ii) Under subs.(2)(b), with the leave of the court, evidence of a matter which could have been put to the maker of the statement in cross-examination and as to which the answer would have been final, *e.g.* that they were expelled from university for cheating in examinations. This might well be redundant and have been included from an abundance of caution—it is difficult to imagine such matters that would satisfy the test of being "important explanatory evidence" or having "substantial probative value" and yet not come under subs.(2)(a).

iii) Under subs.(2)(c), the party can rely, as of right, on evidence of an earlier or later inconsistent statement made by the maker of the statement. This allows a party to prove statements by the absent witness which are inconsistent with the evidence that has been tendered in court. Such statements are a further exception to the rule on finality of answers to collateral issues and may be proved under ss.4 or 5 of the Criminal Procedure Act 1865. They are referred to as 'prior' inconsistent statements since in the normal situation, they are prior to and inconsistent with a witness's present testimony. The impact of ss.116 and 117 makes the term "prior" somewhat strange as s.124 allows the adduction of evidence of inconsistent statements made, both before or after, the statement relied on in court.

When a witness testifies and is present in court, prior inconsistent statements may be put to them. Where proved under the provisions of the Criminal Procedure Act 1865, s.119 of the Criminal Justice Act 2003 makes

---

[6] e.g. *Mendy* (1976) 64 Cr.App.R. 4.
[7] *Toohey v Metropolitan Police Commissioner* [1965] A.C. 595.
[8] These can be proved under s.6 Criminal Procedure Act 1865.
[9] *Richardson* [1969] 1 Q.B. 299.

these prior statements evidence of the matter stated. In other words a court or jury could choose which of the two statements to believe as evidence of the facts. However under s.124(2)(c), if such inconsistent statements are proved, these statements can only be used, "for the purpose of showing that he contradicted himself". In other words, if a court or jury is faced with a choice between prior inconsistent statement and the statement that has been adduced as evidence in court, they cannot use that prior statement as evidence of truth.

There is a potential impasse here—let us imagine that the sole eyewitness makes a statement to the police that the accused was not present but then moves to Spain and writes a letter to the CPS, repudiating that earlier statement and identifying the accused. The witness refuses to return to the UK. The prosecution advance the letter as evidence of guilt under s.119 whereas the defence produce the earlier statement as evidence of innocence, and argue that the letter can only be adduced for the purpose of showing that the witness had contradicted himself—its status as evidence should not be determined by the stage of the trial at which it is introduced.

Where the absent witness's credibility has been attacked under s.124(2), the party introducing the statement is allowed to adduce evidence ". . . for the purposes of denying or answering the allegation" under subs.(3). For example, if the statement is alleged to be a recent fabrication, a prior statement, consistent with the contents of the document, would be admissible.[10]

E. *Section 9 statements*

There are many statutes admitting documentary hearsay as evidence. The most significant of such exceptions is the provision in the Police and Criminal Evidence Act 1984 for the admission of confessions. Others include reports of expert witnesses and evidence by children and other vulnerable witnesses. These are discussed in the relevant chapters. However there are some further examples —these can be found in the context of committal proceedings, but especially in summary proceedings in magistrates' courts. A significant amount of evidence, especially in magistrates' courts, will be through the medium of agreed statements under s.9 of the Criminal Justice Act 1967.

9.—(1) In any criminal proceedings, other than committal proceedings, a written statement by any person shall, if such of the conditions mentioned in the next following subsection as are applicable are satisfied, be admissible evidence to the like extent as oral evidence to the like effect by that person.
(2) The said conditions are—
a) the statement purports to be signed by the person who made it;

---

[10] *Oyesiku* (1971) 56 Cr.App.R. 240—generally see Ch.10.

b) the statement contains a declaration by that person to the effect that it is true to the best of his knowledge and belief and that he made the statement knowing that, if it were tendered in evidence, he would be liable to prosecution if he wilfully stated in it anything which he knew to be false or did not believe to be true;

c) before the hearing at which the statement is tendered in evidence, a copy of the statement is served, by or on behalf of the party proposing to tender it, to each of the other parties to the proceedings; and

d) none of the other parties or their solicitors, within seven days from the service of the copy of the statement, serves a notice on the party so proposing objecting to the statement being tendered in evidence under the section:

Provided that the conditions mentioned in c) and d) of this subsection shall not apply if the parties agree before or during the hearing the statement shall be so tendered

The section should be read in the light of the practice direction[11] regarding the editing of such statements. Statements under s.9 are frequently edited for the court to ensure orderly presentation and the exclusion of irrelevant or prejudicial information.[12] This should be done by a Crown Prosecutor.

Section 9 statements are ones which are agreed by the parties.[13] But agreeing (or not objecting) to the admission of the statement does not mean that the statement is accepted as conclusive evidence and the contents of the statement may still be disputed at trial. In *Lister v Quaife*,[14] the defendant was accused of stealing a dress from Marks and Spencer. She testified that she had bought the dress from another branch on an earlier date and was seeking to exchange it. There were s.9 statements from the M&S head office to the effect that the particular dress could not have been bought at the time and in the shop as suggested by the defendant. The defendant was acquitted and the prosecution argued that, having not objected to the statements, it was not open to the accused to give evidence contradicting those statements and that the magistrates' decision was perverse. The Divisional Court upheld the magistrates' actions.

Lister v Quaife [1983] 2 All E.R. 29 at 32–33, *per* May L.J.:

. . . we have come to the clear conclusion that the answer really lies in a proper appreciation of what section 9 in fact achieves. As I have already said, this is that the contents of the statements read are evidence in the case just as if, and only to the extent as if, the makers of those statements had been called as witnesses in the trial and given the evidence contained in the statements. If that had happened at the hearing before the King's Lynn justices in this case, and there had been no cross-examination about the possibility of mistake, or their evidence had not been chal-

[11] [1986] 2 All E.R. 511.

[12] The weaknesses in the process of recording witness statements are discussed in A. Heaton-Armstrong and D. Wolchover "Recording Witness Statements" [1992] Crim.L.R. 160.

[13] A failure to object within the time limit is not fatal as a party can ask the court to call the witness under s.9(4)(b) of the Act.

[14] [1983] 2 All E.R. 29.

lenged in any way, then when the respondent went into the witness box no doubt strong comment could have been made that nothing had been put to the witnesses about the possibility that the respondent might indeed have been able to and did buy the dress somewhere else . . . .

Although any such comment by those representing the Crown would have had substantial force and might well have led the justices to view the respondent's evidence with a degree of scepticism, the position remains that the burden throughout was on the prosecution and although the proper procedure of putting a defence case to prosecution witnesses had not been followed, it would have been open to the justices, having heard all three witnesses, to have said: 'Well, it may be that that procedure laid down by Marks and Spencer was what should have happened, and it may have happened in at least the majority, if not in every other case concerning a dress of this nature, but we have also seen the respondent. She has given evidence. We cannot say that her evidence cannot be true, and in those circumstances there must be a doubt in our minds and accordingly we must acquit'.

If one realises that that is all that is achieved by a section 9 statement, then notwithstanding that criticism may be made of the fact that the respondent's legal advisers did not give any appropriate notice requiring the makers of the statements to attend at the trial, we do not think that in the end it is right to say that the two halves of that opinion of the justices are necessarily inconsistent and their decision perverse.

In theory the statement has the same weight as oral evidence in the trial and jurors cannot be directed to prefer the oral testimony if it conflicts with the written statement.[15] This is in contrast to statements admitted under ss.116 and 117 of the Criminal Justice Act 2003 which normally require a judicial warning to the jury. In *Abiodun*,[16] defence witnesses were refused visa by the state to enter the country and the prosecution also refused to agree to their statements being read under s.9, leaving the judge with the sole option of admitting them under s.23 of the Criminal Justice Act 1988 and warning the jury, albeit in mild terms, of the danger of relying on witnesses that they had not seen or heard.

---

[15] *Mitchell* [1995] Crim.L.R. 146; *Millen* [1995] Crim.L.R. 568.
[16] [2003] EWCA Crim 2167.

19

HEARSAY IN CIVIL PROCEEDINGS—
THE CIVIL EVIDENCE ACT 1995

I. The New Approach

The rule against hearsay was never absolute. Not only was it affected by the exceptions developed at common law but also by statutory provisions allowing for the admission of hearsay statements. Many of these are concerned with specific cases such as Bankers' Books Evidence Act 1879 or, more recently, section 96 of the Children Act 1989 which sought to apply the more liberal practice of the wardship jurisdiction of the High Court to all courts dealing with matters affecting children.[1] A broader approach was evident in the Evidence Act 1938 which permitted the introduction of certain documentary hearsay into civil proceedings. This statute continued to govern civil proceedings in magistrates' courts until 1995.[2] A more thoroughgoing reform was introduced in the Civil Evidence Act 1968. As a result of this Act, certain hearsay statements became admissible evidence of the facts or opinions[3] contained in them. But the Act in no sense abolished the rule against hearsay, instead creating broad but still limited statutory exceptions, especially for first-hand hearsay (whether oral or in documentary form) and for second-hand documentary hearsay. The principle in 1968 was to maintain the exclusionary rule but establish broad statutory exceptions. But at the same time these reforms were hedged about with a range of restrictions (such as the level of hearsay admissible) and complex procedural safeguards.

The Civil Evidence Act 1995 implements the recommendations of the Law Commission Report.[4] As a result the 1995 legislation adopts a radical approach: principally s.1 abolishes the rule against the admission of hearsay

---

[1] Others include Births and Deaths Registration Acts 1836 to 1953; Marriage Act 1949; Army Act 1955, s.198(5); Solicitors Act 1974, s.18; Inheritance (Provision for Family and Dependants) Act 1975, s.21.

[2] This caused problems in poll tax cases: *R. v Coventry Justices Ex p. Bullard*, *The Times*, February, 24 1992; A. Murdie, "Hearsay Evidence in Poll Tax Cases" [1992] N.L.J. 1551.

[3] The Civil Evidence Act 1972 extended the definition of "statement" to include "representation of opinion" as well as "representation of fact".

[4] Law Commission *The Hearsay Rule in Civil Proceedings* (1993) (Law Comm. No. 216) Cm. 2321— it follows a Consultation Paper, *The Hearsay Rule in Civil Proceedings* (1991) Law Comm. No. 117.

evidence in all civil proceedings. Evidence cannot now be excluded on the ground that it is hearsay. The section also defines the concept of hearsay.[5]

1.—(1) In civil proceedings evidence shall not be excluded on the ground that it is hearsay.

(2) In this Act—

   a) 'hearsay' means a statement otherwise than by a person while giving oral evidence in the proceedings which is tendered as evidence of the matters stated; and

   b) references to hearsay include hearsay of whatever degree.

(3) Nothing in this Act affects the admissibility of evidence admissible apart from this section

(4) The provisions of sections 2 to 6 (safeguards and supplementary provisions relating to hearsay evidence) do not apply in relation to hearsay evidence admissible apart from this section, notwithstanding that it may also be admissible by virtue of this section.

The Act abolishes the rule against admitting hearsay evidence. However, the category of hearsay evidence still remains. There are safeguards in ss.2–6 and under Pt 33 of the Civil Procedure Rules which apply to hearsay evidence and to this limited extent, it is necessary to distinguish between hearsay and non-hearsay evidence.

   i) Section 2 provides for notice to be given to the other party of any intention to adduce hearsay evidence.

   ii) Section 3 allows the other party to call the maker of the hearsay statement and to cross-examine him or her on that statement.

   iii) Section 4 provides a statutory checklist for the court in assessing the weight to be given to hearsay evidence.

   iv) Section 5 ensures that an incompetent witness shall not be made competent through the medium of a hearsay statement. It also allows the opposing party to adduce evidence that would cast doubt on the credibility of the maker of the statement.

   v) Section 6 lays down the conditions for the admissibility of prior consistent statements.

In *Polanski v Conde Nast Publications*,[6] a defamation case, the core issue was whether the claimant should be permitted to testify by video link from France. The claimant, a film director, was concerned that, were he to return to the UK, he would be extradited to the USA where he faced criminal charges. In the context of that main issue, Baroness Hale discussed the impact of the Civil Evidence Act 1995.

Polanski v Conde Nast Publications [2005] All E.R. 945, *per* Baroness Hale:

70. I wish, however, to expand a little on the question of whether the appellant's witness statement should have been admitted if he were not permitted to give oral

---

[5] This is in terms similar to those used by Cross's formulation which was approved by the House of Lords in *Sharp* [1988] 1 All E.R. 65 at 68c as well as to that used in criminal proceedings in to Criminal Justice Act 2003, s.114.

[6] [2005] All E.R. 945.

evidence by VCF. The judge assumed that if he were not called to give evidence, his witness statement would be admitted as hearsay evidence. The Court of Appeal took the view that it would not: indeed they said in terms that if the appellant failed to attend in person to be cross examined on his witness statement, the court would be 'bound' to refuse to admit it . . . . In my view this goes far too far.

71. It remains the general procedural rule that any fact which needs to be proved by the evidence of witnesses is to be proved at trial by their oral evidence: see CPR 32.2(1)(a). But in civil proceedings this is now a matter of procedure rather than substance. The substantive rule is that all relevant evidence is admissible unless there is a rule excluding it. There used to be a rule excluding hearsay evidence, that is, a statement made otherwise than by a person while giving oral evidence in the proceedings which is tendered as evidence of the matters stated: see Civil Evidence Act 1995, s 1(2). To this rule there were numerous exceptions which deprived it of much of its force in civil proceedings. But in 1995 the rule itself was abolished. Section 1(1) of the 1995 Act provides simply that:

"In civil proceedings evidence shall not be excluded on the ground that it is hearsay."

72. This new rule is not made subject to the later provisions of the Act which provide for procedural safeguards where hearsay evidence is to be adduced. Section 2 requires a party proposing to adduce hearsay evidence to give such notice of that fact as is reasonable and practicable in all the circumstances to enable the other party to deal with it. But a failure to comply with this requirement (or with the rules of court dealing with how such notice is to be given) 'does not affect the admissibility of the evidence'; rather it may be penalised in costs and taken into account in assessing weight: see section 2(4).

73. Section 3 gives power for rules of court to provide that if the party adducing hearsay evidence does not call the maker of the statement to give evidence in person, the other party may do so and may cross-examine him as if he had been called by the party adducing the statement; see also CPR 33.4. Nothing in section 3 or in the CPR provides or suggests that if the maker does not attend for cross examination at trial his statement becomes inadmissible. Section 4 provides for the considerations relevant to assessing the weight (if any) to be given to hearsay evidence, the first of which is whether it would have been reasonable or practicable for the maker of the statement to be called as a witness. Section 5(2) provides that the same evidence of credibility or of inconsistent statements is admissible as would be admissible had the maker of the statement been called to give evidence: see also CPR 33.5. Section 6 deals with the treatment of statements made by people who are called as witnesses in the proceedings.

74. The substantive law following the 1995 Act, therefore, is that relevant hearsay is always admissible; there are various procedural safeguards aimed at reducing the prejudice caused to an opposing party if he is not able to cross-examine the maker of the statement; but the principal safeguard is the reduced—even to vanishing—weight to be given to a statement which has not been made in court and subject to cross-examination in the usual way. The court is to be trusted to give the statement such weight as it is worth in all the circumstances of the case.

. . .

78. It is well within this objective[of case management] to seek to get the parties to agree as many facts as possible, to limit the number of witnesses who may be called to give evidence on a particular issue, or to restrict the amount of documentary evidence placed before the court. But it would be a strong thing indeed to use such case management powers to exclude the admissible evidence of one of the parties on the central facts of the case. There may be circumstances in which this could be done. The unreasonable refusal of that party to subject himself to cross examination may be one of them. It might be grossly unjust to the other party, even contrary to his right to a fair trial under article 6 of the European Convention on Human Rights, to decide a claim principally on the untested evidence of a party who had not been subject to cross examination of any sort. But that is not this case. The appellant is quite willing to be

cross-examined by a procedure which is agreed will cause no prejudice to the respondent . . .

II. Admissibility of Hearsay

As Baroness Hale makes clear, s.1 of the 1995 Act takes a liberal approach to the admissibility of previous out-of-court statements but, unlike its 1968 predecessor or the 2003 Criminal Justice Act, it is not a code for the admissibility of hearsay statements. It simply abolishes the exclusionary rule for the purposes of civil proceedings.

A. *Inadmissible for other reasons*

If the statements are inadmissible for reasons other than the fact that they are hearsay, s.1 does not make them admissible. It only cures the vice of hearsay.

14.—(1) Nothing in this Act affects the exclusion of evidence on grounds other than that it is hearsay.
This applies whether the evidence falls to be excluded in pursuance of any enactment or rule of law, for failure to comply with rules of court or an order of the court, or otherwise.

An example of this would be the prohibition on non-expert opinion. In a pre-1995 case, *H v Schering Chemicals*,[7] a personal injury case, where the plaintiffs sought to adduce a series of correspondence and articles from medical journals to prove the harmful effects of drugs, without calling the authors themselves. Bingham J. said:

H v Schering Chemicals [1983] 1 All E.R 849 at 852g, *per* Bingham J.:

If the plaintiffs' submission were right it would, I think, mean that anyone who wrote a letter to "The Times", having done research and summarising the result of that research in his letter, would find his letter admissible as evidence of that research under section 4. That is not, I think, the intent of the section.[8]

The court was dealing with this on the narrow ground of whether a digest or analysis of others' work was itself a "record" within s.4 of 1968 Act so as to circumvent the hearsay rule. While the 1995 legislation has done away with such limitations, the comments are still pertinent—if the writer of the letter or article would not be qualified as an expert witness, then opinions expressed

---

[7] [1983] 1 All E.R. 849.
[8] *ibid.* at 852g.

in whatever newspaper or periodical do not become admissible evidence through the operation of s.1.

B. *Admissible for other reasons*

As s.1(4) makes clear, these safeguards do not apply to hearsay evidence which is admissible independent of s.1(1). This was designed to preserve the effect of other statutory provisions which rendered hearsay admissible as evidence. The Law Commission stated:

> . . . It is not our policy to affect the operation of the existing statutory provisions rendering hearsay admissible, whether for particular purposes or in particular circumstances, or to add procedural burdens where none exist at present, particularly in the case of a statutory code as recent as the Children Act.

Acts such as Bankers' Books Evidence Act 1879 or s.96 of the Children Act 1989 have their own requirements and are not affected by the 1995 legislation.

The 1995 legislation allows for two channels of admissibility. Those are admissibility under s.1(1) and therefore affected by the procedural safeguards; or admissibility under some other statutory provision and therefore unaffected by the 1995 safeguards. But the Act leaves open a third intriguing avenue of admissibility. What is the status and place of the old common law exceptions to hearsay, not specifically preserved in the Act, especially statements by deceased persons and *res gestae*?

Under the 1968 Civil Evidence Act, hearsay was only admissible under the Act. The common law exceptions were either expressly retained by s.9 or otherwise had to conform to the conditions of admissibility laid down in ss.2 and 4. Statements by deceased persons and *res gestae* were both common law exceptions to the hearsay rule but were not preserved by section 9. As categories, they were not abolished but might be seen as put into hibernation. But in the 1995 Act, s.1(3) states.

"Nothing in this Act affects the admissibility of evidence admissible apart from this section".

This allows us to consider whether hearsay statements can be admissible in other, non-statutory, ways. One answer is that hearsay statements for centuries were admissible at common law through a range of exceptions. If we accept the premise that the 1968 Act did not abolish that common law, then, with the repeal of Pt I of that Act, like a phoenix from the ashes, *res gestae* and statements by deceased persons become admissible again as common law exceptions.

Furthermore s.1(3) states that the Act does not affect the admissibility of evidence which is admissible apart from the Act. This might be interpreted to mean that the safeguards of the 1995 legislation do not apply to hearsay admissible through other avenues. Not only would a party not have to give notice under s.2 but as well the opposing party would not have the benefit of s.3 because, although they could call the maker of the statement as a witness, they would not be permitted to treat the maker as a witness called by the other party and thereby cross-examine him or her.

An extension to this argument might be made out with regard to informal admissions. These were specifically provided for in s.(9)(1) and s.9(2)(a) of the 1968 Act. The 1995 legislation regards such statements as coming naturally under s.1 and thus s.7(1) states:

The common law rule effectively preserved by section 9(1) and (2)(a) of the Civil Evidence Act 1968 (admissibility of admissions adverse to a party) is superseded by the provisions of this Act.

Obviously the draftsmen considered that the rule as contained in s.9 of the 1968 Act was superseded by section 1(1). But the repeal of s.9 of the 1968 Act leaves the common law exception on informal admissions alive and kicking and therefore admissible under s.1(3). In such a case, a party relying on an informal admission would not need to give notice of the hearsay statement. Thus hearsay statements are now admissible in civil proceedings:

    i) under s.1 of the Civil Evidence Act 1995;
    ii) under other statutory provisions; and
    iii) where common law exceptions to hearsay apply.[9]

III. Proceedings

Civil proceedings are defined by the 1995 Act.

11. In this Act 'civil proceedings' means civil proceedings, before any tribunal, in relation to which the strict rules of evidence apply, whether as a matter of law or by agreement of the parties.

This provision retains the distinction in s.18(1) of the 1968 Act between those proceedings where the strict rules of evidence apply[10] and those tribunals which use more informal, less court-like procedures. As has been noted, the 1995 Act abolishes the exclusionary rule but retains the category of hearsay evidence to which certain procedural safeguards apply. Whereas tribunals applying "strict rules of evidence" will be bound to apply these procedural safeguards, other, less formal, tribunals will not be affected by the Act.

Prior to the 1995 Act, different rules of evidence applied in magistrates' courts depending on whether the proceedings were licensing applications, family, civil or criminal.[11] The same rules of evidence will now apply in all civil proceedings in magistrates' courts. For example, hearsay evidence is

---

[9] see Ch.17.
[10] These include the Lands Tribunal, the Solicitors Disciplinary Tribunal and the Commissioners of Income Tax. For the position on arbitrations, see Law Commission, *op.cit.*, para.4.44.
[11] Law Commission, *op.cit.*, paras 3.22–3.31.

admissible in proceedings for anti-social behaviour orders in magistrates' courts.[12]

IV. THE NOTICE PROVISIONS

Under the 1968 law, the major safeguard was the requirement to give notice of the intention to adduce hearsay evidence under ss.2, 4 or 5. It was generally recognised to be too complex; not least the requirement that in certain situations, a party had to prove the non-availability of the maker of the statement before the hearsay statement was admissible.[13]

"The Hearsay Rule in Civil Proceedings" (1993) (Law Comm. No.216) Cm.2321, paras 4.11–4.12:

There was general agreement by consultees with the view that the current regime is too elaborate and places unrealistic burdens on parties . . . . The Law Society, for example, commented that the rules are rarely relied on, save where a witness has died, disappeared, or moved overseas. There has also been considerable criticism of the 'beyond the seas' rule which allows, for example, the admission of a statement by a person in Jersey and excludes a statement from a person in Newcastle. There was unanimity that the prescribed time limits were not complied with . . . we were told that this was a matter that was usually left until the pre-trial conferences with counsel . . .[14]

We intend that a major safeguard against abuse of the freedom to adduce hearsay evidence should be found in a new, simplified notice provision . . . . We intend our notice provision to be a departure from the complexity of the current notice rules which require a considerable amount of detail about the statement maker and the circumstances in which the statement was made. We endorse the objectives of the current system which are (a) that all issues arising out of the adduction of hearsay evidence should be dealt with before trial and (b) that there should be no surprises at trial . . .[15]

If a party does not give notice, where it would have been reasonable and practicable in all the circumstances for him to do so, we have decided not to recommend that the courts be allowed to refuse to admit the evidence. We consider that a failure to comply with this safeguard is a matter which should be treated as an abuse of the court's process and not as one which should go to admissibility . . . We believe that the courts' inherent powers to control the conduct of proceedings include the power to rectify prejudice to parties adversely affected by a failure to comply. In these circumstances the relevant powers would be likely to include granting an adjournment to allow the recipient time to deal with the effect of late notification, or to compel the opposing party to perfect an inadequate notice. In extreme cases, it might involve ordering the trial to start again . . .

Section 2 of the Civil Evidence Act 1995 addresses these concerns. Notice is regarded as important and r.33.2 of the Civil Procedure Rules prescribes the

---

[12] *R. (on the application of McCann and others) v Manchester Crown Court* [2002] 4 All E.R. 593.
[13] The reasons were specified in Civil Evidence Act 1968, s.8.
[14] Law Commission, *op.cit.*, paras 3.2–3.3.
[15] *ibid.* para.4.9.

manner of that notice. But a failure to comply with the provisions does not affect admissibility or lead to the evidence being excluded.

2.—(1) A party proposing to adduce hearsay evidence in civil proceedings shall, subject to the following provisions of this section, give to the other party or parties to the proceedings—
  a) such notice (if any) of that fact, and
  b) on request, such particulars of or relating to the evidence,
  as is reasonable and practicable in the circumstances for the purpose of enabling him or them to deal with any matters arising from its being hearsay . . .
  . . . (4) A failure to comply with subsection (1), or with the rules under subsection (2)(b), does not affect the admissibility of the evidence but may be taken into account by the court—
  a) in considering the exercise of its powers with respect to the course of proceedings and costs, and
  b) as a matter adversely affecting the weight to be given to the evidence in accordance with section 4.

Under these provisions, the recipient may request such particulars of the hearsay evidence "as is reasonable and practicable in the circumstances for the purpose of enabling him or them to deal with any matters arising from its being hearsay". The details come under Civil Procedure Rules r.33.2: notice should be given at the same time as witness statements are exchanged; the notice will indicate that the evidence is hearsay, identify the declarant and explain why the declarant will not be called as a witness.

The sanctions for failure to give notice are levied through allocating the costs of the action and, more importantly, by permitting the judge to give more weight to a statement where the proper procedures have been followed than to those hearsay statements where they have not.

V. Responding to a Hearsay Notice

On receiving a hearsay notice, the other party has certain tactical options.

A. Available witnesses—the power to call and to cross-examine

In drafting the 1995 legislation, the Law Commission considered whether hearsay statements ought to be excluded whenever it was reasonable and practicable to call the maker of the statement as a witness. This would have made a broad exception to the principle of general admissibility of hearsay statements, even were it restricted to those situations where there was a failure to give notice. Such an approach was rejected so that hearsay statements have become admissible under section 1 regardless of the availability of the maker of the statement.

The safeguard that has been introduced by s.3 and r.33.4 of the Civil Procedure Rules is to allow the opposing party to call the maker of the statement as a witness. Of course, there is nothing in law to prevent the opposing party from calling the maker of the statement as a witness, if they are available. But they would then be restricted in asking questions since it would not be possible to cross-examine the witness on the contents of the hearsay statement or to call into question their credibility as a witness, unless the witness were, in the opinion of the judge, to prove "adverse".[16] Section 3 addresses this problem.

3. Rules of court may provide that where a party to civil proceedings adduces hearsay evidence of a statement made by a person and does not call that person as a witness, any other party to the proceedings may, with the leave of the court, call that person as a witness and cross-examine him on the statements as if he had been called by the first-mentioned party and as if the hearsay statement were his evidence in chief.

Again the general principle of the admissibility of hearsay evidence is underlined since the availability of a witness does not lead to the exclusion of the hearsay statement. At the same time, a party's right to cross-examine the other party's witnesses is upheld, albeit after obtaining the leave of the court for permission to call and cross-examine the maker of the statement. Total reliance on hearsay statements will not render a finding unfair where the opposing party fails to object to the admission of the hearsay statements and fails to seek permission to call the witnesses in person.[17]

The Law Commission considered it unlikely that this power would be often invoked since parties would wish to rely on "best evidence" and would call their witnesses in person if they were available. Furthermore relying on a hearsay statement of a witness who could have been called to testify will be another factor to be taken account of in evaluating the weight of the evidence under s.4.[18]

B. *Credibility*

One of the major safeguards of adversarial trial is the right to impeach the credibility of the witness. This cannot be undertaken when evidence is through the admission of the hearsay statement. The Civil Evidence Act 1968 provided some protection through s.7(1)(a) which enabled a party adversely affected to adduce evidence which attacked the credibility of the maker of the statement. It also provided that the party relying on the statement could adduce evidence supporting the maker's credibility. The Law Commission and the 1995 Act did not seek to change that position.[19]

5.—(2) Where in civil proceedings hearsay evidence is adduced and the maker of the original statement, or of any statement relied upon to prove another statement, is not called as a witness—
(a) evidence which if he had been so called would be admissible for the purpose of attacking or supporting his credibility as a witness is admissible for that purpose in the proceedings; and

[16] Criminal Procedure Act 1865, s.3—see Ch.13.
[17] *Ryell v Health Professions Council* [2005] EWHC 2797 (Admin).
[18] Law Commission, *op.cit.*, para.4.16.
[19] Law Commission, *op.cit.*, para.4.29 —however it has simplified the language of the section.

(b) evidence tending to prove that, whether before or after he made the statement, he made any other statement inconsistent with it is admissible for the purpose of showing that he had contradicted himself.

Provided that evidence may not be given of any matter of which, if he had been called as a witness and had denied that matter in cross-examination, evidence could not have been adduced by the cross-examining party.

Section 5(2) reflects the distinction between cross-examining on the issues and cross-examining as to credit. When the witness is present in court, this becomes important when counsel wants to introduce evidence in rebuttal of a witness's testimony. If this concerns the issues which the court has to decide, this is possible. But if it concerns a collateral issue, such as the credit of a witness, counsel is bound by the answer given by the witness and cannot call independent evidence in rebuttal.[20] Different scenarios are envisaged.

1. The proviso to the subsection deals with the situation where, in normal cross-examination, witnesses might be asked a question which impeaches their credit. They deny the matter. That is final since counsel cannot introduce evidence to rebut that denial. Where the testimony has been given by means of a hearsay statement, counsel is not permitted to adduce evidence which tends to substantiate the question that counsel has been unable to ask.

2. Paragraphs (a) and (b) allow counsel to adduce evidence in those situations where, even had the witness being normally cross-examined denied the matter, counsel would have been able to rebut that denial. These are the situations which are exceptions to the rule of finality to answers on collateral issues. There are five exceptions to this rule.

    a) Where the witness is present and denies making prior inconsistent statements, these can be proved under ss.3, 4 or 5 of the Criminal Procedure Act 1865. If the testimony has been given by way of hearsay, such statements are admissible by virtue of s.5(2)(b), whether the inconsistent statements were made before or after the statement given in evidence.

    b) Where a witness is present and denies previous convictions, these can be proved under section 6 of the Criminal Procedure Act 1865. If the testimony has been given by way of hearsay, such convictions are able to be proved by virtue of s.5(2)(a).

    c) Where a witness is present and denies bias, evidence rebutting this is admissible.[21] If the testimony has been given by way of hearsay, such bias may be proved by virtue of s.5(2)(a).

---

[20] *Attorney-General v Hitchcock* (1847) 1 Exch. 91.
[21] *Mendy* (1976) 64 Cr.App.R. 4; *Busby* (1981) 75 Cr.App.R. 79 ; *Edwards* [1991] 2 All E.R. 266.

d) Where a witness is present and denies any mental or physical disability, evidence rebutting this is admissible.[22] If the testimony has been given by way of hearsay, such disabilities may be proved by virtue of section 5(2)(a).
e) Where a witness is present and denies having a reputation for untruthfulness, evidence rebutting this is admissible.[23] If the testimony has been given by way of hearsay, such a reputation may be proved by virtue of section 5(2)(a).

Where a party wishes to adduce evidence to attack the credibility of the declarant, notice must be given under the provisions of rule 33.5 of the Civil Procedure Rules.

VI. Competence

Under the 1968 Civil Evidence Act, the admissibility of all categories of hearsay depended on the capacity of the maker of the statement as a competent witness. There was a requirement that ". . . direct oral evidence by [the maker of the statement] would be admissible."[24] This position is not altered by the 1995 Act except that the requirement is spelt out expressly.

5.—(1) Hearsay evidence shall not be admitted in civil proceedings if or to the extent that it is shown to consist of, or to be proved by means of, a statement made by a person who at the time he made the statement was not competent as a witness.

For this purpose 'not competent as a witness' means suffering from such mental or physical infirmity, or lack of understanding as would render a person incompetent as a witness in civil proceedings; but a child shall be treated as competent as a witness if he satisfies the requirements of section 96(2)(a) and (b) of the Children Act 1989 (conditions for reception of unsworn evidence of child[25]).

To avoid doubt on the issue of the date on which the witness has to be competent,[26] the section states expressly that for a hearsay statement to be admissible, the maker of the statement had to be a competent witness on the date that the statement was made.

JC v CC[27] involved breach of a non-molestation order where the mother testified that, after collecting her daughter from the father's home, her daughter had told her that the father had stated that she, the mother, was a prostitute. The father argued that daughter should have been treated as incompetent under s.5(1). The court held that that it was clear that the burden was upon the party who asserted that a witness was not competent to satisfy the court that their evidence was inadmissible. Here, that issue had not

---

[22] *Toohey v Met. Police Commissioner* [1965] A.C. 595.
[23] *Richardson* [1969] 1 Q.B. 299.
[24] Civil Evidence Act 1968, ss.2(1), 3(1) and 4(1).
[25] These conditions are that a child must understand the duty to speak the truth and that he or she has sufficient understanding to justify the evidence being heard—see Ch.9.
[26] Such a doubt arose in Scotland—*F v Kennedy* [1992] S.C.L.R. 139; *M and Another v Kennedy* [1993] S.C.L.R. 69.
[27] [2001] EWCA Civ 1625.

been raised at first instance and it was difficult in any event to be satisfied that such a burden would have been overcome, bearing in mind the daughter's age, which was ten, and the fact that she was doing well in her education.

VII. Weighing the Evidence

Under the 1995 legislation, exclusion of hearsay evidence is not an option. Instead the evidence is admitted and statutory guidelines provided by which the court is able to assess the weight to give to the hearsay statement.

Law Commission "The Hearsay Rule in Civil Proceedings" (1993) (Law Comm. No.2I6) Cm.2321. para.4.18:

The concept of providing guides as to weight is not novel: section 6(3) of the 1968 Act contains guidelines .... We favour developing the use of guidelines for the following reasons. First, having abolished the exclusionary rule, we wish to place extra emphasis on the need for courts to be vigilant in testing the reliability of such evidence. Secondly, we think it important that parties are deterred from abusing the abolition of the rule, for example by deliberately failing to give notice, by giving late and inadequate notice, by relying on hearsay evidence in preference to calling a dubious witness to give direct evidence of a fact, or by attempting to conceal an essential weakness in a case by amassing hearsay statements on a point. As we have mentioned above, the draft Bill also gives an express indication that failure to comply with the duty to give notice may be taken into account at this stage as affecting the weight to be given to hearsay evidence, for instance, where the circumstances in which the evidence is adduced as hearsay are such as to suggest an attempt to prevent a proper evaluation of its weight.

Some of the considerations relevant to weighing of hearsay evidence are specified in s.4.

4.—(1) In estimating the weight (if any) to be given to hearsay evidence in civil proceedings the court shall have regard to any circumstances from which any inference can reasonably be drawn as to the reliability or otherwise of the evidence.
(2) Regard may be had, in particular, to the following—
(a) whether it would have been reasonable and practicable for the party by whom the evidence was adduced to have produced the maker of the original statement as a witness;
(b) whether the original statement was made contemporaneously with the occurrence or existence of the matters stated;
(c) whether the evidence involves multiple hearsay;
(d) whether any person involved had any motive to conceal or misrepresent matters;
(e) whether the original statement was an edited account, or was made in collaboration with another or for a particular purpose;

(f) whether the circumstances in which the evidence is adduced as hearsay are such as to suggest an attempt to prevent proper evaluation of its weight.

It is a checklist of matters of which any court should take account as part of the normal process of assessing the weight of hearsay evidence. To the criticism that the section is self-evident, Lord Donaldson has commented that, as the guidelines became generally known and applied, a climate would continue to be fostered where practitioners would produce the best evidence available. Furthermore the section should concentrate the judicial mind on the issue of weight and, as the then Lord Chancellor, Lord Mackay, has pointed out, the provision is especially useful for magistrates' courts which have not admitted hearsay evidence to the same extent as the higher civil courts.[28]

Other factors may come into play, for example, admissions might be made by persons without personal knowledge of the facts and such statements might be admissible under s.1 of the Act. Where an admission is made which is not based on the personal knowledge of the speaker, it has limited evidential value but is admissible. Precedent suggests that the "personal knowledge" rule affects the probative worth of an admission rather than its admissibility. In *Comptroller of Customs v Western Electric Co. Ltd*,[29] there was an admission that the goods were made in the United States. This was based upon the markings on the goods, markings which were themselves inadmissible hearsay. The admission was of no more value than the information on which it was based. If the admission is based on personal experience, its evidential value is enhanced. In *Bird v Adams*,[30] the defendant was charged with possession of drugs. He admitted that he had 15 tablets of LSD. At the trial the issue arose as to whether there was any evidence of the nature of the tablets. The Divisional Court held that the defendant's past experience and conduct were such that the admission was at least prima facie evidence of its truth.

Bird v Adams [1972] Crim.L.R. 174, *per* Lord Widgery:

If a man admits possession of a substance which he says is a dangerous drug, if he admits it in circumstances like the present where he also admits he has been peddling the drug, it is of course possible that the item in question was not a specific drug at all but the admission in these circumstances is not an admission of some fact about which the admitter knows nothing.

Although a criminal case, it is an approach that fits well within the framework of the 1995 Act.

The issue was raised in *Solon South West Housing Association v James*,[31] a case where the claimant housing association sought the eviction of some tenants.

---

[28] 564 HL Official Reports (5th Series) col. 1051, May 25, 1995.
[29] [1966] A.C. 367.
[30] [1972] Crim.L.R. 174.
[31] [2005] H.L.R. 24 .

There was evidence from police officers, community workers and neighbours that the tenants had behaved in a grossly anti-social manner. Some of the evidence was first-hand but a considerable amount was hearsay from people who felt intimidated by the family and did not want to be identified.

Solon South West Housing Association v James [2005] H.L.R. 24, *per* Mance L.J.:

18. . . . The domestic context is . . . section 4 of the Civil Evidence Act1995. On the face of section 4, the availability of the maker of an original statement to be called is a matter going to weight not admissibility, but there is certainly power under the Civil Procedure Rules to exclude hearsay evidence . . .

19. To my mind, there is very little, if any, relevant difference between asking a judge to exclude evidence (which in this case does not appear to have happened) and asking him not to rely on it, since under section 4 a judge could determine that evidence was not worthy of any particular weight even after it had been admitted. So in one sense it does not matter that there was no application to exclude the evidence. The question is whether the judge put weight on particular evidence and whether he was justified in doing so.

The appellants argued that they were cross-examined about matters which they themselves cannot test by cross-examination places them at a substantial disadvantage. Mance L.J. quoted the trial judge's direction with approval.

25. . . . I recognise that risk and it seems to me that I am in the position envisaged by the Court of Appeal in *Leeds City Council v Harte*.[32] This was a case in which all the evidence was hearsay. The judge at first instance cautioned himself as to the weight which it would be right to place on the hearsay evidence, and then made conclusions of fact adverse to the defendant. The Court of Appeal held that he was entitled so to do . . .

The Court of Appeal held that there was no obligation upon the judge to identify whether or not the oral evidence was of itself sufficient. Moreover, it had been open to the judge to decide what hearsay evidence to rely on and what weight to place upon it. There had been no application to exclude any hearsay evidence and the judge had made clear the parts of that evidence upon which he relied. He had exercised his discretion correctly and in a way that had not impacted adversely on the fairness of the proceedings.

VIII. Previous statements of witnesses

At common law previous statements of witnesses were inadmissible, both because they were hearsay (if a party sought to rely upon the facts they contained) but also because of the rule against narrative which excluded such

[32] [1999] C.L.Y.B. 4069.

statements if they were introduced merely as evidence of a witness's consistency and reliability. Under s.2 of the 1968 Civil Evidence Act, all previous statements of witnesses were admissible as evidence of the facts they contained. Unregulated, such a provision would encourage adducing superfluous evidence and s.2(2) required that, where a person was called as a witness, no previous statement could be adduced without notifying the opposing party and obtaining the leave of the court. In addition the maker of the statement had to testify before the previous statement could be given in evidence.[33] S.2(2) also operated to restore aspects of adversarial trial in civil proceedings that were being circumvented.

The Hearsay Rule in Civil Proceedings' (1993) (Law Comm. No.216) Cm.2321, para.2.17:

. . . to prevent a party from calling a witness simply to adduce evidence of his out-of-court written statement, without taking him through a proper examination-in-chief. It corrected a practice that had grown up under section 1 of the Evidence Act 1938, which allowed for the admission of an out-of-court statement simply by calling the maker to confirm the contents.[34]

The Law Commission's recommendations to maintain this position are included in s.6 of the Civil Evidence Act 1995.

6.—(1) Subject as follows, the provisions of this Act as to hearsay evidence in civil proceedings apply equally (but with any necessary modifications) in relation to a previous statement made by a person called as a witness in the proceedings.

(2) A party who has called or intends to call a person as a witness in civil proceedings may not in those proceedings adduce evidence of a previous statement made by that person, except—

(a) with the leave of the court, or

(b) for the purpose of rebutting a suggestion that his evidence has been fabricated.

This shall not be construed as preventing a witness statement (that is, a written statement of oral evidence which a party to the proceedings intends to lead) from being adopted by a witness in giving evidence or treated as his evidence.

(3) Where in the case of civil proceedings section 3, 4 or 5 of the Criminal Procedure Act 1865 applies, which makes provision as to—

(a) how far a witness may be discredited by the party producing him,

(b) the proof of contradictory statements made by a witness, and

(c) cross-examination as to previous statements in writing,

this Act does not authorise the adducing of evidence of a previous inconsistent or contradictory statement otherwise than in accordance with those sections.

(4) Nothing in this Act affects any of the rules of law as to the circumstances in which, where a person is called as a witness in civil proceedings is cross-examined on a document used by him to refresh his memory, that document may be made evidence in the proceedings.

---

[33] There were some limited exceptions under Civil Evidence Act 1968, s.2(2)(b).

[34] Law Commission *op.cit.*, para.2.17; *Hilton v The Lancashire Dynamo Nevelin Ltd* [1964] 1 W.L.R. 952.

(5) Nothing in this section shall be construed as preventing a statement of any description referred to above from being admissible by virtue of section 1 as evidence of the matters stated

The following points should be noted.

    i) By s.6(2)(b), a previous consistent statement of a witness is only admissible as of right to rebut the suggestion that the witness's testimony has been fabricated.

    ii) In all other cases, the leave of the court must be obtained before a previous consistent statement is advanced in evidence.[35]

    iii) The proviso to s.6(2) of the 1995 Act recognises that where witness statements have been exchanged, under rule 32.5(2) of the Civil Procedure Rules, that statement shall stand as the evidence in chief of the witness unless the court directs otherwise. Many witnesses as a result do not give evidence in chief through oral testimony.

    iv) The Act does not affect the rules whereby a document used to "refresh the memory" can be made evidence in the proceedings.

    v) The section does not affect the rules contained in the Criminal Procedure Act 1865 concerning the treatment of adverse witnesses or the handling of inconsistent statements.[36]

IX. Repetitious Evidence and Case Management

One argument against the relaxation of the hearsay rule was that it would lead to a proliferation of unnecessary evidence. Under the US Federal Rules of Evidence, there is a power to exclude evidence if,

   . . . its probative value is substantially outweighed by . . . considerations of undue delay, waste of time, or needless presentation of cumulative evidence.[37]

The Law Commission decided that a similar provision was not needed,[38] concluding that there were sufficient existing powers of the court to exercise control over evidence adduced by the parties. However, such a power to exclude evidence on this ground in criminal proceedings was introduced by s.126 of the Criminal Justice Act 2003.

At common law, the courts have power to rule evidence that is insufficiently relevant inadmissible. It has in the past been suggested that "needlessly prolix" evidence can be excluded where its production would cause needless vexation, expense or delay.[39] The court has inherent powers in order to be able to "act effectively within its jurisdiction".[40] Such powers have been

---

[35] see Ch.12.
[36] *Denton Hall v Fifield* [2006] EWCA Civ 169; see Ch.13.
[37] Federal Rules of Evidence, r. 403.
[38] Law Commission, *op.cit.*, paras 4.20–4.24, 4.49–4.63.
[39] *Best on Evidence* (12th edn., 1922) para.47.
[40] *per* Lord Morris of Borth-y-Gest in *Connelly v D.P.P.* [1964] A.C. 1255 at 1301 cited in Law Commission, *op.cit.* para.4.53.

rarely invoked but may be changing as the concept of the adversarial trial changes. The Law Commission have argued against the view of the judge's function is to be a "passive umpire" and see this as militating against pro-active judicial intervention. But in cases such as *Mercer v Chief Constable of the Lancashire Constabulary*, there is reason to think that this view of the judge as merely "holding the ring" has undergone a reappraisal.

Mercer v Chief Constable of the Lancashire Constabulary [1991] 1 W.L.R. 367 at 373c, *per* Lord Donaldson M.R.:

Over the last quarter of a century there has been a sea change in legislative and judicial attitudes towards the conduct of litigation, taking the form of increased positive case management by the judiciary and the adoption of procedures designed (a) to identify the real issues in dispute and (b) to enable each party to assess the relative strengths and weaknesses of his own and his opponent's case at the earliest possible moment and well before any trial.[41]

In *A.B. v John Wyeth and Brother Ltd*,[42] Steyn L.J. said that High Court judges assigned to the control of such litigation must depart from traditional procedures and adopt interventionist case management techniques, founding this argument on the inherent jurisdiction of the court.[43]

Not only the Law Commission but also Lord Woolf[44] have argued that civil proceedings require greater pre-trial case management but also increased involvement in the adduction of evidence.

Banque Keyser Ullman S.A. v Skandia (UK) Insurance Co. Ltd [1991] 2 A.C. 249 at 280, *per* Lord Templeman:

The present practice is to allow every litigant unlimited time and unlimited scope so that the litigant and his advisors are able to conduct their case in all respects in the way which seems best to them. The results not infrequently are torrents of words, written and oral, which are oppressive and which the judge must examine in an attempt to eliminate everything which is not relevant, helpful and persuasive. The remedy lies in the judge taking time to read in advance pleadings, documents certified by counsel to be necessary, and short skeleton arguments of counsel.[45]

The Law Commission's conclusion was that the court should be more proactive in preventing the adduction of superfluous evidence but decided that, if such powers were to be made more explicit, this should be done by Rules of Court rather than by primary legislation.

---

[41] [1991] 1 W.L.R. 367 at 373c, *per* Lord Donaldson M.R.
[42] [1993] 4 Med. L.R. 1 at 6.
[43] Law Commission, *op.cit.* paras 4.56.
[44] Lord Woolf, *Access to Justice* (HMSO 1996).
[45] Cited by Law Commission *op.cit.*, para.4.57.

This has been the objective of the Civil Procedure Rules. In *Polanski v Conde Nast Publications*, Baroness Hale discussed the impact of those rules.

Polanski v Conde Nast Publications [2005] All E.R. 945, *per* Baroness Hale:

75. The 1995 Act was the result of the recommendations of the Law Commission in their Report on the Hearsay Rule in Civil Proceedings. The main objection to the proposed abolition of the rule was that it might lead to 'superfluous, repetitious, or prolix evidence prolonging trials unnecessarily'. The Commission had canvassed the possibility of an express rule allowing the exclusion of otherwise admissible evidence if its probative value were outweighed by considerations of undue delay, waste of time, or the needless presentation of cumulative evidence. But they declined to recommend an express statutory provision to that effect . . . Hence if it were thought that the courts' exclusionary powers should be made more explicit, this should be done by rules of court rather than by primary legislation.

Baroness Hale spells out the powers of the court to control evidence in the Civil Procedure Rules.

32.1(1) The court may control the evidence by giving directions as to—
(a) the issues on which it requires evidence;
(b) the nature of the evidence which it requires to decide those issues; and
(c) the way in which the evidence is to be placed before the court.

She stressed that these powers are part of the powers of active case management, subject to the overriding objective of enabling the court to deal with cases justly.

80. The Civil Evidence Act 1995 and the Civil Procedure Rules 1998 are part of a new approach to civil litigation in this country. The court is in charge of how the dispute which the parties have put before it is to be decided. Technicalities which prevent the court from getting the best picture it can of the case are so far as possible to be avoided. The court is to be trusted to evaluate the weight of the relevant evidence for itself. The evidence is to be given in the most efficient and economical way consistent with the object of doing justice between the parties. New technology such as VCF is not a revolutionary departure from the norm to be kept strictly in check but simply another tool for securing effective access to justice for everyone. If we had a rule that people such as the appellant were not entitled to access to justice at all, then of course that tool should be denied him. But we do not and it should not.

X. BUSINESS RECORDS

Most business records are likely to be caught under the definition of hearsay. This was always a problem for civil litigation especially as such records were likely to be very reliable and probative but also central to the case. Previous legislation sought to provide an exception and to ensure the reliability of such records, in particular where it involved multiple hearsay, by references to "record" and "duty". Section 4 of the Civil Evidence Act 1968 is an example:

"record" was not defined but "a person acting under a duty" is defined under s.4(3) to include,

... a person acting in the course of any trade, business, profession or other occupation in which he is engaged or employed or for the purpose of any paid or unpaid office held by him.

Providing an exception to the exclusionary rule was unsatisfactory and the difficulties were shown in cases such as *H. v Schering Chemicals*,[46] in which the plaintiffs sought to admit a file of information about a drug, Primodos. The file contained letters and articles published in *The Lancet* which were summaries of original research reports. Bingham J. held that the purpose of the 1968 Act was to admit evidence that a historian would see as 'original or primary sources', including documents which gave effect to the transaction itself or were a contemporaneous register of information supplied by those with direct knowledge of the facts. A digest of other people's research did not come within this.

The Hearsay Rule in Civil Proceedings' (1993) (Law Comm. No. 216) Cm.2321, para.3.12:

So far as records generally are concerned, consultees commented that the current rules are based on an old fashioned view of business methods and office procedure, where records were largely kept manually and where overall responsibility could be attributed to individual record keepers. Nowadays record keeping is less likely to be a separate function within an organisation and has been largely taken over by technology. The requirement to identify a person with a duty to compile the core information is often unrealistic. Whilst various categories of officialdom may have no difficulty in complying, for example tax inspectors, policemen and people carrying out duties imposed by statute, the rules are increasingly difficult to apply to commerce and industry, where procedures are likely to be less rigid . . .[47]

The abolition of the exclusionary rule by s.1 of the 1995 Act means that business records are generally admissible and subject to the normal notice and weighing procedures. No longer is it necessary to prove a chain of duty linking the suppliers of information to the record in question and requiring personal knowledge by the compiler of the matters recorded. However the Law Commission considered that there should be a simpler regime to make the manner, by which such documents are admitted into evidence easier.

The Hearsay Rule in Civil Proceedings' (1993) (Law Comm. No. 216) Cm.2321, para.4.39:

. . . we consider that steps should be taken to make it easier to get such records admitted in evidence. Once it is accepted that there is often unlikely to be a witness

---

[46] [1983] 1 All E.R. 849; *Savings and Investment Bank v Gasco Investment* [1984] 1 All E.R. 296.
[47] Law Commission, *op.cit.*, para.3.12.

who can give relevant and direct evidence of all or any of the aspects of the compilation of a record, it becomes artificial to require the record to be produced by a witness. We therefore propose that documents certified by an officer of a business or public authority should be capable of being received into evidence without further proof . . . . For the purposes of this section we propose that 'business' be defined widely so as to include 'any activity regularly carried out over a period of time, whether for profit or not, by any body (whether corporate or not) or by an individual'. This is to reflect our view that it is the quality of regularity that lends a business record its reliability, not the existence of a profit motive or the juridical nature of the person carrying on the activity.[48]

This is provided for under the Act,

9.—(1) A document which is shown to form part of the records of a business or public authority may be received in evidence in civil proceedings without further proof.
(2) A document shall be taken to form part of the records of a business or public authority if there is produced to the court a certificate to that effect signed by an officer of the business or authority to which the records belong . . .

Section 9 only provides for the manner by which business or public authority records are to be proved. Such documents are now generally admissible under s.1 and even if the records fail to come within the extended definitions in this section, this does not mean that they are not admissible, simply that they must be proved under the normal s.1 process. The process of proof, under subs.(2), means that a party needs only to produce the document and a statement signed by an officer of the business or authority stating that the document is part of the records of that business or authority.

As a term "record" is a wider concept than under the previous legislation. Section 9(4) states that records means "records in whatever form".

The Hearsay Rule in Civil Proceedings' (1993) (Law Comm. No. 216) Cm.2321. para.4.41:

We have sought to define the term 'records' in a manner which concentrates on the form in which they are kept and which allows for the widest possible admission. We have not sought to define the type of record which is capable of being admitted. However our proposals do not resolve the question . . . of whether a report by a DTI inspector constitutes a record . . .[49]

It is difficult to see that the material in *H. v Schering Chemicals*[50] would come within s.9. But this issue is less important since it only goes to the manner of admission and not to general admissibility. The material should be admissible under s.1.

---

[48] *ibid.* para.4.39.
[49] Law Commission, *op.cit.* para.4.41.
[50] above.

There is some controversy as to whether the absence of an entry in a record constitutes hearsay.[51] In civil proceedings, however, evidence to prove a negative is admissible even if drawing inferences from such evidence is fraught with difficulty. Section 9(3) allows the absence of an entry in such a record to be proved by the affidavit of an officer of the business or authority.

XI. Computer Records

The 1968 legislation revealed a fundamental mistrust of records held on computer and demanded significant safeguards. However it was remarkable that, at that date, this novel form of evidence was considered at all.[52] The safeguards incorporated into s.5 were complex and inappropriate for the proliferation of desk-top computers in the 21st century. The section only applied to hearsay evidence and "real" evidence, such as that produced in the *Statue of Liberty*,[53] was not affected by these provisions. The Law Commission found little disagreement with the position that these provisions were outdated and, more significantly, there was no good reason for distinguishing between different forms of record keeping or for maintaining a different regime for the admissibility of computer-generated documents.[54] As a result, the Civil Evidence Act 1995 contains no special provisions in respect of computerised records which are treated similarly to other records, although the Law Commission Report considered that parties should be encouraged to provide information on the security of their systems.[55]

XII. Human Rights and Civil Evidence Act 1995

A key issue is the extent to which the liberal regime of the Civil Evidence Act 1995 over hearsay evidence infringes a party's rights to a fair trial under Art.6 of the European Convention. These issues have been raised in the use of hearsay evidence to obtain anti-social behaviour orders under the Crime and Disorder Act 1998. In *R. (McCann) v Manchester Crown Court*,[56] Lord Steyn pointed out that these Art.6 points were premature.

R. (McCann) v Manchester Crown Court [2002] 3 W.L.R. 1313, *per* Lord Steyn:

36. It is submitted that, even if the relevant proceedings are civil, words must be implied into the Civil Evidence Act 1995 which give the court a wider power to

---

[51] *Shone* [1983] 76 Cr.App.R. 72; *Shepherd* [1993] 3 All E.R. 225.
[52] Law Reform Committee, 13th Report Hearsay Evidence in Civil Proceedings (1966) Cmnd. 2964 para.10.
[53] [1968] 2 All E.R. 195.
[54] Law Commission, *op.cit.*, para.3.20.
[55] *ibid.* para.4.43.
[56] [2002] 3 W.L.R. 1313.

exclude hearsay evidence. As the Divisional Court judgment makes clear this is unnecessary and unwarranted. [Counsel have] argued that, even if the proceedings are civil, nevertheless the introduction of hearsay evidence infringes a defendants right to a fair trial under article 6(1) 'in the determination of his civil rights and obligations'. This is a misconceived argument. The case has not been heard. Such a challenge is premature. Upon a due consideration of the evidence, direct or hearsay, it may turn out that the defendant has no answer to the case under section 1(1). For the sake of completeness, I need only add that the use of the Civil Evidence Act 1995 and the Rules in cases under the first part of section 1 are not in any way incompatible with the Human Rights Act 1998.

Lord Hope makes a similar point.

R. (McCann) v Manchester Crown Court [2002] 3 W.L.R. 1313, *per* Lord Hope:

"77. For these reasons I do not think that any of the criteria for a finding that proceedings under section 1 of the Crime and Disorder Act 1998 have the character of criminal proceedings for the purposes of article 6 are satisfied. The consequence of so holding is of fundamental importance to the future of this legislation. Cases such as Unterpertinger v Austria,[57] *Kostovski v The Netherlands*[58] and *Saidi v France*[59] illustrate the reluctance of the Strasbourg court to accept that the use of hearsay evidence is compatible with a defendant's right under article 6(3)(d) to examine or have examined witnesses against him. But I would hold that article 6(3) does not apply to these proceedings and that the rules of evidence that are to be applied are the civil evidence rules. This means that hearsay evidence under the Civil Evidence Act 1995, the use of which will be necessary in many cases if the magistrates are to be properly informed about the scale and nature of the anti-social behaviour and the prohibitions that are needed for the protection of the public, is admissible."

Lord Hutton emphasised the need to balance the rights of the defendants with those of the community at large.

R. (McCann) v Manchester Crown Court [2002] 3 W.L.R. 1313, *per* Lord Hutton:

113. The submissions of counsel on behalf of the defendants and on behalf of Liberty have laid stress on the human rights of the defendants. However the European Court has frequently affirmed the principle . . . that the search for the striking of a fair balance 'between the demands of the general interest of the community and the requirements of the protection of the individual's fundamental rights' is inherent in the whole of the Convention. In these cases which your Lordships have held are not criminal cases under the Convention and therefore do not attract the specific

---

[57] [1986] 13 E.H.R.R. 175.
[58] [1989] 12 E.H.R.R. 434.
[59] [1993] 17 E.H.R.R. 251.

protection given by article 6(3)(d) (though even in criminal cases the European Court has recognised that 'principles of fair trial also require that in appropriate cases the interests of the defence are balanced against those of witnesses or victims called upon to testify' . . .)

The issue was raised in *Solon South West Housing Association v James*,[60] a case where the claimant housing association sought the eviction of some tenants. There was evidence from police officers, community workers and neighbours that the tenants had behaved in a grossly anti-social manner. Some of the evidence was first hand but a considerable amount was hearsay from people who felt intimidated by the family and did not want to be identified. In the Court of Appeal, Mance L.J. held that the judge had in mind the relevance of the European Convention on Human Rights.

Solon South West Housing Association v James [2005] H.L.R. 24, *per* Mance L.J.:

29. The judge's admission of hearsay evidence in the present case does not therefore run into any general problem under the European Convention on Human Rights. The issue becomes, rather, the case-specific issue: whether the way in which he addressed the hearsay evidence and the weight which he attached to it was in all the circumstances appropriate and fair, or whether he acted in some way unfairly in its treatment, or attached disproportionate weight to it in such a way as to make the proceedings unfair. It seems to me that in this respect the Convention adds little to what would any way be involved in the proper application of the discretion provided under section 4 of the 1995 Act. Be that as it may, I have, for my part, no doubt that the judge's exercise of his discretion was appropriate and fair, and that he approached the matter correctly and in a way which cannot be regarded as impacting adversely on the overall fairness of the proceedings.

---

[60] [2005] H.L.R. 24.

20

OPINIONS AND THE EVIDENCE OF EXPERTS

I. INTRODUCTION

The final exclusionary rule deals with a witness's opinion. Witnesses are expected to give evidence of what they have seen, heard, smelt, felt or touched—direct evidence of their own perceptions. The inferences or conclusions that witnesses draw from those perceptions are not their perceptions but their opinions or beliefs. These are not evidence. Opinions are not admissible to prove the truth of what is believed or inferred. The rationale for the rule has been put in different ways.

1. Lack of probative weight. Opinions are seen as having little probative weight. In *Kearley*,[1] the accused was charged with possession of drugs with intent to supply. Telephone callers and visitors to the house obviously believed that the accused was a supplier.

Kearley [1992] 2 All E.R. 345 at 370j–371f, *per* Lord Oliver:

What was said—in each case a request for drugs—is, of course, probative of the state of mind of the caller. But the state of mind of the caller is not the fact in issue and is, in itself, irrelevant, for it is not probative of anything other than its own existence. It becomes relevant only if and so far as the existence of other facts can be inferred from it . . . if, at the trial, the prosecution had sought to adduce evidence from a witness not that drugs had been supplied but that it was his opinion or belief that drugs had been or would be supplied, that evidence would be inadmissible as amounting to no more than a statement of belief or opinion unsupported by facts upon which the belief was grounded.

A bare opinion, by itself, has little, if any, probative weight. But an opinion can acquire weight: first, we may be aware that the witness is basing that opinion on knowledge and that witness may be able to testify to those facts on which the opinion is based; secondly, the very status of the witness may cause us to give greater credence to any opinion—but it is only the status as

---

[1] [1992] 2 All E.R. 345.

an "expert" that will allow that opinion to be heard in court; thirdly, the opinion may be commonly held by a number of people. But is an opinion more worthy of belief simply because of the weight of numbers? An opinion held by one person has little weight—does such probative weight increase if there are a dozen witnesses who all share the same opinion? The court in *Kearley* did not think so, considering that cumulatively the callers' statements showed no more than a common reputation.

It is a justifiable rationale to exclude opinion evidence on the basis of the lack of probative weight but should such a principle be expressed as a *rule* of exclusion? Any court has the discretionary power to reject irrelevant and worthless evidence, a power which would suffice to exclude unfounded opinion evidence.

2. Usurping the function of the finder of fact. A further reason for excluding a witness's opinion is that such testimony usurps the function of the finder of fact whose task it is to draw the necessary inferences from the evidence. The trier of fact is free to reject an opinion but the policy behind the rule is to ensure that the trier of fact is not seduced into an easy acceptance of a convincingly-presented opinion. However desirable such a policy may be, it has now been abrogated in civil proceedings.[2] In criminal cases, the threat to the jury's independence as a decision-maker has to be balanced against the exclusion of potentially useful material.

3. The risk of inadmissible evidence. A third reason for exclusion is that a witness's opinion can often be based on evidence which, if stated expressly, would be inadmissible for one reason or another. This is illustrated in *Kearley* in which Lord Oliver suggested that a witness, present in court, who had previously been supplied with drugs by the accused, could give relevant and admissible evidence. But if the witness sought to support any opinion on Kearley's intent to supply by mentioning past drug dealing, this immediately infringes the rule against adducing evidence of bad character and raises difficult problems under s.101(1)(d) of the Criminal Justice Act 2003. The rule against the reception of a witness's opinion guards against the evasion of other exclusionary rules. Is this a necessary safeguard when the trial court can call on s.78 of Police and Criminal Evidence Act 1984 which permits exclusion of evidence which would adversely affect the fairness of the proceedings?

There are two major exceptions to the rule excluding opinion evidence: non-expert opinion is admissible where a strict distinction between perceptions and inference is not possible; and expert testimony is admissible where the information provided is outside the experience and competence of the trier of fact.

II. Non-expert Opinion

Non-expert witnesses are allowed to express their opinion where it would be impossible to separate observed fact from inference, where the opinion is

---

[2] Civil Evidence Act 1972, s.3.

necessary for the coherence and comprehensibility of the testimony and when the opinion involves an everyday matter calling for no special expertise. Even in such cases, the non-expert is not permitted to testify as to the ultimate issue that has to be decided or as to those issues which are within the competence of the trier of fact.

The non-expert witness can give an opinion in relation to those matters where it is almost impossible to separate out the inferences from the perceived facts on which the inferences were based: age,[3] weather, handwriting or the identification of people or objects are all examples. In *Fryer v Gathercole*,[4] a witness testified that she had received a libellous pamphlet from the defendant. She had lent it to other people and gave evidence that that the pamphlet in front of the court was the same one that she had received from the defendant although there were no obvious identifying marks. It was objected that this was mere opinion.

Fryer v Gathercole (1849) 4 Ex 262 at 265, *per* Pollock C.B.:

. . . the question resolved itself into one question of degree only. The witness could say no more than this: 'I believe the copy of the pamphlet produced to be the same with that which I received from the defendant, because when I lent that copy to other persons it was returned to me, and I had no reason to believe it otherwise when I got it back. I then for certainty put my name on it.' If the name had been written in the first instance no doubt could have arisen . . . As has been truly argued, there are many cases of identification where the law would be rendered ridiculous if positive certainty were required from witnesses . . . The evidence in this case was therefore properly received; any objection to it goes merely to its value.

A modern example is a witness's estimation of the speed of a car: legislation provides that a witness can testify as to the speed under the Road Traffic Regulation Act 1984.

89.—(2) A person prosecuted for such an offence shall not be liable to be convicted solely on the evidence of one witness to the effect that, in the opinion of the witness, the person prosecuted was driving the vehicle at a speed exceeding a specified limit.

The section does not allow for conviction 'solely' on the evidence of one person's opinion. Corroboration in the shape of evidence emanating from an independent source is required.[5]

The condition of objects or their general value[6] might also be a suitable subject for a witness's comment. Even an opinion as to the sanity of a person can, in some circumstances, be admissible. In *Wright v Tatham*,[7] the sanity of a

---

[3] *Cox* [1898] 1 Q.B. 179.
[4] (1849) 4 Ex 262.
[5] Inevitably speeding convictions nowadays are obtained on a scientific basis such as speed cameras or hand held speed guns.
[6] *Beckett* (1913) 8 Cr.App.R. 204.
[7] (1838) 4 Bing. N.C. 489.

deceased testator was in issue and it was sought to introduce letters written by acquaintances of the deceased on business matters which implicitly showed the writers' opinion that the testator was sane.

Wright v Tatham (1838) 4 Bing.N.C. 489 at 265, *per* Pollock C.B.:

Each of the three letters, no doubt, indicates that in the opinion of the writer the testator was a rational person. He is spoken of in respectful terms in all. Mr Ellershaw describes him as possessing hospitality and benevolent politeness; and Mr Marton addresses him as competent to do business to the limited extent to which his letter calls on him to act; and there is no question but that, if any one of those writers had been living, his evidence, founded on personal observation, that the testator possessed the qualities which justified the opinion expressed or implied in his letters, would be admissible on this issue.

However in a criminal case, untutored opinion is insufficient for a jury to base a special verdict of not guilty through reason of insanity—the testimony of two medical practitioners is required.[8] There is no similar provision in the legislation providing for the defence of diminished responsibility[9] although the burden of proof is on the defence and expert testimony is essential if the defence is to succeed.

These examples demonstrate the range of non-expert opinion that can be adduced in court. The distinction between the opinion of the non-expert and that of the expert is brought out in *Davies*. The charge at a court martial was driving a vehicle while unfit through drink. The witness testified that the accused had been drinking and was in no condition to handle the car.

Davies [1962] 3 All E.R. 97 at 1112–1113, *per* Lord Parker C.J.:

The defence had strongly taken the stand that the witness should be allowed to speak only as to facts he had seen, because it was for the court to say what was the appellant's condition. Apparently the judge advocate advised the court that the witness could state the impression he formed as to the appellant's condition at the time if he was a witness who knew what was entailed in the driving of a car. It is to observed that the witness was allowed to speak about two matters which are quite distinct; one is what his impression was as to whether drink had been taken by the appellant, and the second was his opinion as to whether as the result of that drink he was fit or unfit to drive a car. The court has come clearly to the conclusion that a witness can quite properly give his general impression as to whether a driver had taken drink. He must describe of course the facts upon which he relies, but it seems to this court that he is perfectly entitled to give his impression as to whether drink had been taken or not. On the other hand, as regards the second matter, it cannot be said,

[8] Criminal Procedure (Insanity and Unfitness to Plead) Act 1991, s.1(1).
[9] Homicide Act 1957, s.2.

as it seems to this court, that a witness, merely because he is a driver himself, is in the expert witness category so that it is proper to ask him his opinion as to fitness or unfitness to drive. That is the very matter which the court itself has to determine . . .

Thus a non-expert witness can testify as to whether somebody has been drinking but only an expert witness could testify as to whether the accused was fit to drive.

The statement of opinion is a convenient method of conveying personal observations. There are limitations. First, the opinion of a non-expert is only admissible when based on facts which are themselves proved by admissible evidence. As a result, non-expert opinions based on inadmissible hearsay evidence are inadmissible. In contrast an expert is entitled to rely on such third party information[10] as a basis for an expert opinion. Secondly, the non-expert witness must avoid the "ultimate issue" rule which prevents both the expert and non-expert witness from expressing an opinion on the very point that the trier of fact has to decide, namely, the ultimate issue. This rule has disappeared in civil proceedings where the role of the non-expert witness is laid down in the Civil Evidence Act 1972.[11]

3.—(2) It is hereby declared that where a person is called as a witness in any civil proceedings, a statement of opinion by him on any relevant matter on which he is not qualified to give expert evidence, if made as a way of conveying relevant facts personally perceived by him, is admissible as evidence of what he perceived.

(3) In this section 'relevant matter' includes an issue in the proceedings in question.

Section 3(3) removes the "ultimate issue" restraint in civil proceedings. This does not give *carte blanche* to witnesses to express opinions—*Liddell v Middleton*[12] concerned a negligence claim arising from a road traffic accident. The Court of Appeal held that even the expert witnesses, having seen the witness statements, were not entitled to draw conclusions as to whether a driver should have sounded his horn or taken evasive action. Those were matters for the trial judge. Non-expert witnesses can express an opinion only as a means of communicating matters perceived by them.

It has been recommended that a similar provision be enacted for criminal trials.[13] This still awaits legislation and in theory, an eyewitness in a dangerous driving case should not be asked whether the driving was dangerous, even where the opinion is rationally based on the speed of the car, the road conditions and the driver's control. In the USA, the rule is put more liberally.

If the witness is not testifying as an expert, the witness's testimony in the form of opinions or inferences is limited to those opinions or inferences which are (a) rationally based on the perception of the witness and (b) helpful to a clear understanding of the witness's testimony or the determination of a fact in issue.[14]

---

[10] *English Exporters (London) Ltd v Eldonwall Ltd* [1973] 1 All E.R. 726.
[11] As amended by Civil Evidence Act 1995, Sch.2.
[12] Unreported July 7, 1995, CA.
[13] 11th Report, Criminal Law Revision Committee (Cmnd. 4991) para.270.
[14] Federal Rules of Evidence, r. 701.

In the USA, non-expert witnesses are allowed to testify that a substance appeared to be a narcotic, so long as they are familiar with the substance. In *US v Westbrook*,[15] two witnesses who were heavy amphetamine users were permitted to testify that a substance was amphetamine, without being qualified as an expert, whereas it was error to permit another witness to make such an identification where she had no experience with amphetamines.

III. Expert Evidence

The key exception to the rule excluding opinion evidence is that regarding expert witnesses. Where an issue in front of a court calls for special skill or knowledge which a judge or jury does not possess, an expert witness will be allowed to present technical information and express an opinion on its significance. For example, in *Mason*,[16] the defence to a charge of murder was that the victim had committed suicide and the issue was whether the doctor could be asked whether the injuries could have been self-inflicted. The Court of Appeal held the answer admissible. But there are significant limitations, discussed below. For example, experts testifying in criminal proceedings are not permitted to give their opinion on issues that are within the competence of the ordinary juror. At common law, no witness was allowed to express an opinion on the ultimate issue but now an expert is permitted to give such evidence as in *Stockwell*,[17] although it must be made clear to the jury that they are not bound to follow that opinion.

The common law always has accepted expert evidence. In *Folkes v Chadd*,[18] the opinion of an engineer was admitted on the issue of whether an embankment had caused the silting up of a harbour.

Folkes v Chadd (1782) 3 Doug K.B. 157 at 158, *per* Lord Mansfield:

The question is, to what has this decay been owing . . . That is a matter of opinion; the whole case is a question of opinion, from facts agreed upon. Nobody can swear that it was the cause; nobody thought that it would produce this mischief when the bank was erected . . . . Mr Smeaton is called . . . . It is objected that Mr Smeaton is going to speak, not as to facts, but as to opinion. That opinion, however, is deduced from facts which are not disputed—the situation of banks, the course of tides and of winds, and the shifting of sands. His opinion deduced from all these facts is that, mathematically speaking, the bank may contribute to the mischief but not sensibly. Mr Smeaton understands the construction of harbours, the causes of their destruction, and how remedied. In matters of science no other witnesses can be called . . . . I cannot believe that where the question is, whether a defect arises from a natural or an artificial cause, the opinions of men of science are not to be received. Handwriting is

---

[15] 896 F.2d 330 (8th Cir. 1990) *cf. Bird v Adams* [1972] Crim.L.R. 174.
[16] (1911) 7 Cr.App.R. 67.
[17] (1993) 97 Cr.App.R. 260 at 265–6; *Gokal* unreported, March 11, 1999, CA.
[18] (1782) 3 Doug. K.B. 157.

proved every day by opinion; and for false evidence on such questions a man may be indicted for perjury . . .'[19]

In the USA, the rule is,

If scientific, technical, or other specialised knowledge will assist the trier of fact to understand the evidence or to determine a fact in issue, a witness qualified as an expert by knowledge, skill, experience, training, or education, may testify thereto in the form of an opinion or otherwise, if (1) the testimony is based upon sufficient facts or data, (2) the testimony is the product of reliable principles and methods, and (3) the witness has applied the principles and methods reliably to the facts of the case.[20]

Expert witnesses may testify to their own findings, the findings of others, to the scientific or other principles relevant to the case and draw relevant inferences from such findings. But their opinions must be restricted to their field of expertise. The most important limiting principle was laid down in *Turner*:[21] if the issue which needs to be decided does not require specialised knowledge and is within the competence of the trier of fact, an expert witness's opinion is inadmissible.

A. *Matters within the competence of the jury—the Turner rule*

The *Turner* rule states that, in criminal cases,[22] an expert witness should not express opinions on those matters which are within the competence of the jury. For example, juries are daily asked to decide whether a defendant intended or foresaw a particular consequence or believed or knew a particular fact. They are expected to reach these conclusions from the accused's behaviour and statements or from the surrounding circumstances, almost certainly testing their conclusions from what they, the jurors, might have known, intended or foreseen in a like situation. The jurors are representatives of the community and are expected to understand how "normal" people behave and react. Expert evidence by psychologists or psychiatrists is not admissible on such issues. Such evidence is only admissible in dealing with the "abnormal" defendant whose actions are assumed to be outside the experience of the jury. This borderline causes problems especially in the area of psychiatric and psychological testimony.

In *Turner*, the accused killed his girl friend by battering her over the head with a hammer. He raised the defence of provocation, arguing that he had lost his self-control when she told him that she had been having affairs with other men while he had been in prison. The judge refused the defence leave

---

[19] *ibid.* at 158 *per* Lord Mansfield.
[20] Federal Rules of Evidence, r. 702.
[21] [1975] 1 All E.R. 70.
[22] This does not apply in civil proceedings since under s.3(1) of the Civil Evidence Act 1972, '. . . where a person is called as a witness . . . his opinion on any relevant matter on which he is qualified to give expert evidence shall be admissible in evidence.'

to call a psychiatrist who would have testified that the accused was not
suffering from mental illness but was likely to have killed her in an
"explosive release of blind rage" at hearing her confession. On appeal, it was
submitted that the witness's opinion as to Turner's personality and mental
make-up was relevant as it showed that he was likely to be easily provoked
and that his account of the killing was likely to be true.

Turner [1975] 1 All E.R. 70 at 74b-e, *per* Lawton L.J.:

Opinions from knowledgeable persons about a man's personality and mental make-
up play a part in many human judgments. In our judgment the psychiatrist's opinion
was relevant. Relevance, however, does not result in evidence being admissible: it is a
condition precedent to admissibility. Our law excludes evidence of many matters
which in life outside the courts sensible people take into consideration when making
decisions. Two broad heads of exclusion are hearsay and opinion . . . .
The foundation of these rules was laid down by Lord Mansfield CJ in Folkes v
Chadd[23] and was well laid: 'The opinion of scientific men upon proven facts', he said,
'may be given by men of science within their own science.' An expert's opinion is
admissible to furnish the court with scientific information which is likely to be outside
the experience and knowledge of a judge or jury. If on the proven facts a judge or jury
can form their own conclusions without help then the opinion of an expert is
unnecessary. In such a case if it is given dressed up in scientific jargon it may make
judgment more difficult. The fact that an expert witness has impressive scientific
qualifications does not by that fact alone make his opinion on matters of human nature
and behaviour within the limits of normality any more helpful than that of the jurors
themselves; but there is a danger that they may think it does.

The Court of Appeal upheld the conviction, arguing that, although mental
illness was within the expert witness's province, Turner's emotional attach-
ment to the victim and his outburst of rage was within ordinary human
experience and the jury did not require the assistance of an expert for them to
assess the defendant's account. The *Turner* rule says that expert evidence is
not admissible:

- when it concerns an issue within the knowledge and experience of
  the jury; or
- when it concerns an issue of human nature and behaviour within
  the bounds of normality

1. The Boundaries of Turner

The courts have consistently policed this line strictly. In *Chard*,[24] the
defendant was accused of murder. The defence was neither diminished
responsibility nor insanity but the defendant sought to introduce the testimony of a psychiatrist as to his mental state at the time of the killing—that is,

[23] (1782) 3 Doug. K.B. 157 at 159.
[24] (1971) 56 Cr.App.R. 268.

whether he was likely to have possessed the intent to kill or to cause grievous bodily harm. The Court of Appeal upheld the trial judge's rejection of such evidence,

Chard (1971) 56 Cr.App.R. 268 at 270–271, *per* Roskill L.J.:

. . . one purpose of jury trials is to bring into the jury box a body of men and women who are able to judge ordinary day-to-day questions by their own standards, that is, the standards in the eyes of the law of theoretically ordinary reasonable men and women. That is something which they are well able by their ordinary experience to judge for themselves. Where the matters in issue go outside that experience and they are invited to deal with someone supposedly abnormal, for example, supposedly suffering from insanity or diminished responsibility, then plainly in such a case they are entitled to the benefit of expert evidence. But where, as in the present case, they are dealing with someone who by concession was on the medical evidence entirely normal, it seems to this Court abundantly plain on first principles of the admissibility of expert evidence, that it is not permissible to call a witness, whatever his personal experience, merely to tell the jury how he thinks an accused man's mind—assumedly a normal mind—operated at the time of the alleged crime with reference to the crucial question of what that man's intention was.

Chard was followed in *Gilfoyle*,[25] a murder case in which the defence was that the victim had committed suicide. The question was whether an expert witness could give evidence about his "psychological autopsy" on the victim where he had reviewed her early experience of the violent deaths around her, the depression and mood swings in her medical records, a study of her diary and direct questioning of her family and friends. His opinion was that this demonstrated convincing support for the deceased having taken her own life. The trial judge and the Court of Appeal rejected this evidence—there were serious questions about the validity of the science employed but the central *Turner* point was made.

Gilfoyle [2001] 2 Cr.App.R. 5 at para.25, *per* Rose L.J.:

. . . we very much doubt whether assessing levels of happiness or unhappiness is a task for an expert rather than jurors and none of the points which he makes about the "suicide" notes is outwith the experience of a jury . . . . The doctor was in no better position to draw an inference on these facts than the jury.

The *Turner* rule depends on the judge's assessment of whether the expert is raising issues of mental illness that go beyond the experience of the jury, of normality versus abnormality. In *Gilfoyle*, the evidence might well have been

---

[25] [2001] 2 Cr.App.R. 5.

admitted if the court had judged it to be about clinical depression rather than happiness or unhappiness. Sometimes this seems an arbitrary line—in *Masih*,[26] the accused was charged with rape and had an IQ of 72. Expert evidence was inadmissible on the issue of whether he realised that the victim was not consenting. The borderline between the normal and abnormal was seen as the arbitrary line of an IQ of 69, below which the defendant would have been a mental defective and expert evidence would have been admissible, "in order to enlighten the jury upon a matter which is abnormal and therefore, ex hypothesi, presumably outside their experience".[27]

Inevitably the rule has led to charges of inconsistency. It is not hard to find such cases—in *Weightman*,[28] a mother killed her child and the appellate court upheld the trial judge's refusal to admit expert evidence of her abnormal and histrionic personality which, however, did not amount to mental illness. However in *Emery*,[29] an unmarried mother of a young child was convicted of failing to protect her child from its father. She was permitted to call expert testimony to the effect that she had been reduced to a state of dependent helplessness, unable to protect her child. The Court of Appeal accepted the trial judge's decision to admit the evidence.

Emery (1993) 14 Cr.App.R. (S.) 394 at 397, *per* Lord Taylor C.J.:

There is potential expert evidence to the effect that if she is right, her will could have been crushed. That would afford her a good defence . . . Therefore, without further explanation or understanding, the jury's lack of understanding might lead to a guilty verdict, whereas if they were to consider the expert evidence which seeks to explain her conduct, they [might] find her not guilty. It follows from that that in my judgment the effects of abuse of the scale and persistence she describes might well not be within the capacity of a jury to understand unassisted by expert evidence.

Yet in *Hegarty*,[30] evidence that the accused was emotionally unstable and especially vulnerable to threats was not accepted. The Court of Appeal considered that to allow such evidence would be to circumvent the objective test of 'a person of reasonable firmness'.

These criticisms have not led to *Turner* being reconsidered. Its boundaries are regularly reinforced—there is a good example in *Ugoh*[31] of those limits. This involved a gang rape of a very drunk woman. The expert witness gave testimony of the capacity of someone so drunk to give informed consent but also said that this would have been evident to anyone who was with her. The

---

[26] [1986] Crim.L.R. 395.

[27] *per* Lane L.C.J.

[28] [1991] Crim.L.R. 204—see *Roberts* [1989] Crim.L.R. 220, evidence was excluded that the defendant was emotionally disturbed and living in a fantasy world and thus would not have formed the *mens rea* for murder; *Wood* [1990] Crim.L.R. 264; *Toner* [1991] 93 Cr.App.R. 382.

[29] (1993) 14 Cr.App.R. (S.) 394.

[30] [1994] Crim.L.R. 353; see also *Horne* [1994] Crim.L.R. 584.

[31] [2001] EWCA Crim 1381.

testimony was admissible so far as it went to the issue of whether a person with that blood-alcohol level could in fact consent. But the witness strayed into *Turner* territory when she also gave an opinion as to what the defendants may or may not have realised about that consent.

2. Exceptions to Turner

There has been one exception to the *Turner* rule: in *Lowery*,[32] the two defendants were charged with a sadistic murder of a young girl. Both accused sought to lay the blame on the other. A clinical psychologist examined both accused and testified on behalf of Lowery's co-defendant, King. He testified that King was immature and emotionally shallow and was likely to be dominated by a more aggressive man. He also testified that Lowery had a strong aggressive drive with weak controls. Such evidence is, on its face, evidence of Lowery's predisposition to the crime and normally inadmissible. But Lowery had testified on his own behalf and had already mentioned his own good character. The psychologist's evidence is admissible in rebuttal. However, even had the defence case not raised the issue of character, the Privy Council held that the evidence would have been admissible.

Lowery [1973] 3 All E.R. 662 at 671b–e, *per* Lord Morris:

If in imaginary circumstances similar to those of this case, it was apparent that one of the accused was a man of great physical strength whereas the other was a weakling it could hardly be doubted that in forming an opinion as to the probabilities it would be relevant to have the disparity between the two in mind. Physical characteristics may often be of considerable relevance: see *Toohey v Metropolitan Police Commissioner*.[33] The evidence of Professor Cox was not related to crime or criminal tendencies: it was scientific evidence as to the respective personalities of the two accused as, and to the extent, revealed by certain well-known tests. Whether it assisted the jury is not a matter that can be known. All that is known is that the jury convicted both the accused. But insofar as it might help in considering the probabilities as to what happened at the spot to which the girl was taken it was not only relevant to and necessary for the case advanced by King but it was made relevant and admissible in view of the case advanced by Lowery and in view of Lowery's assertions against King.

The case put forward by counsel on behalf of King involved posing to the jury the question 'which of these two men is the more likely to have killed this girl?' and inviting the jury to come to the conclusion that it was Lowery. If the crime was one which was committed apparently without any kind of motive unless it was for the sensation experienced in the killing then unless both men acted in concert the deed was that of one of them. It would be unjust to prevent either of them from calling any evidence of probative value which could point to the probability that the perpetrator was the one rather than the other.

This approach has now been supported by the House of Lords in *Randall*,[34] although in relation to the contrasting character evidence of the two accused rather than the contrasting psychiatric profiles.

[32] [1973] 3 All E.R. 662.
[33] [1965] 1 All E.R. 506.
[34] [2004] 1 All E.R. 467—see Ch.15.

3. Turner and witness credibility

An example of an issue within the competence of the jury is the assessment of the creditworthiness of a witness and the weight to be afforded to the testimony. Parties cannot adduce such testimony merely to cast doubt on the reliability of their opponent's witnesses or to suggest that a capable witness was in fact lying. That decision is the jury's. In *Mackenney*,[35] the chief prosecution witness, Childs, refused to undertake a psychiatric examination before the trial. A defence psychologist watched him testify and the defence sought to adduce testimony that Childs was suffering from mental disorder which would affect the reliability of his evidence. The trial judge rejected this evidence and this was upheld on appeal. The principle was that this was an issue within the competence of the jury. In a proper case, medical testimony could be received to show that a witness was *incapable* of telling the truth[36] but here there had been no examination and the expert's credentials were doubted because he had no medical qualifications or diagnostic experience and his expertise was based on an extensive examination of the literature on psychopathy. The defendants served over 20 years in prison before the appeal court quashed the convictions accepting that this was a proper case in which medical testimony should have been received and the psychologist should have been permitted to testify.[37] The appeal court in 1981 and 2004 both manage to remain within the parameters of *Turner*—the former because they understood the evidence merely to going to the issue whether the witness was lying; the latter because they perceived that the witness had an "abnormal" condition.

In *G and H*,[38] the sexual abuse of the victim had occurred many years previously and the appeal was based on the admissibility of fresh evidence on false memory syndrome. The victim had given detailed accounts of the abuse which were challenged by the defence. The expert witness would have testified that memories of early childhood are qualitatively different from memories of later events. Adults cannot usually remember events of early childhood so as to be able to give a coherent narrative account. They may remember an event, and sometimes a visual image, but the recall will be fragmentary, disjointed and idiosyncratic. It was background material that cast considerable doubt on the victim's evidence but was rejected by the trial judge. The Court of Appeal ordered a retrial.

In both *Mackenney* and *G and H*, the evidence cast doubt on the reliability of the witness. It was admissible because in both cases it came within the parameters of *Turner* because it deals with matters outside the competence of the jury. Does the same apply when the evidence supports the credibility of the witness? Should jurors be assisted to understand the victim and other witnesses and their reactions? In a Scottish child sexual abuse case, *H.M. Advocate v Grimmond*,[39] the judge refused permission for expert psychological

---

[35] (1981) 76 Cr.App.R. 271.

[36] *Toohey v Metropolitan Police Commissioner* [1965] A.C. 595.

[37] [2004] 2 Cr.App.R. 5—attitudes towards the reception of such testimony are now much more liberal.

[38] [2005] EWCA Crim 1828.

[39] [2001] S.C.C.R. 708; F. Raitt, "Expert Evidence As Context" (2004) 12 Feminist Legal Studies 233.

evidence to be admitted to the jury about patterns of disclosure by victims in such cases. There was a strict application of the *Turner* rule. Subsequently the Scottish Parliament has passed s.5 of the Vulnerable Witnesses (Scotland) Act 2004 explicitly to cancel the effect of *Grimmond*. It provides:

Expert psychological or psychiatric evidence relating to any subsequent behaviour or statement of the complainer is admissible for the purpose of rebutting any adverse inference to the complainer's credibility or reliability . . .

For example, in sexual abuse cases, the victim may well reveal the story slowly and partially. The defendant might well seize on such reticence to argue that the victim should not be believed and yet post-traumatic stress syndrome may account for the victim's behaviour.[40] The argument against adducing expert testimony on such issues is that it can be seen as simply a collateral matter, a form of oath helping whereby one witness is merely saying to the jury that they should believe what another witness has said. The alternative view may be that this is important explanatory material, in the absence of which the jury without which the jury may find it difficult or impossible to understand the evidence in the case. In English law, such explanatory material is admissible, even where it reveals bad character of the accused or others.[41] Where it is simply explanatory background, there is even less reason to refuse to hear it, as long as it is material that is outside the experience and competence of the jury.[42]

4. Supporters and Critics of Turner

The Turner rule has its supporters, despite the courts' reluctance to admit evidence from psychology, psychiatry and the behavioural sciences. Zuckerman has defended this overall reluctance.

A. Zuckerman, The Principles of Criminal Evidence (OUP, 1989). p.67:

A judge deciding whether expert opinion should be accepted as an arbiter of a certain matter has to consider the state of public opinion on the point. If the community has come to defer to professional standards on the matters in question, the courts will normally follow suit. Medical evidence is admissible on matters of health because we accept the authority of the medical profession in this regard. Psychiatry has not yet obtained a like acceptance. Psychiatric evidence is admissible on the issue

[40] S., Murphy, "Assisting the Jury in Understanding Victimization: Expert Psychological Testimony Battered Women Syndrome and Rape Trauma Syndrome" (1992), 25 Columbia Journal of Law and Social Problems, 277.

[41] s.100(1)(a) and s.101(1)(c) of the Criminal Justice Act 2003

[42] Office for Criminal Justice Reform, Convicting Rapists and Protecting Victims (Home Office March 2006)—this consultative paper suggests legislation to permit the use of expert evidence to explain rape trauma syndrome to juries (App.D).

of insanity but not . . . on the mental state of a normal person. It is argued that the distinction is irrational; for to understand abnormality psychiatry has first to master the normal mental processes. However, as long as the community does not defer to psychiatry on matters such as intention and credibility, the scope for expert evidence on such matters must remain limited . . . . Only when public opinion is clear one way or another can we demand consistency from the courts.

Others have echoed the need to restrict the role of psychological and psychiatric expert witnesses in court.

D. Faust and J. Ziskin, "The expert witness in psychology and psychiatry" Science 24th July 1988 1.31–35:

Studies show that professionals often fail to reach reliable or valid conclusions and that the accuracy of their judgements does not necessarily surpass that of laypersons, thus raising substantial doubt that psychologists or psychiatrists meet the legal standards for expertise.[43]

Others are less sceptical. Are such restrictions on the accused's ability to mount a full defence justified? If there is professional opinion to go before a jury, there is little reason to reject it. Pattenden[44] has suggested that the *Turner* rule rests on three fallacies: that there is a clear demarcation between the normal and the abnormal;[45] that the "common sense" of the jury is a good basis on which to assess the behaviour of a person who is not mentally disordered; and finally that experts only concern themselves with abnormal people. For example, people's reactions and behaviour are often counter-intuitive in response to outside pressures. While jurors recognise external situational causes as contributing to their own actions, they tend to underestimate these factors in the actions of others and to overestimate the importance of internal, dispositional factors.[46]

R. D. Mackay and A. Colman "Excluding Expert Evidence; A Tale of Ordinary Folk and Common Experience" [1991] Crim.L.R. 809:

What might be a reasonable approach to the admissibility of expert psychological and psychiatric evidence? One recent commentator has suggested that, since no clear

---

[43] D. Faust and J. Ziskin, "The expert witness in psychology and psychiatry" *Science* July 24, 1988, 1.31–35.

[44] R. Pattenden, "Conflicting Approaches to Psychiatric Evidence" [1986] Crim.L.R. 92 at 100.

[45] R.D. Mackay and A. Colman "Excluding Expert Evidence; A Tale of Ordinary Folk and Common Experience" [1991] Crim.L.R. 800; R.D. Mackay R.D. and A. Colman "Equivocal Rulings on Expert Psychological and Psychiatric Evidence; Turning a Muddle into a Nonsense" [1991] Crim.L.R. 800; D. Sheldon and M. MacLeod "From Normative to Positive Data: Expert Psychological Evidence Re-examined" [1991] Crim.L.R. 811.

[46] R.D. Mackay and A. Colman [1991] *op.cit* at 807–808.

line can be drawn between the normal and the abnormal, 'all expert evidence as to personality should be admitted subject to its relevance.'[47] We do not advocate such a radical solution, partly because it is the task of the jury to try the facts of a case and it is therefore right that expert testimony should be excluded on matters that are well understood by ordinary people, and partly because we recognise that such a solution would in any event be unacceptable to the judiciary. We advocate instead that expert psychological and psychiatric testimony should be limited but that the range of admissible evidence be extended beyond its present bounds.

It is clear that the *Turner* rule has already been breached by a number of exceptions, but in our view it is still being interpreted too narrowly. The fundamental purpose of the rule is to exclude expert evidence that. in the court's opinion, will not help the jury to understand the accused's state of mind; its reference to 'human nature and behaviour within the limits of normality' is subservient to this purpose. In decisions regarding admissibility, the crucial question ought to be whether or not the expert evidence could make a significant contribution to the jury's understanding of the accused's state of mind. This must depend, of course, on the judge's assessment of the probative value of the evidence. If the expert evidence points to an abnormal state of mind or personality of any degree on the defendant's part at the time of the alleged offence, then we submit that the court ought to exercise its discretion in favour of admitting the evidence. There are many abnormal states of mind brought about by situational forces . . . which, although they do not involve mental disorders in any medical sense, none the less lie demonstrably beyond the understanding of ordinary people, and in relation to which expert evidence could therefore contribute significantly to a jury's understanding. In the spirit of the *Turner* rule, evidence on such matters ought in our view to be admitted, for to exclude it might deprive the jury of evidence that could help them understand the defendant's state of mind at the material time.

The narrow interpretation of *Turner* encourages a futile attempt to divide mental abnormalities into forms that require elucidation by an expert witness and those that do not. In contrast, in a French criminal investigation supervised by a *juge d'instruction*, psychological examination of specific witnesses can be ordered so that the quality of their testimony can be objectively appraised.[48]

B. *The Scope for Expert Testimony*

When an "expert" is presented to the court, the judge has two questions to decide. One of these is whether the witness is indeed qualified in the area but the preliminary issue is about the nature of the specialism itself. Is it proper for the court to accept expert evidence about this field? An illustration might relate to planetary motion where a court might well listen to a qualified astronomer but would reject evidence from an equally qualified astrologer. The field of knowledge is one which must have an objective validity—this might be DNA analysis or literary merit. We must first decide whether the field itself is a proper subject for expert testimony before considering whether the expert is qualified in the subject.

[47] D. Ormerod commenting on *Weightman* [1991] Crim.L.R. 204 at 205.
[48] J. Cooper, "Criminal Investigations in France" [1991] N.L.J. 381.

It would be idle to list areas of knowledge in expert testimony may be received, encompassing matters scientific and medical, architectural and engineering. Bullets, blood and tachographs may all be the subject of expert analysis. Movements in the stock market or market values might all need exposition to the jury. In *Hodges*,[49] an experienced police officer gave expert testimony as to the nature of the heroin market in an English town. In assessing whether expert evidence is admissible, one test may be that of assisting the trier of fact.

M. Ladd "Expert Testimony" 5 V. and L.R. 414 at 418 (1952):

There is no more certain test for determining when experts may be used than the common sense inquiry whether the untrained layman would be qualified to determine intelligently and to the best possible degree the particular issue without enlightenment from those having a specialised understanding of the subject involved in the dispute.[50]

Situations change and in some fields, expert testimony may become unnecessary and judicial knowledge be a more appropriate approach. For example whether a computer has been operated properly, might require expert testimony in the 1980s but be treated as coming within the ordinary competence of the 21st century juror.[51] New forensic techniques and fields of knowledge emerge and the court must be satisfied, not only that the witness is qualified, but whether such evidence should be given. In their time, courts have looked with suspicion at both fingerprints and DNA testing.[52] New forensic techniques, such as ESDA,[53] have been vital element in uncovering miscarriages of justice. In contrast, psychological profiling has yet to be accepted as valid evidence.[54]

In Australian courts, in *Bonython*,[55] King C.J. discussed whether the issue of whether the testimony fell within the area of expert testimony.

Bonython (1984) 38 S.A.S.R. 45, *per* King C.J.:

This . . . may be divided into two parts: (a) whether the subject matter of the opinion is such that a person without instruction or experience in the area of knowledge or human experience would be able to form a sound judgment on the matter without the

---

[49] [2003] 2 Cr.App.R. 15.
[50] M. Ladd, "Expert Testimony" (1952) 5 Vand. L.R. 414 at 418.
[51] *Shephard* [1993] 1 All E.R. 225 at 231b *per* Lord Griffiths.
[52] D. Farington "Unacceptable Evidence" N.L.J. [1993] 806 and 857.
[53] *Wellington* [1991] Crim.L.R. 543.
[54] *Gilfoyle* above, the refusal of the court to accept such testimony led to the collapse of the case against Colin Stagg for the murder of Rachel Nickell—*Guardian* September 15, 1994.
[55] [1984] 38 S.A.S.R. 45.

assistance of witnesses possessing special knowledge or experience in the area, and (b) whether the subject matter of the opinion forms part of a body of knowledge or experience which is sufficiently organized or recognized to be accepted as a reliable body of knowledge or experience, a special acquaintance with which by the witness would render his opinion of assistance to the court.

In English courts, when is a field of scientific knowledge sufficiently established in order that expert evidence is received? What criteria does a judge use to distinguish admissible 'good' science from inadmissible "dubious" science? The position in English law has been liberal—a field need not be generally accepted before expert testimony is admissible but it must be sufficiently established to be reliable. Techniques of voice identification were in issue in *Robb* where the evidence consisted of recordings of ransom demands and control recordings of the accused's voice. The witness concluded that there was no distinction between the two voices. Bingham L.J. accepted that voice identification itself was a field calling for expert testimony.

Robb (1991) 93 Cr.App.R 161 at 164, *per* Bingham L.J.:

This appeal raises questions touched on but not discussed in depth in the authorities: what characterises a field as one in which expertise may exist, and what qualifies, or disentitles, a witness to give evidence of his opinion as an expert? The old-established, academically-based sciences such as medicine, geology or metallurgy, and the established professions such as architecture, quantity surveying or engineering, present no problem. The field will be regarded as one in which expertise may exist and any properly qualified member will be accepted without question as expert. Expert evidence is not, however, limited to these core areas. Expert evidence of finger-prints, hand-writing and accident reconstruction is regularly given. Opinions may be given of the market value of land, ships, pictures or rights. Expert opinions may be given of the quality of commodities, or on the literary, artistic, scientific or other merit of works alleged to be obscene . . . Some of these fields are far removed from anything which could be called a formal scientific discipline. Yet while receiving this evidence the courts would not accept the evidence of an astrologer, a soothsayer, a witch-doctor or an amateur psychologist and might hesitate to receive evidence of attributed authorship based on stylometric analysis.

However the witness's techniques (which involved listening carefully to the tape recordings) were ones which were not scientific or generally respected in the field of phonetics.

Robb (1991) 93 Cr.App.R. 161 at 165–6, *per* Bingham L.J.:

The great weight of informed opinion, including the world leaders in the field, was to the effect that auditory techniques unless supplemented and verified by acoustic analysis were an unreliable basis of speaker identification. Representations to that effect had been made to the Home Secretary and the Director of Public Prosecutions. A unit recently established in Germany under a respected director rejected identification based on auditory techniques alone. Other Western European countries did not receive such evidence. There were only a handful of others, and they were in this country, who shared Dr. Baldwin's opinion. He had published no material which would allow his methods to be tested or his results checked. He had conducted no experiments or tests on the accuracy of his own conclusions . . .

It might not be surprising if the answers given by Dr. Baldwin in cross-examination had led the jury to conclude that they should receive his evidence with caution or that they should place little or no reliance upon it. But that is not the question now before us, which is whether the evidence of Dr. Baldwin was in law admissible at all. We have not found this an entirely easy question. We are alive to the risk that if, in a criminal case, the Crown are permitted to call an expert witness of some but tenuous qualifications the burden of proof may imperceptibly shift and a burden be cast on the defendant to rebut a case which should never have been before the jury at all. A defendant cannot fairly be asked to meet evidence of opinion given by a quack, a charlatan or an enthusiastic amateur. But we do not regard Dr. Baldwin as falling anywhere near these categories. He was entitled to be regarded as a phonetician well qualified by academic training and practical experience to express an opinion on voice identification . . .

The court took a pragmatic approach, accepting the evidence and treating any doubts about the accuracy of the techniques as a question of weight for the jury. The witness had described the features that he paid attention to and it was for the jury to assess the value to give to his opinion. But it is clear that the judgment conflates two issues—the first is whether this particular field has a valid scientific underpinning; the second is whether Dr Baldwin was qualified in the field. The court answers the second question but ignores the first.

There is a different approach taken by the court in *Gilfoyle*.[56] This was a murder case in which the defence was that the victim had committed suicide. The question was whether an expert witness could give evidence about his "psychological autopsy" on the victim which suggested that she was a suicide risk. The expert witness had considerable background and experience in psychological profiling.

Gilfoyle [2001] 2 Cr.App.R. 5, *per* Rose L.J.

24. . . . expert witnesses must furnish the court:

> with the necessary scientific criteria for testing the accuracy of their conclusions, so as to enable the judge or jury to form their own independent judgment by the application of these criteria to the facts proved in evidence[57]

25. In our judgment, although Professor Canter is clearly an expert in his field, the evidence tendered from him was not expert evidence of a kind properly to be placed before the court for a number of reasons. First, although this alone would not necessarily be fatal to the admissibility of his evidence, he had never previously

---

[56] [2001] 2 Cr.App.R. 5.
[57] *Davie v Edinburgh Magistrates*, 1953 S.C. 34 at 40 *per* Lord President Cooper.

embarked on the task which he set himself in this case. Secondly, his reports identify no criteria by reference to which the court could test the quality of his opinions: there is no data base comparing real and questionable suicides and there is no substantial body of academic writing approving his methodology. As Professor Canter says himself in a draft article on psychological autopsy . . . "It has taken off and been used before it has reached the maturity needed to be allowed safely out of the careful confines of its professional birthplace" [H]e says: "there is very little detailed empirical evidence available on many topics that are relevant to preparing psychological autopsies . . . . The scientific literature also indicates the lack of a comprehensive assessment and evaluation of the nature and validity of those investigations which have been carried out . . . . It is therefore most appropriate to consider the psychological autopsy as a relatively unstructured technique". The American Psychology Association Panel has recommended that psychologists conducting a psychological autopsy state in their report that the conclusions drawn are based on a speculative view of events. In our view unstructured and speculative conclusions are not the stuff of which admissible expert evidence is made . . . there is English, Canadian and United States authority which points against the admission of such evidence. In *Chard*[58] it was held that a psychologist may not give evidence of how someone's mind operated at the time of the alleged offence, save in cases of insanity or diminished responsibility. In *Weightman*[59] the evidence of a psychiatrist was held inadmissible when its purpose was to tell the jury how someone not suffering from mental illness is liable to react to the stresses and strains of life.

. . . In the United States, in *Thompson v Mayes*[60] the Texas Court of Appeal upheld a trial judge's ruling excluding evidence of a psychological autopsy in relation to the state of mind of the donee under a will who was said to have killed the donor and then committed suicide: the evidence was tendered to establish that the donee was not responsible for the donor's death. So far as is known, there have been seventeen occasions in the United States when criminal trial judges have admitted evidence of psychological profiling: in each case the decision has been overturned on appeal. The guiding principle in the United States appears to be . . . that evidence based on a developing new brand of science or medicine is not admissible until accepted by the scientific community as being able to provide accurate and reliable opinion.

These are serious questions about the "..criteria by reference to which the court could test the quality of his opinions: there is no data base comparing real and questionable suicides and there is no substantial body of academic writing approving his methodology . . ."[61] This represents a very different view from *Robb*. The court should assess the validity of the science before the expert evidence is admitted—there should be general acceptance in the scientific community, demonstrated, for example, by academic writing which validates the methodology employed.

The possibility that English law might insist on a higher threshold of scientific validity before expert evidence is admitted was dealt a blow in *Dallagher*.[62] The disputed evidence was an earprint left by the killer. Testimony had been given that this print matched that of the defendant. On appeal, fresh evidence about the science behind earprint matches suggested that there was little empirical research or peer review to suggest that such robust conclusions about matches should be drawn. This lack of research in

[58] above.
[59] above.
[60] 707 S.W. 2nd 951.
[61] *ibid.*, at para.25 *per* Rose L.J.
[62] [2003] 1 Cr.App.R. 12.

the field meant that there was no general acceptance in the scientific community. But the court chose to place a great deal of reliance upon the decisions of *Stockwell*[63] and *Clarke*,[64] both of which involved another controversial area of scientific testimony, that of "facial mapping". This involved superimposing photographic images upon one another to assist a jury in determining identity on the basis of such photographs. In both the evidence was accepted. One commentator has pointed out the shortcomings of the *Dallagher* approach.

W. O'Brian 'Scrutiny Of Expert Evidence: Recent Decisions Highlight The Tensions' (2003) Int Jour Evidence and Proof 172 at 175–176:

The court noted that the relevant test was as stated in the most recent edition of Cross and Tapper on Evidence: 'so long as the field is sufficiently well established to pass the ordinary tests of relevance and reliability, then no enhanced test of admissibility should be applied . . .' It concluded that even if the fresh evidence had been presented at trial, the trial judge could not possibly have concluded that the Crown evidence was either irrelevant or so unreliable that it should be excluded.

Kennedy LJ also considered *Gilfoyle*, one of the cases principally relied upon by the defence, and concluded correctly that the *Frye* requirement of general acceptance for expert testimony referred to in that decision was no longer the guiding principle in the United States. Rather, as the US Supreme Court held in *Daubert*, that test was superseded by the adoption of Federal Rule of Evidence 702, which provides that 'if scientific, technical or other specialized knowledge will assist the trier of fact to understand the evidence or to determine a fact in issue, a witness qualified as an expert by knowledge, skill, experience, training or education may testify thereto in the form of an opinion or otherwise'. The judgment might suggest that, after *Daubert*, English law and US law are similar in this area.

However, the Court of Appeal did not discuss the remainder of the *Daubert* decision, in which the Supreme Court concluded that the courts nonetheless had a duty to act as 'gatekeepers' to ensure that any expert testimony presented is both relevant and reliable. This requires them to examine a number of factors before admitting the testimony, including (1) whether the technique at issue is generally accepted in the field to which it relates, as well as (2) whether the technique is testable and has been tested, (3) whether it has a known or potential error rate, (4) whether it has been published and peer-reviewed, and (5) the existence and maintenance of standards controlling its operation. As the case law subsequent to *Daubert* and the extensive commentary on it make clear, Daubert has by no means given the parties *carte blanche* to introduce unproven and untested expert testimony in the United States.

It is difficult to agree with the court in *Dallagher* that scientific testimony should be subject to the "ordinary tests of relevance and reliability". For an ordinary witness, reliability comes from their powers of perception, memory and recall. But for the expert witness, it comes from a combination of the validity of the science involved and the expertise of the person presenting the conclusions. What would "ordinary reliability" mean in testimony, for

---

[63] (1993) 97 Cr.App.R. 260.
[64] (1995) 2 Cr.App.R. 425.

example, about DNA match probabilities? It is for the court to establish a threshold of scientific reliability to decide what expert testimony goes before the jury. For a court to eschew that gate keeping role and to fail to establish robust criteria to assess the validity of the scientific evidence increases the risk of miscarriages of justice: in *Dallagher* itself, the conviction was quashed on other grounds and a retrial ordered. That retrial ended when new DNA evidence from the earprint proved not to match the defendant but another person altogether. The earprint evidence was shown to be unreliable. [65]

How do the courts in the USA police this boundary? The court in *Dallagher* completely misunderstands the law in the USA when it suggests that the position is similar to that in England and Wales. In the USA, until the 1990s, the *Frye*[66] rule was that the theory or technique must be "sufficiently established to have gained general acceptance in the particular field in which it belongs." In 1972 came the introduction of the Federal Rules of Evidence, including rule 702 on expert testimony. This was reviewed by the Supreme Court in the leading case of *Daubert v Merrell Dow Pharmaceuticals*.[67] The Supreme Court draws back from the *Frye* principle of widespread acceptance in the relevant discipline. But *Daubert* went on to impose a more pro-active role on the judge as gatekeeper in relation to scientific testimony.

The case concerned the drug Bendectin, approved by the federal Food and Drugs Administration. The drug was taken to relieve symptoms of nausea during pregnancy and was alleged to have caused birth defects. The claimants employed expert witnesses whose testimony had never been subjected to peer review. The judgment draws on the theories of Karl Popper and in particular, his principle that the criterion of scientific status of a theory is its falsifiability or testability through empirical testing.[68] The Supreme Court considered this principle to be an appropriate approach for assessing the scope for expert evidence. This approach places a heavier burden on the trial judge to determine whether the reasoning or methodology underlying the testimony is scientifically valid. *Daubert* created a non-exclusive checklist for trial courts to use in assessing the reliability of scientific expert testimony. The specific factors are:

a) whether the expert's technique or theory can be or has been tested— that is, whether the expert's theory can be challenged in some objective sense, or whether it is instead simply a subjective approach that cannot reasonably be assessed for reliability;

b) whether the technique or theory has been subject to peer review and publication;

c) the known or potential rate of error of the technique or theory when applied;

[65] Dallagher had already served seven years in prison—R. Ede, "Wrongful convictions put forensic science in the dock". *The Times* February 3, 2004; also see innocent.org.uk/cases/markdallagher/ (accessed February 6, 2006).

[66] *Frye v US* (1923) 54 App.D.C. 46.

[67] 113 S. Ct. 2786 (1993).

[68] K. Popper, *Conjectures and Refutations* (4th edn., Routledge, 1972), pp.36–37.

    d) the existence and maintenance of standards and controls; and

    e) whether the technique or theory has been generally accepted in the scientific community.

Trial judges would have to distinguish good science from bad. But the *Daubert* decision has remained a controversial issue in the USA. A review of the caselaw shows that the rejection of expert testimony has been the exception rather than the rule. *Daubert* did not work a "seachange over federal evidence law" and "the trial court's role as gatekeeper is not intended to serve as a replacement for the adversary system."[69] It has also proved costly for litigants as *Daubert* hearings proved lengthy and expensive. In *US v Mitchell*,[70] the question was the admissibility of latent fingerprint evidence—there was a five day hearing with 1000 pages of testimony.[71]

To assess the admissibility of expert testimony in this way would appear a tall order for the judge faced with the complexities of phonetics and voice identification in *Robb*, the techniques of facial mapping in *Stockwell*[72] or the validity of earprint matching in *Dallagher*. Such difficulties would multiply in the context of expert psychiatric or psychological evidence where controversy surrounds the very existence of certain syndromes and disorders such as recovered memory syndrome, rape trauma syndrome, battered wife or child syndrome, post-traumatic stress disorder or multiple personality disorder, some of which have achieved strong empirical support whereas others have not. It has been argued that such concepts might have therapeutic value but are scientifically unproved and unsuitable for courtroom presentation. But expert evidence on "battered wife syndrome" was considered admissible in *Ahluwalia*.[73] The introduction of a *Daubert* approach in England and Wales might well lead to reconsideration of this position.

There is a further aspect to the reception of expert testimony: this is the issue of the burden and standard of proof. Where the Crown wishes to adduce evidence of any kind, they must (if challenged) prove that the pre-conditions for admissibility exist beyond reasonable doubt. With scientific testimony, a court should be satisfied on that standard that the basic theories and techniques behind that testimony are valid and reliable. This is not a question that can be left to the good sense of the jury. In *Dallagher*, there was the theory that earprints are peculiar to individuals as well as the reliability of the techniques involved in lifting and comparison. There was fresh evidence at the appeal that neither had been properly established nor generally accepted. The court should have considered whether there was a reasonable doubt that earprint evidence was scientifically reliable. If such a doubt existed, it should not have been admitted.

---

[69] For a commentary on the US position, see FRE r. 702 notes.

[70] (2004) 365 F.3d 215.

[71] J. Prescott, *"Speaking in Tongues: The Construction of Science in the Courtroom"* (2005 University of Sussex, DPhil thesis, unpublished) pp.87–88.

[72] above.

[73] [1992] 4 All E.R. 889.

C. Credentials

Once the validity of the science has been established, it is necessary to demonstrate that the witness is an expert in that field. Their credentials may consist of practical experience or professional qualification. The opposing party is entitled to inquire into these. The question whether a witness is an expert is a matter of fact for the judge. If there are some credentials, the evidence is likely to be admitted and the rest would be a matter of weight.[74] In *Silverlock*, a solicitor was accepted as an expert on handwriting though his experience had been picked up as an amateur.

Silverlock [1894] 2 Q.B. 766 at 771, *per* Lord Russell C.J.:

It is true that the witness who is called upon to give evidence founded on a comparison of handwritings must be peritus; he must be skilled in doing so; but we cannot say that he must have become peritus in the way of his business or in any definite way. The question is, is he peritus? Is he skilled? Has he an adequate knowledge? Looking at the matter practically, if a witness is not skilled the judge will tell the jury to disregard his evidence. There is no decision which requires that the evidence of a man who is skilled in comparing handwriting, and who has formed a reliable opinion from past experience, should be excluded because his experience has not been gained in the way of his business.

In Australian courts, in *Bonython*,[75] King C.J. discussed whether the issue of whether the witness qualified as an expert.

Bonython (1984) 38 SASR 45, *per* King C.J.:

An investigation of the methods used by the witness in arriving at his opinion may be pertinent, in certain circumstances, to the answers to both the above questions. If the witness has made use of new or unfamiliar techniques or technology, the court may require to be satisfied that such techniques or technology have a sufficient scientific basis to render results arrived at by that means part of a field of knowledge which is a proper subject of expert evidence . . . Where the witness possesses the relevant formal qualifications to express an opinion on the subject, an investigation on the voir dire of his methods will rarely be permissible on the issue of his qualifications. There may be greater scope for such examination where the alleged qualifications depend upon experience or informal studies . . . . Generally speaking, once the qualifications are established, the methodology will be relevant to the weight of the evidence and not to the competence of the witness to express an opinion . . .

---

[74] *Robb* above; *Clare* [1995] Crim.L.R. 947 and comment R. Munday, "Videotape Evidence and the Advent of the Expert Ad Hoc" (1995) 159 J.P. 547.

[75] above.

If the qualifications of a witness to give expert evidence are in issue, it may be necessary to hear evidence on the voir dire in order to make a finding as to those qualifications. If there is an issue as to whether the subject matter upon which the opinion is sought is a proper subject of expert evidence, any disputed facts relevant to the determination of that issue should be resolved by the reception of evidence on the voir dire.

But if the witness is not qualified, the evidence will be excluded—in *Loake*,[76] the accused was not permitted to call a magistrate who had visited him in his cell to testify as to his sanity. In *Edwards*,[77] the defendant was charged with possession of Class A drugs with intent to supply. He sought to support his defence of possession for personal use by calling a witness who had worked for eight years for a drug advice charity who gave evidence of a user's increasing tolerance. The Crown called a detective sergeant to counter this. Neither witness had any formal medical or toxicological qualification. Both relied on their experience rather than any academic materials. The judge's refusal to treat either as an expert was upheld on appeal.

Experts in Foreign Law

Many cases have considered the qualifications of witnesses called to testify on a point of foreign law which needs establishing as a matter of fact. "The judge has not organs to know and to deal with the text of the foreign law, and therefore requires the assistance of a lawyer who knows how to interpret it."[78] An English court should not conduct its own researches into foreign law[79] and if expert witnesses agree as to the interpretation of the foreign law, the judge is not entitled to reject that evidence.[80] However if the expert witnesses conflict as to the effect of foreign sources, the court is entitled to look at those sources to resolve the conflict.[81] Furthermore the Court of Appeal regards a trial judge's conclusion on a point of foreign law, although a finding of fact, as "a question of fact of a peculiar kind"[82] which may be re-examined on appeal.

At common law the credentials of an expert on foreign law were carefully scrutinised and only a judge or legal practitioner was properly qualified. This exclusive approach was demonstrated in decisions such as *Bristow v Sequeville*[83] although other cases allowed witnesses whose expertise had been gathered in different ways (as an embassy official[84] or through business[85] or banking). Even academics were acceptable.[86] The common law has been consolidated in the Civil Evidence Act 1972.

---

[76] (1911) 7 Cr.App.R. 71.
[77] [2001] EWCA Crim 2185.
[78] *Sussex Peerage Case* (1844) 11 Cl. & F. 85 at 115 *per* Lord Brougham.
[79] *Duchess Di Sora v Phillipps* (1863) 10 HL Cas. 624 at 640.
[80] *Bumper Development v Metropolitan Police Commissioner* [1991] 4 All E.R. 638 at 646.
[81] *Earl Nelson v Lord Bridport.* (1845) 8 Beav. 527 at 537.
[82] *Parkasho v Singh* [1967] 1 All E.R. 737 at 746.
[83] (1850) 5 Ex. 275.
[84] *Re Dost Aly Khan's Goods* (1880) 6 P.D. 65.
[85] *Vander Donckt v Thellusson* (1849) 8 C.B. 812.
[86] *Brailey v Rhodesia Consolidated Ltd* [1910] 2 Ch. 95 but see *Bristow v Sequeville*, above.

4.—(1) It is hereby declared that in civil proceedings a person who is suitably qualified to do so on account of his knowledge or experience is competent to give expert evidence as to the law of any country or territory outside the United Kingdom, or of any part of the United Kingdom other than England and Wales, irrespective of whether he has acted or is entitled to act as a legal practitioner there.

In *Okolie*,[87] the charge was handling stolen goods, namely cars that had been stolen in Germany. The Crown had to prove that the cars were stolen and if they intended to rely on an offence that was committed abroad, they had to provide expert evidence that the behaviour complained of amounted to offences under German law. It is not possible to rely on any rebuttable presumption that foreign law was the same as English law even when the conduct is unequivocally equivalent.

D. *Expert opinion and hearsay*

When witnesses are designated as experts, they testify as to matters of fact that their work and research have revealed; they also draw conclusions from those facts and give their expert opinion on their significance. Experts are not bound by the rule that excludes the opinion of witnesses. Furthermore, although the facts on which an expert may form an opinion should be proved by admissible evidence,[88] they may draw on the work of others to form an opinion. Experts are not bound by the hearsay rule in this regard. Different situations may be envisaged.

a) Facts on which any opinion is based may be based on the witness's own perceptions: the pathologist who performs a post-mortem may testify as to their findings and give an opinion as to the cause of death.

b) Opinions might also be on the basis of assumed facts: the witness might be asked whether, given certain marks on the body, what might be the likely cause of death. In *Mason*,[89] a surgeon who had not seen the body was asked whether, given the nature of the wounds, these could have been self-inflicted. In such cases the expert should state the assumed facts on which the opinion is based so that the trier of fact can assess the weight of the opinion. The opinion is valueless unless the facts themselves are proved.

c) Opinions can also be on the basis of facts supplied by others: the pathologist might well be relying on analyses of stomach contents or body tissues carried out by assistants.

The difficulty comes where expert witnesses rely on facts of which they have no first-hand knowledge and which, if retailed to the court, would be hearsay.

---

[87] *The Times*, June 16, 2000 (CA); *Ofori* (1994) 99 Cr.App.R. 223.
[88] R. Pattenden, "Expert Opinion Based on Hearsay" [1982] Crim.L.R. 85.
[89] (1911) 7 Cr.App.R. 67.

An illustration of this is *Abadom*,[90] where the charge was robbery and the prosecution case rested on evidence that a window had been broken during the robbery and that fragments of glass were found in the accused's shoe. Did the splinters in the shoe come from the scene of the robbery? The expert witness measured the refractive index of the glass from the window and of the glass found in the shoe. The samples matched but what was the probability that the samples had the same source? He referred to Home Office statistics as to how common this kind of glass was. It occurred in only 4 per cent of glass samples investigated and consequently there was a very strong likelihood that the glass in the shoe originated from the window. The expert witness at that time[91] was relying on inadmissible hearsay contained in the Home Office statistics. On appeal it was submitted that he was not entitled to rely on such material and that the case was indistinguishable from *Myers v D.P.P..*[92] The Court of Appeal disagreed.

Abadom [1983] 1 All E.R. 364 at 368e–j, *per* Kerr L.J.:

First, where an expert relies on the existence or non-existence of some fact which is basic to the question on which he is asked to express his opinion, that fact must be proved by admissible evidence: see *English Exporters (London) Ltd v Eldonwall Ltd.*[93] Thus, it would no doubt have been inadmissible if [the witness] had said in the present case that he had been told by somebody else that the refractive index of the fragments of glass and of the control sample was identical, and any opinion expressed by him on this basis would have been based on hearsay. If he had not himself determined the refractive index, it would have been necessary to call the person who had done so before [the witness] could have expressed an opinion based on this determination . . . . Second, where the existence or non-existence of some fact is in issue, a report made by an expert who is not called as a witness is not admissible as evidence of that fact merely by production of the report, even though it was made by an expert: see eg *R v Crayden.*[94]

These, however, are in our judgment the limits of the hearsay rule in relation to evidence of opinion given by experts, both in principle and on the authorities. In other respects their evidence is not subject to the rule against hearsay in the same way as that of witnesses of fact . . . . Once the primary facts on which their opinion have been proved by admissible evidence, they are entitled to draw on the work of others as part of the process of arriving at their conclusion. However, where they have done so, they should refer to this material in their evidence so that the cogency and probative value of their conclusion can be tested and evaluated by reference to it.

This process can also be seen in *Bradshaw*.[95] The accused was charged with murder and the only issue was diminished responsibility. The defence

---

[90] [1983] 1 All E.R. 364; upheld in Hodges, above.
[91] Nowadays the tables would be admissible under s.117 of the Criminal Justice Act 2003 and s.30 of the Criminal Justice Act 1988.
[92] [1964] 2 All E.R. 881.
[93] [1973] 1 All E.R. 726 at 731.
[94] [1978] 2 All E.R. 700 at 702.
[95] (1985) 82 Cr.App.R. 79.

produced medical experts whose opinions were based in part that the defendant had told them that he was "in a state of unreality and confusion". Such statements were hearsay and, while the doctors could not testify to them as proof of their contents, they could testify to them to explain the basis on which they arrived at their conclusions about the defendant's mental condition. This is in contrast to *Abadom* where the primary facts (the refractive index of the pieces of glass) were proved by direct evidence and it was only the secondary information (the statistical tables) that was hearsay. Where the primary information consists mainly or entirely of hearsay, the judge would be justified in warning the jury about the flimsiness of any foundation for that opinion. This was the situation in *Bradshaw* and the judge was justified in ruling that if the truth of what defendant said to the doctors was in question either he must testify or other evidence must be tendered. As a result the accused unwillingly testified. The ruling was upheld.

The English position by and large represents the US position.

The facts or data in the particular case upon which an expert bases an opinion or inference may be those perceived by or made known to the expert at or before the hearing. If of a type reasonably relied upon by experts in the particular field in forming opinions or inferences upon the subject, the facts or data need not be admissible in evidence in order for the opinion or inference to be admitted. Facts or data that are otherwise inadmissible shall not be disclosed to the jury by the proponent of the opinion or inference unless the court determines that their probative value in assisting the jury to evaluate the expert's opinion substantially outweighs their prejudicial effect.[96]

English courts have not expressly stated that the hearsay information which is the foundation of an expert's opinion must be of a type reasonably relied on by experts in the field. However, even if there is general acceptance by experts of the legitimacy of using hearsay evidence as the basis of their opinion, there is still a residual power in the court to exclude evidence which would have an unduly prejudicial effect. For example, in an American case involving an airplane crash, the court refused to allow expert testimony about another accident which involved an identical airplane, since the other accident did not occur under conditions substantially similar to the accident at issue. The introduction of the evidence was seen as likely to have a prejudicial effect on the jury.[97]

There are pragmatic aspects to this—allowing experts to rely on such sources of information saves time and money. One illustration is a doctor who may base a diagnosis on information from numerous sources, including statements by patients and relatives, reports and opinions from nurses, technicians and other doctors, hospital records, and X-rays. Most of them are admissible in evidence, but only with the expenditure of substantial time in producing and examining various authenticating witnesses. In criminal proceedings, s.127 of the Criminal Justice Act 2003 deals this, allowing expert witness testimony to be based on such preparatory material. Where informa-

---

[96] Federal Rules of Evidence, r.703.
[97] *Machtshien v Beech Aircraft Corp.*, 847 F. 2d 1261 (7th Cir. 1988).

tion relied upon by experts is outside their personal experience (for example work undertaken by an assistant) and cannot be proved by other admissible evidence, notice can be given of the people who have prepared the information on which the expert relied. Other parties will be able to apply for a direction that any such person must give evidence in person but a direction will only be given if the court is satisfied that it is in the interests of justice.

E. *The ultimate issue rule*

This traditional rule prevented an expert or non-expert witness from expressing an opinion on the very point that the trier of fact has to decide, namely, the ultimate issue. It has now been abandoned for the expert witness. Under the rule it was impermissible to ask a doctor, as a medical expert in a medical malpractice case, whether the defendant's actions measured up to the standard of the reasonable professional doctor or to ask an eyewitness in a dangerous driving case whether they considered the driving to be dangerous. The rationale is that the finder of fact might be unduly influenced by an expert but in many trials, especially civil, any expert evidence for one party is likely to be countered by expert evidence from the other side; not surprisingly the experts come to diametrically opposed conclusions, favouring the party by whom they are retained. In civil cases, the rule was often evaded so that the expert witness was allowed to express an opinion on the final issue so long as they used different language to that employed by the court.[98] It was finally overturned by the Civil Evidence Act 1972. [99]

> 3.—(1) Subject to any rules of court made in pursuance of this Act, where a person is called as a witness in any civil proceedings, his opinion on any relevant matter on which he is qualified to give expert evidence shall be admissible in evidence.
>
> (2) It is hereby declared that where a person is called as a witness in any civil proceedings, a statement of opinion by him on any relevant matter on which he is not qualified to give expert evidence, if made as a way of conveying relevant facts personally perceived by him, is admissible as evidence of what he perceived.
>
> (3) In this section 'relevant matter' includes an issue in the proceedings in question.

As a result of subsection (3), witnesses, whether expert or not, are able to express an opinion on the facts in issue in the case, although for the non-expert, this is only where the expression of such an opinion is a natural way of expressing what they have seen or heard. It is not a provision that should allow *carte blanche* to the parties to adduce opinions of expert witnesses but the proliferation of opinion evidence has brought considerable criticism.

The position was reviewed in *Barings PLC v Coopers Lybrand,*[1] litigation which arose out of the collapse of a bank as the result of the activities of a

---

[98] In *Rich v Pierpoint* (1862) 3 F.&F. 35, the issue was medical negligence—a doctor who had been present in court throughout the proceedings could not be asked whether the defendant was guilty of any want of skill but might be asked whether anything he heard suggested improper conduct on the defendant's part.

[99] As amended by Civil Evidence Act 1995, Sch.2.

[1] [2001] Lloyd's Rep. 85.

rogue trader. Evans-Lombe J. stated that there was a body of expertise with recognised standards in relation to the managers of investment banks conducting or administering the highly technical and specialised business of futures and derivatives trading. But, having reviewed the authorities, he says,

Barings PLC v Coopers Lybrand [2001] Lloyd's Rep. 85, *per* Evans-Lombe J.:

44. . . . expert evidence is admissible under s 3 of the Civil Evidence Act 1972 in any case where the Court accepts that there exists a recognised expertise governed by recognised standards and rules of conduct capable of influencing the Court's decision on any of the issues which it has to decide and the witness to be called satisfies the Court that he has a sufficient familiarity with and knowledge of the expertise in question to render his opinion potentially of value in resolving any of those issues. Evidence meeting this test can still be excluded by the Court if the Court takes the view that calling it will not be helpful to the Court in resolving any issue in the case justly. Such evidence will not be helpful where the issue to be decided is one of law or is otherwise one on which the Court is able to come to a fully informed decision without hearing such evidence.

Personal injury cases after road traffic accidents take up this theme—in *Liddell v Middleton* there were four eyewitnesses to the accident and also two expert witnesses whose opinions were based on the eyewitness accounts. Stuart-Smith L.J. was robust in his criticisms.

Liddell v Middleton (1996) P.l.Q.R. 36 at 42–43, *per* Stuart-Smith L.J.:

In this case, as I have already indicated, there were four eyewitnesses of the accident, though, as is almost inevitably the case, each of those witnesses saw only part of the scene that unfolded. From their evidence, the Judge had to determine what happened and, based on her findings of fact as to what each of the two parties involved did, decide whether or not their conduct was negligent, and if so whether that negligence caused or contributed to the Plaintiff's injuries. In some cases expert evidence is both necessary and desirable in road traffic cases to assist the judge in reaching his or her primary findings of fact. Examples of such cases include those where there are no witnesses capable of describing what happened, and deductions may have to be made from such circumstantial evidence as there may be at the scene, or where deductions are to be drawn from the position of vehicles after the accident, marks on the road, or damage to the vehicles, as to the speed of a vehicle, or the relative positions of the parties in the moments leading up to the impact.

In such cases the function of the expert is to furnish the judge with the necessary scientific criteria and assistance based upon his special skill and experience not possessed by ordinary laymen to enable the judge to interpret the factual evidence of the marks on the road, the damage or whatever it may be. What he is not entitled to do is to say in effect 'I have considered the statements and/or evidence of the eyewitnesses in this case and I conclude from their evidence that the defendant was going at a certain speed, or that he could have seen the plaintiff at a certain point'. These are facts for the trial judge to find based on the evidence that he accepts and such inferences as he draws from the primary facts found. Still less is the expert entitled to say that in his opinion the defendant should have sounded his horn, seen the plaintiff before he did or taken avoiding action and that in taking some action or failing to take some other action, a party was guilty of negligence. These are matters for the court, on which the experts' opinion is wholly irrelevant and therefore inadmissible.

This was echoed in the Auld Report,

Lord Justice Auld: A Review of the Criminal Courts of England and Wales Ch.11 para.133 (2001):

133 An expert witness is different from other witnesses in a number of respects, an important one of which is that he is permitted to express an opinion on the issue to which his evidence relates. But, at common law, it is for the judge to decide in each case whether the issue is one which is suitable for opinion evidence. Often the issue clearly does justify the calling of an expert. However, there is an increasing tendency, particularly in the criminal courts, for parties to seek to call opinion evidence masquerading as expert evidence on or very close to the factual decision that it is for the court to make. It is for the judges or magistrates to determine whether an issue truly is susceptible to and justifies the calling of expert evidence, in particular whether a proffered expert is likely to be any more expert than anyone else in forming an opinion on separately established facts. In the Crown Court the judge normally directs or indicates at the pre-trial stage whether any particular issue justifies the calling of expert evidence and, if so, of what nature.

There has been no statutory reform in criminal proceedings—misgivings about the rule were voiced by Parker L.C.J. in *D.P.P. v ABC Chewing Gum.*[2] The issue was whether the "battle cards" sold with the chewing gum might deprave and corrupt children contrary to the Obscene Publications Act 1959. The prosecution sought to introduce experts in child psychiatry to testify as to the likely effects on children. The magistrates refused to hear the evidence. The prosecution appeal was upheld by the Divisional Court.

D.P.P. v ABC Chewing Gum [1968]1 Q.B. 159 at 164, *per* Parker L.C.J.:

I myself would go a little further in that I cannot help feeling that with the advance of science more and more inroads have been made into the old common law principles. Those who practice in the criminal courts see every day cases of experts being called on the question of diminished responsibility, and although technically the final question 'Do you think he was suffering from diminished responsibility?' is strictly inadmissible, it is allowed time and again without objection. No doubt when dealing with the effect of certain things on the mind science may still be less exact than evidence as to what effects some particular thing will have on the body, but that, as it seems to me, is purely a question of weight . . . .

[2] [1968] 1 Q.B. 159.

Legislative reform has been advocated for criminal trials without result.[3] But the rule has been, *de facto*, abrogated. The Court of Appeal has recently described the existing rule as "more a matter of form than of substance" and that an expert should be entitled to give an opinion on an issue in the case, although the jury should be warned that such an opinion was not in itself decisive.[4]

In *Gokal*, the charge was conspiracy to defraud and false accounting arising from the collapse of a bank. It was a complex case and an expert investigator from the Serious Fraud Office whose evidence amounted to opinion evidence as to the appellant's guilt given by a prosecution investigator. One of the grounds of the appeal was that the question of dishonesty was critically one within the competence of the jury and the witness should not have been permitted to give evidence of dishonest collusion.

Gokal [1999] 6 Archbold News 2 (CA), *per* Rose L.J.:

In our judgment these criticisms are entirely misconceived. It was common ground at the trial that [the SFO investigator] was an expert. The extent of his independence could go only to weight not admissibility. His opinion was that, as the conduit accounts were in Gulf's control, there had to be collusion between them and BCCI, otherwise money from BCCI paid into those accounts would never have gone back to BCCI. For the reasons already given, the defendant's guilt or otherwise, dependent on his knowledge of what was going on, was a quite separate question from that of collusion between Gulf and BCCI and was so treated by the judge. In any event, we see no difference, in principle, between psychiatric and other expert evidence and there are nowadays, as [counsel for the appellant] conceded, circumstances in which experts can give evidence on the issue which the jury has to decide. (See, for example, *R v Stockwell*). The Judicial Studies Board Specimen Directions cater for that possibility: the judge in summing-up must make clear that the issue is for the jury to decide and they are not bound by the expert's view. In the present case, it was material for the jury to know what BCCI's auditors would be looking for and that this would not generally include re-routing of funds by a compliant third party. Expert evidence on this was properly admissible to help the jury. Indeed [counsel for the appellant] accepted that the jury would need expert help and that such evidence could properly state that the complex mechanics adopted by Gulf and BCCI could have no legitimate purpose and the only purpose was to hide the truth . . .

In *Ugoh*,[5] the Court of Appeal accepted that an expert witness could testify as to whether a rape victim was too drunk to give informed consent. This specifically approved *Stockwell* and *Gokal*.

General acceptance of expert testimony would lengthen trials but criminal trials frequently have significance beyond the immediate parties, especially where the prosecution involves social conflict (such as industrial disputes) or

---

[3] Criminal Law Revision Committee, 11th Report (Cmnd. 4991), para.268; J.C. Smith, *Criminal Evidence* (Sweet and Maxwell, London, 1995), p.116 recommended the abolition of the rule to the Royal Commission on Criminal Justice in 1993 but their final report ignores the issue.

[4] *Stockwell* above.

[5] March 8, 1999 (CA)—p.17 of Lawtel transcript.

unusual charges, especially those of a moral character such as conspiring to outrage public decency.

Knuller v D.P.P. [1972] 3 All E.R. 898 at 936, *per* Lord Simon:

. . . 'outrage', like 'corrupt' is a very strong word. 'Outraging public decency' goes considerably beyond offending the susceptibilities of, or even shocking, reasonable people . . . The offence is concerned with the recognised minimum standards of decency, which are likely to vary from time to time . . . Notwithstanding that 'public' in the offence is used in a locative sense, public decency must be viewed as a whole; and . . . the jury should be invited, where appropriate, to remember that they live in a plural society, with a tradition of tolerance towards minorities, and that this atmosphere of tolerance is itself part of public decency.[6]

Such charges frequently bring in their wake issues of literary merit or contemporary standards of artistic expression: in *Gibson*,[7] the accused exhibited earrings made from freeze-dried human foetuses of three or four months gestation and was charged with outraging public decency. Should expert testimony be permitted in such cases or, tempting as it is, should the issue of the minimum standards of public decency be left to justices of the peace or to a jury? In 1960, Penguin Books published D. H. Lawrence's *Lady Chatterley's Lover* and was prosecuted under section 4 of the Obscene Publications Act 1959. The defence produced 35 witnesses, including bishops and leading literary figures, such as Dame Rebecca West, EM Forster and Richard Hoggart. The prosecution probably lost the case when prosecution counsel Mervyn Griffith-Jones shocked the jury by asking: "Is it a book you would wish your wife or servants to read?" The publishers were acquitted by the jury but the adversarial trial, allied to a liberal approach to expert evidence, had provided a forum for informed debate that changed social attitudes.[8]

F. *Weight Accorded to Expert Testimony*

It is the jury who must decide what weight is to be given to the evidence of an expert witness, making their own independent judgment from the facts and principles proved in evidence. This is obviously the case where there is conflicting expert evidence but also the case where there is no conflict.

    a) Juries should not be directed to accept inevitably the evidence of an expert witness, even where that evidence is not contradicted.[9]

---

[6] *Knuller v D.P.P.* [1972] 3 All E.R. 898 at 936 *per* Lord Simon.
[7] (1991) 91 Cr.App.R. 341.
[8] C. Rolph, *The Trial of Lady Chatterley: Regina v. Penguin Books Limited* (1990)
[9] *Davie v Edinburgh Magistrates* (1953) S.C. 34.

b) Juries should not be invited to disregard the evidence of an expert witness in favour of their own unaided lay opinion. In a notorious obscenity trial, the accused published a "School Kids Issue" of their magazine, Oz, and were charged with a conspiracy to corrupt public morals. The judge was criticised by the appeal court when he invited the jury to disregard expert testimony, referring in his summing up to "so-called experts".[10]

In *Sanders*,[11] the accused relied on the defence of diminished responsibility to a charge of murder. The defence medical experts were uncontested but the Crown contended that, although the defendant had some abnormality of mind, it had not diminished his responsibility and that he had killed his victim in a premeditated fashion, overwhelmed by feelings of bitterness and jealousy. It was clear that, if there were no other circumstances to consider, the uncontradicted medical evidence should be accepted. However those other circumstances need not be medical ones. In *Sanders*, the medical evidence had to be considered in the light of other non-medical circumstances which had been introduced into evidence by the prosecution.

G. *Disclosure of Expert Testimony*

In civil proceedings, a party must obtain the leave of the court to adduce expert testimony.[12] Normally the report will be disclosed to the opposing party—if it is not, then it cannot be used in evidence.[13] But the effect of the Civil Evidence Act 1995 will be to allow a party to rely upon the written statement of an expert witness and not to call that witness in uncontroversial cases. The Civil Procedure Rules allow for written questions to be put to the expert prior to the trial although the opposing party may still call the witness for cross-examination.[14] Failure to call an expert witness in a controversial case would be a factor for the judge in assessing the weight to be given to that evidence.[16] The court has the power to order opposing experts to have pre-trial discussions and also to require a single joint expert.[16]

Disclosure of expert evidence relied on by the parties in criminal proceedings has been required for many years. Initially the obligation was on the prosecution (although only for indictable offences) and the defence were permitted to ambush the prosecution by the surprise production of expert evidence. Reform arose from a recommendation in 1981 from the Royal

---

[10] *Anderson v R* [1972] A.C. 100.
[11] [1991] Crim.L.R. 781.
[12] Civil Procedure Rules, r. 35.4.
[13] *ibid.*, r.35.13; *Derby & Co. Ltd v Weldon (No. 9)* [1991] 2 All E.R. 901 (where report needs not to be disclosed); *Naylor v Preston Area Health Authority* [1987] 2 All E.R. 353 (decision to disclose in medical negligence cases).
[14] Civil Evidence Act 1995, s.3.
[15] *ibid.*, s.4.
[16] Civil Procedure Rules, r.35.8 and r.35.10.

Commission on Criminal Procedure[17] criticising the delay and inconvenience and concluding that placing an obligation on the defence to disclose proposed expert evidence was justified. This was done by s.81 of the Police and Criminal Evidence Act 1984. Nowadays, disclosure of expert witness testimony is dealt with under r.24 of the Criminal Procedure Rules. Under r.24.1, if the prosecution or defence in any criminal proceedings proposes to adduce expert evidence (whether of fact or opinion), they shall,

i) furnish the other party or parties with a statement in writing of any finding or opinion which he proposes to adduce by way of such evidence, and

ii) where a request in writing is made to him in that behalf by any other party, provide that party also with a copy of (or if it appears to the party proposing to adduce the evidence to be more practicable, a reasonable opportunity to examine) the record of any observation, test, calculation or other procedure on which such finding or opinion is based and any document or other thing or substance in respect of which any such procedure has been carried out.

The defendant and the prosecution, in any trial, are entitled both to advance notice, not only of any expert testimony but also, on written request, of the background material on which that expert opinion is based. Any failure to disclose will mean that a party can only rely on that evidence with the leave of the court.[18] Although these rules provide for the mutual disclosure of expert evidence, they do not restrict the prosecution's wider common law obligations.

Ward [1993] 2 All E.R. 577 at 628f–j, *per* Glidewell L.J.:

. . . we believe that the surest way of preventing the misuse of scientific evidence is by ensuring that there is a proper understanding of the nature and scope of the prosecution's duty of disclosure. In our view there was an imperfect understanding of that position in 1974. [The Crown] suggested to us that the problem was solved by the Crown Court (Advance Notice of Expert Evidence) Rules . . . Those rules enable the legal representatives of a defendant in a Crown Court criminal case to require the prosecution by writing to provide in respect of scientific evidence a copy of (or an opportunity to inspect) 'the record of any observation, test, calculation or other procedure on which [any] finding or opinion is based' (r 3(1)(b) The new rules are helpful. But it is a misconception to regard them as exhaustive: they do not in any way supplant or detract from the prosecution's general duty of disclosure in respect of scientific evidence. That duty exists irrespective of any request by the defence. It is also not limited to documentation on which the opinion or findings of an expert is based. It extends to anything which may arguably assist the defence. It is therefore wider in scope than the rule. Moreover it is a positive duty, which in the context of scientific evidence obliges the prosecution to make full and proper inquiries from forensic scientists in order to ascertain whether there is discoverable material. Given the undoubted inequality as between prosecution and defence in access to forensic scientists, we regard it as of paramount importance that the common law of disclosure,

[17] *Report* (1981) Cmnd. 8092 para.8.22.
[18] Criminal Procedure Rules, r.24.3.

as we have explained it, should be appreciated by those who prosecute and defend in criminal cases . . .

Such principles apply to prosecution and defence.

Ward [1993] 2 All E.R. 577 at 632e–g, *per* Glidewell L.J.:

. . . What the rules do not say in terms is that if an expert witness has carried out experiments or tests which tend to disprove or cast doubt upon the opinion he is expressing, or if such experiments or tests have been carried out in his laboratory and are known to him, the party calling him must also disclose the record of such experiments or tests. In our view the rules do not state this in terms because they can only be read as requiring the record of all relevant experiments or tests to be disclosed. It follows that an expert witness who has carried out or knows of experiments or tests which tend to cast doubt on the opinions he is expressing is in our view under a clear obligation to bring the records of such experiments or tests to the attention of the solicitor who is instructing him so that it may be disclosed to the other party.

The common law has recognised a broad duty of disclosure on the prosecution. In the early 1990s that duty extended to revealing all information gathered in the course of a criminal investigation, even where that information undermined the Crown case.[19] There is still no such requirement on the defendant who is very likely to conceal general information relevant to the case. The defence expert witnesses are in a special position—although there is no statement in the rules that they are there to help the court,[20] they must disclose any data or other material which goes counter to the opinion being put forward. The expert witness should be in a fiduciary relationship with the court.

H. *The Role of the Expert Witness*

Issues surrounding expert witnesses and their role have been brought into sharp focus by a series of decisions involving Sudden Infant Death Syndrome (SIDS) or cot deaths. In *Clark*[21] and *Cannings*,[22] mothers were convicted of murdering their children with no conclusive evidence as to the cause of death and considerable reliance on expert testimony. The convictions in both cases were quashed. The court in *Clark* was concerned with the non-disclosure of pertinent medical evidence and misleading testimony about statistical probabilities. In *Cannings*, there was little direct evidence and the court stated that,

---

[19] Now regulated by the Criminal Procedure and Investigations Act 1996 as amended by the Criminal Justice Act 2003—see Ch.6.
[20] Contrast this with Civil Procedure Rules, r.35.
[21] [2003] EWCA Crim 1020.
[22] [2004] 2 Cr.App.R. 7.

although three unexplained deaths in the same family were rare, the case should have proceeded on the basis that if there was nothing to explain them, in the current state of knowledge, they remained unexplained and still possible natural deaths despite the known fact that some parents did smother their infant children. Where there were three deaths, the exclusion of currently known natural causes of infant death did not establish that the deaths resulted from the deliberate infliction of harm.[23]

The publicity surrounding the SIDS cases represented the experts as witnesses who were convinced of the guilt of the defendants. These are problems that have arisen previously as can be seen in Glidewell L.J.'s criticisms of government forensic scientists in *Ward*.

> . . . we have identified the cause of the injustice done to the appellant on the scientific side of this case as stemming from the fact that three senior forensic scientists at RARDE[24] regarded their task as to help the police. They became partisan. It is the clear duty of government forensic scientists to assist in a neutral and impartial way in criminal investigations. They must act in the cause of justice. That duty should be spelt out to all engaged or to be engaged in forensic services in the clearest terms.[25]

In civil cases, the duties of the expert witness are set out in *National Justice Cia Naviera SA v Prudential Assurance Co Ltd Ex p. Ikarian Reefer* where Cresswell J. said,

National Justice Cia Naviera SA v Prudential Assurance Co. Ltd Ex p. Ikarian Reefer [1993] 2 Lloyd's Rep. 68 at 81, *per* Cresswell J.:

The duties and responsibilities of expert witnesses in civil cases include the following:
1. Expert evidence presented to the Court should be, and should be seen to be, the independent product of the expert uninfluenced as to form or content by the exigencies of litigation . . .
2. An expert witness should provide independent assistance to the Court by way of objective unbiased opinion in relation to matters within his expertise . . . An expert witness in the High Court should never assume the role of an advocate.
3. An expert witness should state the facts or assumption upon which his opinion is based. He should not omit to consider material facts which could detract from his concluded opinion . . .
4. An expert witness should make it clear when a particular question or issue falls outside his expertise.
5. If an expert's opinion is not properly researched because he considers that insufficient data is available, then this must be stated with an indication that the opinion is no more than a provisional one . . . In cases where an expert witness who has prepared a report could not assert that the report contained the truth, the whole truth and nothing but the truth without some qualification, that qualification should be stated in the report.

[23] Distinguished in *Kai-Whitewind* [2002] 2 Cr.App.R. 31.
[24] Royal Armaments Research and Development Establishment at Woolwich.
[25] *Ward* above at 628d–f.

6. If, after exchange of reports, an expert witness changes his view on a material matter having read the other side's expert's report or for any other reason, such change of view should be communicated (through legal representatives) to the other side without delay and when appropriate to the Court.
7. Where expert evidence refers to photographs, plans, calculations, analyses, measurements, survey reports or other similar documents, these must be provided to the opposite party at the same time as the exchange of reports . . .

These duties are reinforced by r.35 of the Civil Procedure Rules which state,

(1) It is the duty of an expert to help the court on the matters within his expertise.
(2) This duty overrides any obligation to the person from whom he has received instructions or by whom he is paid.

The duty of the expert is to help the court. The report should be in writing, including a statement that the expert understands that primary duty to the court. These principles are as apposite to criminal proceedings as they are to civil proceedings. Auld recommended that these principles be given the same formal recognition in the Criminal Procedure Rules as they have been given in civil proceedings.

These ideals contrast unfavourably with the realities of criminal investigation or of civil proceedings. When a crime is being investigated, forensic examination may be carried out by private companies or public sector agencies[26] such as the Forensic Science Service which is an executive agency of the Home Office, the Ministry of Defence's Defence Science and Technology Laboratory, or the Laboratory of the Government Chemist which was privatised in 1996 but still retains a statutory role.[27] The Forensic Science Service is the main provider in criminal investigations and dealt with 130,000 cases, attended approximately 1,800 crime scenes, and appeared as expert witnesses in court on 2,500 occasions in 2004/05.[28] The FSS provide services for the police but also for defence solicitors, coroners and the Criminal Cases Review Commission.

The problems of laboratories responsible directly to a government department or to the police are immediately apparent and the Royal Commission recommended the establishment of a new forensic science advisory council which would oversee the effectiveness of the public sector laboratories, developing a code of practice covering professional ethics and duties of disclosure and keeping under review the extent to which the interests of the defence are being properly looked after by the various providers of forensic science services. There is the Council for the Registration of Forensic Practitioners and other professional bodies but the government has not followed the recommendation for an advisory council, despite support for such a reform from Auld.[29]

[26] These are discussed further in Royal Commission on Criminal Justice: *Report* (HMSO, 1993) Cm. 2263, Ch.9; it is based on P. Roberts and C. Willmore, *The Role of Forensic Science Evidence in Criminal Proceedings* (Royal Commission on Criminal Justice Research Study No. 11) (HMSO, 1993).
[27] www.lgc.co.uk.
[28] Reports and information are available at www.forensic.gov.uk.
[29] above, see Ch.11, paras 130–131.

Many of the problems for the expert witness flow from the adversarial nature of trial. For the scientist neither is the courtroom the place nor cross-examination the technique to settle scientific disputes. The Royal Commission recommended compulsory use of informal pre-trial hearings, a recommendation supported by Auld[30] and which is available for civil proceedings. But no formal changes have been introduced. The preparatory hearings introduced by Part III to the Criminal Procedure and Investigations Act 1996 are not empowered to settle such issues.

Where the expert evidence is not controversial, s.30 of the Criminal Justice Act 1988 does permit the report to be introduced without the expert testifying orally.

30.—(1) An expert report shall be admissible as evidence in criminal proceedings, whether or not the person making it attends to give oral evidence in those proceedings

(2) If it is proposed that the person making the report shall not give oral evidence, the report shall only be admissible with the leave of the court

The Royal Commission felt that this provision was underused and that greater use should be made of summaries of expert testimony.[31] Expert witnesses should also be protected to some extent from cross-examination.

Lord Justice Auld: A Review of the Criminal Courts of England and Wales Ch.11 (2001), para.9.73:

. . . many experts feel that they are not always given a proper opportunity to explain what the scientific evidence really means. This may be because counsel stop short of asking vital questions from lack of scientific knowledge or inadequate briefing or because they make inadequate use of the opportunity to re-examine after cross-examination or because they do not want the answer to be heard. We recommend that trial judges, where the evidence is disputed, ask expert witnesses before they leave the witness box whether there is anything else that they wish to say. To avoid inadmissible evidence being heard, the judge should put this question in the absence of the jury and, if the expert witness does indicate a wish to clarify the evidence, it should be heard before the jury returns. If the judge is satisfied that there can be no objection to the evidence, it should be put before the jury . . .

However a more controversial issue was the suggestion that independent court experts should be appointed. The Royal Commission was not in favour.

Royal Commission on Criminal Justice: Report (HMSO, 1993) Cm 2263 para.9.74:

Some of our witnesses would go further . . . In their view expert evidence should be given by a court expert, either instead of or in addition to the experts who appear for

---

[30] Royal Commission, *op.cit.*, para.9.68; Auld *op.cit.*, Ch.11, paras 145–146.
[31] *ibid.* para.9.71.

the prosecution and the defence. Alternatively, some would recommend that judges should sit in the relevant cases with an expert assessor or assessors. We have considered these suggestions but are not in favour of them. A court expert, even if subject to examination and cross-examination, would by implication carry more weight than an expert for the prosecution or the defence. There would, however, be no guarantee that he or she was any nearer to the truth of the matter than the expert witnesses for the parties. A court expert should not in our view be the only expert, since that would deprive the parties of the opportunity of leading their own expert evidence. But to have a court expert in addition to the experts for the parties would greatly extend the amount of time spent in examination and cross-examination of all three experts without making discovery of the truth any more certain. The worse solution of all, in our view, would be to have the expert sitting with the judge as an assessor, since his or her evidence would not be susceptible to examination or cross-examination by either side.[32]

A court-appointed, independent, expert witness is an option in civil proceedings at the application of either party.[33] Either party can cross-examine the witness on the report and adduce their own expert testimony on the same issue. In the USA, both civil and criminal courts have such a power and the trend is increasingly to provide for their use.

The court may on its own motion or on the motion of any party enter an order to show cause why expert witnesses should not be appointed, and may request the parties to submit nominations. The court may appoint any expert witnesses agreed upon by the parties, and may appoint expert witnesses of its own selection . . . . A witness so appointed shall advise the parties of the witness' findings, if any; the witness' deposition may be taken by any party; and the witness may be called to testify by the court or any party. The witness shall be subject to cross-examination by each party, including a party calling the witness.[34]

However in England, such an appointment is not a possibility in criminal proceedings. John Spencer[35] has argued against the current system and for such impartial experts. He argued that the prosecution witnesses can be 'goal directed' towards guilt and conviction; that the defence are free to shop for the 'friendly' expert and that adversarial cross-examination distorts testimony and discourages many experts from acting as witnesses.[36] He points to alternatives such as the French Code of Criminal Procedure where the report of the court expert is circulated to the parties and they then discuss it at a special hearing before the *juge d'instruction*.[37] In both France and Germany, where court experts are used, the defence are entitled to call their own experts as witnesses if they wish. Such arguments did not impress Auld.

---

[32] A fuller argument is put by M. Howard, "The Neutral Expert: a plausible threat to justice" [1991] Crim.L.R. 98.

[33] Civil Procedure Rules, r. 35.10.

[34] Federal Rules of Evidence, r. 706.

[35] J.R. Spencer, "The Neutral Expert: an implausible bogey" [1991] Crim.L.R. 106—his arguments are carried further in J.R. Spencer and R. Flin, *The Evidence of Children—the Law and the Psychology* (2nd edn., Blackstones, 1993), Ch.9.

[36] D.J. Gee, "The Expert Witness in the Criminal Trial" [1987] Crim.L.R. 307.

[37] Stefani, Levasseur and Bouloc, *Precis Dalloz de Procedure Penale* (14th edn., 1990), para.602.

Lord Justice Auld: A Review of the Criminal Courts of England and Wales. (2001), paras 11.140–11.141:

140 Interestingly, the Runciman Royal Commission, despite its drive to introduce a more inquisitorial flavour to the pre-trial stage, showed little interest in court appointed experts in criminal proceedings, either to the exclusion of parties' experts or in addition to them. The overwhelming majority of the many contributors to this Review were against it. Where the court has directed that expert evidence is appropriate, I too cannot see any scope for introduction to criminal trials of a system of court appointed experts to the exclusion, even in the court's discretion, of the right of each party to call its own expert evidence. Even without Article 6, it seems to me that there are fundamental difficulties in denying a criminal defendant that entitlement, particularly where the issue is highly controversial and central to the case and . . . whatever the weight of the case. He would have to instruct an expert to obtain advice as to whether to accept the court expert's view and, if not, he would probably need his assistance for the purpose of cross-examination of the court expert. Yet he would be unable, unless permitted by the judge, to call him to justify the points put in cross-examination or to give his contrary view on which they were based. To leave it to the judge's discretion, as under the Civil Procedure Rules, would, I believe, result in most judges allowing the defendant, or the prosecution for that matter, to call their own expert witness—effectively making the provision a dead letter. Otherwise, the court appointed or selected expert would effectively decide the issue and, depending on its importance, possibly the case.

141 Nor do I believe that it would be helpful for the court to appoint its own expert in addition to any expert witnesses called by the parties, since, in jury cases, the very nature of his appointment might suggest to a jury a greater authority than one or other or both of the parties' experts. Accordingly, where there is an issue on a matter of importance on which expert evidence is required, I can see no justification for empowering the court to appoint or select an expert, whether or not it excludes either party from calling its own expert evidence. Of course, where there is no issue or one in which the parties are content that the matter should be resolved by a single expert, they should be encouraged to deal with it in that way, agreeing his report or a summary of it as part of the evidence in the case.

Reform of the system of giving expert evidence in criminal proceedings, along the lines advocated by Spencer, remains a distant prospect.

21

MATTERS NOT REQUIRING FULL PROOF

I. INTRODUCTION

One of the key characteristics of adversarial trial is the "day in court" at which point all the evidence is put in front of the trier of fact who makes the necessary decisions based on that evidence alone. However,

Thayer, Preliminary Treatise on Evidence 279–280 (1898):

In conducting a process of judicial reasoning, as of other reasoning, not a step can be taken without assuming something which has not been proved; and the capacity to do this with competent judgment and efficiency, is imputed to judges and juries as part of their necessary mental outfit.

In everyday life we constantly make assumptions and use generalisations. We employ such "non–evidence" facts to assess other information that is given to us more directly. This of necessity occurs in court. Obviously there is no need for parties to adduce evidence to prove matters within people's common experience or to tell the trier of fact how to carry out everyday logical operations.

Relevant personal knowledge of the case is a different matter and such knowledge of the immediate facts should disqualify a trier of fact. Nor should they seek to acquire such knowledge away from the courtroom. However the trier may possess knowledge or expertise which is of value in assessing the evidence. In *Wetherall v Harrison*,[1] the accused driver was charged with failing to provide a urine or blood sample without reasonable excuse. He had been taken to a police station where he had apparently had a fit. At the court hearing, one of the magistrates was a doctor who, in the retiring room, gave his views on whether the fit was genuine or simulated. On appeal to the Divisional Court, Lord Widgery saw no problems.

Wetherall v Harrison [1976] 1 All E.R. 241 at 243h–244d, *per* Lord Widgery C.J.:

For my part, I do not think that the position of a justice of the peace is the same, in this regard, as the position of a trained judge. If you have a judge sitting alone, trying

---

[1] [1976] 1 All E.R. 241.

a civil case it is perfectly feasible and sensible that he should be instructed and trained to exclude certain factors from his consideration of the problem. Justices are not so trained. They are much more like jurymen in this respect. I think it would be wrong to start with the proposition that justices' use of their own local or personal knowledge is governed by exactly the same rule as is laid down in the case of trained judges. I do not believe that a serious restriction on a magistrate's use of his own knowledge or the knowledge of his colleagues can really be enforced. Laymen (by which I mean non-lawyers) sitting as justices considering a case which has just been heard before them lack the ability to put out of their minds certain features of the case. In particular, if the magistrate is a specialist, be he a doctor or an engineer or an accountant, or what you will, it is not possible for him to approach the decision in the case as though he had not got that training, and indeed I think it would be a very bad thing if he had to. In a sense, the bench of justices is like a jury, it is a cross-section of people, and one of the advantages which they have is that they bring a lot of varied experience into the courtroom and use it.

So I start with the proposition that it is not improper for a magistrate who has special knowledge of the circumstances forming the background to a particular case to draw on that special knowledge in interpretation of the evidence which he has heard . . .

The specialist knowledge was not to be used as evidence but as a means of considering, weighing up and assessing the evidence before the court. In doing so he could inform the other members of the bench of his views, provided he did not attempt to persuade them to reach a verdict based upon his specialised knowledge. In *Fricker*,[2] the defendant was charged with handling stolen car tyres found in his possession. No date of manufacture was given in evidence but a juror had specialist knowledge of the tyre trade. In the jury room he explained that the date code on the tyres meant that there was such little time between manufacture and the police finding the tyres that they could not have gone through the normal retail process—in other words, that they were likely to have been stolen. This was new evidence that neither party had been able to address and the conviction was quashed.

Similarly jurors must not bring extraneous material into the jury room—in *Karakaya*,[3] the accused was convicted of indecent assault and rape. After the verdict, a court officer found material downloaded from the Internet in the jury room on the difficulties facing complainants in rape trials and suggesting that greater credit should be given to victims.

Karakaya [2005] 2 Cr.App.R. 5, *per* Judge L.J.:

[24] It is easy, but superficial, to dismiss these rules as purely technical or procedural. In truth, they reflect something much more fundamental. If material is obtained or used by the jury privately, whether before or after retirement, two linked principles, bedrocks of the administration of criminal justice, and indeed the rule of law, are contravened. The first is open justice, that the defendant in particular, but the public too, is entitled to know of the evidential material considered by the decision

---

[2] *The Times* July 13, 1999 (CA).
[3] [2005] 2 Cr.App.R. 5.

making body; so indeed should everyone with a responsibility for the outcome of the trial, including counsel and the judge, and in an appropriate case, the Court of Appeal Criminal Division. This leads to the second principle, the entitlement of both the prosecution and the defence to a fair opportunity to address all the material considered by the jury when reaching its verdict. Such an opportunity is essential to our concept of a fair trial. These principles are too basic to require elaboration. Occasionally, however, we need to remind ourselves of them.

Had the juror merely read widely and argued that complainants in such cases should be accorded greater credibility, no complaint could have been made. Was the juror in *Karakaya* going any further than the doctor–magistrate in *Weatherall*?

Beyond common experience and personal knowledge, there are other, more technical, circumstances where there is no need to adduce evidence of a fact or where full presentation of the evidence necessary to prove a fact is dispensed with. The four situations discussed here are:

    i) judicial notice is taken of a fact;
   ii) an estoppel operates to prevent a party denying a fact;
  iii) a previous judicial finding determines the fact; and
  iv) a presumption operates.

II. Judicial Notice

There is no need to adduce evidence where the fact is generally known or is capable of accurate determination so that it is beyond dispute.

Holland v Jones (1917) 23 C.L.E. 149 at 153, *per* Isaacs J.:

. . . whenever a fact is so generally known that every ordinary person may be reasonably presumed to be aware of it, the court 'notices' it, either simpliciter or if it is at once satisfied of the fact without more, or after such information and investigation as it considers reliable and necessary in order to eliminate any reasonable doubt.[4]

Under the US Federal Rules of Evidence,

A judicially noticed fact must be one not subject to reasonable dispute in that it is either (1) generally known within the territorial jurisdiction of the trial court or (2) capable of accurate and ready determination by resort to sources whose accuracy cannot reasonably be questioned.[5]

When judicial notice is taken of a fact, that fact is treated by the court or the jury as having been established, albeit no evidence has been produced and no

---

[4] *Holland v Jones* (1917) 23 C.L.R. 149 at 153 *per* Isaacs J.
[5] Federal Rules of Evidence, r.201(b).

evidence can be given in disproof. In the USA,[6] a judicially noticed fact is conclusive in a civil case but in a criminal trial the jury is not required to accept it as conclusive. Judicial notice can be taken in three ways.

1. Without any inquiry.   These are facts which are so commonly known that there existence is not in dispute. For example, a court will take note of the fact that nine months is the normal term for a pregnancy,[7] that cats are kept for domestic purposes[8] and that universities are established for the advancement of learning.[9] The fact can be generally known but to a small number of people or in a local area—in *Paul v D.P.P.*,[10] the justices were entitled to use their local knowledge that an area was a frequent haunt of prostitutes to infer that the appellant's conduct in "kerb-crawling" was likely to cause a nuisance to others. Similarly in *Mullen v London Borough of Hackney*,[11] the local authority appealed from a fine imposed for failure to carry out an order to repair a tenant's house. In assessing the fine, the judge took into account his knowledge of the council's previous breaches of such orders.

Mullen v London Borough of Hackney [1997] 2 All E.R. 906 at 909a–d, *per* Otton L.J.:

. . . [judges] have a wide discretion and may notice much which they cannot be required to notice. The matters noticeable may include facts which are in issue or relevant to the issue; and the notice is in some cases conclusive and in others merely prima facie and rebuttable . . . Moreover, a judge may rely on his own local knowledge where he does so "properly and within reasonable limits". This judicial function appears to be acceptable where "the type of knowledge is of a quite general character and is not liable to be varied by specific individual characteristics of the individual case". This test allows a judge to use what might be called "special (or local) general knowledge" . . . County courts fall within the scope of the rule relating to courts which have been held to be local courts, and thus courts whose members are not merely permitted to use their local knowledge, but who are regarded as fulfilling a constitutional function if they do so . . . Applying these principles to the present case I am satisfied the judge was entitled to take judicial notice of his "special (or local) knowledge" of how LBH had conducted itself in relation to undertakings given to the court in similar cases.[12]

Judges can refuse to take notice of what might appear to be "notorious" facts. In a Scottish case, *McTear v Imperial Tobacco*,[13] the claimant sought damages from the defendant cigarette manufacturer in respect of the death of

[6] Federal Rules of Evidence, r. 201(g).
[7] *Preston-Jones v Preston-Jones* [1951] A.C. 391.
[8] *Nye v Niblett* [1918] 1 K.B. 23.
[9] *Re Oxford Poor Rate Case* (1857) 8 E.&B. 184.
[10] [1989] Crim.L.R. 660.
[11] [1997] 2 All E.R. 906.
[12] *ibid.* 909a-d *per* Otton L.J.
[13] *The Times* June 14, 2005.

her husband from lung cancer. Whether smoking cigarettes could cause lung cancer was not within judicial knowledge. Therefore, the burden was on the claimant to establish on the balance of probabilities that lung cancer in the general population and in the deceased would not have occurred "but for" the smoking of cigarettes.

Some assumptions made by a court can be problematic. An illustration is *Hawkins v United States*[14] in which the Supreme Court refused to discard the common law rule that one spouse could not testify against the other, saying, "Adverse testimony given in criminal proceedings would, we think, be likely to destroy almost any marriage." This is scarcely indisputable and in such cases should judges take such beliefs into account without hearing evidence?[15]

2. With inquiry. A court can take account of facts after investigation even though such facts are not generally known as long as they can readily be ascertained from authoritative sources. For example, first a court will take judicial notice of certain political facts such as the status of a foreign government[16] or the existence of a state of war.[17] Courts normally act on the certificate of the relevant minister of state. Secondly, a court may refer to authoritative works to ascertain historical or other readily identifiable facts— in *Read v The Bishop of Lincoln*[18] the court investigated whether the practice of mixing communion wine with water was contrary to church law. Thirdly, judicial notice will be taken of professional practices[19] and of general customs which have been proved with some frequency in other cases.[20] This raises the question whether taking judicial notice of a fact constitutes a precedent for inferior courts? An alternative view would be that judicial notice was a substitute for proof and could no more be a precedent than any other finding of fact by a court.

3. By statute. There are many statutes permitting or compelling judicial notice to be taken of certain facts. Evidence is not required to prove the contents of a statute. The Interpretation Act 1978 provides that.

3.—Every Act is a public Act to be judicially noticed as such unless the contrary is expressly provided by the Act.[21]

But private Acts (passed before 1851) and foreign law cannot be the subject of judicial notice and must be proved by evidence.

---

[14] 358 U.S. 74, 79 S.Ct. 136, 3 L.Ed.2d 125 (1958).
[15] The Supreme Court permits parties to introduce material on the social and economic background to the case (a "Brandeis brief")—*Miller v Oregon*, 208 U.S. 412 (1908).
[16] *Carl Zeiss Stiftung v Rayner & Keeler Ltd (No. 2)* [1967] 1 A.C. 853; *Duff Development Co v Government of Kelantan* [1924] A.C. 797.
[17] *Bottrill Ex p. Kuechenmeister* [1946] 2 All E.R. 434.
[18] [1892] A.C. 644.
[19] *Davey v Harrow Corpn.* [1958] 1 Q.B. 60.
[20] *Brandao v Barnett* (1846) 12 Cl. & F. 787, where the House of Lords took notice of the custom of bankers' lien which had been judicially ascertained in earlier cases.
[21] There is a similar provision for the judicial notice of European law under European Communities Act 1972, s.3(2).

The process of judicial notice can appear close to a usurpation of the function of the trier of fact. In *McQuaker v Goddard*,[22] the trial judge consulted books and experts on whether camels were wild by nature and held that they were domestic animals. There was some dispute over that conclusion but the Court of Appeal held that judicial notice could be taken of the matter and that the issue would then be withdrawn from the jury. In his consultations, the judge was not taking evidence in the ordinary sense but conducting an inquiry prior to taking judicial notice of the fact. Best practice might be found in *Thomas v Thomas*,[23] where it was suggested that a judge should give notice of intent to take judicial notice of certain facts, subject to anything the parties might urge to the contrary. Despite the convenience of the doctrine of judicial notice, it needs to be subject to the requirements of procedural fairness.

III. Estoppel

... an excellent and curious kinde of learning .... [I]t is called an estoppel ... because a man's owne act or acceptance stoppeth or closeth up his mouth to alleadge or plead the truth (Lord Coke C.J.)

People act in certain ways or say particular things so that others believe their assertions and perhaps act in reliance on them. The principle of estoppel, in certain circumstances, prevents such people, when they are parties to litigation, from contradicting those assertions. The party relying on the estoppel need only adduce limited proof of the facts whereas the other party is prohibited from leading evidence in disproof. Estoppel arises:

  i) with respect to court judgments when the facts are treated as a matter of *record*;
  ii) when the facts are stated in a *deed*;
  iii) when a clear representation of fact arises as a result of the party's *conduct*.

Whether estoppel is a rule of substantive law or a rule of evidence is debateable. In *Mills v Cooper*[24] Diplock L.J. said,

Mills v Cooper [1967] 2 All E.R. 100 at 104i–105a, *per* Diplock L.J.:

Whatever may be said of other rules of law to which the label of 'estoppel' is attached, 'issue estoppel' is not a rule of evidence. True, subject to the qualifications I have stated, it has the effect of preventing the party 'estopped' from calling evidence to show that the assertion which is the subject of the 'issue estoppel' is incorrect, but

[22] [1940] 1 K.B. 687.
[23] [1961] 1 All E.R. 19.
[24] [1967] 2 All E.R. 100.

that is because the existence of the 'issue estoppel' results in there being no issue in the subsequent civil proceedings to which such evidence would be relevant. Issue estoppel is a particular application of the general rule of public policy that there should be finality in litigation.[25]

It matters little whether we term estoppel a rule of "evidence" or of "law" But estoppel is an example of a technique of proof, analogous to presumptions, by which if a party can prove a secondary fact A, a primary fact B is taken to exist. Thus if you can prove that your opponent executed a deed (Fact A) asserting a state of affairs, the court will presume that that state of affairs (Fact B) in fact exists and will not permit evidence to be given in rebuttal.

This is an evidentiary process, a process which tells us how facts are to be established. Given those facts, substantive rules of law tell us what the rights and duties of parties are. Such substantive rules specify what facts in issue need to be proved. But estoppel does not mean that a fact in issue is no longer an issue; it means that such an issue is taken to be proved irrebuttably by adducing evidence of a court judgment, of a deed or of relevant conduct.

Low v Bouverie [1891] 3 Ch. 82 at 105, *per* Bowen L.J.:

Estoppel is only a rule of evidence; you cannot found an action upon estoppel. Estoppel is only important as being one step in the progress towards relief on the hypothesis that the defendant is estopped from denying the truth of something he has said.

This is supported by Brandon L.J. who suggested, L

Amalgamated Investment and Property Co. Ltd v Texas Commerce International Bank Ltd [1981] 3 All E.R. 577 at 591h, *per* Brandon L.J.:

..the true proposition of law, that, while a party cannot in terms found a cause of action on an estoppel, he may, as a result of being able to rely on an estoppel, succeed on a cause of action on which, without being able to rely on that estoppel, he would necessarily have failed.

It is often said that estoppels cannot override the general law of the land. In *R. Leslie Ltd v Shiell*,[26] a child's misrepresentation as to his age did not estop him from pleading contractual incapacity. In *Re Exchange Securities and Commodities Ltd*,[27] a liquidator was under a statutory duty to distribute the

---

[25] *ibid.* at 104i–105a.
[26] [1914] 3 K.B. 607.
[27] [1987] 2 All E.R. 272.

assets of a company amongst its creditors. The court held that estoppel was only a rule of evidence and was not conclusive in liquidations or bankruptcies when considering the distribution of the statutory estate. Such decisions recall Lord Diplock's comment in *Mills v Cooper* when he said that issue estoppel was only an application of the public policy of finality to litigation. It may be that, although estoppel operates against individual litigants, its boundaries are delimited generally by consideration of the public interest—in *O'Connell v Plymouth City Council*,[28] the claimant lost a harvest of oysters. He brought and lost a claim for financial loss claiming that the loss was the result of the council's negligent dealing with his public health application. Both parties acted on the basis that orders made by the council were valid. They were not. A second claim was seemingly barred as the matter had already been litigated but Clarke L.J. held that it was a question of balancing, on the one hand, real injustice to a litigant by denying him an opportunity for further proceedings and, on the other, the public interest that there should be an end to litigation. In this case, he stated that "justice requires the non-application of the rule."

A. *Estoppel by Record*

Such estoppels exist where there is a judgment of a court.[29] This is conclusive in that, when there is subsequent litigation, it stops the parties from denying the facts on which the judgment was based. However the effect of such an estoppel can be avoided where the initial judgment was obtained by fraud or collusion. In addition, it is only the parties (and their privies[30]) to the judgment who are estopped. This was shown in *The Duchess of Kingston's Case*,[31] where the Duchess was indicted for bigamy and tried in the House of Lords. Her defence was that the Consistory Court of the Bishop of London had already considered the question of her alleged first marriage to the Earl of Bristol. That court had admonished the Earl for wickedly and maliciously boasting and publicly asserting that there was such a marriage. In the House of Lords, de Grey C.J. held that, although a person who was a party to legal proceedings in which a judgment was given is estopped from denying the facts on which the judgment was based, the judgment was not binding on any third party. The Crown was not a party to the proceedings in the Consistory Court and was not prevented from contradicting the facts on which the judgment was based. Furthermore, if it could be shown that the original judgment was based on fraud, this vitiated all judicial acts.[32]

The principles on which the estoppel is based are:

a) that there is a public interest, namely that there should be a finality to litigation; and

b) that nobody should be sued twice on the same grounds.

There are two facets of a judgment that must be distinguished:

a) *Judgments are conclusive against all persons as to the legal state of affairs.* If, for example, there has been a divorce decree, a finding of bankruptcy or a conviction, the whole world is estopped from adducing evidence to deny that legal result.

b) *Judgments can be conclusive against the parties of the facts on which they are based.* This is only in certain circumstances, namely where the same parties or their privies are concerned. In subsequent proceedings, those parties are estopped from adducing evidence to contradict the grounds on which the previous judgement was based.

Judgments are conclusive as to the legal status but not necessarily as to the factual state of affairs, at least in respect of those who were not parties to the action. If a defendant has been acquitted of a crime and brings an action for malicious prosecution against the police, the police would not be estopped from adducing evidence that the claimant had in fact committed the offence. The record is conclusive as to the acquittal, if that is in issue, but not as to whether the claimant committed the offence. A similar case would be where a third party sued for and won damages from an employer for the injuries caused by the negligence of the defendant's employee. If the employer were to sue the employee for recovery of those damages, the employee could not contest the amount of damages which had been awarded but could contest their own negligence.[33]

This distinction requires us to split the discussion of estoppel by record into two: cause of action estoppel and issue estoppel.

1. Cause of action estoppel

Parties are expected to bring forward their whole case at the original hearing. If they bring an action and there is a judgment, they are not permitted to open the same matter against the same party in subsequent litigation.[34]

Henderson v Henderson (1843) 3 Hare 100 at 114, *per* Wigram V.C.:

. . . where a given matter becomes the subject of litigation in, and of adjudication by, a court of competent jurisdiction, the court requires the parties to that litigation to

---

[33] *Green v New River Co.* (1792) 4 Term. Rep. 589.

[34] *Conquer v Boot* [1928] 2 K.B. 336; however cause of action estoppel does not apply in cases of default judgments or similar situations— *New Brunswick Rail Co. v British and French Trust Corporation Ltd* [1938] 4 All E.R. 747.

bring forward their whole case, and will not (except under special circumstances) permit the same parties to open the same subject of litigation in respect of matter which might have been brought forward as part of the subject in contest, but which was not brought forward, only because they have, from negligence, inadvertence, or even accident, omitted part of their case. The plea of res judicata applies, except in special cases, not only to points upon which the court was actually required by the parties to form an opinion and pronounce a judgment, but to every point which properly belonged to the subject of litigation, and which the parties, exercising reasonable diligence, might have brought forward at the time.

These dicta in *Henderson* were approved in the House of Lords in *Arnold v National Westminster Bank plc*[35] which suggested that the bar is absolute in relation to cause of action estoppel unless fraud or collusion is alleged. The plea goes beyond the issues that were determined by the court (*res judicata* in a narrow sense) but also those issues which could have been raised.[36] An issue may be re-opened where further relevant material emerges which could not have been discovered by the parties exercising due diligence at the time of the original litigation. *Henderson* was also applied in *Talbot v Berkshire County Council*,[37] a personal injury case where the passenger in a car sued the driver for negligent driving and sued the local authority for nuisance on the highway. The driver also had a potential claim against the authority arising from the same nuisance but failed to pursue it at that time. The passenger succeeded in both claims. When the driver later issued a writ against the highway authority claiming a contribution, the Court of Appeal held that he was barred by cause of action estoppel since it was a claim which the driver could have brought at the same time as the earlier litigation.

In *Port of Melbourne Authority v Anshun Pty Ltd (No. 2)*,[38] there was a similar situation to *Talbot*. In an original action for negligence, the first defendant, the port authority, had to pay 90 per cent of the damages awarded with the co-defendants paying only 10 per cent. The authority had a defence, an indemnity to which they were entitled, but failed to claim it at the time of the original hearing. In a later action they sought to recover their share of the damages from their co-defendants but were held to be estopped.

Port of Melbourne Authority v Anshun Pty Ltd (No.2) (1981) 147 C.L.R. 589 at 602–604:

In this situation we would prefer to say that there will be no estoppel unless it appears that the matter relied upon as a defence in the second action was so relevant to the subject matter of the first action that it would have been unreasonable not to rely on it. Generally speaking, it would be unreasonable not to plead a defence if, having regard to the nature of the plaintiff's claim, and its subject matter, it would be expected that the defendant would raise the defence and thereby enable the relevant issues to be

---

[35] [1991] 3 All E.R. 41.
[36] *Greenhalgh v Mallard* (1947) 2 All E.R. 255.
[37] [1993] 4 All E.R. 9.
[38] (1981) 147 C.L.R. 589.

determined in the one proceeding. In this respect, we need to recall that there are a variety of circumstances, some referred to in the earlier cases, why a party may justifiably refrain from litigating an issue in one proceeding yet wish to litigate the issue in other proceedings, for example, expense, importance of the particular issue, motives extraneous to the actual litigation, to mention but a few . . .

The likelihood that the omission to plead a defence will contribute to the existence of conflicting judgments is obviously an important factor to be taken into account in deciding whether the omission to plead can found an estoppel against the assertion of the same matter as a foundation for a cause of action in a second proceeding. By 'conflicting' judgments we include judgments which are contradictory, though they may not be pronounced on the same cause of action. It is enough that they appear to declare rights which are inconsistent in respect of the same transaction.

It is for this reason that we regard the judgment that the Authority seeks to obtain as one which would conflict with the existing judgment, though the new judgment would be based on a different cause of action, a contractual indemnity.

Taking into consideration the relevant factors we conclude that the Full Court was right in holding that there was an estoppel . . .

Modern courts view the *Henderson* rule as a species of the modern doctrine of abuse of process and as capable of application where the parties in which the issue is raised are different from those in earlier proceedings. As a general rule, all persons who are to be sued should be sued at the same time and in the same proceedings where such a course is reasonably practicable, and whenever it is so and is not taken then, in an appropriate case the rule may be invoked so as to render the second action an abuse.[39] The House of Lords reviewed the authorities in *Johnson v Gore Wood & Co*,[40]

Johnson v Gore Wood & Co. [2001] 1 All E.R. 481 at 499a–e, *per* Lord Bingham:

. . . abuse of process, as now understood, although separate and distinct from cause of action estoppel and issue estoppel, has much in common with them. The underlying public interest is the same: that there should be finality in litigation and that a party should not be twice vexed in the same matter. This public interest is reinforced by the current emphasis on efficiency and economy in the conduct of litigation, in the interests of the parties and the public as a whole. The bringing of a claim or the raising of a defence in later proceedings may, without more, amount to abuse if the court is satisfied (the onus being on the party alleging abuse) that the claim or defence should have been raised in the earlier proceedings if it was to be raised at all. I would not accept that it is necessary, before abuse may be found, to identify any additional element such as a collateral attack on a previous decision or some dishonesty, but where those elements are present the later proceedings will be much more obviously abusive, and there will rarely be a finding of abuse unless the later proceeding involves what the court regards as unjust harassment of a party. It is, however, wrong to hold that because a matter could have been raised in early proceedings it should have been, so as to render the raising of it in later proceedings necessarily abusive.

---

[39] *Bradford and Bingley Building Society v Seddon* (1999) 4 All E.R. 217 *per* Auld L.J.
[40] [2001] 1 All E.R. 481.

That is to adopt too dogmatic an approach to what should in my opinion be a broad, merits-based judgment which takes account of the public and private interests involved and also takes account of all the facts of the case, focusing attention on the crucial question whether, in all the circumstances, a party is misusing or abusing the process of the court by seeking to raise before it the issue which could have been raised before . . . Properly applied, and whatever the legitimacy of its descent, the rule has in my view a valuable part to play in protecting the interests of justice.

This is a flexible approach, laying down a general and justifiable principle. Estoppel and abuse of process are doctrines which deny litigants right of access to the court. Such access is a major aspect of the right to a fair trial. The very flexibility of the House of Lords should be sufficient to avoid problems with Article 6 requirements under the European Convention on Human Rights.

2. Cause of action estoppel in criminal cases

There are the special pleas of *autrefois acquit* and *autrefois convict* which act in a similar fashion to cause of action estoppel. They are based on the double jeopardy rule and enable defendants in subsequent criminal proceedings to argue that they have been acquitted or convicted of the same offence at an earlier proceeding. The same offence means one for which the defendant could have lawfully been convicted at the original hearing.[41] Thus if the defendant is convicted of causing grievous bodily harm contrary to section 18 of the Offences Against the Person Act 186, there would be a bar to a subsequent charge of malicious wounding under s.20 of that Act but no bar to a homicide prosecution if the victim died subsequent to the GBH conviction. However, under recent legislation, there are now mechanisms by which the prosecution can challenge acquittals:

(i) *Tainted acquittals.*

There is a right of appeal where a person has been convicted of intimidating or interfering with a juror or witness in another trial and that interference has led to an acquittal.[42] This followed a recommendation by the Runciman Commission that there should be the possibility of an appeal and a retrial where the jury can be shown to have been bribed or intimidated. The Commission did not recommend such a course in cases of a "perverse" acquittal or in situations where the accused is convicted because of a mistake by a prosecution witness.[43] This has never been used.

(ii) *Fresh Evidence in Serious Cases.*

The Runciman Commission rejected the idea of a general right of appeal for the prosecution but the MacPherson Report into the death of Steven Law-

---

[41] Criminal Law Act 1967, s.6(3).
[42] Criminal Procedure and Investigations Act 1996, ss.54–57.
[43] Royal Commission on Criminal Justice: Report (HMSO, 1993) Cm. 2263, para.10.72ff.

rence[44] suggested that "consideration should be given to the Court of Appeal being given power to permit prosecution after acquittal where fresh and viable evidence is presented."[45] The Law Commission proposed[46] giving the Court of Appeal power to set aside an acquittal for murder where there is apparently reliable and compelling new evidence of guilt. The Auld Report would have gone further and allow a prosecution right of appeal where the jury verdict was seen as "perverse".[47]

As a consequence, the double jeopardy rule was significantly limited by Part 10 of the Criminal Justice Act 2003 which allows the Court of Appeal to quash acquittals where there is fresh and compelling evidence that the defendant was guilty. The offences include murder, sexual offences, drugs, certain criminal damage offences and war crimes and terrorism.[48] There must be consent by the D.P.P. for an application to the Court of Appeal. The court can quash the acquittal where there is new and compelling evidence which is reliable, substantial and highly probative and if the order is in the interests of justice. The first application was in the case of William Dunlop, acquitted of murdering Julie Hogg.[49]

It is argued that the European Convention protects the rights of defendants who have been "finally" acquitted in accordance with the law. But Protocol 7, Article 4 of the European Convention on Human Rights does not preclude the re-opening of cases in exceptional circumstances.

Right not to be tried or punished twice
1 No one shall be liable to be tried or punished again in criminal proceedings under the jurisdiction of the same State for an offence for which he has already been finally acquitted or convicted in accordance with the law and penal procedure of that State.
2 The provisions of the preceding paragraph shall not prevent the reopening of the case in accordance with the law and penal procedure of the State concerned, if there is evidence of new or newly discovered facts, or if there has been a fundamental defect in the previous proceedings, which could affect the outcome of the case.

The 2003 provisions on their face conform to Convention requirements— the powers are properly established by law and, given the offences to which they apply, are proportional and in the public interest.[50]

3. Issue estoppel

Within an action, once an issue has been raised and distinctly determined between parties, neither party can be allowed to fight that issue all over again. In *Mills v Cooper*,[51] the defendant was charged with camping on the highway, being a *Gypsy* and without lawful excuse. In February 1966 he was

---

[44] *The Stephen Lawrence Inquiry: Report of an Inquiry by Sir William MacPherson* (1999) Cm. 4262.
[45] *ibid.* recommendation 38.
[46] Law Commission *Double Jeopardy and Prosecution Appeals* Report No.267, (2001).
[47] Lord Auld, *Review of the Criminal Courts* (2001), Ch.12 paras 66–67.
[48] Criminal Justice Act 2003, Sd. 5.
[49] "First double jeopardy trial given go-ahead" *Guardian*, November 11, 2005.
[50] R. Pattenden, "Prosecution Appeals" [2000] Cr. L.R. 971.
[51] [1967] 2 All E.R. 100.

acquitted of this charge as the justices were not satisfied that he was a *Gypsy*. Some ten weeks later a similar charge was brought against him. The defendant argued that, since the issue whether he was a *Gypsy* had been decided in his favour in February, there was an issue estoppel debarring the justices from reopening that question.

Mills v Cooper [1967] 2 All E.R. 100 at 104g–105c, *per* Diplock J.:

The doctrine of issue estoppel in civil proceedings is of fairly recent and sporadic development, though none the worse for that. Although *Hoystead v Taxation Commissioner*[52] did not purport to break new ground, it can be regarded as the starting point of the modern common law doctrine, the application of which to different kinds of civil actions is currently being worked out in the courts. That doctrine, so far as it affects civil proceedings, may be stated thus: a party to civil proceedings is not entitled to make, as against the other party, an assertion, whether of fact or of the legal consequences of facts, the correctness of which is an essential element in his cause of action or defence, if the same assertion was an essential element in his previous cause of action or defence in previous civil proceedings between the same parties or their predecessors in title, and was found by a court of competent jurisdiction in such previous civil proceedings to be incorrect, unless further material which is relevant to the correctness or incorrectness of the assertion and could not by reasonable diligence have been adduced by that party in the previous proceedings has since become available to him.

. . . . That general rule applies also to criminal proceedings, but in a form modified by the distinctive character of criminal as compared with civil litigation. Here it takes the form of the rule against double jeopardy, of which the simplest application is to be found in the pleas of autrefois convict and autrefois acquit; but the rule against double jeopardy also applies in circumstances in which those ancient pleas are not strictly available; and it is in connection with the wider application that the High Court of Australia in particular in the cases cited[53] has used the same expression as is used in civil proceedings: 'issue estoppel'. I think with great respect that the use of that expression in criminal and civil proceedings alike may lead to confusion, for there are obvious differences—lack of mutuality is but one—between the application of the rule against double jeopardy in criminal cases, and the rule that there should be finality in civil litigation.

Issue estoppel is less strict than cause of action estoppel:

a) it is only those issues that are in fact raised in the previous proceedings that are subject to an estoppel: the *Henderson* principles relating to cause of action estoppel do not apply to issue estoppel which therefore does not extend to those issues which a party exercising due diligence could have raised.

b) issue estoppel does not apply where significant fresh evidence is available or where the justice of the case requires re-litigation. The test is that the new evidence must be such as "entirely changes the

---

[52] [1926] A.C. 155.
[53] *Wilkes* (1948) 77 C.L.R. 511; *Mraz (No.2)* (1956) 96 C.L.R. 62.

aspect of the case . . . and was not and could not by reasonable diligence have been ascertained before".[54]

In *Arnold v National Westminster Bank plc*,[55] a lease contained a clause for rent review every five years. That rent was to be decided on the basis of a fair market rent for a hypothetical lease for the residue of the term. In 1983, there was a dispute as to whether that hypothetical lease should or should not contain a clause for rent review. This was decided by arbitration and appeal that it should not. However by 1988 subsequent decisions made it clear that this interpretation was wrong. Were the lessees estopped from re-litigating the issue? The landlords appealed to the House of Lords.

Arnold v National Westminster Bank plc [1991] 3 All E.R. 41 at 50b–52d, *per* Lord Keith:

It was argued that there was no logical distinction between cause of action estoppel and issue estoppel and that, if the rule was absolute in the one case as regards points actually decided, so it should be in the other case. But there is room for the view that the underlying principles upon which estoppel is based, public policy and justice, have greater force in cause of action estoppel, the subject matter of the two proceedings being identical, than they do in issue estoppel, where the subject matter is different. Once it is accepted that different considerations apply to issue estoppel, it is hard to perceive any logical distinction between a point which was previously raised and decided and one which might have been but was not. Given that the further material which would have put an entirely different complexion on the point was at the earlier stage unknown to the party and could not by reasonable diligence have been discovered by him, it is hard to see why there should be a different result according to whether he decided not to take the point, thinking it hopeless, or argue it faintly without any real hope of success. In my opinion your Lordships should affirm it to be the law that there may be an exception to issue estoppel in the special circumstance that there has become available to a party further material relevant to the correct determination of a point involved in the earlier proceedings, whether or not that point was specifically raised and decided, being material which could not by reasonable diligence have been adduced in those proceedings . . . .

It is next for consideration whether the further relevant material which a party may be permitted to bring forward in the later proceedings is confined to matters of fact, or whether what may not entirely inappropriately described as a change in the law may result in or be an element in special circumstances enabling an issue to be reopened . . .

. . . I find myself in respectful agreement with the passage in the judgment of [the trial judge] where he said[56]

In my judgment a change in the law subsequent to the first decision is capable of bringing the case within the exception to issue estoppel. If, as I think, the yardstick of whether issue estoppel should be held to apply is the justice to the parties,

---

[54] *Phosphate Sewage Co. v Molleson* (1879) 4 App. Cas. 801 at 814 *per* Earl Cairns L.C. This was approved by Lord Diplock in *Hunter v Chief Constable of West Midlands* [1981] 3 All E.R. 727 at 736c.

[55] [1991] 3 All E.R. 41.

[56] [1988] 3 All E.R. 977 at 983.

injustice can flow as much from a subsequent change in the law as from the subsequent discovery of new facts. In both case the injustice lies in a successful party to the first action being held to have rights which in fact he does not possess. I can, therefore, see no reason for holding that a subsequent change in the law can never be sufficient to bring the case within the exception . . .

There are five basic conditions necessary for issue estoppel to be invoked. These are:

1. that a court of competent jurisdiction must have made a final judgement on the merits of the case;
2. that the parties to the initial proceedings must be the same as the parties to the subsequent proceedings;
3. that the parties to the initial proceedings must be acting in the same capacity;
4. that the same issues must be involved; and
5. that the estoppel must be specifically pleaded.

1. *A court of competent jurisdiction must have made a final judgement on the merits of the case.*   The tribunal can be a foreign court[57] under s.34 of the Civil Jurisdiction and Judgments Act 1982. The question of whether a tribunal is one of competent jurisdiction can be troublesome. In *The Speedlink Vanguard and the European Gateway*,[58] an investigation into a collision at sea had been held under the Merchant Shipping Act 1894. Were the owners of the two ships involved bound by the findings of the court of formal investigation which operated with all the powers of a magistrates' court? The Court of Appeal held that it was necessary to look at the function of the court which in this case was investigatory with its primary aim the safety of life and property at sea and whether in the proceedings there was a defined issue, a lis, between the contending ship owners. As there had been no adjudication of the legal rights of the parties, issue estoppel did not arise. But there is no reason why the decision of an inferior tribunal with a limited jurisdiction and a limited function should not be capable of creating an issue estoppel. In *Crown Estate Commissioners v Dorset County Council*,[59] the court considered the role of the commons commissioner who had a statutory jurisdiction which, inter alia, included the power to decide whether or not road verges should be registered as common land. As part of this function, there was a ruling whether the verges formed part of the highway or not. The Crown Estate was estopped in subsequent litigation from challenging this finding.

A caution administered by the police is not equivalent to a decision by a competent court—in *Abraham v Metropolitan Police Commissioner*,[60] the claimant had been arrested for a breach of the peace. She accepted a police caution

---

[57] *Carl Zeiss Stiftung v Rayner & Keeler Ltd* (No. 2) [1967] 1 A.C. 853; *The Indian Endurance* [1993] 1 All E.R. 998.
[58] [1986] 3 All E.R. 554.
[59] [1990] 1 All E.R. 19.
[60] [2001] 1 W.L.R. 1257.

which requires a defendant to admit the offence. She subsequently sued for damages for unlawful arrest. The defence argued that the caution meant that she was estopped from claiming that the arrest was unlawful. Mantell L.J. reviewed the nature of the caution.

Abraham v Metropolitan Police Commissioner [2001] 1 W.L.R. 1257, *per* Mantell J.:

[14] All the above are characteristics which a formal caution shares with a criminal conviction. Still it is not the same, and the fundamental distinction lies in the fact that it is not brought about by any decision of a court of justice. Consequently, any attack upon the correctness of the admission of guilt is not an attack upon "the correctness of a subsisting judgment of a court of trial" so as to fall foul of the principle of public policy . . . But it may be and indeed is protested that there is in reality no difference between an admission of guilt precedent to the administration of a formal caution and a plea of guilty before a court of trial. Both the admission in the one case and the plea in the other may be false. Why, therefore, should the same policy considerations not apply to the formal caution which is, after all, a valuable feature of our criminal justice system; to which I would answer, firstly, that, even so, the public policy consideration does not arise, in that an attack on the admission to a police officer does not involve an attack on a court of co-ordinate jurisdiction; secondly, that the plea of guilty entered in a criminal court is open to public view and scrutiny and is subject to the supervision of a magistrate or a judge; thirdly, I would say that a conviction based upon a plea of guilty is nonetheless reviewable upon appeal if entered on a false basis or incorrect advice, whereas the only challenge to a formal caution lies by way of judicial review, which Mr Powell concedes would be an inadequate remedy in the present case.

The judgment must be final.

DSV Silo und Verwaltungsgesellschaft mbH v Owners of the Sennar [1985] 2 All E.R. 104 at 106g–h, *per* Lord Diplock:

What it means in the context of judgments delivered by courts of justice is that the court has held that it has jurisdiction to adjudicate on an issue raised in the cause of action to which the particular set of facts give rise, and that its judgment on that cause of action is one that cannot be varied, reopened or set aside by the court that delivered it or any other court of co-ordinate jurisdiction although it may be subject to appeal to a court of higher jurisdiction.

In addition the judgment must be on the merits of the action. No estoppel can arise if the action has been withdrawn, dismissed or terminated for some reason. The rules will be strictly interpreted if there has been a default judgment.[61] However a decision at *voir dire* on the admissibility of evidence

---

[61] *New Brunswick Rail Co. v British and French Trust Corporation Ltd* [1938] 4 All E.R. 747.

will estop a party in any subsequent civil case. In *Hunter v Chief Constable of West Midlands*,[62] Lord Denning in the Court of Appeal held that the Birmingham Six were estopped from raising the issue of the admissibility of their confession, a matter which had been determined against them at their original trial.

Hunter v Chief Constable of West Midlands [1980] 2 all E.R. 227 at 238j, *per* Lord Denning:

... when an issue has been decided by a competent court against a party in an earlier proceeding, it should only be regarded as final if he has had a full and fair opportunity of defending himself therein and the circumstances are such that it would not be fair or just to allow him to re-open it in subsequent proceedings.

2. *Mutuality.* The parties to the initial proceedings must be the same as the parties to the subsequent proceedings. In *Townsend v Bishop*,[63] a father had allowed his son to drive the car. The car was hit by the defendant who was sued by the father for damages to the car. The defendant won on the grounds of contributory negligence by the son, which at that time was a complete defence. Subsequently the son sued the defendant for damages for personal injury and the court held that the son was not a party to the initial action and was thus not estopped from denying his contributory negligence.

This shows a narrow approach to the specific identities of the parties concerned which can have absurd results.[64] *Hunter v Chief Constable of West Midlands*[65] concerned a notorious miscarriage of justice where six men were convicted of bombing pubs in Birmingham. At their criminal trial, the men's confessions were proffered as evidence by the prosecution. The men argued that they had confessed as a result of police violence. After a *voir dire* hearing, the trial judge admitted the confessions into evidence. The men later sued the police in a civil action for the alleged assaults, adducing fresh medical evidence as well as statements from prison officers that they had been assaulted before arriving at prison. The police applied to strike out the action arguing that the claimants were estopped from raising the question of assault since that issue had been determined by the original criminal court. In the Court of Appeal, Lord Denning and Sir George Baker held that the police and the Crown (technically the party in the original criminal trial), although not identical, were in privity, preferring the broader reasoning adopted by the American courts in cases such as *Eagle, Star and British Dominions Insurance Co. v Heller.*[66]

---

[62] [1980] 2 All E.R. 227—the case also is known as McIlkenny v Chief Constable of West Midlands.
[63] [1939] 1 All E.R. 805.
[64] *Petrie v Nuttall* (1856) 11 Ex. 569.
[65] [1981] 3 All E.R. 727; the Court of Appeal judgment is at [1980] 2 All E.R. 227.
[66] (1927) 140 S.E. 314.

Hunter v. Chief Constable of West Midlands [1980] 2 All E.R. 227 at 235j, *per* Lord Denning:

Our friends in the United States have been just as scathing as Jeremy Bentham. They have rejected the doctrine of mutuality altogether, and they have limited the doctrine of privity. They take a distinction between a decision in favour of a man and a decision against him. If a decision has been given against a man on the identical issue arising in the previous proceedings and he had a full and fair opportunity of defending himself in it, then he is estopped from contesting it again in subsequent proceedings. Not only is he estopped but so are those in privity with him. But there is no corresponding estoppel on the person in whose favour it operates.

Thus the claimants were estopped from arguing that they had been assaulted by the police. Goff L.J., dissenting on this point, rejected the argument about identity of parties and issue estoppel, feeling the court was bound by dicta in *Carl-Zeiss-Stiftung* where Lord Upjohn said,

Carl-Zeiss-Stiftung v Rayner and Keeler Ltd (No.2) [1966] 2 All E.R. 536 at 570:

It is clear that a party relying on such a plea must at least prove that the earlier proceedings were determinative of the issues arising in the second proceedings; that the same parties or their privies are common to both proceedings and that the earlier proceedings were within the jurisdiction of the court and were final and conclusive of the relevant issues.

The Crown as state prosecutors and the Chief Constable as a tortfeasor by statute could not be in privity. Instead Goff L.J. struck out the claim on the grounds of abuse of process. The House of Lords rejected the appeal on similar grounds, seeing the action as an abuse of process, being a collateral attack on a final decision, namely the original convictions. Lord Diplock found it unnecessary to discuss estoppel at length, did approve of Goff L.J.'s comments on the characteristics of issue estoppel.[67] It would appear that a litigant is not estopped from raising an issue, decided in earlier proceedings, when they were not a party or privy to those proceedings.

3. *Same capacity.* The parties to the initial proceedings must be acting in the same capacity. In *Marginson v Blackburn Borough Council*,[68] Marginson was in his car being driven by his wife. There was an accident with a bus belonging to the council and being driven by one of their workers. Mrs Marginson was killed and he was injured. Some adjoining houses were damaged. The owners of the houses sued Marginson and the council who were held to be vicariously and equally liable. Marginson then sued the

---

[67] *Hunter* (House of Lords) at 733a-b.
[68] [1939] 1 All E.R. 273.

council, both personally for injuries he himself suffered and as personal representative of his wife's estate. In a personal capacity, he was estopped from denying his wife's contributory negligence (a complete defence at that time) as this issue had been decided at the original hearing where he and the council were parties. But in his role as representative of his wife's estate, he was acting in a different capacity, had not been a party to the original decision and was therefore not estopped.

4. *Same issues.* The same issues must be involved. Usually this does not mean a narrow approach of whether the issues are formally legally identical but whether they are substantially the same with regard to the issues of fact, the evidence to support them and the legal arguments. In *Marginson*, the action by the householders involved proof of the wife's negligent driving whereas in the second case the defendant council raised her contributory negligence as a defence. Formally these are different issues but in substance they are the same. The husband in his personal capacity was estopped from denying that contributory negligence. Similarly in *Bell v Holmes*,[69] where two drivers were involved in an accident. Both were sued by a passenger in one of the cars and both were held liable, although damages were apportioned unequally between them. In subsequent proceedings between the two drivers, the claimant was estopped from denying the apportionment.

But there is a diversity of approach apparent in the cases. The argument that there is a difference (in such road accidents) between the duty of care owed to other drivers and the duty owed to passengers found favour in *Randolph v Tuck*.[70] But in *Wall v Radford*,[71] there was a collision between a Volkswagen and a BMW. A passenger in the VW sued both drivers and damages were apportioned equally. The VW driver subsequently brought an action against the BMW driver for personal injuries arising out of the collision. She argued that the duties owed to the passenger by the drivers were not the same as they owed to each other and to themselves. Consequently there was no room for issue estoppel.

Wall v Radford [1991] 2 All E.R. 741 at 750j–751b, *per* Popplewell J.:

It is, I think, very important to recognise that although a separate duty is owed to another driver from that owed to a passenger, that does not mean in the instant case that the duty is in any way different. The facts giving rise to a breach of that duty are identical and liability for that breach of duty is identical. If two drivers collide in the middle of a wide road, it is quite impossible to see why they should not be found 50% responsible inter se for injury to a passenger, 50% for injury to the other driver and 50% contributorily negligent in respect of their own claim. The duty is to take reasonable care. It is in the absence of special circumstances (which do not apply in the

---

[69] [1956] 3 All E.R. 449.
[70] [1961] 1 All E.R. 814.
[71] [1991] 2 All E.R. 741.

instant case) the same care which has to be taken in respect of the passenger, another driver and the driver himself. In the instant case if he fails to take that reasonable care he will be liable to his passenger, to the other driver and for his own contributory negligence in identical proportions. It is not a different duty. It is the same duty owed to a different person. I am therefore wholly unpersuaded that the alleged difference in duty owed to the third party and that owed to the other driver or to himself plays any part in this case. I prefer the decisions in *Bell v Holmes* and *Wood v Luscombe*,[72] to that of *Randolph v Tuck*.

A similar issue arose in *North West Water v Binnie & Partners*[73] when an explosion occurred in a valve house attached to an underground tunnel link for water distribution. A group of local residents were being shown round at the time and several were killed or injured. The victims sued the water authority, the contractors and the consultant engineers. The Court of Appeal held the latter, Binnies, wholly to blame for the disaster. The water authority then sued the engineers for the damage to tunnelling. The narrow approach would suggest that there is a difference between the duty owed to the original victims and that owed to the authority. The broader approach was again preferred.

North West Water v Binnie & Partners [1990] 3 All E.R. 547 at 561c–d, *per* Drake J.:

I find it unreal to hold that the issues raised in the two actions arising from identical facts are different solely because the parties are different or because the duty of care owed to different persons is in law different. However, I must at once stress my use of the word 'solely'. I think great caution must be exercised before shutting out a party from putting forward his case on the grounds of issue estoppel or abuse of process. Before doing so the court should be quite satisfied that there is no real or practical difference between the issues to be litigated and that already decided, and the evidence which may properly be called on those issues in the new action.

5. *Specifically pleaded.* An estoppel has to be specifically pleaded. In *Vooght v Winch*,[74] the defendant in an action for diverting water from a stream proffered in evidence a judgment in an earlier action between the same parties for the same cause of action. The judge refused to accept that it acted as an estoppel and this decision was upheld.

Vooght v Winch (1819) 2 B. & Ald. 662 at 668, *per* Abbott C.J.:

I am of the opinion that the verdict and judgment obtained for the defendant in the former action was not conclusive evidence against the plaintiff upon the plea of not

---

[72] [1964] 3 All E.R. 972.
[73] [1990] 3 All E.R. 547.
[74] (1819) 2 B. & Ald. 662.

guilty. It would indeed have been conclusive if pleaded in bar to the action by way of estoppel. In that case the plaintiff would not be allowed to discuss the case with the defendant, and for the second time to disturb and vex him by the agitation of the same question. But the defendant has pleaded not guilty, and has thereby elected to submit his case to a jurisdiction. Now if the former verdict was proper to be received in evidence by the learned judge, its effect must be left to the jury. If it were conclusive indeed, the learned judge ought immediately to have nonsuited the plaintiff, or to have told the jury that they were bound, in point of law, to find a verdict for the defendant. It appears to me, however, that the party, by not pleading the former judgment in bar, consents that the whole matter shall go to the jury, and leaves it open to them to inquire into the same upon evidence, and they are to give their verdict upon the whole evidence then submitted to them.[75]

(i) *Issue estoppel in family cases*

In matrimonial matters the court adopts a more investigative role, inquiring into the facts. This means that the ordinary principles of estoppel must be modified. It is said that estoppel binds the parties who have no right to reopen issues but does not bind the court which can, if it sees fit, inquire into the facts.

In *Thompson v Thompson*,[76] the wife applied to the court for an order for maintenance against her husband on the grounds of his wilful neglect to maintain her after she had left him, allegedly because of his cruelty. The husband made a similar charge of cruelty against the wife. The application was dismissed. Subsequently the husband petitioned for divorce, again on the grounds of cruelty. The wife denied this and prayed for judicial separation because of her husband's cruelty. He sought to have this struck out on the grounds that the issue of his cruelty had already been determined in the maintenance proceedings and she was estopped from raising them again.

Thompson v Thompson [1957] 1 All E.R. 161 at 165d–g, *per* Lord Denning:

The situation has been neatly summarised by saying that in the divorce court 'estoppels bind the parties but do not bind the court'; but this is perhaps a little too abbreviated. The full proposition is that, once an issue of a matrimonial offence has been litigated between the parties and decided by a competent court, neither party can claim as of right to reopen the issue and litigate it all over again if the other party objects (that is what is meant by saying that estoppels bind the parties): but the divorce court has the right, and indeed the duty in a proper case, to reopen the issue, or to allow either party to reopen it, despite the objection of the other party (that is what is meant by saying that estoppels do not bind the court). Whether the divorce court should reopen the issue depends on the circumstances. If the court is satisfied that there has already been a full and proper inquiry in the previous litigation, it will often hold that it is not necessary to hold another inquiry all over again: but if the court is

---

[75] Interestingly the court were happy for the trial judge to admit the former judgment as evidence of the facts on which it was based, apparently in contradiction to the rule in *Hollington v Hewthorn* which is discussed later in this chapter.

[76] [1957] 1 All E.R. 161.

not so satisfied it has a right and a duty to inquire into it afresh. If the court does decide to reopen the matter, then there is no longer any estoppel on either party. Each can go into the matter afresh . . .

This is particularly the case in issues relating to children. In *Re B*,[77] the issue was whether the father of two boys in local authority care was fit to take over their care and custody. However there had been a judicial finding that the father had sexually abused two other children. Could the father challenge this finding in the current litigation? The public policy that there should be finality in litigation needs to be balanced against the interests of the child and those interests are rarely served by wrong determinations of fact. The court has a more inquisitorial role and considerable discretion in such cases as to whether any issue of fact should be tried afresh. Flexibility is seen as essential in children's cases and there should be increased control exercised by the court rather than by the parties. However any court will need to consider whether there is some real reason to cast doubt on the earlier findings.

(ii) *Issue estoppel in criminal cases*
To what extent can the Crown or the accused challenge and re-litigate issues which have been decided in earlier proceedings? In *Sambasivam v Malaya Federation Public Prosecutor*,[78] the defendant was charged at the original trial with both possession of ammunition and with carrying firearms. He was acquitted on the first charge and a new trial was ordered on the second charge. At the subsequent trial, the prosecution relied on a statement by the accused in which he admitted carrying a firearm but also admitted being in possession of ammunition. The conviction was quashed since the court failed to direct the two assessors that the prosecution were bound by the acquittal and thus that part of the confession must be regarded as untrue.

Sambasivam v Malaya Federation Public Prosecutor [1950] A.C. 458 at 479, *per* Lord MacDermott:

The effect of a verdict of acquittal pronounced by a competent court on a lawful charge and after a lawful trial is not completely stated by saying that the person acquitted cannot be tried again for the same offence. To that it must be added that the verdict is binding and conclusive in all subsequent proceedings between the parties to the adjudication. The maxim res iudicata pro veritate accipitur is no less applicable to criminal than to civil proceedings. Here, the appellant having been acquitted at the first trial on a charge of having ammunition in his possession, the prosecution was bound to accept the correctness of that verdict and was precluded from taking any step to challenge it at the second trial. And the appellant was no less entitled to rely on his acquittal so far as it might be relevant in his defence.

Is this issue estoppel? The Crown are prevented from re-opening the issue of whether the accused was in possession of ammunition but perhaps the

---

[77] [1997] 2 All E.R. 29; supported by the Court of Appeal in *Re F-K* [2005] EWCA Civ 155.
[78] [1950] A.C. 458.

better view is that the proper ground for setting aside the conviction was that of double jeopardy. The two offences were in fact founded on one and the same incident. The carrying of the revolver and the carrying of the ammunition constituted one and the same incident—the Crown alleged that some of the ammunition was loaded, in the revolver. Having been acquitted of having possession of the ammunition, any conviction for carrying the revolver would be manifestly inconsistent with the previous acquittal.

Sambasivam was supported by the Court of Appeal in *Hay*.[79] The accused made a statement confessing to two offences, arson and burglary, which were tried separately. He was acquitted of arson and in his burglary trial asked for the whole of the statement to be put to the jury. However the trial judge refused an application to adduce evidence of the acquittal on the arson charge in order to show that confession to burglary made on the same occasion was also likely to be unreliable. The jury should have been directed that, in considering the truth of the burglary confession, they should bear in mind the fact that the arson confession was untrue. The accused was entitled to have any independent evidence put before the jury which, if believed, might show a material part of the statement to be false.

These cases suggest that the Crown is estopped from launching collateral attacks which suggest that the accused was guilty of an earlier offence of which they had been acquitted. This was the case in *G v Coltart*[80] where G, a young domestic servant, was charged with two counts of theft, one from her mistress and the other from a guest in the house. No evidence was offered on the latter charge and there was a directed acquittal. But on the first charge the prosecution sought to rebut G's line of defence which was that she had taken the property but intended to return it. They adduced evidence that she had also taken the guest's property and had not returned that. G's conviction was quashed as the prosecution were estopped from arguing that G was guilty of another offence of which she had been acquitted.

A clear case of issue estoppel was *Hogan*[81] where the accused was convicted of GBH. The victim died and there was a subsequent trial for murder—the defendant was held to be estopped from denying that he had the necessary intent. But this has been overturned and the better view is that issue estoppel has no place in criminal proceedings. An acquittal is not conclusive evidence of innocence. Facts alleged in the first proceedings (which end in acquittal) may be advanced as evidence in subsequent proceedings, subject to judicial discretion to ensure the fairness of the proceedings. In *DPP v Humphrys*,[82] the defendant was initially acquitted of driving while disqualified on July 18, 1972. Although a police officer gave evidence of identification, the defendant testified that he had not driven any vehicle in 1972. He was later charged with perjury in relation to that statement. The prosecution had other witnesses as to his driving during the relevant period but also were allowed to re-introduce the evidence of the police officer. The House of Lords upheld the

[79] [1983] Crim.L.R. 390.
[80] [1967] 1 All E.R. 271.
[81] [1974] 2 All E.R. 142.
[82] [1976] 2 All E.R. 497.

conviction, affirming that there is no such thing as issue estoppel in criminal law.

D.P.P. v Humphrys [1976] 2 All E.R. 497 at 523d–523g, *per* Lord Hailsham:

Since this opinion is already long, I venture to summarise it as follows. (1) The doctrine of issue estoppel as it has been developed in civil proceedings is not applicable to criminal proceedings. It follows that the decision in *R v Hogan* was wrong and should not be followed . . . (2) Although the civil doctrine of issue estoppel as it has been developed in civil proceedings is not applicable to criminal proceedings, there is a doctrine applicable to criminal proceedings which is in some ways analogous to issue estoppel, and has sometimes been described by that name. However, (3) the civil doctrine is based on the necessity for finality between private litigants, whereas the doctrine in criminal proceedings is based on the prohibition of double jeopardy, i.e. the maxim nemo debet bis vexari pro una et eadam causa. It follows (4) that whereas the civil doctrine is equally applicable to either of the two civil parties, the criminal doctrine is available to the accused but not to the Crown. (5) Whereas the civil doctrine applies to all cases where an individual issue can be isolated and identified as determined, the criminal doctrine is not so limited but is primarily concerned with verdicts, and applies to verdicts which are either in form or in substance inconsistent. (6) In general, the doctrine in criminal law precludes the Crown from adducing evidence or making suggestions which are inconsistent with a previous verdict of acquittal when its real effect is determined. The doctrine is one of substance rather than form. The court will inquire into realities and not mere technicalities. (7) Where a second charge is brought which is different both in substance and in form from an earlier charge, the mere fact that some of the evidence adduced in support of the second charge is inconsistent with innocence on the earlier charge does not preclude the Crown from adducing that evidence in asserting the truth when considering a verdict on the second charge.

In *Humphrys*, the basis of the prosecution was that the previous acquittal was wrong and had been obtained by perjury. The defendant had given sworn testimony that he had not driven in a particular calendar year. The Crown said that testimony was perjured and it would seem contrary to common sense not to hear the police officer's testimony that was the basis of the allegation. There is finality in relation to the driving offence and the accused is not being 'twice vexed' over that offence.

But to what extent can the prosecution use elements of the earlier acquittal which are probative of their arguments in subsequent proceedings? In *Ollis*,[83] the defendant was acquitted of an offence involving passing a dud cheque to Ramsey on July 5. His defence was that he believed that funds would be paid into the account and the cheque would be honoured. He was later charged with similar offences on 24 and 26 June and 6 July. Ramsey testified as he had at the original trial. The Court for Crown Cases Reserved accepted that this was not re-opening the issue of guilt but that the testimony showed the accused's knowledge about the state of his bank account. The principle is

[83] [1900] 2 Q.B. 758.

clear and probably correct but does the fact that Ollis passed a dud cheque on July 5 show guilty knowledge on the June 24? The chronology leads one to doubt that the testimony logically leads to that particular inference.[84]

This principle was reviewed by the House of Lords in *R. v Z*,[85] where the defendant was charged with rape in 1998. The defence was that he believed the victim consented. The defendant had been tried for rape on four previous occasions. In three of the trials, the defendant was acquitted and in the fourth, he was convicted. In each of the four trials the defendant raised the same defence. The Crown wishes to call the four previous complainants to rebut the defence of belief as to consent. Had the earlier cases all ended in convictions, they would have satisfied the criteria required for them to be admitted as similar fact evidence.[86] The Court of Appeal[87] reluctantly felt bound by *Sambasivam*, and that the significance of a prior acquittal is not merely to preclude a second prosecution for the same offence but extends to preclude the Crown in a subsequent prosecution from asserting that the defendant was actually guilty on the charge in respect of which he was acquitted. The House of Lords reversed this.

R. v Z [2000] 3 All E.R. 385 at 403e–j, *per* Lord Hutton:

1. The principle of double jeopardy operates to cause a criminal court in the exercise of its discretion . . . to stop a prosecution where the defendant is being prosecuted on the same facts or substantially the same facts as gave rise to an earlier prosecution which resulted in his acquittal (or conviction), . . .

2. Provided that a defendant is not placed in double jeopardy as described in (1) above evidence which is relevant on a subsequent prosecution is not inadmissible because it shows or tends to show that the defendant was, in fact, guilty of an offence of which he had earlier been acquitted.

3. It follows from (2) above that a distinction should not be drawn between evidence which shows guilt of an earlier offence of which the defendant had been acquitted and evidence which tends to show guilt of such an offence or which appears to relate to one distinct issue rather than to the issue of guilt of such an offence. Accordingly the judgments in *G (an infant) v Coltart* should not be followed.

The Lords confine *Sambasivam* by dealing with it as an example of true double jeopardy where the prosecution were seeking to re-litigate the same facts. The issue in the immediate case was not whether the defendant is guilty of the other rapes but whether the defendant honestly believed that the victim was consenting. The testimony of the earlier victims is relevant to that issue, without any need to open up the question whether those earlier acquittals were correct.

The difficulties and artificialities created by the rule and preventing evidence from being adduced at a later trial which is inconsistent with an

---

[84] Indeed it appears to be more prejudicial than probative. However *Ollis* is applied in *Caceres-Moreira* [1995] Crim.L.R. 489.

[85] [2000] 3 All E.R. 385.

[86] Now under s.101(1)(d) of the Criminal Justice Act 2003.

[87] [2000] Crim.L.R. 293.

earlier acquittal had been criticised by the Law Commission[88] but in their final report[89] considered that the decision in *Z* has clarified the position so that there was no longer any need for legislative abolition of the *Sambasivam* rule.

In *Colman*,[90] it was the defendant who sought to use acquittals. He was charged with a series of offences of dishonesty. Much of the evidence for all the charges consisted of tape-recorded conversations in a particular car. A voice analyst expert had testified that it was highly probable that the defendant was one of the speakers but that it was a "pre-condition" of her opinion that there was other evidence of his presence. As a result, the prosecution offered no evidence on certain counts and there were directed acquittals. The defendant sought to argue on the remaining counts that the acquittals were conclusive evidence that he had not been in that car. The court held that the outcome of earlier trials arising out of the same events was generally irrelevant but could be admissible when (as here) there was some aspect of evidence that was common to both trials. But the directed acquittals, while relevant and admissible to the issues in front of the jury, were not conclusive evidence.

B. *Estoppel by Deed*

If a person is a party to a deed which asserts a particular fact, that person and those in privity with them are estopped from denying the truth of that fact. This common law rule was put forward in *Bowman v Taylor*,[91] a case in which the claimant sought royalties from the defendant. He had granted the defendant, by deed, a licence to use looms. That deed stated that the claimant was the inventor of certain improvements to the looms, had obtained letters patent and caused a specification to be enrolled. It was held that the defendant was estopped from denying these matters.

Bowman v Taylor (1834) 4 L.J.K.B. 58 at 61, *per* Lord Denman:

An estoppel operates because it concludeth a man to allege the truth by reason of the assertion of the party that that fact is true . . . If a party has by his deed directly asserted a specific fact, it is impossible to say that he shall not be precluded from disputing that fact, thus solemnly admitted by him on the face of his deed . . .

But whether both parties are so bound depends on the intentions of the parties,[92] an issue discussed in *Greer v Kettle*.[93] A company had guaranteed

---

[88] Law Commission, *Double Jeopardy* (Consultation Paper 156) (1999), paras 8.38–8.40.
[89] Law Commission *Double Jeopardy and Prosecution Appeals* (Report No. 267), (2001), para.2.28.
[90] [2005] 2 Cr. App. Rep. 7.
[91] (1834) 4 L.J.K.B. 58.
[92] *Stroughill v Buck* (1850) 14 Q.B. 781.
[93] [1937] 4 All E.R. 396.

under seal a loan from one company to another. In the guarantee document, the lender had recited that the load had been advanced on the security of certain shares but in fact the shares had not been validly issued. Was the guarantor estopped by this?

Greer v Kettle [1937] 4 All E.R. 396 at 404a–f, *per* Lord Maugham:

Estoppel by deed is a rule of evidence founded on the principle that a solemn and unambiguous statement or engagement in a deed must be taken as binding between parties and privies and therefore as not admitting any contradictory proof. It is important to observe that this is a rule of common law, though it may be noted that an exception arises when the deed is fraudulent or illegal. The position in equity is and was always different in this respect, that where there are proper grounds for rectifying a deed, e.g. because it is based upon a common mistake of fact, then to the extent of the rectification there can plainly be no estoppel based on the original form of the instrument. It is at least equally clear that in equity a party to a deed could not set up an estoppel in reliance on a deed in relation to which there is an equitable right to rescission or in reliance on an untrue statement or an untrue recital induced by his own representation, whether innocent or otherwise, to the other party. Authority is scarcely needed for so clear a consequence of a rectification order or an admitted or proved right to such an order. The well-known rule of the Chancery courts in regard to a receipt clause in a deed not effecting an estoppel if the money has not in fact been paid is a good illustration of the equity view . . . The decision of Lord Romilly in *Brooke v Haymes*[94] is even more closely in point, and it may be added that the statement of the law in that case appears never to have been doubted. The headnote being as follows: 'A party to a deed is not estopped in equity from averring against or offering evidence to controvert a recital therein contrary to the fact, which has been introduced into the deed by mistake of fact, and not through fraud or deception on his part'.

C. *Estoppel by Conduct*

In *Freeman v Cooke*,[95] the sheriff had seized goods under a writ of execution which belonged to Benjamin Broadbent. His brother, William, expecting execution against himself, had removed some of his own property to Benjamin's house. When the officers arrived, William assumed the writ was against himself and told them that the goods were Benjamin's whereupon the officers produced their writ against Benjamin. William then claimed the goods belonged to another brother and finally admitted they were his. But the officers still removed the goods. William became bankrupt and his assignees sought to recover the goods. The sheriff as defendant to the action argued that the assignees were estopped by William's statements from denying that the property was Benjamin's.

Freeman v Cooke (1848) 18 L.J. Ex 114 at 119, *per* Parke B.:

The only question is whether it be an estoppel. It is contended that it was, upon the authority of the rule laid down in *Pickard v Sears*.[96] That rule is that 'where one by his

---

[94] (1868) L.R. 6 Eq. 25.
[95] (1848) 18 L.J. Ex. 114.
[96] (1837) 6 A.&E. 469.

words or conduct wilfully causes another to believe in the existence of a certain state of things, and induces him to act on that behalf, or to alter his own previous position, the former is concluded from averring against the latter a different state of things as existing at the time' . . . By the term 'wilfully', however, in that rule, we must understand, if not that the party represents that to be true which he knows to be untrue, at least that he means his representation to be acted upon, and that it is acted upon accordingly; and if, whatever a man's meaning may be, he so conducts himself that a reasonable man would take the representation to be true, and believe that it was meant he should act upon it, and did act upon it as true, the party making the representation would be equally precluded from contesting its truth; and conduct by negligence or omission, when there is a duty cast upon a person by usage of trade, or otherwise, to disclose the truth, may often have the same effect . . . .

Estoppel by conduct comes about when a person by words or conduct causes another to believe in a state of affairs and induces him or her to act on that belief. That person is estopped from denying that state of affairs. As no reasonable person could have had any faith in any of William Broadbent's statements, there was no basis for any estoppel.

There are three[97] forms of such estoppel by conduct.

(i) *Estoppel by representation.* Where a person makes a representation of existing fact, by words or conduct, with the intention, actual or presumed, of inducing another to act on the faith of that representation and alter his or her position to his or her detriment, the representor is estopped from denying the facts as represented. In *Greenwood v Martins Bank Ltd*[98] the claimant's wife forged his signature to cheques drawn on the defendant bank. The husband discovered the forgeries but did not tell the bank. Eventually he confronted his wife, threatening to disclose them. The wife killed herself. The claimant sought to recover from the bank the amounts paid out on the forged cheques.

Greenwood v Martins Bank Ltd [1933] A.C. 51 at 57–58, *per* Lord Tomlin:

Mere silence cannot amount to a representation, but when there is a duty to disclose, deliberate silence may become significant and amount to a representation. The existence of a duty on the part of the customer of a bank to disclose his knowledge of such a forgery as the one in question in this case is rightly admitted . . . The appellant's silence, therefore, was deliberate and intended to produce the effect which it in fact produced—namely the leaving of the respondents in ignorance of the true facts so that no action might be taken by them against the appellant's wife. The deliberate abstention from speaking in those circumstances seems to me to amount to a representation to the respondents that the forged cheques were in fact in order, and assuming that detriment to the respondents followed, there were, it seems to me, present all the elements essential to estoppel ..

In *Greenwood* the husband clearly owed the bank a duty to disclose his wife's misfeasance. A broader approach is apparent in *Taylor Fashions Ltd v*

---

[97] This text will not cover High Trees promissory estoppel: *Central London Property Trust Ltd v High Trees House Ltd* [1947] K.B. 130.
[98] [1933] A.C. 51.

Liverpool Victoria Trustees Co. Ltd.[99] The defendant landlords and the claimant lessees all acquiesced in the assumption that there was a valid option to renew the leases when the original term finished. That option was void for lack of registration but the lessees had altered the frontage and internal layout of the properties in reliance on extending the term of the leases. The claimants sought specific performance of the lease and argued that the defendants were estopped from relying on the invalidity of the option clause. The doctrine of estoppel by acquiescence is not restricted to cases where the representor is aware of their strict rights and where the representee is led to believe that those rights will not be enforced against them. The test is one of unconscionability: here there was a mistake of law common to all the parties and whether the landlords were aware of the true position was just one of the factors to be taken into account in assessing unconscionability.[1]

(ii) *Estoppel by agreement.*   Where the parties have agreed together to base their relationship on an accepted state of affairs, neither party can be allowed to deny that state of affairs. In *Cooke v Loxley*,[2] a landlord sued his tenant for use and occupation of the land. The defendant argued that the claimant had no title to the land but this evidence was rejected.

Cooke v Loxley (1792) 5 T.R 4 at 5, *per* Lord Kcnyon C.J.:

. . . in an action for use and occupation it ought not to be permitted to a tenant, who occupies land by the licence of another, to call upon that other to show the title under which he let the land. This is not a mere technical rule but is founded in public convenience and policy . . . Here the defendant, who occupied the land, did so by the permission of the plaintiff, and then refused to pay his rent under an idea that he might contest the plaintiff's right; but the plaintiff could not be supposed to come to trial prepared to meet such a defence and to make out his title; such an action as the present does not involve the question of title

Similarly an agent or bailee could not deny the title of the principal or bailor. This is an analogous situation to estoppel by representation or acquiescence and the test of unconscionability in *Taylor Fashions Ltd v Liverpool Victoria Trustees Co. Ltd*,[3] discussed above, must be relevant.

(iii) *Estoppel by negligence.* In *Coventry, Sheppard & Co v Great Eastern Railway*,[4] a railway company negligently issued two delivery orders in respect of only one consignment of wheat. As a result, a fraudulent individual was

---

[99] [1981] 1 All E.R. 897.
[1] *Beckingham v Hodgens* (2003) E.M.L.R. 18.
[2] (1792) 5 T.R. 4.
[3] [1981] 1 All E.R. 897.
[4] (1883) 11 Q.B.D. 776.

enabled to obtain two advances from the claimant company. Were GER estopped from denying that there were two consignments?

> The negligence of the defendants was to the prejudice of the plaintiffs and allowed the fraud to be perpetrated upon them. It seems to me, therefore, that the defendants are estopped as against the plaintiffs, their negligence having been the immediate cause of the advance . . .[5]

Where the negligence leads to a state of affairs being incorrectly represented as true and enabling a fraud to be perpetrated, the party responsible is estopped from denying the truth of that state of affairs. Such circumstances can also be seen in *Moorgate Mercantile Co Ltd v Twitchings,*[6] where the claimant was a finance company, the owners of a car that they let on hire-purchase to a third party. That third party purported to sell it to the defendant who, before completing the purchase, checked with an organisation, Hire Purchase Information (HPI), that the vehicle was not subject to an HP agreement. HPI had been set up by finance companies to prevent fraud and the claimant was a member but by oversight the claimant had failed to register their interest in the vehicle. They sought to recover damages from the defendant for conversion as the car had now been sold on to a private person. The defendants argued that the claimants were estopped from asserting their title to the car. The House of Lords held by a majority that there was no duty of care existing.

Moorgate Mercantile Co Ltd v Twitchings [1976] 2 All E.R. 641 at 659a-c, *per* Lord Edmund-Davies:

It is, of course, desirable that finance companies who are members of HPI should promptly and accurately notify HPI of any new agreement entered into, and this both in their own interest and in that of dealer-members of that organisation. But they are, I think, under no sort of obligation to join it at all, though Lord Denning MR[7] went so far as to say that they abstain at their peril, for even non-members may find themselves estopped by their failure to join from asserting title against an innocent buyer or seller. I have to say respectfully that such an approach illustrates the risk of creating legal duties where none was ever contemplated. In most situations it is better to be careful than careless, but it is quite another thing to elevate carelessness into a tort. Liability has to be based on a legal duty not to be careless, and I can find none in this case.

Dissenting, Lord Wilberforce concluded,

Moorgate Mercantile Co. Ltd v Twitchings at 648b-c, *per* Lord Wilberforce:

. . . that a finance company belonging to the HPI scheme is under a duty towards dealers, members of HPI, to take reasonable care to register any hire-purchase

---

[5] *ibid.* at 780 *per* Brett M.R.
[6] [1976] 2 All E.R. 641.
[7] [1975] 3 All E.R. 314 at 325 (Court of Appeal).

agreements to which it is a party so that if in reliance on the absence of any such registration a dealer acts to his prejudice the finance company is estopped from asserting his title against that dealer. In saying this I should make it clear that it does not follow that the finance company is under a similar duty to any other persons, e.g. non-member dealers or members of the public. These are separate categories as to which different considerations may apply . . . [8]

Estoppel by negligence does require a breach of duty to the victim and might well be seen simply as part of the substantive law of negligence. It has been argued that this form of estoppel could and perhaps should be subsumed within the category of estoppel by representation. All that is necessary is proof of intentional words, acts or conduct which can be reasonably construed as a representation by the representor to the representee who need not be in a direct relationship. In *Moorgate Mercantile* this approach was considered and was rejected on the facts.

To constitute an estoppel a representation must be clear and must unequivocally state the fact which, ultimately, the maker is to be prevented from denying. The answer given by HPI to the defendant's enquiry cannot in my opinion bear the meaning for which the defendant must contend. It was simply and carefully drafted . . . . It is quite clear that the answer given by HPI, both intrinsically and as it was understood by this particular motor dealer, conveyed nothing more than information as to the state of the records of HPI; it did not profess to and did not say anything as to the ownership or lack of ownership of any finance house members of HPI . . . [9]

IV. JUDGMENTS AS EVIDENCE OF THE FACTS UPON WHICH THEY WERE BASED

Under the doctrine of estoppel by record, judgments can be conclusive:

  a) against the world as to the legal state of affairs or
  b) against the parties and their privies as to the facts on which a judgment was based

But those who were not parties to an earlier case, although they are unable to dispute the legal state of affairs that case brings about, are not bound by the facts on which any earlier judgment was based. This doctrine is taken further at common law: not only are the parties in subsequent litigation not bound by the facts as found in the previous judgment, they are unable to use that judgment even as evidence of the facts.

This is illustrated by *Hollington v F. Hewthorn & Co. Ltd.*[10] There was a collision between two cars in which the claimant's car was damaged. The drivers were the only eyewitnesses. The driver of the defendant's car was convicted of careless driving. The claimant, who had not been involved in the accident, brought an action against the defendant and the convicted driver. Before the case came to court, the person driving the claimant's car died,

[8] above at 648b.
[9] *ibid.* at 644g–645b.
[10] [1943] 2 All E.R. 35.

depriving the claimant of his only witness. He sought to rely on the conviction to prove his case. The Court of Appeal held that the claimant was not entitled to use the conviction of the defendant driver as evidence of the latter's negligence. The rationale in part was founded on the principle that a later court should not be bound by the earlier court's opinion as to the facts.

The decision has been widely criticised. In *Hunter v Chief Constable of the West Midlands*, Lord Diplock said that it was generally considered to have been wrongly decided.[11] In *Hall v Simons*, Lord Hoffmann, said that the Court of Appeal was generally thought to have taken the technicalities of the matter much too far when it decided that in civil proceedings a conviction was *res inter alios acta* and no evidence whatever that the accused had committed the offence.[12] Although partially reversed by Parliament (below), it has not been overruled by the House of Lords and was treated as authoritative by the Privy Council in *Hui Chi-Ming*.[13]

It was a rule that also applied in criminal proceedings: in *Spinks*,[14] a third party, Fairey, had stabbed the victim and had been convicted under section 18 of the Offences against the Person Act 1861. Spinks, who had played no part in the assault but had hidden the knife, was tried under s.4 of the Criminal Law Act 1967 with doing an act intended to impede the prosecution of a person, knowing or believing that person to be guilty of an arrestable offence. The defendants were tried together but the Court of Appeal were of the opinion that, had Fairey been tried and convicted prior to Spinks, his conviction would not have been admissible evidence that Fairey had committed an arrestable offence.

Spinks [1982] 1 All E.R. 587 at 589b–e, *per* Russell J.:

. . . the only evidence that Fairey had stabbed anyone came from his own admissions to the police, made in the absence of the appellant . . . The short point that is taken, therefore, is that the Crown had no admissible evidence as against the appellant to prove the first ingredient of the offence with which he was charged, namely as alleged in the particulars of offence, that Fairey had committed the arrestable offence of wounding. The only evidence of that fact came from an out of court admission of a co-defendant which was not admissible against the appellant.

For the Crown, it was argued that in some way the admission of Fairey was 'evidence in the case', and that the jury could act on it when considering the case of the appellant. But, as it seems to this court, the fallacy of that argument can be demonstrated in a number of ways. If Fairey had pleaded guilty and had not given evidence against the appellant, or if the appellant had been indicted and tried separately, could the Crown have relied on Fairey's conviction to prove the first ingredient of the offence? The answer must be in the negative. The appellant can be in no worse position because he was being tried alongside Fairey . . .

[11] [1982] A.C. 529 at 543.
[13] [2002] 1 A.C. 615 at 702.
[13] [1992] 1 A.C. 34; for a recent analysis by Toulson, J. see *Lincoln National Life Insurance v Sun Life Insurance* [2004] 1 Lloyd's Rep. 737, para.51 ff.
[14] [1982] 1 All E.R. 587.

This absurd position has now been altered as a result of ss.11–13 of the Civil Evidence Act 1968 and s.74 of the Police and Criminal Evidence Act 1984.

A. *Civil proceedings—convictions*

The narrow ratio of *Hollington* was that in civil proceedings a conviction was not admissible evidence of the fact that the person concerned committed the offence in question. Under the Civil Evidence Act 1968,

> 11.—(1) In any civil proceedings the fact that a person has been convicted of an offence by or before any court in the United Kingdom or by a court-martial there or elsewhere shall (subject to subsection (3) below) be admissible in evidence for the purpose of proving, where to do so is relevant to any issue in those proceedings, that he committed that offence, whether he was so convicted upon plea of guilty or otherwise and whether or not he is a party to the civil proceedings; but no conviction other than a subsisting one shall be admissible in evidence by virtue of this section.
>
> (2) In any civil proceedings in which by virtue of this section a person is proved to have been convicted of an offence by or before any court in the United Kingdom or by a court-martial there or elsewhere—
> (a) he shall be taken to have committed that offence unless the contrary is proved; and
> (b) without prejudice to the reception of any other admissible evidence for the purpose of identifying the facts on which the conviction was based, the contents of any document which is admissible as evidence of the conviction, and the contents of the information, complaint, indictment or charge-sheet on which the person in question was convicted, shall be admissible in evidence for that purpose.

This section overturns *Hollington*. It applies only to subsisting convictions. "Subsisting" excludes those which have been quashed on appeal[15] but not those pending appeal,[16] nor those which are spent under the Rehabilitation of Offenders Act 1974.[17] "Convictions" do not include convictions in foreign courts or any findings of police disciplinary tribunals.[18]

Any party seeking to rely on a previous conviction under the section must, in the pleadings, give particulars of that conviction as well as indicating the issue in the case to which the conviction is relevant.[19] Often the conviction itself will be enough to settle liability but not necessarily give sufficient information on quantum of damages.[20] Section 11(2)(b) admits the contents of the indictment as evidence to identify the facts on which the convictions were based but this does not go into the areas of detail which would normally be required to establish the amount of any civil liability. However the transcript is now admissible under the provisions of the Civil Evidence Act 1995.

It is clear that, where a conviction is proved, s.11 (2) puts the legal burden of disproof onto the party denying the facts on which the conviction was based. This appears to be proof on the balance of probabilities.[21]

---

[15] *Raja v Van Hoogstraten* [2005] EWHC 2890 (Ch).
[16] *Re Raphael Raphael v D'Antin* [1973] 3 All E.R. 19.
[17] s.4.
[18] *Thorpe v Chief Constable of the Greater Manchester Police* [1989] 2 All E.R. 827.
[19] Civil Procedure Rules, Practice Direction 16, para.8.1.
[20] *Microsoft v Alibhai and Bakir* [2004] EWHC 3282 (Ch).
[21] *Sutton v Sutton* [1969] 3 All E.R. 1348.

Taylor v Taylor [1970] 2 All E.R. 609 at 613, *per* Davies L.J.:

[s.11] . . . means that the onus of proof of upsetting the previous conviction is on the person who seems to do so. It is probable . . . that that is an onus of proof on the balance of probabilities. But, having said that, it nevertheless is obvious that, when a man has been convicted by 12 of his fellow countrymen and countrywomen at a criminal trial, the verdict of the jury is a matter which is entitled to very great weight when the convicted person is seeking, in the words of the statute, to prove the contrary.

In *Stupple v Royal Insurance Co Ltd*,[22] the claimant had been convicted of robbing a bank. During a police search, a sum of money had been found in the claimant's possession which had been paid over to the defendants who had indemnified the bank. The claimant now sought the recovery of that money. Buckley L.J. saw the mere fact of conviction in a different light

Stupple v Royal Insurance Co. Ltd [1970] 3 All E.R. 230 at 239h–j, *per* Buckley L.J.:

If the fact of conviction were meant to carry some weight in determining whether the convicted man has successfully discharged the onus under s.11(2)(a) of proving that he did not commit the offence, what weight should it carry? I cannot accept that this should depend on such considerations as, for instance, the status of the court which convicted, or whether the decision was unanimous or a majority verdict of a jury. I cannot discover any measure of the weight which the unexplored fact of conviction should carry. Although the section has made proof of conviction admissible and has given proof of conviction a particular statutory effect under s.11(2)(a), it remains, I think, as true today as before the Act that mere proof of conviction proves nothing relevant to the plaintiff's claim, and it clearly cannot be intended to shut out or, I think, to mitigate the effect of any evidence tending to show that the convicted person did not commit the offence. In my judgment, proof of conviction under this section gives rise to the statutory presumption laid down in s.11(2)(a), which, like any other statutory presumption, will give way to evidence establishing the contrary on the balance of probability, without itself affording any evidential weight to be taken into account in determining whether that onus has been discharged.

In *Hunter v Chief Constable of West Midlands Police*,[23] Lord Denning suggested that the weight given to proof of conviction was much greater, requiring the convicted person to show that the conviction was obtained by fraud or collusion or by adducing fresh and conclusive evidence. In the House of Lords, Lord Diplock disapproved of this, reiterating that the standard of proof was on the balance of probabilities, although after a conviction, that would be an uphill task.[24] As *Hunter* shows, the courts are unsympathetic to convicted defendants seeking to challenge their convictions by collateral means.

[22] [1970] 3 All E.R. 230.
[23] [1980] 2 All E.R. 227.
[24] [1981] 3 All E.R. 727 at 735–6.

This approach was followed in *Cooper v Barry*,[25] where a farmer had been convicted of shooting and injuring gypsies who were hunting rabbits on his land. The victims now sought civil damages on the evidential basis of that conviction. The trial judge found for the defence but the Court of Appeal overturned this and talked of the need of 'cogent and compelling evidence' before rebutting the presumption that the defendant had fired the gun. But the conviction remains a rebuttable presumption—in *J v Oyston*,[26] a rape victim sought damages from her rapist. The defendant claimed that evidence had come to light which was prejudicial to the claimant's credit, and which justified a review of the convictions. He clearly wished to re-litigate the issue as to his guilt and the victim claimed that this challenge was an abuse of process. The judge refused to strike out the defence as abuse of process— although any fresh evidence would need to be very substantial and entirely change the case, to prevent the defendant from having his case re-heard with such new evidence would be to cause manifest unfairness.

B. *Civil proceedings—findings of paternity or adultery*

There are analogous provisions for certain matrimonial matters.

12.—(1) In any civil proceedings—
(a) the fact that a person has been found guilty of adultery in any matrimonial proceedings; and
(b) the fact that a person has been found to be the father of a child in relevant proceedings before any court in England and Wales or has been adjudged to be the father of a child in affiliation proceedings before any court in the United Kingdom,
shall (subject to subsection (3) below) be admissible in evidence for the purpose of proving, where to do so is relevant to any issue in those civil proceedings, that he committed the adultery to which the finding relates or, as the case may be, is (or was) the father of that child, . . .
(2) In any civil proceedings in which by virtue of this section a person is proved to have been found guilty of adultery as mentioned in subsection (1)(a) above or to have been found or adjudged to be the father of a child as mentioned in subsection (1)(b) above —
(a) he shall be taken to have committed the adultery to which the finding relates or, as the case may be, to be (or have been) the father of that child, unless the contrary is proved; and
(b) without prejudice to the reception of any other admissible evidence for the purpose of identifying the facts on which the finding or adjudication was based, the contents of any document which was before the court, or which contains any pronouncement of the court, in the other proceedings in question shall be admissible in evidence for that purpose.[27]

This makes provisions, parallel to those relating to convictions, for findings of adultery or paternity in previous proceedings. Again the effect is to shift the burden of proof onto the party seeking to deny such findings. The making

[25] Unreported, January 18, 1999 (CA).
[26] [1999] 1 W.L.R. 694.
[27] As amended by Family Law Reform Act 1987, s.29.

of a parental responsibility order by a court was relevant proceedings which would place the onus on the person to show that they were not the parent.[28]

C. *Civil proceedings—defamation actions*

Under s.13, a conviction is conclusive in a defamation action. As a matter of public policy, a person should not incur liability for stating that a person is guilty of an offence for which they have been convicted. A convicted person cannot use the libel laws to re-open a conviction, even where there is considerable evidence of innocence which is well known to the defendant.

13.—(1) In an action for libel or slander in which the question whether the plaintiff did or did not commit a criminal offence is relevant to an issue arising in the action, proof that, at the time when that issue falls to be determined, he stands convicted of that offence shall be conclusive evidence that he committed that offence; and his conviction thereof shall be admissible in evidence accordingly.

(2) In any such action as aforesaid in which by virtue of this section the plaintiff is proved to have been convicted of an offence, the contents of any document which is admissible as evidence of the conviction, and the contents of the information, complaint, indictment or charge-sheet on which he was convicted, shall, without prejudice to the reception of any other admissible evidence for the purpose of identifying the facts on which the conviction was based, be admissible in evidence for the purpose of identifying those facts.[29]

In contrast, proof of an acquittal is not admissible evidence.

D. *Civil proceedings—acquittals and other judicial findings*

The general rule is that acquittals are not conclusive evidence of innocence. In *Loughans v Odhams Press*,[30] the claimant brought a libel action against the defendants for publishing a statement that suggested that he had in fact committed a murder twenty years previously although he had been acquitted at the time. The defendants pleaded justification and proved on the balance of probabilities that the claimant was guilty, a finding which is not inconsistent with the result of the original trial where the prosecution failed to prove the defendant guilty beyond reasonable doubt.

But the underlying concerns of the double jeopardy rule, that a person should be 'twice vexed' over the same issue, seem to apply here. Public policy considerations might suggest that those acquitted of a crime should be immune from further allegations that they committed the offence, a position recommended by the Law Reform Committee in 1967.

[28] *R. v Secretary of State for Social Security Ex p. W* [1999] 2 F.L.R. 604.
[29] As amended by Defamation Act 1996, s.12.
[30] [1963] 1 Q.B. 299.

Law Reform Committee: 15th Report (1967) Cmnd. 3391, para.41:

... in defamation actions, where the statement complained of alleges that the plaintiff had been guilty of a criminal offence, proof that he has been convicted of that offence and that the conviction has not been set aside should be conclusive evidence of his guilt, and proof that he was acquitted of that offence should be conclusive evidence of his innocence.[31]

However the European Court of Human Rights in *Ringvold v Norway*,[32] has held that imposing civil liability following a criminal acquittal does not infringe Article 6.

Ringvold v Norway Application No. 34964/97:

38. ... the Court observes that, while the conditions for civil liability could in certain respects overlap, depending on the circumstances, with those for criminal liability, the civil claim was nevertheless to be determined on the basis of the principles that were proper to the civil law of tort. The outcome of the criminal proceedings was not decisive for the compensation case. The victim had a right to claim compensation regardless of whether the defendant was convicted or, as here, acquitted, and the compensation issue was to be the subject of a separate legal assessment based on criteria and evidentiary standards which in several important respects differed from those that applied to criminal liability. This is indeed borne out by the circumstances of the present case, where the compensation matter was the sole issue in the appeal before the Supreme Court, involving private parties only, which was heard in proceedings governed by the provisions of the Code of Civil Procedure, with extensive new evidence being taken on that issue alone.

The Court held that exoneration from criminal liability should not preclude the establishment of civil liability to pay compensation arising out of the same facts on the basis of a less strict burden of proof.

The best view is that acquittals are not admissible evidence. In criminal cases, the acquittals of, for example, third parties alleged to be accomplices of the accused are not admissible evidence—as *Hui Chi-ming*[33] argues, such findings are excluded because they are not relevant. Exceptional features may make them relevant as in *Cooke*[34] where three suspects were alleged to have made admissions to the same detective constable. Two of them were tried first on a charge of robbery and acquitted. There was a clear inference from the acquittal that the jury had disbelieved the detective's evidence. The third was later convicted based on his alleged admissions to the same detective and the Court of Appeal, allowing the appeal, held that his counsel ought to have been allowed to bring out the circumstances in which the first two had been

---

[31] Law Reform Committee: 15th Report (1967) Cmnd. 3391, para.41.
[32] Application No.34964/97, decision February 11, 2003.
[33] [1992] AC 34.
[34] (1986) 84 Cr.App.R. 286.

acquitted because they were so relevant to the credibility of the detective constable.

In civil proceedings, it has been said that acquittals are not evidence of innocence at subsequent trials.[35] But in *Raja v Van Hoogstraten*,[36] a property developer was charged with recruiting accomplices to murder a business rival. The principals were convicted but the developer was acquitted of murder and convicted of manslaughter. This latter conviction was later quashed. The victim's family sought damages—the convictions were clearly evidence under s.11 of the Civil Evidence Act 1968. But the judge also treated the acquittal as admissible but not conclusive, explaining the different considerations applicable to civil as opposed to criminal proceedings.

A broad reading of *Hollington* would exclude not merely convictions but judicial findings generally as evidence of the facts on which they are based. *Hollington* might thus be held to apply to all other judicial findings which do not come within the scope of ss.11–13 of the Act, including acquittals and findings in a civil court. For example, a driver is involved in an accident with another car injuring the other driver and a passenger. The other driver successfully sues for damages on the basis of the first driver's negligence. The passenger on this broad reading may well not be able to rely on that finding of negligence if they brought a later action against the first driver.

Lord Denning's approach to this problem in *Hunter v Chief Constable of West Midlands Police Force*[37] is much more robust, "Beyond doubt, *Hollington v Hewthorn* was wrongly decided. It was done in ignorance of previous authorities. It was done per incuriam."[38] Denning goes beyond the question of using a previous judgment simply as evidence of its underlying facts and states that, in civil or criminal proceedings, where there is a judicial finding *against* a party, that person is estopped from disputing that issue in later actions unless it can be shown that there was collusion or fraud or that there was new evidence. This ratio applied not merely to judgments themselves but to findings such as a holding at *voir dire* that a confession was admissible evidence.

Hunter v Chief Constable of West Midlands Police Force [1980] 2 All E.R. 227 at 238a–d, *per* Lord Denning:

To illustrate my view of the present law, I would take this example. Suppose there is a road accident in which a lorry driver runs down a group of people on the pavement waiting for a bus. One of the injured persons sues the lorry driver for negligence and succeeds. Suppose now that another of the injured persons sues the lorry driver for damages also. Has he to prove the negligence all over again? Can the lorry driver

---

[35] C. Tapper, *Cross and Tapper on Evidence* (10th ed., Butterworths 2004), p.128.

[36] [2005] EWHC 2890 (Ch.), paras 43ff.

[37] [1980] 2 All E.R. 227, reported as *McIlkenny v Chief Constable of West Midlands Police Force*. The House of Lords judgment is at [1981] 3 All E.R. 727.

[38] *ibid.* at 237a.

(*against* whom the previous decision went) dispute his liability to the other injured person? It seems to me that if the lorry driver (with the backing of his employer) has had a full and fair opportunity of contesting the issue of negligence in the first action, he should be estopped from disputing it in the second action. He was a party to the first action and should be bound by the result of it. Not only the lorry driver, but also his employer should be estopped from disputing the issue of negligence in a second action on the ground that the employer was in privity with the lorry driver.

Such a radical approach to issue estoppel would make the debate about the scope of the *Hollington* rule redundant. However Lord Denning's view did not attract the support of the House of Lords although they avoided a direct decision on this point.

E. *Civil proceedings—non-judicial findings*

Many tribunals, formal and informal, hear evidence and come to findings of fact. For example, a rugby player punches another player, injuring him. The assailant is sent off by the referee for violent conduct. The player's county association have formal disciplinary proceedings to determine the punishment, usually a period of suspension from playing the game. But the victim also starts an action for damages for battery. Can either party use the findings of the disciplinary board as evidence in such proceedings? The introduction of such findings might be attacked on the grounds that they are hearsay (although now admissible under the Civil Evidence Act 1995). But should they be excluded under the *Hollington* rule? The broad rationale of that case, however ill-founded, was that a later court should not receive as evidence an earlier court's opinion as to the facts and, right or wrong, this should be the common law position. There is no obvious reason to restrict this to judicial findings. But, were this to be taken to extremes, this would exclude the findings of any sort of inquiry or indeed the conclusions of an expert investigator. Perhaps this reveals the weakness in the *Hollington* decision. Certainly a preferable approach is taken in *Hill v Clifford*[39] where the claimant was seeking dissolution of a dentists' practice on the grounds that his partners had been guilty of professional misconduct. There had been a hearing in front of the General Medical Council, operating in accordance with duty of inquiry under the Dentists Act 1878, who had ordered that the partners should be struck off the Register of Dentists. The Court of Appeal accepted that the order was admissible evidence of the fact that the Cliffords had been guilty of such misconduct.

F. *Criminal proceedings—convictions*

Hollington v Hewthorn applied in full rigour in criminal proceedings. In *Turner*,[40] it was suggested that in a case of receiving stolen property, the

[39] [1907] 2 Ch. 236.
[40] (1832) 1 Mood. C.C. 347.

conviction of the thief would not have been admissible evidence that the goods had been stolen, a fact in issue which would have to be proved by other means.[41] More recently, in *Shepherd*,[42] landlords were charged with harassment of certain tenants. The landlords had been tried and convicted at an earlier hearing of the harassment of the same tenants in the same building. Although the previous convictions of a defendant are normally inadmissible, the prosecution were allowed to adduce evidence of that conviction. The Court of Appeal quashed the conviction on the grounds that the previous conduct did not come within the similar fact rules[43] and was likely to unduly prejudice the jury.[44] The rejection of the conviction as evidence is some authority that the *Hollington* rule applied in criminal cases. *Spinks*[45] and *Hassan*[46] provide additional support. In the latter case, the defendant was charged with living off immoral earnings of a prostitute. Her prior conviction for prostitution was deemed not to be admissible at the defendant's trial. These decisions have now been overturned by s.74 of the Police and Criminal Evidence Act 1984.

74.—(1) In any proceedings the fact that a person other than the accused has been convicted of an offence . . . shall be admissible in evidence for the purpose of proving where to do so is relevant to any issue in those proceedings, that the person committed that offence, whether or not any other evidence of his having committed that offence is given.

(2) In any proceedings in which by virtue of this section a person other than the accused is proved to have been convicted of an offence . . ., he shall be taken to have committed that offence unless the contrary is proved.

(3) In any proceedings where evidence is admissible of the fact that the accused has committed an offence, if the accused is proved to have been convicted of the offence . . . he shall be taken to have committed that offence unless the contrary is proved.[47]

75. Where evidence that a person has been convicted of an offence is admissible by virtue of section 74 above, then without prejudice to the reception of any other admissible evidence for the purpose of identifying the facts on which the conviction was based—

(a) the contents of any document which is admissible as evidence of the conviction, and

(b) the contents of the information, complaint, indictment or charge-sheet on which the person in question was convicted,

shall be admissible in evidence for that purpose . . .

These sections deal with convictions both of the accused and of persons other than the accused, often co-accused. These convictions are admissible[48]

---

[41] Criminal Law Revision Committee 11th Report (Cmnd. 4991), para.218.

[42] [1980] Crim.L.R. 428.

[43] see Ch.14.

[44] But it may be argued that the previous conviction may well have been relevant to rebut a defence of accident or mistake, showing animosity to the tenants, and should have been admitted on analogy with the acquittal which was proved in *Ollis* [1900] 2 Q.B. 758; now it would be admissible under s.101(1)(d) of the Criminal Justice Act 2003.

[45] above.

[46] [1970] 1 Q.B. 423.

[47] As amended by Criminal Justice Act 2003 pt 5, Sd. 37; this subsection ensures that, if prior convictions are proved against the accused under Criminal Justice Act 2003, s.101 or under Theft Act 1968, s.27(3) they are not estopped from denying them although they have the burden of disproof.

[48] The procedure for proving convictions is laid down by Police and Criminal Evidence Act 1984, s.73.

where they are relevant to an issue in the case. When is a conviction '. . . relevant to any issue in those proceedings'? It is clear in *Spinks* where the prosecution had to prove under s.4 of the Criminal Law Act 1967 that the defendant did '. . . an act intended to impede the prosecution of a person, knowing or believing that person to be guilty of an arrestable offence'. Section 74 now allows proof of that earlier conviction for wounding as evidence that there was such an arrestable offence. Similarly in *Hassan*, proof of the conviction for prostitution is directly relevant to the charge faced by the accused, namely living off immoral earnings.

Often the issue is whether the offence has taken place at all. In *Stewart*,[49] the defendant and another person were accused of kidnapping the victim and forcing him to withdraw money from cash machines. The defence was that he was merely collecting a debt from a customer and that the victim had acted voluntarily. The co-accused pleaded guilty and this conviction was admitted as it showed that the offences had taken place and undermined the defence explanation.

Another straightforward example is the area of conspiracy. In *Robertson*,[50] the defendant was charged with conspiracy to commit burglary and the Crown was permitted to adduce evidence of convictions for burglaries carried out by his alleged co-conspirators. These convictions showed that there was such a conspiracy although the Crown still had to prove that the defendant was a party to it.

Robertson [1987] 3 All E.R. 231 at 236a–237c, *per* Lord Lane C.J.:

The heart of the problem is the correct interpretation of the expression 'issue in the proceedings'. Only when that is determined can the court decide what in the particular circumstances is relevant and thus admissible . . . . We think the time has come to attempt to provide some guidance for courts who have the task of applying s.74. The word 'issue' in relation to a trial is apt to cover not only an issue which is an essential ingredient in the offence charged, for instance in a handling case the fact that the goods were stolen (that is the restricted meaning), but also less fundamental issues, for instance evidential issues arising during the course of the proceedings (that is the extended meaning). Section 74 by using the words 'any issue in those proceedings' does not seek to limit the word 'issue' to the restricted meaning indicated above. Although the Report of the Criminal Law Revision Committee is an indication that the committee may have been regarding the matter at least primarily in the restricted sense, it seems to us that we are not entitled to use that possibility as showing that the words of the section mean other than what they plainly state . . . .
So far as the present case is concerned, there was certainly an issue. Indeed it was probably an issue in the restricted sense, namely the issue of whether there was a conspiracy between Poole and Long (of which their joint conviction of burglary was the clearest evidence). It was that conspiracy to which the prosecution sought to prove the appellant was a party . . .

Lord Lane takes a broad view of what is a relevant issue, not confining this to an essential ingredient in the offence charged but more marginal issues. In

[49] [2001] Crim.L.R. 126.
[50] [1987] 3 All E.R. 231; *O'Connor* [1987] Crim.L.R. 260; *Liaquat Ali* [2005] EWCA Crim 87.

Golder,[51] for instance, the accused was charged with robbery at a garage. The prosecution produced a confession which the defendant contested. Two of the co-accused pleaded guilty to that offence and to a previous robbery. The Crown was also permitted to adduce evidence of these pleas.

Golder [1987] 3 All E.R. 231 at 240c–e, *per* Lord Lane C.J.:

The prosecution contended that in the particular circumstances of this case those convictions were relevant. The admissions which he has according to the police made to them were contested. It was suggested to the officers that they had fabricated their story and that no such admission had been made. The prosecution's desire to put the convictions of Moran and Eley in was in order to show that the contents of the alleged confessions by the appellant were in accordance with the facts as they were known and the confessions were therefore more likely to be true . . .

In *Golder*, the key issue was the weight to be accorded to the confession. The accused's statements in that confession provided details about the previous robbery by his co-accused. Proof that the robbery in fact took place went to the issue of the probative weight to be accorded to that confession. In *Castle*,[52] the issue was the strength of the identification evidence. The witness had identified both the accused. The co-accused had pleaded guilty and this was now admissible to support the witness's identification of the defendant.

Under s.74(3), the prior convictions can be those of the accused so long as they are not being admitted simply to demonstrate a disposition to commit such offences. This fitted uneasily alongside the bad character rules at common law but now convictions are more likely to be admissible under s.101 of the Criminal Justice Act 2003. In such cases, they are to be proved under s.73 and the burden of disproof of that conviction is on the accused. Prior to the act, in *Harris*[53] there was a fight involving several people. The defendant was charged on two counts, one of violent disorder and another alleging GBH. The first jury convicted him on the first count but he was re-tried on the second. In the re-trial, the violent disorder conviction was put before the jury. This was admissible under s.74(3) as the conviction was evidence that the defendant was present at the scene of the stabbing. Similarly in *Shanks*,[54] the defendant was charged with murder of an ex-girlfriend and with possessing a firearm with intent to endanger life. The jury was unable to reach a verdict on the first count but convicted on the latter. That conviction was introduced into the retrial for murder—it was evidence that he was in possession of the murder weapon and that at some stage during the day possessed the necessary intent.

But often the conviction can lead to assuming guilt by association. In *Pigram*,[55] two men were arrested transferring video recorders from a car into a

[51] [1987] 3 All E.R. 231.
[5] [1989] Crim L.R. 567.
[53] [2001] Crim.L.R. 227.
[54] [2003] EWCA Crim 689.
[55] [1995] Crim.L.R. 808.

lorry. On a joint charge of handling, one pleaded guilty and the other was convicted after the trial judge admitted the plea of guilty for the purpose of proving that the recorders were stolen goods. But does it? It proves that the co-accused believed the goods to be stolen but that should be an inadequate basis for establishing that the defendant believed the same. The case also raises another point.

> Arguably, section 74 should have been limited by Parliament to convictions upon a plea of not guilty where the matter in question has been contested and decided by the court in the earlier case. The conviction upon a plea of guilty has more weight than the mere admission because of the solemnity of the occasion on which it is made and the consequences for the person pleading guilty; but there may be more than one motive for pleading guilty and the assumptions on which the plea is made may not be well founded.[56]

This sort of problem is illustrated in *Dixon*,[57] where three defendants were charged with attempted burglary. The judge indicated that there would be a non-custodial sentence and two of the accused pleaded guilty. The third denied the offence. The defence was that she had been in the company of one of the accused and that neither of them had never been anywhere near the door which had been damaged. The prosecution met that assertion by putting the co-accused's conviction before the jury and the judge directed the jury to the effect that they had to accept that there had been an attempt at burglary. The Court of Appeal quashed the conviction as the defendant was entitled to challenge the basis of that plea. She had testified that, whatever her co-accused may have said by way of plea, he did not take part in the attempted burglary because he was with her at all material times. Whether the plea represented the truth was something which the jury ought to have been permitted to consider.

The key problem is fairness.[58] A co-accused's out-of-court statements are inadmissible evidence as against another accused for that reason and yet a defendant's case might be contaminated by a co-accused's guilty plea or conviction being admitted into evidence. This was shown in *Hayter*[59] where three accused were convicted of murder. The victim was the husband of B and it was alleged that, with H acting as go-between, she had recruited R to carry out the killing. The key evidence was that of R's girlfriend. R had admitted the killing and identified H as the recruiter and paymaster. This was the main evidence against R but was inadmissible as against H. At the close of the prosecution case, the judge rejected a submission of no case to answer and directed the jury that they had first to consider the case of R. If they convicted R, they could use that finding of guilt as against R as evidence against H under s.74. Had the trials been separate, R's conviction would have been admissible against H but not the hearsay evidence implicating H.

---

[56] *ibid.* at 809—commentary by Professor John Smith. *Golder* decided that a guilty plea is a conviction within the meaning of s.74—above at 240a.

[57] [2001] Crim.L.R. 126.

[58] R. Munday, "Guilt by Association under Section 74 of Police and Criminal Evidence Act 1984" [1990] Crim.L.R. 236.

[59] [2005] 2 All E.R. 209; [2005] Crim.L.R. 720.

Despite this, the House of Lords upheld the conviction. Having admitted the conviction, it was not unfair to allow R's confession to be used as evidence against H. Section 74 has been used to smuggle an accused's out-of-court statements into evidence against another accused and to create another judicial exception to hearsay.

In *Skinner*,[60] one of the accused was charged with aiding and abetting rape. The actual rapist pleaded guilty and the Crown was permitted to introduce evidence of this, as it was relevant to the issue of the accomplice's liability. That aiding and abetting charge foundered at the close of the prosecution case when the judge ruled that there was no case to answer. But the trial continued since there were several defendants charged with rape and indecent assault on the same victim. The men were all convicted and argued that the admission into evidence of the guilty plea was not relevant to any issue affecting their guilt and was prejudicial as the jury might well have concluded that, if one of the men had realised that the victim was incapable of consenting, why should not the other accused have the same knowledge? The Court of Appeal held that under s.78 of the Police and Criminal Evidence Act 1984 the admission of the guilty plea would have had an adverse effect on the fairness of the proceedings and ordered a new trial.

The European Commission of Human Rights has held in *MH v UK*,[61] that, on a charge of conspiracy to commit tax fraud, the admission of a guilty plea by a co-accused did not infringe Art.6. The judge made it clear that the plea did not prove the conspiracy and warned the jury about its relevance. In these circumstances the Commission considered that the judge's ruling that the guilty plea be admitted as the probative value of the guilty plea outweighed the prejudicial effect was not an arbitrary or unreasonable exercise of the discretion conferred upon him.

Domestically the courts have remained concerned about the impact of s.74.

Robertson [1987] 3 All E.R. 231 at 237h–j, *per* Lord Lane C.J.:

Section 74 is a provision which should be sparingly used. There will be occasions where, although the evidence may be technically admissible, its effect is likely to be so slight that it will be wiser not to adduce it. This is particularly so where there is any danger of a contravention of s.78. There is nothing to be gained by adducing evidence of doubtful value at the risk of having the conviction quashed because the admission of that evidence rendered the conviction unsafe or unsatisfactory. Secondly, where the evidence is admitted, the judge should be careful, as the judge was here, to explain to the jury the effect of the evidence and its limitations.

In *O'Connor*,[62] two men were charged with conspiracy to obtain property by deception. Beck pleaded guilty. At O'Connor's trial, the guilty plea was

---

[60] [1995] Crim.L.R. 805.
[61] [1997] E.H.R.L.R. 279.
[62] above.

admitted but Beck was not called to testify for either the prosecution or the defence. The burden of proof was placed on the accused with no opportunity to cross-examine the main witness. The court excluded the evidence under s.78. Similarly in *Mattison*[63] two males were charged with gross indecency. One pleaded guilty while the other denied the offence. Although the plea was obviously relevant evidence, at the same time it was deeply prejudicial and was excluded on that basis.[64]

V. Presumptions

At trial, facts in issue or other relevant facts are only established by some form of judicial evidence, namely witness testimony, documentary evidence or real evidence. As we have seen, the doctrine of judicial notice, estoppels and the use of previous judgments provide shortcuts to full proof. The last of these is the presumption. Presumptions operate where certain facts may be presumed to exist even in the absence of complete proof. For example, there is a presumption that a person is dead if that person has not been heard from for over seven years. As a result, a litigant who needs to prove that the person is dead, need not show that the person is in fact dead but merely that, during seven years, nobody who could be expected to have heard from them has in fact heard from them. An older example would be where a claim rests on being legitimate: there is no need to have blood and DNA tests to show that you are the child of your lawfully married parents. If it is proved that you were born while your parents were still married to each other, you are presumed to be legitimate.

To put it in general terms, where a party is seeking to establish a relevant fact, they may be unable to do so but will be permitted to prove another fact from which that relevant fact will be presumed. There is a *basic* fact (the seven year absence, the birth during wedlock) and a *presumed* fact (the person's death, the claimant's legitimacy). When we use the word "presumption" in an evidentiary sense, this is what is meant.

The effect of applying a presumption is to change the allocation of risk of losing in relation to a particular issue. In the examples above, it would be for the party adversely affected to satisfy the court on the balance of probabilities that the person was still alive or that the claimant was not the biological offspring of their lawfully married parents. The discussion of presumptions is directly bound up with questions of the burden of proof. But the relationship between burden of proof and presumptions is complex as there can be differences in the nature of the burden which is allocated. It is necessary to distinguish between different categories of presumption, although only one of these categories, the rebuttable presumption, is a "true" presumption. The others merely reflect the different senses in which the word is used.

---

[63] [1990] Crim.L.R. 117.
[64] See also *Curry* [1991] Crim.L.R. 274; *Hillier and Farrar* (1993) 97 Cr.App.R. 349; *Kempster* (1990) 90 Cr.App.R. 14.

A. *As a way of stating the burden of proof*

This is not a presumption in the sense being employed here since the allocation of risk is not altered. If we take the example of the presumption of innocence, there is no requirement that a basic fact is proved before the presumption is raised. It is an alternative method of stating that the burden of proof in a criminal trial rests on the prosecution.[65] Where the Crown fails to satisfy the trier of fact of guilt, the accused must be acquitted. Similarly judges talk (loosely?) of the presumptions of sanity, sobriety and volition.

Bratty v Attorney-General for Northern Ireland [1961] 3 All E.R. 523 at 535a–b, *per* Lord Denning:

[W]hilst the ultimate burden rests on the Crown of proving every element essential in the crime, nevertheless in order to prove that the act was a voluntary act, the Crown is entitled to rely on the presumption that every man has sufficient mental capacity to be responsible for his crimes; and that if the defence wish to displace the presumption they must give some evidence from which the contrary may reasonably be inferred. Thus a drunken man is presumed to have the capacity to form the specific intent necessary to constitute the crime, unless evidence is given from which it can be reasonably be inferred that he was incapable of forming it . . . . So it also seems to me that a man's act is presumed to be a voluntary act unless there is evidence from which it can be reasonably be inferred that it was involuntary . . .

The language of presumptions in this context is not helpful since the questions before the court are about allocating the evidential and legal burden of raising particular defences. As we have seen, the defendant has the responsibility of raising particular defences, whether provocation, self-defence or insane or non-insane automatism. Normally defendants bear the evidential burden of proof, namely to adduce sufficient evidence that a reasonable jury properly directed might conclude that there was a reasonable doubt. The legal burden remains on the prosecution although with insanity, the accused bears not only this evidential burden but also the legal burden and must satisfy the jury that they are not sane on the balance of probabilities. Presumptions in the technical sense may be said to have nothing to do with it.[66]

B. *As Conclusive Proof of a Fact*

A second "category" of presumptions is that of irrebuttable or conclusive presumptions. Again it can be argued that these are not 'true' presumptions

---

[65] *Woolmington v DPP* [1935] A.C. 462.
[66] see Ch.3.

but are rules of substantive law which provide that once the basic fact has been proved, the presumed fact is taken as established and no evidence to the contrary is admissible to rebut that conclusion.

Under the common law of defamation, English law presumed that the publication of a defamatory statement was harmful to the person defamed without specific proof of that harm.[67] In *Dow Jones v Jameel*,[68] an Internet article allegedly defamatory of the claimant had been read by, at most three subscribers in the UK. The Court of Appeal held that the presumption that a defamatory publication caused some damage to its victim was, in practice, irrebuttable. Phillips L.J. was not persuaded that the presumption of damage in the law of libel was incompatible with Art.10 of the European Convention on Human Rights. A remedy was found in striking out the claim for abuse of process —"It would be an abuse of process to continue to commit the resources of the English court, including substantial judge and possibly jury time, to an action where so little is now seen to be at stake."

The doctrine of undue influence in equity is another area where irrebuttable presumptions exist. This was described by Lord Nicholls in *Royal Bank of Scotland v Etridge (No.2)*.[69]

Royal Bank of Scotland v Etridge (No.2) [2001] 4 All E.R. 449, *per* Lord Nicholls:

18. . . . The law has adopted a sternly protective attitude towards certain types of relationship in which one party acquires influence over another who is vulnerable and dependent and where, moreover, substantial gifts by the influenced or vulnerable person are not normally to be expected. Examples of relationships within this special class are parent and child, guardian and ward, trustee and beneficiary, solicitor and client, and medical adviser and patient. In these cases the law presumes, irrebuttably, that one party had influence over the other. The complainant need not prove he actually reposed trust and confidence in the other party. It is sufficient for him to prove the existence of the type of relationship.

A traditional example of an irrebuttable presumption is the presumption of innocence under s.50 of the Children and Young Persons Act 1933.

50. It shall be conclusively presumed that no child under the age of ten[70] can be guilty of any offence.

A further presumption was that boys under the age of 14 were conclusively presumed to be incapable of sexual intercourse and therefore could not be convicted of rape or other sexual offences of that nature.[71] This common law presumption was overturned by s.1 of the Sexual Offences Act 1993.

---

[67] *Duke of Brunswick v Harmer* [1849] 14 Q.B. 185; *Shevill v Presse Alliance* [1996] 3 All E.R. 929.
[68] [2005] Q.B. 946.
[69] [2001] 4 All E.R. 449.
[70] Substituted by Children and Young Persons Act 1963, s.16(1).
[71] *Groombridge* (1836) 7 C.&P. 582; *P, Independent*, March 7, 1994.

Recent reforms of sexual offences have brought new conclusive presumptions. Where a person deceives the victim as to the nature of the sexual act or impersonates another person, lack of consent is conclusively presumed. Under s.76 of the Sexual Offences Act 2003,

76 (1) If in proceedings for an offence to which this section applies it is proved that the defendant did the relevant act and that any of the circumstances specified in subsection (2) existed, it is to be conclusively presumed—
(a) that the complainant did not consent to the relevant act, and
(b) that the defendant did not believe that the complainant consented to the relevant act.
(2) The circumstances are that—
(a) the defendant intentionally deceived the complainant as to the nature or purpose of the relevant act;
(b) the defendant intentionally induced the complainant to consent to the relevant act by impersonating a person known personally to the complainant.

This form of "constructive" thought can be a tempting solution for judges and can emerge in unlikely places. In the common law, the doctrine of constructive malice in murder was an example of a conclusive presumption. It existed in two situations: killing an officer while resisting arrest and killing in the course of a felony. The intent to kill was presumed from either the intent to resist arrest or to commit the felony itself. The doctrine was abolished in 1957[72] but judges have long memories! In *D.P.P. v Smith*,[73] the accused was stopped by a police officer who wished to examine his van in which there was stolen property. The accused drove off, seeking to avoid arrest, and the officer jumped on the bonnet, only to be thrown off and killed. Prior to 1957, this would have been murder. It was argued for the appellant that he lacked malice aforethought, in particular that he did not foresee serious harm coming to the officer.

D.P.P. v Smith [1960] 3 All E.R.I61 at 167a–d, *per* Viscount Kilmuir:

The jury must, of course, in such a case as the present make up their minds on the evidence whether the accused was unlawfully and voluntarily doing something to someone. The unlawful and voluntary act must clearly be aimed at someone . . . Once, however, the jury are satisfied as to that, it matters not what the accused in fact contemplated as the probable result or whether he ever contemplated at all, provided he was in law responsible and accountable for his actions, that is, was a man capable of forming an intent, not insane within the M'Naghten Rules and not suffering from diminished responsibility. On the assumption that he is so accountable for his actions, the sole question is whether the unlawful and voluntary act was of such a kind that grievous bodily harm was the natural and probable result. The only test available for this is what the ordinary responsible man would, in all the circumstances of the case, have contemplated as the natural and probable result . . .

Lord Kilmuir came to the unfortunate conclusion that, if a reasonable person would have foreseen serious harm, the accused must be presumed to

[72] Homicide Act 1957, s.1.
[73] [1960] 3 All E.R. 161.

have foreseen the same result, regardless of any evidence to the contrary, an irrebuttable presumption of malice aforethought.[74]

C. *As a Factual Inference*

These again are not presumptions in the technical sense but we are using the language of presumptions to describe the processes of inferential thought. When defendants are shown to have stabbed, shot, raped or stolen, common sense logic leads to the conclusion that they intended those actions. A person is taken to intend the natural consequences of their acts.[75] That conclusion remains provisional and there is no rule of law that the jury must draw that conclusion. In the Court of Appeal decision in *D.P.P. v Smith*,[76] Byrne L.J. put it clearly,

> Although . . . that is an inference which may be drawn, and on the facts in certain circumstances, must inevitably be drawn, yet if on all the facts of a particular case it is not the correct inference, then it should not be drawn.[77]

If a reasonable person would have appreciated the risk and thus intended the consequences, the jury was entitled to infer that the defendant did likewise. But that inference should not be drawn if, in all the circumstances of the case, it was not the correct inference, i.e. if there was evidence that the accused did not intend those consequences. In other words, the fact in issue was the subjective state of mind of the accused. One could draw inferences about that by using common sense objective standards but such inferences were always rebuttable by evidence that the defendant was not, for example, a reasonable person!

Presumptions of fact are provisional inferences that we are willing to make unless and until there is further evidence which makes it necessary to reassess. Again these are not presumptions in the strict sense since this is the normal rational process by which inferences are drawn from evidence. The formal allocation of risk is not changed in any way. Thus, where defendants are provisionally assumed to have intended the offence, they are under neither a legal nor evidential burden to adduce evidence that there was no such intention. They would be entitled to a direction from the judge that the Crown bears the legal burden of proof, namely that they must prove intent beyond reasonable doubt. Of course, informally, once defendants have been proved to have committed the act, they are at increased risk that the jury will find against them unless they adduce some evidence of lack of intent. But this is merely a shift in the tactical balance of the trial.

---

[74] This result was overturned by Criminal Justice Act 1967, s.8. It is arguable that irrebuttable presumptions still infect malice aforethought since intent to cause serious harm is still regarded as sufficient mens rea for murder—*Cunningham* [1981] 2 All E.R. 863. Is this a hidden evidential presumption with the intent to cause GBH being the basic fact and the intent to kill being the presumed fact?

[75] *Steane* [1947] 1 All E.R. 813.

[76] [1960] 2 All E.R. 450.

[77] *ibid*. at 453.

Another factual inference is the continuance of life. In *Lumley*,[78] a woman married her first husband in 1836, left him in 1843 and remarried in 1847. The trial judge held there to be a presumption of law that the first husband was alive at the date of the second marriage. The conviction was quashed.

Lumley (1869) L.R. 1 C.C.R. 196 at 198, *per* Lush J.:

. . . it is incumbent on the prosecution to prove to the satisfaction of the jury that the husband or wife, as the case may be, was alive at the date of the second marriage. This is purely a question of fact. The existence of the party at an antecedent date may, or may not, afford a reasonable inference that he is living at the subsequent date. If, for example, it was proved that he was in good health on the day preceding the marriage, the inference would be strong, almost irresistible, that he was living on the latter day, and the jury would in all probability find that he was so. If, on the other hand, it were proved that he was then in a dying condition, and nothing further was proved, they would probably decline to draw that inference. Thus, the question is entirely for the jury. The law makes no presumption either way.

Another example is proof of guilty knowledge, a necessary element before any conviction on charges of handling stolen property. The jury should be directed that where the accused is found in possession of recently stolen goods, that possession calls for an explanation and, if none is given, they are entitled to infer, according to the circumstances, that the defendant is the handler or the thief.[79] But the burden of proof remains on the prosecution and if the explanation given by the accused leaves the jury in doubt, then the Crown has not proved its case.[80]

The judge is now able to direct the jury that they may draw inferences, probably adverse to the defence, in certain circumstances.

- Under s.34-37 of the Criminal Justice and Public Order Act 1994 where the accused has failed to mention a fact to the police which has later been relied on in the defence; where the accused has failed to testify; where the accused has failed to account for marks or possession of objects which suggests participation in the offence; where the accused has to account for their presence at a particular place which again would suggest participation in the offence.
- Under s.11(3) of the Criminal Procedure and Investigations Act 1996.[81] The statute requires a defendant to disclose the nature of the defence and where that statement of defence is flawed, inferences can be drawn. For example, the statement of defence may be non-existent or late, reveal inconsistent defences or be different from the defence put forward at trial.

---

[78] (1869) LR 1 CCR 196.
[79] *Schama* (1914) 11 Cr.App.R. 45; *Garth* [1949] 1 All E.R. 773.
[80] *Hepworth* [1955] 2 All E.R. 918.
[81] As amended by Criminal Justice Act 2003, s.39.

The jury is entitled to draw such inferences as appear proper in the circumstances. Such inferences may well be about the *weight* that the jury are willing to give to evidence, for example, to a defence which has been advanced for the first time at trial. But the jury can also make *inferences of fact*, such as guilty knowledge from a failure to account to the police or the court for the possession of prohibited articles. Neither statute alters the formal position regarding the burden of proof but informally and tactically the prosecution's position is inevitably strengthened.

D. *As a Rebuttable Proof of a Fact*

This may be described as the true presumption, not as evidence but as a way of dealing with evidence. On the proof of a basic fact, a further fact is presumed to exist in the absence of evidence to the contrary. The allocation of risk shifts so that the party adversely affected by the presumption bears the burden of disproving it. This burden of disproof can be either a legal burden or an evidential burden.

a) If a party proves that they were born while the mother and father were married, the legal burden of satisfying the court that they are illegitimate rests on the other party who must satisfy the court on the balance of probabilities and might, for example, bring in evidence to show that the alleged father was impotent or absent from the country at the relevant time.

b) The presumption of death arises where there is no affirmative evidence by people who are likely to have heard that the person has been alive during a continuous period of seven years. Once this has been demonstrated to the court, this casts a burden on the party seeking to show that that person was or is alive at the relevant time. In this case it is only an evidential burden and not a persuasive one. As long as some evidence to the contrary has been adduced, the persuasive burden still rests on the party who asserts that the person is dead.

In the USA, presumptions simply impose an evidential burden,

In all civil actions and proceedings not otherwise provided for by Acts of Congress or by those rules, a presumption imposes on the party against whom it is directed the burden of going forward with evidence to rebut or meet the presumption, but does not shift to such party the burden of proof in the sense of the risk of nonpersuasion, which remains throughout the trial upon the party on whom it was originally cast.[82]

This distinction between presumptions as evidence of facts as opposed to a change in the allocation of risk and in the burden of proof can be seen in

---

[82] Federal Rules of Evidence, r. 301.

Mobile, J. & K.C.R. Co. v Turnipseed,[83] where the Supreme Court upheld a Mississippi statute which provided that in actions against railroads proof of injury inflicted by the running of trains should be prima facie evidence of negligence by the railroad. The injury in the case had resulted from a derailment. As long as there was a rational connection between the fact proved and the fact presumed, then considerations of public policy arising from the character of the business justified the application of a presumption. But the only effect of the statute was to impose on the railroad the duty of producing some evidence to the contrary. In *Western & Atlantic R. Co. v Henderson*,[84] the jury was instructed that proof of injury raised a presumption of negligence, that the burden shifted to the railroad to prove ordinary care and unless it did so, the jury should find for claimant. This involved a Georgia statute making railroads liable for damages done by trains and was struck down by the Supreme Court, presumably on the grounds that the instruction to the jury was that there was a rebuttable presumption of negligence which shifted the formal burden to the railroad.

Presumptions are mainly common law in origin but can be created by statute —under s.75 of the Sexual Offences Act 2003, there is a rebuttable presumption that the victim in a sexual offence was not consenting where violence or drugs were used or where the victim was asleep, unlawfully detained or suffered from a disability. The defendant in such circumstances would have to produce some evidence that there was in fact consent, before the issue would be left to the jury.

In outline, here are some of the commoner presumptions in common law:

1. Doli Incapax

Under the common law, a child under the age of 14[85] was presumed to have insufficient understanding to distinguish between right and wrong and is therefore incapable of committing a crime. This presumption could only be rebutted by evidence that the child knew that what they were doing was wrong.[86] This rule attracted judicial and academic criticism.[87] One reform which was mooted was the reversal of the presumption so that a child under 14 would be presumed to be capable of crime unless it was shown by the defence that they lacked the ability to distinguish between right and wrong. In *C v DPP*,[88] the Divisional Court ruled that the presumption was no longer good law but the House of Lords rejected this, recognising that there was a case for change. In the light of a long and uncontradicted line of authority, the House declined to abolish the presumption or to tailor it to modern needs, feeling that the imposition of full criminal responsibility from the age of ten was a matter best left to the legislature. In 1997, a government white paper

---

[83] 219 U.S. 35, 31 S.Ct. 136, 55 L.Ed. 78 (1910).

[84] 279 U.S. 639, 49 S.Ct. 445, 73 L.Ed. 884 (1929).

[85] A child under the age of 10 is presumed conclusively to be incapable of crime.

[86] *J.M v Runeckles* (1984) 79 Cr.App.R. 225; evidence of background and character, including previous convictions, is admissible for this purpose: *R v B* [1979] 3 All E.R. 460.

[87] There is a review by Lord Lowry in *C v D.P.P* [1995] 2 All E.R. 43.

[88] above.

asserted that the presumption "flies in the face of common sense" and was archaic, illogical and unfair.[89] Under s.34 of the Crime and Disorder Act 1998, the presumption was abolished.

2. Omnia praesumuntur rite esse acta

This presumption concerns the rightness of official acts. Where a public official is shown to have acted as such, it is presumed that the act has been properly performed in the absence of evidence to the contrary. For example, *Berryman v Wise*[90] concerned an action by an attorney for words spoken of him in the way of his profession and it was held that it was not necessary to prove that he was an attorney by production of his certificate or the roll of attorneys. There is a similar situation with police officers, justices of the peace, and others: it was sufficient to show that they acted in those characters without proving their appointment. In *Roberts*,[91] the rule was applied to a county court judge. The burden appears to be only an evidential burden for the other party to produce some evidence that everything was not as it should be. The prosecution in criminal cases cannot rely on this to establish essential element of an offence. In *Dillon*,[92] a police officer was charged with allowing prisoners lawfully in custody to escape. Could the prosecution rely on the presumption to avoid adducing evidence as to the lawfulness of the custody?

Dillon [1982] 1 All E.R. 1017 at 1019h–1020b, *per* Lord Fraser:

Their Lordships are of opinion that it was essential for the Crown to establish that the arrest and detention were lawful and that the omission to do so was fatal to the conviction of the appellant . . . The lawfulness of the detention was a necessary precondition for the offence of permitting escape, and it is well established that the courts will not presume the existence of facts which are central to an offence . . .

Moreover this particular offence is one which touches the liberty of the subject, and on which there is, for that reason also, no room for presumptions in favour of the Crown. If there were to be a presumption that any person de facto in custody was there lawfully, the scales would be tipped in favour of the fait accompli in a way that might constitute a serious threat to liberty. It has to be remembered that, in every case where a police officer commits the offence of negligently permitting a prisoner to escape from lawful custody, the prisoner himself commits an offence by escaping, and it would be contrary to fundamental principles of law that the onus should be on a prisoner to rebut a presumption that he was being lawfully detained, which he could only do by the (notoriously difficult) process of proving a negative.

3. Presumption of Marriage

There are three presumptions linked to the fact of marriage itself: these are the presumptions of formal validity, essential validity and of marriage through cohabitation.[93]

[89] Home Office, *Tackling Youth Crime* (September 1997) at n.54 paras 3 and 7.
[90] (1791) 4 T.R. 366.
[91] (1878) 14 Cox. 101.
[92] [1982] 1 All E.R. 1017.
[93] A. Borkowski, "The Presumption of Marriage" (2002) 14 Child and Family Law Quarterly 251; R. Probert, "When Are We Married?" (2002) 22 Legal Studies 398.

(i) *presumption of formal validity*

This may be compared to the presumption about the rightness of official acts. While a marriage may be void because of a failure to observe some formality such as the reading of the banns or obtaining a licence, this presumption places the burden of proving such failures onto the person seeking to disprove the validity of the marriage. If two people, who intend to get married, go through a ceremony of marriage, there is a presumption that the marriage is formally valid and the burden of proving its invalidity is cast onto the other party. This is a legal burden. A leading case here is *Piers v Piers*[94] in which a marriage was celebrated in a private house. There was no evidence that a special licence had been obtained but the House of Lords upheld the validity of the marriage. Once there was proof of the ceremony, the marriage was presumed to be valid unless the party contesting that validity can prove that it was not. This also applies to foreign ceremonies of marriage— *Mahadervan v Mahadervan*[95] also suggests that the standard of proof on the contesting party would be that of beyond reasonable doubt. But since that time, section 26 of the Family Law Reform Act 1969 has laid down a lower standard on the balance of probabilities for the presumption of legitimacy and it is difficult to think that different standards could rationally apply.

In *Chief Adjudication Officer v Bath*,[96] the couple married in a Sikh Temple in England which, unknown to the couple, was not registered for marriages. They lived together for 37 years and the issue was whether the widow qualified for a pension on the basis of her "husband's" contributions. This raised two presumptions—the first was raised when the legal requirement laid down a proper form for marriage and that proper form was observed. This presumption could only be displaced by positive and not merely clear evidence. The strength of the evidence needed for rebuttal depended upon the length of the cohabitation. The second presumption was that a marriage could be assumed from long cohabitation. Thus there was the anomaly that a long cohabitation marriage could be assumed where there was no ceremony, but could not be assumed when a bona fide ceremony had taken place which failed to comply with all the requirements of the Act. Where there was an irregular ceremony which was followed by long cohabitation, it would be contrary to the general policy of the law to refuse to extend to the parties the benefit of a presumption which would have applied if there had been no evidence of any ceremony at all.

(ii) *presumption of essential validity*

A marriage is void if the parties lack the capacity to marry, for example, because of lack of age, of being too closely related, or of being already married to another person. The basic fact that there was, on its face, a proper ceremony of marriage raises the presumption that the parties had the capacity to marry. This is a rebuttable presumption with the legal burden on the party

---

[94] (1849) 2 H.L. Cas 331.
[95] [1964] P. 233.
[96] [2000] 1 F.L.R. 8.

who seeks to invalidate the marriage. The standard is the ordinary civil standard of proof. In *Re Peete*,[97] a woman claimed as the testator's widow under the Inheritance Act 1938. There was evidence that she had gone through a ceremony of marriage with the testator in 1919 but also evidence that she had been previously married although she testified that her first husband had been killed in 1916. The presumption of the validity of the 1919 marriage was rebutted by the evidence of the first marriage and the woman's testimony was insufficient to satisfy the burden of proof resting on her.

In *Monckton v Tarr*,[98] H1 married W1 in 1882 only to desert her in 1887. W1 married H2 in 1895, at which time there was no evidence that H1 was still alive. However H2 left W1 and married W2 in 1913, knowing that W1 was still alive. W2 now claimed workmen's compensation as H2's widow. While the claimant can initially rely on the presumption in favour of the 1913 ceremony, this is rebutted by proof of the 1895 marriage and that W1 was still alive in 1913. This puts the burden of proof back onto the claimant who can only succeed by showing that the 1895 ceremony was a nullity and therefore that H2 was free to marry in 1913. In 1895 the first husband had been absent for seven years without contacting his wife and was thus presumed dead. W2 can only succeed by showing some evidence that H1 was alive at that time and this she is unable to do.

(iii) *presumption of marriage from cohabitation*

There is a presumption that, if a couple are shown to have been living together, in the absence of contrary evidence, they are lawfully married. In *Re Taplin*,[99] the claimants sought a declaration that their children were legitimate. The parents alleged that they had been married in Victoria in 1860 where registration was compulsory but there was no record in the Victoria archives. Despite this, the children were still declared legitimate. Where couples have lived together for a lengthy period and presented themselves as married, the law requires compelling evidence to rebut the presumption. In *Al-Mudaris v Al-Mudaris*,[1] the couple had been through Islamic ceremonies in England and in Sharjah.

Al-Mudaris v Al-Mudaris [2001] 2 F.L.R. 6, *per* Hughes J.:

[35] It is important to observe that this is not a presumption which prevails over positive proof of the contrary. Nor does the cohabitation itself constitute the marriage. Rather, the rule is that cohabitation and reputation of this kind together amount to strong evidence that a lawful marriage has taken place and only strong and weighty

---

[97] *Re Peete Peete v Crompton* [1952] 2 All E.R. 599.
[98] (1930) 23 B.W.C.C. 504.
[99] [1981] 1 All E.R. 897.
[1] [2001] 2 F.L.R. 6; see also *De Vire v De Vire* [2001] 1 F.L.R. 460, *Chief Adjudication Officer v Bath* above.

proof that it has not will permit a contrary conclusion. It follows that the presumption will the more readily be applied where the marriage being presumed to have taken place could have occurred with comparatively slight formality. ...

[36] In the present case, if lawful marriage is to be presumed between these parties, it must have occurred in an Islamic country, and it must have been a lawful polygamous marriage. It is common ground between the parties, and I so hold, that the presumption must extend to presuming such a marriage, where the domicile of the parties permits it, since the whole rationale of the rule is to find a lawful occasion for the kind of cohabitation in question whenever that can be done.

4. Presumption of Legitimacy

As a matter of public policy, children born or conceived during marriage are presumed to be the legitimate offspring of the partners in that marriage. The presumption can be rebutted by sufficient evidence to the contrary. This presumption is made even where the parties are living apart or divorce proceedings have been started, although in such cases, evidence of rebuttal might be easier to obtain. The presumption puts a persuasive legal burden on the party seeking to disprove legitimacy. At common law the standard was beyond reasonable doubt but is now on the balance of probabilities as a result of s.26 of the Family Law Reform Act 1969.

Any presumption of law as to the legitimacy or illegitimacy of any person may in any civil proceedings be rebutted by evidence which shows that it is more probable than not that the person is illegitimate or legitimate as the case may be and it shall not be necessary to prove that fact beyond reasonable doubt in order to rebut the presumption.

Although simple evidence of adultery is probably insufficient to rebut the presumption, lack of access of husband to wife at the time of conception, impotence or infertility, cohabitation of wife with another, blood groups, admission by another of paternity may be evidence in rebuttal. There is less significance for this presumption nowadays as reforms in the area of family law have made the distinction between legitimate and illegitimate offspring less important, in addition to which DNA testing can provide conclusive proof of paternity. However the presumption still plays a role—in *Re B*,[2] a woman concealed the fact of her pregnancy and the birth from her husband and family and put the child up for adoption. She said that the pregnancy had been the result of rape. The local authority issued an application for a care order and wished to serve notice of the proceedings on the husband, who was still ignorant of these events. The woman opposed this but the court found that there was a presumption that the baby was the husband's child and that the presumption had not been rebutted by the woman's testimony about the circumstances of the conception.

The longer term value of this presumption was questioned by Thorpe L.J. in *Re H*,[3] where twins had been born to a married woman. The putative

[2] [2004] 1 F.L.R. 527.
[3] [2002] 1 F.L.R. 1145.

father, not the husband, applied for DNA tests on the twins to determine paternity. The Court of Appeal upheld the application.

Re H [2002] 1 F.L.R. 1145, *per* Thorpe L.J.:

30. The judge made it plain that in the absence of scientific evidence then the issue was to be decided on the application of 'a very important, well established principle . . . . that is, the presumption of the legitimacy of children born during the currency of the marriage'. He went on to refer to the case of *Serio v Serio*.[4] Twenty years on I question the relevance of the presumption or the justification for its application. In the nineteenth century, when science had nothing to offer and illegitimacy was a social stigma as well as a depriver of rights, the presumption was a necessary tool, the use of which required no justification. That common law presumption, only rebuttable by proof beyond reasonable doubt, was modified by section 26 of the Family Law Reform Act 1969 by enabling the presumption to be rebutted on the balance of probabilities. But as science has hastened on and as more and more children are born out of marriage it seems to me that the paternity of any child is to be established by science and not by legal presumption or inference.

5. Presumption of Death

Any party wishing to rely on the presumption of death must show that there is no affirmative evidence that the person has been alive during a continuous period of seven years and that there were persons who would have been likely to have heard from that person. In *Chard v Chard*,[5] the husband married his first wife in 1909 and his second wife in 1933. He had last heard from his first wife in 1917 but he had been in prison during the period and was therefore not someone who was likely to have heard.

Chard v Chard [1956] P. 259 at 273, *per* Sachs J.:

By virtue of a long sequence of judicial statements, which either assert or assume such a rule, it appears accepted that there is a convenient presumption of law applicable to certain cases of seven years' absence where no statute applies. That presumption in its modern shape takes effect . . . substantially as follows. Where as regards 'AB' there is no acceptable affirmative evidence that he was alive at some time during a continuous period of seven years or more, then if it can be proved first, that there are persons who would be likely to have heard of him over that period, secondly that those persons have not heard of him, and thirdly that all due inquiries have been made appropriate to the circumstances, 'AB' will be presumed to have died at some time within that period.

The criteria are that the person has been absent for seven years, that there were people who were likely to hear from the person and that those persons

---

[4] [1983] F.L.R. 756.
[5] [1956] P. 259.

have not heard. In *Prudential Assurance Co v Edmonds*,[6] there was a claim on a life insurance policy. Was Robert Nutt dead? He had not been heard of by the family but there was a niece who testified that she had seen him in Melbourne, but did not speak to him as she lost him in the crowd.

Prudential Assurance Co v Edmonds [1877] 2 A.C. 487 at 511 per Lord Blackburn:

Supposing the jurymen had found as a fact that they thought she was mistaken, would or would not the grounds have existed upon which the presumption from a seven years' absence would arise that the man not heard of was dead? I think certainly they would. It seems to me that when she said, 'I have seen the man in the streets of Melbourne,' it upset the presumption arising from the relatives, including herself, never having seen or heard of him, and it turned the onus the other way. It was possible, however, that it might have been proved that the man she saw was not Robert Nutt, but somebody else. If that had been proved, it would have left the matter just as if she had never made the statement. When she said she thought she had seen him, and all the others had heard it from her, although that unexplained and uncontradicted statement affected the onus, yet, as soon as it was made out by satisfactory evidence that she was mistaken, the hearing from her was gone, and the presumption would remain as it was before . . .

Seven years absence creates a presumption of death and there is an evidential burden on the party seeking to show that the person is still alive. The niece's evidence, if believed by the jury, satisfies that and the onus reverts to the party seeking to show that the person is not dead who must persuade the jury of this fact on the balance of probabilities.

The final requirement is that the appropriate inquiries have been made although whether this needs to be proved depends on the circumstances.[7] Failure to make inquiries may be justified but conversely proof of proper investigation may render proof of the other basic facts unnecessary.

Where these conditions are satisfied and death is presumed, the problem arises as to the moment of that death. Is the person presumed to have died seven years before the court hearing or seven years after disappearance? The strict view is that the subject is only dead at the date of the proceedings. In *Chipchase v Chipchase*,[8] Sir Boyd Merriman said,

That presumption—I am taking the statement of it from the judgment of Giffard LJ in *Re Phene's Trusts*,[9]—is that 'the law presumes a person who has not been heard of for over seven years to be dead, but in the absence of special circumstances draws no presumption from the fact as to the particular period at which he died

In *Phene's Trusts* the testator died in January 1861, leaving his estate to his nieces and nephews. One nephew had not been heard of since 1860 when he

---

[6] [1877] 2 A.C. 487.
[7] *Bullock v Bullock* [1960] 2 All E.R. 307.
[8] [1939] P. 391.
[9] (1870) 5 Ch. 139.

deserted from the US Navy. A claim was made for his share of the estate but the court would not presume that he had survived the testator. The court did not apparently consider the strong factual inference that might have been drawn that the nephew was likely to have continued to live from 1860 to 1861. In *Chipchase*, the wife's complaint in front of the magistrates was of her husband's adultery, desertion and failure to maintain. She had gone through a ceremony of marriage with him in 1928, having gone through a previous ceremony with another man in 1915. She testified that she had not heard from her first husband for seven years before the second ceremony. The magistrates dismissed the complaint as there was no evidence that the first husband was dead. The Divisional Court remitted the case to the magistrates to consider whether there was any evidence to rebut the presumption of death which implies a more liberal view that the subject is presumed to have died at a date seven years after the disappearance.

There are various statutory provisions such as s.184 of the Law of Property Act 1925 which provides that where two people die at the same time and in circumstances which make it uncertain which died first, the younger is deemed to have survived the older. In criminal proceedings, under s.57 of the Offences against the Person Act 1861 which defines the offence of bigamy, there is a defence where the spouse has been continually absent for seven years and has not been known to have been alive.

6. Presumption of Negligence—Res Ipsa Loquitur

Where a swab is left in a patient after surgery, a sack of sugar falls from a warehouse crane or a car crosses the central reservation of a dual carriageway and collides with vehicles travelling in the opposite direction, the incident is such that observers assume that the accident has occurred because of the negligence of the surgeon, the warehouse keeper or the driver and will stick to that conclusion in the absence of any contradictory information. The claimant, normally suing for personal injuries, is still under the obligation to prove negligence which can be onerous since the true cause of the accident is often only known to the defendant. However the law adopts a common sense inference: where some thing is shown to have been under the management of the defendants or their employees and the accident which occurred was such that in the ordinary course it would not have happened, there is a presumption that *res ipsa loquitur*, the thing speaks for itself, and that the accident was the result of negligence.

Scott v London and St Katherine Docks Co (1865) 3 H.& C. 596 at 601, *per* **Eric C.J.:**

But where the thing is shown to be under the management of the defendant or his servants, and the accident is such as in the ordinary course of things does not happen if those who have the management use proper care, it affords reasonable evidence, in the absence of explanation by the defendants, that the accident arose from want of care.

The problem is the impact of this maxim. It can be treated in three ways.

a) *as an inference of fact:* were the defendant to adduce no evidence of reasonable care, although tactically unwise, the trier of fact would not be bound to find in the claimant's favour. In some circumstances, the facts raising the presumption may be weaker than in others and even if the defendant produced no evidence, they may still win.

b) *As a persuasive presumption:* the presumption would alter the burden of proof so that the defendant would need to show on the balance of probabilities that he or she was not negligent. In *Barkway v South Wales Transport,*[10] the defendant's bus had fallen down an embankment. The defendant adduced evidence that it had left the road because of a burst tyre.

Barkway v South Wales Transport [1948] 2 All E.R. 460 at 471, *per* Asquith L.J.:

. . . (I) If the defendant's omnibus leaves the road and falls down an embankment, and this without more is proved, then res ipsa loquitur, there is a presumption that the event is caused by negligence on the part of the defendants, and the plaintiff succeeds unless the defendants can rebut this presumption. (ii) It is no rebuttal for the defendants to show, again without more, that the immediate cause of the omnibus leaving the road is a tyre-burst, since a tyre-burst per se is a neutral event consistent, and equally consistent, with negligence or due diligence on the part of the defendants. When a balance has been tilted one way, you cannot redress it by adding an equal weight to each scale. The depressed scale will remain down . . . . (iii) To displace the presumption, the defendants must go further and prove (or it must emerge from the evidence as a whole) either (a) that the burst itself was due to a specific cause which does not connote negligence on their part but points to its absence as more probable, or (b), if they can point to no more such specific cause, that they used all reasonable care in and about the management of their tyres.

c) *As an evidential presumption:* the presumption would not alter the legal burden of proof but merely the evidential burden so that the defendant must adduce some evidence of reasonable diligence. In such circumstances, the legal burden remains on the claimant so that were the probabilities to remain balanced, the claimant would lose. In *Ng Chun Pui v Lee Chuen Tat,*[11] a coach owned by the defendants left the carriageway, crossed the central reservation and collided with a bus being driven in the opposite direction. The claimants relied on the fact of the accident as evidence of negligence under the doctrine of *res ipsa loquitur,*

---

[10] [1948] 2 All E.R. 460; see also *Woods v Duncan* [1946] A.C. 401.
[11] [1988] R.T.R. 298.

Ng Chun Pui v Lee Chuen Tat [1988] R.T.R. 298, *per* Lord Griffiths:

. . . There can be no doubt that the plaintiffs were justified in taking this course. In ordinary circumstances if a well-maintained coach is being properly driven it will not cross the central reservation of a dual carriageway and collide with on-coming traffic in the other carriageway. In the absence of any explanation of the behaviour of the coach the proper inference to draw is that it was not being driven with the standard of care required by the law and that the driver was therefore negligent. If the defendants had called no evidence the plaintiffs would undoubtedly have been entitled to judgment . . .

The judge however was of the view that . . . because the plaintiffs had originally relied upon the doctrine of res ipsa loquitur, the burden of disproving negligence remained upon the defendants and they had failed to discharge it. In their Lordships' opinion this shows a misunderstanding of the so-called doctrine of res ipsa loquitur, which is no more than the use of a Latin maxim to describe a state of the evidence from which it is proper to draw an inference of negligence. Although it had been said in a number of cases, it is misleading to talk of the burden of proof shifting to the defendant in a res ipsa loquitur situation. The burden of proving negligence rests throughout the case on the plaintiff. Where the plaintiff has suffered injuries as a result of an accident which ought not to have happened if the defendant had taken due care, it will often be possible for the plaintiff to discharge the burden of proof by inviting the court to draw the inference that on the balance of probabilities the defendant must have failed to exercise due care, even though the plaintiff does not know in what particular respects the failure occurred . . .

So in an appropriate case the plaintiff establishes a prima facie case by relying upon the fact of the accident. If the defendant adduces no evidence there is nothing to rebut the inference of negligence and the plaintiff will have proved his case. But if the defendant does adduce evidence that evidence must be evaluated to see if it is still reasonable to draw the inference of negligence from the mere fact of the accident. Loosely speaking this may be referred to as a burden on the defendant to show that he was not negligent, but that only means that faced with a prima facie case of negligence the defendant will be found negligent unless he produces evidence that is capable of rebutting the prima facie case. Resort to the burden of proof is a poor way to decide a case; it is the duty of the judge to examine all the evidence at the end of the case and decide whether on the facts he finds to have been proved and on the inferences he is prepared to draw he is satisfied that negligence has been established. In so far as resort is had to the burden of proof the burden remains at the end of the case as it was at the beginning upon the plaintiff to prove that his injury was caused by the negligence of the defendants . . .

English authorities show divergent approaches to the problem, some suggesting that the presumption shifts the legal burden of proof, others that it merely casts an evidential burden on the defendant. However the strength of the presumption necessarily varies with the basic facts which bring it into play and the cases suggest that it has no artificial weight superior to its natural weight. Is it appropriate to label it persuasive, evidential or provisional?

INDEX

(all references are to page number)